Contemporary
Literary Criticism

Guide to Gale Literary Criticism Series

For criticism on	Consult these Gale series
Authors now living or who died after December 31, 1959	*CONTEMPORARY LITERARY CRITICISM (CLC)*
Authors who died between 1900 and 1959	*TWENTIETH-CENTURY LITERARY CRITICISM (TCLC)*
Authors who died between 1800 and 1899	*NINETEENTH-CENTURY LITERATURE CRITICISM (NCLC)*
Authors who died between 1400 and 1799	*LITERATURE CRITICISM FROM 1400 TO 1800 (LC)* *SHAKESPEAREAN CRITICISM (SC)*
Authors who died before 1400	*CLASSICAL AND MEDIEVAL LITERATURE CRITICISM (CMLC)*
Black writers of the past two hundred years	*BLACK LITERATURE CRITICISM (BLC) AND BLACK LITERATURE CRITICISM SUPPLEMENT (BLCS)*
Authors of books for children and young adults	*CHILDREN'S LITERATURE REVIEW (CLR)*
Dramatists	*DRAMA CRITICISM (DC)*
Hispanic writers of the late nineteenth and twentieth centuries	*HISPANIC LITERATURE CRITICISM (HLC)*
Native North American writers and orators of the eighteenth, nineteenth, and twentieth centuries	*NATIVE NORTH AMERICAN LITERATURE (NNAL)*
Poets	*POETRY CRITICISM (PC)*
Short story writers	*SHORT STORY CRITICISM (SSC)*
Major authors from the Renaissance to the present	*WORLD LITERATURE CRITICISM, 1500 TO THE PRESENT (WLC)*
Major authors and works from the Bible to the present	*WORLD LITERATURE CRITICISM SUPPLEMENT (WLCS)*

ISSN 0091-3421

Volume 117

Contemporary Literary Criticism

Criticism of the Works
of Today's Novelists, Poets, Playwrights,
Short Story Writers, Scriptwriters, and
Other Creative Writers

Jeffrey W. Hunter
Timothy J. White
EDITORS

Tim Akers
Angela Y. Jones
Daniel Jones
Deborah A. Schmitt
Polly A. Vedder
Kathleen Wilson
ASSOCIATE EDITORS

The Gale Group

DETROIT • SAN FRANCISCO • LONDON • BOSTON • WOODBRIDGE, CT

STAFF

Jeffrey W. Hunter, Timothy J. White, *Editors*

s, Angela Y. Jones, Daniel Jones, Deborah A. Schmitt,
Polly Vedder, and Kathleen Wilson, *Associate Editors*

Kimberly F. Smilay, *Permissions Specialist*
Kelly Quin, *Permissions Associate*
Sandy Gore, *Permissions Assistant*

Victoria B. Cariappa, *Research Manager*
Julia C. Daniel, Tamara C. Nott, Michele P. Pica, Tracie A. Richardson,
Norma Sawaya, and Cheryl L. Warnock, *Research Associates*
Laura C. Bissey, Alfred A. Gardner I, and Sean R. Smith, *Research Assistants*

Mary Beth Trimper, *Production Director*
Cindy Range, *Production Assistant*

Barbara J. Yarrow, *Graphic Services Manager*
Sherrell Hobbs, *Macintosh Artist*
Randy Bassett, *Image Database Supervisor*
Robert Duncan and Mikal Ansari, *Scanner Operators*
Pamela Reed, *Imaging Coordinator*

Library of Congress Catalog Card Number 76-46132
ISBN 0-7876-3192-2
ISSN 0091-3421

Printed in the United States of America
10 9 8 7 6 5 4 3 2 1

Contents

Preface vii

Acknowledgments xi

Preface

A Comprehensive Information Source
on Contemporary Literature

Named "one of the twenty-five most distinguished reference titles published during the past twenty-five years" by *Reference Quarterly,* the *Contemporary Literary Criticism (CLC)* series provides readers with critical commentary and general information on more than 2,000 authors now living or who died after December 31, 1959. Previous to the publication of the first volume of *CLC* in 1973, there was no ongoing digest monitoring scholarly and popular sources of critical opinion and explication of modern literature. *CLC,* therefore, has fulfilled an essential need, particularly since the complexity and variety of contemporary literature makes the function of criticism especially important to today's reader.

Scope of the Series

CLC presents significant passages from published criticism of works by creative writers. Since many of the authors covered by *CLC* inspire continual critical commentary, writers are often represented in more than one volume. There is, of course, no duplication of reprinted criticism.

Authors are selected for inclusion for a variety of reasons, among them the publication or dramatic production of a critically acclaimed new work, the reception of a major literary award, revival of interest in past writings, or the adaptation of a literary work to film or television.

Attention is also given to several other groups of writers—authors of considerable public interest—about whose work criticism is often difficult to locate. These include mystery and science fiction writers, literary and social critics, foreign writers, and authors who represent particular ethnic groups.

Format of the Book

Each *CLC* volume contains individual essays and reviews taken from hundreds of book review periodicals, general magazines, scholarly journals, monographs, and books. Entries include critical evaluations spanning from the beginning of an author's career to the most current commentary. Interviews, feature articles, and other published writings that offer insight into the author's works are also presented. Students, teachers, librarians, and researchers will find that the generous critical and biographical material in *CLC* provides them with vital information required to write a term paper, analyze a poem, or lead a book discussion group. In addition, complete bibliographical citations note the original source and all of the information necessary for a term paper footnote or bibliography.

Features

A *CLC* author entry consists of the following elements:

- The **Author Heading** cites the author's name in the form under which the author has most commonly published, followed by birth date, and death date when applicable. Uncertainty as to a birth or death date is indicated by a question mark.

- A **Portrait** of the author is included when available.

- A brief **Biographical and Critical Introduction** to the author and his or her work precedes the criticism. The first line of the introduction provides the author's full name, pseudonyms (if applicable), nationality, and a listing of genres in which the author has written. To provide users with easier access to information, the biographical and critical essay included in each author entry is divided into four categories: "Introduction," "Biographical Information," "Major Works," and "Critical Reception." The introductions to single-work entries—entries that focus on well known and frequently studied books, short stories, and poems—are similarly organized to quickly provide readers with information on the plot and major characters of the work being discussed, its major themes, and its critical reception. Previous volumes of *CLC* in which the author has been featured are also listed in the introduction.

- A list of **Principal Works** notes the most important writings by the author. When foreign-language works have been translated into English, the English-language version of the title follows in brackets.

- The **Criticism** represents various kinds of critical writing, ranging in form from the brief review to the scholarly exegesis. Essays are selected by the editors to reflect the spectrum of opinion about a specific work or about an author's literary career in general. The critical and biographical materials are presented chronologically, adding a useful perspective to the entry. All titles by the author featured in the entry are printed in boldface type, which enables the reader to easily identify the works being discussed. Publication information (such as publisher names and book prices) and parenthetical numerical references (such as footnotes or page and line references to specific editions of a work) have been deleted at the editor's discretion to provide smoother reading of the text.

- Critical essays are prefaced by **Explanatory Notes** as an additional aid to readers. These notes may provide several types of valuable information, including: the reputation of the critic, the importance of the work of criticism, the commentator's approach to the author's work, the purpose of the criticism, and changes in critical trends regarding the author.

- A complete **Bibliographical Citation** designed to help the user find the original essay or book precedes each critical piece.

- Whenever possible, a recent **Author Interview** accompanies each entry.

- A concise **Further Reading** section appears at the end of entries on authors for whom a significant amount of criticism exists in addition to the pieces reprinted in *CLC*. Each citation in this section is accompanied by a descriptive annotation describing the content of that article. Materials included in this section are grouped under various headings (e.g., Biography, Bibliography, Criticism, and Interviews) to aid users in their search for additional information. Cross-references to other useful sources published by The Gale Group in which the author has appeared are also included: *Authors in the News, Black Writers, Children's Literature Review, Contemporary Authors, Dictionary of Literary Biography, DISCovering Authors, Drama Criticism, Hispanic Literature Criticism, Hispanic Writers, Native North American Literature, Poetry Criticism, Something about the Author, Short Story Criticism, Contemporary Authors Autobiography Series,* and *Something about the Author Autobiography Series.*

Other Features

CLC also includes the following features:

- An **Acknowledgments** section lists the copyright holders who have granted permission to reprint material in this volume of *CLC*. It does not, however, list every book or periodical reprinted or consulted during the preparation of the volume.

- Each new volume of *CLC* includes a **Cumulative Topic Index,** which lists all literary topics treated in *CLC, NCLC, TCLC,* and *LC 1400-1800.*

- A **Cumulative Author Index** lists all the authors who have appeared in the various literary criticism series published by The Gale Group, with cross-references to Gale's biographical and autobiographical series. A full listing of the series referenced there appears on the first page of the indexes of this volume. Readers will welcome this cumulated author index as a useful tool for locating an author within the various series. The index, which lists birth and death dates when available, will be particularly valuable for those authors who are identified with a certain period but whose death dates cause them to be placed in another, or for those authors whose careers span two periods. For example, Ernest Hemingway is found in *CLC,* yet F. Scott Fitzgerald, a writer often associated with him, is found in *Twentieth-Century Literary Criticism.*

- A **Cumulative Nationality Index** alphabetically lists all authors featured in *CLC* by nationality, followed by numbers corresponding to the volumes in which the authors appear.

- An alphabetical **Title Index** accompanies each volume of *CLC*. Listings are followed by the author's name and the corresponding page numbers where the titles are discussed. English translations of foreign titles and variations of titles are cross-referenced to the title under which a work was originally published. Titles of novels, novellas, dramas, films, record albums, and poetry, short story, and essay collections are printed in italics, while all individual poems, short stories, essays, and songs are printed in roman type within quotation marks; when published separately (e.g., T. S. Eliot's poem *The Waste Land),* the titles of long poems are printed in italics.

- In response to numerous suggestions from librarians, Gale has also produced a **Special Paperbound Edition** of the *CLC* title index. This annual cumulation, which alphabetically lists all titles reviewed in the series, is available to all customers. Additional copies of the index are available upon request. Librarians and patrons will welcome this separate index: it saves shelf space, is easy to use, and is recyclable upon receipt of the next edition.

Citing *Contemporary Literary Criticism*

When writing papers, students who quote directly from any volume in the Literary Criticism Series may use the following general forms to footnote reprinted criticism. The first example pertains to material drawn from periodicals, the second to material reprinted in books:

[1]Alfred Cismaru, "Making the Best of It," *The New Republic,* 207, No. 24, (December 7, 1992), 30, 32; excerpted and reprinted in *Contemporary Literary Criticism,* Vol. 85, ed. Christopher Giroux (Detroit: Gale, 1995), pp. 73-4.

[2]Yvor Winters, *The Post-Symbolist Methods* (Allen Swallow, 1967); excerpted and reprinted in *Contemporary Literary Criticism,* Vol. 85, ed. Christopher Giroux (Detroit: Gale, 1995), pp. 223-26.

Suggestions Are Welcome

The editors hope that readers will find *CLC* a useful reference tool and welcome comments about the work. Send comments and suggestions to: Editors, *Contemporary Literary Criticism,* The Gale Group, 27500 Drake Rd., Farmington Hills, MI 48333-3535.

Acknowledgments

The editors wish to thank the copyright holders of the excerpted criticism included in this volume and the permissions managers of many book and magazine publishing companies for assisting us in securing reproduction rights. We are also grateful to the staffs of the Detroit Public Library, the Library of Congress, the University of Detroit Mercy Library, Wayne State University Purdy/Kresge Library Complex, and the University of Michigan Libraries for making their resources available to us. Following is a list of the copyright holders who have granted us permission to reproduce material in this volume of *CLC*. Every effort has been made to trace copyright, but if omissions have been made, please let us know.

COPYRIGHTED MATERIAL IN *CLC*, VOLUME 117, WERE REPRODUCED FROM THE FOLLOWING PERIODICALS:

American Book Review, v. 7, March-April, 1985; May, 1990; December, 1994. © 1985, 1990, 1994 by *The American Book Review.* All reproduced by permission.—*The American Historical Review,* v. 98, April, 1993. Reproduced by permission.—*Ariel: A Review of International English Literature,* v. 20, April, 1989. Copyright © 1989 The Board of Governors, The University of Calgary. Reproduced by permission of the publisher and the author.—*Arthurian Interpretations,* v. 1, Spring, 1987. Reproduced by permission.—*Australian Literary Studies,* v. 12, October, 1986 for an interview with Thomas Keneally by Laurie Hergenhan; v. 14, October, 1989 for "White Ravens in a World of Violence: German Connections in Thomas Keneally's Fiction" by Irmtraud Petersson; v. 17, May, 1995 for "The Critics Made Me: The Receptions of Thomas Keneally and Australian Literary Culture" by Peter Pierce. All reproduced by permission of the publisher and the respective authors.—*Best Sellers,* v. 27, October 1, 1967. Copyright ©1967, by the University of Scranton. Reproduced by permission .—*Black American Literature Forum,* v. 18, Spring, 1984 for an interview with Nikki Giovanni by Carrington Bonner Copyright © 1984 by the authors. Reproduced by permission of the publisher and the authors.—*The Black Scholar,* v. 1, May, 1970. Copyright 1970 by *The Black Scholar.* Reproduced by permission.—*Book Week—The New York Herald Tribune,* November 14, 1965. © 1965, New York Herald Tribune Inc. All rights reserved. Reproduced by permission.—*Book World—The Washington Post,* for "A Free Spirit of the '60s" by Phillis Crockett. © 1994, Washington Post Book World Service/Washington Post Writers Group. Reproduced by permission of the author, now Noluthando Crockett./ August 16, 1970 for "Wizard Briton" by Sara Blackburn. © 1970, Washington Post Book World Service/Washington Post Writers Group. Reproduced by permission of the author.—*Cambridge Quarterly,* v. IV, Winter, 1969 for "Malcolm X" by R. L. Caserio. Copyright © 1969 by the Editors. Reproduced by permission of the author.—*The CEA Critic,* v. 57, Fall, 1994. Copyright © 1994 by the College English Association, Inc. Reproduced by permission.—*The Centennial Review,* v. XVI, Summer, 1972 for "Autobiography as Fact and Fiction: Franklin, Adams, Malcolm X" by Ross Miller. © 1972 by *The Centennial Review.* Reproduced by permission of the publisher and the author.—*The Chicago Tribune,* October 8, 1995 for "Westward Through the Void" by Allen Barra. © copyrighted 1995, Chicago Tribune Company. All rights reserved. Used by permission of the author.—*Chicago Tribune Books,* April 19, 1987 for "Three Collections Keep Alive the Short Story Renaissance" by Alan Cheuse. © copyrighted 1987, Chicago Tribune Company. All rights reserved. Used by permission of the author.—*The Cimarron Review,* v. 83, April, 1988. Copyright © 1988 by the Board of Regents for Oklahoma State University. Reproduced by permission of the publisher.—*Cineaste,* v. XIX, 1993. Copyright © 1993 by Cineaste Publishers, Inc. Reproduced by permission.—*CLA Journal,* v. XV, September, 1971. Copyright, 1971 by The College Language Association. Used by permission of The College Language Association.—*Columbia University Forum,* v. 9, Spring, 1966. Reproduced by permission.—*Commonweal,* v. CIII, May 7, 1976; July 5, 1992. Copyright © 1976, 1992 Commonweal Publishing Co., Inc. Both reproduced by permission of Commonweal Foundation.—*Commonwealth: Novel in English,* v. 6, Spring and Fall, 1993. Reproduced by permission.—*Critique,* v. 33. Fall, 1991. Copyright © 191991 Helen Dwight Reid Educational Foundation. Reproduced with permission of the Helen Dwight Reid Educational Foundation, published by Heldref Publications, 1319 18th Street, NW, Washington, DC 20036-1802.—*Dalhousie Review,* Fall, 1992 for a review of "White Writing: On the Culture of Letters in South Africa" by Derek Cohen. Reproduced by permission of the publisher and the author.—*Diacritics,* v. 27, Summer, 1997. © 1997. Reproduced by permission of The Johns Hopkins University Press.—*Essence,* v. 12, August, 1981 for "My

of the publisher.

COPYRIGHTED MATERIAL IN *CLC*, VOLUME 117, WERE REPRODUCED FROM THE FOLLOWING BOOKS:

PHOTOGRAPHS AND ILLUSTRATIONS APPEARING IN *CLC,* VOLUME 117, WERE RECEIVED FROM THE FOLLOWING SOURCES:

Frederick Barthelme

1943-

American short story writer and novelist.

The following entry presents an overview of Barthelme's career through 1997. For further information on his life and works, see *CLC*, Volume 36.

INTRODUCTION

Frederick Barthelme is a minimalist writer in the tradition of Ernest Hemingway who has developed a strong cult following. He vividly describes contemporary American urban landscapes, replete with neon signs, strip malls, and fast food joints, and meticulously catalogues the superabundance of brand-name objects to emphasize the depersonalized nature of his characters and their lives.

Biographical Information

Barthelme was born in Houston, Texas, on October 10, 1943, to Donald Barthelme, an architect, and Helen Barthelme, a teacher. Barthelme's initial interest was not in literature; instead, he studied architecture, played in a rock band, and worked as an artist. He studied at Tulane University from 1961 to 1962, the University of Houston from 1962-65, then again in 1966-67, and the Museum of Fine Art in Houston from 1965 to 1966. Barthelme's art work was featured in exhibitions in both Houston and New York City from 1965 until 1974. His early work featured ordinary objects, and then he turned his attention to conceptual art. Barthelme studied creative writing with his older brother Donald and with John Barth, both noted writers of experimental fiction. His first two books, *Rangoon* (1970), a collection of short stories, and *War and War* (1971), a novel, were both very experimental. In 1981 he began publishing short stories in periodicals such as the *New Yorker*. The first of his books to receive critical attention was the short story collection *Moon Deluxe* (1983), which was followed by the acclaimed novel *Second Marriage* (1984).

Major Works

The stories in Barthelme's collection *Moon Deluxe* tackle a theme which runs throughout his fiction: relations between the sexes. The stories focus on middle-aged men struggling as their relationships dissolve and marriages end. The men are lost and lonely, and they become involved in relationships with often bizarre young women. The women in Barthelme's stories are stronger and more aggressive than the male protagonists, and they are often more vibrant and interesting. Barthelme's fiction portrays contemporary American society and the loss of traditional values. Barthelme's characters drift through life without a higher power or moral code to follow—rules are arbitrary and ignored; people are unsure of their own feelings making their relationships casual and tentative. Characters look to the everyday world and ordinary events to fill the void, and Barthelme creates a sense of wonder through his depiction of the commonplace. *Two against One* (1988) follows another of Barthelme's middle-aged protagonists beginning just after his breakup with his wife. There is also the typical Barthelme love triangle involving Edward, his wife Elise, and her lover Roscoe, but the novel represents a departure from Barthelme's usual style as he delves more deeply into his characters inner lives. In *Natural Selection* (1990) Barthelme again focuses on the dissolution of a marriage, but the tone of this novel is darker and more despairing than his earlier work. *The Brothers* (1993) tells the story of Del as he begins a new life following his divorce. First he has an affair with his brother's wife and then begins a relationship with a much younger woman, Jen, who is vibrant and exciting. Barthelme picks up Del and Jen's story again in *Painted Desert* (1995) as the couple searches for meaning while they randomly travel through the American West.

Critical Reception

Reviewers often refer to Barthelme as a minimalist writer. Richard Eder even asserts that *Moon Deluxe* is "a nearly perfect minimalist work." The most often repeated praise concerning Barthelme's work is his ability to portray the contemporary American landscape. Barthelme is also noted for his straightforward style and skillful use of dialogue. In describing Barthelme's writing, Alan Cheuse says, "Barthelme tries time after time to strip away the excess in our lives [and the fat in our rhetoric] to produce a story both usefully spare and accidentally beautiful." Reviewers note that the characters in Barthelme's world are often emotionally ravaged and seem to reappear throughout his fiction with different names. Bette Pesetsky asserts that "Mr. Barthelme's male narrators change names but only occasionally identities. They have no discernible past beyond the woman who left yesterday." In addition to the lack of variety between protagonists from book to book, reviewers complain that the characters are two-dimensional and don't have enough of an inner life. Pesetsky states: "There is no question that Mr. Barthelme creates a landscape that has life. What we want is more of the human spirits who populate this world." As Barthelme's career has progressed, however, reviewers have noticed the addition of more interior reflection in his work, particularly in *Two against One* and *Natural Selection.* Francine Prose notes, "*Two against One* is by far the most powerful, disturbing and interior of Mr. Barthelme's fictions, inviting us to be flies on the wall of a particularly shadowy and unwelcoming corner of its hero's psyche." Despite the many assets reviewers have discovered in Barthelme's fiction, the most sweeping complaint against his work is that it simply skims the surface of things and has no lasting value. Others, however, find Barthelme's ability to portray the lack of depth of contemporary American life as his greatest talent.

PRINCIPAL WORKS

Rangoon (short stories) 1970
War and War (novel) 1971
Moon Deluxe (short stories) 1983
Second Marriage (novel) 1984
Tracer (novel) 1985
Chroma and Other Stories (short stories) 1987
Two against One (novel) 1988
Natural Selection (novel) 1990
The Brothers (novel) 1993
Painted Desert (novel) 1995
Bob the Gambler (novel) 1997

CRITICISM

Ann Hulbert (review date 31 October 1983)

SOURCE: "Welcome the Wimps," in *The New Republic,* October 31, 1983, pp. 35-8.

[*In the following excerpt, Hulbert states that in Barthelme's short story collection* Moon Deluxe, *the author "probes only far enough to note that his characters are always lonely and often nervous."*]

The men in Frederick Barthelme's story collection [*Moon Deluxe*] don't have women they can rely on, and lead irresolute lives as beauties come and go. They are roughly the same age as [Nicholas] Delbanco's characters [in *About My Table*] but the external similarities end there. Single, they live in the Southwest in a garish landscape of bright blue pools, lobster-pink stucco bungalow fast-food places with "oversize foul-color wrapped-in-clear-vinyl menus" worlds away from the natural hues of Delbanco's New England. Those who are employed—and most of these aimless men have no discernible occupation—work for "a company";

what kind of company, or in what kinds of jobs, we never learn. Their main activity consists in puzzling, passive encounters with women.

The interior lives of Barthelme's protagonists are more difficult to describe, even though most of the stories are narrated in the first person. These men are eerily impassive, apparently mesmerized by their gleaming surroundings—especially by sleek women (one man spends days fixated on a succession of gorgeous salesgirls at a mall). In seventeen super-realistically sharp, sometimes funny, but finally inscrutable stories (most of which previously appeared in *The New Yorker*), Barthelme probes only far enough to note that his characters are always lonely and often nervous.

Women are what make them nervous. Generally younger than the narrators, Barthelme's female characters are energetically bizarre where Delbanco's are businesslike, but they too are the assertive figures—not the men. Antonia of the title story is perhaps the most intimidating eyeful of them all:

> . . . she's huge, extraordinary, easily over six feet. Taller than you. Her skin is glass-smooth and her pale eyes are a watery turquoise. Her hair is parted on one side and brushed flat back to her scalp. She [is] . . . wearing khaki shorts and a white T-shirt with "So many men, so little time" silk-screened in two lines across the chest.

As that motto suggests, these women are hungry and in a hurry, and they seem to have Barthelme's quiet men at their mercy. They corral them into cars, jabber at them, impose on them, dump them, while the men nod and feel nervous. Like so many women of yore, the men appear to be ciphers until these manic creatures arrive and rouse them. While the men wait, Barthelme frequently describes them cleaning, like fastidious housewives—emptying the refrigerator, vacuuming the carpet. When they're out with women, they're usually eating, like children—playing with their peas, piling up one-inch squares of roast beef, arranging cream containers into football teams.

What they rarely resemble are grown-up men. They take graphic note of women's bodies, but seem strangely disembodied themselves, conveying no sign of sexual energy. In fact, they're often so aloof that women lose interest (some of them inclining instead to sinister men, or to other women). This female fickleness in turn seems to confirm the men in their cautiousness, although they never reveal their thoughts or hearts. In one story, **"Lumber,"** the subject of relations between the sexes explicitly arises—it's the implicit theme of all of the stories—but the discussion does little to clarify the protagonist's, or Barthelme's, view of the matter. Milby, one of several peripheral brutes in the collection, has just hit his girlfriend Lois and wants to discuss his brutishness with the narrator. "So talk, already," Lois's friend Cherry tells the two men impatiently. "Go get a steak and talk. Be men all over the place. Practice spitting." The docile narrator hardly knows how to rise to this occasion, of course, and he's not sure what to tell Milby, whose anger is so alien to him. "The thing is," Milby sputters over the steak,

> "they take advantage of everything—all the differences—but you can't. You get pissed after a while."

> "Everybody gets pissed." I wonder why I don't tell him what I want to tell him, why he scares me. "Who's this 'they' anyway?"

> "The bitches—what are you, some Holy Ghost or something? I don't need catechism lessons, brother. It's jerks like you screw it up for the rest of us. I'm telling you it just happens, and you're telling me Hail Mary, full of grace. That's a big help."

> "Yeah, O.K.," I say, cutting through my steak. "You're probably right."

It's obvious that he doesn't really think Milby is right, but it's equally clear that this uneasy narrator, like the others in the collection, has no clue about what to expect of women—how much bitchiness, how much sympathy—or of himself.

In their confusion, Barthelme's men generally resort to some version of the gawky nerd gambit: "Hoping for quick intimacy," says the narrator of **"Rain Check,"** "I start telling Lucille the things I'm afraid of." It's hopeless: "Lucille says she's not afraid of anything, so I shut up about loneliness." And when at the very end of the story Lucille apparently decides she's ready for intimacy and asks, "So. What about a shower?" the narrator is as insecure as ever, but cagier now:

> I give her a long look, letting the silence mount up. I stand there with her for a good two minutes, without saying a word, trying to outwait her, trying to see what's what. . . . She smiles at me as if she really does like me. Maybe we've been there longer than two minutes, but when the smile comes, I see her lips a little bit apart and her slightly hooded eyes, and she traces her fingers down my arm from the elbow to the wrist and stops there, loosely hooking her fingernails inside my shirt cuff, pinching my skin with her nails.

However lost and lonely these men may be, they are leery about being found by the reptilian women who abound, and Barthelme doesn't seem to blame them. . . .

Holly Prado (review date 6 October 1985)

SOURCE: A review of *Tracer,* in *Los Angeles Times Book Review,* October 6, 1985, p. 14.

[*In the following review, Prado discusses the emotional landscape of Barthelme's* Tracer.]

Frederick Barthelme's new novel [*Tracer*] is onto some truths about contemporary Americans who exist in emotionally eerie nether worlds. Here, Florida becomes the metaphor for enticements that appear exciting but really have no depth of meaning. At one point, a life-size statue of a horse is trucked into the scene. Great trouble is taken to set the creature on a stretch of beach, but it is, after all, fake; it's only a momentary—and false—diversion.

Martin, "almost" divorced from his wife Alex, finds Alex's sister Dominica a sexual companion, but he also sleeps with Alex when she arrives at Dominica's place on the Gulf. These characters are related to each other, but not truly related at all. They bump into one another's genitals; they talk about sex as if it's vitally important, yet they never fully meet on anything but a fumbling, adolescent level. Dominica tells Martin about an article she's read on "the human parts industry," in which umbilical cords are sold to be used as arteries. In this book, human emotions are transplanted in the same way: Maybe the attachments seem to work for a while, but they don't fit naturally.

Barthelme is terse and scary about this. The vision in *Tracer* is that people damaged by divorce, separations or loss of love never move beyond the damage. They never grow up. They play around.

They seem to make decisions, but the decisions circle back on them. Nobody gets out of anything, although they do eventually exit from Dominica's motel-condo. Martin gets on a plane, just as he arrived on one at the beginning of the novel. Wiser? Freer? Changed? No.

"Maybe I should hang around," he says to Dominica, who replies vaguely, "Maybe I'll call you." He leaves just as lonely, if not lonelier, not unaware of his predicament but seemingly incapable of doing anything about it.

Tracer is full of weary awareness. There's simply not enough energy in this side of the American psyche to ponder large human questions, but people are, at least, direct with one another. They don't have the strength to be anything except pointedly blunt. Dominica asks, "What is this, the end of the known world?"

There's not much fertile past to hold up this kind of literature, and it probably won't be of much importance in the future. But it's important now, a moral lesson in loss of committed romantic love, loss of spirit, loss of self to the extreme where reflections of the self become absurd.

> **There's a sharp eye for contemporary detail at work in the writing [of Tracer], detail that's as soulless as the American dream of love gone sour.**
> **—Holly Prado**

A reader is left with the same unfulfilled longing as the characters: longing for what's really great, what has real value. This makes *Tracer* a cautionary fable about our temptations to defend ourselves against adult life, which is always laced with pain but has to be faced with courage—even battered courage—so that change can occur.

When a child appears, enticingly named Magic, the reader hopes for a moment of vitality, perhaps the discovery of a fresh attitude in Martin. The child even sees a rainbow; surely something will break through now! But Martin's only response is that the little girl "talks a lot."

His defensive emotional state—nothing can awe him—makes change impossible. Barthelme's awfully good at this sort of thing, setting up a moment of possible breakthrough or violence, then snatching it away.

There's a sharp eye for contemporary detail at work in the writing, detail that's as soulless as the American dream of love gone sour. The distances between men and women are chillingly discerned, and the things they notice are impersonal and distanced, too: 800 telephone numbers; "those robot welders on TV news stories"; the popular music that Dominica sways along with, as if it's the only rhythm available to her.

Barthelme has created a world of disenchantment and done it well—even with humor. Not the humor of warm laughter but of maimed feeling pushed to its weirdest shores. It's frightening, but it is, after all, part of what we're about these days.

Roz Kaveney (review date 21 March 1986)

SOURCE: "A Model Muddle," in *Times Literary Supplement*, No. 4329, March 21, 1986, p. 307.

[In the following review, Kaveney asserts that Barthelme's Tracer *provides a "coherent picture of the randomness of contemporary American life."]*

The sheer slimness—sheer as in nylons as well as the merely emphatic—of Frederick Barthelme's second novel [*Tracer*] marks a moderate advance over his already impressive *Second Marriage.* There is here the same seemingly arbitrary proliferation of mildly surreal incidents—a long narrative of sexual paranoia about dwarves, an aggressive hotelier with an electronic box monitoring his brain patterns, a preacher talking of the joys of self-delusion, a small child called Magic who prattles about camels—as top-dressing over the usual sexual muddle of people who have discarded morals but not basic politeness. Here, though, the brevity makes them into a coherent picture of the randomness of contemporary American life, rather than—as seemed to be the case at times in the earlier novel—a lot of good extra bits from abandoned short stories, stuck in as padding.

Like many recent American novels this one deals in a sort of charming amorality whose charm is partly that of freedom from traditional and possibly irrational guilts, partly that of intense tiredness with an existence in which taboos are forgotten rather than ever actually broken. Martin visits, in one of the less fashionable resort towns of Florida, his sister-in-law Dominica, who is trying vaguely to set up a reconciliation between him and her sister Alex before their divorce becomes final; her good intentions in no way preclude her taking him to bed.

Much of the strength of the book comes from Martin's male sense of exclusion from the shared world of the sisters; even Alex's jealous resentment is largely expressed in a private language from which he is essentially and forever excluded. Meanwhile, odd incidents seem to imply that Dominica's ex-husband is trying to pressurize her into abandoning her share of the motel she runs for him; then he turns up on a motorbike and everyone decides that he is so much nicer these days than he used to be that she must be wrong. The campaign of harassment is never traced to source, but Dominica does indeed leave the motel to work on her relationship with Alex, the reconciliation having predictably failed; Martin departs by plane in the same mood of bafflement that he arrived in; accidie and fecklessness seem more closely linked than we had imagined. Quasi-incest and cabbalistic signs in the motel car-park are ultimately not seen as more important to the characters than another motel resident's lectures about pancake-making.

Alan Cheuse (review date 19 April 1987)

SOURCE: "Three Collections Keep Alive the Short Story Renaissance," in *Chicago Tribune Books,* April 19, 1987, p. 6.

[In the following excerpt, Cheuse asserts that the stories in

Barthelme's Chroma, *show "America in hard-edge patterns, colored vividly but with a certain remoteness of the heart."*]

Spring—and the story collections are busting out all over. For those of you who awoke into your lives as serious readers only in this decade you'll believe, upon reading these specific spring books [all of which I recommend], that the recent, much-discussed American short story renaissance is still upon us. For those of you who remember Sherwood Anderson, you'll recall that from early in this century onward American writers turned the genre into multiple worlds in the short form, and a truly national treasure.

Nothing could appear more American than the style Frederick Barthelme has been trying over the last few years to perfect. As in the moment in the story from this collection, [*Chroma,*] called **"Cut Glass"** when a man sits in his Chicago hotel room and studies high-tech architecture magazines with photographs of homes "in which plainness is elevated to unbearable beauty," Barthelme tries time after time to strip away the excess in our lives [and the fat in our rhetoric] to produce a story both usefully spare and accidentally beautiful. Sometimes this works well, as in the lead story in this group **"Driver."** A California couple, now staid and middle-class but once long ago quite wild, recapture some of their old strangeness by trading their Toyota wagon for a low-riding customized Lincoln. "There was an airbrush illustration on the side, between the front and rear wheel wells—a picture of the Blessed Virgin, in aqua-and-white robes, strolling in an orange grove, behind each tree of which was a wolf, lip-curled, saliva shining."

That's about as ferocious as Barthelme's stories get—on the surface. But each sentence is so carefully, so seductively plain and seemingly innocent that the reader doesn't notice the meannness and the madness of this writer's U.S.A. until it's too late. That's in the best stories. In others, the passions of his version of our culture seem so elusive that the writer's passion to put them into narrative remains absent as well, and the reader, like the driver in the short-short **"Trick Scenery,"** discovers that the "splash of your headlights on the road illuminates nothing."

In order to see America in hard-edge patterns, colored vividly but with a certain remoteness of the heart, try these stories. But not too many at one sitting. . . .

Bette Pesetsky (review date 3 May 1987)

SOURCE: "Rites of Shopping," in *New York Times Book Review,* May 3, 1987, p. 12.

[*In the following review, Pesetsky discusses the stories in*

Barthelme's Chroma *and states that "There is no question that Mr. Barthelme creates a landscape that has life. What we want is more of the human spirits who populate this world."*]

Frederick Barthelme, in his second collection of short stories, *Chroma,* drives us through an American urban landscape that has entered folklore. Folklore has a comfortable feeling as we glide past Exxon stations, mall-infested roads, an ex-Dairy Queen reappearing as a Princess Snack. It all sets our charge cards atingle. We are no longer either startled or shocked. We know that Sears will appear, and we nod our heads in recognition. The contemporary reader is too often beset by brand names.

Still, I find an exception in Mr. Barthelme's stories. Consumer passions don't seem pasted on in these stories, but rather create a texture and a spooky land for modern fairy tales. Frederick Barthelme sets this scene with wit and arrow-sharp precision. His object-oriented world is nevertheless a world. In **"Cleo"** we are performing the rite of shopping. "Now the three of us go through a department store at the mall, then split up and agree to meet at the fountain. I head for the mock outdoor cafe and get in line to order a chocolate-filled croissant, but a young guy with ratty hair and a silver shirt open to the waist comes in singing a torch song and pushes in front of me."

Mr. Barthelme's characters stand like skeletons of the urban psyche against this backdrop—they flit, they dawdle, they consume. They perform inexplicable acts. The narrator in **"Driver"** trades in his Toyota for a "killer" car—an ancient Lincoln. In **"Parents"** Agnes yearns for an electric mixer as a symbol of a relationship. We are back in a mall in **"Magic Castle,"** where we find an American Indian. Like the people in his earlier collection, *Moon Deluxe,* the characters in *Chroma* flee, I fear, from one story to the next. Mr. Barthelme's male narrators change names but only occasionally identities. They have no discernible past beyond the woman who left yesterday.

> **There is no question that Mr. Barthelme creates a landscape that has life. What we want is more of the human spirits who populate this world.**
> **—*Betty Pesetsky***

His heroines are jazzy and hyper. They meet conflicts by seeking objects or by withdrawing. In **"Architecture"** Holly wants to get something to eat . . . no, she wants to go shopping . . . no, she wants to go to Virginia. Barring these alternatives, she picks up a hitchhiker and allows him to drive off with her car. Relationships perch on the narrow edges of what you can buy. In **"Perfect Things,"** when Ellen confesses to her husband that she has a lover, the scene moves to all the things they hate, from positioning the window blinds to caring for the lawn, a litany of emotions directed at objects. In the title story people move in and out of one another's lives. "Alicia's taking her weekend with her boyfriend George. It's part of our new deal—she spends every other weekend with him, plus odd nights in between. The rest of the time she's with me. When we started this I thought it'd drive me crazy."

The plots of these stories are slight, the world viewed off-center. Or at the very least, everything is observed through a one-way mirror, where you record what is seen and said, and the connections are to be made later. The reader must infer the meaning from the acutely rendered dialogue. But are we given enough to do this? And does all that desultory conversation mean more than it says? In **"Black Tie"** the couple go for a ride, they come home. "Paul says: 'I like you, Katherine.' 'And why not? I walk, talk, ambulate, somnambulate, fox trot—why not like me?'" I FELT that I knew more about Mr. Barthelme's narrators in two of the shortest of the stories in this collection, **"Trick Scenery"** and **"Restraint."** What marks these stories is the existence of an inner life, free of the elliptical give-and-take that characterizes most of the collection. The male narrators in these stories dream, and yearn for human contact. In **"Trick Scenery"** the narrator's monologue defines his life. "Even without sun the heat of the afternoon, of the early evening, is unbearable, aggravating. With a woman the trees would be pretty and black, silky against the neutral sky—a woman has the power to change things." In **"Restraint"** the narrator is attracted to a woman he passes in the hall. "And the freckles, sweet and off-center, specks floating before her face, under the eyes, hovering like scout ships in advanced mathematical formation, fractals, ready for some mission into this soiled universe." In these two stories the accretion of detail offers us characters with mystery.

There is no question that Mr. Barthelme creates a landscape that has life. What we want is more of the human spirits who populate this world. It is an example of the author's talent that he draws scenes that at first glance appear to be surrealistic; then you carry on and realize that this is our urbanized, wised-up America.

Susan Slocum Hinerfeld (review date 31 May 1987)

SOURCE: A review of *Chroma*, in *Los Angeles Times Book Review*, May 31, 1987, p. 3.

[*In the following review, Slocum Hinerfeld compares the stories in Barthelme's* Chroma *to works of Pop Art.*]

Chroma is purity and intensity of color, and this is indeed a painterly book. Frederick Barthelme's counterparts in the visual arts are Warhol, Lichtenstein, Wesselman—Pop Art iconographers. Theirs is the art of selectivity, the choice of one object, one smile, one gesture, one phrase to represent all others. They are in search of the prototype that epitomizes the universal.

The Pop artist must Stop, Look and Listen. Barthelme is a good listener. He fixes on what he hears and, in a sense, plays it back for us. Is this art? Of course. There is a difference between reality and Realism. One just occurs; the other is created. These creations are vivid.

Barthelme listens to men and women in conversation. Most of it is extraordinary. Women are trying to get tough. "I don't do girl advice anymore," says one. "That's the way I am now. You'd better learn to work around it." "Settle down," orders another, a Lesbian: "Let's don't O.D. on the compassion thing." Men are shaken. An incestuous brother admits, "Getting her married wasn't such a good idea."

It is possible to imagine this whole book told in Lichtenstein comic-strip paintings. Barthelme's characters are flat, deliberately two-dimensional, conventional rather than individual, engaged in a banal present. They have no sentiment or past history, and their future cannot be imagined.

The bursts of dialogue could fit nicely into the bubbles that serve as quotation marks in comics. Everyone appears close-up, outlined, in the foreground—there is no background. The characters—and their cars—fill the frame. Reading Barthelme is a Day-Glo experience.

There is a whole catalogue of lighting effects in *Chroma:* sunlight and moonlight; highlights; fierce contrast between laser-brightness and pitch-dark; striped shadows cast by Levolor blinds. People squint out into the street, and a guy named Ray feels that "Miami Vice" "devalues light."

Like works of Pop Art, these stories are full of brands: Armor-All, Baby Ruth, Cyclone fences, Exxon stations, Danskin, Money and Spin magazines, Pentel, Pez, Pine-Sol, Plexiglas. . . . I could, as Barthelme might say, go on. The point is that we are a society transfixed by advertising; capitalists who are what we buy, stamped with the cachet we can afford.

The brand names lend themselves to games of fantasy and satire. In the middle of the night, a woman who must have as many arms as Shiva brings succor from her bathroom: "a Sucrets, three aspirin, a glass of salt water, a heating pad, a jar of Vicks VapoRub, two Rolaids, a tablespoon of Gelusil, a wet washcloth. . . ." When, in the middle of another night—hardly anyone in this book gets enough sleep—a man stops in "at an off-brand all-night market" for "some liquid refreshment in a sixteen-ounce nonreturnable foam-sleeved bottle," the sudden anonymity is jolting.

Right now, the brand names scintillate on the page. But the effect won't last. What is a D. & H. Red? To quote an S. E. Hinton title, "That Was Then, This Is Now." There will come a time when no man or woman alive will remember the taste of a Baby Ruth.

Meanwhile, the people in this book are hungry. A wandering brother-in-law requests "that chicken thing you do, know the one I'm talking about?" A couple go back to Sears for forgotten popcorn. (Sears is out of popcorn.) A woman driver pulls off the road at a Dairy Queen and says, "Let's get some, want to?" Another woman, looking terrific in the front passenger seat of her husband's lowrider, has a sudden craving for tamales. A gorgeous young wife, discussing her infidelity from the depths of a bubble bath, volunteers to make a cheese ball. "I am dying for cheeseball."

It seems unlikely that this hunger will be assuaged. Life lived on one plane results in nihilism, the sort of emptiness that prompts Peggy Lee to wonder, "Is That All There Is?" Transition between the arts looks easy but isn't. In a strange way, Barthelme's situation is vice versa that of a narrative painter. In that genre of painted emotion, the danger was cloying sweetness. Here it is polyvinyl slickness. In both schools, the art describes the times but cannot transcend them.

Francine Prose (review date 13 November 1988)

SOURCE: "Each Man Hates the Woman He Loves," in *New York Times Book Review,* November 13, 1988, p. 9.

[*In the following review, Prose lauds Barthelme's* Two against One *for its "commitment to plumbing the depths of male ambivalence and sexual confusion."*]

For an alleged minimalist, Frederick Barthelme has always displayed a hearty appetite for the luminous and the extravagant, a faith in the power of serendipity to transform the anesthetized life. His disaffected characters drift through their New South condo complexes, the Hockneyesque poolscapes he has staked out as his turf, their responses so disconnected and elliptical that astonishment has ample room to sneak into the spaces between.

In **"Driver,"** my favorite of his short stories, a young man trades his Toyota for a customized "low rider" decorated with an image of the Virgin Mary surrounded by a pack of wolves; in **"Gila Flambe,"** a man goes to one of those ersatz tropical restaurants that seem perpetually ready to take

Sidney Greenstreet's reservation, and wanders into the middle of some very odd strangers' lives.

What's striking about Frederick Barthelme's third novel, *Two against One,* is how rare these light-filled moments are; to say that is not to criticize the book but simply to observe how his palette has darkened, how his sense of possibility seems drastically to have diminished. His loopy humor and trenchant social observation are still very much in evidence. Yet *Two against One* is by far the most powerful, disturbing and interior of Mr. Barthelme's fictions, inviting us to be flies on the wall of a particularly shadowy and unwelcoming corner of its hero's psyche.

As the novel begins, Edward Lasco—who is celebrating his 40th birthday by "debating with himself the advisability of ordering, from an outfit in California, a complete, prepackaged, do-it-yourself dual-band satellite dish"—receives an unexpected birthday visit from his wife, Elise. Edward and Elise have been living apart for six months, experimenting dispiritedly with what one of their friends calls a "trial sep."

It soon becomes apparent that the rift between them is deeper, more slippery and less hopeful of easy repair than "trial sep" might imply. They are bound by 20 shared years and by what, from moment to moment, seems convincingly like love. Yet there is also hatred, contempt and, most damagingly, Edward's lack of sexual desire for his wife, a near revulsion compounded of irritation, guilt and personal history, of the "things they had done together—arguments, and talk, caring, her needs and his, all the ideas, the moments of heartbreak and hatred, all the opinions, all the fights, all the affections." The result is a complicated and apparently terminal distaste for what Edward experiences as Elise's "her-ness," the smallest manifestations of her psychic and sexual self: "He didn't like her voice sometimes, the way she sounded when she was talking, smoking. The shrillness of it. The artificial excitement. The giggling. . . . He'd spent some time looking at her skin, and little bits of bra. He thought it was tacky when other women let their underclothes show . . . but the same tiny indiscretion in Elise made him loathe her, made him think her tasteless, sloppy, unfit."

Fans of Frederick Barthelme's two previous novels—*Second Marriage* and *Tracer*—will not be entirely surprised when this knot works itself into a love triangle. Actually, *Two against One* includes several intersecting triangles, though the only remotely threatening one connects Edward and Elise and Elise's sometime lover, Roscoe. In the earlier novels such triads were at least partly the result of mischievous and unruly desire, but mischief—and desire—are at a premium here, and it has never been more heartbreakingly transparent that all this romantic geometry is just a symptom of something gone wrong.

As should be clear by now, the combative note and the bad odds of the novel's title refer to the sex war waged unceasingly in its pages. In its determination to pare away the layers of irony, casual self-deception and bravado that obscure the reality of modern marriage, *Two against One* is intermittently shocking and admirably brave. And—at least for this female reader—the book is charged throughout with the voyeuristic fascination of a report from behind enemy lines. Without psychologizing or overstepping the boundaries of its witty fictional world, the novel confronts areas of male sexuality—fear and distrust of women, the compulsion to separate sex from love, to have what Mr. Barthelme calls "the body without the head," and even a certain dislike for the messiness of sex itself—that have rarely been written about so honestly, not for fear of alarming women (when has that ever been a limiting factor?) but because of the challenge these issues pose to men's sense of themselves and to our traditional notions of manhood.

What keeps the novel itself from sounding (consciously or unconsciously) misogynistic is its high degree of awareness. Unlike writers who unthinkingly endorse their heroes' worst prejudices and appear to take it as a given that women truly are loathsome because, at unguarded moments, they let scraps of underwear show, Mr. Barthelme monitors Edward's squeamishness and seems, like Edward, tormented by its implications. Unlike novels in which heroes with marital troubles still manage to have a rollicking good time, *Two against One* is so suffused with loneliness and angst that some sections—most notably, a long scene in which Edward and Elise discuss the reasons she left—are almost unbearably painful to read.

There are some unsteady touches. The portrayal of a rather mulish self-styled feminist feels a bit weighted and suspect. A scene of erotic and quasi-ritualistic closeness between Elise and a woman named Kinta makes reality sound like a worst-case male-paranoid fantasy of female bonding and exclusivity. Nonetheless, it's impressive how—given its risky subject matter—the novel elicits our compassion and dismay, rather than our anger.

Like so much of Mr. Barthelme's fiction, *Two against One* is exceptionally readable—funny, deft and engaging. Yet in this book the bizarre, serendipitous moments have been replaced by moments of insight, by a greater commitment to plumbing the depths of male ambivalence and sexual confusion, which Mr. Barthelme has skated on the surface of for so long. At one point Edward says to Elise, "Some of the stuff we did wasn't pretty." The same, I suppose, could be said for what is revealed in these pages. Frederick Barthelme's portrait of the mid-life late-20th-century American married man is not, as they say, a pretty picture, but rather a strong, unsparing one. Reading it, we keep asking: Has it really come to this? Are men and women really so at

odds? This is very much a novel for these unsettling times, when we are learning to recognize the truth by how deeply we long to disbelieve it.

Lem Coley (review date May 1990)

SOURCE: "So Timely and So Different," in *American Book Review,* May, 1990, pp. 20-1.

[*In the following excerpt, Coley discusses how Barthelme's* Two against One *departs from his previous work.*]

Frederick Barthelme's usual setup—Gulf Coast, passive white male protagonist recently uncoupled from his better half—needs no introduction. But *Two against One* is a departure. While the elements are the same, Barthelme has traded in the polished, elliptical play of surfaces that made his reputation. The new look? Long paragraphs of analysis and exposition. In *Two against One* he has pushed himself to go inside his characters at whatever the cost, and the cost is high.

Time was, heroic writers worked their way into the depths to find images of mythic power. Barthelme comes around the final bend to discover a big neon VACANCY sign blinking on and off. Here's Elise, estranged wife of the passive white male protagonist (PWMP), describing Edward, the PWMP, to himself—and they aren't having a fight, the emotional tone is cool—"I mean, you're a nice guy, and all that, you're an interesting problem, but you're not exactly man of the year. You're a little bit anal, right? And you're not a big romantic. I mean, you give new meaning to the concept of room temperature." That 'little bit anal' is what they used to call litotes. Roscoe, a man Elise wants to be the third leg in a semiplatonic threesome with Edward, makes Edward look like Steerforth. The women are Barthelme's usual quirky, fey types and are the agents who move the story. They're cute but lightweight.

I admire his guts. Before hitting forty-five, Barthelme was successful in both senses of the term: he was getting over, and he was producing distinctive, well-made fiction that worked a significant vein of contemporary experience. Here he tries to move beyond what he has done and achieve something more difficult. Merely to present those important phenomena the empty personality and the make-bit-up-as-you-go-along relationship is one thing; to wrestle with them, confront them in fiction, is another.

In a bitter outburst Edward asks if he should feel inadequate because he doesn't "bust some guy's ass in a business deal, then take a whiskey into the yard and have deep thoughts about America?" Rather, what he likes is "to walk from one room to another, mess around in that room for a while, walk back to the room I came out of, rest a while, then walk into a third room and get a Nestle's Crunch ice cream bar and sit down on the couch for a minute, then go in the bathroom and wash my face, then read a magazine—*Consumer Reports* is good. . . ." Ouch.

Now Barthelme doesn't really think that's all there is to Edward. In the lengthy monologues and dialogues about Edward, Elise, why they split up, why they only made love three times in their final year together, what they should do now, Edward reveals a frozen soul. But that takes us into the land of pop psychology, of how-you-say low self-esteem, blocked anger. That territory has been pretty well picked over. Not much left for the writer there.

Many readers find relationships fascinating—a magazine of that name probably exists already—but for the life of me I can't see what difference it makes whether Edward and Elise get back together or not. Nothing is at stake: no children, no property, no common cause. Where I live hardly a week goes by that a man doesn't shoot his estranged wife and often himself as well. The failure of those relationships made a difference. Edward and Elise will just drift on down the river of time either way—a problem they themselves are aware of.

As is Barthelme. In the November 3, 1988 *New York Times Book Review* he had a lucid, important essay called **"On Being Wrong: Convicted Minimalist Spills Beans."** It explains where he's coming from. It says things like "Events are witnessed, not experienced." Or "People don't froth as much in life as they do in realist fiction." In a brilliant bit of sarcasm it argues that the current incarnation of something like *War and Peace* is CNN.

Well, I dunno. You see his point. I just read Madison Smartt Bell's *Soldier's Joy,* which wants to merge with history, and for all its good prose, good intentions, its heart seems synthetic—a bionic book.

And yet, failure to feel history on the nerve ends is one reason folks who go from suburbs to writing programs to teaching jobs will not write like William Burroughs, Nadine Gordimer, or Toni Morrison. Reading Barthelme's essay I thought of Gyorgy Lukács, who says somewhere that yes, Balzac is melodramatic but history is melodramatic. Barthelme grew up in Texas. When he was twenty, Lee Harvey Oswald and Jack Ruby made the headlines and a governor of Texas was shot most melodramatically. Maybe history is too tough to compete with. What novelist could invent a character as rich, sad, strange, and central to the century as Lee Harvey Oswald? . . .

Richard Eder (review date 19 August 1990)

SOURCE: "Minimalist at Mid-Life," in *Los Angeles Times Book Review,* August 19, 1990, pp. 3, 8.

[*In the following review, Eder discusses the minimalism of Barthelme's* Natural Selection.]

Our minimalist fiction writers, chroniclers of the young urban and suburban middle classes, use deflection to write of their fears and passions. Often ingeniously—some of our best writers are minimalists—they suggest the emotions by muting them: heat by coolness; outcry by silence. It is the silence of Sherlock Holmes' celebrated dog that does not bark.

What would a minimalist dog sound like if it did bark? Frederick Barthelme, whose collection of short stories, ***Moon Deluxe,*** was a nearly perfect minimalist work, has made a fascinating and often moving attempt to find out.

Natural Selection is rich in the oblique ironies and the broken-field talking and thinking that we have come to expect of Barthelme, Ann Beattie, Mary Robison, the late Raymond Carver and so many others, but there is a rupture right down the middle. The skin of control is broken. Awkwardly—Barthelme himself can be awkward attempting it—his characters are turned to stare their anguish in the face instead of in smoked and angled mirrors.

A dozen years ago, Peter and Lily were singles. They lived outside Houston in rented poolside apartments with shag rugs and flimsy plasterboard ceilings. They drove to malls and fern bars and went at 11 p.m. for waffles or beer. Now they are married, have good jobs, an 11-year-old son, Charles—as knowing and rueful-witty as his parents—and a suburban house.

It is a tract house, with barbecue, garden shed and wood deck. But as Peter, the narrator, tells us: "The yard has worn patches you recognize. . . . And the deck looks as old as you are, you don't mind sitting on it."

It is, right at the start, one of those seeded sentences that hint at the transition the book is set in, and the transformations that lie ahead. Minimalist couple glimpse middle-age, and beyond that, growing old and dying.

There are no minimalist deaths; they are all the same size. The recognition and acceptance of time passing requires a wrenching alteration of the language we use for our lives. ***Natural Selection*** is about Peter's painful struggle to learn that alteration.

The book takes place in Peter's early mid-life crisis, with excursions into the past when life and love were easily taken on, and disposed of. Peter is restless, bored, rebellious. Lily and Charles are too precious to be disposed of; realizing this, he realizes he cannot dispose of himself; he feels imprisoned and desperate.

The desperation sways in a balance of acute detail and comedy that sometimes recalls Updike in his suburban period, and sometimes, when Peter's comic soliloquy goes wild, Peter De Vries. The narrator jokes blackly with Lily and Charles and they gamely joke back, but something serious is going on.

The husband and father keeps up a litany of gallows-humor rant about the state of the world and the foolishnesses and conformities of American living. When a man does that, at some point his wife and child will get a different message: Are you angry at us? Fed up? Leaving?

Peter, in fact, is on the borderline of a breakdown, signaled when his intellectual rough-and-tumble with Charles edges past joking into a moment or two of real cruelty. He is not a cruel man; he is a decent man riding on the edge of trouble.

He moves tentatively out of the house, returning every day. To have taken that bit of action clarifies things for him; he is freer to own attachment to his life and to his family. He moves back, not quite as tentatively as he moved out; he may be OK. And then life, perhaps fed up with being learned so tardily and for such low, easy tuition, takes a tragic swipe at him.

It is tempting to spell out the tragedy. It would allow me to give an idea of the distance Barthelme is covering in his own evolution. I will only say that the last 20 pages of this brief but spacious book contain a tautly building horror, followed by a cry of despair and regret as powerful as it is astonishing.

I have stressed theme and form at the expense of detail; if Barthelme is breaking his own new ground with the first two, he is on beautifully cultivated home ground with the last.

Peter's and Lily's first date, in flashback, is a comical minimalist *tour de force*. Each pokes a tentative turtle head out of a protective shell; each says zingy things and apologizes for them. He suggests a movie: "I probably can't be boring in a movie." She hates people who say they're boring, she tells him, and soon she is floundering too. "I do this. I need a verbal skill. Just one: Jesus."

Somehow they get to his apartment; she has cleverly arranged for each to take a car so it will work out. Somehow they not only have sex but, without quite admitting it, they make love. The moment of truth comes in the morning when she has carefully arranged breakfast and is self-conscious about it.

"It was delicious," he says. Turtle head retracts: Has he sounded patronizing? "I mean, I meant it was delicious but I didn't mean the other part—you know what I'm talking about?" "The repellent part?" she asks. He knows they must grow old together.

That is no ending, of course, but a beginning; and it is the battle to grow old that Peter is fighting with himself 10 years later. Barthelme's comedy of detail rarely wavers, but it goes deep until, without apparent transition, we are touched.

He manages to suggest, subtly but without deflections, the pain that Peter's life-crisis is causing. His portrait of the 10-year-old Charles gamely trying to play along with his father's moods while keeping his own independence are funny and moving. Even more remarkable is what he does with Lily.

Wonderfully well-voiced, she is fighting not altogether consciously to bring Peter into life. She will try anything: irony, sympathy, argument. She will even *become* him; at one point, she takes up his angry commentary on the state of the world and out-despairs him.

She will even *dream* for him; it is one of the best fictional dreams in a long time. It is a gathering of philosophers who argue by changing their pants. One dons a green pair; another studies it, reflects, and counters by putting on plaid. It is a rejoinder to Peter's despairing vision of entropy. Lily's vision: "The possibility of good fortune."

Not quite everything works. The last 20 pages are breathtaking, but it is not quite the same breath we have been breathing up to then. Thematically, the shift is justified, but fictionally, though not unprepared, it makes the gears complain.

The main difficulty occurs, now and then, with Peter. His reflections about the state of the world and his own state represent, of course, the minimalist's breakthrough. He is confronting, not evading. But these soliloquies are exceedingly rounded and complete. They can suggest Layman's Sunday in church. The sermon, worked on so hard, is more brilliant than the minister's own average effort, but it fights the occasion a little.

Barthelme's battle with his own literary occasion has these roughnesses. No battle is ever tidy. Some, such as this one, are supremely worthwhile.

Amy Hempel (review date 19 August 1990)

SOURCE: "A Hard Life for the Non-poor," in *New York Times Book Review,* August 19, 1990, p. 13.

[*In the following review, Hempel asserts that "if Mr. Barthelme has not here beat his own best time,* Natural Selection *is still a natural progression from the novels that came before."*]

Since the appearance in 1983 of **Moon Deluxe,** Frederick Barthelme's remarkable first collection of stories, one of the constants in his highly praised fiction has been his dead-on presentation of suburban life, of an apartment-complex and mall culture where, as the Holiday Inn slogan puts it, "the best surprise is no surprise." Another constant has been a quality of fast, fresh exchange that makes the dialogue in so many other novels and stories sound like—dialogue. In addition, there has been a tendency for Mr. Barthelme's estranged and self-mockingly "modern" couples to turn into triangles: husband, former wife and former wife's sister (**Tracer**); husband, wife and wife's boyfriend (**Two against One**); husband, wife and husband's first wife (**Second Marriage**). On television, these folks would star in "I Love Loosely."

In **Natural Selection,** Mr. Barthelme's fourth novel, Peter and Lily Wexler's marriage is more the casualty than the cause of their problems—or, more specifically, of his problems. Peter is a 40-year-old fellow who works in "facilitation consulting" and lives in Lazy Lakes, a lakeless subdivision of Houston, not so far from "the new wish-I-was-designed-by-a-famous-architect convention center." He's the kind of guy who instinctively finds flaws and, as befits a Barthelme character, is characteristically witty about his disillusionment.

Peter's complaints are all-encompassing—"no less real for being middle-class"—and are inspired by everything from unscrupulous politicians to his 15-year practice of correcting the spelling in his wife's shopping lists (never in all that time, he notes, has she spelled "raisin" correctly). Still, he's got to wonder whether he's entitled to these laments. According to the news media, Peter tells us, people like him have "no business being angry. Genuine anger was the province of poor, ignorant, violent people . . . people driven by the elemental. Only poverty, cruelty, and abuse earned the large emotions. . . . Embarrassed by our collective good fortune, the journalists redefined authenticity as the kingdom of the raw." This, Peter adds, makes it "a hard life for the non-poor." "Yeah, you've got it rough," his wife says to him. "Tote that bale." Yet she says she'll wait it out. "Flail away," she tells him.

Thinking that the absence of someone to complain to might slow him down, Peter leaves Lily and their baffled son, Charles, a nearly-10-year-old who is thinking of changing his name to Laramie, and moves into another house in another subdivision 10 miles away—this after an "odd, tough, quick talk" in which he tells his wife he is "tired in a new way." "This isn't about disaffection or disconnection or dysfunction," he informs her, "it's about hiding." Off alone in his new house, he has "no goal except to be more easygoing, to let stuff roll off my back more readily; in the meantime I was going private."

In **Natural Selection,** Mr. Barthelme has once again given us people who are staying together but living apart. Here, though, the extramarital doings are incidental; in the course of the separation, Peter has a brief interlude with the former wife of his brother-in-law, Ray, whom he has earlier described as "the bad brother, given to jumbo concepts and get-garish-quick schemes untainted by the reek of success; I liked him."

Peter tempts fate at one point—and his feelings are echoed by his wife—when he allows that things would be simpler, more obvious and less confusing, if something really awful happened. "When things start to look O.K.," he says, "the problems get intricate and insidious." In the meantime, in a macabre kind of bonding, Peter spends some quality time with his son composing a make-believe suicide note. Charles's advice is to make it gruesome. Peter then tries out a gory, excessive version on the boy. "Way to go, Dad" is his son's response.

There is no one thing, no epiphany, that signals to Peter that reconciliation with Lily is really the way to go. But suddenly he finds that he no longer needs to point out the rampant bad behavior he sees in every direction. "I figured other people learned this at sixteen," he thinks, "but for me it was a breakthrough at forty."

Why, then, did this storm of fault-finding come and go? "Who knew?" says Peter. Maybe this, maybe that. Which, if vague, is at least true to life.

Natural Selection is not as funny or full as **Second Marriage,** nor as odd as **Tracer.** It does not have the interior complexity of **Two against One.** But if Mr. Barthelme has not here beat his own best time, **Natural Selection** is still a natural progression from the novels that came before. Sure we continue to be disillusioned and dispirited. But the shocker of the ending to this latest book serves as an old-fashioned moral. Maybe, Mr. Barthelme seems to say, we don't know how good we've got it. Maybe we had better buckle down.

Janet Burroway (review date 10 October 1993)

SOURCE: "Whatever Happens, Happens," in *New York Times Book Review,* October 10, 1993, pp. 14-15.

[*In the following review, Burroway discusses the arbitrary world of Barthelme's* The Brothers.]

There are by now two full generations of Hemingway progeny. The first—exemplified by James Dickey, Harry Crews and Barry Hannah—has stayed in the wild, testing death, alert to betrayal and the bizarre cruelties of nature. The grandsons are more domesticated, likely to live in suburbia. They are nevertheless tough and soft in the same places. Their characters are almost honorable and never quite defeated; they take the strange in stride, and get on in spite of pain; they talk plain, a signal of their sincerity; they need women, and are baffled by their need. Among the grandsons are Richard Ford, whose characters' bafflement is a style in itself, and Tim O'Brien, who sends the innocents off to war in a prose that swings artfully between parody and homage.

Frederick Barthelme is also of this breed, though he brings his characters and their dogged heroism into a world more arbitrary than alienated (divorce is the dark continent), a place of amiable junk and dangers emerging out of left field, through which they mosey, talking hipster Huck.

In his novel *Tracer,* a recently divorced man goes to the Gulf Coast of Florida and fools around with the sister of his ex-wife. In Mr. Barthelme's fine and funny new novel, *The Brothers,* a recently divorced man goes to the Gulf Coast of Mississippi and fools around with the wife of his brother. Neither affair turns out too well, but the pattern of lust, recrimination and acceptance has a kind of haphazard authenticity for both the reader and the parties concerned. Haphazard is the operative word.

Del Tribute arrives in Biloxi in a 16-foot Ryder rent-a-truck because his former father-in-law has given him a condo as a consolation prize. Del's brother, Bud, lives in Biloxi, teaching college in a desultory sort of way; but at the moment he is in California chasing some phantasm of a film career, and the condo is occupied, so Del settles in for the duration with his sister-in-law, Margaret. The two are mutually attracted; they touch and retreat, approach and avoid, don't quite avoid—a 1950's-style tease fest on the sofa. They aren't sure whether they are doing something wrong or even something likely to cause trouble.

Eventually, Bud comes home, the tenant moves out, Del moves in to the condo and takes up with Jen, a sexy fellow drifter young enough to make him feel his age, which is 44 going on 50. Jen is satiny and sassy. She puts out a Day-Glo news bulletin of the goriest stories she can find on her nifty worldwide computer setup. She does stranglers, shot moms, barbecued dogs, detached thumbs, kittens in Ziploc freezer bags. She can't settle on a name for the magazine, which title-surfs from Blood & Slime Weekly to Organ Meats to Warm Digits, but she understands perfectly well why she publishes it. The stories are "easy to follow, easy to understand. You don't get lost, and you don't have to worry about what things mean all the time."

For Del and Jen and Bud and Margaret, things go O.K.; things go along. The problem is that there's just no telling when Jen or, more threateningly, Bud will stir up the uncertain murk of that quasi-incestuous fooling around. You can't tell if it matters, or if the trouble it caused is over with, or if it ever will be. You have to keep worrying about what it means all the time.

Images of drift, passivity and choicelessness pervade every page and even the most violent events of *The Brothers.* We know very little about the marriage that broke up before the novel began, only that Del thinks of it as "still out there, circling in space but lost to the participants." Nor are we allowed to know the aftermath, immediate or eventual, of the novel's last scene, which balances between the awful and nothing much. The characters know that danger is of the wayward kind: "I'd be afraid to have a gun," Margaret says. "How would you stop yourself from playing with it all the time, pointing it out the window at passers-by and stuff?"

In the meantime things are organized on a principle, as Margaret observes, of "Anarchy Lite." Del works as an electronics salesman, and might or might not give it up. He does a stint as factotum for a college retreat, and might or might not get into teaching something or other (the course on rock video, baseball and Madonna is already taken). He encounters "a young person with a life stretching out in front of her like so many unrented videos," and a priest or former priest who confesses: "I don't actually pay attention; I try to figure what I'm supposed to say. Then I say that."

In a marvelous (surely deliberate) glance back to Papa, Mr. Barthelme makes his characters pay a lot of attention to food, worrying about whether the beer is Grolsch or Stelzig's Wheat, pondering a hot dog, proposing a toast at some crisis point, fixing burgers to settle things down, being unable to get through the night without Vienna sausage.

Hinduism holds that a sacred object may be tin or tinsel; it doesn't matter, the point is that it's sacred. *The Brothers* conveys something of that sense and is an only partly ironic paean to tack and flotsam, the tchotchkes of American enterprise.

"Why are you so worried about phony?" Bud asks at one point. "There's nothing wrong with phony stuff; it's just more stuff."

Mr. Barthelme's eloquence is hard to pin down because it is disguised as boy talk, soaring imagery undercut by two kinds of dumb. He gives us a crew of college-prof beach bums, mouthy modem innocents; and his hero, Del, stands at the wet edge of the world with an exact eye and the syntax of the mall. The effect is wonderful, simultaneously vivid and bewildering.

I once heard Carol Bly inveigh against the kind of metaphor that diminishes the natural world by comparison to manufactured things. But for Frederick Barthelme this is the real world, reconstituted, regurgitated and gorgeous. Pelicans drop like daggers into a gunmetal gray sea. A beautiful woman looks like a catalogue, a man is an enormous Q-Tip.

Del, the more spiritual of the brothers, struggles through our trashed and plastic language to express the fundamental cry of art: "It's just this breathtaking world, that's the point. It's like the story's not important—what's important is the way the world looks. That's what makes you feel the stuff."

David Shields (review date 2 January 1994)

SOURCE: "A Breathtaking World," in *Los Angeles Times Book Review,* January 2, 1994, p. 12.

[*In the following review, Shields complains that Barthelme's* The Brothers *lacks some of the virtues of his earlier work, but asserts that this novel "offers the new and genuine pleasure of seeing a Barthelme protagonist tantalizingly close to celebrating the world."*]

It is often said, with some justification, that most novelists have, finally, only one story to tell and that, in book after book, they ring endless changes on a single essential narrative. Over the last 10 years, Frederick Barthelme has been exploring—with escalating precision, wit and emotional power—the same material (marriage, divorce, middle-aged male ennui), the same territory (Southern suburbia) and similar characters (over-educated protagonists in dead-end jobs and their wry, weary wives, ex-wives and sassy young girlfriends.

Barthelme's new novel, *The Brothers,* his seventh book, is told from the astringent point-of-view of Del Tribute, who moves from Houston "to Biloxi because he'd been given a condominium, outright, by his ex-wife's rich father, a going-away present. It was less than a month since the divorce papers were final." When he arrives in Biloxi, Del discovers that his brother, Bud, has left to pursue an exceedingly vague "movie thing" in Los Angeles. Waiting for the tenant of his condominium to move out, Del stays with and comes perilously close to falling in love with Bud's wife, Margaret.

The real romance of the novel, though, is between Del, a 44-year-old stereo salesman, and Jen, a 24-year-old exhibitionist and satirist who surfs Compuserv for mordant wire service stories for "Blood & Slime Weekly," her one-page "Hi-Speed Terrorzine" that she posts around town. Jen is a wonderfully spirited and funny character. In her combination of youth, beauty, sensuality and intelligence she sometimes seems a little too perfect, less a person than a fantasy figure: "She was a soldier in no army, bought no belief system but her own."

When Bud returns from Los Angeles, he and Del and Margaret and even Jen make much ado throughout the rest of the novel about Del's earlier flirtation with Margaret. This proves to be something of a MacGuffin, as the issue is never really explored or resolved but instead only sporadically re-iterated, and *The Brothers* is not best read as a thorough-going examination of a relationship between two brothers. To the extent that this book is about sibling rivalry, though, it defines that rivalry in starkly Darwinian terms: Del's ascent is Bud's descent. The final image of the book is of Bud, gone slightly mad, "swinging left and right, rocking back and forth, his sheet-wrapped head bobbing like an enormous Q-Tip against the little black sky."

As Del says toward the end of the book, speaking to Jen about the weird wire service articles she culls but referring indirectly to the novel's apparent aesthetic: "There isn't any story. It's not the story. It's just this breathtaking world, that's the point. It's like the story's not important—what's important is the way the world looks. That's what makes you feel the stuff. That's what puts you there."

The novel's true subject is Del's attempt to reclaim his presence in the world by seeing it as breathtaking, as beautiful. In the opening paragraph, "[i]t'd quit raining, and the sunlight was glittery as he crossed the bridge over the bay, but his fellow travelers didn't seem to notice the light." When Del and Jen are at the Singing River Mall, "Del thought it was beautiful. 'Nobody really gets this,' he said. 'Nobody sees how gorgeous this is or knows why.'" At another point, Del says about storms that "[t]hey transform everything instantly. It's like suddenly you're in a different world and the junk of your life slides away and you're left with this rapture, this swoon of well-being and rightness. You get the world in its amazing balance."

This swoon of well-being and rightness—the world in its amazing balance—is what Barthelme's protagonists, from his debut story collection, *Moon Deluxe,* to his most recent novel, *Natural Selection,* have explicitly been seeking. Del, like the protagonist of Richard Ford's *The Sportswriter*—to which this book bears a slight resemblance—believes that he can be content if he can learn to skate lightly on the surface of things. When he waxes self-righteously philosophical, Jen, his instructor in the ineluctable modality of the visible, teases him back to reality: "Whoa. It's Deepman. Deepman in the window."

Although Del remains somewhat prone—as do so many of Barthelme's protagonists—to curmudgeonly media critiques and Rush Limbaugh-like pinnings for the way things once were and are supposed to be, the Jen-cure, in general, takes. The final two chapters offer an instructive contrast between Del and Bud. Bud defines his own mini-breakdown in terms of the fact that he can no longer respond to "the scent of [a woman] as she passes you in an aisle, the light trace of her skirt grazing your thigh, or her blouse on your forearm as you reach for a magazine."

For this reader, a passionate Barthelme fan, *The Brothers* lacks *Moon Deluxe's* verbal and psychic pyrotechnics, *Two against One's* emotional rigor, *Natural Selection's* structural perfection. Here, the protagonist's yearnings are granted more than explored. Perhaps familiar chords are getting struck too routinely. Nevertheless, *The Brothers* offers the new and genuine pleasure of seeing a Barthelme protagonist tantalizingly close to celebrating the world. Never has the world, in a Barthelme novel, looked so lovely, more worth celebrating. By the end of the book, "[i]t was one of those nights when the air is like a glove exactly the shape of your body."

Timothy Peters (essay date Spring 1994)

SOURCE: "'80s Pastoral: Frederick Barthelme's *Moon Deluxe* Ten Years On," in *Studies in Short Fiction,* Vol. 31, No. 2, Spring, 1994, pp. 175-86.

[*In the following essay, Peters argues that Barthelme's best contribution is his direct "confrontation of the contemporary American landscape, the terrain of retail and residential sprawl associated with shopping malls, fast food outlets, tract housing, and television."*]

The suburban dreamscape through which Frederick Barthelme's characters shuffle in *Moon Deluxe,* his 1983 debut collection of short stories, now seems as innocent as that lost America of Nabokov's *Lolita.* The comparison is not altogether gratuitous: many of Barthelme's stories involve relationships between older men and young girls or much younger women. Erika Landson, the beautiful 25-year-old restaurateur of **"Gila Flambé,"** tells the narrator that when she married the rich, middle-aged oddball Warren Pelham, she had been in love with him "since I was a kid." **"Feeders"** offers the creepy Cecil Putnam, at once both anxious father and discarded lover: "That's my baby girl you got upstairs," the fiftyish Putnam tells her landlord. In

"Grapette," Barthelme's standard late-thirty-something narrator spends the evening with a young lady named Carmel whose parents, Margaret and Herman, have just given her a new Peugeot for her seventeenth birthday:

> When she was thirteen and I was thirty-three, we had a little romance. Margaret and Herman wrote it off as a crush, but I wasn't so sure. Carmel looked twenty then; I took her to galleries and movies, and we slept together. One of Margaret's therapist friends wondered if it was such a good idea to encourage this; I told Herman that it was wearing on me, too.

Humbert Humbert's claim in *Lolita* that "the old link between the adult world and the child world has been completely severed nowadays by new customs and new laws" finds ample support in the world of Barthelme's stories, though children make infrequent appearances. More often, his narrators justify the view, popular with American women, that American men are themselves just little boys. Henry Pfeister, the narrator of **"Box Step,"** wears mismatched socks and plays repeatedly with a plastic toy dinosaur he has just purchased: at home, in the presence of his sister and of his co-worker Anne (who is also his emerging love interest), he fills the hollow toy with won ton soup and proceeds to spill it all over the table. Later, over what should be an intimate dinner, Henry presents Anne with, not a ring or a rose, but another toy dinosaur. Similarly, the voyeur-narrator of **"Shopgirls,"** like the deviant Humbert, is childlike in his very obsessiveness, and the dreamy, hypnotic tone of the narrative owes much to Humbert's own perverse lyricism. Readers who recall the latter's clothes-shopping spree in Parkington following the death of Charlotte Haze should be able to recognize the "you" of **"Shopgirls"** as a literary descendant of Nabokov's nympholept:

> You watch the pretty salesgirl slide a box of Halston soap onto a low shelf, watch her braid slip off her shoulder, watch like an adolescent as the vent at the neck of her blouse opens slightly—she is twenty, maybe twenty-two, tan, and greatly freckled; she wears a dark-blue V-neck blouse without a collar, and her skirt is white cotton, calf length, slit up the right side to a point just beneath her thigh. Her hair, a soft blond, is pulled straight and close to the scalp, woven at the back into a single thick strand. In the fluorescent light of the display cabinet her eye shadow shines.

Although his stories are often viewed as wry depictions of looking for love in all the wrong places, it is not the "Lolita" theme as such that I wish to pursue in Barthelme. Rather, I want to argue that the real contribution of his first and best book is its direct confrontation of the contemporary American landscape, the terrain of retail and residential sprawl associated with shopping malls, fast-food outlets, tract housing, and television. My argument takes issue with the point of view typified by John W. Aldridge's recent attack on what he calls "assembly-line-fiction," the authors of which:

> seem remarkably oblivious to the realities of social context and physical milieu in general. They do not indicate in their work that they are aware of the ugliness and vapidity of the contemporary urban and suburban environment. They take no critical attitude toward it. It does not provoke them to raise qualitative questions about it—like those, for example, that Mailer, Vonnegut, Gaddis, Pynchon, and Heller have all been provoked to raise—but as is the case with their response to social issues, they appear to perceive it, if at all, as an abstraction or as an entirely neutral medium, as natural and as invisible as the air they breathe. In the K-Mart fiction of Bobbie Ann Mason and Frederick Barthelme—to take notable instances—the environment typified by the K-Mart is not evaluated as the sleazy and soul-deadening thing it is. It is treated simply as a blank space where the action occurs, as a featureless corridor through which the characters move in their unimpeded progress toward inconsequence.

What is implicit here is that only one response to this physical environment is morally possible: an attack upon it as "ugly," "sleazy and soul-deadening." Aldridge in effect faults Barthelme and Mason for not being satirists, like Don DeLillo who "quite deliberately addresses the more ludicrous and cliched features of contemporary life through comic exaggeration inflates them into prime objects of satire." He goes on to describe this environment as:

> open, bland, uniform, monotonous, and at the same time smoothly functional and accommodative like that of a modern housing development or shopping mall. All one can do with either, besides living badly in it, is find it too dull and depressing to be noticed. If a person has grown up in a development and shopped his whole life in a mall—and in this country over the last thirty years a child of the middle classes could scarcely have avoided that calamity—it would not be surprising if his sensibilities were as atrophied as the optic nerves of fish spawned for centuries in caves.

For the literary righteous, the K-Mart environment is an easy target: to find it either "too depressing to be noticed" or worthy only of satire constitutes a failure of the moral imagination. It is also impractical: this environment is not going to go away, and few Americans have the wherewithal to move to or make a more aesthetically satisfying one. Perhaps the

question becomes that of Robert Frost's Oven Bird: "what to make of a diminished thing."

Critics such as Aldridge and the reviewer of *Moon Deluxe* for *Studies in Short Fiction,* Peter LaSalle, reprimand the *New Yorker* school of fiction for drearily reproducing a name-brand existence devoid of event or principle. Such a view is inadequate to the textures of *Moon Deluxe.* For example, neither Aldridge nor Peter LaSalle comments on the setting for Barthelme's stories: the South—Dallas, San Antonio, New Orleans, Biloxi, Mobile. Surely, the failure of these stories to conform in any way to common expectations of Southern writing is significant, mischievously so, like Richard Ford's praise of Detroit and New Jersey in *The Sportswriter.* Indeed, the demographics of *Moon Deluxe* illustrate just how stylized these settings are: there are, for instance, more African Americans in Woody Allen films than in Barthelme's South. Nor are there Jews, Hispanics, or, for that matter, Episcopalians. He does not exclude minorities from his stories so much as exclude racial, ethnic, or religious consciousness at all. Only an occasional Chinese waiter disturbs the relentless whiteness—or rather, blankness—of his characters, even when they are named, as in the eponymous story, **"The Browns."** Otherwise, blacks, Jews, Hispanics, and gay men are absent, though not, interestingly enough, gay women.

Nor are we ever sure what Barthelme's characters do for a living. Where Jerzy Kosinski's protagonists, like Henry James's, are conveniently rich, Barthelme's narrators have the next best thing to wealth: an office job in America, circa 1981. We rarely know, however, what the company does, or what the narrator's job title is, his salary, qualifications, college, or anything. The office gives him the freedom to come and go more or less at will without the pressing need to accomplish anything particular. Virtually our first image in the book is of Henry Pfeister's feet, in **"Box Step,"** "balanced on the taupe Selectric II." The couple having an affair in **"Trip"** are both, technically, on a business trip, but Barthelme is too honest to claim the adjective even for his title. They begin their courtship by "having long and wistful and detailed telephone conversations on the company WATS line, talking about everything that they can think of, even business." The neurotic, 30-year-old "Browns" are, respectively, lawyer and architect, but the story exhibits no interest in the skills, training, or imagination required to perform these occupations, and we never learn the occupation of the narrator of **"The Browns."** On the other hand, Barthelme's characters are not especially worldly: the female roommates of the title story hardly know the difference between cognac and Ripple, nor do they care. Most of his narrators live in large, modern apartment—not condominium—complexes with the kind of pretentious or predictable names that recall the onomastic litanies of *Lolita:* Casa de Sol, Palm Shadows, Forest Royale, Santa Rosa, and

The Creekside. In short, Barthelme's modestly affluent figures must not be mistaken for that infamous '80s animal the yuppie. They have none of the yuppie's careerist drive or manic materialism: they neither work hard nor play hard.

Thus, Barthelme's stories are no more realistic than Kafka's; his Gulf South as much an invention as Faulkner's Yoknapatawpha county. In this regard, Barthelme parts company from Aldridge's other victim, Bobbie Ann Mason, whose work expresses a painful awareness of the changing landscape of her native Kentucky: farms and fields are jostled by strip malls and condo complexes, while the Eurythmics play in the background. Barthelme eliminates that temporal and spatial perspective, and even the kind of pop culture references to which Mason clings. *His* landscape is not changing at all. The organizing conceit of his narrative mode is that no other world exists. His suburbs are not juxtaposed against any city: references to Dallas or Mobile or Biloxi serve only to identify a geographic base. We never set foot inside these places. Likewise, farms, fields, and forests make rare appearances. The conceit is, in effect, that the entire country looks like this. It is the sly bravery of that conceit I wish to emphasize, a bravery in treating the one subject, the contemporary American landscape, that postmodern American fiction has largely failed to deal with in any way except that licensed by Aldridge—satirically. And it is here, especially, that the model of Nabokov becomes relevant.

Reading *Lolita* today, we find that time has only deepened the richness of the parallel its author engineers between Dolores Haze and America, that "lovely, trustful, dreamy, enormous country," which Humbert admits he only "defiled with a sinuous trail of slime." Nabokov's affectionate if unsentimental picture of postwar American popular and roadside tourist culture affects us today in ways that the reader in 1957 could not have been, in ways that Nabokov himself could not have anticipated. Four decades later, that America can only appear eerily Arcadian. The inventory of ordinary pleasures denied Lolita constitutes a portrait of middle-class American childhood, circa 1948. Subsumed into Humbert's larger account of Truman-era American life, the total picture appears positively quaint to 1990s readers who can forget that their narrator is a child molester. If we itemize what is missing from *Lolita*'s world, we might understand this phenomenon: television, for one thing; as for the world outside, though the endless Komfy Kabins, Pine Manor motels, and dairy bars through which Humbert and his charge pass are meant to embody the vulgar retail landscape of middle-class life, we can only envy the absence of the commercial and cultural uniformity that characterizes our own landscape. There are no Pizza Huts in Nabokov, no McDonalds, no Holiday Inns, no Radio Shacks, no CVSs, no Wal-Marts choking off commerce on Ramsdale's main street, no factory outlets, and no shopping malls. The business establish-

ments in *Lolita* are independently, if not imaginatively, named, owned, and operated: its Wace, Colorado can support four drugstore *cum* soda-fountains. Humbert's Parkington shopping spree (see epigraph) would be impossible now in most of the small cities and towns of the US. From Humbert the alien—artist, madman, European—the temples and tenor of middle-class American life elicit an amused if disdainful fascination. His America, unlike his nymphet, is unchanging: his satire takes for granted an American social and physical environment that we spend millions of tax dollars trying to recreate. The poignant thing about the book now is that we are as much aliens in *Lolita*'s America as was the maniacal Humbert.

Such a gap has already opened up between the reader and the America of **Moon Deluxe**. Again, we need only itemize what is missing from his apartment complex pastoral: crime, AIDS, racism, homelessness, drugs; liquor and cigarettes are almost equally rare, as is rock music, or music of any kind, for that matter. Personal computers, microwaves, and portable phones are starting to turn up, but there is hardly any awareness of the outside world at all—no sense of domestic, environmental, or international crisis. Barthelme has Nabokov's trick of making solipsism seem innocent. The three young engineers from Michigan in **"Grapette"** can drive, without self-consciousness, new Toyota Celicas, which they keep in pristine condition. In effect, Barthelme's stories depict the period in which the United States was losing its economic primacy to Japan and Germany but before it had realized it was doing so. It is here, if anywhere, that Barthelme's stories possess an implicit satirical thrust. Otherwise, his world seems utterly a-historical. We are never encouraged, as we are with Ann Beattie's, for example, to associate Barthelme's characters with the sixties. We never think of his narrators as former campus activists or ex-hippies, even though, by their ages, they are of just that generation. He even avoids offering details of hair length or dress that might evoke a more specific period. In this sense, Barthelme's world is more like Harold Pinter's than Ann Beattie's or Bobbie Ann Mason's: in his work the 1960s seems as far away as the 1860s.

At the same time, there is something heroic about Barthelme's refusal—and the refusal of his characters—to look back, to be nostalgic, or even to scheme for a more aesthetically or materially rewarding future. No character in **Moon Deluxe** longs for that restored Victorian or eighteenth-century carriage-house of the yuppie's imaginings; none of them are killing time until they can move to the country. They do not even acknowledge the possibility. Normally, this should suggest a profound deficiency of imagination or moral energy. Even Russell Banks, in defending Barthelme against Aldridge's book, refers to Barthelme's narrators as almost always "unreliable," and compares his characters to William Burroughs's junkies, "drugged by consumerism."

Put simply, either *Moon Deluxe's* characters are moral dead-beats or Barthelme is. But there is another possibility: Barthelme requires us, if I may cite Nabokov once more, "to learn to discern the delicate beauty ever present in the margin of our undeserving journey." Certainly Ann in **"Box Step"** tries:

> After the movie we stop outside the theatre to look at the coming-attraction posters. It's just beginning to get dark, and the street lights are lime against the pale sky. The store signs have come on, blinking in oranges and blues and bright whites; along Snap Street the cars have amber and red running lights. The parking lot has fresh yellow lines on new black-top, and off to the right clear bulbs dangle on black wires over Portofino's Fine Used Cars.
>
> "Pretty," she says, looping her arm through mine and pulling us off the curb toward her car.

Aldridge faults the authors of "assembly-line-fiction" for possessing "apparently no sense that they belong to a literary tradition that might prove nourishing," but Barthelme is, I would argue, essentially working in a mode, if not a genre, that goes back to the eighteenth century: that of the urban, or town, eclogue, and its cousin the mock-pastoral. The narrator of **"The Browns"** mentions, for example, "the kind of movie Hollywood started making in numbers about five or six years ago, in which ordinary life is made fun of and made mysterious and beautiful at the same time." If a bit glib, the formulation could apply as easily to Pope's *Dunciad* or Swift's "Description of a City Shower" as to **"Moon Deluxe"** or **"Shopgirls."** Like Richard Ford, with his rhapsodies on New Jersey in *The Sportswriter,* Barthelme refuses to be embarrassed by the social environment in which he places his characters. This is, I would suggest, the moral center of his work. By living as if there were no other landscape, his characters repudiate the deadening civic nostalgia that so plagues the US with the ersatz, as in Quincy Market in Boston, or Beale Street in Memphis, where even the police station has its own museum attached. All the historic districts, hardwood floors, and fake gas lamps in the world will not bring back what we have given up: Barthelme's characters know that so well they have internalized it. It is we who, like the son Julian in O'Connor's "Everything That Rises Must Converge," still long for a lost gentility we shall never recover.

This is not say that *Moon Deluxe* is some kind of cyberpunk celebration of shopping malls and concrete. Barthelme's acceptance of the contemporary landscape is as much a stylistic device as an end in itself, but it is a device by which he transforms the ordinary into the dreamlike: for his protagonists, ordinary life still possesses a mystery and a promise, even if it is a mystery they are in no hurry to have solved;

and they are not driven by their hormones. Their very diffidence implies an openness, even generosity of spirit. The narrating "you" of **"Shopgirls"** does not really want to meet the objects of his careful watch: when teased with the idea that it would have been "a dream come true" had one of the shopgirls introduced herself to him earlier, he is decidedly unenthusiastic: "I don't know. Not exactly—maybe."

This openness accounts for the voyeurism motif in Barthelme's stories. In the title piece, for example, the narrator Edward has an awkward encounter with two young women, roommates, one a lively blonde, the other a stunning femme fatale. Elements of dialogue and of setting particularly—lush foliage and winding paths amid a modern apartment complex—produce a mysteriousness about the two women, Lily and Antonia, that defies us to apply to them the labels "lesbian" or "bisexual" even after the relevance of those terms is made clear. Upon leaving the couple, Edward muses, "You wonder what it would be like if they invited you to stay the night, to sleep on the splendid yellow couch, to have a hurried breakfast with them before work, to be part of their routine." Likewise, the narrator of **"Exotic Nile,"** seeing a strip of brick houses off a highway, "wondered how it would feel to live out there, with the highway and the big electrical towers." The 16-year-old Violet, a waitress at **"Pie Country,"** claims to be a runaway when she shows up at the door of one of her regular customers, in effect, going undercover in order to meet him: "'You probably wouldn't know me out of uniform,' she says." The fantasies here are not sexual but rather of participation, of contact with another daily reality. In this regard, Barthelme anticipates the wistful daydreaming of Richard Ford's sportswriter, Frank Bascombe, who hopes for an easy intimacy with his prospective father-in-law, "even if Vicki and I didn't work things out": "If his tire went flat some rainy night in Haddam or Hightstown or any place within my area code, he could call me up, I'd drive out to get him . . . he would go off into the Jersey darkness certain he had a friend worthy of his trust." Here and elsewhere, Ford's Frank Bascombe fantasizes about being, in effect, a regular guy. In Barthelme, sometimes even the talk is about voyeurism, as in this discussion from **"Pool Lights"** between a young woman named Dolores Prince and the story's narrator. Even here, the sexual connotations of "watching" take second place to sheer curiosity about other people:

> "I imagine all these people looking out their windows at me. It makes me nervous."
>
> "Oh you can't think about that," Dolores says. She scans the buildings surrounding the pool. "If they look, they look—who gets hurt?" She says this with a coy smile, as if she suspects you watch poolside parties from the apartment window. She wipes more lotion on her thighs. "Some Saturday afternoons in

summer the sunbathers are irresistible, I guess, especially through a slit in the curtains. . . . I like watching them talk to each other. The way they move around gesturing, making faces—it's interesting."

"I know what you mean. And the women aren't bad either."

Ultimately, Barthelme leaves us uncertain about the fate of his characters and uncertain too, perhaps, about the durability of the delicate tones and narrative methods that sustain his '80s pastoral. His work since *Moon Deluxe,* in the short story and in novels, has been inconsistent, while signaling continuing fascinations. Children become increasingly prominent, though Barthelme and his narrators, like many Americans, have trouble balancing the demands of children and marriage, so much so, in fact, that one of his best novels organizes itself by dividing its attention neatly between the narrator's son and his wife. The title of this novel, *Natural Selection,* hints at an increasingly elegiac, even desperate strain. Its ending, a harrowing catastrophe on the highway, contains two things absent from *Moon Deluxe:* violence and death. That novel and its title might remind us that suggestions of the fragility of life occasionally do surface in the earlier work. The dinosaur of **"Box Step"** alludes to a possibility of extinction that *Natural Selection* only confirms. Indeed, *Moon Deluxe* contains several references to extinct, endangered, or exotic animals: the dying aquarians of **"Fish,"** a wolf in the title story, the reptiles of **"Gila Flambé."** On a more domestic front, the fight between neighboring dogs that inaugurates **"The Browns"** catches the reader by surprise, not only by the reference to fighting, but by the very presence of the dogs themselves, emblematic of a daily world of biology and animality that is itself largely missing from *Moon Deluxe.* With rare exceptions, not only are there no children in these stories, there are no parents. Perhaps the most endangered species in *Moon Deluxe* is its single, childless, male narrator. Henry Pfeister in **"Box Step"** confesses to Ann that he feels "nervous . . . all the time. I don't know why." Later she dances the box step not with Henry but with his toy dinosaur. A photograph in Lily and Antonia's apartment in **"Moon Deluxe"** "shows a man with a black fedora and cane rolled up in a rug in a small room whose only other occupant is a wolf." In both this story and in **"Monster Deal"**—surely, a conscious reworking of the former—the narrator loses out in the competition for a sexual mate to, not a male rival, but a woman. Barthelme's bachelor is frequently confronted with a feminine vitality that overawes him, a vitality invariably signaled by great height. The 16-year-old Violet who shows up mysteriously at the narrator's door is six-feet tall, we're told; later, the two of them encounter a slow-witted if gentle giant, the seven-foot-four Sidney, who seeks only the pleasure of driving the narrator's Rabbit. Antonia, a man-eater of sorts

("So many men, so little time," her T-shirt reads) is "Huge, extraordinary, easily over six feet." Another narrator describes his unexpected guest Tina as "a monster . . . Six feet if she's an inch." Barthelme allows the exotic vitality of his women characters to highlight the limitations of his male protagonists. In a scene near the end of **"Grapette,"** its male narrator loses contact with the earth altogether as he levitates on a La-Z-Boy recliner, "pushing back until I'm horizontal, floating in the middle of the living room." The scene concludes **"Grapette,"** in fact, with one of the few hints of longing and regret in the whole of *Moon Deluxe.* Having returned from a ride in her new car, and spurning an invitation from the party-animal engineers, the narrator catches the curiosity of Carmel when he mentions the eponymous beverage, now, alas, long extinct:

"What is it?"

"The end of the world as we have known it."

"Oh."

"Little purple bottles, six ounces." I wave my hand and twist my head to one side so I can see her on the couch. "Grapette kind of went away, I guess. I hate that."

She's still for a minute, then squirms up on the sofa and pulls the white cushion into her lap turning to face me. "Are you sure? Maybe we ought to go find some, maybe it's still out there."

It is, significantly, the ex-nymphet Carmel and not the narrator who voices that hope, as if the soft drink's childish name suddenly evokes for her an innocence she let go of too soon. But the slightly apocalyptic note here is not the collection's last word. Although its title suggests yet another of the deferred or defused encounters so common in *Moon Deluxe,* the final story, **"Rain Check,"** leaves us with Barthelme's narrator nearing 40, bloodied but unbowed, walking his date (almost half his age) to her door "just the way I've been walking women to their doors for better than twenty years." The narrator might well be bloodied, since his uncomfortable dinner with Lucille is followed by an accident on the road: their car collides with an ASPCA truck. The closing paragraph of the story suggests that there may be hope yet for Barthelme's bachelors; and for readers who remember their Swift, the scene may also justify my allusion earlier to his "Description of a City Shower":

Then, with the garbage men going up and down the street singing some kind of lilting reggae tune, and the cans clanking around and rolling in the gutter when they're thrown from the truck back toward where they were picked up, Lucille says haltingly,

"So. What about a shower?" I give her a long look, letting the silence mount up. I stand there with her for a good two minutes, without saying a word, trying to outwait her, trying to see what's what. It's nearly five o'clock and the light out is delicate and pink. The garbage song dies off up the block, and half a dozen fatigued-looking kids in matching jackets pull up in a green Dodge and pile into the street, making catcalls and whistling and pointing at us. She smiles at me as if she really does like me. Maybe we've been there longer than two minutes, but when the smile comes, I see her lips a little bit apart and her slightly hooded eyes, and she traces her fingers down my arm from the elbow to the wrist and stops there, loosely hooking her fingertips inside my shirt cuff, pinching my skin with her nails.

Robert H. Brinkmeyer, Jr. (essay date Fall 1994)

SOURCE: "Suburban Culture, Imaginative Wonder: The Fiction of Frederick Barthelme," in *Studies in the Literary Imagination,* Vol. XXVII, No. 2, Fall, 1994, pp. 105-14.

[*In the following essay, Brinkmeyer discusses the suburban world of Barthelme's fiction.*]

In Frederick Barthelme's most recent novel, *The Brothers,* a forty-four-year-old divorcee, Del, recounts to his girlfriend Jen a terrifying apocalyptic dream he has had. In a world of huge concrete towers and structures, scores of people are crushed by huge earth equipment, and a remnant of survivors attempts to rebuild the world amidst mountains of rubble and a river of sewage. Jen asks Del what it all means, "What's the story, exactly?" Del responds: "There isn't any story. It's not the story. It's just this breathtaking world, that's the point. It's like the story's not important—what's important is the way the world looks. That's what makes you feel the stuff. That's what puts you there." Aside from what they reveal about his own outlook, Del's suggestive comments call to mind Eudora Welty's observations in her famous essay, "Place in Fiction." There Welty argues that setting, rather than plot, most fundamentally determines the character of a work of fiction. "Every story would be another story, and unrecognizable as art, if it took up its characters and plot and happened somewhere else," Welty writes. "Imagine *Swann's Way* laid in London, or *The Magic Mountain* in Spain, or *Green Mansions* in the Black Forest. The very notion of moving a novel brings ruder havoc to the mind and affections than would a century's alterations in its time." For Welty, only by seeing things in context, placed, can a person focus what she calls "the gigantic, voracious eye of ge-

nius" to recognize the mysterious wonder of life. "The act of focusing itself has beauty and meaning," she writes; "it is the act that, continued in, turns into meditation, into poetry. Indeed, as soon as the least of us stands still, that is the moment something extraordinary is seen to be going on in the world."

Welty's—and Del's—comments on setting and vision in narrative are useful for an understanding of Barthelme's fiction, despite the fact that his fictional world of suburbs and shopping malls is anything but the catastrophic setting of Del's dream and that his postmodernist minimalism shares little with Welty's richly detailed prose. Intriguingly, Barthelme transforms Welty's dynamics of place in a way that Welty, writing in the pre-Sunbelt South, probably never anticipated: he achieves poetry, in Welty's terms, by the detailed evocation of a place—suburbia—that is by its very definition placeless, a place that could be anyplace. By exploiting this fertile contradiction, Barthelme breaks through the seeming sterility of his setting and into a sense of wonder.

Certainly, at first glance, Barthelme's suburban world of apartment complexes, shopping malls, and consumer culture appears far from wondrous. A drab sameness seems to color everything, with most everyone adrift in a world of broken relationships and unsatisfying jobs, gripped by some type of anomie. At their worst, Barthelme's suburban places are ugly consumer strips, as the one described in *Two against One:*

> The highway that split the place in two was bordered on both sides by gas stations and convenience stores and restaurants and nurseries—and these weren't slick, modern, glitzy examples of the breeds. These were low-down, on-the-cheap rehashes: a U-Haul rental place in a former car wash; a video store in a building that still had a purple silhouette of a woman in some kind of aerobics pose on its side; a movie theater in an otherwise empty strip shopping center; a couple of huge blue cedar-sided apartment projects with no cars around them; and hundreds of those tiny prefab wood-siding shacks that you buy off a lot, thrown up along the side of the highway to advertise Bird Heaven, Strings & Things, International Wholesale Outlet, Rug-O-Mania, The Bomb Squad—Edward liked that one—with its "Fireworks to Suit Every Occasion" slogan in Chinese-looking letters under the name, Rent-My-Tux, Hair by Gordie, and the strangest one, a small black building that had "Moose Parts" in crude, handwritten red letters on its roof.

And yet, for all its shoddiness, Barthelme's suburban world always verges on opening into wonder and mystery, visible to those who stand still and look closely. For Martin, the protagonist of *Tracer,* parking lots are sources of endless beauty and mystery:

> I always liked parking lots, especially big ones at dusk, or at night, the way they look, all that open space, the glass in the cars shining, reflecting the lights; different kinds of lots, landscaped ones with cars on different levels, slopes painted with bright directions, boxed trees plum and squat, and wide open ones that stretch hundreds of yards in every direction, punctuated with store signs in harsh colors and careful letters, or curious, circus-like letters that sizzle against dark buildings, or ink-blue sky; and they're wonderful when it rains, or when it has rained, they're even better then than usual because of the way the light splinters and glitters all over the place, and because of how things sound, how it sounds on a cool night when a car rolls through a puddle nearby, or when two or three shoppers walk past, talking, their voices distinct but not quite decipherable, or when there's a breeze going in fits across the blacktop, blowing paper cups in manic half-circles, dragging crumpled cardboard boxes, rolling a soft drink bottle.

Martin's capacity for wonder, his startling response to the ordinary, is precisely what Barthelme's fiction most fundamentally celebrates; and his response can be understood as Barthelme's signpost for how to read his stories and novels about ordinary people in ordinary situations in ordinary settings: keep your eyes posted for the wonder of it all.

Barthelme's celebrations of suburbia signal the tremendous departure his fiction takes from the mainstream Southern literary tradition. Writers of the Southern literary renascence characteristically depicted, with a good deal of regret, the passing of traditional Southern life before the onslaught of modernity. These writers typically foregrounded the loss of cultural stability and identity brought by the demise of traditional culture, and celebrated the heroics of Southerners who sought to transcend the chaos of modernity by affirming traditional values and order. In contrast to their forebears, post-renascent writers, particularly those from the 1960s and after, characteristically have shifted their focus away from matters involving the South's cultural distinctiveness to those involving individuals' existential problems. Few of these later writers have cut themselves off so radically from the previous generation as Barthelme. There is almost nothing of the traditional South left in Barthelme's world: his is the New South, the Sunbelt, an upscale South remade by money and success into a suburban culture that could be just about anywhere in America. It's the Nashville Agrarians' worst nightmare, the Americanization of Dixie. Perhaps most striking in Barthelme's fiction is the absence of Southern self-consciousness. There's no burden of Southern history and

identity because his characters no longer think about such things. Their focus remains fixed almost entirely on present-day matters; if they are haunted at all by the past, it is not by cultural memory but by personal ones, usually those of childhood and early adulthood when life seemed simpler and more vital.

On the level of style, Barthelme also has cut himself loose from mainstream Southern literature, eschewing the rich, elevated language used by so many Southern writers. Fred Hobson has observed that most notable Southern fiction in the twentieth century "has been characterized by a certain elevated sense, a sense . . . of living dramatically, tied both to language and to certain notions about grandeur of person and nobility of purpose, and sometimes both." Barthelme, in contrast, downplays the dramatic, focusing on the quotidian and writing with pared-down rhetoric that has few images and metaphors. This is minimalist literature, close in style to the work of Raymond Carver, Ann Beattie, Bobbie Ann Mason, Tobias Wolff, and others and typified, as Arthur M. Saltzman notes, by "spartan technique and the focus on the tiny fault lines that threaten to open out into violence or defeat." Minimalism is not much in vogue these days, and a number of critics have dismissed Barthelme and other minimalists as writers of the postliterate generation. In this view, minimalism is anorexic, prose stripped of all artfulness portraying weightless characters. It has been derogatorily termed as "Lo-Cal Literature," "Freeze-Dried Fiction," and "Around-the-house-and-in-the-yard Fiction"—that is, writing as dreary as the lives it depicts.

Whatever validity such criticism might have for other writers, it misses an entire realm in Barthelme's fiction. For while Barthelme's work typically focuses on the commonplace, it all the while suggests that the ordinary can be the site of transfiguration. Raymond Carver's observation about portraying the commonplace in fiction certainly applies to Barthelme's depiction of suburban life: "It's possible, in a poem or a short story, to write about commonplace things and objects using commonplace but precise language, and to endow those things—a chair, a window curtain, a fork, a stone, a woman's earring—with immense, even startling power." If Barthelme works for such transformation with his prose, his characters also strive for such regeneration with their lives, seeking to endow the world with mystery and power. This usually occurs when they perceive something familiar—usually a suburban scene, such as a street, shopping mall, parking lot, or apartment complex—from a different angle or in a different light. In *Two against One,* for instance, Edward and Elise sit transfixed before their picture window one night when an ambulance's blue light illuminates the street, their neighborhood transformed before their eyes into a marvelous, pulsating landscape. And later, Edward, on a late-night walk, finds the standing water in a pothole breathtakingly beautiful, which sends him into a reverie about the world around him:

> "Look at this night. It's a beautiful night." He gestured this way and that, pointing out the things he was talking about as he talked about them. "There are some lovely trees. And there are nice houses. There's one, and there's another. And then, above them, the clear night sky, with the twinkling stars twinkling. And below me this fine pavement, pavement of the first quality, fine concrete appropriately curbed, and these handsome street lamps, full of this aggressive blue light that seems to go where no man has gone before, in under the tree limbs, in under the eaves of houses, irradiating the darkness, revealing, revealing. It's a wonderful light."

Reviewers have noted Barthelme's startling evocation of wonder through the commonplace, frequently registering at the same time astonishment at their wonder with his minimalist prose. Francine Prose, for instance, in her review of *Two against One* for the *New York Times Book Review,* writes that

> for an alleged minimalist, Frederick Barthelme has always displayed a hearty appetite for the luminous and the extravagant, a faith in the power of serendipity to transform the anesthetized life. His disaffected characters drift through their New South condo complexes, the Hockneyesque poolscapes he has staked out for his turf, their responses so disconnected and elliptical that astonishment has ample room to sneak into the spaces between.

Critics have also often underscored the unsettling responses to Barthelme's conjoining of the ordinary with the mysterious, pointing to the mixed response of despair and joy that his stories and novels characteristically evoke. In the review cited just above, for instance, Francine Prose writes that *Two against One* elicits "compassion and dismay." *Newsweek's* reviewer of *Second Marriage* observes that Barthelme's "stories may be bleak, but there's a tenderness about them that's both astonishing and pleasing." And David MacFarlane, in a review of *Moon Deluxe* for *MacLeans,* writes that "although Barthelme's effects often have the nightmarish quality of Kafka, there is seldom anything fantastic about his stories"; he finds Barthelme's fictional world "eerie, haunting, strange, but somehow familiar and somehow ordinary."

These unsettled responses to Barthelme's fiction, responses acknowledged but for the most part not analyzed, suggest the extreme power of his fiction, a power that I would suggest resides in the grotesque. Geoffrey Galt Harpham, in *On the Grotesque: Strategies of Contradiction in Art and Lit-*

erature, locates the disturbing power of the grotesque, what he calls "a species of confusion," in its merging of categories normally kept discrete. "Broadly speaking," Harpham writes,

> we apprehend the grotesque in the presence of an entity—an image, object, or experience—simultaneously justifying multiple and mutually exclusive interpretations which commonly stand in relation of high to low, human to subhuman, divine to human, normative to abnormal, with the unifying principle sensed but occluded and imperfectly perceived.

By this reading, the grotesque, found in the gaps between the known and the unknown, knots together the alien with the familiar and challenges the beholder to resolve the ambivalence that this intermingling evokes. Harpham writes of the generative power of the grotesque:

> Fragmented, jumbled, or corrupted representation leads us into the grotesque; and it leads us out of it as well, generating the interpretive activity that seeks closure, either in the discovery of a novel form or in a metaphorical, analogical, or allegorical explanation.

Harpham's reading of the grotesque goes far in explaining the unsettling power of Barthelme's fiction, a fiction that in depicting a world at once surreal and familiar, dreamlike and ordinary, startling and quotidian, challenges the reader to work through his or her ambivalence by generating novel ways of understanding it.

Barthelme's characters, who typically find themselves at some point in their lives overwhelmed by conflicting feelings and confusion, face a similar challenge. Their struggles to come to terms with their ambivalence, usually about love and relationships, form the heart of his fiction. Edward's conflicted feelings toward his estranged wife Elise in *Two against One* typify the struggles of Barthelme's characters: "It was typical of his life with Elise, when he'd had a life with Elise, that he would like her one minute and dislike her the next, that he would find her heartbreaking and lovable and then turn around moments later and find her repellent." Barthelme's characters are generally at such a loss because the old rules of living, those of simple cause and effect, of having obvious problems and obvious solutions, no longer seem to apply to their lives. Peter's discontent in *Natural Selection* is endemic to Barthelme's fictional world:

> "What's wrong is we don't have an obvious problem, something to make it simple. The good thing about misfortune, about being poor, addicted, cut up with a knife, sick with some high-profile disease, is that everything's easy as long as you're under

pressure—it's easy to know what to do, what to think, how to act, what to feel. It's like TV. There are no additional complications. On the other hand you take us, no obvious problems, plenty of food, shelter, a healthy child, a decent life, house, cars, a future of some kind—we should be happy. But when things start to look O.K., the problems get intricate and insidious—it's not easy to figure things out anymore."

The simplicity of which Peter speaks is precisely what most of Barthelme's characters seek; it is a way out of their confusion. But ultimately whatever clarity a character discovers is later mired in ambivalence—the end of the search generates another quest in a continuous process of growing insight and frustration.

The pleasure of even momentary clarity defines the appeal—and the limits—of the gruesome and bizarre stories that Jen in *The Brothers* posts all over bulletin boards and store windows. To the comment from one of her friends that the stories are grotesque, Jen responds:

"Yeah, but they're clear. There's no mistaking them. They're grotesque enough so there's no disguising what goes on in them. It's like all the cartoony plot stuff in books and movies—it makes them easy to follow, easy to understand. You don't get lost, and you don't have to worry about what things mean all the time."

Clearly Jen's stories are not grotesque in Harpham's sense; they are merely exaggerated tales that elicit clear rather than ambivalent responses and so shut down rather than prompt interpretive activity. This simplistic clarity stands out dramatically against the confusing yet generative world—the grotesque world—in which Barthelme's characters flounder.

In his discussion of the grotesque, Harpham suggests that its uncanny, evocative power is located in the interval, or the frontier, between two opposing realms of order and understanding. Barthelme's suburban world, frequently set along the Gulf Coast, is such an interval, the frontier between city and country, land and sea. This frontier world lacks the coherence of a stable society (it lacks a generally-held, historically-based tradition), and most of the people who live there are pulled alternately—and at times simultaneously—toward an ideal of ultimate freedom (embodied in the act of escape, in the unbounded wilderness) and ultimate community (embodied in the security of conformity, in the hierarchy of structured society). Barthelme's suburbs mix together both ideals, with characters being pulled this way and that in their discontent and in their searches for happiness.

At the one extreme, Barthelme's characters seek out the security of a place in a neatly structured and organized world. They characteristically take great joy in organizing their homes and in keeping things in order. The precision of neatly laid-out subdivisions delights them. In *Two against One,* one of Edward's fondest memories of his marriage with Elise is their weekday evening drives through the suburbs, "where all the houses were alike, and all the office buildings were middle-sized and clad in green or bronze-tinted glass, and the shopping centers were new, with pristine asphalt and bright yellow parking spines patterning the smooth black lots like erratic backbones." On these drives Edward radiates with contentment, awash with

a sense of a world properly ordered, appropriately in control, and at bay. Edward liked looking at the homes they passed, homes where small hopes had been effectively met, thinking of himself both as an integral part of that world, of having a home like that himself, where the warm yellow light from the interior laced the edges of the leaves of the chinaberry tree that stood just outside the glass, and somehow, too, as a glider in that world, a planetary traveler with no exceptional powers or capacities, and every good intention.

Edward's joyful sense of being part of a community—but not being utterly subsumed in it—is echoed throughout Barthelme's fiction when characters delight in living in apartment complexes, where they feel, as Peter does in *Natural Selection,* the "odd comfort of being close to people with whom you have almost nothing in common, the community feeling even though you never talk to these people, and only rarely see them."

Too much community, too much order and stability, however, leads Barthelme's characters into despair. Lurking at all times beneath their joy in suburban order is their fear of the stultifying routine to which such order frequently leads. At its extreme, suburban order becomes the crushing sameness found in the exclusive and restricted retirement community where Jen's parents (in *The Brothers*) live, a community Del terms as "Empty World." Jen characterizes the development as "the kind of place where you only have to print the newspaper once, because nothing ever happens. Everything is cookie-cuttered." Almost all of Barthelme's protagonists are haunted by the fear that their lives are becoming or have become like those who live in such retirement communities: secure but routine, ordered but repetitious, without worry but without wonder. Usually the focus of this discontent is the protagonist's relationship with his or her spouse or lover, a relationship that has not come undone in violence and anger but has devolved from joyous spontaneity into quiet desperation. Some, like Margaret in *The Brothers,* find security in the predictable repetition of such a relationship. "I would die and go to heaven before I'd let Bud go," she says of her husband. "You get sick and tired of everything—every breath, gesture, every nasal note in the voice—but you get over it, and after a while it's like having a big pet around, a dog, a giant monkey lizard." More typically, however, Barthelme's characters come to rage against the everyday details of their marriages or relationships, frequently leaving home to embark on quests to rediscover lost joy and wonder.

Barthelme's suburban world, as a number of critics have pointed out, is a world of things, of artificial objects, not a modernist world of universals, but a postmodernist world of surfaces, textures, and signs. What's most important are not the things themselves, but what one makes of them: it's matter of not being immobilized by one's vision—that is, by thinking in essences, by falling prey to established patterns—but being invigorated by the wonder of the most commonplace object.
—*Robert H. Brinkmeyer, Jr.*

These characters' quests involve breaking out of their everyday routines and living instead by whim and accident. They long for new possibilities and wonder in their lives. Lily's words to Peter in *Natural Selection* suggest what Barthelme's questers seek: "It's all about risk and possibility, it's about love, it's about hope, excitement." For Peter, the complex interweavings of interstate cloverleafs, where at great speeds instantaneous decisions must be made, embody the thrill of danger and possibility that he so desperately wants in his life:

> I knew this part of the freeway, of course, we'd been through it a hundred times, five hundred times, but it never failed to stun me with its complexity, its grace, the danger of its intersections, the quirkiness of the linkages drivers routinely made, day after day, the quickness with which decisions came upon you. One moment you were on track, moving forward at freeway speeds, knowing exactly where you were and where you were going, where you were supposed to be in this elaborate set of intersections, and the next moment was a chaos of possibilities, of exits flashing by faster than you could figure which they were, where they went, of ramps cantilevered off in odd directions, of stacked and clustered signs pointing out connections to Interstate 59, 75, 31 East. . . .

As Peter suggests here, there is both joy in the routine, in

knowing one's way, and joy in the possibility of cutting loose, of spontaneously setting off in new directions. Most of Barthelme's characters seek this mix of order and disorder in their lives, an interweaving that mirrors Peter's reading of the interstate and more generally the suburbs in which they live. On a more profound level, it is an interweaving suggestive of Harpham's grotesque, a generative confusion.

How Barthelme's characters respond to the ambivalence generated by suburban life in large part determines whether or not they reinscribe wonder back into their lives. Only by embracing their confusion and attempting to work through it does a person invigorate his or her vision to the mysterious beauty of the commonplace. In *The Brothers,* an ex-priest, Marco D'Lo, describes how when he was in religious life the outside world looked fresh and alive. "When you're in there you think there's a whole world out here, a whole range of experiences, a fabulous array of things to do, ideas to have, women to meet," he says. "It's all bullshit. You get out, and there's nothing out here." But as Barthelme's fiction makes clear, Marco is wrong; there is something out there, the suburbs, a grotesque interval of order and disorder cluttered with things and spaces not of themselves mysterious and wondrous, but regenerative in their challenge to the active imagination to make them so. Barthelme's suburban world, as a number of critics have pointed out, is a world of things, of artificial objects, not a modernist world of universals, but a postmodernist world of surfaces, textures, and signs. What's most important are not the things themselves, but what one makes of them: it's matter of not being immobilized by one's vision—that is, by thinking in essences, by falling prey to established patterns—but being invigorated by the wonder of the most commonplace object. In rupturing everyday routine and celebrating everyday matters, a person delights in the festive play of the imagination. Even such a mundane occurrence as lamb chops on the grill, as we see in *Natural Selection,* can inspire festive wonder. "Lamb chops," Peter muses as he thinks about dinner, "and suddenly the world was new, a place of mystery and possibility."

At first glance, it is tempting to dismiss Barthelme's (and indeed all of America's) suburbia as an ugly hodge-podge of subdivisions, shopping strips, and malls where everyday life has lost vitality and significance. But as becomes apparent with closer examination, Barthelme suggests that even in this world of surfaces and commodification, and indeed in part because of these conditions, the human imagination still possesses the power to transfix and transfigure, to remake anew. That a simple object can inspire such imaginative mystery may in fact be largely explained by the possibility that the creation of imaginative wonder in the mind mirrors the production of material things in the world. As Elaine Scarry demonstrates in *The Body in Pain: The Making and Unmaking of the World,* the creation of artifact, be it poem or chair, involves an arc of action, a projection of imaginative vision by the maker and then, because of the power of the artifact to remake sentience (a poem alters the way we see things, a chair the way we sit), a return back to the maker who is remade in the process. "It is this total, self-amplifying arc of action," Scarry writes,

> rather than the discrete object, that the human maker makes: the made object is simply the made-locus across which the power of creation is magnified and redirected back onto its human agents who are now caught up in the cascade of self-revision they have themselves authored.

In their abundance of objects and signs, Barthelme's suburbs everywhere announce themselves as constructed, as artifacts, by Scarry's reading as sites of wonder—and so they are appropriate sites for Barthelme's characters to construct their lives by imaginative wonder.

The natural world in Barthelme's fiction also can inspire creative remaking, but generally only when it is perceived as something made, when it is seen metaphorically as a constructed object—for instance, when clouds are seen as plates or spills of Cool Whip. Such metaphors do not diminish Barthelme's characters' appreciation of the world but actually enrich it; as Janet Burroway writes in her review of *The Brothers,* the natural world understood as the man-made is for Barthelme "the real world, reconstituted, regurgitated and gorgeous." Reconstituted, regurgitated, and gorgeous is also a way for us to understand Barthelme's suburbia, a grotesque world clustered with the everyday objects of modern life and remade by the imagination into a world of possibility and joy.

Robert Siegle (review date December 1994)

SOURCE: "While (Big) Brother Sleeps," in *American Book Review,* December, 1994, pp. 16, 29-30.

[*In the following excerpt, Siegle asserts that Barthelme's* The Brothers *"tempts sarcasm, since the utterly pathetic and vapid imaginations of its self-indulgent video-victims spill an emptiness that invades the prose of its third-person 'omniscient' narrator."*]

Any novel sounds ridiculous in summary. (1) A rich girl is abducted, raped, and dies; the guy is sorry afterward. (2) A young kid assumes the whole world is to be his; when he ends up broke and alone, he's grateful to become a multinational's gofer. (3) A small town girl marries an old guy and gets bored, but he dies and she marries Mr. Right. (4) A college kid can't handle his sister's unplanned pregnancy and kills himself; the family is bummed out. (5) A pair of brothers get stuck in mid-life crises; one finds himself a young chick, the other winds up pacing the balcony with his head wrapped up with sheets into a big blind ball. [(1) *Clarissa;* (2) *Great Expectations;* (3) *Middlemarch;* (4) *The Sound and the Fury;* (5) *The Brothers.*] You have to hope something happens along the way to redeem the always bad idea of a coherent narrative line.

The last of these cruel summaries reduces Frederick Barthelme's *The Brothers* by almost 262 pages. In those pages we learn more about the titular fellows. Younger brother Del dallies with his sister-in-law (Margaret) and shacks up with "a younger, thinner, pastier" surrogate (Jen) who "made him enviable when they went down the street together" and therefore "produced a feeling of power, inescapably." Older brother Bud wants the American dream machine (literally: he tries to cash in on a former student's Hollywood connections on a blind sojourn at The Coast, but produces only the *cinema verité* of himself working furiously, on nothing, at his desk—it's Del and Margaret's prime entertainment during their almost-affair); Bud gives Del the new machines he buys and doesn't like, gives his department head a hard time, ogles "the lovely Vietnamese girl" working as a bartender at the faculty club.

What do they worry about? Computer peripherals, channel-switching on the cable, whether people will think Jen wears no pants under her long t-shirt, "having a bad hair day," whether a dog or even a baby might be in their future. Del sells stereos; wants to be in his own (tame) remake of *Blue Velvet,* dreams something like *Brazil*'s city landscape vision, gathers grotesque news stories off the Internet for Jen's one-page newsletter (called *Warm Digit* . . .), and begins the novel patronizing the beer sucking kid-popping stringy-haired Pinto crowd (his adjectives) from the comfort of his "riding high in the Vibra-Matic cabin of a sixteen-foot Ryder rent-a-truck with his car and everything he owned or wanted to own, just about, in the back of him and the rest of his life somewhere out in front." Father Marco d'Lo (get it?), on vacation from The Order, wishes he'd stayed inside the cloister: "When you're in there you think there's a whole world out here, a whole range of experiences, a fabulous array of things to do, ideas to have, women to meet. It's all bullshit. You get out, and there's nothing out here."

And Bud, also aptly named, tells us "there's nothing wrong with phony stuff; it's just more stuff," and ends the novel wrapped up in his childhood game (of Invisible Man), "bobbing like an enormous Q-Tip against the little black sky." This novel tempts sarcasm, since the utterly pathetic and vapid imaginations of its self-indulgent video-victims spill an emptiness that invades the prose of its third-person "omniscient" narrator (it's the narrator who actually says "bad hair day," who allows an endless catalog of what they've seen on their drive along the Gulf Coast, as if obsessive-compulsive reality-avoidance syndrome required a realtime recording of whatever happened to be out there on a journal-filling roadtrip). The narrator doesn't wince when Jen interrupts its notion of generation X-speak to say, "That film stuff ruins it for me, disauthenticates it." It all reads sometimes as if it were a malicious trick offered to an *Iron Man* weekend workshop, as if this were all meant to be "just more stuff" in an era when most fiction-for-profit were itself Vibra-Matic, as if the swelled head in the Q-tip image were meant to be Mobius Dick come to clean out our collective ears from the culture machine's Ryder rent-a-life.

Perhaps it simply comes down to what you expect from a "novel." My generation came to Novels from the movies, from comic books, from heroic romances. Novels were amazing to discover, at the right age, because they made their stories connect to the way their societies were wired. From wanting things to work out in the end, we (1) shifted to wanting to see how characters wanting utopia were exercised by the constraints peculiar to their time and place. Timeless tales (the Heroic Thing projected in varying costumes and scenery) still felt like fun, but you didn't try to think with them. When, late into the night, I read Conrad while my big brother slept, I knew I was into something different, something I'd have to think about, something I didn't yet know *how* to think about.

Then there was Ionesco, the *nouveau roman,* Beckett, Burroughs, in no particular order, just as they happened to surface through a friend or someone else's casual reference. And of course others, those who began where Conrad's most marginal "asides" to his "proper" narrative left off, who were themselves left off the syllabi and out of the anthologies, who nonetheless had something to do with life outside the classrooms and suburbs. Once you had learned to read the Novel, you learned to read the para-novel, the novel woven into whatever was not high culture, that used the novel to play out not E=MC2 but something like *energia is matter* multiplied by the exponentiated variable of, well, whatever, it was multiplicity and variability that mattered in a way that would wait around for Deleuze and Guattari to formalize. The Novel, read straight, came to sound like a special case of "the Heroic Thing," but read for self-difference it did something else altogether.

Readers who resent my tone in these paragraphs, for whom "heroic" is a term without stigma ("I *like* Western Culture," a colleague says; "all that other stuff just doesn't *speak* to me." I am thanking this trans-Atlantic traveler for the comment, thinking how many others, in/out of the geographic boundaries, will stay invisible along this itinerary of "Western Culture")—readers for whom the novel is honed on the quotidian grindstone with as little as possible of the oil of alien tongues, with scarcely a notion traceable outside the literary canon, with but a whisper against the grand conjunc-

tion of middle class ethics and trickle-down economies and the more cherished of cultural continuities, such readers will find Barthelme's novel undisturbing, a rearticulation of mid-century American Fiction with a bit of the Bellow/Updike/Percy tilt from neurotic narration. *The Brothers* is not a novel with which to think difference, or even to think differently, though this fact may be relevant only to those readers who recognize some version of their own experience in my literary autobiography paragraphs. . . .

Tom De Haven (review date 24 September 1995)

SOURCE: "Drive, She Said," in *New York Times Book Review,* September 24, 1995, p. 11.

[*In the following review, De Haven complains that while the travel episodes in Barthelme's* Painted Desert *"present some of Mr. Barthelme's best descriptive writing . . . they also contain his weakest, least persuasive fiction."*]

In Frederick Barthelme's new novel, **Painted Desert,** no matter where Del Tribute and his girlfriend, Jen, happen to be—at a coffee shop, a restaurant, the Holiday Inn—they seem also to be at some make-believe broadcasting studio, giving a frank interview. These are the grown children (he's 47, she's 27) of "Nightline" and "Larry King Live," both speaking in premeditatively reckless bursts meant to capture attention and glamorize their complaints. ("We're so cynical that our cynicism takes paint off warships.") These mediaholics are so painfully conscious of the planet—and so convinced that every aspect of it demands an epigrammatic opinion—that it's become a daily struggle just to keep abreast, to stay current. "If we're not actually going to participate in the world," Jen says, "If we're not going to do anything but watch it, then we might as well be good spectators."

It is June 1994, the week O. J. Simpson takes off in the white Bronco. Del, who's on vacation from his "dinky" teaching job at a junior college in Biloxi, agrees to drive to Baton Rouge to meet Jen's father, Mike. It's an awkward visit. A retired insurance man, Mike keeps bringing up the fact that Del is only six years younger than he is. "Doesn't that seem a little odd to you?" Mike says. Whenever he can, Del, hardly the most confrontational of men, slips away—to nap, to brood, to check what's on television.

As a narrator, Del Tribute—who, like Jen, appeared in Mr. Barthelme's previous novel, *The Brothers*—is a mixed blessing. He's witty and likable, personally kind and fully alert to detail, but his obsession with car crashes, plane wrecks, homicides and fires—what he calls "wonderful stuff"—can turn your stomach. Though Del is blind to his ghoulish pro-clivities, at least he's honest about the source of his politi-cal disgust. "Things weren't going to be fixed, and maybe I didn't want them fixed," he tells us. "I needed the mess to complain about, to point to when I wanted to devalue the system, or protect myself with a kind of alibi for my lim-ited prosperity."

One evening at Mike's, while Del and Jen are watching a documentary, they see a videotape from the 1992 Los An-geles riots in which a truck driver's genitals are spray-painted by an assailant. While Del is mostly just amazed that he's never seen this footage before, Jen is outraged by it. On the spot, she decides to leave for California. She's not sure why, but it's—like, you know—a moral compulsion. Sort of. Be-sides, she and Del don't have anything else to do. And while they're out in L. A., they can go see Nicole Simpson's house. O. J.'s, too. And "where Rodney King got it."

Sounds like a plan.

To Del's chagrin, Mike—who also doesn't have anything else to do—asks to come along for the ride. He even offers the use of his big black Lincoln Town Car. Then Jen sug-gests a side trip to Shreveport, where they pick up her mo-rose girlfriend Penny Gibson. At last they're off, California bound.

As so often happens in Mr. Barthelme's stories, events don't follow human intention. Destination doesn't either. Jen's an-gry pilgrimage, a muddled venture from the start, turns into a meandering, touristy swing through the Southwest, with impulse visits to Dallas (Dealey Plaza, of course); Roswell, N.M. (a U.F.O. museum); White Sands; the Grand Canyon, and finally the Painted Desert. Oddly, while these episodes present some of Mr. Barthelme's best descriptive writing (much of it could be excerpted without tinkering for a su-perb travel article), they also contain his weakest, least per-suasive fiction.

Because of Del's lack of access to Mike and Penny's pri-vate moments, their budding romance seems almost perfunc-tory, while Jen's on-the-road E-mail correspondence with a homicidal maniac raises ethical and legal issues the novel has no thought of seriously addressing. But it's the conclu-sion that is most disappointing—and disingenuous.

Mr. Barthelme strongly and seductively suggests that for sheer weirdness, exhilaration and fun, the information su-perhighway is still no match for the old-fashioned mac-adam one, but it would take more than "a little bit of first-order experience, a little bit of contact with the ground, a little reminder of the wonder of things" to make a pair of hard-wired pessimists like Del and Jen suddenly

"feel like saints" and decide to get married. Call me un-romantic, call me a killjoy, but I just don't believe it.

Allen Barra (review date 8 October 1995)

SOURCE: "Westward Through the Void," in *Chicago Tri-bune Books,* October 8, 1995, p. 6.

[*In the following review, Barra complains that "there's noth-ing much at stake" in Barthelme's* Painted Desert, *and that he finds himself "closing [Barthelme's] books with a sense of admiration for his craft but still a little hungry for a novel."*]

Frederick Barthelme is a wonderfully entertaining writer who has built, over the last ten years, a large cult following. It's easy to see why. If you're tuned to Barthelme's wavelength, reading his mildly surreal accounts of Mississippi Gulf middle-class folk, rendered in smooth, dialogue-driven prose, is like gliding along one of those water slides they spread on summer lawns for kids to play on. In fact, read-ing Barthelme anywhere gives you the feeling of reading from your back yard chair in the summer sun. Only, like any-thing you read in the summer sun, Barthelme's fiction is hard to focus on. There's a little too much light, a little too much glare.

The main character in *Painted Desert* is Del Tribute, a part-time communications teacher who Barthelme fans will re-call from his 1993 novel, *The Brothers.* In fact, the two books kind of meld together in the mind, as both do with Barthelme's *Second Marriage.*

This time out, a middle-aged divorced male Barthelme char-acter is given a hot young college-age girlfriend to fool with. (Unlike the middle-aged divorced males in Richard Ford's novels, Barthelme's Del knows something life-sustaining when he smacks into it.) The young woman, Jen, is a "cybermuckraker"—editor of a one-page "magazine" that actually is a randomly distributed collection of horrors culled from tabloid papers. Jen, as they say in that part of the coun-try, is a hoot—good-natured and curious, she wisecracks like Lauren Bacall in a '40s Warner Brothers flick but with a '60s thrust. She also has a snappy way of summing up places and people.

"He likes everything real neat," she says of a neighbor. "No-tice how neat the house is? The neighborhood? He's deeply neat."

Painted Desert wouldn't get much of anywhere without her—not across Mississippi, not to Dealey Plaza in Dallas, not to the Arizona Painted Desert of the title, where Jen and

Del go on a vacation-odyssey in pursuit of the American zeit-geist. Along the way, there's much talk of the O. J. trial and the L. A. riots, all of which fills the air with that vague dread that American novelists as different as Joseph Heller and Don DeLillo are always trying to get to the heart of. They never do, of course, and neither does Barthelme. But with Barthelme you get the unsettling feeling that behind all the jokiness his characters really yearn for some kind of apoca-lypse, if only to stir things up in what otherwise seems like a void. As Del says, "In a sense, I've had an easy life. But in another way it's a punishment, an absence of grand events."

Painted Desert could use a grand event or two; there's noth-ing much at stake in the book. For some readers, this is the heart of Barthelme's appeal—the dialogue is clever, the char-acters are always enjoyably quirky and there's nothing too serious going on to distract one from those pleasures. Oth-ers, like me, find themselves closing his books with a sense of admiration for his craft but still a little hungry for a novel.

When Barthelme is on a roll, the seemingly random events in his fiction add up to a plausible picture of an incoherent world. But we're never given the author's vision of that in-coherence. It's been said that the virtue of Barthelme's style is that he doesn't tell us how we're supposed to feel, but he also doesn't give us any guideposts as to how *he* feels. His obliqueness isn't meant to be a style; it's meant to be a vir-tue.

Because it moves from place to place, *Painted Desert* is even more oblique than his previous books. Barthelme's charac-ters are so stumblingly, amusingly inarticulate that we're of-ten unprepared for the shards of poetic precision the otherwise impersonal author greets us with. One character, glimpsed in passing, is "so thin and pale that he looked like a chapstick with ink on top." A burg Del and Jen pass through is "a ratty little town that dangled off the highway the way a broken leg hangs off a dog that's been hit by a car." A rain is "the lightest rain imaginable" as if it "was slightly embarrassed by being there."

But despite the fine writing, when Jen and Del finally get somewhere, there is, to quote Gertrude Stein on Oakland, no there there. Or perhaps it's that when they get there, they're there—all the there's being much the same.

In Barthelme's world, one place, one situation, one decision offers much the same payoff as any other. What he cannot tell us, though, is why, given such a world, he wants to write novels about it.

***Publishers Weekly* (review date 25 August 1997)**

SOURCE: A review of *Bob the Gambler,* in *Publishers Weekly,* August 25, 1997, p. 42.

[*In the following review, the critic asserts that "the narra-tion* [*of Barthelme's* Bob the Gambler] *is pitch-perfect and the plot is clever, surprising and vibrant with immediacy."*]

Clear-sighted, decent Ray Kaiser narrates his sudden capitu-lation to the allure of Biloxi's Paradise Casino in Barthelme's deftly comic and gently melancholic 11th book [***Bob the Gambler***]. Abandoning his unremunerative architecture firm (running Ray Kaiser Design "is kind of like being a pro bongo player"), he becomes intoxicated by the rituals and the heady promises of big payoffs at the blackjack tables and the slot machines: "It was a joy to see the money move at a sedate pace back and forth the table, as if it had a life of its own, or was reacting to my will, or the dealer's, or even the magic in the cards." His thoroughgoing investment in the casino prompts him to reevaluate everything—looking askance at the architecture profession even as he takes jobs "a little south on the food chain." With bracing good humor and moral nuance, the novel makes this familiar tale fresh again: Ray is as much a husband and father as he is (in his stepdaughter's sardonic parlance) "Bob the Gambler." His relationships with her, his parents and his wife, Jewel, are beguiling and carefully delineated. The unpredictable and morally ambiguous outcome of the tug-of-war between these relationships and the casino distinguish this rueful comedy, in which the narration is pitch-perfect and the plot is clever, surprising and vibrant with immediacy.

FURTHER READING

Criticism

Ingoldby, Grace. "Without a View." *New Statesman* 108, No. 2803 (7 December 1984): 34-5.
>   States that "Barthelme concentrates on suburbia's slip-pery surfaces amusingly and with alarming observation" in the stories of *Moon Deluxe.*

Kaveney, Roz. "Making Themselves Over." *Times Literary Supplement,* No. 4511 (15-21 September 1989): 998.
>   Discusses the relationships in Barthelme's *Two against One.*

A review of *Bob the Gambler. Kirkus Reviews* LXV, No. 17 (1 September 1997): 1323.
>   Calls Barthelme's *Bob the Gambler* "a novel of surpris-ing heart and soul."

Williams, Joan. "All the Lonely People." *Washington Post Book World* XIII, No. 35 (28 August 1983): 9.

Discusses Barthelme's use of characterization in the stories in *Moon Deluxe.*

Additional coverage of Barthelme's life and career is contained in the following sources published by Gale: *Contemporary Authors,* **Vols. 114, and 122; and** *Dictionary of Literary Biography Yearbook,* **Vol. 85.**

J. M. Coetzee

1940-

(Full name John Michael Coetzee) South African novelist, essayist, critic, editor, and translator.

The following entry presents an overview of Coetzee's career through 1997. For further information on his life and works, see *CLC*, Volumes 23, 33, and 66.

INTRODUCTION

Regarded as one of South Africa's most accomplished contemporary novelists, Coetzee examines the effects of racism and colonial oppression in his works. While addressing the brutalities and contradictions associated with the South African policy of apartheid, Coetzee writes from an apolitical viewpoint that extends beyond geographic and social boundaries to achieve universal significance. This effect is enhanced through his use of such literary devices as allegory, unreliable narrators, and enigmatic symbolic settings.

Biographical Information

Coetzee has lived in numerous small towns in rural Cape Province as well as the suburbs of Cape Town, where he was born. He attended the University of Cape Town, where he received undergraduate degrees in mathematics and English by 1961. Moving to London, Coetzee worked for International Business Machines (IBM) as a computer programmer while writing poetry and studying literature in his spare time. "[I spent] the evenings in the British Museum reading Ford Madox Ford," Coetzee wrote, "and the rest of the time tramping the cold streets of London seeking the meaning of life." He eventually gave up computer programming and traveled to the United States to complete his graduate studies in English at the University of Texas; he earned a Ph.D. in 1969. There he became troubled by such events as the Vietnam War and the assassination of South African Prime Minister H. F. Verwoerd. In his first major published work, *Dusklands* (1974), Coetzee addressed the underlying imperialism he sensed in the Vietnam War and applied its meaning to the ongoing sociopolitical situation in South Africa.

Major Works

In the Heart of the Country (1977) was the first of Coetzee's works to be published in both South Africa and the United States. Presented in stream-of-consciousness form, the novel relates the story of Magda, a troubled white woman who murders her father, ostensibly because of his affair with a

young black woman. Unable to adjust to change and doomed by her isolation, Magda is usually considered by critics to represent the stagnant policies of apartheid. Coetzee's strong international reputation was solidified with his next novel, *Waiting for the Barbarians* (1980). Set along the frontier of an unspecified empire, this work addresses oppression through its depiction of a magistrate who must choose between helping to dominate a group of natives known as "the Barbarians" and his desire to ally himself with them. *Waiting for the Barbarians* also examines the poststructuralist theoretical discussion of the meaning of language and signs, particularly within an imperialist context, as the magistrate becomes obsessed with interpreting the meaning of the scars on the body of a young barbarian woman who has been tortured by authorities. *Life and Times of Michael K* (1983) corresponds thematically to Coetzee's earlier works but includes a new dimension in its focus on the oppression of a single character. Michael K is a slow-witted outcast who searches with his mother for a home during a turbulent period of an unnamed country's civil war. Although Coetzee has denied any similarities, critics frequently compare Michael K with the character K in Franz Kafka's novel *The Trial.* In *Foe* (1987) Coetzee returned to an examination of how language contributes to oppression. A retelling of the story of *Robinson Crusoe*, Coetzee's *Foe* features a woman who comes to the writer Foe—actually Daniel Defoe—with her story of Crusoe and the native Friday. When writing the story himself, Foe alters it by presenting its characters as idealistic and enterprising rather than indigent and depressed as the woman had originally described. Coetzee thus addresses the notion that written history can itself be a method of oppression because it is controlled by those who write it. Coetzee's next novel, *Age of Iron* (1990), traces the experiences of Elizabeth Curren, a white South African woman suffering from cancer who writes long letters to her daughter in the United States. Some critics considered this to be Coetzee's most brutal and pessimistic novel because of its detailed explication of the viciousness of apartheid and of the physical deterioration of disease; however, several note that Elizabeth's sentimental musings on childhood and maternal love signify rebirth and human continuity. *The Master of Petersburg* (1994) is an account of Russian novelist Fyodor Dostoyevsky's reaction to his stepson's mysterious fictional involvement with a group of political nihilists and subsequent death. As Dostoyevsky returns to Petersburg from his exile in Dresden in order to find the truth about his stepson's death, he becomes entangled in an increasingly totalitarian political system. Coetzee raises questions about the nature of authoritarianism and truth itself within such a system. Coetzee's essay collections—*White Writing* (1988), *Doubling the Point* (1992), and *Giving Offense* (1996)—all contain his work pertaining to theoretical poststructuralism. In *Giving Offense* Coetzee takes a controversial stance on questions of censorship. Coetzee's memoir, *Boyhood* (1997), is unusual in its third-person present tense style, which allows Coetzee to take an objective, reportorial, tone when discussing the events of his early life.

Critical Reception

Coetzee is widely considered one of the most important contemporary writers exploring the effects of Western imperialism on native culture. Critics have found his focus on the relationship between authorship and authority to be particularly pertinent in the postcolonial, late twentieth century, when questions have been raised by historians and literary theorists about the so-called ownership of history. Many commentators have praised Coetzee's commitment to giving marginalized people a voice in his fiction rather than telling his stories from the expected points of view. Some critics, however, find Coetzee's novels to be lacking a substantial social or political stance. Rather, they argue that Coetzee's avoidance of definite geographical settings and refusal to advocate revolutionary tactics reflects only the conflicted situation of the white middle and upper classes and, as such, actually reinforces the status quo.

PRINCIPAL WORKS

Dusklands (novellas) 1974
In the Heart of the Country (novel) 1977
Waiting for the Barbarians (novel) 1980
Life and Times of Michael K (novel) 1983
Foe (novel) 1987
White Writing: On the Culture of Letters in South Africa (essays) 1988
Age of Iron (novel) 1990
Doubling the Point: Essays and Interviews [edited by David Attwell] (essays and interviews) 1992
The Master of Petersburg (novel) 1994
Giving Offense: Essays on Censorship (essays) 1996
Boyhood: Scenes from Provincial Life (memoir) 1997

CRITICISM

J. M. Coetzee with Tony Morphet (interview date 1983)

SOURCE: "Two Interviews with J. M. Coetzee, 1983 and 1987," in *TriQuarterly,* No. 69, Spring-Summer, 1987, pp. 454-64.

[*In the following excerpted interview, which was conducted in 1983, Coetzee discusses his novel* Life and Times of Michael K.]

[*Morphet:*] *The most immediately striking fact is the omission of "the" from the title* [*of* **Life and Times of Michael K**]. *I have puzzled over this, not without pleasure, but I cannot find a substantial answer to the riddle. Do you have any comment?*

[Coetzee:] To my ear, "The Life" implies that the life is over, whereas "Life" does not commit itself.

The location of the story is very highly specified. Cape Town—Stellenbosch—Prince Albert—somewhere between 1985-1990. This puts it very close to us, closer than any of your previous work. Were you looking for a more direct and immediate conversation with South African readers? Or is it part of another strategy?

The geography is, I fear, less trustworthy than you imagine—not because I deliberately set about altering the reality of Sea Point or Prince Albert but because I don't have much interest in, or can't seriously engage myself with, the kind of realism that takes pride in copying the "real" world. The option was, of course, open to me to invent a world out of place and time and situate the action there, as I did in *Wait-*

ing for the Barbarians; but that side of *Waiting for the Barbarians* was an immense labor, and what would have been the point, this time round?

How did you "find" Michael K? Where did he come from and how and why did he make his way into your mind as an heroic figure?

I don't remember how I found Michael K. I have no recollection at all. I wonder whether the forgetting is deliberate.

Did you at all feel that you were taking big risks by placing Michael at the center of your fiction? He has a very limited consciousness and it seems that it is for that reason precisely, that he becomes the central figure. It seems a very austere and risky procedure for a novelist to adopt. Are you happy with the result?

Yes, I certainly saw that I was taking a risk by putting K at the center of the book, or at least at the center of most of it. But then it didn't turn out to be a book about *becoming* (which might have required that K have the ability to adapt, more of what we usually call intelligence) but a book about *being,* which merely entailed that K go on being himself, despite everything.

You must not forget the doctor in the second part of the book. He is by no means a person of limited consciousness. But where does his consciousness get him?

Would it be fair and accurate to say that the novel is built on the structural opposition between "the camp" *in all its hideous variety (from Huis Norenius through Jakkalsdrif, Brandvlei and the Kenilworth Race Course to the implied horrors of the penal camps), and* "the garden," *principally Michael's cultivation of the land around the pump in the Karoo, but including also De Waal Park and the Sea Point room?*

I suppose you might say that there is an opposition between camp and garden. But I wouldn't lump De Wall Park and the Sea Point room with the garden in the Karoo. Nor, I think, should one forget how terribly transitory that garden life of K's is: he can't hope to keep the garden because, finally, the whole surface of South Africa has been surveyed and mapped and disposed of. So, despite K's desires, the opposition that the garden provides to the camps is at most at a conceptual level.

Michael's harvest of, and feast upon, the pumpkins provides us with something relatively rare in your work—a powerful positive celebration. It is a very moving and beautiful scene. Did you have anything like the ceremonies of the first fruits in mind when you composed it? Is there anything further you would like to say about it?

K discovers or recreates some of the rituals of agricultural life, if only because he has to live by the cycle of the seasons. As for positive celebration, isn't there a fair amount of celebration (of elementary freedoms) in *Waiting for the Barbarians?*

The great "given," or "taken-for-granted," fact in the story is the war. No South African reader will be able to take his eye off the details which the story gives. Did you see it as an important purpose of the novel to take South African readers into the knowledge of what war here will mean?

> **I am hesitant to accept that my books are addressed to readers. Or at least I would argue that the concept of the reader in literature is a vastly more problematic one than one might at first think.**
> **—J. M. Coetzee**

I am hesitant to accept that my books are addressed to readers. Or at least I would argue that the concept of the reader in literature is a vastly more problematic one than one might at first think. Anyhow, it is important to me to assert that *Michael K* is not "addressed" to anyone. But the picture of war given in the book is, I would hope, a plausible picture of what a state of war might be like.

The narrator in Part Two—the pharmacist turned medic at the Kenilworth camp—mythologizes Michael. He sees him as Adam, the gardener of paradise and in fantasy he follows Michael away from the camp, pursuing him for his "meaning." Is this figure the crisis-ridden liberal of the time? He participates in the camp system but does what he can to alleviate its horrors and stupidities. He is burdened with guilt and with a complex consciousness but he is unable to act on his understanding. He is important to the development of meanings in the novel but his fate is to be swallowed by the facts of war and the camps. Would you like to comment on this figure?

You say that the doctor is "unable to act." But of course he does act, all the time. He heals people, he helps people, he protects people. Does it matter that his actions don't satisfy him? Maybe the world would be a better place if there were more people like him around. Maybe. I put the question, anyhow.

Maybe it isn't helpful to think of the doctor *primarily* as "the liberal." First of all he seems to me a person who believes (or wants) Michael K to have a meaning. I don't think that K believes (or wants) the doctor to have a meaning.

The closing sequence in Sea Point seems in some ways gra-

tuitous—particularly the sexual incidents. Michael's own interpretation that this is people's "charity" is unconvincing. Can you throw further light on your purposes in this sequence—leaving aside the wonderful closing pages in which Michael characterizes himself as a mole or an earthworm.

If the closing sequence doesn't work, that's a pity. Obviously it would be a cop-out for the book to end after Part Two. It is important that K should not emerge from the book as an angel.

The image of the teaspoon and the windmill shaft is so specific and potent that it is almost emblematic with the effect that it tends to displace the density of the preceding sequences. Did you feel you were taking particular risks in using it?

I thought that the prose had been subdued enough for 250 pages to earn that last gesture.

The novel clearly speaks to a range of literary texts—your own books first and foremost but also obviously through the letter K to Kafka. Would you like to comment on your use of Kafka?

I don't believe that Kafka has an exclusive right to the letter K. Nor is Prague the center of the universe.

The story resonates powerfully within the context of your own writing. To explore just one line of inquiry, can we focus on the mind/body split. In **Dusklands** *in particular this is a powerful theme in which the mind is dominant. Jacobus Coetzee and Eugene Dawn each in their own way are engaged in raping the world to satisfy the imperatives of the mind. In* **Life & Times** *you appear to be reversing the dominance. Michael complies in his mind to the demands of the war/camp system—it is his body that will not submit. It yearns for its food—the food of "the garden." It is this dumb imperative which gives his claim to being a gardener such force—even to the point where the camp medic's invocation of paradise seems trite since Michael's experience with the pumpkins is the experience of which the Garden of Eden is an image. He is an ingester of the earth—literally an earthworm, whereas Jacobus is an exploder of the earth. The radical and profound nature of these fictions (if I am not wholly mistaken) imposes great pressure on your readers. Do you pursue the logic of the fiction for your own sake or your readers?*

I hope that I pursue the logic of the story for its own sake. That is what is means to me to engage with a subject.

Setting your story in the near future will inevitably draw comparisons with Gordimer's July's People. *I do not like her*

work but I wonder whether you were conscious of the comparison and what it meant to you.

Fortunately Michael K had been born and was living his own life by the time I read *July's People,* so I didn't have to worry about questions of influence. Also, Gordimer writes about a Transvaal which is practically a foreign country to me. I don't recognize important similarities between the books.

Does it make any sense to you to recall Marvell—the poet who in the midst of civil war wrote consistently of both the war and gardens?

I had forgotten that about Marvell.

Would you describe your work as structuralist and, if so, what meanings would you want to attach to the term?

No, I wouldn't describe my work as structuralist, mainly because I prefer to give a quite strictly delimited meaning to the word "structuralist." But obviously I have learned a lot from contemporary French thought about the mediations that systems of signs provide.

Your fiction is, you must be aware, vulnerable to critique from both the political right and left. Both are in effect saying "Don't interfere—allow us to finish our tasks and there will be a time for what you want later. The making of a society is a fierce and brutal business and requires conscience to be silent." How would you answer such a joint voice?

Yes, my work is certainly open to attack from right and left, though how vulnerable it is we have yet to see. But would the right really join the left in expressing the sentiments you have attributed to it? I think there are more telling attacks that might be made. But the question remains: who is going to feed the glorious opposing armies?

The left, which in one or another form shares with you a common perception of the life of "camps," is likely to be especially angry at Michael's implicit answer to the guerrillas "in the mountains":

> There must be men to stay behind and keep garden-
> ing alive, or at least the idea of gardening; because
> once that cord was broken, the earth would grow
> hard and forget her children.

The left will charge you with furthering the liberal fantasy of the politics of innocence and so obstructing progressive action. They will, possibly, question the final clause of the quotation most closely, "How will the earth forget her children?," and accuse you of mystificatory categories. Do you have a sense of how you will answer the objection?

I have no wish to enter the lists as a defender of Michael K. If war is the father of all things, let the objection you voice go to war with the book, which has now had its say, and let us see who wins.

You have always taken unusual care in creating your reader and in managing your relations with him. (The double death of Klawer is not easily forgotten.) Whom are you seeking to create as the ideal reader of **Life & Times***? And has your sense of the readers changed as a result of achieving such widespread international recognition?*

I wasn't aware that I have ever taken care over my readers. My ideal reader is, I would hope, myself. But I know something of the insidious pressures faced by South African writers to simplify and explain for a foreign audience.

Did you conceive of the novel as in any way a task presented to you by history—the history of South Africa specifically?

Perhaps that is my fate. On the other hand, I sometimes wonder whether it isn't simply that vast and wholly ideological superstructure constituted by publishing, reviewing and criticism that is forcing on me the fate of being a "South African novelist."

If we can take it that **Dusklands** *records the interior imagination of colonial conquest,* **The Heart of the Country** *the intricate ferocities of the master-slave relationship,* **Waiting for the Barbarians** *the mind of an empire in decline,* **Life & Times of Michael K** *the meaning of war and resistance, then your total project appears to record the drama of the ruling South African consciousness. Would you accept this description?*

I don't know. It sounds very grand, the way you put it. There never was a master plan, though obviously certain subjects get written out and one has to move on. But then, meaning is so often something one half-discovers, half-creates in retrospect. So maybe there is a plan, now.

I don't know what you mean by "the ruling South African consciousness." Is it meant to describe me? Is that who I am?

As a writer you are working in cultural terms. Your fictions however, as we have them, present a puzzling double face. They articulate intensely within themselves, and to each other, but they also have a dramatic referential capacity. Sometimes the impression is that you write to satisfy cruel and exacting "internal" criteria and that any references external to the work are arbitrary and the creations of chance—at other times, especially in **Life & Times,** *one gains the sense that you are conducting a very precise dialogue with the South African reality. Would you like to comment?*

You have half-asked the question before, in a different form.

I don't know what "the South African reality" is, but I suspect that you are unlikely to discover it by reading newspapers, if only because what you read in a newspaper (of whatever "orientation") has been mediated through the epistemological framework called "news." I have never found anything about Michael K in the newspapers. If I was conducting any dialogue in *Life & Times,* it was with Michael K.

. . . . .

At points in the story—particularly for some reason when Michael is taken to work on the railway—it seems that you are writing your own way out of an intolerable realization. The structure of the book builds this sense. The opening sequences are exceedingly painful to read because one cannot deal with Michael's vulnerability to the horrors around him. But as the story proceeds, one begins gradually to realize the extraordinary strength and submerged purpose in Michael. As the terms "camp" and "garden" begin to deepen and clarify one realises that at a particular and intense cost there is a meaning deeper than, beyond, and ultimately more powerful than "the camps." Are you in a sense writing yourself (and your readers) into a future?

There is a sense in which Michael K cannot die.

Do you see yourself as exploring the deep structures of the South African imagination? (I can't think of a better phrasing to capture my sense of the meanings of **Dusklands, Heart of the Country, Waiting for the Barbarians** *and* **Life & Times of Michael K.**)

The imagination is my own. If not, I am really in the soup.

Allan Gardiner (essay date Autumn 1987)

SOURCE: "J. M. Coetzee's *Dusklands*: Colonial Encounters of the Robinsonian Kind," in *World Literature Written in English,* Vol. 27, No. 2, Autumn, 1987, pp. 174-84.

[*In the following essay, Gardiner explores the ways in which Coetzee's novella "The Narrative of Jacobus Coetzee" resembles Daniel Defoe's novel* Robinson Crusoe *in its textual codification of European imperialism.*]

Although post-colonial criticism has been primarily concerned with comparisons between the various post-colonial literatures, it has recently turned to establishing crucial differences between particular texts and their European analogues. The works of Cape Town author and scholar J. M.

Coetzee have all subversively inscribed Daniel Defoe's *Robinson Crusoe* with the deliberate aim of rejecting its canonical formulation of the colonial encounter. Coetzee's longstanding interest in *Robinson Crusoe* is overtly declared in his latest novel, where the connections between his work and "De/Foe's" themselves become the subject of the text. Entitled *Foe,* it is set on the island of the castaways Friday and Cruso and in the England of the writer Daniel Foe. Coetzee's earlier novels do not signal their engagement with Defoe's text quite so directly, but they have *Robinson Crusoe* as their "thematic ancestor" in their explorations of colonialism. This paper describes the South African "translation" of *Robinson Crusoe* that occurs in the first novel, ***Dusklands,*** and it is guided by Coetzee's assertion that his aim is to expose historical contrasts, and that his purpose is to criticize.

The title of ***Dusklands*** invokes a revealing metaphor traditionally associated with European imperialism. The "dusk" in question is that of the long "day" of empire. The "lands" are Europe's colonies and all places that exist in this symbolic time-frame. The time of empire, unlike concepts of temporality in other real or theoretically possible social arrangements, has a beginning and therefore, by definition, its span is finite. The forces which impose the beginning of the imperial period on each new "unconquered" place simultaneously invoke those that will bring about its demise. In this sense, every moment of empire since the first takes place at dusk. Consequently, moments in colonial history that are distant in time and space have much in common. Although ***Dusklands*** comprises two apparently separate narratives, set two hundred years apart, they are episodes in the same story of the playing out of the fatal contradictions within European imperialism.

"The Vietnam Project," set in the United States, is narrated by Eugene Dawn, a propagandist in a government department responsible for psychological warfare. He is employed in a project called "New Dawn" that has intentional similarities to the U.S.'s "hearts and minds" and "pacification" policies. Dawn's contribution to the project is a piece of writing, an analysis of the "mythic" status of the war in Southeast Asia. This report, which appears as the centrepiece of Dawn's narrative, casts the Vietnamese as rebel "sons" of the United States, itself conceived of as a deathless "father." Dawn recommends a terrorist campaign aimed at destroying what he sees as the pre-Cartesian, unalienated community of the Vietnamese, which is the sign of their alliance with a "mother earth" deity. The report is the expression of Dawn's own socially induced psychopathology, and he subsequently becomes "possessed" by his "text-child."

In the second story, **"The Narrative of Jacobus Coetzee,"** a Boer farmer becomes an explorer, and hence an agent in the van of colonialism. In making the first European contact with the Namaqua tribe, Jacobus experiences deep hu-

miliation, which leads to his insanity and to his massacre of the tribe on a return journey. I have limited my remarks to **"The Narrative."** My aim is not to show how these stories repeat a pattern, but to study the pattern itself and its relation to *Robinson Crusoe.*

Robinson Crusoe is characterized by its narrative techniques, which are the foundation of many of the codes of the realist novel, and by the allegorical and metaphorical significations that it gives to motifs of exploration. It is the first English novel that portrays the expansion of European capitalist arrangements into non-European, non-capitalist settings. As powerful tools in the hands of the European side of that encounter, texts such as *Robinson Crusoe* are themselves part of the colonization process, in that they capture the meeting within European ideology and thereby set the terms in which it will occur in future encounters. These terms reject, by assimilation or exclusion, the *difference* of the non-European by reacting to its alterity with a complex of processes which Gayatri Chakravorti Spivak has analyzed as "othering." The narrative and the allegory of *Robinson Crusoe* present the European version of the colonial situation, simultaneously silencing alternative versions by appropriating its terms as absolute or axiomatic.

A comparison of the narrative methods of **"The Narrative of Jacobus Coetzee"** and *Robinson Crusoe* (a comparison Coetzee's text deliberately invokes) raises questions of history, truth, authorship and epistemology. The explanation of **"The Narrative"** given in the "Translator's Preface" by the semi-fictional "J. M. Coetzee" is as follows:

> *Her relaas van Jacobus Coetzee, Janszoon* was first published in 1951 in an edition by my father, the late Dr. S. J. Coetzee, for the Van Plettenberg Society. This volume consisted of the text of the *Relaas* and an Introduction, which was drawn from a course of lectures on the early explorers of South Africa . . . The present publication is an integral translation of the Dutch of Jacobus Coetzee's narrative and the Afrikaans of my father's Introduction, which I have taken the liberty of placing after the text in the form of an Afterword. In an Appendix I have added a translation of Coetzee's official 1760 deposition. . . .

So **"The Narrative"** comprises three accounts of the same journey. The first is in the form of a journal, told in the first person by Jacobus. The commentary of "S. J." is a third person narrative with exaggerated intrusions of the "authorial" consciousness, as in "I hope I have succeeded in conveying something of the reality of this extraordinary man." The last is a translation, apparently unmodified, of the genuine deposition dictated by the historical Jacobus Coetzee to a colonial secretary in 1760, and transcribed in the third person.

With its bracketing of a central text by scholarly glosses and original documents, **"The Narrative"** recalls the format of a typical modern edition of *Robinson Crusoe.* It mimics the editorial practice of publishing Defoe's text with others inspired by Alexander Selkirk's experiences. Jacobus' official deposition corresponds to the report by Woods Rogers, Selkirk's rescuer (included in the 1983 Penguin) and there are further parallels between the various authors, editors and narrators in **"The Narrative"** and those in an edition of *Robinson Crusoe.* By combining objective and fictional discourses, an editor of *Robinson Crusoe* becomes a *de facto* collaborator with Defoe in his creation of illusionistic fiction. But where *Robinson Crusoe* encourages readers to comply in suspending their disbelief in the fictionality of the narrative and to construe the imaginative as the objective, **"The Narrative of Jacobus Coetzee"** prevents this complicity by strategically inscribed paradoxes.

The official deposition was dictated, not written, by the real Jacobus because he was illiterate, so the first narrative is "unofficial" because it is the result of what "S. J." calls his "positive act of the imagination." He is not merely its editor but its author. That this is so is easily inferred from the statements of "J. M." and "S. J." but only if the reader steps outside of the mode for reading objective discourse. The paradox calls attention to the ways in which colonial literature involves an incest between the texts that record personal experience and those that gloss that experience, and between these texts and their readers.

Another paradox occurs in the treatment of the distinction between the written and the non-written. **"The Narrative of Jacobus Coetzee"** and *Robinson Crusoe* are both presented as memoirs, each containing a journal as a text-within-a-text. *Robinson Crusoe* emphatically presents both the memoir and the journal as *written,* not spoken or thought, by the narrator. In the framing narrative, the old Crusoe is the writer of his story. He allows himself digressions but retains the linear, chronological structure of rationalist discourse. In the journal he is again a writer, one whose proximity to the events he describes is much greater, such that the descriptions appropriate the authority of empiricism. This narrative strategy which presents the narrating character as the author of the words on the page is another means by which European modes of perception are privileged and their objectivity over-determined in *Robinson Crusoe.* By contrast, Jacobus the illiterate (or "S. J." his creator) cannot make statements about where and when he writes. Other codes associated with the narrator-as-writer convention are used, but without explicit "lies" about the origin of the words on the page, they cannot consistently support the narrative superstructure. In the absence of an adequate formal boundary between the memoir and the journal, the single consciousness that underlies both of them and that speaks through Jacobus is unmasked. The inscription of Defoe's formal techniques within **"The Narrative"** exposes the narrative conventions of realism, showing their intentionally equivocal relation to factual discourse and their dependence on the complicity of a reading community that has a vested interest in accepting the validity of textual representations of colonialism, whether they are fictional or not.

> **"The Narrative of Jacobus Coetzee" takes its cue from *Robinson Crusoe* and raises questions of the material function of the ideology of colonial literature.**
> —*Allan Gardiner*

As with narrative structure, so too with its treatment of the theme of exploration. **"The Narrative of Jacobus Coetzee"** takes its cue from *Robinson Crusoe* and raises questions of the material function of the ideology of colonial literature. "If Defoe hadn't found and used Selkirk's story," says Angus Ross, "he would have found something of the same kind." In the context of slavery-based economics, European fiction is almost compelled to represent a culture hero lost in an alien landscape and contacting the unenslaved Other. Jacobus is a figure "of the same sort" as Selkirk, and ***Dusklands*** as a whole is an acknowledgement of the importance of the "explorer story" as a means by which the material realities of colonialism have been converted to literary myth and automatized thought.

The cosmology of *Robinson Crusoe* is established by the pronouncement on social class by Crusoe's father:

> He bid me observe . . . that the calamities of life were shared among the upper and lower classes of mankind, but that the middle station had the fewest disasters. . . .

Coetzee has commented on how the passive voice in this passage entrenches the proposition that social "stations" are, and always were, universal phenomena and that a purposive agent made them so. Crusoe becomes a special kind of rebel from this cosmological order. His transgression is to become a sailor-merchant, and thereby to enter a lower station than the one chosen for him within the pattern of class and commerce. His punishment, like that of Adam in the Christian allegory that underlies *Robinson Crusoe,* is to be sent out into "the World." It is this penitent state that Defoe associates with that of an explorer. But the Fall is fortunate because the explorer can contribute to the progress of the divine plan whose vehicle is commerce.

By using this allegory to convert exploration into fiction, Defoe makes exploration a matter of journey, fear and destiny. The presentation of a journey is not an inescapable motif of fiction about colonialism, but it is a mode frequently adopted. (As Chinua Achebe's and Olive Schreiner's fiction shows, however colonialism can be experienced and expressed as a static narrative of staying at home and being visited and annihilated.) The appeal of the journey motif is to a European audience that is predisposed to reading and decoding allegorical journeys. The motif of fear is consistent with these predispositions. Alien territories are seen not only metaphorically but literally as the realm of Satanic forces. But Defoe's presentation of "the World" and the terror that it contains is not a simple transposition of the Christian allegory, for it also incorporates Enlightenment ideas of the individual and his/her relation to others. In addition to its *availability,* the metaphysical system by which Defoe presents colonial exploration has the advantage of directing attention away from unpleasant facts. For example, when Crusoe makes his first trading voyages, the details of the missions show that they were slaving enterprises. Yet Defoe never gives this information directly, focusing instead on the details of profit and loss (and thereby, on the state of Crusoe's "spiritual development"). A similar occlusion results from the assumption that the economic and social arrangements of Europe were divinely ordained as static structures, altering only in the direction of improvement and increase. This myth elides the fact that a radical social upheaval associated with the plunder and exploitation of South America and Africa was occurring.

For Defoe, the propagandist of a period of expansion and change, humanity's climb back to the unfallen state of the first man was accelerating. The proof that his evolution of humanity was God's plan could be seen in the economic ascendency of bourgeois European culture over those races and classes who had remained in the unregenerate state.

The preamble of **"The Narrative"** performs the same operations as do the preliminary sequences of *Robinson Crusoe.* The difference is that Defoe's narrative works through its hidden assumptions, whereas Coetzee's re-invocation of a similar apparatus brings those assumptions, and the moments at which they become socially functional, into full view. **"The Narrative"** begins with Jacobus' reflections on his conditions of life as a colonist. These reflections form a kind of genesis story that identifies the primal elements of South African colonialism; the roots, so to speak, from which South African society grows.

The first primal element is a system of property that uses human beings as currency or as property itself. A rich man, for instance, is said to own land, cattle, and a "stable full of women." Dutch wives "carry an aura of property with them. They are first of all property themselves." Like Crusoe, however, Jacobus avoids explicit references to race slavery by describing selectively the mercantile practices of which it is a part. In effect, this means that slavery is the subject of the

absences in Jacobus' preamble, but it exists in an uneasy balance with a second important element. This is the economic and geographical link that is forged between diverse peoples in a colonial context and which, in Jacobus' view, threatens to *unite* the whites and the detribalized blacks under the monopolist Company.

Detribalization is an atrocity of capitalist imperialism, but, after it has become a fact, capitalist forces in their early stages can seem to have some liberating potential. The interrelation of racism and capitalism is imperfect enough, in Jacobus' world of eighteenth-century southern Africa, to allow some blacks who follow the rules of capitalism to overcome the secondary forces of racism. At the same time whites may lose their position in a class with more privileges than blacks:

> The days are past when Hottentots would come to the back door begging for a crust of bread while we dressed in silver knee-buckles and sold wine to the Company. There are those of our people who live like Hottentots, pulling up their tents when the pasture gives out and following the cattle after new grass. Our children play with the servants' children, and who is to say who copies whom? In hard times how can differences be maintained?

There are two answers available to Jacobus' question. Further expansion by whites offers the chance to repeat the process by which the original colonists escaped the limitations of a rigid class system. By finding new populations that can be conscripted into the lowest position in the European economic hierarchy and by finding new sources of land, wealth, and labour, a new wave of colonizers can transform all these things into property by the deployment of their weapons, chief among which are the gun and a special mode of thought. But until such material differences between the races are established, and by way of making the colonial form of capitalism a servant of racism, a symbolic separation can be enforced by means of the idea of destiny in a Christian framework; which is to say, the theological justification of apartheid. "The one gulf that divides us from the Hottentots," says Jacobus, "is our Christianity. We are Christians, a folk with a destiny."

In *Robinson Crusoe* the idea of destiny flows into concepts of individualism which in turn involve the conflation of blacks with "nature." Peter Knox-Shaw has noted how closely Defoe ties his story of exploration to the problem of maintaining the boundaries of the self. Crusoe nears the ultimate goal of Protestant history whenever his faith is strongest that everything external to himself exists to satisfy his needs. To show "the World" responding to Crusoe's "ventriloquism," Defoe carefully manipulates his depictions of natural phenomena, or which blacks and animals are indistinguishable examples. Jacobus also moves from the idea of destiny to an association of blacks with animals:

> The Bushman is a different creature, a wild animal with an animal's soul . . . Heartless as baboons they are, and the only way to treat them is like beasts.

A captive escaping the basest slavery becomes, in Jacobus' mind, an animal manifesting its ability to take the stamp of civilization:

> The only way of taming a Bushman is to catch him when he is young . . . not older than seven or eight. Older than that he is too restless.

Between the lines of Jacobus' descriptions of Bushmen it is possible to read an account of a people defending themselves against the genocidal whites, and doing so resourcefully and (despite the cowardice, the chilling ruthlessness and the superior technology of their enemy) effectively. But J. M. Coetzee's wider interest is in the terms of Jacobus' account and their patterns. Jacobus' belief in the animality of blacks leads him into adopting the novelistic codes by which the reader (conceived as a Cartesian subject) is encouraged to identify with the (Cartesian) hero. Thus, he says: "*You* have perhaps thirty yards to get *your* shot off" and "If there are two of *you* it is, of course, easier." And of the rape of native women: "Her response to *you* is absolutely congruent with *your* will."

As these quotations suggest, the link between black "animalism" and the affirmation of the white subject's individuality and superiority is violence, and again *Robinson Crusoe* is the model. As Crusoe oscillates between losing and regaining his moral will, the corresponding events on the level of plot involve violence to blacks. A case in point is Crusoe's lengthy consideration of the morality of murdering, en masse, a group of natives in order to procure a guide to take him off the island, and the consumation of these plans. Crusoe's effectiveness of will benefits from these violent meditations whether or not he acts on them. The fear of others, which plagues Crusoe from the moment of finding the footprint in the sand and which causes his loss of will, is reversed by his knowledge that he has the capacity to turn the lives and deaths of natives to his own purposes. The high moral tone of his deliberations is belied by the exuberant tone of his descriptions of the eventual slaughter. Each death is posed by Defoe with the imaginative care that is lavished on pornographic images, and the sequences are charged with an underlying Hobbesian fantasy of the uninhibited savagery of the isolated self in a "natural" or asocial environment. Earlier in *Robinson Crusoe,* Crusoe's behaviour towards Moley and Xury, his fellows in enslavement to a Moor, is also characterized by compensatory aggression.

This pattern, in which Crusoe oscillates between the loss of self through the intrusion of otherness and the independence of self through the negation of external phenomena, is formalized as a metaphysical law of exploration in the scenes of Crusoe's fevered delirium and Christian conversion. The conversion is presented as a direct imparting of knowledge to him by God through a vision, so the emphasis is on the absolute truth of the content of the vision. The "proof" is that it is an explanation of life that originates outside individual consciousness. What has been *felt* becomes the known absolute. Further to validate the vision, Defoe has Crusoe experience it during the time of his journal-keeping so that the objectivity of writing can be doubly invoked. The content of the vision is an interpretation of Crusoe's shipwreck, which, according to the angel of the dream, is a matter of his election by God as His agent. All the phenomena that Crusoe experiences (earthquakes, stormy seas and so on) are staged to prepare his soul for this purpose. That the purpose is to do the groundwork for the advance of European colonialism is left as an inference to be drawn from the subsequent events leading to the "taming" of Friday and establishment of a penal colony to take Crusoe's place on the island.

By the time Crusoe finds the footprint, and when Jacobus meets the Namaqua, their existential need to deny the subjecthood of others and their technological and metaphysical apparatus for doing so have been established. Common to both novels is the exaggerated shock of the first contact, and a response to the shock that involves questions of the nature of being and of perception, and the difference between "savagery" and "civilization." Jacobus' "sojourn" with the Nama leads him also into loss of self-containment and to a delirium in which metaphysical purposes for his "suffering," related to the role of the pioneer, dawn upon him as if from outside his consciousness. But is not "God" Coetzee suggests, but the structures of culture, embodied in the ideology of language and therefore reproduced in miniature in the consciousness of each speaker, that determine the revelations gained introspectively by these explorers. It is not "God's" independent intervention but the material pressures on the agents of colonial domination that trigger the "insights."

The Nama, however, refuse to adopt the role that Jacobus expects of them. Acting out of playfulness and an innocent greediness and curiosity, they turn Jacobus' heroic moment into farce. The true confrontation with radical difference occurs during the "minutes of confusion in which the paths of shamefaced friend, grinning foe and scrambling beast were forever confused." His tranquility gives way to a state of shock, in which he tries to maintain his belief in his manichean separateness from the natives by multiplying his self-delusions. At this point the eighteenth-century Boer suddenly has access to nineteenth-century fictions and twentieth-century jargon. Jacobus prepares himself for the meeting by "tracing in my heart the forking paths of the endless inner adventure. . . these forking paths across that true wilderness without policy called the land of the Great Namaqua where everything, I was to find, was possible." The four paths or scenarios that he outlines are amusing reductions of the plots of typical imperial adventure stories of the Haggard/Kipling kind. This anachronism is appropriate and suggestive because the fictional response to the moment of first contact is so predictable. It also suggests that this aspect of colonial discourse does not originate as a representation of actual colonial experience, but rather is generated from the (European) public symbolic order. Although the actions of the Nama do not fit into any of the four scenarios, Jacobus nevertheless finds a way in time of interpreting them in terms of his inner adventure.

Jacobus begins his sojourn with the Nama and is confronted with one proof after another of a world that does not conform to his metaphysical scheme. His feeling of God-imitating detachment and godlike superiority is evident only to himself. For the Nama, these concepts lack all meaning: "Perhaps on my horse and with the sun over my right shoulder I looked like a god, a god of the kind they did not yet have." Moreover, the smoke holes in their huts have no religious significance, at least in the binary terms of upper/lower or heavenly/earthly that Jacobus can recognize as religious. Their head-man bears no relation to the patriarchal symbol at the head of the explorer's cosmology. As the Nama continue, not to reject their inferior place within his scheme, but to disregard it completely, the foundations of Jacobus' sense of separateness are undermined. He experiences a "terror" of the "communal life" of the Nama that centres on their huts. Yet it is into one of these huts that Jacobus is swallowed when fever makes him dependent on the tribe's hospitality.

Significantly, it is a hut for menstruating women. The scenes of Jacobus' fever recall the free-associations with which he began his narrative: "Adam Wijnand, a Bastard . . . his mother was a Hottentot . . . Adam Wijnand, that woman's son, is a rich man." A powerful black, a half-caste whose very person signals the removal of absolute separateness on the level of race, and whose condition of conception and birth denies the primacy of paternity over maternity; this is the figure which prompts Jacobus to speak, which provides the point of generation of his narrative. As a symbol of the destruction of separateness, Adam Wijnand is functional in a manner similar to a rule of syntax from which many sentences may be generated. The social realities of Jacobus' colonial world continue to thrust such representations of relative, as opposed to rigid, values into Jacobus' story, and his need to deny them becomes the fuel that continues to generate the narrative. The pervasive presence of *Robinson Crusoe* in *Dusklands* is an invitation to the reader to see that the novel form itself is driven by this kind of motor; that its very nature and origin is in a textual response to the encounter with other cultures.

It is at this point that Jacobus experiences his Robinsonian vision. His fever brings on a state of mind in which he makes part visionary, part insane speculations on his being, using jargon and concepts that, again, were not available to an eighteenth-century Boer. By this means he maintains his delusions of manichean separateness from the Nama and of the existence of everything outside him as contingent upon his conceptions of it. These speculations are a means of naming the Other as harmless. His dependence on the Nama and the farcical scene of first contact are reconstructed by his speculative story of himself as an explorer, and declared to be unreal in comparison with the larger "reality" of his transcendent power. But to convince himself of his power he must, like Crusoe, meditate psychotically on his gun as he does in the story of hunting Bushmen. The only real superiority that Jacobus possesses is the superior ability to murder. He returns to the myth of Christian destiny to reinforce his delusions, and arrives at the conviction that "the transformation of savage into enigmatic follower" is a thing decreed from above which "we feel as a fated pattern and a condition of life." Significantly, this pattern is "felt" as fated. *Dusklands* shows how that sense of inevitability flows from a power-functional mind set, manifested through texts such as *Robinson Crusoe,* which expresses the fear that others may "have a history in which I shall be a term." Ultimately, the gun can be the only hedge against the fear of equality or inferiority.

The motif of the gun in **"The Narrative,"** then, is used to deconstruct the specific role of violence in Defoe's schema of exploration. In *Robinson Crusoe* the gun is the tool of the colonist hero, who uses it as an instrument of separation against the threat of the absorbtion of the one into the many. **"The Narrative"** situates this structure of aggression within a society that is marked everywhere by the exploitation of a majority by a minority and which therefore needs to make a distinction between the individual person and a plenum of humanity. Since Coetzee is dealing with Defoe's creation of a morphology of different kinds of violence, it is misleading to suppose, as some writers have, that he is depicting violence as an historical, universal, "categorical imperative." The link between the two stories in *Dusklands* is forged as much by the way that they illustrate a decrease in the effectiveness of imperialist tools of aggression over time as by their illustration of the continuity in the operation of those tools. In **"The Vietnam Project"** the active resistance by the Vietnamese people, even more than that of the Bushmen in **"The Narrative,"** signals a refusal to be negated or captured within the terms of colonialist ideology, just as in history a signal victory was won over the technological weapons of imperialism. Eugene Dawn's mythography, like its thematic ancestor, Defoe's allegory, becomes startingly unconvincing in the late twentieth century.

For Jacobus (and S. J. Coetzee), the explorer myth of violence remains functional. Jacobus links violence and destiny by deciding that his role is not merely the exploration of land but the metaphysical entering and plundering of any interior. He overcomes his fear of being eaten/equal by fetishizing his eye, the instrument of exploration, and imagining its power to "eat" the other instead. Thus he can foil any "representative of that out there which my eye once enfolded and ingested and which now promises to enfold, ingest, and project me through itself as a speck on a field which we may call annihilation or alternatively history." His self-preserving rationalization for his work becomes the rationalization for his sadistic slaughter of the Nama. He wonders: "Are they not perhaps fictions, these lures of interiors for rape" but undercuts that possibility with: ". . . that the Universe uses to draw out its explorers?" Coetzee presents these sophistries to show how much the materiality of exploration and cultural contact can be and have been denied in favour of an allegory of its "deeper meaning." That it is one of the most pervasive metaphors in the English language is unintentionally illustrated by the publishers of **Dusklands,** who have printed on its jacket a quotation from a review: "J. M. Coetzee's vision goes to the nerve centre of being. What he finds there. . . ." Such claims invoke those very assimilative metaphors of explorer stories that Coetzee's text attacks for their ideological validation of white minority rule in South Africa.

> ... **Coetzee writes texts that are necessarily allegorical, but like similar post-colonial texts, they are direct engagements with, rather than escapes from history, reflexively "conscious" of their place within textual production, and of the supreme importance of texts in the capture and annihilation of "the others."**
> —*Allan Gardiner*

In spite of the continuing similarities in the nature of European imperialism, the world out of which Defoe wrote may be contrasted with the contemporary world. Defoe's account of the presence of European power in other lands and its role and function there was compatible with the philosophical currents of his time. Now, thanks in large part to the peoples against whom it becomes a weapon, this depiction of an "archetypal" relationship is threatened by the relativity of the truths which anchor it. The confidence of European thought has given way to desperation. Coetzee's "translation" of *Robinson Crusoe* exploits these contrasts as part of a critical exploration of the colonial encounter, but it also acknowl-

edges the continuing relevance of the theme of isolation, and therefore of the motif of "the island," as the site of this exploration. Writing directly out of his South African experience, Coetzee confronts an intellectual environment that is tied to its stagnant place in colonial history. In their structures and metaphors, the literary expressions of this intellectual milieu frequently contribute to the textual colonization of which *Robinson Crusoe* is an example. While many liberal South African novels are willing to question the degree to which the culture of the ruling class is any more "civilized" than that of the black majority, even these retain the ethnocentric intellectual baggage that comes with the term "civilization," and hence they also tend to repeat the patterns of fiction that were pioneered by Defoe.

By taking as his subject the representations by which South African colonialism has interpreted itself to itself, Coetzee writes texts that are necessarily allegorical, but like similar post-colonial texts, they are direct engagements with, rather than escapes from history, reflexively "conscious" of their place within textual production, and of the supreme importance of texts in the capture and annihilation of "the others."

Rosemary Jane Jolly (essay date April 1989)

SOURCE: "Territorial Metaphor in Coetzee's 'Waiting for the Barbarians'," in *Ariel,* Vol. 20, No. 2, April, 1989, pp. 69-79.

[*In the following essay, Jolly discusses the physical territory of both geographical locations and of the human body as a metaphor for colonial invasion in* Waiting for the Barbarians.]

When J. M. Coetzee's third novel, **Waiting for the Barbarians,** appeared in 1980 it elicited a number of interesting responses which have to do—whether the reviewers realize this or not—with the implications of the setting of the novel. Leon Whiteson criticizes it for an apparent lack of mimetic accuracy: "The geography is garbled; there is desert and snow, lizards and bears. The story is told in that most awkward tense; the historic present. The dialogue is stiff, the writing has the air of a translation. . . . Coetzee's bad dreams have not been earned by any truth. . . . The heart of this novel is not darkness but mush." Irving Howe, in a generally favourable article published in *The New York Times Book Review,* comments that "one possible loss is bite and pain, the urgency that a specified historical place and time may provide." Finally, in an extremely revealing review of *The Life and Times of Michael K.* (Coetzee's fourth novel, published in 1983) Nadine Gordimer praises this novel for its depiction of the reality of violence, but criticizes it for its "revulsion" from history, its lack of recognition of the primacy of politics in a scheme of historical determinacy. She goes on to observe that Coetzee

> chose allegory for his first few novels. It seemed he did so out of a kind of opposing desire to hold himself clear of events and their daily, grubby, tragic consequences in which, like everyone else living in South Africa, he is up to the neck, and about which he had an inner compulsion to write. So here was allegory as stately fastidiousness; or a state of shock. He seemed able to deal with the horror he saw written on the sun only—if brilliantly—if this were to be projected into another time and plane. His *Waiting For the Barbarians* was the North Pole to which the agitprop of agonized black writers (and some white ones hitching a lift to the bookmart on the armoured car) was the South Pole: a world to be dealt with lies in between.

I have quoted Gordimer's remarks at such length because, in referring to the indeterminate "time" and "plane" of the novel, she raises not only the question of the setting of *Waiting for the Barbarians,* but also the larger question of what literature can, or in this case, even *should,* be expected to do; what kind of territory it undertakes to explore.

The ambiguities of time and place to which Whiteson in particular has shown such aversion are clearly deliberate. In a rare comment on his own work, Coetzee stated that "The setting is not specified for *Barbarians,* and very specifically is not specified . . . I just put together a variety of locales and left a lot of things vague with a very definite intention that it shouldn't be pinned down to some specific place." The fact that Coetzee ensures that the Empire remains unnamed, the time unspecific (sunglasses are a new invention, but horses are the means of transportation) and the geography indeterminate, indicates that the setting of the novel is something of a key to the working of the narrative.

The geography of the fiction may not correspond to an identifiable geo-political entity, but its depiction is both detailed and comprehensible. To the north of the settlement the river runs into the lake; there is a road that runs from the settlement to the lake, turning north-west along its coast. South of the lake are marsh-lands and salt flats, and beyond them "a blue-grey line of barren hills." To the north of the lake is the desert. Colonel Joll takes the north-west road to find the nomads; the narrator takes a short cut to the barbarians when he returns the girl, a track that leads off the river road to the east, skirting the lake to the south and then heading off to the north-east, to the valleys of the ranges where the nomads winter. "Two miles due south of the town" are a cluster of dunes, which are stable owing to the vegetation on their surface and the timber ruins which they shroud, ruins that date back to the time before the Empire annexed the

western provinces and built the fort. The frontier settlement, for which the narrator is responsible as magistrate of the Empire, is not only the focus of the geographical surroundings: it is also central to the action of the novel. Colonel Joll comes to the settlement from the interior of the Empire, from the Third Bureau, "the most important division of the Civil Guard nowadays"; both Colonel Joll and the narrator make excursions from it into the land of the barbarians. Most importantly, the settlement is the home of the narrator.

To reject the strange geography of the novel, to desire it to be immediately recognizable, is to reject the narrative itself, to diminish the fiction. As Lance Olsen points out, any such reading "implies a refusal on the part of the reader to take the fiction as itself," which in turn implies a desire to "change the fiction into something it cannot or will not be." We, as his readers, have to accept the narrator's landscape. After all, it is the narrator's charts Colonel Joll uses to make his first raid on the barbarians: he is the mapmaker; his descriptions of his surroundings are as meticulous as he can make them. We need to inhabit his narrative.

What is the nature of that narrative? The controlling metaphor is again territorial. Just as his home, the settlement, is situated on the frontier of the Empire, facing the land of the barbarians, so the narrator is positioned on the fringes of the Empire's authority, confronted by those who are subject to it. The narrator is obsessed with discovering the meaning of his situation. He tries to explore what it is to be of the Empire, what is to be of the barbarians. He reflects on Joll after the Colonel's torturing of the boy and his father:

> Looking at him [Joll] I wonder how he felt the very first time: did he, invited as an apprentice to twist the pincers or turn the screw or whatever it is they do, shudder even a little to know that at that instant he was trespassing into the forbidden? I find myself wondering too whether he has a private ritual of purification, carried out behind closed doors, to enable him to return and break bread with other men. Does he wash his hands very carefully, perhaps, or change all his clothes; or has the Bureau created new men who can pass without disquiet between the unclean and the clean?

This passage is sprinkled with territorial metaphors. The narrator imagines Joll in the moment of transition, (tres)passing from the one region to another, from the "clean" to the "unclean," from the innocent to the "forbidden." Later, when Warrant Officer Mandel sets him free, the magistrate asks the torturer how he finds it possible to eat after he has "been . . . working with people." When Mandel turns from him, the narrator appeals to him: "'No listen!' I say. 'Do not misunderstand me, I am not blaming you or accusing you, I am long past that. . . . I am only trying to understand the *zone* in which you live. I am trying to imagine how you breathe and eat and live from day to day. But I Cannot!'" (emphasis added).

With the same urgency the narrator tries to understand the barbarians: where they come from, what they are, what they think of the Empire. His fascination for the blind barbarian girl stems from this curiosity: he treats her body as a surface, a map of a surface, a text. He washes her body, finding in the exploration of her features an ecstasy. Often he falls asleep "as if poleaxed," oblivious, and wakes an hour or so later "dizzy, confused, thirsty." These spells are to him like "death," or "enchantment." When he discovers the torture mark at the corner of the girl's eye, he observes: "It has been growing more and more clear to me that until the marks on this girl's body are deciphered and understood I cannot let go of her." He is not unaware of the position in which he places her by treating her in this manner: "The distance between myself and her torturers, I realize, is negligible, I shudder." He wants to know of her people, her family; she offers him little information. Whatever he discovers of her, he does so by examining her, by "reading" her as one would a map. The dream in which he tries to remember her as she was before Joll got hold of her, is a measure, a scale of his progress in exploring her.

Eventually the narrator reaches a certain recognition of the "interior" of the barbarian girl, even if it is only that this "interior" exists:

> While I have not ceased to see her as a body maimed, scarred, harmed, she has perhaps by now grown into and become that new deficient body, feeling no more deformed than a cat feels deformed for having claws instead of fingers. I would do well to take these thoughts seriously. More ordinary than I like to think, she may have ways of finding me ordinary too.

Instead of the worshipping of a surface—the denial of substance which the washing ritual portrayed—he gains a sense of the girl in her entirety; her form has an essence which is yet to be discovered. Whereas before, in his dream of the child building a snow-/sandcastle, he could not envision the child's face, he now remembers for the first time the girl's face before its mutilation: she becomes the child of his dream vision. Having come this far, he realizes the need—his need—to take the girl back to barbarian land. It is during this journey, when they reach the bed of the ancient lagoon which lies between the sand dunes and the mountains of the barbarians on the far side, that the narrator finally consummates his relationship with her: "I am with her," he says, "not for whatever raptures she may promise or yield but for other reasons, which remain as obscure to me as ever." The reunion of girl and territory is the turning point of the fiction:

the narrator returns, resigned, to the settlement as prisoner—not agent—of the Empire. What precisely has been realized?

In his "Author's Note" to the Faber and Faber edition of *The Whole Armour and The Secret Ladder,* Wilson Harris identifies Melville's *Benito Cereno* and Conrad's *Heart of Darkness* as "prophetic" novels. He discusses the strange juxtapositions in the image of Negro slaves mistaken for "Black Friars" by Captain Delano and in "Kurtz's manifesto of moral beauty . . . which almost overshadowed the small script at the bottom of the page—'Exterminate all the brutes'" as "expressionist" or "symbolic" devices, pointing to "a transplanted value or faith which had become such a dominant persona that it ceased to be a homogeneous value or enactment of identity and freedom, and turned into an all-consuming bias." We are reminded of the nature of Colonel Joll's quest for truth. When the narrator asks him how he can tell when he is told the truth, Joll replies that "there is a certain tone." The narrator responds:

> "The tone of truth! Can you pick up this tone in everyday speech? Can you hear whether I am telling the truth?"
>
> This is the most intimate moment we have yet had, which he [Colonel Joll] brushes off with a little wave of the hand. "No, you misunderstand me. I am speaking only of a special situation now, I am speaking of a situation in which I am probing for the truth, in which I have to exert pressure to find it. First I get lies, you see—this is what happens—first lies, then pressure, then more lies, then more pressure, then the truth. That is how you get the truth.

Colonel Joll's process of divining the truth corresponds to the historical process of colonization, to the relationship between conqueror and conquered: his quest is conquest. In his "Author's Note" Harris describes the implications of "a landscape saturated by the traumas of conquest." He is referring to the particular history and geography of Guyana as he represents it in his novels, but again his observations apply to *Waiting for the Barbarians,* and specifically to the position which Colonel Joll occupies:

> A bitter thread or scale runs through Carib and Arawak pre-Columbian vestiges capable now of relating themselves afresh to the value-turned-bias-structures of twentieth-century man. Thus, it would seem, we are involved in a peculiar juxtaposition at the heart of our age—renascent savagery and conquest-ridden civilization.

This juxtaposition is the product of historical consequence: to conquer, to colonize, to turn the "transplanted value" into the "all-consuming bias," requires the use of a complex violence, that violence which the Empire represents and with whose meaning our narrator is so obsessed.

From the beginning the narrator is intrigued by violence and anxious to understand the meaning behind the marks it leaves. He caresses the barbarian girl's broken feet, and observes in detail the wound the torturers have left near her eye: ". . . I notice in the corner of one eye a greyish puckering as though a caterpillar lay there with its head under her eyelid, grazing. . . . Between thumb and forefinger I part her eyelids. The caterpillar comes to an end, decapitated, at the pink inner rim of the eyelid. There is no other mark. The eye is whole." He investigates the room where the girl's feet were broken and her eye blinded—the same room where her father was tortured to death. He observes that it is a clean room, marked only by soot on the ceiling above the fireplace and on the wall. He asks her how they blinded her, and she describes to him the instrument they used. Later, once he has returned to the settlement, he reflects on the undeniable desire to violate. He longs for his impression on the barbarian girl to be as great as Colonel Joll's conquest of her is:

> Our loving leaves no mark. Whom will that other
> girl with the blind face remember: me with my silk
> robe and my dim lights and my perfumes and oils
> and my unhappy pleasures, or that other cold man
> with the mask over his eyes who gave the orders
> and pondered the sounds of her intimate pain?
> Whose face was the last face she saw plainly on this
> earth but the face behind the glowing iron? Though
> I cringe with shame, even here and now, I must ask
> myself whether, when I lay head to foot with her,
> fondling and kissing those broken ankles, I was not
> in my heart of hearts regretting that I could not en-
> grave myself on her as deeply.

In this desire for violence resides the will to bring both poles of Harris's juxtaposition—"renascent savagery" and "conquest-ridden civilization"—together in the act of violence. How far does the narrator come in interpreting t(his) desire? How do we understand the act of it?

The title of Coetzee's novel comes, of course, from Constantin Cavafy's poem "Waiting for the Barbarians," which depicts a decadent Roman Empire awaiting a barbarian conquest which never happens. The border guards report that "there are no barbarians any longer." The narrator concludes: "Now what's going to happen to us without barbarians? / Those people were a kind of solution." The realization that there are no barbarians impresses the problem of the existence of the Empire on the Empire. So in Coetzee's novel. When the narrator explains to the young officer of the new detachment—who thinks that he and his troops have been followed by barbarians *en route* to the

settlement—that the barbarians have no plans to destroy the town, that they know that the town will peter out by itself as the lake-water grows more salty, the officer refuses to believe that the imperial troops will ever leave: "'But we are not going,' the young man says quietly. 'Even if it became necessary to supply the settlement by convoy, we would not go'." Ultimately, of course, the troops do desert the frontier town. The point, however, is not only that without the barbarians the Empire has nothing against which to rally, against which it has to defend its territory; if, in addition, the barbarians are not responsible for the decline of Empire—and we are told by one of the few survivors of Joll's final campaign that "We froze in the mountains! We starved in the desert! . . . *We were not beaten*—they [the barbarians] led us out into the desert and then they vanished!" (emphasis added)—who is responsible?

When the narrator is taken into custody on his return to the settlement, he hears of a fire along the river. He surmises that someone has decided that the brush on the river-banks provides too much cover for the barbarians. However, he tells us, the brush is broken by patches of barren land, so someone must be following the fire down the river, rekindling it when it dies out: "They do not care that once the ground is cleared the wind begins to eat at the soil and the desert advances. Thus the expeditionary force against the barbarians prepares for its campaign, ravaging the earth, wasting our patrimony." In addition, the antagonism of the force provokes an attack, allegedly by the barbarians ("No one saw them. They came in the night"), on the irrigation wall, which causes the fields to flood. "How can we win such a war?" the narrator asks. "What is the use of textbook military operations, sweeps and punitive raids into the enemy's heartland when we can be bled to death at home?"

When, also on his return to the settlement, the magistrate is immediately charged with "treasonously consorting with the enemy," he responds to the accusation with the same insight that he uses to evaluate the physical deterioration of his domain: "'We are at peace here,' I say, 'we have no enemies.' There is silence. 'Unless I make a mistake,' I say. 'Unless we are the enemy'." After Colonel Joll has marked the backs of his barbarian prisoners, their hands wired to their faces through their cheeks, with the word "ENEMY" in charcoal, the narrator accuses Joll:

> "Those pitiable prisoners you brought in—are *they*
> the enemy I must fear? Is that what you say? *You*
> are the enemy, Colonel! . . . You are the enemy, *you*
> have made the war, and *you* have given them all the
> martyrs they need—starting not now but a year ago
> when you committed your first filthy barbarities
> here! History will bear me out!"

The magistrate has come to identify that which is barbarian

with the signatures of his own civilization. He has read the signs of violence on the surface, and realizes that, as fellow South African novelist André Brink puts it, "violence denies not only the humanity of the person against which it is directed but also that of the person who practises it."

This reading of the relationship between violator and violated ties Colonel Joll, the barbarian girl and the narrator together just as surely as if Colonel Joll had connected himself to the other two with the wire he uses to subdue his prisoners. In Harris's terms, the juxtaposition of "renascent savagery" and "conquest-ridden civilization" constitute a kind of synthesis. On the surface this "marriage" appears to be "sinister," but it may become a synthesis which is related to the dire need of the twentieth century for new vision—"vision as capacity to resense or rediscover a scale of community":

> That scale, I would think, needs to relate itself afresh to the "monsters" which have been constellated in the cradle of a civilisation—projected outwards from the nursery or cradle thus promoting a polarization, the threat of ceaseless conflict and the necessity for a self-defensive apparatus against the world *out there*.
>
> In some degree, therefore, we need to retrieve or bring those "monsters" back into ourselves as native to the psyche, native to a quest for unity through contrasting elements, through the ceaseless tasks of the creative imagination to digest and liberate contrasting spaces rather than succumb to implacable polarizations.
>
> Such retrieval is vision.

This quest for vision is the quest of the narrator. He moves between Empire and barbarian territory, between present and past, trying desperately to retrieve some sense of original unity in order to liberate his future from history and his territory from conquest. He knows that something from the past needs to be recovered. He digs among the ruins for artifacts that will enlighten him: he never gives up trying to understand the characters on the wooden slips he finds in the bag buried below the floor level of the excavation. When Colonel Joll asks him for the meaning of the slips, the magistrate tells him how to find the signs:

> It is recommended that you simply dig at random: perhaps at the very spot where you stand you will come upon scraps, shards, reminders of the dead. Also the air: the air is full of sighs and cries. These are never lost: if you listen carefully, with a sympathetic ear, you can hear them echoing forever within the second sphere.

He also works against the limits imposed on him by the Empire, but just as he never does learn the language of the signs, he does not learn the language of the barbarians from the girl before she leaves him. When he asks her, after her return to the barbarians, to come back with him to the settlement, both stand on the same frontier, each on the fringe of their own territory. But the narrator, as yet, does not understand the depth of his desire for the girl; and she has no way of conceiving it as anything other than that of the conqueror for the conquered. She goes back to her people, but there is one sense in which she stays with the narrator—she continues to appear to him in his dreams, in the vision of her as a child.

The realm of the novel is both familiar and unfamiliar; it is both South Africa and everywhere else; it is the present trying to redeem the past in anticipation of the future.
—*Rosemary Jane Jolly*

Nadine Gordimer's criticism of *Waiting for the Barbarians* seems to undermine to some degree the value of the fiction in its focus on frontiers. The novel deals metaphorically with the meeting point between two territories. The realm of the novel is both familiar and unfamiliar; it is both South Africa and everywhere else; it is the present trying to redeem the past in anticipation of the future. The fiction is not an "allegory" in Gordimer's sense of the word. In its representation it is true to the violent domain of conquest in the present; but it remains faithful to the future in that its crucial locations are those which suggest the potential for transition—not those which make the fiction a "historical allegory . . . —a matter of ticking off fictional events against their literal counterparts" (Shrimpton). This fluidity is necessary to dislocate, to "liberate" the reader from claims of temporal and geographic specificity by confronting her/him with the possibility of transition. The narrator himself is unable to make the transition, to make a new time and a new place for himself—when the possibility presents itself in the desert, "things fall apart": thereafter his only access to the possibility of a new vision, a new "territory," is through his dream-visions. But the reader *is* left with the possibility. The narrator's dream-visions, which indicate his imaginative involvement with the barbarian girl, and less specifically the possibility of a new community, represent the imaginative potential of the reader who is prepared to take a novel such as Coetzee's on its own terms. The relation and distinction or boundary between character/narrator and reader, the material and the visionary, is revealed in the territorial metaphor of the frontier. The language of a fiction of transition, concerned as it is with the potential rather than the representative, is perhaps a far cry from the language of a

Gordimer novel; but the attempt to categorize it as an "allegory" may constitute a dismissal of a crucial development in the form of the novel, a denial of a certain kind of frontier which the *genre* may undertake to explore.

Derek Wright (essay date Summer 1989)

SOURCE: "Fiction as Foe: The Novels of J. M. Coetzee," in *International Fiction Review*, Vol. 16, No. 2, Summer, 1989, pp. 113-18.

[*In the following essay, Wright examines Coetzee's fiction as representative of a hostile colonial act in itself.*]

The settings of J. M. Coetzee's five novels are, at first glance, unusual for a contemporary South-African writer. They are, respectively, the United States, undefined parts of the South-African hinterland of the eighteenth and nineteenth centuries, the frontier of an unnamed country on "the roof of the world," a war-ravaged Cape Town and Karoo of the future, and the fictional-cum-metafictional territory of the Robinson Crusoe fable. In fact, each of the novels is, not surprisingly, a fictional extrapolation from South Africa's current historical crisis. In these fictional projections, however, the very fictional properties of myth, ideology, and history—and finally fiction itself—are themselves targeted as a principal source of hostility to human values in the colonial context.

Coetzee's first experiment in damaging and deranged fictions, *Dusklands* (1974), couples two megalomaniacal narratives. The first, **"The Vietnam Project,"** is that of Eugene Dawn, a "mythographer" employed by the American military in a Californian research station to explore the potential of radio broadcasting for psychological warfare against Vietnam. The second, **"The Narrative of Jacobus Coetzee,"** purports to be a translation of an eighteenth-century frontier narrative of a brutal punitive expedition against the Namaqua Bushmen. The first is, by implication, a modern version of the colonial frontier narrative insofar as the American occupation of Vietnam is a continuation of the processes of Western imperialism, and both men are revealed to be paranoid victims of the colonial mentality. Both mythologize their war into the pattern of benign fathers putting down rebellious children who are incapable of taking care of themselves (the American authorities finally discover Dawn, at the peak of his madness, torturing his young son in a hotel room). Both condemn their subjects to death in the name of some higher power, each regarding himself as an instrument of God or a "tool in the hands of history," though for Jacobus the gun is the major instrument and symbol of control, for Eugene the word. Like his historical Afrikaans counterpart, the latter has an exploring temperament:

"Had I lived two hundred years ago I would have had a continent to explore, to map, to open to colonization. In that vertiginous freedom I might have expanded to my true potential." Like the Magistrate in Coetzee's third novel, *Waiting for the Barbarians* (1980), he likes to record the customs and decipher the relics of the people he is involved in destroying. To the power of the gun is added that of the pen, camera, and radio-speaker, through which academic writers and media men presume to speak for the obscure, remote people whose right of speech they in fact deny and who, as in the living analogue of contemporary South Africa, are still unable to speak for themselves. *Dusklands* challenges the idea that the exploring social scientist—the ethnographer and mythographer—can neutralize his stance towards, and distance himself objectively from, the colonized subjects of his exploration. Rather, his own mental fictions are imposed upon them, locking them into a foreign code of consciousness, and Coetzee refuses to exempt the novelist himself from the colonization process. Coetzee situates himself at the edge of Dawn's narrative by giving his own name to the director of the propaganda program, ironically called the "New Life Project," and Jacobus Coetzee's eighteenth-century narrative is supplemented by a critical afterword from an "S. J. Coetzee" and is translated by one "J. M. Coetzee," thus linking the author with his Afrikaans ancestors. Since both of the narrators are mad, it is difficult to distinguish what happens from what they imagine, to mark off what is "real" from what is invented, but the novel does not stay for long even within the elastic bounds of a deranged psychological realism. As Teresa Dovey has observed the self-implicating strategies of Coetzee's fiction, by candidly announcing its fictionality, take self-consciously into account the material circumstances of the book's composition, the conditions for the production of narratives like this, and the processes by which particular modes of narrative and discourse that have been tied up with the colonization process are officially institutionalized and constitutionalized. The very arbitrariness with which the two narratives are conjoined implies that their relation to historical reality is problematical and is not a straightforward matter of representation. Behind *Dusklands* are the implications that "Realism" is simply a product of one limiting kind of language code, and that, as Stephen Watson has argued, it is not only through violent military conquest that we are colonized but through language itself, through conventional sign systems passing themselves off as "natural" and "universal." To the extent that historical realism is the favored mode of the frontier and colonial narrative, the literary deconstruction of traditional realism is simultaneously a political act of decolonization, and Coetzee attempts both of these in his first novel.

Coetzee's second novel, *In the Heart of the Country* (1977), is sited in the nightmarish world and murderous fantasies of another "mad" person, Magda, a vaguely nineteenth-century spinster living on a farm out in the veld, "totally outside human society, almost outside humanity." In her fantasy Magda is perpetually killing and burying her father Johannes, one of the mythic fathers of the Afrikaans government who refuses to be got rid of in spite of her imaginative efforts to "fold him away for the night." "If I intend to settle him in this grave there is no way to do so but to pull him in, to climb in first and pull him in after me," she concludes. "But now I think that for some days after my death he will still lie here breathing, waiting for his nourishment." Her desire to be rid of her father, and the regime he represents, springs from her white liberal impulse to communicate with and befriend her slave servants Klein Anna and Hendrick. Magda, as suffering white female, empathizes with the oppressed blacks to the point where she virtually thinks herself black: "From wearing black too long I have grown into a black person." She wears white only at night and black by day, and imagines both her "black" daytime self and her "white" nighttime self as being raped by Hendrick. She is barren and, like the blacks in the scheme of the official colonial fiction, is viewed as sexless by a white paternal authority which considers itself as the supreme embodiment of potency. The father's codes, however, have also entrapped the daughter, who finds her behavior circumscribed by the inherited patterns of dominance and subservience. A female colonial Crusoe, she insists on renaming her "Friday" and, like her father, resorts to the gun when willpower fails and refuses to let the African take charge of his own destiny. But Magda is caught up in fictional codes of a sociolinguistic as well as a historical order, for the nineteenth-century colonial spinster in her historical backwater is, amazingly, familiar with the commonplaces of structural linguistics: "Words alienate. Language is no medium for desire. Desire is rapture, not exchange. It is only by alienating the desired that language masters it." As in *Dusklands,* the madness/reality frontier is also the site of a debate between postmodernism's and traditional realism's approaches to language, and the novel, by thrusting its heroine and an implied nostalgia for realism into the heart of the postmodernist breakdown, acquires an often painfully reflexive awareness of the contemporary contexts of its composition.

Waiting for the Barbarians, Coetzee's third novel, is a timeless parable of Empire, set on the frontier of an anonymous country, in the fort of an unnamed imperial power, and focuses on the moral dilemma of a liberal-minded Magistrate who takes the side of the nomadic people occupying the wilderness on the other side of the "barbarous frontier." The dominant enemy-fictions in this novel are the "barbarians" of the title and the "fisherfolk" with whom the undiscriminating imperial power frequently confuses them. The real nomads and hunters behind the labels desire only, it seems, to be left alone in peaceful coexistence with the frontier people on land which they consider theirs to traverse. The imperial power, however, persuades itself into believing that

it is under threat and sends out an army to kill or imprison and torture the "barbarians," who respond by destroying crops and leading the garrison into the desert where the soldiers die of starvation and exposure. The military of the "civilized" power, who are of course the real barbarians, then proceeds to inflict a terrible and hideous revenge. The barbarians, who are basically innocent, are really a mental fiction born of colonial paranoia and a political convenience: their invention has become indispensable for the maintenance of a blind, insane power which sucks everything into its vortex and for the antithetical definition of the Empire as a force for "civilization," which presupposes the existence of barbarism. The title is taken from a poem by Cavafy: "And now what will become of us without Barbarians? / Those people were some sort of solution." Civilization cannot exist without an enemy. A compassionate man who always "believed in civilized behaviour," the Magistrate is thrown into jail and tortured for his treasonable kindness to a crippled barbarian woman whom he nurses back to health and then returns to her people. By taking the side of the oppressed, the Magistrate—much more than Magda—effectively becomes one of them and at his eventual release is left stranded between two camps, "a man who lost his way long ago but presses on along a road that may lead nowhere." His muddled minority position makes him a common figure in Coetzee's work: the reluctant colonizer who can no longer bear the burden of an arbitrary historical role which condemns him to treat others as things and himself to a state of murderous self-hatred. He tries, the narrator says, "to live outside of history."

What the Magistrate attempts, the protagonist of the next novel, *Life and Times of Michael K* (1983), does. Michael K, concludes the hospital doctor into whose care he drifts, is "a human soul above and beneath classification." He is "untouched by history . . . a creature left over from an earlier age." The novel depicts the strange peregrination of Michael, a municipal gardens laborer, from the Cape to the Karoo with the sick body, and then the ashes, of his mother: a pilgrimage which is blocked at every border by army and military police, and which leads to his triple internment as vagrant and suspected guerrilla in prison, camp, and hospital. There is a war, civil or revolutionary, going on in the background of his journey but it remains vague: it is fought, according to the camp commandant, "so that minorities will have a say in their destinies," which probably refers to the ruling white minority keeping their "say." K, who "barely knows there is a war on," is out of it because he is busy existing on his own marginal terms, unresponsive to historical determinants which to him are unreal. In *Waiting for the Barbarians* the ruling abstraction, the hostile fiction preoccupying the paranoid mind of the oppressor was the barbarian. In *Michael K,* however, there is a sense in which the prevailing "fiction" is extended beyond the guerrillas—the "friends" Michael is accused of collaborating with by growing them food on his improvised allotment in the Karoo—to take in the whole unreal, insane historical situation of South Africa which has issued in Civil War. The keynote is again sounded by the doctor, who sees Michael not as part of the substantial historical world which he himself believes in but as "scuffled together" from "a handful of dust . . . into the shape of a rudimentary man." He is a "genuine little man of earth," his fingers hooked and bent, ready "for a life of burrowing, a creature that spends its waking life stooped over the soil, that when at last its time comes digs its own grave and slips quietly in and draws the heavy earth over its head like a blanket and cracks a last smile and turns over and descends into sleep, home at last, while unnoticed as ever somewhere far away the grinding of the wheels of history continues."

Continually lapsing out of and back into consciousness, less a human being than a spirit of ecological endurance, Michael K is a creature not of human history but of earth, his true literary ancestors Lear's "naked unaccommodated man" and those rocklike, purely elemental Wordsworthian presences, the Leech-Gatherer and the Old Cumberland Beggar, rather than Voltaire's Candide (who also "works in the garden"). Disenfranchised from a human existence on the earth's surface, he is directed back towards the earth itself and goes literally underground like an animal, insect, or grub, leaving no trace of himself; he is ploughed back into the soil and, after surviving three dungeon-like incarcerations, rises, as if from the dead, from the element to which he has rooted himself. Earth is a constant touchstone and referent for his existence. He burrows, grubs, plants, and hides in it, he carries his mother's ashes to the part of it from whence she came, and he will take back as food only what he has put into it: his family of sister-melons and brother-pumpkins, the fruit of his real mother, to which he is umbilically connected by an invisible "cord of tenderness." It keeps him barely alive and adumbrates his grave, for his desire to grow food is inversely proportionate to his need to consume it: "As he tended the seeds and watched and waited for the earth to bear food, his own need for food grew slighter and slighter . . . When food comes out of this earth, he told himself, I will recover my appetite, for it will have savor." He plants for posterity, not for the present, and, as Nadine Gordimer has noticed, to keep the earth, not himself, alive. Planting is K's, and the earth's, positive alternative to history as War: "Enough men had gone off to war saying the time for gardening was when the war was over; whereas there must be men to stay behind and keep gardening alive, or at least the idea of gardening; because once that cord was broken, the earth would grow hard and forget her children." Thus K makes his own kind of history: the earth man does not ponder the meaning of his existence but creates and becomes it. For those who live moment by moment there is, as K claims at the close, "time enough for everything": for the tender of earth who transcends the historical, suspended time

of war, time is as full at one time as at any other, being ever geared to the fruitful eventfulness of nature. At the end of the book he is bound for earth again, without money for food but with half a packet of seeds to reestablish his connection with his element.

Coetzee dramatizes the complicity of colonial settler narratives with exploitative politico-historical processes: the enemy is the imperial text through which the white author shuts the racial and cultural otherness of colonized peoples into closed European myth systems and codes of interpretation.

—Derek Wright

Coetzee does not provide his protagonist with a surname that would particularize him as a Cape Colored but chooses instead to surround him with Kafkaesque trappings—like the "K."s of *The Castle* and *The Trial,* he has no permit to be where he is so is moved restlessly on by authority derived from "the Castle," and is made to feel unspecified guilt over an unnamed crime—and the author, remarkably, draws our attention on the first page not to Michael's color but to the harelip which so hampers his speech that he is barely articulate. Of course, everything in K's circumstances insists that he isn't white. Coetzee's silence and apparent color-blindness, Kelly Hewson has argued, immediately betokens a refusal to label him in any way—black, white, or colored—because that is precisely what the dehumanizing classifications of apartheid do, but more important than this is K's representation of something so elemental and irreducible that it is beyond formulation in any of the existing historical codes: he is chthonic man, outside of language and history, as inarticulate as the seeds, plants, and humus of the earth cycle into which he is locked. Equally important, K is allowed only a minimal articulacy precisely because he is black and because it is dangerous for a white author, a composer of self-conscious fictions from the enemy camp, to presume to speak for him: a dilemma which Coetzee resolves in a different way in his most recent and startling novel, *Foe* (1986).

Commenting on Gordimer's achievements in the mode of critical realism, Coetzee has said, "I would like to think that today the novel is after bigger game" and, during the composition of *Michael K,* expressed feelings of dissatisfaction with the limitations of traditional form. In *Foe,* he does away with conventional realism almost altogether, dismantling his own fictions and stripping his fictional practice to the bone. *Foe* is simultaneously a retelling of the Robinson Crusoe fable, an allegory of South Africa's racial dilemmas, and a meditation on the art of fiction. In this version of the "Cruso" story the hero is a sullen boor without energy, imagination, or desire. Susan Barton, another shipwrecked voyager who is washed up on his island and into his dull celibate existence, is amazed that he has kept no journal of his island life—"Nothing I have forgotten is worth remembering"—and has frittered away his time building, with Friday's help, stone terraces for the planting of nonexistent seeds. Reluctantly rescued, Cruso dies at sea a few days from Bristol, and Susan takes his story and his black servant to one Mr. Foe (the novelist Daniel Defoe). At his quarters she slips into his bed and, in the fashion of the Muse, begets upon him the tale which he later pours forth as "Robinson Crusoe."

Through all this, Friday remains mute (his tongue was cut out, either by slavers or Cruso himself) and all attempts at communication with him come to nothing, principally because they are founded—and therefore founder—on erroneous European cultural assumptions. When Friday plays his flute, Susan can make nothing of the repetitive six-note melody of his African scales, and when she teaches him to write, can make no sense of what he puts to paper. The attempt is abandoned and it is only in the surreal last scene of the book, when a visitor from the future encounters the wraiths of Defoe, Susan, and Friday, that the black slave's mouth is prised open and from it issues "a slow stream, without breath, without interruption . . . it runs northward and southward to the ends of the earth." As Michael K's harelip is correctable and articulation restorable, so Friday's dumbness, a culturally enforced rather than a physical condition, is remediable. But we do not hear, because Coetzee does not and cannot know, what Friday says. Friday, if he could speak, would speak only in the colonial language of Cruso; and Coetzee, who can speak, is no longer prepared to speak for him, thus abandoning the token narrative and psychological realism of *Michael K.* Instead, as Helen Tiffin has cogently argued, he has demonstrated the oppressive structures—in this case, colonial narratives—that render blacks voiceless. Coetzee dramatizes the complicity of colonial settler narratives with exploitative politico-historical processes: the enemy is the imperial text through which the white author shuts the racial and cultural otherness of colonized peoples into closed European myth systems and codes of interpretation. It is not (and never was) tenable for such an author to write either about or on behalf of anyone who, like the South-African black, is still denied a voice of his own. In *Foe* Coetzee candidly abdicates from the fictionalizing process which the earlier novels are either about or participate in. In his deepening and darkening vision, the white fiction, by virtue of its privileged existence in the context of black oppression, is always the "foe," whether its author's name is Defoe or Coetzee.

G. Scott Bishop (essay date Winter 1990)

SOURCE: "J. M. Coetzee's *Foe*: A Culmination and a Solution to a Problem of White Identity," in *World Literature Today,* Vol. 64, No. 1, Winter, 1990, pp. 54-7.

[*In the following essay, Bishop questions the veracity of the authorial voice in postcolonial literature written in English and pinpoints* Foe *as a successful example of this questioning in a textual context.*]

Ngugi wa Thiong'o, in "The Language of African Literature," argues that African children should be taught African literature in their own African languages to preserve the cultural identity that colonization sought to destroy. A paradoxically similar assertion can be made for students of English literature. If by studying English literature we are studying our cultural identity, then we must also read postcolonial literature written in English. As Michel Foucault, Edward Said, and many feminists including Nina Auerbach, Margaret Homans, Sandra Gilbert, and Susan Gubar have shown, our cultural identity has resulted in our seeing the non-Western, nonwhite, nonmale, non-Christian, non-English-speaking world as other, as deviant. The Western, white Christian world, so confident of its identity, has imposed itself on the world of others, and from that world a new English-language literature is emerging. In contrast to Ngugi's concern that the colonial mind, through the literature of the colonizers, is being "exposed to images of his world as mirrored in the written languages of his colonizers," the colonizer is now, in his or her own language, being exposed to images of the usurper and the usurped world as mirrored in the literature of the colonized, the oppressed. Postcolonial literature shows us the post-colonial world's "way of looking at the world at its place in the making of that world." If it is not our moral duty, it is at least our duty as students of English literature to study postcolonial literature.

> **J. M. Coetzee's novels offer the privileged, predominantly white world an illuminating if not disconcerting picture of the political and moral entanglements in the complex postcolonial world.**
> **—G. Scott Bishop**

J. M. Coetzee's novels offer the privileged, predominantly white world an illuminating if not disconcerting picture of the political and moral entanglements in the complex postcolonial world. Coetzee is an Afrikaner born in Cape Town in 1940. He was educated in South Africa and the United States and is now a professor at the University of Cape Town. He has written five novels: *Dusklands* (1974), *In the Heart of the Country* (1977), *Waiting for the Barbarians* (1980), *The Life and Times of Michael K* (1983), and *Foe* (1986). He has won a number of prestigious awards including South Africa's premier literary honor, the CAN prize, as well as the Geoffrey Faber Memorial Prize, the James Tait Black Memorial Prize, and the Booker McConnell Prize.

Coetzee's success is significant, I think, because it can be attributed to our ability, as members of the privileged world, to identify more readily with Coetzee, who is an Afrikaner, a descendant of colonizers, than with black Africans who are writing and publishing alongside Coetzee. Besides his political sympathy for blacks, his work reflects a concern for the whites' precarious position at the top of the social order. In the 9 March 1986 *New York Times Magazine* Coetzee's article **"Tales of Afrikaners"** appeared. In it he said, "Many Afrikaners, more moderate than their stereotype, still don't understand that they live on a lip of a volcano." That volcano encompasses South Africa's political realities.

These political realities, which necessarily mediate the conscious voice of any writer in South Africa, direct Coetzee's voice, a voice in conflict with itself. Coetzee reveals the power of language as a political tool, but at the same time he questions the validity of that power. He tells the story of oppression without pretending to speak for the oppressed. As a white man, an Afrikaner, he illustrates and questions his own voice as spokesman for the oppressed. Coetzee's doctoral dissertation, **"The English Fiction of Samuel Beckett: An Essay in Stylistic Analysis,"** explores why Beckett gave up English to write in French. During Coetzee's analysis of *Watt* he says:

> I began this excursus by asking why it is that language is pushed to the foreground in *Watt*. It now seems clear that when all is called into doubt no assertion can be made; yet the process of doubt, uttered by the doubter, remains on the page. We read, so to speak, a sequence of sentences that have been scored through: they form no statement because they have been cancelled, yet we read them all the same.

I think this Derridian idea of erasure, this process of pushing language to the forefront to record thoughts in "sentences which have been scored through," is an important aspect of Coetzee's own fiction.

Three of Coetzee's novels, *Life and Times of Michael K* and especially *In the Heart of the Country* and *Foe,* in form and content destabilize the reader's sense that any particular telling of events can be trusted. As Denis Donoghue said of Coetzee's books, "There is a certain fictive haze between the events and their local reference." Donoghue argues that it is the "fictive haze" which gives Coetzee's novels "a suggestion of ancestral lore and balladry." As I see it, the "haze"

is accomplished through plot and language, but increasingly by a displacement of authorial voice.

All three of the novels to some degree are presented as compilations of texts, letters, and diaries, which tell both a story and the story of that story. The reader is at times forced to read the book as a series of documents which reveal their own credible or incredible stories. In such cases the voice presented in the documents usurps the authorial voice, which becomes little more than that of an editor. The authorial voice is displaced into an abyss. It is as if we were standing on the lip of the volcano listening to the detached voices echoing out of darkness.

Besides the critical self-canceling voice, there is also an aspect of Coetzee's voice that agrees with Derrida's contention that the tradition around which Western thought has had "to organize itself" is that the "order of the signified is never contemporary, is at best subtly discrepant inverse or parallel—discrepant by the time of a breath—from the order of the signifier." Especially in his white female characters, the discrepancy between the signifier, or the Dasein—the Heideggerian notion of particular human existence, the concept of the self—and the signified, the actual self, is an unnerving and unresolved issue. Linguistically, the speaker whose language is the language of oppression is as shackled to the system of oppression as is the oppressed. The displacement of authorial voice is logically tied to this self-alienated speaker and is emotionally tied to what Donoghue expresses when he asserts that "the novels seem to say . . . that there was a time, in South Africa and elsewhere, when life was agreeable, a matter of local customs and drift of seasons, the productive earth, the beginning and the end." Within that sense of the past there is a sense of longing for a time like that to be restored, and restored for those who no longer wish to be identified as oppressors but who wish to have a tenable identity in a country which is their only home.

I see Magda from *In the Heart of the Country* and Michael from *Life and Times of Michael K* as prototypes for Susan Barton and Friday in Coetzee's most recent novel, *Foe.* In both cases the movement from the earlier to the later personage is toward a character shaped for a more clearly political reason. Susan is a far less sympathetic figure than Magda. Magda is mad not only from loneliness and alienation, but also from her philosophic understanding of her predicament. Magda stands at her window looking out as one of the servants crosses the yard at dusk.

> If I am an emblem then I am an emblem. I am incomplete, I am a being with a hole inside me. I signify something, I do not know what, I am dumb, I stare out through a sheet of glass into a darkness that is complete, that lives in itself, bats, bushes,

predators and all, that merely do no regard me, that
is blind, that does not signify but merely is. . . .
There is no act I know of that will liberate me into
the world.

Susan has many of the same problems that Magda has. Besides being, like Magda, an unwitting author in a language
which for various reasons she does not trust, Susan also believes, as Magda does, that she should be able to communicate across the racial bar. Both women naïvely believe that
women can communicate with blacks more easily than white
men can because blacks are more closely related to nature
than white men. Blacks are members of that world that
"merely is." Susan and Magda's misunderstanding is symptomatic of their whole problem. They have preconceived
notions of what blacks are like at the same time that they
do not understand their own roles as oppressors. Susan differs from Magda, however, because she is saner and therefore more competent to change her political circumstances.
However, she lacks Magda's philosophic insight. Susan tries
to free Friday by hanging a written proclamation signed with
Cruso's name in her hand around Friday's neck. She is be-
wildered to find that the proclamation only opens Friday to
those who would get the document, and thus Friday. Her
naïveté is carried further to her misunderstanding about the
truth of stories. Susan truly believes and continues to believe
that Daniel Foe, because of his identity as an author, can
write stories that tell the truth about experience, that give
experience "substance." In a letter to Foe she pleads with
him to write the story of the island.

> When I reflect on my story I seem to exist only as
> the one who came, the one who witnessed, the one
> who longed to be gone: a being without substance,
> a ghost beside the true body of Cruso. The island
> was Cruso's (yet by what right? By the law of the
> islands). . . . Return me to my substance Mr. Foe:
> that is my entreaty. For though my story gives the
> truth, it doesn't give the substance of the truth.

In short, Susan has a naïve belief that there is a rightful authority, someone who knows the Truth. She is like the
Afrikaners Coetzee mentions who "still don't know that they
live on the lip of a volcano." She believes there is someone
who represents authority just by nature of his identity, and
she does not see the volatile silence that authority so poorly
speaks for and to.

Whereas Susan is a more moderate figure than her prototype, Magda, Friday is a more extreme version of Michael.
The obvious connection between Michael and Friday is clear.
Although we do not know if Michael is black, we do know
that he is nonwhite. Friday is black. Michael's harelip symbolizes his crippled political voice. Friday's tongue has been
cut out by slave traders or by Cruso; we do not know by
whom. Just as Friday's physical impairment is more extreme

(is indeed horrific), so is Friday, as a symbol of oppression,
more extreme than Michael. Michael's bane is the regulations that control his rights to travel and have residence in
the country, and those regulations come to him in the form
of paperwork, permits, bureaucratic paraphernalia designed
to control his life. Friday's freedom is completely entrenched
in his inability to use language, and he is impotent against
any language. Whereas we learn very little about Michael
despite his being the central figure in *Life and Times of
Michael K,* we learn almost nothing about Friday. He is reduced to the barest frame of a man. We know nothing of his
past or of his thoughts. He is an unmediated being, and his
story is an unmediated story. Still, both Michael and Friday
become not only the subject of the interpretation (and therefore the subject of the authority) of other characters in the
books, but also the subject of the reader's interpretation.
Coetzee puts us, as readers, in the very position he finds so
questionable. We see Michael's and Friday's presence as literary and political issues, and we try to interpret the meaning of them as characters; but Coetzee has made Michael
and especially Friday resistant to interpretation. That is their
nature as figures in the novels: they suggest that the reader
should interpret, but they thwart any interpretation. They remain steadfastly silent.

The movement of the characters from their prototypes to
their culmination in Susan and Friday shows that Coetzee's
concern for political identity becomes increasingly evident
throughout the course of his work. Issues of personal identity and political power have been increasingly expressed in
issues of language. Susan, Friday, and *Foe* are a culmination of Coetzee's attempt to tell a story without asserting
himself in the novel. He displaces authorial voice for reasons simultaneously political and moral. Recognizing language as the tool of oppression it can be, Coetzee dissipates
the voice which could be mistakenly identified as authority.
Having dissipated the voice, he calls into question the authority it is mistaken for, and by that very act he suggests
the possibility of revolution and the subsequent reestablish-
ment of a valid moral system.

Using the torture room as a metaphor for South Africa,
Coetzee says of postrevolutionary South Africa that in such
a society

> . . . it will once again be *meaningful* for the gaze
> of the author, the gaze of authority and authorita-
> tive judgment, to turn upon scenes of torture. When
> the choice is no longer limited to *either* looking on
> in horrified fascination as the blows fall or turning
> one's eyes away, then the novel can once again take
> as its province the whole of life.

Coetzee, as a writer, is morally compelled to speak at the
same time that he is aware of the suspect nature of repre-

sentation, authorial voice, and even language. The figures of Magda and Susan deal most directly with the divided identity of the oppressor and the paradoxical nature of authorship. The figures of Michael and Friday illustrate the effectiveness of language as a political tool and deal with the nature of the blacks' unspoken and unmediated story. *Foe* finally presses the novel to unprecedented limits as it deals with the silence of the blacks' story, the identity of the oppressor, the questionable political power of language, and the nature of authorship and authority. Because the authorial voice has been so thoroughly displaced, Coetzee seems to be trying and self-consciously failing to assert the idea that Roland Barthes discusses in "The Death of the Author": "It is language that speaks, not the author; to write is to read, through preliminary impersonality—which we can at no moment identify with the realistic novelist's castrating 'objectivity'—that point where not 'I' but language, performs." At the same time that language does "perform" so as to usurp any power Susan might have over the purpose of her writing, we find out more about Susan through the text than we do about what happened on the island. Still, even though in *Foe* we do not recognize Daniel Foe as the "I" of the novel, Susan trusts him as the author of *Foe.* Coetzee is saying that even though language does function beyond the "I," there is always an implied "I" just beneath the surface of the ink on the page, because writing is an authoritative act. In *Foe* Daniel Foe and Coetzee are almost the same person. Through his identity as author of *Foe* Coetzee has brought his own political identity into question.

Left doubting author and genre, we are entrenched in doubt, and it is that experience which makes *Foe* so effective. It is a distinctly political novel which forces the reader into the political experience of doubting author, authorial voice, and authority.
—*G. Scott Bishop*

Since Coetzee has displaced authorial voice and has done so in form as well as in content, we not only see that "when all is called into doubt no assertion can be made," but by reading "a sequence of sentences that have been scored through," we *experience* the doubt of the doubter. We are made leery of language as a tool for self-expression, because we see it as a tool of oppression. We doubt the ability of language to tell a story because we doubt if it can express identity, and if it cannot express identity, it cannot relate the experience of the speaker. Faced with the form of *Foe*—a compilation of documents, some within quotation marks— we begin to doubt if the book can properly be called a novel.

Left doubting author and genre, we are entrenched in doubt,

and it is that experience which makes *Foe* so effective. It is a distinctly political novel which forces the reader into the political experience of doubting author, authorial voice, and authority. At the end of *Foe,* when Cruso's formal robe and wig, when the pen and paper have been handed over to Friday, one can imagine Coetzee scoring through his last words and laying his finger against his own lips. When a reader finishes *Foe,* she does not long for Coetzee's next novel before she wonders if in *Foe* Coetzee has not effectively silenced himself.

Derek Cohen (review date Fall 1992)

SOURCE: Review of *White Writing: On the Culture of Letters in South Africa,* in *Dalhousie Review,* Fall, 1992, pp. 425-27.

[*In the following review, Cohen praises* White Writing *as a valuable addition to the study of post-colonial and post-revolutionary South African culture, although he finds in many of the essays a "rather heavy-handed solemnity of purpose."*]

It is not cheering or easy to reconcile the author of some of the most exciting and wrenching fiction of recent years with the careful academic who produced this book of essays [*White Writing: On the Culture of Letters in South Africa*]. Certainly the essays have their value, and they supply criticisms and readings of much neglected and misread South African white writing. But they are somewhat off-puttingly and self-consciously postmodernist, larded with snazzy phrases like "poetics of blood," which sounds good, but ends up meaning what we have always known as racial theory. And yet, while he loves the sound of the new or the neo, he also is amongst the most cautious and careful writers of academic prose one is likely to find, scrupulous almost to a fault. One longs, in reading this book, for some of the vibrations and earthquakes Coetzee can set off in his fiction. His critical tact can also be questionable, as when he writes in an essay on Sarah Gertrude Millin, "It is a mistake to ask whether Millin is for or against the attitudes toward genetic inheritance that make if impossible for Barry to live a normal life with this English wife in South Africa: or at least it is a procedural error to ask the question too soon." We may be forgiven for wondering what this overprecise legalese means, and whether, in art—or life—it is ever a mistake to ask a question.

Nevertheless, despite its rather heavy-handed solemnity of purpose, the book possesses real value for those who wish to understand the culture of the white settlers of South Africa in their historical, political and cultural contexts. *White Writing* is Coetzee's attempt to give a context to those works of white South Africans that have shaped the white South African—English and Afrikaans—political culture. He is a storehouse of information and knowledge of the works that have shaped white thinking, and, in addition, has a rather ostentatiously capacious familiarity with the nineteenth-century European traditions which informed the sometimes too-receptive and willing white writers of South Africa. He uses his familiarity with the more recent theorists, especially the French, fairly tactfully and always usefully, and manages to supply a kind of postmodernist cast to his mostly critical-historical essays. Though, with his fascination with these writers, the book becomes rather weighty with phrases like "the Discourse of the Cape" that ends up sounding better than it means.

The flagship essay of the book, **"Idleness in South Africa"** is also, in some ways, the least satisfying. On the one hand it is an audacious and serious attempt to write the history of Cape colonialism around those terms which have invaded and transformed the concept of racism. On the other, and less successfully, Coetzee rather arbitrarily chooses idleness as his touchstone of cultural differentiation when, virtually by his own admission, he might as well have chosen a plethora of other criteria as frequently and characteristically deployed through the literature of his white European examplars. The essay makes the fascinating point that idleness became the identifying mark of racial inferiority of the inhabitants of the Cape, of the non-white people and the Afrikaans settlers alike. The taint of idleness became, to the white minds which constructed it, the index of the inferiority of the peoples whom the dominant culture and political authority determined to oppress. The white conception of black idleness was used to justify oppression of the Hottentots, whose perceived characteristics permeated the white way of thinking, writing about, and seeing them. The Hottentots were perceived from a white perspective as idle, smelly, incestuous, promiscuous, improvident, etc. It is Coetzee's contention that it was their perceived idleness above all that determined for the whites the *difference* of the Hottentots and smoothed the way to their subjugation and eventual extermination. For me, one of the problems with this interesting argument—and it is a problem one keeps encountering in the essay—is the fact that idleness, by Coetzee's own criteria and references, is merely one of the categories of debility with which the whites branded the Hottentots. Their odoriferousness, for example, or their sexual permissiveness seem to loom as largely in the argument as their idleness, and, one feels, could as convincingly have been documented and levelled against them as their propensity to lie in the sun and do nothing. What is truly fascinating about the essay is the way the author places the white war against the Hottentot people of South Africa in the context of the ferocious European war on the beggars and how notions of the South African indigenous people were imported into the language and culture of European

settlers in a characteristic travesty. It is intriguing to see how the idleness of the Boers does not create the same crisis of recognition for the writers on idleness. The question of whether black idleness is prelapsarian innocence or evidence of depravity is tackled when the habit of indolence begins to be noticed amongst the Boers whose idleness is directly proportional to their use of the non-white people for their easy way of life. The crime of capitalism, both early and present, looms large in most of the essays of the book as one of the compelling sources of the evil of racism.

A major contribution to South African English cultural studies made by *White Writing* is the long overdue inclusion of Afrikaans writing as one of the many shaping phenomena of South African cultures of race and racism. Coetzee's essay on the Afrikaans writer, C. M. van den Heever, truly the D. H. Lawrence of South Africa, with his equally ludicrous blood consciousness, goes a long way to explaining and describing the deep vein of sentimentality in Afrikaans culture and the bond to the land as an almost preconscious feature of that culture. His essay on the outrageous racial writing of the Jewish writer Sarah Gertrude Millin establishes the literary and historical contexts for the ballyhoo that white culture was for too long willing to accept as scientific, with its roots in Zola and the Goncourts. Millin's importation of these Realist theories into the South African context engraved these notions in the granite of High Art. It may be suggested that white South Africa has never recovered.

There are interesting essays on various other themes. All are subversive and radical in the best senses of those words. And though I began with a qualification, by which I stand, the pieces that make up *White Writing* supply a refreshing and vigorous means of entry to South African culture.

Mike Marais (essay date 1993)

SOURCE: "'Omnipotent Fantasies' of a Solitary Self: J. M. Coetzee's 'The Narrative of Jacobus Coetzee'," in *The Journal of Commonwealth Literature*, Vol. XXVIII, No. 2, 1993, pp. 48-65.

[*In the following essay, Marais argues "that J. M. Coetzee's novella 'The Narrative of Jacobus Coetzee' . . . suggests as much about the ethnocentricity of early South African travel writing" as does early colonial literature.*]

Referring to early colonialist literature in general, Abdul JanMohammed makes the point that "Instead of being an exploration of the racial Other, such literature merely affirms its own ethnocentric assumptions, instead of actually depicting the outer limits of 'civilization', it simply codifies and preserves the structures of its own mentality". In this paper,

I shall argue that J. M. Coetzee's novella **"The Narrative of Jacobus Coetzee"**, which is presented as a travelogue from "the great age of exploration when the White man first made contact with the Native peoples of *our* interior" (emphasis added), suggests as much about the ethnocentricity of early South African travel writing. Being a profoundly metarepresentational work, it foregrounds those strategies by which Europeans represent to themselves their others. In arguing this case, I shall trace the novella's thematization of the mediation of the contact between the European self and the African other by language and the narrative systems of western culture. I shall also demonstrate the part played by the text's dislocated temporal structure in relating the consequences of this mediation to the contemporary South African reader.

When Jacobus Coetzee leaves "civilization" and ventures forth into the unsettled wilderness, he encounters a world of things, what he refers to as an "undifferentiated plenum" without polity. This world, elsewhere referred to as consisting of "interspersed plena and vacua", is depicted as a void, the antithesis of all human sign-systems. In order to comprehend this chaos of raw African matter, Jacobus Coetzee transforms it into human constructs, a transformation described as follows: "In his way Coetzee rode like a god through a world only partly named, differentiating and bringing into existence". The analogy here between colonization and divine creation *ex nihilo* suggests that the Africa which Jacobus Coetzee encounters and explores in the course of his expedition has been invented rather than found; instead of exploring a new world, he creates a discursive world on the base of a natural one. The linguistic terms in which this analogy is couched imply that the natural African reality is contingent and can only be rendered accessible to European minds by being settled conceptually through language. In relating the incomprehensible and inexpressible African space to European systems of order, language provides the European mind with purchase on this landscape. It follows, then, that in his account of his travels, Jacobus Coetzee does not represent Africa as much as present it for the first time and constitute it in his European reader's mind as a verbal construct, an artefact.

This act of linguistic and conceptual transformation is not just Empire's hubristic emulation of a divine feat: it forms the basis of an active scheme of mediation and settlement by other, secondary systems of social ordering. So, for example, Jacobus Coetzee, who describes himself as "a hunter, a domesticator of the wilderness, a hero of enumeration", comments on the imperial enterprise as follows:

> We cannot count the wild. The wild is one because it is boundless. We can count fig-trees, we can count sheep because the orchard and the farm are bounded. The essence of orchard tree and farm

sheep is number. Our commerce with the wild is a tireless enterprise of turning it into orchard and farm. When we cannot fence it and count it we reduce it to number by other means.

In this context, linguistic settlement can be seen as a covert form of colonization, the first step in a process of overt colonization aimed at containing the land, subordinating it to human will and rendering its infinitude finite by reducing it to an assortment of computable acres. Even the introduction of orchard trees and stock animals forms part of this scheme of settlement, since they constitute a means of Europeanizing the land which sustains them. Plantation is thus both an act of enclosure and an act of creation.

The African landscape, then, is perceived in terms of a scheme of social and economic use. This mode of perception is particularly evident in the following description of Jacobus Coetzee's "discovery" of the Orange River:

> And so on 24 August Coetzee arrived at the Great River (Gariep, Orange). The sight which greeted him was majestic, the waters flowing broad and strong, the cliffs resounding with their roar . . . He saw that the banks, clothed in trees (*zwartebast, kareehout*), might furnish timber for all the wants of colonization . . . He dreamed a father-dream of rafts laden with produce sailing down to the sea and the waiting schooners.

As this mercantile reverie makes clear, the wilderness is not expressed in terms of its *dasein* but in terms of the human principles of profit and gain.

At stake here, though, is not simply the conceptual settlement of African territory through language and its mediation by European categories of trade and social use but the extent to which such mediation implies a certain conception of time and history. In being mediated, colonial space which is unordered in the present of observation is transformed and given a "prefigurative order", that is, it is codified in the terms of a Euro-expansionist, capitalist future. Thus it is clear in the examples cited above that for Jacobus Coetzee the future consummation of the colonial project and with it the victory of European order in Africa is always extant in the moment of observation: instead of seeing wilderness, he sees orchards; instead of a river, a channel of trade. The act of seeing, then, projects European hegemony into the future—hence Jacobus Coetzee's boast that his journey implicates the "discovered" world in history: "Every territory through which I march with my gun becomes a territory cast loose from the past and bound to the future". Upon being "bound to the future" in this way, the raw colonial matter, which is contingent and unapproachable on its own terms, becomes part of a larger pattern and process and accordingly gains significance. The colonial habit of perception evinced by Jacobus Coetzee thus narrativizes Africa and implicates it in the European plot of colonial history.

Once narrativized in this fashion, Africa becomes a term in a highly deterministic plot, since the syncopation of time which occurs with the conflation of present and future in the colonial mode of perception prospectively determines the course of history in predicating a fixed, teleological line of development. Since there can be no deviation from this narrative line, all possibility of change is eliminated and history becomes a relatively simple affair, an inexorably advancing narrative which seeks its own end, that is, its *telos*—the realization of imperial intention in Africa. Any colonial material which challenges this comic ending to the colonial story is consequently elided from the narrative.

Nowhere in the novella does this conception of colonial history emerge more clearly than in Jacobus Coetzee's encounter with the Khoi. Describing himself as a "tool in the hands of history", he makes it very clear that the Khoi threaten the European story in Africa with teleological disorientation and must therefore be removed from it: "If the Hottentots comprise an immense world of delight, it is an impenetrable world, impenetrable to men like men, who must either skirt it, which is to evade our mission, or clear it out of the way". African raw material which cannot be narrativized must thus be annihilated. Not having been absorbed into, and thus given significance by, the pattern of meaning formed by the European design in Africa, the murdered Khoi can be dismissed off-handedly by Jacobus Coetzee as "nonentities swept away on the tide of history". In other words, only a term in a history can be deemed an entity, a "thing that has real existence". The plot of colonial history does not only confer significance, then, but also reality; and since they are bereft of reality or mere insubstantial figments in his eyes, Jacobus Coetzee, agent of European order in Africa, can also assert of the Khoi that "They died the day I cast them out of my head".

So, in order to preserve the *telos* of the ideal European plot in Africa, Jacobus Coetzee resorts to prospective plotting, a process which culminates in the elision of corrosive material from the tale. The fixation with its own completion which the European plot in Africa manifests here, is foregrounded by the iterative structure of the novella. In the text, Jacobus Coetzee's travelogue is followed by an afterward in which S. J. Coetzee, a historian who is presented as a twentieth-century descendant of Jacobus Coetzee, repeats his ancestor's actions by effacing all rival views from his own account of Jacobus Coetzee's expedition:

> The present work ventures to present a more complete and therefore more just view of Jacobus Coetzee. It is a work of piety but also a work of his-

tory: a work of piety toward an ancestor and one of the founders of our people, a work which offers the evidence of history to correct certain of the anti-heroic distortions that have been creeping into our conception of the great age of exploration when the White man first made contact with the native peoples of our interior.

By eliminating "anti-heroic distortions" from his record, S. J. Coetzee protects the colonial plot from dissenting histories which challenge its centricity. Where his forebear, the frontiersman, engages in prospective plotting by mapping out future events, S. J. Coetzee, the historiographer, engages in "retrospective plotting" by ordering events that have already occurred. In both cases the ordering process aestheticizes history by rejecting material which does not fall into the ideal pattern of European experience in Africa.

These exercises in retrospective and prospective plotting reduce the dialogic nature of history to a monologic story in which the subject of Empire acts upon and predicates docile colonial objects. The imperial syntax which underpins this story and which installs this binaric relation between the European self and the colonial other is laid bare in the novella by Jacobus Coetzee's following description of his allegorical journey:

> I become a spherical reflecting eye moving through the wilderness and ingesting it. Destroyer of the wilderness, I move through the land cutting a devouring path from horizon to horizon. There is nothing from which my eye turns, I am all that I see".

The image of the travelling, disembodied eye and the pun on "eye" and "I" here, suggest that the collocations of subjects, verbs and objects in the text are thematically significant, and that the plot is informed by an imperial syntax in which the subject of the narrative sentences is the explorer, the journey the verb, and African matter the direct object. This imperial grammar is not only confined to the particular story of European reaction to African space which the novella recounts, but also informs a much larger process. After all, the story of Jacobus Coetzee clearly allegorizes the entire colonial project by presenting an explorer-hero as embodiment of European order on a journey of discovery which instead of "discovering" anything merely subsumes raw colonial matter into prior categories and so confirms and celebrates the ability of European cognitive structures to contain African events and objects. Since it contains the seed in which can be detected the outlines of the concluded story, the imperial syntax could be said to constitute the narrative formula which informs the entire colonial effort. If adhered to, this formula regulates colonial history by excluding mordant matter from its plot and by placing those events which it does subsume in an acceptable relation to others, thus making them part of a single, inclusive line of action which leads inexorably to the *telos* of European success in Africa.

J. M. Coetzee's point here seems to be that colonial representations of Africa and aestheticizations of history are dictated by this imperial grammar of narrative. The iterative structure of the novella, for example, shows that it is the basic formula to which both Jacobus and S. J. Coetzee reduce the infinite variety of Africa. Moreover, the temporal gap of two centuries with which J. M. Coetzee separates the documents of this explorer and historiographer in the novella is calculated to show that this formula has been re-enacted in various permutations over the centuries in European representations of Africa. The novella's shifting temporal perspective therefore focuses the reader's attention on the processes which have mediated these representations. Accordingly, it becomes clear that the imperial syntax and systems of language in general create their referent rather than offer direct access to it. In other words, rather than represent the actual Africa, they systematize it, constitute it in the European's mind as a verbal construct with a specular function, namely to reflect the cognitive framework of his/her own language and culture and thus affirm his/her experience of that culture.

In producing Africa and its indigenous population as Europe's other, the imperial narrative sentence thus enables Europe to imagine *itself* into being, that is, to secure its *own* representation in its communal consciousness. This self-constituting function of narrative strategies of representation is parodied throughout the novella, the putative documents of which construct their assumed readers as Europeans. While ostensibly a travelogue from the "great age of exploration", Jacobus Coetzee's account for instance, presupposes the inscription of an encounter between European and African cultures intended for, in Mary Louise Pratt's terms, the "domestic audience of imperialism". Indeed, by opening with a description of the differences between Khoi and colonial societies, it appeals to the reader to align him/herself with the subject of the enunciation: "The one gulf that divides *us* from the Hottentots is our Christianity. *We* are Christians, a folk with a destiny. *They* become Christians too, but *their* Christianity is an empty word" (emphasis added). While othering the Khoi, this description valorizes the identity contained in the subject position which it inscribes, namely white, European. In this way the text engages the reader, the "domestic subject of Empire", in a ritual of ideological recognition through which his/her apprehension of European superiority and African inferiority is sustained and reinforced.

Although S. J. Coetzee's historical document serves a similar ideological function, its construction of its reader suggests that the European colonialist's conception of selfhood has changed slightly in the two centuries which separate this document from that of Jacobus Coetzee. So while the reader is, in Louis Althusser's sense of the word, "hailed" by the text and created as a subject in the references to the land that "*we* had inherited" (emphasis added), "*our* early history" (emphasis added), and *our* people" as opposed to "the native peoples of *our* interior" (emphasis added), the identity implicit in the subject position here is not simply white European but, more specifically, white republican Afrikaner. In this regard it is significant that the Afterword is presented as a series of lectures delivered by S. J. Coetzee between 1934 and 1948 and first published in 1951—dates which coincide with that period of Afrikaner nationalism which culminated in the National Party's accession to power in 1948. The suggestion in this parody of foundational historiographical texts is that European colonizers are in the process of imagining themselves as citizens of a southern African republic, in other words, Europe now conceives of itself as being indigenous. At the same time, however, tangled constructions like "the *native* peoples of *our* interior" (emphasis added) expose the ironies inherent in this attempt at naturalizing colonial relations and racial hierarchy by insinuating that the "Afrikaner" has possessed the southern African interior by dispossessing the true "natives", and that s/he, even while establishing a purportedly independent South African society and culture, still retains and relies on European-based assumptions of white supremacy, power relations and strategies of self-invention.

Ultimately, then, S. J. Coetzee's document implies that, rather than collapsing during the Afrikaner's attempt to found a decolonized culture and conception of selfhood, the imperial syntax informs this attempt at negotiating new modes of self-understanding and therefore still mediates the dynamics of self-representation in the supposedly post-colonial society. The Afrikaner founding vision thus produces no new self. On the contrary, the colonialist's self-image is bolstered by S. J. Coetzee's aestheticization of history, his invention of a national narrative of origin for the nascent Afrikaner nation. As the repeated appeals to a common language, past, and race in this document show, the reader is invited to become, through identification with the unified subject of the enunciation, part of a coherent narrative which is self-sustaining to the extent that it makes the individual part of some larger set of projects which includes the past and the future. The *telos* which inscribes this coherent and continuous subjectivity, however, is merely a minor variant of the European expansionist *telos* of colonial history as a whole.

II

In focusing on self-sustaining aestheticizations of south African history and on the way in which they routinely re-enact the narcissistic narrative sentence, J. M. Coetzee directs his reader to the repression of another aesthetic, one governed by another syntax. The structural juxtaposition of Jacobus Coetzee's document with that of S. J. Coetzee, for instance, foregrounds the historiographer's elision of the explorer's "sojourn" with the Khoi from his account of the expedition. Upon closer examination, the reader is able to see that S. J. Coetzee's dismissal of this episode as an "historical irrelevance" can be ascribed to the fact that it constitutes a momentary departure from the grammar which informs the rest of Jacobus Coetzee's travelogue. As has already been established, Jacobus Coetzee, the putative author and hero of his account, is for the most part the subject and his journey the verb of the imperial sentences which form the document. That section of the report which recounts his "sojourn" with the Khoi, however, constitutes a hiatus in which the journey is suspended and the subject loses control over the world of objects which surrounds it and which it hopes to order. Ignored by both the villagers and his servants, Jacobus Coetzee spends his time convalescing from illness in a hut reserved for menstruating women. This passive position inverts the highly active, heroic role he assumes in the various scenarios he imagines upon first meeting the Khoi:

> Tranquilly I traced in my heart the forking paths of the endless inner adventure: the order to follow, the inner debate (resist? submit?), underlings rolling their eyeballs, words of moderation, calm, swift march, the hidden defile, the encampment, the graybeard chieftain, the curious throng, words of greeting, firm tones, Peace! Tobacco!, demonstration of firearms, murmurs of awe, gifts, the vengeful wizard, the feast, glut, nightfall, murder foiled, dawn, farewell, trundling wheels.

This scenario and the ones which follow it are easily recognizable as standard variations on the formulaic plot which characterizes frontier writing, a plot in which the imperial syntax clearly manifests itself. Jacobus Coetzee thus positions himself in relation to the Khoi according to expectations created by European colonial discourse. In this regard it is significant that the entire encounter between explorer and native is described in aesthetic rather than existential terms, a description which constructs a reflexive analogy between the colonial encounter and the literary encounter of reader and text: just as the reader's approach to the text is conditioned by the codes and conventions of the literary intertext, so too is the colonizer's contact with the native conditioned by the corpus of colonial discourse. Given this mediation, no direct contact takes place when Jacobus Coetzee meets the Great Namaqua. Instead of the actual Khoi, he encounters the verbal construct constituted in his mind by colonial discourse, a construct which occludes them. It is therefore quite obvious that he expects his meeting with the Khoi to ritualistically re-enact the classic plot of European expansionism.

In marked contrast to this expectation, however, Jacobus Coetzee is reduced by this encounter to a figure of endurance rather than one of achievement, a process which starts when the Khoi do not adopt the position of submissive colonial objects. Rather than confirming the expectations contained in the various interaction he imagines, they act contrarily to them and therefore undermine them. Thus, when he addresses the Namaqua "as befitted negotiations with possibly unfriendly powers", they merely become bored and drift "out of [his] firm but friendly line of vision"; when he anticipates an attack, he finds that they display "no organized antagonism"; when he thinks that they probably regard him as a god and pictures himself as "an equestrian statue", he finds that they call him "Long-Nose"; and, instead of the "greybeard chieftain" of his expectations, he finds that the Khoi have "only perfunctory reverence for authority" and can only show him a dying man quite incapable of according him the ceremonious welcome that he expects. Finally, the epic flight which he envisages in one of his scenarios, becomes an abject scramble in which he is debased to a caricature of the intrepid "tamer of the wild" that he imagines himself to be: "Held in position by Klawer I evacuated myself heroically over the tailgate". The incongruous use of the adverb "heroically" in this context advertises Jacobus Coetzee's transformation from active agency and hero of the report to passive nonentity.

This disjunction between the treatment he expects from the Khoi and that which he actually receives is a measure of the extent to which Jacobus Coetzee's encounter with the Khoi differs from the ideal plot of European success in Africa, from the ritualistic celebration of the victory of western order over African space. Instead of confirming the heroic themes that it sets out to affirm, his journey threatens the colonial plot with teleological disorientation. Not, surprisingly, then, S. J. Pretorious, despite the fact that Jacobus Coetzee's eventual annihilation of the Khoi village reasserts the imperial syntax and thus constitutes a return to the original design of European intentions in Africa, deems it necessary not only to exorcize this evidence of radical discontinuity in the coherent colonial plot, but to rewrite the record in such a way that it reproduces the imperial syntax:

> On the fifth [day] he emerged upon a flat and grassy plain, the land of the Great Namaqua. He parleyed with their leaders, assuring them that his only intention was to hunt elephants and reminding them that he came under the protection of the Governor. Pacified by this intelligence they allowed him to pass.

Thus rewritten, this episode becomes syntactically identical to the formulaic plot which generates Jacobus Coetzee's expectations in his encounter with the Khoi. So, through the historian's intervention and artifice, that which did not match and promote the ideal plot in fact, is made to do so in fiction.

Although the original pattern of the colonial narrative is reasserted following Jacobus Coetzee's encounter with the Khoi, this momentary lapse from its imperial syntax is enough to foreground a dissonance between the contingent space of the African wilderness and the imported schema of European order. For a moment, the resistance to reification of the Khoi, whom Jacobus Coetzee refers to as being "representative of that out there", transforms the plot of history from one that represents Africa as a realm of imperial success to one that speaks of an-other Africa which blocks artificial, European designs and which denaturalizes the seemingly seamless connection between the verbal construct "Africa" constituted by colonial discourse and its referent. The consequence of this frustration of European intention is that the appearance of totality produced by the system of language and the teleology of colonial history disintegrates, discovering that which has been misrepresented and repressed, namely the unconfined world in which the Khoi live. Jacobus Coetzee describes this complex plural reality as "an immense world of delight" without polity: "What evidence was there, indeed, that they had a way of life of any coherence? I had lived in their midst and I had seen no government, no laws, no religion, no arts". It is only after he fails to comprehend them narratively, fails to "find a place for them in [his] history", that Jacobus Coetzee is able to see and describe the Namaqua in this way. Since it is unmediated by the schemes of European order, this is his first contact with the actual Khoi and thus his first real discovery.

The consequence of discovering this world of unconfined Dionysian flux is the exposure of the artificiality of the Apollonian forms of order which repress and seek to contain it. Once demystified in this way, the European plot in Africa collapses. And since Jacobus Coetzee's sense of self depends on the subject position which he occupies in this plot, its failure reduces him to a "pallid symbol", an unrealized nonentity. Ultimately, then, the Khoi's passive resistance to being reduced to malleable objects in a foreign plot decentres the subject of the imperial narrative sentence, discovering it as a construction of a textualized world.

Thus denarrativized, the explorer who requires a temporal world for the realization of his dreams of empire, one in which he can set *teloi* and commit himself to a certain continuity over time, is forced to occupy a wholly uncharacteristic, passive and inert position in a seemingly timeless realm completely antithetical to western conceptions of selfhood and history. In the context of such temporal deprivation, Jacobus Coetzee's desperate longing to be killed by the Khoi could be read as a desire for renarrativization. Thus he indulges in the following fantasies in which he is a term in a Khoi history:

I would gladly have expired in battle, stabbed to the heart, surrounded by mounds of fallen foes. I would have acceded to dying of fevers, wasted in body but on fire to the end with omnipotent fantasies. I might even have consented to die at the sacrificial stake . . . I might, yes, I might have enjoyed it, I might have entered into the spirit of the thing, given myself to the ritual, become the sacrifice, and died with a feeling of having belonged to a satisfying aesthetic whole, if feelings are any longer possible at the end of such aesthetic wholes as these.

Apart from pointing to the irony of having a character in a narrative seek narrativization, the self-reflexive references in this passage indicate that a coherent identity is rooted in narrative continuity. Thus Jacobus Coetzee comes to see that that which he initially feared, namely that the Khoi "have a history in which [he will] be a term", is far preferable to being treated as a mere "irrelevance". His desire to be taken "more seriously" is therefore underpinned by the hope that, as a term in their history, he would recuperate a sense of identity.

Since such an interpolation in a Khoi "history" would lead to a radical restructuring of his identity, Jacobus Coetzee's apparent willingness to submit to an alterior syntax initially suggests a readiness to rethink old imperial forms. Indeed, his fantasies of narrativization by the Khoi initially seem to involve a reversal of roles in which the Khoi adopt the subject position and reduce him to an object of antagonistic verbs in their plot of history. Ultimately, though, these "omnipotent fantasies" point to a desire to reassert the subject-object cognition of the imperial syntax. In this regard, it is significant that Jacobus Coetzee is the author and therefore actual subject of what he presents as Khoi plots. Thus, although he depicts the Khoi as subjects who reduce him to an object, the role he constructs for them in these narratives eventually affirms rather than challenges his culturally-conferred sense of self. The reason for this, of course, is that he represents not the actual Khoi, but reproduces their image in colonial discourse. This emerges when it is considered that their projection in these fantasies of an alternative plot is no different from that in the various scenarios he imagines upon first meeting them. In other words, it is the standard representation of the colonial native as barbarous other that occurs in frontier writing, a representation which negates the native but allows the colonizer to position himself in opposition to it and thus affirm his experience of his own culture, his sense of European superiority. Ultimately, then, that which is presented as a Khoi history proves to be just another aestheticization of Africa from the European point of view.

Since the Khoi eventually oust rather than narrativize him, it goes without saying that the content of Jacobus Coetzee's omnipotent fantasies is ironic. Furthermore, these fantasies are also ironic in shape for, as Jacobus Coetzee realizes, the Khoi live in a world to which a narrative form is entirely inappropriate: "To these people to whom life was nothing but a sequence of accidents had I not been simply another accident?" This world does not recognize the oppositions, such as that between subject and object, from which history erects itself, and therefore treats European man seeking his *telos* as an irrelevance. The Khoi's resistance to Jacobus Coetzee's imperial endeavours is therefore not premised on adopting an oppositional position, as his omnipotent fantasies suggest. The corollary is that they do not see him as an object and this, in turn, suggests that their structures of perception are informed by an alterior grammar, one entirely different to the imperial syntax. In this regard, J. M. Coetzee's description of a middle-voice practice which situates itself between the active and the passive voice is of interest. According to Coetzee, middle-voice practice does not construct the sharp divisions "between subject and verb, verb and object, subject and object" that transitive and active voice syntax does. The importance of this difference is that the blurring of these divisions prevents the self from assuming the subject position necessary to predicate the other. This distinction between a syntax based on a clearly differentiated subject and object and one based on their interconnectedness also emerges in the novella when Jacobus Coetzee, in an attempt to define himself in opposition to the Khoi, does so by singing the following ditty: "Hottentot, Hottentot, / I am not a Hottentot". He tells his reader that he chooses Dutch as the medium for this exercise in self-affirmation because "It was neater in Dutch than in Nama, which still lived in the flowering-time of inflexion". Since it erects divisions between subject verb and object, the syntactical structure of the European language accommodates notions of cultural superiority and inferiority more readily than does the highly inflected structure of Nama.

If Jacobus Coetzee's encounter with a syntax and structure of perception appropriate to Africa, such as that of the Namaqua, were to culminate in a rejection of the imperial syntax, Africa would become a site of regeneration; instead of being filled with the recognizable forms of European understanding by the European mind, it would prompt a decolonization of that mind, a restructuring of its cognitive character and so induce a new epistemology, a new way of seeing, understanding and imagining. Following his expulsion by the Khoi, it at first seems that Jacobus Coetzee will accept the rhetorical challenge of devising an alterior syntax. Alone in an open, limitless world vastly disproportionate to himself, he realizes that his self is fading; "In a life without rules I could explode to the four corners of the universe". Indeed, his stance in relation to colonial matter indicates that the divisions between subject, verb and object are collapsing and that he is dissolving into the wilderness:

> I was alone . . . Here I was, free to initiate myself into the desert. I yodelled, I growled, I hissed, I roared, I screamed, I clucked, I whistled . . .

However, the very existence of his travelogue, in presupposing his agoraphobic retreat to European society and reaffirmation of its social orders, indicates that rather than

> set[ting] out down a new path [and] implicat[ing] [him]self in a new life . . . the life of the white Bushman that had been hinting itself to [him],

he suffers a failure of the imagination. So while the metafictional play at this stage of this novella suggests that Jacobus Coetzee, in a world "without rules", a *tabula rasa,* becomes an author of sorts: "I played [my games] against an indifferent universe, inventing rules as I went", the nature of these "games" and "rules" shows that rather than being an *auctor,* in the sense of an originator who devises a new aesthetic and identity, he is an author in the demystified post-structuralist sense, one whose choice is dictated by the closures of the form of narrative history and who is consequently not a creator but a function of discourse. This becomes apparent when he itemizes as "games" four possible endings for the plot of his journey of discovery. It soon becomes clear that these "games" are all designed to restore his sense of identity by once again making him part of a narrative and therefore enabling him, in his own words, "to translate [him]self soberly across the told tale". As he puts it, "In each game the challenge was to undergo the history and victory was mine if I survived it".

The content of the third section of Jacobus Coetzee's narrative, that is, the genocide of the Namaqua tribe, indicates that he eventually chooses the second of the four possible endings to the plot of his journey, namely "to call up an expeditionary force and return in triumph to punish [his] depredators and recover [his] property". Furthermore, the success of this endeavour to recuperate his self narratively is suggested by the stylistic features of this section. Grammatically speaking, the difference between it and the previous section dealing with his "sojourn" with the Namaqua could hardly be more marked. While his presence as an agent in the first section is virtually effaced and he becomes a receptor rather than initiator in a static account in which passive constructions abound, in the second he constructs himself as the hero of an epic account in which he reduces the Khoi to the object of aggressive verbs. Indeed, the following citation invites the reader to read the genocide of the Khoi tribe as an epic battle in which Jacobus Coetzee is the hero: "WE DESCENDED on their camp at dawn, the hour recommended by the classic writers on warfare". This section thus clearly constitutes a syntactical transformation of the previous one, it rewrites Jacobus Coetzee's encounter with the Namaqua according to the dictates of the imperial syntax. In so doing, it reconstitutes him as a subject and eliminates all "anti-heroic distortions" from the account.

This reassertion of the imperial idiom obviously means that Africa's potential for becoming a site of regeneration which could stimulate the dialogic ideal of a re-negotiation of western conceptions of culture and identity is repressed by the monologic colonial plot. Accordingly, Africa remains a site of conquest and the critical historical juncture at which its unconfined and complex plural reality presents itself is relegated to a minor episode in the eventual success of European intention. It is, of course, precisely through this occlusion of the actual Khoi and construction of them as his barbarous other, that the imperial syntax reconstitutes Jacobus Coetzee as a subject. As the following passage makes clear, the image of the Khoi as a fiendish, indigenous horde enables him to re-imagine his self into being:

> Through [the Khois'] death I, who after they had expelled me had wandered the desert like a pallid symbol, again asserted my reality. No more than any other man do I enjoy killing; but I have taken it upon myself to be the one to pull the trigger, performing this sacrifice for myself and my countrymen, *who exist,* and committing upon the dark folk the murders we have all wished. (emphasis added)

The fact that Jacobus Coetzee should ultimately account for his choice in terms of a reassertion not only of his own identity, but also that of his "countrymen" indicates that he exercized the imperially correct option. Any deviation from the predetermined plot of his journey would undermine not simply his own enterprise but the entire European plot in Africa as well. And when an old plot fails, the identity of its postulated community is lost or, in terms of Jacobus Coetzee's assertion of his reality and that of his countrymen, unrealized.

III

The point of the novella is not only that Jacobus Coetzee's failure of the imagination before the void of colonial space determines his identity and that of his countrymen in the present, but also that it attempts to determine that of future white South Africans since it constitutes an act of prospective plotting which strives to ensure the realization in future history of the original design of the colonial plot of history. By rehabilitating the imperial syntax, he entrenches a single, inclusive, converging action which cuts through the centuries and leads to the present. The suggestion here that Jacobus Coetzee's actions may provide the narrative germ or blueprint for the twentieth-century South African reader's times and identity and that he, in a sense, "authors" the reader challenges the latter's ontological reality. In a metaleptic reversal, the reader is confronted with the thought that s/he may be a character in the narrative of Jacobus Coetzee, a product of his "father dream" and "omnipotent fantasies".

The novella's temporal and genealogical structure contributes to this metaleptic effect. For the most part the text consists of a succession of documents purportedly written by members of the Coetzee family over a period of two centuries. The fact that these characters all share the same name does not simply signify a familial affinity, it also indicates that the corporate identity which Jacobus Coetzee restored by reinstating the colonial plot has remained stable and intact over the centuries. The name "Coetzee" thus comes to signify the white, European identity inscribed in colonial history. Indeed, Dorian Haarhof, in referring to the recurrence of this name in the text, contends that "These Coetzees constitute the family frontier lineage of white South Africa incorporating space and zone over three hundred years of colonisation". Significantly, in this regard, Jacobus Coetzee is referred to by S. J. Coetzee as "one of the founders of our people". The question which the genealogical structure of the novella poses for the white South African reader in the late twentieth century is therefore whether his/her identity forms part of the genealogical line established by Jacobus Coetzee, that is, whether s/he is a character inscribed in the plot of white conquest.

In a final metaleptic manoeuvre calculated to implicate the ever-shifting present of reading, J. M. Coetzee allows the reader to assume that the date of the Translator's Preface which frames all the other documents is also the date of publication of the novella, that is, 1974. This period in South African history was distinguished by the rise of the Black consciousness movement, a movement which, as Stephen Biko's following words show, was intensely aware of the extent to which discursive practices inform oppression: "attention has to be paid to our history if we as blacks want to aid each other in our coming into consciousness. We have to rewrite our history and produce in it the heroes that formed the core of our resistance to the white invaders". The fact that this novella, which emphasizes the importance of narrative continuity to the national plot, should ostensibly both originate and conclude in the early 1970's, a period which constituted the emergence of a threat of discontinuity to that plot, should be deemed significant. In intimating a departure from the ideal plot of colonial history, it suggests that this plot may be a truncated tale, a tale which, given its obsession with its own completion, is therefore ironic in form. Ultimately, however, the novella, in an ateleological gesture, leaves it to the reader to determine the outcome of this dislocation of the *telos* of the colonial plot. In so doing, it positions him/her as the author of history—his/her actions or lack thereof in the arena of history will decide whether this deviation from the original design of the European plot in Africa constitutes its ultimate perversion and collapse or whether it is simply another minor episode in the eventual success of white intention. With regard to the white South African reader, the novella thus places him/her in a position which is analogous to that of Jacobus Coetzee, that is, s/he is prompted into making a choice which will help determine the future course of history. If this parallel between Jacobus Coetzee and the white reader were to hold and s/he were to re-enact Jacobus Coetzee's failure of the imagination by rehabilitating the monologic plot of colonial history, s/he would answer the question posed by the novella's structure by becoming part of its genealogy. Like Jacobus and S. J. Coetzee, s/he would be an author (in the post-structuralist sense) engaged in the preservation of the colonial plot, an interchangeable "tool in the hands of history". And since history plays a constitutive role in the text, this authoring of history, if successful, would provide an ending for the novella, an ending which would continue its iterative structure, its seemingly endless replication and therefore validation of the imperial syntax.

Another ending, however, is possible, one to which the course of the South African national narrative over the nineteen years since 1974 has tended. In a manner of speaking, then the rest is history. Rather than being a momentary lapse in the teleological momentum of the white plot, the trends of the early 'seventies led to Africa's sustained obstruction of the apartheid State's unreal designs. So, for example, they were followed by the Soweto uprising of 1976-78 which initiated a period of low intensity guerilla warfare in South Africa in the 'seventies and 'eighties. The State's response to this period of teleological disorientation was, of course, to attempt through physical and verbal exorcism to recuperate the *telos* of white history. Thus, in successive states of emergency, black political organizations were banned, their leaders detained, tortured and in many cases killed. A concerted effort was made to stifle black expression in general by banning the work of black writers, by restricting their publishers, by closing down newspapers directed at a black audience, and by silencing the media in general—restricting in particular their coverage of political unrest in the black townships. In effect, then, these material realities of apartheid point to a discursive intent, that is, to delete competing stories from the coherently single plot of the national narrative.

These other tales, however, have proved inerasable and, following the release of Nelson Mandela and the unbanning of the African National Congress and Pan-Africanist Congress in 1990, the potential for a vastly different national plot has become evident. In responding to the novella's ending from the perspective of 1993, one can therefore say that white history is indeed a truncated tale, an unfulfilled design, for the present is clearly a time of interregnum in which the old plot is dying and a new one is struggling to be born. Nevertheless, despite the fact that the contours of a better and alternative tale can be detected, a failure of the imagination is still possible. After all, an interregnum is, by definition, an open period with numerous aesthetic possibilities. Confronted with a large, diverse and complex order in which competing views abound, it remains for the contemporary South African reader and his/her compatriots to originate an aesthetic which represents the multiplicity of centres in southern African experience instead of replicating yet another exclusionary scheme of cultural dominance. In other words, a truly different nationhood and identity have yet to be imagined. And that is another journey, a difficult one along which alter Africa still awaits discovery.

Mark D. Hawthorne (essay date Spring and Fall 1993)

SOURCE: "A Storyteller without Words: J. M. Coetzee's *Life & Times of Michael K,*" in *Commonwealth: Novel in English,* Vol. 6, Nos. 1 and 2, Spring and Fall, 1993, pp. 121-32.

[*In the following essay, Hawthorne examines the meaning of Michael K's silence in* Life and Times of Michael K.]

While many critics have examined J. M. Coetzee's *Foe* (1986) for its intertextuality, treatment of women's issues, and use of fiction theory, few have examined his *Life & Times Of Michael K.* Those who have looked at this equally interesting novel have discussed Coetzee's use of myth and history or analyzed his use of starvation and his definition of the heroic or the mythic. While such studies help to clarify Coetzee's place in the development of the novel and in the development of the South African novel in particular, none has looked at what I believe is one of its central themes, the dilemma of the storyteller who distrusts the very words that he must use because social disintegration has resulted in semiotic systems that he neither understands nor, when he comprehends, accepts. In short, not dealing specifically with the making of fiction, Michael K examines some of the same kind of issues that Coetzee explored three years later in *Foe.*

In *Waiting for the Barbarians* (1980) Coetzee used straightforward first-person narration; he polished this sort of narration in *Age of Iron* (1990), where first-person narration takes the shape of a letter that Mrs. Curren, the narrator, writes over many months to her daughter in America. *Waiting for the Barbarians* lacks an immediate audience, the complexity of the narration arising from character portrayal, not narrative technique, but in *Age of Iron* Coetzee ironically understates the action, forcing the reader to explore the implied value systems of the mother and daughter in order to determine why Mrs. Curren includes certain events and to ask when Mrs. Curren has, indeed, been straight-forward and when she writes knowing that her words will be read by her daughter after her death. In the first two sections of *Foe,* Coetzee also used an epistolary technique although, as Gallagher has observed, the use of quotation marks seems to indicate a spoken voice, thus developing the writer-reader irony later implicit in *Age of Iron,* but Coetzee changed to third-person narration in the third section, giving the appearance of narrative simplicity that we find in *Waiting for the Barbarians,* a narrative simplicity sharply contrasted by the strange final section where he seems to have used interior monolog. *Michael K,* written between *Barbarians* and *Foe,* shares the latter's narrative complexity and may be read as a metafiction (Attwell) without weakening its "naturalistic" or "realistic" directness (Pinner).

Coetzee divides the narration between chapters told by an unspecified third-person narrator, who describes K with dispassionate, often clinical objectivity, and a middle chapter, related by an anonymous medical officer in Kenilworth, a rehabilitation camp. The K described by the narrator, while simple, seems to be functionally literate: for example, stuck by the news item on the Khamieskroon killer, he "stuck the page *with the story* on the refrigerator door" (emphasis mine). He figures how to keep the wheels of his cart from wobbling off the axle and knows to release water from the pump so that it will neither dry up the borehole nor reveal his presence to others. Scrupulously honest, this K apparently has no great difficulty either assessing the value of money when he shops or finding Prince Albert, the Visagie farm, or—on his final trip—the Côte d' Azur. This narration is not simplistic or mere "free indirect speech" (Dovey): it sometimes slips from third person to first person as if the distance between narrator and character were tenuous, and K's actions sometimes seem to originate from a much simpler person than the one suggested by the narrator's first-person accounts of his thinking.

In contrast, the K described by the medical officer is slow witted, maybe even seriously retarded, a mental condition physically symbolized by his hare-lip. As unable and, sometimes, unwilling to speak as Beckett's Watt, he frequently does not answer when directly addressed and consistently creates the appearance that he is an "idiot" or, at least, "a person of feeble mind who drifted by chance into a war zone and didn't have the sense to get out." Confronting a person free from the confusions forced on him by the war and desperate to fit him into his own preconceived categories, the medical officer finally abstracts K into an icon of the primitive innocent morally superior to the educated but corrupt bureaucrats who control South Africa. From the view of the medical officer, K is like the filthy, ignorant, and drunken Vercueil, who fascinates Mrs. Curren as she dies of cancer, or like Friday, whom Susan Barton believes might hold the secret of exactly what happened on the island before she arrived. In all three cases, the character who does not or cannot speak for himself most significantly influences the articulate narrator.

The structure of *Michael K* is strikingly similar to that of Beckett's *Watt,* a novel that Coetzee intimately knows as he has illustrated both through his dissertation and through several scholarly articles. In both novels, the first and last sections are narrated in third person by an unnamed narrator (who in *Watt* may be Sam) who shifts between external objectivity and a direct relation of the character's thinking. In both, the middle section is told in first person by a character who attempts to unlock the titular character's silence and to speak for him. In both, the titular character has a story to tell but is unable to articulate, and in both, the authors force the reader to harmonize, or at least to balance between, the character as described by the third-person and the first-person narrators.

The double focus builds a character who lacks spoken verbal skills but seems to have well-developed, or at least competent, internal verbal and mechanical skills. Even the medical officer's view of K suggests that his verbal deficiency may, indeed, be his hare-lip in that two different medical men claim that it can be corrected if he wants. Nonetheless, Coetzee forces on his readers the conflicting images of a thirty-year-old mentally deficient child in a man's body who seems to answer the confusion of modern life by ignoring it and a man mechanically competent but so distrustful of language that he inadvertently (and probably unconsciously) cultivates the appearance of a child. Further, K's thoughts, especially after his escape from Jakkalsdrif, seem to mature as he loses interest in his body, as if, contrary to usual physiological experience, he becomes more mentally alert as his body starves. Like Kafka's Hunger Artist, who might figure as a major subtext, K's freedom from the ordinary demands of the flesh sets him apart; however, K, who never starves himself with the conscious intent of the Hunger Artist, has found the food that he truly wants in the melons and pumpkins.

The narrator clinically describes the inner man; the medical officer passionately describes the outward appearance. The narrator, as it were, *invents K,* constructing a product that causes the reader occasional uneasiness when the distance between the two seems to fluctuate, the narrator sometimes seeming to know everything that K feels and thinks and other times seeming to know only the externals of K's actions. In contrast, the medical officer—and the reader who learns with him—*discovers K,* a shocking process that disrupts any formulate that he/she might have generated as ways of coming to terms with K and finally tries to turn him into an allegory of the unattainable in modern life. In the final part of *Michael K,* Coetzee brings the reader, who has already been shocked by the abrupt transition from one view point to the other, back to the third-person narration, but the medical officer's interpretation of K colors whatever the reader might think of the character. While putting K in the larger framework of social disorder, the return to the narrator's voice again shocks the reader. Now the medical officer's conclusions seem facile, a depersonalization that inadvertently obscures the real K behind his intellectually satisfying abstractions. To abstract K either as "less a human being than a spirit of ecological endurance" or as an emblem of "a poor working-man's mind and soul" seems to limit him; the attempt, like that of the medical officer, is to make him fit into a rational scheme that disregards his humanity.

In the first part of the narrator's account K is fully defined by his mother and his schooling at Huis Norenius. At Huis Norenius, the "godforsaken institution" that he thinks of as his father, he learned to be a gardener, to follow rules, and silently to endure hunger. Before his mother's death, he had someone to tell him what to do. Anna decides to go to Prince Albert and tells him to quit his job although he makes the cart, talks his mother into moving into the Buhrmann's apartment, and finally decides to leave Cape Town when the permits do not arrive.

After his mother's death, however, he becomes inarticulate, unable to understand the "code" in the language of the people at the hospital; he neither understands euphemisms for death nor knows how to act or speak when there is no familial authority to command his actions. The death of Anna is to K what the diagnosis of cancer is to Mrs. Curren in *Age of Iron:* in each case, the force that causes or motivates change in the main character comes outside, fully beyond the character's control. Suddenly K has no one to think for him but does not know how to respond to direct questions. For example, when one nurse gives him the parcels containing the ashes of his mother and some clothes and toiletries, he challenges her with "how do I know?" and receiving no answer opens the larger parcel and asks why they gave him the clothes. The nurse's lack of any direct answer confuses him.

While he takes his mother's ashes to Prince Albert, whoever meets him tries to limit him or to regulate him to a socially accepted niche by labeling him. K consistently refuses to fit into these limiting labels. When arrested after arriving in Prince Albert, he has no paper—in other words, no labels—and is too sick to speak to the police; therefore, the police creates labels for him: "Michael Visagie—CM—40—NFA—Unemployed," a mixture of half-truths and suppositions that seem to satisfy their need for clearly defined labels. Later, the medical officer, at first a man who needs to force his experiences into clear categories to understand them, also tries to reduce K to a series of labels:

> There is a new patient in the ward, a little old man who collapsed during physical training and was brought in with a very low respiration and heartbeat. There is every evidence of prolonged malnutrition: cracks in his skin, sores on his hands and feet, bleeding gums. His joints protrude, he weighs less then forty kilos.

As the medical officer later realizes, these observations do little except fit K's physical appearance into categories that preclude his having to face with what K might represent. Even after he begins to discard such labels, he refuses to accept that the patient is named "Michael," not "Michaels," a form of the name that lets the medical officer speak about K while maintaining distance while still ignoring his actual name.

In the first and last chapters K repeatedly questions the meanings of labels and, by his actions, rejects them. Though simple, he deconstructs the semiotic systems of an oppressive society: by not understanding how the power elite uses words, he cuts through the pretenses of that world with simple-minded directness. For example, in describing K's exchange with the soldier who steals the purses that contain Anna's savings, the narrator relates the incident by first showing K's initial confusion:

> K licked his lips. "That's not my money," he said thickly. "That's my mother's money, that she worked for." It was not true: his mother was dead, she had no need for money. Nevertheless. There was a silence. "What do you think the war is for?" K said. "For taking other people's money?"
>
> "*What do you think the war is for,*" said the soldier, parodying the movements of K's mouth. "Thief. Watch it. You could be lying in the bushes with flies all over you. Don't you tell me about war."

K's "silence" begins as a moment of philosophical confusion: if the purse is Anna's, then it is not K's; furthermore, either Anna did not clarify to him that he was to inherit the purse after her death, or he is incapable of understanding an abstract concept like "inheritance." Because he cannot resolve this philosophical dilemma, he briefly experiences semantic stutter that shifts the basis of the exchange: war should not be an excuse for oppressing civilians, i.e., taking their savings.

Unknowingly, K has cut to the core of the exchange; the soldier defends himself by mocking and then threatening, returning to the label he originally used to justify his forcing K to open the suitcase. The soldier labels him "thief" even while robbing him, thus ironically reversing the word and effectively silencing him. The exchange ends with the soldier's giving K a ten-rand note from the purse and telling him to buy himself an ice cream; in other words, obviously knowing that he is wrong and that his victim has pinpointed the nature of his crime, the soldier tries to soften its effect.

K acquiesces without further argument, but as soon as he is free, he evaluates the encounter: "It did not seem to him that he had been a coward."

In a closely following episode, the narrator shows K's measuring his own action of taking vegetables from a well-cultivated garden: "It is God's earth, he thought, I am not a thief." Having moved through the first exchange with its confusion, K reinterprets the label, making it *define,* not *limit:* because a thief takes the possessions of another person, the soldier is a thief; because K takes vegetables from a garden and gardens belong to God, K is not a thief. The simplistic logic frees K from the label, though he still fears the retribution of the gardeners; it lets K sift through the accusation and redefine the label that the soldier used to limit him.

The interrogation at Kenilworth moves through a similar pattern. Noel demands that K tell "the whole truth" about his friends from the mountains although they are not his friends and he knows nothing about their activities. Not understanding, K "crouched perceptibly, clutching the blanket about his throat," a defensive posture that indicates his confusion. The medical officer, who uses K's correct name, tries to get through to him by adding, "Come on, my friend!" That he would use the same word as Noel but with patently different connotation confuses K, who again sinks into linguistic silence until the medical officer pushes him in a new direction:

> "Come on, Michaels," I said, "we haven't got all day, there's a war on!"

> At last he spoke: "I am not in the war."

As with the soldier, he seems to experience a moment of semantic stuttering before he sharply changes the topic, but after the medical officer angrily replies to his response, he simply adds, "I am not clever with words." K cannot speak because he will not lie; the medical officer cannot understand him because he does not realize that his use of words is confusing and untrue.

To give the police the report that they expect, the medical officer and Noel fabricate the story that the police want to hear, using language as that K does not understand. From the untruth of concocting a story for K, however, the medical officer has learned that he cannot limit K with the usual labels; the section ends with his thinking, "No papers, no money, no friends, no sense of who you are. The obscurest of the obscure, so obscure as to be a prodigy." As in the case of the label "thief," the condition of war makes the definer

inaccurate: the medical officer, who first limits K as a "prisoner" along with the police, later redefines "prisoner" to describe himself and his situation at the rehabilitation camp.

This process of redefinition colors all three sections of ***Michael K.*** Sometimes K contrasts the received signification of words such as "freedom" and the actions of the people who use such words. At Jakkalsdrif, a work camp patrolled by the "Free Corps," he is told that he is free, but the guard tells him that, if he tries to leave at any time other than on a work party, he will be shot. After saboteurs destroy the town's cultural history museum, he does not comprehend the police captain's label that Jakkalsdrif is a "nest of criminals" and that the Free Corps guards are "monkeys" to be caged; after all, "nest" signifies something comfortable, a haven against disorder, and "Free Corps guard" signifies someone in power, not a person who needs to be caged and guarded. Other times the narrator indicates that K reflects on words by logically deducing they can have different meanings for different people; thus he determines that the police captain's label "parasite" is truthful only because he can force his opinion on others.

The "unimaginable bureaucracy" forces all its citizens into preconceived limiting definitions. Typically identifying people by impersonal labels, it places all people into the same categories that the police imposed on K—name (and family), sex, ethnic origin (place of birth, race, and place of childhood), age, political and religious affiliations, employment, moral or legal record. Thus Coetzee identifies the mainstream society of South Africa, (or, for that matter, of any modern bureaucracy) with the camps, places that identify people and mold them into socially acceptable patterns. As K clearly realizes by the end of the novel, there are camps for anyone who fails to fulfill society's image of what constitutes a good citizen. Thus Jakkalsdrif was built so that the "good" citizens of Prince Albert could not see it because they do not want to admit that the homeless and unemployed exist, and Kenilworth is to "effect a change in men's souls," turning social misfits into productive conformists. Like reflections of the greater society outside the barbed wire, the camps have rules and regulations; in Jakkalsdrif, for example, K is expected to follow these rules, but before Robert takes him under wing, no one has explained just what the rules might be. He is a non-conformist, not because he is a rebel with a mission but because he escapes other people's definition of who he is and what he should do by not resisting. If he resisted, he would become "man who resists" and thus fit into a socially limiting label. As it is, the only labels that the medical officer can finally use to identify him define or describe him such as "escape artist" or "gardener."

In the first chapter Coetzee suggests that the fictional Cape Town of the "near future" still has a functioning infrastructure. K has a job with Parks and Gardens and rides a bus to Somerset Hospital to get his mother. The bureaucracy functions however much it dehumanizes. The police quickly respond to the sniper however brutally they might attack innocent bystanders. Guards prevent looting and protect the property of those who have been displaced, however negligent they might be in overlooking K and his mother. With water and electricity K and his mother make the Burhrmanns' apartment into a comfortable hiding place. Apparently the mail is still delivered, though none comes for K.

By the last chapter, however, merely a year or so later, the infrastructure seems to have failed. Though K seems to hear the distant "tinkle of an ice-cream vendor's bell," traffic is not moving and a burned out, stripped car blocks the road. Broken glass and garbage litter lawns, and no water runs in the public lavatory. Instead of a bureaucracy, police, or soldiers, K meets derelicts. In this part of **Michael K** language itself has become as disorganized and empty as the war-torn city. The people whom K meets have lost the remnants of civilized behavior: the stranger and his two "sisters" sharply contrast Robert's attempt to maintain law and order for his family in Jakkalsdrif and the medical officer's original belief that somehow law and order needed to be preserved.

In his language as well as in his actions, the stranger is a man of many labels, none of them truthful. He introduces himself as having "plenty of sisters . . . [a] big family" though it is more probable that he is a pimp; he gets his "sister" to tell K where he lives, though he is only a squatter; he calls K "Mister Treefeller," the name on the overalls that he took from Kenilworth; and he refers to K as "brother," though he tries to rob him during the night. Even basic labels such as "thief" have no meaning: after the stranger takes K's seeds during the night, K only asks, "Can I have my packet?"

But in this social and linguistic chaos, K finally finds a label that he can apply to himself and fully accept:

> It excited him, he found, to say, recklessly, *the truth, the truth about me. "I am a gardener,"* he said again, aloud. . . . I am more like an earthworm, he thought. Which is also a kind of gardener. Or a mole, also a gardener, that does not tell stories because it lives in silence.

Whenever K refers to himself with an image, he uses similes. Uncertain about words either because they seem foreign to him as in the case when the nurse "sounded as if she were reading the words from a card" or because they "Would not come" to him, K avoids metaphors because they more directly infringe on his self-identity. The narrator, seemingly uncertain himself how far to push K's growing self-awareness in chapter one, also describes K in terms of similes such

as "chewing quickly as a rabbit." It is as if both the narrator and K distrust the language when words that may describe can also seem to categorize or contain. Thus the reader finds that K is *like* "a termite boring its way through a rock" or an "ant that does not know where its hole is," but both insects hardly describe him because both are usually female identified with hives or communities (at least in the twentieth century). His later image of himself—"I am like a woman whose children have left the house"—humanizes the notion of a mother (analogous to the female insect) now separated from the home (analogous to the incest's hive). That K thinks of himself with such sexual ambiguity parallels his refusal to fall into socially acceptable labels; he does not identify the tags whereby his society can classify and thus easily dismiss him.

In contrast, the medical officer, who begins with a direct limiting description—"a little old man"—quickly discovers that usual labels are inappropriate: "Though he looks like an old man, he claims to be only thirty-two." Moving from clinical description to poetic trope, the medical officer vacillates between comfortable labels whereby he can limit K and poetic describers that give him insight without confining:

> He is like a stone, a pebble, that, having lain around quietly minding its own business since the dawn of time, is now suddenly picked up and tossed randomly from hand to hand. A hard little stone, barely aware of its own surroundings enveloped in itself and its interior life. He passes through these institutions and camps and hospitals and God knows what else like a stone. Through the intestines of the war. An unbearing, unborn creature.

As reluctant to use similes as the narrator is reluctant to use metaphors, the medical officers dilemma is that K's very existence makes him question himself, a process that finally makes him vulnerable to the war and to his own insignificance and inability to act.

Though the medical officer at first dismissed him as an "idiot," a "simpleton," or a "clown," Michael K is a storyteller who cannot find the right words because, in his opinion, his story is too important to muddle and because he distrusts the very medium that he must use to communicate it. When he first tries to tell his story at Jakkalsdrif, he falls into silence while he thinks, "Now I must speak about the ashes, . . . so as to be complete, so as to have told the whole story," but before he can translate his feelings into words, his audience has drifted away. Later, during the interrogation at Kenilworth, he has an audience, eager to hear his story, but to tell the story that the medical officer expects would be dishonest. His problem in telling his story, however, does not rest solely with his audience:

Always, when he tried to explain himself to himself, there remained a gap, a hole, a darkness before which his understanding balked, into which it was useless to put words. The words were eaten up, the gap remained. His was always a story with a hole in it: a wrong story, always wrong.

Unwilling or unable to falsify or to accept limiting labels, K confuses himself and stammers over his words.

When the medical officer tries to get him to tell his story, he cannot initially understand K's abrupt shifts in logic and reference:

"Where is your mother now?" I asked. "She makes the plants grow," he replied, evading my eyes. "You mean she has passed away?" I said (pushing up the daisies?). He shook his head. "They burned her," he said. "Her hair was burning round her head like a halo."

He deduces that K is the pathetic result of bad education, a convenient diagnosis that with a less sensitive man might have let him dismiss the patient as an incurable. It is precisely this interpretation that he foists on Noel to justify the fabrication of a story for the Prince Albert police: "there is nothing there, no story of the slightest interest to rational people." Only after K has escaped from Kenilworth and a new shipment of prisoners threatens to overwhelm the facilities, does the medical officer come to see that "Michaels means something, and the meaning he has is not private" to him, for

if Michaels himself were no more than what he seems to be . . . a skin-and-bones man with a crumpled lip . . . , then I would have every justification for . . . putting a bullet through my head.

In his final imaginative pursuit of a conversation with K, he still attempts to reduce him to an object that he can understand and by understanding rationalize, even though he seems aware that his attempts to "allegorize" will ultimately fail.

Obsessed with discovering K's purpose partly because he is himself disillusioned by the war and believing that society must have rational or, at least, orderly grounds, he attempts to force K into teleological constructs that speak to his confusion; in other words, he consistently romanticizes K's story. But when he imagines "following" K, because he wants him to answer his final question, the children, who accepted K throughout the narrator's story, intercept and prevent his getting an answer. The medical officer, who has an inkling into K's nature, cannot divorce himself from his belief in his own rationality and purpose. The reader, who has briefly identi-

fied with the medical officer intellectually and verbally, is left with no certainty; there is no clue from K or the narrator to help either the medical officer or the reader categorize him.

Throughout, K thinks about telling his story. At Jakkalsdrif he tries but finds that "he could not, or could not yet." At Kenilworth he obviously talked with the medical officer, who thus knew many of the parts of his history, but Coetzee only shows K's full telling of his own story in the final section. For the stranger and his two women on Signal Hill, he sums up his life in seven "paltry" sentences:

I was three months in the camp at Kenilworth, till last night. . . . I was gardener once, for the Council. That was a long time ago. Then I had to leave and take my mother into the country, for her health. My mother used to work at Sea Point, she had a room there, we passed it on the way. . . . She dies in Stellenbosch, on the way up-country. . . . I didn't always get enough to eat.

As in his attempts to speak to the soldier, the people at Jakkalsdrif, or the medical officer, words confuse and silence him; the attempt to tell his story nauseates him, breaking him out in a cold sweat. The narrator adds that K either thought "his story was paltry, not worth the telling" or "he simply did not know how to tell a story, how to keep interest alive." Distrustful of language and, in his own simplicity, caught in "the self-relexive process of meaning-making which highlights the continuous deconstruction of established meaning," K is reduced to silence. Whether the narrator is, indeed, echoing K's thoughts at this moment or guessing what K actually thought, the moment quickly passes with K's leaving his story untold. In the end, he chooses silence over articulation: the telling of his story would have falsified it.

In his final analysis he reconciles himself by thinking, "I was mute and stupid in the beginning, I will be mute and stupid at the end." Unbounded by any of the camps and, therefore, free, he has escaped from all limiters. To talk about him— even for him to talk about his own history—is to force him into those labels that he has managed to evade. Words have failed him, but, at the same time, words have been his salvation, for without words he can return to Sea Point without having been categorized into a pawn for the government or into an intellectual abstraction by the medical officer. He has learned, and perhaps the narrator has learned as well, that "there is time enough for everything." Though K is apparently close to death at the end of the novel, the last word of the novel is "live," as if K will, indeed, have the time that both the medical officer and the narrator lack.

Ironically, K's story has been told. The narrator and the medical man, from their different perspectives, each of which limits K by transforming him into a verbal rather than onto-logical experience, have transformed him into their "stories." Like Susan Barton, only K knows the truth of his experiences; unlike Susan, he is almost as inarticulate as Friday, who literally has no tongue. Foe rewrites Susan's story, falsifying it though there is still a strange truth in the published tale of a man's survival on an island visited only by cannibals; without the narrator and the medical man, maybe "[i]t would have been better if his mother has quietly suffocated him when she saw what he was, and put him in the trash can." These storytellers save K from that oblivion though he does not tell his story himself.

Rita Barnard (essay date Winter 1994)

SOURCE: "Dream Topographies: J. M. Coetzee and the South African Pastoral," in *South Atlantic Quarterly,* Vol. 93, No. 1, Winter, 1994, pp. 33-58.

[*In the following essay, Barnard examines the significance of place in Coetzee's novels and critical essays, arguing that his settings are not dystopian, as has been suggested by some critics, but rather "atopian," embodying a feeling of constant displacement.*]

In his recent edition of essays by and interviews with J. M. Coetzee, David Attwell notes that Coetzee's return to South Africa in 1976, and his second novel, *In the Heart of the Country,* marked the emergence of a new concern with *place* in his work. This concern has, in fact, been an enduring one for Coetzee: his criticism and fiction have been profoundly affected by an interest in such geographically or topographically defined genres as the exploration narrative and the pastoral, as well as in such politically significant spaces as the imperial border, the labor camp, and the torture chamber. Even the titles of his first two novels, *Dusklands* and *In the Heart of the Country,* suggest this fascination, referring as they do to strangely elusive and yet symbolically resonant places. It is possible that the structuralist and therefore synchronic orientation of Coetzee's academic training as a linguist might have something to do with his interest in spatial organization; but, as Attwell's observation suggests, this interest also seems to have the experiential and personal dimension of a skeptically and rigorously examined attachment to the South African landscape: Coetzee once remarked, after all, that people can be in love with only one landscape in their lifetime.

Coetzee's increasing discomfort in recent years with the dominance of the discourse of history (or, more exactly, a Marxian historicism) in South African academic circles may also, in part, be connected to a concern with the spatial. I say "in part" since, in a polemical essay like **"The Novel Today,"** it is clear that Coetzee's impatience with the all-"swallowing" tendency of historical master-narratives comes from his sense of himself specifically as a *novelist:* a sense that in times of political pressure the novel becomes reduced to a mere supplement to or illustration of the discourse of the historical "real." Even so, it seems worth noting that there have been other contemporary social theorists interested in the critical analysis of space who, like Coetzee, have challenged the explanatory privilege of historicism. The geographer Edward Soja, for one, has polemicized vigorously against the marginalization of the spatial by the historical discourse of Western Marxism and has posited that, in contemporary forms of capitalism, spatial relations have become as mystified as the commodity form once seemed to Marx—and thus require renewed attention. This argument urges us to consider, for instance, the degree to which the erasure of the conditions of labor in today's world depends on the geography of late capitalism: the fact that the impoverished workers who produce our glossy commodities live far out of sight, in Mexico, in the Philippines, or in a South African township, and that their invisibility perpetuates the illusion of historical progress in the economic centers. I think that we can say, without falling into a new trap of "swallowing up" Coetzee's novels in the discourse of a critical geography, that this line of thought resonates with certain moments in his writing, both academic and fictional: he is concerned with how people inhabit, how they imagine, and how they represent the physical terrain that surrounds them.

The literary possibilities of a critical geography are suggested in an intriguing passage by John Berger (which Soja cites in his opening chapter):

> Prophecy now involves a geographical rather than historical projection; it is space and not time that hides consequences from us. To prophesy today it is only necessary to know men [and women] as they are throughout the whole world in all their inequality. Any contemporary narrative which ignores the urgency of this dimension is incomplete and acquires the oversimplified character of a fable.

The notion that it is space that hides inequalities from us, in particular, calls to mind Coetzee's comments on the political geography of South Africa:

> If people are starving, let them starve far away in the bush, where their thin bodies will not be a reproach. If they have no work, if they migrate to the cities, let there be roadblocks, let there be curfews, let there be laws against vagrancy, begging, and squatting, and let offenders be locked away so that no one has to hear or see them. If the black townships are in flames, let cameras be banned from them. . . . Certainly there are many lands where pris-

ons are used as dumping-places for people who smell wrong and look unsightly and do not have the decency to hide themselves away. In South Africa the law sees to it as far as it can that not only such people but also the prisons in which they are held become invisible.

These ideas have significant implications for those who strive to understand (and change) the inequality of South African men and women. Apartheid, as Coetzee so clearly understands, operates from day to day as a means of distributing people in space and, in the process, of controlling the way they see the world. The system perpetuates itself by decreeing that certain spaces be invisible: homelands, prisons, torture chambers, and black cities are deliberately hidden, removed from view. The beneficiaries of apartheid are, after all, not particularly sadistic; they (we) would simply rather not see the "consequences" of which Berger speaks. The ideal—and in some sense actual—social topography for those in power would be the one described by a vagrant in Coetzee's **Life & Times of Michael K:** a workers' camp placed hundreds of miles away, "in the middle of the Koup" or some such arid waste, from which they could "come on tiptoe in the middle of the night like fairies and do their work, dig their gardens, wash their pots, and be gone in the morning leaving everything nice and clean."

I would suggest that in moments like these his writing offers us something of that demystifying "geographical projection" or even "prophecy" (though Coetzee would certainly balk at this term) of which Berger speaks. In such instances, Coetzee renders visible the places that the system would rather keep out of sight and mind. Elsewhere, his examination of the spatial seems more literary, as in his implicit critique of the reiterative codes that have shaped descriptions of South African landscapes: the descriptive catalogue, for instance, in which "the Karoo has been done to death in a century of writing and overwriting (drab bushes, stunted trees, heat-stunned flats, shrilling of cicadas, and so forth)." Perhaps most importantly, he forces us to examine our automatic responses to "place" (for example, white South Africans' passionate and often proclaimed love of the country's vast landscapes): to ask what political and imaginative failure such a passion might conceal.

The notion of place has not been completely ignored by South African literary critics: Stephen Gray, for one, has suggested that the notion of a "sense of place" could be used as a crude but serviceable means of mapping the successive phases of a South African (and a more generally postcolonial) literary historiography. In the first phase, the colony offers what Richard Rive has called a "Scenic Special": the exotic appeal of a distant place. Its landscape is presented to readers in the centers of power as *different,* a novel entertainment for the armchair traveler back "home." It offers

a kind of verbal safari, entirely Eurocentric in its assumptions. Although its historical origins (as Gray points out) lie in the Renaissance, this kind of literature remains enormously influential: it is still evident in writers like Lawrence Durrell, in TV documentaries, and, I would add, in such profitable exports as Jamie Uys's film *The Gods Must Be Crazy.* (The Disney film A *Far-Off Place,* based on the work of Laurens van der Post, is perhaps the genre's most recent avatar.)

The second phase is more distinctively and assertively "colonial" and emerges with such exceptional figures as Olive Schreiner. (Miles Franklin, the author of *My Brilliant Career,* would be her Australian counterpart.) In such isolated and singular texts as Schreiner's *Story of an African Farm,* "phase two" literature reacts to the cultural tourism of the first phase by asserting an inescapable rootedness in the landscape and the emotional horizon of the colony; in Schreiner's case that setting is, of course, the vast and stony desert of the Great Karoo, which has become (perhaps because of her novel) the archetypal South African landscape. It is ironic, as Gray points out, that this literature was received in the metropolitan center (where Schreiner had to find her readers) as indistinct from "phase one" writing: *The Story of an African Farm* was largely seen as bringing an entertainingly novel and fresh "sense of place" to English literature, and Schreiner's critique, from her forbidding marginal vantage point in the South African desert, of the aridity of European ideas and values was readily overlooked.

In its third phase South African writing becomes, for Gray, much less vulnerable to such Eurocentric misreading, since it is associated not only with a full-fledged sense of national identity, but with the emergence of a cultural nexus that supports a national literature: a publishing industry, a community of local readers and critics, and a self-referring use of language, norms, and values. Place remains, or so the argument goes, a defining feature, but it is no longer—as it was with "phase two" writers—a cultural battlefield on which the rights to an indigenous identity must be fought. It becomes, in Gray's view, more of a shared and felt milieu, a familiar backdrop from which writers as different as Athol Fugard, for instance, writing from his home in the Eastern Cape, or Sipho Sepamla, writing from the vantage point of the explosive Soweto scene, can stage their distinct literary projects.

There are clearly a number of theoretical problems with this outline. It is, for instance, open to the objection that it defines place as the "single variable" that generates the distinctiveness of South African writing: "The elements of plot, character, action, use of dialogue, rhythm, and all the other techniques of making literature, remain the same" as in the great tradition of the British canon. This pre-supposition surely minimizes the thematic and stylistic inventiveness of postcolonial writing and ignores the effects of political determinants on literary forms and genres. But the most important weakness vexing Gray's schema is the fact that he relies on an all too empirically conceived notion of "place" (which is used interchangeably with "setting"); the implicit notion of artistic representation, consequently, is straightforwardly mimetic and bears the implication that South African literature must represent the South African land. It is no accident, then, that Gray makes no reference to the work of J. M. Coetzee: the first part of **Dusklands** and **Waiting for the Barbarians** (**Foe** had not yet appeared by then) are not set in South Africa at all. But the exclusion is also symptomatic: Gray's historiographic schema could not accommodate Coetzee's treatment of place, which in effect swallows up and explodes all of its categories. Coetzee's work, as Stephen Watson has observed, seems to "float free of time and place, even in the act of alluding to a time and place which is specifically South African." What is at stake for him is not place or landscape as an object of mimesis, but the discursive and generic and political codes that inform our understanding and knowledge of place. There is a deliberate analytical unsettledness in Coetzee, which deconstructs, rather than assimilates to, any South African literary tradition, or any South African "sense of place."

> There is a deliberate analytical unsettledness in Coetzee, which deconstructs, rather than assimilates to, any South African literary tradition, or any South African "sense of place."
> —*Rita Barnard*

This tendency is emphasized by Teresa Dovey (the author of the first full-length study of Coetzee's novels) when she deftly selects, as one of the keywords of her study, Roland Barthes's notion of "atopia": *drifting habitation.* The word evokes, in appropriately spatial (or perhaps antispatial) terms, the deconstructive and "writerly" quality of Coetzee's texts: his formal shiftiness, the fact that his novels, like hermit crabs, inhabit, but only to abandon, the shells of various fictional genres, such as the narrative of exploration, the pastoral, and so forth. "Atopia," in short, identifies Coetzee's project as one of displacement. It is a refusal to settle in a space that is conventionally and ideologically given, a critical gesture which Dovey explains (in the Lacanian terminology she privileges) as "a constant deferral of the position available to the subject in language." While I shall eventually take issue with Dovey's readings, the idea of "atopia" provides a useful rubric under which we may briefly consider one way that Coetzee problematizes the notion of a "sense of place": the metafictional aspects of his novelistic topographies.

The idea of "drifting habitation" is perhaps most applicable to **In the Heart of the Country** and is most readily illustrated in those instances where the text seems to offer a scenic description. This is, of course, a novel whose problematic temporality strikes us immediately: we are never allowed to be certain about *when* the events take place (the narrator is never sure if she is in a time of donkey carts or bicycles or airplanes), nor are we sure what "really happens"—the sequence and effects of events are always in doubt. The same is true about the novel's ostensible setting—despite the realistic details of stone, the whitewashed homestead, the gravelly yard, the chickens, the dust, and the gleaming copperware. The title itself initiates a kind of ironic instability: it appears to allude to a symbolically resonant location, but the narrative, with its rapid succession of often self-cancelling segments, seems really to have nothing at its "heart." The text continually reminds us that the farm is entirely fictive, that there is, properly speaking, no "setting," no "stone desert," but only "stony monologue." Magda, the narrator of this monologue, repeatedly, and regretfully, insists that the panorama before her depends entirely upon her consciousness, her words:

> Seated here I hold the goats and stones, the entire farm and even its environs, as far as I know them, suspended in this cool, alienating medium of mine, exchanging them item by item for my word-counters. A hot gust lifts and drops a flap of ochre dust. The landscape recomposes itself and settles.

Yet it would also be incorrect—and too safe—to think of this consciousness as in any way settled or "central"; Magda thinks of herself as a void, a hole, and frequently seems on the verge of dissolving into a complete insubstantiality: "a ghost or a vapour," she muses, "floating at the intersection of a certain latitude and a certain longitude," an intersection that remains a purely hypothetical location. The farm is not just set in the proverbial "middle of nowhere" (such remoteness would accord with the realist notion of the vastness of the Karoo range): it is nowhere, "on the road from no A to no B in the world, if such a fate is topologically possible"; it is configured almost as a kind of antispace: "a turbulence, a vortex, a black hole," a swallowing up of any presence.

Considering all this, what seems curious is the extent to which the novel remains so visual in its effect, how much it remains concerned with description. Even the highly self-reflexive passage cited above seems just for a moment, when a gust of wind raising the dust appears to disturb the "suspended" verbal landscape, to flirt with a more conventional realism. And there are certainly moments when the narrative offers, albeit ironically, a conventional South African "sense of place"—a rural "scenic special" of sorts. We might think, for instance, of the evocation of the impoverished settlement, Armoede, where the servant, Hendrik, goes to fetch his bride. The description is offered in the form of a list, the slightly weary tone of which emphasizes the famil-iarity and typicality of the details (once again the reader who knows the code, or so the very form suggests, can extend the catalogue): "the bleak windswept hill, the iron shanties with hessian in the doorways, the chickens, doomed, scratch-ing in the dust, the cold snot-nosed children toiling back from the dam with buckets of water, the same chickens scat-tering now before the donkey-cart." But despite the vivid-ness of detail, the context does not permit this scene of "local color" to attain a lasting mimetic effect. The narrator merely imagines this scene, admitting that she has never been to Armoede. (Indeed, she "seem[s] never to have been any-where": a confession that explains the curiously improvisa-tional quality of even her descriptions of her own home—her ignorance, for instance, of whether or not she happens to have any neighbors.) The place name "Armoede" also seems to work in a complicated and contradictory way, debunking, as it were, its own suggestion of referentiality, its own South Africanness. To anyone familiar with the country, the name Armoede (Poverty) could seem "realistically" typical, call-ing to mind any number of those curiously morbid place names that dot the South African map: Weenen (Weeping), Lydenburg (Town of Suffering), Put-Sonder-Water (Water-less Well), or Misgund (Begrudged). But this reality effect is undercut, one feels, by the all too perfect, too allegorical, match between the name and the scene; the appellation seems to bear the mark of the literary, or at least to draw attention to the linguistic label: it is all, as Magda laments, a matter of "names, names, names."

In the absence of any resistance to this process of naming, and of the linguistic reciprocity of which Magda dreams, all becomes solipsistic, improvisational: the landscape is a fig-ment of Magda's narratorial consciousness, her "speculative . . . geography," one might say; but her consciousness seems equally determined by this fictive, composed land. Her "speculative bias," her radical, though somehow insubstan-tial freedom, has its origin, Magda tells us, in the vast dis-tances of the land into which she must stare. "I make it all up in order that it shall make me up": such are the unstable, shifting operations, the "lapidary paradoxes," that make up this fiction.

It is easy to see why this novel in particular has provided grounds for the Lacanian reading offered by Dovey: her as-sociation of the narrating self with the hermit crab, scuttling from shell to shell, or code to code, or signifier to signifier, is in many ways compelling and accurate. But it seems to me that in the matter of genre, which is central to Dovey's understanding of Coetzee's "fiction-as-criticism," the purely deconstructive reading reveals certain limitations. It is true, of course, that a generic instability and self-consciousness is perhaps the most telling characteristic of self-reflexive fic-tion. Coetzee himself notes that what clearly distinguishes the postmodern text from the realist novels of, say, Defoe

or Hardy, is that Moll Flanders and Jude never pause to pon-der what kind of text they seem to be inhabiting. And *In the Heart of the Country* is no exception: Magda is constantly questioning what kind of action or event might justify her insubstantial presence in the elusive heart of that country: not Greek tragedy, despite the imagined axe-murder and the surrounding "theatre of stone"; nor gothic romance, despite her brief fantasy of waiting for "a castle [to] crumble into a tarn"; nor even the colonial idyll, with its dreary possibili-ties of marriage to a neighbor's second son or dalliance with an itinerant schoolmaster. Yet the seductions of the more lyric aspects of the pastoral are ever present in the novel and are, I think, not so easily dismissed. When Magda asserts that she would not be herself if she did not "feel the seduc-tions of the cool stone house, the comfortable old ways, the antique feudal language," it is still possible to take the re-mark as just another momentary, self-cancelling speculation. But by the end of the novel, the tone seems to have shifted. The monologue concludes on a note which suggests that Coetzee's fictional strategies are perhaps not fully explained by an "atopian" reading. This lyrical finale, however self-consciously announced as "closing plangencies," expresses a desire that seems rather more specific, rather more local than the universal linguistic condition of desire and defer-ral that is figured for Dovey by the hermit crab:

> There are poems, I am sure, about the heart that aches for Verlore Vlakte, about the melancholy of the sunset over the koppies, the sheep beginning to huddle against the first evening chill, the faraway boom of the windmill, the first chirrup of the first cricket, the last twitterings of the birds in the thorn-trees, the stones of the farmhouse wall still hold-ing the sun's warmth, the kitchen lamp glowing steady. They are poems I could write myself. It takes generations of life in the cities to drive that nostal-gia for country ways from the heart. I will never live it down, nor do I want to. I am corrupted to the bone with the beauty of this forsaken world. . . . I have chosen at every moment my own destiny, which is to die here in the petrified garden, behind locked gates, near my father's bones, in a space echoing with hymns I could have written but did not because (I thought) it was too easy.

As Peter Strauss has argued, those nostalgic poems on Verlore Vlakte (Lost Valley), which are remembered but not parodied in these lyrical lines, preserve a certain pastoral possibility, which the reader is allowed—barely—to discern, but in which the narrative voice never fully indulges. While it would be reductive to ascribe the passion of these lines to the author, there is surely in the passage a kind of uni-son—or at least a kind of homology—between narrator and author. (And I shall resist speculating on an intriguing com-ment in the final interview of *Doubling the Point,* where

Coetzee notes, in describing the person he was as an adolescent, that "for a variety of reasons" he ceased visiting the family farm, "the place on earth he has defined, imagined, constructed, as his place of origin.") In the same way that Magda has up to this point scrupulously resisted, and still resists, the pastoral possibility, Coetzee's work resists the easy option of creating a fictional dwelling place, a fictional utopia—"that heady expansion into the as-if," as Magda calls it. Coetzee's work in general suggests a reluctant abnegation of certain artistic forms, a gesture that is also evident in his uncharacteristically revealing comments (again, in **Doubling the Point**) on the situation of the contemporary author. He speaks of "the pathos—in a humdrum sense of the word—of our position: like children shut in the playroom, the room of textual play, looking out wistfully through the bars at the enticing world of the grownups, one that we have been instructed to think of as the mere phantasmal world of *realism* but that we stubbornly can't help thinking of as the *real*." Coetzee is, in short, anything but enamored of the antimimetic and deconstructive techniques that he himself deploys: he speaks of the "impasse" of "anti-illusionism" while recognizing—almost regretfully—the necessity for such techniques. In the history of the novel, he argues, metafiction is a "marking of time." It is surely no coincidence that this condition of marking time, of waiting, is the same morbid condition so often associated with white South Africans, living in the uncertain age of what Nadine Gordimer (following Gramsci) has called the "interregnum." It seems to me, therefore, that we must, while acknowledging the paradoxical nature of such a move, situate and *localize* his atopian strategies; we must also recognize not only a historical but an ethical impulse behind Coetzee's anti-illusionism. For it is specifically as a white South African that Coetzee feels he must refrain from the pastoral, and it is as a novelist writing within a certain troubling historical configuration that he must avoid producing what he calls, in an essay on Beckett, "the daydream gratification of fiction."

> **Coetzee is, in short, anything but enamored of the antimimetic and deconstructive techniques that he himself deploys: he speaks of the "impasse" of "anti-illusionism" while recognizing—almost regretfully—the necessity for such techniques.**
> —*Rita Barnard*

The problem with Teresa Dovey's determinedly deconstructive reading of Coetzee's work is that it is not balanced by a consciousness of the contingency and historicity of cultural forms. Most notably, there is no sense that the Western psychoanalytic and deconstructive theories she deploys may themselves be destabilized, slipping into different nuances and creating different meanings and allegiances when they are invoked in different contexts, deployed at some remove from their original source. This critique has been suggested in general terms by David Attwell, who notes that in Dovey's discussion of **In the Heart of the Country** the Hegelian master/slave dialectic is entirely stripped of its historical-political aspect, that is, of the implication that such goals as freedom and self-realization are attainable only *in a just society.* The problem becomes even clearer if one looks closely at some of Dovey's curiously reductive readings of passages from Coetzee's work. A characteristic instance occurs when she glosses a key moment in **Life & Times of Michael K,** a passage in which the starving Michael K meditates on the minimal and ahistorical way he would like to live on the land—refusing to be a settler:

> I am not building a house out here by the dam to pass on to other generations. What I make ought to be careless, makeshift, a shelter to be abandoned without a tugging at the heartstrings. . . . The worst mistake, he told himself, would be to try to found a new house, a rival line, on his small beginnings out at the dam.

Dovey's reading of this rather touching passage renders it almost mechanically self-referential. Michael K's improvised dwelling place becomes nothing but an allegory for the operations of this novel: "This text in particular [i.e., **Life & Times of Michael K**] must not be too closely bound to Coetzee's own meanings; he must be able to abandon it, without a tugging at the heartstrings, to the successive meanings which each new reading will generate." For all its apparent openness, this is precisely the kind of comment that makes one hesitate to offer a more specific interpretation. But even if we take K's invisible, traceless, self-erasing mode of living on the land as a figure for a mode of writing, we must remember that K himself (not the quickest mind around) sadly recognizes that it is the context of war, the *times* of Michael K, if you will, that demands this strategy:

> What a pity that to live in times like these a man must be ready to live like a beast. A man who wants to live cannot live in a house with lights in the window. He must live in a hole and hide by day. A man must live so that he leaves no trace of his living. That is what it has come to.

"Drifting habitation" as a literary strategy must likewise be seen as a historical condition.

A similar point can be made in relation to Dovey's reading of another important meditation in **Michael K,** when, after a vicious assault on the Jakkalsdrif labor camp, K ponders the relationship between parasite and host:

Parasite was the word the police captain had used: the camp at Jakkalsdrif, a nest of parasites hanging from the neat sunlit town, eating its substance, giving no nourishment back. Yet to K lying idle in his bed, thinking without passion (What is it to me, after all? he thought), it was no longer obvious which was host and which parasite, camp or town. . . . What if the hosts were far out-numbered by the parasites, the parasites of idleness and the other secret parasites in the army and the police force and the schools and factories and offices, the parasites of the heart? Could the parasites then still be called parasites? Parasites too had flesh and substance; parasites too could be preyed upon. Perhaps in truth whether the camp was declared a parasite on the town or the town a parasite on the camp depended on no more than on who made his voice heard loudest.

Dovey relates this passage, as we could surely have predicted, to J. Hillis Miller's argument in "The Critic as Host": "[T]he term 'parasite,'" she ventures, "comes to signify as a locus of substitution, and refers to the way in which Coetzee's novel, which is parasitic in relation to the previous texts which it deconstructs, will in turn become the host to successive parasitic readings." While it is certainly possible to understand the relationship of host and parasite in terms of acts of reading and interpretation (acts that are thematized in section 2 of the novel, where the medical officer creates rather than "reads" the story of Michael K), I find myself wanting to insist that the atopian reading, the punning etymology which turns the "parasite" into a (dare I say mere?) "locus of substitution," misses something. It universalizes, and in so doing flattens out the operations of a text that seems to ask questions with urgent ethical implications for South Africa in particular: Who eats whom? Who lives off whom? Who lives in the town and who in the camp? Who lives in the city and who in Soweto? In other words, the host/parasite opposition carries a certain local potency: the atopian slippage, the "endlessness of textuality," as Attwell puts it, is halted by "the brute facticity of power." And that power manifests itself in a certain socially and materially constructed topography.

I would like, then, to move from the keyword "atopia" to the phrase "dream topography": an idea that can enable us to give the ethical and political dimensions of Coetzee's novels their due, without recourse to any kind of naive empiricism. The term emerges from Coetzee's discussion of the South African pastoral in *White Writing,* where the notion of genre becomes not so much a metafictional strategy—a temporary home for the writerly hermit crab—but a kind of social dreamwork, expressing desires and maintaining silences that are profoundly political in origin. The idea of the generic and ideological topography offers us a spatial concept that is more stable and historical than "drifting habitation": not a "sense of place," but a sense of discursive and cultural maps.

The essays in *White Writing* are mainly concerned with two rival "dream topographies," both of which are aspects of the pastoral: they are the maps and the ideological blueprints that this genre has projected on the land. Both of these projections are sketched out in Coetzee's 1977 review of Ross Devenish and Athol Fugard's film, *The Guest* (the plot of which is based on an incident in the life of the Afrikaans poet Eugène Marais—an almost life-long morphine addict—who is sent to go cold turkey on a Transvaal farm). To the dismay of the well-meaning director, Coetzee observed that the film's representations of the white man's relation to the land were patched together from flattering myths designed—however unconsciously—to keep certain unresolvable inconsistencies from view. The Afrikaner family is presented via a visually seductive mise-en-scène of "whitewashed walls, . . . dark verticals of doors and windowframes," a dinner table in the glow of lamplight: interiors reminiscent, or so Coetzee claims, "of the classic Dutch painters," settings that gleam "with Rembrandt browns and golds." The compelling visual image, he points out, suggests that the Meyers are "not rootless colonials" but, simultaneously, "rude children of the African earth and heirs to a venerable European tradition." The limited contexts in which we see the family also make it difficult to raise certain troubling questions about the running of this African farm. Coetzee spells out some of these: "If the Meyers run a cattle farm, why do they never talk about cattle? . . . Where do the African farm laborers who materialize out of nowhere for a single fifteen-second sequence live? How do the Meyer men spend their time when they are not eating?" The film confines itself to the terrain permitted by the ideological horSizons of the South African pastoral, within which the Meyers and their farm, Steenkampskraal, stand as emblems of simplicity and permanence. As far as the film's presentation of the poet goes, Coetzee argues, another myth applies: that of the Genius in Africa, the man for whom consciousness is pain, and for whom the African landscape is "a murderous mother-goddess," silently rejecting the alienated poet-supplicant who tragically adores her stony bosom. This glamorously dystopian relationship with the land is no less ideologically fraught than the rough-hewn arcadia of the (non-genius) Boers. The essay raises for the first time an idea that will become a major theme of *White Writing:* that is, to the majority in South Africa, for whom "Africa is a mother who has nourished them and their forebears for millions of years," this stoic lyricism would make no sense at all. "South Africa, mother of pain, can have meaning only to people who can find it meaningful to ascribe their 'pain' ('alienation' is here a better word) to the failure of Africa to love them enough." An apparently aesthetic preoccupation with the land can mask a resistance to thinking about South Africa in social terms.

In *White Writing,* the two ideological positions discovered earlier, in *The Guest,* are described in more elaborate and more generally (generically) applicable terms. Coetzee maps out the first "dream topography" as follows: "[A] network of boundaries crisscrossing the surface of the land, marking off thousands of farms, each a separate kingdom ruled over by a benign patriarch with, beneath him, a pyramid of contented and industrious children, grandchildren, and serfs." In this map of the land, the farm—the soil—characteristically becomes a kind of wife to the father and sons who all merge into a single mythic husband/man. With the notable exception of the English writer Pauline Smith, it is fair to identify this "dream topography" with the more nostalgic and romantic aspects of the Afrikaner *volkskultuur.* It is the mythic space not only of novelists like Van Bruggen or Van den Heever (whom Coetzee discusses), but also of countless movies, stories from popular magazines like *Huisgenoot,* and old soaps from Springbok Radio. I can recall such titles as *Uit Juffrou se Dagboek* (From the Schoolmistress's Diary), *Die Du Ploois van Soetmelksvlei* (The Du Ploois of Sweetmilk Valley), or *Die Geheim van Nantes* (The Secret of Nantes)—"Nantes" and "Soetmelksvlei" are, to an Afrikaans speaker, immediately recognizable toponyms: the names of family farms. While Coetzee does not mention these subliterary examples of the genre in *White Writing,* they confirm its thoroughly ideological status. Key to Coetzee's approach, however, is the understanding that this topography is a mode of writing, that it is not only of a literary or a mass-cultural sort, but also of a material one: the furrows of the plow, in this social text, assume the character of a signature, a deed of ownership, a title to the land. The pastoral activities of digging, building, fence-making—even the construction of those Cape Dutch houses in the classic shape of the letter H—are acts of ideological inscription.

The second and rival "dream topography" is South Africa

> as a vast, empty, silent space, older than man, older than the dinosaurs whose bones lie bedded in its rocks, and destined to be vast, empty, and unchanged long after man has passed from its face. Under such a conception of Africa—"Africa, oldest of the continents"—the task of the human imagination is to conceive not a social order capable of domesticating the landscape, but any kind of relation at all that consciousness can have with it.

This stoic and defeatist lyricism—this poetry of empty space—originates with the antipastoral of Schreiner's *Story of an African Farm* and is continued by a succession of English-language poets (Sidney Clouts stands, for Coetzee, at the end of this line). Although the key trope here is absence,

silence, the failure of language, it is again imperative that this naturalistic topography of desolation should also be apprehended as writing: it does not inscribe the land, as in the Afrikaans pastoral, with the obvious signatures of culture and cultivation, but rather projects a kind of blankness onto the land. In that blankness—the same blankness that Marlow discovers on the map of Africa in *Heart of Darkness,* that imposed emptiness which so fascinated him as a boy—Coetzee reads a certain "historical will to see as silent and empty, a land that has been, if not full of human figures, not empty of them either; that is arid and inflexible, perhaps, but not inhospitable to human life, and certainly not uninhabited." Erasure is also an act of writing—and not simply its binary opposite. Indeed, the message of silence that the lone poet encounters in the empty landscape bears an uncomfortable resemblance, or so Coetzee concludes, to the "writing" of those official historiographers who claimed that the land settled by the Voortrekker pioneers in the nineteenth century was open, empty, and unpeopled.

The critical point is that in both dream topographies the black man, whether as the farmer of an earlier age, or the agricultural worker, or even just as human presence, is obscured. As in his review of *The Guest,* Coetzee's analysis in *White Writing* leads to a series of profoundly uncomfortable questions—questions that strike at the heart of the South African political system and that these apparently pacific ideological landscapes are designed to avoid. Does the poet's inevitable failure to hear the language of the stones "stand for, or stand in the place of, another failure, by no means inevitable: a failure to imagine a peopled landscape, . . . to conceive a society in South Africa in which there is a place for the self?" Or even more pointedly: "Was there no time before the time of the forefathers, and whose was the land then? Do white hands truly pick the fruit, reap the grain, milk the cows, shear the sheep in these bucolic retreats? Who truly creates wealth?" *White Writing* illuminates the crucial, embarrassing blindness implicit in the white man's dream about the land: its necessary "blindness to the colour black." It also reveals a characteristic and consistent critical procedure: an effort on Coetzee's part not to read the "writing," but to ask what it occludes, and to find the truth not in the utterance, but in the evasions and omissions. It is a method of demystification, of revealing the textual and cultural unconscious.

The themes and methods of *White Writing* are also evident in Coetzee's fiction. *Life & Times of Michael K,* for instance, is at least in part a meditation on the ideological function of the pastoral and an example of the critical strategy of subverting the dominant—of listening to silences. That there should be connections between these two texts is hardly surprising since the novel was written concurrently with some of the essays in *White Writing.* Even the lines from Ovid's *Metamorphoses* that serve as the epigraph to *White*

Writing indicate certain overlapping concerns. They symbolically capture the conditions that beset the life of Michael K, the gardener, and that have historically beset South Africa, the troubled garden colony. (The settlement at the Cape of Good Hope was originally intended as a garden and a supply station for the ships of the Dutch East India Company.)

> Pressing his lips to foreign soil, greeting the unfamiliar mountains and plains, Cadmus gave thanks. . . . Descending from above, Pallas told him to plow and sow the earth with the serpent's teeth, which would grow into a future nation.

From the beginning, the epigraph suggests, the settler's pastoral efforts have been productive of, and indeed synonymous with, war and strife. The context in which K finds himself likewise conflates the ideas of gardening and war, or at least forces them into an uncomfortable oxymoronic embrace: in the novel people dig to plant mines, or march in prison camps with spades over their shoulders.

Michael K sets out with a desire to escape the war and capture a pastoral dream: "a whitewashed cottage in the broad veld with smoke curling from its chimney." But his experience soon teaches him that the land is mapped and gridlocked in such a way that the pastoral fantasy, let alone an idyllic rural life, is proscribed for a person who is officially classed as "coloured": "CM-40-NFA-Unemployed." He can live freely in this terrain only by being simultaneously a trespasser and an escapee. Coetzee's use of a black protagonist is essential to the novel's demystificatory operations. The perspective of one like K allows Coetzee to reveal the dystopian dimensions of the Afrikaner's dream topography of beloved farms and fences—those enclosures by which the Visagies of the novel (like the real-life Van der Merwes, Bothas, Coetzees, Malherbes, and Barnards) have staked out their "miles and miles of silence . . . to bequeath . . . to their children and grandchildren in perpetuity." The novel's allegorical strategies represent this landscape in a photographic negative, showing its exact homology with the Foucauldian "carceral archipelago." K's South Africa is a place where one can only dream of "forgotten corners and angles and corridors between the fences, land that belonged to no one yet." What one actually experiences, however, is a proliferation of "camps":

> camps for children whose parents run away, camps for people who kick and foam at the mouth, camps for people with big heads and people with little heads, camps for people with no visible means of support, camps for people chased off the land, camps for people they find living in storm-water drains.

For those outside, and, indeed, for those inside the landed

clans, the map of the Afrikaner's pastoral merges with the map of a vast prison comprising innumerable cells—a society in which everybody is either fenced in or guarding a gate. The scandalous force of this image can be grasped only if one recalls the repeated and utterly conventional association of the vast South African landscape with notions of freedom, a commonplace of innumerable patriotic songs, such as "Die Lied van Jong Suid-Afrika" (The Song of Young South Africa):

> Die hoogland is ons woning, die land van son en
>   veld,
> Waar woeste vryheidswinde waai oor graf van
>   menig held,
> Die ruimtes het ons siel gevoed, ons kan geen
>   slawe wees,
> Want vryer as die arendsvlug is die vlugte van ons
>   gees.
>
> (The highland is our dwelling place, the land of
>   sun and veld,
> Where wild winds of freedom blow over the
>   graves of many heroes.
>
> The open space has fed our souls, we cannot ever
>   be slaves,
> For freer than the eagle's flight are the flights of
>   our spirit.)

One of Magda's more profound insights from *In the Heart of the Country* comes to mind here: one can be imprisoned just as readily in a large place "as in a small." And, as Coetzee points out in his Jerusalem Prize acceptance speech, liberty "comes in a package" with equality and fraternity; and in a land without that fraternity, it is therefore inevitable that a "literature of vastness" should carry undertones—the undertones that Coetzee turns into the dominant tones of this novel—of "feelings of entrapment, entrapment in infinitudes."

In the light of this discussion, it seems all the more significant that we should discover in Coetzee's fictional meditations on the South African pastoral the one scene which must, above all, remain hidden if the Afrikaner's dream topography is to be sustained (sustained, that is, in its mythical virtue). This scene appears in Magda's "speculative history"—or "speculative geography":

> Hendrik's [the servant's] forebears in the olden days crisscrossed the desert with their flocks and their chattels, heading from A to B or from X to Y, sniffing for water, abandoning stragglers, making forced marches. Then one day fences began to go up . . . men on horseback rode up and from shadowed faces issued invitations to stop and settle that might also

have been orders and might have been threats, one does not know, and so one became a herdsman, and one's children after one, and one's women took in washing.

The erased presence of those earlier nomads represents a challenge to the birthright of the "Boer." The lines remind us vividly that the history of agricultural enclosure, as Raymond Williams demonstrates so well in *The Country and the City,* is not just a history of settlement, but one of displacement: the first herder-farmers became temporary sojourners, or, like Robert in *Life & Times of Michael K,* persons of "no fixed abode." This displacement is the secret historical precondition of the Afrikaner's idyllic map of rural homesteading: the old tracings "from A to B" are the submerged and erased text that challenges the settlers' elaborately inscribed title to the land.

The logic of the pastoral topography imposed on this originary scene requires that the black man's inscriptive acts of digging and plowing should leave no trace—should be legally and culturally invisible. This idea is, I would argue, played upon throughout *Life & Times of Michael K.* It is perhaps most powerfully and frighteningly expressed in a passage where K imagines that all the dispossessed might be sent off to dig precisely in order to erase themselves: to scoop out a mass grave into which they can then be thrown, by means of which their presence becomes not just obscured, but permanently deleted.

The brilliance of Michael K's own strategy is that he finds a way to reclaim displacement, invisibility, tracklessness as a form of freedom. He turns the social condition prescribed for him—to work the land without owning it, without having a story—into something else, something to be desired. The significance of his solution is prefigured in a memory he retains from his school days:

> One of the teachers used to make the class sit with their hands on their heads, their lips pressed tightly together and their eyes closed, while he patrolled the rows with his long ruler. In time, to K, the posture grew to lose its meaning as punishment and became an avenue of reverie.

K's mode of farming rewrites (despite and because of its invisibility) the rules of the game of the South African pastoral. He keeps alive "the idea of gardening" almost by its negation: the idea of plenty through starvation, the idea of self-affirmation in self-erasure, the idea of rural dwelling and settlement in "drifting habitation."

The same can be said of Coetzee's artistic practice. The capacity for changing the rules of the game is precisely what he values most in a work of art. One might say, moreover,

that he too proceeds by negation and, if need be, invisibly. This connection with K is delicately suggested, I think, in one of the interviews from *Doubling the Point,* where Attwell and Coetzee discuss a quotation from Rilke which Coetzee had cited in a 1974 essay on Nabokov: "It is our task to imprint this provisional, perishable earth so deeply, so patiently and passionately in ourselves that its reality shall arise in us again invisibly. *We are the bees of the invisible.*" The impulse here is strikingly lyrical; but Coetzee responds to it cautiously, commenting on the nostalgic qualities of Nabokov's desire for the past, and observing that one must look at the past with a cruel enough eye to see what made that joy and that innocence possible. The observation clearly applies not just to the past, but also to the pastoral, and to the poetry of empty space that celebrates South Africa's vast landscapes. Coetzee's position in this regard is, one might say, dialectical. As he has indicated both in *White Writing* and in his Jerusalem Prize acceptance speech, it is no longer possible to love the land in unreflective "sincerity": white South Africans have claimed all too often that they love the mountains, the earth, the trees and flowers—all those things that cannot return love. This kind of poetry can no longer be written. And yet it seems that one must, secretly and invisibly, continue to "imprint" the "provisional, perishable earth" in oneself, in the manner suggested by Rilke, so that, as Michael K says in one of his naively wise meditations, the thread that binds man to the earth should not be entirely broken.

It is appropriate, then, that such critics as Neil Lazarus and (at times) David Attwell should have associated Coetzee's work not so much with that of other postmodern fabulists as with the modernist critical theory of Theodor Adorno; Coetzee's works, in the words of Adorno's essay on commitment, "point to a practice from which they abstain: the creation of a just life." This connection raises the following question: If Coetzee's fiction is in the main antipastoral and dystopian, then isn't our task as critics (following his own example) to read dialectically, to subvert the dominant, to discover in his work the utopian possibility, the pastoral impulse which cannot be written directly? One of the most remarkable and virtuosic passages in *White Writing* suggests that this approach is exactly what is called for. Here, Coetzee seems to address his fellow critics directly: "Our craft," he says, "is all in reading *the other*: gaps, inverses, undersides; the veiled; the dark, the buried, the feminine; alterities." But then he poses the following question: "Is it a version of utopianism (or pastoralism) to look forward (or backward) to the day when the truth will be (or was) what is said, not what is not said, when we will hear (or heard) music as sound upon silence, not silence between sounds?" These surprisingly wistful lines in many ways resemble the lyrical conclusion to *In the Heart of the Country;* one detects, in both instances, a regretful, minimalist lyricism, a yearning to come right out and sing "the beauty of this forsaken world." But we should not underestimate the cautiousness of Coetzee's language—a language that is, as Strauss puts it, "forever on guard against itself." The *White Writing* passage admits only in the form of a rhetorical question to a desire for the pastoral (utopian) possibility and indicates a strong awareness of the untimeliness, indeed the scandalousness, of this desire. It asserts, in a way that certainly does recall Adorno, the necessarily negative stance of the contemporary work of art, the refusal of easy "daydream gratification," so that the utopian impulse may be preserved for a later, less bleak time.

It is therefore not only possible, but necessary, to read the outlines of this utopian desire in Coetzee's fiction and in his criticism. Like the Magistrate of *Waiting for the Barbarians,* who in a dream urges the barbarian girl to put people in the empty city she builds out of snow, Coetzee's texts ask, especially in their silences, for a landscape full of people, a society of reciprocity and fraternity. A more explicit moment can be found in the essay **"Into the Dark Chamber,"** where Coetzee notes that Rosa Burger (in Gordimer's novel *Burger's Daughter*) "suffers and waits for . . . a time when humanity will be restored across the face of society, and therefore when all human acts, including the flogging of an animal, will be returned to the ambit of moral judgment." In such a space and in such a time, Coetzee notes, the novel would once again be able to "take as its province the whole of life," and only under such circumstances could the ultimately dystopian, the ultimately secretive space of the torture chamber, "be accorded a place in the design." We could easily extend this logic and say that at such a place and in such a time the novel could again invoke, not ironically but lyrically, the "country ways" of the pastoral: the "whole of life," which, after all, includes digging, includes planting, includes the cultivation of one's garden.

Patrick McGrath (review date 20 November 1994)

SOURCE: "To Be Conscious Is to Suffer," in *New York Times Book Review,* November 29, 1994, p. 9.

[*In the following review, McGrath finds* The Master of Petersburg *"dense and difficult, a novel that frustrates at every turn," but a worthy addition to Coetzee's canon.*]

A ferociously bleak sense of human isolation has characterized the work of the South African writer J. M. Coetzee. In each of his novels he has created figures who stand starkly silhouetted against a vast, harsh landscape and an equally harsh political system; they are belittled and dehumanized by both. His prime concern has been with survival, spiritual and physical, the scraping of meaning and sustenance from

the most hostile of environments. There is no comfort to be had from this experience; for Mr. Coetzee's characters, to be conscious is to suffer.

That theme is Dostoyevskian, and in his strong, strange seventh novel, *The Master of Petersburg,* Mr. Coetzee has gone directly to the source. He has imagined Dostoyevsky returning to St. Petersburg from Dresden after the death of a stepson, Pavel. It is Mr. Coetzee's grimmest book yet, and suggests a new degree of darkness in an outlook that has yet to find much to celebrate in the human condition. The backdrop that here casts its brooding shadow over the characters is of course Russia. And like the South Africa that has provided the setting of most of his novels, this is a Russia poised on the brink of upheaval.

> **His prime concern has been with survival, spiritual and physical, the scraping of meaning and sustenance from the most hostile of environments. There is no comfort to be had from this experience; for Mr. Coetzee's characters, to be conscious is to suffer.**
> **—Patrick McGrath**

In a sense, Mr. Coetzee has written of Russia before. *Waiting for the Barbarians,* a novel published in 1980, is set in a garrison town on the border of a nameless empire apparently threatened by barbarian incursions from the north. It has a definite Central Asian feeling, with the distinct suggestion of Mongol hordes massing for pillage. The relevance of this political allegory to apartheid-era South Africa, and the increasingly vicious response of a doomed regime to what it perceives as the enemy at its gates, is clear at once. But what gives the story its universality is the inspired simplicity of the central image, that of a border region between the known and the unknown, and the associated human tendency to demonize what we do not know and then attack the demons.

The Master of Petersburg is an obscure book by comparison, its plot labyrinthine, its tone relentlessly melancholy. Much of the difference can be attributed to the protagonists. The narrator of *Waiting for the Barbarians,* a district magistrate, is a man of humane and self-indulgent disposition who bobs like a cork on his sea of troubles and gives the book its zest and flavor. Mr. Coetzee has never written another character like the magistrate, and this is a pity. Certainly as a companion, as a narrator, the magistrate is better company than the depressive Dostoyevsky who tramps and glooms through the pages of *The Master of Petersburg.* The magistrate is a bon viveur, a fat man who frankly enjoys his food and wine and sex, and for him the so-called barbarians pose no threat because he understands the threat to be illusory. Stoically, he endures torture and humiliation for his heretical sympathies.

The position of Mr. Coetzee's Dostoyevsky is by contrast one of tortuous complexity. Adrift in the perilous political currents of late-czarist St. Petersburg, he is compromised in the eyes of the authorities by his stepson's having been a member of a revolutionary gang led by a sinister character called Nechayev. (Sergei Nechayev was in fact a revolutionary who fascinated Dostoyevsky, and it might be noted that Nechayev was the maiden name of Dostoyevsky's mother.) It is because of this connection that the great writer runs into difficulties with a police investigator called Maximov, himself a most Dostoyevskian character. Maximov tells him that among his stepson's papers he has found a list of people to be assassinated as a prelude to a general uprising leading to the overthrow of the state.

The weary, aging Dostoyevsky of these pages has as little appetite for revolutionary violence as he does for the status quo; this political apathy earns the disdain of Nechayev himself, who soon makes an appearance, and other former accomplices of Pavel. In these scenes the political dimension of generational strife emerges strongly, as the caution and conservation of maturity are derided by the fierce insurrectionary fervor of youth. It seems that for Mr. Coetzee everything must be defined anew in a totalitarian society on the point of disintegration. The fissures that divide the powerful from the powerless make all human connections tenuous and difficult, particularly the parent-child relationship.

This is an idea he has explored before. In his novel *Life & Times of Michael K,* which won Britain's Booker Prize in 1983, it is the attempt of Michael K to take his ailing mother home to die that brings him into conflict with the police state. Unlike either the magistrate or Dostoyevsky, however, Michael K has nothing with which to combat the forces ranged against him, and so withdraws utterly from society and scratches a living from a patch of earth on a deserted farm.

Then in *Age of Iron,* published in 1990, an old white woman dying of cancer in a comfortable suburb of Cape Town finds her maternal sympathies aroused by her black housekeeper's son when she sees him brutalized by the police. Surrogate parenthood gradually opens her eyes to the vicious realities of the apartheid state; ironically, it is to her daughter, who has long since fled to America, that she pours out her thoughts in writing. Her real children, she begins to see, are the black youths being murdered by the security forces under her nose. The personal and the political are most elegantly conflated in this novel.

But for poor Dostoyevsky, engaged in a futile attempt to be reconciled with his stepson, or the ghost of his stepson, noth-

ing can ever be so simple. He stays in the room Pavel rented from a widow called Anna Sergeyevna, who lives next door with her young daughter. Anna comes to him in the night, and together they do "fiery, dangerous work," with the child asleep in the next room. However, when the wily Nechayev, on the run from the police and dressed as a woman to escape detection, comes to the apartment and asks Anna's daughter for money, and despite Dostoyevsky's objections gets it, it seems that everyone and everything in the writer's world is conspiring against him. Nechayev takes him to a cellar and there, after a lengthy argument, shows him a printing press and demands that he write for the revolutionaries. Dostoyevsky realizes he has fallen into a trap: "Pavel's death was merely the bait to lure him from Dresden to Petersburg. He has been the quarry all the time."

At this point we seem to have reached some sort of narrative junction, for all the elements of the story are brought together in this dramatic revelation. For the first time we detect the shape of the plot, in both senses of the word: it is a plot that turns on Dostoyevsky's identity as a writer. Mr. Coetzee, a professor of literature at the University of Cape Town and the author of extensive literary criticism, including a book of essays called *White Writing,* has consistently returned in his fiction to the linkage of language and power, the idea that those without voices cease to signify, figuratively and literally. His most explicit expression of the theme is the novel *Foe,* published in 1987, where he reimagines the writing of *Robinson Crusoe,* and in the process creates a woman who brings the story to Daniel Defoe and so is its "true author." She, not alone among Mr. Coetzee's characters, loses her voice in history, and thus her identity.

The act of writing, and written work in the form of diaries and stories, play a central role in *The Master of Petersburg.* Writing, for Mr. Coetzee's Dostoyevsky, is not so much a tool of power, however, as a means of identification with his dead stepson, and that identification a means in turn to his own salvation. It is this complex chain of ideas that Mr. Coetzee pursues in the last chapters of the book, veering sharply from the implications of Nechayev's trap, and thus from any clear narrative resolution. So the book's momentum is dependent finally on idea rather than incident, with the significance of events contingent on one's grasp of Dostoyevsky's complex frame of beliefs.

All of which makes *The Master of Petersburg* dense and difficult, a novel that frustrates at every turn. But despite that difficulty, the figure who emerges from these pages, the master himself, in his tortured unhappiness, his terror of the next epileptic seizure, his restless sexuality and his desperate gambling with God, will seize any imagination still susceptible to the complicated passions of the Slav soul. He will reveal himself as a profound man in the throes of a furious struggle to wring meaning and redemption from the death of a son.

Joseph Frank (review date 16 October 1995)

SOURCE: A review of *The Master of Petersburg*, in *New Republic*, Vol. 213, No. 16, October 16, 1995, pp. 53-57.

[*In the following review, Frank contends that* The Master of Petersburg *is an "enigmatic and rather puzzling book" and that Coetzee is one of the most important contemporary English-language writers.*]

J. M. Coetzee is a subtle and complex writer whose works invariably contain more than appears on their seemingly pellucid surfaces. He made his reputation with novels that focused on the psychological tension created in the white South African psyche by the social and human anomalies of apartheid. But his special gift is to raise this particular conflict, through a certain starkness of treatment and careful choice of detail, into a parable of the master/slave relationship in all colonial circumstances, in all unjust structures of power. In addition to such works, Coetzee also produced a strange little book called *Foe,* which was essentially a rewriting of *Robinson Crusoe* by a female narrator washed ashore on the island of the original Crusoe, who sees many things not contained in the first version, and who unsuccessfully struggles to persuade Defoe to convey her version of events after she returns to England accompanied by the silent Friday, whose thoughts and feelings she tries to fathom.

Such a work reminds us that Coetzee, who teaches literature at the University of Capetown, is a professional linguist and literary scholar as well as a novelist. He sometimes prefers to express his ideas by means of literary pastiche as well as through his highly stylized treatment of contemporary South African life; and his new book is another contribution to this genre of pastiche. *The Master of Petersburg* draws not on the beginnings of the English novel but on the mid-nineteenth-century Russian novel, in particular on a number of Dostoevsky's creations, great and small. The central figure of the novel is Dostoevsky himself. Another important protagonist is the revolutionary Sergey Nechaev, whom Dostoevsky portrayed, though with no attempt at literal exactitude, in *The Devils,* and so it might be thought that *The Devils* is Coetzee's most important source; but he has culled from many places for his own purposes.

Coetzee's story begins in 1869, when Dostoevsky began the writing of *The Devils* and was living in Dresden with his second wife, afraid to return to Russia because he might be thrown into debtors' prison. In the novel, though, he returns to St. Petersburg with a false passport because he is notified that his stepson, Pavel Isaev, has died. Dostoevsky did have a stepson, the child of his first wife, whom he brought up as his son, and who was a rather feckless though by no means delinquent young man. Pavel, or Pasha, held a number of clerical jobs until his death in 1900. Coetzee thus

plays fast and loose with the historical record by killing off Pavel Isaev in 1869; and this raises a more general problem about the book.

Other events that are simply recorded in Coetzee's novel, such as Dostoevsky's adulterous affair in St. Petersburg, or his supposedly catching a glimpse of Nechaev and Bakunin together at a meeting of the League for Peace and Freedom in Geneva, have no basis in fact. Coetzee is a novelist, of course, and he has the novelist's right to play with history. Still, it is regrettable that he did not include a warning to his readers, many of whom will be unfamiliar with the details of Dostoevsky's biography, not to take his fiction as fact. Many will no doubt do so, for the same reason that, as Dostoevsky complained, people thought he had murdered his wife because this was the crime imputed to the narrator of *House of the Dead.*

The fictional Dostoevsky thus arrived in St. Petersburg to gather up Pasha's effects and to look into the causes of his death. Coetzee's opening pages, rather than reminiscent of *The Devils,* recall the atmosphere of Dostoevsky's little-known early story "The Landlady," which is somewhat atypical of his work and written in a garishly Romantic style in imitation of Gogol's Ukrainian tales.

Coetzee's Dostoevsky moves into the rooming house in which Pasha lived, and soon enters into a passionate love affair with the enigmatic landlady, much like the young intellectual Ordynov in Dostoevsky's story. And though Coetzee's tonality is a good bit more subdued, his fictional Dostoevsky drifts through the action in much the same semi-hypnotic fashion as Ordynov drifts through "The Landlady," which some critics have taken to be (mistakenly, in my view) a dream-like hallucination of the main character. *The Master of Petersburg* is written in a very similar register, and Coetzee makes no attempt to provide any realistic psychological motivation for his figures and their actions. Rather than a novel, one might use a musical analogy and call Coetzee's book a poetic fantasia on Dostoevskian themes; it should be read as such a work, and not approached with more conventional expectations as a work of fiction.

The fictional Dostoevsky is portrayed as obsessed by Pasha's death (like so many other Coetzee characters in the grip of different obsessions), and in some obscure way refusing to surrender him to the oblivion of the grave. Motifs from Dostoevsky's work are interwoven with the character's attempt to cope with the sensation of loss produced by Pasha's death, which he feels as really his own. "I am the one who is dead, he thinks; or rather, I died but my death failed to arrive." Just as Prince Myshkin is haunted by the thought of what a condemned man feels in the few moments before the fall of the guillotine, so Dostoevsky here cannot bear . . . the thought that, for the last fraction of the last instant of his fall, [Pavel jumped, or was pushed, from a height] Pavel knew that nothing could save him, that he was dead. He wants to believe Pavel was protected from that certainty . . . [but] he wants to believe in order to etherize himself against the knowledge that Pavel, falling, knew everything. By thinking such a thought, Dostoevsky imagines that he is identifying himself completely with Pavel, who is "thinking in him, he thinking . . . in Pavel. The thought keeps Pavel alive suspended in this fall."

When he goes to pick up Pavel's confiscated papers at the police station, Dostoevsky is informed of Pavel's connection with the Nechaev conspiracy, an underground revolutionary group which murdered one of their members for suspected treason. Readers will think of Raskolnikov's visits to a similar police station, and Coetzee teases them (and amuses himself) by allowing his fictitious Dostoevsky to clarify an obscure sense of having once been in an exactly similar situation. "Somewhere to the side falls the nagging shadow of a memory: surely he has been here before, in this very anteroom or one like it, and had an attack or a fainting fit!" Yes, indeed! He had been here before as Raskolnikov, summoned to pay an IOU and fainting when he hears talk of the murder he has just committed.

Pasha's papers contain a list of people condemned to execution by Nechaev's revolutionary group, "The People's Vengeance"; and the councillor Maximov, who physically resembles the magistrate in *Crime and Punishment* ("a bald man with the tubby figure of a peasant woman"), suggests that perhaps Pavel's death, rather than an accident or suicide, was a murder by the Nechaev group. Dostoevsky expresses horror and then revulsion at Pasha's links with Nechaev but at the same time sees the revolutionary as the embodiment of a much larger force. What moves Nechaev and accounts for his uncanny influence is not "ideas" (the historical Dostoevsky would have contested this formulation), but "a spirit, and Nechaev himself is not its embodiment but its host; or rather, he is under possession by it." For all his historically accurate hatred of Nechaev, Dostoevsky is finally stirred to protest by Maximov's scornfully detached reading of an awkwardly romantic story written by Pasha, which contains a note of social protest by including the murder of a lecherous landowner about to rape a young peasant girl.

Dostoevsky instinctively springs to Pasha's defense against Maximov's amused contempt, and his tirade broaches what will soon become an important thematic motif. For Dostoevsky accuses Maximov of suppressing his enjoyment of everything that, as an upholder of the law, he presumably wishes to combat and destroy. Of the murdered landowner, Dostoevsky says: "[D]o you suffer with him, or do you secretly exult behind the arm that swings the axe? You don't answer? Let me tell you then: reading is being the arm and

being the axe and being the skull; reading is giving yourself up, not holding yourself at a distance and jeering."

As for Maximov's pretense of merely enforcing the law: "Do you not truly want to chop off his [Nechaev's] head and stamp your feet in his blood?"

Literature here, for Coetzee's Dostoevsky, involves a total imaginative participation with all the figures of the story, not only with the victim but also with the murderer revenging an injustice; and Maximov has no right to feel morally superior to the ruthless revolutionary he is pursuing. The fictional Dostoevsky in this way reveals both his view of literature as a surrender to every facet of good and evil projected in a text, and his own capacity to transcend his hatred of Nechaev by viewing Maximov as equally guilty of reveling in bloodshed. One suspects here the influence of Mikhail Bakhtin's suggestive (but somewhat exaggerated) view that the source of Dostoevsky's greatness as a writer is precisely this ability to identify with all his characters to an equal degree, and to allow them unlimited freedom to express their own point of view.

The theme that dominates Coetzee's early chapters—Dostoevsky's desire somehow to keep Pavel alive in memory and his guilty despair at his failure as a father—becomes quite tedious after a while, and less and less artistically persuasive. Luckily, it is taken up and fused with the Nechaev theme, which is far more interesting. Nechaev's group finally contacts Dostoevsky, first through a roly-poly female emissary and then through a transvestite Nechaev, incongruously clad and carefully powdered but with hairs sprouting on his chin. Nechaev insists that the police killed Pavel, and appeals to Dostoevsky, as an ex-revolutionary, to take up the struggle again on the side of his murdered son. Nechaev's passionate plea makes Dostoevsky think of "Christ in his wrath. . . . The Christ of the Old Testament, the Christ who scourged the usurers out of the temple." But he replies to Nechaev's accusation that "all you can do is mumble and shake your head and cry," with a telling retort. "Is it the voice of the people you obey, or just your own voice, a little disguised so that you need not recognize it?"

The fictional Dostoevsky becomes more and more involved with Nechaev, whom he describes in terms used by the historical Dostoevsky for Stavrogin. "He is a sensualist. He is an extremist of the senses. He wants to live in a body at the limits of sensation, at the limits of bodily knowledge." Nechaev takes him to the decrepit tower in Petersburg from which Pavel fell (or was thrown), and they climb it in a storm-tossed night with "the roofs of St. Petersburg glinting in the rain, the row of tiny lamps along the quayside." Nechaev accuses Dostoevsky of having neglected Pasha, unerringly touching the sorest spot of his conscience ("We were his family when he had no family"); and as the two men shriek in the howling wind while they clamber above the city Coetzee craftily anticipates the reader's reaction to the staginess of this effects. "In fact the whole scene—two men on a moonlit platform high above the streets struggling against the elements, shouting over the wind, denouncing each other—is false, melodramatic": these words are supposed to transcribe Dostoevsky's reaction to what he is experiencing.

The final chapters in which Nechaev and Dostoevsky verbally cross swords constitute the ideological climax of the book, and set "the spirit of justice" against what might be called the spirit of freedom. What will happen, Dostoevsky asks, "once the tempest of the people's vengeance has done its work and everyone has been levelled? Will you still be free to be whom you wish? Will each of us be free to be whom we wish, at last?" Dostoevsky invokes Shigalov's theory of equality praised by Peter Verkhovensky in the *The Devils* ("if another Copernicus were to arise he should have his eyes gouged out"); but Nechaev replies with an apocalyptic image of total destruction, as a prelude to a perpetual regeneration, which radicalizes even the historical Nechaev and his mentor Bakunin.

The future, for Nechaev, is a revolution "when everything is reinvented, everything erased and reborn: law, morality, the family, everything." The "old way of thinking" will be abolished and (anticipating Mao) "the peasants will be the teachers and the professors will be the students. . . . Everyone will be reborn with a new heart." When Dostoevsky mentions God, Nechaev rapturously replies that "God will be envious . . . [and] the angels will stand around us in circles singing their hosannas." Even more, the souls of the dead, the soul of Pavel Isaev, will arise and walk the earth again. Imitating the Christ of the "Legend of the Grand Inquisitor," Dostoevsky embraces Nechaev, "breathing the sour smell of his carbuncular flesh, sobbing, laughing, he kisses him on the left cheek and on the right." Still, in a last feeble effort to resist being swept away, he threatens Nechaev with eternal damnation. But Nechaev charges him with ignorance of theology and invokes the apocryphal legend of the Mother of God who, making "a pilgrimage to hell to plead for the damned," refuses to desist until all have been forgiven (the historical Dostoevsky uses this legend in *The Brothers Karamazov*).

Finally, at the end of Coetzee's book, street fighting between the students and police has broken out, fires are burning, and "a cloud of smoke hangs over the city." (Coetzee may have been thinking of, and magnifying, what occurred in St. Petersburg in 1862.) Dostoevsky feels that he has been defeated by Nechaev, that he "has lost because, in this debate, he does not believe himself." He leafs through Pavel's papers, and we are met for the first time by Dostoevsky's self-awareness as a writer. For what Pavel (or his master Nechaev, as well

as the landlady) did not understand is that "I pay too . . . I pay and I sell: that is my life. Sell my life, sell the lives of those around me. . . . Sell you, sell your daughter [Matryona], sell all those I love. . . . A life without honour; treachery without limit; confession without end." All this has led to a terrifying awareness of his own uncertainty, which requires him, if he is to continue to create, "to put aside all that he himself is, all he has become, down to his very features, and become as a babe again."

By the end of the book, in the chapter significantly called "Stavrogin," Coetzee seems to equate Dostoevsky as a writer—or writing in general—with the efforts of this Byronic dandy transformed into metaphysical rebel to wipe out the boundaries of good and evil. Dostoevsky does not appear as a writer at all until this last chapter, but finally he sits down to compose in Pavel's room, determined to "refuse the chloroform of terror or unconsciousness," and instead, "to live in Russia and hear the voices of Russia murmuring within him. To hold it all within him: Russia, Pavel, death." No longer merely the victim of epilepsy or madness, he willfully becomes their vehicle: "not to emerge from the fall unscathed . . . to wrestle with the whistling darkness, to absorb it, to make it his medium; to turn the falling into a flying, even if a flying as slow and old and clumsy as a turtle." But he also feels, as he unpacks his writing-case, that he is engaging in an act of betrayal.

What Dostoevsky writes, in the empty pages in Pavel's notebook, is a re-constitution of Pavel's life in the landlady's apartment, garnished with details taken from Stavrogin's confession, the suppressed chapter of *The Devils* published only after Dostoevsky's death, which recounts his seduction and violation of a young girl. What he has written is "an assault upon the innocence of a child. It is an act for which he can expect no forgiveness," and is in effect a temptation of God. "Now God must speak, now God dare no longer remain silent." He imagines himself standing outside his own soul, "somewhere he stands and watches while he and God circle each other." Writing thus involves the loss of one's soul, it is a challenge to God, and he feels again that "he has betrayed everyone; nor does he see that his betrayal could go deeper." The book ends with the action unresolved; we do not know how or why Pavel died, or whether the fictional Dostoevsky returns to Dresden. And Dostoevsky is left only with a sense of complete emptiness and dispossession, his mouth filled with the bitter taste of gall. "They pay him lots of money for writing books, said the child [Matryona], repeating the dead child [Pavel]. What they failed to say was that he had to give up his soul in return."

This is an enigmatic and rather puzzling book whose aim is difficult to unravel. Clearly Coetzee is not attempting, like a historical novelist, to convey any sort of historically correct image of Dostoevsky's life in 1869; he prefers to make use of his writer's liberties and to invent his own details. He makes only a very perfunctory stab at filling in the St. Petersburg background, and the effect that he creates is more somnambulistic than realistic. What, then, is he trying to do?

Coetzee, one must remember, is a South African writer, and it may be that he felt himself to be living (until very recently) in a society even more repressive than that of Russia in the nineteenth century, and poised like Russia on the edge of a revolutionary upheaval. Dostoevsky is the greatest novelist of modern revolutionary crisis, of the clash of values that such a crisis involves. It is not difficult to understand why Coetzee, who has used the pastiche of *Foe* to dramatize the issues of feminism and multiculturalism, should use Dostoevsky in the same way to express the dilemmas racking his own society. Coetzee may well have lived the clash between the spirit of justice and the spirit of freedom with all the intensity of Dostoevsky.

But there is also, as we have seen, the problem of writing and the writer, which Coetzee presents so poignantly; and here perhaps he is obliquely taking into account his own personal situation in South African literature. There has never been any ambiguity about his unswerving hostility to the abominations of apartheid, now happily a thing of the past; but he has been harshly criticized in his homeland because his novels did not attack these evils in any overt, socially propagandistic manner. A typical charge, made in 1982, accused him of giving "privileged attention to the predicament of a liberally petty bourgeois intelligentsia." Even the publication, a year later, of his intensely moving *Life and Times of Michael K,* whose central character is black or a person of color vainly seeking to lead a normal, peaceful life, did not put an end to such brickbats. In 1986, another critic attributed Coetzee's increasing international fame "to the muddled pathos of the position of the white South Africans," which gives such fiction as his its worldwide appeal. Coetzee himself has commented somewhat sadly on the difference in his status at home and abroad.

The Master of Petersburg, then, may be an implicit act of self-defense, a defense of the writer's obligation in an explosive revolutionary period to participate creatively in all sides of the human bedlam, even at the cost of personal self-abandonment. Such an obligation seems to stir Dostoevsky when he rewards Nechaev with the kiss of Christian forgiveness, while being left himself only with a tragic sense of loss and self-betrayal. Is this novel more a self-revelation than may appear at first sight? We can only speculate. One thing, though, can be stated unequivocally: Coetzee is an intriguing and ingenious writer.

T. Kai Norris Easton (essay date December 1995)

SOURCE: "Text and Hinterland: J. M. Coetzee and the South African Novel," in *Journal of Southern African Studies,* Vol. 21, No. 4, December, 1995, pp. 585-99.

[*In the following essay, Easton suggests that Coetzee places his novels in settings other than South Africa in order to symbolically emphasize himself as a "regional" writer, highlighting as he does the feelings of displacement of most South Africans.*]

There is a certain paradox in placing a writer in a national or regional context, especially a writer like J. M. Coetzee who has distanced himself from such a reading. However, as much as his novels and scholarly criticism range well beyond a South African terrain, they also track this course—at times—quite deliberately. Think only of **'The Narrative of Jacobus Coetzee'** in the second half of *Dusklands* or his collection of essays, *White Writing.* This article will explore the ambivalent space of Coetzee's fiction with particular reference to *Life & Times of Michael K* and *Age of Iron.* His novels retreat and roam; like Michael K, they root themselves 'nowhere'. But the South African base is there—in the Cape, from which his stories emigrate. As such, Coetzee's oeuvre might be seen as a series of 'travelling texts' which reinscribes, by dislocation, a South African topography. Indeed, Coetzee's work carries a double tendency towards the South African landscape: one which is concurrently removed and engaged. If it draws heavily from a European tradition, it also drifts in and out of a local one. The question I wish to pose is this: Is there a way to discuss Coetzee's narratives as 'South African' without reducing his novels to a reading of the 'nation'? Or to phrase it differently, can his novels be read as 'national' texts precisely for their fragmented South Africanness—a 'nationality' which presupposes diversity and a mingling of cultures and forms? The discussion which follows makes use of a dispersal of spatial terms. They are not, in any way, meant to contain Coetzee's fiction in a South African context, nor to imply that his fiction is self-containing. Rather, it will be argued that—perhaps against all intentions—his novels offer a new kind of mapmaking which opens up the space of South African fiction.

Introduction

J. M. Coetzee's fiction-writing career spans two decades and seven novels. Since the publication of *Dusklands* in 1974 to *The Master of Petersburg,* released last year, Coetzee has consistently written against the grain, purposefully evasive of commitment to any particular mode of discourse—be it academic, political, intellectual, or literary. Instead, his fiction has crossed boundaries, twisting and bending South Africa's literary frontiers. He has parodied the explorer narrative, the farm novel (or *plaasroman*) and the traveller's tale, interrogating in his fiction, as well as in his criticism, colonial and apartheid mythologies of land and settlement, possession and ownership.

What is significant is the way in which Coetzee's textual practices and literary landscapes are constantly on the move. His most recent work, for example, published in the year of apartheid's collapse, is set in the late years of tsarist Russia.

That Coetzee steers clear of a South African setting at the height of its most historic political reforms is not surprising, considering that while his sixth novel, *Age of Iron,* gave us a realist locale—Cape Town in the 1980s—*Foe,* as its predecessor, had taken on Daniel Defoe's eighteenth-century England and Robinson Crusoe's island. In terms of the South African literary debate, then, where exactly do the novels of J. M. Coetzee fit in?

The *Times Literary Supplement* marked South Africa's first all-race elections with a special issue focussing, as one might expect, on the anticipated changes to come, on the new politics and the new literature. On the latter, Elleke Boehmer wrote, 'What South African fiction could use more of is narrative structure that embraces choice or, if you will, stories that juggle generic options'. A decade earlier, Njabulo S. Ndebele had called for writers to be 'storytellers, not just casemakers'.

Many others have echoed Ndebele's words. Bessie Head tried to imagine worlds beyond, writing in *Tales of Tenderness and Power:* 'Possibly too, southern Africa might one day become the home of the storyteller and dreamer. . .'. It was Albie Sachs, however, in his revolutionary 'Preparing Ourselves for Freedom' address to the ANC in 1989, who made the debate popular—or, at least, controversial—in his proposal that writers should refrain from saying, 'Culture is a weapon of the struggle' for a minimum period of five years. More recently he tells Christopher Hope in a BBC Radio 3 programme, 'There are things to celebrate now, as well as to decry'. But there are writers on the other side of the debate, like Mongane Wally Serote and Keorapetse Kgositsile, who argue that a direct engagement with South African realities is absolutely crucial. The writer and critic 'must be steeped in reality', says Kgositsile, for this is the 'point of departure for any hardnosed imaginative search or exploration'.

How then to decide what aesthetic criteria should be, what the level of relevance? How do realism and postmodernism accommodate a changing society—and is either mode more suitable than the other? In a 'new' South Africa, after so many years of apartheid, of banning and censorship, the question is whether now isn't the time, as Ian Steadman says, to move into 'new terrain'. But if this new terrain is to embrace all cultures, can writing be subject to prescription, can

there be a single form and a single view? J. M. Coetzee rejects the notion that there is a certain role the writer should play. 'The alternative which he would have us consider is "whether there might not be a whole spectrum of valid literature open to Africa"'. Within this debate, then, Coetzee would seem to occupy a more inclusive middle ground. In terms of his own work, however, he would have a closer affinity with the first group of writers. A remarkable craftsman, Coetzee is careful and deliberate in his writing, candid and provocative in his interview responses. What we see is a very self-conscious, highly allusive, and playful approach to language and literature—playful in irony and understatement, his dry humour subtly pervading his texts and commentary—but there is an utter seriousness and attentiveness there as well. As Debra Castillo notes in an article on *Dusklands:*

> Thus this game theorist clearly, casually, and brutally articulates the underlying theoretical debate about the role of fiction in South African reality and suggestively positions the novel within that debate.

Not everyone, however, is enamoured with Coetzee's style or technique. A writing which tends towards the metafictional and the non-specific, his 'aesthetics of ambiguity' has disgruntled some critics, who see his work as overrun with 'strategies' and 'gaming'. James Booth applauds Paul Rich's article, 'Apartheid and the Decline of Civilization Idea' for its 'definitive debunking of Coetzee's self-indulgent and grossly overrated book' (i.e. *Waiting for the Barbarians*). In his view Coetzee has 'absolutely no conception of any positive values outside his own "civilisation"'.

Is Coetzee caught up in his own 'civilisation'—is he too removed from civilisation at large? In an interview with the author, Richard Begam asks a question regarding the state of the novel today: 'The effect—so the argument goes—is a literature which has cut itself off from a general reading public, a literature which is of interest only to the academic'. Both Begam's question and Coetzee's answer are given in general terms; Coetzee's response, though not directly related to his own work, is interesting for its implications. His words are typically provisional:

> I suppose that . . . writers ought to be wary and ask themselves every now and again whether they are not cutting themselves off from real human concerns. But, when we look around who are in fact the writers who have lost themselves in narcissism? Few that I can name. And to take the point one step further, I think it is possible to ask oneself that very question and come back with a perfectly serious answer: yes, I may indeed be cutting myself off, at least from today's readers: nevertheless, what I am

engaged in doing is more important than maintaining that contact.

The engagement Coetzee is describing here may sound, on the surface, elitist, but at the basis of it seems to be a moral code. The suggestion is for a more lasting type of relevance, for something more substantial, for something which goes beyond the immediate present. Mazisi Kunene's maxim might apply: one should write, he says, 'as though reporting to somebody who will be here in a thousand years from now . . .'. David Attwell positions Coetzee's work as an attempt to project a 'post-humanist, reconstructed ethics'. Indeed, there is an ethical underpinning to Coetzee's work, and an arguably *conscious* effort not to follow 'established' codes of liberalism and fiction; he chooses instead to cross or redefine the boundaries, maintaining, at the same time, the distance of doubt. Bessie Head once asked, 'If one is a part of it, through being born there, how does one communicate with the horrible?'. The answer given by Coetzee's character, Mrs Curren in *Age of Iron,* suggests the near impossibility of that communication: 'To speak of this', she says, 'you would need the tongue of a god'—or, perhaps, the missing tongue of Friday in *Foe.*

Each of Coetzee's novels, through its play on land, language, and identity, interrogates—to use Susan Barton's term in *Foe*—the 'father-born' epistemologies of history, geography, and categorisation. In the Foucauldian sense, the question is, 'What rules, for instance, allow the construction of a map, model, or classificatory system?'. And as Said reminds us in *Orientalism:*

> We must take seriously Vico's great observation that men make their own history, that what they can know is what they have made, and extend it to geography: as both geographical and cultural entities—to say nothing of historical entities. . . .

'Rival Topographies'

As Coetzee's discussion in **White Writing** delineates, the white South African literary landscape consisted of two rival 'dream topographies': one which was 'a network of boundaries crisscrossing the surface of the land, marking off thousands of farms, each a separate kingdom ruled over by a benign patriarch . . .'; the other which portrayed South Africa 'as a vast, empty, silent space . . . . The imperial-born myth of the 'unsettled' land is thus the origin of a literature which is just as empty: white pastoral inscribes itself on the colonial South African imagination, but exhibits only a superficial topography—an economic one where black labour is but a 'shadowy presence' to the settlers' farms.

Evoked through the genre of the Afrikaans *plaasroman* (and to a lesser extent its English counterpart, the farm novel),

the literature of white pastoral, with its idealised rural order and insularity, gave rise to nationalist sentiment. Published in 1883, Olive Schreiner's *The Story of an African Farm* was perhaps the first work of fiction in white South African literature to reject the pastoral. She initiates a more sceptical vision of white settlement in South Africa, putting the terrain, a 'merciless' and 'monstrous' one, at the centre of her narrative.

A century after Schreiner's story was published, South African literature showed signs of a different kind of settlement. Writers were struggling not against colonial modes such as the white pastoral, but against the modes imposed on the imagination under an increasingly brutal system of apartheid. As Coetzee described it in his 1987 Jerusalem Prize acceptance speech, South African literature was 'a literature in bondage'; it was 'exactly the kind of literature you would expect people to write from a prison'. In an article published the same year, Neil Lazarus called it an 'obsessional literature. . . . It tracks relentlessly and more or less pitilessly over the ever more restricted terrain to which, by virtue of its situation, it is condemned'.

What we keep seeing, in historical and literary representations of South Africa, are boundaries, in effect, that confine geographies, people, fiction. At the time of this speech, as an author of five novels, J. M. Coetzee had fully established himself as a writer. Of these five novels, the first two, *Dusklands* and *In the Heart of the Country,* can be seen 'as deliberate revisions of two of the most common South African genres: the travel narrative and the farm novel'. His fourth novel, *Life & Times of Michael K,* roams around the southwestern Cape—from Cape Town to the Karoo and back again, while his sixth novel, *Age of Iron,* is set in a Cape Town suburb in riot-ridden late 1980s South Africa.

The third, fifth, and seventh novels situate themselves elsewhere: *Waiting for the Barbarians* is an invented, non-specific landscape (a remote frontier 'oasis' of Empire); *Foe*'s location moves from an unnamed island to Bristol and London and other bits of England in between; and *The Master of Petersburg* travels back in time to Dostoevsky's nineteenth-century Russia.

Despite Coetzee's obvious engagement with ideas, theories, and literatures of the West, as well as his reluctance to take on the label of a 'South African novelist', the influence of the country is clearly there: it is enough so that Attwell actually refers to him as a 'regional writer'. Certainly, in the Jerusalem address, Coetzee is speaking for himself as well as other South African writers: 'How *we* long to quit a world of pathological attachments and abstract forces, of anger and violence', he says, 'and take up residence in a world where a living play of feelings and ideas is possible . . .

In a different address at the 1987 *Weekly Mail* book festival, Coetzee's response was less one of lament, more a certain kind of call to literary action. In this speech, he proposed the freedom of the novel, the novel to '*rival* history':

> . . . a novel that operates in terms of its own procedures and issues in its own conclusions, not one that operates in terms of the procedures of history . . . a novel that evolves its own paradigms and myths . . . perhaps going so far as to show up the mythic status of history—in other words, demythologising history.

'Cape Inscription'—Coetzee's Altered Geographies

> The Cape of Good Hope was one of the few places in Africa where Northern Europeans had access to the continental interior. It was a magnet both for settlers and for explorers eager to make their mark.

Coetzee's demythologising tackles history and its colonial mappings, most notably in the region of the Cape. On 'writing' the Cape, the following example from Paul Carter's excellent study, *The Road to Botany Bay,* makes for an interesting comparison.

In 1801, the name 'Cape Inscription' was given to a spot on the north-west coast of Australia by a Captain Emmanuel Hamelin, who found on this particular piece of earth a pewter plate. On the plate were inscriptions of two explorers, both Dutch, who had 'discovered' this Cape on separate excursions. Hamelin's name for this bit of coast is surprisingly apt, linking as it does with the act he is performing. As Carter writes, ' . . . Such a name . . . belongs firmly to the history of travelling . . . It suggests a kind of history which is neither static nor mindlessly mobile, but which incorporates both possibilities'.

Carter creates his own use for the name 'Cape Inscription', saying it is emblematic of the approach he took in writing his book. His discussion of Captain Cook's naming process observes a similar notion, describing the names Cook offered as 'means, not of settling, but of travelling on'. Carter has hit on a crucial question: Is there a way to 'write' the Cape (or any place) without replicating a colonial 'script of possession'? And, if so, what is behind the writing?

J. M. Coetzee's reinscription of the Cape reveals a cartography closer to Carter's. As Rita Barnard writes:

> What is at stake for him is not place or landscape as an object of mimesis, but the discursive and generic and political codes that inform our understanding and knowledge of place. There is a deliberate analytical unsettledness in Coetzee, which deconstructs, rather than assimilates to, any South

African literary tradition, or any South African 'sense of place'.

Two of Coetzee's novels are set in Cape Town itself. But while *Age of Iron* situates itself definitively there, *Life & Times of Michael K* resists complete enclosure. One striking geographical detail is omitted from this text: the name of the country itself. As such, it might be read, to use Attwell's term for *Waiting for the Barbarians,* as a 'pivotal' one in Coetzee's corpus: its ambiguous space and shifting narrative, not to mention the elusiveness of Michael K himself, are in many ways representative of Coetzee's narrative practice as a whole. Coetzee places himself geographically, but only provisionally—although consider his comments below:

> I do believe that people can only be in love with one landscape in their lifetime. One can appreciate and enjoy many geographies, but there is only one that one feels in one's bones. And I certainly know from experience that I don't respond to Europe or the United States in the same way as I do to South Africa. And I would probably feel a certain sense of artificial background construction if I were to write a fiction set in another environment.

This statement made by Coetzee in a 1984 interview holds up Susan VanZanten Gallagher's theory—perhaps South Africa influences Coetzee's fiction more than he (otherwise) admits. For what is it except a certain kind of 'artificial background construction' in his third novel *Waiting for the Barbarians?* And what does this say for his response to Tony Morphet regarding the geography of *Michael K?* When asked whether the 'highly specified' location of this novel was an attempt for a 'more direct and immediate conversation with South African readers' or, indeed, 'part of another strategy', Coetzee replied:

> The geography is, I fear, less trustworthy than you imagine—not because I deliberately set about altering the reality of Sea Point or Prince Albert but because I don't have much interest in, or can't seriously engage myself with, the kind of realism that takes pride in copying the 'real' world. The option was, of course, open to me to invent a world out of place and time and situate the action there, as I did in *Waiting for the Barbarians;* but that side of *Waiting for the Barbarians* was an immense labor, and what would have been the point, this time round?

It is very appropriate that Coetzee invents his imperial landscape in *Waiting for the Barbarians,* for it represents both the artificial (i.e. imaginary) war that the 'barbarians' are engaged in and the artificial possession by Empire of their land. Rosemary Jolly, in her article, 'Territorial Metaphor', demonstrates the central place that the setting has both in Coetzee's purpose for the book and in critics' reception of it, including this comment by Leon Whiteson:

> The geography is garbled; there is desert and snow, lizards and bears. The story is told in that most awkward tense; the historic present. The dialogue is stiff, the writing has the air of translation . . . . Coetzee's bad dreams have not been earned by any truth . . . . The heart of this novel is not darkness but mush.

Whiteson's idea of a novel involves a geography as superficial as that marked by settler colonialism: a geography of sameness rather than variety, of the identical rather than the diversified. Coetzee's fiction puts this uniform space into question. In so doing, his maps do not duplicate what is already there—but neither are they as patchy as Whiteson seems to indicate. As Jolly notes, 'The geography of his fiction may not correspond to an identifiable geographical political entity, but its depiction is both detailed and comprehensible'. In a comment Coetzee himself makes to David Attwell more recently, he acknowledges that '*Barbarians* is more accommodating toward nature description' than either of his first two novels: 'But of course what is "described" in *Barbarians* is a landscape I have never seen; whereas I know the landscape of the other two books, to say nothing of *Michael K,* all too well'.

Life & Times of Michael K

Life & Times of Michael K, his fourth novel and winner of the 1983 Booker Prize, is indeed more familiar terrain for Coetzee; it is set in what is not only a recognisable South Africa, but returns to his home region—Cape Town and the Karoo. But the Cape Coetzee comes back to is no longer the site of imperial narratives, as in the **'Narrative of Jacobus Coetzee'** in *Dusklands,* where the archetypal hunter-explorer treks through the wilderness, naming it and claiming it as he goes along; nor is it the numbered entries of the 'locked diary' of Magda, the lonely spinster and reluctant 'daughter of the colonies' in *In the Heart of the Country,* who lives out a stultifying existence in the aridity of this desert. In each of his first two novels we have protagonists who are left on a surface, *exterior* Cape landscape. But in *Life & Times of Michael K,* the main character is neither trying to explore nor settle, mock nor imitate the pastoral. Michael K's relationship is one of *affinity* with the stony ground; he is virtually 'lodged within the landscape' as he burrows himself into the soil.

From *Waiting for the Barbarians,* the 'Other' has moved into the forefront: K is the primary focus of the thoughts of two separate voices: one unnamed 'limited omniscient' narrator; the other, in part 2 of the novel, by the medical officer at Kenilworth. In this dual address to K's story, what comes across is a resistance to the fabrication and objectification of the 'Other'. Unlike the 'Hottentots' in Jacobus Coetzee's narrative, or the servants Hendrik and 'Klein-Anna' in Magda's diary, Michael K is hardly in the background. Even within these 'Other' narratives, K is self-defined; and his assertiveness comes through in his frequent escapes, in his suggestive silences, in his crafting and cleverness, in his unyielding to any type of colonisation, either mental or physical.

Sea Point is the site with which the novel begins and ends. The narrative travels full circle, following Michael K on a journey to take his ill mother, by the wheelbarrow cart of his own invention, from Cape Town to the rural home of her childhood in the Karoo. The structure of the book consists of three parts, the first and third of which are told in *style indirect libre*. Part 1 comprises the bulk of the story with the life and times thus far of Michael K, a gardener for the municipal parks, and his mother Anna K, as they try to escape to the country.

The flat desert Karoo over which K travels is cut through by the 'national road'. Like Jacobus Coetzee's 'devouring path' in *Dusklands,* the road is the symbol of the state's occupation and defence line during war-time; it is full of roadblocks and checkpoints—barriers which prevent Michael and his mother, who do not have the required permit, from travelling beyond Cape Town on their first expedition to Prince Albert. K imagines there must be less controlled spaces: '. . . next time we'll go by the back roads. They can't block every road out'. K's travels are not unencumbered, but the possibility is posed: has the mapping out of national roads and blockades left any areas unoccupied? Have they crisscrossed the entire country or are there areas yet uncontained, unclaimed—areas not yet 'parcelled and possessed'?

On his second expedition, K does manage to counter the bureaucratic barriers, travelling without a permit and getting as far as Stellenbosch, but he later refers to it as a 'place of ill-luck', for it is where his mother dies in hospital. From here, K's devotion will be to his mother *earth:* he will continue the journey to Prince Albert and occupy himself in a new garden, beginning with the cultivation of his mother's ashes at what he thinks is the farm of her birthplace. 'Now I am here, he thought, Or at least I am somewhere'.

The war landscape, if not explicitly descriptive, is more pronounced in this novel than in *Waiting for the Barbarians.* The epigraph from Heraclitus immediately defines the opposition: the war in Michael K has been constructed by the 'founding fathers'—the founding colonisers:

> War is the father of all and kind of all.

Some he shows as gods, others as men.
Some he makes slaves, and other free.

In this war, however, the enemy is no longer the Empire's construction. Here the state is having to battle with a real enemy, the majority population whom they have thus far controlled and oppressed. Nöel's reply to the medical officer in part 2: 'We are fighting this war . . . so that minorities will have a say in their destinies', is the only hint we have of the *politics* of this war. The symbolism, which Stephen Clingman speaks of below, points to an apocalyptic vision:

> In *Life & Times* virtually the entire setting is symbolic—a symbolic landscape as much as a real one traversed by Michael K. Here the function of the symbolism is also specific, having to do with the confrontation of various choices in the landscape of the future.

Security measures have intensified. Military jeeps, riot troops, police vans, looters and guards, shots and sirens, shuttered windows and abandoned houses are the signs of the 'local' war in the city. As K and his mother huddle together in the Buhrmanns' devastated flat in Cape Town, 'the conviction grew in them that the real war had come to Sea Point and found them out'.

But the real war, the scenes of warfare, are very much left in the background. The focus is rather on this fringe character, Michael K, who keeps to the sides of the road, to the slopes and mountains. Disfigured by his hare lip, and described by others as a 'simpleton' or an 'idiot', Michael K is nevertheless a clever and adaptable person, who creates space for himself as he ranges over the landscapes of Cape Town and the Karoo.

> He thought: Now surely I have come as far as a man can come; surely no one will be mad enough to cross these plains, climb these mountains, search these rocks to find me; surely now that in all the world only I know where I am, I can think of myself as lost. (*Life & Times of Michael K*)

Unlike Magda in *In the Heart of the Country,* K does want to be one of the 'forgotten ones of history'. In his makeshift existence at the dam, when he returns for the second time, he wishes to leave no trace of himself; and thus he will not inscribe history like a castaway or a prisoner, for '. . . his life by the dam was not a sentence that he had to serve out'. He uses materials and tools that will disintegrate into the earth; and, unlike the 'founding fathers', K refutes the idea of patrimony: '. . . I am not building a house out here by the dam to pass on to other generations', for 'The worst mistake, he told himself, would be to try to found a new house, a rival line . . .'.

But the garden spot does rival the farmhouse: precisely because K's existence by the dam is *not* an imitation of that structure, but one which is based on completely different terms. And when the guerrillas come to the farm, there is that much-quoted moment when he considers joining the war effort:

> Yet in the same instant that he reached down to check that his shoelaces were tied, K knew that he would not crawl out and stand up and cross from darkness into firelight to announce himself. He even knew the reason why: because enough men had gone off to war saying the time for gardening was when the war was over, whereas there must be men to stay behind and keep gardening alive, or at least the idea of gardening. . . .

The garden is thus a site of *resistance,* for K is defining his own role. He is not a fighter, but a cultivator. One must also remember that he makes the 'deserted farm bloom', which, when he arrived, was simply a 'rockery garden in which nothing was growing'. Additionally, in order to make these pumpkins grow, K must work in a very disciplined and *strategical* fashion: he is not cultivating an open and abundant garden. He uses the pump sparingly and only at night; he has only a certain number of seeds, and only two kinds: pumpkins and melons. Having to hide out from the enemy as it were, he camouflages his existence. And realising he could be betrayed by his pumpkins, which he first piled 'in a pyramid near his burrow; it looked like a beacon', he than goes through elaborate measures to disguise them, painting 'each shell in a mottled pattern' with a mud paste. Earlier, when a helicopter flies above him, he realises the absurdity of cultivating such visible vegetables. He muses: 'They can see everything from the air, everything that by its nature does not hide underground. I should be growing onions'.

But lest we start to glorify Michael K and his garden, and write our own version of the pastoral or an adventure tale, it is clear that his existence is minimalist; it is not romantic: '. . . a man must be ready to live like a beast', he says; and then, 'One cannot live like this'. Coetzee himself emphasises 'how terribly transitory that garden life of K's is: he can't hope to keep the garden because, finally, the whole surface of South Africa has been surveyed and mapped and disposed of'.

At odds with Voltaire's romantic credo from *Candide:* 'Il faut cultiver le jardin', is the reality of Michael's lot. As a member of the 'multitude in the second class' (as the medical officer calls him), K lives within certain restrictions. In what seems to be a South African landscape, we have a character who *seems* to be a member of the majority oppressed class. But, with the exception of the medical officer's reference above, and his charge sheet designation of 'CM', which may or may not refer to 'Coloured Male', Michael K is classified, within the first paragraph of the text, not by his race, as Kelly Hewson notes, but by his *disfigurement.*

K will be put in his first 'camp' at Huis Norenius, an orphanage for afflicted children, for his supposed simple-mindedness, at the expense of the state. Now, during war-time, the state will fund other camps for Michael K. After his one-day stint in a labour gang on the railroad tracks near Touws River, he will have more extended stays in Jakkalsdrif, a 'resettlement camp', (what he had thought, from his view in the mountains, was a 'construction site') and then at the old racecourse Kenilworth, the 'rehabilitation camp'/hospital in part 2. They try to contain K within these bits of barbed wire, the guards on duty; and others try to contain him with euphemisms, renaming the sites: 'This isn't a prison', said the man. 'Didn't you hear the policeman tell you it isn't a prison? This is Jakkalsdrif. This is a camp', even going so far as to say, 'You climb the fence . . . and you have left your place of abode. Jakkalsdrif is your place of abode now. Welcome'.

Throughout the text, Michael K is creating his own environment. He is a resilient figure, despite his bouts of hunger and fever and confinement in various camps. But is his garden life a 'rival topography' in this state of civil war?

There is first the distinction, which K himself makes, between the garden he cultivated in Cape Town at Wynberg Park and the garden he cultivates in the Karoo: '. . . he was no longer sure that he would choose green lawns and oak-trees to live among. . . . It is no longer the green and the brown that I want but the yellow and the red. . . .'. Secondly, there is Coetzee's reply to Tony Morphet that if there is a 'structural opposition' between 'camp' and 'garden', it is 'at most at a conceptual level'.

Coetzee's answer is based on the ephemeral nature of K's garden existence; but perhaps K's own 'dream topography', which closes the novel, closes down the camp sites as well.

Fences and Fictions

> He could understand that people should have retreated here and fenced themselves in with miles and miles of silence; he could understand that they should have wanted to bequeath the privilege of so much silence to their children and grandchildren in perpetuity (though by what right he was not sure) . . . (*Life & Times of Michael K*)

As Michael K's movements show, fences are simply signs of an outward, exterior story: they cannot, in the end, enclose him. Moreover, K proves himself to be both good at escaping them and, ironically, talented at *making* them. As the farmer in one of his Jakkalsdrif work gang assignments tells him, he has 'a feel for wire' and 'should go into fencing. There will always be a need for good fencers in this country, no matter what'. Later, running through the 'almost empty' landscape upon his escape from Jakkalsdrif, he feels a 'craftsman's pleasure' in the taut wire of the fences he is ducking. But K has never been the entrepreneur, never the proprietor, and 'he could not imagine himself spending his life driving stakes into the ground, erecting fences, dividing up the land'.

Fence posts, barbed wire and the national roads dot the landscape—within these enclosures are the farms captured by settlers. The fences both exclude and isolate, and Magda, in the heart of the country with too much land, is sceptical of her inheritance: 'But how real is our possession? . . . *the land knows nothing of fences,* the stones will be here when I have crumbled away. . . .'

The interior of the land resists capture, finally, like Michael K. It insists on identification, not exploration, so that even Jacobus Coetzee questions in his narrative whether he is truly able to penetrate the interior, 'Are they not perhaps fictions, these lures of interiors for rape which the universe uses to draw out its explorers?'

Age of Iron

Age of Iron (1990), Coetzee's sixth novel, is an even more identifiable and contemporary South Africa then *Life & Times of Michael K,* where, as Cynthia Ozick writes, 'Except for the reference to Cape Town and to place-names that are recognizably Afrikaans, we are not even told that this is the physical and moral landscape of South Africa.' Indeed, there is no textual reference to 'South Africa' in *Michael K,* although the back cover blurb of the Penguin edition designates the setting as a 'South Africa torn by civil war'.

In *Age of Iron,* there are not such geographical gaps: we know this is South Africa, but the topography has shifted— both in Coetzee's narrative style and in the novel's landscape. Not since *Dusklands* (the dated narratives of both Eugene Dawn and Jacobus Coetzee) have any of Coetzee's novels been assigned such a particular time and place. And from the *imagined* apocalyptic vision in *Life & Times of Michael K,* here is something even more tangible: the 'emergency years' of 1986-1989, during which Coetzee was writing the novel, are the context for the novel itself.

The desert Karoo of much of *Michael K* has given way to the seascape of Cape Town; K left us in Sea Point, but Mrs Curren's sea brings us to False Bay, and it is just as empty as the sea which surrounds Susan Barton's desert isle in *Foe.* It is neither a source of inspiration nor a site of activity, but a symbol of the 'sluggish, half asleep' minority population. Here, South Africa is not a land of beauty or mystery, but is 'Fixed in the mind as a place of flat, hard light, without shadows, without depth'. As Benita Parry says in her review of the book, '. . . the drably named False Bay is redesignated a "bay of false hope"; and a land renowned for its scenery and sunshine . . . is derided for its "uninspired name"'.

Mill Street of the suburbs is not described for its comforts or its opulence, but for its slow decay. Mrs Curren's own house 'is tired of waiting for the day, tried of holding itself together'. The sagging of the gutters, the clogging of pipes—the house itself represents the country's malaise:

> A house built solidly but without love, cold, inert now, ready to die. Whose walls the sun, even the African sun, has never succeeded in warming, as though the very bricks, made by the hands of convicts, radiate an intractable sullenness.

Constructed by the labour of prisoners, the house is not a home, nor a landmark of history, but a 'site without a human past . . .'. The orders of the 'patricians of Cape Town' a hundred years earlier that 'there be erected spacious homes for themselves and their descendants in perpetuity . . .' are thus empty of promise. In this 'age of iron', white patrimony and pastoral no longer have a place. Echoing Coetzee's 'failure of love' theme in his Jerusalem Prize acceptance speech, Mrs Curren's words, this time, carry some weight:

> A land in the process of being repossessed, it heirs quietly announcing themselves. A land taken by force, used, despoiled, spoiled, abandoned in its barren late years. Loved too, perhaps, by its ravishers, but loved only in the bloomtime of its youth and therefore, in the verdict of history, not loved enough.

The landscape itself recoils, rendering Mrs Curren's own version of the pastoral obsolete. She has rested her roots in South Africa on her mother's story of the early days of settlement—'in the age of ox-wagons'. But the site of her 'natal earth', the Piesangs River, 'Such a lovely golden name! I was sure it must be the most beautiful place on earth', becomes—in Mrs Curren's own adulthood—'Not a river at all, just a trickle of water choked with reeds. . . . Not Paradise at all'.

Pastoral is seen to be an old, old story—the old story of the 'shadowy presence', like the gardener who is missing from her family photo: 'Who are the ghosts and who the presences? . . . No longer does the picture show who were in the garden frame that day, but who were not there'.

'After [the] Bigger Game'

> The feel of writing fiction is one of freedom, of irresponsibility, or better, of responsibility toward something that has not yet emerged . . . .

In an 'emerging' South Africa, Coetzee's literary landscapes are landscapes in the making; boundaries are renegotiated, erased, or ever-shifting. Like Michael K, who 'wondered whether there were not forgotten corners and angles and corridors between the fences, land that belonged to one yet', Coetzee's novels speak from spatial margins which *question*—rather than reclaim—notions of space.

Since territory, in the South African context, is such an explosive term, the seemingly 'marginal' concerns in his fiction have in the past provoked charges against him of 'evasiveness' and 'ambivalence'. These very positions or conditions of Coetzee's work, however, *are* the nature of his commitment: contestation rather than rigid fixity and unthinking acceptance; arbitrariness and alternative narratives instead of confining literatures and methodologies.

> **In an 'emerging' South Africa, Coetzee's literary landscapes are landscapes in the making; boundaries are renegotiated, erased, or ever-shifting. . . . Coetzee's novels speak from spatial margins which *question*—rather than reclaim—notions of space.**
> **—T. Kai Norris Easton**

Taken together, the terrain of Coetzee's fiction shows movement: there are gradations in the landscape as well as gradations in his fictional technique. But the 'ruptures' within his novelistic corpus demonstrate a dual concern: there is a commitment to craft, to the play of writing; and there is a deeper, ethical sense which is not bound in liberal-humanism, but which might be more accurately recognised as the '*rational humanism*' to which Neil Lazarus refers in terms of T. W. Adorno's model of modernism: '. . . however problematical and problematized—[it] might well exist as the only aesthetic on the side of freedom.'

Coetzee's aesthetic preferences would indicate a need to find different approaches, imagine new scenes—and new scenery, perhaps. For not only is he not interested in 'copying the "real" world', as he tells Morphet, it would appear that he is not interested in copying himself. Regarding the change-over in *Michael K* to a more 'specified' location as compared with the 'invented' landscape of *Waiting for the Barbarians,* he says (as quoted earlier): '. . . *and what would have been the point, this time round*?'

Coetzee is, however, *consistently* wary of language and entrapment. His attitude toward literary discourses—academic and fictional—are, as with his politics, non-committal. There is a tendency to subsume him under a 'postmodernist' heading, it seems, because he writes in a postmodernist *fashion*. Attwell also places him as 'working within the culture of postmodernism', but with the qualifier that 'he certainly does not do so in the spirit of abandonment that seems to typify much of what goes on under the name'.

His attitude towards realist modes of fiction is generally known, and otherwise evident, for the most part, from his novels. In a 1978 interview with Stephen Watson, he commented that he admired Nadine Gordimer's work but 'would like to think that today the novel is after a bigger game [than the critical realist type]'. This 'bigger game', however, doesn't simply carry the label of 'postmodernism'. Despite the fact that he sometimes plays within it, 'pilfering' and 'adapting' what he can, Coetzee is sceptical of the trend—or at least some of its conventions. As he tells Attwell:

> Anti-illusionism—displaying the tricks you are using instead of hiding them—is a common ploy of postmodernism. But in the end there is only so much mileage to get out of the ploy. Anti-illusionism is, I suspect, only a marking of time, a phase of recuperation, in the history of the novel. *The question is, what next?*

What is to *emerge,* rather, in Coetzee's own fiction?

Conclusion

If, as a writer, Coetzee has placed himself outside a narrowly defined 'national' field, it could also be argued that the progressions and digressions in his oeuvre are essential to the multivocality of a 'new' South Africa. Through parody and irony, plays on genre and geography, and elaborate intertextuality, Coetzee's novels perform cultural leaps. One could say that the 'South Africanness' of his narratives comes only from this '"doubleness" in writing'. That is, as Homi Bhabha has discussed in his seminal piece, 'DissemiNation', referring to an essay by John Barrell '. . . a discourse that was *at the same time* obsessively fixed upon, and uncertain of, the boundaries of society, and the margins of the text'.

In his paper, 'Reading for the Nation', Anthony Vital says he chose to focus his discussion on *Michael K* and *Age of Iron*

> because of all Coetzee's novels to date, by drawing conspicuously on conventions of realism, they insist on their South African location. Through techniques of both naming and plotting, each constructs

a space that is identifiably Cape Town and surrounding regions.

Interestingly, what follows each of these novels—*Foe* and *The Master of Petersburg*—are revisions of earlier texts from other empires. If Coetzee is sceptical about the 'newness' of South Africa as a nation, his fiction proves that the 'South African' novel is far from being exhausted. Rather, it shows, as Graham Huggan and John Noyes have used the term, vivid signs of '*re*-territorialisation'.

Long ago begun by Jacobus Coetzee and his ilk, 'the outward story', in an ironic twist, has been reclaimed by a descendant, who shows a different sort of exploration at work. It belongs not to the colonial trek of possession, but to the post-colonial route of configuration. Through his migratory maps, Coetzee contributes to a radical remaking of South African literature and history—a nomadic discourse—which works to displace any static notion of what constitutes (or has constituted) South Africa as a space.

Mike Marais (essay date 1996)

SOURCE: "Places of Pigs: The Tension between Implication and Transcendence in J. M. Coetzee's *Age of Iron* and *The Master of Petersburg*," in *Journal of Commonwealth Literature*, Vol. XXXI, No. 1, 1996, pp. 83-95.

[In the following essay, Marais contrasts relations of power in Age of Iron *and* The Master of Petersburg.*]*

I

In a recent article on J. M. Coetzee's *The Master of Petersburg,* Stephen Watson observes that "the bulk of South African literature gives much evidence of that atheism of the imagination which is always conspicuous when a writer has set up barriers between human beings and the crucial questions of existence, such as their very awareness of themselves as spiritual beings". Watson maintains, however, that Coetzee's novels do not exhibit this form of "truncated imagination":

> There are times in his recent fiction, particularly *The Master of Petersburg,* when it really does seem as if the spiritual needs of human beings are not simply the alienated form of their longing for justice and fraternity; when these emerge, clearly, as an expression of ineradicable psychic drives as well as the consequence of facts about our human situation which no amount of social engineering can hope to change.

This remark overlooks an aspect of *The Master of Petersburg* which is a key feature of Coetzee's recent fiction: its thematization of the inevitable implication of literature in the relations of power which determine the social context in which it is produced. By extension, then, the "truncated imagination" to which Watson refers is a condition of writing in a politically-fraught social context, one which Coetzee's novels cannot escape. Despite this oversight, however, Watson's remark does touch on a significant and paradoxical dimension of these novels which runs counter to this self-conscious admission of implication, that is, the desire which they evince to become a more human literature by transcending the stultifying politics of their social context. It would seem, then, that Coetzee's recent fiction is grounded in a paradox, one which this article will examine by means of a comparison of *Age of Iron* and *The Master of Petersburg.*

II

Set in Petersburg in late 1869, *The Master of Petersburg* focuses on the murder of a young student, Ivanov, by a group of nihilists led by Sergei Nechaev. The killing of Ivanov by this group of student revolutionaries is probably best remembered as the historical event which inspired Dostoevsky to write *The Devils,* a novel which explores the political implications of the ethical problem posed in *Crime and Punishment,* that is, the indifference of the amoral superman, in the absence of a spiritual essence, to issues of good and evil. Coetzee's decision to focus on the above-mentioned incident suggests that he too, like Dostoevsky, wishes to examine the ethical ramifications of political nihilism in his novel. Furthermore, the fact that he departs from history by making the murdered student Dostoevsky's stepson, and by fabricating Dostoevsky's return from exile to Petersburg following the murder, suggests, in addition, that he wishes to explore the latter writer's personal and artistic response to the amorality of these revolutionaries.

Dostoevsky's literary response to revolutionary nihilism revolves around the biblical story of the Gadarene swine, a tale in which unclean devils, having been exorcized from a sick man by Christ, enter a herd of swine. This story serves as the structural metaphor through which Dostoevsky explores and ultimately condemns political nihilism in *The Devils.* As the following comparisons drawn by one of the nihilists in the novel indicate, the story generates a series of analogies which suggests that Russia is a "sick man" possessed by devils, and that the swine which the devils enter upon being exorcized are the revolutionaries:

> These devils who go out of the sick man and enter the swine—those are all the sores, all the poisonous exhalations, all the impurities, all the big and little devils, that have accumulated in our great and

> beloved invalid, in our Russia, for centuries. . . . all those devils, all those impurities, all those abominations that were festering on the surface . . . will themselves ask to enter into swine. . . . They are we . . . and we shall cast ourselves down, the raving and the possessed, from the cliff into the sea and shall all be drowned, and serves us right, for that is all we are good for.

It is misguided to conclude, as David Coad does, that since Dostoevsky implies "that the [nihilists] are possessed by the devil, pervaded by evil", Coetzee simply shares this conviction. It is true that he employs the parallels created by *The Devils* when his own character, Dostoevsky, argues that it is futile to imprison revolutionaries such as Sergei Nechaev since nihilism is a "spirit" for which the individual is merely a "vehicle", a "host". However, he applies the story of the Gadarene swine not only to Russia and the phenomenon of revolutionary nihilism, but also to Dostoevsky himself and his literary response to this phenomenon. So, in *The Master of Petersburg,* Dostoevsky is depicted as a "sick man" possessed by devils. The outward sign of this affliction is his epilepsy, a sickness which the novel relates to demon possession. Indeed, he speculates that not "seizure" but "possession" would be "the right word" to describe the fits from which he suffers. Coetzee's application of the story of the Gadarene swine to Dostoevsky's artistic response to nihilism emerges when this character is described as shaking "his head as if to rid it of a plague of devils". Elsewhere, Anna Sergeyevna tells him that he is "in the grip of something quite beyond [her]" and while engaging in sexual intercourse with him, at the onset of climax, she utters the word "*devil*". Significantly, in this scene the sexual act is depicted as both an inspiration and an exorcism, with Anna Sergeyevna occupying the dual role of muse and exorcist. As the novel ends shortly afterwards with Dostoevsky commencing work on *The Devils,* the implication, therefore, is that this text is also to be equated with the exorcized spirits in the story of the Gadarene swine. Clearly, this equation gives the title of Dostoevsky's text fresh significance. A further inference now also surfaces, namely that the readers within whom copies of the novel can be said to take up residence correspond to the swine in the biblical study.

I read Coetzee's reworking of the story of the Gadarene swine in *The Master of Petersburg* as a comment on the implication of writer and literature in the power dynamics or "sickness" of the social context in which they are located. Through applying the story to the artist and the artistic process itself, Coetzee suggests that Dostoevsky and his work are not immune to the "sickness" of Russia. Both are a part of Russia and are therefore also "sick". It is significant, for example, that as the novel develops, the boundaries between this character and his social context are increasingly blurred. He refers, for example, to epilepsy as "the emblematic sickness of the age" and earlier equates himself with Russia: "I am required to live . . . a Russian life: a life inside Russia, or with Russia inside me".

Clearly, "sickness" and devilry in this novel therefore serve as a metaphor for a destructive force at work in Russian society. The nature of this force is never clearly revealed in *The Master of Petersburg* but can be deduced when this novel is compared with *Age of Iron.* In both novels, a strong affinity emerges between the protagonist and his/her social and physical context—in the latter case, South Africa. Thus Mrs Curren describes the country as her "mother", "the place of the navel, the place where [she] join[s] the world". Moreover, like Dostoevsky, she too is ill and her illness, cancer, serves as a correlative of the diseased and deformed nature of South African society. In this regard, Mrs Curren often refers to South Africans as being ugly, deformed or virtually inhuman. As the novel proceeds, it gradually emerges from Coetzee's use of mythological analogies that it is the apartheid state's structures of power that exert this deforming influence on its citizens. So, for example, Mrs Curren claims that her tumours have been "sent by Saturn" or Cronus, the archetypal political father. Furthermore, the state and its ideological apparatuses are on various occasions likened to the Gorgons and to Circe, myths which deal with the metamorphosis of human beings into stone and swine. The implication here, then, is that the state's power relations have dehumanized South African people.

> **In both *Age of Iron* and *The Master of Petersburg*, Coetzee's point seems to be that the networks of power within the societies in question pervade and pervert every aspect of life, including art.**
> —*Mike Maraias*

In both *Age of Iron* and *The Master of Petersburg*, Coetzee's point seems to be that the networks of power within the societies in question pervade and pervert every aspect of life, including art. "Power", as Mrs Curren puts it, "is power, after all. It invades. That is its nature". A less cryptic statement on the corrosive aspect of power can be found in Coetzee's **"Jerusalem Prize Acceptance Speech":**

> About these [unnatural] structures of power [that define the South African state] there is a great deal to be said. . . . The deformed and stunted relations between human beings that were created under colonialism and exacerbated under what is loosely called apartheid have their psychic representation in a deformed and stunted inner life. All expressions of that inner life, no matter how intense, no matter how pierced with exultation or despair, suffer from

the same stuntedness and deformity. I make this observation with due deliberation, and in the fullest awareness that it applies to myself and my own writing as much as to anyone else.

Although Coetzee is specifically referring to the South African context here, the parallels which I have traced between *Age of Iron* and *The Master of Petersburg* suggest that his point holds for *all* societies which have been "defined" by "unnatural structures of power" and for their literatures since these are inevitably preoccupied with "power and the torsions of power".

It is because of their representation, and therefore replication, of these "deformed and stunted relations" that South African and Russian writing are depicted as being disfigured in both *Age of Iron* and *The Master of Petersburg*. In the earlier novel, for example, Mrs Curren refers to the words of her diary as "the issue of a shrunken heart", and as "words vomited up from the belly of the whale, misshapen, mysterious". And in the later novel, as Coetzee's broadening of the application of the story of the Gadarene swine to include the artistic process indicates, Dostoevsky's *The Devils* is not detached from but a part of "all the poisonous exhalations, all the impurities, all the big and little devils, that have accumulated in our great and beloved invalid, in our Russia, for centuries". In the societies portrayed in these novels, then, the literature produced is cast as a literature which, to appropriate Coetzee's term, "supplements" history by reproducing those oppositions related to class, race and gender conflict "out of which history and the historical disciplines erect themselves". Being "unable to move from [such] elementary relations of contestation, domination, and subjugation to the vast and complex human world that lies beyond them", it is, to use Coetzee's description of South African literature in his **"Jerusalem Prize Acceptance Speech"**, "a less than fully human literature".

The "relations of contestation, domination, and subjugation" to which Coetzee refers here, can readily be detected in both of the novels under discussion. Indeed, upon comparison it becomes evident that the two texts share a basic pattern in this regard. Both depict societies which, temporally, find themselves in the interregnum between a decaying, old political order and a new one seeking to establish itself. In each novel, a protagonist who embodies the values of Western society confronts revolutionary nihilists who challenge his/her ethical assumptions. In the conflictual relationship which then develops, each protagonist condemns his/her antagonist's nihilism in ethical terms. Finally, the protagonists of both novels embark on literary exercises which reflect the assumptions that underpin their relationships with the nihilists.

The basic structure of the relationship which is depicted between protagonist and nihilist-antagonist in both of these novels is oppositional: the former—be it consciously or unconsciously—endeavours to adopt a subject position in relation to the latter, a position from which s/he then attempts to define and reify him/her. Significantly, these attempts at reification are conducted in terms of the dyadic structure of the Western ethical system. In *Age of Iron,* for instance, Mrs Curren's confrontation with the nihilism of John leads to an ethical judgement being passed on him and his political cohorts: "Comradeship is nothing but a mystique of death, of killing and dying. . . . I have no sympathy with this comradeship. . . . It is just another of those icy, exclusive, death-driven male constructions". And, in *The Master of Petersburg,* the character Dostoevsky echoes this judgment in his condemnation of the nihilism of Sergei Nechaev and his associates: "Nechaevism is not an idea. . . . It is a spirit. . . . It is a dull, resentful and murderous spirit". When asked to assign a name to this spirit, he responds with the word "Baal".

Clearly, the oppositions of God/Devil, heaven/hell, elect/reprobate, Christian/heathen, good/evil, right/wrong, life-directed/death-directedand, ultimately, self/other which inform these judgements, assist in establishing those relations of domination and subjugation which "contaminate" society. The oppositional structure of the ethical system which Mrs Curren and Dostoevsky employ to judge and thereby define their antagonists thus colludes with the state's networks of power. As with all oppositional constructions, it facilitates the process of othering in which subject defines object by integrating the latter into its interpretive framework.

This complicity of conventional Western morality in the state's power structures is made especially clear at the end of *The Master of Petersburg* when the fictional Dostoevsky starts writing *The Devils.* By presenting his novel, as the pretext of *The Devils,* Coetzee contrives to make his reader evaluate the historical Dostoevsky's novel in terms of the fictional Dostoevsky's relationship with the nihilists in *The Master of Petersburg.* Against this background, *The Devils* has to be seen as a continuation of its author's attempt to other the nihilists, that is, to condemn nihilism in terms of the Manichean dualism of conventional morality—as E. H. Carr argues, it is a fairly transparent attempt to "demonstrate the fundamental identity of moral evil and political nihilism". The metafictional dialogue which Coetzee sets up between his novel and *The Devils* suggests, therefore, that Dostoevsky and his novel remain locked in the oppositional mode of the contestatory relations that define Russian society. It also implies that, in depicting the nihilists as being possessed by devils, Dostoevsky not only endorses these relations, but also places them in a transcendental realm, thus providing them with a secure metaphysical foundation.

In failing to move beyond the power relations which per-

vade the society in which it is produced, the literary text which the character Dostoevsky settles down to write at the end of *The Master of Petersburg* (ostensibly *The Devils*) is, in Coetzee's terms, "less than fully human". In representing the deformed and stunted relations created by the state's hegemonic strategies, it reinforces them and thus colludes with the state's dehumanization of its citizens. This point emerges clearly when the imagery used to depict the state's dehumanization of South Africans in *Age of Iron* is compared with the imagery applied to Dostoevsky's writing in *The Master of Petersburg.* As I have indicated, in the earlier novel the impact of the apartheid state's manipulative power relations is depicted by means of an analogy between the state and Circe: like Circe, the state dehumanizes people or turns them into 'swine'. And, in the later novel, Coetzee's reworking of the story of the Gadarene swine constructs a link between the readers of Dostoevsky's novel and swine. The parallel which exists, here, in the portrayal of the brutalizing effect on society of state structures and the similar effect produced by literature suggests that the latter merely replicates the operation of the former, and thus collaborates in the state's dehumanization of its citizens.

III

In the passage from the **"Jerusalem Prize Acceptance Speech"** quoted earlier, Coetzee indicates that literature's implication in the network of power relations which defines a society such as South Africa is inevitable. His argument in this regard is very similar to Said's contention that "texts are worldly, to some degree they are events, and, even when they appear to deny it, they are nevertheless a part of the social world, human life, and of course the historical moments in which they are located and interpreted". Despite maintaining this position in the above speech and enacting it in his fiction, Coetzee has on occasion suggested, paradoxically, that it *is* possible for literature "to move from elementary relations of contestation, domination, and subjugation to the vast and complex human world that lies beyond them". For instance, in **"The Novel Today"**, after having referred to fiction which "supplements" history, he refers to *another* fictional mode that "occupies an autonomous place" and "operates in terms of its own procedures and issues" and not those of history. And, in **"Into the Dark Chamber"**, he argues that the writer should not "allow himself to be impaled on the dilemma proposed by the state, namely, either to ignore its obscenities or else to produce representations of them". Instead, the challenge for the writer should be "how not to play the game by the rules of the state, how to establish one's own authority, how to imagine torture and death on one's own terms".

In *Age of Iron,* Coetzee takes up this challenge and explores the possibility of transcending the power relations which define South African society. This exploration marks the point at which the pattern of similarities which I have thus far traced between this novel and *The Master of Petersburg* ends. Differences between these novels begin to manifest themselves in the development which Mrs Curren's relationship with John undergoes following her initial condemnation of his nihilism. As I have indicated, her initial moral condemnation of John may be compared with Dostoevsky's response to Nechaev. After Bheki's death and her visit to Guguletu, however, Mrs Curren appears to realize that the system of Western values and ethics in terms of which she judges and acts has lost all validity and relevance in the historical context in which she finds herself. Thus, she comes to question her right and ability to judge at all:

> "But now I ask myself: What right have I to opinions about comradeship or anything else? What right have I to wish Bheki and his friend had kept out of trouble? To have opinions in a vacuum, opinions that touch no one, is, it seems to me, nothing. Opinions must be heard by others, heard and weighed, not merely listened to out of politeness".

At this stage in the novel, it becomes clear that the references to the Furies which occur throughout suggest that, just as these mythical creatures lost their ability to protect Classical Greek society when that society ceased to believe in them, so too the Western system of ethics in modern South Africa has become obsolete. By juxtaposing in this way an archaic ethical system with one in the process of losing currency, the novel shows that ethics are socially and historically relative.

Her realization that the conventional system of Western ethics has lost its legitimacy in South Africa is the point in the novel at which Mrs Curren attempts to break out of the relations of contestation to which the dualism of that ethical system predisposes her. The procedure which she decides upon in her attempt to "rise above" these power relations is quite clearly articulated in the novel in the following passage:

> I want to be saved. How shall I be saved? By doing what I do not want to do. That is the first step: that I know, I must love, first of all, the unlovable. I must love, for instance, this child. . . . He is here for a reason. He is part of my salvation.

In other words, she strives to overcome the deformed relations between human beings entrenched by the South African apartheid state's politics of dominance and subservience through learning to love the "children of iron"—those, such as John and, indeed, herself, who have been brutalized by these very power relations.

The efficacy of this strategy emerges in the way in which it enables Mrs Curren to reconstruct her relationship with John: "Yet something went out from me to him. I ached to embrace him, to protect him". The allusion, here, to a restoration of the umbilical bond between mother and child indicates that love is an emotion which is based on relationship and connection rather than separation and objectivity. Accordingly, it may be deduced that in this novel, "love" signifies a form of consciousness which, in acknowledging "our formation out of an interdependence with other human beings", points to the possibility of developing a relational mode which subverts the divisive power relationship in which subject defines object. And, in subverting the boundary between subject and object, self and other, it holds out the hope of constructing an ethical system which is grounded not in subject-centred consciousness, but in intersubjectivity.

Since it is the relations of contestation imposed by the state which dehumanize people, it follows that "love", in undermining the subject-centred consciousness which underpins such relations of power, has the ability to humanize that which has been brutalized. Indeed, this point emerges in the novel when, in an allusion to the analogy between the state and Circe, Mrs Curren comments as follows: "Metamorphosis, that thickens our speech, dulls our feelings, turns us into beasts. Where on these shores does the herb grow that will preserve us from it?". From this analogy it may be inferred that "love", which subverts the subject-object relation of dominance and subservience, is the equivalent of the herb *moly* through which Odysseus breaks Circe's spell and restores to his men their humanity.

The humanizing ability of "love" is also apparent in the novel's designs on its South African reader. In this respect, the effect of the change which Mrs Curren's relationship with the "children of iron" undergoes on the letter which she writes to her estranged daughter—who is also characterized as a child of iron—is significant. In contrast with the text on which Dostoevsky commences work at the end of *The Master of Petersburg* (a text which "supplements" history and so endorses oppositional relations and, accordingly, brutalizes its readers), Mrs Curren's text represents a mode of relationship which is grounded in affinity rather than division. Thus it is presented as an intimate letter from the writer-as-mother to the reader-as-daughter, a letter in which the writer attempts to restore the broken "filial" connection. Being a letter of "love", and therefore the product of a reconstructed ethical consciousness, it constitutes an attempt to represent a mode of intersubjectivity which undermines the state's oppositional relations and, after the manner of *moly,* restores to the reader—also a victim of the Circe-like state—her humanity.

IV

There lies a danger in drawing too absolute a distinction between *Age of Iron* and *The Master of Petersburg* on the grounds of the potential of the former to humanize the reader, since in certain significant respects this novel questions its own ability to achieve this end. By identifying the South African reader with Mrs Curren's estranged daughter, the novel constructs as its reader someone who is somewhat indifferent to its content. Furthermore, Susan VanZanten Gallagher is correct when she argues that in presenting itself as a letter which has to be conveyed to its reader by an inebriate, the novel advertises the possibility that the words which form it "may remain dead leaves" and "never even find an audience", and thus seriously "questions its own basis for existence". This self-reflexive questioning can, in part, be ascribed to the fact that it is impossible for the novel and, indeed, for Mrs Curren to "rise above [their] times", that is, to transcend the relations of contestation which have underpinned those times. (As I have already indicated, an admission to this effect is contained in Coetzee's **"Jerusalem Prize Acceptance Speech".**) Paradoxically, then, even as it thematizes the notion that the text, through transcending its temporal context, can provide a representation of a relational mode which is able to humanize its brutalized South African reader, the novel seriously questions the feasibility of this endeavour.

This strategy of nurturing the impossible can be observed throughout Coetzee's *oeuvre* and is, perhaps, most clearly articulated in *Life and Times of Michael K* in the medical officer's description of K's stay in the Kenilworth camp as an "allegory . . . of how scandalously, how outrageously a meaning can take up residence in a system without becoming a term in it". It amounts to what Julia Kristeva has called "strategic essentialism"—in this context, a practice through which the text, whilst acknowledging their validity, self-consciously disregards social constructionist notions that the subject is constructed through and determined by insensible social relations of power. In *Age of Iron,* for instance, Mrs Curren, after becoming aware of the extent to which she has been brutalized by the state, comments as follows:

> I have intimations . . . that once upon a time I was alive. Was alive and then was stolen from life. From the cradle a theft took place: a child was taken and a doll left in its place to be nursed and reared, and that doll is what I call I.

These "intimations" of an original identity which pre-date her state-conferred, artificial sense of self inspire her to *rewrite* her identity through reconstructing her relation with John. In the novel, this process of self-reconstruction is couched in terms usually reserved for fiction-writing, a fact which suggests that Mrs Curren, rather than excavating an original self, becomes the *author* of her self—engages, that is, in the Nietzschean paradox of discovering her self through

creation. Instead of affirming the existence of transcendental essences, then, such "intimations" of an original identity and a primal relation based on connection and not separation function strategically in Coetzee's fiction. After all, being "intimations", they cannot "affirm", only allude, hint or insinuate. Accordingly, they serve primarily as an incentive to and stimulus for change.

Coetzee's general observation on the Buberian I-Thou relation is significant in this latter regard: "Intimations of the lost relation . . . inspire our efforts to reconstitute again and again the 'between' of the primal *I-Thou*". Apart from being manifest in characters such as Michael K and Mrs Curren, whose attempts to reconstitute the primal I-Thou are dramatized on the presentational surface of the respective novels themselves, this process of inspiration by intimation is frequently extended to include the reader of the text. In attempting to transcend the relations of contestation which define the society in which it was produced, *Age of Iron,* for instance, provides the reader with an "intimation" of "love"—that emotion which bridges the gap between the subject-object power relation. So, for example, Mrs Curren describes her letter and, by implication, the novel to her daughter and, by further implication, the actual reader of the novel in the following manner: "In this letter from elsewhere . . . truth and love together at last. In every *you* that I pen love flickers and trembles like St Elmo's fire". The suggestion here is that, like Mrs Curren's house, the novel is a "museum" which not only preserves the idea of the "lost relation", but also, as the etymology of the word "museum" suggests, inspires the reader with "intimations" of love to recreate his/her times and so convert South African history from a static realm of being into a dynamic realm of becoming.

Of course, being intimations, such prompts are easily overlooked or ignored. Indeed, it is the nebulous and minimalist nature of these "intimations", which can either be responded to or overlooked by the protagonists and readers of his novels, that accounts for the fluctuations in Coetzee's *oeuvre* between the guarded optimism of texts like *Age of Iron* and the bleak pessimism of *The Master of Petersburg.* Like the protagonist of the former novel, who is inspired by "intimations" of an original identity to reconstruct the "'between' of the primal *I-Thou*" in her relation with John, the character Dostoevsky, in the latter novel, receives "intimations"— in the form of the visions which he has of trying to communicate with his son underwater—which initially encourage him to reconstitute the filial bond. As the novel advances, however, these "intimations" are progressively blocked out by the exigencies of the dynamics of power in Russian society. So, towards the end of the novel, Dostoevsky comes to feel that "he has lost touch with Pavel and with the logic that tells him why, because Pavel died here, he is tied to Petersburg".

With the loss of the inspiration which comes from these "intimations", Dostoevsky is unable to humanize and resurrect his son, a son who, it earlier becomes clear (in an obvious allusion to the fate of the Gadarene swine), has flung himself or been pushed from a tower and who, it is also frequently suggested, has drowned. Indeed, the novel ends with Dostoevsky writing a text in which, as Watson puts it, "he proceeds to take an evidently true story about his dead stepson, one in which the latter is shown in a particularly good light, and rewrites it so that it is transformed into an episode of gratuitous cruelty". In other words, he writes a text inspired not by "intimations" of the primal I-Thou relation, but by the reality of the "deformed and stunted relations between human beings" created by the structures of power that define the Russian state. He produces, that is, the kind of text which, to use again the distinction which Coetzee's draws in **"The Novel Today"**, "supplements" history, rather than that which "rivals" it by operating "in terms of its own procedures and issues". In so doing, he endorses those very hegemonic strategies which caused his son's death. When it is kept in mind that Coetzee's reworking of the story of the Gadarene swine equates Dostoevsky's *The Devils* with the devils who possess the swine and force them to hurl themselves from a cliff, the final perverse irony in this novel may be appreciated. In a complete metaleptic inversion of linear narrative, *The Master of Petersburg* ends by suggesting that Dostoevsky—who at the beginning returns to Petersburg to establish, among other details, whether it was the police or the revolutionaries who pushed his son from the tower—sired "the devils" who were responsible for this act.

In conclusion, then, one finds in Coetzee's fiction a minimalist programme for prompting change which is, quite literally, undermined even as it is articulated. Convinced of the need for change in the society in which he writes but, at the same time, aware of the compromising nature of the ineluctable "worldliness" of the literary text, this writer has had to choose between subsiding into silence and adopting a strategy of paradox. Premised as it is on this uneasy balance between knowledge of implication and hope for transcendence, this strategy can, at best, generate only "intimations" of an alternative to the *status quo,* intimations which are therefore often either overlooked or ignored.

World Literature Today (interview date Winter 1996)

SOURCE: "An Interview with J. M. Coetzee," in *World Literature Today,* Vol. 70, No. 1, Winter, 1996, pp. 107-11.

[*In the following interview, Coetzee discusses his book* Giving Offense *and his position on key issues in the debate on censorship.*]

J. M. Coetzee's new book, *Giving Offense: Essays on Censorship* discusses both writers and theorists from D. H. Lawrence to Geoffrey Cronje. It also covers a variety of concepts from feminist protest against pornography to South African apartheid opposition. Coetzee's stance does not take the binary oppositional Either/Or except in voting against censorship. On the whole, the ethical and philosophical question presented is whether or not one respects the act of taking offense by those whose convictions one does not share.

[*World Literature Today:*] *Your new book has chapters on a wide range of writers—D. H. Lawrence, Desiderius Erasmus, Osip Mandelstam, Aleksandr Solzhenitsyn, Zbigniew Herbert, Andre Brink, Breyten Breytenbach—as well as on people who aren't usually thought of as writers—the apartheid theorist Geoffrey Cronje—and on a variety of topics in the field of censorship: the feminist critique of pornography, the history of so-called publications control in South Africa, your personal experience of working under censorship. Obviously there is a certain South African bias to the book, and secondarily perhaps a bias toward the Russian or East European experience; but beyond expressing your general opposition to censorship (which won't be news to anyone, I am sure), I wonder whether you can say what the general thesis of the book is.*

[J. M. Coetzee:] This is not a book with a general thesis. Its substance lies in the chapters on individual writers, rather than in the chapters that deal—unavoidably—with generalities. In fact, I am even dubious about accepting your comment that the book expresses a general opposition to censorship. I don't dispute your statement that a distaste for censorship—even a strong distaste—emerges from the book. What I am reluctant to endorse is the statement that the book is written to express an opposition to censorship. I would rather say that the book explores, in theory and in practice, opposition to censorship—explores that opposition not only in studies of several writers working under censorship, but also in my own case: what does it mean for a person of my kind, a rather disaffiliated intellectual whose heritage is largely European, or European-in-Africa, to be in opposition?

A certain ambivalence toward your own position certainly does emerge in the first chapter. I think, for example, of a passage in which you seem to be favoring a stance of liberal tolerance, but then say that, "depending on how you look at it," this tolerance is "either deeply civilized or complacent, hypocritical, and patronizing." Which is it? Is liberal tolerance deeply civilized or is it in fact the expression of a rather myopic point of view, in certain of its facets misogynist and imperialistic?

You raise a number of questions, not all of which I can deal with satisfactorily here—not all of which I can deal with to your satisfaction or to my own—but which I hope are at least approached in the book itself. Let me simply say that I am not enamored of the Either-Or. I hope that I don't simply evade the Either-Or whenever I am confronted with it. I hope that I at least try to work out what "underlies" it in each case (if I can use that foundationalist metaphor); and that this response of working-out on the Either-Or isn't read simply as evasion. (If it is, I have been wasting my time.)

Giving Offense is not a polemic. Polemic is not its genre and, I would hope, not its spirit. I have seen too many writers and intellectuals shift into the mode of polemic when they confront censorship, and in my opinion the results do not do them credit. In fact, one of the things I try to point out is that a regime of censorship creates among the intelligentsia an atmosphere of antagonism and anger which may be as bad for the spiritual life of the community as any of the more obviously repressive acts that the censor carries out.

Am I a liberal? Am I "merely" a liberal? Does *Giving Offense* espouse a liberal position? Do I think a liberal position on censorship is civilized or patronizing? I hope I am not "merely" a liberal. But then, no liberal today is merely a liberal: all liberals have careful qualifications of themselves that set them apart, however slightly, from "mere" (or "classic") liberalism. We have to do here with the phenomenon, the act, of naming, characterizing, and correspondingly with the experience of being-named. I am not espousing a position, or not setting out to espouse a position; but that does not mean that a position does not get espoused. I do not fly a banner, but that does not mean that a banner will not get attached to the book. That is how time works, how opinion works.

If this response to your questions seems vague, I can only say that in my chapter on Desiderius Erasmus I try to talk about the Either-Or and about vagueness or slipperiness or other stances (or non-stances) toward the Either-Or in a more philosophical way. A more philosophical way which (in a chapter on "The Praise of Folly") must also be an appropriately foolish way.

Is Erasmus then a hero of yours?

A hero insofar as a fool and a coward can be a hero. It must be clear to you that a range of attitudes get expressed in the various essays constituting the book. For instance, I don't have an immediate, intuitive sympathy toward someone like Solzhenitsyn, who is too much of a polemicist for my taste. At the same time, he is a world-historical figure. He has also, I think, undertaken some terrifying self-searchings in his books, self-searchings that have been a little obscured by his larger political, or politico-religious, project. In the case of Breyten Breytenbach, too, I think a complex attitude emerges in the book. There is something savage in Breytenbach, sav-

agely self-rending, that I retreat from. At the same time his confrontations of himself are exemplary, particularly for South Africans of his generation and his background—among whom I number myself.

But it must also be clear to you that the most sympathetically treated figures in the book are Erasmus and Zbigniew Herbert. Erasmus in a sense maps out the ground I have to traverse in the face of the Either-Or. Luce Irigaray, who is otherwise not a central figure in the book, plays a similar guiding role when I take up the feminist critique of the law. As for Herbert, there is a kind of moral steadiness to him that stands as a light to me.

But Herbert has not suffered particularly under censorship. Some of the writers you deal with have been at the center of the struggle against censorship in our times. Either they have chosen of their own accord to be at the center—like Solzhenitsyn—or they have simply landed up at the center of censorship rows—I think of D. H. Lawrence and Lady Chatterley. *But in the lives of other writers—like Herbert—censorship has been a rather peripheral matter.*

Maybe. But that is because they have made it peripheral. They have put the censors in their place, which is a peripheral place.

I was going on to say: the censor has been rather peripheral in Herbert's life, and he (or she?) has been rather peripheral in your own life too. Were any of your books banned in South Africa?

No. Nor do I want to say that I suffered under the South African censorship. I do not want to minimize the impact of censorship on those South African writers to whom it was applied in its full rigor, particularly those black writers who stood absolutely no chance of publishing a word in their native country. At the same time, the metaphorics of suffering (the suffering writer), like the metaphorics of battle (the writer battling against the censor), seem to me to belong to structures of opposition, of Either-Or, which I take it as my task to evade.

I did not "suffer" in this sense. On the other hand, I would contend that we all suffered, together. We lived an impoverished intellectual life, just as we lived an impoverished cultural life and an impoverished spiritual life. If there is any general thesis in the book, it is that the unintended or not-fully-intended consequences of censorship tend to be more significant than the intended consequences. From that point of view, the spectacle of what is going on in South Africa right now, as new censorship laws are formulated to replace the old ones, is profoundly depressing. The past is being relived as though it had never occurred. "Pornography is bad (for us, for our children), therefore it must be banned"—that is the form that one side of the debate takes. And on the other side the form it takes is: "Is pornography really bad (for us, for our children)? If it is indeed bad, is it bad enough to be banned?" What does not enter the debate is the question: "What does it entail, to ban?" In the old South Africa we had bans; in the new South Africa it seems we are going to have bans again. What is banned is, to my mind, a secondary question. Regimes of banning are all alike.

You devote a lot of space in your book to South Africa, but not to the present, not to the issues you have just been talking about.

No, I don't. But in the light of what I have to say, not only about Publications Control in the 1970s and 1980s but about bans on pornography in general, I think you can predict what I would say about the present agitation for controls on pornography, on insult, and so forth.

What would you say?

What would I say as a citizen, or what would I say in a book to be published by a university press?

Both.

As a citizen I would vote against controls. That is the nature of the vote: Yes or No, Either-Or. In a book I don't think I would add anything to what I already say. There is nothing novel in the present South African situation. That, in a sense, is what is disappointing about it.

What you have said thus far centers very much on pornography. Yet one could argue that censorship on moral grounds is very much a side issue, that what ought to concern us, in the case of South Africa as much as in the case of the Soviet Union, is political censorship.

The theoretical case for distinguishing political from moral censorship, and for elevating the first over the second, at least in our times, is massive. However, the fact, the peculiar fact, is that regimes of censorship usually frame their legislation to cover both fields and entrust the role of watchdog over both fields to the same set of officials (though, I grant, there is sometimes a higher-echelon political censorship set over the bread-and-butter censors). This may be a mere accident—totalitarian regimes are usually conservative in morals as well—but the fact remains that the consequences for people in general are much the same: a kind of bleakening, if I may invent a word, of the landscape.

A book that is very much about political censorship in South Africa—*A Culture of Secrecy* by Christopher Merrett—has recently come out. It is not the kind of book I would have any interest in writing. A chronicle of instances with a strong polemical bias. But then, Merrett has no interest in literature that I can detect.

How does your long chapter on Geoffrey Cronje fit into what you have been saying? I haven't read any more of Cronje than what you quote here, but on the basis of that evidence I wouldn't want to.

Cronje wasn't a writer, a "literary" writer, he was an academic sociologist in one part of his life, and a propagandist of apartheid in the other. Nevertheless, I would hope that contemporary literary theory, if it has achieved nothing else, has opened up ways for us to talk about peripheral discourses—academic, political—in useful ways.

The chapter on Cronje sits rather uneasily with the rest of the book, I agree. Nevertheless, approaching Cronje with questions about censorship at the back of our minds allows us to see interesting things about him. To begin with, Cronje delivers strong hints that the censorship exerted by public opinion in the immediate post-World War II years makes it impossible for him to say just what he means: the reader is invited to fill in the blank spaces, so to speak. Nevertheless, Cronje does go on to express deep racial antipathies in a way that would certainly not be possible in public discourse today. To such an extent that his successors in the National Party intellectual establishment found him an embarrassment.

And then, finally, there is the silence of contemporary scholarship about the deeper currents that flow in the writing of Cronje and his fellows (who include influential political figures like Nico Diedrichs, Piet Meyer, H. F. Verwoerd). The historians and political scientists to whom we assign the task of comprehending apartheid—of comprehending our immediate past in South Africa—have nothing to say about it that interests me. It is as a response to their silence that my chapter on Cronje emerges.

I'd like to turn back to pornography, and to your critique of the feminist critique of pornography. There is a passage where you distinguish between erotic art and pornography. If that is a distinction you accept, then why don't you accept the position that, while erotic art—films, books, et cetera—may be valid, a line needs to be drawn when it comes to the deliberate denigration and humiliation of people, to the portrayal of violence against women and perhaps even the sexualization of violence against women, to the encouragement of the sexual abuse of children? That seems to me the kernel of feminist opposition to pornography.

But that isn't just a feminist position that you have been expressing. It's much older.

No, it isn't. But it is expressed most clearly today by feminists.

A complicated question. First, you ask whether I accept a distinction between the erotic and the pornographic. But it isn't a matter of whether I accept the distinction: it is a fact of life that people make that distinction, and act in terms of it. That is to say, writers, filmmakers, whatever, advance their productions under the banner of the erotic or the pornographic as they choose, very often with specific commercial ends, specific markets, in view. The question is therefore what I make of the distinction.

By claiming to be working in an erotic rather than a pornographic mode, on the grounds that sexual materials are being handled with imagination, intelligence, taste, et cetera, the producer, in the range of cases I am interested in, intends to invoke the protection of the law. What I point out is that it is not in the erotic mode but in the pornographic mode (for instance, by people like Sade) that real assaults have taken place, not only on moral norms and indeed on norms of human conduct, but on the limits of representation itself, or at least on the idea that representation must have limits.

Whether you are happy to have assaults take place on these targets, whether you think assaults on them ought to be allowed, is another question, a question with a strong political dimension. For the moment, let me simply stress that if you stand for a ban on such assaults, then you are standing for the protection of, among other things, standards of representation. To this extent opposition to pornography is and must be conservative.

Is that the essence of your opposition to Catharine MacKinnon—that she is an unacknowledged conservative?

I would hesitate to say so. I am by no means the first person to point out that MacKinnon has landed herself with some uncomfortable bedfellows from the moral right wing in the United States. But in fact I would hesitate to say that I am opposed to MacKinnon. Or to put it slightly differently, I don't believe the point of my chapter on MacKinnon is to express opposition to her. It is rather to explore the foundations of her outrage. In the process I find that there are concepts that illuminate her outrage more satisfactorily, to me, than the moral-political vocabulary she herself uses: the concepts of honor and shame, for instance.

You mention outrage. I would like to return, finally, to what you have to say about offense and outrage, and particularly about your own inability to take seriously the outrage of other people—of religious groups, for instance, or perhaps ethnic groups, though you don't actually mention them. Let me formulate my question in the strongest terms, which would be something like this: Don't you think that a scholar who, in today's world, can't take outrage at ethnic or religious insults seriously is not competent to write a book with a title like **Giving Offense,** *which presents itself as a discussion of such phenomena—psychological phenomena, perhaps, but profoundly important social and political phenomena too—as giving offense and taking offense?*

If I didn't take offense seriously, I wouldn't be spending years of my life writing about it. Let me try to respond as clearly and precisely as possible. I take offense itself seriously. It is a fact of life. The question is whether I respect the motion of taking offense. To be more precise, the question is not whether I, in person, respect this motion: the question is, what does it mean to respect—really respect—the taking-offense of others when you do not share the religious convictions or ethnic sensitivities from which this taking-offense emerges? This seems to me a properly philosophical question, and I hope that in the book I give it a philosophical answer, to the best of my abilities. Therefore, to answer your question finally, if I am incompetent to write the book I have written, it can only mean that I am philosophically incompetent.

Jennifer Wenzel (essay date Spring 1996)

SOURCE: "Keys to the Labyrinth: Writing, Torture, and Coetzee's Barbarian Girl," in *Tulsa Studies in Women's Literature,* Vol. 15, No. 1, Spring, 1996, pp. 61-71.

[*In the following essay, Wenzel argues that although* Waiting for the Barbarians *does not deal explicitly with sociopolitical issues of South Africa, the image of the tortured human body around which the novel revolves represents "a nexus of the political and the poststructural, the historic and the linguistic," which necessarily includes events in South Africa.*]

In a 1987 address in Cape Town, J. M. Coetzee denounced what he called

> a powerful tendency . . . to subsume the novel under history, to read novels as what I will loosely call imaginative investigations of real historical forces and real historical circumstances; and conversely, to treat novels that do not perform this investigation of what are deemed to be real historical forces and circumstances as lacking in seriousness.

Coetzee's interest in maintaining the autonomy of the novel from history is especially significant in terms of his position as a white South African novelist whose novels, for the most part, are not set in the contemporary turmoil that is South Africa. Since Coetzee's fiction explicitly engages questions of language and the difficulties of constructing truth or a story, the novels invite poststructuralist readings that in their insistence on the indeterminacy of truth could suggest an abdication of political responsibility. The magistrate in *Waiting for the Barbarians* becomes obsessed with the telling of a story, but the object around which his frustrations with language revolve is a broken human body, tortured into silence under an imperial regime. When the structure of torture is examined alongside the play of language, Coetzee's seriousness about language, politics, and the human body becomes clear. *Waiting for the Barbarians* cannot be read as an explicit investigation of South African history, but the silence of the tortured body in the novel does provide a nexus of the political and the poststructural, the historic and the linguistic.

In describing the treatment of Coetzee's fiction in criticism, David Attwell speaks of "a considerably oversimplified polarization between, on the one hand, those registering the claims of political resistance and historical representation (who argue that Coetzee has little to offer) and, on the other, those responsive to postmodernism and poststructuralism, to whom Coetzee . . . seems to have much to provide." Critics who do find political significance in Coetzee's novels too often resort to simplistic allegory by mapping his plots onto the surface of South African politics; yet the ambiguity of Coetzee's language provides no "moral" for a story of South Africa. The indeterminacy of language also tends to forestall questions of historical significance for those critics responsive to poststructuralism. If language is a "self-referring system of signs," as Paul Williams maintains, then a literary text cannot speak about reality or South Africa. Thus Coetzee's novels are read as politically and historically irrelevant or irresponsible, depending on a critic's agenda. But Barbara Eckstein questions the inviolability of the opposition of poststructuralist language and political responsibility:

> The method of deconstruction which questions certainty, scrutinizes authority . . . and undoes the rigidity of binary oppositions can serve serious political concern and analysis of politics in texts. When a critic practicing a deconstructive method leaps to conclusions of irresponsibility and despair, it is not because those conclusions are inherent in the method.

Eckstein, by allowing for a critical methodology that reveals not only indeterminacy but also oppression, explores a discursive space at the center of the critical opposition. This space is much like what Teresa Dovey terms "the potential area between the [political and the poststructural], which is concerned to theorize the ways in which discourses emerging from diverse contexts, and exhibiting different formal assumptions, may produce *different* forms of historical en-

gagement. . . ." The alternative historical engagement that Dovey calls for would combine the South African story and Coetzee's characters' inability to tell their stories, without resorting to allegory or irresponsibility.

One "discourse" that may allow for an exploration, grounded in language, of the political dimension of Coetzee's fiction is that surrounding the practice of torture, which is undeniably a part of the South African story. The definition of torture in the United Nations' Declaration against Torture, adopted in 1975, reads:

> torture means any act by which severe pain or suffering, whether physical or mental, is intentionally inflicted by or at the instigation of a public official on a person for such purposes as obtaining from him or a third person information or confession, punishing him for an act he has committed, or intimidating him or other persons.

Inflicting pain to obtain information has long been the justification for judicial torture; the third-century jurist, Ulpian, provides an early definition of torture: "By *quaestio* [torture] we are to understand the torment and suffering of the body in order to elicit the truth." But a further investigation of the structure of torture reveals, with remarkable resonance to the tropes of poststructuralist theory, the elusiveness of the truth that torture seeks.

On the surface, torture appears to be a kind of conversation in which physical and mental pain are used by one person to encourage another person to speak. The means of "encouragement," of course, represent the inequity of power in the verbal and physical exchange between tortured and torturer. In *The Body in Pain*, Elaine Scarry calls into question the truth-value of the information obtained in this exchange. Scarry argues that physical pain has the ability to destroy the voice that would express it in language; furthermore, she suggests that this is precisely the motive of torture: "it is in part the obsessive display of agency that permits one person's body to be translated into another person's voice, that allows real human pain to be converted into a regime's fiction of power." If the pain of torture eliminates the voice of the victim, the traditional guise of torture as a means of eliciting the truth is unmasked. Still, the conception of torture as enforced truth-telling must remain in order for the practice to continue. Ñacuñán Sáez explains that "executioners think that *ideally* torture is a way to find out the truth, but . . . they also admit that the *practice* of torture gives rise to many distortions." Attending to Scarry, Sáez argues:

> The threat of pain does link in the mind of the victim the experience of the self and the recognition of truth, but only through their negation. . . . Scarry

has argued that torture destroys language and the self; I am contending, instead, that it produces them as negative, as absent, as disembodied images. . . . Torture forces pain to become something like a "transcendental signifier," the dominant element in the system of language. . . . I will stop making sense so that they stop the pain.

Far more explicitly than Scarry, Sáez makes clear the connection between the practice of torture and poststructuralist theory. For the victim, truth is negated along with the voice of an integrated self, although torturing continues to demand truth while further destroying the victim's ability to speak, or even to know, truth.

Sáez writes of the fascination of the discourses of both torture and post-structuralism with "language, the body, the absence of truth" as a "strange coincidence." This coincidence proves extremely useful in reconciling the abstraction of language with the reality of oppressive political regimes:

> The recognition . . . of that coincidence . . . does not expose the guilt, or even the responsibility, of the postmodern mind; it merely points to its limits. To venture beyond those limits (to stop before torture), does not mean to take refuge once again in the old myths of subjectivity and truth. It means, on the contrary, to subject those myths to a more ruthless theoretical attack. It also means, it means perhaps above all, that the most ruthless attack has to be more than just theoretical.

If torture represents the limits of the postmodern mind, it also represents a discursive space between language and history in which Coetzee's historical engagement can be considered, with the understanding further that in addition to that discursive space are many geographical, physical, bodily spaces where torture is practiced, as Eckstein says, "from Chile to Pakistan; from history's beginning to this minute." Eckstein insists upon holding in mind the fact that torture (and not only the discourse of torture) exists now everywhere; and the unnamed, unhistoricized empire of Coetzee's *Waiting for the Barbarians,* far from representing an avoidance of the story of South Africa, allows torture to be examined as a phenomenon that could (and does) occur not only in South Africa, but in any place where political power imposes itself upon the human body.

Coetzee does not name South Africa as the empire in *Waiting for the Barbarians,* but one may wonder how writing a novel about torture and imperialism could be construed as shirking political responsibility. Coetzee's protagonist, a frontier civil magistrate, confronts torture when the perceived threat of a barbarian invasion brings Colonel Joll, a military interrogator, to the frontier from the capital. But one of the

magistrate's frustrations in the novel is that he is not given the details of events in Joll's torture chamber; the magistrate finds himself compelled to elicit from a tortured barbarian girl the story of her experience. In the first part of the novel, torture is named but not described, allowing it to be potentially absent to critical eyes. Coetzee himself provides a possible explanation for this absence that implies that the telling of a story of torture is not necessarily an act of political resistance. In **"Into the Dark Chamber,"** Coetzee admits the South African writer's fascination with torture, and he wonders "how to treat something that, in truth, because it is offered like the Gorgon's head to terrorize the populace and paralyze resistance, deserves to be ignored." Coetzee obviously cannot and does not ignore torture, but in choosing to represent torture, he must face the challenge of "how not to play the game by the rules of the state, how to establish one's own authority, how to imagine torture and death on one's own terms." The terms for torture that Coetzee employs are deeply embedded in language, a language that tells not of beatings or shocks but instead of the difficulty of talking about the body in pain. By examining torture in a language separate from that of historical discourse, however, the unspecified geographical setting of the novel can become a merely theoretical space in which the political implications of the novel are subsumed into the poststructural; Susan Gallagher writes, "With his combination of sexual and authorial images, his antonymic articulations, and his failure to discover meaning in words, the Magistrate *seems to be wandering in the wilderness of deconstructive criticism*" (emphasis added). Out of history and into language, the magistrate is suddenly more poststructural literary critic than fictional political figure. But if the magistrate is lost in a poststructuralist "wilderness," one way to locate him (if not for him to position himself) may be to forge through the wilderness using its terms in an attempt to reveal how a deconstructive criticism can also be a criticism of the state.

The magistrate recalls a dream in which he is "carrying the girl, the only key I have to the labyrinth"; it is the relationship between the magistrate and the tortured barbarian girl that offers a way out of the magistrate's struggles with his relation to both language and power. The magistrate finds the blinded and lamed barbarian girl begging by the barracks wall after Joll's departure; as he brings her first into his house and then into his household, the magistrate finds himself increasingly compelled to find out from the barbarian girl exactly what Joll has done to her. Torture has transformed her into a text to be read: the magistrate admits, "It has been growing more and more clear to me that until the marks on this girl's body are deciphered and understood I cannot let go of her." The magistrate finds the girl's body impenetrable, unwilling to yield its secrets, and as such he experiences it as wholly other, unknowable, to the point that he cannot even remember what the girl looks like when he is away from her. It is this sense of otherness that allows torturers to ignore the pain of their victims; the magistrate seeks to eliminate his sense of the girl's otherness and to understand the pain of her torture as he verbally and physically probes the girl in an effort to read the signs of torture written on her body. Eckstein explains the magistrate's linguistic disposition: "As a man of the 'first world,' [the magistrate] is accustomed to assigning meaning to sentient signs, particularly signs of the (barbarian) 'third world.' He can make presence or absence as he chooses."

Eckstein's argument holds also for the magistrate's fascination with the hieroglyphic poplar slips he finds outside the fortress: he can admit to himself that he cannot read them, or he can provide his own strategic reading of imperial injustice when Joll demands that he interpret them. "Reading" one of the slips for Joll, the magistrate says, "It is the barbarian character *war,* but it has other senses too. It can stand for *vengeance,* and, if you turn it upside down like this, it can be made to read *justice.* There is no knowing which sense is intended. That is part of barbarian cunning." Likewise, Joll has the political power to inscribe "ENEMY" into the flesh of his barbarian victims in front of a gathering of the outpost residents; he beats them until "their backs are washed clean" by sweat and blood, the act of torture literally erasing their threat to the empire.

But Joll cannot "read" the potentially fictional nature of that threat; his public staging of torture makes the threat seem so real that even the skeptical magistrate helps to prepare the fortress against the barbarian attack. Joll does not understand that he may be writing, and not reading, the threat of the barbarians. Similarly, the magistrate does not have the linguistic power to read meaningful presence in the tortured body of the girl or the ability to approach her in any other way:

> Is it . . . the case that it is the whole woman I want, that my pleasure in her is spoiled until these marks on her are erased and she is restored to herself; or is it the case . . . that it is the marks on her which drew me to her but which, to my disappointment, I find, do not go deep enough? Too much or too little: is it she I want or the traces of a history her body bears?

In a way, torture has domesticated the other so that it cannot be perceived in and of itself. The magistrate exerts intellectual and physical energy trying to read the hieroglyphic inscription of force on the body of the girl, but she does not provide him with any satisfactory answers. Frustration at his inability to read her only makes his desire more like Joll's writing of her: he asks himself "whether, when I lay head to foot with her, fondling and kissing those broken ankles, I was not in my heart of hearts regretting that I could not engrave myself on her as deeply [as Joll]."

Both Joll and the magistrate fail to understand how the experience of torture has transformed the girl's relationship to language. Just as there is no answer the girl could give to satisfy Joll's need for the "truth," there is no story the girl could tell that would make the magistrate certain of her pain. By not allowing her tortured body to be translated into language, she prevents the othering that the magistrate's categorizations would impose in transforming her story into his own. Although the magistrate falls into the old trap of locating truth in the body of woman, the relationship between the magistrate and the girl becomes a "key . . . to the labyrinth." Furthermore, in allowing the girl to refuse translation of her tortured body into language, Coetzee presents the body as a "key to the labyrinth" and a way out of the deconstructive wilderness.

Because he can neither read the girl's body nor inscribe his own meaning onto it, the magistrate is able neither to determine his own position within the imperialist regime nor to pen the history of his outpost. The magistrate admits: "It seems appropriate that a man who does not know what to do with the woman in his bed should not know what to write." The magistrate only fully recognizes the resistance of the body to linguistic significance, however, after his own aging body is subjected to a torturous interrogation. He finds, contrary to Joll's confident assertions about his craft, that pain is *not* truth, that the only "truth" of torture is the truth of the body, that, as Attwell says, "the body sets clear limits to what can be endured or claimed on behalf of ideals or principles."

After his own experience of torture, the magistrate finds himself in a position similar to that he had imposed on the girl. A blow to his face leaves a "caterpillar"-like scar under the magistrate's eye: the scar is not only nearly identical to those on the girl's damaged eyes, but the magistrate also discovers that "people are surreptitiously fascinated" by the marks on his body. Just as the girl, because "[she] did not have a choice," had found shelter and sustenance in the company of several men before the magistrate took her in, the broken magistrate finds himself "sing[ing] for [his] keep" when he learns that "I am not without friends, particularly among women, who can barely conceal their eagerness to hear my side of the story." The gendered parallelism of the barbarian girl's and the magistrate's reintegration into the community after torture extends even to sexual activity: while the sympathetic men and women play a rather parental role by feeding, bathing, and clothing these victims of torture, it is the girl and the magistrate (as victim) who escalate physical contact with their respective nurturers to a sexual level, thereby signaling their return to the adult realm.

The status of the barbarian girl and the magistrate in the outpost community is transformed after torture into something like that of children; gender differences play a role only in terms of the parallel (un)conventional heterosexual relationships in which Coetzee's characters find recuperation. Examining the process of torture in *The Politics of Cruelty: An Essay on the Literature of Political Imprisonment,* Kate Millett writes, "Under torture one is first reduced to a woman, then to a child, and as the torture creates a woman out of any human material being tortured, he also creates a child, the citizen as child, frightened before the great, all-powerful . . . state." While the experiences of the barbarian girl and the magistrate after torture are indeed initially childlike, the forms of torture they endure move beyond the gendered terms of Millett's analysis. The assumptions lurking behind Millett's pronoun choices betray the rather antifeminist (though common) conception of the role of gender in torture that the rest of her words confirm: (male) torturers humiliate (male) victims by "reducing" them to women. The barbarian girl's torture is seemingly ungendered: her eyes and her feet are the areas that Joll targets for mutilation. A reader following Millett's argument might assume that Joll has no need to "reduce . . . [the girl] to a woman," that "unfortunate" task already having been accomplished by her birth. When the magistrate is subjected to a mock hanging and then suspended by his wrists from a tree, his torturer offers him the choice between wearing a woman's smock or nothing: he can be symbolically "reduced" either to a woman or an animal. The magistrate accepts the smock; but the pain inside of his body, the "body that knows itself damaged perhaps beyond repair," so overshadows the intended patriarchal shame of the feminine clothing covering the body that the magistrate subsequently describes himself as a "beast," rather than as a woman. Regardless of the intentions of the torturers in the novel, the pain that the girl and the magistrate experience effectively erases the significance of gender at the moment of their torture; both are subjected to pain that lies at the limits of human experience. To conclude that torture reduces the (hu)man to woman is thus to deny the pain of the body and to acknowledge and embrace the shame of the smock offered by the torturer.

The magistrate understands the pain inscribed onto his body by the regime as much more significant than the clothes it forces him to wear, and only then can he read his own bruises and scars as signs of his position within the empire. He attempts to distance himself from the crowd watching, and thus participating in, the public torture of the barbarians in order to extricate himself from responsibility:

> For me, at this moment, striding away from the crowd, what has become important above all is that I should neither be contaminated by the atrocity that is about to be committed nor poison myself with impotent hatred of its perpetrators. I cannot save the prisoners, therefore let me save myself. Let it at the very least be said, if it ever comes to be said . . . that in this farthest outpost of the empire of light

there existed one man who in his heart was not a barbarian.

Yet the magistrate finds that he cannot go far in distancing himself from the empire that he serves. When he imagines alternative possibilities for the shape of his society, empire remains at the center: "It would be best if this obscure chapter in the history of the world were terminated at once, if these ugly people were obliterated from the face of the earth and we swore to make a new start, to run an empire in which there would be no more injustice, no more pain." When the magistrate ventures outside of the walls of the imperial fortress, he soon recognizes that a space outside of the empire is no place at all; he finds "nothing for me outside the walls but to starve." The magistrate's experience confirms Edward Peters's words on torture: "a society which voluntarily or indifferently includes among its members both victims and torturers ultimately leaves no conceptual or practical room for anyone who insists upon being neither." The magistrate, like the girl whose story he sought, wants to be neither victim nor torturer, and it is only after he has been in both positions that he can understand the girl's inability to tell her story.

Subsequently, the magistrate acknowledges his inability to write a history of his outpost that can account both for his aversion to and his complicity with empire. It is in the anguished cries the magistrate utters while being hung from the tree—cries that the spectators call "barbarian language"—that he comes closest to the truth of his position in the worlds of language and history. The suffering body cannot be reduced to "civilized" language, and civilization itself obstructs any protest made within its structure. The history remains unwritten, except in the magistrate's private monologue that is *Waiting for the Barbarians.* At the end of the novel, the magistrate dreams of children building an armless snowman: he walks away instead of trying to translate the body into a fully realized form. In this final image is an awareness that just as the tortured body cannot be subsumed to linguistic structures, the political systems supported by those structures are incapable of completely appropriating the vulnerable human body and its voice, incapable of silencing the voice of protest, however implicated within the structure it may be. The hope implicit in this view is conditional on the recognition of the body as partly autonomous from, but nonetheless vulnerable to, the totalizing abstraction of language.

Coetzee insists on holding the substantial body, the body in pain, on equal terms with the abstraction of language; in doing so he broaches alternative frameworks for reconciling language with history. In *Waiting for the Barbarians,* the tortured body serves as a marker for what Sáez terms the limits of the postmodern mind, while at the same time a postmodern sensibility reminds us of the difficulty of making oversimplified appeals to truth in the face of historical oppression. Yet the problems that the magistrate, Coetzee's would-be storyteller, faces are to some extent Coetzee's own. Coetzee, like the magistrate, is implicated in an imperial regime that, as Peters argues, leaves no room beyond being either torturer or tortured. Coetzee's struggle is then, as Anne Waldron Neumann says, a struggle "with how best to tell the history of oppression, without imposing that history on anyone else (particularly on those most directly oppressed) . . . a struggle to determine the value of that telling, to determine the value literary art can have in the context of a political struggle that is itself all too present." Attwell argues that it is Coetzee's insistence on maintaining the autonomy of fiction from history that imbues his work with both literary and historical value and allows him to imagine, if not to speak from, a position outside of the imperial structure: "the brute facticity of power can halt the endlessness of textuality; but . . . if authority is ultimately a function of power, then it ought to be possible, through the rediscovery of fiction's capacity to reconfigure the rules of discourse, to find a position *outside* current power relations from which to speak." It is precisely because Coetzee (unlike the magistrate) is a literary and not a political/historical figure that he can write an imaginative imperial history that explores the issue of complicity without becoming co-opted by it.

Coetzee's fiction, in terms of his desire to prevent the appropriation of the novel by the discourse of history, represents an engagement with history on his own terms, terms that can blur the distinctions between self and other, between oppressor and oppressed.
—*Jennifer Wenzel*

Coetzee's fiction, in terms of his desire to prevent the appropriation of the novel by the discourse of history, represents an engagement with history on his own terms, terms that can blur the distinctions between self and other, between oppressor and oppressed. *Waiting for the Barbarians* presents the reader with an interpretive choice, but that choice is not necessarily between historical seriousness and poststructuralist indeterminacy. The language of Coetzee's novels reveals both the liberation and the oppression latent in theoretical discourse and reminds us as readers that we are all, like the magistrate, like Coetzee himself, people of "language in a world of pain."

Martha Bayles (review date 22 September 1996)

SOURCE: "The Silencers," in *New York Times,* September 22, 1996, p. 33.

[*In the following review, Bayles praises Coetzee's approach to questions of censorship in* Giving Offense.]

"Of all the pathologies," J. M. Coetzee writes, "paranoia has been the most amenable to artificial simulation." The workings of the paranoid mind, Mr. Coetzee explains, can be programmed into a computer so that "qualified psychiatrists have been unable to tell whether what is being relayed to them is the verbal behaviour of a human being or an automaton." Not surprisingly for a dissident South African novelist, Mr. Coetzee finds a similar narrow, predictable "automatism" in state censorship.

Yet in *Giving Offense,* an extraordinary collection of essays written over the past eight years, Mr. Coetzee does not cast himself as the noble, freedom-loving artist; he finds this role almost as narrow and predictable. He rejects the melodrama (he does not call it that) of heroic artist and foul villain censor because it is simpleminded, and like all simple—mindedness leads back toward censorship. Instead, he seeks to demonstrate the complexity and insidiousness of censorship's harm.

At the book's core is a somewhat cryptic reading of Erasmus's *Praise of Folly* that is basically a tour-de-force defense of humanist "weakness" against every kind of radical certainty—including those bequeathed by the progenitors of post-modernism. Mr. Coetzee does not dismiss Michel Foucault, Jacques Lacan or Rene Girard, but he does not embrace them as uncritically as has, say, the American academic establishment. Perhaps, having lived in a police state, he hesitates over the Foucaultian proposition that liberal democracy is just another kind of prison.

What Mr. Coetzee does do is squeeze a drop of wisdom from these theorists. For example, his essay on Aleksandr Solzhenitsyn begins with an account of Mr. Girard's theory of the politics of desire. Here Mr. Coetzee finds a metaphor for the struggle of the writer with the censor. Instead of the usual Freudian scenario of the son in revolt, Mr. Girard posits the image of rival brothers. Thus, the grandiose, intolerant, polemical face of Mr. Solzhenitsyn strikes even his admirers as that of "a secret Stalinist . . . his own enemy, rival, twin."

Despite his erudite commitment to free speech, Mr. Coetzee stands at a certain remove from the concerns of most Americans. Consider his discussion of pornography. As a South African, he complains that though "there is a world of difference between subversive ideas and morally repugnant representations," this difference is not recognized in law: "The same censors patrol the boundaries of both politics and esthetics." Therefore, Mr. Coetzee declares, he will not bother drawing a "sharp line between censorship on political and on moral grounds."

Yet this is precisely the line that in the American context separates protected from unprotected speech. Indeed, for some American artists, one way of getting acquitted of obscenity charges for "morally repugnant representations" is to argue (in the language of the 1973 Supreme Court decision Miller v. California) that the work possesses "serious political value." Even, in some cases, that it expresses "subversive ideas." From Robert Mapplethorpe to 2 Live Crew, this strategy has expanded the definition of political speech to encompass material that in a different era, or a different polity, would unquestioningly be judged obscene.

South Africa is obviously such a polity—or has been until recently. Doubtless this is why Mr. Coetzee writes, "I am not sure . . . what to think about artists who break taboos and yet claim the protection of the law." For him, the thorny question of constitutional protection for morally repugnant material is not yet salient. Yet by the same token, Mr. Coetzee's dissection of the totalizing arguments of the feminist antipornography crusader Catharine MacKinnon is cogent, witty and salted with good sense. And his warning—that if censorship returns, it will be down such paths of righteousness—is well worth heeding.

Michiko Kakutani (review date 7 October 1997)

SOURCE: "Childhood Hurt and Fear as a Writer's Inspiration," in *New York Times,* October 7, 1997, p. E8.

[*In the following review, Kakutani discusses the early elements of Coetzee's life, as described in* Boyhood, *that led to his later writing career.*]

Though **Boyhood** has the stylized, fablelike quality of so much of J. M. Coetzee's fiction, it is not a coming-of-age novel, but a memoir that happens to be told in the third person and the present tense. It is a fiercely revealing, bluntly unsentimental work that both creates a telling portrait of the artist as a young man and illuminates the hidden courses of his art.

[Boyhood] is a fiercely revealing, bluntly unsentimental work that both creates a telling portrait of the artist as a young man and illuminates the hidden courses of his art.
—*Michiko Kakutani*

Indeed, the seeds of Mr. Coetzee's mature work—**Waiting for the Barbarians, Life and Times of Michael K, Foe** and **Age of Iron**—can all be found in this slim volume. Mr.

Coetzee's fascination with power and the Darwinian equation it draws between those with authority and those without, his sympathy for the disenfranchised and dispossessed and his concern with the struggle that isolated individuals wage for emotional and physical survival—all, we learn, have very specific roots in his childhood, in his tempestuous relationship with his parents, in his fearful experience of school and in his youthful apprehension of race under the apartheid laws of South Africa.

The young Mr. Coetzee, referred to throughout this volume as "he," and only once, obliquely, as John, grew up in the years after World War II in a dismal housing project outside the town of Worcester, a place where the streets "have tree-names but no trees yet." Although his family's name was Afrikaans, English was spoken at home, and John always felt like an outsider at school, set apart by his family's lack of religion and his parents' failure to fit in with their neighbors. At once fearful and contemptuous of his classmates and teachers, he came to see school as a microcosm of "the cruelty and pain and hatred raging beneath the everyday surface of things," a place where beatings and humiliation could be randomly dispensed by others.

John's sense of isolation seems to have nourished a sympathy, even a sense of identification, with "the Natives." "In the stories that have left the deepest mark on him," Mr. Coetzee writes, "It is the third brother, the humblest and most derided, who, after the first and second brothers have disdainfully passed by, helps the old woman to carry her heavy load or draws the thorn from the lion's paw. The third brother is kind and honest and courageous while the first and second brothers are boastful, arrogant, uncharitable. At the end of the story the third brother is crowned prince, while the first and second brothers are disgraced and sent packing.

"There are white people and Colored people and Natives, of whom the Natives are the lowest and most derided. The parallel is inescapable: the Natives are the third brother."

Like Michael K, the young John is endowed with the clearsightedness of innocence, a child's common sense that enables him to intuitively understand the injustice of apartheid and the corruption of the system. "He does not see the point of having elections if the party that wins can change the rules," Mr. Coetzee writes. "It is like the batsman deciding who may and who may not bowl."

John's skepticism, however, also gives him a highly cynical take on his own family, goading him to see love as just another form of politics. Even before his weak, ineffectual father returned home from the war, he says, he decided "he was not going to like him": he decided "he does not want to have a father, or at least does not want a father who stays in the same house."

As for his doting, protective mother, he regards her with a mixture of adoration, resentment and Marcel-like dependence. Her self-sacrificing love for him, he realizes, means he will never be able to pay her back: "The thought of a lifetime bowed under a debt of love baffles and infuriates him to the point where he will not kiss her, refuses to be touched by her. When she turns away in silent hurt, he deliberately hardens his heart against her, refusing to give in."

John's wariness of the claims of others makes him a furtive, secretive child, quick to worry, quicker to dissemble. This watchfulness, combined with a grandiosity—he thinks of himself as special, capable of achieving whatever he wants to do—will turn his heart "dark and hard." It will also make him into an observer and storyteller who will transform the raw hurt, fear and anxiety of his childhood into such remarkable works as *Waiting for the Barbarians* and *Life & Times of Michael K.*

Though this book does not possess those novels' artistry or mythic power, it provides a potent emotional blueprint for them, even as it reveals how their creator became a writer to begin with.

FURTHER READING

Criticism

Gitzen, Julian. "The Voice of History in the Novels of J. M. Coetzee." *Critique* XXXV, No. 1 (Fall 1993): 3-15.

Examines the "history-conscious characters" in Coetzee's novels.

Moses, Michael Valdez. "The Mark of Empire: Writing, History, and Torture in Coetzee's *Waiting for the Barbarians.*" *Kenyon Review* XV, No. 1 (Winter 1993): 115-27.

Discusses the place of the written word within an imperial context.

Rody, Caroline. "The Mad Colonial Daughter's Revolt: J. M. Coetzee's *In the Heart of the Country.*" *South Atlantic Quarterly* 93, No. 1 (Winter 1994): 157-80.

Posits the character Magda in *In the Heart of the Country* as an answer and solution to the problem of disempowered but colonizing white women in postcolonial literature.

Wohlpart, James. "A (Sub)Version of the Language of Power: Narrative and Narrative Technique in J. M. Coetzee's *In the Heart of the Country.*" *Critique* XXXV, No. 4 (Summer 1994): 219-28.

Proposes a reading of *In the Heart of the Country* that "engages and subverts the traditional uses of language that encode the ideology of power."

Interview

Wood, Philip R. "Aporias of the Postcolonial Subject: Correspondence with J. M. Coetzee." *South Atlantic Quarterly* 93, No. 1 (Winter 1994): 181-95.

Contains excerpts from a written interview carried on between the author and Coetzee.

Additional coverage of Coetzee's life and career is contained in the following sources published by Gale: *Contemporary Authors,* Vol. 77-80; *Contemporary Authors New Revision Series,* Vols. 41, and 54; *DISCovering Authors Modules: Novelists*; and *Major Twentieth Century Writers.*

Bret Easton Ellis
1964-

American novelist.

The following entry provides an overview of Ellis's career through 1998. For further information on his life and works, see *CLC*, Volumes 39 and 71.

INTRODUCTION

Brett Easton Ellis has been called the voice of a new generation by some critics, and accused by others as being "superficial." He leaves few readers indifferent to his work. Critics compare Ellis's frank representations of rich but desensitized young Americans to the works of authors Ernest Hemingway and F. Scott Fitzgerald. Ellis's novels also share affinities with the work of Raymond Chandler and Joan Didion, the latter an author Ellis acknowledges as an important influence. Music-video and film aesthetics also mark Ellis's style and themes. *American Psycho* (1991), arguably his most notorious work, has been the subject of extended critical discussion and the object of public scorn for its graphic rendering of violence against women. Ellis has enjoyed commercial success, but the artistic and sociological value of his work is a source of ongoing debate.

Biographical Information

Born and raised in Los Angeles, Ellis's early novels focus on events similar to experiences in his own life. Ellis graduated with a B.A. from Bennington College in Vermont in 1986. A year earlier, he made a sudden and spectacular appearance on the literary scene with his novel *Less Than Zero* (1985), at the age of twenty-one. The novel grew out of a writing course at Bennington, and was reworked over a period of several years. Ellis's second novel, *Rules of Attraction* (1987), continued in the same vein as his first, focusing on thrill seeking teen-agers, and is infused with MTV imagery and allusions to suggestive commercial slogans and rock band titles. *Rules of Attraction* drew mixed reviews, and was not as successful as *Less Than Zero*. *American Psycho* was published by Random House after it was rejected by Simon and Schuster, and the book provoked a violent reaction from many sources, including reviewers who urged readers to avoid the novel. The Los Angeles Chapter of the National Organization for Women (NOW) objected to its vivid depiction of violence against women. NOW mounted a boycott of Random House, and Gloria Steinem publicly promoted the idea that Ellis should be held accountable for acts of violence against women that were inspired by the novel's misogynist narrator. Ellis's next book, *The Informers* was published in 1994.

Major Works

Ellis' novel *Less Than Zero* focuses on the experiences of the young narrator, Clay, a wealthy student from Los Angeles who attends college on the East Coast. The novel recounts a trip home for the Christmas holidays which plunges him into a world where young teenagers buy Porsches, indulge in casual sex, abuse drugs, and watch music videos and pornography with the same detachment as their parents. Ellis has observed that his novels portray a lifestyle that "a lot of teenagers hunger to be in." *Less Than Zero* was praised for its cool prose and critics admired Ellis's ear for language. *The Rules of Attraction* covers similar territory. One reviewer summarized the characters' lives and the plot in the following manner: "they drink, get high, get tranquilized, spend a great deal of their parents' money, and practice junk-food sex." The values underlying this lifestyle are dramatically represented in Ellis's best known work, *American Psycho*—the narrative of Patrick Bateman, a character introduced in

Rules of Attraction. Bateman is a twenty-six-year-old investment banker, serial killer and quintessential citizen of consumer society who consumes the victims of his madness, all with the same detached obsession he uses in choosing outfits advertised in magazines. Many commentators view *American Psycho* as dangerously exploitative and irresponsibly reliant on shock-value. Others read *American Psycho* as a metaphor, seeing in Bateman's story a symbolic criticism of greed and "inhumanity" of the American upper class whose victims are the disadvantaged underclass. In *The Informers,* Ellis returns to focusing on rich and beautiful college students, and incorporates deadpan prose and scenes of horror similar to that seen in his early work. In the novel, a multitude of friends and acquaintances find their lives uprooted by several random murders and mutilations. The murderers are revealed to be Dirk and Jamie, two of the friends in the group who turn out to be vampires. Ellis weaves thematic and narrative features of his other novels into this work, and also includes an experimental element that drew a comparison to William Faulkner's *The Sound and the Fury.*

Critical Reception

Heated critical debate surrounds Ellis's relatively small oeuvre. It centers around the shocking qualities of his characters' actions and attitudes. Scott Spenser praises Ellis's use of deadpan humor: "There are flashes of wit that can lead you to suspect he sees and even recoils from the hollowness of the young lives he writes about." However, Spenser derides Ellis for his passivity in his regard for social malaise, stating: " . . .it [is] within his grasp to become a satirist, but for now his method of aping the attitudes of the burnt-out works against him." In a review of *American Psycho,* Alberto Manguel suggests that the book produces "a revulsion not of the senses but of the gut, like that produced by shoving a finger down one's throat." Norman Mailer, a writer similarly known for vivid depictions of brutality, finds it difficult to defend Ellis's approach to writing, due to its apparent lack of moral purpose. Nevertheless, defenders of Ellis's work abound. Gore Vidal feels *American Psycho* is "a wonderfully comic novel," and other positive critical commentary centers on the metaphorical dimension that was missed by those who, compelled to act on the outrage the work provokes, are quick to ban and censor the book. *American Psycho* is seen by these defenders as an indictment of unprincipled materialistic consumerism. Richard Eder commends Ellis's sharp "ear and eye for the patter and drift of his contemporaries" and the satirical thrust of his work, but complains of the lack of contrast due to the absence of "an alternative . . . standpoint."

PRINCIPAL WORKS

Less Than Zero (novel) 1985

The Rules of Attraction (novel) 1987
American Psycho (novel) 1991
The Informers (novel) 1994
Glamorama (novel) 1999

CRITICISM

Richard Eder (review date 13 September 1987)

SOURCE: "Flopsy, Mopsy, Paul, Sean and Lauren," in *Los Angeles Times Book Review,* September 13, 1987, pp. 3, 8.

[*In the following review of* The Rules of Attraction, *Eder critiques Ellis's style and examines the author's themes.*]

Bret Easton Ellis' characters have an odd resemblance to Beatrix Potter's.

True, they drink, get high, get tranquilized, spend a great deal of their parents' money, and practice junk-food sex. The comparison with the chaste Miss Potter may seem farfetched. Furthermore her rabbits and squirrels are more human than Ellis' college kids, and livelier.

But the resemblance is there. Both groups live snugly in burrows, do their things, pay each other visits, and have infrequent contact with the outside world. Adults appear rarely, and, when one does, it is a Mr. MacGregor, whose vegetable patch is briefly and perilously raided (Ellis' is a rich parent appearing now and then to moo and be milked). Afterward, they scamper home for tea (Ellis: cocaine and tacos).

Of course, Potter's point is the coziness of small, furred things who set their table with real Spode. Ellis' point is the bleakness of a lost generation with platinum credit cards. But both the coziness and the bleakness are laid on; neither is earned.

It is only human to prefer unearned coziness. It is harder to accept Ellis' post-adolescent bleakness, subsidized—if you cost out the tuitions and the consumption of expensive goods and services—at five or six grand a page.

Ellis' first novel, **Less Than Zero,** was set in Los Angeles, though its protagonist was a New England college student back home for the summer. **The Rules of Attraction** is New England college life on the spot.

College life, in a manner of speaking. We actually catch a glimpse of one professor—though we hear about two or three others—and he is asleep on his office couch and reeks of pot. The tutorial he was supposed to give—only one student shows up—is "The Postmodern Condition." Ellis' pegs in **Rules** tend to fit into familiar satirical holes. One student changes his schedule from "Flute Tutorial" to "Advanced Video."

Classes and term papers have barely the force of a premonition. The function of college is to provide a setting, free of past, future or an external reality. One student may or may not have lost her virginity to a townie—there were several revelers present—if so, it is a faintly embarrassing social misstep. Within the setting, the barely distinguishable inhabitants grasp at each other with a form of desire that is briefly urgent and permanently hazy.

There are no parties, there is only partying. There are no real characters; there are only names, supplied with clothes, activities—mostly sexual—and a kind of sated neediness.

One of the names cuts her throat in the bathtub, which is no great surprise since she has been flitting in and out with a plain case of schizophrenic dementia. The subsequent color of the bath water is more vivid than she is.

Ellis supplies three of the names with rudimentary feelings and a story of sorts. One is Paul, a handsome homosexual, with a passion for exploring bisexual possibilities among the better-looking men students.

His main interest is Sean, who drifts among serial encounters—as many as four on one particular night—with the women. Paul's narration proudly recounts his success at seducing Sean. Sean's own recital mentions only the most casual meetings with Paul, whom he regards as a pest.

The reader inclines to believe Paul, although he is vain and foggy enough to be making it up. On the other hand, Sean is equally foggy, what with drugs and his own delusions. More important, Ellis suggests that the characters in *Rules* are so cut off from their own as well as others' feelings that the reality or unreality of any particular relationship is irrelevant.

Sean's delusions concern Lauren, with whom he imagines himself to be having a passionate affair. For her part, she has sex with everyone, including Sean, but her own obsession is with a student whom she no longer sees. At one point she has an abortion, as shadowy as everything else.

Ellis' theme, traditional to social satirists, is "How We Live Now" or, given the anomie of his young people, "How We Fail to Live Now." His ear and eye for the patter and drift of his contemporaries in the rich college set are sharp; his surfaces are sometimes, though not always, convincing.

But he never departs from surface. Satire needs contrast; an alternative or at least an innocent standpoint to let it register. Without Gulliver, Lilliput would be meaningless; without George Winston, *1984* would be noise. Ellis, both here as in his first book, lacks the strength—or perhaps the courage or desire—to precipitate his swirling materials.

The materials themselves are not of the first water. Ellis' sketch of a pretentious literary gathering is a tired cliché; someone actually murmurs: "Seminal, seminal." A gay student, taken to the hospital after overdosing himself, argues groggily with a doctor who insists that he is clinically dead.

The scene tries for absurdity; it is no more than dumb. Even the French in a French student's love letter is clumsy and dotted with mistakes.

Ellis is a graduate of Bennington College, and the affluent and freeform student body in *Rules* is presumably based on his own recollections. I doubt that Bennington will sue him over its portrayal as a marsh of plaintive hedonism. Perhaps he, or whoever paid his bills, could sue Bennington for a spotty education.

Scott Spenser (review date 13 September 1987)

SOURCE: "Love Me, Love My Porsche," in *New York Times Book Review,* September 13, 1987, p. 14.

[*In the following review, Spenser critiques the superficiality of Ellis' characters in* The Rules of Attraction.]

With his first novel, *Less Than Zero,* Bret Easton Ellis made a name for himself here and abroad with an account of life among the overdrugged, underloved rich kids of southern California. It was a kind of *Valley of the Dolls* for the 80's, but it had its own oblique power, and there was something remarkable in the fact that the author was merely 20 years old. Now, two years later, Mr. Ellis gives us *The Rules of Attraction*—maybe the first expose of what really goes on in the coed dorms we've heard about. It serves to establish Mr. Ellis's reputation further as one of the primary inside sources in upper-middle-class America's continuing investigation of what has happened to its children.

The Rules of Attraction is a not-quite-random collection of voices, all of them giving their points of view about the sexual rites and rivalries in a place called Camden College. As in *Less Than Zero,* Mr. Ellis isn't concerned about constructing a novel with a plot. His interest is in misbehavior patterns, and it could be that some of his older readers are experiencing his work on the level of social psychology. Here, threaded through the indistinct mixture of narrators, is the story of a girl named Lauren, who is more or less in love with a boy named Victor, who is traveling and not really aware of her feelings. Lauren, on the other hand, is pursued by a boy named Sean, who is being sent love letters by a girl named Mary—letters he thinks are from Lauren. (Mary, a minor character, commits suicide.) Sean, in turn, is being pursued by a boy named Paul, who eventually tires of him, though he does continue to chase after him in a half-hearted way.

The students court and reject one another not so much with the frenzy of youthful eros as with the swaggering, petulant whine of entitlement. They yearn for each other the way they pine for Porsches, and Mr. Ellis is successful in portraying the shallowness of their desires.

They live in a world of conspicuous and compulsive consumption—consuming first one another, and then drugs, and then anything else they can lay their hands on. This consumerist impulse, however, doesn't seem to function on the level of social satire, but as a way of locating and even glamorizing the characters. Their choices of product are not only expensive but up-to-the-minute and refined. One character, recounting a night of dissipation, sighs, "Somewhere along the line I lose my Concord quartz watch," with the clear implication that this is more poignant than losing a Timex. Elsewhere we read: "The Polynesian bartender gives me a dirty look. I flash him a gold American Express card. He makes the drink." Privilege is the shield these characters use to defend their attenuated sensibilities and their right to be left alone.

At times, the writing reaches the name-dropping proficiency of a Judith Krantz. "He's also wearing a bowtie he bought today when we went shopping but I don't remember where it was he bought it. It could have been Paul Stewart or Brooks Brothers or Barney's or Charivari or Armani—somewhere." (The "somewhere" is presumably meant to existentialize the parade of plugs.) Naturally, a narration so obsessed with making the correct purchases must take a rather dim view of those without the means to buy chic things. One of the narrators, relating a night in New York, tells us, "Up on 92nd we sat at a cafe and cursed a waitress. Then taking a cab downtown we got into an argument with our driver and he made us get out. Twenty-ninth Street, hassled by prostitutes. . . . Three in the morning. P.J. Clarke's. [Mitchell] complains the eggs are too runny." There is a raunchy tradition in literature—the young man lurching around the lower depths, short on cash, long on nerve, taking his knocks and writing about it. But here we have an odd afterburn of that once-hot topic—young men and women spending their parents' dough and feeling victimized by the help.

At one point, Mr. Ellis tries to have a character pose and answer the question most readers will have been snarling at the characters from the very beginning: What is wrong with you? "The Talking Heads record was scratched maybe or

perhaps Dad hadn't sent the check yet. That was all this girl was worried about. . . . Other people might not sympathize with this couple's problems and maybe they didn't really matter in the larger realm of things—but they still mattered to Jeff and Susie; these problems hurt them, these things stung."

It remains ambiguous where Mr. Ellis locates his own intelligence in this book. There are flashes of wit that can lead you to suspect he sees and even recoils from the hollowness of the young lives he writes about. One character, for instance, in a snit, decides to "take a crate of singles I own and make sure I have them on tape before I snap them all into two. . . . I kick at the walls on roommate's side." Yet these moments of humor are infrequent. Mr. Ellis has it within his grasp to become a satirist, but for now his method of aping the attitudes of the burnt-out works against him. He seems as passive in his regard of social rot as, say, the editors of *Interview.* Nothing seems to surprise, disturb or even affect him, and though this deadpan effect is surely deliberate and is in large part the reason for Mr. Ellis's popularity and warm critical reception, one closes the book feeling that this time out the author has stumbled over the line separating cool from cold. Where we ought to be saying, "Oh my God, no," we are, instead, saying, "Who cares?"

Steeped in the anticulture of fashion photography and cable television, *The Rules of Attraction* eventually lulls us into a kind of dreary complacency, until we feel we've been sitting in an unkempt little room watching those Hanna-Barbera cartoons his characters relax with—one-dimensional squiggles one stares at not for pleasure but for the memories they vaguely stir about how bored you were the first time you saw them.

David Pan (essay date Summer 1988)

SOURCE: "Wishing for More," in *Telos,* No. 76, Summer, 1988, pp. 143-54.

[*In the following essay, Pan looks at the stylistic features of* Less Than Zero *in relationship to the visual media of television, video and film.*]

The first question which comes to mind in reading Ellis' bestseller, *Less Than Zero,* is "Is Los Angeles really like that?" This astonishment betrays not only the vague feeling that one has somehow missed out on all the action in Los Angeles, but also the compulsion to continue reading in order to experience, at least vicariously, all the sordid details of life in the American "elite." This voyeuristic query fits perfectly into the framework of a book in which the closest thing to a plot is the attempt of Clay, the first person narrator, "to see the worst" and in which the characters continually try to certify the authenticity of their experiences. After watching a snuff film, the characters voice the same concern as the readers:

> "Yeah, I think it's real too," the other boy says, easing himself into the jacuzzi. "It's gotta be."

> "Yeah?" Trent asks, a little hopefully.

> "I mean, like how can you fake a castration? They cut the balls off that guy real slowly. You can't fake that," the boy says.

The voyeuristic impulse which grips the snuff film viewers and forces the question, "Is it real?" is the same impulse which propelled *Less Than Zero* to its bestseller status, fueling suspicions of its essentially trashy novel character. But the question "Is it real?" in addition to revealing the voyeuristic stance of the questioner, also expresses a certain incredulity that the scenes depicted might not be fiction, but reality. *Less Than Zero* might really be a journalistic account. Either way, both the pulp fiction and journalistic qualities of the book tend to disqualify it from being real "literature." Yet, even though it has succeeded as a pulp novel and has become, in its abysmal Hollywood filming, a piece of journalistic evidence for crusaders in the war on drugs, it is clear that *Less Than Zero* is not just pulp fiction or journalism. It is also a critique. Whether this critique is successful hinges on the question constantly haunting critics of culture of how to criticize the banal without becoming it. For the primary reason for studying the products of mass culture is their popularity, and to the extent that critics do not share the enthusiasm of the populace, they are also excluded from a true understanding of the influence and significance of mass culture. The successful critic must both identify with the duped cultural consumer and also maintain a reflective stance. Though unable to achieve a satisfactory solution, *Less Than Zero* does make the attempt.

In the novel, the first person narrator, Clay, continuously high on drugs, alcohol or both, wanders from nightclub to nightclub and party to party, mingling with "blond-haired pretty male models," standing mesmerized before video screens, and sleeping with most anybody, male or female, who seems to take a passing interest in him. He is less a character than a spectator of all that happens to him, passively and indifferently accepting everything around him as if he were watching it on TV. The prose style underlines Clay's virtual lack of individual identity. Though Clay is the first person narrator throughout the novel, his consciousness is at times so inobtrusive that most passages read as if written in the third person. That the reader loses track of the first person narrator in the midst of the action does not merely demonstrate the unreflecting mentality of "Clay" who, presumably faithful to the name, compliantly accepts any situation he happens to find himself in. The indifferent flow of images and events resembles the stream of flat images seen on television. Ellis' prose shares television's drive to continually change the image, to relentlessly keep up the pace of the action, a drive which ultimately debases the image and trivializes the action. Clay's own identity and consciousness is replaced by the string of events which, like the video images before his eyes, he seems to have no control over, and which in the end perhaps entertain for a while, but can never really satisfy. Accordingly, Clay's displays of discontent correspond to the sort of dazed and disgusted feeling one has after having sat in front of the television until three in the morning, and which, if one is like Clay, can quickly be remedied by taking another Valium.

Yet, Clay is not always a passive observer without a conscious perspective of his own. In sharp contrast to this virtual absence of consciousness, Clay at other times demonstrates the same ironic distance which Ellis himself expresses in describing his peers at Bennington College. This attitude becomes obvious in passages where the ironic tone is unmistakable, but at the same time, entirely incompatible with the passive attitude which Clay otherwise displays. Sensing that his MTV prose style threatens to become as banal as MTV itself, Ellis attempts to use such ironic passages to make Clay into a critic. Not only is Clay the example of the passive television viewer who lives his life like he watches a video, he is also the critic of this same attitude, ironically describing the teenagers bathed in images. By combining both perspectives in one character, Ellis attempts an "immanent" critique of mass culture, i.e., from the "inside." This "insider," however, has an implausibly schizophrenic consciousness. Clay as the passive spectator accepts his surroundings as real and submits to their logic, no matter how artificial, distorted, or manipulative. Clay as critic takes the exact opposite tack by completely rejecting through irony the very same object which the spectator so uncritically accepts. Ellis' depiction of Clay as a totally passive media construct takes the logic of the spectator too seriously by denying Clay the participation and feeling which the culture industry manipulates, but never completely eliminates. On the other hand, Clay's rejection of the media world is a failure to take it seriously. The rejection is too facile, as if his critical self could simply erase his voyeuristic self without a trace and his return to an Eastern college at the end of the book could leave "LA decadence" far behind.

Finally, *Less Than Zero*'s deadpan, state-of-the-art "MTV" prose demonstrates a problem which is shared by a specific sector of 1980s American culture, the David Byrne mixture of parody and hip cynicism. A conversation in *Less Than Zero* illustrates the problem:

"Yeah, *Beastman!* that was pretty good," the film student says to me. "See it?"

I nod, looking over at Blair. I didn't like *Beastman!* and I ask the film student, "Didn't it bother you the way they just kept dropping characters out of the film for no reason at all?"

The film student pauses and says, "Kind of, but that happens in real life. . ."

A characteristic of the film which would normally be considered "bad art" acquires new meaning because it turns out to be a characteristic of "bad reality." But whether the film reproduces bad reality because it is simply unconscious of its inadequacy or it is actually trying to parody reality, the film, as well as *Less Than Zero* itself, falls prey to the same problem. In either case, the resort to a reproduction of clichés in reality demonstrates both a lack of inventiveness and a fascination with the inane which numbs one's sense for the healthy. For even as parody, such a film would contribute to the omni-presence of that which it should resist by failing in its representation of reality to present positive aspects and alternatives within the dominant order. As much as the present media environment might testify to the contrary, reality is not merely "less than zero." Positive elements exist as well, both in reality and as not yet fulfilled possibilities. *Less Than Zero's* suppression of those elements is a capitulation before the media's depiction.

Though he never gets beyond a clichéd description of the two extremes of voyeur and critic and his attempt at combining them in Clay fails to illuminate the complexity of the problem, Ellis' attempt at problematizing the relationship between the two attitudes, whether successful or not, demonstrates the present quandary of American media critics. For as Christa Bürger notes, "even in cases where they find themselves in opposition to contemporary society and culture, they see this society and culture simultaneously as a history which they seek to appropriate as their own." These critics attempt to combine the perspectives of the media "voyeur" and the media "critic." The voyeur is fascinated by that which he sees and allows himself to be led along by the images and the action. The engendering of a voyeuristic attitude is the sign of all successful forms of mass culture: e.g., Hollywood movies, network broadcasting and bestseller novels. Their success lies in their ability to indeed tap real desires and needs and give them expression. At the same time their insidiousness lies in their channeling of the expression of these desires into forms which end up preventing their fulfillment. The critic on the other hand remains distant from the images and refuses to become caught up in the fascination. The critic seeks thereby to expose the subjugation which this fascination means for both viewer and viewed alike. But it is precisely the distance of the critic from

the object of criticism which often makes the criticism, on the one hand, unfeeling, and, on the other hand, uninformed. Clay, as ruthless critic of mass media, is certainly guilty of the first charge, and, in spite of his complicity with the captive spectators, voices a critique which is extraordinarily oblivious of their situation. By depicting its characters as totally subsumed within their lifestyle and impossible to differentiate from each other, *Less Than Zero* confirms rather than resists the stereotyped images. But even a critique of mass media which begins as an informed analysis of the spectator often denies the voyeuristic impulse which threatens the analysis. For this analysis has as its basis the same frustrated desire to attain something real which compels the voyeur. The critic after all seeks the "realization" of that which he finds lacking in the object of criticism.

Which brings us back to the question "Is it real?" At first, this question which the boys in *Less Than Zero* pose about the snuff film does not seem to fit into the logic of voyeurism at all. A voyeur is supposed to be so fascinated by the images and the action that the constructedness and artificiality of what is being viewed remain unconsidered and, in the end, irrelevant. So long as the desired effect (emotional high, suspense, excitement, shock, sexual stimulation, thirst, hunger) is achieved in the receiver, the image has been successful, regardless of whether there is any "reality" to the image. This should apply as well to the snuff film as it does to a TV thriller, a Hollywood movie, a Coca-Cola commercial, or a network news broadcast. In all these examples the images are oriented toward drawing in their viewers and riveting their attention, thereby maintaining sales and improving ratings. The question of the reality behind the images is of secondary concern, often times even irrelevant.

For the critic as well, the question of an outside reality does not seem to always be an issue. In *Amusing Ourselves to Death,* Postman argues that the very logic of the video medium, independent of any other outside factors, threatens to destroy the possibility of rational debate and argumentation in practically every area of public society. In Postman's eyes, the video medium dictates the characteristics of that which is shown through it. The emphasis on immediate images, the need to constantly change the images, and the compulsion to pull elements out of their contexts are unavoidable characteristics of television programming. These properties prevent sustained thought on the part of the viewer and even dissolve the fundamental concept of contradiction upon which all logical thinking is based. According to Postman, the inevitable consequence of the rise of the video media has been the deterioration of political debate in the US. As evidence, Postman contrasts the televised debates between Reagan and Mondale in the 1984 presidential elections with the 1858 Lincoln-Douglas debates in Illinois. Whereas the Lincoln-Douglas debates were marked by complex argumentation and positions which could be critically studied and further discussed, the emphasis in the Reagan-Mondale debates was on appearances and on a rhetoric reminiscent of television advertising. Postman contends that the change in the character of political debate is a result of the rise of the electronic media. As clear as the contrast is which Postman demonstrates, the conclusion which he draws fails to penetrate to the core of the problem. Because Postman ascribes such overwhelming power to the video medium and holds the medium itself principally responsible for the deterioration of American politics and education, he never discusses the relationship between the television image and an outside reality, a relationship which is crucial for the role of television images in our society. For as Noam Chomsky has pointed out, the spectators of televised sporting events, for example, are extremely well-informed, intellectually sophisticated, and not at all interested in appearances, but rather in concrete results. "I think this concentration on such topics as sports [wrote Noam Chomsky, in *The Progressive*, July, 1987] makes a certain degree of sense. The way the system is set up there is virtually nothing people can do anyway, without a degree of organization that's far beyond anything that exists now, to influence the real world. They might as well live in a fantasy world, and that's in fact what they do. I'm sure they're using their common sense and intellectual skills, but in an area which has no meaning and probably thrives because it has no meaning. . ." The problem lies not with a medium which in itself leads to the imbecility of its users, but in the structuring of this medium in a way which excludes the populace from participation in debate about real social issues.

Television in the US demonstrates the absence of such active participation. Whatever the viewers might think or do, their thoughts and actions will have virtually no effect upon that which happens on the screen, in "TV land." However, this lack of participation is not caused by the medium itself, but by the current implementation of this medium within a context of decreasing public debate. The lack of active participation on the part of the typical television viewer in fact mirrors and reinforces the lack of active participation within which typical US "citizens" exist within their society. For the fascination of television viewers is predicated upon their boredom, a boredom which is a result of their exclusion from a participatory role, both in the action on the screen and in their society. The failure of society to provide its members with opportunities for active participation—the state and corporate bureaucratization of modern society—leads to a permanent state of boredom which drives a person to turn on the television set. Bureaucratization of society is the precondition for the development and expansion of the culture industry.

But because the television does not offer anything essentially different than a passive relationship to uncontrollable events either, the boredom which turned on the television in the first place constantly threatens to overtake the viewer again while watching. Consequently, the first rule of American television programming is that the images must constantly entertain the viewer to the point where not only the boredom of the viewer's passive position in front of the television is forgotten, but also the initial boredom in society which drove the viewer to buy the television and turn it on in the first place. This obligation to entertain is not inherent to the video medium itself, as Postman argues, but to the specific situation of American television programming, manifesting itself in its most successful forms as an ability to fascinate viewers, turning them into "voyeurs." For what separates a normal "viewer" from a true "voyeur" is this fascination which allows the voyeur to vicariously participate in the images and the action. This participation remains, however, on the level of voyeurism—the fascination functions, on the one hand, as a passive participation of the viewer with the viewed object which, on the other hand, is based upon the viewer's exclusion from a truly active participatory relationship to this same object. The inability of the typical citizen to influence decision-making in society is the prerequisite for the power the image attains by providing a replacement for such true participation. The citizen, frustrated in the attempt to achieve this goal, accepts the artificial media substitute which distracts the viewer from the original desire for participation to such an extent that it is displaced into a desire for spectacles and diversionary entertainment.

This voyeuristic attitude has become so far-reaching that it has overtaken not only the television viewer but also the television critic. Neil Postman directs his criticism against the medium and does not consider the programming at all. According to Postman, the programming itself cannot be successfully criticized because it has no other alternative but to create the fascination which is demanded by the logic of its medium. He compares the advent of television to the invention of the printing press. Both are technological advances which actually change the character of truth, according to Postman's invocation of Marshall McLuhan's slogan, "the medium is the message." In Postman's perspective, if the invention of a written language and the Gutenberg press necessarily made truth into something written, expository, and argumentative instead of oral, mnemonic, and aphoristic, the invention of television has made truth into something necessarily visual, spectacular, and entertaining. At this point, Postman's argument, in its attempt to be a strict analysis of the video medium, demonstrates its own participation in the same passive, voyeuristic attitude which it should be criticizing. Postman's description of the development of human technology from the alphabet to the television set, as well as his excusing of television programming because it is merely obeying the logic of its medium, recalls the same attitude which prevails over the television viewer. By viewing both the development of technology and of television programming as if they were occurring on a screen, totally beyond the control of the viewer, he fails to recognize possibilities for interaction with other aspects of society, possibilities which can radically alter the "logic" of television. He in effect affirms these developments by participating in them in the same passive, fascinated way that voyeurs "participate" vicariously in that which they are watching. In both cases the participation is an affirmation of the object which questions neither the relation of the viewer to the object—Postman himself never mentions the voyeuristic quality of this relationship—nor the extent to which the object both hides and betrays a reality more important than the object itself.

The failure of Postman and the television voyeur to perceive this reality leads in both cases to the assumption that this reality does not exist. With the television voyeur this assumption takes the form of a fascination with the image which considers the question of the reality of this image as either irrelevant or senseless. The level of fascination is the primary interest. With Postman this assumption expresses itself in the belief that truth itself changes according to the medium. "The medium is the message," and there is no reality behind the medium. Hence Postman cannot even conceive of the possibility that television's fascination might be grounded in a reality separate from it—the bureaucratization of modern society.

In spite of such denials, however, the question "Is it real?" continues to recur. For the television viewers, the question is an expression of the inadequacy of the pure image in satisfying their desires. For Postman, who implicitly asks a similar question by undertaking a critique of television at all, this question signals the sense of loss remaining after the disappearance of the message in the medium and the withering of public debate in society. If it were not for this sense of loss, Postman would have to embrace television as the bringer of a new age in truth, and all his humanist worries about a society without political debate would be obsolete concerns from out of the antiquated medium of written language. A critique of television would be senseless because the advent of the video medium would be inevitable and unstoppable, as open to criticism and human decision as the movement of the stars in the sky or, in Postman's perspective, the play of images on the screen.

That Postman senses such a loss in spite of his own argument is to be explained by the fact that the phenomenon he is describing is only a part of a larger process of bureaucratization in American society. But Postman's fascination with the logic of the video medium itself causes him to overlook the social prerequisites for television's exploitation of a passive voyeuristic attitude. It is also this oversight which explains his lame liberal solution to the problem which he sees as being confined to the effects of television. His solution is a change in educational policy which would teach children to be "critical viewers." Postman fails to demand changes in television programming and in the bureaucratic organization of both the television industry and American society in general. He thus demonstrates the same paralyzing despair in the face of the power of technological developments and the bureaucratization of society as the despair which draws the voyeur to the image.

An article in the *New York Times* describing a shootout in Miami between FBI agents and two suspected robbers reported that "A few cars traveling on the street merely slowed and steered around the stalled vehicles as the agents and the robbery suspects exchanged fire. Several witnesses later said they had believed at first they had come across the filming of a scene from the television show *Miami Vice*. Because the witnesses consider reality as if it were an image, the actual shootout is no longer a part of direct experience which has any consequences for those experiencing the event. The motorists could ignore the shooting and steer around just as if it were a television show to be switched off. The stance toward reality becomes a passive one. According to Susan Sontag, whereas "philosophers since Plato" have insisted upon the distinction between image and reality, both a "primitive" sensibility and the "modern" one do without such a distinction. "But the true modern primitivism is not to regard the image as a real thing; photographic images are hardly that real. It is common now for people to insist about their experience of a violent event in which they were caught up—a plane crash, a shoot-out, a terrorist bombing—that 'it seemed like a movie'." As the "Miami Vice" incident demonstrates, Sontag's observation about the transformation of reality into an image is certainly to be taken seriously. The actual development of the video media and the resultant change in the way reality is actually perceived implacably demonstrate that the relationship between image and reality has fundamentally changed since the advent of photographic images. But in her ardor to show that the "powers of photography have in effect de-Platonized our understanding of reality, making it less and less plausible to reflect upon our experience according to the distinction between images and things, between copies and originals," she neglects to develop the distinction between the "primitive" treatment of images as reality and the "modern" treatment of reality as image. For the "primitive," by elevating image to the level of reality, maintains an active relationship to both image and reality and is a participant in both, subject to their influence and able to influence them in turn. An image is not merely an imitation, but an emblem, a talisman, which embodies otherwise unseen powers and which is to be respected as such. The "modern primitive," however, by reducing both reality and image to the level of a TV image, maintains a passive relationship to both reality and image and is a helpless spectator of both. Not only is "Miami Vice" an imitation, but the actual shootout cannot be taken seriously either. Instead of being able to consider both images and thereby also the metaphysical as serious components of a heterogeneous reality, the "modern primitive" reduces everything to the level of impotent images, shorn of any real significance.

This repression of an active relationship to both image and reality eventually feeds into a latent aggression. The resulting violence comes to light in the fascination of the snuff film viewers in **Less Than Zero.** The passive fascination of these viewers at first fits in with the earlier model of alienation from real participation. The viewers embrace a passive voyeuristic stance which robs them of a direct participation in reality. The boy being castrated and the boy watching the castration do not stand in direct relation to each other. It is only the relationship of their roles which influences each of them. The first boy is not being castrated because one particular boy wanted to watch, but because of the general existence of such a desire. He does not ever see the real viewer, but only the camera, an abstraction of this viewer. The boy who watches is not fascinated by the castration of a particular boy, but by the thought of such a thing happening at all. The original castration was an act of violence performed for the benefit of the camera and, ultimately, of the viewers. Once the event is transferred to the screen, it becomes a spectacle and the questions of intervention, practical action, and morality become irrelevant. Instead, the effects of the images on the viewer become the primary concern.

The frightening aspect of this development is that, together with the stimulation which the snuff film viewers in **Less Than Zero** experience in watching the film is a nonchalance which carries over into their reactions to "real" events. The characters discover a dead body in an alley and carry out the gang rape of a 12-year-old girl with the same detached and yet rapt fascination with which they view a film. Not only that, but their actions actually mimic the actions which they originally see on film. Not only does pure stimulation become the primary concern in watching a film, stimulation, not participation, becomes the essential characteristic of all experience. This change in the character of experience leads in turn to a horrifying revision of the meaning of participation for the snuff film viewers. Whereas the television viewer's passive fascination provides a replacement for direct experience, and the underlying longing for a participatory situation is thus forgotten, the snuff film viewers have reached the point where participation has been redefined as subjugation. In this new sense, the snuff film viewers push for more participation. The thrill which accompanies the young boys' hope in **Less Than Zero** that the castration was "real" is the horrifying expression of a desire on the part of the voyeur to stop being a voyeur and become a participant. For if a young boy had truly been castrated in order to make the snuff film, then the voyeurs have the assurance that their collective gaze, by creating the demand for such a castration, actually did have a real effect on that which they see.

The absolute boundary which the screen creates between viewer and viewed, preventing the development of any direct relationship between the two, would have been overcome. But in the case of our snuff film viewers, the breakdown of the absolute boundary between viewer and viewed, far from being the fulfillment of the dream of a participatory democracy, becomes the blueprint for the torture chamber.

The move from passive fascination to active aggression can be traced in the historical development of the forms of mass culture. [Russell] Berman [in *Telos,* Winter 1984-85] has provided a detailed analysis of this development. Without going into details, it will suffice to note that, in the 1980s, the passification which the image once enforced becomes coupled with a simultaneous unleashing of latent aggression. "The increasingly violent character of culture industrial manipulation is evident not only in the bloodlust of films like *Friday the Thirteenth* and *Halloween,* but in the murderous sociability portrayed in daytime soap operas or prime time series (*Dallas, Dynasty*) in contrast with which the television figures of the 1950s and 1960s seem endearing in their naive accounts of humanistic values." What differentiates the snuff film viewer from the previous description of the television viewer is that the television viewer's passive and "naive" identification derives from an empathy with the characters or the action. Such empathy, the most "endearing" aspect of the television viewer, is missing from the snuff film viewer, as it is from the sadist-torturer. *Leave It to Beaver, Friday the Thirteenth,* and the snuff film are stages in a development in which the viewer gains more and more distance from the action—at first totally empathizing with the characters, and by the end deriving only stimulation from the effects of the images. In this development there remains an essential tie between the voyeur who must settle for a vicarious fulfillment of desire and the snuff film viewer who, unsatisfied with vicarious fulfillment, begins to demand a direct participation which takes the form of a violent subjugation. The fulfillment of desire expresses itself as violent aggression. As Berman argues, "the attack on erotic restriction has turned into its opposite: the restriction of eros to universal competitiveness and a weakening of the structures with which eros held thanatos in check. The modernist promise of unlimited pleasure has been realized as a constantly increasing aggressive potential. . ." While Berman here emphasizes the proximity of eros and thanatos—the voyeur and the snuff film viewer—he also relates how this aggressive potential feeds into bureaucratic structures which contain equally destructive impulses.

It turns out, however, that this aggressive potential is also an element of the critic. The element of empathy differentiating the naiveté of the television viewer from the violence of the snuff film viewer, a sign of compassion, was what also caused the television viewers to lose themselves in the television plot in the first place, thereby giving up on social action in reality. The empathy and identification with another's situation, a sign of compassion, leads in this case to both an alienation from one's own situation and a consequent inability to actively criticize this situation. It was precisely this problem against which modernists such as Benjamin and Brecht directed their aesthetics. Through the use of techniques such as montage, distraction, or interruption of dialogue, they sought to break down the identification of the viewer with the characters in order that the viewer might develop a critical stance. But the elimination of identification in the fostering of a critical audience corresponds with the elimination of empathy in the genesis of the snuff film viewer.

This unexpected congruence underlines the fact that the problem of the spectator is twofold and paradoxical. For in both the case of the voyeur and that of the critic, the result is "less than zero." On the one hand, when images become "larger than life," as they do for the voyeur, reality becomes less than the "zero" of the televised image. On the other hand, when the voyeur has no sympathy in the eyes of the critic, the critic's lack of feeling, his cold castration of the voyeur, is even less appealing than the "zero" of the voyeur's passive fascination. But this cold contempt which the critic too often directs against the voyeur, resulting in a cynical despair, is primarily a result of the critic's failure to identify with and encourage those aspects of the voyeur which are not determined by the video medium. Analyses of film and video which do not recognize the primary role of an outside reality for the development and logic of video must remain trapped within the strict dichotomy of spectator and critic. The successful merging of these two poles and the attainment of something more than that which is being presented on the screen can only come about when this basic question concerning video, "Is it real?" is answered with "Of course not. It's only Hollywood."

Peter Freese (essay date 1990)

SOURCE: "Bret Easton Ellis, *Less Than Zero:* Entropy in the 'MTV Novel'?" in *Modes of Narrative,* Königshausen & Neumann, 1990, pp. 68-87.

[In the following essay, Freese contemplates the narrative qualities and social commentary of Less Than Zero.*]*

In 1985, a twenty-year-old Bennington College undergraduate named Bret Easton Ellis published a book which, as rumour has it, he had typed on his bedroom floor in about a month and which he entitled *Less Than Zero.* The young man, who had grown up in Sherman Oaks as the son of a well-to-do real estate analyst, wrote about what he seemed to know well from personal experience: the aimlessness and *angst* of rich Los Angeles youngsters in their hectic world of drugs, casual sex and violence. In a surprisingly short time his lurid tale about "the seamy underside of the preppy handbook" turned into a craze in Los Angeles and a must on many American campuses. The movie rights were secured by independent producer Marvin Worth before the novel had even appeared in the stores, and Penguin Books bought the paperback rights for $100,000. Meanwhile the film has been released, and the book is out in a fast-selling German translation. Ellis has followed his successful debut with a second novel, *The Rules of Attraction* (1987), which the blurb of the paperback edition describes as dealing with "the couplings and capitulations, the dramas and the downfalls of American college life in the 1980s" and which reads like a fictional confirmation of Allan Bloom's crushing diagnosis of contemporary student life in his controversial bestseller *The Closing of the American Mind.*

The reviews of Ellis' first novel were extremely mixed. While one group of critics expressed their outraged rejection of the book's juvenile sensationalism conveyed, as one aggravated reviewer put it, "in the inarticulate style of a petulant suburban punk," another group celebrated the novel as "a weirdly fascinating book" and greeted it as the authentic literary expression of a new generation. However drastically the critical estimations diverged, two statements were frequently repeated: *Less Than Zero* was understood as *The Catcher in the Rye* updated for the eighties, and the slim book was classified as an 'MTV novel.'

> **Quite obviously, *Less Than Zero* is no masterpiece, but, apart from its significance as a cultural document, it deserves closer scrutiny as a narrative which is more artfully structured than a first reading reveals.**
> **—*Peter Freese***

Whereas the first argument can be easily disproved—Ellis' protagonist is definitely no new Holden Caulfield but rather a latter-day male Sally Hayes—the second argument raises some intriguing questions. Has the ubiquitous mass medium of Music Television with its incessant flow of video clips, its devotion to glittering surfaces, its limitation to the immediate present, and the reduction of its 'stories' to the short attention span of contemporary youth really found its verbal equivalent in a new narrative style? Is it feasible to say that "you don't so much read [*Less Than Zero*] as you watch and listen to it unfold"? and is "reading it [. . .] like watching MTV"? Has the young debutante actually managed to develop a new narrative voice geared to the lifestyle and the experiential reality of a particular segment of today's young generation?

Since so far no critic has subjected the supposedly ephemeral novel to the close scrutiny necessary to either confirm or disprove the trendy phrases of hurried reviewers, these questions remain as yet unanswered. And they are difficult to answer because the referential context within which Ellis' novel unfolds combines the hero worship, fashion cults and behavioural codes of a rapidly changing youth culture with the hermetic habits and expressions of an underground drug scene. Consequently, the traditional literary critic has a hard time unravelling the significance of rock lyrics and behavioural or conversational gambits which do not belong to his cultural code and he is too easily tempted to dismiss the laconically understated first-person narration of Ellis' protagonist as just another example of pervasive triviality and cultural decay. Quite obviously, *Less Than Zero* is no masterpiece, but, apart from its significance as a cultural document, it deserves closer scrutiny as a narrative which is more artfully structured than a first reading reveals.

*

"Where are we going?" I asked.
"I don't know," he said. "Just driving." "But this road doesn't go anywhere," I told him.
"That doesn't matter."
"What does?" I asked, after a little while.
"Just that we're on it, dude," he said.

(Bret Easton Ellis, *Less Than Zero*)

The action of *Less Than Zero* can be easily summarized: Clay, an eighteen-year-old freshman, comes back from his first term at a college in New Hampshire to spend his Christmas vacation with his broken-up wealthy family in Los Angeles. During the month he stays in his hometown, he whiles away his time at endless parties and in fashionable restaurants and nightspots, sleeps indiscriminately with the boys and girls that belong to his overprivileged set of bored adolescents, constantly drinks and smokes, sniffs cocaine to get high and takes Valium to come down again, aimlessly drives around sprawling Los Angeles in his expensive car, mindlessly watches television, listens to pop songs on the ubiquitous stereos, and plays senseless games in video arcades. In between he visits his fashionable psychiatrist, who cannot help him, and tries to avoid contact with his parents, with whom he cannot communicate. Clay's frantic search for cheap thrills leads to nothing but boredom and a pervasive sense of anomie and desperation.

Clay's aimless meandering between beach houses in Malibu and extravagant villas in the Hollywood Hills, guarded mansions in Bel Air and expensive bungalows in Palm Springs conveys an image of a world which is characterized by frantic hedonism and pathetic futility. The interchangeable members of his clique turn out to be alienated youths who have nothing to look forward to because they know and own everything. They take their Porsches, BMWs and Mercedes for granted, assume that it is their natural right to go to the most expensive colleges and universities, and have tried every sexual variation and experimented with every available drug. These boys and girls, whose lives revolve around the newest fads, who talk about the state of their suntan with the intensity of theologians discussing God, and whose cultural horizon is confined to current pop songs and movies, are deprived of the stability provided by functioning families. Their parents, divorced or separated, occupied by their passing affairs, intent on their success in the Hollywood industry, and obsessed by their futile attempts at preserving eternal youth, have no time for and no interest in their children, have never provided them with a functioning value system, and try to absolve themselves of their responsibility by generously writing cheques. Consequently, their children enjoy every privilege money can buy, but their anarchic liberty is tainted by rootlessness and the complete absence of any sense of belonging. For all the young drifters contact with their dealer is much more important than any other relationship. Human decency and care are unknown factors in this world of drug-induced euphoria, and the ever-changing partners for both hetero-and homosexual sex are either shown off as status symbols or simply used as objects of instant gratification.

The young men and women with their well-tanned bodies and stylish clothes pretend to themselves and others that they are rebels against the money-orientated life of their parents. But they are rebels without a cause, who shy away from bodily labour, intellectual exertion and emotional commitment alike and who act out their phony rebellion by spending the money of those they pretend to despise. All they finally manage to effect is their physical and psychological self-destruction through drugs and prostitution, and thus it turns out that although they appear to have everything, they really have "less than zero."

Clay's dealer Rip, for example, who had earlier complained that "there's not a whole lot to do anymore", tries to get some new 'kick' by drugging and sexually abusing a twelve-year-old girl in the most sadistic fashion. When Clay half-heartedly remonstrates that this is not right, Rip states, "If you want something, you have the right to take it. If you want to do something, you have the right to do it"; he dismisses Clay's objection that he has everything with the plaintive assertion: "I don't have anything to lose". Young Alana, who has just gone through an abortion, knowledgeably confides in Clay, "I think we've all lost some sort of feeling". Lindsay reports to his exhilarated peers "how he hasn't met anyone for the past four months who's over nineteen", and Kim tells Clay that she had thought her mother was in England but she recently read in *Variety* that she is actually in Hawaii. Julian, the spoilt youngster with his expensive Porsche who peddles drugs to children to finance his costly habit, ambiguously observes, "I'm just so sick of dealing with people", and Clay, after looking for new records in a well-stocked store, comes to the realization, "I don't find anything I want that I don't already have".

These statements illustrate a lifestyle which is both repellent and pitiable. They demonstrate that, as a cultural document about the consequences of affluence and permissiveness, the ceaseless search for success and the influence of sensation-seeking mass media, *Less Than Zero* is a frightening admission of social failure. To cultural critics of shirt-sleeved free enterprise the novel offers devastating proof of their charges, and it strikingly illustrates Neil Postman's thesis that we are amusing ourselves to death in our mendacious age of show business.

*

"The young Americans [. . .] have abandoned all concealment; and when they are most themselves, nearest to their central concerns, turn frankly to Pop forms—[. . .] they choose the genre most associated with exploitation by the mass media: notably, the Western, Science Fiction and Pornography."

(Leslie Fiedler, "Cross the Border— Close That Gap: Post-Modernism")

Considered as a 'literary' text, Ellis' novel appears to be a rather artless tale, which makes use of the genuinely American tradition of vernacular first-person narration, employs the elementary storyline of a chronological sequence of events in the form of a loosely structured urban picaresque, and limits itself to a simple concatenation of brief narrative passages and extended dialogues rendered in direct speech. The reader's initial impression of formlessness and contingency is underscored by the fact that the 208 pages of the novel are divided into 108 very short chapters with an average length of less than two pages. These chapters are obviously geared to the limited attention span of both the drug-impaired narrator himself and the readers he addresses. Each chapter presents a self-sufficient slice-of-life, a short 'take,' as it were, defined in space and time and unfolding as a visible action, with the available 'actions' limited to partying, watching television, driving around, taking drugs, having sex, eating out, and talking at cross purposes. The chapters often switch abruptly from one place and time of action to another, and as it is up to the reader to connect them, they provide the necessary orientation by opening with exact temporal and/or spatial pointers like "it's two in the morning and hot and we're at the Edge" or "I'm sitting in

my psychiatrist's office the next day". Thus the outward pattern of the novel might well be compared to the rapid sequence of video clips as they abruptly and unceasingly follow each other on Music Television.

> **Considered as a 'literary' text, Ellis' novel appears to be a rather artless tale, which makes use of the genuinely American tradition of vernacular first-person narration, employs the elementary storyline of a chronological sequence of events in the form of a loosely structured urban picaresque, and limits itself to a simple concatenation of brief narrative passages and extended dialogues rendered in direct speech.**
> —*Peter Freese*

Behind the artless surface of Clay's fast-paced tale, however, lies a structure that provides the novel with some unexpected coherence and additional meaning. Ellis makes his eighteen-year-old protagonist tell his story in the present tense. This strategy is meant to enhance the immediacy and confessional urgency of Clay's tale. While it certainly achieves the desired effect, it necessarily deprives the story of historical depth and disconnects Clay's frantic present from the past which alone could help to explain it. Such a lack of continuity characterizes the hedonistic existence of all the novel's actors with their hectic search for instant gratification, and thus Ellis' choice of narrative tense turns out to be an appropriate formal correlative of his *sujet*. But obviously Ellis knows that a novel is supposed to deal with life in its developmental unfolding, and he achieves at least some semblance of temporal depth by presenting 12 of his 108 chapters as 'memory' chapters which deal with selected aspects of Clay's earlier life. In deference to the uninitiated reader, these chapters, which necessarily use the past tense, are printed in italics and thus made immediately recognizable as 'inserts' providing some explanatory material which the reader has to relate to the present state of affairs. These chapters also announce their function by opening with temporal pointers like "during the end of my senior year" or "last summer". They deal with "the way things were" and thereby conjure up some vague image of a time when the family was still intact—with the grandparents alive, the parents not yet separated, and Clay's love affair with Blair still flourishing. But the 'memory' chapters are already suffused with ominous signs and intimations of bad things to come. They thus serve the double function of providing a foil against which to understand Clay's present malaise and of offering some tentative explanation why an erstwhile happy youth has turned into a passive wreck haunted by disorientation, anxiety and despair.

While the outwardly unstructured sequence of chapters in the present tense turns out to be the appropriate formal equivalent of the fact that in spite of all the actors' hectic activities nothing significant can happen in their lives, the twelve interspersed 'memory' chapters in the past tense suggest a historical dimension and introduce a developmental aspect into the novel. Of course, this rather superficial attempt at a point-and-counterpoint structure is hardly a great achievement, but it points to a group of structural strategies which are meant to translate a sequence of chapters merely added to one another into a causally unfolding whole and which therefore deserve a detailed investigation.

On closer scrutiny, the dizzying spiral of Clay's desperate search for pleasure and diversion in the metropolitan purgatory of *ennui* and *angst* reveals some inner logic. This logic depends on the two strands of the novel's kaleidoscopic action which are concerned with the gradual breakup of Clay's relationship with his girlfriend Blair and with his witnessing the development of his erstwhile school friend Julian into a drug addict and male prostitute. The loss of the only person Clay felt close to and the frightening decline of his best friend constitute the two strands which dominate the action of the novel. Although these strands are often interrupted and superseded by other events, they provide the threads which keep the action together and give the four weeks of Clay's life to which **Less Than Zero** is limited some coherence and meaning. Thus, it is no accident that at the very beginning of the novel Clay is picked up at LAX by Blair and that the first thing he finds in his room is a message from Julian asking him to phone back. And thus it is equally logical that the last conversation he has before leaving is his 'final' talk with Blair and that the last important event during his holiday is his witnessing of Julian's degradation.

Since it would go against the grimly 'cool' attitude sported by Clay and his group to discuss personal problems in detail and to show true feelings openly, the ritualistically understated verbal and gestural delivery of both the narrator and the novel's actors prevents the real issues of the book from being expressed directly. Consequently, the reader has to proceed on mere hints and oblique clues. It is against this background that Ellis artfully employs a set of iterative images and muted references to make his point. Here again an analogy to the video clips of MTV and the patterns of rock lyrics proves helpful, because these iterative images work like the refrains of songs and convey their messages through repetition and variation.

The opening sentence of the novel—"People are afraid to merge on freeways in Los Angeles"—an observation made by Blair which "stays in [Clay's] mind for an uncomfortably long time" and occupies him for reasons he cannot name, is an outstanding example of Ellis' associative technique. Given a prominent position at the very beginning of the novel, the sentence is soon repeated verbatim and then taken up again with "on freeways in Los Angeles" left out. Thus, right at the beginning, the conversational remark about people's behaviour in traffic turns into a general comment on the human situation—"people are afraid to merge"—and thereby assumes a more general significance. When Blair drops Clay at his house, "nobody's home" (*ibid.*): his mother and sisters have gone shopping instead of waiting for him on his first return from an eastern college. They are "afraid to merge," and when Clay goes to his room in the empty house, it is small wonder that he "still can hear that people are afraid to merge and tr[ies] to get over the sentence, blank it out".

Seven short chapters later, Clay is returning from a shopping trip with his mother and sisters and listening to their gossip. Talking about a young man, they mention that his house is for sale, and the older sister nastily remarks, "I wonder if he's for sale". For the moment, this is just a passing slanderous remark, but two chapters later Clay, sitting in a restaurant, feels he is being stared at by a stranger and comments, "all I can think is either he doesn't see me or I'm not here. I don't know why I think that. People are afraid to merge. *Wonder if he's for sale*". Here two hitherto unrelated observations are brought together and suddenly acquire a new meaning. The general comment about people's fear to communicate and the nasty quip about a young man's sexual availability for money are applied to a stranger whose insistent stare Clay interprets as an attempt to make a pass at him. In connection these statements render the insight that people might try to buy sexual contact unencumbered by personal commitment for the very reason that they are afraid to 'merge.' Two chapters later, Clay stops at a traffic light on Sunset Boulevard and sees a billboard. "All it says is 'Disappear Here' and even though it's probably an ad for some resort, it still freaks me out a little". In the context established so far, the slogan 'Disappear Here' can be understood as referring back to Clay's observation under the gaze of the staring stranger that possibly "I'm not here", and while the link is yet rather tentative, it soon becomes obvious.

A few days later, a sleepless Clay thinks "about the billboard on Sunset and the way Julian looked past me at Cafe Casino". By now he has not only heard nasty comments about Julian's state but has also met him without being able to find out from his strangely reluctant friend what his message had been about. He has deduced from Julian's behaviour and his way of avoiding eye-contact that his unrevealed problems might have to do with his drug addiction and that he might already be selling himself to acquire the money for his habit. The probability of such a development—and this is another of Ellis' strategies—is obliquely insinuated when Julian tells Clay that he has been to a Tom Petty concert and heard him sing a former favourite song of theirs—*"Straight into darkness, we went straight into darkness, out over that line"*.

Thus, the different and initially unrelated images can begin to coalesce when Clay spends Christmas Eve with his embarrassed parents in an expensive restaurant. Bored by the phony familiarity of the two strangers claiming to be his parents and "semistoned" on cocaine, he falls into an associative reverie: "I think about Blair alone in her bed stroking that stupid black cat and the billboard that says 'Disappear Here' and Julian's eyes and wonder if he's for sale and people are afraid to merge" (*ibid.*). Here, then, Clay thinks about his former girlfriend Blair with whom he would like to 'merge,' and about Julian who might be "for sale," that is, willing to 'merge' for money because he has gone "straight into darkness," crossed "that line" of drug addiction and therefore is well on his way towards 'disappearing here.'

A few days later, Clay is lying listlessly on the beach and staring "out at the expanse of sand that meets the water, where the land ends. Disappear here". By now the clever advertising slogan has assumed crucial significance and turned into an obsessive concern for Clay. And when one relates the young man's unhappy stare into nothingness to one of the mottos of the novel, a quotation from a Led Zeppelin song that reads "There's a feeling I get when I look to the West. . . ," the extent of Clay's hopelessness becomes painfully obvious. Walt Whitman, "facing west from California's shores," could still seek "what is yet unfound" and speculate about "the circle almost circled"; a century later the heroine of Thomas Pynchon's *The Crying of Lot 49,* a novel about the Californian subcultures of the sixties, was sustained by her belief in "some principle of the sea as redemption for Southern California" in spite of her recognition that the American Dream had turned into a nightmare. For Clay, however, the traditional promise of westward expansion has completely evaporated. Having substituted the last, the inner frontier to be reached only on drug-induced 'trips,' for the vanished frontier of the West, all he can see is an "expanse of sand that meets the water" and all he can think of is "Disappear Here".

After the combination of 'disappearing' and being 'for sale' has been mentioned once more and is thus kept alive even for the undiscerning reader, the cluster of images gains its final impact in the two crucial scenes which deal with Julian's downfall. Driven by his "need to see the worst", Clay accompanies his friend to a hotel to watch a stranger make love to Julian: "The man rolls Julian over. *Wonder if he's for sale.* I don't close my eyes. You can disappear here without knowing it". This is the ultimate degradation brought about by the need for drugs. Julian's 'disappearing' into the abyss of sexual exploitation, his self-betrayal through prostitution and the loss of his human dignity graphically illus-

trate what happens when one goes "*straight into darkness, out over that line*". A little later on the same day, Julian makes a final and desperate attempt to rebel against his drug-dealing pimp. But cynical Finn, on whose desk stands "this glass paperweight with a small fish trapped in it, its eyes staring out helplessly", knows his power and easily quenches his employee's rebellion by giving him an injection: "Disappear Here. The syringe fills with blood. [. . .] Wonder if he's for sale. People are afraid to merge. To merge". By now the three originally unrelated phrases about disappearing, being for sale and fearing to merge have acquired manifold meanings through repetition and variation within different contexts. By simply combining them Clay can express his terror and despair about the hopelessness of a self-destructive generation suffocating on the terrible combination of spiritual poverty and material abundance.

But this does not end Ellis' artful manipulation of his few simple but effective images. When Clay meets Blair for a last time before his return to the East, their meeting takes place in a restaurant on Sunset. And while Blair takes her former boyfriend to account for his negligent behaviour, "I look at her, waiting for her to go on, looking up at the billboard. Disappear Here". On the surface, Clay will soon follow the injunction of the advertising slogan and 'disappear'—"After I left" are the final words of the novel—but on a metaphorical level he has 'left' long ago by withdrawing into the narcissistic no-man's-land of drug-induced apathy and self-pity. Ellis obliquely conveys this fact by making Blair reproach her former boyfriend that "it was like you weren't there. [. . .] You were never there".

From Clay's casual comment on a stranger's stare at the beginning of the novel—"either he doesn't see me or I'm not here"—to the book's final scene in which "for one blinding moment [Clay] see[s] [him]self clearly" and the person closest to him charges him with never being there, he has been afraid to 'merge,' has run away from the risks and problems of human companionship and 'disappeared' into the dream world of cocaine and the false security of tranquillizers. The billboard slogan, then, supposedly advertising "some resort," proves true in an unexpected way. Functioning like the refrain of a pop song to which some new meaning accrues after every stanza, it sums up the cowardly retreat of Clay and his clique into the escape world of drugs and 'kicks,' their withdrawal from a socially useful and fulfilled existence into "some resort" of their sick imagination. It proves a highly effective strategy of providing the understated and scarcely verbalized problems of the rather incoherent narrator and his peers with some deeper meaning.

Another variation of the point-and-counterpoint strategy is Ellis' use of a background of ominous signs and catastrophes serving as a foil against which to evaluate the hectic foreground activities of Clay and his friends. Coming home, the first thing Clay sees are some workmen "lifting the remains of palm trees that have fallen during the winds". This is an early and as yet inconspicuous reminder of the ubiquity of death and decay, which is taken up when Clay reminisces about the old house in Palm Springs as full of "empty beer cans that were scattered all over the dead lawn and the windows that were all smashed and broken". In the nocturnal silence of the Hollywood hills Clay can "hear the sound of coyotes howling and dogs barking and palm trees shaking in the wind up in the hills" (pp. 62f.). Time and again there are passing references to the "damage the storm caused", the sudden torrential rains that wash houses down, the fact that cats cannot be let out at night because "there's a chance that the coyotes will eat them", or someone finding "a rattlesnake floating" in his swimming pool. Nature cannot be domesticated and will lash back at the thoughtless humans who exploit and ruin it. An earthquake is the most obvious reminder of the fact that Los Angeles is situated on the San Andreas Fault and that the pleasure-seeking activities of its rich denizens are a dance on the volcano.

But society is also in a state of threatening unrest and imbalance. When Clay and Rip have a talk about the quality of their suntans, "an old woman, holding an umbrella, falls to her knees on the other side of the street". On their way to yet another party, the young drifters "pass a poor woman with dirty, wild hair and a Bullock's bag sitting by her side full of yellowed newspapers. She's squatting on a sidewalk by the freeway"—by the freeway, that is, on which people are afraid to 'merge.' When the clique goes to the City Cafe, "there's an old man in ragged clothing and an old black hat on, talking to himself, standing in front and when we pull up, he scowls at us". Shopping-bag ladies, loitering bums and elderly people breaking down in the streets are a constant reminder of poverty and misery, pain and illness; and throughout the novel one hears ambulances passing by and police sirens howling in the distance.

Clay remembers driving around Palm Springs and coming upon "a Toyota parked at this strange, crooked angle, its hood open, flames pouring out of the engine," and for a long time he has "these visions of a child, not yet dead, lying across the flames, burning". This is when he starts collecting newspaper clippings about violent accidents, sadistic cruelties, and brutal crimes. He collects "a lot of clippings [. . .] because, I guess, there were a lot to be collected". This aspect of a society driven by violence and brutality is obvious in the novel. The pornographic activities of Clay's clique find their equivalent in the daily crime statistics of Los Angeles. When Clay buys some magazines, "the checkout clerk is talking about murder statistics"; when the family comes home from their expensive Christmas dinner, "on Little Santa Monica, a car lays overturned, its windows broken"; when Rip and Clay drive along winding Mulholland, Rip gleefully points out "the number of wrecked cars at the bottom of the

hill"; and before Clay leaves his hometown, he coolly enumerates the following incidents:

> Before I left, a woman had her throat slit and was thrown from a moving car in Venice; a series of fires raged out of control in Chatsworth, the work of an arsonist; a man in Encino killed his wife and two children. Four teenagers, none of whom I knew, died in a car accident on Pacific Coast Highway.

All through the novel, then, there are constant reminders of natural catastrophes and disasters, of violent crimes and terrible accidents, of old age, illness and death. They conjure up the general state of a society divided into the obscenely rich and the unspeakably poor and provide the overall background against which the hedonistic dance of pleasure and withdrawal of Clay and his clique has to be seen.

*

> "For Los Angeles, more than any other city, belongs to the mass media. What is known around the nation as the L.A. Scene exists chiefly as images on a screen or TV tube, as four-color magazine photos, as old radio jokes, as new songs that survive only a matter of weeks."

(Thomas Pynchon, "A Journey Into the Mind of Watts")

Of crucial importance to a better understanding of the youngsters' thoughtlessness and inconsideration, their ruthless pursuit of pleasure, and their violence and inhumanity is the formative influence exerted upon them by the ubiquitous mass media devoted to the lurid, the sensational, the gruesome and the horrible in their cynical attempt to reach a surfeited audience. As early as 1961, Philip Roth observed that "the American writer in the middle of the 20th century has his hands full in trying to understand, and then describe, and then make *credible* much of the American reality" and complained that "the actuality is continually outdoing our talents, and [that] the culture tosses up figures almost daily that are the envy of any novelist." A few years later Bruce Jay Friedman spoke of "a fading line between fantasy and reality," stated that *The New York Times* with its daily reports on the most unbelievable events had become "the source and fountain and bible of black humour," and concluded that a writer who wanted to reach a "surprise-proof generation" needed to use a "new, one-foot-in-the-asylum style of fiction" to catch the attention of his audience.

These observations certainly apply to **Less Than Zero,** and whoever thinks that Ellis' novel is given to undue exaggerations just needs to read the *Los Angeles Times* to learn better. The list of drugs consumed by Clay and his friends offers a faithful replica of the existing drug scene and testifies to the fact that in Hollywood "the white kid digs hallucination simply because he is conditioned to believe so much in escape, escape as an integral part of life, because the white L.A. Scene makes accessible to him so many different forms of it." Then too, the countless references to films, television plays, video clips and pop songs conjure up an actual youth culture with its hectic media events. The general atmosphere evoked by these references is one of abandonment, revolt and brutality, even bestiality, of a vicarious release of aggression and sadistic urges through fantasies of violence and pornography, and of an all-pervasive ecstasy of doom and destruction.

> **. . . whoever thinks that Ellis' novel is given to undue exaggerations just needs to read the *Los Angeles Times* to learn better. The list of drugs consumed by Clay and his friends offers a faithful replica of the existing drug scene . . .**
> **—*Peter Freese***

Clay's thirteen- and fifteen-year-old sisters habitually watch "porno films on the Betamax". Clay buys porno magazines, and his aroused clique gleefully watch a sadistic blue movie and agree that the mutilations and castrations it shows must be "real" because somebody "paid fifteen thousand for it". Kim and Blair insist on going to a movie "about this group of young pretty sorority girls who get their throats slit and are thrown into a pool," but bored Clay watches "just the gory parts". Pornography, then, is ubiquitous: Rip's sadistic violation of a twelve-year-old girl is just his individual acting out of the media events to which he is constantly exposed; and the animalization of humans which results from this exposure is graphically illustrated when Clay says about one of the girls waiting to be admitted to a nightclub that she "stares at me and smiles, her wet lips, covered with this pink garish lipstick, part and she bares her upper teeth like she was some sort of dog or wolf, growling, about to attack".

On the car radio a group called "Killer Pussy" sings a song entitled "Teenage Enema Nurses in Bondage", and when Clay's outraged mother asks whether they have to hear this, her under-age daughters insist on listening to it. At a concert of The Grimsoles, the singers throw live rats out into the audience. One day Clay wakes up to a song entitled "Artificial Insemination", and he frequently listens to songs like "Do You Really Want to Hurt Me?", "Hungry Like the Wolf" or "Tainted Love". The Clash sing about "Somebody Got Murdered"; and at a party everybody expectantly waits for the songs "Sex and Dying in High Society" and "Adult Books" to be performed. A video bootleg of *Indiana Jones and the Temple of Doom* is traded for high prices (pp. 34, 90). Other films or TV plays referred to are *Alien, The In-*

vasion of the Body Snatchers, Beastman!, Star Raider, War of the Worlds, The Twilight Zone, and "the new *Friday the 13th* movie". Even the video games with which Clay and his friends while away their time seem only to "deal with beetles and bees and moths and snakes and mosquitoes and frogs drowning and mad spiders eating large purple video flies [. . .] and the images are hard to shake off". Small wonder, then, that when somebody disappears in Bel Air there are hysterical speculations about "some kind of monster, [. . .] a werewolf"; that Spit, who wears "a skull earring," assures a friend, "You know I don't keep dead animals in my room anymore"; and that Rip "carries a plastic eyeball in his mouth". The unceasing onslaught of outrageous science-fiction horrors and ever more violent pornography has made people callous and insensitive. A "huge green skull leering at drivers from a billboard on Sunset, hooded, holding a pyx, bony fingers beckoning" advertises some new 'kick'; "little girls" sing about an earthquake in Los Angeles and announce "*My surfboard's ready for the tidal wave* [. . .] *Smack, smack, I fell in a crack* [. . .] *Now I'm part of the debris*". When Clay, whose first action is to switch on MTV whenever he is alone, refers in passing to "a video on cable of buildings being blown up in slow motion and in black and white", or when he enters somebody else's house and finds a girl "watching some movie about cave men" and describes his exit by saying, "Some caveman gets thrown off a cliff and I split" (*ibid.*), the continual presence of images of violence and destruction is quite incidentally evoked as something which everybody takes for granted.

The ubiquitous presence of sensational films and videos that thrive on sadistic violence and all-encompassing destruction, on gruesome fantasies of man-animal transformations and intergalactic warfare, on outrageous sexual abuse and the thrills of a final cataclysm pervades ***Less Than Zero,*** and this presence becomes all the more striking as it stands in absurd contrast to such faddish accessories of wealth as Giorgio Armani sweaters and Calvin Klein jeans, Gucci loafers, Louis Vuitton luggage, and Wayfarers sunglasses. Leslie Fiedler's assertion that the new 'Pop novel' thrives on the genres most associated with exploitation by the mass media, namely the Western, Science Fiction, and Pornography, is fully borne out by Ellis' tale, which makes use of these fields not only as the 'cultural' background to its foreground action, but also as the target of its obliquely presented exposure of social grievances.

*

> "[. . .] she thinks of the Heat Death of the Universe. A logarithmic of those late summer days, [. . .] the heat pressing, bloating, doing violence. The Los Angeles sky becomes so filled and bleached with detritus that it loses all colour and silvers like a mir-

ror, reflecting back the fricasseeing earth. [. . .] She imagines the whole of New York City melting like a Dali into a great chocolate mass, a great soup, the Great Soup of New York."

(Pamela Zoline, "The Heat Death of the Universe")

"What it is is, most of the things we say, I guess, are mostly noise."

(Thomas Pynchon, "Entropy")

It is obvious that the manifold references to a spiritually sick culture and the illnesses it has bred in a sizeable segment of its affluent young generation create a pervasive sense of impending doom, a cataclysmic feeling of last days which Clay and his friends use as an alibi for their refusal to grow up and face reality. This sense of doom is related to the traditional notion of the Christian apocalypse when Clay starts "watching religious programs on cable TV because [he is] tired of watching videos". The first show he sees happens to be especially pertinent to his world because it presents some fervent preachers "talking about Led Zeppelin records, saying that, if they're played backwards, they 'possess alarming passages about the devil'" (*ibid.*). Again, this is no invention of Ellis' but the show depicts an actual record-burning campaign of a Pentecostal group. The programme is ironically related to the novel's action when the worried preacher declares that he will go on fighting satanic rock music since it is detrimental to youth and "the young are the future of this country" (*ibid.*). At another occasion a televangelist promises that Jesus "will come through the eye of that television screen" and thereby involuntarily reveals that even the Christian message has been commercialized and trivialized by the mass media. Clay is desperate enough to wait "for something to happen" (*ibid.*), but, of course, nothing happens; and again it is highly ironic that all the helpless youth can remember are the preacher's words "Let this be a night of Deliverance".

The apocalyptic implications of *Less Than Zero,* however, are only of marginal importance, because Ellis' kaleidoscopic whirl of disparate 'takes' and the iterative images relating them is infused with a competing motif providing his verbal "videos [. . .] flash[ing] by" with some deeper significance. This motif is that of entropy in both its thermodynamic sense of the 'heat death' of the universe and its cybernetic sense of increasing informational attrition. One day, Clay and a friend of his meet the girl Ronnette. She tells them that she had

> this dream, see, where I saw the whole world melt. I was standing on La Cienega and from there I could see the whole world and it was melting and it was just so strong and realistic like. And so I thought,

Well, if this dream comes true, how can I stop it, you know?

On the surface, of course, this is just a drug-induced hallucination, but it so obviously points to the traditional motif of the 'heat death' of the universe that it becomes an indicator of some larger significance. Such an assumption is borne out by many further references. Clay remembers, for example, "last Christmas" in Palm Springs when it was so unbelievably hot that "the metal grids in the crosswalk signs were twisting, writhing, actually melting in the heat" (pp. 68f.). When he witnesses a car accident, he is haunted by a vision of "a kid burning, melting, on the engine". Going out into the oppressive heat, he experiences the sun as "huge and burning, an orange monster", and on another occasion he stands on a hill, "overlooking the smog-soaked, baking Valley and feeling the hot winds returning and the dust swirling at my feet and the sun, gigantic, a ball of fire, rising over it". He reads the paper, "at twilight," and finds "a story about how a local man tried to bury himself alive in his backyard because it was 'so hot, too hot'". And when he hears a harsh and bitter song about Los Angeles, he hallucinates "images of people, teenagers my own age, looking up from the asphalt and being blinded by the sun". At the house of Finn, the pimp, he sees a young surfer dividing his attention between reading the back of a Captain Crunch cereal box and watching *The Twilight Zone* on television, and on the huge screen "Rod Serling's staring at us and tells us that we have just entered The Twilight Zone and though I don't want to believe it, it's just so surreal that I know it's true".

It is a genuine achievement of Ellis' novel that its whirl of interrelated 'clips' is so surreal that it achieves the frightening impact of authenticity and truth. It is a world in which, in a fashionable nightspot, someone has "written 'Help Me' over and over in red crayon on the table in a childish scrawl", thus revealing the amount of loneliness and despair behind the glittering facade of mindless pleasure; in which the vanity numberplates of rich people's cars read "CLIMAXX" and "DECLINE", thus achieving a significance their owners are probably unaware of; and in which bathroom graffiti spell out "Gloom Rules"—such a world has already entered the 'twilight zone' of chaos and inertia, in which the available energy has been spent and the entropy of the system is moving towards a maximum. Therefore, the atmosphere which pervades *Less Than Zero* is not that of apocalypse, that is, of an impending Last Judgment which will bring both death and rebirth, an end and a new beginning, but that of entropy with its irreversible movement towards final chaos and decay.

On the informational level, as worked out by Shannon and Brillouin, popularized by Wiener and brilliantly put to literary use by Thomas Pynchon, the concept of entropy as a gradual reduction of communicable information is also implemented in Ellis' novel. The numerous dialogues between Clay and his friends never become a real exchange of ideas or opinions. They constitute frightening examples of the speechlessness of an almost autistic generation living in a world in which true meaning has long been buried under the relentless onslaught of never-ceasing 'information.' The entropic movement from diversity to similarity, from difference to sameness is strikingly illustrated by the uniformity and interchangeability of the young people.

In Clay's circles, one of the most important prerequisites for being 'in' is the correct tan: Blair's U.S.C. friends, "all tan and blond", Blair's father's boyfriend, who is "really young and blond and tan", Clay's father, who is "completely tan and has had a hair transplant", Dimitri, who "is really tan and has short blond hair", and Clay himself, who comes back from the East looking "pale" and quickly decides that he "need[s] to work on [his] tan"—anybody who wants to be accepted has to have the correct complexion. When Clay goes to a party, he comments, "There are mostly young boys in the house and they seem to be in every room and they all look the same: thin, tan bodies, short blond hair, blank look in the blue eyes, same empty toneless voices, and then I start to wonder if I look exactly like them". Of course, he does. The similarity and interchangeability of the standardized youths is not only another indication of the failure of their phony revolt in the name of liberation from social pressures, but also the sign of a far advanced entropic movement from difference to sameness. On a deeper level, then, the frantic punk-yuppie-video hunt for instant pleasure on a volcano that can erupt any moment, under a sun which is a gigantic "ball of fire" and "an orange monster" threatening to melt the whole world, is revealed as a last desperate exertion before the final and imminent onset of maximum entropy and the appearance of the ultimate chaos of inertia.

In Thomas Pynchon's *Gravity's Rainbow* there is a reference to "those emptying days brilliant and deep, especially at dawn, with blue shadows to seal its passage, to try to bring events to Absolute Zero," which occurs in the first book entitled "Beyond the Zero." With Pynchon one can safely assume that this is a reference to Walther Hermann Nernst's Third Law of Thermodynamics, concerning the zero entropy to be achieved at a temperature of absolute zero which, however, one cannot reach. With Ellis, however, the "Zero" appears to be just a metaphor of ultimacy indicating that the irresistible movement from distinction and differentiation to sameness and interchangeability has run its course, that an irreversible and universal 'merging' other than the desirable one of human interaction is about to occur, and that the energy necessary for survival is on the verge of 'disappearing here.'

It is in this context that the novel's title achieves its metaphorical significance, which is underscored by a fact which is not mentioned but which the youthful reader is expected to know. In his room Clay has "the promotional poster for an old Elvis Costello record [. . .] on the wall above [his] bed". This record is one of the most successful songs Costello ever produced, namely, "Less Than Zero." The novel's title, then, is an unacknowledged quotation, and its allusion to a song by a leading representative of the British punk and new wave explosion is another indication that Ellis' referential context is not that of 'mainstream' literature but of contemporary pop culture. Costello's song refers to "Mr Oswald with his swastika tattoo" and obliquely relates President Kennedy's assassination to general social decay by stating that "Mr Oswald said he had an understanding with the law / He said he heard about a couple living in the USA / He said they traded in their baby for a Chevrolet." The refrain of the song reads:

> Turn out the TV,
> No one of them will suspect it.
> Then your mother won't detect it,
> So your father won't know.
> They think that I got no respect,
> But every film means less than zero.

Costello's song, then, conjures up the very atmosphere of a world violently out of joint and drifting towards ultimate chaos, filled with the ubiquitous 'noise' of the mass media and pervaded by a desire for the release of death, which also pervades *Less Than Zero.* Consequently, the novel's title is a programmatic statement which places the book within the wider context of a youthful punk and rock revolt.

*

> "The facts even when beaded on a chain, still did not have real order. Events did not flow. The facts were separate and haphazard and random even as they happened, episodic, broken, no smooth transitions, no sense of events unfolding from prior events."
>
> (Tim O'Brien, *Going After Cacciato*)

When Salinger's Holden Caulfield declared his rebellion against a "phony" adult world in the name of the few things he considered "nice," his position constituted a psychologically believable stance in spite of his adolescent obfuscation. This is why a whole young generation could identify with him and venerate him as their spokesman. With Ellis' Clay, however, the situation is different. Paul Gray was certainly right when he observed in his *Time* review that Ellis' "efforts to distance Clay, the narrator, from all the other zombies is unsuccessful" and that "ultimately, Ellis' novel is anchored to a hero who stands for nothing." Clay is bound to remain an unconvincing character because his creator's choice of the present tense deprives him of historical depth and results in a complete lack of narrative distance between Clay's behaviour as 'experiencing I' and his stance as 'narrative I.' Moreover, there is a disturbing tension between his languidly understated, indifferent and drug-impaired registering of his and his clique's meaningless life on the one hand and the rare instances in which he achieves the distance necessary for meaningful narration on the other. Admittedly, he has, rather inexplicably, mustered enough energy to leave his group and attempt a new beginning at an eastern college, he is content with 'only' sniffing cocaine and has not yet "mainlined"; he chides Rip for his sadistic behaviour, cannot stand the pornographic movie to its cruel end, and rejects the invitation to rape the drugged girl. His recurring crying fits are obviously meant to indicate that he is conscious of his malaise, and in the end he knows that "it was time to go back. I had been home a long time". But the tension between his unprepared assertions of self-recognition—"the sun bursts into my eyes and for one blinding moment I see myself clearly"—and his immediately adjacent expressions of indifference and inertia—"Nothing makes me happy. I like nothing"—remains unresolved, and he never assumes the stature of a rounded personality.

Such shortcomings are typical of a first novel and are the necessary corollaries of the narrative perspective chosen by Ellis. Nevertheless, *Less Than Zero* is not only an expressive cultural document but also an accomplished narrative. It authentically expresses the lifestyle of a generation nourished on the ubiquitous products of a sensation-bent entertainment industry, a generation in love with the violent and rebellious music of rock and punk, conversant with the escapist underground culture of drugs, abandoned by their pleasure-hunting, success-orientated and irresponsible parents, and haunted by a sense of impending doom. *Less Than Zero,* then, is no *Catcher in the Rye* of the eighties. But the unwarranted comparison can alert us to the enormous and frightening changes that have occurred in the less than four decades between the appearance of Salinger's and Ellis' novels. And despite the reviewers' rash assertions, *Less Than Zero* is no 'MTV novel,' a genre which due to the differences between visual and verbal texts will remain impossible. But it is a tale which manages to translate the fast-paced urgency, the total lack of historical awareness, the additive impact and the macabre glitter of musical television into narrative strategies which deserve to be taken seriously as expressions of a contemporary lifestyle and indications of future literary developments.

Nicki Sahlin (essay date Fall 1991)

SOURCE: "'But This Road Doesn't Go Anywhere': The

Existential Dilemma in *Less Than Zero,*" in *Critique,* Vol. 33, No. 1, Fall, 1991, pp. 23-42.

[*In the following essay, Sahlin considers Ellis's* Less Than Zero *in the existential tradition of writers such as Franz Kafka, Albert Camus, Jean-Paul Sartre, Ernest Hemingway and F. Scott Fitzgerald.*]

In *Less Than Zero* (1985), Bret Easton Ellis joins the tradition of Hollywood writers who have been capitalizing on southern California, its landscape, and its lifestyle for more than fifty years. That group includes writers such as Nathanael West, James M. Cain, Raymond Chandler, and, more recently, Joan Didion and John Gregory Dunne. Hollywood has long served as a setting for fiction that reveals the corruption lurking behind glamorous lifestyles or, in the case of crime and detective novels, the intrigue and masquerade so suited to a city whose business is a form of deception. By the time Joan Didion published *Play It As It Lays* (1970), the Hollywood tradition had dispensed with a large portion of the glitter, moving toward heavier doses of cynicism, which Didion parlayed into her own brand of existentialism or even nihilism. Yet even as early as Nathanael West's *The Day of the Locust* (1939), "the absurdist tradition" was putting down roots in Hollywood, and, for the next few decades, major novelists hired as screenwriters were expressing their disillusion in "nihilistic novels which have made the Hollywood antimyth a permanent part of our national folklore." [Mark Royden Winchell, 1984.] By now, Hollywood has a fifty-year history as a setting for varying levels of disillusionment and various kinds of revelation, and existentialist readings of Hollywood novels are to some degree inevitable.

> *Less Than Zero,* **narrated in deadpan style by an eighteen-year-old named Clay, takes its place in the Hollywood scenario so naturally, with the book's overprivileged cast of characters playing their roles so convincingly, that reviewers have regarded the book as no more than an adolescent novel, an updated version of *The Catcher in the Rye* that just happens to take place on the West Coast rather than the East.**
> —*Nicki Sahlin*

Less Than Zero, narrated in deadpan style by an eighteen-year-old named Clay, takes its place in the Hollywood scenario so naturally, with the book's overprivileged cast of characters playing their roles so convincingly, that reviewers have regarded the book as no more than an adolescent novel, an updated version of *The Catcher in the Rye* that just happens to take place on the West Coast rather than the East.

Perhaps because of the author's youth—Ellis was just twenty-one at the time of the novel's publication—reviewers have treated the book as if it were a quasi-fictional rendition of Ellis's personal history and have labeled its author a member of the "brat pack," a specialist in "the lifestyles of the young and naughty." That these lifestyles might have been consciously shaped by the author and might have symbolic or philosophical implications are possibilities that were hardly considered by reviewers of the novel.

Ellis's writing is most often viewed as a kind of effortless self-indulgence. ". . . [Y]ou sometimes get the feeling that chunks of this book were lifted whole from the high melodrama and adolescent angst of Ellis's diary," comments one reviewer. Moreover, Ellis's fiction is not generally regarded as a genuinely fictional, or even fictitious, creation. "*Less Than Zero* is almost more interesting as a cultural document than as a novel," observes one reviewer, whereas another, admitting that Ellis "clearly possesses talent," claims that *Less Than Zero* ". . . ends up feeling more like a *60 Minutes* documentary on desperate youth than a full-fledged novel. A critic less responsive to the inherent interest of Ellis's material characterizes the novel as "a rather juvenile attempt to capture the sense of purposelessness that seems to afflict so many young people these days."

Reviewers accuse Ellis, on the one hand, of owing too large a literary debt—". . . his descriptions of Los Angeles carry a few too many echoes of Raymond Chandler, Joan Didion and Nathanael West"—or, on the other, of possessing no literary ties at all—"Reading [the novel] is like watching MTV." One reviewer finds that the novel's tone is marked by "an obvious indebtedness to . . . Hemingway"; another maintains that it is "[w]ritten in the inarticulate style of a petulant suburban punk." A reviewer who feels that Ellis draws his material too directly from reality wishes the young novelist would "write a story that doesn't merely depress us with sociological reports"; another suggests that his characters seem too little in touch with reality: "Prematurely world-weary, these martyrs of anomie and non-existential alienation go from party to party looking for cheap thrills. . . ." In one way or another, all of these critics use Ellis's youth as a basis for their complaints, dismissing his clean style as inarticulate and his philosophical effects as "non-existential," or, at best, strictly "documentary." One wonders whether an identical first novel by a middle-aged author might not have received more credit for its art and fewer accusations of artifice.

In any case, after the rash of reviews that appeared when it hit the best-seller list, *Less Than Zero* never received further critical attention. A factor contributing to the neglect may have been the failure of Ellis's second novel, *The Rules of Attraction* (1987), to live up to the promise of the first. A mediocre, if technically accomplished novel, based too much in the trivia of college life, *The Rules of Attraction* should not detract from the power of Ellis's first work. Firmly in the Hollywood tradition, *Less Than Zero* is far from being a random, diary-style pastiche of minutiae drawn from the decadent life-styles of Los Angeles youth; it is stylistically accomplished, carefully crafted, close to the bone in its use of telling detail. First acting on the advice of his Bennington teacher, Joe McGinnis, and then under the supervision of his editor, Ellis spent between two-and-a-half and three years revising and paring down the original version of his novel. The patterns of symbolism and imagery in *Less Than Zero* are remarkably consistent, contributing to the overwhelming sense of dread that pervades the book and finally giving it an existential dimension that goes beyond the limits of verisimilitude.

It is unlikely that Ellis was writing as a disciple of any specific existentialist philosophy; it is highly probable that his unsparing portrayals of absurdity and nothingness in the Hollywood setting owe a great deal to American literary influences. Ellis has acknowledged his indebtedness to Nathanael West, Joan Didion, Raymond Chandler, and, of course, Ernest Hemingway. There can be little doubt that within the usual purview of a liberal arts education and within the range of influences available in writing workshops, Ellis would also have been exposed to more explicit existentialist outlooks on life.

Whatever the immediate influences, the elements of existentialism evident in *Less Than Zero* are most readily seen as a mixture stemming from both Camus and Sartre. Like the "stranger" or "outsider" portrayed in Camus's *L'étranger* (1942), Ellis's narrator feels intensely alienated, a stranger even in familiar territory. Moreover, he feels compelled to confront and question the absurd; he becomes aware of the absurd in its existential sense as his month-long experience tells him that all the practices and values that he has previously accepted actually have no meaning. He is finally brought to the kind of awakening described in *The Myth of Sisyphus* (1942) when "the stage sets collapse," and the "easily followed" path is questioned, when ". . . [O]ne day the 'why' arises and everything begins in that weariness tinged with amazement."

Ellis's protagonist also becomes painfully aware of the void or "nothingness" (Sartre's *le néant*), and the resulting anxiety brings him the burden of freedom and responsibility, a burden that is part of both Camus's and Sartre's existential schemes. At times, particularly in scenes with his own family, Ellis's narrator bears a fleeting resemblance to Kafka's characters, for whom life seems painfully absurd and whose very existence seems to them to be without value. For the most part, a reliance on the most familiar elements of existentialism—alienation and anxiety, increasing awareness of the absurd and of nothingness, then, more positively, the awakening to individual responsibility—serves as the best way to approach a novel that is consistently existential in its outlook without being highly sophisticated in a philosophical sense.

Ellis's narrator, Clay, is a third- or fourth-generation Hollywood adolescent, eighteen at the time of his return from a college in New Hampshire for Christmas break. Although the novel is not fully plotted—one might complain that it does indeed consist of an endless round of parties, clubs, and restaurants, with intervals grudgingly spent with family—its subplot shapes both chronology and theme. The novel's foreground reveals that Clay has nothing to gain from his family, his girlfriend Blair, his psychiatrist, the drugs he takes, or the Los Angeles milieu in general. The novel's darker subplot, in which Clay plays a kind of passive detective role in discovering what has become of his close friend Julian, lends a vague air of mystery and suspense, shows what could happen to Clay should he follow the same path, and adds to the novel's existential dimension, as Clay becomes aware of the power of nothingness in Julian's life.

Clay's sense of threat and menace, the dread he feels upon his return to Los Angeles, are not without identifiable roots. Though his feelings range from depression to existential despair and though he often stays up at night worrying, feels sick or tense, or lacks appetite, Clay is not portrayed as an oversensitive adolescent. His emotions are not a sign of self-indulgence but an indication that he is making a choice, whether or not he is yet aware of it. Indeed, Clay may be viewed as embarking on an involuntary existential quest, embodying Camus's "absurd man" who is keenly aware of the meaninglessness around him, while others go on acting as if everything makes sense. The rather anticlimactic resolution of the novel, Clay's decision to return to college in the East, is a natural manifestation of the will to survive, both physically and spiritually, after having endured a month-long revelation. The focus of the novel is on how even an initially passive perspective can yield to a kind of revelation; certainly the book is about more than a college kid's weary decision to return to classes. In analyzing Didion's *Play It As It Lays,* David J. Geherin makes an observation that applies just as well to **Less Than Zero:** ". . . [T]he novel is as much 'about' Hollywood as *Heart of Darkness* is 'about' Africa or *The Stranger* is 'about' Algeria." Indeed, Ellis's novel, like Didion's, is about man confronting the void. It is not a novel of initiation, for there is no society of substance into which Clay might reasonably expect to be initiated. His responsibility is to bear witness to the moment-to-moment absurdity of the place he had heretofore considered home.

Less Than Zero may be taken as a realistic novel only to a certain extent. Ellis has created a dense pattern of images and symbolic events that often bear more resemblance to Gothic than to realistic fiction. The descriptions of Los Angeles and its surroundings are surrealistic in their intensity. As a backdrop for the novel's events, Los Angeles is given an air of menace, with destruction or disaster constantly on the horizon. Clay's first sight upon his return home is of "remains of palm trees that have fallen during the winds." The sounds of nature here are not peaceful but consist of "coyotes howling and dogs barking and palm trees shaking in the wind up in the hills" (62-63). Earthquakes, rainstorms, and mudslides are also part of the picture. Most ominous is the sun itself, described variously as an "orange monster" (172) or a "gigantic . . . ball of fire" that rises over a "smog-soaked, baking Valley" while dust swirls at Clay's feet (195). The wasteland imagery, reminiscent of Fitzgerald's "valley of ashes," is unmistakable. A tee-shirt Clay notices bears the phrase "Under the Big Black Sun" (185). In **Less Than Zero,** the Los Angeles sun is not a life force but a destructive power.

Unlike Nathanael West or Raymond Chandler, but like Joan Didion, Ellis has chosen to focus not so much on the superficial and deceptive glitter of Hollywood as on its more telling geographical features. The claustrophobic, windy, overheated atmosphere is anxiety provoking for Clay and Gothic in its threat of entrapment. When Clay has nightmares, the horror arises from the California earth itself, the mud filling his mouth, nose, and eyes and finally burying him (114); the image of live burial is another familiar Gothic element, reminiscent of Poe's "The Premature Burial." The image reinforces the pervasive feelings of menace and dread while also showing symbolically that Clay's way of life is directed toward death. The real horror for Clay is not Gothic, however, but existential. The mud of his nightmare is also a reminder of the Bouville or "Mudville" of Sartre's *La Nausée* (1938), suggesting that Clay, like Roquentin, must confront horrors to which his unquestioning companions remain blind.

Dispensing entirely with Hollywood glamour, Ellis suggests through nearly every scene in the novel that in reaching the edge of the continent, one also approaches the abyss. Anxiety, meaninglessness, and nothingness become themes that combine toward an existential effect. Each of these themes is developed by means of events, symbols, and a variety of minor emblems or leitmotifs that consistently echo the larger themes. Anxiety and meaninglessness begin in the shambles that is left of family structure, and the drugs that offer escape add instead to the feelings of panic and purposelessness. The nothingness theme extends to outright fears of nonbeing, with a number of references to darkness or disappearing. Considerable emphasis is given to the word "nothing," which often translates as "nothingness."

Ellis's portrayal of the anxiety integral to the Hollywood family ranges from the pathetic to the bizarre. The sense of nonbeing begins at home. The parents' failure to provide a firm foundation establishes visible sources, if not excuses, for the younger generation's shortcomings. That these characters are virtually abandoned by their parents, while hardly registering the fact consciously, accounts for some of their more generalized feelings of anxiety and malaise. Stereotypically spoiled in material terms, they are nevertheless neglected emotionally.

Clay's first encounter with his family after an entire semester away at college is with a note, for "Nobody's home" (10). Practically speaking, the absence is understandable—his mother and sisters are Christmas shopping—but it is emblematic of how unimportant Clay's return is to them. For most of Clay's friends, Christmas is a time not of traditional family gatherings but of abandonment and depersonalization. Keeping in mind that the characters are eighteen or nineteen years old, one might consider their possible responses to the question, "It's Christmas. Do you know where your parents are?" Griffin invites Clay to come to his house after a party because his parents are in Rome for Christmas (37). Daniel thinks his parents are in Japan, "Shopping,'" or maybe in Aspen. "'Does it make any difference?'" (55), he asks, meaning that he is alone in either case. Daniel's is the kind of rhetorical question often asked by Clay's friends, and its message is hopelessness, a defensive nihilism posing as sophisticated indifference. Kim gives a New Year's Eve party in an unfurnished house while her mother is away in England with someone named Milo. "'At least that's what I read in *Variety*'" (82), she explains, apparently unaware of the irony that she must consult a publication, for lack of personal communication, to determine her mother's whereabouts.

When Blair gives a Christmas party, both parents are present, as is Blair's father's boyfriend. Blair's friend Alana, in a fine bit of role reversal, expresses her concern about how drunk Blair's mother is becoming and engages the other young people in a solemn discussion about how much better it would have been had Blair's father waited until the next week and seen "Jared" on location (16-17). Clearly, the holiday activities of Blair's parents constitute another form of abandonment. On Christmas morning, Clay's father is present but impersonal, looking "neat and hard" (72) as he writes out checks while Clay wonders why he couldn't have prepared them beforehand. The message conveyed is that family ties are no more than financial, even on holidays. One would expect Christmas in Hollywood to lack religious connotations; Ellis portrays it as devoid of all tradition and emotion, the holiday season itself a symbol of an existential world completely lacking in values.

The depiction of Clay's family covers three generations, his grandparents being portrayed in some of the italicized flashbacks that appear periodically throughout the novel. The function of the extended family picture seems to be not to create nostalgia for better times but rather to show how deeply alienated the family members are from each other. Because his family has been in the movie industry for several generations, the Hollywood setting is for Clay not a place of dreams but an ordinary home base lacking in glamour. His grandfather is portrayed not as a source of warmth or security but as a dubious character, forming a memorable image as he sits by a pool, wearing only a straw hat and a jock strap, opening his fifth beer (123-24). That Clay has counted the beers is perhaps meant to show his lack of any deep trust for his family, a lack of roots in anything but a family history of anxiety and alienation. Certainly this is a world without values.

Clay's parents are separated, and their approach is not so much to ignore him totally as to ignore selectively the areas in which he most needs guidance. Clay's father gives the appearance of expressing concern when he tells his son that he looks thin and pale, but when Clay mumbles, "It's the drugs,'" his father replies, "'I didn't quite hear that'" (43), an obvious way of conveying that he does not want to hear it, that he won't address any serious problems of Clay's. Seemingly bland and harmless in the way they communicate, both of Clay's parents abdicate their responsibilities to their children.

Clay's father is portrayed with an irony that is humorous at times. His appearance—"My father looks pretty healthy if you don't look at him for too long" (42)—is emblematic of all the families portrayed in *Less Than Zero:* don't give them more than a glance, or you will see that they aren't healthy. Of course, Clay's father's tan, face-lift, and hair transplant also indicate a nearly adolescent concern with his appearance. The father has a way of shaking Clay's sense of identity, introducing him to one business acquaintance after another only as "'my son'" (42), as if he had no name. The character who should be Clay's strongest source of identity is instead a depersonalizing force. Like some of Kafka's characters, Clay accepts the situation rather passively. "It doesn't bother me that my father leaves me waiting . . . for thirty minutes while he's in some meeting and then asks me why I'm late" (41), he comments, also claiming that his father's treating him as if he were nameless "doesn't really make me angry" (42).

At another lunch with Clay, his father appears in a new Ferrari, wearing a cowboy hat that, to Clay's relief, he does not wear into the restaurant. Once again, the father's concern with material things is shown; he doesn't say much to Clay but "keeps looking out the window, eyeing the fire-hydrant-red Ferrari" (145). This is the only scene in which Clay's father, or any parent in the novel, for that matter, offers his child direct advice and guidance: "He wants me to see his astrologer and advises me to buy the Leo Astroscope for the upcoming year. . .'Those planetary vibes work on

your body in weird ways'" (144). As advice, this bit of fa-
ther-knows-best wisdom is pathetic and absurd, yet Clay has
no choice but to receive it politely. The values presented by
his father are patently transient, and Clay clearly must look
elsewhere for any meaning in his life.

Occasionally, Ellis uses humor to convey the sense of confusion and anxiety that his characters absorb from their own
parents, as in the following exchange:

> "Jesus, Clay, you look like you're on acid or some-
> thing," Blair says, lighting another cigarette.
>
> "I just had dinner with my mother," I tell her.

Contact with one's mother or father is not a stabilizing factor for Clay and his friends; it is disorienting, a "trip" in itself. Without saying so explicitly, Ellis shows that Clay's
parental encounters are at best empty of useable values and
at worst more like confrontations with the existential void.

Whether or not most Hollywood parents are emotional adolescents who neglect their children is not the issue at hand.
The point is that through a stylized portrayal of estranged
parents and children, Ellis has established a clear source of
the intimations of nonbeing that haunt the novel's young
characters. Taking the place of the parents so ready to abandon their offspring both physically and emotionally is an array of ironic surrogates who appear to compensate for
parental shortcomings while actually exploiting the young.

Clay's parents have provided him with a young psychiatrist
who, rather than helping Clay asks for his help in writing a
screenplay (109). When Clay finally admits that he has problems with his parents, his friends, and drugs, the doctor's
response is to start an aimless conversation about Elvis
Costello (122-23). When Clay finally asks, three times, the
desperate question, "What about me?" the psychiatrist's response is "'Come on, Clay . . . Don't be so . . . mundane'"
(123). The caretaker assigned to Clay's emotional well-being is so indifferent that he considers Clay's fears and anxiety boring and treats his survival instinct as a kind of
absurdity. As with the indifference of the parents, the effect
here is negation of the self, the brief scene reinforcing the
fact that Clay is totally alone in his quest for meaning.

Parent surrogates are presented with darker irony in the subplot involving Clay's friend Julian, who embodies what
could become of Clay should he remain in Los Angeles.
Finn, the drug dealer to whom Julian is in debt, has him paying off the debt by serving as a male prostitute. Finn asks
Julian how his parents are (170), as if to emphasize their in-
accessibility, and as he injects him with heroin croons,
"'Now, you know that you're my best boy and you know that
I care for you. Just like my own kid. Just like my own son

. . .'" (171). Finn's gentle words are a mockery, in view of
his predatory nature. His name evokes the image of a shark's
fin; he is in fact a particularly vicious loan shark.

Finn hires Julian out to a businessman from Indiana who
calls him "son" (173-74), an especially ironic label, given
the nature of their interaction. It is when the established order uses endearments in the interest of destruction and perversion that Ellis's writing most resembles Kafka's, for here
the sense of menace becomes nearly surrealistic. Clay's last
encounter with Finn is a chance meeting in a supermarket,
and Finn's seemingly friendly farewell is "'Catch ya later,'"
which he says while "cocking his fingers as if they were a
gun" (197). Here, near the end of the novel, the sense of
menace has become so palpable that without any explanation from Clay, the reader senses the feeling of threat that
the commonplace, normally affectionate gesture conveys.
The surreal quality is in familiar mannerisms taking on
heightened connotations; momentarily, the mock gun becomes real.

The novel's young characters have absorbed from their families the idea that their own existence and actions are of very
little import. The only value system that has been handed
down to them is materialism, and they apply the ethic freely,
sometimes viewing even themselves as material goods. A
refrain that is repeated several times in the course of the
novel is "Wonder if he's for sale." The question comes up
twice with regard to Julian (176, 183), who has literally done
just that. As the businessman from Indiana tells Julian, "'Yes,
you're a very beautiful boy . . . and here, that's all that matters'" (175). An obsession with physical appearance is normal for adolescents, but these characters are learning from
adults that appearance, the self as raw material, is "*all* that
matters."

Young boys who all look the same—"thin, tan bodies, short
blond hair, blank look in the blue eyes, same empty toneless voices"—are an everpresent commodity, and Clay begins to fear that he might "look exactly like them" (152). In
sharing the commonly acceptable appearance associated with
membership in a privileged class, Clay actually becomes part
of a minority, and an exploitable minority at that. His fear
is existential as well as pragmatic, for he sees no evidence
that he has an identity distinct from any of the tan, blond
others. His state of anxiety seems close to that described by
Camus, who points out that when ". . . fear becomes conscious of itself, it becomes anguish, the perpetual climate of
the lucid man 'in whom existence is concentrated.'" From
this perspective, Clay's frequent anxiety is an admirable trait,
a milestone on the existential quest that is making him a "lucid man."

By contrast, most of the other characters in the novel seem
free of fear and anxiety even though they face possible de-

struction. The actual agents of destruction are nearly always drugs and alcohol, indulged in due to limitless leisure and wealth. It is worth noting that Ellis rarely depicts these substances as giving pleasure or even as relieving anxiety. When Blair meets Daniel at a party that he is giving, her question is "'Is he alive?'" (56), and the next day Daniel tells Clay that the reason for his stuporous condition was "a bad Quaalude" (63). A character named Sophie mentions that she slept through a concert because "her brother slipped her a bad lude before the show" (136). (The unthinking use of the word "bad" here implies that there are "good" Quaaludes that have benevolent effects. This is an example of the subtle irony Ellis employs to show his characters accepting an absurd value-system.) Another minor character named Dmitri sticks his hand through a window, cutting it so badly he has to go to an emergency room (139-40), an event that occurs only because he is drunk. A death caused by a drug overdose is depicted when the body of an eighteen- or nineteen-year-old boy is discovered behind a nightclub (185-86).

Ellis's intention seems to be to portray drugs and alcohol as anywhere from partially to absolutely destructive, as pathways to oblivion, and certainly not as aids to having a good time. Yet the message is more existential than it is corrective, for the characters operate in a sort of vacuum where there seems to be no alternative but to continue with the destructive behavior. Even the names of the clubs that they frequent are suggestive of risk or impending doom: The Wire, Nowhere Club, Land's End, the Edge (106).

Two characters in particular, Julian and Muriel, epitomize the devastating effects of drugs, for the two have in effect ceased to struggle and have submitted to a state of nonbeing. Clay confronts nothingness or the void partly through his interactions with these characters. When Clay responds to a message to meet Julian, finding him only after missing him a couple of times, Julian looks "almost dead" (91), obviously an effect of his drug addiction. Julian's only use for Clay now is to borrow money from him, purportedly for someone's abortion. The image most clearly connecting Julian to death is a paperweight Clay sees in Finn's office:

> . . . [S]itting on the desk is this glass paperweight
> with a small fish trapped in it, its eyes staring out
> helplessly, almost as if it was begging to be freed,
> and I start to wonder, If the fish is already dead,
> does it even matter?

Julian, of course, is the fish; his wish to be released unvoiced; and the concern that Clay expresses as to whether or not this dilemma matters is existential. In this milieu, the degree to which anything matters becomes reductionistic. If appearance is "all that matters," the question must be whether Julian—or anyone else—and his plight "even matter." It is because Clay is already engaged in an existential

quest that he cannot ignore such questions and cannot remain content with seeking oblivion himself.

Muriel's dilemma also involves a rather dramatic cluster of themes. Clay visits her at Cedars-Sinai, where she has been hospitalized for anorexia, and sees issues of *Glamour* and *Vogue* lying by her bed (45). The obsessive concern with appearance commonly acknowledged to be a factor in anorexia is embodied in these magazines, while Muriel herself is, ironically, pale white with dark circles under her eyes. Later on, at her New Year's Eve party, Kim tells Clay and Blair that Muriel's mother has just given her "a fifty-five-thousand-dollar Porsche" (80), a material "fix" for problems that are not material in nature. It would seem that in addition to her anorexia, Muriel also has an alcohol problem; Kim confides, "'. . .[O]nce she gets drunk, she's fine. She's just a little strung out'" (80). Muriel may have a death fixation, as is apparent in her begging to wear Clay's vest, which is gray and white with just one dark red triangle: "'It looks as if you got stabbed or something. Please let me wear it,' Muriel pleads . . ." (82). As if all this were not enough, Muriel has a heroin habit, and, at this party, Clay watches her shoot up, witnessing the immediate aftereffects:

> Muriel begins to cry and Kim strokes her head, but
> Muriel keeps crying and drooling all over, looking
> like she's laughing really and her lipstick's smeared
> all over her lips and nose and her mascara's run-
> ning down her cheeks.

Hardly a picture out of *Vogue* or *Glamour:* Ellis's ironic portrayal of Muriel's clown-like state and of her incredible gamut of problems may be heavy-handed, but it serves as a paradigm of the "bad faith" of Sartre's existential philosophy, the meaningless life that results when one abdicates personal responsibility and carries an array of false values to their logical limits. Obsession with appearance and material acquisitions, addiction to chemical substances, and an unreflective attraction to death combine in Muriel to form a picture of existence devoted to, rather than questioning, the absurd. In sum, both Julian and Muriel are symbols of the death-in-life that Clay is beginning to recognize. He alone seems to see this absurdity: his friends accept as paths to pleasure practices that are actually paths to destruction. The conventional values of this milieu are potentially fatal; Clay is up against more than just the petty values of an unthinking *bourgeoisie.*

When one's family has not given one an adequate sense of personal identity, when one's goal in life is to achieve not so much pleasure as a kind of numbness, one is not so much living as courting death, Ellis suggests. The potential for self-destruction that lies insidiously at the heart of the Hollywood value-system gives Clay's existential quest a believable urgency. Within this perspective, the frequency of references to death in *Less Than Zero*—perhaps fifty, roughly one every four pages—appears thematically logical. The references range from the oblique to the graphic, with a noticeable increase in both frequency and intensity in the second half of the novel. The death images make general thematic sense, but they also function to define the narrator's sensibility. Clay's sense of existential dread builds with his increasing sensitivity to suggestions of death all around him; as his anxiety deepens, the images of death intensify. His reportorial manner of noting death images and actual deaths may at first seem obsessive and ritualistic, but it also may be seen as part of the existential quest. One of Ellis's primary influences, Hemingway, has been analyzed in an existential context as a writer who "has been more ritualistic about death-seeking than almost any other figure in the modern world," creating heroes who "have seen real life, vital, authentic life, through the trauma of death, and they must continually recreate it."

Many of Ellis's images are not tied to death in a literal sense but are merely suggestive of death. These include, to mention a few, Death Valley (16); Cliff Notes to *As I Lay Dying* (22); a skull earring (79); a movie "about this group of young pretty sorority girls who get their throats slit" (97); a billboard showing a "huge green skull" (106); a dealer Clay thinks is named Ed but whose name turns out to be "Dead" (127); a song called "Somebody Got Murdered" (181); a song called "Sex and Dying in High Society" (184); and games played by Clay's sisters, in which they compete to see who "can look dead the longest" and "who can look drowned the longest" (198). The movie's subject, the choice of a nickname, the popular song titles, and most of all the sisters' "games" are all suggestive of numbed sensibilities attracted to death as the only stimulating concept. In the cumulative effect of such images, the novel's death theme gathers force.

References to actual deaths are also numerous, and the collective impact of these deaths on Clay's state of mind is substantial. He is told that the family of Trent's maid "was killed in El Salvador" (52); Clay's father "mentions that one of his business associates died of pancreatic cancer recently" (66); a checkout clerk happens to be "talking about murder statistics" (74); Clay hears on the news that "four people were beaten to death in the hills" (78); Clay is shown a snuff film, in which two young people are killed at a party in Malibu (153-54); he remembers the deaths of his own grandmother (163) and great-grandfather (173); and he remembers learning of the brutal murder and mutilation of a young girl one summer (190-91). Just before Clay leaves Los Angeles, he hears of a series of recent deaths:

> Before I left, a woman had her throat slit and was thrown from a moving car in Venice . . . a man in Encino killed his wife and two children. Four teenagers, none of whom I knew, died in a car accident

on Pacific Coast Highway. . . . A guy, nicknamed Conan, killed himself at a fraternity party at U.C.L.A.

Few of the deaths mentioned involve natural causes, and a disproportionate number of the dead are young people; Clay has developed a morbid obsession that is more a warning than it is a neurotic symptom.

In one of the novel's dozen flashbacks, Clay remembers when he was fifteen years old:

> . . . *collecting all these newspaper clippings; one about some twelve-year-old kid who accidentally shot his brother in Chino; another about a guy in Indio who nailed his kid to a wall, or a door, I can't remember, and then shot him, point-blank in the face, and one about a fire at a home for the elderly that killed twenty and one about a housewife who while driving her children home from school flew off this eighty-foot embankment near San Diego, instantly killing herself and the three kids and one about a man who calmly and purposefully ran over his ex-wife somewhere near Reno, paralyzing her below the neck. I collected a lot of clippings during that time because, I guess, there were a lot to be collected.*

Clay's rationale for collecting the clippings cannot cover up the fact that his own frame of mind attracts him to the activity. The enumeration of these deaths has a ritualistic quality more reminiscent of Didion than of Hemingway; the confrontation with nothingness is more meditative than aggressive, and the deaths after all were at a safe distance. It is worth nothing that most of these deaths involve not random violence but rather one family member killing another. The death theme in *Less Than Zero* thus dovetails with the theme of parental neglect. A man's crucifying his own child or a housewife's driving her children to their deaths may be viewed as carrying to extremes the parental neglect and abandonment with which Clay's circle of friends is already so familiar.

At the novel's end, in a scene that is sheerly thematic, Clay discusses the images that a song called "Los Angeles" creates for him:

> The images, I later found out, were personal and no one I knew shared them. The images I had were of people being driven mad by living in the city. Images of parents who were so hungry and unfulfilled that they ate their own children.

A large part of the psychic horror forming a strong undercurrent in the novel is the tendency of those who should be protectors and caretakers to act instead as predators and destroyers. The sensationalistic, "fast-lane" qualities of *Less Than Zero* are in fact subordinate to the crucial pattern of the strong turning on the weak. The characters in the novel are barely past childhood, still dependent upon the adults in their lives. This aspect of the book more than any of its shocking events gives the novel a valid claim to its atmosphere of existential dread and despair. The future awaiting these young characters is itself an absurdity; their use of drugs only postpones their awareness of the void before them. Rip "keeps screaming happily" while using cocaine, "'What's gonna happen to all of us?'" (128), but within the context of the novel, his question is rhetorical. Spin's repeated reply, "'All of who, dude? All of who?'" (128) is not so much a question as an answer, showing that most of these characters have given so little attention to their own identities that they are already in a vacuum of nonbeing.

The theme that forms the understructure of the novel is the theme of caretakers as predators, a pattern that increases the young characters' readiness to abandon any search for identity. At times the parental abdication of responsibility lends a poignancy to the tough cynicism of the young and wealthy in the novel. In Blair's room, for instance, Clay notices "all these stuffed animals on the floor and at the foot of the bed" (58), reminders that Blair is still really a child. With parental affection unavailable, Blair turns to inanimate surrogates for comfort. While watching Julian begin his session with the Indiana businessman, Clay calls to mind "[a]n image of Julian in fifth grade, kicking a soccer ball across a green field" (175). This simple image has a freshness and innocence that evoke in the reader Clay's unvoiced questions as to how such horror and despair have arisen out of such promising, hopeful beginnings.

The adult world's readiness to utilize beautiful youth as a commodity has no limits and in fact is imitated by the young themselves. Late in the novel, just after Clay has been shown the corpse of the eighteen-or nineteen-year-old boy, Rip announces, "'I've got something at my place that will blow your mind'" (188). The dehumanizing attitude of the characters is clear when the "something" turns out to be a twelve-year-old girl who has been sexually abused by both Spin and Rip while drugged and tied to a bed. When Clay objects, "'Oh God, Rip, come on, she's eleven'" (189), Rip responds, "'Twelve,'" as if the added year would justify his actions. Clay argues, in what may be the only statement of any kind of morality in the novel, "'It's . . . I don't think it's right,'" provoking from Rip a statement encapsulating the principles of his group of friends: "'What's right? If you want something, you have the right to take it. If you want to do something, you have the right to do it'" (189). To Clay, "right" has moral connotations; to Rip, the word connotes only privilege or demand. While Clay is at least tentatively searching for values, most of his friends are openly nihilistic.

It must be noted, however, that Clay does not finally emerge as a moral protagonist who is repulsed by the immorality of his friends. The snuff film revolts him; the abuse of the young girl sickens him; but to a degree he is also fascinated by violence and cruelty. He shares with the others the symptom of having emotions so anesthetized that it takes something extreme to interest him or to reawaken his feelings. Thus, when he goes to the movie in which sorority girls are killed, he watches "just the gory parts" (97). The only sex scene with Blair occurs just after she has run over a coyote, and Clay watches it die (142-43). Although Clay's admitting "I've never wanted her more" (143) is not overtly connected to the coyote's violent death, it is clear that the juxtaposition of the animal's gruesomely depicted last moments with the lovemaking scene is not accidental. Clay's sudden desire has been prompted by witnessing a death, which makes him temporarily capable of strong feelings.

While the reader may have been aware of Clay's distorted perceptions for some time, Clay himself shows an increase in self-awareness only after going with Julian to meet Finn and agreeing to accompany Julian to an assignment:

> . . . [I]n the elevator on the way down to Julian's car, I say, "Why didn't you tell me the money was for this?" and Julian, his eyes all glassy, sad grin on his face, says, "Who cares? Do you? Do you really care?" and I don't say anything and realize that I really don't care and suddenly feel foolish, stupid. I also realize that I'll go with Julian to the Saint Marquis. That I want to see if things like this can actually happen. And as the elevator descends, passing the second floor, going even farther down, I realize that the money doesn't matter. That all that does is that I want to see the worst.

The elevator's movement seems intended, perhaps too didactically, as a symbolic descent into hell; a valid part of this "hell" is Clay's encounter with his own twisted emotions. Julian's situation has brought Clay to a realization in several stages. He realizes that he lacks feelings for even his closest friend, that his curiosity outweighs any concern he might feel, and that he has developed an appetite for depravity. One might question the logic behind "all that [matters] is that I want to see the worst," and Clay is not a narrator who provides answers or analysis. At the moment of this realization, he is of two minds, witnessing and appalled by his immediate impulses, yet not ready to pull away from the situation that excites his warped sensibility. What "matters" is not that he must immediately get the morbid thrill he is seeking—though this will happen—but rather that he must register and eventually act upon the epiphany he has just experienced. Usually a passive observer, he cannot avoid the implications of the active "I want." He cannot pretend to be unaffected by the devastating events he sees; what he had perceived all along as disgust or boredom suddenly takes on larger proportions. In existential terms, he has realized that everything that happens matters, that even observing is not a passive activity, that man is defined by the events of his life.

Clay's experience, rooted though it may be in parental neglect and chemical dependency, consists more basically of a confrontation with the absurd and nothingness. The problem with nothingness, for Clay, is that it is simultaneously fascinating and horrifying, seductive and repulsive. In the context of his encounter with the void, many of the seemingly vacant or random comments earlier in the novel make thematic sense. One sees that the existential dilemma has been foreshadowed from the opening scenes, when Blair, dropping Clay off at home, asks, "'What's wrong?'" and he says, "'Nothing'" (10). What is wrong is "nothingness," the sense Clay has immediately upon returning to Los Angeles that spiritual annihilation is at hand. Camus's interpretation of "nothing" seems applicable:

> In certain situations, replying 'nothing' when asked what one is thinking about may well be pretense in a man. . . . But if that reply is sincere, if it symbolizes that odd state of soul in which the void becomes eloquent, in which the chain of daily gestures is broken, in which the heart vainly seeks the link that will connect it again, then it is as it were the first sign of absurdity.

The same double meaning of the word may be read into a flashback to Christmases spent with the family at Palm Springs, when Clay's grandfather would tell Clay "*that he heard strange things at night*" and when asked what he heard would "*finally say that it must have been his imagination, probably nothing*" (70). Perhaps there are strange noises to be heard in the "*insane heat*" (69) of the desert nights, but it is more likely that Clay's grandfather also had intimations of what was "probably" nothingness. One is reminded of the "*nada*" experienced by the older waiter in Hemingway's "A Clean, Well-Lighted Place."

For someone as young as Clay, existential dread has a personal immediacy. Thus, when Clay sees a new billboard bearing the invitation, "'Disappear Here,'" he overreacts: "even though it's probably an ad for some resort, it still freaks me out a little and I step on the gas really hard . . ." (38). Other incidents that would seem like random diary entries make sense when informed by Camus's concept of nothing:

> On Beverly Glen I'm behind a red Jaguar with a license plate that reads DECLINE and I have to pull over.

"What's wrong, Clay?" Trent asks me, this edge in his voice.

"Nothing," I manage to say.

Again, the problem is "nothingness," Clay's awareness that he is confronting the void. By this point in the novel, he is oversensitized to the degree that the slightest reminder makes him nearly sick with awareness of the dilemma.

Julian recalls, and sings, a song he and Clay used to listen to: "'*Straight into darkness, we went straight into darkness, out over that line, yeah straight into darkness, straight into night*'" (48). "'Love that song,'" he remarks, and because Clay agrees with him in the past tense, "'Yeah, so did I'" (49), one sees that it is only Julian, and no longer Clay himself, who finds oblivion a seductive idea. The danger Julian embodies is not of growing up too fast but of passing from childhood straight into nothingness. All of these characters are walking a thin line, in the sense that death itself may overtake them before they have any chance to contemplate the more philosophical connotations of nothingness. The novel's existential dimension lies in the condition embodied by Julian and to a degree even by Clay himself, a condition in which spiritual death precedes physical death. Clay might be said to have flirted with nothingness from the novel's beginning. Asked by both his mother and then his father what he wants for Christmas, his answer is the same, "'Nothing'" (18, 43). During the course of his Christmas vacation, he does indeed "get" Nothing, in the sense that he finally grasps the concept.

Indeed, the title of the novel, taken from an Elvis Costello song title, suggests that the real subject of the book is the confrontation with absolute nothingness.
—*Nicki Sahlin*

Indeed, the title of the novel, taken from an Elvis Costello song title, suggests that the real subject of the book is the confrontation with absolute nothingness. The refrain of the song "Less Than Zero" mentions a "mother" and a "father" and states, "They think that I got no respect, but / Everything means less than zero." The claim is certainly reminiscent of Clay's situation. Although he would appear on the surface to have a disrespectful attitude and a questionable lifestyle, he is actually grappling with his deep sense of the meaninglessness of life.

A religious program that Clay watches promises deliverance from the whole dilemma. Clay listens to a man declare: "'You feel confused. You feel frustrated . . . You don't know what's going on. That's why you feel hopeless, helpless.

That's why you feel there is no way out of the situation. But Jesus will come'" (140). The man talks on and on, promising "'Deliverance,'" and Clay's desperation is shown by his waiting for "close to an hour" for "something to happen." The outcome is put simply: "Nothing does" (140). In the only instance in the novel where the actual promise of an answer is made, the answer that arrives is nothingness. The absence of God is a factor in most existential literature; it is fitting that in *Less Than Zero,* with the parents conveying no values, God's absence becomes clearest through that ubiquitous babysitter and parent-substitute, TV.

After receiving "nothing" from the religious program, Clay's reaction is to avoid the message by taking cocaine. It is only after the crucial episode with Julian that the implications of nothingness begin to distress Clay. The two of them meet the Indiana businessman in the San Marquis in "room 001" (173), as close to nothing as a room number can get. The realization that emerges from the scene is found in its last line, in Clay's understanding that "You can disappear here without knowing it" (176). Clay is beginning to understand that the power of nothingness is insidious; the same thing that has happened to Julian could happen to him "without [his] knowing it." Though Clay feels pity for Julian, he is unable to intervene and save Julian. He does, however, feel the burden of his own freedom; having seen the destructive direction of Julian's life, he cannot accept it for himself.

During Clay's last week at home, his dealer, Rip, takes him for a ride and stops to show him a scene:

> He pointed out the number of wrecked cars at the bottom of the hill. Some were rusted and burnt, some new and crushed, their bright colors almost obscene in the glittering sunshine. I tried to count the cars; there must have been twenty or thirty cars down there. Rip told me about friends of his who died on that curve; people who misunderstood the road. People who made a mistake late in the night and who sailed off into nothingness.

It is obvious that driving off the road is not the only "mistake" possible in *Less Than Zero;* symbolically, the "people who misunderstood the road" could be any of Clay's acquaintances. Some, like Muriel, are courting death, while others, like Julian, have already made their fatal mistakes. Still others, perhaps Blair for one, are headed for a meaningless existence while believing themselves to be pursuing pleasure. When they begin to drive again, Clay warns Rip that he may be heading down a dead-end street, provoking a symbolic exchange:

> "Where are we going?" I asked.
> "I don't know," he said. "Just driving."
> "But this road doesn't go anywhere," I told him.

"That doesn't matter."
"What does?" I asked, after a little while.
"Just that we're on it, dude," he said.

For Clay, the critical question is always what matters, and Rip's seemingly existential answer is unsatisfactory and in fact nihilistic. Clay has already tacitly concluded that to exist without regard for the quality of life is not enough. Once having become aware of the void, Clay must fight its attraction and exert force of will to recoil from it. Time and again, the signs that he must get off the directionless road are offered by those who are content just to be on that road, headed either nowhere or to their own destruction.

It is obvious that driving off the road is not the only "mistake" possible in *Less Than Zero;* symbolically, the "people who misunderstood the road" could be any of Clay's acquaintances.
—Nicki Sahlin

How deeply the nothingness of the Hollywood environment has affected Clay is apparent in the final scene with Blair. She is the character with whom he should be having the most meaningful relationship, but he avoids her the most; even her name suggests that communication between loved ones has become nothing more than a meaningless "blare." Their final face-to-face encounter at a restaurant resonates with nothingness. Blair asks Clay about his weekend, and he replies, "'I don't remember. Nothing'" (203). In justifying going back to school, he reasons, "'There's nothing here'" (203), quite possibly a reference to the nothingness he has encountered in Los Angeles. The simple statement encapsulates the state of awareness he has reached. While his companions remain prey to their dangerous way of life, he has become "a prey to his truths," having reached the state described by Camus: "A man who has become conscious of the absurd is forever bound to it."

The ensuing conversation revolves around Blair's question as to whether Clay has ever loved her, a question he evades, and her repeated accusation, "'You were never there'" (204). At this moment, Clay thinks of the billboard refrain, "Disappear Here." Clay has been even closer to nothingness than he imagined, and the emotional absence about which Blair complains reflects how close he has come to losing himself. Blair adds, in what is probably meant as reassurance, "'You're a beautiful boy, Clay, but that's about it'" (204), a particularly ill-timed echo of the businessman's words to Julian, a suggestion that Clay, too, could become nothing but a commodity.

Near the end of their conversation, in response to Blair's

"'What makes you happy?'" (205), Clay declares, "'Nothing. Nothing makes me happy. I like nothing.'" (205). Such a statement is not merely an indication of a negative attitude but is more like a triple affirmation of nothingness. Syntactically, "I like nothing" is not a statement anyone would naturally utter; it reads more clearly as "I like nothingness" and might be seen as further testimony to Clay's long-standing attraction to oblivion. In the aftermath of his epiphany, though, the statement acquires more depth. "Nothing" makes Clay "happy" in the sense that it has satisfied him by making him an absurd man, finally self-aware if by no means content. The revelation of nothingness in the Hollywood way of life has both enlightened and freed him; it has also given him the responsibility to leave when it might be easier to stay.

The novel's last section consists of Clay's free association with the lyrics of the song "Los Angeles"; the book ends, "These images stayed with me even after I left the city. Images so violent and malicious that they seemed to be my only point of reference for a long time afterwards. After I left" (208). The existential solution to Clay's dilemma is not far-reaching. His answer, after having seen the horror and emptiness around him, is to leave the scene. He has no ability to change the lives of others and no particular plans for the future. Clay has, however, taken the clearest possible look at what life at home offers him, found that the answer is nothing, and taken the step that is his only honest reaction to an unanswerable problem.

By making Clay's final choice survival rather than oblivion, Ellis offers redemption in a nearly hopeless situation. For some readers, the circumstances surrounding Clay's confrontation with the void may strike a dismayingly minor note in terms of existential possibilities, but given the nihilistic alternatives, *Less Than Zero* holds its own. Ellis has created a character who is in realistic terms no hero but who has nevertheless grappled with a fundamental question. Clay has become aware of his own anxiety and alienation, as well as the meaninglessness around him; and though he has found no solution, he has found the courage to continue to live. In having faced the absurd as he finds it, Clay takes on the proportions of an existential hero.

Elizabeth Young (essay date 1992)

SOURCE: "The Beast in the Jungle, the Figure in the Carpet," in *Shopping in Space,* Atlantic Monthly Press, 1992, pp. 85-129.

[*In the following essay, Young appraises* American Psycho *as a postmodern text.*]

The publication of Bret Easton Ellis's *American Psycho* in 1991 was replete with ironies. It seemed as if the world had decided to add to the book all the old-fashioned fictional qualities that it so conspicuously lacked: melodrama, plot, characterization, irony, hubris. The story *of* the book—its publication history, its author, its controversial aspects, its fashionability—had to stand in for the lack of story *in* the book which no one seemed to bother to read in any detail.

> **The publication of Bret Easton Ellis's *American Psycho* in 1991 was replete with ironies. It seemed as if the world had decided to add to the book all the old-fashioned fictional qualities that it so conspicuously lacked: melodrama, plot, characterization, irony, hubris.**
> —*Elizabeth Young*

Bret Easton Ellis started making notes for his third novel, which he intended to be the monologue of a serial killer, whilst still working on the proofs of *The Rules of Attraction.* The publishing house Simon and Schuster offer a $300,000 advance for the book only to withdraw from publication in the autumn of 1990 after some exceptionally violent, gory excerpts from what is now known as *American Psycho* appear in *Spy* and *Time* magazines. Sonny Mehta immediately acquires the manuscript for Vintage Books. It is published as a trade paperback in America in February 1991 and in Britain, under the Picador imprint, in April of the same year. Its publication was attended in America by furious psychodrama. Roger Rosenblatt in *The New York Times,* under the heading "Snuff This Book", described it as "the most loathsome offering of the season". *Time* spoke of "the most appalling acts of torture, murder and dismemberment ever described in a book targeted for the Best-Seller lists". Tammy Bruce of NOW said it was "a how-to manual on the torture and dismemberment of women" and called for a national boycott of the book. Gloria Steinem suggested that Ellis would have to take responsibility for any women tortured and killed in the same manner as described in the novel. Ellis made some attempt to respond to all this furore in interviews with *The New York Times and Rolling Stone,* pointing out that he didn't expect anything better of critics anyway. ("Do most critics' taste extend beyond the hopelessly middlebrow?") He said what might be expected, that the book was a work of fiction and should speak for itself. He was quite clear about his position: "The acts described in the book are truly, indisputably vile. The book itself is not. Patrick Bateman is a monster. I am not. The outrage that has been expressed is totally disconnected from what the book is about." America even wheeled on Norman Mailer, their iconic emblem of Literature, for one last go-round with art and censorship in *Vanity Fair.* Mailer, whose own book

An American Dream is, as a straightforwardly "realist" novel, far more offensive towards women than Ellis's comic-strip hyperreality, sounded lost. He noted wearily that: "*American Psycho* is saying that the eighties were spiritually disgusting and the author's presentation is the crystallization of such horror." Mailer went on to strike a blow for that old ghost, the classic realist novel: "Since we are going to have a monstrous book with a monstrous thesis, the author must rise to the occasion by having a murderer with enough inner life for us to apprehend him?" Why? In all this media fall-out, these shrieks of "the literary equivalent of a snuff film" and "pure trash" there is a notable absence of any *literary* criticism; the most recent authors mentioned, apart from Tom Wolfe and his *The Bonfire of the Vanities* are Kafka and Beckett. In *The Village Voice,* Mim Udovitch manages after a great deal of work to decide that "this is a good old-fashioned Beckett-esque anti-novel, with all the attendant no-frills—flat characters, monotonously detailed surface description, no plot to speak of and endless repetitions." It is as if no one had written anything in between.

In Britain critics were able to distinguish themselves by exhibiting a near-total ignorance of Ellis's intentions and of contemporary American fiction in general. Along with their counterparts in America they were obsessed with context rather than text. John Walsh in *The Sunday Times* and Fay Weldon in *The Guardian* were almost the only commentators to even attempt a defence. Some critics reacted as though the novel were virtually autobiographical. It was said that Ellis "chose to sit in his apartment month after month imagining unoriginal ways of torturing women (not to mention dogs, gays and homeless people)"—as if he were some demented Son of Sam and not a novelist at all. Feminist groups again behaved as though this were not fiction but a manifesto, a statement of intent. Ellis was accused of making a killing in more ways than one. It was said that he had chosen repulsive sensationalism as a way of ensuring the commercial success that had eluded his novel *The Rules of Attraction*—a wholly unfounded suggestion in that, as mentioned, he started writing *American Psycho* before his second novel was even published. And what seemed to fuel critical rage more than anything was the $300,000 advance retained by Ellis when Simon and Schuster refused to publish the book. This was the familiar British primal scream of hatred at the artist who was not only doing something that they did not like and could not understand but was actually *being paid a lot of money for it.* The unashamed greed and envy that lay behind many of these accusations was typical of the decade and ironically, one of the principal themes in the novel itself. The mass media, in fact, behaved exactly as Ellis and countless other postmodern theorists had already noted they did, leeching away all the drama into their own arena, re-writing the script and re-presenting it to the consumer hordes. The story of *American Psycho*—as opposed to the book itself—uncannily paralleled the fictive themes

it explored; it was treated as a fashion statement—controversial, emotive, urgent, very NOW! Early copies became *the* essential fashion accessory amongst the hip cognoscenti and then, as it was disseminated amongst the uncool masses, it was swiftly dropped. Within months it was media history, yawn time. Don DeLillo has commented on the way in which the media consumes and fictionalizes events so that the media itself becomes the source of our fictions. Where once people turned to fiction for plot and character, drama and action they now turn to the filmic or televisual. The ability to ghost-dance freely between the factual and the imaginary is an essential strategy for contemporary psychic survival, as Andy Warhol understood when he decided to treat his entire life "as a movie". DeLillo has also commented on the role of the novelist in such a psychically cannibalistic culture, saying that the writer was now merely "part of the background noise—part of the buzz of celebrity and consumerism" in a world where: "Everything seeks its own heightened version. Nothing happens till it is consumed."

It soon became impossible for anyone to focus on the novel at all, let alone pay any attention whatsoever to "the language, the structure, the details". Had they done so it would have forestalled many of their criticisms. Not since *The Satanic Verses* had a book been so poorly read. It was dismally revealing of the low quality of cultural commentary in England and America. Ellis himself was perfectly aware of the extravagant inanities of the media tirade. "Most of them haven't read it and those who have, I think, have missed it in a big way."

American Psycho is of course a classic of the 1980s. In a sense it is the 1980s. It embodies the decade and all the clichés of the decade in the West—the rampant self-serving greed, relentless aggression and one-upmanship; the manic consumer overdrive, exhaustion, wipe-out and terror. The book arrived in Britain at a time when much of this furious, doomed drive towards success and perfection was still dominant. The media had just started wildly signalling that it was over, that it was time to lower our moral hemlines and become gentle and caring for a bit. However, having been activated, the tread-mill kept spinning. People have lives, not life-styles and they cannot be dismantled at the whim of the Sunday supplement. It was hardly surprising that a novel which unequivocally condemned a way of life to which many people had sacrificed their youth and energy was tepidly received; journalists were as much at the mercy of the status-driven conspicuous consumption of the eighties as anyone else and the froth over the book's alleged violence may have concealed a hideous disquiet that the leotards and Agnès B. leggings, the enormous mortgages and obscene restaurant bills were . . . just . . . not worth it.

Don DeLillo had unwittingly described something of the strange, hushed arena in which the book really functioned when he said: "I think everything we do in the West is so easily absorbed by the culture that it is very difficult for art to become dangerous. There is something in the culture that absorbs danger." The critics tried very hard to defuse ***American Psycho*** by focusing on one aspect of the book—the violence, which turns out, on close reading, to be something of a chimera—and ignoring the rest or dismissing it as boring. Naomi Wolf's assertion that "It was the single most boring book I have ever had to endure" was typical. It probably does seem boring to the careless reader. This is irrelevant because tedium has never prevented art from having an impact. The films of Andy Warhol, one of the single most important artistic influences of the century, are undoubtedly boring. It did not stop them from being dangerous in that they were incapable of being absorbed by the dominant culture. ***American Psycho*** was a dangerous book. It was not alone in this—it was not even the most dangerous book published that spring. Dennis Cooper's *Frisk,* discussed later, is infinitely more disturbing. What unites Warhol's work and Ellis's novel is that, despite receiving the concentrated attention of the mediatized culture, their art remained unassimilated precisely because it was comprised of subversive elements so cleverly interwoven with the cultural attitudes of the time that to have fully recognized them, *at the time,* would have proved destabilizing to the commentators.

For the record, *Frisk* attracted minimal attention upon publication in the USA. It was a homosexual-murder novel and thus unimportant, ghetto-ized. When asked if he could understand the feminist horror at his novel, Ellis commented: "But would it offend you if he [Patrick Bateman, the 'hero'] committed the same actions on young men? If they were mutilated, tortured in the same manner, would you be boycotting the publisher?" (Apparently not.) Women have the stage right now and rightly so but Ellis says that he feels no responsibility to write what they consider a "socially acceptable book": "Buy Alice Walker if it makes you feel better. Buy Amy Tan. I don't care what you read . . . "

The literary establishment retains its hegemony by marginalizing threatening material. There is almost nothing published in Britain that both receives attention and could remotely be considered dangerous. When something struggles through, like the novels of Kathy Acker, it is to widespread abuse and misunderstanding. There are various other strategies for rendering potentially inflammable material impotent. The most usual is just to ignore it. The novels of Dennis Cooper and Juan Goytisolo remain mired in the small press underground, admired by the few, ignored by the many, until time or age has tamed them. The works of, say, Jean Genet or Georges Bataille passed almost seamlessly from being small press rarities to modern classics, without ever spending time in the media spotlight or getting the attention they deserved. William Burroughs was received, albeit reluctantly, by the American Institute of Art

and Letters, when his work was de-fanged by age. The most telling example of all is that of Hubert Selby, a serious and influential artist, whose ground-breaking work in confronting contemporary urban reality, media fantasy and even, in *The Demon,* ur-yuppiedom has not escaped any of the younger Manhattan writers. The British establishment was forced into a ludicrous trial over *Last Exit to Brooklyn* which nearly broke down when the jury found the book unreadable—and presumably very boring indeed.

The fuss and froth over ***American Psycho,*** when seen in the context of other unnerving literature seems ever more pitiful. In the two years previously translations of de Sade's *120 Days of Sodom,* Guillaume Apollinaire's *Les Onze Milles Verges* and Octave Mirbeau's *The Torture Garden* had appeared in Britain to a resounding chorus of apathy, although de Sade eventually ran into a bit of trouble. This was largely seen for the nonsense it was—but only because de Sade and the other French authors had been neutered by time. Their rantings were not *relevant* to the present—or not perceived to be. Even so, the Apollinaire text was trimmed by the publishers, Peter Owen. The most offensive bits were cut and rendered in po-faced précis at the bottom of the page. This quiet editorial abbreviation is another little British publishing strategy; the most improbable American texts arrive here strangely shorn, from Richard Price's *The Wanderers sans* its infamous "venereal sandwich" to Pamela Des Barres groupie memoirs. Literary censorship operates in other covert ways. The independent London bookshops—radical, gay, horror/fantasy—will all admit now to a careful buying policy when it comes to questionable books and comics, following years of persecution by the police and customs.

When exclusion, censorship or prosecution won't work, ghettoization probably will. Many of the most subversive writers working now operate entirely within genre; SF, horror, fantasy, crime, true crime and comics. That these fields receive so little attention is indicative of the contempt in which they are held—for no good reason—by the literary and cultural establishment. Such writers gain a great deal of freedom and, if they are in the Stephen King class, money, alongside a lifelong loss of reputation as serious artists. Occasionally writers of some quality like Thomas Harris—mega-successful after the film of *The Silence of the Lambs*—Ruth Rendell or Patricia Highsmith will achieve something approaching respect as well as popular success but more usually they are left to scrape along on the lean pickings of cult appeal. A writer of the calibre of Derek Raymond (a.k.a. Robin Cook), with his bestial, wrenching vision of modern London is likely to remain relatively ignored on the crime shelves until some media smart-ass films his "Factory" series novels.

In short, what distinguished ***American Psycho*** was not that it was unusual in depicting scenes of extreme sexual violence. Much, much worse can easily be found in small press publications, in genre or in the past. Not to mention, of course, the success and sycophancy surrounding psychotics and killers in films and television. *The Silence of the Lambs,* Jonathan Demme's film in which Anthony Hopkins played the psychotic psychiatrist Hannibal "The Cannibal" Lecter, was showered with Oscars. Criminal trials in America draw huge television audiences. "When Charles Manson is eventually paroled," wrote John Waters, "will *he* have to stand in line outside some crummy, trendy, New York nightclub? . . . Ha! Are you kidding? Right this way, Mr. Manson. Free drink tickets? . . . Yessir!" When Ellis talks of "How desensitized our culture has become towards violence" and how this necessitated the extremes of his novel, he is stating a fact. But it was the combination of overt sexual violence and Ellis's status as a "serious" novelist—young, relevant, living, mainstream—that determined all the hysteria. What was unusual was that such a provocative book should come from a writer who had already been accepted—indeed, groomed—by the most high-toned, respectable arm of the publishing industry. Some of the depressing reaction to the book may lie in the fact that Ellis had transgressed the unwritten contract, had bitten the hand that fed him, had *gone too far.* If he was going to write such filth why wasn't he dead, or underground, or in the ghetto? This isn't to say that there wasn't a frisson of plain commercial joy and excitement at a writer who was effortlessly garnering so much publicity and presumably was going to sell so very many books. Ellis was there; he had to be reviewed, he had to be taken seriously or at least appear to be taken seriously. However the media played their old trick of substituting the image for the actuality and it remains for the street-cleaners of literature, the academics, to come along now and try and soothe everyone with a spot of textual analysis. Bret Easton Ellis spent three years writing this novel, and it *is* a novel—not a "How-to-manual", nor true-crime, not a manifesto or a tract—and it seems reasonable to give it more than three minutes consideration.

In the context of Ellis's other two novels, *American Psycho* is a natural, even an inevitable development. The all-prevailing *kenosis* of his previous work—the evacuation of content, the numbing-out of feeling and sense—together with his interest in social trends, and his expressed belief that only the most extreme and disruptive images or experiences can penetrate the bland vacuity of his generation seem to make the combination of serial killer and the yuppie meritocracy of eighties New York an obvious choice of subject. However, right from the start there are curious tensions and oppositions within the text.

It is an extraordinarily *fictional* text, an over-fictionalized, overly structuralized book. And yet, simultaneously it actually comes closer to being a manifesto, a rhetorical device, than those who accused it of such qualities seemed to real-

ize. From the first line, "Abandon all hope ye who enter here", to the last, "This is not an exit," we are *signed,* we are entered in to what is really a *circle* of hell. Once we have given ourselves up to the text, made the choice to "abandon hope", we have no way out. It is a closed system. These imprisoning, claustrophobic qualities are deftly manipulated in order, not only to force us to live as close to Patrick as is possible in a fictional sense, but to imprint the reader with such force that we cannot ever get out. This is an act of great aggression and confidence on the part of the author revealing a controlling ego which asserts its rights over both characters and readers. It is a gesture of defiance in the face of all post-Barthesian erosions of the authorial actuality. Furthermore it is successful; the reader does not ever get out in the sense that it is thereafter impossible to apprehend the eighties without some reference to their memories of the book.

> **In the context of Ellis's other two novels, *American Psycho* is a natural, even an inevitable development. The all-prevailing *kenosis* of his previous work—the evacuation of content, the numbing-out of feeling and sense—together with his interest in social trends, and his expressed belief that only the most extreme and disruptive images or experiences can penetrate the bland vacuity of his generation seem to make the combination of serial killer and the yuppie meritocracy of eighties New York an obvious choice of subject.**
> **—Elizbeth Young**

Ellis's work seems to be on a search-and-destroy mission. In *Less Than Zero* the otherness of the text, the *hope* of the text, lay on the East Coast, in college education, all of which was systematically destroyed and revealed as depthless and banal in *The Rules of Attraction.* The rules of attraction themselves were at hopeless cross purposes and the characters were, emotionally, on the road to nowhere. The otherness in this book, the hope, was adult life, work and mature relationships. And so, in the first chapter of *American Psycho,* Ellis, very explicitly, very distinctively says goodbye to college life, to bohemian life and moves us deliberately into his previously signalled other, the adult, world.

The opening chapter of *American Psycho* is a tour-de-force during which all the ground rules of the rest of the book—the rules of repulsion—are laid out. Patrick Bateman and his friend Timothy Price, both Young, Urban Professionals, leave work and go to dinner at the house of Patrick's girlfriend, Evelyn. Patrick is the narrator, but the author who titles the chapter "April Fools" is immediately asserting himself as the controlling voice and creating a dissonance between Patrick's words and authorial meaning. The struggle between Patrick and the author continues, more subtly, throughout the book, underlining its fictionality and providing a counter-point in direct opposition to the stated text. The authorial voice—or rather, the authorial language—constantly foregrounds the fictionality and rhetoricity—the artificiality—of the book.

We all once knew the narrator, Patrick Bateman. Looking back we can see that he is wearing a two-button wool gabardine suit with notched lapels by Gian Marco Venturi, a cotton shirt by Ike Behar, a tie by Luciano Berbera and cap-toed leather lace-ups by Ferragamo. His hair is slicked back, he has redwood-framed non-prescription glasses by Oliver Peoples and a Tumi leather attaché case. He works at Pierce & Pierce on Wall Street. He is eating a meal of blackened lobster with strawberry sauce, quail sashimi with grilled brioche and cherimoya sorbet. He is a Yuppie, a Clone. He is also an extremely unreliable narrator.

In this first chapter "April Fools", little happens but we receive a great deal of information. In that it acts as a microcosm of the rest of the book "April Fools" is worth examining in some detail. Even the title can be read in two directly oppositional ways and has this in common with all the major events of the novel.

The first line: "ABANDON ALL HOPE YE WHO ENTER HERE is scrawled in blood red lettering on the side of the Chemical Bank. . ." neatly conjoins the primary themes of blood, despair and banking as well as sub-textually noting our entrance to the novel, as previously discussed. At this stage in the novel some of Ellis's literary devices are a bit brash, a bit crude. He is painting in broad strokes.

We are in New York, in the 1980s. The city is littered with posters for the hit show of those years, *Les Misérables,* forcing us to contrast Hugo's spirited starvelings with the bloated, spiritually impoverished characters of the text. Simultaneously this signals the contemporary "miserables" strewn like rag-dolls over the city-scape; the bums, the homeless, the mental patients, the dispossessed and the disinherited.

In the cab with Bateman, Tim Price—whose very name denotes value—mentions that he has counted already twenty-six beggars that day. Reading from newspapers they discuss the ways in which the city is falling apart: "the trash, the garbage, the disease", Tim, whipping himself into a savage heartless parody of media overkill chants: "Nazis, gridlock, gridlock, baby-sellers . . . AIDS babies, baby junkies . . . maniac baby, gridlock, bridge collapses", cutting quickly to:

"Why aren't you wearing the worsted navy blue blazer with the grey pants?"

On the third page is the first mention of violence and murder. Critics have generally asserted that Bateman does not kill until page 131 but any careful reading will reveal that he claims to have disposed of three, or possibly four people before then. In this opening chapter a newspaper report mentions two people who disappear, leaving bloodstains, at a socialite party on a yacht. Bateman reveals shortly that he has recently been at a yacht party and by the end of the book, the bodies, three in fact, have been recovered and are claimed as victims by Patrick. The discrepancy between the original two who vanish and the three who re-appear is only the first example of the myriad discrepancies in Patrick's account. Or did the newspapers get it wrong, as they so often do? Ellis is right to talk of "details". The text is littered with detailed clues, every single one of which can be plausibly countered by an alternative explanation and all of which underline the trickery of the fictional process.

Returning to "April Fools", Price rants on about disease, claiming, in a particularly fine example of mindless vacuity, that you can get "dyslexia from pussy". Before they arrive at Evelyn's house (a brownstone, bought for her by her father) there are already *two* cases of mistaken identity—guys with slicked-back hair, suspenders and horn-rimmed glasses who look exactly like other people they know. Ellis has no intention of deserting his obsession with deindividualization. It is extended so that it functions as the primary plot device.

Evelyn and her girlfriend Courtney are also wearing absolutely identical clothes: Krizia cream blouse, Krizia rust-tweed skirt and silk-satin d'Orsay pumps from Manolo Blahnik. Evelyn, in an hysterical state of tension—eating in is a sort of penance for her restaurant-crazed peers—is arranging a stunning display of sushi; tuna, yellowtail, mackerel, shrimp, eel and *bonito* with piles of wasabi and ginger.

Evelyn, much to the disapproval of Patrick and Tim Price, has guests from downtown; an artist, Stash and Vanden, his girlfriend. Vanden attends Camden, the fictional equivalent of Ellis's own college, Bennington, and the setting for *The Rules of Attraction.* Vanden has green streaks in her hair, is wearing leather, is watching a heavy-metal video on MTV and—horror of horrors—smoking a cigarette. Stash is pale and lumpy, with a poorly cropped haircut and dressed all in black, ill-fitting clothes. They are unmistakably refugees from the adolescent world of the previous two novels. Patrick notes glumly that Stash looks nothing at all like the other men in the room; he has no muscle tone, he has no suspenders, no horn-rimmed glasses and his hair isn't slicked back. In short he is worthless.

Patrick is further repulsed by Stash's behaviour at dinner. Rather than eating a piece of yellowtail he impales it with a chopstick, which he leaves standing straight up in the fish. He soon points accusingly at it and asserts that, "It moved!" On leaving the house Stash pockets his animated sushi and Patrick is sufficiently distressed by this bizarre, arty behaviour to raise the matter later. "Am I the only one who grasped the fact that Stash assumed his piece of sushi was"— I cough, then resume—"a pet?" The implications of Stash's behaviour (so reminiscent of the moment in *The Rules of Attraction* when "Resin wakes up and starts talking to the ashtray") as far as Patrick *et al* are concerned are clear—it is totally unacceptable. Such artistic weirdness is *demode,* old-fashioned, tasteless and worthless. Ellis further semaphores his intentions by having Vanden read an article in "some East Village rag" entitled THE DEATH OF DOWNTOWN.

Patrick launches into an extraordinary, lengthy speech about American domestic and foreign policy indicating the ludicrous contradictions and oppositions therein. We have, he says, to slow down the nuclear arms race *and* ensure a strong national defense, prevent the spread of communism *and* prevent US military involvement overseas. We have to improve health care, social security and education, clean up environmental damage and at the same time promote economic growth and business expansion. He continues, saying that it is necessary to provide food and shelter for the homeless, to combat racial discrimination and promote civil rights whilst taking care to support women's rights and at the same time changing the abortion laws to protect the right to life whilst somehow maintaining women's freedom of choice. He concludes: "Most importantly we have to promote general social concern and less materialism in young people."

Patrick doesn't seem to notice that his speech is nonsensical. Normally it would be read as being terminally cynical. He and Price have already demonstrated all too vividly their attitude to social problems in their taunting and abuse of the street bums. They are materialists to the bone. However what is deeply chilling about the speech is the implication that it is dead-pan. Patrick is incapable of thinking about these issues and noting their contradictions. It is delivered in a media monotone and denotes an abyss between Patrick's daily life and any apprehension of the political realities behind it. This dissociation between life as it is lived on the city streets, between this and the media avalanche that snows us, soothes us, providing a seamless, self-contained, *meaningless* background commentary, this dissociation *is* the reality—for Patrick and for everyone else.

Stash and Vanden leave to "score" in SoHo. This leaves Tim Price, Evelyn and Patrick. The designer litany continues: "I'm lying on Evelyn's bed holding a tapestry pillow from Jenny B. Goode, nursing a cranberry and Absolut."

Tim moans about Evelyn's "artiste" friends, saying he's sick of being the only one at dinner who hasn't talked to an extra-terrestrial. They sneer at Vanden's stupidity; she thinks that Sri Lanka is "a cool club in the Village" and *High Noon* a film about marijuana farmers. They are so much wiser, so much more adult. Evelyn accuses Tim of gaining weight and losing hair. He retaliates by raising the status stakes and saying that she uses Q.T. Instantan—a very low-rent product. Tim flirts. Patrick tells the reader that Tim is the only interesting person he knows. Evelyn keeps repeating vacuously that Patrick is "the boy next door" and that he, unlike Tim, is no cynic. Patrick whispers to himself, "I'm a fucking evil psychopath," the first of numberless similar statements throughout the book all of which are ignored, misheard, or laughed at.

Finally, Tim leaves and Patrick asks Evelyn why she doesn't have an affair with him, pointing out that he is rich, good-looking and has a great body. She retorts that *everybody* is rich, and good-looking and has a great body.

The central premises have been established: small world exclusivity, status frenzy, high-toned snobbery, conspicuous consumption.

Evelyn states that Stash has tested positive for the HIV virus and she believes he is going to sleep with Vanden that night.

"'Good', I say."

Evelyn finds this exciting. In this way Stash and Vanden are killed off. They are dead, gone from the text. They never reappear. It's goodbye to Camden College and the East Village, goodbye to bohemianism, art, poetry, whimsy, creativity and—ostensibly—to drugs.

This is up-town, this is the modern world, the adult world— money, status, pragmatism, skills, market-value.

Thus, in one short chapter, all the major thematic constituents of the book are carefully delineated and intertwined. It's an adult world, an amoral world, a status-driven, food-obsessed world, a world of interchangeable people, a misogynistic world despite its apparent equal opportunities for women and finally a brutal, violent and terrified world.

Ultimately it is Stash, the embodiment of Ellis's earlier fictional *Zeitgeist* who signifies the opposition between Patrick's narrative and authorial intention. His crazy remarks, his affectedly artistic behaviour might just be dumb or they might, all together, provide a sneering, provocative commentary on his up-town night out. Just who, exactly, are the April Fools here?

The text of *American Psycho* also functions as a maze or puzzle. In order for the critical intelligence to breathe within this particular prison-house of language it is essential for the reader to crack the codes of a narrative that is richly littered with clues. In this respect the book works at times as a parodic deconstruction of the thriller, or serial-killer mystery novel. However, in *American Psycho,* the "clues" are all entirely linguistic rather than the unselfconscious plot-based devices of the popular mystery thriller wherein the reader is never required to consider the "artificial" linguistic formations of the text.

While the performative aspects of *American Psycho* directly reflect its content, there is, sub-textually, the counterpoint of authorial condemnation—or so we are forced to assume lest we find ourselves blandly approving of Bateman's actions. In his earlier books, Ellis's critique of character and values was constantly signalled. In *Less Than Zero* such criticisms are very evident and they still exist, to a lesser extent in *The Rules of Attraction.* However in *American Psycho* there is absolutely nothing stated that implies a critique of Bateman's world and his actions, beyond his own jejune philosophical agonizings which, paradoxically serve to render the character less, rather than more, plausible. Critics, noting the lack of overt condemnation in the text, excoriated Ellis for what they assumed was violent misogyny. Of course they could not allow themselves to conclude that the author was condoning acts of mutilation and murder. Here we have again an act of authorial aggression in that the onus is on the reader to interject the moral values so conspicuously lacking in the text. The critic has to decide when to jump ship. For example, many readers would have internalized the aggressive, money-making values of the decade—who is to say that an honest job as a Wall Street broker is such an evil thing? However these same readers might swiftly be revolted by Bateman's attitudes to women, or to the homeless, and at this point would have to dissociate themselves from the narrative and register dissent, assuming that the author shared their disgust or else—and this a trap for the unwary—roundly scold the author for his unsound attitudes, as many critics did. However that still leaves the problem of trying to define when the author himself had decided to distance himself from events. He might, for example, mistrust women but presumably he wasn't in favour of popping out people's eyeballs? This put the critic in the ludicrous position of, firstly, supplying the moral framework to the book and arguing, in effect, for dualism and old-fashioned fictive ambiguity and secondly, of having to tangle with the autobiographical element in fiction—of defining the author's own feelings, intentions and standards. This has the effect of turning the tables on the reader; rather than being presented with a well-ordered fictive universe, secure in its moral delineation, the reader is, forced to engage personally with the text, to fill in the blanks, as it were, if he is not to produce a completely coarse and slip-shod reading. The

reader is forced to scrutinize his own values and beliefs, rather than those being provided for him within a Good-Evil fictive universe. The alternative is to reject these misleading binary oppositions that Jacques Derrida has defined as intrinsic to Western thinking and to immerse oneself in the free play of signifiers within the text. Ellis himself does not achieve judgement and closure in the text but an endless circularity and *deferral of meaning.*

This leads us to another of the deepest ironies in the novel, the difference between *apparent* and *actual* writing. The book is written as if to be skimmed. It is written largely in brochure-speak, ad-speak, in the mindless, soporific commentary of the catwalk or the soapy soft-sell of the marketplace; the sort of writing that comes up with phrases like "an attractive two-piece with matching accessories", or "As for dining out, the Caribbean island cuisine has mixed well with the European culture." Ellis has said that Bateman is: "A mixture of *GQ* and *Stereo Review* and *Fangoria* . . . and *Vanity Fair.*" Yet, ironically, all this demands the very closest of readings. By situating this mall-speak within a serious novel Ellis destabilizes genres and suggests that, in general, a close study of our cultural debris might reveal clues. However, more seriously for the reader of *American Psycho,* the only way out of the all-imprisoning text is a minutely close reading of the book which will definitely establish Patrick Bateman's fallibility. Only by decisively admitting Patrick's unreliability—and the scales are very evenly weighted—can the critical imagination be freed and an approximation of interpretation allowed to begin.

American Psycho continues with its scatter-gun itemization of Patrick's way of life. The chapters are generally short and have blandly factual headings: "Office", "Christmas Party", "Lunch". They function again, as did the chapters in *Less Than Zero* as Polaroids or sound-bites, providing a brief glimpse of what the author wishes to convey. The artificiality of this structure is intrusive. The reader is given no chance to sink back mindlessly into a warm bath of narrative. This is underlined by the fact that the chapters are not, even when they seem to be, sequential. A "Morning" may be followed by an "Afternoon" but close reading—usually of Patrick's wardrobe—will always indicate that we are on a completely different day. Thus the seamless monotone of Patrick's life, which is indeed positively robotic in its round of office, restaurant, gym and bed, is subtly undermined and fragmented by continual narrative jump-cuts.

Ellis continues to describe, in detail, the clothes and accessories of each character as they appear. Again this is a device more complex than it might seem. It irritated many critics because they found it boring, whereas it is of course no more boring than the constant consumer hum emanating from magazines, media and advertising. It is only when this media mantra is foregrounded and heavily concentrated, as it is in the novel, when it is in fact, decontextualized, that it has the ability to annoy, as Ellis was no doubt aware. The novelist is usually expected to rummage among the cornucopia of contemporary information and to extract the telling detail, the revealing style, the right tie, hair-do or sunglasses and to conscientiously apply them to a character in order to accentuate type and motivation, in short, to assemble the outerwear of the character in accordance with the personality and spiritual framework that is simultaneously being assembled in exactly the same way. Ellis absolutely refuses to participate in this process of "constructing" character and in rejecting it makes us overly aware of the "normal" fictional process as encouraged in Creative Writing class. By adorning his characters, as if they were Barbie dolls, in more or less interchangeable haute couture, and, moreover, by duplicating the self-important intonations of the fashion magazine as he does so, he ably deconstructs much of what we mean by "character" in fiction and forces on us an awareness of the surreal qualities of consumer-speak. Douglas Crimp, writing about the use of reproduction and parody in Pop Art says: "The fiction of the creating subject gives way to the frank confiscation, quotation, excerptation, accumulation and repetition of already existing images. Notions of originality, authenticity and presence . . . are undermined." Towards the end of the book, when Patrick's narrative increasingly tends to shiver and shake around the edges, the litany of designer names begins to falter: shoes by "Susan Warren Bennis Edwards" becomes shoes by "Warren Susan Allen Edmonds" and then shoes by "Edward Susan Bennis Allen". For such a tiny detail this is conspicuous in its effects. What ego-madness possesses a designer (and she's certainly not the only one) that she will inflict an insanely complex name on an entire retinue of stockists, advertisers, fashion-journalists and consumers? Why do we meekly accept and repeatedly intone such a vast array of fancy, complex, weirdly spelt (Manolo Blahnik) and obviously self-assumed names? What drives Patrick crazy is driving us all crazy—why don't we all just crack up and start screaming about brand-names and up-town pizza recipes, like he does? Thus, detail by detail, as if bricking up a tomb, Ellis defines Patrick's insanity and our own place within it.

In addition, by his rigid adherence to an adspeak dress-code for his characters, Ellis continues his emphasis upon deindividualization in contemporary society. Finally, and very ironically, Ellis's use of detailed dress-code to obliterate rather than to define character in the traditional sense ends up contributing to the mechanics of the plot in an *entirely* traditional sense—the "plot" such as it is, eventually turns upon the impossibility of anyone distinguishing one character from another.

All the other accoutrements of Patrick's daily life are delineated in the same stun-gun detail as the clothes in the book.

Patrick's apartment is a temple to status frenzy and state-of-the-art living. Let us pass briefly over his Toshiba VCR, his Sansui stereo, his Wurlitzer and his Steuben glass animals. From the start Patrick is a cipher, rather than a "character". He is Everyyuppie, indifferent to art, originality or even pleasure except in so far as his possessions are the newest, brightest, best, most expensive and most fashionable. By implication, Patrick's absorption in the minutiae of the moment colludes with the author's intention of negating him as a character. At every step he is being rubbed out because, as the author must be aware, every mention of "real" brand-names and designer clothes dates as quickly as the ink can dry.

Patrick also details for us his *levée* during which he utilises a mind-boggling array of products including: anti-plaque, floss, ice-pack mask, deep-pore cleanser, herb-mint facial mask, spearmint face-scrub, water-activated gel-cleanser, honey-almond body scrub, exfoliating scruffing lotion, shampoo, conditioner, nutrient complex, mousse, moisturiser, alcohol-free anti-bacterial toner, emollient lotion, clarifying lotion, anti-ageing eye-balm, "protective" lotion. All this in a book that Blake Morrison managed to describe as a work "of Zola-esque naturalism"! Beyond the obvious point that no one—not even a girl—could go through this beauty routine every morning and still get to work and the concomitant implication that men have now been herded into the highly lucrative cosmetic market, Ellis's relentless hyperbole here is leading inexorably towards one of the central lines in the novel. A little later in the book, Patrick, in the video store screams: "*There are too many fucking movies to choose from.*" This is a notably unsubtle evocation of the unsubtle sensory overload that effects us all. Daily the cry goes up, the anguished scream from the never-ending moment: "There are too many fucking . . . to choose from." Yams or paw-paws, Clinique or Clarins, am I up-town girl or down-town slob tonight? In this embarrassing plethora of image and reality, we cringe as we gobble and consume, we try to give with one hand and grab with the other (queues in Russia, kwashiorkor in Ethiopia), what shall we buy, take, eat, consume, shit, who are we? This is the boring, mundane heart of postwar consumer capitalism, the hamburger that ate the world, this is it—too much, too soon.

Within consumer capitalism we are offered a surfeit of commodities, an abundance of commodity choices, but this image of plenty is illusory. Our desires are mediated by ideas about roles and lifestyles which are themselves constructed as commodities and our "choices" are propelled by these constructs. In a world in which the only relations are economic we remain alienated from any "authenticity" of choice or desire. Patrick has been so fragmented and divided by his insane consumerism that he cannot "exist" as a person. Literature has been surprisingly coy about tackling the subject of "I shop therefore I am", as one of the girls in the film

Heathers says. Bateman's full-throated cry is a fact, a dead-end, a full-stop. The beyond—be it apocalyptic, climatic, atomic, political—remains fantastical and although Bateman's world might now, in the nineties, be fraying at the edges, the consumer spectacle continues to accelerate. The same critic, Blake Morrison, went on to complain that a book need not mirror all the faults it portrays in order to represent them accurately; boredom need not be boring, nor crudity crude. This is the old debate: William Carlos Williams, Charles Olsen and "form and content". Text and context. We have come to accept that the intervention of authorial language must *always* renegotiate the experience portrayed. In Paul de Man's words: "A fundamental discrepancy always prevents the observer from coinciding fully with the consciousness he is observing." This is particularly evident in **American Psycho** where language is actually used against itself, to distort the narrative. However, in his lists of consumer products Ellis does no more than utilize simple rhetorical devices to ludicrously exaggerate, cartoon-fashion, the experience of consumerism and bring it more fully to our consciousness. At its most basic level, this reduces Bateman's reliability as a narrator and any "realist" reading of the novel.

The best example of this process is seen in Patrick's description of a TV show to which he is addicted and which airs every morning. *The Patty Winters Show* is presented as a talk show not unlike that of Oprah Winfrey and throughout the novel Patrick laconically records the subject of the latest Winters show, frequently interposing his observation against the most incongruous scenes, be they murder or mergers, just as the show itself with its melodramatic content is inappropriately dumped in a million homes. During the novel Patrick tells us that the show covers such subjects as multiple personalities, autism, nuclear war, Nazis, mastectomy, dwarf-tossing, Teenage Girls who Trade Sex for Crack, how to make your Pet a Movie-Star, Princess Di's beauty tips, and many more. As a simple example of the daily fragmentation of our consciousnesses by tabloid mentality, Ellis's use of the show is competent, if uninspired. However, Patrick also tells us that the show featured an interview with a boy who fell in love with a box of soap and an interview with Bigfoot—"to my surprise I found him surprisingly articulate and charming." Also, Patrick tells us, one day on the show a Cheerio sat in a very small chair and was interviewed for an hour. Now these assertions raise much more interesting issues. First, the reader is again called upon to intervene, to supply, in this case, not the moral framework of the book but the sanity. At which point does Patrick's sanity diverge from the general insanity of the show? Out there in tabloid heaven it is certainly possible that someone might believe themselves in love with a box of Ariel and want to tell the world about it. But surely they couldn't have talked to Bigfoot—this is television, not print. And even the most flexible reader must discount the possibility that a small cereal

was interviewed for an hour. So, Patrick is not watching what's on television? At what point did he diverge and start misleading us about the show? Some of the earlier episodes are "authenticated" by Patrick's workmates. But after that—Psycho City. Of such small puzzles is **American Psycho** composed and therein lies much of the humour and pleasure of the book.

Once the tenor of Bateman's days has been established we get some closer glimpses of his social life—drinking sessions with the boys, much jolly racist, sexist bantering coupled with nervous status frenzy as they try to outdo each other in the matter of acquisitions—be they women or engraved business cards. Money remains the bottom line at all times and everyone has difficulty distinguishing their friends. They all look interchangeable and as Ellis has largely refrained from providing any detail of character the "human" element is consistently devalued adding to the impression of an author manipulating robotic puppets. Much energy is expended in securing reservations to fashionable, ludicrously expensive restaurants where food is tortured into iconic artefacts. Food functions as art in the book, paintings themselves being no more than an investment. One of Patrick's first hysterical outbursts occurs in a restaurant where he starts screaming, in a frenzy, about the perfect pizza: "a pizza should be yeasty and slightly bready and have a cheesy crust!"—with all the passion that one might usually reserve for art or politics. This hysteria, besides being funny, defines the miserable limitations of Patrick's world and confirms the fragility of his mental state—anyone who has that much invested in a pizza recipe has to be seriously disturbed.

The first event of importance occurs during a visit the boys make to a nightclub called Tunnel. The gimmick in this club is a set of train tracks which vanish—into a tunnel. After the usual business of scoring poor quality cocaine and trying to pick up girls, with Patrick announcing, as always, unheard: "You are a fucking ugly bitch I want to stab to death and play around with your cunt," Tim Price shouts to Patrick that he is leaving. He stresses it, "I'm getting out . . . leaving." He starts screaming, "I . . . am . . . leaving". Where to, Patrick wants to know, "Morgan Stanley? Rehab?" but Tim "just keeps staring past the railings, trying to find the point where the tracks come to an end, find what lies behind the blackness." And Tim does leave, leaping onto the tracks, running through the flashes of the strobe lights and receding into the tunnel. Tim, who is the "only interesting person" Patrick knows vanishes right into the book, into the text. Tim cannot "leave" the book as his only "existence" is within its pages but he can vanish deeper into the black *tunnel* of the authorial imagination. In cancelling the only character with some pretension to personality, Ellis again emphasizes his artistic control and his decision to people a book with characters whom he resolutely refuses to (con)form into "interesting" representations of human beings. In addition, of course, Tim's vanishing determinedly re-locates Patrick in a joyless, tedious world where panic boredom is never far away.

More than ever now, "everyone looks the same". Patrick's sick sadism is increasingly mentioned. He has rented the *Body Double* video thirty-seven times so that he can masturbate over the scene where a woman is drilled to death by a power drill. He reads endless true crime biographies, Ted Bundy, Son of Sam, Charles Manson. A crack appears in his apartment ceiling. His narrative has its weird slippages—can an "Italian-Thai" restaurant exist? Patrick's narrative is deadpan and such observations destabilize it further. Mim Udovitch pointed out in *The Village Voice* many of the innumerable mis-attributions of pop songs in the book; "Be my Baby" attributed to the Crystals rather than the Ronettes and so on until the *Voice* critic here is finally able to gasp out: "SLOW. UNRELIABLE NARRATOR WORKING." This was actually an achievement considering how few other critics had even managed to reach this simple decision.

When Patrick next returns to Tunnel he finds it empty; the avalanche of fashion-crazed revellers has swept on to new sensations. Tunnel has swallowed Tim only to be emptied itself. Patrick's progress is marked by the continual "death" or wiping-out of whatever has gone immediately before. There is no continuity either in his "self" or his surroundings. There is just the endless circularity of text and an incessant *re*-creation within text. His narrative continues, at times, to collapse into near-meaningless fragments, a blur of obsessions and possessions: "Glass of J&B in my right hand I am thinking. Hand I am thinking . . . Porsche 911. A sharpei I am thinking." Patrick takes what he claims to be blood-stained clothes to the dry-cleaners. Meeting a friend there he claims that the stains are cranapple juice or Hershey's Syrup and indeed, they could be. This is the first of numerous occasions where one can either accept Patrick's version of events or choose an alternative, and quite ordinary explanation.

One of Patrick's acquaintances mistakes him for a man called Marcus Halberstam; he is constantly mis-recognized. The question begins to arise: Who is Patrick? We know of his *fictional* existence. He is the big brother of Sean Bateman in *The Rules of Attraction* and has already made an appearance in that book. He works at Pierce and Pierce which was Sherman McCoy's investment firm in *The Bonfire of the Vanities*. He knows people from other "brat-pack" novels; Stash could be the person of the same name in *Slaves of New York*. Patrick tells of a chilling encounter with Alison Poole, heroine of Jay McInerney's *Story of My Life*. It seems as though Ellis is re-inforcing the fact that Patrick's only "existence" is within fiction. And we know from Roland Barthes just how bizarre is the fictional construct, how illogical, incongruous and contradictory is the contract between writer and reader. We know too how much time postmodern fiction has spent in deconstructing and disentangling the implicit agreements that lie behind fictive "realism". Ellis, in one of his interviews, has challenged the expectation "That novels must have traditional narrative structure . . . You would think that most writers in their twenties would want to fool around a little bit—would want to be a little experimental—would want to write something a little bit subversive." Any reading of **American Psycho** must take these intentions into account.

By the time Patrick describes a murder in detail he has already claimed to have murdered a number of people: guests on the yacht, Evelyn's neighbour whose head, he says, he kept in his refrigerator, and two black kids. He now kills a poor black bum, slowly and sadistically, in a scene whose terrible pathos is inescapable. Ellis may have intended this in order to highlight Patrick's increasing zombiefication as the murders progress and the most repulsive of acts are described in an affectless monotone. The existence of increasing numbers of homeless people throughout the eighties aroused strong, conflicting responses in the more fortunate, responses compounded of hate, dread and pity. Throughout **American Psycho** the spectre of the homeless is constant; they hover, *les misérables,* like ghosts on the edge of consciousness, a reproach, a reproof, a warning.

> **Ellis has sound reasons for his sensationalism and, moreover, it is inextricably intertwined with the technical sophistication of the book. Unfortunately the violence overpowered critical response to a point where few were able to see the humour of the novel.**
> **—Elizabeth Young**

Ellis has sound reasons for his sensationalism and, moreover, it is inextricably intertwined with the technical sophistication of the book. Unfortunately the violence overpowered critical response to a point where few were able to see the humour of the novel. This is understandable perhaps, but the book is, in parts, extremely funny. Ellis has said: "I used comedy to get at the absolute banality of the violence of a perverse decade." Two of the characters, Luis Carruthers and his girlfriend Courtney Lawrence, seem to evolve, almost against the author's will, into fairly animated personalities and as it is Luis whom Patrick next attempts to murder, it is worth examining the couple in slightly more detail.

Courtney is a ditzy, romantic beauty, strung-out on lithium who shows traces of sensibility and loyalty from within her tranked-out haze. Patrick goes to bed with her while Luis is out of town, a highly comic coupling. While Patrick builds furiously towards his orgasm he realizes there is . . . some sort of problem and, pulling out, goes stumbling around the apartment. He is looking for the medicine cabinet. He needs the . . . water-soluble spermicidal lubricant! He needs it badly—he absolutely cannot have sex unless his obsessive-compulsive need for the correct consumer product is satisfied. He dabs on the lubricant, reapplies his latex sheath and bounces back onto Courtney who gasps, "Luis is a despicable twit." No. Someone has misheard again. Similarly product-dazed, what she moaned was: "Is it a receptacle tip?" It isn't. They have to sit up and discuss the *force of the ejaculate.* They manage to half-heartedly complete a sex act that is completely bedeviled by consumer products, with Courtney wittering on to the end about Norma Kamali bikinis, "antique cutting boards and the sterling silver cheese grater and muffin tin she left at Harry's.

Similarly, any encounter with Luis tends towards the farcical. When he returns from his business trip to Phoenix he describes the dinner he had with his client, a routine-sounding affair of roasted chicken and cheesecake. Patrick gets anxious, confused "by this alien, plain-sounding list". He asks feverishly, "What sauce or fruits were on the roasted chicken? What shapes was it cut into?" Luis is confused. "It was . . . roasted," he says. Patrick demands to know what the client's bimbo had. Scallops, apparently. "The scallops were grilled? Were they sashimi scallops? In a ceviche of sorts? . . . Or were they gratinized?" "No, Patrick", Luis says. "They were . . . broiled." Patrick then thinks for a while. "What's broiled, Luis?" "I'm not sure," he says. "I think it involves . . . a pan." There lies the gulf between the yuppies and the rest of the known world.

Even Patrick's attempt to *murder* Luis is farcical. When Patrick decides to kill Luis it is in the vague, unrealistic hope that Courtney who might be a "shallow bitch" but is a "physically superior, near-perfect shallow bitch" might spend more time with him if Luis were dead. Mindlessly he asks himself: "Would I ruin things by strangling Luis?" Deciding that he wouldn't he follows Luis to the men's room and puts his hands round Luis's neck, hoping to crunch his trachea. However Luis, who is known to be bisexual, totally misreads Patrick's intentions. He kisses Patrick's left wrist and looks up at him shyly and awkwardly. "'God, Patrick', he whispers . . . 'I've noticed your'—he gulps—'hot body.'" He speaks in "a low, faggoty whisper" and begs Patrick not to be shy.

Despite the comic aspects of Patrick's discomfiture, this and later scenes with Luis where Luis expresses his hopeless love have an oddly tender and touching quality.

From when Patrick tries to murder Luis, the book becomes darker and more relentless as the body-count mounts inexorably. Patrick has already announced once, in a restaurant,

"My life is a living hell," but no one responds. He has had a sort of breakdown where he staggers around town, "sweating and moaning and pushing people out of the way, foam pouring out of my mouth . . ." He shoplifts a ham, eats it, throws it up and meets some friend from Wall Street who greets him as "Kinsley". "I belch into his face, my eyes rolling back into my head, greenish bile dripping in strings from my bared fangs." The man is unfazed which suggests that either, once again, Patrick's narrative is seriously askew, or that the legendary tolerance of New Yorkers for terminal weirdness is well deserved.

Patrick kills a sharpei, he kills an old gay man, he hires whores and tortures them. He endures a nightmare Christmas, describing shops crammed with "bookends and lightweight luggage, electric shoepolishers and heated towelstands and silver-plated carafes" and so on and on in passages reminiscent of Nicole Diver's celebrated consumer binge in *Tender Is the Night.* Evelyn's Christmas party involves guests wearing antlers on their heads and bar-tender elves singing "O Tannenbaum". The pressure mounts.

The following summer he kills a broker he envies, Paul Owen, dining with him first under the name Marcus Halberstam, which is who Owen thinks he is anyway. Imitating the victim's voice he leaves a message on the answering machine saying that Owen has gone to London. After a revoltingly explicit ax murder he puts Paul's body in a sleeping-bag, drags it past the night doorman and down the block. He runs into two friends, one of whom asks him what the general rules for wearing a white dinner jacket are. Is any reader still taking him seriously? He next kills an ex-girlfriend from college, Bethany, in a fit of furious jealousy. He nails her to the floor with a nail-gun. We learn a little of Patrick's background from Bethany: the fact that he is independently wealthy and doesn't have to work, only doing so because "I want to fit in". Patrick's psychological profile is in general, so slight and muddled as to deliberately reject the pleas of all the Norman Mailers of fiction for an "inner life".

After each of the major killings—those of the black bum Al, Bethany and the several in the chapter "Chase, Manhattan"—there follows, either immediately or very shortly afterwards, an extremely strange, bland analysis of pop music. Al's murder is followed by a chapter on Genesis, Bethany's by a chapter on Whitney Houston and the mass murders in "Chase, Manhattan" by one on Huey Lewis and the News. The change in tone is so marked, so extreme that at first it seems impossible that "Patrick", not known for organized thinking has "written" them. Written in the style of middlebrow AOR rock journalism they use the first person so any straightforward reading of the text would assume that they were indeed intended to have been "written" by Patrick. However their entire presence is so at odds with Patrick's narrative performance that one is tempted to read them as further evidence for the non-reality, the not-thereness of Patrick, as they seem to indicate, through the narrative voice, an entirely different personality. The language is sophisticated and emotional—"It's an epic meditation on intangibility, at the same time it depends and enriches the meaning of the preceeding three albums . . ."—and much concerned with feeling and maturity. Each of the chapters, but particularly the one on Huey Lewis, concerns the maturation of a creative artist and in this there might be a clue as to what comprises the "absence" in *American Psycho*. As previously noted, *Less Than Zero* was postulated against an absent "other", in its case education and the East. *The Rules of Attraction* moved on to deal with and destroy that particular illusion and in this second novel the "absent presence" was adult life. *American Psycho* moves us into that life, into the grown-up world but what is now absent is maturity, growth, successful relationships, marriage and parenthood. Ellis, in these rock-critic chapters, suggests firstly that there is another "personality" in the book, not Patrick, not, except by default, the author, and secondly that this personality defines, particularly in his analysis of the career of Huey Lewis, the absence of personal growth and maturity in the novel as a whole. Towards the climax of *American Psycho* a sort of salvation is offered to Patrick in the form of the love of his devoted secretary, Jean, and although this is an utterly mawkish, clichéd device and intended to be seen as such, nevertheless, it is to Jean that Patrick makes remarks such as, "I just want to have a meaningful relationship with someone special." Some part of his personality is striving towards maturity.

Eventually Paul Owen's fiancée hires a private detective, Donald Kimball, to investigate Owen's disappearance. Patrick is able to offer useful insights along the lines of: "He. . .ate a balanced diet." Paul's diary of course states that he was having dinner with Marcus Halberstam but Marcus has been interviewed and found to be telling the truth when he said he spent the evening at a club with a group of friends, all named and . . . including Patrick Bateman.

Patrick spends the summer with Evelyn in Tim Price's house in East Hampton. It is the classic romantic idyll which swiftly degenerates—all too soon Patrick is microwaving jellyfish— and as such closely reminiscent of Clay's doomed holiday with Blair in *Less Than Zero*. The hopeless and rather sad black comedy of Patrick's relationship with Evelyn is epitomized by his presenting her with a gift-wrapped, chocolate frosted urinal-cake in a restaurant which she gamely, innocently tries to eat, gasping at intervals, "It's just . . . so minty." Patrick then claims to have terminated the relationship (without killing her).

Patrick continues to kill girls and to desecrate their bodies. It is these torture murders and the killing of a child at a zoo

that, naturally, attracted most critical attention, but in fact Patrick is a thoroughly democratic killer and by the end of the book the body-count, by my reckoning stands at thirty-three and covers the entire cross-section of race, class, age and gender in New York society. At one point he takes two prostitutes to Paul Owen's "ridiculous-looking condo", tortures and kills them there. In blood he scrawls the words "I AM BACK" on the wall above the faux-cowhide panelling and follows them with a "scary drawing" which he says "looks that this". A blank space follows.

The novel now rapidly approaches its climax. The sex murders become more extreme and Patrick claims to torture a girl to death with a starving rat. These killings are robotically described: "I'm wearing a Joseph Abboud suit, a tie by Paul Stuart, shoes by J. Crew, a vest by someone Italian and I'm kneeling on the floor beside a corpse, eating the girl's brain, gobbling it down, spreading Grey Poupon over hunks of the pink, fleshy meat." Real murderers *have* been known to behave in such ways towards their victims but the way this is presented is such an extreme manifestation of blanket blank that it can only be read as a parodically hyperbolic comment on affectlessness and a further destabilizing of Patrick's competence as a narrator. Boundaries are being eroded. Even if we believe it to be remotely possible that someone might try to grind a woman into meat patties and cook her, sobbing all the while, "I just want to be loved," we can only respond, in this context, with sick hilarity. "I guess you walk a very thin line when you try and write about a serial killer in a very satirical way," says Ellis. "There's this new sensitivity. You cannot risk offending anyone."

In the seminal "Chase, Manhattan" chapter Patrick goes completely berserk. He rages through Manhattan killing first a busker, then an Iranian cab-driver and then, just after the narrative goes into the third person, he kills some cops. At this point the novel seems to enter into a parodic version of a cop-killer thriller: "he returns their gunfire from his belly, getting a glimpse of both cops behind the open door of the squad car" and so on. Patrick flees towards Wall Street, shooting a night watchman and then, as the narrative reverts to the first person, he is "safe in the anonymity of my office". A helicopter appears, a SWAT team leaps out, a half-dozen armed men make towards the entrance on the roof, flares are lined up everywhere and Patrick has phoned a friend, Harold Carnes, who predictably, isn't in. Patrick leaves a message confessing to "thirty, forty, a hundred murders". The cops are all approaching, police cars and ambulances surround the base of the building and "night turns into day so fast it's like some kind of optical illusion. . ." It *is* some kind of optical illusion. The next chapter opens with the sane, sensible account of Huey Lewis and the News and the one after that finds Patrick back in bed with Courtney.

This chapter must be the final nail in the coffin of Patrick's credibility. Ellis has already created a most unusual creature, a serial sex-killer who is also, at the same time, prepared to kill absolutely anyone. (In his *Rolling Stone* interview Ellis claims, weirdly: "I thought maybe serial killers would protest the book.") Killers have their *modus operandi* and in "Chase, Manhattan", Ellis compounds the absurdity by making Patrick both a serial-killer and a mass murderer, two quite distinct types who have never been known to co-exist in one person. Mass murderers (Charles Whiteman, James Huberty) blow up suddenly, kill as many people as possible in a single incidence and are invariably shot by police. Serial killers (Ted Bundy, John Wayne Gacy, the Yorkshire Ripper) are usually sexually motivated, careful and cunning and can remain in action for many years. However, lest anyone actually believes that Patrick Bateman could have continued with his everyday life after this rampage, we are given several more quite distinct opportunities to make up our minds.

One hundred and sixty-one days after he left the two escort girls dead in Paul Owen's apartment, Patrick returns to find the apartment, which is extremely valuable, up for sale. A real-estate agent, "distressingly *real*-looking" and a yuppie couple are present. There is no trace of "the torrents of blood and gore that washed over the apartment". The place stinks of roses. There are dozens of bouquets. After Patrick has asked about Paul Owen, the estate agent warns him to leave, saying, "Don't make any trouble." Can it be possible that a dreadful double murder was concealed for the sake of a grasping real-estate sale?

Patrick runs into Harold Carnes, the person to whom he made his confession on an answering machine. During the conversation Carnes manages to address Patrick as "Davies" and as "Donaldson" and apparently believes that the message about "Bateman" was a joke. "But come on, man, you had one fatal flaw: Bateman's such a bloody ass-kisser, such a brown-nosing goody-goody, that I couldn't fully appreciate it." Carnes also mentions that Evelyn dumped Bateman. Patrick starts to shout, insisting, "I killed Paul Owen. I did it, Carnes. I chopped Owen's fucking head off. I tortured dozens of girls," although, interestingly, he doesn't mention what might have seemed necessary which is that he *is* Bateman. Carnes brushes him off saying that his assertions are simply not possible he—had *dinner* with Paul Owen—*twice*—in London just ten days ago.

This might *finally* seem conclusive but we must still remember the constant confusion of identity throughout the novel.

Lastly a cab-driver attacks Patrick saying that he killed his friend Solly, another cab-driver and that Patrick's picture is on a WANTED poster downtown. Patrick recalls killing a foreign cab-driver, an Armenian he thinks now, not an Iranian, during the chase sequence, but certainly not a Solly.

The driver steals Patrick's Rolex and Wayfarers, which is probably all he wanted to do anyway.

Thus we are given three distinct opportunities to weigh up Patrick's narrative, with evidence assembled both for and against its authenticity, as in a court of law. That so many critics accepted Patrick as a "real" killer in the face of all this is a massive testimony to careless reading. However, and this is the most important question raised by Patrick's narrative, what difference does it make whether we believe Patrick committed some, any or all of the murders, or not? We have still had to read all the detailed descriptions of the killings and the effect on us is exactly the same. Whether Patrick's murders are fantasies or not, within fiction, they are all fictional. Thus we are forced by the author to confront the definition and function of fictionality itself.

This leads on to an even more basic question about Patrick's role. At around the time that all this comes to a head, Patrick is being offered pure, untainted love by his secretary, Jean. In a chapter entitled "End of the 1980s" he indulges in some heavy-duty musing about the tragic nature of contemporary reality: "Individuality no longer an issue . . . Fear, recrimination, innocence, sympathy, guilt, waste, failure, grief, were things, emotions that no one really felt anymore. Reflection is useless, the world is senseless. Evil is its only permanence. God is not alive. Love cannot be trusted. Surface, surface, surface was all that anyone found meaning in . . ." This sophomoric philosophizing appears to be delivered seriously, although it is nonsensical placed against the enormity of the crimes Patrick has claimed to have committed. As he talks to Jean about her feelings for him he continues to think, this time about himself: "My personality is sketchy and unformed, my pain is constant and sharp . . . This confession has meant nothing." He also states to himself: "*I simply am not there*", and it is tempting to take him at his word. Perhaps the Patrick we know simply does not exist and the person talking to Jean, tentatively accepting her love and experiencing an "epiphany" is another Patrick, the real Patrick, the one who Carnes sees as a "goody-goody", whom Evelyn rejects, who is given to thoughtful, if somewhat cloying considerations of popular music and who kills no one? He and Jean see a baby. "I feel I'm moving towards as well as away from something and anything is possible."

Anything *is* possible. Around this time Patrick, although he seems to have stopped saying he kills people after his conversation with Jean, appears to be going madder and madder. He has started drinking his own urine, laughing at nothing, sleeping under his futon and flossing his teeth constantly. His automated bank teller has started speaking to him and "I was freaked out by the park bench that followed me for six blocks last Monday evening."

Ellis also writes: "And, for the sake of form, Tim Price resurfaces, or at least I'm pretty sure he does." *For the sake of form? I'm pretty sure he does?* With the authenticity of Patrick's narrative in shreds, with Patrick operating as at least two and possibly three personalities and with statements like this one we are forced to ask who is Patrick, really? The "Bateman" known to the guys and to Carnes is seemingly not the person who tells the story of the book. Who *is* Patrick? *I simply am not there.* Is he perhaps Tim Price who vanishes so deeply into the book, whose East Hampton house Patrick stays in and who now re-appears, strangely elusive on the subject of his absence. ("It was . . . surprising" "It was . . . depressing". Where has he been? Inside the book, in Patrick's brain?) Is Patrick one of the *other* guys in the book, fleetingly mentioned, always around? Might Patrick be Paul Owen whose apartment he appropriates? Could he possibly even be . . . Marcus Halberstam?! Who knows? The person who tells the story, who fantasizes about impossible murders does not "exist" in any traditional fictional sense. We might as well consider him a spirit; the *Zeitgeist,* all-yuppie, all-corrupt. Or we could regard him as the sense of humour so notably lacking in his circles, created in Patrick's voice to render black comedy from the intolerable. Patrick is device. He is never the author and at the same time, like all fictional devices, he is always the author.

> **American Psycho is what Roland Barthes called a "writerly" text. It invites the reader in to play amongst its games and inconsistencies.**
> —*Elizabeth Young*

Much of the frustration felt by critics as they tried to grapple with the book's apparent context stemmed from a vague sense of Patrick's *insubstantiality* as a "character". It was impossible to get to grips with him—because he wasn't really there. Ellis talks of "becoming" Patrick for hours at a time while he was writing and it seems as if while in this state of possession Bateman started to "write" Ellis. Patrick is annihilated in language and it is impossible to tell when the rigid authorial control may have ceded "meaning" to the involuntary forces of language itself. Patrick is "wiped-out" between the two spheres of life, the public and the private. His agony consists of the way his interior life keeps leaking into the public arena only to be inauthenticated, so that he has to reinforce his "self", his "identity", in ever more extreme and violent ways. It is a basic tenet of postmodernism that the public and private spaces of life are being eroded, are blending—blanding—into one hyperreal theatre. It could be that Patrick is annihilated at precisely this juncture, is unable to realize his "self" without a collision of the public and private which then destroys any autonomous "ego". Of course the interplay between the public and private spheres mimics the fictional process itself; an author always extrudes

the interior into the public arena. However, in Bateman's case, within the text the juxtaposition and erosion of the public and private worlds seems exceptionally central to his story and accounts for much of Bateman's confusion and incomprehension in relation to the world. He does not understand the boundaries of the appropriate and inappropriate, the acceptable and the unacceptable; his "personality" debouches haphazardly along a spectrum from the most secret and interior desires to the mannered conventions of a highly-sophisticated society. This is postmodernity in process, knowing no limits, uniting desire and entertainment within spectacle. An individual "personality" cannot sustain these contradictions; an individual "personality" in which Id, Ego and Super-Ego go into melt-down is doomed. It is doomed to psychosis, schizophrenia, gibberish non-language—and we see this happening to Patrick before he implodes completely within the text. Patrick *is* a cipher; a sign in language and it is in language that he disintegrates, slips out of our grasp. Patrick is Void. He is the Abyss. He is a textual impossibility, written out, elided until there is no "Patrick" other than the sign or signifier that sets in motion the process that must destroy him and thus at the end the book must go back to its beginnings and start again. This process reveals his invisibility and re-signs him to a circle of hell where he can never find resolution or autonomy in that he "exists" only to disintegrate. Patrick becomes in effect, feminized, excluded from "existing" in language; he is the void, the mystery, the threat of dreadful desires, the uncontrolled libido, the unconscious, the dark side of the moon. As "nothing" Patrick is dangerous. As a person, as a consumer, he cannot exist; he is an impossibility.

American Psycho is what Roland Barthes called a "writerly" text. It invites the reader in to play amongst its games and inconsistencies. Unusually however, unlike most "writerly" texts it is not deeply subversive or dislocating. It has nothing in it of what Barthes termed rapture, "bliss" or *jouissance.* For all the fuss it lacks the "shock, disturbance, even loss, which are proper to ecstasy, to bliss". Texts of bliss are extreme, threatening, they bring us towards death or annihilation; Barthes mentions Georges Bataille. *American Psycho* might seem, superficially, to be such a text but in fact it is not at all. It is far closer to what Barthes termed a "text of pleasure": "the text that comes from culture and does not break with it." Ellis might be very critical of his culture, his text may be an experimentation in many ways but he comes from deep within that culture and cannot be said to pose anything of an anarchic threat towards it. The faults Ellis perceives in contemporary culture come from an old-fashioned, straightforwardly moralistic reading of it. His books present terrible amoral deviations, which, if rectified, would restore to society all the moral values it has lost and would revive a more wholesome dominant culture. Ellis's vision is conformist and conventional. He is skilled at presenting disintegration within postmodernity and his energies are straightforwardly judgemental and condemnatory. He is denunciatory, a supporter of the status quo and in relation to this it is ironic to what a large extent he has been depicted as some sort of literary tearaway. Insofar as Patrick Bateman is allowed to operate as a unified entity, before his persona is totally shredded, he functions as a rhetorical device, the Devil's Advocate whose consumer manifesto merely highlights what Ellis has referred to as the "spiritual" malaise and ugliness of the eighties. Like David Lynch, Ellis is merely "weird on top" not "wild at heart". Just as in *Twin Peaks* the "identity" or "meaning" of the murderer behaved like language, slipping from signifier to signifier, so Ellis too is inventive, deconstructing within language the existence or "meaning" of *his* fictive murderer. Both Patrick Bateman and "Bob" from *Twin Peaks* through their actions "murder" the order of a moral universe and slide us into postmodern chaos. Behind them lies the conventional nostalgic vision of a lost world where actions were not random, where emotion was authentic and where everything once made sense.

American Psycho should be taken seriously; if it is as blunt and simplistic as its critics claim how have they managed to miss everything of significance within the book? It is an important text. Ellis manages to take his obsession with deindividualization in consumer society to its extreme and demonstrate that Patrick's in his role of ultimate consumer, someone who is composed entirely of inauthentic commodity-related desires *cannot* exist as a person. He is doomed to fragmentation and disintegration.

> *American Psycho* **represents all that we mean by Post-Punk or Blank Generation writing in that it is written from deep within consumer culture by an author who has never known anything else and who consequently lacks much of the critical ambivalence and the political disquiet about popular culture evinced by older novelists and theoreticians.**
> *—Elizabeth Young*

American Psycho represents all that we mean by Post-Punk or Blank Generation writing in that it is written from deep within consumer culture by an author who has never known anything else and who consequently lacks much of the critical ambivalence and the political disquiet about popular culture evinced by older novelists and theoreticians. At the same time it has its own agenda which is anything but blank. Despite his unease with moral absolutes the author is determined not to flinch from representing that which he undoubtedly condemns. Although Ellis is skilled at representing contemporary society it would seem that, unlike many postmodern theorists, he maintains a belief in a "real-

ity" or morality somewhere beyond the spectacular blandishments of the hyperreal consumer circus. As it seems unlikely that he inclines towards revolutionary politics, it is natural to assume that like David Lynch he might have a vision of some more edenic moral universe, pre-postmodern fragmentation and commodity fetishism. At the same time *American Psycho* is a sophisticated high postmodern text. All the theoretical constituents of postmodern culture are there—the commodity fixation, the focus on image, codes and style, the proliferation of surfaces and the deindividualization of neofogey characters who "play" with the past—"I'm pro-family and anti-drug"—and in doing so embody irony and paradox. The text itself participates fully in the "conventions" of postmodern literature: the unreliable narrator, the lack of closure, Eco's "game of irony", double-distancing, a refusal to mirror "reality" and a constant examination of the ways in which fiction is ordered, ever aware of its own status as discourse and construct. Thus *American Psycho* can be seen as a classic text at the end of the high postmodern period and simultaneously as playing its part in the slow emergence of an American renaissance that attempts to transcend these fictional games, and re-establish, from deep within consumer culture, other ways of writing fiction and apprehending American society as it approaches the millennium.

Neal Karlen (review date 21 August 1994)

SOURCE: "Attack of the Anti-Heroes," in *Los Angeles Times Book Review,* August 8, 1994, pp. 3, 8.

[*In the following review of* The Informers, *Karlen critiques the development of Ellis's work.*]

Joe McGinniss' gravest crime against literature was not *The Last Brother,* the author's recent and ridiculous faux-biography of Ted Kennedy. Rather, McGinniss' worst felony was rushing Bret Easton Ellis, his fiction-writing student at Bennington College, to publish *Less Than Zero* at age 21.

Ironically, the 1985 first novel was an excellent beginning for an obviously talented writer; *Less Than Zero* provided a provocative snapshot of a time when the anomic ditherings of idle, rich, drug-addled, white-bread Los Angeles young adults was considered fresh material. Bearing a canny journalist's eye for detail and dialogue, Ellis' storytelling already carried the complete lack of sentiment and empathy of a seasoned nihilistic novelist.

Ellis became a famous, best-selling young writer and was touted as the voice of a generation. But like a rookie phenom pitcher without a second pitch, Ellis immediately ran out of what ballplayers call *stuff.*

Ernest Hemingway and Norman Mailer earned their material and early anomie through actual life experience; both had been to war by the time they were famous writers in their early 20s. Bret Easton Ellis, however, had only been, apparently, to Bennington. Walled in by his own youth and too early fame from any adult life experience, he refused to learn any new pitch beyond the Reagan-era ditherings of idle, rich, drug addled young Los Angeles adults.

Sadly and predictably, during the years Ellis should have been apprenticing his skills and honing his chops, he wrote the same novel over, calling the 1987 volume *The Rules of Attraction.* This time, however, the insights were rarer, the humor almost absent, the prose as flat as a day-old *latke.* His characters, meantime, had degenerated into half-dimensional Barbie and Ken dolls.

Ellis was writing worse and acting stupid. In time, his Manhattan nightclub shenanigans, constantly and mockingly detailed by *Spy* magazine, provided a much more tragic story than anything he was typing.

By the time *American Psycho,* his last novel, was published in 1991, Ellis was largely a joke among the young cognoscenti who'd once made him famous. That book, filled with the excruciating, affectless murderings of a serial killer, became a *cause célèbre* when it was boycotted by feminists as misogynistic pornography. The book was indeed a horror; by now Ellis had seemed to give up even the pretense of writing, and was content to simply transcribe lists of tony clothing manufacturers from the back pages of *GQ.*

Sadly, the publication of *The Informers,* Ellis' newest book, is not a case of a literary comeback of a written-off one-hit wonder, but a further slide down for an author who long ago had it. Ostensibly a novel, the book is a plotless collage of short stories alternately narrated by a rogues' gallery of human monsters whose characters are developed with technical dexterity.

There is, for example, the club-hopping vampire who drains his bimbo pickups' blood dry; the dazed-on-downers studio wife who sleeps with her kids' friends; the rock star who makes underage prostitutes eat Kleenex; the young man who unashamedly rifles his just-dead friend's pockets for salvageable marijuana seconds after a hideous car accident. For a point, one must turn to the novel's publicity write-up, where we learn that the characters are "all suffering, whether they admit it or not, from no disease other than the death of the soul."

Unfortunately, Ellis' publicist is a more interesting writer than Ellis, whose anti-heroes swim in swamps duller than bongwater. His notorious sex passages are often detailed with the kind of plodding, leering, badly described scenes published in Penthouse Forum: "The girl is pretty, blond, dark tan, large wide blue eyes, Californian, a T-shirt with my name on it, faded tight cutoff jeans. Her lips are red, shiny, and she puts the magazine down as I slowly move toward her, almost tripping over a used dildo that Roger calls the Enabler."

When Ellis isn't writing about brutal sex or casual murder—which isn't often—his scenes can sound like the product of an introductory fiction-writing workshop where students are told to record exactly a banal, everyday scene. "The Librium I took at dawn has worn off and my mouth feels thick and dry and I am thirsty," Ellis writes. "I get up, slowly, and walk into the bathroom and as I turn on the faucet I look into the mirror for a long time until I am forced to notice the new lines beginning around the eyes. I avert my gaze and concentrate on the cold water rushing out of the faucet and filling the cup my hands have made."

And then there are the sex-and-slice passages so nauseating that it doesn't matter if a joke is intended. At one point, the vampire relates in a relatively mild scene in *The Informers* how "I begin to lick and chew at the skin on her neck, panting, slavering, finding the jugular vein with my tongue, and I start bleeding her and she's laughing and moaning . . . and blood is spurting into my mouth, splashing the roof, and then something weird starts to happen. . . ."

There is a rancid phoniness to Ellis's delivery of his chosen demimonde. Again, one suspects the author's early suffocation by fame. While William Burroughs and Charles Bukowski spent anonymous decades on the fringes living the perverse material they turned into art, Ellis had spent the better part of his waning youth playing the buffoon at Nell's.

Los Angeles, meantime, is rendered in just the kind of soggy clichés that Ellis dissected so neatly in *Less Than Zero.* It's not just that he's hopelessly mired all of his novels in the pre-riots, pre-O.J. 1980s. After all, decades after they were published, Nathanael West's *The Day of the Locust* and Alison Lurie's *The Nowhere City* still capture the city's unique brand of status-driven dread with the timeliness of a new episode of "Entertainment Tonight."

Ellis, however, is unable to transcend his chosen decade, to make his relentless name-dropping of mediocre 1980s rock groups somehow bring his story alive for the latest generation of disaffected youth for whom Duran Duran is of no more cultural relevance than Mario Lanza.

Ellis, at 31, is still young enough to be the voice of Generation X, and it is a mantle he still seems to covet. But he long ago lost that race—and to a rock singer no less. The late Kurt Cobain of Nirvana wrote the poetry that will be remembered as the "Howl" of the twentysomething slacker army; his words, "*Here we are now / entertain us,*" long ago swamped Ellis's entry—the once famous opening line to *Less Than Zero:* "People are afraid to merge on freeways in Los Angeles."

Yet even after his precipitous fall from the ranks of America's most promising young writers, Ellis apparently has not learned the lesson of empathy, either on the page or in life. In the August issue of *Vanity Fair,* Ellis commented on the real voice of his generation: "The thing that struck me about Kurt Cobain's suicide is not that I was sad but that it wasn't Kathie Lee Gifford."

Like Ellis' late *oeuvre,* the statement was opaque and bitter, devoid of both humanity and meaning. One hopes he will spend the coming years working on the craft he abandoned after *Less Than Zero.*

Alexander Star (review date 5 September 1994)

SOURCE: A review of *The Informers,* in *New York Times Book Review,* Vol. 211, No. 10, September 5, 1994, pp. 46-7.

[*In the following review, Star identifies Ellis's themes and his stylistic contributions to the "L.A. novel."*]

As if to make up for the city's incessant boosterism, the Los Angeles novel carries a strong current of disaffection. Brooding despair mocks buoyant dreams; cynicism poisons the sunshine. This tradition distilled itself in Joan Didion's *Play It as It Lays,* where the entire metropolis was coolly reduced to a few locations (restaurants, hotel rooms, the freeway) and an even smaller number of emotions (anxiety, disengagement). *Play It as It Lays* may have been intentionally fatigued, designed to sound like the last book of its kind. But it inspired a legion of imitators. For many Californian writers, the L.A. novel became a trip to Didionland.

Bret Easton Ellis's *Less Than Zero,* which appeared in 1985, cleverly adapted Didion's narrow range and brittle style to the age of MTV. Not surprisingly, Ellis became an instant object of emulation as young writers everywhere began composing their own stripped-down novels about drugs, sex and driving. And then, his ambitions inflated by early success, Ellis saw his stock fall. *American Psycho,* his third book, was intended as a nightmarish indictment of Wall Street, serial killers and the American way, but its lurid violence and its colorless prose prompted an avalanche of ill will.

Four years later Ellis is back in L.A., stringing together stories about kids who don't know if they've been pampered or abused by their affluent parents. The barely linked mono-

logues of *The Informers* are set in the early '80s, which means that synth-pop and breakdancing dominate the cultural landscape and MTV is new enough to be worth mentioning. There are the usual divorced entertainment executives, bored teenagers and ravenous party-goers. As ever, the pills (Thorazine, Nembutal, Librium) have more personality than the characters (Bruce, Martin, Tim). The closest thing to a political theme is the danger of corporate jets.

Ellis's L.A. is a city bordered on one side by boredom and on the other by disaster. In one episode, four teenagers mark the anniversary of a friend's death by taunting each other and avoiding the subject. In another, a young woman travels across the country by train; horrified that her stepmother-to-be has seen Flashdance five times and that her parents don't talk, she decides to stay on the train and keep traveling. Meanwhile, ominous portents suggest that a team of vampires is at work in the hills. After a brutal episode in which a child is kidnapped and stabbed to death, the book returns to quieter scenes. Someone pleads with her boyfriend at the zoo. A girl sits on the beach all day, succumbing to a fatal disease, while her friends observe that "she's looking pretty shitty."

What is this all about? Ellis might not be the most intellectually demanding of writers, but he does have a plan, which is to expose the nihilism and depersonalization of the well-financed young. (Someone has to do it.) This was most evident in the despised *American Psycho.* As that book proceeds, its narrator, the yuppie stockbroker Patrick Bateman, comes apart. His self is vacated of identity and inhabited by a series of brand names, talk show topics and fashionable restaurants. Then he starts to kill people.

The book's greatest fault was that Ellis seemed to think no better of his readers than of his characters. Desperate to impress something onto his jaded audience, he resorted to stiff caricature and gruesome violence. His Manhattan epic became a jumble of severed tongues and gouged-out breasts, staple guns and jumper cables. Still, Ellis's demonization wasn't entirely deserved. His primary subject was not brutality (about which he had little to say). It was another venerable theme: the tyranny of surfaces in a culture ruled by status symbols. In *The Bonfire of the Vanities,* Tom Wolfe perched himself high above his turbulent, position-crazed Manhattanites; Ellis simply abandoned himself to their consumer madness.

Though Ellis didn't seem to fully appreciate it, this is a dangerous act; it's hard to tell the difference between writing about anonymity and writing anonymously. Like his anti-hero, Ellis often seemed bewitched by the consumer carnival. Yet Ellis did approach depersonalization with a paradoxical kind of intimacy, setting Bateman's disintegration against a detailed background of maddening gadgets and mindless conversation. He was especially prescient about the small irritations that new technology can provoke; one elaborate scene is choreographed around the impossibility of two people making dinner plans while being interrupted by call-waiting. In Bateman's flawlessly up-to-date apartment, the CD player is always skipping.

Many readers complained of the endlessly reiterated brand names and disposable goods ("paisley ties and crystal water pitchers, tumbler sets and office clocks that measure temperature and humidity and barometric pressure, electric calling card address books and margarita glasses . . ."). They certainly didn't make for graceful writing. But these catalogs were not the artless attempts at specificity typical of '80s fiction. The main accomplishment of *American Psycho* was to give its glittering artifacts a mysterious, and threatening, presence. As Bateman vanishes from the story, they acquire a hallucinatory energy of their own; they are the dismal residue of his soul.

> **With *The Informers,* a chastened Ellis returns to a safer, and more familiar, zone of alienation. Unlike *American Psycho,* the new novel never attempts much in the way of development; the typical passage begins with a flat, declarative statement . . . and ends with a shrug . . .**
> —*Alexander Star*

With *The Informers,* a chastened Ellis returns to a safer, and more familiar, zone of alienation. Unlike *American Psycho,* the new novel never attempts much in the way of development; the typical passage begins with a flat, declarative statement ("I drive to the Beverly Center and wander around . . .") and ends with a shrug ("I hang up, pass out"). As in Didion, Ellis's characters are invariably numb on the surface, agitated underneath. Their stories are intended as miniature dramas of dissociation. No one gets anyone else's jokes; telephone conversations meander ("Is the connection, like, clear?"); every human encounter is interrupted by random distractions. Long, uninflected sentences mirror blank, uninflected lives.

To compensate for the lack of momentum, Ellis tries to maintain an edgy tone of coolness and control, rising up to the edge of feeling but never beyond it. Quite often, however, he intrudes himself into the void; and then his stark monologues quickly devolve into stagy set-pieces or blatant editorializing. In one chapter, a divorced father tries to get to know his son on a Hawaiian vacation, and fails. Ellis isn't content just to show the distance between parent and child. "Looking at Tim," the father muses, "one cannot help feel-ing great waves of uncertainty, an absence of aim, of purpose. . . ." In a final scene, the father imagines Tim "looking out past the horizon, his eyes disappointed at finding even more of the same flatness."

Ellis's even, unmodulated prose looks like the kind of writing style that anyone can operate. But it isn't, and Ellis doesn't have the tact and the precision to make it work. Every time disaster strikes, a distracted or evasive response follows. When Jamie dies in a car crash, Dirk shuffles through his dead friend's pockets, looking for a joint. When Danny tells Cheryl the anchorwoman that Rickie is dead, she berates him for forgetting to "tape the newscast tonight." When Graham hears shots being fired inside an apartment building on Wilshire Boulevard, he approaches a nearby doorman who is listening to a good song on his Walkman. This sort of anti-drama can be effective: Malcolm Cowley once compared Hemingway's writing to a widow's cleaning the house on the morning after her husband died. But Ellis is no Hemingway; he doesn't trust his culturally damaged readers, and so he repeats his point over and over again until it loses its charge.

The Informers isn't as edgy as *American Psycho,* but it is modestly more humane. Not all of the characters here are as odious as Bateman and his stupid, cynical friends. In one scene, Cheryl finds herself alone at a deli, strung out between a departing lover and a disconsolate ex-husband. When a group of smirking punks asks for her autograph, she becomes the target of their ridicule and abuse. As these unfamiliar people intrude into her well-protected life, she's no longer certain of her bearings. Her dependable public image undoes itself. In response, she clings tightly to her cigarettes and Diet Coke.

In this collision between sadness and consumerism, Ellis nearly makes depersonalization plausible. The real L.A. flashes by for a moment, a fragmented jurisdiction of jostling parts and confused identities. It is a great subject. Richard Riordan's domain is a kaleidoscope of anger, billboards and cultural diversity, an ideal tableau for an alienated young novelist who is eager to put aside Didionesque minimalism. But Ellis largely retreats from the challenge, setting his novel in the sullen and insulated recent past. No riots, no anti-immigrant backlash, no celebrity lawyers. *The Informers* is a subdued, nostalgic book. It looks back fondly on the 1980s, when the L.A. elite could enjoy its anxiety in peace.

George Stade (review date 18 September 1994)

SOURCE: "Hopping, Popping and Copping," in *New York Times Book Review,* Vol. 99, p. 14.

[*In the following review of* The Informers, *Stade links features of Ellis's novels and addresses the author's thematic concerns.*]

The setting of Bret Easton Ellis's fourth novel is that of his first, *Less Than Zero* (1985), a critical and popular success made into a movie that was neither. In these two novels, the setting, Los Angeles and environs, has more motive force than any character. But the method of the new novel is pretty much that of Mr. Ellis's second, *The Rules of Attraction* (1987), set in the fictional and farcical Camden College in New Hampshire. In these two novels, affectless voices (to which names are attached) speak directly to the reader of their party hopping, narcotics popping and sexual copping, all of it joyless. In those three novels, the main characters are well-off college students who spend little time studying.

In that respect, they differ from Mr. Ellis's third, the notorious *American Psycho* (1991), set among New York wheeler-dealers a few years farther into Reaganomics. The publication of *American Psycho* was at first forestalled and then denounced by our cultural commissars and professional hand-wringers. What mainly aroused their censorious zeal was a tone of moral neutrality and the particularized descriptions of some especially nasty mutilations and murders (as hallucinated by the psycho), descriptions for which Mr. Ellis has a flair.

Although there are American psychos who mutilate and murder near the end of *The Informers,* in this novel Mr. Ellis mostly returns to the material of his first, the method of his second and a few characters from each, as though this time to get them exactly right. And so he does, given his outlook and esthetics, both of which are exacting. *The Informers* is spare, austere, elegantly designed, telling in detail, coolly ferocious, sardonic in its humor, every vestige of authorial sentiment expunged.

The action (or inaction) takes place from 1982 to 1985. The hub of characters around whom a couple of dozen others circle is mostly male, absurdly rich, blond, assiduously tanned and with marvelous abs. "All these beautiful blond tan people (specimens!)," says a young woman visiting from Camden College, "staring into outer space." They are objects of desire to young women, to older women, to older men, to each other and each to himself, for Narcissus is their totem. They are nominal students at U.C.L.A., U.C. San Diego, the University of Southern California or Pepperdine, but they are pig ignorant of everything that does not stroke their senses. If they read at all it is *GQ* and *Vanity Fair.* "I never read. Boring," says one. They have heard of Reagan only because their parents attend fund-raisers in his behalf.

They are, however, educated consumers. They drive around aimlessly in Ferraris, Mercedes-Benzes, Porsches, Rolls-Royces, Jaguars, gorgeous machines that somehow always break down—when they don't crash. They wear Armani and Gucci and Yves Saint Laurent; they pick at their salads and sip on their Tabs in Le Dome and the Polo Lounge; they are connoisseurs of pot and coke and occasionally heroin. But they also know their Valium and Librium, their Nembutal and Demerol and Seconal, their Dalmane and Darvocet, although some go for nitrous oxide and animal tranquilizers, or even heavy doses of vitamin pills. Above all, they know their rock-and-roll, sounds of the silence within them. "Songs sometimes are uncannily appropriate," writes the Camden visitor.

They one-up each other by dropping names of the rock groups whose concerts they have recently attended; entering their cars, they immediately turn on rock radio stations or slip in a tape; entering their rooms, they turn on MTV or slide in a cassette; tanning themselves by pool or beach, they wear their Walkmans—the idea being not to hear themselves think. For similar reasons, they go to all the new movies or endlessly watch videos, however their bodies are otherwise engaged. And that's it, except for the hopping, popping and copping. "Basically her emptiness thrills me," says one of them about another.

Who's to blame? Mr. Ellis does not say, for his practice is to present, rather than to explain. Certainly, the older generation, those swingers in the record industry, in the studios, in television and real estate, are not what you would call good role models. Relations between parents or step-parents and children are bad: after a father dies in a plane crash, his son gambles away the funerary ashes in a gesture of good riddance. The parents are too involved in attending to their own addictions, their face lifts and serial marriages and predatory affairs, to tend their kids, who are unforgiving. But if the older generation's self-absorbed behavior is a cause, it is also a result—of an ambiance that includes the weather, wealth, the electronic reproduction of fantasy all around them: "I guess we can't escape being a product of the times, can we?"

That ambiance is colored, increasingly darkened, by images and motifs that accumulate on the periphery of the reader's field of vision: servants high on pot, dead rats in the pool filter, helicopters hovering, tumbleweed blowing across deserted streets. In casual asides, we hear of suicidal and anorexic daughters, of sons dying in car accidents, of someone's "hideous" mother whose "throat was slashed by some maniac," of overdoses, of drug dealers stabbed to death, of somebody shot in the head and skinned, of Carlos's arms found in a bag, of Tommy's body (or was that Monty's?) found empty of blood and vital organs, of Corey found sealed in a metal drum buried in the desert, of sundry disappearances, of body parts along the freeway. "There are a lot of frightened people in this town, dude." In a cluster of truly unsettling final scenes, the metaphors of vampirism and body-snatching that have been flickering through the novel become literal, for if those blond, suntanned beauties are like the Eloi of H.G. Wells's *Time Machine,* there are Morlocks around to tend and devour them.

As in Mr. Ellis's other fiction, as in the fiction of most satirists, the emphasis is less on what individuates his characters or on what unites them with the whole of humankind than it is on the aberrations that unite them with a milieu. We get not so much rounded characters as a group consciousness careering into dissolution. For all that, for all of his studied neutrality, Mr. Ellis provides his readers with grounds for judgment and occasions for feelings other than dread and repulsion, as when parents falsify memories of those happy days when their kids were still kids, while their offspring remember only parental squabbling and self regard.

In fact, a case could be made for Mr. Ellis as a covert moralist and closet sentimentalist, the best kind, the kind who leaves you space in which to respond as your predispositions nudge you, whether as a commissar or hand-wringer or, like me, as an admirer of his intelligence and craft.

James Gardner (review date 17 June 1996)

SOURCE: A review of *American Psycho,* in *National Review,* Vol. 48, No. 11, June 17, 1996, pp. 54-7.

[*In the following review, Gardner considers* American Psycho *among a group of other "transgressive novels."*]

Thirty years ago the art of fiction began to undergo a change similar to one that had already befallen the theatrical arts. Though theater had once been the best loved form of mass entertainment, it yielded that title to film and then turned inward, catering to an elite taste that saw theater as art rather than diversion. As a result, these two factors, which had formerly been united, increasingly went their separate ways. Fiction also used to fulfill the Horatian injunction to delight as well as to edify. But in recent years it too has split, not into different media, as theater and film have done, but into different forms of fiction. On the one hand Stephen King and Jackie Collins are widely read for their entertainment value. On the other, novelists like Thomas Pynchon and William Gass intentionally and provocatively suppress the element of pleasure, as if it were incompatible with serious fiction.

The logical consequence of this latter trend, and easily the most hyped novel of the decade, is David Foster Wallace's *Infinite Jest,* a thousand densely printed pages of plotless abstrusity punctuated by a series of brainless pratfalls. These are followed by a hundred more pages of notes which man-

age to be semi-literate in four languages and whose purpose, to this critic at least, is entirely inscrutable. There have been rumors that Little, Brown, the publisher, actually pressed Mr. Wallace to make the book even longer than he had intended, in order to increase its "stunt" value. As it is, everyone is talking about the book and no one so far has actually read it.

Fortunately, most contemporary fiction of the artistic kind is somewhat more rewarding. Often its vanguardism consists less in the sorts of formal difficulty that were characteristic of Gass and Pynchon than in the freshness of the authors' identities. Amy Tan, for example, writes about being a Chinese-American woman, Bharati Mukherjee about being an Indian woman in Iowa, Dale Peck about being homosexual, and Ernest J. Gaines about being black. Such literature falls within the modern liberal tradition of embracing difference and being open to other experiences. But both of these undertakings imply a core of shared values, so that, even as this literature asserts the difference between author and reader, it usually has the reassuring subtext of a common humanity that unites us all.

Despite the primacy of this kind of "nice" literature, there is another kind of literature that increasingly exhibits, and sometimes even advocates, very different values. Such fiction is often termed "transgressive," and there are correlative developments in film and the visual arts. Like the humanistic literature of Amy Tan, it is seen as being somehow liberal or leftist because it seeks the distinction of radical "otherness" and because it aspires to threaten the status quo that writers like Amy Tan and Bharati Mukherjee seek only to correct. The two strains converge from different angles of assault on a center allegedly dominated by a white, Anglo-Saxon, heterosexual, right-handed patriarchy.

The roots of transgressive literature, of literature that violently attacks the center of a culture, are ancient, reaching all the way from Euripides's *Bacchae,* through Marlowe and Webster and the Marquis de Sade, to Huysmans and Celine. This literature of self-defined immorality, anguish, and degradation is constantly waxing and waning in our culture, as, for its part, is the humanistic strain. Thus the ages of Fielding, George Eliot, Sinclair Lewis, and Saul Bellow were in a general way humanistic, whereas those of Byron and Wilde and the Surrealists tended in the other direction. At the present time—and this is perhaps a unique occurrence—the two strains exist side by side, as different faces of the same coin. Four recent and critically celebrated novels—Susanna Moore's *In the Cut,* A. M. Holmes's *The End of Alice,* Dennis Cooper's *Try,* and Bret Easton Ellis's ***American Psycho***—exemplify this development, each from a different angle.

What unites all these novels, aside from their almost unimaginable gruesomeness, is the peculiar relation in which they stand to the straitlaced center of society. Reading *In the Cut,* a polished performance with a gripping plot and some humor, we immediately recognize the protagonist as "one of us," that is, a liberally inclined citizen of the center. This slightly dowdy but attractive English teacher is well-intentioned in a schoolmarmish sort of way, eager to bring literature to the inner city. Though she is, to all appearances, the sort of person who would read the novels of Amy Tan and Bharati Mukherjee, each of the subordinate characters she encounters is at variance with her. They do not read quality fiction. They do not sip white wine and herbal teas. They are either working class or underclass. Cornelius, whom she is struggling to teach English, is a black high-school student whose hidden literary talents derive precisely from his authenticity as a member of a minority. Detective Molloy and Detective Rodriguez are as casually racist and as foul-mouthed as the narrator is enlightened and reserved. Yes, they are men, and Molloy is even a white man. But because they are working-class they are outside the narrator's intuitively perceived center, and this provides them too with authenticity.

The novel begins with the narrator witnessing a murder, one in a series. The central question of the novel concerns the identity of the killer. Each of the three men mentioned is suspected by the narrator. But in the end what is surprising is not the killer's identity so much as the transformation that the prim and reserved narrator undergoes. In the name of her awakened desire for sexual fulfillment, she seems implicitly to endorse the murder's misogyny, inhumanity, and vulgarity. In the final scene, we realize that everything we have been reading until now has been the voice of the narrator just as she is about to be slain by the serial killer. The preliminary act of mutilation—since the murderer always takes a "token" from his victims—is described in sensuous terms: "He grabbed me by the back of the neck, pressing the razor against my breast . . . cutting smoothly, easily through the taut cloth, through the skin, the delicate blue skein of netted veins in flood, the nipple cut round, then the breast, opening, the dark blood running like the dark river."

Here we meet one of the main conflicts in contemporary feminism, as represented by Catharine MacKinnon and Suzie Bright—that is, between those women who see sexuality as essentially a masculine invasion of women, and those who believe that women are and should be as sexually predaceous as men. The development of Susanna Moore's protagonist consists in her increasing awareness of the primacy of sexuality, which she has repressed in herself and for which, almost as a point of morality, she will have to be punished. For sexuality is an anarchic catalyst, cutting through all the hypocrisy and manners of the center.

In contrast to the sexual awakening of the narrator which is

the main theme of *In the Cut,* we see in *The End of Alice* by A. M. Holmes, another woman writer, and in Dennis Cooper's *Try,* sexual license presented not as a dilemma but as an accepted fact. The protagonist of the former novel is a 56-year-old man who has spent the past 23 years in prison and whose affected utterances recall Hannibal Lector minus the cannibalism. The plot is fairly simple: this murderous pedophile recounts his past adventures in a correspondence with a young woman who sees him as a role model, except that she is interested in young boys whereas he is interested in young girls. Many graphic scenes of child molestation, sodomy, and murder, follow. "All three boys," the female correspondent recalls, in a fairly typical passage, "were at that age of supreme softness where muscles waiting to grow are coated in a medium-thick layer of flesh, highly squeezable. They were at the point where if someone were to take such a child, to roast or bake him, he would be most flavorful."

If anything, Dennis Cooper's *Try* manifests an even greater level of sexualized violence, but this time from the perspective of male homosexuality. The protagonist, Ziggy, is a victim of child abuse at the hands of the gay couple who adopted him. Though child abuse is very much in the news these days and is always reprehended in the strongest terms, Cooper's take on the problem is one of ambivalence, when not verging on enthusiastic endorsement. *Try* is an extended fantasy of unbridled sexual license in which those whom society sees as the victims are willingly acquiescent if not entirely complicit in their own sexual exploitation. In this voided world, there is no family structure to speak of. Parents are absent, or else they are ersatz, like Ziggy's. Likewise, school is only a place for trysting and for the purchase of drugs. Crimes go shockingly unpunished. When, in a subplot, Uncle Ken sodomizes the corpse of a 13-year-old who overdoses on the drugs Ken supplied, he simply disposes of the body and that's that. There would be little point in attempting to cite a passage, as it would not get past the judicious editors of this publication.

These two novels are intended for two groups of readers, pedophiles on the one hand, and "normal" people on the other. This loaded term "normal" is used advisedly for the simple reason that the authors themselves implicitly draw the same distinction. One senses that their gaze is always steadily fixed on the reader, as though asking, "Are you revolted yet? Are you shocked?" If this work were marketed as pornography, the term being used not in reproach but simply for purposes of description, we should be forced to acknowledge its usefulness to those whose fantasy life comprises the sodomizing of children, necrophilia, and coprophilia. What is entirely unpalatable is the squeamishness of *Try*'s reviewers, squeamish not in the sense of opposing so off-color a work, but in the sense of being too timid to call it by its name. The reviewer for the *New York Times* states that "Dennis Cooper has written a love story, all the more poignant because it is so brutally crushed." The reviewer for *Spin* calls it "Painfully poignant . . . beneath the queasy surface, no novelist empathizes more with the pathos of put-upon youth." Of course opinions may differ. But suffice it to say that I found no trace of poignancy at any level.

What is it then about the three books I have discussed that has granted them absolution from the censure that ordinarily would accompany such unbridled lubricity? The answer is clear. Sexual aggressiveness is traditionally defined in our society as the province of the straight white male. To the extent that each of these books attacks this center, it appears to acquire a contemporary relevance which exempts it from the moral scrutiny that a straight white male would receive. Furthermore, in its implicit threat to the patriarchy, and all that this threat implies of traditional liberal egalitarianism, it seems to take the moral high-ground. Susanna Moore and A. M. Holmes display women who are as sexually predaceous as any man. Dennis Cooper displays homosexuals and even child molesters as spirited crusaders against a hypocritical middle class. It is in this light that they gain their relevance for those who read "quality literature," and it is this that makes them morphologically identical to Amy Tan and Bharati Mukherjee, however different their content.

The fact that, in the eyes of their many admiring critics, it is this perceived quality that alone redeems them will be made more apparent by studying the fate of Bret Easton Ellis's *American Psycho*. This book is not nearly as bad as many had supposed or hoped without having really read it. To be sure, there are problems with the book. More often than not its violence is gratuitous; its characters are too realistic for satire and too unbelievable for realism; long passages are meant to be monotonous—and they are; the book proceeds by repetition rather than by development and is never satisfactorily resolved, even if we accept that it is supposed to end on a note of irresolution. With these reservations it should be said that the book's virtues—its swift narrative, its dead-pan humor, and its eye for detail—have generally been ignored. For example, the Vintage paperback, from a series that is traditionally bedecked on front, back, and end papers with blurbs and raves, is devoid of any comment whatever. As readers may recall, the book was originally scheduled for publication by Simon & Schuster, which withdrew at the last moment under pressure from feminist groups, so that it was finally brought out in hardcover by Knopf.

The protagonist, Patrick Bateman, is an arrogant, spoiled super-yuppie who has everything. He is young, handsome, Harvard-educated, and incalculably wealthy. From the first page, the yuppie creed is articulated by one of the subordinate characters. "I'm resourceful, I'm creative, I'm young, unscrupulous, highly motivated, highly skilled. In essence what I'm saying is that society cannot afford to lose me. I'm an asset." Bateman is also a serial killer, and it is a main conceit of the novel to suggest that yuppie-dom, with its arrogant egomania, is one step on the way to serial murder. In one scene Bateman is having problems with an unresponsive salesgirl in a video store. "The things I could do to this girl's body with a hammer," he muses, "the words I could carve into her with an ice pick." Another woman he describes as "too ugly to rape." Then he reveals the most brutal insensitivity to centrist attitudes. He sees a "bum lounging below the *Les Miserables* poster and holding a sign that reads: I'VE LOST MY JOB I AM HUNGRY I HAVE NO MONEY PLEASE HELP, whose eyes tear after I pull the tease-the-bum-with-a-dollar trick and tell him,'. . . will you get a f—ing shave, please . . ." He is similarly insensitive to homosexuals and to animals. He is, in short, politically incorrect to the point of psychosis.

The three previous novels implicitly attacked the center, but in a manner acceptable to liberals. *American Psycho,* by contrast, has been emphatically rejected by the same liberals, and it is easy to see why. This book makes fun precisely of the center's attempt to assimilate those who are outside of the center, whether homosexuals, the homeless, Koreans, or animals. Ellis seems to perceive a gust of bad faith in liberal discourse, and it is the relentless vigor with which he goes after liberals' hypocrisy, with which he tramples all over their self-serving sensiblerie, that is the most valuable thing in this novel. What cannot be explained away or mitigated by this reading, however, is the extremeness of the violence, to which no nobler purpose can be ascribed than simple sadism.

Aside from that, there is an element of bad faith, if not of downright hypocrisy, in these novels, one from which even *American Psycho* is not exempt. It comes in the form of the seemingly irresistible need of the authors to attribute to their private preoccupations a larger social message, which is really only window dressing. Thus in the chapter titled, "The End of the Eighties," near the end of *American Psycho,* Bateman sums up what is intended as the heavy message of the book. "Justice is dead. Fear, recrimination, innocence, sympathy, guilt, waste, failure, grief, [were] things, emotions, that no one really felt any more. Reflection is useless, the world is senseless. Evil is its only permanence, God is not alive. Love cannot be trusted. Surface, surface, surface, was all that anyone found meaning in . . . this was civilization as I saw it, colossal and jagged."

In a similar mood, the child-molesting narrator in *The End of Alice* turns at one point to the reader and says, "I am no better or worse than you. A conspiracy, a social construct supported by judge, jury, and tattle-tales, has put me away because I threaten them. I implore you not to be such a scaredy-cat." This attitude—disabused, amoral, and implacably opposed to the civics of the center—is the recurring theme of all the current transgressive novels, not to mention contemporary rock bands like Nine Inch Nails and contemporary art like that of Joel Peter Witkin and contemporary films like Quentin Tarantino's *Reservoir Dogs.*

One crucial difference between these authors and the authors of ordinary novels, such as Stephen King and Jackie Collins, is that, whereas the latter are content to preserve the traditional protocols of fiction, these newcomers would have us believe, as they themselves believe, that they have penetrated to an all-important and long-hidden truth about human society. And in a general way we, their readers, do believe them. We believe them because in our relativistic age, we have lost the spiritual resources to confront that potent error which they lack either the intellectual honesty or the intellectual power to oppose: the error of supposing that, because everything indeed is not right with the world, everything must accordingly be wrong with the world; the error of supposing that, because we are plainly not a race of angels, we must perforce be a race of beasts. But in the end, they are still fiction writers after all, and this morbid fascination of theirs, this confidence that the center cannot hold, that all of morality is a sham, is the supreme fiction.

Carla Freccero (essay date Summer 1997)

SOURCE: "Historical Violence, Censorship, and the Serial Killer: The Case of *American Psycho*," in *Diacritics,* Vol. 27, No. 2, Summer, 1997, pp. 44-58.

[*In the following essay, Freccero discusses reactions to* American Psycho *and explores the significance of the novel's violence.*]

US mass media has become a much-publicized target of censorious commentary within American public culture in recent years. Censorship, as E. S. Burt notes, may take at least two forms: philosophical censorship, such as that discussed by Leo Strauss's *Persecution and the Art of Writing,* and the more commonly applied form of US censorship enacted against "pornography" or "obscenity." Philosophical censorship, in this reading, entails the state's persecution of message-bearing texts or utterances that counter the *doxa* and threaten to disrupt the state, while the second form of censorship involves "a language use that falls outside the interpretive scheme defining the work as the intentional act of a moral being". In the United States, state censorship of the first kind may perhaps be practiced through the "incitement to riot" escape clause provision in the First Amendment, while obscenity censorship—in certain forms—is explicitly written into legislation as excluded from speech protection.

Extending Strauss's argument to the liberal state, Burt suggests in effect that these two forms of censorship become related insofar as the state's censorious intent is directed not so much at the content of the expression as at the degree to which it confirms the axiom, what Burt calls the "very fundamental, convening assumption of the. . .liberal state" that "virtue is knowledge". Thus obscenity is a form of expression that cannot be interpreted as productive knowledge but instead as a certain repetitive excess, "dirt for dirt's sake". The problem here, of course, is that such distinctions do not apply comfortably to that category of utterance termed the literary, and especially to the use of figurative language, where "art for art's sake" can be seen precisely to resemble the nonproductivity of obscenity. The text I am going to discuss in depth here, Bret Easton Ellis's ***American Psycho,*** has been attacked on both grounds—as an active (and violent) disruption of the *doxa* that is also obscenely nonproductive of knowledge—and as such, it serves as an illustrative, and I will argue, noncoincidental, case of "censorship" in the liberal state.

It may be useful here to begin by surveying and making distinctions among the various popular and popularized censorships in recent US media: Ice-T's "Cop Killer" was probably the most authentic case of "philosophical" censorship, even though its silencing did not derive directly from the state (the liberal state often does not function in some of the ways supposed when the definition of censorship is restricted to state censorship). "Cop Killer" is a song about killing policemen, and thus came closest—in the list I am going to propose of silenced works—to tempting the state's retaliation. It was written and sung by a black man (a black man who often plays a gangster and a cop in popular films), in a genre already regarded as threateningly disruptive to the state: rap. The result is that the CD containing this song was pulled from the shelves of music stores and can no longer be purchased. There was no trial. The author withdrew his work from public circulation in the face of death threats and informal police retaliation. Another instance involving a rap group was a case of censorship on the grounds of obscenity. 2 Live Crew were arrested at a live concert, and so was a man selling their CD, "As Nasty as They Wanna Be," in a record store in Florida. The group went to trial in a latter-day instance of the more famous obscenity trials of the literary work of James Joyce and Arthur Miller.

Michael Jackson's "Black or White" was also in a sense censored: the scene where "he" (the actor, singer, protagonist of the mini-narrative) expressed rage inside the prison of race was excised from the MTV-aired video, so that what we remember instead is the Benetton-like display of high tech digitalized morphing back and forth among beautiful, racially differentiated, multiply gendered faces, a serene version of the technology used in the film *Terminator 2.* But the original video is available for purchase or rental in stores.

Here, the censoring apparatus took a classic liberal form: consumption of the commodity in question was confined to more restrictive venues, so that "thoughtful men [*sic*]" who are "careful readers" would continue to have access to the text.

Madonna, whose career has been forged in the courting of censorship, has had three famous brushes with the problem of silencing: the first involved a Pepsi commercial, aired once and thereafter buried when the lyrics to the song turned out to have as their full-length video a shocking combination of sexual, interracial, and religious commingling that disturbed and outraged the Catholic and fundamentalist establishments in the US. The Pepsi commercial is unavailable for viewing. The second incident involved live performance, the rendering of "Like a Virgin" as a song about masturbation, where Canadian officials, invoking that country's obscenity laws, threatened to close down the show. The third incident involved MTV's refusal to air "Justify My Love," one of Madonna's videos, for the reason, presumably, that the video exposes an occasional breast and that television's federal arm prohibits such exposures on stations like MTV. Madonna, however, has found a way to advertise censorship: "Like A Prayer" spawned an unprecedented amount of academic inquiry and analysis, while the concert tape of the Blonde Ambition tour and the video of "Justify My Love" assumed a life of their own at the video stores (though Madonna still profits less this way than she would have if both of these videos had been aired continuously on MTV). Indeed, the production of "veiled" spectacles, the striptease performed around selected works within an artist's ample corpus, the production of scarcity, and the marketing of censorship as a technique to spur consumption have proven profitable as long as the artist continued to remain visible through the sheer volume of his/her other, easily circulating work.

The Internet has become one of the most recent targets of censorship efforts; here comparisons might be drawn with the infamous senate debates regarding Robert Mapplethorpe and state funding for "obscene, indecent, and offensive" art. One of the proposed solutions to the distress occasioned by Internet pornography is to make the Internet a more highly privatized domain; indeed, censorship in the United States seems to have drifted once again toward the question—in popular or populist arenas—of public versus private. The language of public and private succeeds in evading questions of censorship and silencing, focusing instead on regulation and restraint, as in the cases of the Jackson and Madonna videos, so that what emerges is a benign paternalism that reinstates the elite/popular distinction in the domain of culture.

I perform this survey of recent mass media/popular cultural artifacts and their conflicts with the law or with public standards in order to move toward another popular artifact whose

encounter with an effort to silence may seem more surprising in late twentieth-century America by virtue of the medium in which it is presented: writing. The examples above are aural or visual (indeed even the hairsplitting around Internet regulation suggests that "freedom of expression" is to be taken rather anachronistically and that words—by virtue of their already elite status and limited access—are to be protected more than pictures; symptomatically, the Communications Decency Act compares the Internet not to written text but to telephone and telecommunications). They are also artifacts of mass media whose circulation is massive, for they are ubiquitously accessible via electronic technology—perhaps the most difficult of all technologies developed so far to cordon off, control, effectively regulate and confine—across the United States and internationally. Finally, these are all works of art produced by citizens markedly marginalized in other ways in US public culture: they are African American males, a white female coded as sexually dangerous, a white gay man who died of AIDS, and in the case of the Internet: youth.

One might assume, then, that a novel, a work of fiction, would suffer the benign consequences of neglect, if for no other reason than that its circulation does not benefit from the mass distribution available for video or audio artifacts. Furthermore, a book published by what are called "respectable" (middle-brow?) publishers (Random House) ordinarily would not be expected to be as familiar to the public as Madonna's videos or Ice-T's songs. Finally, it is a book written by a white man (of indeterminate sexual "orientation") who, even in the opinion of the conservative writer George Will, is "conventionally dressed and barbered". Yet Bret Easton Ellis's ***American Psycho*** occasioned a minor outburst in the publishing industry in the US in 1990 and 1991, which produced in its wake a weighing-in by culture critics and magazines across the political spectrum, from *Time* and *Spy* magazines to the *New York Times, Vanity Fair, Rolling Stone,* the *Nation, Commentary,* the *New Republic,* and library and publishing journals. Well-known writers and commentators joined the fray: Norman Mailer, Fay Weldon, Roger Rosenblatt, George Will, and Roger Kimball. To Simone de Beauvoir's famous question, "Must We Burn Sade?," which was a considered and serious defense of the man and his writing, this country answered, regarding Ellis, yes, we must, at one extreme; and no, we mustn't, at the other, but let's not read him either. The *New York Times,* somewhat uncharacteristically, weighed in on the side of bonfires, for Roger Rosenblatt's prepublication review was (humorously?) entitled "Snuff This Book!"

The story, in brief, is this: Ellis's manuscript, ***American Psycho,*** was accepted for publication, and its author was given an advance by Simon and Schuster. After the book had been advertised, announced in catalogs, and a press packet had been mailed around the country in anticipation of a publicity tour, prepublication proofs came under the scrutiny of *Time* and *Spy* magazines, each of which published particularly explicit excerpts of the novel accompanied by reviews decrying the decision to publish the book. The publisher at Simon and Schuster subsequently read the manuscript and decided to withdraw the offer of publication. Within forty-eight hours, Random House bought the publishing rights, and the novel appeared the next year in Random House's Vintage series.

American Psycho is narrated for the most part in the first-person voice of a serial killer. The serial killer is a popular American figure of dementia, universally regarded as unthreatening precisely because of his singularity, the nonrationality of his pathology, and the individualized and eccentric nature of his violence. A serial killer is not the oppressed masses, and although his murders are usually lurid, his reach is limited. In this sense, the serial killer serves the function of a fetish in public culture: he is the means of the disavowal of institutionalized violence, while the "seriality" of his acts of violence marks the place of recognition in this disavowal. Through the serial killer, then, we recognize and simultaneously refuse the violence-saturated quality of the culture, by situating its source in an individual with a psychosexual dysfunction. We are thus able to locate the violence in his disorder rather than in ourselves or in the social order. As Amy Taubin, in *Sight and Sound,* puts it:

> With just 5 per cent of the world's population, the US is believed to have about 75 per cent of the world's serial killers.

> Disturbing as these figures are, the fact is that the number of people who will die at the hands of serial killers doesn't even bear comparison with, for example, the number of women who will die because they don't have access to breast screening, or even know it exists. But institutionalised violence—the destruction of millions of lives through poverty and neglect, the abuse practised against women and children, the slaughter of 100,000 Iraqis—has no easy representation. The image of the serial killer acts as a substitute and a shield for a situation so incomprehensible and threatening it must be disavowed.

Serial killers also typify an individualistic conception of violence, singularly embodied and psychically caused. In serial killer stories the sources of pathology lie in a decontextualized family romance separable from the social order. What is somatized in the figure of the serial killer, then, is also an ideology of violence that presents violence as something originating in the private sphere. Taubin concludes, "Bred in the heartlands, he's the deformed version of the American dream of the individual". Yet the "deformation"

of the American dream—that which we *do* recognize and avow—is located not in corrupt government, or economic institutions that exploit us, but in an individual. The solution to the problem of violence then also becomes relatively simple: kill the serial killer and your problem goes away.

In "Burning Acts: Injurious Speech," Judith Butler traces how the polity elides or effaces the violence of history (a continuative, iterated process of wounding, a transitivity not imaginable as originating from a singular source), by establishing a moral framework of accountability whereby a subject is brought into being, in Nietzschean fashion, to stand as the cause of an injurious "deed" ("For Nietzsche, the subject appears only as a consequence of a demand for accountability"). She notes that this process, the process of demanding accountability for injury, not only produces a subject as an effect that then stands in as the cause, but also produces from action a discrete act, a singular deed that can be isolated and can serve as an object of prosecution. The Nietzschean formulation presupposes, however, a prior, sovereign subject or supreme being capable of deeming—or judging—as she puts it, the "injurious consequence". This prior subject is the law, and Butler here questions the wisdom of conferring power on the (presumably neutral) domain of the juridical to assign blame for and to prosecute injurious action. One way in which hate speech prosecution has been understood to be possible is by assigning to citizens the power to enact violence normally assigned to the state through the "state action doctrine". The suspension of this doctrine in the prosecution of hate speech has the potential to displace state power "onto the citizen, figured as a kind of sovereign, and the citizenry, figured as sovereigns whose speech now carries a power that operates like state power to deprive other 'sovereigns' of fundamental rights and liberties".

Butler suggests that not only does such a shift of emphasis from the state to its citizenry as "sovereign" agents risk "a suspension of critical insight into state power and state violence", but also that "the juridicalization of history . . . is achieved precisely through the search for subjects to prosecute, who might be held accountable and, hence, temporarily resolve the problem of a fundamentally unprosecutable history", given that the utterance that produces injury does so "through a transitivity that cannot be reduced to a causal or intentional process originating in a singular subject"; in other words, through the iterability (citationality) of the violence of history itself.

The political power of this analysis lies in questioning the notion that injury, such as the injury produced by utterances, can be in any sense simply and finally attributed to a singular subject and its act, for when it is, it becomes a juridical matter of assigning blame rather than a political matter of analysis and opposition. "Indeed," Butler writes, "when political discourse is fully collapsed into juridical discourse, the meaning of political opposition runs the risk of being reduced to the act of prosecution. How is the analysis of the discursive historicity of power unwittingly restricted when the subject is presumed as the point of departure for such an analysis?".

This analysis may go a long way toward explaining the consoling fantasy of the serial killer as a condensation of the violence of American historicity into a singular subject who performs discrete, singular injurious acts. If such is the case, and if the popularity of the vehicle of the serial killer as sign of social disease is any indication, it also illustrates the degree to which history is already successfully censored in the manner Strauss suggests, since we figure history's violence, and the violence of the state, in the sovereign citizen-subject of the serial killer. Furthermore, as the case of *American Psycho* illustrates, the critics who respond to the violence "depicted" and—according to the censors—"enacted" within it, have also internalized the censor, internalized the law, the juridical, by assigning the blame for the harm produced to an agent, the author, and an act, the writing of a novel.

Hate speech is not too farfetched an analogy in considering the case of *American Psycho* and those who most vigorously protested its existence, the Los Angeles Chapter of the National Organization for Women. Indeed, NOW's response to the novel construes it as act of incitement, as hate speech, in other words. I want to ask Butler's question, "How is the analysis of the discursive historicity of power unwittingly restricted when the subject is presumed as the point of departure for such an analysis?," in part because I think it is a matter of political urgency in liberal feminist political analyses that have recently targeted pornography and in liberal political analyses that have targeted hate speech as objects of prosecution. As a feminist interested in the interventionary power of the political analysis of culture, I want to explore the (in) adequacies of the discourse of injury and accountability invoked by denunciations of this novel.

NOW called for a boycott of Random House, the publisher that picked up Ellis's book after Simon and Schuster dropped it in a breach of contract with the author. In a January 1991 resolution, NOW stated that "the publication of *American Psycho* is socially irresponsible and legitimizes inhuman and savage violence masquerading as sexuality. *This is totally unacceptable*". The book was referred to as a "how-to novel on the torture and dismemberment of women." In a move similar to that of Andrea Dworkin's *Intercourse,* which transcribes the pornographic passages that it then denounces, NOW's hotline phone message included a recording—in a woman's voice—of one of the passages of rape and dismemberment from *American Psycho* (as the *New Republic* put it, "the phone number is sure to fall into the wrong lonely hands").

NOW seems to acknowledge the citationality of the novel's violence, though not its own, when it follows the recording with a statement that crimes of rape and violence against women are epidemic and on the rise. The hotline tape concludes by calling for a boycott. "'We are not telling them not to publish,'" says Tammy Bruce, president of the Los Angeles Chapter, in an interview with the *New York Times*; rather, NOW hopes the publisher "will learn [that] violence against women in any form is no longer socially acceptable" [see McDowell]. One might be tempted to ridicule this exercise first for the patent falsity of the statement that somehow violence against women is not socially acceptable, and second for refusing the possibility that, just as its own gesture of citation is not to be construed as a misogynist act of violence, so too perhaps the passage quoted may bear a complicated—and willfully citational—relation to the violence it depicts. But it is worth noting that NOW's response is not atypical of public culture's responses to popular cultural artifacts: representation is construed as advocacy, and figuration is construed as performativity. Furthermore, the emotional denunciations, uttered in horror and disgust, inevitably cite—obsessively and in detail—the target of their denunciation, thus betraying the perverse or pornographic investments of the censors themselves.

Here, then, is another consoling fantasy: Bret Easton Ellis and Random House are the serial killers, they are the agents of the injurious act of misogyny that is the novel. At least one very obvious political limitation ensues: George Will, author of numerous misogynistic social analyses of the family, is confirmed in his self-congratulatory denunciation of this book and all of popular culture on the grounds of "today's depraved appetite for imaginary violence against women," while continuing to dismiss that very "real" social violence with the inclusion of the emphatic term "imaginary".

> **Yet the other reason for which *American Psycho* was denounced and dismissed, namely "taste," demonstrates the ways in which liberal intellectuals engaged in artistic evaluation also relinquished analysis; indeed, their response may be said to resemble censorship on the grounds of "indecency" or "obscenity."**
> —*Carla Freccero*

NOW may be an easy target for liberal "freedom of expression" intellectuals; its response seems a straightforward call for censorship in the interests of protecting the public—women in particular—from the violence enacted by the novel. Yet the other reason for which *American Psycho* was denounced and dismissed, namely "taste," demonstrates the ways in which liberal intellectuals engaged in artistic evaluation also relinquished analysis; indeed, their response may be said to resemble censorship on the grounds of "indecency" or "obscenity." The refusal to defend the novel on the grounds of its content and its style was, in this case, also symptomatic, betraying a longing for the consoling fantasy of the serial killer to narrate and contain the trauma of historicity.

American Psycho does not offer its readers the serial killer as consoling fantasy; instead, as the narrator/killer/protagonist Patrick Bateman himself remarks, in a moment of near-revelation at the end of the novel: "Surface, surface, surface was all that anyone found meaning in. . . ." Ellis explains: "'I was writing about a society in which the surface became the only thing. Everything was surface—food, clothes—that is what defined people. So I wrote a book that is all surface action; no narrative, no characters to latch onto, flat, endlessly repetitive'" [see Cohen]. Christopher Lehmann-Haupt best illustrates Burt's contention that the liberal state insists on the positive productivity of knowledge in expression when he complains that *American Psycho* does "violence to an organic idea of art," by collapsing form and content and by eliminating a "moral framework" for the depiction of "monstrous criminality" in the novel. He thus rejects as self-evidently impossible the aesthetic of surface deployed in the text: "The trouble with *American Psycho* is, of course, that you can't create a meaningless world out of meaninglessness. Surface, surface, surface cannot serve to define substance". A related critique involves Ellis's use of formal mimesis: "Mr. Ellis's true offense is to imply that the human mind . . . can no longer distinguish between form and content", and "But to write superficially about superficiality and disgustingly about the disgusting and call it, as Ellis does, a challenge to his readers' complacency, does violence to his audience and to the fundamental nature of his craft". Not only do these critics explicitly reject the MTV-style postmodernist aesthetics of surface adopted by Generation X (for which Ellis has been dubbed a spokesperson), but they also inadvertently miss Ellis's citation of what is perhaps the most famous and time-worn literary deployment of mimetic violence, known to Dante scholars as "infernal irony," for the novel's first words are: "Abandon All Hope Ye Who Enter Here is scrawled in blood red lettering on the side of the Chemical Bank. . . ." As Norman Mailer, to his credit, points out: "Bateman is living in a hell where no hell is external to ourselves and so all of existence is hell".

The aesthetic critique of the absence of a formal or stylistic surface/depth model in the novel is echoed by a critique of the absence of a metaphorical surface/depth model in Ellis's character portrayal. What critics reproach Ellis for is that he precisely does not provide a psychologized narrative of origins, a comforting etiology for his killer's illness; we do not hear that he was a sexually abused child or that he had a domineering mother. Indeed the novel inserts the mother—for, in serial killer stories, at least since Hitchcock's *Psycho,* the mother has to be there—in one chapter toward the end, when Bateman goes to visit her in a nursing home, where she lives out her days heavily sedated. She seems like quite a nice person, really, and no clues are provided that would suggest a tortured relationship between the two. Rather, the chapter concludes tantalizingly (but inconclusively) with a line about Patrick's father in a photograph: "He's standing next to one of the topiary animals a long time ago at his father's estate in Connecticut and there's something the matter with his eyes", hinting, in interestingly feminist terms, that, if there is an etiology, it is patrilineal, and thus located squarely within the dominant social order itself.

Ellis is thus taken to task—and negatively compared to Thomas Harris, author of *Silence of the Lambs*—for failing to provide a "moral framework" for his tale of the twenty-six-year-old Harvard graduate, Patrick Bateman (Norman Bates? Batman?), an independently wealthy Wall Street investment banker who works for Pierce and Pierce(!), the company his father owns, and who is devastatingly handsome, beautifully dressed, "hardbodied," and a psychopath. Mailer, who defends the concept but not the execution of the book, writes: "Since we are going to have a monstrous book with a monstrous thesis, the author must rise to the occasion by having a murderer with enough inner life for us to comprehend him". "Can he emerge," Mailer asks, "entirely out of no more than vapidity, cupidity, and social meaninglessness?" And again: "We cannot go out on such a trip unless we believe we will end up knowing more about extreme acts of violence, know a little more, that is, of the real inner life of the murderer".

For these critics, there needs to be an inner truth, and the truth of "extreme acts of violence" needs to be located in the psyche of the serial killer. Yet it is precisely the violence of this kind of search for truth that the mainstream cultural critics decry in (what they view as the current spate of) novels and movies that eviscerate women. For example, Lorrie Moore recounts how in her writing classes twenty-year-old boys are producing more and more stories of "hacked-up women": "It's like David Lynch, the boys say now. It's getting to the truth, the difficult, hidden core, they say". And Lehmann-Haupt, who at one turn denounces *American Psycho*'s superficiality, its lack of depth, also claims that the novel suggests that "the human soul is something to be sought with knives and hatchets and drills." In *Torture and Truth: The New Ancient World,* Page du Bois writes:

> The female body—among others—is still represented as a locus of truth . . . and th[e] philosophical subject needs to find the truth, needs to locate truth elsewhere in the body of another, employs torture or sexual abuse against the other, because he

finds that he does not know truth, because truth has been defined as a secret, as the thing not known, not accessible to consciousness . . . a hidden truth, one that eludes the subject, must be discovered, uncovered, unveiled, and can always be located in the dark, in the irrational, in the unknown, in the other. And that truth will continue to beckon the torturer, the sexual abuser, who will find in the other—slave, woman, revolutionary—silent or not, secret or not, the receding phantasm of a truth that must be hunted down, extracted, torn out in torture.

She concludes pithily that "the psychotic pursues women's truth through torture". Critics who denounce *American Psycho*'s refusal to provide an inner truth for his character's monstrosity insist upon precisely a model of truth, and its disclosure and/or recovery, that, du Bois argues, produces the desperate monstrosity of the psychopath in the first place: that somehow the truth must be there, lurking beneath a surface—of skin. Indeed, this is what distinguishes the author Ellis from his serial killer protagonist, for the novel demonstrates that there is no truth to be found beneath appearances, and the accumulation of Bateman's successful, unnoticed, and ultimately deeply unsatisfying torture-murders that do not teach him—or the rest of us—anything, proves this point.

Even Bateman's confession, a moment in the novel that teases us with Foucauldian irony, succeeds in revealing absolutely nothing, not because anything remains hidden, but because there is no truth to be revealed, extracted, and expiated in confession. No one is listening to him (he speaks to a telephone answering machine) and, since proper names correspond interchangeably to bodies, no one can tell who is who; nor does anyone (except the protagonist) notice that fact, and no one, including Patrick, cares. As Fay Weldon notes, to explain why "you got so squeamish all of a sudden":

> I'll tell you why. It's because there's always been someone in the other books to play [sic] lip service to respectability; to the myth that the world we now live in is still capable of affect. The serial killer gets discovered, punished, stopped. There are people around to throw up their hands in horror, who can still distinguish between what is psychotic and what is not. Justice is done. There is remorse.

Not in *American Psycho*. And we hate him for saying it. In *American Psycho*, nobody cares. Slaughtered bodies lie undiscovered. The city has fallen apart. Nobody takes much notice. The police have other things to do. Those who are killed don't rate— they are the powerless, the poor, the wretched, the sick in mind, the sellers of flesh for money: their own and other people's. The tides of the city wash over them, erase their traces. The landlady, seeing her blood-spattered walls, is vexed because she needs to re-let quick. She doesn't want a fuss, she wants her rent.

Gilles Deleuze's "Coldness and Cruelty" analyzes the literary symptomatology of the clinical terms *sadism* and *masochism* and points to some of the reasons for the massive prosecutorial defenses that have been erected to fend off the cultural analysis that *American Psycho* proposes. The first point he makes about the practice of sadism as a literary mode, via Bataille, is that its language is paradoxical, for normally the description of torture (as in testimonials) is the language of the victim and not the torturer, who usually invokes the hypocritical language of established power to rationalize and justify his actions, but not to describe. Elaborate descriptions of torture, then, are the victim's strategy. Thus, as victim, Bateman establishes a relation of identification with the reader. Furthermore, Deleuze notes that the sadist's intention is not to persuade or convince his reader, but to demonstrate: to demonstrate that reason itself is violence through the cold impersonality and singularity of its demonstration. He argues that what is at work in sadism is the attempt to arrive at the thought of pure negation through a totalization and transcendence of the partial and repeated negating of what is outside the self: "There is a progression in sadism from the negative to negation, that is, from the negative as a partial process of destruction endlessly reiterated, to negation as an absolute idea of reason". In psychoanalytic terms, the sadist identifies so exclusively with the superego that his ego no longer exists except as it is externalized onto the other. "What normally confers a moral character on the superego is the internal and complementary ego upon which it exerts its severity"; the relation of judgment and punishment that normally exists between the superego and the ego becomes an intersubjective, rather than an intrasubjective relation, and the superego then exercises its cruelty upon the externalized other, as ego. The sadist thus both projects his ego onto the external world and, simultaneously, the external world becomes nothing but his ego.

The story sadism tells, writes Deleuze, is of

> how the ego, in an entirely different context and in a different struggle [from that of masochism], is beaten and expelled; how the unrestrained superego assumes an exclusive role, modeled on an inflated conception of the father's role. . . . Desexualization, now represented by the superego, ceases to be of a moral or moralizing character, since it is no longer directed upon an inner ego but is turned outward, upon external victims who take on the quality of the rejected ego. . . . The Death Instinct now assumes the character of a Thought of a fearful nature, the idea of demonstrative reason.

The story *American Psycho* tells is the story of the super-ego, the father, the law. The sadism and violence of the law are enacted upon the bodily ego of the self (this is how we and he are victims), a self now externalized as other: a dog, a beggar, a child, some prostitutes, a gay man, some women, and a colleague—all of them are him, all of them are us, and we are him. Weldon puts it this way: "Look, I didn't want you to actually read Ellis's work. I did it for you. I expect you have enough trouble with your own fantasies of revenge, as you wonder whether you're brave enough to walk down your street late at night".

Within what Foucault has described as our social order's medico-juridical regime, there is little recognition of the literariness of a discourse that proposes not etiologies but symptomatologies, and, in delineating an uncanny symptomatology, *American Psycho* has articulated an unbearable—but lucid, but rigidly logical—antihumanism as the mundane and mannerly order of the day.

—*Carla Freccero*

Deleuze concludes his discussion of Sade and Sacher-Masoch by pointing out that pathologies are often defined first from their symptoms and only later as a function of their causes and that, while scientific or clinical medicine seeks the etiology of disease, etiology is subordinated to symptomatology, the artistic and literary, or interpretive, aspect of such inquiry. Within what Foucault has described as our social order's medico-juridical regime, there is little recognition of the literariness of a discourse that proposes not etiologies but symptomatologies, and, in delineating an uncanny symptomatology, *American Psycho* has articulated an unbearable—but lucid, but rigidly logical—antihumanism as the mundane and mannerly order of the day. One of the epigraphs to *American Psycho* features a quotation from Judith Martin, better known as Miss Manners. In the first part of this passage, Martin declares: "One of the major mistakes people make is that they think manners are only the expression of happy ideas. There's a whole range of behavior that can be expressed in a mannerly way. That's what civilization is all about—doing it in a mannerly and not an antagonistic way."

The political loss for progressives, in denouncing *American Psycho,* has been a victory for conservatives, who decry modern popular culture and the "twentysomething" Generation X's postmodern approach, which they interpret as a relativization of values, a lack of a moral framework, and as producing a world without civilization, without decency. Carol Iannone, writing in *Commentary,* focuses instead on

the second half of Judith Martin's statement, which seems, in Iannone's view, to invoke the Sixties as the "immoral" beginning that culminated in the decline of civilization represented by Generation X. Here is Martin: "One of the places we went wrong was the naturalistic Rousseauean movement of the Sixties in which people said, 'Why can't you just say what's on your mind?' In civilization there have to be some restraints. If we followed every impulse, we'd be killing one another." Iannone quotes this second half of the epigraph and continues, in an extravagant indictment of "postmodernism" as the culmination of the sixties:

> In one way or another, then, Ellis seems to have absorbed a sense of our age as one in which a deluded permissiveness has badly misread human nature and the contingencies surrounding the human condition. In this light, his caricature of Reaganite America becomes a mere epiphenomenon of a deeper cultural holocaust. Indeed, when Patrick Bateman speaks his mind, he invokes not the culture of Reagan, which for better or worse is only the culture of middle-class America, but rather a phantasmagoric, quintessentially post-modernist landscape from which all traditional structures, values, truths, have been eliminated. . . . In a deconstructed world of jagged surfaces, devoid of hierarchies of meaning, there are no depths to cry out of, and none to receive the cry. . . .

> . . . we are witnessing: a novel that both seeks to portray and at the same time is itself a manifestation of extreme cultural breakdown. As such it inadvertently forces a number of politically incorrect truths on our attention—that civilization does not cause barbarism, it controls it; that the weakening of civilized restraints does not mean the flowering of the individual but the rise of savagery; that when we deny the moral law, people will just go farther to hit bottom, to feel, if only negatively, the boundaries of their humanity.

Yet it is precisely that "civilization"—which Iannone refers to as "only the culture of middle-class America"—that is being indicted by the twentysomething perspective Ellis represents. In an essay for the Arts and Leisure section of the *New York Times* far "bleaker" than the fictional philosophies of *American Psycho,* "The Twentysomethings: Adrift in a Pop Landscape," Ellis invokes history as the primal trauma of his generation: "Few of my generation were alive for, much less remember, the assassination of John F. Kennedy, but the oldest of us, even at age 2, could sense something had gone wrong". And Ted Rall, describing a generation on the cusp of thirty-and twenty-somethings, remarks:

> These are heady days for those of us who always suspected that treating people like dog meat is a

recipe for a better breed of citizen. No more will weak-willed social engineers and their fellow travelers in Government fall for the trap of "caring," "helping" or other outmoded social policies. All over the nation, we "twirtysomethings"—Americans 25 to 35 years old—decide elections, set trends and fall behind no faster than other people. We're saving the United States from itself, and we're doing it by being neglected, mistreated, and ignored!

Liberals, in arguing for a moral framework and an etiology with which to turn Patrick Bateman and the novel *American Psycho* into a consoling fantasy of an evil agent as the cause of evil, want a humanist resolution to the monstrosity of the world Ellis presents, want to continue to believe that the killer will be caught and punished, rather than, as Ellis proposes, quoting Talking Heads in the epigraph to the novel: "And as things fell apart / Nobody paid much attention." Thus they collude with the right wing in their condemnation of the writer's symptomatic "inadvertency," while refusing—unlike the right, whose diagnosis is ready and true—to take up the question of history the writer poses. Ellis, who is here analyzing and demonstrating the philosophical insights of Generation X, is instead criticized for juvenile cynicism and the "bad taste" of the younger generation. Thus the generational perspective is trivialized—as "grown-ups" are wont to do—or else, indeed, rendered tragic (as in the case of liberal laments about violence, teen suicide, and AIDS).

What the critics and censors have done, then, is to denounce a symptomatology—antihumanism, or rather the total negation of humanism—in despair of ever being able to locate a cause, at least in this serial killer. The violence of history, its transitivity, its temporality, may be ungraspable as such, as Butler says, but in figuring that violence as a handsome, successful, upper-middle-class white male serial killer—an individual—and then refusing to confer upon that American icon of the serial killer an inner truth that would explain the cause of evil, that would provide some sort of moral accountability for that evil—Ellis responds to what Mailer argues is our postmodern condition:

> Art is no longer the great love who is wise, witty, strengthening, tender, wholesomely passionate, secure, life-giving . . . no we are far beyond that moral universe—art has now become our need to be terrified. We live in the fear that we are destroying the universe, even as we mine deeper into its secrets. So art may be needed now to provide us with just those fearful insights that the uneasy complacencies of our leaders do their best to avoid.

In doing so, Ellis refuses us a consoling fantasy, a fetish for

our disavowals; instead he returns us to that history, to the violence of historicity and to the historicity of violence.

The last words of the novel are a sign, written in red like the red of the sign scribbled on the Chemical Bank wall in the opening lines of the novel:

> Someone has already taken out a Minolta cellular phone and called for a car, and then, when I'm not really listening, watching instead someone who looks remarkably like Marcus Halberstam paying a check, someone asks, simply, not in relation to anything, "Why?" and though I'm very proud that I have cold blood and that I can keep my nerve and do what I'm supposed to do, I catch something, then realize it: Why? and automatically answering, out of the blue, for no reason, just opening my mouth, words coming out, summarizing for the idiots: "Well, though I know I should have done that instead of not doing it, I'm twenty-seven for Christ sakes and this is, uh, how life presents itself in a bar or in a club in New York, maybe anywhere, at the end of the century and how people, you know, me, behave, and this is what being Patrick means to me, I guess, so, well, yup, uh . . . " and this is followed by a sigh, then a slight shrug and another sigh, and above one of the doors covered by red velvet drapes in Harry's is a sign and on the sign in letters that match the drapes' color are the words THIS IS NOT AN EXIT.

From Dante to Sartre, from Europe's premodernity to its late modernity, from theology to existentialism, *American Psycho* charts its affinity with, and fragmentation of, a history of hellish visions of history. It does so, however, without necessarily seeking redemption from knowledge, without, that is, consenting to the positive productivity mandated by censors in the liberal state.

FURTHER READING

Criticism

Barnes, Hugh. "Young Ones." *London Review of Books* 8, No. 10 (5 June 1986): 22.
    A review of *Less Than Zero* that considers the novel alongside "postpunk" writing by Julie Burchill.

Brown, Rosellen. "The Emperor's New Fiction." *Boston Review* 11, No. 4 (August 1986): 7-8.
    Looks at the style and content of "postsixties" fiction, including Ellis's *Less Than Zero*.

Hendin, Josephine. "Fictions of Acquisition." *Culture in an Age of Money,* edited by Nicolaus Mills, pp. 216-33. Chicago: Ivan R. Dee, 1990.

Presents an overview of "youthcult fiction" of the 1980s, including that of Bret Easton Ellis.

Irving, John. "Pornography and the New Puritans." *New York Times Book Review* (29 March 1992): 1, 24-25, 27.

Discusses *American Psycho* in the context of censorship and the relationship between writing and criminal acts.

Klavan, Andrew. "The Shrieking of the Lambs." *Boston Review* 19, Nos. 3 & 4 (June 1994): 30-4.

A defense of violence in fiction that discusses several violent works and includes a consideration of *American Psycho.*

Additional coverage of Ellis' life and career is contained in the following sources published by Gale: *Authors and Artists for Young Adults,* Vol. 2; *Contemporary Authors,* Vols. 118, and 123; *Contemporary Authors New Revision Series,* Vol. 51; and *DISCovering Authors Modules: Popular Fiction and Genre Authors.*

Nikki Giovanni

1943-

(Born Yolande Cornelia Giovanni) American poet, essayist, autobiographer, editor, and author of children's books.

The following entry presents an overview of Giovanni's career through 1998. For further information on her life and works, see *CLC*, Volumes 2, 4, 19, and 64.

INTRODUCTION

One of the premier twentieth-century African-American poets, Giovanni achieved such popularity in the 1960s that she has become known as "The Princess of Black Popularity." Gaining fame with her revolutionary poetry in *Black Feeling, Black Talk* (1968) and *Black Judgement* (1968), Giovanni built on this popularity through readings of her work set to gospel music, and even issued several recordings. Throughout her career, Giovanni has produced strongly oral poems, employing blues rhythms and conversational language. She has focused on themes of family, blackness, womanhood, and sex. In addition, she has written numerous essays and several critically acclaimed children's books.

Biographical Information

Giovanni was born in Knoxville, Tennessee in 1943. Her family soon moved to Lincoln Heights, Ohio, a predominantly black community. Her happy childhood, spent in part with her grandparents in Tennessee, became a major theme of Giovanni's poetry. At the age of seventeen she entered Frisk University but was asked to leave for a rules infraction. She returned in 1964 and pursued a degree in History while participating in many university activities, including the creative writing workshop led by novelist John Oliver Killens. Out of her political protest experiences of the 1960s, Giovanni wrote her first two volumes of poetry *Black Feeling, Black Talk* and *Black Judgement*. In 1968 Giovanni accepted a teaching position at Rutgers University. About this time she also gave birth to a son. Throughout the 1970s Giovanni shifted the focus of her writing away from revolutionary politics and towards personal observations and domestic experiences. She published her first children's book *Spin a Soft Black Song* in 1971. She won the Mademoiselle outstanding achievement award in 1971, the Ladies' Home Journal Woman of the Year Youth Leadership Award in 1972, was nominated for a National Book Award in 1973 for *Gemini* (1971), and won the Langston Hughes Award in 1996.

Major Works

Giovanni gained widespread popularity during the 1960s for her revolutionary poems in *Black Feeling, Black Talk* and *Black Judgement,* two works which feature rhythmic, often angry verse. One of Giovanni's best-known poems, "The True Import of the Present Dialogue, Black vs. Negro," is a call to African Americans to destroy both the whites who oppress them and blacks whose passivity and compliance contribute to their own oppression. "Nikki Rosa," from *Black Judgement,* which recounts Giovanni's childhood, is often considered the author's signature poem. Affectionately recalling her supportive family, the poet asserts that happiness is dependent on love, not material possessions, and this love is the staple of unity within the black community. Both of these works were well received both critically and publicly, launching Giovanni's career as a noted American poet. Giovanni's next two works, *Re:Creation* (1970) and *Gemini* (1971) reflected more personal themes and observations and mark a significant transition in Giovanni's style. The poems, influenced by Giovanni's love of rhythm and blues music, are less angry, reflecting black experience from a personal viewpoint rather than the collective movement. In her 1972 collection, *My House,* Giovanni depicted personal and public lives as complementary forces working together toward change. Giovanni shifts from this focus on society to themes of isolation in *Cotton Candy on a Rainy Day* (1978). Poems such as "The Rose Bush" are somber and bleak observations about estrangement and dislocation. *Those Who Ride the Night Winds* (1983) features tributes to various historical figures such as John Lennon, Martin Luther King, Jr., and Rosa Parks. In addition, Giovanni has published several volumes of children's poetry which is at times angry, poignant, and humorous.

Critical Reception

Critics praised Giovanni's early work for its raw emotions, energy, and her commitment to black issues. However, with her publication of *Re:Creation* and then *Gemini,* formerly enthusiastic critics questioned her shift from political to personal. Critics such as Ruth Rambo McClain felt that she had abandoned the black movement. However, other critics praised the work, noting that Giovanni appeals to an audience who feels disconnected with the more radical and violent protest poetry and that her work still reflects the black experience, albeit from a more personal side. Margaret McDowell argues that critics have misunderstood Giovanni's work, stating that Giovanni "has tended to focus on a single individual, situation, or idea, often with a brief narrative thread present in the poem." Martha Cook writes, "[t]he best of [Giovanni's] poetry throughout her career has been concrete, with references to specific places, rooms, furniture, people, colors, quantities of light and dark." Cook argues that Giovanni is less successful when her poetry is more abstract. While Giovanni's emphasis on orality and the sound of language in her poetry has earned her considerable attention, some critics have questioned whether the emphasis on rhythms have undermined the structure of her poems. Criticizing *Cotton Candy,* William J. Harris writes, "Giovanni is a frustrating poet . . . She clearly has talent that she refuses to discipline. She just doesn't seem to try hard enough." He argues she is too dependent on her strong personality and ego. Other critics, however, such as Duffy, argue that this strong persona gives strength to her works.

PRINCIPAL WORKS

Black Feeling, Black Talk (poetry) 1968

Black Judgement (poetry) 1968

Night Comes Softly: An Anthology of Black Female Voices (editor) 1970

Re:Creation (poetry) 1970

Ego Tripping and Other Poems for Children (poetry) 1971

Gemini: An Extended Autobiographical Statement on My
First Twenty-five Years of Being a Black Poet (autobiography) 1971

Spin a Soft Black Song: Poems for Children (poetry) 1971

My House (poetry) 1972

A Dialogue: James Baldwin and Nikki Giovanni (essays) 1973

A Poetic Equation: Conversations between Nikki Giovanni and Margaret Walker (essays) 1974

The Women and the Men (poetry) 1975

Cotton Candy on a Rainy Day (poetry) 1978

Vacation Time: Poems for Children (poetry) 1980

Those Who Ride the Night Winds (poetry) 1983

Sacred Cows . . . and Other Edibles (essays) 1988

Racism 101 (autobiographical essays) 1994

The Genie in the Jar (poetry) 1996

The Sun Is So Quiet: Poems (poetry) 1996

Love Poems (poetry) 1997

CRITICISM

Bernard W. Bell (essay date September 1971)

SOURCE: "New Black Poetry: A Double-Edged Sword," in *CLA Journal,* Vol. XV, No. 1, September, 1971, pp. 37-43.

[*In the following essay, Bell analyzes African-American poetry, discussing its influences and its agenda.*]

Perhaps the most phenomenal cultural development in the nation during the 1960's was the renaissance in Afro-American art, especially poetry. Naturally this development, like the Vietnam War, did not come about overnight nor in a social vacuum. Rather, it was an outgrowth of the cultural frustrations and political exigencies of black Americans in their struggle for self-determination if not their very survival. More specifically, it was directly related to LeRoi Jones' baptism in blackness and his remarkable achievements in drama and poetry.

As early as 1962 in "The Myth of Negro Literature" Jones had lashed out at black writers for imitating "the useless ugly inelegance of the stunted middle-class mind," an updated version of Richard Wright's 1937 animadversions in "Blueprint for Negro Literature." But it is in subsequent poems like "Black Dada Nihilismus," "Black Art," and his third volume of verse, *Black Magic: Collected Poetry 1961-1967,* that Jones actually begins blazing the path toward a new aesthetic and a new nation, the frequently avowed goals of most contemporary Afro-American poets. But LeRoi Jones was not the only force responsible for the direction and flowering of recent black poetry. In 1965-1966 John O. Killens's writing workshops and conferences in New York and Tennessee provided the forum; Hoyt Fuller's 1966-1967 joint sponsorship of the OBAC writers of Chicago (the late Conrad Kent Rivers and Gerald McWhorter were the other co-sponsors) and his editorial policy in *Black World* (formerly *Negro Digest*) offered the popular vehicle; Dudley Randall's extraordinarily successful Broadside Press, founded in 1966, the commercial outlet; and Gwendolyn Brooks, the artistic encouragement necessary to foster a revolutionary generation of talented, race-conscious black poets.

Because of their scathing indictment of anything considered detrimental to the advancement of black people, some critics believe that the generating spirit of these new black poets is hatred. But I submit that their hatred is a valid though increasingly ineffective poetic stance and that on a deeper level the new black poetry is rooted in a love of black people and an affirmation of life. "You see," says poet Don Lee in the *Negro Digest,* "black poetry will not, necessarily, teach the people how to die, but will teach the people how to live. We must live, we must show those who control the world how to live. Re-define man and put man in his proper perspective in relation to other men and to the world." It is this tension between hatred and love, life and death that constitutes much of the vitality of the new black poetry.

This brings us to the central question of this essay: just how revolutionary is the new black poetry? In a sense, the Black Consciousness poets are bearers of the legacy of the New Negro movement of the twenties and, at the same time, rebels without a past. Generally speaking, the giants of the New Negro movement—James Weldon Johnson, Claude McKay, Langston Hughes, Countee Cullen, Sterling Brown—turned to Africa and Afro-American folklore as well as England for a sense of tradition. In the immediate background of that movement were the Pan-African Congresses convened by W. E. B. Du Bois, the pioneering studies on Africa by Carter G. Woodson, and the Back-to-Africa movement of Marcus Garvey. Equally important in giving impetus and direction to young black artists of the era was Dr. Alain Locke, a professor of philosophy at Howard University. Literary historians have come to view his anthology, *The New Negro* (1925), as the manifesto of the movement. Containing essays by black and white scholars as well as representative selections of creative writing by young Afro-Americans, *The New Negro* celebrates what Professor Locke optimistically considered "the attainment of a significant and satisfying new phase of group development" by Americans of African descent.

As in the Black Consciousness movement of the sixties, the acknowledged standard bearers of the New Negro movement were the poets. Following the appearance of Jean Toomer's poetic novel in 1923, books of black poetry began pouring from the presses: Cullen's *Color* (1925), *Copper Sun* (1927), *Caroling Dusk* (1927) and *Black Christ and Other Poems*

(1929); Hughes' *The Weary Blues* (1926) and *Fine Clothes to the Jew* (1927); Johnson's *The Book of American Negro Poetry* (1922) and *God's Trombones* (1927); and Brown's *Southern Road* (1932). The avowed intention of most New Negro artists was to write honestly—to explore, not to exploit the roots of Afro-American culture. But many of their white admirers were more interested in the exotic qualities of their work. As a result, the young black poets soon found themselves impaled on the horns of a dilemma. On one side were the white patrons and publishers encouraging them to highlight the primitiveness of Harlem life, while on the other were members of the black gentility frequently condemning them for not using their talents to portray the intellectual and social parity of the race.

At this point, it is important to remember that the thrust of the Harlem movement, as Robert Hayden has stated in the Introduction to the Atheneum reprint of *The New Negro,* was "more aesthetic and philosophical . . . than political." Langston Hughes in his well-known essay "The Negro Artist and the Racial Mountain," forcefully addresses himself to this issue:

> We younger Negro artists who create now intend to express our individual dark-skinned selves without fear or shame. We know we are beautiful. And ugly too. The tom-tom cries and the tom-tom laughs. If colored people are pleased, we are glad. If they are not, their displeasure doesn't matter either. We build our temples for tomorrow, strong as we know how, and we stand on top of the mountain, free within ourselves.

Toward the achievement of this freedom of expression and faith in the future, the contests and prizes sponsored by the *Crisis* and *Opportunity,* the journals of the NAACP and Urban League, were of invaluable service.

During the Depression, the Harlem Renaissance came to a close. In retrospect, the primary accomplishment of the literary movement of the twenties was to provide a national showcase for a newly awakened sense of racial pride. In the absence of a formal organization or literary school, the black poets of the day found a common bond in their race-consciousness and desire to become their own image-makers. A close examination of their poetry reveals 1) a nostalgic interest in Africa, 2) a rediscovery and reevaluation of black folk values, 3) the elevation of members of the black masses, especially the working class, as heroes, and 4) the introduction and validation of the blues, jazz, ballads, sermons and black idiom as poetic material. This is the literary legacy that the present generation of black poets has inherited. And a quick glance at the poems of LeRoi Jones, Don Lee, A. B. Spellman, Sonia Sanchez, Carolyn Rodgers, Nikki Giovanni and David Henderson confirms the current interest in Africa, Afro-American music, and the urban black idiom.

On the other hand, a serious study of the new black poetry gives evidence of an unprecedented revolutionary fervor and commitment to the concept of art as weapon. "We want 'poems that kill'," says Jones in "Black Art." ". . . . Clean out the world for virtue and love, / Let there be no love poem written / until love can exist freely and clearly. . . ./ We want a black poem. And a / Black World." The sound and sense of this poem is clear. Black art must be a double-edged sword: the instrument of the Day of Judgment and the new Black Jerusalem. Written back around the time of the Harlem conflagration, "Black Art" is a chillingly effective frontal attack on the myth that white is right. More importantly, in stripping away the sham of outmoded academic poetic conventions and challenging the primacy of Western values, it helped to liberate the minds and voices of many new black poets.

Looking neither to white critics nor posterity for fame and fortune, these poets raise their voices in song for the black man on the street. Their spirits have been tempered by the eloquent defiance and charisma of Malcolm X, the self-reliance and religious faith of the Nation of Islam, the rising star of the independent nations of Africa and the incisive psychological studies on the nature of oppression by Frantz Fanon. Their aesthetic theories and the rudiments of their craftsmanship have been developed in the writing workshops of John Oliver Killens, Hoyt Fuller, LeRoi Jones, and Gwendolyn Brooks. Their poems, essays and fiction are published by small black presses like Broadside, Third World and Jihad and appear in the pages of the *Journal of Black Poetry, Black World, Black Expression, Nommo, Black Dialogue* and *Liberator.* In contrast to the writers of the Harlem Renaissance, they are largely supported by the grass-roots elements of black urban communities in Chicago, Detroit, San Francisco, New York and Newark. For instance, Don Lee has published his four books of poetry exclusively with black presses without advertising in the mass media yet his sales hover around the 100,000 mark. For these economic and political reasons as well as those related to their preoccupation with racial themes the most popular new poets are members of the Black Consciousness movement.

The service that Alain Locke's anthology performed for the New Negro movement, LeRoi Jones and Larry Neal's *Black Fire* (1968) accomplished for the Black Consciousness movement. A collection of essays, poems, short stories and plays by over seventy black writers, *Black Fire* is, as its book jacket states, "a naked indictment of American prejudice and a flaming prophecy of future turmoil. . . . addressed primarily to black people and the Third World of Africa, Asia and Latin America." At the same time, *Black Fire* is a soul-bear-

ing "search for a definition of the black sensibility" and an expression of love for black people.

Most of the new black poetry, then, is a celebration of blackness, both physical and spiritual. In "my beige mom," for instance, Ed Spriggs sings of his "tall, strong-boned / beige & bruised" mother, whose inherited strength he lays "at the third world's door." In the title poem of Mari Evans' *I Am A Black Woman* the black woman speaker looms majestically "tall as a cypress" in defiance of historical circumstances, proudly proclaiming to the world: "Look / on me and be / renewed." The symbolic strength of the black matriarch is also the redemptive force of Lance Jeffers' "My Blackness is the Beauty of this Land," but this time the central figure is a "drawling black grandmother" whose love and hate "shall civilize this land" and be its salvation. In "to all sisters" Sonia Sanchez strikes a different chord as she croons "there ain't / no MAN like a / black man. / he puts it where it is / and makes u / turn in / side out." And for the girl whose Afro "without words speaks of black and blues and boogaloo" Bob Bennet says, "(She is my sister: I am her brother) / Without romance there is love."

And so it goes, with older poets like Langston Hughes, Gwendolyn Brooks, Dudley Randall, Margaret Walker and Mari Evans influencing and being influenced by the looser style and self-assertiveness of the younger generation of prophets of a new world order. The sections on "The Blackstone Rangers" in Miss Brooks' *In the Mecca* and "A Black Oneness, A Black Strength" in Miss Evans' *I Am A Black Woman* immediately come to mind as exquisite examples of the new wine of Black Consciousness in the old bottles of traditional yet more relaxed forms. Moreover, in such memorable lines as Lucille Clifton's "My Mama moved among the days / like a dreamwalker in a field," Audre Lorde's "Earth is still sweet, for autumn teachers bearing / And new sun will warm our proud and cautions feet," and Etheridge Knight's "I do not expect the spirit of Penelope / To enter your breast, for I am not mighty / Or fearless . . ." we discover poetic sensibilities that are as refreshingly responsive to the human soul as those of their literary progenitors.

Thus, contrary to the opinion of some older critics, the new black poets do not march in lock step to the same revolutionary tune. More important than the obscenity, name-calling, guns and bombs of the new black poetry is its Soul Power. Soul, writes Lerone Bennett in *The Negro Mood,* is

> a distinct quality of Negro-ness growing out of the Negro's experience and not his genes. *Soul* is a metaphorical evocation of Negro being as expressed in the Negro tradition. It is the feeling with which an artist invests his creation, the style with which a man lives his life. It is, above all, the spirit rather

than the letter: a certain way of feeling, a certain way of expressing oneself, a certain way of being.

This is the potent black myth that energizes the slender volumes of verse by Don Lee, Carolyn Rodgers, Nikki Giovanni, Keorapetse W. Kgositsile and a host of other black poets. This does not mean that they have all mastered their craft or that they all strive for the same levels of black consciousness. They are all committed to the struggle for black liberation, yet differences in emphasis and approach characterize their best poems. From the subtle touch of Mari Evans to the hard-hitting street idiom of Sonia Sanchez, we see the handwriting on the wall and hear the trumpeting voices of prophets of a new world order. Ironically, the techniques of new black poetry that some critics decry as gimmickry and others consider exclusively black in origin—unconventional capitalization, line and word spacing, abbreviations, unclosed parentheses and quotation marks, esoteric images and the like—are actually derivative of E. E. Cummings, T. S. Eliot, Ezra Pound, William Carlos Williams, and Charles Olson á la LeRoi Jones. But regardless of whether they self-consciously turn to Western or African sources, these mythmakers and visionaries of a better tomorrow should be heard in full. Then and only then can we meaningfully evaluate the role they have played in broadening the scope of poetry, revitalizing the American language and bringing about a spiritual if not political regeneration of the nation.

Martha Duffy (review date 17 January 1972)

SOURCE: "Hustler and Fabulist," in *Time,* Vol. 99, No. 3, January 17, 1972, pp. 63-4.

[*In the following review of* Gemini, *Duffy argues that Giovanni has crafted both a memoir and a manifesto about her life.*]

> I really hope no white person
>   ever has cause
> to write about me
> because they never understand
> Black love is Black wealth
>   and they'll
> probably talk about my hard
>   childhood
> and never understand that
> all the while I was quite happy.

These proud words come from Nikki Giovanni's best-known poem, *Nikki-Rosa.* At 28, she is one of the most talented and promising black poets. She is also one of the most visible, not only because she is beautiful but because she is a

shrewd and energetic propagandist. In this interim autobiography, both poet and propagandist underscore that point about black love and happiness. Part memoir and part manifesto, it is a plain-spoken, lively, provocative, confusing book.

The memoir part deals with growing up in a tightly knit, loyal family of social workers in Cincinnati and Knoxville. As a child she had two idols, her glamorous older sister Gary and her grandmother Louvenia. Nikki did all Gary's fighting for her for the excellent reason that Gary was a musician who argued that if her hands were "maimed," the families of her music teachers might starve. Protecting Louvenia was a harder assignment. Nikki's childhood ended the day she realized that her grandmother was dying. Uprooted from her old house by a spurious urban-renewal scheme in Knoxville, Louvenia had lost the will to live. She was "gone, not even to a major highway but to a cutoff of a cutoff."

On the subject of her childhood, Miss Giovanni is magical. She meanders along with every appearance of artlessness, but one might as well say that Mark Twain wrote shaggy-dog stories. The little figure in the center—"big, brown eyes, three pigtails and high-top shoes"—is a classic American child, pelting rocks at her enemies from the roof, lining up for all-day movies, eating her liverwurst on raisin bread with mayonnaise.

The later chapters are less autobiography than polemic. The tone swings wildly from bitterness to defiance, from humor to cant, from wisdom to frenzy. The gentlest statement about whites is that "all white people need to be taken out of power, but they all clearly are not evil." The only white leaders to whom any quarter is offered are the dead Kennedy brothers and John Lindsay.

If Nikki Giovanni has ever suffered personally from the color of her skin, she does not admit it. An honor graduate of Fisk (in history) who nearly went into social work too, she has instead taught creative writing at Rutgers and become a major figure in the black oral poetry movement. Hers is a committed social rage. She is capable of scalding rhetoric, but the artist in her keeps interrupting. For one thing, she is a natural fabulist. A tirade on colonialism turns into a series of irresistible parables about the wise and natural black man faced with the petty, scheming honky. Also, she cares too much about language not to kid her own fire breathing, at least occasionally: "I'm essentially a hustler because I'm essentially Black American and that carries essentially a hustling mentality (if you can essentially follow that)."

One feels that *Gemini* will not be her last autobiography. For one thing, she is determined to keep publishing. One of her few deep criticisms of a black is directed at Novelist Ralph Ellison, because he has published no novel since *The Invisible Man* in 1952. "He can put us down and say we are not writers, who are persistently exposing our insides and trying to create a reality."

That is Nikki Giovanni's approach. She keeps sending out bulletins—in poetry, prose, children's books—whether they are neat or messy, rash or reasoned. But one senses a dynamic intelligence behind the shrillest page of *Gemini.* It is a report about a life in progress that demands to be seen.

Nancy Rosenberg (review date 5 May 1974)

SOURCE: "A Tree Grows in Print," in *New York Times Book Review,* May 5, 1974, p. 38.

[*In the following review, Rosenberg praises Giovanni's style and skill in* Ego-Tripping.]

In a previous book, *Spin a Soft Black Song,* Miss Giovanni used warm, unaffected language to describe being young and black. In *Ego-Tripping,* which has George Ford's illustrations reflecting strength and good feeling, the poems are directed at older readers able to handle heavier subjects and more ambitious poetry. Several are familiar from anthologies and previous works while others are published here for the first time. They are sly and seductive, freewheeling and winsome, tough, sure and proud. Miss Giovanni pursues both personal and cultural matters: loneliness, private dreams, love and survival, all with a boundless enthusiasm for the essences of black life. In the best poems, language and spirit rebound and join forces. The title poem is a celebration of African heritage and modern dignity.

> I was born in the congo
> I walked to the fertile crescent and built the sphinx
> I designed a pyramid so
>   tough that a star that
>   only glows every one
>   hundred years falls into
>   the center giving divine
>   perfect light
> I am bad

She can chide herself for "radical dreams," joke about more common ones, admit with wry humor

> . . . as i grew and matured
> i became more sensible
> and decided i would
> settle down
> and just become

a sweet inspiration

Throughout the book Miss Giovanni shares her razor-sharp perceptions with energy and passion.

Stephanie J. Stokes (essay date August 1981)

SOURCE: "My House," in *Essence,* Vol. 12, No. 4, August, 1981, pp. 84-8.

[*In the following essay based on an interview with Giovanni, Stokes remarks on Giovanni's home and family.*]

"Now don't expect to find me in a fancy mansion," Nikki Giovanni said when told the *Essence* crew was on its way to Cincinnati to share a day in her busy life. "But if you want someone who lives like everyone else, then you're coming to the right place."

We couldn't imagine Nikki's house as anything less than wonderful. Sure, she lives in an average, middle-class Black community called Lincoln Heights. And yes, her house looks much like others on her block; it's nice, although in passing one wouldn't look twice. But once inside you feel there's a lot of care and love in this house. One of Nikki's poems does say that Black love is Black wealth. Our expectations were confirmed.

But what's Nikki Giovanni doing in *Cincinnati:* She recalls that once when she was washing her car a brother recognized her and asked in amazement, "Nikki Giovanni? What're *you* doing *here*?" Her reply: "Washing my car. Want to help?"

The true answer to his question lies deep in the love Nikki has for her family. Three years ago, after her father had a stroke, Nikki and her son, Thomas, moved from New York City to be with her parents.

"The stroke was so serious that there was some question as to whether he was going to live," Nikki explains. "I thought, 'If he dies, somebody's going to have to be here with my mother. If he doesn't, somebody's going to have to be here with him.' So the decision wasn't difficult and didn't bother me. I like New York but I don't feel like 'Oh God, I've made this great sacrifice for these people.' If I did I wouldn't have come." Nikki's father is now convalescing in California with Nikki's older sister, Gary. And Nikki is enjoying living in her old hometown.

The day we spent with Nikki, she had just returned from a 90-day lecture tour. Yet the hectic pace had not diminished her energy one bit. She washed clothes, answered correspondence, took her latest memorabilia went to the framer, went to the bookstore, the cleaners and the post office. When 11-year-old Tommy came home from school, she played football with him, then cooked dinner.

Most days she works on a new volume of poetry and a book of "nonpoetic faction." She also writes free-lance for newspapers and magazines. "I'm a writer that likes to be topical," she explains. "Some poems are topical, but the nature of poetry is not topical; it's emotional. So I like journalism too. I'm not very good at who, what, when, where and how; I'm more interested in discussing 'What does it really mean?'"

One writing obligation Nikki doesn't overlook is answering her loads of mail. She comments that she often gets requests to provide more information about her poems. Not one to live in the past by explaining how or why she wrote her poems, Nikki says, "I'm not the critic. If I have to give information that will enable someone to write a critique, then I should write the critique. And if I have to write the critique, then I've failed in 14 books to make a statement."

"I don't think I have to backtrack," she adds. "I definitely stand behind all my poems. There's not one that I can say I regret. My poetry is as much a part of me as kindergarten—I'm not denying it, but I'm not going back."

She has gone back to living in her parents home, however, and that has required some adjustments. "No matter what the situation is or what the financial arrangements are you are always their child," she says. "If you're in your parents' house or they're in yours, it's still a parent-child relationship. When I get tired of being a child, I go to the small apartment I maintain in New York. But essentially, I don't have any problems living with my parents."

Actually, Nikki has made a special place for herself, a kind of apartment, right in her parents' basement. It's a gold mine of wall-to-wall bookshelves, Afro-American memorabilia and antique furniture. The books and records are in alphabetical order. The memorabilia is framed and hung or neatly displayed. Everything is organized and has its own place. When Nikki describes how the basement used to look, with a large cocktail bar and room for dancing, the renovation seems especially astounding.

"I like to do renovations," Nikki says, sitting in her library retreat. "So I looked around this house and thought. 'Well, we have a lot to do here.' I thought it would take about a year. It turned out to be a three-year job."

The project took longer than she had anticipated because the workers she called were slow to start. "In Manhattan, if you call for something you get it right away," she explains. "I called here and the guy said. 'Well, I'll have to call you back in about a week.' The slowness took an adjustment." As a result, Nikki took on many of the jobs herself. "I have a girlfriend who's forever in awe of me because of the things that I do" she says, smiling. "I'm amazed that women sit around and don't do things, saying. "I have to wait on my husband.'"

In her renovation, Nikki considered the needs of everyone living in the house. "I wanted to make a home that everyone could function in. My father likes to sit on the front porch and holler at his neighbors, so we made the front porch larger. I took the garage and turned it into a gazebo for Tommy and his good friend Brian. Since they're into records now, in the summer I put a record player in the driveway and they dance outside. I like to barbecue and sit in the backyard, so I put up an awning. And so that I wouldn't have to walk my dogs, I built a fence for them to have the run of the yard. I've enjoyed playing with the house. It's fun."

As Nikki talks about the birthday party she threw for her father, the small field she's clearing for her son and his friends to play soccer and the relationship between her mother and Tommy, a smile of satisfaction crosses her face.

"I don't think I have a lifestyle," she says, turning serious. "I have a life. It's not a style. Lifestyles are transitory. For example, one moved to Paris if one happened to be a Black artist in the thirties or forties. Or one moved to California in the late fifties, early sixties. I'm sure that's charming, but that's not what I am about. I'm about my life."

Nikki's life doesn't include role playing or following a formula. "I'm not into roles," she states firmly. "When I lecture, the kids keep asking, 'What's the role of the woman? What's the role of this or that?' This is no job. This is our life. It's reality, and I think you do what has to be done. Some people wait for the sink to be fixed, because, after all, they're a woman and they don't do that. That means nothing. Working together to build a common homestead—that works.

"I think all the concern about the family in the eighties is slightly overblown," Nikki adds. "Or maybe I'm in an awkward position because I am personally fond of my family. I think we get along—although not without effort. I mean, a family member's like any other friend. That's where people miss. They expect a family to take the worst of them and their friends to get the best. They don't work at a good relationship. I think familial relationships are very delicate and should be treated as you would any other love affair.

"I've been seeing articles that ask, What's causing the breakup of the family? Well, it's not surprising it's breaking up—the nuclear family doesn't work. Many of us are divorced already. Many of us will be stepparents. Some of us will rear our brothers or live with aunts and uncles. Some of us are adopted. And we make this big deal. 'Oh, this is a different child. It's adopted.' If you tell me you're family, I take your word for it."

Nikki lives by her philosophy. It was her choice 11 years ago to have a baby and not marry the child's father. To her, the concept of extended family is real. And even though her parents have been married 43 years, she's not interested in living her life based on theirs.

"I don't think anybody should stay on the job that long. Just for the exercise of it there should be a separation. I'm glad my parents like each other.

"I just think that we're responsible for our own happiness." Nikki adds that one way to start being responsible is to change the wording of the marriage ceremony toward an equitable living situation. "In the old days," she muses, "it was 'I now pronounce you gender and role.'"

"This is not my soapbox," she adds. "I'm not saying that I won't wake up ten years down the pike and say, I really think I want to get married.' I'll be as happy to get married as I am to be single now."

> i mean i want to keep you warm
> and my windows might be dirty
> but it's my house
> and if i can't see out sometimes
> they can't see in either
>
> i'm saying its my house
> and i'll make fudge and call
> it love and touch my lips
> to the chocolate warmth
> and smile at old men and call
> it revolution cause what's real
> is really real
> and i still like men in tight
> pants cause everybody has some
> thing to give and more
> important need something to take
>
> and this is my house and you make me happy
> so this is your poem

Nikki Giovanni with Arlene Elder (interview date Winter 1982)

SOURCE: "A *MELUS* Interview: Nikki Giovanni," in *MELUS*, Vol. 9, No. 3, Winter, 1982, pp. 61-75.

[*In the following interview, Giovanni discusses her travels to Africa, the role of the writer in society, and writers she admires.*]

Throughout her career, Nikki Giovanni's poetry has been valued, at least in part, as a touchstone to the latest political and artistic ideas in Black American writing. She, however, never considered herself a spokesperson for any group. She says she is a "we" poet whose work might reflect the thoughts of others but judges it the height of "arrogance" to assume one is the "voice" of a people; people, she is confident, can speak perfectly well for themselves. She feels that her poetry is richer now because she understands more than she did when she was younger; as if to accommodate that fuller understanding, she is experimenting with longer pieces, some of 1200 to 1500 lines. Her forthcoming book is *Those Who Ride The Night Winds,* to be published later this year by William Morrow.

[*Elder:*] *I was interested in your trip to Africa. Have you been there several times?*

[Giovanni:] I've been there three times.

. . . interested particularly in terms of your poetry and if you found that it affected your poetry in ways other than as subject matter. I am thinking of perhaps more of an emphasis on orality than you were conscious of previously.

No. No more than Mexico or Europe, or, probably, the moon. No. Of course, you are always conscious, just because of the nature of the African continent, that you are on the oldest continent and the richest, and that you're with the first people on earth who were, in fact, civilized, but you don't all of a sudden say, "Oh, now I'm a part of that; there's a tradition here." No, I don't think so.

First of all, it would be very difficult for me to be anything other than western, you know, because I am. I'm not wedded to tradition. I think that when we consider poetry, period, the nature of poetry, if we go pre-biblical, of course, we are going to get right into the African experience. And, of course, the oral arts in Africa are at an extremely high level. So you do have this involvement with the spoken word. I think that that is important, but I also think it's important to be able to write something down, so I don't have any conflict. It doesn't make my day, and it doesn't break it.

Has your attitude toward your relationship to Africa changed over the years, after your firsthand experience there?

I really don't think I have a relationship with Africa. I think I have a relationship with my mother, my son, a number of other things; I don't think I have a relationship with the continent. I enjoy traveling in Africa. I'm so happy: from the first time I went in 1972, until now, it's much cheaper to go, and one is more capable of going. And you don't really have to go through Europe; you can actually go from New York to Dakar without having to stop over, make what amounts to a courtesy stop in Europe. And I think that probably anybody who likes to travel would choose to travel to Africa at some point. I think to not go is a great loss. You are, as I said, on the richest continent, and you are among the first of civilized man. And I think that's an important part of your experience. I also feel, though, it's equally important to do other parts of the earth. I'm really looking forward to going to Antarctica. It's environmentally sound. I don't want you, or anyone, to think that I am denigrating Africa. Some people say, "Well, why doesn't she have a relationship with Africa?" or "why doesn't she have her day made by going?" What I'm just trying to say is that you have to recognize, first of all, in 1982, Earth is a very small planet, and what we do is involve ourselves so that we are properly educated. I would still be remiss in my intellectual growth if I only did Africa. I would certainly be remiss if I did *not* do it. But it is not sufficient unto itself. We have to move around and utilize the best of all cultures.

I happen to be in an art that is almost overwhelmingly African because the poets started there. The first codification, of course, that western man recognizes is the Bible, and of course, we're still on the African continent—never understood how that became the Middle East, when the map says to me that it is Africa. You can see that, and we're very proud of it, but we also recognize that there are changes that have been made in the profession, and that those changes also are necessary to the life of the profession, in order for art to be serious, if I can use that—there must be a better word—to be viable. It had to remain alive; it has to remain adaptive to whatever forms. I have, of course, recorded some of my poetry: to gospel music in one case, and contemporary music, and some other albums just as a straight reading. It would be ridiculous, the only word I can think of, that I would live in an electronic age and not choose to electronically transmit my voice. That doesn't mean that I'm going to have the number-one-best-selling record. It's not likely at all; if I did, it would certainly be a fluke. But you do seek to use the tools that are available to you at that time. Always. You can't be so, I think the term is, purist. You get those people that say, "I would never print a book," and I'm sure that when the printing press came, "that's not the way you do it." And people continue to think that. I think that our obligation is to use whatever technology is available, because whether or not art is able to be translated tells us something about whether or not it's, in fact, living, whether or not it's part of us.

Whether it can be translated from one form to another, you mean?

To some degree. That's not the test of it, but to some degree. We were talking about a Shakespeare or a *Don Quixote*, particularly *Don Quixote*, but it has lasted so long. Not to denigrate *Don Quixote*, but essentially it's your basic soap opera. Every evening, the Spanish Court would gather, and somebody would read it. Well, it had to be interesting; it had to be true; it had to be something that people could connect to. And that's what you try to do. Now, I don't know that *Don Quixote* would make a great movie. Of course we did make it into a play, and I think we've done variations on the theme. I'm saying that you don't write for one medium to turn it into another. What I'm trying to say is that, as we are evolving, as the species evolves, we try to make use of all media. So if I were a poet when Gutenberg invented his press, I would say, "let me recite this, and you write it down, and we'll get it printed. And we'll see what this becomes," because you don't want to ignore the possibilities.

And if I understand you correctly, what you see remaining is that human quality that you said is essential for vital art to continue.

Well, people have made changes. You take a poem like the *Iliad* which was composed over some 400 years by a variety of people. We give Homer credit because Homer started it, and I'm sure Homer is delighted to take credit for it. But it kept evolving, because it was a poem being recited. And just a mere translation, just coming from Greek into anything else, just coming from Athens into Sparta would change it as much as coming from New York into Atlanta. So that what you have is something that, in fact, is alive. And it is alive because it has met the test of people.

It's curious, isn't it, that something like the Aeneid *or the* Odyssey, *maybe even something like* Don Quixote, *meets the definition of what we now call "folk art," in the very real sense. And yet, "folk art" is not considered serious. Folk art is not important; it's not high art. What do you think happened in the course of our, as a people, listening to poetry, participating in poetry, that changed somebody's mind, anyway, about what was serious and what was not?*

The rise of the merchant class. I really do. They did a lot for art. I don't take that away, because they were essentially an unlettered group, and what they did was to go out and purchase it, and at some points they were purchasing that which they understood. And as we got into "keeping up with the Joneses," it would almost be: "Well, *my* poet read this *poem* last night"; "Well, *my* poet read this *poem!*" Neither one of them gave a damn. . . . But what we got into was more and more exotic, and the poets began, of course, to read for each other: "Anybody can do what *you* did. Let me show you what *I've* done."

We were talking about *V*. And I have nothing against *V* and that kind of exotic novel, that most people won't read. They won't have the patience or, really, the interest in wading through it. But you take something that almost every kid on Earth reads, science fiction, which is not considered literature. If we charted science fiction on the *New York Times* best-seller list, I'm sure they would have the first nine without looking back. Or your mysteries. Which is somehow, again, not considered literature. So then, we also got the rise of the merchants who made money off the poets who were making money off of the merchants. So you got into this publisher class, right? Again, I'm kind of simplifying it. But, then, the publishers were saying, "okay, then, now we shall determine what is real art." And of course that would be determined by how difficult it is to meet the test of people. Because, therefore, they would have to buy the book. You're forced to.

And of course there's a marvelous story by an Ohio writer, Charles Chesnutt, whom you probably know, "Baxter's Procrustus." And, of course, Baxter bought this book and raved and raved and raved about it, and finally one day the guy opened it, and of course there was nothing inside. And I think to some degree, publishers have played that game historically. And I think to some degree, it is being played now. The publishers, of course, having kept up with the technology, are now playing the game on even a cheaper level, because what they're saying is not that we're bringing you something uniquely different that you cannot understand, but that we're bringing you crap, and what we're going to do is make use of the electronic media to make you want it.

I looked at Sy Hirsch sitting on the *Today* show the other morning. He's got a piece in the *Atlantic* on Kissinger. Now that happens to have some worth. I don't want you to think that I don't think Sy Hirsch has any worth. It's just that he had to go to the electronic media to sell the competition, really. We can keep saying, television doesn't have to be in competition, but television *is* in competition with books. And what you're saying is, "we're conceding that you have my audience, and now can I have a piece of it back?" And I just find it fascinating. We sell crap all day long, though. Sy Hirsch would be one of the better examples.

Whom do you read now, who is obviously not crap? Whom do you really like?

I happen to like my fellow Ohio authors. I'm particularly fond of Toni Morrison, of course, because Toni continues to confound people by continuing to strike a different pose every time. Everybody says, "well, okay, so you wrote *The Bluest Eye* . . ."; well, everybody was looking for her next book, and they thought, "well, this is going to be the formula, and she's gonna put it out," and she came back with *Sula.* "Oh, well, that must be an accident." Then she came

back with *Song of Solomon,* and we don't understand. So, she's in danger right now, because *Tar Baby,* which is, absolutely, I think, an incredible novel, is now being considered trivial, because nobody can write four brilliant books. That is not possible; therefore, it couldn't be brilliant. I mean that's the way the critics have been sort of going at that, and, of course, the Black press has been going at her with that, and this is not each and every, but the Black intellectuals are saying "*well* she just writes best sellers." Well, that's not really true at all. What she does is write extremely well. I talked to Toni recently, and I said, "we're living in the age of Toni Morrison." And I'm not, have no interest really in trying to flatter her, but the reality is that Toni writes so well that the rest of us who write will have to come up to that. And I think it is frightening to, especially, that group of white men—the Philip Roths, Norman Mailers—who have dominated literature for some unknown reason, because it certainly was not based on talent, that all of a sudden, they're coming up against a Black woman from the Midwest who is clearly, clearly brilliant. And if we were going to compare Toni to somebody in terms of literature, we would probably have to go to South America, the *One Hundred Years of Solitude.* Marquez. You get into that level. Americans and Europeans have considered themselves quite fine with the novel. I think that they're really devoid of ideas.

And, again, some of the lovelier novels that have been written lately have been done, in fact, by women, not only Toni, but a woman, Elizabeth Forsyth Hale, *A Woman of Independent Means*. It's gotten ripped off eight thousand different ways: "A woman of substance," "A woman in a corner pigging"; they picked it off. It was a collection of letters about a woman, from her first camp letters. Her great-granddaughter found her trunk, and she had kept all these letters. It's nothing but literature; that's one of the problems. You can't turn it into a movie; it won't be a hit song; you have to read the book. But it's absolutely, absolutely gorgeous. And, of course, it had a very difficult time finding a publisher, because nobody understood it.

Judith Krantz was, I think, lucky if you can use that term, because *Ordinary People* was quite an extraordinary novel, and it just so happens that Bob Redford is literate, which many, many people are not. And it seemed that he thought, "well, I should make a movie out of it," which, of course, helped to move that along. But, you know, that came over the transom. That was, "I wrote this book. Would you consider it?" And now, "we don't know you: where's your agent?" And you wonder what we're losing. *A Woman of Independent Means* went out of print. It only sold everything, right? I think the publisher must have put out about 1500 copies, and they went, whoosh, and all of a sudden he says, "Oh thank God I got out of that!" It was the independent book sellers, who I think are very, very important to all of us. Independents were saying, "but we're recommending this book, and we can't get it." And he's saying, "there's no market for a middle book." A book either, right now, gets at least $250,000 to a half-million dollars in advance, you know, in terms of a paperback, or there's no room. So, you have a book that's coming in at a $20,000 advance, and they don't know what they're going to do with it. So, finally, it got picked up, because somebody, some place—I'm sure it's some little old gray-haired lady—read it and said, "well why don't we buy this?"

Which poets do you read?

Most of us, most of the time. It's probably not fair to say it like this, but I don't really think that I read poetry for the pleasure of it. I'm interested in the profession. So I don't look at poetry the way I do the novel, for example, because I'm not basically a novel reader. So, it has to be something to really capture me. I read mostly nonfiction.

A particular category?

History.

I thought you were going to say that.

Yes, I really have a great love of history and, of course, as you can see, politics. I do a lot with history and politics, which are not all that different.

I bear special affection for the poetry of Anne Sexton. I think "Her Kind" is just one of the most outstanding single poems I've ever read. And I like a young poet, who in my opinion does not write enough, named Carolyn Rodgers, a Chicago poet. But for the most part, you read most poets because you should have some awareness of the profession.

I don't know if you know this or not, but you're being taught in a course at the University of Tennessee in Knoxville as an Appalachian writer.

Oh, that's fine. I was born in Knoxville. I think that's marvelous.

Do you ever think of yourself that way? You're being taught by a novelist named Wilma Dykeman, who is herself an Appalachian writer.

No, I didn't know that. I think that's great. You know, Agee is from Knoxville also, James Agee. Knoxville, for a little city, has produced a number of people that have done—I think—extremely well. I don't have any problem with being an Appalachian. I don't think of myself—I'm not particularly outdoorsy. We were talking about my nephew earlier. That would make his day, because he is off backpacking to Montana or something. I basically consider myself pretty urban, but because of birth I'm a Southerner, or in this particular case, I'm an Appalachian, actually, because the Tennesseeans are very different from the rest of the South. Well, Tennessee is the Volunteer State, because Tennessee went with the Union. So you go up into the mountains, and you've got a whole other situation altogether. So you had West Virginia seceding from Virginia, you know; you get into that kind of thing. I think it's interesting.

I think that birth largely has to be considered an accident; I don't know another way around it. It's just a way of identifying. If it's not going to be positive, then it's pointless, because nobody chose the circumstances under which they were born, nor the place, nor the parents to whom they were born, nor their gender, nor any of that. So if it's not going to be a positive identification, then you really should let it go.

And yet it's so hard to let go for many people, isn't it?

Well, there is *something* you can do about it; you can change your behavior, if not your attitude. But I think, yes, we as a species need to let go, because it's enough that we do in life what we are responsible for. Somebody said, "we were calling you into account. Certainly we should not call you into account for your race, or your age, or your gender. You had nothing at all to do with that. You just happened to have survived. And the only reason we can complain about that is that you are alive. Because, if you weren't we wouldn't." On the other hand, I certainly see no reason that we should reward you, particularly for any of those three things. It's unacceptable that we continue to reward men for having been male. They didn't sit up in babyland and say, "well I think I'll be a boy, or I think I'll be a girl." It doesn't work out that way, so that we cannot continue to punish and reward people based upon something that they have absolutely no control over. It's illogical, just one of the things that human beings need to learn, and I should imagine at some point we will let go.

I hope so, but we were speaking earlier about the illogicality of human beings.

The rather interesting thing to me—I am a "Trekkie"—is that either we're going to come to a basic new understanding of what it is to be a human being, or we're going to destroy ourselves. So, I'm not blasé, but we would have to move away from a lot of things and pretty much all at once. We're talking race, gender, and age. It's not my fault I was born in the United States, and I shouldn't be disproportionately rewarded as to the world's minerals because of that. If that's the case, then everybody, all the little babies sitting up in baby heaven, will say, "well, I'm not gonna do Southeast Asia; I'm not gonna do Latin America. I want to go to the United States where I can disproportionately use up resources." It just doesn't happen. And I think it's time that we shut down the industrial age. We are really quite capable right now. We're moving into robotics and cybernetics, and it's time that we let go. I'm not picking on the industrial age, but that's when you've got your little machine, and then you run out, and you get your colonies so that you can take their raw materials, and then you can send the manufactured goods back. And all of that is just tiresome. It's moved us along, and I don't have a quarrel with history, otherwise you'd spend all of your time debating whether or not your mother should have had you. But if it did move us along, it cannot now. What it does, it leads to irreconcilable conflicts which frequently erupt into some level of war, which increases the possibility of a great error.

Of total destruction?

I don't think that writers ever changed the mind of anybody. I think we always preach to the saved.
                                        —*Nikki Giovanni*

Oh sure. Which would not surprise me. I'm much too cynical and much too aware of the nature of human beings to be surprised, but it would be a disappointment, because it is not necessary. For what we are trying to hold on to and what that offers us, as opposed to what we can possibly become, it's just not necessary to hold on to the 15th century the way that we're doing it.

Do you think it's possible for writers to express their convictions strongly enough or imaginatively enough to change the mind of anybody?

I don't think that writers ever changed the mind of anybody. I think we always preach to the saved. Someone from the *Post* asked me, how would I describe myself, and I said, "I'm a preacher to the saved." And I don't think that anybody's mind has ever been changed. It has been enhanced by an already-meeting-of-the-minds. When the reader picks up the book and proceeds to begin a relationship, it will proceed based upon how that book and that reader are already in agreement. Because almost nobody really reads anything that they are totally . . . I mean, I couldn't read a position paper about the *Ku Klux Klan.*

You mean, you, literally, could not get through it?

I wouldn't even try. Why? Because I already know. To me it's like reading—which I guess I shouldn't say to you like this—, but it's like reading anti-abortion literature. I'm totally in opposition to their position. Unless I can read a headline that says they bring something new to the table, then

no, I'm not going to do that, because I already know where they are, and what I'm going to do is look for a strengthening of my position, where I am. And everybody does that.

And again, I'm out of the tradition of the sixties that sort of crazily believed that there would be the poem that would free everybody. You would say to those people, "listen, fellows, that's not going to happen." The big term, of course, was "sell out," and everybody that didn't do what certain groups wanted—you know, Leroi Jones and all of them—everybody that didn't sort of hew the Black aesthetic line had "soldout." No. There will never be the poem that will free mankind. We would be fools . . . anybody that thinks that is a fool. And I don't really know another term for that.

Anybody that thinks any one thing or one person can make a difference in your life. . . . If we could crucify Jesus, you know, whom we recognize in the western world as being the Son of God, then you know we would shoot down everybody. Now there are people who charismatically do make a difference. We were talking about holding two [opposing] thoughts, but I do that a lot. There are people who charismatically embody an age. But they didn't create the age. They personified it, and people often overlook that. They really think somebody . . . they really think Disraeli made [his age]. He didn't. He was the one who could personify it. Or Jack Kennedy. Now, I happen to like the Kennedys. I find them interesting people to read about. But Jack didn't make the sixties. Nor did Martin Luther King. We honor them, and we recognize them, because they personify the best within us. But they didn't create it. It was the little old ladies that said. "I'll walk," that made Martin Luther King. It was the kind that said, "even after his death we're antiwar. We're going to move even this image that we will maintain, but we're going to move it and make it much more." People overlook that, because they think that *you* could do something. They'll tell you, "Fidel Castro liberated Cuba." I'll be damned if he did, whatever you feel about Cuba. Fidel personifies that liberation. Therefore, to the Cuban people, it would probably be a loss had he been killed, say twenty years ago. I'm sure that they're ready to accept it now, not because Fidel was a loss, though of course it would be a loss to whomever loved him, but because he was the embodiment.

The same thing with our community. It was so unnecessary to shoot down Martin Luther King. And what happened there was that a man lost his life, but it was a message. And what it said was, "since we can't shoot a million people, we'll shoot this one, so that the million people will know that this is where we are." And of course what you got from that was a perfectly logical response: "Mother Fucker, since you did that, we will get you." So that you got, of course, the riots coming. There was no question that the Black community was going to respond to the white community. You sent the message, and we sent the answer. So that everybody said, "okay, well, tell you what, since I can't bring back my cities, and you can't bring back King, why don't we try peace." And you just wish that people would function on that a little bit, and earlier. We recognize that at some point if the message is sent, and an answer is sent, that we still have to come back to peace.

Sounds to me, and correct me if I misunderstood you, that in all that, the role of the writer is very much like that of the historian rather than the prophet. Or possibly, the prophecy comes in—and I used the word, "role," again, I realize, the function of the writer—is that the writer recognizes what you just expressed and communicates the meaning of some chaotic event or historical circumstance in whatever way he does it, and people read that because they recognize the writer as someone in whom they trust and believe, and possibly as a result of reading the meaning of what has happened, they are going to understand a little bit more of what's going to take place next, or, they will understand a little bit more of the consequences of behaviour the next time something comes up. Not that they necessarily agree with what the writer said, but they understand a little bit more. And that's about all the writer can expect?

About all the writer can expect is to be read. That would probably be what most of us get. I think the word I was looking for is "vitality." You were using "role" and changed it to "function." But I think that the *vitality* of the writer, for those of us who are contemporary writers, who are writing contemporaneously—because some of us are literary writers who are not,—is that we are just a little bit of both. We're a little bit of a prophet, and we are a little bit of the historian. And we're saying, "this is the meaning that we find. You have to take what you can." We are not Marx; we're not sitting there saying, "A is A." We're not Ayn Rand either. We're sitting there saying, "I saw this through my eyes."

The word that you used that I do like is, "trust." There are certain writers that no matter what they have to say, no matter how much in agreement you would be with them, you simply don't trust the writer. I hate a damned liar. I really don't care what you have to say, or how awful you might think it is, or how awful I might think it is, but I hate a damned liar. Once you have given up that, once you have given up your basic integrity, then you have given up that, once you have given up your basic integrity, then you really have nothing else to offer. And maybe that's harsh, and I don't intend to be harsh. But when Norman Mailer, for example, had to pay off *Marilyn,* the book *Marilyn,* because it was plagiarized, I don't know what Mailer could write that I would read. It was hard enough to be bothered with his chauvinism and his crap before that, but to recognize that the man would be in a profession, but would take the work of somebody else. . . . There's just no way. It couldn't happen. I mean, Norman's

spirit could descend in this room, and he could start to read from something, and I'd say, "well I have to leave."

Because the only thing you bring, the only thing any of us, any professional brings, is your honesty. You don't mind that the patient died on the table, as long as the surgeon wasn't drunk. It's sad if he did. It's sad to you; it's sad to the patient. It's probably sad to the surgeon. But you feel like, "well he tried." And in my profession, if you're not going to be honest. . . . It's not that you ask the reader to spend, which I think is ridiculous, 15 dollars upwards for a book, but that you're asking them for their time. Because they can go get another 15 dollars. That's not hard to do. You really cannot give back time; you think about the time you spend with a book. I mean, I'm a reader. You'd feel raped to think that you involved your heart and your mind and your time, that there were things you could have been doing, and you were sitting there reading a book to find out that it's essentially dishonest. You honestly came to that book. You chose it, and that it's a lie? I mean, it's not acceptable. Absolutely unacceptable. The profession is not really strong enough to me on your basic plagiarism. I know lawyers who worry about lawyers who are essentially dishonest. Because you can't always win. Those of us who are writers can't always be prescient, but we can always be honest. So that if we make a mistake, if we misunderstand something, if we're journalists and don't see something, that's all right, because we know that what was brought to bear there is the best that we have. That's all any of us are going to do, because you're going to miss a few calls there. One reason you don't shoot the umpire is that you know the guy is watching the ball. Now if you have to feel that other team gave him 10 bucks, then there's no game. There's absolutely no way that we can play the game. And life I think is like that.

It's tremendously fragile, isn't it, because it is back to "trust." We talked before about the formula, learning how to write the formula and just repeating it, repeating it. It takes a while for the reader to catch on that that's happening especially if that reader has read that writer before and has developed his trust and liking and is willing to invest not only 15 dollars, as you say, but the time and the emotional energy. And so it's really a very fragile kind of delicate thing between writer and reader.

I honestly think,—we were talking formula,—I think that formula is essentially dishonest. I'm not fighting with my fellow writers who are formula writers. I think it's essentially dishonest, but so is the circus, so is the Hall of Mirrors. And one of the things that I think happens to you when you are involved in that level of lazy writing is that you know what you're giving, and they know what they're getting. And I don't think that is a lack of trust. If I pick up a Frank Yerby, it's my fault. I'm not picking on Yerby, but it is, because I know exactly what he's going to do; What does the song say, "you knew I was a snake when you brought me in,"? I knew that. I happened to like Jacqueline Susann when I'm doing junk-like reading. I can pick up a Jackie Susann and know exactly what I'm going to get. I don't feel misused.

I think that is true of all of us. You kind of know what you're getting when you pick up a certain level of book. What I do have a serious problem with, though, is your basic plagiarism, because that is actually taking someone else's work and putting it off as yours. What we are saying here is that, if I'm Steven King, ninety percent of my writing is going to be macabre. Take it or leave it. I'm sure that he considers that he writes as honestly and as well as any of the rest of us. As a matter of fact, he has a lot more money to show for it. What I'm saying is, I don't think that's your basic rape, because it's Steven King. You might say that someone was unaware that all his books are just alike. But that is very, very hard to do. That is like saying I didn't learn anything from "LaVerne & Shirley" this week; I'm disappointed. You know damn well you are not going to learn anything from "LaVerne & Shirley" or whatever it is that you're doing on TV. That is not to say that all of television is a waste. It's just that you know if you turn on TV, seven to ten, you're going to get mostly crap, unless it's Thursday night and there is a show called "Fame," which somehow or another is surviving; which makes my Thursdays. It's a great little show. I'm just saying, you've got to know that, and I don't think that's the same level as your basic lie.

There is a distinction.

Sure. It's like your professor who reads the same notes every year. He's not lying. He says, "this is, for the level of energy that I'm willing to invest in this class, what you need to know. And if my notes have not changed in 5 years, that is not my problem. My subject hasn't changed, or at least it hasn't involved me." But that is not a lie. That's not the guy who stands in the lab and manufactures results that he knows never came up. Sure. You get into that, and I think that has to be dealt with much more stringently. A professor of medieval poetry might be dull, but he's not lying.

It seems as if a very mysterious relationship exists between the reader and the writer, which is one, frequently, and I think, charmingly, of awe; that this person has the ability to use language that makes me put down my $15 or makes me take that book out of the library. And there is a love that develops there, because that person has that power over you, and trust, because any time you love, you want to trust.

I think that what essentially makes art so potentially dangerous is that it is totally egalitarian.

Explain that a little more.

Well, the term you use is "power," that the person has power over you. I don't think so. As a matter of fact, the writer is totally vulnerable to people that we shall never see. We sit someplace and create something, or explain something, research, and develop certain ideas. We convince a publisher to publish it, or a museum to hang it, or a producer to put it on Broadway, and we are subject to the judgment of people who never even knew us. We could have been dead 800 years before somebody discovered us.

Last year, here in Cincinnati, last September, October, and I think a little bit in November, I did a program. I don't know really how to express it, but I was invited, and I went to a number of elementary schools here in Cincinnati. And the thing that surprised the kids was that I was alive. It may sound strange, but that was the biggest thing, and when you think about how many dead authors we read, it was really not unusual. Just last night, I was at Morehead State. Even going there, people are really looking at you like, "she's really alive," and it's kind of strange. And, again, I think that the dangerous position is that we recognize not our power but people's power for themselves. The same way that I can sit here and decide whether or not Sy Hirsch, for Christ's sake, has written a creditable piece on Kissinger. That is a level of egalitarianism that most people don't have. Most people don't have to be bothered with that. Sy Hirsch should not have to worry about what some poet in Cincinnati thinks about his work. And I'm not saying that he does. I am just saying that I can make that judgment.

That certainly is a factor, but don't you feel power over your own interpretation of the world which really is not dependent upon how well someone else is going to agree with that?

Well, it really is, because if you are Ezra Pound and your interpretation of the world is markedly different from the country in which you happened to be born, you will find yourself adjudged insane, which is quite unfair. Do you understand? And that does happen, I think, frequently enough to make us take pause. You get into the whole thing with the Soviets and their writers and, of course, we with ours. We don't do ours the same way as the Soviets do, because what we do with ours is just buy them out. The end result is the same thing, and if we can't buy them out, we simply refuse to publish them; we kind of hound them out of the country, essentially. But it all amounts to the same thing. I think that I have a view of the world, that I have an obligation, if not just your basic right, to share. But I don't consider that, in any respect, that that connotes any power. I still have to go upstairs [even though] they're locking CETA out. I still have to go to IGA.

You know, the artist is not a god, and I mention Mailer because he's such a prototypical, awful artist. Of all the real dumb things that he's said recently, the most stupid had to be on the Jack Abbott case. As a writer, you just simply cringe that somebody is justifying murder because the guy can put three words together. It's totally unacceptable. The writer is not god. It's what we do for a living. It's not who we are. And I have a great resentment—you haven't ruffled my feathers on that one at all, but you will see the hairs on the back of my neck rise—because writing is not who I am. It is what I do. And I think that anybody who fails to separate what they do from who they are, and that is from Ronald Reagan to Lyndon Johnson to Pope John Paul to whomever, is in serious, mental trouble. You've got to separate yourself; unfortunately, a lot of people don't.

And a lot of the people who don't are Reagan, and Pope John, the people who are in power.

But, hey, lot of people don't.—The only reason we talk about the people in power is because that is who we know. You want to chart mental illness? We can go right up I-75 to Detroit and see a guy who has been laid off for six months who was a mechanic: who is nothing more. Now, we just don't talk about him, unless we are Studs Terkel. That appears to be a very human trait, but it also appears to be one that we have learned, because if we go back—again we are talking Africa or we go back to Chinese history, for two quickies and two good ones—you will see people and artisans, and what you did was not who you were.

Nikki Giovanni with Carrington Bonner (interview date Spring 1984)

SOURCE: "An Interview with Nikki Giovanni," in *Black American Literature Forum*, Vol. 18, No. 1, Spring, 1984, pp. 29-30.

[*In the interview below, Giovanni offers her views on modern culture and writing.*]

Nikki Giovanni wants to make it clear: "I did not perform in South Africa. I think that's ridiculous. I mean what would I do: sing, dance, recite **'Nigger Can You Kill'**? It's either a misunderstanding or a lie, whichever comes first. It's just ridiculous. My books are banned in South Africa."

The princess of Black poetry has returned to the road, on tour in the midst of controversy, and is offering thoughts. Commenting on Black writers she says, "Toni Morrison has taken the American novel to stage five, and people are asking, 'Where are stages two and three?' She's riding the night wind. She's not playing it safe. Every time they say Toni can't write she comes out with another book. . . . I think

Shange's *for colored girls* . . . was brilliant. I can't say enough how brilliant it is." She goes on, "Black writers are not helping each other. We don't encourage our artists to grow."

Nikki Giovanni is riding the night winds and "those who ride the night winds/must learn to love the stars/those who live on the edge must get used to the cuts." ***Those Who Ride the Night Winds*** is a book of twenty-eight new poems separated into two sections, "Night Winds" and "Day Trippers." Her recurring reminder of Emmett Till's past in her poems reminds us that we have gone full circle with the children's murders of '81/82 in Atlanta. Giovanni's sweet memories, mixed with cunning wit, are captured in such poems as **"I Wrote a Good Omelet"** and **"Love Thoughts."** The reflective **"A Word For Me . . . Also"** is not only a poem about and for herself but one for all poets.

There are others who ride the night winds, like the late musician John Lennon ("He was the first to say, 'We didn't do anything new; it was Little Richard and Chuck Berry'"), tennis player Billie Jean King ("I admire her courage"), the Eagles, and the late painter Charles White. After the heat from the South African controversy was cooled somewhat, Nikki felt more ready for an interview than she'd been at first. Our conversation occurred at the Common Concerns Bookstore in Washington, D.C., on April 10, 1983.

[*Bonner:*] *How did you come up with the title of your book?*

[Giovanni:] I've never been asked that before. It came up out of the John Lennon poem.

Was the John Lennon poem spontaneous, or did it take time to seep in?

It took a little time. A friend called me about midnight and told me, "If ever there was a senseless death, it was John Lennon's." I mean for some so-called scribble scrabble a life was taken.

You wrote two powerful poems for Lorraine Hansberry, Rosa Parks, and others. How did they come about?

I think it's time we pay homage to those who are courageous.

Who are some of the painters you like besides the late Charles White?

Jacob Lawrence.

Do you plan to do any more albums?

No, books are my heart. Records are not.

Did you know you are on the International Dishonor Roll along with Ray Charles, Liza Minelli, Cher, and others?

I think it's ridiculous. People who came up three days ago have the authority to tell you what to do with your life. It's really a shame. [A New York gang member] told me about this list and came to me saying, "I know it's not true." . . . They have a plane leaving from Kennedy Airport every day going to Johannesburg. It's not full of entertainers. It's full of White businessmen who exploit Black workers.

Ray Charles was stoned in South Africa.

Ray Charles has a history of involvement. Should that history be ignored because he went to South Africa? Come on. He's a singer. In the Sixties, when Bull Conners said, "We don't want to niggers down here in Mississippi," if we had signed a petition saying we refused to perform down there do you think things would've changed? Bull Conners would have loved it. I'm not going to South Africa. I don't have to sign a petition saying I'm not going to perform. You want me to sign a petition not to commit rape? One not to beat my mother? Boycotting Millie Jackson is not helping South Africans.

Is it difficult separating writing from the business?

I don't have that problem. Poetry is not a big business.

A lot of people think you can do much to save the world. How do you deal with that pressure?

I'm not here to convince you I'm all right. We have to believe in each other's dreams.

You use the periods and dots in your latest book. Why?

I thought it was a good way to have human breath breaks on the page, without intimidation to the reader. James Baldwin is a master with the dash and comma.

Do you plan to get into any other forms of writing?

I like journalism. I think it's important.

What are you working on now?

I'm not working on anything.

You haven't been out with a book for a while.

I come out with one every two years.

Oh yeah, **Vacation Time.**

That's a book. People think children books are easy. It's a

discipline as hard as poetry. You're teaching to read and reaching to children.

How do you relate your own writing in relation to contemporary writing like that of Ntozake Shange, Marge Piercy, Lucille Clifton, etc.?

I don't know if I understand that question. . . . There's no competition. This is not a dance. Writers write what they see and feel.

What kind of vibes do you get from today's college population?

I don't relate to the term *vibes* too well, but I think today's college students are a bright group and hard workers. It would be nice if the current administration would give them a break.

Do you owe Amiri Baraka some money, or did you say no to a serious question?

What?

Baraka wrote a tasteless poem about you, and I was wondering why.

I don't let things like that worry me. Life is too short. Baraka hasn't written a good book since *Black Music.* He's got a nerve. Have you seen his latest work? He runs out of ideas and puts an anthology together. Have you read it? He's got a lot of nerve.

Does William Morrow publish any other Black poets?

Mari Evans and, as a matter of fact, Baraka. . . . He should just leave me alone.

When you published with Broadside, there was a lot of activity among Black writers.

Broadside didn't publish me. They distributed my books. I published myself. **Black Feeling/Black Talk** and **Black Judgement** were published by me, along with an anthology of women writers. I was in debt, and William Morrow asked to publish me. They did—got me out of debt and have done a good job since.

Young Black writers coming up are not as well acknowledged.

They have to do it themselves. When we get together and form publishing companies, the money has to go back into the product, not cigarettes, a new ride or shoes. . . .

Why is the Black woman's interest in the feminist movement small?

The interest is there. There can't be a woman's movement without Black women. The feminist movement didn't recruit or have Black women in leadership roles. They were arguing to be bank executives while we wanted to be in a position to have a bank account. So many Black women are dying in Detroit it's becoming a scandal. One out of three dies from childbirth, and you have to get records of this from the British. Yeah, for real.

James Watt?

He doesn't know what's going on. He should have Prince playing on the 4th of July in the Mall. . . . It's ridiculous that they still penalize Mexicans for crossing the border but don't penalize the people who exploit Mexicans. . . . Two percent of Wisconsin's population is Indian, but twenty percent of the prison population is Indian. Come on.

Prince?

There's a lot of talent there. We worried about everything but his music. If he dies it'll be our fault.

Like Jimi Hendrix?

Like Hendrix.

What other things are you listening to?

Nona Hendrix' new album is fabulous. If there's one album to get, that's the one.

Some parents say Marvin Gaye is too x-rated for kids.

Are you kidding? Have you ever been sexually healed? I mean really. Parents are passing their fears. Leave Marvin on. I love Marvin.

What qualities do you look for in men?

What? . . .

Margaret B. McDowell (essay date 1986)

SOURCE: "Groundwork for a More Comprehensive Criticism of Nikki Giovanni," in *Studies in Black American Literature, Volume II: Belief vs. Theory in Black American Literary Criticism*, edited by Joe Weixlmann and Chester J. Fontenot, Penkevill Publishing Co., 1986, pp. 135-60.

[*In the following essay, McDowell argues that critics have failed to adequately analyze the whole of Giovanni's poetry.*]

The nature of Nikki Giovanni's poetry cannot be fully understood nor its significance in recent literary history be established unless critics provide more perceptive interpretations and assessments of her work than they have done in the first fifteen years of her career. Such informed appraisals are long overdue, and her reputation has suffered from the neglect of her work by serious critics. Those who would contribute now to more comprehensive and open-minded judgments of her work will undoubtedly wish to consider the early contradictory appraisals of her poetry to ascertain what is genuine in them as a basis for this more comprehensive undertaking. I shall summarize, accordingly, the extreme reactions which Giovanni's poetry evoked primarily during the first five years of her career (1969-1974). And I will speculate on possible explanations for these contradictory responses and mediate among the early conflicting judgments, because they significantly affect her reputation to this day.

It is my general conclusion that much of the writing on Giovanni's poetry has been predicated on the critics' misperceptions, their insistence on half-truths, or their rigid and demanding political and personal convictions. Academic literary critics have been inclined to generalize about Black poetry and have failed to recognize the relationships present between the poetry and Black speech or Black music. They have tended also to discover aesthetic excellence only in poetry of intricate symbolic or intellectual complexity. On the other hand, political reviewers of Giovanni's work have overestimated the necessary function of poetry in the furtherance of Black Cultural Nationalism and Pan-Africanism, and they have underestimated her poetry affirmation of Afro-American culture and her realistic portrayals of individual Afro-Americans and their experience. In writing of her poetry, critics have allowed personal and political attitudes not merely to affect their judgment but to dominate it. For example, they have used, in place of objective criteria, the tenet that poets should subordinate their individual creativity to the rhetorical needs of the political or racial group. They have placed excessive value on consistency in the views expressed from poem to poem and book to book as if the persona of a poem is always the author herself and the experience depicted is autobiographical. They have demanded that the author's personal behavior be approved if her poetry is to be judged favorably. Some reviewers have sought in Giovanni's poetry an ideal for Black womanhood and been disappointed either by the assertiveness, impudence, and strength they found in the poetry or, conversely, by the acknowledgment of emotional vulnerability, disillusionment, and fatigue which can also be found in it. The written response to Giovanni's poetry shows relatively little evidence of the application of objective criteria or of clearly formulated critical postulates. In the total body of criticism on her, no systematic, career-long examination of her techniques, her development, or the shifts in her interests and viewpoint can be found. In the reviews, one finds ardent enthusiasm for "the Princess of Black Poetry" and also cutting and humiliating attacks on both the poet and her poetry, but only a handful of writings reflect an open-minded, sensitive, and careful reading of all her work.

The written response to Giovanni's poetry shows relatively little evidence of the application of objective criteria or of clearly formulated critical postulates.
—*Margaret B. McDowell*

The judgments one infers from the popular response to Nikki Giovanni's poetry may ultimately provide more reliable critical assessment than that gleaned from "professional" sources, because such popular judgments are often made by listeners as well as readers and depend on reactions to the immediate clarity of lines; the impact of tone, rhythm, and language; and the integrity of the realism in Giovanni's depiction of Afro-Americans and their experience. The response at the popular level reflects the views of large numbers of people from a wide variety of backgrounds. However, such judgment comes, in part, from the shared enthusiasm of the crowd and the charismatic personality of the poet as well as from the poetry itself, and while the emphasis on the poetry's orality is important in criticism of Giovanni, the listener cannot fully assess the damage done to a poem by a single flawed line or by an awkward beginning, and he or she is equally likely to overlook the rich ambiguities and ironies found in the best of Giovanni's lyrics.

In the past, Giovanni claimed that the criticism of her work was irrelevant. But her attitude appears to have changed. Recently, she has implied that "harder questions" than those asked last year challenge her work this year. Her statements in recent interviews with Claudia Tate and Arlene Elder may, in themselves, provide guidance for an effective critique of an author's achievement throughout a career—particularly of an author like Giovanni, who is still experimenting with technique, growing as an artist, and broadening her vision.

A consideration of the difficulties which Giovanni experienced in the 1970s in establishing her early reputation and of her own recently expressed views on the criticism she has received to the present time might serve to indicate those aspects of her work which call for further scrutiny. Among the subjects that have never had full discussion and that demand considerable systematic and reasonable criticism are (1) an identification of her goals, (2) a definition of her techniques, (3) discrimination among her aesthetic successes and

failures, (4) an analysis of the changes in her processes of invention and of revision, (5) an identification of the objects of her satire and its purposes, (6) an analysis of her use of folk materials, (7) the compilation of a history of the oral presentations of her poetry (before various kinds of audiences in stage performances, on records, and on television), (8) an examination of her status as a writer of books for children, (9) a determination of the shifts in her interests as related to the forms that she has used, (10) an exploration of the alleged inconsistencies in her work, and (11) a sensitive analysis of the flexibility, the ironies, and the ambiguities that add grace and substance to her poems—particularly those in which she develops "the women and the men" themes. Her use of Black music (jazz, blues, spirituals, folk, and popular), which enriches the patterns to be found in her poetry, and her recourse to stylized elements in Black conversation are also important features of her work that contribute to the "orality" for which she is famous, and these subjects need further investigation.

Each of Giovanni's successive volumes has been marred by the inclusion of some misbegotten poems or prosaic or sentimental lines (which usually occur at the beginnings or ends of poems). These failures repeatedly have claimed disproportionate attention in reviews, blurred the focus of her critics, and delayed the acknowledgment of her developing stature. Consequently, I would view as a first priority in the building of a comprehensive criticism of Giovanni the publication of a collection of her poems, selected with exceeding care. Such a volume seems crucial to the serious assessment of her achievement from 1968 to the present and to a more general awareness of her continued promise as a mature poet. With such an ordered and trimmed presentation of her work, critics might begin to see her poetry in its proper place in the history of Afro-American poetry and in its relation to the work of other American poets of the present time. Her critics, acting largely upon personal and political beliefs and preferences, have delayed such observation of Giovanni's work from the perspective of American literary history. While a chronological presentation of the selected poems could encourage developmental studies of the poet, arguments could be made for arrangement by topic, theme, or form.

If Giovanni is eventually to receive her merited place in the history of American literature, it is time for critics to examine the marked division in the response that her work has elicited (a division that began in 1971 and that widened greatly in 1972 and 1973). In 1972 the audiences for her poetry and its readers were highly enthusiastic; academic critics ignored her; radical Black critics, having praised her a year or two earlier, attacked her, mostly on ideological and personal grounds; and newspaper and magazine reviewers wrote brief generalizations and seemed to be reading each other's reviews rather than her poems. A disinterested consideration of her work as literary art appeared impossible when those who read her work praised it extravagantly, sharply attacked it, disregarded it, or commented on it in general formulas. Nor did it seem possible later in the 1970s for writers to consider her career in its totality in order that they might ascertain her development as a thinker and an artist as each new volume appeared and that they might appraise her achievement for what it had gradually become. On the basis of her first widely-read collection, *Black Feeling/Black Talk/Black Judgement* (1970), critics casually placed her in the context of current Afro-American poetry by classifying her with "the Black revolutionary poets" and by referring to her work as representative of "the new Black poetry of hate." Following the reactions which met *My House* (1972) and later volumes, wherein she includes few political poems, no critic has seriously confronted the whole body of her poetry and its relationship to the developments in Afro-American poetry since 1960, and to modern poetry in general.

Before she gained the attention of the critics and the public with *Black Feeling/Black Talk/Black Judgement,* Giovanni had attained a modicum of distinction as a promising scholar and writer, receiving honors from universities and grants from funding agencies for the humanities. She graduated in 1967 from Fisk University (her maternal grandfather, a Latin teacher, had earlier graduated from Fisk; her parents, both social workers, had graduated from Knoxville College, also in Tennessee). At her graduation she received honors in history, a formative discipline in her life. She has continued to read history as her recreation, and it has influenced her perspective on many contemporary issues. In 1967 she won a Ford Foundation Fellowship to study at the University of Pennsylvania; in 1968, a National Foundation of the Arts grant to study at the School of Fine Arts, Columbia University; and in 1969, a grant from the Harlem Council of the Arts.

She had also by 1970 grown in political and racial perspicacity and had gone through several phases of awareness of, and commitment to, Black causes. From early childhood she knew that her grandfather had changed teaching jobs and smuggled her grandmother, Louvenia, out of Georgia to Knoxville, Tennessee, one night, after hiding her under blankets. Louvenia had, as an "uppity" pioneer member of the NAACP, offended white people with her outspoken assertion of her rights. Nikki Giovanni's moving portrayal of Louvenia in *Gemini* (1970) suggests convincingly the effect of her independent, yet emotionally vulnerable, ancestor upon her. In Cincinnati, where her parents worked in social services, Giovanni learned as a child about urban poverty, the difficulties that Blacks face in attaining equal justice, and the struggles that Blacks undergo for economic survival in a Northern industrial city. During the times she lived in Knoxville, Tennessee, she saw, through her grandmother's eyes, the relative powerlessness of Blacks in confronting the racism of the white population in a smaller Southern town. For example Giovanni in 1967 thought Louvenia had been figuratively "assassinated" by the people who so wanted "progress" in Knoxville that they re-routed a little-used road, necessitating the displacement of her grandmother and her neighbors from the houses in which they had lived most of their lives. She felt that the elderly people grieved to death in alien surroundings.

In *Gemini* Giovanni tells an anecdote about herself at age four. She threw rocks from the porch roof at enemies who chased her older sister from school. She thought her sister should not fight her own battle: she might "maim" her hands, not be able to take her music lessons, and, as a consequence, the music teacher's family might starve. The story anticipates Giovanni's willingness and energy to enter the fight at hand (as in Black Cultural Nationalist enterprises between 1967 and 1969), but it also suggests that the motivation for her militance lay in helping the Black community rather than in gaining power for herself. In college her political activism intensified. Her ambivalence about the politically moderate family heroes—Martin Luther King, Jr., and Roy Wilkins— led her to found a campus chapter of SNCC during the period of Stokely Carmichael's leadership of that organization. As a graduate student at the University of Pennsylvania and then at Columbia (and simultaneously as a teacher at Queen's College and then at Rutgers University) for about two and a half years before the birth of her son (Thomas Watson Giovanni), she supported the Black activists in the leftist and radical Black Arts, Black Theater, and Black History groups; and she spoke at conferences in Detroit, Newark, Wilmington, and New York during the time that Amiri Baraka, Larry Neal, and Ron Karenga became leaders of Black Cultural Nationalism. Although she has consistently retained her commitment to the Black Aesthetic principles that all genuine Black art explore and affirm the Afro-American experience, she has always been ambivalent and cautious about the expectation that noteworthy Black art be "useful" in promoting the struggle for social and political power–and especially about the mixing of para-military activity with poetry. She has never believed that self-determination for a people negated the need for individual self-determination.

By 1969 she had openly dissociated her work from the demands that prescriptive didacticism was making upon her as an artist. By that time, Baraka and his associates had gained national domination of the Black Liberation Movement through para-military means in the Committee for a Unified New Ark, had violently challenged the supremacy of parallel California groups and their leaders, and, between 1970 and 1974, had fought for the support of major coalitions in the Pan-African organizations. Giovanni retreated from such extreme political action, and, as her dialogue with James Baldwin (1973) and some later poems show, she had begun again to appreciate the effectiveness of Martin Luther King. Only occasionally in the 1970s did she write about Black revolution, and then she addressed in prose issues related to equal justice, as in the cases of Angela Davis and H. Rapp Brown.

Giovanni still sees the need for continuing the Black revolution, but she contends that the revolution started four hundred years ago in America rather than in the 1960s and that one confronts its struggles, and experiences its victories, constantly. In frequent public and printed remarks, she undoubtedly alienated certain younger Black critics in the early 1970s as she dissociated her goals for Afro-American power from the more radical politics of the Black Nationalists and the Pan-African liberation groups. In her interview with Arlene Elder, Giovanni describes Africa as the world's richest continent and oldest civilization but indicates that she does not feel a closer relationship to it than to all of the other places on "this little earth" in which she wishes to travel everywhere freely with her son. She regards her poetry as having been little influenced by African culture, because she is Western by birth and no traditionalist. (Curiously, because she views the Near East as an extension of the African continent, she sees the influence of the Bible upon her poetry as African in origin.) The subject matter of her poems has consistently been Afro-*American*.

Giovanni's willingness to limit her political efforts to Afro-American causes has continued to bring her negative criticism, even today, partly because she so openly calls herself a Black American "chauvinist." Since the feminist movement has increasingly linked American women with those in developing nations, some feminist critics of Giovanni have also seen her focus as self-centered. The evidence that political disapproval of her exclusive focus on Afro-American needs, and not on African needs, *still* affects her literary reputation can be seen in the exclusion of her poems from the fine anthology, *Confirmation: An Anthology of African American Women*, edited by Amiri and Amina Baraka. The book includes works by forty-nine practicing women poets, and since Giovanni is frequently considered to be today's most widely-read Black American woman poet, perhaps the most widely-read living Black American poet, period, her absence from this volume is startling. A terse footnote in the prefatory material states that Giovanni's contributions were rejected at press time because she traveled in South Africa in 1982.

The most significant development in Giovanni's career has been her evolution from a strongly committed political consciousness prior to 1969 to a more inclusive consciousness which does not repudiate political concern and commitment, but which regards a revolutionary ethos as only one aspect of the totality of Black experience. Her earlier political as-

sociates and favorable reviewers of the late 1960s often regarded her development after 1970 with consternation, as representing a repudiation of her racial roots and of political commitment, without perhaps fully understanding the basis for her widened concerns and interests. Giovanni's shift in interest from revolutionary politics and race as a collective matter towards love and race as they affect personal development and relationships brought strong reviewer reaction. (The shift to less favorable criticism, which is apparent in the reviews of *My House,* is also evident in the late notices of *Gemini,* Giovanni's most widely reviewed book.) The problems involved in studying the relationship between this shift in her poetry and the somewhat delayed shift from favorable to less favorable criticism, as her artistry grew, are complex. And they are further complicated by the fact that, at the very time the negative reviews of her poetry markedly increased, her popularity with readers surged dramatically ahead. Witness the late sales of *Gemini* (1971) and *Black Feeling/Black Talk/Black Judgement* (1970), the new sales of *My House* (1972), and the record-breaking sales of two of her early albums of recorded poetry. Her audiences around the country grew markedly in size and enthusiasm in 1972, and feature articles and cover stories on "the Princess of Black Poetry" appeared in over a dozen popular magazines in 1972 and 1973.

Studying the relationships between the positive and negative reviews and between the opinions of reviewers and popular audiences is made more difficult by an anomaly presented by Giovanni's *Black Feeling/Black Talk/Black Judgement:* two-thirds of the poems in this 1970 volume are brief, introspective lyrics which are political only in the most peripheral sense—that they mention a lover as someone the speaker met at a conference, for instance. The remaining third, poems which are strongly political and often militant, received practically all the attention of reviewers. Critics ignored almost completely the poems that foreshadow nearly all the poetry Giovanni was to write in the next thirteen years. In short, the wave of literary reviews that established Giovanni's national reputation as a poet also established her image as a radical. Yet, by the summer of 1970, when these reviews began to appear, Giovanni had been writing solely non-political, lyric poetry for a year. The label "the poet of the Black revolution" which characterized her in the popular media was already a misnomer in 1970, when it began to be popularly used.

The change in stance had, in fact, appeared by 1969, when Giovanni published an article criticizing the leaders of Black Cultural Nationalism. In it, she also rejected the rigidity and the prescriptiveness of the Black Aesthetic, the proponents of which insisted that committed Black writers like herself could only write about changing the Black situation in America in terms of power. She further charged that Black Arts groups had become exclusive and snobbish, and she attacked the Movement's male activists for demanding the sub-servience of Black women to the male leaders of the cause. In general, she concluded that she could no longer as an artist subordinate her poetry to the politics of revolution. Entitled **"Black Poets, *Poseurs,* and Power,"** the essay appeared first in the June, 1969, issue of *Black World.* The aggressive Black leaders of the revolution must surely have read it, but apparently few of her other readers knew of the essay. Since Giovanni had no popular following prior to 1970, her 1969 essay did not become a widely discussed matter in the literary world.

At least initially, readers also seem to have paid scant attention to the philosophical conclusions that Giovanni had arrived at and had announced in her casually organized and conversational essay when it was reprinted in *Gemini,* a collection of prose pieces, in 1971. Most would have been more interested in her angrily expressed charge that the Black Cultural Nationalists "have made Black women the new Jews." Black readers of *Gemini* would have focused, too, on her reaction to the 1968 electoral campaign in Newark: the Black citizens of Newark, she contends, seemed more fearful of their "liberators" than they did the corrupt white politicians who had oppressed them in the past. That Giovanni had, by 1971, felt some repercussions from the publication of her article might account for her remark, in *A Dialogue: James Baldwin and Nikki Giovanni,* that "the young Black critics are, I think just trying to hurt people, and the white critics don't understand."

Ruth Rambo McClain, reviewing Giovanni's 1970 poetry collection *Re: Creation* in the February, 1971, issue of *Black World,* is one of the first critics to recognize the change in Giovanni's subject and form. McClain regards the many lyrics in *Re:Creation* as "tight controlled, clean—too clean" and sees in Giovanni not only "a new classical lyrical Nikki, exploring her new feeling," but "an almost declawed tamed panther." *Re:Creation,* a small collection, contains a few poems on revolution, the imprisonment of Blacks, and the hatred of white oppressors (perhaps written prior to having arrived at the conclusions Giovanni presents in **"Black Poets, *Poseurs,* and Power"**). Most of those who reviewed her two 1970 books of poetry wanted more poems of this sort and referred to them as *sharp, vital, energetic,* or *non-sentimental.* A few more detached critics saw the rhetoric in them as somewhat posed and artificial but did not object on political grounds.

Most of the reviews and essays on Giovanni in 1971 recognized no impending change in her work. For example, A. Russell Brooks, writing on "The Motifs of Dynamic Change in Black Revolutionary Poetry" in the September, 1971, issue of *CLA Journal,* includes Giovanni in his list of nine poets "in the forefront" of revolutionary poetry, and he identifies her as "one of the first two or three most popular black

poets." Placing his comments on her between those on Don L. Lee (Haki Madhubuti) and LeRoi Jones (Amiri Baraka), he refers to Lee as the most impatient, Giovanni as the most popular, and Jones as "the Dean of Black Revolutionary Artists." However, in a later review of *A Dialogue,* Brooks speaks of Giovanni's "marked change in her mode of looking at the world and writing about it" as reflected not only in *My House* but "fairly well indicated" in *Re:Creation* and *Gemini.* In a 1971 article entitled "The Poetry of Three Revolutionists: Don L. Lee, Sonia Sanchez, and Nikki Giovanni", R. Roderick Palmer failed to acknowledge Giovanni's shift in vision, seeing her, among these three figures, as the *true* revolutionary: "the most polemic, the most incendiary; the poet most impatient for change, who . . . advocates open violence." Palmer, like many other readers, failed to recognize the preponderance of the lyric mode in the collections of 1970, the preponderance of poems devoted to self-analysis, love, and the exploration of personal relationships; he mistakenly remarks that she "occasionally lends herself to less explosive themes."

On February 13, 1972, June Jordan, herself a Black poet, reviewed *Gemini* in the *New York Times Book Review* in a generally favorable way. She notes that the paragraphs of Giovanni's prose "slide about and loosely switch tracks" but feels that two essays are "unusual for their serious, held focus and for their clarity." She singles out for special comment the 1969 article **"Black Poets, *Poseurs,* and Power"** and the last essay in *Gemini,* **"Gemini—A Prolonged Autobiographical Statement on Why,"** which closes with the statement "I really like to think a Black, beautiful, loving world is possible." More directly than had McClain, Jordan remarks on what she also identifies as an impending transition in Giovanni's work—because of the attitudes she sees revealed in these two essays. She agrees with Giovanni that the growing militarism in the Black Arts Movement is deplorable and that the Black community itself is the loser when violent strategies pit Black against Black and leave the real enemies "laughing at the sidelines." She observes that Giovanni, in **"Black Poets, *Poseurs,* and Power,"** was telling the world in 1969 of a change occurring in her poetry and in herself. In speaking of the closing essay in the book, Jordan concludes: "When you compare the poetry [apparently she refers here to the revolutionary poems included in the 1970 volumes] with the ambivalence and wants expressed in this essay, it becomes clear that a transition is taking place inside the artist. . . . She is writing, 'I don't want my son to be a George or a Jonathan Jackson!'" A few months later, the publication of *My House,* without revolutionary poems and with most of its lyrics written after 1969, proved June Jordan's careful and perceptive interpretation of Giovanni's intent to have been accurate.

Two of Giovanni's friends wrote positively of her new emphasis on personal values in 1972. Howard University Press editor Paula Giddings, who provided the preface for Giovanni's *Cotton Candy on a Rainy Day* (1978), in a brief review of *Gemini* in *Black World,* contends that Giovanni's concern for individual Black self-determination places her in a longn-standing tradition of Black literature. Ida Lewis, Editor of *Encore,* a magazine for which Giovanni wrote a twice-monthly column beginning in 1975 (as well as many other articles), mentions in her preface to *My House* that Giovanni already "has been reproached for her independent attitudes by her critics. . . . But Nikki Giovanni's greatness is not derived from following leaders, nor has she ever accepted the burden of carrying the revolution. Her struggle is a personal search for individual values. . . . She jealously guards her right to be judged as an individual." These two sets of remarks make it evident that Giovanni had heard that attacks on her work were soon to appear in print. In the preface to *My House,* Lewis quotes Giovanni as saying of such Black critics: "We are the *only* people who will read someone out of the race—the entire nation—because we don't agree with them."

In the same month that Jordan's review appeared, Black critic Peter Bailey published a favorable feature story in *Ebony* on Giovanni's rapidly growing popular reputation, but he ominously suggested, as did Lewis, that the negative reaction from certain Black artists and politicians loomed just ahead for Giovanni and her poetry. Unlike Jordan, Giddings, and Lewis, however, Bailey saw her popular reputation as a partial *cause* for the accelerating attack on her work, whereas Jordan had referred to it as a "guarantee" of the interests of her work: "Like it or not," writes Bailey, "—and some people don't like it—she has become a cultural force to be dealt with. She's a much-anthologized poet and she's a lecturer who commands a vast audience. . . . There are black artists—those in what she called 'the black-power literary establishment'—who are convinced that Nikki's emergence as a 'star' will hinder her development as a *black* poet."

Since the bulk of Giovanni's Black political associates and fellow artists did not understand the basis for her widened concerns as a poet and saw only her apparent retreat from revolutionary politics, few critics who supported the Black Aesthetic applauded her. Dudley Randall (editor of the Broadside Press), Ida Lewis, Paula Giddings, and probably June Jordan recognized the imperative of the artist to follow her or his own vision if one's imaginative poetry is to flourish. Most others regarded Giovanni's new position as a failure in nerve, even a betrayal. In their reviews they commented disapprovingly about her diminished political and racial commitment in turning to the lyric and away from revolutionary themes, and they judged harshly the poems that dealt with sex, love, and family relationships.

These critics seldom attacked either specific poems or specific lines; they simply opposed Giovanni's new ideological orientation. Repeatedly, they stereotyped her unfavorably—as a woman crying for a lover she could not hold, as a mother abandoned with a baby—frustrated and resentful, longing for the return of her man. While she was insultingly derided for "singing the blues," she was almost as often stereotyped as a frivolous woman, joking, laughing, enjoying herself when serious issues of race and revolution needed to be addressed, and as an overly ambitious and successful woman, who had compromised to accommodate and please everyone in order to gain popularity, wealth, and applause. This second stereotype—the too-happy woman—was labeled the "ego-tripper." (**"Ego-Tripping"** is the name of one of her most popular poems which she often reads to audiences. It derives from folk origins—the tall-tale, the amusing boaster whose exaggeration increases throughout the story or song and has no bounds as explicit details accumulate into a semblance of invulnerable realism. *Ego-Tripping* is also the name of her 1973 book for young people.)

Those reviewers who promoted the stereotype of Giovanni's crying the blues for a lost love said that her poems were sad and lacking in energy; those promoting the ego-tripper stereotype complained that her poems were irrelevant, frivolous, trivial, and derived from European lyric traditions. Giovanni's son was five when this kind of attack was most blatantly made—certainly not an infant—; in 1969 and 1970 when he *was* an infant and when her revolutionary poetry was occupying reviewers, no such references were made. The image of the woman sitting alone and weeping over a sacrificed future must have seemed strange to the crowds who knew of the strenuous speaking and travel schedule which she maintained in the early '70s. In addition, she was writing the poems published in *The Women and the Men* in 1975, and both preparing her dialogues with Margaret Walker and with James Baldwin for publication in 1973 and 1974, respectively, and producing two books of children's poems, written for her son. During part of this time she also continued to teach at Rutgers University.

In any event, whether critics' animosity arose from their disapproval of independent motherhood, envy of Giovanni's success and popularity, or anger at her political withdrawal from the Black Cultural Nationalist activity and failure to support Pan-African groups, the bitterness of their reviews is startling. They are as extreme in their negation as were the crowds which welcomed Giovanni wherever she spoke or read her poetry extreme in their enthusiasm. Hilda-Njoki McElroy prefaces her review of *A Dialogue* in the December, 1973, issue of *Black World* by satirizing the book as "Who's Afraid of James Baldwin and Nikki Giovanni: A Comedy for White Audiences," starring N. Giovanni who, as a "super cool, funny woman [,] reveals her vulnerability." McElroy then refers to Giovanni's recent honors as "accolades and awards from the enemy."

Kalamu ya Salaam (Val Ferdinand) launched a still harsher attack upon Giovanni's integrity in an essay which purports to be a late review of *My House* and of her record album *Like a Ripple in the Pond.* This critic—who edits the *Black Collegian,* is associated with the Nkombo Press in New Orleans, and writes essays, poetry, and plays—had won the Richard Wright Prize for Criticism in 1970. He was active in the Congress of Afrikan People and the Afrikan Liberation Support Committee, and a few months later published a long report on his assessment of African Liberation Day entitled "Tell No Lies, Claim No Easy Victories." He is obviously sympathetic to Baraka's progress in the early 1970s towards dominance in the Pan-African groups as he won strength also for the CFUN (Committee for a Unified New Ark). Given Salaam's political background, it is not surprising that he disapproved of Giovanni's 1969 statement on the Black Cultural Nationalists and her refusal to participate in the African liberation groups. Nevertheless, the sense of shock which he expresses in his review rings false, because he is writing about a change that occurred in her work five years before and should have been clear to everyone two years earlier with the publication of *My House.*

Giovanni has been viewed by some of her politically ardent contemporaries in the liberation groups as having deserted the movement with which she was at first visibly associated.
—*Margaret B. McDowell*

In his essay Salaam centers on a quotation from Baraka which describes the Black actress Ruby Dee in a mournful pose, sitting at a window on a rainy day. (Ruby Dee had, since 1940, played roles in *Agamemnon, King Lear, Boesman and Lena,* and *A Raisin in the Sun* and taken other parts in stage plays, films, and television dramas. Like Giovanni, she had produced poetry readings against a background of jazz and gospel music.) Quoting Baraka, "Ruby Dee weeps at the window . . . lost in her life . . . sentimental bitter frustrated deprived of her fullest light. . . ." Salaam continues, "This describes *Nikki* perfectly." He then contends that Giovanni has moved from revolutionary poetry to sad lyricism in *My House* because she is lamenting a lover who has abandoned her, and she now is, like "a whole lot of Ruby Dees, sitting . . . waiting . . . the footsteps of us brothers come back home." His supposed pity for her suddenly assumes a harsher tone: "Nikki has gone quietly crazy." Referring to her lyric about the experience of being a bridesmaid, he taunts her by saying, "A lot of the seeming insanity and nonsense that Nikki verbalizes . . . must be understood for what it is: Broken dreams. Misses. Efforts that failed. I betcha Nikki wanted to be married. . . ." This fictionalized biography completed, Salaam attacks Giovanni's

poetry for its sentimentality, its romanticism, and its being influenced by European tradition ("strictly European literature regurgitated"). He scolds her for turning from the unremitting analysis of "collective oppression" in order to "sing the blues" about personal problems. She should have known that "just love" is not an appropriate theme for poetry, because love is an intensely personal experience between only two individuals and, thus, is counter-revolutionary. He concludes that Giovanni does not have the right to "do whatever . . . she feels like doing" because she is, as a Black, still "in captivity." She should see the limits of her poetry within the message "The revolution is, and must be, for land and self-control. And good government."

It is my contention that Giovanni's rejection of the pressure to write primarily a didactic, "useful" political poetry was not only a sign of her integrity but an inevitable sign of her development. A truly comprehensive criticism of her work must be willing to recognize both her continuing commitment to the attainment by Black people of power in America and a commitment to personal freedom for herself as a woman and an artist. Critics need not only to see the importance of politics in her life but to perceive also that a commitment to politics, pursued with ideological rigor, inevitably becomes constricting to an artist. That Giovanni still writes political poetry can be understood by attending to the anger which she expresses in each volume at the oppression of Blacks, women, and the elderly; she continually deplores also the violence which oppression spawns. She illustrates the conflict between ideological commitment, exacted by political beliefs, and the demands of the artistic sensibility which tend to find such commitment confining and stultifying. She illustrates in her own work and career the same arc that the poets of the Auden generation in England illustrated: the passing beyond a doctrinal basis for one's poetry to a work responsive to an illuminating of the whole of the individual's experience. Giovanni's case is both complicated and made clearer by her connections with the Black Liberation Movement, which has not yet won all its objectives, particularly her affinities to the work of those closely tied to Marxist-Leninist ideology and Pan-African goals.

Giovanni has been viewed by some of her politically ardent contemporaries in the liberation groups as having deserted the movement with which she was at first visibly associated. Her revolutionary poem in ***Black Feeling/Black Talk/Black Judgement*** made her into a heroic figure for some Blacks, and the myth of her fiery opposition to tyranny was slow to die—even though she had moved away from Black Cultural Nationalism before most of those who hailed the strenuous and dominant voice in her poems knew that she existed. A more comprehensive criticism would permit critics to consider that Giovanni may have gained rather than lost as a result of the development of a personal idiom and of a more lyrical stance in her post-1970 work. In her response to Peter Bailey's questions early in 1972 about the "reproach" from Black activists that was gathering about her and her work, Giovanni displayed again the defiance and staunch independence captured in the anecdote from *Gemini* which features the four-year-old Nikki holding the fort with stones on her porch roof, ready to fight back against detractors: "I'm not about telling people what they should do. . . . The fight in the world today is the fight to be an individual, the fight to live out your own damn ego in your own damn way. . . . If I allow you to be yourself and you allow me to be myself, then we can come together and build a strong union. . . . I'm an arrogant bitch, culturally speaking."

In her poetry Giovanni has chosen to communicate with the common reader, as well as with artists and critics; consequently, she has used graphic images from everyday Afro-American life and stressed the "orality" of her usually short poems, often by assimilating into them the rhythms of Black conversation and the heritage from jazz, blues, and the spirituals—reflecting these origins both in rhythmic patterns and borrowed phrases. She has tended to focus on a single individual, situation, or idea, often with a brief narrative thread present in the poem. Her choice of such simple forms has meant that academic critics might well be less interested in her work than in that of the more complex and intellectualized poets most often associated with modernism, such as T. S. Eliot, Ezra Pound, and W. H. Auden. She avoids the allusions to classical literature and mythology, the relatively obscure symbolism, the involved syntax, the densely-packed idiom, and the elliptical diction often characteristic of such poets. If the verbal and structural forthrightness of Giovanni's poetry in some measure accounts for the paucity of academic criticism of it, this elemental quality accounts also for her popular acclaim by thousands who come to hear her read her work. Like a folksinger, she senses the close relationship of poetry with music, since her poetry, like music, depends on sound and rhythm and is incomplete without oral performance and without an audience. (At times, especially in her children's poetry, she relates her poems to a third such art, dance.)

Throughout the 1970s Giovanni read her poetry and lectured on campuses, at churches, and on radio and television. Paula Giddings reported in the preface to Giovanni's *Cotton Candy on a Rainy Day* (1978) that Giovanni appeared before as many as two hundred audiences a year during the 1970s, commanding substantial speaking fees. Today she continues to make public appearances but on a less strenuous schedule. As a poet of the people, Giovanni renews the tradition of the bard, prophet, or witness who sings or chants to inform the people, to subvert tyranny, and to bring an audience together as a community to celebrate a cause or person or a heritage, or to establish a basis for sympathy and understanding of one another's suffering or problems. For Giovanni's audience participation at a poetry reading can be

as much a part of the aesthetic experience as congregational expression may be part of worship experience.

Giovanni's acceptance by the public was strong in 1970 and grew in 1971 with the publication of *Gemini,* and in 1972 and 1973 it greatly increased, in counterpoint to the negative reviews of *My House* during those years. In 1969 the *Amsterdam News,* a Black New York weekly found in 1909, listed her as one of the ten most admired Black women in America. By 1970 and 1971 journalists and television speakers generally referred to her as "the star" or "the Princess of Black Poetry." June Jordan, in reviewing *Gemini,* commented in 1972 that the book's interests were "guaranteed by Miss Giovanni's status as a leading black poet and celebrity," and she referred to Giovanni's "plentiful followers" who claimed her as "*their* poet," so directly did she speak to them.

The popular media both reflected her burgeoning popular reputation and strengthened its further growth. Besides the many feature articles on her poetry and personality in major popular magazines, over a dozen in 1972 and 1973 alone, she frequently appeared on late-night television talk shows, and she read her poetry regularly on *Soul,* a one-hour television show of music, dance, drama, and literature for young people (sponsored by the Ford Foundation). In 1970 she established her own company, NikTom Records, Ltd., and then recorded albums on which she read her poetry against a musical background—first, gospel; and later, blues, jazz, rock, and folk. Two early albums were best-sellers, and one received the national AFTRA Award for Best Spoken Album in 1972.

Giovanni says that she speaks for no one but herself, but she actually has become, in her poems, the speaker for many diverse groups and individuals. She has revealed a sincere interest in the people from many backgrounds who come to hear her or who write to her. Though in her early work she made use of a militant rhetoric with images of violence, she deplored—even in her first major volume—the actual violence seemingly endemic to American life. In one of her first poems, **"Love Poem: For Real,"** she mourned the fact that "the sixties have been one long funeral day." In her poetry she is ardently sympathetic to those who have died uselessly and goes on in each new volume to lament the senselessness of the results of prejudice and intolerance, the public tragedy that she makes personal tragedy in her poetry—from the Ku Klux Klan murders of civil rights workers in Philadelphia, Mississippi, through the assassinations of public leaders in the 1960s, to the murders of kidnapped children in Atlanta.

She has attracted feminists with her portrayals of the women in her family and of elderly Black women. They have noted her frequent dedications of poems to women and have been impressed by her courageous assertion that she had her baby in 1969 because she wanted a baby, could *afford* to, and didn't want a husband. The more traditional leadership of the National Council of Negro Women, moreover, has honored her with a life membership, and she has praised their inclusive program of advocacy and membership policy. Young protesters against the draft and Viet Nam involvement crowded her campus lectures, but she also encouraged high school students at assemblies (often Black students) to avoid an alignment with "hippie" groups and to follow a disciplined life—to aim higher, work harder, and demand bigger rewards. After the inmates of the Cook County Jail presented her with a plaque, she boasted that prisoners and students were her best supporters. She relished ceremonies in which mayors from Gary, Indiana, to Dallas, Texas, gave her keys to their cities. With more somber pomp and ceremony, she was in three years (1972-1975) awarded four honorary doctorates.

One example of the acclaim Giovanni received in 1972 and 1973 can be found in an event honoring her which combined the setting of the Kennedy Center for the Performing Arts, a formally attired audience of government dignitaries and other celebrities, a several-month-long publicity promotion in the *Ladies' Home Journal,* and the financial backing of Clairol (a large manufacturer of hair products) with a one-hour television extravaganza which pre-empted network programs. In 1972 Giovanni received one of seven "Highest Achievement Awards" from *Mademoiselle* as "one of the most listened to of the younger poets." In the more highly publicized *Ladies' Home Journal* "Women of the Year" contest in 1973, she became one of the eight winners (from among eighty nominees on ballots printed in the magazine, which thirty thousand subscribers clipped, marked, signed, and mailed that month). A jury of prestigious women who made the final choices for the list included Shirley Temple Black; Margaret Truman Daniels; Eunice Kennedy Shriver; the presidents of the National Organization for Women, the General Federation of Women's Clubs, the National Council of Negro Women, Women in Communications, and two women's colleges; the dean of a medical college; a recruiter for high-level positions in the Nixon administration; and a woman Brigadier General in the U.S. Air Force. Besides Giovanni, the list itself included such famous women as Katharine Graham, publisher of the Washington *Post*; Shirley Chisholm, recently a Presidential candidate; and actress Helen Hayes. Other nominees included Coretta King; Dorothy Day; Judge Shirley Hofstedler; sculptor Louise Nevelson; historian Barbara Tuchman; authors Joyce Carol Oates, Anne Sexton, and Pearl Buck; musicians Beverly Sills, Joan Baez, Carly Simon, and Ethel Waters; athletes Billie Jean King, Chris Evert, and Peggy Fleming; feminists Bella Abzug, Betty Friedan, Gloria Steinem, and Aileen Hernandez; former ambassador Patricia Harris; sex researcher Virginia Masters; Patricia Nixon; Julie Nixon

Eisenhower; and Rose Kennedy. The awards (pendant-pins with three diamonds, specially designed for the occasion by Tiffany's) were presented by Mamie Eisenhower, news commentator Barbara Walters, and Senator Margaret Chase Smith. The ceremony, hosted by actress Rosalind Russell, was viewed by an estimated television audience of thirty million.

The nomination ballots had identified Giovanni as a "Black consciousness poet," and the award presentation statement cited her as "a symbol of Black awareness." Although it also described her somewhat patronizingly as a person "rising above her environment to seek the truth and tell it," readers of her poetry know that its "truth" derives not from her rising above her environment but from her having remained so close to it. This mass-media event offers evidence of the poet's rapid rise to celebrity and provides evidence of the widespread recognition of her and her poetry. This popular acclaim would seem to be an affirmation of her decision four years earlier to write on a wide variety of subjects and to reach as wide a number of people of differing backgrounds and personal characteristics as possible.

The problems arising from Giovanni's early critical reception linger. As we move in the direction of providing a more adequate base of understanding and assessment of her work, it is fortunate that three good sources of Giovanni's own views on the criticism of poetry (particularly her own work) have appeared in the last two years: the verse preface to Giovanni's *Those Who Ride the Night Winds* (1983), the 1983 interview with Claudia Tate in *Black Women Writers at Work,* and the 1982 interview with Arlene Elder.

As I mentioned earlier, negative criticism of Giovanni—often based on personal or political bias rather than sound literary assessment—gains strength by pointing to a particularly poor poem or an unfortunate line. Giovanni's process of revision (or discarding all or part of a poem), therefore, has special relevance in her continued development. As she describes her process of revision to Claudia Tate, she essentially discards an entire poem if it appears to present several problems or a major problem. Otherwise, when she discovers a recalcitrant line or two, she "starts at the top" and rewrites the entire poem—perhaps a dozen times—rather than working on a particular line or phrase. She finds this radical rewriting necessary to insure the poem's unity: "A poem's got to be a single stroke." It is particularly important to understand this characteristic process, established over fifteen years, as one begins to criticize Giovanni's forthcoming works. According to Arlene Elder's introduction to her interview with Giovanni, the poet is about to embark on an experiment with much longer poems (1,200-1,500 lines) after a career of writing short poems. Since one cannot rewrite a long poem a dozen times upon encountering problems in a few lines, Giovanni's revision process may radically change.

One already sees changes of probable significance between Giovanni's most recent book, *Those Who Ride the Night Winds,* and her books of the 1970s. In many of the poems she is using a "lineless" form: the rhythmic effects come from measured groups of words or phrases of fairly regular length separated from each other by ellipses, but appearing otherwise to be prose paragraphs. Except for works before 1970, she has (more than other contemporary Black poets, such as Sonia Sanchez or Haki Madhubuti) avoided such unconventional typographical devices as capitalizing all the words in a line, separating a single syllable between lines (Bl-Ack), or spelling for the sake of puns (hue-man, Spear-o-Agnew, master-bate). She has probably done so, in part, because of the artificiality of these tricks—but more often because she stresses the oral nature of her poetry, and such typography has little effect on the spoken word. One wonders, then, whether she is, in her latest volume, moving away from the emphasis on the oral. She may also be seeking a bridge between the freedom of prose and the more exact structuring of poetry. In this book she also includes a number of poems about individual white people—John Lennon, John F. Kennedy, and Billie Jean King, for example. New critics of Giovanni will need to know her earlier work and the nature of its development to understand and evaluate the changes that appear to be approaching in her career.

From the Tate interview, one learns much that is significant about Giovanni's views on good criticism. She now claims that she does not care whether her critic is black or white, but the individual should understand her work, or try to do so, before writing on it. In her view critics must not permanently "brand" a work so that other critics unconsciously embrace that judgment. They should not expect consistency within an author's canon, since such an expectation denies the fact that an artist may grow and change. In reviewing a book, they should place it in the context of the rest of the author's work. They should not assume that the voice ordering the poem and the experience described in the poem are necessarily autobiographical. They should not aim to injure an author personally by referring to private matters instead of concentrating on the work apart from the author's life. They should not question a writer's integrity because they happen to disagree with the ideas expressed in the work. Giovanni's comments, though offhanded, are pithy: "There would be no point to having me go three-fourths of the way around the world if I couldn't create an inconsistency, if I hadn't *learned* anything." "You're only as good as your last book. . . . God wrote one book. The rest of us are forced to do a little better." "You can't quote the last book as if it were the first."

In her preface to *Those Who Ride the Night Winds,*

Giovanni invites her readers to hurry along with her as she flies the uncharted night winds, because she is *changing,* and because—as the Walrus said—the time has come to talk of *many things.* If she still feels distrust of critics, in this preface she suggests a willingness to listen, as in the interviews she suggests a desire to be energized as a poet by "better questions this year than last." In spite of her mixed experience with critics, she does not see herself as their victim, because she knows that she was free to choose a safer occupation than that of writer and did not do so. In the "lineless" poetry she uses in her new book—the first unconventional typography she has used since 1970—she puns on the "bookmaker" as a professional gambler and her own game of chance as a "maker of books": "Bookmaking is shooting craps . . . with the white boys . . . downtown on the stock exchange . . . is betting a dime you can win . . . And that's as it should be . . . If you wanted to be safe . . . you would have walked into the Post Office . . . or taken a graduate degree in Educational Administration . . . you pick up your pen . . . And take your chances . . ."

Giovanni's critics, who often limit themselves to reviews of her separate books, devote little attention to her development from year to year and provide little specific analysis of the significant aspects of the form and structure of her poetry. No critic has fully discussed the variety of her subjects and her techniques. Beyond this, personal bias and political needs, rather than a commitment to judgments based on sound theoretical postulates, dominate much of the criticism which does exist on her work. Those who have attacked her poetry most severely have failed to understand Giovanni's compulsion to follow her own artistic vision as well as her continued commitment to Afro-American culture. Her great popularity among readers of many ages, classes, races, and economic backgrounds is at variance with the neglect of her work by critics or their tendency to patronize her and her work. Sympathetic and sophisticated studies of her work are a prime necessity if she is to achieve the recognition due her as a literary artist. Such studies, it is hoped, would encourage her to achieve her full potential as a poet and would also attain for her the reputation that the corpus of her work calls for.

Don McDermott (review date April 1988)

SOURCE: "Unedibles," in *Cimarron Review,* Vol. 83, April, 1988, pp. 94-5.

[*In the following review of* Sacred Cows . . . and Other Edibles, *McDermott criticizes Giovanni's monotony and lack of wit.*]

On February 19th William Morrow and Company will publish what it defines as a collection of essays by Nikki Giovanni, but this designation seems a bit inaccurate. The term "essay" suggests an attempt to order and shape material to a particular topic or collection of closely related topics. *Sacred Cows . . . and Other Edibles* is almost exclusively an exercise of glib incoherence. What is recommended by her publisher as her irreverence, her shamelessness, is nothing more than her audacity in attempting to chat about everything and nothing, almost simultaneously. And yet it is not discursive. To call her work discursive is to suggest that at some point it is on track. There are no tracks—no destination, merely large unmapped areas of speculative discourse. But hers is perhaps a studied, or at least affected, incoherence, and for those who are admirers of Sterne's *Tristram Shandy,* this refusal to get to the point or stick with the subject might be to your taste. Consider her range in this entire paragraph from **"In Sympathy With Another Motherless Child (One View of the Profession of Writing)":**

> I really don't know what to say about myself. I like music, there is something very special about capping my headphones and drowning in a vision of sound. Someone once asked me if I played an instrument and I replied, "My stereo." It's not surprising that man's first musical instrument was a drum; the image of the heart had to be manifest. The African people made use of the ability of the drum to both inform and incite; for over two hundred years of the American experience drumming was outlawed. A people, though, are rarely stopped in their legitimate desire for either knowledge or pleasure. Whether the Eighteenth Amendment would outlaw alcohol or the Miss America Pageant would desire the clothing of their Black Venus, a people, through individual risk or simply aesthetic innocence, will bring word of a new day.

This style reflects an interesting prose experiment, much the way Molly's soliloquy represents the direct reflections of Molly as she waits for Bloom and approaches the gates of la-la-land. But can you imagine the entire *Ulysses* transcribed from the interior walls of Molly's slipping consciousness? Imagine, then the monotony of the above Giovanni style for 163 pages.

But Giovanni's collection is also lauded by the publisher as a witty book. Is it?

> Recently, a friend of mine, through no lack of sensitivity, on a rainy day in Florida, pulled into a handicapped parking place. Well, the parking space wasn't handicapped, it was simply so designated.

The sacred cow at stake here will be, of course, handicapped

privileges. This, in one of her more pointed discussions after a momentary lapse, will reach the witty barb:

> But hey. We were discussing designated handicapped parking. At the risk of sounding a bit cold—if they can drive, they can take their chances like the rest of us. Or I'm going to ask James Meredith to initiate a march demanding designated COLORED parking spots. Then, of course, the militant gays will demand designated gay spots, ...

Has the initial joke crawled too far? Is this wit, seething with delicious sarcasm? What ever it is, it is a sort of formula wit that she employs again and again:

> I am totally shocked by the Cincinnati father who raped his five-month-old baby while his wife was out shopping. Guess that will teach his wife to ask him to babysit.

But ultimately, it is wit without content. And her serious prose stance is, if not pedestrian, sometimes confused as in this opening passage from **"An Answer to Some Questions on How I Write":**

> It's always a bit intimidating to try to tell how I write since I, like most writers, I think, am not at all sure that I do what I do in the way that I think I do it. *In other words,* (italics are mine) I was always told not to look a gift horse in the mouth.

Is there any sort of mirror relationship between the first passage and the second that follows upon the qualifier "In other words"? Perhaps this is unfair to ask that her words say literally what she would like to say—which in this case is "Besides." But is there any significance or content to justify this paragraph or the following confessional insight:

> . . . I do pick my nose when I'm afraid. It's gotten so bad, in fact, that now I know that I'm afraid because I find myself picking my nose.

Perhaps my standards for the genre designation "collection of essays" is too high. There are reputable critics who maintain that *Tristram Shandy* is not a novel. Be that as it may, *Tristram Shandy's* existence is insured by its brilliance. *Sacred Cows . . . and Other Edibles* has no such insurance policy.

Martha Cook (essay date 1990)

SOURCE: "Nikki Giovanni: Place and Sense of Place in Her Poetry," in *Southern Women Writers: The New Generation,* edited by Tonette Bond Inge, University of Alabama Press, 1990, pp. 279-300.

[*In the essay below, Cook considers the influence of the Southern writing tradition on Giovanni's writing.*]

Nikki Giovanni's poetry has been most often viewed by literary critics in the tradition of militant black poetry; the first serious critical article on her work, in fact, is R. Roderick Palmer's "The Poetry of Three Revolutionists: Don L. Lee, Sonia Sanchez, and Nikki Giovanni." More recent critics, especially Suzanne Juhasz in her *Naked and Fiery Forms: Modern American Poetry by Women, A New Tradition* (1976) have emphasized the developing feminism in Giovanni's poems. No critic has yet focused on what I see as the key to reading Giovanni, her position in the rich tradition of Southern poetry, proceeding unbroken from Richard Lewis in the eighteenth century through Poe, Henry Timrod, and Sidney Lanier, on through the Fugitives and Jean Toomer, down to James Dickey and Ishmael Reed today. By focusing specifically on the sense of place, a vital element in Southern literature, I have identified a group of poems that represent Giovanni at her best, technically and thematically.

> **No critic has yet focused on what I see as the key to reading Giovanni, her position in the rich tradition of Southern poetry, proceeding unbroken from Richard Lewis in the eighteenth century through Poe, Henry Timrod, and Sidney Lanier, on through the Fugitives and Jean Toomer, down to James Dickey and Ishmael Reed today.**
>
> —*Martha Cook*

Before looking at specific themes, subjects, images, and symbols, I should survey the significant aspects of Nikki Giovanni's life and career. She was born on 7 June 1943 in Knoxville, Tennessee, to a middle-class black couple, Jones Giovanni, a probation officer, and his wife, Yolande, a social worker. It is clearly a mark of Giovanni's respect for her mother that she sometimes gives her formal name as Yolande Cornelia Giovanni, Jr. When she was young, the family lived "in Wyoming, Ohio, which is a suburb of Cincinnati, which some say is a suburb of Lexington, Kentucky." Later they moved to the black community of Lincoln Heights. Nikki often visited her much-beloved Watson grandparents in Knoxville and attended Austin High School there. She closely identified her grandparents with their home on Mulvancy Street; when her grandmother Louvenia was forced by urban renewal to move to Linden Avenue, Giovanni explained her own feelings of displacement:

"There was no familiar smell in that house." Giovanni's Southern roots were further strengthened during her years at Fisk University in Nashville. She began college immediately after high school; though difficulties in maturing during the turbulence of the 1960s resulted in a gap in her college work, she eventually graduated with honors in history in 1967. She is remembered for her radical activities on campus, especially her role in reestablishing the Fisk chapter of the Student Nonviolent Coordinating Committee. She also studied with John Killens and edited the Fisk literary magazine.

Giovanni continued her involvement in the civil rights movement of the 1960s, primarily through her writing. Right out of college, she began publishing articles, poems, and book reviews in journals such as *Negro Digest* and *Black World*. Consistently attacking elitism in the black arts movement, she praised writers whom she viewed as presenting a realistic yet positive picture of black life, both new voices, such as Louise Meriwether, author of the 1970 novel *Daddy Was a Number Runner,* and established ones, such as Dudley Randall. During the late 1960s, she worked to organize the first Cincinnati Black Arts Festival and the New Theatre in that city, as well as a black history group in Wilmington, Delaware. She also took courses at the University of Pennsylvania School of Social Work and the Columbia University School of Fine Arts and taught at Queens College of the City University of New York and Livingston College of Rutgers University.

Randall's Broadside Press, invaluable for its support and encouragement of black poetry, brought out two small collections of Giovanni's poems, ***Black Feeling, Black Talk*** (1968), which she had first printed privately, and ***Black Judgement*** (1969), including many poems that contributed to Giovanni's early reputation as a militant poet who advocated the violent overthrow of the white power structure in America. Many readers found these poems exciting and inspiring, and the poet Don L. Lee pointed to "lines that suggest the writer has a real, serious commitment to her people and to the institutions that are working toward the liberation of Black people." However, he goes on, "when the Black poet chooses to serve as political seer, he must display a keen sophistication. Sometimes Nikki oversimplifies and therefore sounds rather naive politically." Giovanni offered further support for fellow black writers by founding a publishing cooperative, NikTom, Ltd. One of its significant projects is her edition of a collection of poems by black women, ***Night Comes Softly: Anthology of Black Female Voices*** (1970), with contributors ranging in age from seventeen to eighty-four, from unknowns to Sonia Sanchez to Gwendolyn Brooks.

In addition to her literary creations, Giovanni marked her twenty-fifth year by having a child, though she did not marry his father. She was living in New York, where she was writing poetry and serving on the editorial board of the journal *Black Dialogue.* One suspects that the humor used to describe her pregnancy and the birth of her son in the essay **"Don't Have a Baby Till You Read This"** masks to some degree the fears and uneasiness with which she faced life as a single parent. However, she amusingly recounts planning for a daughter's birth in New York, but giving birth prematurely to a son while visiting her parents in Ohio. Through this experience, she learns that one is always a child to one's parents; finally, she asserts herself and goes "home" to New York with her own child. Of her decision to have a child alone, she said later, " 'I had a baby at 25 because I *wanted* to have a baby and I could *afford* to have a baby. I did not get married because I didn't *want* to get married and I could *afford* not to get married.'" Giovanni has remained unmarried and has consistently viewed her single motherhood as a positive choice.

By 1969, Sheila Weller had called Giovanni "one of the most powerful figures on the new black poetry scene—both in language and appeal." Weller goes on to indicate that the woman she is interviewing is not the woman she expected from reading her poetry: "The tense anger that wires many of Nikki's poems is in direct contrast to the warm calm she generates." Giovanni said of herself at the time of the interview, "'I've changed a lot over the last few months.'" When her next volume of poetry, *Re:Creation* (1970), was published by Broadside, a reviewer for *Black World* was concerned that the poems were not so radical and militant as those in Giovanni's earlier volumes, describing the poet as transformed "into an almost declawed, tamed Panther with bad teeth," yet conceding, "a Panther with bad teeth is still quite deadly." Seeing her changes as positive rather than negative, as strengthening her work rather than weakening it, *Time* noted in a 1970 article on black writers that "already some, like Nikki Giovanni, are moving away from extreme political activism toward more compassionate and universal themes."

In 1970, the firm William Morrow issued Giovanni's first two Broadside books under the title **Black Feeling, Black Talk/Black Judgement.** This publication, followed in 1971 by the prose volume *Gemini: An Extended Autobiographical Statement on My First Twenty-Five Years of Being a Black Poet,* brought her such attention as a lengthy review by Martha Duffy in *Time.* Duffy particularly praises the autobiographical sections of *Gemini,* emphasizing: "On the subject of her childhood, Miss Giovanni is magical. She meanders along with every appearance of artlessness, but one might as well say that Mark Twain wrote shaggy-dog stories." Of Giovanni's propagandistic writing, Duffy observes: "Hers is a committed social rage. She is capable of scalding rhetoric, but the artist in her keeps interrupting."

The year 1971 also marked the publication of Giovanni's first volume of poetry for children, *Spin a Soft Black Song.* The poems, enhanced by excellent illustrations by Charles Bible, offer realistic images of black urban life and positive images of black identity. The same year, she recorded the first of several poetry readings combined with gospel music or jazz. **"Truth Is on Its Way"** includes a number of poems from Giovanni's Broadside volumes, with music by the New York Community Choir under the direction of Benny Diggs. According to *Harper's Bazaar,* Giovanni introduced the album at a free concert in a church in Harlem. Following her performance, "the audience shouted its appreciation.

Peter Bailey summed up Giovanni's public role as follows: "Nikki, the poet, has become a personality, a *star.*" At that time, in 1972, Giovanni seemed to see herself in the tradition of confessional poetry, like so many twentieth-century American women poets, but with the particular perspective of the black American: "' When I write poetry, . . . I write out of my own experiences—which also happen to be the experiences of my people. But if I had to choose between my people's experiences and mine, I'd choose mine, because that's what I know best.'" Her next volume of poems is entitled *My House* (1972). In the introduction, Ida Lewis, editor and publisher of *Encore,* for which Giovanni was serving as an editorial consultant, calls her "the Princess of Black Poetry," saying lightheartedly: "I've seen Nikki mobbed in Bloomingdale's department store by Black and white customers; I've walked with her down Fifth Avenue and watched a man who was saying 'hi' to her walk into an oncoming taxi." Yet Lewis concludes in a serious vein, emphasizing that Giovanni "writes about the central themes of our times, in which thirty million Blacks search for self-identification and self-love." The star, the princess, at the age of twenty-nine was taken seriously enough to be awarded an honorary doctorate by Wilberforce University, the oldest black institution of higher education in America. Even after the publication of her next two volumes of poetry, Alex Batman considered *My House* her "finest work."

Giovanni's next album, **"Like a Ripple on a Pond,"** again with the New York Community Choir, features selections from *My House.* The volume and the album were criticized by *Black World* reviewer Kalamu ya Salaam for failing to live up to the promise of Giovanni's earlier work. Salaam is particularly hard on the poems, citing their sentimentality and romanticism. He is accurate in some cases, yet he is harshly critical of the sequence of African poems that other critics have seen as one of the strongest elements of the volume. Giovanni's next volume of poetry for children, *Ego-Tripping and Other Poems for Young People* (1973), includes a selection of previously published poems illustrated by George Ford. The title poem is an especially good example of her theme of racial pride and her interest in the places associated with her African heritage.

In 1971, Giovanni had taped a program for the WNET series "Soul!"; this appearance was transcribed, edited, and published in 1973 as *A Dialogue: James Baldwin/Nikki Giovanni.* The volume offers insight into both the works and the personal lives of these two important black writers, as does a similar volume apparently inspired by that experience, *A Poetic Equation: Conversations between Nikki Giovanni and Margaret Walker,* published by Howard University Press in 1974. The latter is perhaps the more interesting, as it gives these black women writers of succeeding generations the opportunity to react to contemporary political and literary issues.

The early 1970s were clearly a period of change and growth for Giovanni, as she was coming to terms with the legacy of civil rights activism and her own personal concerns as a woman and a mother. In 1973, a number of public figures were asked by *Mademoiselle* to describe their views of the previous decade in a so-called epitaph. Giovanni's contribution, a mock radio-drama called **"Racism: The Continuing Saga of the American Dream,"** was obviously a difficult chore; she commented, "'I had to use a light touch. To approach the '60s any other way right now would be too painful.'" A warmer side of Giovanni is seen in her contribution to a *Mademoiselle* feature entitled **"A Christmas Memory,"** where she concludes, "Christmas to me is a special link to the past and a ritual for our future."

> **The early 1970s were clearly a period of change and growth for Giovanni, as she was coming to terms with the legacy of civil rights activism and her own personal concerns as a woman and a mother.**
> *–Martha Cook*

During this period of increasing strength in the feminist movement in America, Giovanni seems to have become more aware of the personal and political significance of sex roles and of sex discrimination. "'Roles between men and women are changing. . . . We no longer need categories,'" she said in an interview. "'There is no reason why my son can't cook and rock with his teddy bear as well as swim and play ball.'" Giovanni's next volume of poetry, *The Women and the Men* (1975), reflects her growing awareness of such issues but also hints at difficulties in the creative process. Three years after *My House,* she offers a volume including a number of poems from the 1970 *Re:Creation* (which did deserve wider circulation than it had received); the new poems do not generally demonstrate meaningful development

in theme or technique. Yet *The Women and the Men* brought Giovanni further attention in the media, including pre-publication of three poems in *Mademoiselle* (September 1975). Jay S. Paul has called it "her richest collection of poems." The mid-seventies also produced another album, **"The Way I Feel,"** with accompanying music by Arif Mardin and liner notes by Roberta Flack.

In addition to Giovanni's growing concern with feminist themes, in the 1970s, she further explored her heritage as a black American. In *Gemini,* she writes of her father's journey from Ohio to Knoxville College as a journey to his "spiritual roots"—his grandfather had been a slave in eastern Tennessee—and also tells the story of how her maternal grandparents were forced to leave Georgia because her grandmother refused to submit to white domination. Another essay in the volume describes her own trip to Haiti in search of "sunshine and Black people"; feeling like a foreigner, she went on to Barbados, where she gained a deeper understanding of the sense of displacement of West Indian immigrants in American society, clearly analogous to the position of blacks who were brought to this country as slaves. In 1975, she traveled to Africa, where she spoke in several countries, including Ghana, Zambia, Tanzania, and Nigeria.

Giovanni continued to receive recognition in the mid-1970s, with, for example, honorary doctorates from the University of Maryland, Princess Anne Campus, Ripon University, and Smith College. Another honor was more controversial. According to Jeanne Noble, "Nikki's winning the Ladies' Home Journal Woman of the Year Award in 1974 meant to some young revolutionaries that she was joining forces with the very people she often considered foes. But, she does not shun confrontation or even violence if whites provoke it." In fact, Giovanni had for some time been more concerned with broader themes of identity and self-knowledge than with her earlier militancy, though she remained politically active. "While her poetry is full of Black pride," *African Woman* explains, "she transcends colour to deal with the challenge of being human."

Giovanni's next volume of poetry, *Cotton Candy on a Rainy Day* (1978), represents a definite, if not wholly positive, change. Paula Giddings's introduction emphasizes the development she sees in Giovanni and her work: "If Nikki, in her idealism, was a child of the sixties then now, in her realism, she is a woman of the seventies." She also notes, "*Cotton Candy* is the most introspective book to date, and the most plaintive." Alex Batman describes the distinctive features of this volume in a similar way: "One feels throughout that here is a child of the 1960s mourning the passing of a decade of conflict, of violence, but most of all, of hope. Such an attitude, of course, may lend itself too readily to sentimentality and chauvinism, but Giovanni is capable of countering the problems with a kind of hard matter-of-factness about the world that has passed away from her and the world she now faces."

Giddings further says of the **Cotton Candy** volume that it represents "the private moments: of coming to terms with oneself—of living with oneself. Taken in the context of Nikki's work it completes the circle: of dealing with society, others and finally oneself." Giddings's description of Giovanni's work may reveal why her development of new themes and techniques was slow. Perhaps she had to come to terms with herself, doing so to a certain degree through her poetry, before she could truly deal with others and with society. Indeed, her poetry is in many ways a mirror of the social consciousness of the 1960s, followed by the self-centeredness of the 1970s. Yet Giddings's comments do not predict what might follow such an inwardly focused collection, what one might expect from Giovanni's poetry in the 1980s. Anna T. Robinson, in a short monograph entitled *Nikki Giovanni: From Revolution to Revelation,* believes that **Cotton Candy** is "a pivotal work in Nikki Giovanni's career. It will mandate that she be evaluated as a poet rather than a voice for a cause."

The title of the volume **Cotton Candy on a Rainy Day** is ironic; the poems are not lighthearted or optimistic, as the positive connotations of cotton candy suggest. Giovanni's next volume has an ambiguous and perhaps also ironic title, **Those Who Ride the Night Winds** (1983). Having read **Cotton Candy on a Rainy Day,** one might anticipate a journey into the further gloom night can symbolize. However, the dedication indicates that night may offer possibilities not readily apparent: "This book is dedicated to the courage and fortitude of those who ride the night winds—who are the day trippers and midnight cowboys—who in sonic solitude or the hazy hell of habit know—that for all the devils and gods—for all the illnesses and drugs to cure them—Life is a marvelous, transitory adventure—and are determined to push us into the next century, galaxy—possibility." The form of the poems shows an interesting development in technique. Most are written in long verse paragraphs with abundant ellipsis marks, a stream-of-consciousness form that is not traditionally "poetic" but produces a sense of openness and forward movement with thematic significance.

The reasons behind the changes in Giovanni's poetry between the 1978 and 1983 volumes may well lie in her decision to move back to Lincoln Heights with her son and share her parents' home after her father suffered a stroke. Although she maintained an apartment in New York City, she devoted time, energy, and money to making a place for herself in Ohio again. She has more than once spoken of the difficulties she has encountered in this situation, not to complain, but simply to explain. For example, she said in 1981, "'No matter what the situation is or what the financial arrangements are, you are always their child. . . . If you're in your

parents' house or they're in yours, it's still a parent-child relationship.'" When her son was born, Giovanni apparently needed to assert her independence, but she had matured enough not to feel her sense of identity threatened by her family. Though she spoke of the need "to feel at home in order to write," she seems to have made the adjustment rapidly, for during that period, she published her third volume for children, new poems with the title *Vacation Time* (1980).

The poems in **Those Who Ride the Night Winds** transcend such categories as black/white, male/female, reality/fantasy. "In this book," Mozella G. Mitchell points out, "Giovanni has adopted a new and innovative form; and the poetry reflects her heightened self knowledge and imagination." A look down the table of contents reveals new kinds of subjects, with poems to Billie Jean King, John Lennon, and Robert F. Kennedy, as well as to Lorraine Hansberry, Martin Luther King, Jr., and Rosa Parks. Having once stated that she wrote primarily from personal or at least from racial experiences, Giovanni recently contradicted herself in the best Emersonian sense: "I resent people who say writers write from experience. Writers don't write from experience, though many are hesitant to admit that they don't. I want to be very clear about this. If you wrote from experience, you'd get maybe one book, maybe three poems. Writers write from empathy. . . . Writers write because they empathize with the general human condition." **Those Who Ride the Night Winds** is an impressive illustration of the effectiveness of that kind of empathy and the value of change. "'Only a fool doesn't change,'" Giovanni once commented. In the preface to this volume of poems, she alludes to both Lewis Carroll and the Beatles as she announces: "I changed . . . I chart the night winds . . . glide with me . . . I am the walrus . . . the time has come . . . to speak of many things. . . ." Having changed, Giovanni has reached maturity as a poet, with a volume that satisfies the reader, yet promises more complex and challenging poems in the future.

Giovanni has continued to receive recognition for her work in the 1980s in the academic world, with honorary doctorates from the College of Mount St. Joseph on-the-Ohio and Mount St. Mary College, and with teaching positions at Ohio State University, Mount St. Joseph, and Virginia Polytechnic Institute and State University. She also continues to reach the larger world outside the academy, as indicated by her being named to the Ohio Women's Hall of Fame and as the Outstanding Woman of Tennessee, both in 1985. She was chosen co-chairperson of the Literary Arts Festival for Homecoming '86 in Tennessee, the Duncanson Artist-in-Residence of the Taft Museum in Cincinnati in 1986, and a member of the Ohio Humanities Council in 1987.

Some of these honors and positions indicate that Nikki Giovanni has maintained close ties with the South of her birthplace, despite having lived more years away from the

South than in it. What the South as a place means to her is of considerable significance in looking at the body of her poetry. Like many writers of the Southern Literary Renaissance before her, Giovanni left the South after her graduation from college. Louis D. Rubin, Jr., speaking of earlier writers such as Allen Tate and Robert Penn Warren, has pointed out: "Almost all the young Southern writers at one time or another packed their suitcases and headed for the cities of the Northeast, toward the center of modernity, toward the new. Some turned around and came back to stay; others remained." These remarks apply to succeeding generations of Southern writers, such as William Styron and Ralph Ellison, and on to Alice Walker and Nikki Giovanni, who continue to be influenced by the South and their often ambivalent feelings toward it, even though they may have felt compelled to leave.

The ambivalence of black Southerners toward the region has been in the past compared to the way Jews might feel about Germany: "They love the South . . . for its beauty, its climate, its fecundity and its better ways of life; but they hate, with a bitter corroding hatred, the color prejudice, the discrimination, the violence, the crudities, the insults and humiliations, and the racial segregation of the South, and they hate all those who keep these evils alive." Though the South has changed, there has been much in Giovanni's lifetime to cause pain for the black Southerner. Still she has acknowledged the South as a symbolic home, commenting earthily: "I can deal with the South because I love it. And it's the love of someone who lived there, who was born there, who lost her cherry there and loved the land. . . ." In the opening essay of *Gemini,* Giovanni describes "going home" to speak in Knoxville, Tennessee, and looking for familiar places—Vine Street, the Gem Theatre, Mulvaney Street. "All of that is gone now," she realizes. Even so, after a tour of the city, "I was exhausted but feeling quite high from being once again in a place where no matter what I belong. And Knoxville belongs to me. I was born there in Old Knoxville General and I am buried there with Louvenia. . . . And I thought Tommy, my son, must know about this. He must know we come from somewhere. That we belong."

This theme of belonging has occurred in Giovanni's poetry since the beginning, in poems set in the South and in other places as well. The best of her poetry throughout her career has been concrete, with references to specific places, rooms, furniture, people, colors, qualities of light and dark. When she is abstract, her poetry is sometimes still successful in a political but not a critical sense. This kind of concreteness has been identified as one of the essential elements in Southern literature by Robert B. Heilman, in a seminal study entitled "The Southern Temper," where he distinguishes between what he terms "a sense of the concrete" and merely employing concrete images. The overriding importance of place in Southern literature has often been noted, for ex-

ample, by Frederick J. Hoffman, whose essay "The Sense of Place" is a landmark in the criticism of modern Southern poetry and fiction. Looking closely at the body of Giovanni's poetry, one finds places large and small, houses and continents, places she has lived in or traveled to, places important in the history of black people, places from the past and in the present, metaphorical places, places of fantasy, symbolic places. To emphasize this sense of place in her work is to see it, along with the best literature of the South, not as provincial but as universal.

While Giovanni has received more attention first for her militant poems on racial themes and later for her feminist writing, the poems that will finally determine her position in the canon of American poetry are, almost without exception, ones in which place functions not only as a vehicle, but also as a theme. In her most recent work, her themes are becoming increasingly complex, reflecting her maturity as a woman and as a writer. Traditionally in Southern writing, place has been associated with themes of the past and the family; these themes are seen in Giovanni's poems of the late 1960s and the early 1970s, with the added dimension of a desire to understand the faraway places from which black slaves were brought to the American South. Her later poetry reflects a changing consciousness of her role in society as a single woman, the need to adjust her concept of home and family and of the importance of smaller places, such as houses and rooms, to fit her own life, a life that many American women and men, black and white, can identify with. In her best poems, places grow into themes that convey the universal situation of modern humanity, a sense of placelessness and a need for security.

In her first collection of poems, Giovanni expresses themes anticipated by the title *Black Feeling, Black Talk.* But already she demonstrates occasionally her gift for the original, individual image, for example, as she evokes the days and places of childhood in **"Poem (For BMC No. 2)"**:

> There were fields where once we walked
> Among the clover and crab grass and those
> Funny little things that look like cotton candy
>
> There were liquids expanding and contracting
> In which we swam with amoebas and other Afro-
> Americans

This poem is a striking contrast to the best-known poem from this volume, **"The True Import of Present Dialogue, Black vs. Negro (For Peppe, Who Will Ultimately Judge Our Efforts),"** with its repetition of the lines "Nigger / Can you kill." Like **"Nikki-Rosa"** and **"Knoxville, Tennessee"** from her next volume, **"Poem (For BMC No. 2)"** recalls a time and place that endure in memory, even in the face of violence and hatred.

One of Giovanni's finest poems is set in this homeland of the past. **"Knoxville, Tennessee,"** written at the height of the unrest of the civil rights movement of the 1960s, develops a theme of security, of belonging, through simple yet highly effective images of nature, of family, of religion. Although it is almost imagistic, it builds to an explicit thematic statement:

> I always like summer
> best
> you can eat fresh corn
> from daddy's garden
> and okra
> and greens
> and cabbage
> and lots of
> barbecue
> . . . .
> and be warm
> all the time
> not only when you go to bed
> and sleep

The simple diction, the soothing alliteration, the short lines to emphasize each word, all create a feeling of love for this place and these people that transcends topical issues.

Giovanni later wrote a prose description of Christmas in Knoxville using images of winter rather than summer, yet conveying the same feeling of warmth: "Christmas in Knoxville was the smell of turnip greens and fatback, perfume blending with good Kentucky bourbon, cigars and cigarettes, bread rising on the new electric stove, the inexplicable smell of meat hanging in the smokehouse (though we owned no smokehouse), and, somehow, the sweet taste of tasteless snow." As Roger Whitlow notes, though, this kind of warmth is "rare" in Giovanni's early work. Still, Giovanni's use of this Southern place from her past speaks to the same aspects of Southern life as poems by James Dickey or prose by Eudora Welty.

Most of the poems in *Black Judgement* are militant in subject and theme; one of the most effective is **"Adulthood (For Claudia),"** in which Giovanni catalogs the violence of the decade, the deaths of leaders from Patrice Lumumba to John F. Kennedy to Martin Luther King, Jr., and of lesser-known civil rights workers such as Viola Liuzzo. In another poem from this volume, **"For Saundra,"** Giovanni seems to explain why poems of political rhetoric dominate her first two volumes. The persona speaks of the difficulty of composing poems in revolutionary times; for example,

> so i thought
> i'll write a beautiful green tree poem
> peeked from my window

> to check the image
> noticed the schoolyard was covered
> with asphalt
> no green—no trees grow
> in manhattan

She concludes that "perhaps these are not poetic / times / at all." Although the thrust of the poem is toward the civil rights strife of the late 1960s, the reader also senses something of the alienation and displacement of a Southerner in the urban North.

Giovanni uses the South and its people to develop the specific theme of the past in **"Alabama Poem"** from her next collection, *Re:Creation.* A student at Tuskegee Institute meets an old black man and then an old black woman whose remarks indicate that knowledge must be gained through experience, must be inherited from the past. The persona speculates in conclusion: "if trees would talk / wonder what they'd tell me." Her words do not seem ironic; rather she seems to have learned a valuable lesson in her walk along this Southern country road. Though the images in this poem are sparse, the rural place and its people are seen to be of vital significance to one who seeks knowledge. The theme of the necessity of learning from the past what one needs to live in the present links this poem by Nikki Giovanni to a rich tradition in Southern writing, especially from the Fugitive poets of the 1920s to the present.

A more challenging use of the concreteness of place and the thematic significance of the past can be seen in the complex, ironic poem **"Walking Down Park,"** also from *Re:Creation.* Speculating about the history of New York City, the speaker wonders what a street such as Park Avenue looked like "before it was an avenue," "what grass was like before / they rolled it / into a ball and called / it central park." She even thinks:

> ever look south
> on a clear day and not see
> time's squares but see
> tall birch trees with sycamores
> touching hands

Questioning why men destroy their environment, she returns to days of the past, musing, "probably so we would forget / the Iroquois, Algonquin / and Mohicans who could caress / the earth." Possibly this relationship with nature, which characterized the Indians of an earlier time, can be recaptured:

> ever think what Harlem would be
> like if our herbs and roots and elephant cars
> grew sending
> a cacophony of sound to us

Here through a complex set of images Giovanni connects the situation of blacks in contemporary America with the past of the American Indian, another oppressed minority group, as well as with their African heritage. **"Walking Down Park"** thus becomes a statement of a longing for happiness, related in the mind of the speaker not only to life in the past, which allowed for a closeness to nature lost in contemporary urban life, but also to a specific place from the past—Africa.

One of the most important examples of the ways Giovanni employs places in her poetry is her use of houses, both literal and metaphorical, from the past and in the present. In **"Housecleaning,"** another poem from *Re:Creation,* the persona speaks first of her pleasure in ordinary chores essential to maintaining a house, then turns tidying up into a metaphor to describe aptly the chores necessary in human relationships as well. The growing sense of independence and identity in this poem anticipates the major themes of Giovanni's next volume, *My House.*

At this point, in the early 1970s, Giovanni is still using the lowercase "i," which R. Roderick Palmer identifies as a common device in revolutionary poetry, more then the uppercase. Perhaps she intends to symbolize the concept she has often invoked, that one retains qualities of childhood, even when striving for maturity. She uses this device in a poem from *My House* set, as is **"Knoxville, Tennessee,"** in a place that now exists only in memory. In **"Mothers,"** Giovanni depicts a woman remembering her mother sitting in a kitchen at night:

> she was sitting on a chair
> the room was bathed in moonlight diffused
>   through
> those thousands of panes landlords who rented
> to people with children were prone to put in
>   windows

Recalling a poem her mother taught her on this particular night, the persona determines to teach the same poem to her son, to establish with him the relationship she had with her mother. This relationship is re-created for the reader in the simple description of a place remembered, especially in the quality of light Giovanni uses as the central image of the poem.

In the title poem, Giovanni uses homes and houses to represent the movement toward maturity, symbolized by the movement away from the places, homes, of one's childhood toward establishing a home for oneself, or an identity as a mature person. Like Giovanni's poems about childhood, **"My House"** is characterized by images of warmth and security, emphasizing that in her house the speaker is in complete control:

> i mean it's my house
> and i want to fry pork chops
> and bake sweet potatoes
> and call them yams
> cause i run the kitchen
> and i can stand the heat
>
> . . . .
>
> and my windows might be dirty
> but it's my house
> and if i can't see out sometimes
> they can't see   in either

As Suzanne Juhasz emphasizes, the woman speaker "orders experience and controls it. . . . She controls not only through need and desire, but through strength, ability. . . . In contrast to the child persona of **"Knoxville, Tennessee,"** the "i" here has discovered that she is an autonomous being who can shape at least the smaller places of her world to suit her own needs and desires; at the same time, the "i" is willing to take responsibility for her actions, to pay the price for such control.

In this context, the title poem of the volume *My House* takes on a deeper level of meaning. In fact, Erlene Stetson has identified the house as a dominant symbol in poetry by women, especially black women, explaining: "The house represents the historic quest by black women for homes of their own—apart from the house of slavery, the common house of bondage, the house of the patriarchy. The house embodies women's search for place and belonging and for a whole and complete identity. . . . In addition, the house is a symbol for place—heaven, haven, home, the heart, women's estate, the earthly tenement, the hearth—and for region—Africa, the West Indies, America, Asia, the North, and the South." Stetson does not emphasize, as she might, that this use of place as symbol is particularly significant in the tradition of Southern literature to which Nikki Giovanni and a number of other black women poets belong.

Many of Giovanni's poems are set, as I have mentioned, in Africa. For Giovanni, as for black Southerners and other black Americans in the twentieth century, the significance of this place lies mostly in the past—a past with which each individual must come to terms. Like other Southern writers in the period since World War I, Giovanni recognizes that no one can live in the past or relive the past, yet there is no meaningful life in the present or the future without an understanding of, often involving a confrontation with, the past. In a three-poem sequence in *My House,* she creates powerful images of the displacement of a people who in their racial past were forced to leave their homeland involuntarily.

The first poem in the group, **"Africa I,"** describes a plane journey to Africa. During the flight, the speaker dreams of seeing a lion from the plane but is jarred by the statement of a companion that "there are no lions / in this part of africa." Her response is quick: "it's my dream dammit." The poem closes at the journey's end, with the following thoughts:

> we landed in accra and the people
> clapped and i almost cried wake up
> we're home
> and something in me said shout
> and something else said quietly
> your mother may be glad to see you
> but she may also remember why
> you went away

Seeing Africa as a woman, a mother, as she did in the fantasy poem **"Ego-Tripping,"** Giovanni movingly illustrates how the significance of this place relates to the past of these tourists, visitors, just as the significance of an adult's mother usually lies more in the past than in the present. In one's personal past as well as in one's racial past may exist harsh memories difficult to confront. Yet coming to terms with the past is necessary in order to grow and mature, as an individual or as a people.

"They Clapped," the third poem in this sequence, demonstrates even more explicitly that the dream of Africa and the reality, the past and the present, are not the same. The black American tourists clap because they are so happy to be landing in "the mother land"; then they see the realities of poverty and disease, as well as of their own foreignness. As they leave to return to America, they appear to have come to terms with the past in a way that frees them for their lives now and later. Giovanni uses the metaphor of possession, a subtle allusion to the horrors of slavery in the past, to convey the theme of displacement:

> they brought out their cameras and bought out
>   africa's drums
> when they finally realized they are strangers all
>   over
> and love is only and always about the lover not the
>   beloved
> they marveled at the beauty of the people and the
>   richness
> of the land knowing they could never possess
>   either
>
> they clapped when they took off
> for home despite the dead
> dream they saw a free future

So the physical confrontation with this place serves to make these tourists aware of their historical past as past rather than

as present or future. They have learned too that, as modern men and women, they are "strangers all over," that in a very important sense they do not belong anywhere except in the place they must create for themselves as individuals. Thus Giovanni reminds the reader that the visitors to Africa are returning home, to America.

Many of the best poems in Giovanni's next volume, *The Women and the Men,* such as **"Ego-Tripping"** and **"Walking Down Park,"** originally appeared in *Re:Creation.* The new African poems, including **"Africa"** and **"Swaziland,"** are less successful than the Africa sequence in *My House* because they depend more on abstract diction than concrete images to convey themes. Yet one new symbolic poem, **"Night,"** uses complex metaphorical language to contrast New York City with Africa and the Caribbean. The latter are both portrayed as places where the night is strong, natural, black:

> in africa night walks
> into day as quickly
> as a moth is extinguished
> by its desire for flame
>
> the clouds in the caribbean carry
> night like a young man
> with a proud erection dripping
> black dots across the blue sky
> the wind a mistress of the sun howls
> her displeasure at the involuntary
> fertilization

In contrast, the night in New York is seen to be unnaturally white, with humans being unable to adjust to their environment:

> but nights are white
> in new york
> the shrouds of displeasure
> mask our fear of facing
> ourselves between the lonely
> sheets

Again Giovanni contrasts the natural environment of the warm Southern country and continent with the literal and metaphorical cold of the urbanized northeastern United States, dominated by white culture. The images of masking and of death suggest that no one, black or white, can live a meaningful life in a place like New York. However, the negative images in the earlier sections of the poem—death, rape—reveal the generally grim situation for modern man or woman in Africa, in the Caribbean, anywhere.

The volume *Cotton Candy on a Rainy Day* contains mostly poems relying on images of placelessness or homelessness rather than security, or dominated by ideas rather than strong central images. The title poem sets a fairly pessimistic tone for the volume yet hints at what may follow in Nikki Giovanni's career. Characterizing the seventies as a decade of loneliness, Giovanni uses the image of cotton candy poignantly:

> But since it is life   it is
> > Cotton Candy
> > on a rainy day
> The sweet soft essence
> > of possibility
> Never quite maturing

Though she speaks of a lack of maturity, in this poem Giovanni uses an uppercase "I" to define the speaker, acknowledging perhaps unconsciously a certain kind of maturity that seems to have been missing in earlier poems such as **"My House,"** regardless of their bravado.

At any rate, the speaker is characterized as a lonely, placeless person, yet one who can write a prescription to improve her own condition:

> Everything   some say   will change
> I need a change
> > of pace   face   attitude and life
> Though I long for my loneliness
> I know I need something
> Or someone
> Or . . . . . .

Perhaps acknowledging the desire to succumb to loneliness, to the temptations of the solitary life, allowed Giovanni herself to move forward, to change in a way that profoundly affected her poetic subject matter and technique.

This sense of placelessness is perhaps seen most clearly in an urban poem different from those in Giovanni's earlier volumes. **"The New Yorkers"** focuses on the so-called bag people, "night people" who seem to "evaporate during the light of day," others who are seen during the day but appear to have nowhere to go at night. Of these placeless people, she comments:

> How odd to also see the people
> of New York City living
> in the doorways of public buildings
> as if this is an emerging nation
> though of course it is

In addition to its commentary on American society in the 1970s, the poem provides a commentary on the persona's shaky self-image, as "an old blind Black woman" says on hearing her voice, "You that Eyetalian poet ain't you? I know

yo voice. I seen you on television." Yet the old woman feels the poet's hair and determines that she is truly black; symbolically, her identity is intact.

Among the innovations in *Those Who Ride the Night Winds* is a different sense of place, a sense of space, of openness, as well as a concern with "inner" rather than "outer" space, both striking contrasts with earlier uses of place in Giovanni's work. For example, in **"This Is Not for John Lennon (And This Is Not a Poem),"** the speaker implores:

> . . . Don't cry for John Lennon cry for ourselves . . .
> He was an astronaut of inner space . . . He cel-
> ebrated happiness . . . soothed the lonely . . . braced
> the weary . . . gave word to the deaf . . . vision to
> the insensitive . . . sang a long low note when he
> reached the edge of this universe and saw the Black-
> ness . . .

This view of John Lennon leads to the conclusion that "those who ride the night winds do learn to love the stars . . . even while crying in the darkness. . . ." In other words, only those who travel far enough, metaphorically, to confront the harshness of reality are able to transcend it, as Lennon did.

An extreme example of this philosophy is seen in **"Flying Underground."** Dedicated to the children of Atlanta who died in the mass murders of the early 1980s, the poem develops the idea that in death these innocent children "can make the earth move . . . flying underground. . . ." Giovanni thus takes the entrapment of the place "underground"—literally, the grave—and transforms it into a sense of freedom and possibility. The reader is reminded of the old slave's cry so often invoked by Martin Luther King, "Free at last," a phrase Giovanni used with effective irony in a poem on his death, published in *Black Judgement.*

The concluding poem in *Those Who Ride the Night Winds,* **"A Song for New-Ark,"** is an appropriate end to an impressive volume. Giovanni characterizes the city of Newark, New Jersey, where she once lived, in predominantly negative terms, stressing, as she did in the earlier poem **"Walking Down Park,"** the destruction of nature to create this urban environment: "I never saw old/jersey . . . or old/ark . . . Old/ark was a forest . . . felled for concrete . . . and asphalt . . . and bridges to Manhattan. . . ." After drawing analogies between city dwellers and the rats that plague them, the poet-persona closes:

> When I write I want to write . . . in rhythm . . . regu-
> larizing the moontides . . . to the heart/beats . . . of
> the twinkling stars . . . sending an S.O.S. . . . to day
> trippers . . . urging them to turn back . . . toward the
> Darkness . . . to ride the night winds . . . to tomor-
> row . . .

She moves from the confinement of a physical, earthly place to the openness and freedom of outer space and places of fantasy.

> **[For Giovanni], place is more than an image, more than a surface used to develop a narrative or a theme. . . .**
> —*Martha Cook*

In addition to this new sense of place, Giovanni displays a new sense of herself as a poet in *Those Who Ride the Night Winds.* In **"A Song for New-Ark"** and also in **"I Am She,"** Giovanni seems confident of the role she has chosen for herself, secure in her place in society. As she says in the latter poem, "I am she . . . who writes . . . the poems. . . ." Again the ellipses give the sense of openness, of more to come from this poetic talent. While the poems in this volume seem to reflect Giovanni's own feeling that she has reached maturity as a poet, there are still indications of the necessity of coping with the demands of modern life. She acknowledges the presence of loneliness, not as she did through the poems in the volume *Cotton Candy on a Rainy Day,* where loneliness seemed to be a problem for which she could at the time see no solution, but in a way that indicates the strength of her inner resources. In the poem **"The Room with the Tapestry Rug,"** she creates a persona who confronts loneliness by seeking out "the room . . . where all who lived . . . knew her well. . . ." The room holds memories of the past, symbolized by a garment created by a member of her family who was important in her childhood, used in a literal and metaphorical way to keep out the cold.

But Giovanni moves beyond this fairly traditional symbol, refusing to let the room be only a place of confinement and protection from the larger world; it becomes a place where she can also find comfort in the cool air from outside, while luxuriating in the security of her own space:

> If it was cold . . . she would wrap herself . . . in the natted blue sweater . . . knitted by a grandmother . . . so many years ago . . . If warm . . . the windows were opened . . . to allow the wind . . . to partake of their pleasure . . .

The closing paragraph of the poem indicates the resources of the persona beyond her memories of the past: "Her books . . . her secret life . . . in the room with the tapestry rug. . . ." Here she shows not only the need for but the fact of control over the places in her own life.

In the 1970s, such poems as **"My House"** conveyed an important theme of the development of a strengthening identity as a single woman; in the 1980s, such poems as **"The Room with the Tapestry Rug"** and **"I Am She"** illustrate not only the strength but also the depth and range of that identity. It is appropriate that a volume that so strongly exhibits Giovanni's talents as a writer should also attest to the importance of literature and art in her life, an importance reflected as well in her continued involvement in efforts to bring people and the arts together.

These examples from Nikki Giovanni's poetry—and her prose as well—demonstrate that, for her, place is more than an image, more than a surface used to develop a narrative or a theme, just as place functions in the best poetry of the Southern tradition lying behind her work. Further, the changing sense of place in these poems can be seen to reveal Giovanni's developing sense of herself as a woman and as a poet. Suzanne Juhasz, Anna T. Robinson, and Erlene Stetson all emphasize in their recent critical discussions the growing feminist consciousness they find in Giovanni's work. Her use of place is broader than simply a feminist symbol, though, just as her poetry has developed beyond purely racial themes. The relationships of people to places and the ways people have responded to and tried to control places are important themes for Giovanni, as are the ways places sometimes control people. Greatest in thematic significance are the need to belong to a place or in a place and the necessity of moving beyond physical places to spiritual or metaphysical ones.

Looking at Giovanni's poetry in the context of Southern literature expands rather than limits the possibilities for interpretation and analysis. In fact, this approach reveals that within the body of her work lies a solid core of poems that do not rely on political or personal situations for their success. Rather, they develop universal themes, such as coming to terms with the past and with the present so that one may move into the future—again, themes that have been and continue to be of particular significance in Southern poetry. These themes mark her work as a contribution to the canon not just of Southern poetry, of black poetry, of feminist poetry, but also of contemporary American poetry. However, Giovanni's response to any generalization, any categorization, would probably echo the closing line of her poem **"Categories,"** from *My House.* Emphasizing her uniqueness as an individual, she might well proclaim, "i'm bored with categories."

Phyllis Crockett (review date 13 February 1994)

SOURCE: "A Free Spirit of the '60s," in *Washington Post Book World,* February 13, 1994, pp. 4-5.

[*In the following review of* Racism 101, *Crockett argues that*

Giovanni accurately reflects African-American views on race.]

Poet Nikki Giovanni is caught up in the past and the future at the same time. In *Racism 101,* her latest collection of largely autobiographical essays, she describes herself as a '60s woman and a Star Trek fanatic. These two obsessions are like highway markers on her life's path, pointing the way to where she's been and where she's headed. Giovanni first captured the nation's attention as one of the most powerful voices in the black culture movement of the 1960s. Her work, then as now, is all about perspective—first as a black, next as a woman, then as an American, but ultimately as a human being in a complex universe.

Talking about Shakespeare in **"I Plant Geraniums,"** she reflects: "Shouldn't we hold him to the same standards as the Constitution and Bible and bring him 'up to date'? I think not. I think we should leave him in the brilliance of his expression. We need, we modern artists and critics, to do exactly what Shakespeare did. Write for now. Think for now."

Before the '60s, most African Americans simply accepted our invisibility as a fact of life. During the '60s, voices like Giovanni's helped blacks and whites understand black contributions to the world. This was a new and an important revelation to the masses of blacks, and we took it personally in a way most whites could not. Virtually every black person in the U.S. who is old enough to remember the '60s, no matter where they hail from in the diaspora—the U.S., the Caribbean, Africa—fondly reminisces about those times.

Giovanni captures that spirit in *Racism 101.* Many whites may remember those days in negative terms—turmoil, civil unrest, deaths. While all that is true, many if not most blacks recall those days as a time when we did what we had to do to make America live up to its promises. "You must do, say and write that which you believe to be true," Giovanni notes. "What others think can be of no significance."

In *Racism 101,* Giovanni is teaching history. She reminds us that Rosa Parks; the catalyst in the Montgomery bus boycott that launched Dr. Martin Luther King Jr.'s civil rights career and the modern-day protest movement, "was not just a little old lady with tired feet. She was a moving force in the Montgomery NAACP." Giovanni recounts the authentic horror story of Emmett Till's death—the black boy from Chicago brutally lynched by whites in Mississippi. His mother insisted on an open casket, saying "I want the world to see what they did to my boy. . . . And the world was ashamed."

Giovanni bemoans black conservatives like Thomas Sowell, Shelby Steele and Clarence Thomas who've criticized affirmative action. "Clarence is against affirmative action? Shelby is against affirmative action? Since when? Since the

people fought so that neither of these men would have to die for their choice of wives? So that Yale would admit a poor boy from Pin Point, Georgia? When did affirmative action become an insult? Shortly after you were granted tenure at your university? You don't like being made to feel you can't honestly do your job because affirmative action made someone hire you? There is a solution. Quit."

Giovanni says she laughs at the critics who say she is bitter and full of hate. She responds, "Nothing could be further from the truth. I am not envious or jealous either. I am just me . . . I do not measure my soul by the tape of the white world."

In various essays she delivers a message to African-American collegians, explores campus racism, and talks about her struggle for tenure. "Why did I agree to fight against those who so glibly dismissed my achievements—to whom my 16 books, my honors and awards, my 20 years in public life, simply didn't count? . . . Had I had the meager credentials that some of my tenured colleagues have, I would have been turned down . . . The biggest stumbling block to progress in America is still racism." Giovanni writes what most blacks know: Despite white denials to the contrary (after all, how would they know?), if you are black in America, no matter your economic standing, it's virtually impossible not to deal with racism at some point even in the 1990s.

Giovanni reminds us that as a people, we haven't reached our destination of equal opportunity. Here she's at her best, describing the achievements of the first black woman astronaut, Mae Carol Jemuson, or searching for answers to better understand lost youth. She is less convincing when she lambastes Spike Lee and gives him specific directions for rewriting his movie "X."

For an accomplished writer who celebrated her 50th birthday last year, Giovanni sometimes comes across as incredibly insecure. This is the same woman who gave us the signature poem **"Ego Tripping"**? But perhaps we're all entitled to our insecurities. She muses about why she has not yet received a "major" poetry award, and in one essay she continues, "I plant geraniums. No one will remember that. I have an allergy to tomato fuzz. No one will care. I write poetry and sometimes prose. No one will know me . . ." Surely that will never be true. We lovers of words and black culture will keep Nikki Giovanni alive and see that she gets her wish to have her work become required reading in colleges—and that she even becomes a question on "Jeopardy."

Effie J. Boldridge (essay date Spring 1995)

SOURCE: "Windmills or Giants? The Quixotic Motif and

Vision in the Poetry of Nikki Giovanni," in *The Griot,* Vol. 14, No. 1, Spring, 1995, pp. 18-25.

[*In the following essay, Boldridge explores the relation between Miguel de Cervantes's character Don Quixote and Giovanni's world view.*]

Of the generation of black poets that emerged in the volatile sixties, as Paula Giddings notes, Nikki Giovanni is among that select group "whose career has defied the odds." Certainly, her writing has been the subject of ongoing, extensive critical commentary. Among the many topics noted in this body of work, the kinship between Nikki Giovanni and Don Quixote, the legendary protagonist of Miguel de Cervantes' remarkable baroque novel, has been alluded to by a few scholars. In the "Introduction" to *Gemini* (1971), Barbara Cosby makes reference to a certain relation between the contemporary poet and the immortal knight when she describes Giovanni as ". . . the most sensitive, slowest to anger, most quixotic . . ." woman she knows. Publisher and editor Ida Lewis submits that the highly independent writer, as the self-reliant Don Quixote does, trusts her own sensibilities to define her reality. She maintains that in the frequently cited lines from the poem **"nikki-rosa":** ". . . I really hope no white person ever has cause / to write about me / . . . they'll probably / talk about my hard childhood / and never understand that / all the while I was quite happy", Nikki Giovanni makes a "quixotic judgment" as to the quality of her formative years, disavowing any external interpretation. Apart from these references to a likeness between Miguel de Cervantes' mythical main character and the prominent poet, Giovanni's own remarks about the master work and its renown literary persona are noteworthy:

> It is a big, clumsily written book about a dude fighting windmills for the love of some chick who didn't dig him . . . It deals with chivalry and knighthood and stuff. In other words, it describes the standards of a lifestyle that no western man could afford to live.

Despite Giovanni's apparent dismissal of the novel as little more than a farcical work and even though the relationship between the modern poet and Cervantes, who articulates his personal philosophy via his extraordinary fictional character, has only been touched on, it is a connection that, as this paper intends to show, undoubtedly deserves more attention than it has been given.

A good starting point for exploring what the baroque novelist and the contemporary poet have in common is the windmill episode that Giovanni mentions in her commentary on *Don Quixote.* Of the many ventures of the knight, this incident in which he "engages in righteous warfare" with what he believes are "thirty or more lawless giants", the problem

of the nature of reality is still very much alive. Like other major writers, Giovanni addresses this issue in her work. A brief consideration of the poet's definition of reality illustrates that her notion mirrors Cervantes' definition, one of several affinities between the two writers.

According to the respected critic Samuel Putnam, ". . . the basis of Cervantes' art is an essential realism based on verisimilitude and the imitation of nature" . . . "the truth that our senses give us. . . ." The seventeenth century novelist's concept of "an essential realism", as Putnam defines it, is clearly acknowledged by Giovanni in various poems. In **"Nothing Makes Sense",** in a baroque fashion play on words and theory, she comes to terms with Cervantes' "truth behind the show of things", submitting that:

> the outline of a face on a picture isn't really a face or an image of a face but the idea of an image of a dream that once was dreamed by some artist who never knew how much more real is a dream than reality.

"The imitation of nature" and "the truth that our senses give us" that the humanist novelist ascertains is the primary state the poet apprehends in **"Revolutionary Dreams"** when she "dreams of being a natural / women doing what a women / does when she's natural. . ."

Not only do Giovanni and Cervantes discern a natural order, a genuine state of being based on changeless truths, they both see man as deeply alienated from his harmonious condition in a ravaged world. The starkly realistic view of their societies and times that they share is an important component of their correspondence as a look at their perception of their eras reveals. Cervantes' treatment of the Spanish national character at the time he conceived Don Quixote is unmistakably human and socially incisive. Historically, the Spain that gave rise to Cervantes' works was the Spain of Phillip II, the Counter Reformation, a political and military disaster. As deputy purveyor for the Spanish Armada, Cervantes toured the country seeking provisions for the Spanish fleet. From a wide range of novelistic experiences, he acquired firsthand knowledge of his compatriots and their circumstances. Consequently, his understanding of human nature deepened, inspiring his successful depiction of flesh-and-blood characters.

Giovanni's keen observation of modern man and society is no less sensitive and informed than Cervantes' insightful view of his fellow countrymen and epoch. In her poetry and prose, she lays bare the oppressive conditions of contemporary existence. Indeed, her delineation of the ills of the life today is unquestionably sobering. The present-day human experience, as she sees it, is overwhelmingly solitary.

If loneliness were a grape/she observes, "the wine would be vintage." Earmarking the adverse effect that the welfare system has on self-esteem, she stresses that "Institutions still haven't found a way to give service and to leave the ego intact."

In today's dehumanizing social climate, the solicitous writer points out that "the most gentle of the species are pruned," "the imagination of children is stifled," and ". . . people speak more personally of their dogs or cats than they do of their children." Since there is little regard for human life in modern civilization, she further notes that, ". . . we kill each other at a very high rate." In the final analysis, the poet concludes that we live in a world where: "Nothing is easy; nothing is sacred."

Even though Cervantes and Giovanni are deeply troubled by the crises of their times, the outlook of both writers is essentially positive. Although Giovanni scoffingly refers to the lofty standards of the knight of La Mancha as "a lifestyle that no western man could afford to live," she holds that man can live nobly and effect a better world. Undergirding the optimism of the novelist and the poet is their abiding faith in the natural goodness of man. Though highly conscious of humankind's spiritual impoverishment, at the same time they firmly believe that man can redeem himself and his world if he fully commits himself to that enterprise. The relationship between Cervantes and Giovanni undoubtedly broadens when their common attitude regarding personal engagement, as disclosed in the course of their texts, is explored.

That Cervantes subscribes to the concept that every man, as a part of the human race, should take part in shaping a world built on large and noble lines, resonates throughout his great work. The matter of individual obligation is, however, patently addressed in a conversation that ensues between the Knight of the Sorrowful Countenance and his niece. After one of the Knight's misadventures, his concerned niece affords him the option of accepting things as they are, the status-quo:

> But tell me, uncle, who is responsible for your being involved in these quarrels?" she questions the frail Quixote, then rhetorically asks, "Would it not be better to remain peacefully here at home and not go roaming through the world in search of better bread than is made from wheat, without taking into consideration than many who go for wool come back shorn."

The apprehensive woman's dissuasive words, as is true of similar advice from the level-headed Bachelor Carrasco and the well-meaning curate, go unheeded. The commanding knight remains firm in his resolve to realize a poetic world.

That Giovanni likewise maintains that sincere concern about the ignoble condition of man in a debased world must be translated into revolutionary action, as with Cervantes' masterpiece, permeates her work. Pointedly, where she stands concerning each man's accountability to himself, his fellow man and his world is voiced in the poem **"Charles White."** In the grown-up world she posits, ". . . we are all in some measure responsible / for the life we live and the world / we live in." Emerging from the unconventional poet's compelling sense of obligation to human kind and society are protestations of the causes of the crises of modern life. In as much as protest is an exemplary theme in *Don Quixote,* it is another link between the two writers that appropriately deserves consideration.

As regards Cervantes' protest stance, the iconoclastic writer, by means of his ingenious knight, passes sentence on all that constricts man's courage, aspirations and vision. The windmills that Don Quixote is convinced are giants, the inns that he believes to be castles, and the flocks of sheep that he thinks are armies are all telling episodes that illustrate Cervantes' disdain for the unimaginative. Adhering to this point of view, it is not surprising that the enlightened novelist attacks ideologies, conventions and distortions that undermine man's creativity, dignity, and spirituality.

Giovanni's indictment of all that diminishes human potential and compassion is no less zealous than Cervantes'. Her "maverick attitude" and "a confessed fallibility in the face of humorless ideological dictates" has been addressed extensively. In a number of her poems, such as **"Categories"**, she challenges the unnatural restrictions imposed by an inflexible social system. Overall, to sum up Giovanni's relentless opposition to oppressive imperatives, it can be said that the assertive poet takes to task all the forces that sustain a reality where "everything controlling can be justified: everything liberating denied." Similarly, from the Golden Age novelist's and the twentieth century poet's remonstrations emerge some critical questions about life and its meaning, issues that, upon examination, shed further light on the writers' relationship.

In his great social novel, Cervantes asks questions that are still very much alive today. How should man live? Where will he find his true greatness? Can man fashion a world that will serve his soul's needs? Giovanni comes to terms with some comparable matters of importance in her writing as exemplified in *Poetic Equations.* In her candid conversation with Margaret Walker, she contends that "What makes a person, what makes a man and what makes a woman" are definitions that subvert the full expression of individuals. Moreover, "in order to be a fulfilled person," she maintains that one "must do what is necessary regardless of predetermined roles." Notably, in the aforesaid dialogue, she concludes that ultimately, the only true question is "How shall we live?"

The questions that Cervantes and Giovanni raise and unresolved controversies that, as both assert, confuse, hamper, and desensitize men. Yet, as caring and committed artists, as might be expected, they do not limit themselves to a grim discourse on the moral horror of their realities and the desolation of humankind. To the contrary, Cervantes, through his romantic character, and the spirited poet accord man a pathway to the fulfillment of his true self and the actualization of a society that does not abort his dreams or as Giovanni sums it up, a world "where all are endowed with the inviolate right . . . to perceive the limitlessness of their possibilities unencumbered. . . ." In a like manner, Cervantes and Giovanni uncompromisingly maintain that pursuing a life centered in love is the only means for man to redress his fallen nature and rediscover his human self. Of the many parallels between the two writers, nowhere is their conformity clearer than in their shared belief in love as the antidote against the problems that plague and demoralize the human species.

Cervantes' notion of the transformational force of love, is manifest in his tenderhearted knight's adoration of his lady, Dulcinea del Tobosco. Much attention has been given to Don Quixote's "heart interest" who is primarily intended to be "a glorification of love, as the only means of knowing we are alive . . . the very image of love, of love that is our reason for being." The bleakness of life without love is articulated early in the narrative by Don Quixote himself who dramatically points out that "a knight errant without a lady is like a tree without leaves or fruit / a body without a soul." During the course of his often foiled but well intended, exploits, the fearless knight frequently invokes the name of the "lady of his fancies." To prove himself worthy of her, he persists in his grand mission to restore a world of chivalry.

That the human capacity to love is the wellspring of a meaningful, benevolent life experience is a leitmotif in Giovanni's body of work. After pinpointing, "How shall we live" as the primary dilemma of contemporary existence, the apprehensive poet mindfully added that "if there was a corollary to that question, it was: And will there be love?" In the poem, **"Love: Is a Human Condition"**, as Quixote pays tribute to his lady who is the inspiration for his exalted endeavors, Giovanni celebrates love "as the only true adventure." In **"Statement of Conservation"**, she echoes the Knight of the Sorrowful Countenance's faith in the power of love to prevail in face of the most adverse circumstances. Assuredly, she explains why she is not disquieted by the flux and uncertainties of modern times. "I don't mind the cold or heat / and I've got a reason / Love when it's spread all around / can tackle any season".

To embrace love, and kindled and empowered by it, to set out on a venture to uplift man and society is not a charge that Cervantes' hero nor the activist poet see solely as a matter of personal duty. In fact, both hold that every man can attempt to live a life grounded in love and work towards the betterment of the human race. Spain's greatest Golden Age prose writer as well as the distinguished Afro-American poet invoke others to undertake the romantic enterprise of restoring order, meaning, and beauty to a world that has lost these resources. Looking at who are the visionaries that Cervantes and Giovanni acknowledge and their significance contributes to a fuller appreciation of the correlation between the two authors.

> **As to the fundamental character of black people, Giovanni unwaveringly insists that they are vital human beings enriched by a creative disposition, "a spiritual, emotional nature reaching back to their African roots."**
> *—Effie J. Boldridge*

In response to his niece's admonition regarding the perils of his nobly aimed adventures, the unassailable Don Quixote simply tells her that the world needs more knight-errants. The resourceful gentleman of La Mancha does indeed convince one man to share his dream and join him in his quest of opportunities to redress "all manner of wrongs". Although the peasant man, Sancho Panza, who sallies forth with him agrees to do so solely for material reasons: riches, fame, and the promise of the governorship of an island, in the course of his master's foolhardy escapades, he becomes an idealist. His transformation, which Salvador de Madariaga calls quixotification of Sancho, is manifest when he, as Don Quixote does, begins to see "things as they should be and not as they are." As is true of the characterization of the peerless Dulcinea del Tobosco, Sancho Panza's symbolical meaning has been widely commented upon. Primarily, however, Sancho is seen as the practical man who, illustrating the "sublime quality that the masses possess, embraces 'an honored and good cause.'"

Nikki Giovanni, no doubt, would agree with the perspicacious Quixote's observation that there is a need for more knight-errants to address what she sees as "the lack of class this nation is showing" and the "big chill" that has settled into present-day living. As a result, and in keeping with the "pragmatic-existential idealism" that Ida Lewis claims is characteristic of the poet, she sets apart those who are beacons of hope in a spiritual wasteland. The modern day utopians that she recognizes are the masses, the black race, black women, artists, and children. A brief discussion, respectively, of the revolutionary role these torchbearers play in effecting an ideal society reemphasizes a central analogy between Cervantes and Giovanni: their enduring faith in man's heroic nature and in his capacity to bridge the gap between his inner and outer self, and thus, consummate his true existence.

Just as Cervantes called upon the common people of Spain, figuratively through the inimitable Sancho Panza, to embrace the chivalric principle, the energetic poet urges the masses to respond courageously to the destructive experiences of pain and loss in their lives. "Ordinary people like myself," she contends in her prose selection, **"CITIZEN RESPONSIBILITY (Hey! I'm Running for Office!)"**, must endeavor to fulfill the dream. Accordingly, the trusting poet makes the unqualified statement that "everyone can gather into themselves the subjective feelings needed to place the world in its natural order." To bring about the restitution of all things, she establishes some guidelines to follow:

> Love those with whom you sleep, share the happiness of those whom you call friend, encourage those among you who are visionary, and remove from your life those who offer you depression, despair, and disrespect.

Giovanni's eulogy of the black race is a refrain in her writing. The "Princess of Black Poetry" as she has been identified consistently, holds that black people are singularly endowed to forge a humanitarian world "a people who through / individual risk or simply aesthetic innocence will bring word of a new day." She supports her posture by routinely directing attention to the inner grace of blacks, their humanitarian lifestyle, and their survival of horrendous circumstances. As to the fundamental character of black people, Giovanni unwaveringly insists that they are vital human beings enriched by a creative disposition, "a spiritual, emotional nature reaching back to their African roots." In reference to the modus vivendi and operandi of African descendants, the poet highlights the magnanimous conduct of blacks in spite of being ruthlessly disfranchised. In **"An Answer to Some Questions On How I Write"**, she reviews the principles that have prevailed in the black community:

> Our politics have been the standing for that which is right and good; for the desegregation of society; for the equitable distribution of goods and services; for the free movement of a free people: for the respect of the old and the love of the young.

Perhaps Giovanni's conviction that black people are caretakers and apostles of an affirmative vision is best supported, as she emphasizes, by their amazing survival of a dehumanizing plight. With obvious pride, she points out that the history of black people is a paradigm of human triumph, a

testimony to the truth that "the human spirit can not be tamed and should not be trained."

Apart from recognizing the black race as whole as a visionary culture, Giovanni avows that black women are remarkable individuals. "Who else but the black woman," the prideful poet asks, "could not only survive slavery but thrive and grow stronger". Without reservations, she asserts: "we black women are the single group in the West intact . . . We are . . . the only group that derives its identity from itself . . . we measure ourselves by ourselves. . . ." Since the black woman, although discredited, has not compromised her integrity, Giovanni maintains that her fortitude, attests to the power of the spirit to overcome the most erosive forces.

The conventional notion of artists as divinely gifted individuals whose fuller insight enables them to illuminate the inner recesses of the human psyche is clearly seen in Cervantes' and Giovanni's work. That the Spanish novelist adhered to this viewpoint is apparent in how Don Quixote sees the love of his life, Dulcinea. Through imaginative perception, love's eyes, the homely, course peasant girl becomes a gracious, beautiful woman. That the enamored knight is under no illusion regarding his lady is evidenced in the knight's own words regarding her transfiguration. "I see her as she needs must be", he outrightly admits and readily adds, "I will act as if the world were that I would have it to be."

The creative perception that allows Don Quixote to see Dulcinea "as she needs must be" is also apparent in Giovanni's writing. In *Poetic Equation,* she comments specifically on the transformative nature of poetry and the aesthetic end it accomplishes, describing it as "the art of making beautiful that which never was." Echoing Cervantes' and the traditional perspective of artists as a select population that comes close to unveiling truth, she suggests that "we who write our dreams . . . confess our fears . . . and witness our times . . . are not so far from the root . . . the heart of the matter." Although Giovanni sets apart all artists as couriers of truth and craftsmen of a higher vision, it would be remiss not to mention that she pays special tribute to black poets as envoys of timeless principles and prophets of cheer. Openly, she states why she regards them so highly: "I think a lot of the Black poets because we honor the tradition of the griotes. We have traveled the length and the breadth of the planets singing our songs of the news of the day, trying to bring people closer to the truth."

Perhaps those closest to the truth, and, thus the real evangelists of the advent of an utopian society, as set forth in Giovanni's work, are the children. Their experience is recurrently represented by the poet as intact, untouched by the fragmentation, dislocations, and uncertainties of the modern age. Whether children are observed or whether they are the onlookers, their portrayal plainly shows that they live in har-

mony with themselves, with others, and with their environment. This kind of state of grace that envelopes children is
the subject of several of Giovanni's poems. **"Jonathan Sitting in Mud"** in which a young boy's contended existence
is contrasted with the distressful and demanding reality of
his parents is a good example:

> Jonathan sat in the mud
> all day
> Jonathan sat in the mud
> His Mother cried
> His Father tried
> But Jonathan sat in the mud
> And Jonathan said
> as he stretched out for bed
> "I'm happy where I am."

In spite of Cervantes' and Giovanni's belief that heroic individuals can effect a better way of life and that a fuller, truer
existence is attainable, it can not be denied that a mood of
disillusionment comes out in their texts that seemingly be-
lies their affirmative outlook. This disheartenment, so discernible in each's work, is certainly a connection between
the two writers that should be taken into account. The disillusionment, dequixotization, of Cervantes' madman-philoso-
pher character, as he comes to terms with the destructive
operatives of day-to-day living so unworthy of his high-
mindedness, is regularly noted by specialists in relation to
the knight's final days. The heartrending deathbed scene in
the novel is at times regarded as the despondent Quixote's
submission to a base reality. Yet, even today, how to interpret the dispirited Knight's return to La Mancha is open to
discussion. There are those that argue that when the weary
gentleman came home to his village, he returned victorious
over himself. They support their viewpoint alleging that
Cervantes, who survived an inordinately tedious life, would
not have brought his spokesperson to such a disastrous end.
Such specialists hold that the protagonist's triumph is, in effect, achieved when he determines that "it is fitting and necessary to become a knight-errant" . . . "for he could not but
blame himself for what the world was losing for his delay"
. . . "so many were the wrongs that were to be righted, the
grievances to be redressed, the abuses to be done away with,
the duties to be performed.

The low-spiritedness that comes out in Giovanni's work, as
with Cervantes' disenchantment, has elicited varied commentary. Specifically, *Cotton Candy on a Rainy Day* (1978),
considered the poet's bleakest book of verses, prompted the
critical assessment that the poet's optimism that came from
believing that the ideal was possible was gone. In her analysis of the text, Virginia Fowler explains that its' themes of
disillusionment, disappointment and diminishment reflect
"the poet's responses to events in her own personal life as
well as to those in the social and political life." Paula

Giddings note that "the book is immersed in world-weary
cynicism" and that "it is the rain dampening the spirit of another time that prevails" . . . "the consequences of an emotional compromise to a bleak reality." The poet herself,
acknowledging the gap between the ideal and the actual, concedes, "I am cotton candy on a rainy day / the unrealized
dream of and ideal unborn."

Apparently, there is no question that Cervantes' central
character's and the romantic poet's dreams and ideals are
shaken when confronted with the distance between illusion
and reality. Yet neither's optimism is crushed by that realization owing greatly to their conception of victory. If
Cervantes is indeed saying as has been noted to be the viewpoint of many scholars, that victory is gained when each of
us recognizes and fulfills his cycle of obligations, Giovanni's
notion of triumph is analogous. Throughout her work, the
prestigious poet maintains that the prize is won man rises
to heroic behavior and "goes in search of better bread." In
Those Who Ride the Night Winds, she pays tribute particularly to all who display moral and spiritual determination and
invites them as fellow passengers to answer the upward call.
She applauds the intention of those who take the risk inherent in enhancing the quality of life rather than focusing on
the possibility of failure. Straightfowardly she acknowledges
her own fallibility, but, at the same time makes the point that
failing to attain the ideal in no way lessens the value of the
effort.

> "Life is only about the I-tried-to-do", she espouses,
> and, on a personal note, adds, "I don't mind the fail-
> ure, but I can't imagine that I'd forgive myself if I
> didn't try."

The substratum of Cervantes' and Giovanni's celebration of
the intention to shape a poetic reality, as an alternative to
an adverse one, is their conviction that life, despite its te-
diousness, is a wondrous adventure. Both writers fervently
believe that living is a stimulating experience and both refuse
to reconcile themselves to an insipid and oppressive existence. As the critic Aubrey G. Bell points out,

> "It would . . . be contrary to all that we know of
> Cervantes to assume that a long succession of hard-
> ships, disappointments, vexations and disillusions
> had reduced the least morbid of men to a state of
> apathy, idleness, and gloom. He remained gay and
> active to the end. . . ."

That Giovanni regards life similarly is plainly seen in her
denotation of life as a "marvelous transitory experience." As
such, she exuberantly insists, "I don't have a lifestyle, I have
a life."

Critics disagree as to whether the life-battered Cervantes,

facing death, was conscious of the magnitude of his creation. Notwithstanding, today it is generally acknowledged that "... the most important of the world's writers ... in one way or another ... have felt the breath of the Cervantine spirit." As I have attempted to show in this paper, Nikki Giovanni is among those profoundly human writers whose work reflects the Quixotic outlook upon the world. Her dream of the "best of all possible worlds" mirrors the uncompromising knight-errant's vision of a world where "there would be ample scope for love, truth, and beauty." Although she is at times disconcerted by the horrifying conditions of our restless, discontented age, her idealism and hope are the bedrock of her life and work. Early in her professional career, she shared her positive regard for man and optimistic worldview with her readers:

> think we are all capable of tremendous beauty once we decide we are beautiful, of giving a lot of love once we understand love is possible, and we are capable of making the world over in that image ... I really think that a ... beautiful loving world is possible.

Nikki Giovanni's belief in the consummation of a higher ground way of life centered in love and her lasting faith in the true goodness and greatness of man is the Quixotic refrain and vision given body and substance in her work. In a world ravaged by demoralization and factionalism, she charges modern man, as Cervantes endearing knight did, to resurrect love and trust, to keep the doors open to the possibilities of the human soul, "to take a chance on being human" "to earn our right to be called men and women". In the final analysis, she reminds us that "what one person does ... makes a difference".

FURTHER READING

Criticism

Review of *Sacred Cows ... and Other Edibles. The Antioch Review* 46, No. 3 (Summer 1988): 397.
States that Giovanni covers many subjects in a variety of tones.

Buchanan, Carol. Review of *Shimmy Shimmy Shimmy Like My Sister Kate,* edited by Nikki Giovanni. *Voya* 19, No. 4 (October 1996): 229-30.
Remarks favorably on the collection and praises Giovanni's commentary.

Cook, William W. "The Black Arts Poets." In *The Columbia History of American Poetry,* edited by Jay Parini and Brett C. Millier, pp. 674-706. New York: Columbia University Press, 1993.
Describes Giovanni's role within the modern black poetry movement.

Cotter, James Finn. Review of *Those Who Ride the Night Winds,* by Nikki Giovanni. *The Hudson Review* XXXVII, No. 3 (Autumn 1984): 499-500.
Unfavorable review of Giovanni's poetry in *Those Who Ride the Night Winds.*

Millar, Neil. "Dancing Poetry, Chantable Verse." *Christian Science Monitor* 66, No. 110 (1 May 1974): F5.
Reviews *Ego Tripping* and argues that while the poems are original and zesty, some are full of hatred.

Ostriker, Alicia. "Of Being Numerous." *Partisan Review* XXXIX, No. 2 (Spring 1972): 270-75.
Discusses the revolutionary nature of the poems in *Black Feeling, Black Talk,* and *Black Judgement.*

Smith, Dale Edwyna. "The Mother Tongue." *Belles Lettres* 10, No. 2 (Spring 1995): 68-70.
Reviews the work of several African-American writers and praises Giovanni's *Racism 101.*

Additional coverage of Giovanni's life and career is contained in the following sources published by Gale: *Authors and Artists for Young Adults,* Vol. 22; *Authors in the News,* Vol. 1; *Black Literature Criticism,* Vol. 2; *Black Writers,* Vol. 2; *Children's Literature Review,* Vol. 6; *Contemporary Authors,* Vols. 29-32R; *Contemporary Authors Autobiography Series,* Vols. 6; *Contemporary Authors New Revision Series,* Vols. 18, 41, and 60; *Dictionary of Literary Biography,* Vols. 5, and 41; *DISCovering Authors; DISCovering Authors: British; DISCovering Authors: Canadian; DISCovering Authors Modules: Most-studied, Multicultural, Poets; Major Authors and Illustrators for Children and Young Adults; Major Twentieth-Century Writers; Poetry Criticism,* Vol. 19; *Something about the Author,* Vol. 24; and *World Literature Criticism Supplement.*

Thomas Keneally
1935-

(Full name Thomas Michael Keneally) Australian novelist, playwright, nonfiction writer, and author of children's books.

The following entry provides an overview of Keneally's career through 1996. For additional information on his life and works, see *CLC*, Volumes 5, 8, 10, 14, 19, 27, and 43.

INTRODUCTION

Since the publication of *The Place at Whitton* in 1965, Keneally has published over thirty novels, plays, and nonfiction books. His work is noted for being as diverse as it is prolific. The settings of his fiction range from Australia and Europe to America and cover such topics as the settlement of Australia, the life of Joan of Arc, the First and Second World Wars, and issues of contemporary life. Keneally's writings often focus on the role of faith and religion in society, and human interactions in time of war.

Biographical Information

Keneally was born October 7, 1935, in Sydney, Australia. His parents, Edmund Thomas and Elsie Margaret (Coyle) Keneally, were of Irish Catholic descent; Keneally entered the seminary, but he left two weeks short of taking orders. Two of his early novels—*The Place at Whitton* and *Three Cheers for the Paraclete* (1969)—are set in seminaries and reflect Keneally's conflict with church dogma. In 1965 he married Judith Martin, and they had two children, Margaret Ann and Jane Rebecca. Keneally taught high school, then college in Australia, then at the University of California at Irvine and New York University. He served on the board of several literary and cultural organizations, and became involved in the movement for Australian independence. He was an advisor to the Australian Constitutional Committee in 1985-88, and Chairman (1991-93), then Director (1994—) of the Australian Republic Movement, a political organization with the goal of Australian independence from Great Britain.

Major Works

Keneally's first novel, *The Place at Whitton,* is a Gothic horror set in a seminary. The play *Halloran's Little Boat* (1966) was expanded into the novel *Bring Larks and Heroes* (1967). Both works deal with moral and ethical conflicts in the early convict settlements of Australia. Ethical conflict is also the subject of *Three Cheers for the Paraclete,* the story of a young, idealistic priest teaching in a seminary. Keneally ex-

plores race relations and the effects of power and poverty in Australia in *The Chant of Jimmie Blacksmith* (1972), the story of a young aborigine turned outlaw. The backdrop of war is used in several Keneally novels as a setting for the exploration of stress, conflict and hard ethical choices. In *Blood Red, Sister Rose* (1974), Keneally uses the story of Joan of Arc to examine conflict and ethics. *Gossip from the Forest* (1975) looks at the difficult compromises involved in negotiating the armistice at the end of World War I. Matthias Erzberger, head of the German delegation, recognizes the compelling need to end the conflict. Pressured by both sides, he accepts the ruinous terms demanded by the French. These conditions, Keneally suggests, lead to the disastrous economic conditions which follow in Germany, and ultimately sow the seeds of World War II. *Confederates* (1979) uses the United States Civil War as a setting for a more personal conflict between neighbors. In the midst of the war's climactic battle—Antietam—another conflict is underway. Ephie Bumpass' husband Usaph and Ephie's lover Decatur Cate are thrown together to fight in the Shenandoah Volunteers. Cate's emasculating injury in the battle is a symbolic punishment for his sin. In *Schindler's List* (1982),

Keneally examines war, man's inhumanity, and the complex moral and ethical issues present in difficult and perilous times. The novel focuses on the story of Oskar Schindler, a less-than-perfect hero who saves the lives of over a thousand Jews through clever manipulation of the Nazi war machine. In *Woman of the Inner Sea* (1992), Keneally's protagonist, Kate, is an urban housewife who loses, in rapid succession, her husband to another woman and her children to a tragic accident. Lost in her grief, Kate travels to Myambagh, a small town in the Outback. Every year the area is ravaged by terrible floods, and the time in between is spent repairing damage and preparing for the next flood. Kate is comforted by this repetitive cycle, wherein disaster is made routine, and she finds a renewed ability to face life. Keneally's non-fiction support of Australian independence, delineated in *Memoirs from a Young Republic* (1993), generated a great deal of political as well as literary criticism. Set in turn-of-the-century Australia, *A River Town* (1995) is the story of a young Irish immigrant, Tim Shea, who is trying to leave behind the restrictive social structure of his native land, but finds many of the same difficulties in his new country. Shea suffers financially for his refusal to support the Boer War and for not signing a blanket oath of support to the goals of Great Britain. Most critics see this novel as an extended metaphor on the subject of Australia's independence.

Critical Reception

One measure of the controversy generated by much of Keneally's work is the amount that has been written by critics about other critics of his writing. This is to be expected when a writer takes a controversial political stand, such as Keneally did with *Memoirs of a Young Republic,* and by acting as Chairman of the Australian Republican Movement. But diverse critical reaction to Keneally's work preceded this book. He has been both criticized and praised for his portrayal of female characters (*Blood Red, Sister Rose, A Dutiful Daughter,* 1971); the graphic nature of his portrayals of violence in his war novels (*Schindler's List, Confederates*); and his novelization of historical fact (*Schindler's List, Gossip from the Forest*). Keneally, defending his approach to the historical novel, says that the best ones are "really about the present and uses the past as a sort of working model . . . in which the human issues are the same as those we have now, and have always had to face." Keneally's characters are complex, full of internal conflict and torn by mixed emotions that make it difficult for readers to simply summarize his position. As Janet Turner Hospital says, "His protagonists, men and women who have a yen for ordinary unremarkable lives but who are compelled by circumstances and by some hard inconvenient kernel of integrity to be exceptional, are torn by self-doubt, they are hyper-conscious of mixed motives, they are distrustful of certainties." Some critics see these conflicted, marginal heroes, such as Phelim

Halloran (*Bring Larks and Heroes*) and Oskar Schindler as representative of a pessimistic view of history, in which a savage system only allows for small moral victories of exceptional people. Many critics, however, praise Keneally's ability, through these deep, complicated, conflicted characters, to make a strong moral statement. They characterize Keneally's message as hopeful, that average, imperfect individuals can take action against unjust systems and have tangible, positive effect. Keneally is praised for taking a moral position without resorting to standing on a soapbox. This is, as Hospital says, "one of the consistent strengths of the entire (and considerable) body of Keneally's work. Though he has a passionate moral vision, he is not didactic."

PRINCIPAL WORKS

The Place at Whitton (novel) 1965
The Fear (novel) 1965
Halloran's Little Boat (drama) 1966
Bring Larks and Heroes (novel) 1967
Childermass (drama) 1968
Three Cheers for the Paraclete (novel) 1969
The Survivor (novel) 1969
A Dutiful Daughter (novel) 1971
An Awful Rose (drama) 1972
The Chant of Jimmie Blacksmith (novel) 1972
Blood Red, Sister Rose: A Novel of the Maid of New Orleans (novel) 1974
Gossip from the Forest (novel) 1975
Moses the Lawgiver (novel) 1975
Season in Purgatory (novel) 1977
A Victim ofthe Aurora (novel) 1977
Ned Kelly and the City of the Bees (juvenile novel) 1978
Passenger (novel) 1979
Confederates (novel) 1979
The Cut-Rate Kingdom (novel) 1980
Bullie's House (novel) 1981
Schindler's List (novel) 1982; also published in Europe as *Schindler's Ark*
Outback (nonfiction) 1983
A Family Madness (novel) 1985
Australia (nonfiction) 1987
The Playmaker (novel) 1987
To Asmara: A Novel of Africa (novel) 1989; also published in Australia as *Towards Asmara*
By the Line (novel) 1989
Flying Hero Class (novel) 1991
Now and in Time to Be: Ireland & the Irish (nonfiction) 1992
The Place Where Souls Are Born: A Journey into the Southwest (nonfiction) 1992
Woman of the Inner Sea (novel) 1992

Memoirs from a Young Republic (nonfiction) 1993
Jacko the Great Intruder (novel) 1994
A River Town (novel) 1995

CRITICISM

Kerin Cantrell (essay date 1968)

SOURCE: "Perspectives on Thomas Keneally," in *Southerly,* Vol. 28, No. 1, 1968, pp. 54-67.

[In the following essay, Cantrell traces the development of Keneally's novels through Bring Larks and Heroes.*]*

Thomas Keneally was born in Sydney in 1935. He has written two plays and three novels, and though his work has usually been favorably received, it is only with his latest novel, **Bring Larks and Heroes** (1967), that he has suddenly been acclaimed as the author of the "long-sought Great Australian Novel". His first book, **The Place at Whitton** (1964), Mr. Keneally is reported as having "intended . . . as a pure thriller but (he) feels now that the book couldn't make up its mind what to be". It reveals the interest in Catholicism that is to persist in the later novels (Mr. Keneally studied for the priesthood to within months of taking orders) and it seems not unfair to suggest that in **The Place at Whitton** the author is partly reviewing his own attitudes to the priesthood. The perspective is a critical one. The vocation of priesthood is seen as attracting a fair proportion of psychically disordered personalities, and though this is not a profound insight it is well conveyed. Mr. Keneally creates with skill the smoothly functioning administration of seminary life, beneath which is concealed a host of doubts and frustrations.

Singled out for particular attention are the exceptional candidates for the priesthood, such as the visionary Verissimo and the homicidal Pontifex. But because Mr. Keneally seems, in all his works, more interested in men in a social situation than in the men themselves, none of his analyses is characterized by particular insight. The author has a conception of character as being simply anchored in social and environmental determinants, as with the priest Buchanan, who is said to suffer from a fear of thirst because he witnessed in his youth the grotesque antics of an alcoholic uncle. Moreover, the action tends to bog down a little in the "case histories" of the priests which are related one after the other (see particularly chapters 8 and 9).

Yet, as the author seems now to concede, the novel lacks direction. It tends on the one hand towards the "whodunit", and on the other towards the probing of the priestly psyche. Not that these elements are essentially incompatible in the one work; it is simply that the "whodunit" elements lack the conviction that informs the rest of the novel. Mr. Keneally establishes a link between the two tendencies by making the priest-murderer at Whitton the *mauvais-prêtre* necessary to the completion of the rites of a sophisticated young witch, Agnes. Except for the concluding thirty pages, the depiction of the witch's King's Cross world is contrived and mundane, and the author finally betrays his own lack of assurance by mocking it. Hence the uncertainty of the scene in which Agnes and her witch associates are celebrating, in Grecian costume, the initiation into their circle of the lawyer Townsend:

> "Mark him!" a Greek chorus chanted. "Mark him!"

> The iron was ready, blazing in his sight. It wavered before him, its two red prongs quavering with heat. Then it sped forward and bit the flesh of his forehead. Like some type of leech, it sucked and mouthed the flesh away.

> "Augh!" Townsend yelled.

Mr. Keneally shows a tendency to graft his personal dislikes on to his material. This results in some trite commentary and in stereotyped characterization, observable in the treatment of the lawyer Townsend, of Agnes, and the policeman Ptolemy, who is in charge of investigations of the murder at Whitton. The following account is that of the typical "mug cop":

> "Well, I'm not used to violent death," [the priest] Cyril said. It was a quiet statement of neutral tone, but Ptolemy felt it as an assault on his authority.

> "If you're not, Father," he said hotly, not caring if Cyril deserved the title or not, and happier if he didn't, "if you're not used to violent death, I am. I mightn't be a clergyman, I mightn't be a believer of any description, but unlike a centipede beneath a rock, I deserve human respect. Whatever you may think, a policeman is not lower than a grub. He's a poor coot whom all despise yet all fly to. Everyone suspects him of bribery and corruption, but he's the bloke who arrests the homicidal maniac who's got everyone scared."

This is prentice-work caricature, as is the following out-of-keeping outburst of Verissimo's "vision woman", Joan of Arc. The visionary Verissimo expresses dissatisfaction with the poor food and accommodation at the seminary. Joan tartly delivers a homily:

> "Hah," said Joan. "But the people who eat well and sleep warm aren't happy. They live a shadow life.

They imitate happiness. They travel parallel to it and go through all its functions. Yet somewhere, in a moment of passion or deceit, they lost the way or the key or whatever you want to call it."

The author also airs his irritation with the Australian absorption in football, and with the standard of reading matter to be found in a physician's waiting room. Fortunately this tendency to swipe at easy targets is not evident in his later works, although *Bring Larks and Heroes* suffers a little from unshaped detail and from the same inability to handle women as was evident in the treatment of Agnes.

Keneally's mastery lies in the depiction of men in social situations, and in descriptions of physical rather than mental landscapes.
—*Kerin Cantrell*

But if *The Place at Whitton* reveals Mr. Keneally's weaknesses it also indicates his strengths. Mr. Keneally's mastery lies in the depiction of men in social situations, and in descriptions of physical rather than mental landscapes. The old seminary at Whitton is fondly described:

> The main doors of the place at Whitton were . . . archaic and bulky, held on by large iron hinges as long as a bayonet. A glossy electric button near the right-hand handle gave them a surprised look—like that of a dignitary discovered with his navel showing.

And Mr. Keneally's interest in language (more evident in *Bring Larks and Heroes*) shows itself in his aptitude for happy images: "the three of them waded across fields crumbling like wet biscuit."

Mr. Keneally displays in all his work a marked talent for the macabre incident. The notable instance in *The Place at Whitton* is the splendid burial alive with which the novel concludes. Pontifex finds another victim in Agnes. He drives a stake straight through her, and with this stake secures her in a shallow grave which he then calmly proceeds to fill in. Surprisingly enough, the force of this conclusion is not at all diminished by the very clumsy incidents which immediately precede it. It would seem that the author came to realize toward the end of the novel that the negative emphasis laid on the place at Whitton (which is hardly shown as a fruitful, life-giving institution), needed a positive counterpart.

First there is the brief anecdote of Whitton's Ghost, the ghost of a member of the seminary who died shortly before ordination, and whose abortive career speaks for the achievement of several of the inmates under scrutiny. Then on . . . we are introduced to two characters who will correct this impression. The local schoolteacher, Dawes, is pursuing a "bloody virgin queen" named Colette. The tedium of their days is mapped out at a length much too considerable for their importance to the plot, which lies in their meeting with Agnes and Pontifex on a deserted beach. Dawes has persuaded the timid Colette to accompany him on a day's fishing, while Pontifex, having fled Whitton after another attempt at murder, is using the beach as a hideout at Agnes's suggestion. The two couples meet on the beach, and to Dawes, Pontifex appears as a sort of father-figure. Possibly Dawes also experienced a sudden desire to be alone with Agnes for a while; his instinct urges him to leave Pontifex and Colette together. Pontifex quickly takes an interest in Colette and draws from her the fears she harbors about marriage. Pontifex points out Dawes's loneliness and urges that though marriage is a lottery, "in a world of rotten motives and twisted passions, you have to give everything into someone else's keeping. If you survive the giving, you come to flower. That's the odds." Pontifex's words hit home, for three pages later we are told that

> in some way the talk and the companionship of the day had made the world whole for (Collette). For the first time, she was overtaken by a starting emotion of trust, trust for Dawes.

As Colette's morbid fear of all males has been so insisted on, this sudden conversion is hardly convincing. The author's fault lies in failing to show his character in a depth sufficient for the reader to be able to accept such a change. I believe Mr. Keneally repeats this error in the concluding pages of *Bring Larks and Heroes.*

The point of the Colette-Dawes episode is to adjust a balance, to point out that no man, not even a multiple-murdering candidate for the priesthood, is wholly bad. The point is trite, and tritely made. Nor does Mr. Keneally manage to bring Colette and Dawes alive, to make of them anything more than the "two lukewarm personalities" he has himself dubbed them.

The second novel, *The Fear* (1965), does not mark such a development on *The Place at Whitton* as does *Bring Larks and Heroes* on both the earlier works. The measure of the achievement in *Bring Larks and Heroes* (1967) may perhaps be taken by a single instance. In this novel and in *The Place at Whitton,* the author portrays the impulse to barbarity, barely under the surface, that can take a man by surprise. In *Whitton,* the explanation of this impulse is long and repetitive (see chapters 8 and 22). The rendering of the similar impulse in *Bring Larks and Heroes* is far more precise and forceful.

In the latter work, Mr. Keneally heightens tension by dramatizing not only this impulse to let blood, but also a conflict of loyalties. Captain Allen is in charge of a disciplinary attack, by conscripted Irish troops, on insurgent Irish transports. The bitterness of the brother-against-brother situation has already been insisted on, particularly in the affair between Corporal Halloran and the Irish felon Quinn. Halloran now avoids attacking his kin by merely pretending to strike the insurgents, but Halloran's mate, Terry Byrne, is paralyzed by the prospect of attacking fellow Irishmen. Captain Allen tries to force the petrified Byrne to take action:

> The (battle) was nearly over now, except that a little way uphill and across the narrow valley, low comedy was in progress, as Allen chased Byrne who chased a felon. It *was* like a play, like a bad play, the way Halloran heard it later and over and over from Byrne. Byrne sprinting, the Irishman falling on his knees constantly saying. "In the name of God!" And like a farce figure was Allen, striking the turf with his sword three times, roaring "Kill him!"

> Byrne gaped because he knew he would bayonet this angular young man yelling, "In the name of God!" There seemed no good reason to desist. Byrne saw him fully enough to know that he was brother-man and that the bayonet would viper him, craggy as he was, with a small head and curls close down on his forehead. When he rose and broke away again, Allen tried to get him by these curls and hack him with the sword. But he was away, and for some seconds, Allen and Byrne stood still, as if the matter was solved. Allen realized first that it hadn't been solved at all. He changed his sword to his left hand and struck Byrne across the jaw. The yellow blindness all but put an end to the affair for Byrne and for the Irishman, and even for Allen. Because Byrne made off uphill in quite frenzied style and found the boy trying to hide in under the limbs of a native fig fairly spacious and concealing in the dark. Byrne was thinking, *I'm only doing soldier's work,* yet he was bitter against himself, thinking also how if you're no good in the first place, you'll be no good in the melting pot, in the furnace, in the womb of wild events. He ducked under the branches and walked to the young fellow. "Jesus, Mary, Joseph," said the young fellow, louder and louder the closer Byrne got. The Holy Family couldn't do the job tonight, Byrne thought. They depended on him, and he had no mercy. The bayonet gestured softly at the boy, who turned his back and took it in the buttocks. He began a whining, too, that cringed on a rising note, back into the mousiest corners of sound. The iron went into his belly, high up because

> he was rolling; and he was so close to death then that, under the double bark of the fig, his breath sounded more like a felled bird than like true breath. Byrne was enthralled by the barbarous fluidity of his bayonet going in. He actually felt for the man's softer parts with his boot and spiked him a last time.

There is a grim comedy of the grotesque operating here, which adds to the macabreness of the situation where terror becomes a fascination with the act of killing. The sexual overtones of the final few lines deliberately recall that other, persistent Byrne, the Byrne who commits sodomy and makes bawdy jests about Halloran's "secret bride".

This is Keneally at his best, but it is a best that is not always sustained. The profundities which reviewers have detected in *Bring Larks and Heroes* may be due in part to a confusion within the work itself, although there does seem to be an attempt in the novel to probe issues which have a pertinency beyond it, as it were. Some confusion arises from the author's tendency to introduce ideas that are given too large an airing for their effect in the work as a whole. Mr. Keneally's speculations tend to run away with him at times.

There is for instance the long description of books dealing with the ethics of suicide in *The Place at Whitton,* or the debates, in *Bring Larks and Heroes,* on the propriety of a marriage that is consecrated only by the mutual exchange of vows between partners, owing to the absence of a priest. In presenting Halloran's introspections about the ethics of his "secret marriage", Mr. Keneally shapes his material to show that there is a discernible direction in Halloran's thought. Halloran has a concern with truth and propriety, but tends to romanticize issues and always remains a little perplexed. But the emphasis placed in the first thirty pages on the ethics of Halloran's situation is a repetitive rather than an intensifying device. The situation is not used to probe deeper into Halloran's mind.

In a sense, the author cannot probe deeply, for Halloran is shown to be a fairly limited person, whose perceptions are never impressive. His naive idealism is pointed to time and again: he has, for instance, an idea as to what constitutes the "artistic type". When he is rowing upstream with the artist Ewers, Halloran observes

> the artist's gaze . . . (which) could have taken in two raw damned little men with sweat in their sternums and hairy navels and nubbly feet gripping the foothold either side of his boots. Halloran, who had seen some of the flabbergasting but redeemed ugliness in Leonardo's sketch-book, tended to expect that these two would delight an artist, send him grabbing for his transforming charcoal.

The boat is beached, and Halloran asks Ewers if he feels moved (as Halloran expects he ought), to paint the landscape. Ewers replies in the negative; a picture, he says, would give a false impression of this harsh country:

> "If I painted this landscape," Ewers explained, "those who ever saw it would think that the forests behind the beaches were teeming with fruit and game. They would think that this river led to a kingly town, that Eden lay at the headwaters."
>
> *Eden lay at the head-waters* was such a nice phrase that Halloran suspected he was listening to a recitation, perhaps part of the artist's private journal.

There is also the instance where Halloran brutally kicks the queer soldier, Miles. This is a seemingly motiveless attack, and most probably springs from the fact of Miles's homosexuality. Immediately prior to the kicking, Halloran had been obliged to settle a lovers' quarrel between Miles and his regular friend, a quarrel sparked off by Byrne's interference.

Finally there is the presentation of Halloran in his disputes with Hearn, the gentleman felon who likens himself to the Savior—"like one greater, I had wounds to show" he grandly announces. Hearn challenges Halloran's conscience on matters of loyalty to God and King. He hopes to prove Halloran's allegiances groundless and so persuade him to join in an escape to Europe, where the 1789 uprising has occurred. Halloran's allegiances are shaken but not destroyed, and in the altercations his wit is seen as inferior to Hearn's. Halloran adopts therefore a pompous defense, only to have it crumpled by Byrne, who has been won over by Hearn's zeal and who suddenly announces, "'Your nose is starting to run.' It made Halloran furious to have his nose so thoroughly betray his mortality. He became noticeably taut." There is a similar debunking effect soon after, when Halloran "tried to look ironic, but a sneeze scattered his efforts."

Halloran is certainly more sensitive than his fellows, but it is his essential *ordinariness* that is stressed. It is necessary to insist on this since some reviewers see Halloran as a sort of Christ-figure, and such a reading ignores the qualifications that events and Mr. Keneally place on him. One reviewer remarks for instance that

> Halloran looks towards an agony which will not only be his but will also be a summation of the violence which the despised and rejected must suffer at the hands of those who sit in the high places of this earth in all times and places. His suffering is representative, as Christ's was, because it is so in-

tense, so lonely and he is so conscious of it, as a process, a path to be walked, a grave ceremony (*sic*). Impressive in this sort of rumination is the tight holding to, the stoic guarding, the refusal to spare one's self an atom of the knowledge of what will be. The refusal to cry out is the more impressive in the light of the fact that Halloran not only is a good man, but he is to suffer all this as the direct result of his actions as a good man.

The main justification for such a reading seems to me to rest on the novel's final lines. As the gallows-rope breaks Halloran's neck he asks himself "Am I perhaps *God?*" Most clearly he is not, but the effect of the remark is uncertain. Possibly Mr. Keneally is attempting to enhance the importance of his protagonist's suffering, and the remark is to be read without ironic implication. Though I doubt this, Halloran's final perception remains unconvincing, for he has been shown to be limited in perception, with neither exceptional ruminative power nor spiritual status. Further, he is an essentially humble person. For his remark to strike the reader as convincing, the author would have needed to show Halloran's capacity for life as being enlarged by what he undergoes. Mr. Keneally does not show any such development, hence the change in Halloran is too sudden and the remark fails to convince.

Another reading seems more plausible, which is that this is the final irony in the career of Halloran, a man who "has the illusion of knowing where he's going", as the novel very early announces. Halloran married Ann "to ward off oblivion", yet both meet an early death. Further, Halloran fails every person who looks to him for help, and it is his own nature which contributes to such failures, as well as the circumstances of his existence. Halloran realizes this, and Hearn's hold over Halloran is possible only because he strikes Halloran on a vulnerable point. Might not Halloran have done something for the luckless Ewers, who is accused of and hanged for rape, and who Halloran knows to be a eunuch? The confusion in Halloran's notions that the debates with Hearn bring out, indicate that this final notion, "Am I perhaps *God?*", may be the most misguided of all.

The reading I am advancing receives further support from the parallel drawn between Halloran and the Reverend Calverly. These two are early associated: "only (Calverly) and Halloran, perhaps, in that whole town, did not resent the grotesque land, did not call it evil because it was weird." Both come to rejoice in the mercy of death, both experience mental and physical suffering. Most pertinently, both fail those who depend on them for relief. Calverly's sermonizing in the cell where Halloran awaits the gallows with two other soldiers brings down on him a volley of abuse and mockery, while Halloran's failure in respect of Quinn brings that Irishman's bitter curses raining on his head.

Such speculation may however distort the main emphasis of the novel, which is essentially concerned with the penal *system,* rather than with a stroke-by-stroke analysis of a single character. Mr. Keneally continues the line of Australian novels of the convict system, and there are a couple of stylistic touches that recall Hal Porter, though he and Keneally are literary stylists of a very different kind. In *The Tilted Cross,* Porter was primarily concerned with the effect of the penal system on the individual, but Mr. Keneally does not primarily use the "system" to make an exploratory study of human experience. Emphasis throughout is on the *system,* and it is in depictions of men in a community, and in rendering physical rather than mental landscapes, that Mr. Keneally excels. Ultimately, the "system" is more memorable than the persons that comprise it; the physical world by which Halloran lives is more strongly imagined than his inner experience.

The brutality and decay (of justice) in the settlement are touched in lightly at several points. Government House is described thus:

> At the top of the town stood a Government House whose thatch roof was being replaced by shingles of blackbutt. Transports moved in and out and about the hole in its distant roof with the effective indolence of maggots in a skull.

Or the measure of the expectations of the colony's inhabitants is taken by the incident in which the artist Ewers has his hand painfully slashed by a caged bird for which he is attempting to provide some shade. And always there is the landscape, its stunted growth providing a physical counterpart for the failure of hopes and ideals. The sense that Mr. Keneally conveys of the dreadful inevitableness of events is created partly by pertinent detail in the landscape. Ann and Halloran spend their precious half day a week together, near the sea. They waded through

> a matting of shrubs stripped and cuffed westward by the prevailing wind. Once the green shoals could be seen under the cliff, he sat Ann down on a hump of granite. The cliff-top was sown with partly revealed clods of the rock and was not unlike a half-buried grave-yard, with the names and scraps of remembrance having wasted into the crystals of the stones.

Small touches such as this prepare for harsher brutalities, such as the description of the back of a youth flogged three-quarters to death. There is "a seam in the boy's purple back and a herd of flies, whose bite is maggots, drinking from it".

Keneally is a master at rendering the manner in which men will use one another to work off frustration. Twice, felons are flogged in the capacity of scapegoats for an officer who wishes to thwart a superior and relieve irritation: Rowley's flogging of Quinn, and Captain Howard's of Hearn, follow this pattern.

One of the novel's most interesting situations is that between Ann and Mrs. Blythe, mistress of the house in which Ann serves as kitchenmaid. Ulcerated Mrs. Blythe is the possessor of a "pious gut" which her husband is endeavoring to crack by starvation. She also possesses a curious concern for her servant's chastity, and her ostensible reason, that she does not wish to see Ann fat with Halloran's bastard, hardly suffices in the face of the elation she experiences when Ann is executed. Mrs. Blythe identifies directly with Ann when she discovers that the latter is no longer a virgin ([she knew] "that Halloran had involved her in the Fall"), and on the occasion of Ann's death, experiences a sudden surge of energy. She rises awkwardly and performs on ulcerated legs a grotesque sort of can-can.

This morbid relationship is highlighted to excellent effect in the novel's stage version, **Halloran's Little Boat** (reappearing at the Independent Theatre, Sydney, at the time of writing). The play also brings out the tendency to disintegration of structure which results from too free speculation, speculation which is not closely rooted in the work. Ann's resentful doubts about the existence of God in such a country as this, and her exchanges with Halloran about the "secret bride" ethic, with which most of Act One is concerned, have slipped from the memory by the time of the final act which is dominated by the much more arresting Mr. and Mrs. Blythe. To adjust this balance, Mr. Keneally has curiously romanticized the play's finale by bringing back on stage the executed Ann and Halloran, who confirm, in heavenly trappings, their eternal happiness.

I wish to comment only briefly on **The Fear** (1965). "Joseph, the boy caught up in the battle between Catholic and Communist, and in an escape in Australia of Japanese prisoners of World War II, is brought face to face with evil in the clear Australian sunlight". Thus incorrectly and misleadingly reads the publisher's blurb on the back of the recent Sun Books edition. It is not Joseph but Daniel who confronts the Japanese, and further, the novel is not concerned with any "battle between Catholic and Communist". **The Fear** is instead more of an autobiography, being partly based on incidents from Mr. Keneally's youth.

The eight-year-old Catholic boy, Daniel Jordan, is both protagonist and part narrator of this novel; the other narrative voice is that of the mature Daniel Jordan. Neighbors to the Jordans are a Communist family, the Mantles, and it is Mr. Mantle, "the Comrade", who is the source of the fear that Daniel experiences. Daniel becomes entwined in the Mantles' affairs and the upshot is a tragedy resulting in the death of two of Daniel's friends. The Comrade brings home and enthrones on a dresser in the dining room, a grenade which he threatens, in his more belligerent moods, to explode in the house. Daniel, the Mantles' two sons and Dolph Conlon steal the grenade and explode it early one morning at a rubbish tip. This results in the deaths of Len Mantle and Dolph Conlon, and shortly afterwards Mrs. Mantle commits suicide and takes with her the crippled son Joseph. The Jordan family then moves to the Cape, where, after an interval of some months, the Comrade reappears, having fled his former surroundings and the rumors of his responsibility for the deaths of the two lads and of his wife and elder son. Daniel and the Comrade are among those involved as hostages in an escape of Japanese prisoners-of-war. This incident costs the Comrade his life, and Daniel expresses relief at a feeling of release that the Comrade's death effects in him.

The mass of events is given very little shape beyond the arrangement of a chronological sequence. Mr. Keneally has drawn some parallels in the two situations in which Daniel finds himself (i.e. in the incidents prior to and following the move to the Cape). At the Cape Daniel becomes the third member of a group which, prior to his arrival, was an established twosome, and this recalls his association with the Mantle boys. The drinking and whoring Comrade has his Cape counterpart in the alcoholic schoolteacher, John Oakley, who professes a platonic love for Daniel's mother and who has to be warned away from the Jordan's home in much the same manner as the Comrade's whore had to be ordered off the Jordan premises previously.

I cannot believe, however, that Mr. Keneally intends any serious comment on Communists, or Catholics, in this novel. The portrait of Mr. Mantle is true to the stereotype of the whoring, wife-beating drunkard, who confides in those much younger than himself in order to gain the esteem denied him by his peers. But there are some indications that we are meant to take events as pointing to certain truths, as for instance the desire of the Comrade's crippled son, Joseph, to be baptized. Daniel's talk of the Catholic faith arouses in Joseph a desire for salvation, despite the Comrade's instruction to the contrary. The childish prattle on this issue becomes tedious, and I fail to see why it is included unless to suggest that the rigors of Communist doctrine, as exemplified by Mr. Mantle, cannot overcome a fundamental human desire for assurance of some sort of after-life.

The events of the novel are registered through the eyes of Daniel, and the mode of narration is a little disturbing, as Mr. Keneally freely interchanges the idiom appropriate to an eight-year-old ([Stell] "was *mad* with me," my italics), with that appropriate to the more reflective adult: "the Mantles' narrow little brick place . . . seemed to be subsiding crookedly into the earth like an ill laid tombstone". This

is a pertinent comparison since the Mantles' son Joseph is dying of a disease that is turning his neuro-muscular system to jelly.

Mr. Keneally has not chosen to show the development of the protagonist-narrator. He is content to evoke the world of childhood for its own sake, though some adverse light cannot but be shed on Daniel at certain points. Mr. Keneally is in none of his works at his most assured when handling character development; he cannot extend a character in depth, in order to trace a change in attitude or an increasing capacity for experiencing life to the full. Since in *The Fear* hardly any development in character is sustained, the incidents tend to become a catalogue with no reflective narrator to focus their influence on the developing child. Daniel remains of ordinary perception, basically unaffected by the events he experiences.

Hence when Daniel expresses "a feeling of grief" that the Comrade is dead and that he, Daniel, is now without the Comrade's "peculiar brand of menace", it is a matter of statement rather than of demonstration, for there is very little of *menace* in anything that happens to Daniel. It is perhaps as a consequence of registering everything through the eyes of a not very outstanding eight-year-old, that the whole novel takes on the tone of a schoolboy adventure story. The incidents themselves are grim enough, but the manner of narration reduces them to extended escapade.

Although the Comrade is responsible for four deaths, he remains a somewhat pathetic figure who disturbs Daniel's consciousness (and conscience) only when the latter is visibly reminded of the Comrade's existence. Though there is an occasional touch of irony in the author's treatment of Daniel, the latter's perceptions are on the whole endorsed. There is nothing comparable in *The Fear* to the pervading irony which attends the depiction of the protagonist in *Bring Larks and Heroes*.

The Fear remains then, the relating of a period of childhood, a period tinged, for the protagonist, with some unease, but more predominantly with much of the color of high adventure. The prose fiction breaks down at times into mere reportage, particularly in the account of the Japanese prisoners' escape. The apology to the reader that "one thing that you'll no doubt say of this random coverage of ten months of childhood is that it's shambling," is certainly warranted. However the novel shows, in small incidents and touches, the mastery of the author of *Bring Larks and Heroes*. The actual throwing of the hand-grenade is particularly well described, as is the account of the traveling country pastor's congregation:

> In Gilbert, Father Mullally was said to be a deep man, which meant that no one understood his ser-

mons. That morning he spoke of John Calvin and free will. A comatose generation slumped on the benches before him, one ear open for his cadences. They did not know John Calvin. There was no resentment against the man when the priest named him as the greatest enemy of the sovereign soul of man. Their eyes did not turn blazing with pity to inspect the millions of shackled souls lined up century by century—according to the preacher's gesture—between the tea urns at the back of the hall. The massive self-dialogue rolled on and over our heads, intimidated the terribly ordinary fibro walls. And the people seemed content, as did the priest himself.

Suddenly we could hear the Gilbert-Cape bus grinding over Warialda with the day's picnickers. The priest brought the sermon to a close by unleashing on it a sign of the Cross which was like three or four smart judo chops. He couldn't have our Protestant brethren hanging around the surf shed slaking their Protestant curiosity or getting good Catholic dogma without putting anything in the plate.

The Fear evokes as distinctly an Australian landscape as that in *Bring Larks and Heroes,* and in all three novels the sea plays an important part, as a symbol of refuge and release. The claims made by reviewers for *The Fear* (such as "the fascination that Keneally holds for Australian readers lies in his deep sense of tragedy and the cold proximity of sin, death and darkness"), were premature, and are more applicable to *Bring Larks and Heroes,* which contains the author's most perceptive writing to date.

This article has been an attempt to refocus Mr. Keneally's reputation, in the face of too extreme a critical reception. Although there is a frequent lack of assurance about his work, with *Bring Larks and Heroes* Mr. Keneally shows himself a novelist of distinction.

Janette T. Hospital (essay/interview date 7 May 1976)

SOURCE: "Keneally's Reluctant Prophets," in *Commonweal,* Vol. CIII, No. 10, May 7, 1976, pp. 295-300.

[*In the following essay, Hospital characterizes Keneally's protagonists as movern-day Jeremiahs, interspersing her analysis with an interview of Keneally, in which he discusses political aspects of religion and authobiographical elements of his writings.*]

Thomas Keneally is an Australian novelist who has won high critical acclaim in his own country, Great Britain and America. He was born in Sydney in 1935, and trained for several years for the Catholic priesthood but did not take Orders. His novels include *Bring Larks and Heroes* (1967) which won the Miles Franklin Award for the best Australian novel of that year; *Three Cheers for the Paraclete* (1968) which the *New York Times Book Review* noted was "rich in unexpected visions and sudden epiphanies. [Keneally] writes like an angel"; *The Survivor* (1969) which was the joint winner of the Captain Cook Literary Award; *A Dutiful Daughter* (1971); *The Chant of Jimmie Blacksmith* (1972) which was on the short list for the Booker Prize; *Blood Red, Sister Rose* (1974); *Gossip from the Forest* (1975). Mr. Keneally lives in Sydney, but is currently spending two years in Connecticut with his wife and daughters while working on two novels for his American publishers, Harcourt Brace.

When the word of the Lord first came to Jeremiah he demurred: "Ah, Lord God! behold, I cannot speak: for I am a child." The Lord God insisted: "Before thou camest forth out of the womb I sanctified thee, and I ordained thee a prophet unto the nations." Humbled by such proof, and driven by the persistent voice of the Almighty, Jeremiah obeyed, roaring the wrath of God up and down the streets of Jerusalem—but not without protest, not without a very human smarting at the ridicule and hostility, not without attempts to wrench free of the divine destiny:

> O Lord, thou hast deceived me,
> and I was deceived;
> thou art stronger than I,
> and thou hast prevailed:
> I have become a laughingstock all the day;
> every one mocks me. (R.S.V. Jer. 20:7)

Yet he is trapped, the puppet of the inexorable will of God, and of his own inner drivenness:

> If I say, "I will not mention him,
> or speak any more in his name,"
> there is in my heart
> as it were a burning fire shut up in my bones,
> and I am weary with holding it in,
> and I cannot. (R.S.V. Jer. 20:9)

The protagonists of the novels of Thomas Keneally are Jeremiahs of a sort, reluctant prophets or messiahs. A form of sainthood is thrust willy nilly upon them. At times they court it, romanticize it, flaunt the exceptional nature of their chosenness; at times they fight it, struggling to escape, knowing the price of sainthood to be martyrdom, victimization; at times they mock it, demythologizing their own aureoles, revealing themselves as ordinary men and women with fears, lusts, greeds, impure motives—prophets by random circumstance only.

The contexts of their election vary greatly. There is Halloran of *Bring Larks and Heroes,* educated in the Bishop's school in Wexford, Ireland, destined for the Sulpicians in Paris, but consigned to the "world's worse end" as a felon for having attended a meeting of the Land Tenure Committee. As a Corporal of Marines in the late eighteenth century penal colony of Sydney, where life is raw and brutalized, he is forced to make a choice between his military oath and his humanity, in effect a choice between probable military promotion with eventual return to the world's civilized hemisphere—and a felon's death by hanging.

> The protagonists of the novels of Thomas Keneally are Jeremiahs of a sort, reluctant prophets or messiahs. A form of sainthood is thrust willy nilly upon them.
> —*Janette T. Hospital*

In *Three Cheers for the Paraclete,* Maitland is a scholarly priest with a hankering for the quietude of uninterrupted research. He has no taste for the role which takes him by surprise—the storm center of theological and political controversy in St. Peter's House of Studies in Sydney, a bastion of orthodoxy and conservatism. He tries earnestly *not* to be a rebel, to submit humbly to discipline, but falls casualty to his burning conscience—and his hasty temper (sainthood never being unalloyed with tangled human psychology in Keneally's novels).

In *The Survivor* there are two candidates for the status of uneasy prophet. The leader of a 1924 Antarctic Expedition looms gigantic in the memory of a surviving member of the team who was forced to leave his leader dead in the wasteland of ice. Now an aging small-town academic, Alec Ramsey is tormented by guilt: can he be certain that Leeming was actually dead when he abandoned him with a few crude burial rites—a broken ski made into a cross and carved with Leeming's initials? And was Leeming God-like or Satanic, a moral giant, an arrogant bastard, or simply a "rather shrunken man"? Ramsey's own role as a survivor is ambiguous—a sort of self-imposed destiny. "I was a polar monk and Leeming was my abbot." He is the "professional survivor" of Rotary Club speaking engagements, by turns self-mocking and righteously outraged that his callow audiences have no awareness of the massively heroic significance of Leeming.

Leeming has, for Ramsey, the quality of a sacrament as potent as the word that compelled Jeremiah. At an academic party he is suddenly asked by a drunken poet:

"Well, question is, did you and that Dr. Lloyd eat of Leeming?"

"I beg your pardon." If Alec was not straightaway outraged it was because the stressed preposition came to his ear with an almost biblical sound, innocuous to the sixty-two-year-old son of a Presbyterian pastor. *Unless you eat of the flesh* . . . "How did you get back to the coast then?" the poet was insisting . . . . Ramsey dared not move. That indigestible leader and unswallowable death flooded and exposed him at the one time; very like the similar vertigo and smotheration caused by the Antarctic phenomenon called white-out . . .

After a time he remembered that he had not in fact eaten Leeming, but the poet's suggestion seemed to him one that he must urgently blend into what he already knew of Leeming and himself.

Finally his gnawing guilt is both exposed and expiated by the unexpected "resurrection" of the dead leader. Forty years later another expedition finds the body frozen and preserved in the polar ice-cap. Ramsey's shock is considerable.

His fear of the resurrection, of the mere event, recurred.

He fought it with his reason . . .

He felt frightened too that Leeming's reappearance would bend and incite him powerfully towards publicly saying *the truth*.

And he thought of *the truth* as of an unknown baggage that would be forced on him by this last ploy of Leeming's, this resurgence. He seemed to be afraid, therefore, of matters yet unknown to him, matters for which he would feel culpable yet which would surprise him as much as they would surprise anyone.

It is an apocalypse he tries frantically to prevent. "For it seemed to him then that he had always been consoled by Leeming's incorruptibility in the ice. It was as crude an intuition as this: he sensed that it diminished his guilt. Now he thought instantly that they must not force those pitiful remains to make any deferred payment of decay."

Although in a state of dread, Ramsey cannot refrain from returning to the Antarctic to witness the removal of the body, though he fears "a change in the essence of his life, a change as absolute as death." The body is removed from its crevice by a winch in a macabre parody of ascension:

As the bundle eked a slow semi-circle above the heads of the people Ramsey saw how he had based his world on guilt for the quite transcendent wrongs done against Leeming. But now the ordinariness of the bundle spurred him to acknowledge the ordinariness of Leeming and the pedestrian nature of his sins against Leeming. Ramsey was so angered at the years he had wasted on shame that a demand rose in him to tear his own flesh.

In **The Chant of Jimmie Blacksmith,** a fictional treatment of actual incidents, Jimmie is a half-blooded Aborigine living on a reservation. He is singled out by the Methodist missionary for education, for imbuement with European ideals. The time is 1900-1901, the fermenting years of Australia's federation as a nation.

Jimmie self-consciously accepts his chosenness. He sets out to disprove the image of the black man as shiftless, drunken, incapable of learning or of holding a steady job. He becomes more educated than the constables and farmers in the small rural towns where he works, he labors hard and diligently, he is Christian rather than a worshiper of the ancient tribal spirit gods, he marries a white girl in a Methodist church. And he is hated and spurned with an intensity greater than the indifferent contempt reserved for his tribal relatives. Quite suddenly, by a random conjunction of an instance of insulting discrimination with the limits of Jimmie's hopes and endurance, he becomes an apostle of black vengeance and violence, a black Jeremiah crying woe to the white oppressors. His rampage is not indiscriminate. With passionate but calculated method he brutally murders men, women and children from the long list of the families who have wronged him.

He knows that he must sustain his hatred and anger at a fervid and religious pitch to justify his butcheries, but is unable to do so. Jimmie Blacksmith, "lost beyond repair somewhere between the Lord God of Hosts and the shrunken cosmogony of his people" is doomed to spend the rest of his life "in tenuous elation and solid desolation between self-knowledge and delirium." He eludes capture for months, is shot and wounded, slips into a convent while the nuns are at vespers, and, ironically, it is the bishop's bed in which he almost bleeds to death before being discovered by the Mother Superior. He is nursed back to sufficient health for hanging.

Blood Red, Sister Rose is the story of Joan of Arc. Keneally's Jehanne—with the compulsion of her Voices, her dread of the martyrdom she foresees, her vacillation between a craving for the peaceful life of a peasant's wife and the thrill of leading the king's armies—has much in common with Jeremiah. As King Zedekiah both needs and fears Jeremiah, keeping him as a privileged prisoner until he is expendable because no longer useful, so Charles needs and fears Jehanne, who is kept on the leash of political expediency until her purpose has been served. She has the same abrasive and aggressive courage as Jeremiah.

* * *

[Hospital:] *Mr. Keneally, your Jehanne is very much a fifteenth-century feminist. Was this a conscious political characterization on your part?*

[Keneally:] Yes. I characterized Jehanne as a rough Australian country girl. As a matter of fact, she was modeled after Germaine Greer.

Does Germaine Greer know that?

No, I'm not at all sure she'd be flattered. She might well be outraged.

I take it you are an admirer?

Yes, but I also find her terrifying. I had to interview her on TV in Sydney in 1972. I was extremely nervous, and well primed with alcoholic courage to face her verbal sharpshooting. But I suddenly had a sense of the almost animal panic in her, of her vulnerability to attack—a feeling for the loneliness of her role—a "somebody has to do this but why me?" aura. I sensed her being pulled in two directions—between determination and anguish.

Did this interview give you the idea to write about Joan of Arc?

No. The subject matter had fascinated me for some time. Jehanne changed the very nature of warfare almost single-handedly. But Germaine Greer gave the shape and style to the character.

I feel sure that Ms. Greer (and all feminists, including myself) would share Jehanne's outrage when her success is put down in a very well-worn sexist way after *all the battles have been won and the king crowned:*

De la Tremoille: *And such a new way of proceeding on the matter of prisoners! One would think you were trying to destroy the rules of knighthood.*

Jehanne: *In my tiny knowledge of the business, my lord, they look stupid without any help from me.*

He did his high laugh and began climbing the stairs again.

De la Tremoille: *Well, a great day for everyone. I*

didn't think I'd see it . . . And now it's all done I suppose you can wear skirts again.

When she put weight on the ball of her foot her whole leg trembled. She thought that fat man would crucify me this morning if he could.

Most of your protagonists seem caught in the grip of either some divine force or their own consciences to act politically and socially. If Halloran and Jimmie Blacksmith do not bring about any changes, they at least function as the conscience of their societies. Maitland and Jehanne actively intervene in their societies politically, and do bring about social and political change. I assume then that your theology would be in agreement with that of the Theology of Liberation writers, such as Rubem Alves and Rosemary Ruether?

I don't really know. I don't read theology as such any more.

But you yourself still consider what Andrew Greeley calls "the God question" worth asking?

Oh certainly. But not in an orthodox or institutional way. And I no longer think of God as a personal being.

How long were you in seminary?

Six and a half years, from 1953 to 1959. Training in Sydney as a diocesan priest.

When would you have been ordained?

Two weeks after I pulled out.

Why did you pull out?

It was not a crisis of conscience or faith. It was a crisis of emotional suppression. I still feel much anger at the responsibility of the church as an institution for the stifling of the intellect, of talent, of love, of the possibility of love, of the possibility of forming any intimate relationship with any other human being.

* * *

In *Bring Larks and Heroes,* Halloran suffers from this learned stifling of love as he recalls his schooling in the Bishop's house at Wexford. He remembers the Dean's Latin anatomizing of love, from the divine, down through the affection between the spouses for the purpose of begetting children, descending finally to "love only in a debased sense of the word, love by analogy only, love execrable in a tipsy ditch with a dirty, racy vagrant woman." Halloran explained to his secret wife, Ann, that his purpose, "whenever he lay with her, was to keep matters as close to God and as far away from the vagrant woman as he could." But when Ann proves to be "as racy as any vagrant woman" Halloran is "delighted but baffled."

His mind would intervene as an arbiter and try to reorganize his motives according to the rules as laid down by Dean Hannon. And his ardor would die, and he would see doubt all over Ann's face.

In *Three Cheers for the Paraclete,* Maitland is celebrating Mass on a windy headland for a group of graduate students. He preaches a short sermon which subsequently causes him much trouble with his superiors, although it endears him to the students. Even as he preaches he is tormented with self-doubt, with fears of his own hypocrisy, afraid that he sounds "like a fashionable priest, the glib kind."

"There are historical causes why European Christianity gave Eros poison to drink, took a confused view of him, placed him under a subtle ban."

He said what the causes were, he touched lightly on centuries and found them pliant to his touch. It was a false pliancy . . . "What have you been told from childhood, again and again? You've been told that Eros is a source of danger. So he is. Yet it must have seemed that if he did not have a hand in the propagation of little Catholics, he wouldn't be given standing room. For Eros is a filthy little pagan with dirty habits. One comes to see that he has been maligned. His presence generates in a person those decent human enthusiasms without which life and even religion are lost. You complain of the pallid cast of soul of this or that priest? But he lacks the self-surrender imposed by Eros to help men to enthusiasm. The priest's way is harder because he does not have this ready means of keeping his personality malleable. As you pity all sapless humans, you must pity and have understanding for the sapless priest. For some of us have been betrayed into a frame of mind that is justly expressed in the saying: 'Because they love no one, they imagine that they love God'."

* * *

[Hospital:] *Maitland is conscious of this stifling of human love, of the intellect, of his scholarly articles and books. Did you experience any specific suppression of your writing?*

[Keneally:] Yes. My articles, short stories, poetry were all censored.

You are, then, Maitland?

Yes and no. I didn't have the guts or the maturity of Maitland. Like Maitland (and Halloran and Jehanne) I feel a tremendous pull toward the conservative prosaic life, a yen for the peaceful and ordinary.

* * *

All Keneally's protagonists try to escape their destinies, to quiet their consciences, to cling to the ordinary life. Halloran dreads a felon's death; he has seen hideous hangings; yet his humanity and conscience compel him to steal food to aid the convict Hearn (like Leeming, an enigmatic Prophet-Satanic figure). Hearn is a Wicklow Protestant, and is convinced his escape plan is "God's scheme."

> "Yes," Halloran said, "I can imagine the Almighty dodging up and down this part of the world, grinding his axe with a Wicklow Protestant . . ." In fact, he was terrified that there might be something on the divine agenda to cut straight across the cramped sphere of tenderness where he and Ann lived . . . He detested prophets, prophets were a great danger. This prophet had had two raw nights to succumb to, but here he was, voluble with prophecy, muttering omens in the bushes. They don't feed you enough to take these shocks, Halloran told himself.

Maitland detests his own prison of doubt, hankers after the old certainties:

> The cold fust of old books assailed him in the dark; devotional books, Dublin 1913, a good year for unalloyed faith. Why couldn't he have been alive and priested then? Saving up indulgences, averting tumors of the throat with a St. Blaise candle, uttering arcane litanies . . . dying in 1924 of dropsy, rosaries and the certainty of Paradise.

Jehanne's divine destiny seems part biological chance; she is an embarrassment to her family because she has never menstruated. To herself, this seems to single her out for a more absolute virginity. Perhaps she is the virgin of Merlin's prophecy, the virgin from Lorraine who will deliver the king. She longs to be normal, to marry, to have children; she grieves for the abnormality of her womb. But she also yearns to be special; she does not want to join in the country adolescent body games and "vanish into some pattern of family and kinship." Then there are her Voices—but there is also her *decision*. "I'm *that* virgin. The one in Merlin." A local gentlewoman responds: "For God's sake, Jehannette, how could you be *that* damned virgin?" Jehanne replies: "Someone has to be. If someone wasn't chosen, someone would have to choose herself." What Jehanne needs, says the lady, is a husband. To which Jehanne retorts with irritation: "Do

you think I want to be that virgin? Do you think there are rewards for it?"

All Keneally's protagonists try to escape their destinies, to quiet their consciences, to cling to the ordinary life.
—*Janette T. Hospital*

Like Jeremiah ("Cursed be the day that I was born") Jehanne is terrified of her own victimhood. Both beg their God and their king for a release from the destiny and from martyrdom. Jehanne wrestles with her Voices:

> *Messire:* Little he-rose, little she-soldier, when the king is anointed . . .
>
> *Jehanne:* What? What, Messire?
>
> *Messire:* The steel goes in, the heat blasts, the rose bleeds.
>
> *Jehanne:* Holy Jesus!
>
> *Messire:* You'll never be alone.
>
> *Jehanne:* But when the steel goes in . . .
>
> *Messire:* There's no consolation.
>
> She woke yelling *I deserve better*!

* * *

[Hospital:] *In spite of the yen for the ordinary of your protagonists and yourself, you, like them, did become politically involved, didn't you?*

[Keneally:] Yes, I was one of the sponsors of the Australian Vietnam Moratorium in 1970. I marched in demonstrations. But my political involvement did not begin until after I left the seminary. When I left I was mentally and emotionally strung out. I worked for six months as a builder's laborer. No one showed any interest in my welfare. No one cared what had become of me. I felt an enormous sense of betrayal, of the inhumanity of the church as an institution toward individual people. I began for the first time to think politically, to see the church as one more corrupt institution among many in a corrupt society.

In 1966, I did a TV documentary in Sydney on the corruption of the corporations and institutions of Australian society, including the institutional church which functioned like any other commercial corporation. It appalled the church, of course, and brought down wrath upon my head.

Just like Maitland?

* * *

Maitland's working-class cousin, Joe, has been cheated out of his small savings by the misleading advertising and devious legal contracts of a housing development corporation. Maitland protests to the corporation on Joe's behalf.

> [He was shown] into the office of the Allied Projects Development Company's chief accountant. He was greeted in a manner he had come to hate by a man of about forty. The greeting said, "We're all professional men together and know the price of fish. Besides which, some of my best friends are Catholics and Monsignor X has money invested in us. Your *company,* if I can call it that, and ours are two of the pillars that keep the sky up."

The company refuses to refund Joe's money. Maitland preaches a sermon in a fashionable church on the readiness of the church to condone social evils. It is reported on the front page of a city newspaper under the headline "A Power in the Pulpit." His superiors are furious. There are so many safe topics one could preach on. "It's the patently artificial things a priest can safely attack. The mass media, materialism, advertising, the threat of Communism, paganism in the arts. Add all that to faith and morals and you've enough for a lifetime of sermons."

The newspaper subsequently publishes seven letters from people who have suffered under the same company, and also the announcement by the managing director of Allied Projects that the archdiocese owns shares in both itself and its mother-sister-company, Investment General. Maitland receives a phone call from the Archbishop:

> "James, I detest this sort of embarrassment, you know, the type that gives hint that the Church is economically entrenched . . . Of course, there are still people who feel that way, who imagine that an archdiocese can be run without revenue, where an oil company can't."

> . . . "Your Grace," he said trembling, "is the archdiocese going to back me up by selling its holdings in both those companies?"

> There was silence at His Grace's end . . .

> "My heaven, *that's* called turning the flank," His Grace decided, not without some hint of approval.

> "However, Mr. Boyle [a papal knight, and auditor of the company] . . . assures me that the companies are respectable and in no way depart from the norms of the business world."

Nevertheless, a few days later His Grace telephones again with the news that having sought legal advice, the archdiocese will be getting rid of its stock.

A century and a half earlier, in the same city, Halloran had less success with, and more bitterness for, the institutional church. Four Irish Catholic convicts have been condemned to hanging for stealing from government stores to aid another convict in escaping. The Protestant chaplain comes to the condemned hut where Halloran and his three fellow convicts are chained like animals awaiting execution.

The Reverend Mr. Calverley begins to preach about the wrath of God to sinners. The men "pelt him with the best blasphemies they had." The noise brings a Constable with a chain in his hand. He swings it round the hut, beating "at the four man-soft corners. The chain clattered and plopped across wood and flesh, hissed along Halloran's scalp one way, then another." The chaplain is appalled, and orders the Constable to stop, "but he thought that stripes these four deserved, and stripes they would get in their pit in hell."

> "There is no other name but the name of Jesus given in heaven or on earth by which it behooveth a man to be saved," proclaimed the chaplain quietly.

> "And *he* works for Government House," John McHugh called, feeling out his chain wounds and crying over them.

* * *

> **I must make it clear that my distrust of the church's left-wing political endeavors is not a rational one. It is still a reaction of personal and instinctual anger.**
> **—*Thomas Keneally***

[Hospital:] *Although all your protagonists find themselves in opposition to an institutionalized God, they are all supported by an inner (sometimes mystical) religion. And they act on the authority of this religious conscience. So although you do not read the theologians of liberation, I assume you would approve of their political activity.*

[Keneally:] With reservations. I have a great distrust of the church's history of co-operation, of its ability to exploit legitimate impulses of rebellion for its own ends.

Yet surely people like Camillo Torres, Paulo Freire, Helder Camara are like the heroes/heroines of your novels? They have stayed within the institution of the church, risked their lives in political involvement.

Yes. I must make it clear that my distrust of the church's left-wing political endeavors is not a rational one. It is still a reaction of personal and instinctual anger.

Yet Maitland submitted completely to his superiors in the end—to the censorship of his sermons, the ban on publishing and a disciplinary transfer to a rural parish. If you were writing **Three Cheers for the Paraclete** *now, eight years later, would you still have Maitland remain a priest?*

No. I'd have him get out into politics. Or writing.

Patricia Monk (essay date Summer 1982)

SOURCE: "Eden Upside Down: Thomas Keneally's *Bring Larks and Heroes* as Anti-pastoral," in *World Literature Written in English,* Vol. 21, No. 2, Summer, 1982, pp. 297-303.

[*In the following essay, Monk traces the progress of Halloren's apotheosis in* Bring Larks and Heroes *as a function of the narrative's inversion of conventional and pastoral tropes, related to characters, settings, and moral tone.*]

Thomas Keneally can justifiably lay claim to an important place in Australian literature. If, however, there were a single moment in his works by which he might be best remembered, I suspect that moment would be the final paragraph of **Bring Larks and Heroes,** in which he describes the death agonies of Phelim Halloran:

> It was as he had foretold. Every prayer, curse and snatch of song unleased itself up the vent of his body. Oh, the yawning shriek of his breathlessness, above him like a massive bird, flogging him with its black wings; the loneliness ripping his belly up like pavingstones. On his almost closed lids, six-sided pillars of light came down with terrible hurtfulness. It was with such a surpassing crack that his head split open, he being borne presiding through so many constellations, that he asked himself, panicstriken, "Am I perhaps *God?*"

Halloran's apotheosis—the apotheosis of a spoiled priest from a poor Irish family into a Christ figure—is the final

act of a pastoral tragedy set among the transported felons of an early settlement "not meant to be identified with" Sydney, according to the author's note.

Keneally's primary concern in **Bring Larks and Heroes** is with the culture shock awaiting new colonists whose expectations of a return to Eden are shattered by encounters with the foreignness of trees that shed bark rather than leaves, mammals that lay eggs, and the phenomenon of summer in December. Eden has thus become demonic, and "the busy compilers of journals called it evil at some length." Consequently Halloran, who does not "call it evil because it [is] weird," becomes estranged from the community, and eventually becomes the scapegoat for a crime committed by others. Halloran's inexorable progress towards his sacrificial death and apotheosis can be traced as a symbolic corollary of his steady progress towards his final understanding that the landscape surrounding him is not, in fact, demonic, but only Eden upside-down.

Before I trace that progress of Halloran towards his apotheosis I want to look briefly at what I consider to be the keys to Keneally's inversion of the pastoral convention in **Bring Larks and Heroes.** There are, in fact, two complementary patterns of inversion existing simultaneously in the novel: the inversion of the picture of the early settlers as the inhabitants of a pastoral setting, and the inversion of the concept of the landscape of that setting as a type of Eden. In the first of the patterns, the settlers, free or transported, see themselves as the innocent inhabitants of a pastoral world, frustrated only by the ugliness, hostility, and inhospitability of the physical aspects of that world. Keneally's inversion shows us that the settlers themselves are the demonic element, bringing death and disease into the landscape. The conventional pastoral, concerned as it is with the depiction of an ideal society, uses the trope of the sheep to represent the people under the benevolent protection of their aristocratic or ecclesiastical rulers, the shepherds. In **Bring Larks and Heroes,** however, the relationship takes on a thoroughly demonic aspect as the role of sheep is given to convicted felons, and that of the shepherds to their military guards. Benevolence is replaced by bloody and brutal tyranny. Hence society itself is shown not as idealized but as demonic.

The second pattern of inversion concerns itself with an apparently demonic landscape: crops fail, the weather is bad, stock dies, and the settlement is very close to starvation. However, in this case the point of the inversion is to show that this landscape, in its beauty and fertility, is the hoped for and elusive Eden. The key to the understanding of this process of inversion is found in the passage where Byrne catches a sea gull. As the narrator oxymoronically states, "Byrne ate the inedible bird." If you can eat something safely and gain nourishment from it, as does Byrne, then it is by definition *not* "inedible." Here Keneally points directly to a truth that is also made clear elsewhere in the novel, with regard to Halloran's understanding of his relationship with the natural world: the land can provide food if one is willing to revise one's ideas of food. The Aboriginals survive because their idea of food conforms to what the land provides (gulls or grubs); the Europeans almost starve because their idea of food (cheese, beef, bread) does not conform to what is provided. The wasteland is paradoxically the fertile garden, if only one can learn to recognize its fruits.

The most prominent patterns of inversion, then, are those of character and setting. There is another kind of inversion present, however, albeit one implied to a somewhat lesser extent: the inversion of choice in one's moral actions. Halloran, when we first meet him, is carrying a gun, but without any hope of killing game, because "the full-time game-killers, three men chosen from amongst the transported felons, had not brought in anything since the New Year." The crime for which they have been transported is not named, but the skills required for full-time game-killing would be almost identical with those required in poaching. Poachers, therefore, become licensed hunters on behalf of the community—and the definition of crime is changed to suit the needs of the community. But the inversion here is not simple, for although the poaching/game-killing inversion turns a crime into a community service, the crime of stealing food from the community remains a crime, one which is in fact less unjustifiably punishable in the circumstances of the settlement than in the country from which they have come. Keneally's point is not that circumstances change morality, but that people change it, usually for their own benefit—a suitably demonic concept for a demonic society.

It is Halloran's triumph that he recognize all these truths: that the settlers are the demonic element, that the landscape is really edenic, and that a demonic society produces a demonic morality. It is also his tragedy, for the community cannot tolerate someone who sees things differently. Consequently, he is killed for his vision. This vision is not a sudden revelation but one which develops slowly in the course of Halloran's relationship with the natural world, and with his fellow human beings in the settlement.

> **Keneally's point is not that circumstances change morality, but that people change it, usually for their own benefit—a suitably demonic concept for a demonic society.**
> —*Patricia Monk*

To return to the inversion of setting: the novel begins in an apparently demonic landscape, "the world's wrong end," which is, to borrow [Northrop] Frye's definition, "the world that desire totally rejects: the world of the nightmare . . . as

it is . . . before any image of human desire, such as the city or the garden, has been solidly established." The natural features of the landscape are, however, "far too open to a bland, immense, and oriental sky," and consequently the settlers are also exposed. Yet in spite of this evident vulnerability, the settlers' response is to resist assimilation, and to impose their will upon the land:

> although nothing but the worm of death seemed to flourish in this obdurate land, it was the duty of those who served the King . . . to outstubborn the wayward earth.

Halloran, however, in the midst of this apparently demonic land, is confronted by the possibility, indeed the necessity, of developing a new set of standards by which new values might be determined, for "it seemed that in these poor scrubby woods, all his judgements on what a forest should look like were being scarcely tolerated by the whole pantheon of the gods of this, the world's wrong end."

Halloran's visit to Ann releases her from the "God-abandoned" hutch of Blythe's, for the divine center no longer rests in human dwellings or society, into the temporary freedom of the woods presided over by a new pantheon. Here she is "transmuted by something very close . . . to pure animal joy"— a transmutation into something more in tune with the land, and one which Halloran (who is described as feeling "cubbish") shares with her. It should be noted, however, that at this point Halloran is still identified with the demonic settlers insofar as the symbol of his superiority, which he has chosen to carry through "this forest," is a gun. His notion of his own superiority to the blacks who are "dying of smallpox" rests on his perception of his superior ability to kill and to resist death.

Having established Halloran's initial identification with human society, Keneally proceeds to present a series of juxtaposed visions of the land as actually edenic (although apparently demonic) and white humanity as actually demonic (although apparently innocently pastoral). The first of these occurs when, standing on the cliff, Halloran sees

> set in the jelly-blue, a fleet of jew-fish tend[ing] slowly north. It did make one angry, to see such placid manna a foot or two below the sea-top, passing by the hungry town without a flick of their tails.

Set in juxtaposition to the colonists' indifference to this "placid manna" (no fishing boats are out) is their frantic activity in the lime hunt; considerable time is spent looking for mussel-shells left behind by generations of native people. Ironically, these shells are intended to be used, by the military rulers of the settlement, in the making of the mortar necessary to the construction of a real "brick" building, a building designed to make its inhabitants feel more at home. The hungry colonists ignore the fish, which would satisfy and nourish them, in order to try to make the land conform rather more to what they think it should be like.

The second of these juxtapositions occurs during Halloran's expedition upriver to "the Crescent" with the transported forger Ewers. Here the land begins to seem hospitable to Halloran, even beautiful:

> The land looked promising from the jolly-boat, the river went west quite royally, spangled with sun, miles wide. Before its massive kindliness, the coves and beaches, cliffs and islands stood back.

Ewers, with the artist's eye, sees this beauty more immediately than Halloran, to whom he remarks:

> If I painted this landscape . . . those who ever saw it would think that the forests behind the beaches were teeming with fruit and game. They would think that this river led to a kingly town, that Eden lay at the headwaters.

However, Ewers' hubristic vision of the true nature of the land, away from the colony, as edenic, and his ability to make others see it his way, founders at once on his confrontation with Mrs. Daker; the death of his vision is recorded in his recognition that the two of them appear, this time, as a part of a "caricature of the Pastoral landscape." As the bird he is painting, and the beauty of the land which it represents, dies in her crazy hands, it prefigures his own death, described in terms of a "ravaged animal spill[ing] dirt and water down its legs." Although Ewers' death acts as a foreshadowing of Halloran's, the full vision of demonic humanity, as opposed to the edenic land, is presented not through Mrs. Daker but in the scenes in the hospital at the Crescent.

Here the cruelty, filth, and irrational sexuality of demonic humanity is exposed as Halloran, separating the couple copulating on the filthy floor in a ring of bystanders, makes his way to the bed of the criminal patient he has been ordered to escort to headquarters; looking down at the man, he sees his back and upper legs to be a mass of stinking, gangrenous flesh. Later, when he sees this flesh encrusted with flies, Halloran can only rush outside in order that the "clean astringency" of nature can provide some kind of antidote to the effects of demonic humanity. Breathing in the fragrance of crushed eucalyptus leaves, he comes to the moment of unconscious choice—when he aligns himself with the land. It is worth noting, however, that by this point he already has begun to think of it as "the world's south end" rather than as its worse end.

A further such juxtaposition provides the turning point of the novel, for here Keneally presents Halloran's *conscious* alignment with the forces of the land. This takes place on the occasion of Captain Allen's expedition into the wilderness, an expedition which, although designed to conquer, only proves its own incapacity. The members of the expedition, including Halloran, are in such poor condition that they can only cover fourteen miles the first day, "although the country was easy." Their lack of stamina is made particularly evident in their encounter with a family of natives:

> In the early afternoon of that first day, they found themselves being watched by a stock-still native family not unlike denuded acacias at a distance of a quarter of a mile. They were very thin, that family, but loped easily away. The crooked grey thickets consumed them like mist.

The natives are thin, admittedly, but fit; they survive because, in their likeness to trees, they shape themselves to the land. Some time later a moment of conscious choice presents itself, to Halloran, as a kind of "transfiguration":

> The generous morning continued to gild them all with an heroic light. Halloran himself gazed across the river, across mangroves to a tableland as blue and hazed and comfortable as chimney-smoke. He felt himself to be very much the center of this world. With his hat off, he found that the tawny drench of light through his eye-lashes was made of gold rods all bearing on him. He was the focus, he was the central screw. Take him out and the hills would fall apart. He contained the world and was not contained by it.

Here he identifies consciously with the land, most significantly with the light which is so conspicuous a feature of it. Yet, it is "an heroic light," and consequently Halloran's identification with it points forward to the "heroic" death he must suffer.

That heroic death is the occasion for the final juxtaposition of land (now revealed as truly edenic) against humanity (now revealed as truly demonic). In the previous episode I have mentioned, it is of considerable significance that the natives are likened to trees rather than to any other natural feature. Not only is the image visually attractive and apt, but also it adds a further item to the sequence of tree images in the novel; one is led steadily forward from the opening scene where Anne, visited by joy, leans against a tree, to the final, symbolic juxtaposition of the tree of life and the tree of death. In this scene, Halloran perceives the trees outside the "death-hut" as part of a single tree of life: "Outside, the white eucalyptus grew, five trees from the one bole, gusting outwards from each other, very much a conclave . . . . Life arrogant there, outside the death-hut; life astringent in white trees."

At the final moment Halloran dies on the gallows, his neck broken in the drop, Keneally ends with Halloran's question, "Am I perhaps *God*?" The answer implied by the novel is, I believe, yes. For in this upside-down, hardly recognizable Eden, the tree of knowledge and the tree of life are the same. Halloran has tasted the "cool astringency" of the eucalyptus which has brought him both knowledge and life. At the moment of his physical death he is raised in an apotheosis in which he becomes identified with the natural world. "Borne presiding through so many constellations" and therefore immortal, he passes beyond both demonic and human comprehension, a dying and a living god.

Thomas Keneally with Laurie Hergenhan (interview date October 1986)

SOURCE: An interview in *Australian Literary Studies,* Vol. 12, No. 4, October, 1986, pp. 453-57.

[*In the following interview, Keneally discusses the function of history in his fiction, the significance of his non-Australian settings, and his fictional use of historical facts.*]

[*Hergenhan:*] *A number of your novels have been concerned with history and war. They have been set wholly or partly outside Australia often with no overt Australian element [Keneally interpolates: 'the sin against the Holy Spirit']. How would you account for this, do you see any recurrent concerns and associated aesthetic problems?*

[Keneally:] The whole business of historical novels is that for a time I found history an easier model—paradigm to use that fashionable word—to work with than the present is. Unfortunately though, the reading public have problems with working out what sort of historical novel a novel is. As I said in an article in *New Republic* when I was reviewing Gore Vidal's *Lincoln* the best sort of historical novel is not the tempestuous sagas of bygone ages or the bodice-rippers that you see in newsagents. These have certainly a great commercial value but ultimately many of them debase history. The best sort of historical novel is the one which is really about the present and uses the past as a sort of working model for the present. Or, to put it another way, the best sort of historical novels are novels in which the human issues are the same as those we have now, and have always had to face. I went through a phase in my writing when the model I worked with was the past in one way or another. Mind you I have to say that of course there are a number of my novels which are contemporary and set in Australia as well. *The Chant of Jimmie Blacksmith* wasn't one of them because

it was set in the year of Federation but such novels as *Three Cheers for the Paraclete, The Survivor, Passenger* and *Family Madness* are all Australian centered though in *Family Madness* you see the interest in history again, in European history, specifically the history of Belorussia during World War II. Notice that there is suspicion there that Australia is twice as interesting if placed in that rather vivid historic context. The migrant is more interesting if you know the history he comes from and it may be an ancient history, of course older than World War I, older than Joan of Arc. We see such a history operating in Australia in 1984 on a family of Belorussian migrants. If you take a book like *Gossip from the Forest* which is about the signing of the Armistice in 1918, it admittedly has not a lot to do with Australia and yet on the other hand it has. There had been for Australians between 1788 and my generation a tendency to look upon Europe as a place where the other half of your soul was, particularly to look upon somewhere in the British Isles as the place where the other half of your soul was. But one of the greatest 'future shock' sort of events of our lifetime has been the decline of Britain and the decline of Europe. My grandparents used to look upon Britain as something admittedly satanic but enormously powerful, ramified, megalithic, as something that was immutable. There was a great comfort both for the English and the Irish in that picture of things and to my amazement in the space of my early adolescence Britain virtually withered and became an increasingly impoverished nation and I suppose in *Gossip from the Forest* I am looking at some of the causes of this withering. I imagine that I write both as an amateur historian and as an Australian of my generation who used to sit in my childhood round family gatherings where uncles would show the shrapnel wounds in their legs, or would be visibly affected from gassings which had happened more than a quarter of a century before at Paschendale or Ypres or some such place. It is inevitable that that war should seem to me to be the event which signaled the end of innocence and the end of freshness and power for Europe.

Now about recurrent concerns I think there is a recurrent concern in the novels in men of decency, the central characters often being men, fighting historic causes on which they can't quite get a grip. It happens with Erzberger in *Gossip from the Forest,* the German politician who tries to bring sanity to the negotiations and who has a sense of being the only one there who can foresee the ultimate results for Europe in what is happening in that railway carriage, and you see it too in Delaney an innocent Australian lad, quite charming, who is trying to rescue a girl he loves, Danielle from White Russian history—a history he doesn't understand and whose power he is ill equipped to deal with.

About associated aesthetic problems that run through the novels: I am not aware of any, although every novelist has enormous aesthetic problems to deal with. I'm not aware of any to be honest that arise specifically out of the historical aspects of the work I do. The continuing aesthetic problem is to make the human being real and immediate and that is not the problem which the bodice-ripper type of historical novelist has. His main aim is to make the person exotic either through dress, speech, preposterous wealth, preposterous cruelty, etc. A distancing mechanism is quite deliberately employed in the Gothic romance and the historical romance. The opposite is true of historical novels which wish to pass as novels as such, but that observation is true of all serious writing.

How would you relate these novels to those set in Australia?

I find that the work is pretty well a continuum. You have in say Corporal Halloran in *Bring Larks and Heroes* of long, long ago, or in Delaney in *A Family Madness,* the same sort of pilgrim voyager though I like Delaney rather better than Corporal Halloran because I think he's more fully developed than Halloran, not more fully developed as a character but certainly as a human being. I suppose the critical debate about the body of my work if there is one or if there is to be one would be concerned about this question of whether the body of work is a continuum or whether it is a set of jerky new directions continually embarked upon. I hope it won't seem special pleading if I say that the historical novels, the ones set outside Australia, were the equivalent of the Australians' trip overseas which in my youth was generally sanctioned by the dictum that you could only get perspective on Australia by seeing it from outside and I think that is the case, I think that we have been so little subject to outside scrutiny that we have got to do it to ourselves, we have been so little objects of interest and there has always been this gulf peculiar to small countries and ex-colonies, I suppose, between what seem to be eternal verities and important issues here and the way those same issues and verities look when they are reviewed from a distance of 12,000 miles. So if those historic novels like *Gossip from the Forest, Confederates* and so on were my sort of literary overseas trip then of course the difference between them and my Australian preoccupations are more apparent than substantial. I remember a publishing executive a few years ago advising me to stop being a literary bikie, thundering off down unexpected and unprecedented alleys and dragging my readership with me like a semi-willing bikie's moll. But I think that some writers are simply like that temperamentally, they prefer to jump about. There is more of this in the American writing tradition, in Mark Twain or Gore Vidal or others than there is in the Australian tradition. Just the same you have it in a nascent way in Blanche D'Alpuget who has written about Asia and now about Israel. Continuity comes from the perceptions and values of the main characters, so basically, I see my work as a continuous and relatively homogenous thing, although it can't ever *seem* to be as homogenous as

the work of those novelists who generally write out of intimate personal experience.

Do you think your fiction about war stands apart from other fiction about war written by Australian authors?

The different settings go without saying because we have the south in *Confederates* and we have the signing of the Armistice in *Gossip from the Forest* and in that other book *Season in Purgatory* we have Croatia, but I think theme and treatment are more or less the same as those in such works as *1915.* You are dealing with innocents trying to prove their honor against the background of massive movements of history and massive items of technology and out of that comes the poignancy of most of this sort of fiction. When I am writing that sort of book, whether it be *Confederates* with the central character, Usaph Bumpass, or whether it be my favorite work, *Cut Rate Kingdom,* in which a labor politician deals with the realities of Australia's position vis-a-vis Asia in 1942, whichever it is, you always show the myths that the individual takes with him into the fray and the way these are ultimately swamped and overwhelmed by (I have probably used the phrase before) the realities of history. The myths that Johnny Mulhall takes into his dealings with the Americans in *Cut Rate Kingdom* have to do with Australian socialism, Australian utopianism, the Australian warrior—whether, that's a political or a battle field warrior as the gamest, the flashiest, the one with the most panache; and of course such local and tribal mythologies get gobbled up by forces vaster than them. But that's something that I think all writers about war and history also deal with, so that apart from the mere differences of the settings, once again I see a continuity in terms of theme and treatment with other fiction written by other Australians on this sort of theme. Perhaps there is a greater stress on those forces of history moving in the background, and perhaps there is a greater stress on that rather than the mere comradeship or the intimate events of the group of men who are undergoing this experience.

> **The recurrent flaws and strengths of a personality such as Schindler's give his life an artistic form of the type you have to make up for a fictional character. The most remarkable coincidence between life and art lies in that phenomenon, that lives often have what appears to be an artistic neatness to them.**
> **—*Thomas Keneally***

I think one of the reasons Australians write about this sort of subject, particularly Australian males (it's very much what your feminist would call Anglo-Celtic and rather sexist) is that most of Australian life has been fairly safe and that, for Australian males anyhow, it is quite obvious that the battles they experienced are the supreme events of their lives. Maybe this says a lot about the impoverishment of male experience. I think that may be too glib a judgment but that there is none the less a great deal of truth in it. I am pleased to be out of that phase of my career now and moving onto other matters.

Would you care to comment on the use of fact as a basis or departure point or whatever in your fiction?

The only book I have written which purported to be based to a strict degree on fact is *Schindler's Ark.* The reason it had to be so written was that I had a duty to the people who gave me interviews and who had been Schindler's prisoners which no doubt accounts for this or that small error of fact in the book but the point is that these errors do not occur for any aesthetic or technical reason but are a mere lapse. In an historic novel errors can be deliberately courted. By error here I mean the deliberate imposition on an historical character of a vision he or she may not have had or of a particular linking of events which may not have taken place but which has that prevailing artistic truth of something which *should* have happened.

Let's talk about that terrible word 'faction'. *Schindler's Ark* was such a book and I thought it an appropriate mode to use since it had been used so well by Tom Wolfe in *The Right Stuff.* The writer of 'faction' has a great deal of artistic liberty in interpreting what the events mean, in finding their linking symbolism, in the use of language and metaphor, in providing a piquancy to the characterization. It is a valid genre, again much more honored in the United States than it is here, though Bryson's *Evil Angels* was a fine example of it and it is in a way technically easier to write, though in research terms it is more demanding. Why it is technically easy is that the recurrent flaws and strengths of a personality such as Schindler's give his life an artistic form of the type you have to make up for a fictional character. The most remarkable coincidence between life and art lies in that phenomenon, that lives often have what appears to be an artistic neatness to them. The same faults that do us in during youth become terminal in age. The only reason that lives aren't quite as neatly arranged in the real world as they are in a novel is that in the real world accidents occur which are genuine accidents whereas in a novel accidents should only occur if they have already somehow been caused by the action and by the excesses of the characters. The point about 'faction' though is that it is in some ways too limiting. You are bound by the realities of the exterior world. You cannot have an essential inventive experience which goes with writing true novels like *Family Madness.* You certainly can't have what you have in *A Dutiful Daughter,* an adolescent girl who turns her parents into cattle creatures, and

you can't have a journal-keeping foetus like you have in *Passenger.* So 'faction' is one decent direction for writing to take but the fantastic is another. I think in my future work I shall veer towards the fantastic.

David English (essay date 1987)

SOURCE: "History and the Refuge of Art: Thomas Keneally's Sense of the Past," in *The Writer's Sense of the Past: Essays on Southeast Asian and Australian Literature,* edited by Kerpal Singh, Singapore University Press, 1987, pp. 160-69.

[*In the following essay, English examines the subjective bases of the authorial consciousness that informs Keneally's novels, emphasizing specifically the textual connections between his own biography, his sense of history, and other written texts..*]

In every aspect of his published writing and commentary, Thomas Keneally presents a consistent and uniform consciousness: he lives in a world of unresolved dualisms. The primary dualism is that which distinguishes the sacred potential of the will from the profane, finite betrayal of all bodies, or forms, most importantly the human body.

Keneally presumes that to be an author is to accept the task of eliminating these dualisms. He regards himself as a mediator in the eschatological struggle. He venerates and translates what he regards as authoritative, and he attempts to consecrate what he regards as mere form. He doesn't regard himself as a source or an authority. He once said "Order is beyond me" when referring to his research techniques, which is fortuitously emblematic of his total state of consciousness. Keneally is unable to accept the idea that truth, or analogues for truth, in the form of literary structures, might emanate from him and live independently of him in a life of their own. Such a situation would imply that we are alone in a fatherless universe and, since our product can live independently of us, mortal as well.

His need for what he himself calls "repositories of immortality" manifests itself as a general inability to relinquish authorship. While the "author" is in communication with the product of his imagination then *finitude,* an ending, is temporarily deferred. He remains an omniscient, self-conscious writer and his product becomes a self-created momentary order with which he can have a reflexive dialogue. With Keneally there can never be a created reality existing beyond the narrator's consciousness—there can be no true characterization, no arbitrary fate, no "past" if that means an entity existing in its own terms to which he must subject himself.

It is a commonplace paradox that the dualistic uncertainty of an author like Keneally which prevents him from relinquishing control, terminating his art, or accepting reminders of mortality, is the same uncertainty which prevents him from being truly an "author", if that is taken to mean the origin of authority. Patrick White, for example, is not self-conscious. He submits himself to his own vision with no idea of the outcome and no attempt to retain authority over the significance of what he says. As a result White is repetitive, or *insistent* as Don Anderson has put it, but he is truly original, an *origin,* whereas Keneally who avoids repetition because it becomes an analogue for the pointlessness of life, also remains profoundly unoriginal.

Keneally finds certitudes, or origins beyond his unresolved consciousness, in three major areas: (i) his own biography, and immediate experience, and the act of writing, because in this subjectivist world one's self is the most tangible entity, and the words on the page are miraculous objects which have precipitated in a sea of subjectivism; (ii) what he calls "the past" because it seems to have a neat order; and (iii) other written documents or literary works, because they offer, like one's own language, a defining point or authorising agent which calls out a reaction and relieves consciousness from the burden of finding its own literary-creative direction.

> **It is a commonplace paradox that the dualistic uncertainty of an author like Keneally which prevents him from relinquishing control, terminating his art, or accepting reminders of mortality, is the same uncertainty which prevents him from being truly an "author", if that is taken to mean the origin of authority.**
> **—*David English***

Keneally's reliance on the certainties of subjective experience has resulted in two novels which are obviously autobiographic, *The Place at Whitton* and *Three Cheers For the Paraclete,* as well as two novels which revisit the themes and text of previous works of his own, *A Victim of the Aurora* and *Passenger.* Perhaps more significantly, Keneally's reliance on his own vision or subjective perception for authority leads him to resort to surrealist fantasy of the sort in *A Dutiful Daughter,* which breaks out from time to time in otherwise realist narratives like *Confederates, Blood Red, Sister Rose* or *Schindler's Ark.*

The condition which constantly eludes Keneally is ordinariness, both in terms of event and narrative stance, because to sustain a created sense of ordinary reality requires him to engage in illusionism, to erect an analogical edifice which

suggests the real through the intangible. The unseen is a threat for a consciousness like Keneally's, so that he is able to engage directly only with his own language, or alternatively to produce convulsive surreal fantasy, another version of subjectivism. As he puts it himself:

> I've been reading Marshall McLuhan, and I've come to realise that print is only the most artificial repository of immortality—and that's what we're involved in, immortality. I'm wondering whether to cast off into a sea of pure fantasy.

One of the happiest outcomes of Keneally's need to use himself as an authorised source of information is the portrait of Phelim Halloran in *Bring Larks and Heroes,* his second historical novel. It is a brilliantly confessional novel, and a true autobiography. The unrecognised achievement in this novel is how, with sentence-by-sentence precision, Keneally fits Halloran into a biographic scheme or proposition. The imagery, logic, vocabulary and event-sequence around this personality never deviates from the thesis that authoritarian belief systems produce a personality which is self-conscious, irresolute, fearful, dualistic, marginalised, morbid, fatalistic, powerless, superstitious—the complete victim.

All of Keneally's characters are framed inside this master-victim dualism, and he has broken no new ground in characterisation since *Bring Larks and Heroes,* because, I would suggest, he is not interested in being *informed* by the world beyond himself.

II

It should come as no surprise to find that a writer with Keneally's preoccupations should find the past more congenial than what he calls "the perilous moment in which we live". The "perils", of course, lurk in the uncertainties of the present. With the exception of the autobiographic and surrealist novels, along with the highly self-conscious *Passenger,* all of Keneally's novels are "historical" if that means set in the past.

Certainly the *idea* of the past is very reassuring for Keneally. As he said in 1975 when referring to the perilous present:

> Writers will always be attracted by the past, it is less confusing than the present. Historians have already reduced it to some understandable unity for us. Their gift is beyond estimation.

He goes on to make another characteristic dualist claim that the past is merely "the present rendered fabulous", that is, the past offers a rock-like certitude against which he can project his irresolute consciousness; it is he as author who constructs the fable.

There are three aspects of Keneally's sense of the historical in his novels which are consistent with his own formulation. Perhaps most obviously, there is no sense in Keneally's historical novels that any one period is different from another, nor could there be if the past is merely the present, (that is, Keneally's present), rendered fabulous.

Keneally's portrayal of life in the past automatically, almost obsessively, dismisses the intractable, the foreign, the social structure, the determining context, in favor of an anachronist, knowing-humanist view in which all men and women of all nations and times have the same personality. The victims, Halloran, Jimmy Blacksmith, Jehanne, Usaph Bumpass, Poldeck Pfefferberg have mental processes, even occasionally speech mannerisms, which are indistinguishable: as do the masters—Major Sabian, Dowie Stead, Stonewall Jackson, or Sir Jean D'Aulon in 1422:

> D'Aulon: They call me honest Jean. By that they mean I'm the poorest knight banneret in the army. I'm not married because no girl's old man is very interested in estates that have been in the keeping of the Goddams for the last eleven years . . . .
>
> Jehanne: Sir Jean, this is my page Minguet.
>
> D'Aulon: Hello Sunshine!

Of course this passage has many elements familiar to readers of Keneally. There is the knowing compound allusiveness available to an author with time to construct it, (but not to a participant feeling his way through the perilous present), and the verbal play ("honest Jean"), and the outrageous piece of triumphalist authorial wit ("Hello Sunshine!"). However, while there may be a respectable view of History to suggest that "there's nothing new under the sun" and all people in all cultures are the same, or while the Christian view of man, which Keneally presumably represents, might presume that there is an a-historical integrity of the individual soul before God and therefore historical periods are only constructs, there is still the possibility that Keneally needs to invade and demystify, or appropriate "the past", since the existence of the past indicates transience. If an event, an entity or an order of things is allowed to have existed beyond the narrator, then the narrator himself is threatened with mortality.

One only need think again of Patrick White's sense of the past, by comparison, to understand what Keneally finds difficult. White, the illusionist, traces out in *The Twyborn Affair* a series of intensely nostalgic sketches of the Edwardian South of France, Australia between the wars and London in the blitz. The places and periods are *allowed to have existed* and then relinquished.

If the first aspect of Keneally's sense of history is that he won't permit the past to exist outside his own consciousness, then the second is that his historical novels only ever concern themselves with war and violence. There may be a view of history which relates war to key social and economic changes, but this is not Keneally's reason for always writing about war. For him the intensities of acts of violence and military behavior are the extraordinary modes which he hopes will give meaning to the ordinary.

War or Civil Disturbance is one of the great certitudes. While a country or district is under arms the imponderable ordinariness of peacetime can be shelved. Action is *required by* the circumstance, life has a purpose and a given order. As a writer Keneally can take voyeuristic sustenance from the immediacy of the event without being threatened as he might have been in real life. From the tranquillity, the refuge, of his armchair and his omniscience, he can imagine his way into the bush with Jimmie Blacksmith, or into the Confederate army, or the carriage in which the Armistice is signed. He can be a General, fantasizing about rolling an army up this way or that, or *he* can think of the timely expedient of hosing down the hot cattle trucks carrying Jewish prisoners on their way to Auschwitz. It was actually a character called Sandie, but it could just as easily have been Keneally in ***Confederates*** who thinks, as he rides out behind Stonewall Jackson, "This is what it is to live . . . with a man who sees his job as being to whip history into shape".

Keneally also tends to behave as the omniscient repository of technical details, terms, and incidental observations which are placed, almost precipitated, into the narrative, presumably to add authenticity. The effect however, is often a voyeuristic fetishism, a suggestion that his fascination with the caliber and names of guns, the branches and anabranches of rivers, the precise ranks and army equivalents of officers of the S.S., compels in him an ambiguous boyish fascination. When Oskar Schindler is watching from what is literally his refuge, the shade of trees on the hill overlooking Krakusa Street, he notice that:

> An armed S.S. man intervened. Beside the nondescript mass of Ghettomenschen, such a being, in his freshly pressed summer uniform, looked superbly fed and fresh. And from the hill you could see the oil on the machine pistol in his hand.

Of course Oskar could not have seen the oil, it is Keneally who imagines it, just as in ***Blood Red, Sister Rose*** it is not Sir Jean D'Aulon but Keneally who is interested in the precise place in the hierarchy occupied by a "knight banneret."

However, it is Keneally's specific obsession with violence that allows him to make what I think is his real contribution to historical understanding. Keneally is not one who wishes evil, pain or suffering on anybody; his interest in violence is merely one version of a larger morbid preoccupation with the relationship between significant and insignificant form, and in particular the moment of transgression, or violation, when the secrets of that most significant of forms, the body, might be revealed.

Keneally is an acknowledged master of the art of representing violence. His "technique" is not as deliberate as the term implies. His automatic and unvarying way of representing violence is to separate physical cause from conscious effect. Invariably the subjective consciousness learns, by observing that its mortal vessel the body is no longer intact, that it, the consciousness, is a function of another agent, the body. Keneally sees an act of violence as an eschatological experiment, a search for the essence in the form. Often, as in *The Chant of Jimmie Blacksmith,* a ripeness is split. Often death is administered by a probing bayonet, as it is by Terry Byrne in *Bring Larks and Heroes* who is enthralled by "the barbarous fluidity of his bayonet going in". The same bayonet is run into Albert in *Confederates* although Usaph Bumpass has, like Terry Byrne's victim, turned his buttocks to Albert expecting his own end. The murderers of Navaille in *Blood Red, Sister Rose* also have delving swords and later in the novel Jehanne wonders how she'll feel "When—to use Messire's phrase—the steel went in". It's Keneally's phrase, of course, but then Messire is also a deity.

In preparing this present study I've become conscious of how important a trigger for Keneally's imagination has been Joseph Heller's *Catch-22.* While he was researching *Schindler's Ark* he suggested that *Schindler's Ark* would be the Jewish version of *Catch-22.* Oskar Schindler is certainly the Axis answer to Milo Minderbinder, but the more urgent metaphor in *Catch-22* that "The spirit gone, man is garbage", the message in Snowden's entrails, is one that infects Keneally like a disease; it may be that each of his novels is a version of *Catch-22.* Hunter Maguire in *Confederates* gets off his horse at the Culpeper pike to attend to Snowdon Andrews. He lifts the blanket to find that a "great mess of Snowdon's viscera was tumbled into the dust", and when Jehanne comes across an Englishman at Orleans whose "guts flopped red and grey out of a long belly wound", she wonders about how to tuck them back.

However it is perhaps Keneally's more general morbidity which helps him and his reader to fantasize into events of the past. Keneally gravitates towards the moment of "transubstantiation", when significance or essence leaves or enters a given form. The wider dualism at work in his military historical novels is the balance between the rarefied diverting abnormality of a civil emergency and the unsanctified ordinariness of everyday life.

Schindler's Ark, for example, is a monumental and thoroughly engrossing treatment of the Second World War be-

cause, thoroughly in accord with Keneally's minimalist smart-aleck view of historical cause and effect, most of the creative energy is spent establishing that the shooting and battlefield maneuvering has only a small place in the texture of the routine life of a country at war. Keneally replaces our adventure-film view of war as shooting with another kind of fantasising detail—what it was like to walk down a Cracow street in 1943, go shopping, catch a tram. How running a prison camp meant procuring permits for this that and the other, installing machinery, buying food, dealing with the Armaments Inspectorate. What Keneally in fact does is force together the two modes—decisive violence and everyday details of life, so that author and reader alike become engrossed by the obscenity of the process whereby something as horrendous as the final solution can be expressed in terms of supply and demand, train timetables, consignment notes.

A third aspect of Keneally's representation of history is that he does remain omniscient, not simply as the ordering intelligence which any historian will bring to his narrative, but as an all-knowing arbiter or deity. He enjoys the sense that as author the outcome is in his hands. He regards his novel as a world of his own creation, and his characters as beings whose lives are terminated at his will, not by the workings of an independent fate. Keneally enjoys being the repository of the future; he likes the suggestion that he has the prescience of a God when in fact all he has is the privilege of being the narrator. For example, in *Confederates* Horace Searcy, who is a journalist and spy, both attributes that make him an author-figure in this novel, is leaving on his mission to steal army battle orders, and we're told that:

> . . . he and young Angus were riding through the shuttered town. It looked finally shuttered now, as if it knew the army and all its needs were going to vanish overnight, as if it were now money-counting time and time to take thought about what attitudes to strike whenever the Union army should arrive, as it would surely soon do, pursuing Lee.

And it is in *Bring Larks and Heroes,* the Keneally proto-novel which is at once an analysis of the victim personality, the *product* of the dualistic self-conscious narrator, and the literary "mesh of sunlight and shade" from which the artist can conduct his arcane craft, that Halloran feels "above himself and Ann, the mercy of a story-teller".

III

Which brings us to the third of those experiences offering Keneally a resolving authority beyond himself. If his own subjectivity and "the past" each in their own way free Keneally from the burden of true authorship, he also relies heavily on a received order from other authors and documents. There is in fact a level of engagement in the historical novels which has nothing to do with the past at all. Keneally engages *directly* with his historical and literary sources because they at least are tangible; in the end however, he finds it difficult to take any received structure seriously.

In the 1975 statement in which he claims that the past "is less confusing than the present" Keneally also remarks of the past that it is the historians who "have already reduced it to some understandable unity for us", and he goes on perhaps archly to say that "their gift is beyond estimation". "Their gift" is certainly important for Keneally. It seems to me that his historical research is not directed towards finding out "the truth" about the past—it often seems superficial and too reliant on popular interpretation. What Keneally seems to need is a range of actual texts to play off as a kind of latent model: they provide the pre-existent order which allows him to achieve his tone of easy omniscient matter-of-factness. As he puts it himself:

> With Jean and *Blood Red, Sister Rose* I had both the notes and four very good biographies of the lady to chart my course by. Anatole France, Regine Pernoud, Viola Sackville-West and Andrew Lang were continually consulted and read—I hope not for the purposes of plagiarism but because they provide ideas to expand or fight against.

Keneally is not a plagiarist, but he does enter into a dialogue with the source text to the point where its ordinary content and purpose can no longer hold his attention. The ironic suggestiveness of the French pronunciation of "Jean" which allows him to coin the phrase "honest Jean" is one example. Another is the growing suspicion in *Blood Red, Sister Rose* that Jehanne, having been called a duckling right through the novel has become in the epilogue a roast duckling for Keneally. And yet another is the unexpected insistence on the phrase "It's time" in *Blood Red, Sister Rose,* published in 1974, two years after the Australian Labour Party swept to power under the famous slogan "It's time." He certainly cannot sustain serious engagement with sober human reality for too long, as Veronica Brady points out when she accuses Keneally of being Apollonian, shrinking "from the Dionysian spirit" and points out that in *Blood Red, Sister Rose* "Novelist and reader stand off, voyeurs of decay, not participants in the human drama involved . . .".

The examples with which I'm most familiar in which Keneally practises a secret art and engages with neither the past, nor the ostensible story nor the historical documents are *Bring Larks and Heroes* and *The Chant of Jimmie Blacksmith.* For each of these novels he has a "profane" literary model which he "reacts against" to give himself a sort of naughty-boy's minimalist joy in consecrating them.

For *Bring Larks and Heroes* the "profane" model is Hal Porter's *The Tilted Cross* and for *Jimmie Blacksmith* it is Frank Clune's *Jimmy Governor.* He derives much of the basic story for each of his novels from these two pre-existing models, but he also enters into a dialogue with them. Frank Clune's stolid misunderstandings of criminality, and his genteel evasiveness, are corrected and satirised time and time again by Keneally. Similarly while Porter's Queely Sheil has most of the characteristics of Halloran, Porter's rococo flights of fancy are mercilessly sent up either by being rewritten or alluded to. He also, with both sources, relies on them to define the parameters and referents of each story, choosing himself often only to vary, invert or otherwise comment on the detail.

Interestingly, too, for each of these novels there is a second antecedent model, one which in each case Keneally feels is worthy of appropriation, veneration or, to use his own term, is something "to expand". For *Jimmie Blacksmith* it is Dostoevsky's *Crime and Punishment* and for *Bring Larks and Heroes* it is Nabokov's *Lolita.* In this case he relies heavily on the thematic and metaphoric structures of the antecedent novels. *Crime and Punishment* lends Keneally in *Jimmie Blacksmith* a ready-made kit for discussions of "madness", "guilt", and identity, not to mention the axe-murder itself. It also offers things like the surreal school teacher McCready, who is modeled on Porfiry, plus the opportunity for jokes about Napoleon, Wellington boots and Dulcie, who in Jimmie's dream is both mother and religious sister, and finally the observation from Mr. Hyberry, (who is having trouble with his Grand Master) that "sewage was less contingent than crime and punishment" which makes sense if it is realized that while "CRAP" might only be the initials of a book title, it can certainly make its presence felt.

Similarly, *Lolita* provides Keneally with themes about authorship, identity and authenticity, the nature of art, the artist as voyeur observing from his refuge, the concept of two selves and the idea of the omniscient author being the deity who can both terminate life and the novel. It also provides some specific metaphors and events which otherwise give the novel an unspecified density. The surreal involvement of the Blythes in the hanging of Halloran and Ann derives much of its creative energy from the confrontation between Clare Quilty and Humbert Humbert at the end of *Lolita.* Halloran "has the illusion of closing the door on so many rooms" in his life just as Humbert "lucidly insane, crazily calm" goes about trying to close the doors in Quilty's house. The Blythes and Humbert and Quilty argue about potency. Mr. Blythe and Humbert are both toting pistols, they are both locked out and manage to get in, they both cause their better halves to rise up; while Clare plays the piano and dances in the air Mrs. Blythe hears wet leaves outside "tinkling with chandelier music" which she wants to dance to, and so on.

All this is what Veronica Brady might think of as a profound *disengagement from* the ordinary realities of events in an actual historical past, or for that matter the present. Keneally, like Jean Farlow in *Lolita,* gravitates towards "a place of green concealment, spying on nature," where he joins the robed author Quilty, and his own squadron of author-prophets, Hearn and Halloran on their wooded hills, Gilda's baby and McCreadie in *Jimmie Blacksmith,* both in hoods, Private William Hood up a tree in *Confederates* spying on the Union army, Joan of Arc in her red thigh cloak, or Oskar Schindler watching from the woods as the toddler in Krakusa Street "dressed in a small scarlet coat and cap" makes a "scarlet node" in the street. But then in this case as Oskar watched from the woods above the ghetto, and as we might expect if the tranquil safety of a Breughel canvas suddenly came to life:

> Everything seemed speeded-up, difficult for the viewers on the hill to keep pace with. Those who had emerged were shot where they stood on the pavement, flying out over the gutters from the impact of the bullets, gushing blood into the drains.

Irmtraud Petersson (essay date October 1989)

SOURCE: "'White Ravens' in a World of Violence: German Connections in Thomas Keneally's Fiction," in *Australian Literary Studies,* Vol. 14, No. 2, October, 1989, pp. 160-73.

[*In the essay below, Petersson investigates the parallels between Keneally's use of German imagery and the Australian cultural experience, correlating German traits to similar Australian values.*]

Despite an increasing diversity in both modes of, and critical approaches to Australian writing, the question of cultural specificity has remained one of the foremost issues. How do we see and represent ourselves? What distinguishes us from other cultures? What do we want to be? These are some of the major questions raised. The debate about 'radical/nationalist' vs. 'universalist' positions and their 'postcolonial' variants may have become more refined, but hardly less self-conscious. Cultural independence comprises the readiness to look for similarities as well as differences, for models and anti-models 'out there'. Perhaps cosmopolitan rather than universalist, Thomas Keneally is one of those novelists who have addressed national issues in an international framework, and contemporary problems in an historical perspective. Keneally says that he has found history an easier paradigm to work with than the present, and that the best sort of historical novel is 'the one which is really about the present and uses the past as a sort of working model', a novel 'in which the human issues are the same as those we have now, and have always had to face'. In analogy to the use of the past as 'a parable for the present', Keneally's use of foreign settings and characters can be assumed to be paradigmatic, providing reference points for Australia, and raising questions about both human behavior in general and Australian issues in particular.

Among the cultural 'hetero-images' in Australian writing of the past four decades, German images have, for obvious reasons, been mostly unfavorable. They have usually emphasized the pretensions of 'high culture' and the incomprehensible transition from civilization to the barbarity of Nazism. By and large, German-speaking societies have been set off as 'the others', representing what Australians do not want to be. In a sense, therefore, Keneally's German images are an exception. Two major characters in his novels are Germans, Matthias Erzberger in *Gossip from the Forest* (1975) and Oskar Schindler in *Schindler's Ark* (1982), and so are some minor characters in *A Family Madness* (1985). Linking up with Keneally's preoccupation with war, violence and times of crisis, and with individual behavior in extreme situations, the two world wars provide the historical context for his German images: the armistice after the First World War in *Gossip,* events of the Second in the other novels.

There are some striking similarities between the German characters in Keneally's novels. They are outsiders who come from the periphery of the German *Reich,* both regionally and culturally. Though publicly functioning within the ideological and social system, or even representing it officially (a system which is either disintegrating or proves to be downright evil), these men are at odds with its mainstream developments. Within a merciless environment, they retain an unusual sense of human responsibility. None of them is portrayed as a 'flawless innocent' or a larger-than-life-sized idealist; in fact, they all are rather ambivalent. This applies to Erzberger, whom Keneally sees as 'a classic contradictory character', to Willi Ganz (of *A Family Madness*) and, most obviously, to Oskar Schindler, whose story has fascinated Keneally and who, in his own words, 'was such a fantastic character that it's hard to imagine making up a character who would be as contradictory, picaresque and large'. Keneally himself has emphasized the concern in his novels with 'men of decency' who fight historic causes 'on which they can't quite get a grip', and he says that he finds it more and more striking 'how every generation seems to produce independent spirits, the people who evade conditioning'. Erzberger, Schindler and Ganz (and some of the other minor German characters) have in common such an independence of spirit, a nonconformity which is all the more striking when set off against a background of extreme relentlessness or even barbarity.

Matthias Erzberger, leader of the German armistice delegation, is the center of attention in *Gossip from the Forest,* and even more obviously so in the dramatised version of the novel. Erzberger is a tragic figure. A moderate politician, he is dispatched by a collapsing political system that is hardly able to back him up any more. It is he, a civilian, who is expected to end the sufferings of war, whereas the military shun their responsibility. What he observes of the situation of soldiers and civilians on both sides, spurs him on to accomplish a truce ('All the fathers had abandoned the front and left their children behind'). But this compels him to accept the ruinous and humiliating terms on which Marshal Foch insists. These terms would increase poverty and famine in Germany and eventually, as foreshadowed in the novel, fuel the nationalistic and anti-democratic forces and help to establish Nazi tyranny. Erzberger knows the implications: the enemies despise him on the one hand for being one of the monsters 'liable for the mustard-gassed and the torpedoed corpses', and on the other for being weak and indulgent, a compassionate humanist ('Wemyss: Imagine those chaps trying the *starving-children* line?).' His compatriots, for their part, despise him for his way of ending the chaotic war situation. They will blame him for the disastrous outcome, call him and his companions the 'November criminals' and finally murder him.

Keneally's novel informs the reader extensively about the historical implications of Erzberger's career and, through it, about the German (and European) situation, by including documented facts and comments, but also through a poetic subtext of reverberating imagery. When one compares Keneally's portrayal of Erzberger with a scholarly study on the politician such as Klaus Epstein's *Matthias Erzberger and the Dilemma of German Democracy,* one realises that Keneally followed closely the results of research regarding both the personal and the political situation. Like the biography, the novel stresses Erzberger's Swabian peasant background which so markedly distinguished him from the ruling upper classes in the capital Berlin in various ways: in dialect and religion, appearance and manners, education and refinement. Erzberger, a southerner and a bright country boy, is constantly aware of the condescension and contempt with which the Prussian aristocrats and officers regard him, the outsider: 'He had never got used to facing the blue eyes and sculptured faces of the *vons* of the earth; there were still movements of bumpkin disquiet in his stomach, the belly calling him back to his peasant state'. The novel highlights a sense of inferiority that makes Erzberger wonder whether he can live up to the greatness of his task: 'He thought, we won't get far because this is long traveling, it's Dante's hell and all we can expect is a further circle. And the worst thing is I have no Alighieri stature. I'm just a happy glutton with a head for figures and a little wife'. Although the novel, more than the biography, suggests an ambivalence of character ('His motives were both opportunist and visionary: that was

Erzberger's nature'), it construes as predominant qualities Erzberger's incorruptible conscience, and his compassion and sympathy for the simple people. Rather than presenting a German character as the enemy, or as the embodiment of odious German imperial pretensions, the novel focuses on a man with a humble background, a basic decency and a sense of responsibility for the ordinary human causes. That he may appear petty in the eyes of the great and powerful adds to his qualities, and also to the sense that he is constructed to comprise some traditional Australian values. In emphasising those idiosyncrasies which originate from his social and ethnic provenance, the characterisation of Erzberger implicitly draws parallels to Australian cultural experience. There is firstly an association with postcolonial white Australians who lived at the periphery of the British Empire, as the Southern Germans did with regard to the Prussian dominance in the German *Reich*. There is also the parallel to an aspect of Australian society: Erzberger's Catholicism and his Swabian ethnicity put him in a marginal position similar to that of the Irish-Catholic minority in Australia (a theme treated in Keneally's *Bring Larks and Heroes*). The author's sympathies would certainly be with the outsider.

> **In analogy to the use of the past as 'a parable for the present', Keneally's use of foreign settings and characters can be assumed to be paradigmatic, providing reference points for Australia, and raising questions about both human behavior in general and Australian issues in particular.**
> **—Irmtraud Peterson**

In an obvious departure from historical sources, the name of one of the German delegates is changed from Count Alfred Oberndorff (still used in the first edition) to Count von Maiberling. Considerations involving the Oberndorff family prompted the author to rename this character, who seems constructed more freely than others, as a contrast to Erzberger on the one hand, and a symbol of a general decadence on the other. Another, at first glance minor, divergence is the novel's treatment of the umbrella connected with Erzberger's death. In Epstein's detailed account of the assassination, it is Erzberger's companion Diez who carried an umbrella on the fatal walk in the Black Forest. *Gossip* equips Erzberger with the umbrella and transforms it into one of the symbolic or allusive elements of imagery used to intensify the significance of events. In Erzberger's premonitory dream the umbrella is urged on him by his wife against his will, a 'treacherous', 'terrible' and 'sickening' umbrella, one which threatens rather than protects. From its bulletholes, pale young soldiers struggle and attack Erzberger. The corresponding murder scene at the end of the novel reads:

Erzberger had forgotten his dream of 1918. All he had was the normal sense of *déjà-vu.* Impelled by it he opened his umbrella. Diez hit them with his. But Erzberger yielded to his supine nub and blotted them out with black silk.

Through this *false hemisphere* he was shot in the chest and forehead. (my emphasis)

In this scene Erzberger is presented as fatalistically prepared, as both unwilling and unable to defend himself. However, the umbrella image also carries geographical and historical overtones. The soldiers rising from the 'blood-bespattered' bullet-holes point towards the future war (as do also the Nazi arm bands the murderers put on in Keneally's playtext), and the metaphoric umbrella as a 'false hemisphere' suggests the old world as a terrible, treacherous place which can no longer protect the decent or innocent.

To be sure, Keneally's novel does not promote the southern hemisphere as a better alternative, nor does it refer explicitly to any Australian participation in the 'Great War'. But there is an Australian subtext in the novel, although Australia as a place figures only in a marginal episode where the British Admiral Lord Wemyss remembers a voyage around the world in the 1870s, visiting the distant parts of the British Empire with the future King. Wemyss's nostalgic retrospection to the 'benign imperial concept', 'the empire which was not only a geographical reality but a resonant abstraction also' evokes the decline of the British Empire and the 'collapse' of Europe. These the author sees as one of the most disturbing events for the Australian consciousness, and their effects on Australia underlie many of his books. Thus the links with Australia in *Gossip* are implied, for one thing, in the historical consequences. The choice of Erzberger as a protagonist and his characterisation provide another, more subtle link.

Whereas Erzberger eventually loses—personally when he is murdered, politically because his working for a peaceful democratic Germany will prove to have been in vain—Oskar Schindler is obviously more successful. Most critics and reviewers have emphasised the sense of hope that prevails in *Schindler's Ark* and sets it off from Keneally's earlier, more pessimistic novels. However, the novel's optimism is not based on the perception of an encouraging progress in humankind or societies at large, but rather on what the author sees as manifestations of independence and grandeur of spirit in individual human beings such as Schindler, 'an ordinary German who evaded the conditioning of his culture, his childhood and the politics, in a highly individualistic way'. In *Schindler's Ark,* a documentary novel described as 'imaginative historical journalism', the German protagonist once more functions as the outsider. Like Erzberger, Schindler comes from the periphery, and because of his background, his life-style and his attitudes, the respectable and powerful treat him with patronising condescension: 'He was Sudeten German, Arkansas to their Manhattan, Liverpool to their Cambridge'. Schindler is 'virtuous' in a strange sense. He provides a sanctuary for Jewish prisoners and saves many of them from death at the risk of his own life, but he 'worked within or, at least, on the strength of, a corrupt and savage scheme'. This scheme is reminiscent of the penal colony in Keneally's *Bring Larks and Heroes,* but it is more outrageous and horrific in its dimensions, 'one which filled Europe with camps of varying but consistent inhumanity and created a submerged, unspoken-of nation of prisoners'. And, as in *Bring Larks and Heroes,* 'the gaoler actively conspires with the gaoled in order to subvert the system'.

Keneally's novel depicts several other positive characters besides Schindler, people who try to relieve the suffering and undermine the monstrous machine of mass-murder. The narrator tells their stories, but seems fascinated only by Schindler. One dissenter of kindred spirit, *Wachtmeister* Bosko, helps Schindler to smuggle Jewish children out of the ghetto. When he turns his back on the system completely and joins the partisans, the book stresses that he remains ineffective. He 'secretly despised himself and had contempt for partial rescues', the narrator comments, and 'Bosko wanted to save everyone, and would soon try to, and perish for it'. Only jovial Schindler with his playboy exterior, the apolitical capitalist, one who drinks and plays cards with the devil, succeeds in saving many victims because he is cunning and makes use of the oppressors' own modes and manners. The question of motivation underlies Keneally's reconstruction of Schindler's amazing story. Some critics in Australia and overseas argue that the book gives no satisfactory answers, others have questioned its ideological implications. Comments on its protagonist range from 'a man chosen by some divine force for its own ends', to an anti-intellectual, a 'Voss in the 80s, on the rebound from the Australian desert, back in his home patch, shorn of idealism'. The puzzling ambivalence of Schindler's character certainly pervades the novel as an informing theme. When Schindler is juxtaposed with his cruel opponent Amon Goeth, the commandant 'who went to the work of murder as calmly as a clerk goes to his office', the novel evokes a Jungian dichotomy of good and evil, with Goeth as the shadow of Schindler's persona ('the reflection can hardly be avoided that Amon was Oskar's dark brother, was the berserk and fanatic executioner Oskar might, by some unhappy reversal of his appetites, have become'). In Keneally's narrative Schindler has integrated the polar opposites within himself to a practical, social and humane wholeness. He becomes what in German is called a *weisser Rabe,* an exceptional 'white raven' who, aware of the evil intentions of his peers and familiar with their fatal methods, acts for deliverance and life instead of suffering and death. However, by concentrating hope on an exceptional person who can outwit a savage system only on a small scale, Keneally's novel puts forward an individualist and basically pessimistic view of history.

> **Accentuated by keywords such as madness, lunacy, insanity, savagery, violence, corruption or brutality, the world presented in Keneally's writing continues to be a world of terror despite the occasional 'white raven', Australian or European.**
> **—Irmtraud Peterson**

In examining representational patterns in Australian narrative, Graeme Turner fits *Schindler's Ark* into that section of literary treatment of imprisonment ('our most enduring literary and mythic image') which presents 'moral criticism of the gaolers in order to propose the moral superiority of those incarcerated'. Another critic, Michael Hollington, argues that Keneally's novel owes more to 'the mythology of the bush than to that of Central Europe'. Investigating the novel's 'subterranean connection with Australia', Hollington finds that Schindler represents features of the Australian bush hero and outlaw and calls him 'the Ned Kelly of Cracow'. Referring to the Schweik stereotype in the characterisation of Schindler, he evokes Brecht as a contrast: 'Brecht's 'red statements' about Nazi Germany remain superior: his Schweiks are not heroes, but they at least grasp that you get somewhere only when the office of "just man" is abolished'; and, '"Australia," read as the natural impulse of the heart, isn't ultimately an effective counterweight to "Europe."' However, Brecht believed that humankind could learn and 'get somewhere', that change is possible (and that the artist can contribute to this educational process)—but Keneally obviously does not, nor does he believe in 'salvation through a political system'. He rather admits an instinctive and strong belief in original sin, or, in his own words, assumes that there is 'a problem at man's core that can't be overcome by any particular system'. Accentuated by keywords such as madness, lunacy, insanity, savagery, violence, corruption or brutality, the world presented in Keneally's writing continues to be a world of terror despite the occasional 'white raven', Australian or European. It is this lack of hope in historical progress that Keneally's portrayals of the Germans Erzberger and Schindler have in common with some of his more revolutionary characters such as Jehanne in *Blood Red, Sister Rose* or Halloran in *Bring Larks and Heroes*.

At this point it is worthwhile to look at some problematic aspects of the relation between the use of fact (or documented material) and fiction in Keneally's writing. One issue has already been mentioned in connection with the

changing of the name of Count Oberndorff in *Gossip from the Forest,* that is, the sensitivities of living 'characters' or their relatives towards possible distortions. For *Schindler's Ark,* Keneally did thorough research. He interviewed a great many witnesses all over the world, and tried to be as exact or 'documentary' as possible. This method, on the one hand, attracted the criticism of those who did not consider the book a 'novel', a work of fiction and creative imagination, when Keneally was to be awarded the Booker Prize. But it also attracted criticism from some who felt there was too much fictional embellishment or courting of effects in the book, at the cost of a more reliable documentation of historical evidence and facts. (In the case of transcribing oral history, it would, however, always be difficult to decide who does the 'construing' of events—those who tell their story from memory, or those who structure it into written form.) During a recent stay in Germany, I spoke to one of the Jewish survivors saved by Schindler, who was interviewed by Keneally and included as a character in his book. I must respect his wish to remain anonymous for his own reasons, but some of his general remarks are important enough to be noted. Although this person did not question the overall value and quality of Keneally's book, he had some objections and proposed some corrections concerning particular (though minor) details described, which he remembers differently and regards as unrealistic fictional adornments. The importance of such questionable details lies not in their relevance for the story by and large, the witness pointed out, but rather in the fact that inaccuracies play into the hands of reactionists who have doubted the measure of Nazi atrocities and have even tried, for defensive purposes, to discredit reports from extermination camps as untruthful exaggerations. (And one is reminded of a recent trend in Germany towards national apologetics in connection with the so-called *Historikerstreit.*) Perhaps the implications of these controversies can only be fully appreciated in a society confronted with such a terrible history. The problematic relation between 'real' and 'realistic' remains, and also between the 'imaginative' and the 'documentary' rendering of historical truth in writing. Is Schindler's story, presented in a realist mode and based on witness accounts and documents, more real, true or credible than, for instance, Himmelfarb's story in Patrick White's *Riders in the Chariot,* 'created' as fiction and lacking a realistic description of the brutality involved? And, to carry the question further, is the sensational presentation of savagery, e.g. in *The White Hotel* by D. M. Thomas, more likely to shake up complacency than the quiet, laconic and ostensibly distanced approach of Claude Lanzmann's film *Shoah*?

With *A Family Madness* Keneally moves closer back to the mainstream fictional genre, although this book, too, is based on historical material (and on an Australian incident). The novel combines two strands of narrative, one set in Europe around the time of the Second World War, the other in Australia of the 1980s. The two parts are interwoven by thematic and structural devices, thus providing an obvious illustration of Keneally's concept of linking history with the present. The Belorussian immigrant family Kabbelski/Kabbel serve as an external connection. Forty years after the war, the Kabbels are still unable to lay to rest the ghosts of a savage past, gradually revealed as the Australian story develops. This haunting past is juxtaposed with the reality of a contemporary Australia in the process of losing the qualities of a sanctuary. Through a network of parallels and associations, imagery and comments, the narrative suggests that events, settings and situations may be different, but basic human predicaments resemble one another; that humankind finds itself placed dangerously at 'the cutting edge of history'; and that the belief in possible safety is an illusion.

Focusing on the fate of the Kabbelski family, the European part of the novel also portrays two German characters who swim against the tide, trying to preserve some decency in a savage environment: the SS *Oberführer* Willi Ganz and, a minor character, the young *Wehrmacht* sergeant Jasper. The novel picks up motifs from *Gossip* and from *Schindler's Ark*. Willi Ganz is an outsider like Erzberger and Schindler, but one of a different kind. As the German provincial governor in an occupied Belorussian town, he represents the 'white raven' within the black flock of German SS officials whose brutal ambitions are aimed at complete extermination of the Jewish population and of political enemies. His attempts to bring about a policy of moderation and to protect some of the victims fail completely and let him become the target of a murder plot, executed by Russian partisans, but contrived by his own superiors. Ganz is modeled on the German *Generalkommissar* in Belorussia, Wilhelm Kube, a 'civilian' administrator and thus a rival of the SS. In comparing the representations of Kube in historical, and Ganz in fictional writing, the latter emerges as a much more human and positive figure than the former—perhaps an indication of the author's tendency to explore both sides of the coin in his fiction?

There is no sense of hope in Keneally's representation of the Belorussian world. As in *Season in Purgatory,* all participating sides act with utmost brutality: occupiers and partisans, Germans, Poles, Soviet Russians and Belorussians. An aesthete and artist, Ganz does not really fit into that scheme, but he is too vulnerable to be effective or even to survive. Unlike Schindler's, his individualism is esoteric, elitist and escapist, and unlike Schindler, Ganz fails to recognize that 'no one could find refuge any more behind the idea of German culture' (*Schindler's Ark*) and that the values of enlightenment are vain in an age of darkness, where 'both Germans and Russians behave like savages' and the locals assist for the sake of nationalism. Ganz commits himself through his compassion and thereby courts danger, but he can save no one. The novel presents his attempts to escape into a world of art and refined culture, of friendship, children and domestic peacefulness, as an attitude of resignation, a retreat into a utopian dream that can never cope with the brutal reality. The 'Bavarian sentimentalist' Jasper, presented as a more genuinely 'innocent' character than Ganz, is 'a representative of that generation of Europeans who were all forced at great pace to learn a fierce amount about themselves and their fellows during those years in the furnace'. But, like Bosko in *Schindler's Ark,* he is eliminated before his resistance to the system has any effect. Like some of the German soldiers in *Season in Purgatory*, Jasper is a victim himself, conscripted and exploited by the regime.

Despite an occasional ambivalence towards the character Ganz, the novel uses him and Jasper to point up the helplessness of the decent individual within an evil or deteriorating world. Thus he is thematically related to the Australian protagonist, Delaney, who also tries to save others, but fails to prevent the decline in his mate's and his lover's lives and in his own. Though the consequences are of a different scale, a sense of resignation in the face of the inevitable, but also of guilt and confusion connects both parts of the narrative. The madness of the title is not restricted to the story of the Kabbel family and their past, but echoed in aspects of societal developments in contemporary urban Australia. Like Delaney, several of the foreign characters are ordinary people, with ordinary hopes and expectations. There is nothing megalomaniac about them, and they become guilty in pursuit of such aims as nationalism, patriotism, self-preservation, family protection—aims with positive connotations as Australian values.

One of the narrative devices of linking Australian and European experience in *A Family Madness* is the literary reference to *The Tin Drum* by Günter Grass. Keneally admires the experimental qualities of Grass's novel, and he may have found in the German author's work attitudes, concerns and topics both congenial and challenging to his own views, e.g., a strong though critical affinity with Catholic tradition, combined with a kind of social and political 'moralism', a preference for realistic descriptions of lower-middle-class surroundings, and for the interweaving of the fictitious private foreground with the historical public events in the background. Both authors share a boldness in verbally attacking (or ignoring) sexual taboos (often to unmask bourgeois hypocrisy), an ironic tone and (occasionally grim) humor, and a taste for the picaresque. *The Tin Drum* covers the same time span as the Kabbelski accounts in *A Family Madness,* and both novels evoke the history of Europe in the first half of this century, dwelling particularly on the time of the Third Reich. There are some parallels between the fictitious narrators Oskar Matzerath and Rudi Kabbel. Their recollections present history through the perspective of a child endowed with the understanding of an adult. Both are exiles, and both are victims who are eventually driven into madness by the insanity of their environment. Whereas Oskar's refusal to grow up is a visible protest, Rudi's refusal to accept the world as it is, manifests itself in his vision and in his depending on voices and the imaginary uncle. The most interesting aspect of this literary connection concerns the way in which Keneally's book presents the German novel to the (Australian) readers; that is, for one thing, which themes from *The Tin Drum* are highlighted and how they are related to the narrative, and, for another, the impression the book makes on the Australian protagonist of *A Family Madness.* By having Delaney read some of the explanatory course notes to *The Tin Drum,* several central themes are outlined which, though referring to Grass's novel, also allude to themes in Delaney's own story. The connections with the Kabbelski story and with the terrible consequences of nationalism in occupied Belorussia are obvious; those with Australia are more allusive. When Delaney starts to read the novel, he is conscious only of the girl behind the book, but already he senses an imminent threat. The danger implied works on two levels: in private life the love affair jeopardising his marriage and career, in public life an increasing societal instability. The allusion to the 'Glass Night' in the notes foreshadows a subsequent incident of violence connected with the urban 'guerilla warfare',where windows are broken and a bag of glass is emptied on the car park, an incident that points to some disturbing features of contemporary urban development. Whereas Oskar's dwarfism as a trope for deliberately retarded consciousness is made explicit, the consequences of another (albeit less devastating) retarded consciousness in the Australian reality of Delaney and his mates reveal themselves only gradually and less conspicuously. Thus the early juxtaposing of the *Tin Drum* notes and Delaney's Rugby League diary operates like a warning: later in the novel, Delaney's world of sport, this 'perfect model of an imperfect world', will be infected by increasing brutality.

A further reference to *The Tin Drum* is used to contrast European and Australian perceptions. Delaney is impressed and confused by the opening chapter of *The Tin Drum,* 'The Wide Skirt', which tells the story of Oskar's grandfather who, persecuted by the police, escapes under the skirts of Anna in a potato field. The setting of the episode, 'somewhere around the borders of Poland and Germany', does not really interest Delaney. He 'preferred in fact for the young fugitive's politics to be vague and for the location to be a no-man's-land, a land still to be invented'—there is an association with a Utopia, an Australian topos. Whereas in Grass's novel there is an immediate motivation for the persecution, Delaney in his dreams associates it more generally with a Kafkaesque situation of the alienated individual in a threatening world. The wish for security found under Anna's skirts is a recurrent motif in Grass's novel, as is, in Keneally's, the wish for ultimate security. Delaney relates

the skirt image to his almost pious longing for the ideal love, the ideal woman embodied by a medieval picture of a woman with a unicorn, symbolising chastity and faithfulness—ironically just the qualities Delaney is about to destroy. His wish to find 'the woman at the middle of things' informs his love for Danielle, and he tries to adapt her European strangeness to his sphere, by imagining her as the woman surrounded not only by unicorn and lion but also by kangaroos and emus. For the 'innocent' Australian, Delaney, the world evoked in *The Tin Drum* and the 'dark atmosphere of *that* book' remain alien and frightening. He feels relieved when Danielle in her course moves on to a novel more lucid and familiar to him, *Our Man in Havana,* where the atmosphere is homely and humane because there are heroes and villains, whereas 'in *The Tin Drum* there were escapees sheltering in weird and joyous places; a mother and an uncle loved each other; midgets could break glass with their voices; horses' heads squirmed with eels; and a woman ate herself to death with fish oil'. Delaney's reaction indicates that the Australian reader might find it difficult to understand Grass's novel and the (un-British) European world it presents, therefore its images remain meaningless to him. But there is an irony in the novel's use of art as an indicator of innocence or decadence. Grass's *The Tin Drum* apparently does not appeal to Delaney, nor does it suit his 'Australian ethos'. Yet by exposing the mounting violence endangering society, the Australian part of the narrative also creates a 'dark atmosphere', one without a clear-cut division between heroes and villains. Delaney's own story evokes, among other things, an Australian wish for Utopia not fulfilled.

I have suggested that Keneally uses the German images in his fiction to explore a different kind of experience but at the same time to relate them to aspects of specifically Australian issues. By treating such issues in another cultural and historical context, Keneally's narratives indirectly also complement, expand and comment on problems of Australian self-definition. Some positive traits of the German characters correspond to positive values of Australian self-images, and are therefore affirmative. The negative ones serve to correct or change self-images and draw attention to inherent dangers in Australian society. Referring to a dictum, common in his youth, that one 'could only get perspective on Australia by seeing it from outside', Keneally calls those of his historical novels set outside Australia the equivalents of a 'literary overseas trip'. This links up with the notion of an 'accidental Australianness' which Keneally shares with Malouf and other writers, and of the alternatives that can at least be written out, if not lived out. The European world of violence in Keneally's writing could be read as a reversal of an 'antipodean' myth, implying that hell is over there. More than this, however, it is a way of fictionally distancing fundamental human issues which also affect Australian self-understanding. Many of Keneally's characters have a utopian dream, an insight that there are better possibilities worth striving for. But as a small nation such as Australia seems helpless against the influence of overwhelming powers, some of the protagonists in Keneally's fiction, including several German characters, seem helpless before the terrific task of changing the course of things—be it history, the system, or simply humankind's cruelty. Keneally sees the Germans as 'a fit study for anyone interested in humanity'. Thus the German characters in his fiction are presented not so much as 'ogres', but rather as exemplifying more widespread trends which in turn mirror 'what always goes on'.

Thomas Swick (review date 5 June 1992)

SOURCE: A review of *The Place Where Souls Are Born*, in *Commonweal*, June 5, 1992, pp. 22-3.

[*In the following review, Swickfaults* The Place Where Souls are Born *for its "confused mosiac" of Native American history and for Keneally's dependence on secondary sources.*]

Here is an interesting idea: A book by an Australian, introduced by a Welsh woman, about the least "European" region of the United States.

It helps your natural dubiousness to learn that the Australian is the highly regarded Thomas Keneally (author of, among other books, *Schindler's List*) and the Welsh woman is the doyenne of contemporary travel writers, Jan Morris, who over the last few years has enlisted some of her favorite authors as contributors to a travel series called "Destinations." With *The Place Where Souls Are Born,* Keneally joins an impressive list that includes M. F. K. Fisher, Herbert Gold, and William Murray.

I am sorry to report, however, that his book is not as engaging as the others in the series. My suspicions were aroused when I turned to the acknowledgments page at the back. (New books, like new cars, should be looked over carefully, front and back, before being started.) Almost the entire page is taken up with the titles of the books that helped Keneally along the way, while four lines are given to the names of the people. This, I thought to myself, could be a long haul.

The journey covers four states: Colorado, Utah, Arizona, and New Mexico (all decoratively mapped in the front). But the book is not concerned with the mechanics of travel—we hear little about the long drives from state to state and almost nothing about the author's wife and daughter who are accompanying him—but rather the ravages of history.

Keneally starts off, outside Denver, with some recreational skiing and lengthy ruminations on the Ute Indians. From the former activity, we get: "Aerobics at high and lovely altitudes have a very humanizing influence on a marriage"— an observation that is felicitous even while being somewhat pompous.

But Keneally's real interest is with the Indians. "The Ute were intransigent nomads. . . . They were dangerous fellows, a peril to European livestock and to European stock. Like the Celts, they honored warriorhood. They were stub-born."

This passage sets the tone for the rest of the book, which is replete with historical vignettes, culled from the books listed on the acknowledgments page, interlaced with personal reflections. By the time we get to New Mexico, having made a counter-clockwise loop from Denver, we have read about more tribes than we can remember. Keneally, apart from his obvious respect for these peoples, seems to delight in the very mention of their names and the names of their settlements. "A pause was thereby brought to the essential Eagle Clan and Arrow Shaft ceremonies. Other Hopi in Oraibi, Waipi, Shungopovi, and Mishongnovi, so that they could take over the ceremonies and continue the cycle, decided that the population of Awatobi should be massacred."

There seem to be two fundamental problems with Keneally's approach. A travel book—especially one built, like this one, around a journey (as opposed to the "sedentary" travel books of Gerald Brenan and Elliot Paul)—is by nature cursory and impressionistic. The history of the native peoples of the American Southwest is ancient and complex, and so does not lend itself to this sort of passing glance. Instead of a revealing portrait, we get a confused mosaic.

Considering this handicap, it might have made more sense to focus on how Native Americans are faring in the "European" Southwest of today. In fact, that Southwest is curiously absent from these pages. Apart from some brief descriptions of the suburban sprawl of Phoenix and Albuquerque, there is little sense of contemporary life. Too many passages, with their recollections of the past, sound as if they were written—or at least could have been—back home in Sydney.

One of the most interesting parts of the book, for me, is the discussion of D. H. Lawrence—a superb travel writer himself—and his relationship to this part of the world. "We cannot go back to the savages," he wrote, "not a stride. We can be in sympathy with them. We can take a great curve in their direction. . . . But we cannot turn the current of our life backwards. . . . So many 'reformers' and 'idealists' who glorify the savages in America. They are death-birds, life-haters. Renegades." Keneally, calling Lawrence "an unrepentant Caucasian," claims that his point is "the crucial debate in our relationship to tribal people and is still being argued in New Mexico and elsewhere." But, sad to say, it is not much argued in these pages.

The other problem with the book is that Keneally depends so heavily on secondary sources. He spends entirely too much time with his history books, especially for a man who is so seemingly enamored of the intuitive ways of native peoples. Rarely are we introduced to living people, and when we are, rarely do they speak. There is virtually no dialogue—a critical failing for a travel book.

I suspect that the culprits here are Keneally's wife and daughter. Though, as I've said, we hardly hear of them, they are always silently present, keeping the author from getting around and meeting the people who would give his book life. Last year at the Key West Literary Seminar on Travel Writing, a distinguished panel was asked if travel writing had to be a solitary pursuit. The unanimous answer was yes. "Sad but true," added Jan Morris.

My advice to Keneally: Next time, leave home without them.

Susan Fromberg Schaeffer (review date 18 April 1993)

SOURCE: "The Woman Who Lost Her Children," in *New York Times Book Review,* April 18, 1993, p. 9.

[*In the following review, Schaeffer outlines the plot and themes of* Woman of the Inner Sea.]

What would you do if you were a happily married woman whose husband had an affair with a woman who came to obsess him—and then a mysterious catastrophe took your two beloved children from you forever? Would you have the emotional stamina to survive? If you are one of those fortunate people who hasn't experienced this kind of tragedy, you don't know. Kate Gaffney-Kozinski, the heroine of Thomas Keneally's 20th novel, *Woman of the Inner Sea,* doesn't know either—even though it has all happened to her—but she is about to find out.

Kate was raised as a modern woman, trained to think of the frenzy of motherhood as something primitive. Wealthy and privileged in her beach house near Sydney, she came to believe that life would be one long, sun-drenched idyll. When her marriage collapsed and her children were gone, she became, according to her uncle, the roguish Rev. Frank O'Brien, the "Queen of Sorrows." She needs to rediscover how to live, needs to learn "what is required of me now."

Kate is looking for a personal myth or fable that can explain her own life and give her purpose. She is convinced, as is her Uncle Frank, who has carefully passed his own beliefs along to her, that it does not matter what gods you believe in as long as you have gods to believe in, gods that can give you faith to see you through a life all too often disfigured by suffering. It is not necessary, according to Uncle Frank, to worship only "the Other. The Dressed-up One."

Kate does not seek wisdom in the "big, loud, mad cities" where, she believes, there is no truth to be found; instead, she sets off for the outback. Acting as a "free traveler," she decides to let the "wide-spaced towns educate her," then randomly settles in Myambagh, in central Australia, because it "looked most eminently a town of habit," a town tailored exactly to her requirements: "She wanted to be amongst those country faces anyhow. She wanted to *feed* numbly on them. From the present, poisoned world, she wanted to track back with the help of those faces to the safer Australia . . . where people called lunch *dinner* and dinner *tea.*"

Kate takes up residence in Murchison's Railway Hotel and quickly comes to see the hotel bar as a kind of church, a sacred place "of holiness and taboo like other places of this nature: the weighing room at racecourses, the middle box of a confessional." In this bar are men who have also become holy. Each one, the owner tells her, is "bloody famous for something." Each, in other words, has a purpose and knows what it is. Sitting at the bar, "they thought they were pleasing themselves but in fact were at a kind of work, fulfilling a function, occupying spaces which had to be occupied to insure that things lasted and that constellations stayed in place."

Kate herself is soon ordained as a barmaid in this holy place. And when one of the floods that periodically threaten Myambagh arrives, Kate, who has begun an odd affair with a man called Jelly (not for his weight, but because he handles gelignite, an explosive he has learned to use in the construction business) goes with him on his sacred mission to dynamite the railway levee that is trapping the flood waters near the town. They are joined by a bar mate, Gus Schulberger, and his pets, an emu named Menzies and a kangaroo named Chifley. But all are led by Jelly, who after dying in his effort to save the town "would have such renown in Myambagh tomorrow, a man who would have rounded the circle of his own appointed fable."

With Jelly gone, Kate turns to Gus—and to Chifley, the tame kangaroo, whose ability to leap through the air restores her faith in salvation. Weighed down as she is by guilt, which has slowed and trapped her, she sees Chifley as something of a god, perhaps as her own child, certainly a symbol of freedom.

Before Kate's adventures in the outback end, her dead lover, Jelly, is transformed from a mere hero of Myambagh into someone of truly mythic stature, and Gus, who has rescued the emu and the kangaroo, has become a folk hero. When Kate returns to Sydney, she has learned what she needs to know: that suffering is in the nature of things; that the worst catastrophe that can occur is merely one among many; and that no crisis, however enormous, justifies expending everything on it.

These are, as Kate's Uncle Frank tells her, simple truths, but hard to grasp. Yet now that she knows them, she is free to revenge herself on her husband, free to solve the riddle of her children's deaths, free to lift the undeserved burden of guilt from her own shoulders. She reaches, as Mr. Keneally tells us in his final passage, "the illusorily static point appropriate to the closure of a tale." In his concluding line— "We all wish her nothing but well"—he underscores his theme: life does not always leave us happy. Trouble never ends. And Kate, like everyone else, will need our good wishes.

Woman of the Inner Sea succeeds on many fronts. It is a picaresque and often hilarious adventure story, recounting one woman's unforgettable if improbable travels. It is a series of love stories, as Kate meets the man who is appropriate for her at each stage of her life, and it is a mystery story as well. But the novel is also very much an exploration of ethics. What is a good person? asks Mr. Keneally. And what is good behavior? A good life? Does an individual existence have a purpose and, if so, what is it?

"Kate is in her way a strong character," Mr. Keneally tells us. "She's not like someone out of Ionesco." And, he adds, "it is all very well for novelists not to believe in character, but what if the characters themselves have been raised to believe in it?" This question gives us a strong insight into Mr. Keneally's own purpose. He regards modern urban life as a wasteland where people no longer speak the truth. In *Woman of the Inner Sea,* he stands up for his own verities.

The world we live in is, according to Mr. Keneally, "poisoned" and overcivilized materially, while spiritually it is dangerously undernourished. Using all his novelistic skills (including uproarious humor) he asserts and makes convincing the very serious belief that each of us has a necessary place — and that our most important task is to find it. *Woman of the Inner Sea* is a magical fable about how this can be done.

Donna Rifkind (review date 16 May 1993)

SOURCE: "Is There Birth After Death" in *Los Angeles Times Book Review,* May 16, 1993, p. 7.

[*In the following review of* Woman of the Inner Sea, *Rifkind focuses on the characterization of the book's heroine.*]

Australia, like America, was built on the promise of reinvention. Live here, it urged its immigrants, and be someone your old world would never permit. Thomas Keneally's 20th novel, *Woman of the Inner Sea,* reinvents the theme of reinvention. Set in the heart of Australia, the book asks a universal question. Is it possible to transform yourself after you have suffered the greatest loss you could ever imagine?

Keneally is an impeccable writer with a longstanding international reputation whose books have had settings as various as Nazi-dominated Europe (*Schindler's List*) and the interior of a hijacked airplane (*Flying Hero Class*). He has written about his native country many times as well. But, the contemporary Australia of this new novel has a particular dual purpose. Its miles of empty red earth, stringybark and eucalyptus, savage storms and eccentric wildlife represent more than just the external landscape through which the book's main character, Kate Gaffney-Kozinski, travels; the fluid unpredictability of the land also mirrors Kate's transformation as she makes her way from the coast toward the country's interior.

In her former life Kate had been the pampered but neglected wife of a Sydney real-estate tycoon. Lacking her husband's affection, she had poured all her resources—a beautiful home on the beach, limitless money, fine taste and the best intentions—into the art of motherhood. No matter that Paul spent more time with his mistress than with his two children; Kate made up for it by being the kind of mother who enrolls her toddler son in a class to learn to catch a ball, who rejoices in her agile daughter's swimming speed, who perches near their rooms at night to feel "the voiceless motors of her children's sleep."

In the space of a tragic afternoon Kate's maternity is erased. A house charred to its foundations, a husband screaming accusations and two small coffins are evidence of how completely her conscientiousness has come to nothing. She boards a train for the interior, hoping to lose herself in the country's great yawning center, to be "breathed in by the great antipodean stupefaction." The place Kate chooses for her self-annihilation is the "three-minute town" of Myambagh, where she finds work as a barmaid at Murchison's Railway hotel and concentrates the rest of her numb energy on getting as anonymously fat as possible on the pub's steady supply of steak and beer.

Myambagh, built on the hard flat rock of what was once an immense inland sea, is a town where a four-wheel drive is the key to survival, not a suburban affectation. The local economy relies on the certainty of brutal annual rains, which cause floods of biblical proportions: the time between yearly inundations is spent nailing, patching and plastering the town back together in preparation for the next disaster.

Kate likes Myambagh's soothing guarantees of loss made routine and unsurprising. She also likes the regulars at Murchison's, who have made a liturgy out of the strict unspoken code of pub behavior. These include Jelly, an obese pensioner with a hero's reputation for using dynamite to blast back the floods; Guthega, a loudmouth whose son holds the local championship for sheep-shearing; and Gus a crackerjack mechanic.

Despite the town's preparations, the inevitable rains come, and Myambagh is once again swallowed by flood. At the height of the well-publicized catastrophe, fearing that the news cameras will betray her hiding place to her family in Sydney, Kate escapes westward again, closer to the country's obscuring core. This time she's not alone: Gus travels with her, attended by his pet emu and kangaroo.

Keneally's characters are archetypes to a man and woman, not to mention those two hugely symbolic animals, who happen to appear on the coat of arms of the commonwealth of Australia. His purpose is to invoke the Australian frontier tradition which, like all frontier cultures, seeks to reinvent ordinary people as icons and mythic figures.

While the major Australian icons have always been men, Keneally augments his country's tradition by making Kate the story's hero. In the tragedy of her dead children and her subsequent pilgrimage, Kate represents a nation on a perpetual search for reinvention, a nation hardened by countless histories of cash hunger, tough luck and untimely death; by the principle, as Keneally writes, "that the order of the world is loss followed by loss" in an unpredictable, unforgiving landscape.

Yet Kate is, to the author's credit, an utterly believable individual as well as an icon. Outlining the vastness of a mother's grief is one of literature's hardest challenges. The very outlandishness of Kate's pilgrimage (at one point, she and Gus pose as animal wranglers on a movie set with the emu and the kangaroo in tow) is made plausible by her bereavement: after suffering like hers, Keneally is suggesting, nothing surprises.

Woman of the Inner Sea is not a long book, but it has a wealth of complex characterization and action of a kind that few contemporary novels provide in any length. Keneally is a born storyteller whose writing becomes more clean and purposeful with every book. The experience of reading his latest work provides more grateful pleasure than the usual vocabulary of promotional cliches could ever begin to describe.

Peter Conrad (review date 12 September 1993)

SOURCE: "Wizard of Oz with Jet Lag and Too Busy for His Own Good," in *The Observer,* September 12, 1993, p. 53.

[*In the review below, Conrad finds the arguments and production values of* Memoirs from a Young Republic *"shockingly amateurish."*]

Writers are the makers and the keepers of a nation's identity. Thomas Keneally (or Tom, as he now matily styles himself) has done as much as any living writer to identify and extol Australia. He deals with the bogus ceremonial of its European settlement in *The Playmaker,* and with the suppressed tragedy of aboriginal dispossession in *The Chant of Jimmie Blacksmith;* in *Outback* he tramps across its dusty, torrid, adored terrain.

He was an inevitable choice as chairman of the Australian Republican Movement, which aims to make the country at long last its own master by severing constitutional links with Britain before the centenary of federation in 2001. Why then has he now disgraced himself and degraded the cause by writing such a shoddy, ill-argued book about it?

Please don't mistake me for an expatriate loyalist. The republican cause is as dear to me as it is to Keneally, and in my wallet I carry one of the ARM's trinkets, an unspendable five dollar bill from which the Queen's face has been meticulously expunged by nail polish remover. I too will feel proud when I finally have a passport which treats me as a citizen rather than the subject of a non-resident and increasingly unmajestic Majesty. But before I accept the jumble of anecdote and propaganda in *Memoirs from a Young Republic* as an emotional and intellectual justification for this epochal change, I'll drop a curtsy in the main street of Wagga Wagga.

Keneally's conviction of historical inevitability absolves him from having to do anything except repeat that the republic is coming, whether the Windsors are ready or not. Paraphrasing law books, he works through the iniquities of the current Australian constitution; he also recites the usual list of local gripes against Britain, which commandeered colonial troops for use as cannon fodder at Gallipoli in 1916 but declined to defend Australia against the Japanese in 1942.

His own contribution to the debate consists of a claim that 'Jenny Kee, the couturier' can't market her wares in Asia because Australia is still perceived to be a 'white supremacist' bastion, and a lament that, during his own promotional junkets across America, he has had difficulty explaining the monarchical connection to 'deconstructionists like Harold Bloom and Jacques Derrida' (who, given the self-centeredness of Yale and its cabalistic high priests, probably suffer from a more basic bemusement about where and what Australia is). There have to better reasons than facilitation of the rag trade and a spanielling desire to earn Derrida's approbation!

Keneally's analysis of Australia's ancient servility towards Britain, recycled from a review of Robert Hughes's *The Fatal Shore,* is interesting; he blames it on 'our penal origins', which encouraged Australians to see themselves as 'the fallen, the spiritually defeated', requiring redemption by a mystical White Goddess like Elizabeth II.

The same demoralization is probably responsible for the economic malaise of a country which can no longer lazily trot to prosperity on the back of its merino sheep. Keneally trusts that affluence will return, along with self-respect, when the 'mercantile protectorate' is ended. This surely over-estimates the curative powers of a quick constitutional fix. Keneally's case is not helped by a quote from the poet Les Murray, who windily prophesies 'a surge of creative energy' the moment the Union Jack is lowered. Australia needs entrepreneurs, not more state-subsidised novelists.

The fuzziness of Keneally's thinking might be forgivable if his book weren't so sloppily put together. Grammar and syntax frequently slump out of control, and he manages to misspell the names of Randolph Stow and Peter Shaffer, colleagues he professes to admire.

He is, admittedly, a busy man. He casually mentions that in 1990 he wrote three books and a screenplay simultaneously, and reveals that while compiling **Memoirs from a Young Republic** he worked on a new novel and ghosted the autobiography of 'the great Manly Warringah utility player Des Hasler' (a footballer, in case you were wondering). He now commutes between continents as well as projects, hopping from Sydney to California, where he teaches creative writing, with detours every few months to England to promote the latest of those mass-produced books. Recently there have been diversions to Prague, where Spielberg was filming **Schindler's Ark,** and humanitarian expeditions to Eritrea. 'I work a lot on planes', Keneally confesses. Alas, it shows.

He tends to excuse political blunders by pleading jet lag. On one return to Australia, when his body arrived in advance of his brain, an interviewer asked him for a short list of presidential candidates. Keneally provoked a scandal by blurting out the names of 'a number of women: Ita Buttrose, Geraldine Doogue, Faith Bandler. . . .' Not exactly world-class ladies: after considerable research I ascertained that the first used to edit the *Australian Women's Weekly*; the second is that most unbearably light-headed of beings, a television personality; and the third has the fortune—in the grievance-culture of political correctness—to be the daughter of an enslaved plantation worker from the New Hebrides. If the plangent question of the cultural cringers is 'Who

among us is worthy, Lord?', then I'm afraid the answer is 'None of the above'.

Meanwhile Joan Sutherland—the only woman with the proper theatrical training for the post-regal role, though disqualified by her DBE and OM—was faxing support to the royal resistance from her tax-free fastness above Montreux ('in the Helvetian Republic', as Keneally tartly comments), and declaring that the republicans deserved transportation to Australia, which is where they were already. This shockingly amateurish book makes me feel, in spite of my own sympathies, that she has a point. Cry, the beloved country.

Bruce King (review date Autumn 1994)

SOURCE: A review of *Jacko the Great Intruder,* in *World Literature Today,* Vol. 68, No. 4, Autumn, 1994, pp. 879-80.

[*In the review below, King praises the cultural insights and narrative strategies of* Jacko the Great Intrude.]

Jacko the Great Intruder is the most complicated novel Thomas Keneally has written and the most exciting to read. While it will not get the same attention as **Schindler's Ark** or **Confederates,** it is probably even a better novel and would make an excellent film, provided that a way could be found to treat the many flashbacks, the changes in place, and the multiple strands of the narrative, which are essential to the story.

Jacko is one of Keneally's studies in the strange ways of goodness and evil in this world. A product of Australia's immense, largely uninhabited, remote Northern Territory, he is a contradictory mixture of ambition, energy, roughness, cunning, bad taste, good will, sentimentality, and enthusiasms, who lives dangerously, carelessly, as likely to shock with his disregard for the feelings of others as unexpectedly to do good. Seemingly unrooted, except in Australian matesmanship, he belongs to a crude, hardy, still lawless culture, in which toughness, survival, and individuality produce larger-than-life characters with few of the social refinements, liberal guilts, or squeamishness of the cities.

The novel follows Jacko's career as a television interviewer, itself analogous to the increasing international role of Australia in the communications and arts industries, from Australia to New York to California. Jacko has a more vulgar kind of Australian low taste, lack of propriety, and imprudence which makes even American television appear inhibited, but he can have moments of bravery and moral obsessions which endanger his career and life and which, by contrast, show how hardened others, especially Americans, have become to the evils of modern life. If this is a novel about cultural contrasts, it is also, surprisingly for Keneally, a story about manners and morals in which the most sensitive, compassionate, and conscious are not necessarily the best. If Jacko is the great intruder, invading homes to interview people, invading lives to get what he can, carelessly breaking legal contracts, careless of his marriage, he leads demonstrators in destroying the Berlin Wall while other television reporters get the best footage. He spends months tracing a missing person and, finding her in slavery in California, is so overcome with her condition that he throws away the best program of his life and then pays from his own pocket to send her to Australia to recover. *Jacko the Great Intruder* is a complex novel, but one of its themes concerns a brash, naive innocence still found in parts of Australia in contrast to a jaded, equivocating, refined high seriousness and political correctness which has left much of the West without active moral courage.

The novel involves various times, moves between continents, and shifts of focus between the lives of many characters, including a novelist narrator who resembles Keneally and a Nobel Prize laureate who resembles Patrick White. Still, the stories and lives are so interesting that the book reads like a collection of Australian yarns. A realist who bases his material on the recognizable, Keneally now has the mastery of form that many critics associate with magical realism or the postmodern, yet he remains a Catholic novelist concerned with good and evil and an Australian writer who tells a good tale.

Peter Pierce (essay date May 1995)

SOURCE: "'The Critics Made Me': The Receptions of Thomas Keneally and Australian Literary Culture," in *Australian Literary Studies,* Vol. 17, No. 1, May, 1995, pp. 99-103.

[*In the essay below, Pierce examines the motives of Keneally's detractors.*]

While Thomas Keneally himself generously acknowledges that 'the critics made me', few Australian authors—in the course of long, productive and internationally acclaimed careers—have suffered such critical opprobrium in their own country. His perception of causes soon to be fashionable (such as the treatment of Australian Aborigines), his insistence on how the Australian present can be traced to its European social and intellectual origins, his espousal of an Australian republic, have held up a mirror to a generation of Australian readers. Nevertheless he has been subject to censure by some academic critics without losing a loyal general readership, in Australia and overseas.

It is received wisdom in some quarters that Keneally's work has steadily fallen off in quality since the early 1970s; that his treatment of female characters has been misogynist; that his novels show an inordinate interest in, and relish for, violence; that—in the case of *Season in Purgatory* (1976)—Keneally was a plagiarist; that his Irish origins and republican affiliations (properly separate matters, between which Keneally at least is capable of distinguishing) somehow discredit, or diminish, his literary achievements; finally that his art has suffered from success and excess, from the prolific and profitable professional career which Keneally has established. If these charges cohered, let alone if all of them could be sustained, they would amount to a weightier indictment than any ever previously brought against an Australian author. Investigating why this is so, why Keneally has apparently caused such grievous and abiding offence to some critics, will illuminate murky aspects of the literary culture of this country.

In the last year, the most vicious assault on Keneally's reputation came in the course of a 5AN radio discussion, broadcast on 26 July 1994. Christopher Pearson, a pro-monarchist and editor of the *Adelaide Review* offered this gambit:

> I remember learning about a St. Patrick's Day speech where Tom Keneally described the Queen as 'a colostomy bag on the Australian body politic'. It's a memorable phrase and it seems to me to suggest the quality of the passion that drives him.

Keneally denied that his simile had been so colorful. Instead he recalled a tamer offering: 'like a briefcase carried at arm's length or . . . the constitutional equivalent of a colostomy bag'. And he pleaded 'a few Guinesses too many'. That convivial admission further incited his adversary, who moved savagely sideways from a consideration of Keneally's support for an Australian republic to damn him as a novelist. Belittling Keneally's literary credentials was presumably intended to deride, by association, the political cause of republicanism.

This commentator continued:

> the best that the Republic Movement can do is to trot out a novelist who's burnt out basically, who's done his best work early and who's never overcome the plagiarism charges of *Season in Purgatory* and is now writing warm, fuzzy holocaust novels and who's obviously in a sense looking for rehabilitation, to rediscover a role for himself as a man of public affairs.

These intemperate and inaccurate charges indicate the depth of rancor which exists in some recesses of Australian cultural life, when Keneally is at issue. While Pearson's invective scarcely deserves rebuttal, one can remark that, in the last decade, this burnt-out case has written his finest and funniest anatomics of Australian contemporary life—*A Family Madness* (1985) and *Woman of the Inner Sea* (1992)—besides brilliantly revisiting his first critical success, **Bring Larks and Heroes** (1967), in the altogether more benign tale of our European origins, **The Playmaker** (1987). The 'plagiarism charges' are now forgotten, and the matter of Keneally's guilt was at best ambiguous. Nor is Keneally now 'writing warm, fuzzy holocaust novels'. He has never written one. And **Schindler's Ark** (if that is the book meant) was published thirteen years ago.

No honour was satisfied by this exchange, nor could any conclusions be reached from it, except as concerns the pathology of some Australian monarchists. But larger questions were raised: why has criticism of Keneally's work (as novelist and public figure) been so vexed and bitter? What have the effects of this been on his career? What cultural problems in Australia do the attacks on him, and his responses to them, expose?

An answer to these linked questions suggests that Pearson's spleen was extreme, but not exceptional. Keneally has suffered from the high expectations that critics foisted on him in the late 1960s. As long afterwards as March 1991, the anonymous author of the 'Shelf Life' column in the *Sunday Age* sadly intoned that:

> There was a time when he looked the natural successor to Patrick White. Over the years, however, Thomas Keneally has done his best to turn himself into our one popular international writer.

Forget Carey, West, McCullough for the moment, Keneally is being slighted here not only for not succeeding White, but for securing acclaim overseas. A writer's pardonable ambitions (to be distinctive, and successful) are disdained. The source of resentment of Keneally is obscure, but the caricature offered of the author is a potent one. Keneally has been described as 'the most notable Australian example of a not unfamiliar type: the potentially major talent which dissipates itself in commercialism' (Craven). Such a comment leaves no escape for the author, whose financial rewards are disparaged as the waste of a talent with which evidently they have no connection.

Recognizing the currency of this parody of himself, Keneally was finally goaded into responding to his Australian critics. On 13 November 1993 he had a letter published in the *Weekend Australian* where he expressed 'a genuine anguish and bemusement'. He had been especially upset by reviews of two of his books that year: the novel *Jacko* (by Michael Sharkey) and **Our Republic** (by Imré Salusinszky). Keneally's response was to recount the literary awards which

he had won, at home and abroad; the critical and commercial success he had had overseas; the honors bestowed upon him, for instance a Distinguished Professorship for Life in the University of California system. Accordingly Keneally wondered what he had to prove to certain Australian critics, as distinct from his reading public? How was he to square parochial pundits' views of his falling away with 'the experience of having every novel published during the period of my supposed decline praised by literary figures in the *New York Times Review of Books* and elsewhere'. Why was it, Keneally continued, that no foreign review was ever 'as bitter and intimately rancorous as the ones I frequently received in Australia?'

Critical opprobrium towards Keneally began in earnest in the 1970s, after the publication of **The Chant of Jimmie Blacksmith.** Keneally concedes that he courted trouble. Reminiscing two decades later, he admitted: 'part of it is my folly. I attacked academics. I was a real smart-arse when I was young'. Some of these academics did not forget. Historian Henry Reynolds characterised the novel reductively as 'very much a book of its time'. Reynolds contended that 'at worst', it

> shared faults with some contemporary Government policies which, though superficially well-meaning, were paternalistic in execution and burdened with an unconscious legacy of ancestral racism.

How Keneally, with his deeply imbued memories of the history of the Irish at home and in Australia, responded to this presumptuous charge is not recorded. Not for the last time he was suffering from the confusion of the political agenda of others with an evaluation of his fiction; suffering, too, because he is a cultural barometer, who draws for his art on the most contentious issues just before their season of wider publicity.

In 1974 Keneally found himself the subject of an astonishing commentary. Under attack was his alleged relish for violence. Purportedly reviewing **The Chant of Jimmie Blacksmith,** a critic ventured *ad hominem* speculations of an unpleasant, unwarranted kind:

> One gets the impression ... that Keneally turns to the past not out of historical interest but for the opportunity that a more brutal past affords him to express his taste for blood.

Off-handed psychoanalysis of Keneally's vampirism consorted with the hand-me-down terms of Leavisite critical reproof as the reviewer concluded:

> The chief obstacle in the way of his development now is the violence within himself which he must

renounce before he can enter the vast world of productive human relationships . . . An angry writer can achieve power and intensity; but he rarely grows.

This anticipated other occasions when Keneally's character would be insulted in the guise of literary judgment, and critics arrogate the right to dictate the course his career should take.

As that career progressed, Keneally was subject to one of the more insidious tactics of marginalization practiced in Australian literary circles. This is a pseudo-argument that affects to demonstrate how local writers of once splendid talents often suffer a lamentable decline in their powers. Envy appears in the guise of invidious comparisons, made in sorrowing tones. Writers such as Williamson, Murray and Carey, besides Keneally, have had later works disparaged by comparison with all that their earlier ones supposedly promised. Williamson commented on this phenomenon with a rueful wit:

> You were discovered, given premature canonization, the artistic hopes of Australia were placed on your shoulders, then if you happened to have a critical reverse you were subjected to savage retribution and you spent the rest of your life wandering from bar to bar wondering why you weren't Dostoevsky.

Keneally has had plenty of experience of this treatment. One commentator opined that 'the early stuff was remarkable, the later stuff less demanding'. No specific instances were given. Another claimed that

> his artistic career is paradigmatic of the path of so much creative talent and so many people in this country: from potential excellence to ineluctable mediocrity; from daring and excitement to chafing comfort; from passion to anomie.

O'Hearn begged questions. Why should there be an 'ineluctable' path to mediocrity for Australian writers? Does this indicate an ingrained pessimism among certain critics as to the worth of the Australian product? Or is it that they cannot forgive their early enthusiasms for authors whose subsequent development has failed to please them? And if a writer seeks 'comfort', and this is conceived in terms of material rewards, why should it chafe?

As David Marr's recent edition of *Patrick White Letters* (1994) shows, the novelist he was once deemed likely to succeed attacked Keneally viciously in private. On 18 March 1968 he wrote to James Stern, an American critic, that he would:

> like to write about *Larks and Heroes,* but I am

prejudiced by all the publicity from this rather revolting little bog-Irish almost priest married to a renegade nun.

Snobbery apart, we will never know (but would not previously have been inclined to suspect) whether jealousy of a potential rival was one motive for White's response to the novel which he had just read. More acrid is his undisguised sectarianism. Keneally would find that sentiment resurfacing in an attempt to discredit his espousal of republicanism.

With evident reluctance, Keneally has developed ways of responding to critical assaults upon him. The letter to the *Weekend Australian* was a blunt, exasperated reaction. His strategies have usually been subtler. One has been his willingness to give interviews, cannily crafted to set the terms for an appraisal of his writing. For many years Keneally has responded generously to requests from around the world for accounts of his work practices, recently to Zhang Wei-hong, who wrote a PhD thesis on "Thomas Keneally's Work as a Continuum" for the Beijing Foreign Studies University. Peter Quartermaine, in his monograph *Thomas Keneally* (1991), represented the author as "a man of the people," who yet "remains a very private person in his concerns, and wary of the effects of publicity". Less "wary" than cunning perhaps: several of the epigraphs in Quartermaine's book are drawn directly from interviews with or essays by Keneally.

Another of Keneally's responses to attack has been the pose of indifference to criticism, and the assertion that he is determined to write on regardless. Keneally is sensible of what the Australian Prime Minister, Paul Keating, styled "the Paris option"—exile abroad, as a gesture of contempt for ungrateful local critics. That exile is literal, in that Keneally spends lengthy periods each year absent from Australia, making himself less frequently "a motley to the view" and resigning from the Chair of the Australian Republican Movement. It is also a metaphorical (if intermittent) withdrawal from Australia, into the solace of an overseas reception of his work that continues to be warm, in contrast with his Australian reception.

Publicity kits, such as Heinemann produced for *Jacko,* included encomia of his previous work by Bernard Levin and Graham Greene. But there is a risk in advertising, or depending on, praise from abroad. The comparison of his favourable reception overseas with what he now perceives as an entrenched hostility among some Australian critics becomes sterile, as Keneally surely knows. Moreover, his appeal to international arbitration can be attacked on the very grounds of national independence which—when concerned with Australian sovereignty—he would strongly espouse. Keneally has provided his adversaries with weapons to use against him. For instance, writing as much as he does guarantees that some of his novels will be more highly wrought than others.

By making his public profile more than that of an author, Keneally has also invited attacks on his politics which, once made, have been used to tarnish his credentials as a writer. Keneally has never claimed that his stature as a novelist underwrites his opinions on an Australian republic. Nor has he heeded those (with whose interests at heart?) who have called on him to write less, and spend more time instead on revision. Or perhaps he has listened. After three books in 1993, none appeared in 1994, not even under the pseudonym, 'William Coyle', which Keneally adopted for two novels of the Second World War.

Keneally's critical reputation has been so fiercely disputed for so long that any diagnostician of Australian culture must speculate why this is so. Both the genius of the national literature and—less fortunately—the sovereign temper of literary history and criticism in Australia are melodramatic. The manifestations of such a temper are many, and usually pernicious. In a melodramatic action and setting, the villainous prey on the virtuous. A heightened, hysterical and adversarial language characterises, at the same time as it disables discourse. The argumentative habit of dichotomy, so often truculent and embattled, prevails. As it happens, Keneally is one of the most acute analysts of the national melodrama. To the extent that he is a victim, however, he has had to endure persecution without sufficient warrant; has seen his career divided into lopsided parts, with the consequent critical neglect of his fine work during the last decade. With a growing and pardonable testiness, Keneally has endured attempts to dispossess him, to remove him from an academically if not generally approved canon of Australian literature.

> **It is a tribute to Keneally's moral resilience, to the equability and generosity of his temperament, to an apprehension that he can appeal over the head of critics to the people, and—of course—to his continuing dedication to his craft that he has survived what may look increasingly to him like systematic persecution from some Australian critics.**
>
> —*Peter Pierce*

The melodramatic vision is paranoid. The hero-victim feels persecuted beyond any reasonable measure of offence. It is a tribute to Keneally's moral resilience, to the equability and generosity of his temperament, to an apprehension that he can appeal over the head of critics to the people, and—of course—to his continuing dedication to his craft that he has

survived what may look increasingly to him like systematic persecution from some Australian critics. The critical reception of Thomas Keneally is by now a complicated and contradictory business that is three decades old. He has had loyal, long-term advocates (for all that they have occasionally been disappointed): David English, Brian Kiernan, Leonie Kramer and Adrian Mitchell among them. That his reception nevertheless seems to be narrower and more prejudiced these days is an indication of cultural malaise rather than the exhaustion of the author. One wonders whether critics have made of Keneally the scapegoat for their own distaste for, or lack of confidence in, Australian culture, so that attacks on his art, subjects, politics signify a cultural deathwish?

But that is too negative a note, Keneally's relationship with the critics who once 'made' him has always been dynamic. Reckoning with their strictures, he has made amends, however wryly, for his earlier portrayals of women, for which he was taken to task in the 1980s by Shirley Walker and Frances McInherny. More importantly, Keneally has engineered a seismic shift in his career between "alienation" and "affirmation," as he told Zhang Wei-hong (173). Criticism of Keneally's fiction may in the end have been more creative than destructive, in that it released the rejoicing side of his imagination; led him from **Bring Larks and Heroes** to **The Playmaker,** from his first novel, **The Place at Whitton,** which features a literal witch, to **Woman of the Inner Sea,** where the unhistrionic bravery of a woman is explored. Criticism did not discourage Keneally's desire to write a *comédie humaine* in the antipodes, although he has never thought of Australia as anything but part of one world, where we are all in the same boat, or ark, and where we all hang together.

David Willis McCullough (review date 14 May 1995)

SOURCE: "A Hard Life in Haunted Spaces," in *New York Times Book Review*, May 14, 1995, p. 12.

[*In the following review, McCullough assesses the narrative style of* A River Town.]

Traditionally, the annual announcement of the Booker Prize, Britain's most famous fiction award, comes accompanied by ready-made controversy. But when Thomas Keneally won in 1982 for **Schindler's Ark** (published in the United States as **Schindler's List**), the outcry was over an issue more basic than the usual squabble over quality. The book was nonfiction, the protesters said, and not a novel at all.

Such confusion over the line that separates fiction and nonfiction seems to be a typical problem for Mr. Keneally. But then few novelists are quite so invisible as he is. Like a master character actor, he disappears into his subjects. Whether he is dealing with Joan of Arc or the American Civil War or the negotiations leading up to the end of World War I or revolt and famine in contemporary East Africa, the grace and clarity of his writing style—not to mention his facility as a story teller—often get overlooked because he works so magically with such mundane things as facts.

Which is why I am sorry Mr. Keneally has let it slip with hints on the dedication page and in prepublication interviews that his impassioned new novel—his 21st—is based on events in the lives of his grandparents, real Irish immigrants who ran a real grocery store in a raw little Australian river town back at the turn of the century. This simply opens the way for the kind of speculation that always hounds Mr. Keneally. That any of *A River Town* is "real" or "true" or "based on fact" should be beside the point. It is a wonderfully rich novel, and readers should appreciate Mr. Keneally—who has never as a writer been emotionally more visible—not as an especially clever cryptohistorian but as a novelist with a vision of his own.

The name of the river town is Kempsey, an isolated village on the banks of the Macleay River, hundreds of miles north of Sydney. The year is 1899. The Victorian era is about to end. An aging British Empire is feeling the strains of civil war in South Africa and appealing to its colonies for help (or perhaps simply for cannon fodder). An infant Australia is debating its future: how unified does it want to be, how independent of that distant island so many of its residents still call home? In Kempsey, the future is embodied in the pilings of a bridge being built across the Macleay that promises to unite a handful of scattered villages into a city.

At present, though, it is a divided little town, with English and Irish—few think of themselves as Australians—maintaining an uneasy and distrustful peace. Tim Shea, from County Cork, owns one of the town's general stores, one that can count on its Irish clientele but needs some wealthy English customers to prosper.

Tim is a good man trying to do an honest job, extending more credit than is probably wise, but he is haunted by dreams and memories and what he considers his responsibilities. He regrets losing a successful pub he was unable to buy because his arranged bride from home, Kitty, did not arrive in time (pub owners must be married men). He daydreams about the beautiful wife of one of his wealthiest customers. Although he cannot afford to, he secretly takes on the financial care of an orphaned farm girl simply because he was one of the first to arrive at the scene of her father's fatal accident.

Most of all, he is haunted by a dead young woman. No one knows her name; no one remembers having ever seen her. She died during an illegal abortion. Her body was buried in a local graveyard, but her head has been placed in an alcohol-filled jar that is being shown around the countryside (although not to "respectable" women) by an especially inept policeman.

Inexorably, step by step, always by doing what he believes to be the good or right thing, Tim digs himself deeper into trouble. Often he is accompanied, against his better judgment, by a traveling Punjabi herbalist, someone even lower on the social scale than an Irishman. At his lowest ebb, Tim is even suspected of introducing bubonic plague to the Macleay Valley.

A River Town is hardly a lyrical novel. There is a curious stillness about it. The relentless heat is palpable. Smoke from wildfires in the nearby mountains clouds the sky. The countryside around Kempsey, places with names like Euroka and Dongdingalong, seems drab and featureless. As Mr. Keneally describes it, only the river—the community's link to the outside world—is alive and moving, relentlessly sweeping with a force that just recently cut a new path to the sea.

This is a truly compassionate novel, full of vividly portrayed outcasts. They are outsiders in a nation of outsiders who are only beginning to define themselves in their new home, people who thought that "if they traveled 12,000 miles, they might outrun original sin." Instead, Mr. Keneally writes, they found that "the old Adam was already waiting for them on the new shores. Met every damned boat."

The final pages seem a bit hurried, as if the characters, having met this crisis, were in a rush to get on with their lives. Or perhaps the author realized that in the conclusion of Tim Shea's heroic, seemingly predestined story are the seeds of a broader, even more complex tale that needs to be written as soon as possible. Either way, *A River Town* is a finely told novel. It is fired with the passion and hidden poetry that only a sure and experienced novelist can bring to fiction.

Janette Turner Hospital (review date 25 May 1995)

SOURCE: "Grand Gestures," in *London Review of Books*, Vol. 17, No. 10, May 25, 1995, pp. 22-3.

[*In the following review, Hospital emphasizes the millennial tone of* A River Town, *comparing the novel's themes on Australia in 1900 to comtemporary Australian experience.*]

There is something about a millennium, something about the clicking over of zeros on the odometer of history that sends a frowsy doomsday swell welling up from under, Good round numbers beget both end-of-an-age unease and unreasonable hopes. They breed signs and wonders. They inspire large gestures towards New Beginnings.

In 1900, the year in which Thomas Keneally's most recent novel situates itself, the separate Australian colonies were reeling from economic depression and the worst drought since European settlement began in 1788. There were catastrophic losses of cattle and sheep, wheat plummeted to less than one-tenth of pre-drought yield, dustbowl conditions prevailed, bushfires raged, farmers and squatters were forced to abandon their land. Far away, the sons of these hard-pressed farmers were dying under British generals in other people's wars: the Boer War in South Africa, the suppression of the Boxer Rebellion in China. And above and beyond all this, most ominous of doomsday signs in that apocalyptic year, there was an outbreak of bubonic plague in Sydney.

In 1900, in short, death was swift and common in the six Australian colonies: from drought, bushfire, battle, accident, disease. And yet for most settlers, compared to what was left behind—the dreary lives of the impoverished and the excluded of London, Glasgow, rural Ireland—Australia was still the promised land. Indeed, the revellers of 26 January 1900, celebrating the centenary of the First Fleet's arrival, had a jubilant and self-confident view of themselves, not as the transplanted pawns of empire in exile at the 'world's worse end', but as Australians, a lucky people, fiercely independent, with hope and initiative in their tucker bags.

In spite of plague and hard times, grand gestures toward a new age were definitely in order, and on 1 January 1901, federation of the six colonies as the Commonwealth of Australia took place. An editorial in the *Worker* (Brisbane) on 5 January 1901 reflected the messianic optimism:

> For good or ill the several Australian colonies now constitute what is known as the Australian Commonwealth ... and what was a group of colonies steps upwards and onwards to the dignity of a Nation. Victorians, Queenslanders, or Westralians will be unknown, and every child born of the soil, or approved and naturalised colonist, will in future be an Australian. An Australian; a citizen of a nation whose realm is a continent and whose destiny is— what? ...

Australia has ever been an exemplar to the old lands. From the first establishment of responsible government within its borders it has steadily forged ahead, initiating and perfecting, experimenting and legislating, on new lines. By a happy fortune it sprang up free of most of the superstitions, traditions, class distinctions, and sanctified fables and fallacies of the older nations. What few of them were bound about it it has shaken itself free of, and stands on the threshold of the future with its fate in its own hands.

Nevertheless there were, in the small bastions of transplanted gentry, fierce voices raised against "disloyalty" to Britain. Irish settlers were deemed particularly culpable, their motives and their Australian patriotism suspect. No one, needless to say, so much as consulted the indigenous population on the question. The dark underside of 1900 has been powerfully explored in another Keneally novel set in the same millennial year, *The Chant of Jimmie Blacksmith.*

All this sounds oddly familiar as Australia approaches the year 2000, staggering out from under economic recession and from the worst drought of the century, the old millennial urge for a New Beginning still running strong. It is the promise of Prime Minister Paul Keating of the Labour Party, of the Australian Republican Movement, as well as the majority wish of the populations as sounded by pollsters, that on Australia Day 2000—or at the latest by 1 January 2001, the anniversary of Federation—Australia will cease to be a constitutional monarchy owing allegiance to the British Crown, and will become a republic. There has been much airing of a 1900 refrain: that republican fervour is a species of treason toward the past, that the ARM is an Irish-Australian plot (and indeed, the Prime Minister and the leading lights of the ARM are conspicuously of Irish descent). But the appeal of the republic is far wider than this. Although debates still rage, there is general acceptance of its inevitability, and over the past year public discussion has moved from whether Australia should become a republic to what sort of republic it should become.

It is of course no accident that *A River Town* should seem to be so eerily about the present. The allegory is intentional, the intention passionate. Thomas Keneally was first chairman of the Australian Republican Movement and is now a member of the National Management Committee. His grandparents, to whose memory the novel is dedicated, were Irish immigrants who kept a store in the Macleay Valley, north of Sydney, a store identical in its location and lineaments to the store owned and run by Tim Shea, protagonist of the novel. When the characters of *A River Town* debate Britain's needs and Australia's duty in the Boer War, or when Irish Tim is blacklisted by certain establishment gentry for his unwillingness to swear an oath to 'support without equivocation the aims of the British Empire in Southern Africa, including the extinction of all Boer pretensions of sovereignty', the reader is being offered the hindsight of history as a glass through which to look at today's political agenda. ('How in hell's name,' Tim asks himself, 'could you vote casually for the death of the young?')

The novel opens in January 1900, in the town of Kempsey, in the valley of the Macleay, 'on the lush and humid north coast of New South Wales'. Almost everyone in town except Tim Shea, proprietor of the general store, has gone downriver by steamer to celebrate the national holiday. Hope is in the air. 'Hard times were said to be ending.'

But doomsday signs and wonders also abound. On the holiday, at the edge of the empty town, there is a horrible horse-and-sulky accident. Shea, in an impulsive though futile rescue attempt, is witness to the ghastly sight of wild pigs goring and devouring the crushed driver's head. The driver's orphaned children are also frightened observers. Later, still on the national holiday itself, Tim is shown by the local constable the severed head of a young woman, unnamed, unidentified, victim of a bungled abortion. The head floats ghoulishly in a flask of alcohol 'in accordance with long police practice in such affairs.' Before the imprisoned abortionists can be prosecuted for murder, their victim must be identified, and so the head is carted around by the constable who keeps it in a preserving jar wrapped in blue gingham in a picnic basket. 'We call her Missy. She was only young . . . You'll see, she was lovely in life'. The severed head, with its eyes not quite shut, its lips parted, haunts Tim Shea. He sees 'a serious child, making serious claims'. From the first glimpse, he feels marked, chosen, senses that she makes moral demands of him, seeking the restoration of her name and the calling to account of the man (clearly someone powerful, someone affluent) who discreetly arranged the abortion of the child he had fathered. For Tim, Missy is dreadfully everywhere', particularly in his nightmares.

And then there are the orphaned children of the accident, for whom Tim feels responsible. The disaster has particularly disturbing effects on Lucy who has a strange power to infect other children with her detachment and her death-defying urges. More signs and wonders: children fly, they scale lunatic heights, they leap off cliffs.

A severed head, another head gored by pigs, untamable orphaned children; these are weighty symbols, suggesting parallels in the body politic (a distant head of state, alien to its imperial limbs; an orphaned colony bent on self-destruction), though their allegorical import runs curiously counter to the protagonist's sympathies. Such slippage gives the book a richly ambiguous texture. Here, in fact, lies one of the consistent strengths of the entire (and considerable) body of Keneally's work. Though he has a passionate moral vision, he is not didactic. (Spielberg, yes; Keneally, no; the rose-tinted light of moral sentimentality that Spielberg has cast on Keneally has skewed the perception of the novelist's work in some quarters. Perhaps Keneally will come to wish that he had done as Art Spiegelman, author of the Pulitzer prize winning *Maus,* has done: turned down Spielberg's film offer.) Keneally is one of those rare writers whose work is widely accessible yet also of real sinew and complexity. He is too fine a novelist not to subvert any narrow moral or political intention. His images skitter in several directions at once, their import is provocatively and fruitfully multivalent.

Like all his protagonists, deeply reluctant prophets and heroes every last one of them, Keneally has a heightened awareness of the contradictions inherent in characters and in issues. His protagonists, men and women who have a yen for ordinary unremarkable lives but who are compelled by circumstances and by some hard inconvenient kernel of integrity to be exceptional, are torn by self-doubt, they are hyper-conscious of mixed motives, they are distrustful of certainties.

Long before Oskar Schindler, by random encounter, had caught Keneally's attention with his imponderable life and ambiguous sainthood, the novelist had been exploring the hubris and the vulnerability of the kind of flawed hero whose archetype is the Biblical prophet Jeremiah. ('Oh Lord, thou hast deceived me, and I was deceived . . . I have become a laughingstock all the day; everyone mocks me . . . But if I say "I will not mention him, or speak any more in his name," there is in my heart as it were a burning fire shut up in my bones, and I am weary with holding it in, and I cannot.')

From Halloran of *Bring Larks and Heroes* (the early novel of Australia's convict days, winner of the Miles Franklin Award in 1967) to Leeming, the Antarctic explorer in *The Survivor* (1969), to Jimmie the Aboriginal rebel pushed beyond endurance in *The Chant of Jimmie Blacksmith* (1972), to Joan of Arc in *Blood Red, Sister Rose* (1974), to Oskar Schindler, to Tim Shea, rebel in spite of himself, Keneally has given us a gallery of extraordinarily memorable, complex, deeply flawed heroes-by-accident.

Tim Shea's life seems proof that no good deed goes unpunished. His inconvenient conscience and his generosity (of finances and of compassion) almost destroy him. Taking ten year-old Lucy to his own home after the accident, he feels morally and financially responsible for her, a stance he can ill afford, being in more or less perpetual debt because of his unwillingness to demand payment from hard-pressed customers. Further, and in spite of an astringent attitude toward his Catholic heritage and the Church hierarchy, he also feels compelled to pay for intercessory masses for Missy of the severed head. Not only is this financial lunacy, it renders him suspect in the eyes of the constable. Is Tim the guilty lover who arranged the abortion?

Of even more serious consequence is his behavior at a jingoistic meeting to drum up a Patriotic Fund for the Boer War. Tim has no intention of completely ruining his precarious business by any public posturing. He feels irritation for the newspaper editor who is much 'taken by the surface glitter of injustices. That was the great fault of writers. Injustice never penetrated their skins too deeply, put them off a meal, or the next drink which waited for them in the bar of the Commercial'.

Though Tim 'was willing to risk being poor for the sake of everyone thinking him open-handed, he didn't want to risk it for the sake of politics'. He listens with wary admiration to the dairy farmer Borger who speaks out against the war, but is catcalled down. Borger reminds Tim of 'his own *political* uncle from Glenlara, a family secret. Uncle Johnny was Fenian "Centre"—they said at his trial in Tim's infancy—for the whole of Cork. Denied absolution by most priests . . . Stuck by his ideas, like Borger, and was shipped on the last convict ship to Western Australia . . . A soul like Borger's. A soul Tim didn't want to have.' And yet, in spite of his fixed intention, Tim finds himself applauding Borger and making his own speech. 'It was the first public display he had given, and he could feel the blood prickling its way along his arms and legs. For there was some rare gesture building in him. He was excited by such occasional rushes of courage, but loathed them too, the way they exposed him.'

Tim is blacklisted, his business brought within a whisker of ruin. It is through the shipping negligence of his principal opponent, prosperous merchant and chairman of multiple civic bodies, Ernie Malcolm, that the plague comes upriver from Sydney, first striking at Ernie Malcolm's own wife. And through an impulsive and wholly typical act of compassion, which he furiously regrets, Tim himself risks infection and is quarantined in the same barracks as his foe. More secrets than either anticipated come tumbling out of this closeted time. In an unexpected way, a kind of justice is done, a kind of right order restored.

> He directs, as always, bracing satire and astringent wit towards the Church, but also reveals a nostalgia that is soft at the center. The Irish-Australians and the Catholics in Keneally's novels may be larrikins, they may be faulty and flawed, but none of them is ever mean at the core.
> —*Janette Turner Hospital*

Such a resolution, even with the bittersweet edge, is rare in Keneally (victory is usually Pyrrhic, frequently posthumous), though it is historically in keeping with the millennial optimisms of 1900 and 2000. *A River Town* is not without weaknesses, veering as it does towards political fable, political romance. There are times when Keneally's lapsed-Catholic sensibility and his not-at-all-lapsed Irish sensibility turn mawkish, a recurrent sin (venial, to be sure) in his work, more under acerbic control in the early novels, less so in the

later ones. It is as though he were still furtively yearning for absolution from Manly Seminary (which he left two weeks before his ordination to the priesthood) and from the unbending Christian Brothers of his schooldays. He directs, as always, bracing satire and astringent wit towards the Church, but also reveals a nostalgia that is soft at the center. The Irish-Australians and the Catholics in Keneally's novels may be larrikins, they may be faulty and flawed, but none of them is ever mean at the core. One can never say the same for the non-Irish and the non-Catholic.

Nevertheless, Keneally's lapses are redeemed and overshadowed by his meticulous attention to psychological details which have nothing to do with his political agendas and which in fact subvert them, diverting and dispersing focus. He is truly catholic in the non-sectarian sense of the term in the breadth of his empathy, in the nuanced observation of private and social relations (between a policeman and other drinkers in a bar, for example), and in the sheer delicacy and affection lavished on the portrayal of even minor characters.

Above all there is the quite extraordinary portrait of orphaned Lucy, ten years old going on fifty, somber and wise beyond her years, needy as an infant, gifted manipulator, both self-sufficient and desperate, a wild child, a cynical and alarmingly intelligent all-seeing observer. Only in Henry James does one encounter another such riveting portrait of cursed innocence, and Keneally's Lucy is a more vibrantly warm flesh-and-blood waif than any of the little lost souls in James. Think what you will of the republic and the politics of Australia, past and present, you will not easily forget Missy's severed head or Lucy's spreading of her tragic little wings for her brave flight into the new century. The meaning of these images are multiple, unclear, unassimilated, unforgettable.

Judith Ryan (essay date 1996)

SOURCE: "Shrunk to an Interloper," in *Field Work: Sites in Literary and Cultural Studies,* edited by Marjorie Garber, Paul B. Franklin, and Rebecca L. Walkowitz, Routledge, 1996, pp. 113-19.

[*In the following essay, Ryan compares the authorial perspectives of* Schindler's List, *Günter Grass's* Show Your Tongue, *and Marguerite Duras's* The Lover, *to account for the ways their national identities influence their attitudes toward multicultural relations.*]

In one of my very earliest classrooms—it must have been at nursery school—hung a large map of the world. In the lower middle part of the map, a big reddish-pink island swam in a blue sea; at both upper corners small reddish-pink shapes hovered like guardian angels on either hand; in the center a large reddish-pink triangle pointed downward from an amorphous and multicolored land mass; and the whole map was satisfyingly unified by patches of ruddy color distributed over a substantial portion of its surface. I did not know then that what I was experiencing was the aesthetics of Empire.

"Two souls, alas! reside within my breast," declares Goethe's Faust. Within my breast reside, however, not two, but at least three souls. Teaching German and comparative literature would seem to place me equally on the side of the "national" and the "global." Yet I also happen to be Australian. The Australian self—my "third soul"—subverts conventional relations between the smaller and the larger worlds.

Hence I've conceived this paper from the viewpoint of what Australia's great poet, Ern Malley, has described as a "black swan of trespass on alien waters." In Australia, we were taught from the beginning to internalize a Eurocentric view while at the same time defiantly creating an Australian one. When we learned French and German, we had to memorize the words for scores of trees, plants, and flowers, along with their English translations—but practically none of this vegetation actually grew in Australia. I still don't know what a nightingale sounds like—though the mere thought of its song is enough to move me quite profoundly.

To place myself as an Australian is to feel myself—again in the words of Ern Malley—"shrunk to an interloper," yet also conveniently located off to the side of an argument in which it is only too easy to take one side or the other. If you ask me whether "national literatures" should be eliminated in favor of "global" perspectives, I'm inclined to say "yes"—as long as I don't specifically think about Australian literature and its long and ultimately successful struggle for an identity of its own.

Let me talk now about some literary texts of our time in which a great writer has tried to come to grips with the problem of the national versus the global viewpoint. My first example is Thomas Keneally's novel *Schindler's List,* of 1982; my second is Günter Grass's travelogue *Show Your Tongue,* of 1988; the third, Marguerite Duras's novel *The Lover,* of 1984. In a more conventional presentation, I would have felt obliged to treat these works chronologically; but what interests me here is the gradation in complexity with which they explore the ways in which one's national identity affects the position one takes toward complex cultural relations. I will try to show that even in the apparently dualistic worlds of these works, another, more complicated "soul" leaves an important trace—a trace that might even be regarded as the principal message of these difficult and troubling texts.

Schindler's List is the story of a man who saves numerous Jews from the Nazi death camps for motives that are by no means unmixed and irreproachable. In the novel, as opposed to the movie, the ambiguous nature of Schindler's actions is highlighted at every turn. Schindler is a Faustian figure with two souls in his breast, genuinely caring, in some sense, about the Jews entrusted to his care, but at the same time driven by economic motives and his desire to succeed as a big businessman. After the war, the Jews Schindler saved from the Nazis are scattered over the face of the Earth among what the "Author's Note" at the beginning of the book describes as "seven nations—Australia, Israel, West Germany, Austria, the United States, Argentina, and Brazil." The Schindler survivors, a nation in the psychological sense, are disseminated throughout a range of other nations in the political sense of the word. But this duality of psychological versus political nationhood is only one way of seeing what is at work in the formulation of the "Author's Note." This prefatory explanation also subtly disturbs most customary hierarchies, arranging the various nations neither alphabetically nor in order of their relative political power. In this list, Australia is named first.

Another important trace of a "third soul" occurs in this text at the point where Oskar Schindler decides to move his enamel factory from Cracow to Brinnlitz. On returning to Cracow from a preliminary visit to the Brinnlitz site, Schindler finds the charred wreckage of a downed Stirling bomber. The men in the plane, he discovers, were Australian. "If Oskar had wanted some sort of confirmation [of his plans to move away from Cracow], this was it. That men should come all this way from unimaginable little towns in the Australian Outback to hasten the end in Cracow." Whereas the writer who names Australia first in his list of seven nations can only be an Australian, the speaker in this passage about the Stirling bomber shifts into the consciousness of someone for whom Australia is quite remote from the familiar. No Australian would speak of "unimaginable little towns in the Australian Outback"; even if we have never actually seen outback towns, Australians have no trouble imagining them. Keneally's novel, despite its subsequent entry into the "global world" by means of the Steven Spielberg movie, is nonetheless a text that secretly insists on its Australianness—while overtly distancing itself from Australia by treating World War II from a perspective that appears to transcend what might otherwise have seemed, to the "global" world, a far too limited one.

The implications of *Schindler's List* for Australians go beyond the events of German racism in the nineteen-thirties and -forties, though this has rarely been noted in connection with the book. Most Australians would prefer, after all, not to think about their country's own racist past as exemplified in the notorious "White Australia" policy, the aim of which was to prohibit the immigration of Asians and Pacific Islanders into Australia and to deport workers of Asian origin from the sugarcane fields of Queensland. When the original bill (called the Immigration Restriction Act) was enacted in 1901, one newspaper wrote, for example, that the policy would save Australia "from the colored curse" and from becoming "a mongrel nation torn with racial dissension." The Immigration Restriction Act was not rescinded until 1973. Only those familiar with the history of Australian nationalism can fully understand the irony of that little scene in *Schindler's List* (the novel) where Australian bombers descend upon Cracow in an attempt to drop supplies for the partisans fighting against Nazism and where the charred remains of one pilot are found in the destroyed plane, still firmly clutching "an English Bible." The novel's final sentence about Oskar Schindler, "he was mourned on every continent," thus acquires a peculiar resonance for readers from Keneally's homeland.

Günter Grass's *Show Your Tongue* is, as it were, the other face of *Schindler's List.* Written not from the point of view of an ex-colonial, but from that of a former colonizing nation, the book is contemporaneous with Grass's 1988 proposal for a Pan-European cultural union. In large measure, *Show Your Tongue* is about the crossing of borders and the partitioning of nations. Grass's visit to India—the ostensible subject of the book—also permits a side trip to Bangladesh, a divided country whose citizens repeatedly urge him to draw the comparison with Germany, which at the time of course was still divided. In Grass's view, only one thing unites the split Bengali nation: its admiration for its lost leader Subhas Chandra Bose. The novel opens with a discussion of a bronze statute of Bose in Calcutta, and later notes the existence of statues of him in other cities. Traveling around the subcontinent, Günter and Ilse Grass learn the story of Bose's attempt to free India from British domination by allying himself in turn with Nazi Germany, Imperial Japan, and Stalinist Russia; they learn of the plane accident that caused his death and of his continued popularity in India and Bangladesh as a "Führer" and "holy man" who is thought to be hiding out in the hills and will reputedly return, at the age of one hundred, to rescue his fellow Bengali from their fate. In Grass's view, the numerous monuments to Bose crowd out memorials to his polar opposite, Gandhi, the "other soul"—to use my Faustian terminology—of the country the two Germans are touring.

Subverting this easy dualism are the narrator's repeated references to Ilse's uninterrupted preoccupation with the nineteenth-century German realist Theodor Fontane, whose novels she reads obsessively throughout their travels. The presence of this literary precursor in the minds of the two travelers gives an additional twist to their response to Indian cultural history. Fontane's comments on the Scottish regiments' defense of Calcutta during the Sepoy uprising, which took place while he was living in Britain as press

attaché for Prussia, the similarities between present-day traces of Victorian India and the nineteenth-century country estates described in Fontane's novels, and finally Grass's embarrassed discovery of Fontane's "ironic, patronizing amiability when dealing with Jews," serve to cast an icon much cherished in the German literary tradition into a highly questionable light. Grass's book about India complicates the insider-outsider problematic of traditional travel writing by insisting on its Germanness and criticizing it at one and the same time, distinguishing between home and abroad, past and present while simultaneously conflating these seeming oppositions. An early note in the travelogue articulates the difficulties of this complicated perspective: "What I am flying away from: repetition that claims to be news; from Germany and Germany, the way two deadly foes, armed to the teeth, grow ever more alike; from insights achieved from too close up; from my own perplexity, admitted only sotto voce, flying with me."

Marguerite Duras's novel *The Lover* is an even more complex attempt to deal with these issues. Narrated by a woman who, like Duras herself, grew up as the daughter of a French schoolteacher in Vietnam but has now reversed her parents' emigration and returned to live in France, it tells the story of an adolescent who moves among what seem at first to be three cultures: her French family, the Vietnamese world around her, and the young Chinese businessman who becomes the partner in her first erotic experiences. The intrusion of the Chinese lover troubles the fifteen-and-a-half-year-old's adolescent self-image, a deliberately ambiguous amalgam of apparent oppositions. We first see her dressed in gold lamé sandals and man's flat-brimmed hat, a privileged white girl on her way to school who nonetheless looks and acts in many ways like a child prostitute. Dualisms of male and female, mother country and colony, educated and uneducated classes, age and youth—among others—are set up in this opening passage, only to be undermined by the Chinese lover, who cannot be identified by any of these conventional rubrics. Other elements in the novel also work to subvert the binary structures of colonialism: the narrator's retarded classmate, Hélène Lagonelle, who belongs to the privileged boarding-school world but can never be completely integrated into it; the narrator's mother, whose psyche combines activist ambitions with passivity and melancholia; and the violent older brother who is at once a wild beast in the Vietnamese jungle, a viciously oppressive representative of the male sex and the colonizing nation, and the ultimate symbol of the decline of empire and (conflated but not necessarily identical with it) the modern collapse of reason. Finally, the retrospective narration that comprehends the past not as a factual reality but as an imaginative and constantly metamorphosing construct that must continually be subjected to questioning, subverts the conventional autobiographical compact as it is usually described by literary theorists. Couched in deceptively simple language, the novel increasingly gathers complexity. Its insistence on what is not said, not written, not photographed, is much more than a call for the reader to recover what has been repressed—or suppressed, according to one's perspective. Nor is it an attempt to hold oppositions in suspension by converting them first into ambiguities, and then, by sheer multiplication, into what is fashionably termed "indeterminacy." Rather, Duras's novel is quite literally a demonstration of the resistance put up by linguistic and cultural structures to representation when even an individual viewpoint can only be understood as inherently multiple.

Many of us who move easily between "national" and "global" traditions have tended to ignore what remains in our psyches of a colonial or otherwise subjugated existence. Rescued from its repression, this "third soul" can become a powerful tool to undermine an opposition between the "national" and the "global" that should long since have become outmoded. And yet it is surely an affront to those who have been more clearly and outrageously oppressed to suggest that a postcolonial like myself is peculiarly equipped to dissolve binarisms. For this reason, I do not propose that we should all adopt in some sense a position on the margins—that is precisely what my literary examples do *not* do. Rather, they show the complexities of contemporary cultural situations in which the opposition between center and periphery is no longer adequate. But neither is it enough, they imply, merely to activate a third perspective in addition to the familiar two. Rather, they suggest that we should experiment more freely with an array of different positions, discarding conventional dualisms, but also avoiding "indeterminacies" that swallow up fine distinctions and nuances that mark relational experience in all its exhilaration and despair. Even when the languages we speak and the traditions in which we move prevent us from freeing ourselves entirely from oppositional thinking, we should at least become more aware of the interplay of multiple perspectives that informs our understanding of culture and that makes it impossible for any individual, whatever his or her actual intention, to be reduced to a spokesperson simply for the "national" or the "global."

Reading literary texts, and observing ourselves as we read them, is one of the best ways we have of understanding this intricate problem.

FURTHER READING

Bibliography

Chernekoff, Janice. "Thomas Keneally: An Annotated, Secondary Bibliography, 1979-1984" *Bulletin of Bibliography* 43, No. 4 (December 1986): pp. 221-27.
　　Identifies secondary sources, including articles, essays, and reviews.

Criticism

Beston, John B. "An Awful Rose: Thomas Keneally as a Dramatist" *Southerly* 33, No. 1 (1973): 36-42.
　　Examines Keneally's effectiveness as a playwright.

Burns, Robert. "Out of Context: A Study of Thomas Keneally's Novels" *Australian Literary Studies* 4, No. 1 (1969): 31-42.
　　Praises Keneally's development through his first four novels, citing several examples.

Frow, John. "The Chant of Thomas Keneally" *Australian Literary Studies* 10, No. 3 (1982): 291-99.
　　Studies Keneally's presentation of Australian aboriginal culture in *The Chant of Jimmie Blacksmith.*

O'Hearn, Tim. "*Schindler's Ark* and *Schindler's List*—One for the Price of Two" *Contemporary Novel in English* 5, No. 2 (1992): 9-15.
　　Refutes the contention that textual differences exist between the European and American versions of *Schindler's List.*

Additional coverage of Keneally's life and career is contained in the following sources published by Gale: *Contemporary Authors,* Vols. 85-88; *Contemporary Authors New Revision Series,* Vols. 10 and 50; *Discovering Authors: Novelists Module;* and *Major Twentieth-Century Writers.*

Tadeusz Konwicki

1926-

Polish novelist, journalist, essayist, screenwriter, and memoirist.

The following entry presents an overview of Konwicki's career through 1994. For further information on his life and works, see *CLC,* Volumes 8, 28, and 54.

INTRODUCTION

A leading literary figure in post-World War II Poland, Konwicki is a novelist and self-described "essayistic prose" writer. Best known to readers in English-speaking countries as the author of the novels *Sennik wspólczesny* (1963; *A Dreambook for Our Time*) and *Kompleks polski* (1977; *The Polish Complex*), Konwicki wrote many other novels that have remained unavailable in translation. In his fiction, he combined elements of satire, irony, and surrealism with political analysis, philosophical rumination, and social commentary about the significance of historical events. Konwicki's forced emigration from his homeland during World War II profoundly influenced the thematic unity of his writing. Except for his initial, minor works which affirm the quality of postwar Polish life in compliance with the dictates of socialist realism, nearly every work concerns in some degree various aspects of war, sweeping criticism of contemporary life, and nostalgia for the scenes of his native landscape and the lost culture of his youth. In addition, Konwicki directed and wrote scripts for several films between the late 1950s and the early 1970s, some of which won prizes at prestigious European film festivals. In both his writings and films, he examined the grim realities of twentieth-century Polish life, including the devastating effects and lingering memories of World War II, the subsequent Communist domination, and the social spasms resulting from the imposition of martial law and the rise of the Solidarity labor movement in the late 1970s and early 1980s. Critics have admired Konwicki's analysis of what he has termed "the Polish complex," a state of alienation and despair induced by both the romantic idealism and the tragic events of Poland's past which stunts the development of individual expression. Moreover, Konwicki framed his definition of "the Polish complex" in terms of his tendency to view Polish history as a series of failed attempts to gain freedom and independence. Lamenting the paucity of translated editions of Konwicki's prose, Michael Hofmann has observed that his books "give a fascinating picture of Poland—no, they *are* Poland, as Juan Rulfo is Mexico, or Patrick White Australia."

Biographical Information

The son of a Polish metalworker, Konwicki was born and raised in Nowa Wilejka, an ethnically diverse village of Lithuanians, Jews, Poles, Russians, and other "Asiatics" near Wilno in what was then northeastern Poland (present-day Vilnius, Lithuania). According to Konwicki, he is "a hideous hybrid formed at the boundaries of [the Polish and Russian] worlds." As World War II ravaged Europe, he completed high school by attending underground study sessions. In 1944, Konwicki joined and fought with the Polish underground resistance movement, Armia Krajowa (Home Army), which liberated Wilno from Nazi occupation. When Russian troops entered the conflict, Polish guerrillas were arrested, imprisoned, then either executed or deported to concentration camps in Siberia. Konwicki, however, escaped deportation and resumed fighting against the Communists, until further resistance became futile, and his native land—as most of Eastern Europe—eventually fell under Soviet control. In 1945, Konwicki escaped to central Poland, living first in Krakow, where he studied Polish literature at Jagellonian University, then resettling in Warsaw, where he pursued a career in journalism and literature. Konwicki won the Polish State Prize for Literature twice—first in 1950 for his literary journalism collected in *Przy budowie* and again in 1954 for the novel *Wladza,* both of which exalt heroic workers who support the Communist agenda. By 1956, when state-imposed restrictions on artistic expression relaxed somewhat for the Polish movie industry, Konwicki found a new medium and began a career as a film director and screenwriter. His films either presage or illumine such themes as self-destructive guilt and deep sexual frustration that appear in his prose works. With the publication of *Rojsty,* written in the late 1940s but not published until 1956 and widely viewed as the watershed of his literary career, Konwicki completely repudiated the principles of socialist-realism and began to experiment with other modern literary models, most notably in *A Dreambook for Our Time,* which brought him international recognition. In 1977, the "official" publishing house Czytelnik turned down *The Polish Complex,* and censors banned both the novel and Konwicki's name from the press for ten years. Despite such efforts to silence him, Konwicki found an outlet for his writings in the *drugi obieg,* the Polish expression for the Russian *samizdat* system, or the underground press. Subsequently, three other novels clandestinely appeared: *Mala apokalipsa* (1979; *A Minor Apocalypse*), *Wschody i zachody ksiezyca* (1982; *Moonrise, Moonset*), and *Rzeka podziemna, podziemne ptaki* (1984). By the late 1980s, Konwicki returned to the "official" press with the publication of the lyrical novel *Bohin* (1987; *Bohin Manor*).

Major Works

Suffused with doubt, guilt, and skepticism, Konwicki's prose repeats several narrative constants, including similar situations, settings, episodes, and characters. A satire based on Konwicki's experiences with the Polish resistance in Wilno, *Rojsty* depicts a young man who desperately seeks hero status while attempting to prevent the communist takeover of Poland, but instead he dies anonymously. This novel examines concerns and motifs that Konwicki explored in his subsequent work, including themes related to banished hope and vain ambition. *A Dreambook for Our Time,* a terrifying study of a war-shattered mind trying to cope with a bleak, godless existence, relies on garish episodes and inner monologue to lend a surrealistic quality to the narrative. Oldster, the protagonist, a tormented survivor of World War II, engages in a futile attempt to come to terms with his past. Alternating between Oldster's random, blurred memories of his war experiences and the dreamlike events of his present life, this novel features a series of connected flashbacks, nightmarish images, and shifting realities. Published in the underground literary magazine *Zapis, The Polish Complex* tells the stories of a group of Poles waiting in line on Christmas Eve for a shipment of gold rings from Russia; the people represent various types of Polish personalities and their situations reflect diverse living conditions in pre-Solidarity Poland. The narrative digressions to historical conditions of

Poland in 1863, when a popular rebellion against czarist rule failed, underscore an unending cycle of thwarted ambitions and hypocritical complacency that define "the Polish complex" for Konwicki. *Nowy Swait i okolice* (1986) comprises a collection of over fifty self-illustrated essays that alternate between childhood memories in prewar Wilno and his present-day life in Warsaw. In contrast to the tone of Konwicki's other works, *Bohin Manor* adheres to romance conventions well-established by the late-nineteenth century. Set on a Lithuanian manor farm in 1875, this novel recounts the resolve of a young, female protagonist to wed an elderly count in order to relieve her isolation and to regain the standard of life to which she was accustomed prior to the 1863 Polish revolt against Czarist Russia that had cost her family its wealth. Instead, she enters a romantic though mutually unwanted relationship with a working-class Jew. At the same time, *Bohin Manor* also represents the genealogy of Konwicki's grandmother and features characters linked to actual historical figures, which plays with the distinction between reality and illusion.

Critical Reception

Echoing the sentiments of many critics, the Polish, Nobel Prize-winning author Czeslaw Milosz has called *A Dreambook for Our Time* "a major literary sensation" and "one of the most terrifying novels of postwar Polish literature." Reviewers usually noted the stoic tone of the novel; however, some commentators have found that the novel is "nihilistic and gloomy" and incapable of arousing reader sympathy. As they did to *A Dreambook for Our Time,* Western critics warmly responded to *The Polish Complex,* and most have concurred that this novel presents Konwicki's finest literary qualities—a skillful use of surrealist techniques, distinctive Polish character types, and an ability to show the influence of historical forces in shaping the modern Polish psyche. Scholars have suggested that *The Polish Complex* powerfully states the degrading effects of a totalitarian regime yet offers a poignant analysis of the Polish condition. According to some critics, the image of the Polish queue symbolically represents the passive faith of the Polish people in an idealized homeland as well as their implicit cooperation in an organized process of victimization and oppression. Jerzy R. Krzysanowski has said that "even if Konwicki's novel might fade away with time, as often happens with contemporary novels, that single [image of the queue] . . . will remain in the history of Polish literature as the most shocking and tragic document of the years of violence and oppression." In retrospective light of developments in Polish society, some critics have complained that Konwicki's works lack political understanding and underestimate the determination and power of Polish workers. Still, "Konwicki has modernized Polish perceptions about art and literature; he has brought them, so to speak, up to date," Mozejko has asserted, adding that in this achievement "lies his originality and very important contribution to the Polish cultural scene."

PRINCIPAL WORKS

Przy budowie (journalism) 1950
Wladza (novel) 1954
Klucz (novel) 1955
Rojsty (novel) 1956
Zoblezonego miasta (novel) 1956
Dziura w niebie (novel) 1959
Sennik wspólczesny [*A Dreambook for Our Time*] (novel)
    1963
Ostatni dzien lata (screenplays) 1966
Wniebowstapienie (novel) 1967
Zwierzoczlekoupior [*The Anthropos-Specter-Beast*] (novel)
    1969
Nic albo nic (novel) 1971
Kronika wypadkow milosnych (novel) 1974
Kalendarz i klepsydra (prose) 1976
Kompleks polski [*The Polish Complex*] (novel) 1977
Mala apokalipsa [*A Minor Apocalypse*] (novel) 1979
Wschody i zachody ksiezyca [*Moonrise, Moonset*] (prose)
    1982
Rzeka podziemna, podziemne ptaki (prose) 1984
Nowy Swait i okolice [*New World Avenue and Vicinity*]
    (memoir) 1986
Bohin [*Bohin Manor*] (novel) 1987
Zorze wieczorne (novel) 1991

*This work contains the screenplays *Zimowy smierzch, Ostatni dzien lata, Zaduszki, Salto,* and *Matura*; an enlarged edition (1973) also includes *Jak daleko stad, jak blisko.*

CRITICISM

Abraham Rothberg (review date 17 May 1970)

SOURCE: "Still the Poles Go on Living," in *New York Times Book Review,* May 17, 1970, pp. 4-5, 20.

[*In the following excerpt, Rothberg considers the themes of stoicism and endurance as represented by* A Dreambook for Our Time.]

For more than 200 years Poland has lived between the hammer of Germany and the anvil of Russia, cloven by partition after partition, inflamed by insurrection after insurrection, molded by anguish, tribulation and death. Still the Poles go on living, making love, drinking vodka—oh yes, drinking vodka!—and occasionally and sporadically work-

ing to rebuild their war-torn country. They seem to be a people without incentive, their lives without luster, their spirits without hope. And yet, though over all of them hangs the pall of physical desolation and spiritual despair, the most interesting writing in Communist Europe—including the Soviet Union—has emerged from postwar Poland. These three novels [Leopold Buczkowski's *Black Torrent,* Tadeusz Konwicki's *A Dreambook for Our Time* and Stanislaw Dygat's *Cloak of Illusion*], newly translated into English by David Welsh, are an excellent introduction to contemporary Polish letters. In them one almost has a capsule history of the temper of Polish life in the past three decades. . . .

Tadeusz Konwicki's *A Dreambook for Our Time* might almost be a sequel to *Black Torrent,* with similar characters living in the postwar decade, and haunted by the events of the war. Set somewhere in what Poles like to call the "recovered territories," land taken in the West from the Germans after the war and given to them in exchange for areas annexed by the Soviet Union, the actual place, the valley and forest, are kept deliberately vague, but symbolically clear—near Powstancza Gorka, which in Polish means "Insurrection Mountain."

The antihero of the book, known only as Mister Paul or Oldster, his partisan pseudonym, has come here to find forgiveness for his past. He is persuaded that in this remote valley and forest he committed the deed which forever put him beyond communion with mankind: he was assigned to execute a Pole who had betrayed some partisans to the Germans, and he shot the man in cold blood before the eyes of the man's small daughter. Oldster is not certain the man died, because he did not shoot to kill; as he later explains to a postwar Communist party investigation, "At that time I'd already stopped wanting to kill people." He believes the man he shot is still living in the valley, and he is also persuaded that the partisan chief who gave him the order to kill is still hiding in the nearby forest. Whether this is delusion, obsession, mania, is never made clear.

Constantly reminded of and living in the past, Oldster can find no forgiveness in the valley, no grace, no love. He does not even have the strength to leave or to try suicide. One of the characters finally gives him some perspective by telling him: "During the war too, I kept to the political average. Most of the nation neither fought at the front, nor hid in the forests, nor suffered in concentration camps. The ordinary majority stayed in their badly heated houses, ate frozen potatoes and dealt a little in the black market. I did the same. Nobody gave me a medal for what I did during the occupation, but nobody reproved me either. I didn't gain anything, but I didn't lose anything."

At last Oldster realizes that the present, however unheroic and boring, must be lived in and endured. After giving up the nightmare of the past, both its horror and heroism, half-willing, half-pushed, half-knowing, half-duped, he is constrained to leave the valley, saying, in the very last lines of the book: ". . . I would scramble with the remains of my strength out of these seething depths to the edge of reality, and would get up to an ordinary, commonplace day, with its usual troubles, its everyday toil, its so well-known, familiar drudgery." . . .

Polish literature has always assumed the task of holding the often partitioned nation together, of defining its identity, preserving its history and heritage. It is still doing so in a continuing process of redefining values, subtly shaping the ideas of what constitutes duty, sacrifice, courage and commitment in an especially drab and difficult time. Most important, Polish literature must now delineate the necessary stoicisms and endurance, the saving ironic detachment and scalding humor, the eschewing of romantic illusions about the (truly) heroic past and its bloody insurrections that have so often decimated the people and devastated the land. These three novels are a worthy part of that effort and that tradition.

Jerzy R. Krzyzanowski (review date 1980)

SOURCE: "The Polish Complex," in *The Polish Review,* Vol. XXV, No. 1, 1980, pp. 98-110.

[*In the following review, Krzyzanowski discusses* The Polish Complex *in the context of Konwicki's canon, describing common themes, techniques, and contemporary and historical allusions.*]

Tadeusz Konwicki, whose works only recently entered the American book market, hardly needs an introduction to his Polish readers but a few words about his literary career might be helpful to those who have not read his novels in the original language. As the author of many contemporary novels, producer and director of well-known movies, a winner of many international prizes and readers' plebiscites in Poland, Konwicki was among those writers whose names had been mentioned often enough to make him well known to many readers, viewers, and radio-listeners. He had been—and the past perfect tense used here is fully justified, since he had been in the limelight until 1976 but in the last three years his name has appeared in the Polish press only casually or only in some critical contexts such as Wlodzimierz Sokorski's press conference in March, 1978 meant to discredit the literary opposition in Poland. The reason for that "conspiracy of silence" was the publication of Konwicki's novel, **The Polish Complex,** which appeared in *Zapis* 3 of July, 1977, and subsequently a *zapis,* i.e., a black mark by the official censorship banning Konwicki's name from the Polish literary press. And since the novel has been reprinted

in the West, in a series "Index on Censorship," and hopefully will appear in English translation, there seems to be a need to discuss it in some detail, to look at it from the historical and literary perspective, to devote some thought to its symptomatic features reflecting both Konwicki's own work and contemporary Polish literature at large.

It should be noted, however, that **The Polish Complex** is neither surprising nor exceptional, in certain aspects, when read as a part of Konwicki's work. It appears to be a logical consequence of the author's thirty years of creative work, a summary of many of his experiences and thoughts, a conclusion of many premises toward which Konwicki has gradually moved ever since 1948. Hence, it seems only proper first to discuss his novels, scenarios, and movies before **The Polish Complex,** and only later to elaborate the contents and significance of that particular novel.

The period of thirty years just mentioned began in 1948 when Konwicki wrote his first novel **Rojsty** (*The Marshes*) which was to wait another eight years, until October 1956, when the Polish thaw created an atmosphere more conducive to the publication of his novel. And although it was in the early 1950s when his name was first officially introduced with the publication of his unfinished novel **Wladza** (*The Power*), his actual work deserving a critical discussion has developed from **Rojsty** to **The Polish Complex,** leaving aside his works of the socialist-realist period as insignificant. They represented the results of all sorts of pressures hardly related to literature, and they should remain in bibliographical notes and in the sad history of the Stalinist period, together with hundreds of books written by young writers between 1949 and 1955. As much as they may interest a historian or a sociologist of literary movements, those books represent a testimony to the period of "mistakes and vitiations"—as Stalinism is officially called in Poland—although that particular term better applies to literature than to politics which was neither mistaken nor vitiated anything; quite to the contrary, it consistently followed the Stalinist program of pressure and terror.

The place **Rojsty** occupies in Konwicki's work is as important as its place in the history of contemporary Polish literature. Presenting a complex image of the experiences of a boy who joins the Polish guerrillas fighting against the Soviet occupation of the Wilno region in 1944, Konwicki has not only placed a firm foundation for the autobiographical character of all his later novels but also introduced in it all the basic motifs which would find their climax in **The Polish Complex.** One can find there, then, the problem of an overwhelming power of history over the fate of an individual, the guilt complex, the feeling of alienation, erotic frustrations, ideological misgivings, a lyrical image of the land of the childhood and the realization of a final loss of that land, irony and humor, satire and bitterness; all those motifs surfaced in that early novel. Its significance in the history of contemporary Polish fiction, on the other hand, lies in the fact that **Rojsty** represents the first, and so far the only artistic document of the anti-Soviet resistance in the eastern Polish territories in 1944-45, passed over in silence by official Polish history. Instead of depicting "the reactionary underground," Konwicki succeeded in presenting the tragedy and heroism of the young men who fought their forgotten war without any hope for either a victory, or even recognition, motivated by a deep patriotic duty to defend their country against the Russian invasion. One might parenthetically mention here that a novel, *Graves Without Crosses,* published by an Estonian writer, Arved Viirlaid, in Canada in 1972, has become an international bestseller thanks to an almost identical topic of resistance and fight against the Soviets in the Baltic states.

But the theme of resistance, presented by Konwicki in a satirical vain for psychological as well as historical reasons, gave way to some other problems probed by the author in his next novels. And although the motifs of the Soviet menace reappear in **Sennik współczesny** (1963, English tr.: *A Dreambook for Our Time,* 1970) and in Konwicki's movies, the land of his childhood, the Wilno region, will replace them in sharp contrast with the infernal images of life in central Poland after the war. Those contrasts are particularly strong in **Wniebowstapienie** (1967, **The Ascension**) and in **Jak daleko stad, jak blisko** (1972, **How Far It Is From Here, How Near**); a pure lyricism of **Kronika wypadków milosnych** (1974, *A Chronicle of Love Affairs*) and a nostalgic happy valley in **Dziura w niebie** (1959, *A Hole in the Sky*) are juxtaposed with a bitter, tragic overtone in **Kalendarz i klepsydra** (1976, *A Calendar and an Hourglass*) indicating a deep gap between those two worlds between which Konwicki's fiction has been stretched. Such a phenomenon is not entirely unique in contemporary Polish literature. Suffice it to list here the names of Kusniewicz, Stojowski, Auderska, or Buczkowski, Stryjkowski, and Iwaszkiewicz among the authors living in Poland, or Milosz, Odojewski, and Haupt among the writers in exile to see that contrast ever emerging and making it into a chapter in a "Great Book of *Kresy*" yet to be written. But none of those authors makes those problems as contrasting and as consequent as Tadeusz Konwicki.

Those problems, of course, reach much farther than literature alone. In spite of the official reports published in the Polish press about all sorts of "Polish Days" in Lithuania, Byelorussia, and Ukraine, the question of the Polish population there remains as tragic and painful as it has ever been. Cut off from Poland, forgotten, and exposed to the ever increasing Russification, the Poles left east of the river Bug represent one of the most tragic chapters in the post-war Polish history. And although Konwicki and the rest of the authors mentioned above keep returning to those territories in their fiction and memoirs, the official silence still prevails. The Communist authorities, having abandoned their countrymen thirty-five years ago, do not want to re-open the case once and for all solved by the Russians. Needless to say that Konwicki, who in the concluding scenes of **Kalendarz i klepsydra** presents such a process of Russification almost openly, has become quite an embarrassing author for the authorities, and their watchful eye has begun to scrutinize his work more and more closely. "The lost valley of childhood," writes a young Polish critic Jan Walc, "when seen from a distance seems to appear as a happy and bucolic one, and the protagonists return there, but then the causes which made them leave it before begin to appear with extreme harshness." And from there there is just one step to pass a judgment on those causes, a step made in **The Polish Complex.**

Another set of problems, perhaps less controversial for the censorship but certainly no less delicate to handle, is Konwicki's realism in presenting the realities of life in contemporary Poland. His realism, often hidden in a satirical form, often heightened to a symbolic vision, particularly evident in his scenarios and movies, leaves little doubt that Poland today is a police state, a country on the brink of moral collapse, a country populated with people in a desperate search for some valid set of values, for something permanent, or even a hope for the better future. Such a presentation of daily life in Poland is particularly striking when seen from a distance, e.g., by a foreign reader, but it seems almost certain that a reader in Poland who, after all, experiences those problems every day must also be painfully aware of the acuteness of Konwicki's image. And that fact, perhaps, accounts for voting **Wniebowstapienie** a book-of-the-year in a readers' plebiscite, while *A Dreambook for Our Time* enjoys an international reputation in many translations. And if Andrzejewski's novel *Ashes and Diamonds* remains the most dramatic literary document of the Communist seizure of power, the novels written by Konwicki represent a similarly important document of the 1960s and 1970s in Poland.

> **Ever since he created his metaphoric valley doomed to damnation and populated by a group of wrecks in *A Dreambook for Our Time* . . . Konwicki has become more and more vocal in his dialogue with life in contemporary Poland, more and more openly and in an ever more aggressive manner asking questions about the sense of our life in the existing conditions.**
> —*Jerzy R. Krzyzanowski*

Ever since he created his metaphoric valley doomed to damnation and populated by a group of wrecks in *A Dreambook for Our Time,* through the bitter realism in *Wniebowstapienie* and *Nic albo nic* (1971, *Nothing or Nothing*), up to an open polemic with contemporary times in *Kalendarz i kelpsydra,* Konwicki has become more and more vocal in his dialogue with life in contemporary Poland, more and more openly and in an ever more aggressive manner asking questions about the sense of our life in the existing conditions. At the same time he comes closer and closer to a perfection in his means of artistic expression, develops his own poetics, entirely individual and quite different from the style and forms prevailing in contemporary Polish fiction. It was only logical then, that all those features listed above have led to a logical climax which would create a coherent image of the past and the present, of history and politics, of tragedy and satire, a modern novel and a philosophical essay, disclosing, at the same time, the roots of national complexes together with those personal ones tormenting the author for the last thirty years. Such an image resulted in a novel entitled *The Polish Complex.*

II

The Polish Complex is a contemporary novel in every sense of that word. The action takes place at a jewelry store "Jubiler" in Warsaw, "at a huge circular plaza on the intersection of large avenues," near the dominating structure of The Palace of Culture; its time—a Christmas Eve in the mid-seventies; the time duration—11 A.M. till midnight. The narrator's name is Tadeusz Konwicki, he is a writer, was born near Wilno, in short, the identification of the narrator with the author is almost complete, adding to the novel's realism. Those who know the society circles in Warsaw could easily recognize some characters as portraits of some well-known personalities in the same way as they could recognize them in the previous novels by Konwicki who has been coming closer and closer to an authentic presentation of authentic people and events, as, for instance, in *Kalendarz i klepsydra* where full names of his friends and colleagues were given. In other words, realism, authenticity, and contemporariness make *The Polish Complex* almost a documentary, a fact which in turn gives the novel its specific character. Because if it takes place at a given moment, and in a given place, if it is told by a given narrator, one could hardly doubt the fictitious character of the matters discussed in it— on the contrary, they should be as real and authentic as the factors anyone can prove really exist.

These matters which taken all together create a complete image of a phenomenon called "the Polish complex" are so many that one must assume they are not merely authentic but symptomatic, key problems of life in contemporary Poland. Beginning with the opening scene of a patient waiting in a line for goods, and ending with a collection for the Committee to Defend the Workers (KOR), the novel about a usual—and yet quite unusual—Christmas Eve in Warsaw sums up and points to all basic problems existing in Poland in a deceptively simple way. Deceptive, for it proves to be deeper, more probing, and more open than any other contemporary Polish novel so far.

Let us discuss first the most obvious, realistic features in the novel. And so, there is that commonplace line in front of a closed jewelry store in Warsaw. The narrator stands there, he is the twenty-third person in line; he warms himself up in his sheepskin coat, he stamps his feet, he looks around in a snow-covered street. "Large crowds of passers-by move along the walls without interruption. Once in a while someone runs into someone else and moves further without saying 'sorry,' immersed in his thoughts. Once in a while someone hits someone else with a Christmas-tree stand and curses with a bad word, once in a while someone tipsy slips onto the pavement, but he gets up and goes his way. A common Christmas Eve day".

But at this point, in the third paragraph on the first page of the novel, there occurs a digression, the first among many which will interrupt and supplement the realistic plot. Such digressions, largely implemented before in *Kalendarz i klepsydra,* let the narrator leave the Warsaw street for a while, and look at the problems from above, as it were, from a distant and universal perspective; at the same time they provide some sort of conclusions, generalizations, and climactic points, thus, in the course of the novel, creating a second, higher level of discussion with contemporary times. What's more important, perhaps, they seem to be intended for a foreign reader who might not be entirely familiar with life in Poland, and thus become signals desperately sent to the wide world outside of the borders of the country. "I expect," writes Konwicki, "that a copy of this book which I have been painstakingly writing will reach the hands, the antennae, or the computers of another kind of rational creatures who by chance will enter our galaxy, those rational creatures from the central regions of the universe, from the elegant quarters of God's metropolises, creatures wiser and better than us, noble supermen thought-out and dreamt-up by man." This image, only slightly camouflaged, of creatures from another planet who might bring hope and a change for the better, will once more appear in the novel as a spaceship "levitating above the avenue and looking at an incomprehensible city in the middle of Europe." This "space probe or an American balloon" hovering over the red lights of The Palace of Culture—"Why American?", asks a lady in an over-size coat. "And what else?"—lightening the Warsaw night on the last pages of the novel is sharply contrasted with another, more realistic sight: "A new light hits my eyes. Those are the headlights of an invisible truck. A militiaman emerges from under a tarpaulin: 'Shut up, or else I'll come down to you.'" Generalizing digressions, symbolic visions, and gloomy realism merge into one tight entity of the external features of the Polish complex.

But so far that common Christmas Eve day has only begun, and the narrator, still stamping his frozen feet, has plenty of time to look at his companions patiently waiting for the opening of the jewelry store. From among some forty people he chooses those who are standing near him, and who will remain in the center of his attention throughout the day and the night. There is a fellow countryman from Wilno, Kojran, who is just about to leave for the United States, there is a former secret policeman, Duszek, there is Grzesio, an *agent-provocateur,* a Christ-like looking student with his French friend, an anarchist, and there are some women, too: a lady in an over-sized coat, a pseudo-farmer lady wearing a Persian lamb coat, and an old lady who eventually turns out to be not old at all. And from behind the display window glass there looks at the waiting crowd "a dark-haired girl with a slightly indecent mouth," and "sepia-like eyes." And, for the time being, "the snowy wind hurls a huge spruce made into a Christmas tree at the great circular plaza on the intersection of large avenues. The forest tree jerks in all directions as if bowing to the four corners of the world, as if trying to break off from its confinement, from this stony captivity." Some snow, red from neon signs, falls down. And the narrator concludes: "Yes . . . I am waiting for a miracle."

Such a metaphoric imagery not only gives Konwicki's novel some specific style but it also slowly unveils a second, basic meaning of daily existence in Warsaw to its most minute details. The goods people in line have been waiting for turn out to be golden wedding rings imported from Russia, and the narrator will eventually call them "the symbol of shackles," but when the people finally enter the store after a long period of waiting, and the manager brings in the first cartons, instead of rings they contain "electric Soviet samovars" which, incidentally, will once more reappear in the novel "covered with Grzesio's or the student's blood" as a result of a scuffle between the *provocateur* and the student who represents KOR, a young man "unscathed by the roughness of life."

The waiting line represents, of course, yet another pretext to expose the roots of the Polish complex. When the customers reach the counter "there pushes into the salon a crowd of people wearing fur hats," and disregarding the local customers takes places in front of them. Once more, it is worth noticing "the double bottom" of Konwicki's prose: he manages to create images which instantly result in far-reaching implications. The obviousness of the situation, and its generalizing meaning—a crowd of savages entering "a salon"—do not leave any doubts as to the real meaning of the metaphor, even before the newcomers will be identified as "better customers." "Those are better customers," explains the manager to enraged Kojran. "Those are our guests from the Soviet Union." The Polish version emphasizes that contrast on its linguistic level too, using an emotional differentiation between two terms denoting anything Soviet, the

adjectives *sowiecki,* usually employed by anti-Soviet speakers, and *radziecki,* an officially approved term. The Polish customers have to reconcile, and Kojran concludes: "Well, if the Soviets (*sowieci*) are waiting, it means the goods will arrive for sure." "And indeed," adds the narrator, "the Soviet tourists (*radzieccy*) made themselves at home in the salon for good."

As it turns out, there is even a link between the two groups: among the newcomers there is the narrator's relative, Kaziuk, who "smells with a home-grown tobacco and a sheepskin coat," while the narrator, as we remember, wears an identical coat but he smells "probably with an aftershave Green Water" (English in the original). The relative from Wilno, one of the many doubles of the narrator in this novel, does not complain. "Money there is plenty but there is no life," he says in a complacent mood, although this "positive hero," or "polozhitel'nyj geroj" as the narrator calls him using Russian words to underscore the ironic meaning of that cliché, does not appear to be a resigned man. "I sit near Oszmiana," he says, "and watch over our land, our forests, our prayers. And I don't know about anything else. Everything else is just a *jerunda*" (Russian for nonsense). And on this note a meeting with the past suddenly resurrected in a Warsaw street ends. The narrator has a heart attack, he falls down and becomes unconscious, and when he wakes up he finds himself in the arms of a strange girl from the store, Iwona or Basia, who represents the new generation without complexes whatsoever as proven by the scene of a hasty love-making in a room behind the store, on a crumbled bed lighted with a naked lightbulb covered only with a piece of newspaper. Clearly, she is a girl liberated from any ties with the past as demonstrated by her sexual liberation.

But even this sex scene does not liberate the narrator from the problems making the Polish complex. Looking for a cigarette he finds in his pocket a letter from a friend from the good old days, a letter representing one more digression in the novel. The letter was sent from a fictitious country "on another continent," a country which "might resemble my lost homeland just a little bit." In fact, the country run by a totalitarian monoparty is nothing else but a true picture of contemporary Poland. We shall return to all those digressions later on, for the time being following the contemporary plot line, although the structure of **The Polish Complex** is based on a constant intertwining of the current events with such digressions.

The Christmas Eve day passes away, they close the store and seal it with "a beer bottle cap filled with a modeling clay and a piece of string" but people in the line do not give up their hope for the transport of wedding rings. They move to the staircase of a nearby apartment house, and only there, at the lights of an incidental Christmas tree, the characters become better acquainted with each other, and some mutual ties are established. And more and more often there intervenes the ever-present militia, the Warsaw landscape is threatened with a vision of a new holocaust, the student who collects money "for those who fight for freedom" is juxtaposed with a picture of banners announcing "the Moscow days in Warsaw," whereupon the narrator comments: "Well, Moscow is going to visit us, too?" And then, on the last page of that strange story about a common Christmas Eve in Warsaw, he adds a concluding comment, paraphrasing a saying used by one of the characters throughout the novel: "When a Pole gets mad, beware you blind, lazy, corrupted Europe." On this ominous note pronounced against an image of a red glow resembling "an open abyss of hell" over the city one should end the discussion of the realistic level of the novel.

III

The realistic plot in **The Polish Complex** is written in the present tense in a manner well known from Konwicki's previous novels and scenarios. Such a method has a certain advantage thanks to some specific features of Polish grammar: there is no distinction between the simple present and the continuous present tenses. Thus the opening sentence *stojê w ogonku* can actually mean either "I am standing in line" or "I stand in line," implying that the situation presented can be occurring right now as well as be a permanent, everyday occurrence. Those implications are far-reaching for they tend to generalize certain situations and states, showing them not only as phenomena present in today's Poland but also as conditions existing permanently and contributing to the development of "the Polish complex" in its various stages.

It would be erroneous to assume that those conditions have been in existence only for the last thirty-five years, i.e., since The July Manifesto of 1944, ranging from a seizure of power by the Communist Party up to the apocalyptic vision at the end of Konwicki's novel. For the Polish complex is not merely an anti-Soviet complex but the deepest—two hundred years old at least—anti-Russian complex. Its roots as well as its present manifestations are shown in Konwicki's novel in the contemporary plot and in the two large historical digressions which make a basic structural element of that thoroughly contemporary novel. They should be discussed here in the context of the contemporary plot.

Tired with waiting in the line, three characters whose fates have been closely intertwined—the narrator, one of his doubles Tadeusz Kojran, and his former tormentor from the Security Police named Duszek (a Polish term indicating either an elf or a diminutive of the word *duch,* a ghost)—decide to "make the Christmas Eve fish swim a little" in "a helping of a transparent narcotic made out of the mild Mazovian potatoes." The alcohol, Christmas carols played by a street band, some memories from the Wilno region and from the post-war years blur over the present time when even

a TV set "joyfully blinking with distortions" works without electric current—"such an obnoxious machine." And suddenly, into that world blurred with memories, vodka, and an all-covering snow storm there comes a story addressed to a man who lived more than a hundred years ago, a nineteen-year-old freedom fighter from Oszmiana, Zygmunt Mineyko.

The Mineyko story which makes a forty-page-long digression in a hundred-and-sixty-page-long novel we may call an addressed story for it is written in a form different from the contemporary plot: while the latter uses the first person narrative and the present tense, the former employs second person form and the past tense thus creating the effect of a direct address to its protagonist. And yet it maintains a close relationship to the narrator's own fate: throughout the story he interjects personal reminiscences or remarks such as "and I remember that kitchen, too," or "and that Wanda resembled very much our liaison girl, Jaskólka, who was arrested in 1944." Here the past and the present become one, perhaps even more than in Konwicki's previous novels, with all the consequences of that continuity affecting a contemporary citizen of Poland.

The name of Zygmunt Mineyko was hard to find in Polish historiography until 1971 when his memoir *Z tajgi pod Akropol (From the Taiga to Acropolis)* was published in Warsaw. Out of this colorful story of an insurgent in 1863, an exile to Siberia, and finally a member of the Greek General Staff, Konwicki took just one short episode and developed it in an independent story of idealism, fight, and treason. The episode which in Mineyko's own memoir occupies some 30 pages out of a five hundred pages long book comes alive under Konwicki's pen with complete and dramatic characters, and having a bearing on the historical past on the one hand, and the narrator's future on the other hand. Because in the structure of **The Polish Complex** the Mineyko story appears right after a short reminiscence of the narrator's trip to the United States completed a few years before. In a conversation with Kojran he tells him about his meeting with "an elderly gentleman, extremely emaciated, invalid man with sorrowful eyes." He had been, as it turns out, the commander of "a guerrilla unit in the first months of 1945," to whom the narrator reports after all those years about his "war nobody remembers anymore, nobody remembers so much that perhaps it had never existed." From some other sources we know that Tadeusz Konwicki, while visiting in the United States in 1975, indeed met with Captain Stanislaw Szabunia, the former commander of the 2nd Company 77 Infantry Regiment, so ironically depicted in **Rojsty,** and that fact adds to **The Polish Complex** some more authentic features. But it is less important than the sequence of the two episodes which culminate in a question Mineyko sees in the eyes of the traitor who gave him up to the Russians, "a question always familiar to us: was it worth it?"

Konwicki does not answer that question directly but one can find it in the shortest biography of a Warsaw beggar introduced earlier in the novel. That invalid lost both his legs "just like that, simply. In forty four. Poetically minded girls used to kiss my stumps. I rose because of my downfall. To have no legs was like having four legs. Lovely time. Well, now it isn't bad either. But we won't change the world anymore." This motif of giving up the idea of "changing the world" appears both in the American episode and in Mineyko's story with a vision of the country which is "just, noble, rational, making an example for the whole Europe, born out of the blood of her best sons"; furthermore, it is ironically juxtaposed with the character of that invalid from the Warsaw Uprising, a man who "scares sensitive passersby" with his artificial limbs right from the very first page of the novel. "I guess we are going to lose this set by a walkover," concludes the invalid as if answering the question asked by Mineyko. And yet when the student collecting for KOR approaches the narrator, he, instead of money gives him the most precious gift, just received from his relative, a malachite stamp with a Polish eagle, made by an exile to Siberia a hundred years ago. "For your freedom and ours," he whispers handing over this symbol of a freedom fight to a representative of a new generation who takes over without ever questioning whether it was worth it or not.

This particular scene in the novel is immediately followed by another historical digression, a ten-page-long episode on Romuald Traugutt on the eve of his dictatorship in the 1863 Uprising. And once more, in Traugutt's dialogue with his wife there returns the same question: "Was there any sense to rise against such a power?". "I don't know, whether there was any sense or not," he answers his wife, himself, and, at the same time giving an answer to Mineyko, the insurgent from Warsaw in '44, and to the student collecting for KOR. "I know it was a must."

Parenthetically, one wonders how incredibly little we know about that unusual man from literary works. Except for some half-forgotten stories in a collection *Gloria victis* (1910) by Eliza Orzeszkowa, and two contemporary historical novels by Jan Dobraczynski and Stanislaw Strumpf-Wojtkiewicz, there is no literary work which would depict that complicated road traveled by the tsarist lieutenant colonel and the hero of Sebastopol who ended up as a Polish national hero hanged by the Russians in front of the Warsaw citadel. Thus a little portrayal created by Konwicki in an episode which begins and ends with a phrase, "it could have been like that," becomes even more precious.

Actually the episode consists of just one scene, a meeting between Traugutt and his beloved wife in bed, in a casual hotel room, in a moment of weakness, both spiritual and purely physical. That last characteristic creates a jarring contrast with the sexual prowess of the narrator, demonstrated earlier in the novel when he met with a partner whose name he did not even know. The juxtaposition of both scenes is quite obvious: where a contemporary narrator succeeds in a dubious situation, the historic hero fails, but when the historic hero proves his greatness, a contemporary man covers up his emptiness with cosmological dialogues and fantasies concocted together with the casual partner of his sexual adventure. Critics who regard the historical digressions in the novel a nuisance have been clearly mistaken, because both fragments firmly belong in the structure of the novel, support it, develop, and enlarge.

Critics who regard the historical digressions in [*The Polish Complex*] a nuisance have been clearly mistaken, because both fragments firmly belong in the structure of the novel, support it, develop, and enlarge.
—Jerzy R. Krzyzanowski

In both digressions the Russians represent the main theme. While in the contemporary plot the Russian tourists "push forward to the counter like deaf-mutes, and only thick puffs of steam emerging from their mouths indicate how nervous they are," the Russians in the Mineyko story are shown as a group of volunteers joining the uprising, and as cruel henchmen torturing their Polish captive. In the original Mineyko's memoir a Russian, Major N., who had brought in ten volunteers, starts running away as soon as the shooting starts, but in Konwicki's novel thwe same major, called Nawalkiewicz, seems to be modeled on good-natured characters borrowed from Pushkin, Lermontov, and Tolstoy; most of all he resembles Major Woldemar Hawrylowicz in *Fantazy* by Juliusz Slowacki. And only in Traugutt's story do the Russian officers dining in an adjoining hotel room achieve terrifying dimension symbolizing a cruel, blind, and savage foreign power. Even though one of them begins to sing a forbidden song and the second stanza "has been picked up by several voices more boldly" the image of the Russians is horrifying, from the initial meeting with an officer of the gendarmes, through a brief encounter with a "fierce governor," up to a wild orgy of the drunken officers and a cry resounding in a deserted street "*Karaul! Karaul!*" (Police! Police!).

As an ironic supplement to that image there appears at the end of the novel a group of "tipsy tourists . . . waving to the sides like in a Tyrolian waltz," their yodeling mixed with a carol *Heilige Nacht, stille Nacht* in a Warsaw street. Comments the narrator: "They too have an appetite for us. Just waiting in line." Needless to say that the German tourists "move along to a nearby hotel erected on the place of executions." Without such a scene no image of a Polish complex could have been complete.

Thus the role of both historical digressions is obvious and carries some important weight in diagnosing the Polish complex. They point out the sources of all those problems which result in such a complex. Now it can be named: it is Russia.

IV

We have discussed so far two levels of *The Polish Complex:* the level of contemporary plot, and the level of historical digressions both of which refer to the 1863 uprising. Both levels, intrinsically interrelated, supplement and enrich each other in the main motif of the Polish complex, and both of them create the basic fictional plot line in the novel. But there exists in it also a third level supplying a commentary with a series of essayistic digressions, generalizing and often abstract in character, seemingly related to the fictitious plot only in a loose manner, and yet representing a higher, perhaps the most important level of the novel's structure. For that particular reason those commentaries often take the form of an open, sometimes ruthless criticism of the political system existing in Poland, and deserve a close scrutiny here.

As it has already been mentioned, those comments appear from the very beginning of the novel, and are to be found in every key moment of the plot. So, for instance, a sentence closing the second paragraph of the first chapter "a common Christmas Eve day" is immediately followed by a broad, panoramic view of that day "creeping through a small planet in a tiny solar system"; having completed a cosmic circle it ends with a sober notion returning the reader to a realistic level with a statement: "on that day I am standing there, tucked in a warm sheepskin coat, in front of a jewelry store named, somewhat without a particular sophistication 'Jubiler.'" The development of the plot, however, and a gradual disclosure of the narrator's experiences and feelings lead to a more open character of the comments, referring to the reality seen not so much from a cosmic perspective as from the perspective of a man imprisoned in that reality. And not only in the existential sense of that term but also in a very real one. The narrator named Tadeusz Konwicki gives place to the author, a contemporary Polish writer Tadeusz Konwicki, who is deeply concerned for his country and its people.

Let us consider some of the most important comments dealing with the Polish complex as we have tried to diagnose it on the evidence discussed above. "I read a lot of historical studies," writes Konwicki, "I follow the lives of nations and single men. I wade through our history back and forth, one way or another. Sometimes I am subjected to the affections

and exultant levitations, sometimes I hit the bottom of humiliations and despairs. Then I reach for the curriculum vitae of our great sister, Russia. She has really made it having an uninterrupted run of luck." And comparing the histories of both countries Konwicki goes on: "The whole social, economic, and cultural structure should have led, pushed, and brought the Russian state to an abyss of annihilation and nonexistence. Dark, obscurant despotism, rowdiness of the higher social classes, the poverty of the population, the license of the stupid and corrupted officials, incredible indolence of the military leaders, the most reactionary laws and customs, barbarity in human relations—all those factors instead of sinking the state, instead of expelling the Russian nation from the European community, all those factors laboriously built up the power of old-time Russia, her supremacy, her greatness among the nations of the old continent. Our nobility of educated monarchs, the energy of wise ministers, good will of citizens, profession of the high ideas of humanity, all those positive, exemplary, text-book values suddenly depreciated. All of a sudden they whored and like a millstone pulled the venerable corpse of the Republic of Two Nations to the bottom."

"Do I have to be ashamed of loving freedom?" asks the author. "Even if it were a stupid, foolish, total, anarchic, provincial freedom, even if it were a freedom leading to destruction?" And he concludes: "Nobility will always be defeated by baseness for virtue will surrender to crime, and freedom will perish by the hand of captivity. But one may also say that the law will conquer sin, that the good will win over the evil, that freedom will triumph over captivity. Nonetheless let us remember that goodness is slow like a cloud in the sky while evil is as fast as lightning"

In a letter from a friend already mentioned, a letter written in an almost Orwellian tone, its author devotes his attention to the problems of a totalitarian system introduced "by a junta supplied by a categorical neighbor, brought in coffers, or rather in military trains." The character of a monoparty is quite explicit: "Our regime is being kept in its agonal movement by a magic neighborhood of a northern power." "We are forced to love officially our northern neighbor and our own country. But that love for our own country, this patriotism of ours, is a quality so far unknown to anybody that far, it is a discovery in the region of higher rank feelings. The main part, and as a part which comes first, of that patriotism of ours is a hysterical, debauched, and slightly perverted love for our northern neighbor, and only as a supplement, as it were, as a luxurious condiment, comes our attachment to our own country. And so both loves in the final result are very much alike for in both the cornerstone, or rather a coal consists of a bitchy lust for our unscrupulous neighbor." It should be explained here that in the last sentence Konwicki uses a play on words: "corner stone" in Polish is *kamien wêgielny* while "coal" means *wêgiel kamienny*; the reference to the Soviet exploitation of Polish coal supplies is quite obvious.

Making a comparison between ideology and religion Konwicki refers directly to the censorship: "We all live in state of a savage fear of the word. The word horrifies the Party and the ministries, the word awakes fears in the generals and the censors, the word haunts in the listening devices, and in the still insufficiently controlled dreams of the citizens. But the worst is the written word, the word made permanent in orthographic signs or phonetic signs on paper, on a celluloid tape, or in marble. And for that reason I am scribbling these sentences furtively, in this foggy lake of pain and misfortune, in this refuge of a second-long freedom before an annihilation." Next he directs his attack against the Party for which "our expression of gratitude is the goal of our life," the Party obsessed with power, "the cancer of power, an amok of power, an abyss of power. An abyss engulfing millions of consciences and millions of souls."

Equally explicit is the presentation of the relationship between the citizens and the authorities: "If they had only tortured us with their brash ever-presence, if they had only buried us in prisons, if they had only bothered us with their ideological nagging, if they had only dehumanized us with their everyday lies, treason and corruption, if they had only denationalized us making us an anonymous horde of a steppe cattle, but they bother us, bother to death, tire us, fool us, twaddle us, piss on us with a boring bore from tip to top. A boredom descends upon us from the skies, from the trees and country fields, from the seas and oceans, from the newspapers and theaters, from the laboratories and strip-teases, from the buildings and the official limousines, from entertainment and from the seriousness, from the school kids and from the faces of the dignitaries. The boredom is a secret elixir of our regime. The boredom is their mistress and mother. The boredom is their natural scent. The boredom evaporates from the administration brains and from the administration mugs. The boredom emanates from the military, the police, and the listening devices. The boredom oozes from prisons and torture chambers. The boredom is their own curse. They are ashamed of that boredom, they fear it, they choke with it, and they will never be free of it. The boredom is a boundless gulf in which they are drowning, and we are drowning together with them. The boredom is the satan in his worldly incarnation."

But the most dramatic and most outspoken among many such commentaries scattered throughout the novel appears to be the fragment which, as we have assumed, represents a message to "those rational creatures from the central regions of the universe . . . creatures wiser and better than us," to all those who could not comprehend the Polish complex or the Polish realities. This rather extensive fragment appears in the novel right after a scene of confession, i.e., after the mo-

ment of the deepest introspection, and deserves to be quoted here at some length:

> Modern captivity resembles certain situations from the gangster movies: the telephone rings, and the gangster orders his blackmailed victim to pick up the receiver and with a normal, social tone of voice converse with the person calling about just anything. Or, somebody has entered a house taken over by the gangsters. The owner of the house with the bandits' pistol aimed at him, receives his guest as if nothing happened, offers him a drink, tries to behave normally and to get rid of the only man who could help him. Or, the gangsters escape from the bank leading in front of them a terrorized teller, under the cover of her body run to a car, and the woman begs of the custodians of justice not to shoot and give the gangsters a chance to escape safely.

> The same happens to whole nations in the contemporary world. Where are the beautiful times of the old-fashioned captivity? Where is the lofty fight of the invader with the language of the captives, with their national emblems, where is the open and ceremonial pursuit of the patriots, where are the solemn executions of the heroes? That captivity in a retro style used to be open, theatrical, celebrated. And everybody knew who violated the weaker ones, and who would respond for such violations before the tribunal of history.

> Today captivity has become invisible. Some poor nation seems to act naturally, listens to its anthem with reverence, elects a parliament, dispatches its envoys, takes its place in the Security Council, in a word behaves as any independent and sovereign state. And nobody sees that it has a revolver stuck at its back, a cocked revolver of its neighbor, or perhaps not even a neighbor. Such a nation pronounces words which are matter-of-fact, rational, deep, such and such, pronounces them with a poker face, and nobody can even guess that that nation would like to roar like a slaughtered animal, with all its might, from the bottom of its guts, to howl like a skinned rabbit, to yelp to God for help before the unavoidable doom.

> In the old times a slave had the right to scream, today slaves are granted the right to be silent, mute. A scream brought about a relief, hardened the health like it is with the babies, hardened for the future. A silence, muteness degenerates, suffocates, kills. In the old days a slave, when freed, could join the great family of nations without any hindrance. Today, when freed by accident, he will not be fit for

life. He will die from poisons he had accumulated during the black night of interdiction.

Rarely in world literature can one find a confession written with such a powerful expression, so moving and desperate. Perhaps only Solzhenitsyn, the bravest of the brave, can speak with such a courage, so movingly and accurately at the same time.

And even if Konwicki's novel might fade away with time, as often happens with contemporary novels, that single part of it will remain in the history of Polish literature as the most shocking and tragic document of the years of violence and oppression.

World Literature Today (review date Autumn 1982)

SOURCE: A review of *The Polish Complex,* in *World Literature Today,* Vol. 56, No. 4, Autumn, 1982, p. 720.

[*In the following review, the critic delineates the historical significance of the setting, plot, and characters of* The Polish Complex.]

A prolific and talented novelist (who has also worked effectively in film), Konwicki has recently felt it necessary to express through fiction his most passionately held socio-political views. *The Polish Complex,* first published in London by "Index on Censorship" (1977) after limited *samizdat* circulation at home, points an accusing finger at Russia, the age-old enemy which has dominated, exploited and repressed Poland for almost two centuries. The writer comes from Vilno (the former capital of Polish Lithuania); as a very young man he joined the partisans and fought against the occupying Germans and later the Russians (for which he was sentenced to jail). Now, apparently, he has been again arrested by the new military authorities in his country.

In his work Konwicki returns almost obsessively to Vilno and to Lithuania's forests and marshes. Memories of the past, shimmering eerily, merge with feelings of guilt and disillusion from that now-shadowy war. The narrator K., an alter ego, propels us on a train of free association back and forth in time and space. He probes with irony the depths of bathos—the pedestrian absurdity of contemporary Polish life. The past is rendered with romantic pathos; the future is pathetic too, in a disturbing though unoriginal vision of a triumphant One-State.

The main plot is intentionally anti-climactic: on the day before Christmas a group of Varsovians wait in line at the central state-run jewelry store. Anticipating the arrival of a shipment of gold rings from the Soviet Union, they brave the raw weather, converse, quarrel, even fall in love. Ironically, the shipment turns out to contain only electric samovars; however, the assembled fortune hunters remain undeterred. After the store's closing, they repair to the hallway of a neighboring apartment building. When they part company, the first star hovers above the Palace of Culture irradiating light like a UFO. In the finale a black man and his Polish wife enter carrying their newborn infant.

The characters are aptly chosen to represent social diversity: a worker, a student, an affluent countrywoman, a seedy Laurel and Hardy twosome (one of whom was once ordered by the underground command to kill the narrator), a young police spy clad in fashionable denims, a youthful French anarchist (naively infatuated with Poland) and a languorous brunette store employee whose fresh beauty brings the ailing, aging narrator erotic stimulation and temporary fulfillment.

In essence the novel forms a mosaic in which digressive passages counterbalance and sometimes eclipse the story being told in the present tense. The digressions, often narrated as interior monologues, examine the way Poles see themselves and the world. Are they romantic, irresponsible mythmakers who transmit their "complexes" to future generations, or are they the innocent victims of brutal historical currents? Have their repeated self-sacrifices tended to preclude the practical acceptance of hard realities? Konwicki feels that, as a writer, he must show his country's travail, ultimately to place it within larger perspectives. The novel's main leitmotiv depicts, in turgid prose, an eternally dark, cosmic landscape marred by the excrescences of modern civilization, a faithless world lacking in moral fiber but rich in banality.

Ewa Kuryluk (review date March-April 1985)

SOURCE: "In Eastern Poland . . . ," in *American Book Review,* Vol. 7, No. 3, March-April, 1985, pp. 21-2.

[*In the review below, Kuryluk examines elements of time and setting in* A Minor Apocalypse, *suggesting analogies to contemporary Polish-Soviet relations.*]

One of the best ideas in Tadeusz Konwicki's *Minor Apocalypse* is the uncertainty of time. All actions of the novel take place in Warsaw between the morning and the evening of one day, but none of the characters is sure which day, month or year that is. Different dates are suggested by different people, newspapers and calendars. Supposedly the occasion is a festive one and a banner reads: "Long live the fortieth anniversary of the Polish People's Republic."

The Polish People's Republic was proclaimed on July 22,

1944 in Lublin, a small town in Eastern Poland, by the Communist government set up by the Soviets. Thus, by means of a simple addition, the reader is led to 1984, a year that unmistakably points to Orwell's famous novel. It deals, among other things, with the perpetual concealment and alteration of facts in a totalitarian society. What cannot be interpreted in accordance with the newest line, becomes unavailable. In all Communist countries there is a permanent shortage of maps, guide-books and calendars. But without a calendar the monolithic stream of time cannot be divided into smaller, individual entities and people drown in it.

In Konwicki's novel not only dates are uncertain but even the weather is completely mixed up; summer heat is followed by snow. This way the confusion of human minds is matched by the visible disorder of nature. This apocalyptic disturbance of climate might have been inspired by a popular anecdote that comments on agricultural disasters. They happen every year and are always explained as being caused by the weather. Accordingly, the saying goes: once Communism has been established, even the climate goes wrong.

On the uncertain day that possibly coincides with the anniversary of the Communist rule, Poland is supposed to apply for membership in the U.S.S.R. Though under Konwicki's eyes the country looks already like a Soviet colony, the last and rather nominal step is still opposed by a group of dissidents. They decide to disturb the celebration of the annexation by staging a suicidal event in front of the party headquarters. After the 1968 invasion of Czechoslovakia a student set himself on fire in Prague. Now a Pole is selected for the same purpose. He is a writer and the narrator of the story.

The novel starts in the morning. Two friends wake up the to-be-hero and inform him about his expected death in the evening. They instruct him also how to get gas and matches unavailable on the market. The material basis of life is provided everywhere by women and even more so in a Communist country. While men drink vodka and plot, women stand in line and are responsible for emotional support. And indeed, one woman, a matter-of-fact Polish activist, equips the writer with the instruments of his future death, another, a romantic Russian, offers him love.

Both the nationality and the name of the second girl ("Nadezda" means "Hope" in Russian) are meant to be symbolic. Her copulation with the narrator mirrors the political fusion. The moment they embrace, the television screen shows the first secretaries of the Polish and Soviet parties kissing each other. But Nadezda impersonates also another Russia, soft-spoken, cultured and full of charm, that for centuries has attracted the Polish intelligentsia. Her affair with the narrator reflects, thus, the ancient love-hatred relationship between the two countries.

The tone of the novel is sinister and slightly cynical. Konwicki conveys the feeling that all actions are not only futile but also infinitely banal. The best passages of the novel describe the bad quality of everything. Houses fall apart and people get worn out and corrupted. Poland in 1984 looks like one big slum where people have stopped to care for life. Though Konwicki wrote his novel in the relatively prosperous seventies, the picture is close to present reality. His ability to foresee the complete breakdown of economy and liberalism adds to his book a prophetic quality. He is less successful with the love-story which offers nothing but stereotypes. However, one could argue—and probably Konwicki would—that at a certain level of deprivation and exhaustion even the erotic vibrance and originality must get lost.

> **[Konwicki's] ability to foresee the complete breakdown of economy and liberalism adds to his book a prophetic quality.**
> —*Ewa Kuryluk*

The Minor Apocalypse makes a most depressing reading. But, though hard to grasp, a grain of hope is buried between the lines of the novel. The hope consists of the very fact that somebody at all dares to protest the annexation, that somebody at all is against the Big Brother. Over sixty years ago the very same hope was expressed in the first and still most relevant vision of a totalitarian Soviet society. In 1920 Yevgeny Zamyatin wrote *We,* a novel on which not only Orwell based *1984,* published more than 25 years later, but to which Konwicki is indebted as well.

The key chapter of Zamyatin's book is entitled "Descent from Heaven. The Great Catastrophe in History. The Known Is Ended" and it plays on "Unanimity Day." On this day the Benefactor is to be elected for the forty-eighth time in an "unanimous vote." People are supposed to answer the question "who is against?" by continuing to sit "motionless, joylessly bowing" their heads "to the beneficent yoke of the Number of Numbers." However, in this very vote suddenly "thousands of hands swing up—'against'—and drop."

Not thousands but millions of Poles voted "against" and helped Solidarity to rise. And they are evoked, out of all hopelessness and cynicism, in the last words of the hero as he begins walking toward the stone platform to kill himself: "People, give me strength. People, give strength to everyone in this world who is, at this very moment, going, as I am, to make a burnt offering of himself."

Wanda Urbanska (review date 15 November 1987)

SOURCE: "Poland Has 50 Good Years Coming," in *Los Angeles Times Book Review,* November 15, 1987, pp. 2, 11.

[*In the following review, Urbanska comments on the thematic diversity and frank tone of* Moonrise, Moonset.]

At first glance, it might seem that Tadeusz Konwicki had an ax to grind with his Poland. In *Moonrise, Moonset,* Konwicki's irreverent memoir of the fateful year 1981, the author spars with such sacred cows as Radio Free Europe, Solidarity followers and Czeslaw Milosz, the 1980 Nobel Prize laureate for literature. "I had an itch to give certain people a real thrashing," he writes, "but I lost the urge."

Don't believe him. In this alternately somber and zany ride through modern Polish history—with forays into the West, the East and the past—what the author states definitively one minute he contradicts the next. Just when you think you have a bead on the man, he'll zap you with the verbal equivalent of a stun gun.

"Yes, the German occupation was beautiful," writes Konwicki, who was born in 1926 in Wilno, Lithuania. "Beautiful because it was my youth, my one and only youth. There won't be any other."

In *Moonrise, Moonset*—set against the backdrop of the country's fling with freedom during Solidarity's heyday—Konwicki tackles such diverse themes as the need for the young to feel superior to the old, Poland's potential role in the undoing of the Soviet empire, the cost to an author of failing memory and the superiority of a fountain pen over ball-point. Two novel fragments are folded into the narrative.

Spinning in all directions, a book without a central thematic thrust stands the risk of literary entropy. With the possible exception of the digressive novel fragments, this book manages to hold its center by force of Konwicki's engaging chivalry. He disarms you by confronting your doubts head-on. "An enormous number of readers are incapable of reading even seven pages of my prose," he writes. "My prose infuriates many people, it causes eyes to wander and sudden foaming at the mouth."

For any Polonophile, there is much juicy stuff here, well worth the trouble. Konwicki documents his 1981 effort to mount the film version of Milosz's 1955 novel, *The Issa Valley.* Initially lukewarm to the project, Milosz later comes 'round with a vengeance and begins issuing "thousands of pointers. That [the lead character] Thomas will not be tall but, rather, squarely built, naive but not stupid, more male than angelic, and so forth and so on." Milosz becomes, in a

word, precious with his literary darling, leaving Konwicki "not altogether sure that the laureate has ever been inside a movie theater." His creative hands tied, Konwicki makes a film that does not go over.

What makes Konwicki's confessions work—and rise above the self-serving—is his willingness to expose his own flaws.
—*Wanda Urbanska*

What makes Konwicki's confessions work—and rise above the self-serving—is his willingness to expose his own flaws. In the zealous atmosphere of truth-seeking Solidarity, younger writers held Konwicki's record—especially his card-carrying Communist phase—up for account. Finding he "couldn't satisfy" minds bent on indictment, Konwicki arrives at the universal conclusion that the strength of young writers "depends on their dissatisfaction with me.... With our criminal past held constantly up to us by the young, we would be more lenient in negotiating their place in literature with them."

Elsewhere in the book Konwicki chastises himself for similar misdeeds against his elders. After Poland's wrenching defeat in 1945, "I had turned my childish wrath" on Home Army leaders, he writes. "None of us knew that this was how the river of history had to flow, that our will was the will of a drop of water dissolved in that river."

Nevertheless protective of his war memories, Konwicki accuses *Ashes and Diamonds*—Andrzej Wadja's famous 1958 film depicting the last day of the war in Poland—of being derivative from American film and mores. "Home Army bumpkin that I am, it stuck in my throat," writes Konwicki. "Yes, we had our fashions, fads, modes. But our fashions did not include blue jeans, sunglasses, excessive drinking, neurotic kicks, hysterical sobbing and short-term love affairs.... We were coarse, common, we wore knickers; we were punctual, reliable, restrained, embarrassed, hungry for death."

Beneath his acerbic tongue—fired by that characteristic Polish mixture of pride, shame, rage, ambivalence, romanticism, stubbornness and frivolity—lies the heart of a Polish partisan. Konwicki relates the recent prophecy of an aging priest whose clairvoyance was awakened while in Nazi captivity.

"'Poland has 50 good years coming'—he held his thumb up—'Poland's time is coming and so is her enemies' decline.'"

Moonrise, Moonset comes to its natural conclusion in December, 1981, when martial law has been imposed and

Konwicki is called into police headquarters to sign a loyalty oath. Making light of it all, Konwicki decides the questioning officer is a character he created in an earlier novel. Konwicki has been around the block too many times to be overwhelmed by the peaks and valleys in his or his country's life. Such is the privilege of age and seasoning.

Patricia Hampl (review date 15 July 1990)

SOURCE: A review of *Bohin Manor*, in *New York Times Book Review*, July 15, 1990, Sec. 7, p. 7.

[*In the review below, Hampl traces the autobiographical and historical significance of the narrative design of* Bohin Manor.]

This beautiful, grave book [**Bohin Manor**] begins not once, but twice. It opens first, guilelessly, as a novel: "Miss Helena Konwicka rose that day right after dawn, as she usually did during the week."

On the next page it starts up again, this time in the voice of a memoir: "Miss Helena Konwicka, my grandmother, stopped in front of her window, and once again glanced at a dewdrop containing a likeness of the holiday morning's light."

From the moment Tadeusz Konwicki casually introduces his possessive pronoun—"my grandmother"—the ground shifts powerfully under the novel. Its pastoral assumptions are uprooted, and the book ceases to be simply a story. It turns into a lyric antiphon, a call between Central Europe's 19th century and its lurid 20th.

"I am working my way through the back streets of time," Mr. Konwicki writes shortly after introducing his grandmother on her 30th birthday in the last quarter of the 19th century. He is also working his way, he says, "through the numbness of the imagination, through my own river of pain, and I must make it to that other shore, to my grandmother Helena Konwicka, a young lady slowly aging in a sad time, a dreary era, a hopeless hour of dispassionate history which floods behind us, beside us, ahead of us."

Mr. Konwicki wisely allows his own "river of pain" to remain unspecified. This canny reticence avoids an autobiographical dead end; instead, the anonymous pain achieves the authority of a national or historical emotion. Yet, he never forfeits the intimacy of the personal voice. The relation of the historical point of view and this personal voice gives the book a haunting brilliance.

But there is a real story here; that is, a 19th-century realist story: Helena Konwicka, who worries that talking to herself (something she is in the habit of doing) is "one sign of spinsterhood," feels pressured to marry Alexander Broel-Plater, a neighboring landowner whose lovemaking consists of pointing out to her that neither of them is getting any younger.

The curious enervation of her life encourages Helena to cave in to this dispiriting suitor—even when she learns that his natural affections tend toward his rifleman, the sulky Ildefons.

Into this airless world of humiliated Polish gentry appears Elias Szyra, "a Jew boy from Bujwidze," as Helena at one point calls him in a frantic attempt to let her native anti-Semitism protect her from a fateful passion.

Elias fought in the failed 1863 uprising against the Russians and is a hunted man. He is, implicitly, a hero. He appears out of nowhere, his red hair flaming like a signal. And of course, with Mr. Konwicki's habit of murmuring from his very 20th-century perch, this hunted Polish Jew evokes millions.

Elias's erotic certainty is calamitous for Helena, who lives in a world of small moves and suspended action. He tells her he used to watch from afar as she went by in her carriage. "I came back here to see you," he says simply.

His clarity mesmerizes and claims her. "We're fated for each other," he says. But the languid landowner Plater has also invoked fate as the trump card in his courtship. Helena's romantic dilemma sustains the tension of Mr. Konwicki's 19th-century story.

Helena is not the only one suffering from fate—or inertia. The countryside itself is caught in the depression of oppression. For this is Polish Lithuania, 10 years after the failed uprising, now forcibly annexed to Russia. Helena sees that her old country priest, to whom she goes for counsel, has even lost his faith.

And Helena's father, Michal Konwicki (or, sometimes, "Michal Konwicki, my great-grandfather"), hasn't uttered a word since the suppression of the uprising. The only sounds he makes come in the night when, from his solitary room, Helena hears his screams, strangled protestations of guilt and love.

This penance may be for his lost country, or perhaps as an act of mourning for his dead wife, about whom Helena knows only one chilling fact: she asked to be buried not in the family cemetery but by the side of the road, "like one of Napoleon's soldiers who had fallen in battle."

So, while Mr. Konwicki is trying to locate his grandmother, Helena (and, like any author, his heroine), Helena is trying to locate her own mother, swallowed by death and history—the very fate that bedevils her grandson author in his quest for her.

The novel is rich in such echoes. The great pleasure—and achievement—of the book is that these calls and replies across the centuries are not arch literary gestures. They always feel urgent and as real as the imagination always makes memory. The entanglement of the author's voice and Helena's story, like the collision of the two centuries, seems inevitable.

The book is wholly animate, in the way fairy tales are. From the first page, the novel is ruled by the disarming assumption that all of the world is alive, even sentient. "The whole house was still asleep," Mr. Konwicki writes. "The white-washed walls were still sleeping, as were the mahogany wardrobes, the muslin curtains on the windows, and the floorboards. . . . The servants were asleep and so was Helena's father."

This belief in an animating spirit in all things - in dewdrops that sparkle "like a fortune-teller's crystal ball" and roe deer that stand by the road ready to take to the woods at the least indication of hostility - encourages the novel's most daring leaps. For it is not only her 20th-century grandson who is invading Helena's 19th-century story.

Helena's Lithuanian countryside is also peopled with the makers of the next century's troubles. The spirits of Stalin and Hitler are alive in the land, and even Lenin makes a cameo appearance. Mr. Konwicki's time machine runs the other way too, allowing Aleksandr Pushkin and Adam Mickiewicz to appear from earlier in Helena's century.

"For so many days and nights," Mr. Konwicki writes at the end of the book, after Helena has made her fateful choice and has discovered what fate really is, "I have kept an idea in store in my soul, a warning or words of farewell, for the time of farewells is close at hand; I wanted to scratch something onto the wall of common memory."

In this fine translation by Richard Lourie—accompanied by a most helpful essay—Tadeusz Konwicki has accomplished this most profound of literary tasks. And the epitaph he has carved so deftly honors not only Helena, the grandmother he never knew, but our own century, which, it seems, he has known all too well.

K. J. Phillips (essay date 1990)

SOURCE: "Sacrificing to Baal," in *Dying Gods in Twenti-*eth-*Century Fiction,* Bucknell University Press, 1990, pp. 82-107.

[*In the following excerpt, Phillips analyzes various mythical rituals enacted by the narrative of* A Minor Apocalypse, *emphasizing their significance in the context of the Polish resistance movement.*]

A Minor Apocalypse (1979) is the ninth novel by Tadeusz Konwicki and his second to be published in *samizdat,* the Polish underground system for circulating dissident literature. When the narrator tries to dispel his waking thoughts about death—his own mortality, his country's subjection, the planet's extinction—with "gestures of ritual," he means only his morning routine and the habit of writing, that "narcotic of the wounded individual." The narrator's friends Hubert and Rysio arrive just at this point to recommend a much more primitive ritual, one that could, in fact, come straight out of [James] Frazer's chapter on "The Burned God." The "friends" politely propose that "tonight at eight o'clock you set yourself on fire in front of the Party Central Committee building," as a protest against Soviet domination of Poland. Naturally nonplused, the narrator puts off a direct reply. Nevertheless, he seriously considers the plan. As he walks around the city for the rest of the book, blue plastic gasoline can in hand, the suspense builds: first, whether he will go through with the terrible suggestion and, second, whether such immolation in a kind of balefire can actually do any good.

As "mysterious hierophants . . . of the last people who suffer insomnia in this sleeping country," Hubert and Rysio still link sacrifice with the well-being of the community in the same way ancient people derived the good of the group from the demise of the god or his human surrogate. "Your death will bring them back to life or redeem them," the friends insist. Moreover, Konwicki echoes several other ritual effects of the type described by Frazer: the victim can revive the plants as well as the spiritual health of the community; he may be killed when his sexual powers fail; an effigy made out of plants may be thrown into a body of water as a rain charm; and he may enact a theogamy to make the vegetation thrive. Konwicki shrewdly matches several of these "rites," which the narrator bungles through pathetically, with competing versions conducted by the state, as if the government were claiming that communism, not this single citizen, has by its institutions already ushered the divine into life.

According to Frazer, ritual death was supposed to end winter or waste, and Konwicki paints a traditional wasteland. As the narrator wakes, he hears elderly delivery women knock over some milk crates, while an armored refrigerator truck carrying food for Party Secretaries races through the milk puddles. Only officials enjoy plenty—at the people's expense. The impression of dearth for ordinary folks intensifies when successive workmen arrive during Hubert and

Rysio's visit to warn that they will be shutting off the water and gas supply. When a worker advises the narrator to save a tubful of water, he protests, in obvious untruth, "I don't need any water." He is still desperately trying to dissociate himself from the wasteland and from his delegated role in ending it, whether as grail quester releasing the waters or as Frazerian priest-king dying to ensure fertility.

In addition to depicting communist Poland as a wasteland deprived of food, warmth, and water, Konwicki wryly parodies Frazer's claim that the man-god on whom the health of the community depends is sometimes killed at the first sign that his physical powers are beginning to wane, particularly at any sign of "incapacity to satisfy the sexual passions of his wives." Just as the narrator receives the ominous visit, "A sudden hailstorm rattled past the balcony, knocking a condom withering on the iron balustrade off into the abyss. Those condoms were bouquets of violets bestowed on me by my neighbors from the upper floors on their days off." Because Frazer associates violets with the blood of Attis, the traditional bouquets combine with the withering signs of past potency (and infertility) to hint to the reluctant narrator that it is time for his demise.

If such a failing priest-king did bow out after any indication of aging, the vegetation was supposed to rejoice. No sooner have the friends given breath to their grim plan when the house plants revive: "My jade plant was on the windowsill. Only then did I notice how much it had shot up lately and how thick its young, strong leaves had grown. It had been sickly for many years and now suddenly, without any external cause, it had surged upward, sending out a large number of powerful, knotty branches." This minor, natural flourishing seems to promise that the narrator might successfully carry out his mandate to revive the community. Any good he could do beyond encouraging the house plants, however, remains far from proved.

As these references to waning powers, violets, and reinvigorated plants echo rites for primitive dying gods, Konwicki also alludes to Christianity's dying god when the narrator announces "one last kilometer of my Golgotha" or when he circles the "Square of the Three Crosses." Richard Lourie, in the "Translator's Note" to an earlier novel by Konwicki, notes that "Poland in its darkest century was identified by its Romantic poets as the Christ of nations. The term evoked both the fact of crucifixion and the promise of rebirth. The Polish imagination felt itself summoned both to the unpleasant cunning of survival and to exalted martyrdom."

Some allusions in *A Minor Apocalypse* sound both Christian and pagan. The narrator, for example, goes to a river where "My sins, my pains, my shame flowed away to the distant sea like the wreaths on St. John's Day. To leap into the water forever, that would be good. But my miserable brothers want me to leap into the fire." Frazer records celebrations for St. John's Day in which people burn effigies in bonfires or throw them into streams. He believes that human victims at one time underwent the god's sacrifice, with effigies only gradually replacing the live offering and Christian holidays eventually taking over old pagan ceremonies. Although folk wreaths released into the Polish rivers may have come to symbolize washing away sin, in the manner of Christian baptism, Konwicki senses an older, grimmer intention of drowning the sinner—or the sinless, as long as someone suffers. The narrator derives scant comfort from the thought of rinsing away shame because he faces only the "choice" between death by water or death by fire.

The narrator must not only try to equal the old dying god according to the plan proposed by the dissidents. He also has to outdo the communist state, which has competitively set itself up as the new idol. Replacing wreaths and effigies both pagan and Christian, the government floats the slogan "we have built socialism," made out of wreaths and lit candles, down the Vistula River. But, Konwicki intimates, the state is a tattered and unreliable savior, since a bridge disaster has already mauled the letters: "seized by an eddy, the exclamation point was sinking." The pretensions of the bureaucracy to be the new god, commemorated in eternal wreaths, explain why the narrator sometimes varies his self-definition from Christ to Antichrist. As Christ he can mount the hill of Golgotha to suffer, while as Antichrist he would signal the termination of a communist millennium.

Although the narrator seems to inherit only the doubtful prerogatives of the priest-king, like the right to throw himself into the river or onto a pyre, he does get to enjoy a kind of sacred marriage between impersonators of the god and goddess. Frazer details how wily kings marked for death came up with the brilliant idea of choosing a substitute, who would, after his brief, unexpected glory, be put to death. Such a king-for-a-day might be given as many slave women as he wished. The Polish underground allows the narrator—perplexed, ordinary, shoved unwillingly to the spotlight—to meet up with the "perfect woman," Nadezhda or "Hope," on his last day.

The narrator may characterize their intercourse as "a rite of magic," but Konwicki deflates such rhapsody. Nadezhda's mystic recognition of the narrator turns out to be more flattery than affinity: she claims to have read all the narrator's books but later waffles, "I said that? All Poles and Russians are writers." The fact that the couple meet twice also recalls the periodic nature of sacred marriages, though the narrator admits that repetition in his life is more likely to signal failed earlier attempts than reassuring recurrence.

Both lovemakings are interrupted, once by a man collecting taxes on sex in a public building, and once by a telephone call from the dissidents, wanting to know what color gas can the narrator prefers for his burning. Thus Konwicki shows how mythic theogamy, transposed to the modern, faithless world, acquires new triviality to go with the continued deadliness of the god's rites.

> **Konwicki shows how mythic theogamy, transposed to the modern, faithless world, acquires new triviality to go with the continued deadliness of the god's rites.**
> —*K. J. Phillips*

Despite the shoddiness of their theogamies, the second meeting between Nadezhda and the narrator occurs in a primordial "enchanted garden," where they can stand waist deep in ferns "which were strewn with white, mysterious seeds left to them from the good old days when they had been trees on this earth." By force of ardor the couple may temporarily seem to cause sympathetic nature to bear seed, but basically they inhabit a ruined world in which ordinary forests, let alone paradisiacal trees, have long since disappeared.

Just as the state matches St. John's Day wreaths with those of its own, it also stages parodic theogamies and opens a garden to compete with the narrator's ferns. The government offers its grotesque version of divine bride and bridegroom in a pair of Party Secretaries, Russian and Polish. The narrator glances at them all day on various televisions: the Secretaries, at different moments in the replays of a ceremony, are clasped in a hug, holding hands, or kissing each other on the mouth. The fact that the viewers have invariably turned down the sound brings out the ritual nature of these embraces, not to mention their ludicrousness and sterility. Moreover, if the narrator is supposed to burn himself near the Palace of Culture to promote fertility, the state has preceded him in fashioning fertility symbols of its own. The Palace of Culture "shone like an indecent erection against the low, cloudy sky. The first test rocket burst over the Vistula." This building also appears "bleached white by searchlights and shedding its stone slabs like some gigantic fish." The fish has long been a sign of life and sexuality. The state's stone fish joins the "amorous" Party Secretaries to preempt the narrator's claim to give life.

Proclaiming that its divinely ordained, millennial marriage between Russia and Poland has been perfectly fruitful, the state offers as evidence a garden, which is actually a shallow paradise over a reclaimed parking lot. Right before the narrator decides what to do with that gasoline can, he wanders into the official, stunted orchard: "The army searchlights by the Palace of Culture gave off a violet glow like a flash of light that had just died out forever. We walked past currant and raspberry bushes, and mounted beds of cauliflower,

carrots, and garlic. We passed trees so small there wasn't room on them for a single pigeon." In these inauspicious surroundings, where the violet glow might remind him of his earlier depressing "bouquet of violets," the narrator—as the proverbial dying man seeing his life flash before his eyes—discovers all fifteen women to whom he has ever made love. The dismal atmosphere of the state's garden overshadows the earlier idyll with Nadezhda, as these women wittily trounce any hope he may nurse to rival the god who releases the springtime:

"The nerve of him."

"Blaming us."

"That's the limit."

"The hell with him."

I pulled a torch-like firebrand from the flames. A little bit for show, a little for self-defense. The wind fluttered the meager flame like a scrap of silk.

"My dears, my darlings. We have the whole night ahead of us. Remember those springs, those summers, those autumns, even those winters. The mornings, the afternoons, the evenings. The silk sheets, the mossy forests, the little rooms off the kitchen. Weigh everything fairly, and only then should your kangaroo court pass sentence on me."

"But I hardly know him," said Rena after a moment.

"And I only know him by sight," added Rysia.

"He's more smoke than fire."

"Let's drink to ourselves, girls."

"To spring."

"To the new year."

"To tomorrow."

As he meets this series of women who fill the role of priestess—only partially satisfactorily in Nadezhda, wholly sardonically in these fifteen scoffers—the narrator also encounters a series of old or dying men who resemble the long line of guardian priests at Nemi. For the narrator is actually only one of a number of stubborn Poles who have resisted the government in subtle ways: "Jan, why did you kill yourself all these years?". Like the guardians of the Nemian grove, these men of conscience—Hubert, the paralytic white-bearded veteran, the renegade party official, Jan in a bathtub, and Caban—show hostility to the new arrival on the killing ground. Hubert, for example, prefers a movie director to the scorned narrator as the favorite son to stand by his deathbed. The green corpse glare in Hubert's hospital room does not augur well for the green of spring, which the narrator hopes to infuse into the world by his own death.

Other clues abound that the narrator will not be able to inaugurate a new season, either natural or political. He cannot pin down the correct year, let alone distinguish equinox from solstice. He notices contradictory placards that proclaim the city is celebrating an anniversary: the thirty-fifth, fortieth, fiftieth, or sixtieth. Konwicki probably alludes to George Orwell's *1984,* in which officials rewrite history to foster a dangerous forgetting of past alternative governments and of past wrongs. By confusing the number of the present anniversary, Konwicki may also parody the primitive idea that rituals merge historical time with the original "sacred time" at the beginning of the world, abolishing intervening centuries. The state abolishes only accountability, not alienating distance from a golden age. The seasons have spun erratically all day for the narrator, who wakes on an autumnal morning, registers many summery moments, but sees the snow starting to fall when he approaches the place of immolation. . . .

Does the narrator finally decide to go through with this hideous burning? Yes. Can it do any good, personally or communally? No. Personally, he'll be dead, and he has already used up his one facetious chance for revival. Earlier in the day he feels like a new man when a surge of flirtatiousness digs him out of a hangover. Beside market stalls that look like "ancient pagan Slavic temples," he tries for a date, but his companion, intent only on buying matches for his pagan bonfire, soon dashes his briefly reawakened self:

> "Maybe we could go for a coffee, Halina," I asked.
> "I'm not feeling well. I had some sort of accident yesterday but I can't remember anything about it."
>
> "But now you've come back to life?"
>
> "No. I liked you right from the start. I was looking at your legs when we were walking up the escarpment.". . .
>
> "Old fart," Halinka [Halina] muttered, looking at me without anger.

If he cannot come back to life after too much booze, he is even less likely to do so after making himself into fuel for bonfire.

Nor can he take comfort, personally, from the thought of a hero's adulation from his fellow dissidents, who will prob-

ably ferret out base motives. A man who trails him around, hoping to write up a sensational newspaper story about suicide, mocks the narrator's artistic career: "You want to take your own life because you've had no success." Assuming similar motives for protest (pique or vanity), someone accuses the character "Konwicki" in the fictionalized autobiography *The Polish Complex:* "Your cunning is that of a minister of police, a great provocateur who wants to die on the cross. Your cunning is vile, elusive, exalted, dripping with sincerity, a foul sentimental attempt at sanctity aspiring to the tragic."

As for aiding the community, the "sanctimonious" deeds in either book—from refusing a state-sponsored book contract to burning oneself alive—do not topple the government. From the very first pages of *A Minor Apocalypse,* the Polish authorities and the Polish resistance blur: the narrator's friends, not the secret police, present the gasoline can. If dissidents cannot effectively change anything, they just further the suffering begun by the totalitarian system. But despite his lack of effect on the regime or even on the underground, whose members will probably sneer at his vanity rather than applaud his heroism, the narrator lights his match. Without effective ritual, he still makes the fruitless gesture. He does so for the sake of a modicum of self-respect, doubt-laden but precious. The dying god and individual surrogates go down, but only the secular, corporate state reasserts itself.

Tadeusz Konwicki with Dorota Sobieska (interview date 7 January 1991)

SOURCE: "'Everything comes from what I said at the beginning, from this territory': An Interview with Tadeusz Konwicki," in *Review of Contemporary Fiction,* Vol. XIV, No. 3, Fall, 1994, pp. 112-23.

[*In the following interview, originally conducted on January 7, 1991, Konwicki discusses geographical influences of his native territory on his writings and thought, his storytelling methods, the significance of animal symbolism in his works, the poetic quality of his prose, and his views on women.*]

[Dorota Sobieska:] *I have plenty of questions but would prefer this to be more of a conversation.*

[Tadeusz Konwicki:] Yes, but I have to have something to start with, and the best questions are silly because they give one a chance to say something. Clever questions always contain the answers themselves. Those very ambitious Polish scholars ask a question which goes on for ten minutes. . .

To which you answer "Yes" or "No."

That's right. Or, trying to be equal to a task, I begin to repeat myself, talk nonsense, things like that. So silly questions are the best.

In your writing about the territory you are from, there are usually two sides: the ideal one and the one full of conflicts between the nationalities living there. For instance, in **A Dreambook for Our Time** *you show the conflict between the Poles and the Lithuanians during the Second World War. What is happening there now and how do you feel about it?*

I don't feel particularly good about it; that is, I experience contradictory emotions because I root for both the Lithuanians and the Poles there, and they are in continuous strife against each other. This conflict subsides and then becomes aggravated again, and it is very painful to me because it is a result of various petty political games both in Lithuania and in Poland. And these matters are easy to solve, but only when there is good will on both sides. The case is very dramatic because the Poles there were under double occupation for fifty years: Soviet, but also to some extent Lithuanian. The whole Polish intelligentsia left this place—all the more active, more educated social classes repatriated themselves. Only peasants and workers stayed there, or that part of the intelligentsia that deteriorated because of persecutions. That is why they are weak, and that is why they opted for the Soviet system. On the other hand, Lithuanians were not in the best situation either. They were terribly persecuted right after the Second World War. Almost one third of their population was taken to Siberia. They put themselves together with great difficulty. But this is a very strong, hardened nation. These people are not at all like the Polish, but more like Scandinavians: hard-working, moderate, taciturn, stubborn, reliable. And of course, clearly, after those years of persecution, nationalism had to burst out, especially because their past is troubling from our point of view. After all, they opted for Germany in the last war. Their reasons of State could have been such that they had to hold with the Germans, but from the European point of view, and especially ours, it is troubling. So, both sides have their faults, various old hostilities. But when it comes down to the real conflict, it is like a quarrel between two villages. I come from the Wilno Colony, and there were the Upper and the Lower Colony. The Upper Colony was always rumbling with the Lower Colony. And this conflict with Lithuanians is, in fact, a domestic one because we are so intertwined ethnically, historically, culturally, and even, though it may not seem so, linguistically, because in Eastern Polish there are a great number of Lithuanian borrowings. I even take delight in using them. For instance, in the Wilno area, to say that we wanted "to ride on a sled," we used to say *wazyniac sie,* when *vaziuoti* in Lithuanian means "to travel, to ride." I use the word *dyrwan* for a "wasteland," to say that the boys are running or the geese are waddling on a *dyrwan.* This is

simply Lithuanian *dirvonas. Rojsty,* the title of one of my books, is simply *raistai,* which means "marshes, bogs." Similarly, in Lithuanian there are many Polish borrowings, and understandably so. All in all, everything compels us to become reconciled, to accept each other, and to make use of Wilno. Wilno in European culture means "so much." And I will remind America that many outstanding Americans, I am thinking here about movie directors, writers, journalists, actors, admit the descent which we can roughly call the tradition of the Grand Duchy of Lithuania.

You were there after the war.

I was. In 1956. I was there two days by a miracle because then the Soviet Union was still closed to us.

This is in **Kalendarz i Klepsydra,** *on your way back from China.*

That's right. It was the most unpleasant stay of all for me because Wilno was then completely Soviet, that is, an Asiatic city in which I recognized some architectonic traces dear to me. Even the natural surroundings were familiar. All of it, though, was swarming with Asiatics, this most unpleasant Russia, the czar's, from the end of the nineteenth century. My impressions then were terrible. It seemed to me that it was a lost cause. Years later, in 1988, I was there because of my film **Lava,** which is based on Adam Mickiewicz's *Forefathers,* and I saw Wilno a little recovered, in a somewhat better condition but still with obtrusive, importunate Russianness, which appears not only in the language, signs, clothes but in certain manners quite disagreeable to us. I was there a year later when I showed my finished **Lava** in the fall, and I saw a more Lithuanian city. On the streets one could see young Lithuanians perhaps even in the majority and could hear their language. Good-looking young people, with European aspirations, dressed like the rest of Europe. These were the good signs that I saw from the Lithuanian point of view. But from my point of view, I do not see any good signs; and I think that I will not be returning to Wilno if I don't have to. No . . . no, I won't be going because this city, or its appearance, is recorded in my memory as different. Even if it were supposedly a Polish city, and I visited it after a few decades, it would seem to me somehow alien. And because it is after all Lithuanian—even with these Polish, Jewish, or Belorussian enclaves—it is a city whose character is changed. This Wilno, which I remember, passed to the memory, to our European cultural archives. At the same time, I have to stress here that it lives splendidly in its new circumstances. There is a tremendous scholarly interest, especially among Slavists, Polish scholars from Europe, and European historians. Every so often they devote conferences to the culture of the prewar Polish Eastern borderland, where Europe clashed with what we used to call Asia, where the Latin culture met the Byzantine. This borderland was extremely fertile. And we know that all borderline territories are interesting. If we look at America, I, as an unprofessional observer, see that the American South is closest to this ethos. Why? Because of a mixture, a clash of cultures.

Every so often [scholars] devote conferences to the culture of the prewar Polish Eastern borderland, where Europe clashed with what we used to call Asia, where the Latin culture met the Byzantine. This borderland was extremely fertile. And we know that all borderline territories are interesting. If we look at America, I, as an unprofessional observer, see that the American South is closest to this ethos. Why? Because of a mixture, a clash of cultures.

—Tadeusz Konwicki

I am thinking even of the mentality based on a certain tradition: manor houses, large families, and family ties.

Here you extend the comparison which I talked about: that is, a certain form of feudalism met and interacted with contemporary capitalism, if we allow ourselves some Marxist ambitions to use these terms. Those similarities exist and I can feel them. When I watch American films that take place in the South or read books or even listen to their music, I can see traits of custom, some kind of distinct resemblances to our ethos, to our moral and cultural syndrome.

You often speak about yourself as "a guest," someone passing by. Is this connected with your place of birth or the passing of generations or what?

There are many reasons for that. First of all, you have to consider this geographical territory, this borderline, certain customs and morals connected to a certain mentality, and, even more, certain ethics. I am an orphan, and to be an orphan carried a special status there—even, in a way, a kind of profession. Families were interrelated, entangled; half of the Wilno country, I may say, were my relatives. So I was at someone else's house all of the time, at an aunt's or uncle's or grandparent's. This must have developed in me the habits of a vagrant. Another thing, when we observe these people's customs, we can see that in terms of civilization it was a backward European region—very fertile culturally but not at all industrially. Long distances scattered human settlements, difficult communication among people—all these formed certain attributes of one's character. For instance, self-restraint, a kind of asceticism. Religious life—I am thinking of my Catholic environment—was very austere. This religiousness was perhaps even more stern than the

Protestant. All this shaped a certain kind of man, his character, dignity, as well as his sense of humor, but above all asceticism. What is it? A lack of appetite of the kind that middle-class societies have, restraining, controlling it as something reprehensible. Pushing one's way through to be first or lying to show off was disgraceful. That's why I have no motives, like possessiveness, that middle-class societies have. I was relatively free here even in the worst times [the Stalinist period] because there was nothing to punish me with, there was nothing to take away from me—because I am not greedy, grasping, possessive, because I don't care about most things. That gives me freedom. That's why I can say that I am only passing by. I am not entangled in affairs, coteries, cliques, lobbies which fight for literary position and money. And in Poland there is always an especially fierce fight for the seat of the bard, the poet-prophet, the father of the nation.

But unlike in America, in Poland such a position exists.

Literature there does not have the national and messianic significance that it has in Poland, because in Poland literature's life-history is the life-history of maintaining this society's identity. Thanks to literature, this society somehow survived all its bad fortune, but this situation brought upon it awful habits, such as servility or the obligation that, like the Catholic church, it has to fight with fists raised against all enemies. Such a position lent literature wings, honor, position, but at the same time restricted it to expectations. So, summing up, with my disposition, I am outside the game of interests. I am an exceptional outsider, even though I show up in the city, make jokes, and so on; but I am excluded from the game, from all this. I do not participate in the exchange, the races. But it is not a bad position, and it's a voluntary one. I am in a way independent, though showing off one's independence is stupid because we all are dependent on the climate, Bush's whims, and I am even dependent on my wife of whom I am a little afraid. So the only thing is to diminish the degree of dependence.

You went through so many changes, periods like Wilno, partisan war, Stalinism, Gomulka, and so on. Now, with all the recent changes in Poland, a certain world has ended and a new epoch has begun. How do you feel in this new system of values?

As always. I was always the same. I felt the same before the war and in the partisan troops. I was also an outsider. Even though once I was in the Party, I was never a brilliant activist, but rather a nobody. But what's important is the question of what is happening apart from these political changes—it's astounding! We see that the so-called evil empire, which seemed impossible to shake or to crack, collapsed under its own weight. No American bombs or Marines crushed this empire; it fell under its own weight.

Yet another important thing is that the end of the century is coming and, what's worse, the end of the millennium. Those numbers are obviously arbitrary, but people nevertheless are influenced by them—the phenomenon of autosuggestion. And this affects our frame of mind, our decadence. But I think that the greatest influence on the second half of the twentieth century was World War II. And I think that the holocaust produced a continuous sense of guilt and despair, which is manifested in moral nihilism. All anarchistic movements, all trends of liberation from moral conventions—hippies and other movements of young people, women's or homosexuals' protests—all these resulted from the moral crash which happened during the war. All that edifice of human thought and morality which we had built for 2000 years suddenly tumbled down because of the Nazi genocide. And even you, the young, are born with the thread of hunger containing the sense of guilt that we all have, a sense that something happened not quite right, that these 2000 years of human efforts were wasted if such a catastrophe could occur. All these factors create the general unrest that we feel—that values are changing, that certain habits are breaking down, that generations appear that want to articulate something new but are unable. But we remember what Roitschwantz says in Ehrenburg's novel: if they dismiss one, it means that they will accept a new one—that if certain values break down, it means that right away new ones will appear because this is how the market of life operates. So I do not see any magical meanings in this time, do not exaggerate. I do not think that anything extraordinary is going on but only what always has happened in human destiny. I think that all generations that enter life resemble in their psychological profile individual people. I mean, there are hysterical generations and there are sober ones, ones with exuberant imagination and ones without any. It is as if you looked through the last hundred years and observed all these ways to live connected with the generation's frame of mind. That is why I do not believe in canons in art. There are none! This is chaos! Every generation creates its own canons. One generation likes this, and the next comes and likes something else. And we see it even in fashion, clothes. Now I watch films from the sixties and women's clothes appear to me terrible, but in fifteen, twenty years they will be attractive again.

Except, perhaps, shoes. They rarely come back.

As for shoes, I have a very peculiar attitude. Shoes were my childhood and youth complex. Why? Because we had immense snows in the Wilno country, and I was a passionate sportsman, and because of my boots, my feet were always wet from skiing or skating.

*In **Rojsty** (Marshes) this motif is omnipresent, like the young nurse whose feet are frozen.*

Where I lived, shoes had a biological-practical function.

They were necessary for life, whereas nowadays shoes are like gloves: chosen to match the clothes and thrown away after a while. They have moved from the practical sphere to the aesthetic.

But American shoes still tend to look practical.

That's right, because their civilization is a few centuries late. Their pioneers had to have solid boots, unlike Parisians who in the eighteenth century had pavements.

It doesn't befit you, an American, to accuse me, a Pole from Warsaw, of a money motif. All American art is based on the money syndrome—a little bit about sex, but money is the real issue.
— *Tadeusz Konwicki*

Coming back to the new system of values in Poland which is geared towards money. . .

It doesn't befit you, an American, to accuse me, a Pole from Warsaw, of a money motif. All American art is based on the money syndrome—a little bit about sex, but money is the real issue. So it is quite normal that money begins to play an important part here now. But I am anxious about something else, and that is the changes in our thinking conditioned by the Catholic church and even by rationalistic circles which were hidden, persecuted, inactive for decades and now have a chance to demonstrate themselves. These are unwelcome signs in a world afraid of nationalisms, smugness, and quarrelsome parochialism. But this seems to be temporary, too. This society was uncorked, like a bottle with a terribly fermented liquid. All the bubbles, gases, have to escape from this society. I think that the Polish intelligentsia, thanks to its tradition, is strong, and we are able to take control of our society's mentality, unlike the Russians who are afraid—the Russian intelligentsia still feels weak, though in my opinion it is strong. But its self-confidence is not very dynamic. They are afraid of these vast territories, these crowds which no rational thought can subdue. But we are not in such a bad position because we never lost strong ties with the West, with European and world thought.

Recently I read a long report by Ryszard Kapuscinski (a Polish journalist), who visited Russia, traveled there, and went to a mine because its workers were on strike. Then he came back to his friends who belonged to the Russian intelligentsia and asked them why they weren't there, why they did not formulate the workers' demands. They were puzzled at his questions. In Poland there were always some ties between the intelligentsia and the workers, but not in Russia.

That's what I am talking about. I think that the Russian intelligentsia is already strong, and only has to be more decided, has to have the will to want it. But we have to remember that there is a kind of global consciousness. Scientists already know about it, that we are like TV or radio sets connected with this global consciousness. And this global consciousness also affects Russia, and Russia has to yield to global moral, social, and intellectual processes. So it must not be too bad. Because if it is bad, the world will end. The so-called end of the world will come if we continually slide down. But because those biped mammals—those humans—are an awfully vital and resourceful species, I think that they will manage to persist and still pollute the air.

Coming back to some of the things you have said before, could we say that you are a Pole from the East?

It sounds better to me . . . but please hold this question because it is a good one. I would prefer to call myself a European from the East because of all my biography, my coming from this borderland. I am not a particularly zealous patriot, which is something that rankles the people here. But already public opinion has become somewhat used to my not being constantly serviceable in these matters. Of course I sympathize with those people who live by the Vistula river. I am very ambitious for them and often defend them when I see them suffering from injustice done them by other nations. But I am not a particularly fervent patriot. I feel myself to be a European, an inhabitant of this little piece of the big continent where so much started. I even feel emotional ties with America. In *Rzeka podziemna, podziemne ptaki* I write about Manhattan, which seems to me a torn-away piece of my Wilno country, a piece that sailed the ocean and now hangs beneath America's belly. I do not feel that America is strange or alien to me. Of course, this is also connected to the fact that America was created by immigrants and especially my countrymen, that is Belorussians, Jews, Poles, and others; whoever emigrated from these territories founded big movie companies, newspapers, theaters, business, clothes production. . .

So you say, your countrymen Belorussians, Lithuanians. . .

Tartars. . .

Jews, Karaites. . .

That's right.

Russians?

Here an ignorant Pole awakes in me. Here, I feel a certain reserve . . . even more so because Russian culture is captivating, and I am under its huge influence.

As you wrote in **Moonrise, Moonset,** *you are a "hideous hybrid formed at the boundary of two worlds," that is Polish and Russian.*

I like Russianness. I feel an unhealthy attraction to it, and that is why I recoil from saying such things, because this Russianness was a mortal threat to us. That is why I hesitated here, and restrained my enthusiasm for Russia. But indeed yes! Indeed yes! I remember once I was in San Francisco, invited by the Department of State. They ask me, "What would you like to see? There is a film festival in San Francisco." "What do they show?" "Tarkowski's *Rublov.*" I never saw it before and was not really inclined to. I say, "Of course," and go. Some kind of a hall divided by a cherry-red curtain. The festival was very modest, to say the least. The audience stands waiting. A thousand White Russians stand in their coats with their velvet collars from the czar's times. They chat. They came to see a Russian film. I am there alone, unexpectedly, because the only Americans are ushers. And I almost cannot resist shouting "Hey, there, listen! I am your man, I am one of you!" So this is clear proof of how many threads intertwine in me. And, I have to confess, I think that's good . . . that's good. This is where Europe is going. That is, I would have liked it best if we had a Europe of regions, so that villages would fight rather than countries, like the Upper Colony with the Lower Colony—those from the other village pick up our girls, so we have to beat them black and blue—not that wars are fought for some bombastic ideological principles.

I have a couple of questions connected with Mickiewicz and his Polish national epic Pan Tadeusz. *Let's take the very beginning of it: "Lithuania, my fatherland!" A Pole will say that, of course, it is Polish, and so is Mickiewicz, whereas a Lithuanian will say without hesitation that he is Lithuanian.*

Aleksander Malachowski, a journalist and a member of the Parliament, once said very nicely about Mickiewicz: half-Jew, half-Belorussian, the greatest Polish poet, begins his epic with the words "Lithuania, my fatherland!" And that is the essence of what I am telling you from the very beginning about all these matters and myself.

While reading your **Bohin Manor,** *I had a feeling that it was written in direct relation to* Pan Tadeusz, *perhaps because of a manor house, a Jew who is an important character.*

Elias here is, in fact, a test. I wanted to see how our public opinion would receive this love story, how deep our anti-Semitism runs. The test came out all right. The novel was well received even though I designed the love story somewhat disturbingly: a woman from Polish nobility with a Jew. But of course all these circumstances, landscapes, moods.

The action takes place several decades after Mickiewicz's times. In this territory things didn't change so fast, not civilization nor custom nor ways of thinking. I didn't have to do any research, check what dishes they used or how they traveled because I still remember from my childhood Mickiewicz's world and because the nineteenth century in the Wilno country ended in 1939.

I had a similar feeling reading a book of interviews with Milosz when he spoke about this territory.

He is a stray! He is from the Kowno region in Lithuania! From the Niewiaza river. He came to Wilno as a grown boy. So he is not a native of Wilno. He is a Lithuanian.

You see, I can't see the difference.

How's that? Because you, poor Poles, when you hear his poem about his homeland to which he will never come back, you think that he writes about Poland. No! He writes about Lithuania from the thirties! The homeland to which he will never come back is the Kowno Lithuania, the country on the Niewiaza.

With Poles, it is like this: whoever speaks Polish is a Pole. But where you come from, because so many languages coexist, perhaps the territory defines one's belonging.

Of course language determines man somehow, his homeland, but not necessarily his nationality. Anyway, all this will not matter in the future when probably all of us will have to speak in English, in this terrible pidgin language of languages. In that language everything is upside down. You can't pronounce one word normally, not even *Jesus Christ.* A certain Englishman told my friend who had a speech defect that he would speak English well because he didn't open his mouth.

Are you biased against this language?

No, I just cannot learn it! I passionately tried, and the more I studied English, the better I spoke Russian.

To change the subject, what is Puszkarnia in your books?

You see, everybody invents magic places, like the Mormons who have their mountain where, they believe, the world will end; and I've got from them a piece of rock from this mountain. Every society tries to make its life more magical, to grant it a greater value than the obvious, and they especially do it to some places. And this is, in fact, justified by history. Certain places that were considered magic proved to be volcanic or, like the Suwalki region, spread over uranium deposits. They affected human life. The belief that the earth influences human life is called tellurism. Every civilization creates for itself such magic places, like Mount Sinai. And I, sinfully, allowed myself to invent a few places, like the Wilno Colony, Puszkarnia, the French Mill, which is already starting to catch on in Europe, and I am very proud of it. Some English and French think that Puszkarnia exists and that something good is there.

That God dwells there?

Once I heard the greatest compliment. A reader of mine wrote to me that after one of my films, her four-year-old son said: "Mom, at night I dreamed of Puszkarnia," which he didn't know, never was there, but his imagination was inspired in the direction so dear to me.

But factually, what was Puszkarnia?

Probably it is an old place of manufacture, a primitive factory from precapitalist times. They must have produced artillery there in the eighteenth century. And this name survived even though Puszkarnia now bears only traces of something old. Besides, all these symbolic places are our nostalgia for the passing of time. We enjoy finding signs of old life.

Staying with this territory, I would like to ask you about the storytelling that you mention in **New World Avenue and Vicinity.**

This is my audacity of a sort which comes from my belief that I invented a new literary genre or subgenre. I am so used to diaries, memoirs, journals in literature. So I invented an intermediate form, a loose stream of memories, quotations, sudden recollections and digressions. They also have their justification relating to the customs and geography. If you imagine a wooded area where human settlements are scattered over several miles, where the nearest train station is forty miles away, where communication is so difficult, where everywhere around is a forest, where mail is always late, where you have no bookstores, theaters, gramophones, then forms of entertainment are restricted. People visit one another during holidays, come for Christmas or a wedding or a name day, and it lasts for a week. Then, what is the most enjoyable way to cheat time, apart from music? A talent to tell stories. There is always someone who was somewhere far away in the world or rather who knows circulating stories about legendary figures. I spend my vacation on the Hel Peninsula. One of the houses there is called America, and the guy who lives there, a Kashubian, is called America because he was in America and came back. He got a label for life. Somebody was in America, somebody else was in France or fought in Caucasus—they were substitutes for books, readings, radio programs, or even movies. So this form, this ability to confabulate, was common. And also, the language was bewitching, compared to central literary Polish, because it had all these influences—Lithuanian,

Belorussian, Jewish, and even Russian. It was melodious, from the borderland, gaining some sounds that central Polish never had, as the disappearance of nasal vowels. It was a language, so to say, not quarrelsome, not verbose, in love with detail, with an extremely musical, songlike intonation. All this constituted the form that I ingeniously attribute to myself but that was used by Wankowicz and many others, not to mention our dear Adam Mickiewicz, who in *Pan Tadeusz* created a model for the following generations. Period.

*In your novels you seem to use repetitively certain short expressions, such as "Achilles who some day will be a superb professor," or "a man who was eating a hard-boiled egg" in **Nic albo nic**. A name is followed by a short expression identifying this person. Were such formulaic expressions used in the storytelling you speak about?*

The point is that my generation is aware of its fate all at once. There is no way to forget the whole biography and no way to avoid saying about the man who was eating a hard-boiled egg that he had been in Auschwitz or that this woman, so well-dressed and perfumed with Chanel, survived a Siberian labor camp. So the seal of our biography, complicated and stormy, dictates such style and even the collage form.

Your personal biography or historical?

Of our generation. I mean biographies with war, the ideological change, crucial questions, constant wrestling with the ultimate, which an American middle-class man never faces. He can only have his house burned, or a car can hit him on a street.

But they also have such literary forms as a collage.

Yes, but for them these forms are only a literary fashion. There is no dread behind them, no real life experience.

Perhaps I should have been more specific about the storytelling you talked about. Such a folk tradition. . .

Of nobility, gentry.

There was a tradition of storytelling in Yugoslavia, a tradition of long epic poems recited from memory. There are records and books about it. These poems used formulaic expressions that remind me of the ones you sometimes use.

I invented all this to make things more interesting. I never followed any storytelling model. It is characteristic of my style to charm, chat, contradict, leap, question, speak with self-irony, and just to make it look nice, I couch it in a literary-historical thesis. It doesn't pay off to make much of my stories.

How's that?

I am very convincing even when I pull your leg.

So there was nothing like that at all?

See, I said it so well that now you defend it. Go ahead, we have to finish.

All right . . . three more questions. The first one is about animals which so often show up in your novels, especially in **The Anthropos-Specter-Beast.** *What are the reasons for your feeling toward animals? Your past?*

Of course. Everything comes from what I said at the beginning, from this territory. We were afraid of wolves all my childhood and youth. As a partisan in the winter of 1944-45, I still heard those packs of howling wolves around in the woods. Household animals were real members of the household. They were people, even though our stern religion forbade us to anthropomorphize animals. It was even a serious sin from the canonical point of view. But we anthropomorphized them anyway because those animals lived with us all the time. They were not like your dandy, doted-on lap dogs, but they worked together with us. A dog was guarding a house or drove the cows to pastures, a cat was catching mice, horses worked, cows gave milk. These animals shared our fate. That is why our approach to animals is not like yours, Western Europeans, not patronizing or falsely sentimental, but matter-of-fact. I could hit a dog with a stone, but a dog could bite my calf. We were equals; that is, we didn't hold mutual grudges. So the presence of animals was very important, including wild animals that had magic meaning connected with the woods. You have to remember that Lithuania received baptism by the end of the fourteenth century, four centuries later than Poland, even more than that. And paganism in custom and the subconscious is still there in certain relics. The woods, for instance, were sacred. Oaks, snakes, streams, marshes, forest vapors—all these things were very significant in our life. Even today, I live very well with trees. To me, every tree has its own personality. One is wounded, another rustles with melancholy, another is brisk, full of life. I've read *Perpetual Motion,* a book by a Canadian writer, Graeme Gibson, and was struck by elements of nature similar to *Wuthering Heights.* The same thing was revived among inhabitants of Canada. So we have something in common, as opposed to the townspeople, who don't see trees or even birds.

The acacia in your books has its own life.

That's right.

I am thinking again of what you've said in **New World Avenue and Vicinity:** *"I can't break away from that Wilno,* *from that hybrid land that is both Lithuania and Belorussia and neither" or "If any time in my future life I am caught mentioning the Wilno Colony, the Wilno country, or Lithuania once more, let the nearest passerby shoot me without mercy."*

True, but no one wants to. They nag me all the time to speak on those topics.

So there may be real value in them.

I said, I am a European, and I don't want to be a regional bandore player.

But I don't see any contradiction.

Exactly, you said it right. I want those topics to be universally relevant.

A British poet, Philip Larkin, said once that he quit writing novels because novels are about other people whereas poetry is about oneself. If we go with this distinction, can we call your books poetic?

Technically, yes. I write about myself because I came to the conclusion that I am most competent in this sphere. Even if I create various characters, make a plot, some chain of events, everything is saturated with me. I am present all the time, to formulate, mold, remind the reader that it's me. I staked my writing on that. I think that, in the terrible chaos we have now, objective, transparent prose has to perish because it will be replaced by more perfect forms, like film or television. Only a person can arouse other people's interest in societal relations. Some people are fascinating, others are old bores. We want to be with some, and we run away from others. So I charm the reader all the time and satiate him with myself, and in this way I use poetic technique. And that's the only thing worth doing, as opposed to describing the world that we get every day from millions of TV news programs, journalists, photographs, newspaper reports. We know this world inside out. We have enough dead bodies in Yugoslavia, Georgia, Palestine, or anywhere else. Finally we are haunted by a thirst to find some universal sense in all that happens. And that's what poetry likes.

My last question is really a set of questions about the portrait of women in your. . .

Women are an element of beauty, loveliness, and pleasantness in the world. And many people, I don't say all, need beauty in life. For some, valuables, trumpery, and golden glare are enough, but not for others. I talked about trees or the sky. A woman also, in her gesture, movements, silhouette, has something that makes a man stop, arrested, and look. Of course what I am saying is very old-fashioned. Now we have "unisex," and a woman loses her femininity. Maybe this is a defense mechanism against excessive population. Something happened, and maybe it's God's gift, that women today have a different function, more utilitarian. For my generation, a woman was first of all a mystery. Secondly, she had her inscrutable dignity. And that is why for my generation, love was not just copulative acts but a whole big procedure, strife, the magic of winning this loveliness, this drop of beauty in our world, to use great words. I belong to the generation intrigued by women. To give a vulgar example, if I see beautiful women on our sidewalk, which is the New World Avenue, I, as an elderly man, look after her, unlike young men. So it's a pity that the magic place of women in our life got lost. We only have women friends, buddies, guardians, stepmothers, foster mothers. The world lost so much, but I suppose only for a while. As I said, together with Roitschwantz, if they dismiss one, they will accept a new one. If they lost their interest, then maybe they will soon start to love women hysterically.

But from the point of view of American feminism. . .

Why spoil this nice final note! Why look for what feminists. . . . I will tell you the truth. Feminists will die a natural death because they are ugly, ungainly, and won't have children and will become extinct. And only beautiful girls will remain who will be feminists only so much as need be. Thank you, we have to go.

Thank you, too.

Stanislaw Baranczak (review date 27 January 1991)

SOURCE: "Poland's Jester in Chief," in *New York Times Book Review*, January 27, 1991, p. 25.

[*In the following review, Baranczak locates the tenor of Konwicki's views in* New World Avenue *in the tradition of the jester role, focusing on the paradoxical thematic and stylistic tone of the memoir.*]

In 1959 the Polish philosopher Leszek Kolakowski published a trailblazing essay, "The Priest and the Jester." The two personifications stood for the two opposed strategies of modern intellectuals—conservative celebration of absolute values and critical questioning of them. Mr. Kolakowski himself chose the jester because, in his view, the jester's seemingly insolent and cynical "vigilance against any absolute" offered, paradoxically, the only chance to save humanity's endangered values, to provide for "goodness without universal toleration, courage without fanaticism, intelligence without discouragement, and hope without blindness."

Now that three decades have passed since Mr. Kolakowski's pronouncement, his coeval and compatriot, Tadeusz Konwicki, looms as Jester in Chief of Polish literature, an almost perfect embodiment of those four qualities. To be sure, the attitude of "vigilance against any absolute," along with its stylistic counterparts—a characteristically deflated tone, ironic detachment and propensity for the grotesque— have served as an identifying mark not just for him but for a much larger trend that dominated Polish letters during the last decades of Communist rule. Mr. Konwicki, however, has given this attitude its most memorable expression. He has done so mostly in his fiction: no history of literature of the now defunct People's Poland will ever omit *The Polish Complex* or *A Minor Apocalypse,* with their unforgettably absurd images of a mile-long queue functioning as society in miniature or of a dissident writer roaming Warsaw in search of matches needed for his self-immolation on the steps of the Palace of Culture. But Mr. Konwicki has also written several books of nonfiction, or, to be exact, books that at least pretend to belong in the category of "literature of fact."

"Literature of fact. I am the fact of my literature," Mr. Konwicki remarks curtly in *New World Avenue and Vicinity,* and this minimalist definition is true of each of his non-novelistic works. Within their sequence—which before *New World Avenue* included [*Kalendarz i klepsydra* (*The Calendar and the Hourglass*)], which has not been translated yet; [*Rzeka podziemna, podziemne ptaki* (*Underground River, Underground Birds*)], and *Moonrise, Moonset,* all four originally published over the 10-year span of 1976 to 1986—each book represents, more than anything else, the genre of a writer's diary, in the capacious and flexible sense given this term in the Polish modern tradition by the legendary *Diary* of Witold Gombrowicz.

The only two stable characteristics of this sort of diary are its formal diversity on one hand and its strictly subjective thematic focus and narrative perspective on the other. Just like Gombrowicz, who famously began his diary with the impudent *"Monday:* Me. *Tuesday:* Me. *Wednesday:* Me. *Thursday:* Me," Mr. Konwicki never lets us forget that his writing, all its apparent thematic variety notwithstanding, revolves constantly around the subject he knows best: himself. He can be provocatively, if not downright obnoxiously, self-centered, whimsical, obsessive, moody, inconsistent, even repetitive and overly emotional; but he never pretends to impose on us any truth other than the truth of his own individual perception.

But this does not mean that from his egotistic perspective only the inner landscape of his soul can be scanned. On the contrary, the central paradox of his diaristic nonfiction lies in the fact that instead of narrowing the field of observation, such an individualistic point of view broadens it remarkably.

While reading *New World Avenue* in Walter Arndt's excellent translation, we are in Mr. Konwicki's company without a moment's respite, but that would be wearisome only if he were a boring interlocutor.

He is anything but. True, he does his best to irritate us with his grouchy tone and general disgust with outside reality. This attitude, however, seems justified enough when we realize that Mr. Konwicki's book was written in Warsaw in the mid-1980's. Its obsessively self-centered nature seems to result at least in part from the author's agoraphobic reaction to the hostility seething in the surrounding world. His apartment is near the downtown street called in the optimistic 18th century—certainly with no irony intended—New World Avenue. But it is enough for Mr. Konwicki to step outside to see unmistakably what the Polish new world has come to at this last stage of the decline of the 20th-century utopia: he risks either being drenched by a water cannon spraying still another street demonstration, or mugged by one of the neighborhood junkies desperately in need of a high. It is no accident that the book's only positive hero is the author's cat; apart from isolated figures of relatives and friends from the past, the human inhabitants of the sick country and the sick world of the present do not arouse much sympathy in him.

Yet Mr. Konwicki's grumpiness, at times perilously near to whining, turns out to be just the outward sign of his usual "vigilance against any absolute." *Any* absolute, not just the dubious dogmas of declining Communism but also the most sacred stereotypes of its nationalistic or theocratic potential replacements. He may be a grim and despairing jester, but he never resigns the jester's privilege to say aloud what others pass over in safe silence, however unpleasant such truths may be.

[Konwicki's] idiosyncratic viewpoint allows him to address freely—precisely in a manner of a jester who does not care whether he offends anybody—the most urgent political and moral issues of the 80's.
—*Stanislaw Baranczak*

He by no means turns away from the disgusting reality; rather, like a student of anatomy dissecting an odious frog, he cuts through its slimy surface to examine how its muscles and inner organs work. His idiosyncratic viewpoint allows him to address freely—precisely in a manner of a jester who does not care whether he offends anybody—the most urgent political and moral issues of the 80's. And to emphasize that he is oblivious to offense, he occasionally ridicules or lampoons the Government censor himself: "I know that Mr. Censor has been squirming on his stool for a good while now.

Every moment he reaches for his blue pencil to put an exclamation mark here, underline a whole sentence there, mark a spot of pollution at the margin elsewhere. I know that Mr. Censor is now wrestling with competing thoughts: to take out the whole section or only delete what might offend or incense somebody or even provoke a telephone call."

The apparently hopeless predicament of Poland, whose martial-law rulers painted themselves into a corner of prolonged social crisis, is just the most immediate of those issues. Another is "the great paroxysm of democracy which runs through the world" and may not only bring relief to the enslaved nations but also unleash the dark forces of hatred lurking in their midst. The People's Poland, as well as the rest of the old East bloc, is happily gone; yet Mr. Konwicki's remarks on what may happen to Central European nations as a side effect of "the great paroxysm of democracy" sound almost prophetic today. This book's diagnoses and warnings, tied down so strongly to a specific time and place, have by no means lost their validity with the disappearance of the last water cannon from New World Avenue.

Reuel K. Wilson (review date Summer 1991)

SOURCE: A review of *Bohin Manor,* in *World Literature Today,* Vol. 65, No. 3, Summer, 1991, p. 514.

[*In the following review, Wilson draws thematic parallels between* Bohin Manor *and Konwicki's other works.*]

Tadeusz Konwicki, a prolific writer with a tendency obsessively to return to his roots in formerly Polish Lithuania, has in the last decade become a major spokesman for his compatriots' sense of collective despair and impotence. Now that the Soviet Union is no longer inclined to play its traditional role of oppressor vis-à-vis its long-suffering but always unbending western neighbor, one wonders what will become the new target for Konwicki's acerbic wit and biting irony. *Bohin Manor* represents a daring attempt to conjure up a person, the writer's own grandmother Helena Konwicki, and a past epoch. The genre he chooses resembles the historical romance; the sometimes turgid style recalls modernism, as does the imagery, which also suggests magic realism; and the vocabulary, abundant in quaint and often Belorussified regionalisms, strikes a genuinely authentic note (which cannot, unhappily, be captured in translation). Konwicki knows how to set the stage well, for he has a keen sense of the apt cinematic moment. (Nota bene: Konwicki has for years gravitated in and out of time, both as writer and director.)

The novel's viewpoint is primarily that of the author's grandmother as he would imagine her at age thirty. As the novel opens, she is a handsome and thoughtful virgin whom life

has bypassed since the death of her fiancé in the insurrection of 1863. As the story unfolds, Konwicki the narrator occasionally interrupts to voice his own opinions on Poland's destiny, his role as narrator, or the meaninglessness of existence. Almost inevitably, his sense of taedium vitae coincides with that of his persona; in addition both share a sense of cosmic consciousness, which intuits an existential void in the cold, jarring confines of intergalactic space—a motif perhaps all too familiar to readers of Konwicki's other recent work.

Helena inhabits a rural backwater that is haunted by the ghosts of the past and menaced by the dark forces of the evil to come. Both Stalin and Hitler have roles to play within the novel's surrealist framework. Helena belongs to the rural gentry which is, at the same time, an ethnic minority: i.e., the Poles in Lithuania, whom history has marked for persecution and eventual banishment. Perhaps these Polish gentlefolk partly deserve their fate, Konwicki implies by showing Helena's aristocratic suitor Alexander Broel-Plater as a cynical degenerate and portraying her father Michael as a proud, self-martyrizing fanatic. All live under the shadow of the unsuccessful rebellion against Russia in 1863, and many (including the wealthy neighbor who has Russified his name as a mark of his collaboration with the Russian authorities and now, half-crazed, seeks for a way to expunge his guilt) bear the permanent scars of defeat, humiliation, and reprisal.

For Helena the horizon looms darkly with portents of apocalyptic events, and her sense of bitter futility closely parallels the narrator's own. Imminent apocalypse is also the central theme of Konwicki's two previous novels, *The Polish Complex* and *A Minor Apocalypse* (see respectively *WLT* 56:4 and 54:2). The dreamlike atmosphere, a trademark of Konwicki's style, can be evocative and spellbinding: as in the novels of Thomas Hardy (whose black pessimism Konwicki shares), nature plays an important role, reflecting human emotions, providing symbolic accompaniment to the action, but never affording respite or solace.

In making Elias Szyra, a young Jewish wanderer, the hero (and a very romantic one at that), Konwicki reflects a preoccupation with Jewish themes, to be found as well in two outstanding Polish novels also published in the second half of the last decade. These are: Pawel Huelle's *Weisser Dawidek* and Hanna Krall's *Sublokatorka.* All three writers deal with the conflicting nature of Jewish and Polish identities. The two groups are shown as inseparably bound yet irreconcilably different; both resort to extravagant and creative mythmaking in the struggle for self-preservation and assertion. Konwicki has his grandmother Helena bear a child (his future parent) by Szyra, thereby implying a solidarity, sealed by affinity, with the star-crossed fates of Polish Jewry.

All in all, the novel's characters work well within the very intentionally structured universe of the writer's literary imagination. They represent a loving re-creation of a patriarchal and cruel past. Seen from the vantage point of Warsaw in the 1980s, they are neither to be pitied nor to be envied.

Reuel K. Wilson (review date Autumn 1991)

SOURCE: A review of *New World Avenue and Vicinity,* in *World Literature Today,* Vol. 65, No. 4, Autumn, 1991, p. 734.

[*In the review below, Wilson describes the subject, tone, and style of* New World Avenue.]

Today Tadeusz Konwicki is one of Poland's most respected literary personalities. He loves conversation and is known for his acerbic wit, often expressed over coffee at the little café located in the basement of his Warsaw publisher, Czytelnik. Czytelnik's offices are a hop, skip, and a jump away from the Nowy Swiat (New World Avenue), the focal point of the writer's present existence. The busy thoroughfare with its old-fashioned charm and modern vitality contrasts with Konwicki's other main creative axis: prewar Wilno (Vilnius) and its environs, where the writer grew up and which he left in 1945 after participating in the underground resistance movement. When Konwicki evokes nature in his work, he tends to re-create (and idealize) the eastern landscape of his youth. The miscellaneous sketches collected here, numbering over fifty and all written in the first person, are anecdotal. Some recall his childhood in Polish Lithuania and his adoptive parents, great-uncle and -aunt Blinstrub; others remember with affection such departed colleagues and friends as Slonimski and Dygat.

Unlike most of Konwicki's recent work, which appeared underground in Poland and above ground only in the West, *New World Avenue* was first published by Czytelnik in 1986. The author wrote it for official publication, and he often turns to the censor, perhaps his most demanding reader, with disingenuous apologies for remarks critical of the then-reigning Communist Party and its failed policies. Autocensorship, he suggests, is the most invidious of all, for it turns the writer into a silent partner to authoritarian power. Konwicki's sense of taedium vitae comes from alienation and isolation. He is purportedly writing after his wife has left to visit their daughter in the United States. He remains behind to take care of the family cat Ivan. Like his aging master, Ivan accepts with equanimity the encroachments of time upon his physical powers. Living in the grim days of the middle 1980s, Konwicki finds solace in stoic pessimism. The world around him offers few blandishments: natural beauty is rapidly succumbing to rampant commercialism; free thought is stifled by the harsh exigencies of martial law. For Konwicki the meaning of life is unknowable, at least in the short term. He inhabits a world where all the previous fixed ethical codes have failed in one way or another. Unhappy with an unraveling present and lacking a cohesive vision for the future, he grins sardonically and rails against the ignorance and weakness of his fellows. He also seeks escape from the absurd of the present in imaginary re-creations of the past or childish fantasies of erotic adventure (**"She"**) or exotic travel (**"The Southern Cross"**). The writer warns us against taking him too seriously: he pokes fun at his readers, deprecates himself in order to amuse them.

When moved to do so, Konwicki can write very powerfully. The piece entitled **"Resurrection"** shows him at his narrative best. The scene is the intensive-care cardiac section of a Warsaw hospital. Konwicki, a patient in the ward, witnesses the miraculous reanimation of a beefy metalworker whose heart stops beating shortly after his arrival. Using outmoded and unreliable equipment, the staff works over the patient with incredible speed, efficiency, and determination. The tone moves effortlessly from bathos to pathos, from grotesque exaggeration to poetic hyperbole. The narrator marvels at the doctors' and nurses' selfless dedication to saving human life, yet the last sentence reads: "Unwittingly, he [the patient] had already been where one awaits the Last Judgement, and unwittingly he had made the leap back into the chill fires of our hell." In **"The Southern Cross,"** the book's final chapter, Konwicki tempers his pessimism by affirming the power of reason and human intellect—qualities that may someday unlock the mysteries of the universe.

The author's little pen-and-ink sketches fit in nicely with the text. The unpretentious, somewhat idealizing drawings portray the writer, his cat, New World Avenue, and other people and places that have been significant to him over the years. A word on the translation, which is accurate and fairly well replicates the writer's rhetorical tonalities: unfortunately it does not always reflect Konwicki's preference for lexical simplicity. Walter Arndt likes to substitute recherché words for simple direct ones: *ksialeczki* (little books) becomes "little screeds"; *kurwy* (whores) becomes "trollops"; *dziki* (wild) becomes "feral"; *nowy czlowiek* becomes "tyro" when "novice" would have served; and so on. Some of the vocabulary sounds British to the American ear, yet the translator occasionally resorts to Americanisms to render the colloquial prose of the original. Finally, the chapter entitled **"Portret epizodzisty"** has been misinterpreted to read **"Portrait of a Short Story Writer."** Since the central figure here is not a writer but an actor with a genius for creating episodic roles, especially off camera, perhaps "Portrait of a Great Minor Actor" would be more appropriate.

Henry Dasko (essay date Fall 1994)

SOURCE: "A Note on Konwicki's Filmmaking," in *Review of Contemporary Fiction,* Vol. XIV, No. 3, Fall, 1994, pp. 197-200.

[*In the essay below, Dasko provides an overview of Konwicki's filmmaking.*]

Tadeusz Konwicki's filmmaking adventure, now well into its fourth decade, is not a common scenario. While film directors frequently cross over into literature, if only to coauthor a screenplay, few novelists are ever offered a chance to stand behind a camera. In neither craft is Konwicki a journeyman; in fact, his accomplishments as a writer place him firmly in the august circle of those European men of letters whose voices ring with unchallenged spiritual and artistic authority. Yet, time after time, he would continue to reach beyond his traditional, verbal universe and seek to express himself within the world of the visual.

Konwicki's arrival into the international film community could not pass unnoticed; while he had previously written two screenplays of no special merit, his directorial debut, *Ostatni dzien lata* (*The Last Day of Summer*), unexpectedly took top honors at the 1958 International Short Film Festival in Venice. A Polish film critic remembered a decade later, "They sent the worst print available, and the credits didn't even get translated. There was no advertising of any kind and nobody had any information about this film."

The tersely scripted drama synthesized the elements of Europe's existentialist torment of the late fifties: the scars of a not-so-distant war and the fear of a nuclear future. Shot in stark black and white, it featured only two characters, both unnamed. Curiously, of all the films he was to later direct, *Ostatni dzien lata* remains Konwicki's only truly universal work, unburdened by cultural symbols and historical references only Poles are able to decipher.

Curiously, of all the films he was to later direct, *Ostatni dzien lata* remains Konwicki's only truly universal work, unburdened by cultural symbols and historical references only Poles are able to decipher.
—Henry Dasko

Throughout the sixties and early seventies, Konwicki's literary and film endeavors were generally homogeneous: to a large extent, his films from that period are a visual exposition of his literary projects. Like the novels, the movies reflect the author's own biography and Poland's tortured history. In fact, the leitmotivs within three of Konwicki's films from that period are clearly traceable to the subplots within his seminal 1963 novel *A Dreambook for Our Time.*

Both as a novelist and as a filmmaker, Konwicki believes in being defined by one's past and origins. Thus, he repeatedly and obsessively recalls Poland's Eastern Borderlands, where he spent childhood and adolescence, World War II, in which he fought with the underground resistance movement, against first the Germans, then the Russians, and, equally important, the complex years of postwar Stalinist Poland.

The three films Konwicki directed during that period, *Zaduszki* (*All Souls' Day,* 1961), *Salto* (*Somersault,* 1965), and *Jak daleko stad, jak blisko* (*So Far and Yet So Near,* 1971), are a commentary on the complex fate of his generation. Critics agree that events from his own biography play a major and recurring role in all three pictures. The same visitors and episodes from the time long gone repeatedly intrude into the present; the past, a shadow one cannot outrun, continues to explode in memories of life's crucial events. As Konwicki commented in a 1985 interview, "There are perhaps no more than five or six important moments in anyone's life."

With each subsequent picture, Konwicki's plots appear less and less linear, the structures more meandering, the protagonists harder to name and define. Because all of his heroes are evocative of the director himself, they too continue living in constant awareness of the past, sharing the nightmares and demons Konwicki is unable to leave behind.

In *Zaduszki* the two principal characters, a man and a woman, find their ability to love each other crippled by recollections of tragic, youthful love affairs they each experienced during the war. In *Salto* the memories of a wartime execution are no longer flashbacks but appear as a series of nightmarish dreams, edging closer and closer to reality. In *Jak daleko stad, jak blisko,* his last film of the series, Konwicki freely transcends the limits of time and space. Orthodox Jews from a pre-Holocaust shtetl populate 1970s Warsaw; the protagonist, perhaps the director's alter ego, moves through the city dressed impeccably in a shirt and tie but with a partisan's submachine gun concealed underneath a Harris-tweed sportcoat. As one Polish critic points out, Konwicki's films are the last requiem for a world that has gone out without a farewell yet is kept alive by the process of artistic narrative.

Since the mid-sixties, Konwicki has made his voice heard with clarity and strength on the side of Poland's fledgling opposition movement, in which intellectuals play a prominent role. This resulted in his films being only grudgingly allowed into distribution in the state-owned theater network;

Jak daleko stad, Jak blisko, hailed by film critics as his finest, received hardly any public screenings at all. Consequently, Konwicki's popularity as a director never really matched his status as a writer. His elitist movies were never destined to become major box-office hits, although *Salto* and *Jak daleko stad, jak blisko* developed a cultlike following among Konwicki's army of aficionados.

During the late seventies, Konwicki no longer submitted his books to Poland's official publishing houses, and several of his novels were brought out by underground publishers. This meant an automatic ban on any independent film work in a severely censored, government-sponsored industry. It was only after the emergence of Solidarity that Konwicki was able to return to filmmaking.

In the eighties Konwicki no longer adapted his own original material but instead brought to the screen two important works belonging to the canon of Polish literature. In 1982 he directed *Dolina Issy* (*The Issa Valley*), based on Czeslaw Milosz's semi-autobiographical novel. Like Konwicki, Milosz grew up in the Wilno region, now Lithuania but before World War II a part of Poland's Eastern Borderlands, which were ceded to the Soviet Union in 1944.

Loss of the Borderlands, a territory over which the Poles fought innumerable wars for half of their recorded history, has left a deep, unhealed wound in the Polish national psyche. A nonsubject in communist Poland, it nevertheless reverberates throughout Konwicki's entire literary output. *Dolina Issy,* a dark film of extraordinary beauty, combines Konwicki's narrative skill with Milosz's poetic vision of a mystical world suspended in an almost pagan past, oblivious of the storms blown in by the twentieth century.

Konwicki's most recent picture *Lawa* (*Lava,* 1989), is a screen adaptation of *Forefathers,* a nineteenth-century drama by Adam Mickiewicz, which to Poles remains a patriotic icon of unparalleled magnitude. Mickiewicz's work depicts Poland under the Russian rule during the nineteenth century; Konwicki's *Lawa,* produced during the final months of communist rule in Poland, carried both a message of hope and a powerful historical analogy.

Konwicki has said repeatedly that he is tired of making films and has no plans to return to directing. Still, his books continue to attract other filmmakers. In 1985 Andrzej Wajda filmed *Kronika wypadków milosnych* (*Chronicle of Love Events*), with Konwicki himself appearing in the movie. Konwicki's 1985 political novel, *A Minor Apocalypse,* is presently being filmed with an international cast by Constantin Costa-Gavras.

Konwicki is a symbolist, and the subject of his narrative is individual memory. He offers no happy endings and, usu-

ally, no solutions to the moral dilemmas his protagonists face. Unquestionably, he is an artist of splendid technical skills. Yet it isn't the sheer technique but rather his ability to make the most individual, subtle, and private experience relevant to the collective that has brought Konwicki his fame.

Edward Mozejko　(essay date Fall 1994)

SOURCE: "Beyond Ideology: The Prose of Tadeusz Konwicki," in *Review of Contemporary Fiction,* Vol. XIV, No. 3, Fall, 1994, pp. 139-55.

[*In the following essay, Mozejko traces the evolution of Konwicki's literary career, outlining the thematic and formal features that define his narrative discourse.*]

In many ways Tadeusz Konwicki (born in 1926) is a typical example of a writer who entered mature life in Poland after the establishment of the communist dictatorship in 1945. His writing underwent a gradual transformation from socialist realism, which he embraced as his "creative method" in the late forties and early fifties, to a complete rejection of socialist principles and adoption of a new independent aesthetic. In one respect, however, his biography seems to differ from many others of his generation. Born near Wilno (Vilnius), the present capital of Lithuania, Konwicki completed high school by attending clandestine study classes. On the eve of the German retreat in 1944, he joined the Polish underground resistance movement, Armia Krajowa (the Home Army), which remained under the orders of the Polish government-in-exile in London. After the Soviets recaptured the region, the Home Army turned its arms against them. It considered the Red Army to be a new occupying force, more dangerous to true Polish independence than the previous invader. As a soldier of the Home Army who swore allegiance to its goals and ideals, Konwicki served in a unit which fought the Soviets. The outcome of this conflict was a foregone conclusion: patriotic motivation could not match Soviet military power. He described the agony of this experience in the novel *Rojsty* (*Marshes*). After the defeat, thousands of Home Army soldiers were captured, imprisoned, executed, or left to perish in the concentration camps of Siberia. The country that Konwicki thought of as his native land was handed over to the so-called Socialist Republic of Lithuania or, in other words, became part of the Soviet Union. He managed to escape to Poland, living first in Krakow, where he studied Polish literature, and shortly afterwards settling in Warsaw. Seemingly, Konwicki could celebrate: he came out of the ordeal safe and sound. Yet the painful loss of his homeland and forced emigration left an indelible mark on his personality. He perceived this change as something that could not be rationally explained, as something that shattered his sense of security. It also left him, a young man, with unfulfilled dreams. Later, in the novel *A Minor Apocalypse,* the main character—who in some episodes and statements can be recognized as the writer's alter ego—makes the following admission: "Fate only drove me a few hundred kilometers, but it separated me from my unfulfilled life by an entire eternity of reincarnation." This traumatic experience exerted a lasting impact on Konwicki's writing and lent to it a peculiar stamp of thematic unity: all his works are permeated with the retentive memory of the past, and, as if to cure himself from its burden, he leads the reader to a beautiful valley (the site of Nowa Wilejka where he was born), obsessively depicted throughout his whole prose and symbolizing the time and place of his lost adolescence.

By and large it can be said that Konwicki went through three basic stages of creative evolution. Early in his career he published a piece of literary reporting, *Przy budowie (At the Building Site,* 1950), and a few volumes of fiction, among which the most significant was probably the novel *Wladza (The Power,* 1953). Both of these books offered an optimistic view of postwar Poland ruled by the newly established communist order and complied with the norms of socialist realism, which had been imposed on Polish writers in 1949 as "the only correct method of artistic creativity." The second stage can be called a period of doubt and skepticism. It begins after 1956 and is characterized by an intense literary experimentation; now the author tries not only to reassess or even redefine his relation to the political and social conditions of his country but also to find new means of artistic expression to enhance his specificity as a writer. This period was opened by the publication of *Dziura w niebie (A Hole in the Sky,* 1959), but it began in earnest with the novel *Sennik współczesny (A Dreambook for Our Time,* 1963) and ended with *Kalendarz i klepsydra (The Calendar and the Hourglass,* 1976)—a volume of what the author himself defined as "essayistic prose." Shortly afterwards, Konwicki's evolution as a writer took yet another turn: in 1977 the official publishing house Czytelnik refused to accept his novel *The Polish Complex,* and the author decided to publish it in the "second circulation" or *drugi obieg,* also known as *niezalezny obieg* (independent circulation), the Polish terms for *samizdat* or *tamizdat.* Apart from *The Polish Complex,* three other books appeared in the underground press: *A Minor Apocalypse, Moonrise, Moonset,* and *Rzeka podziemna, podziemne ptaki (Underground River, Underground Birds,* 1984). For ten years Konwicki's name remained absent from official publications and banned from the press. While Konwicki steadfastly defended his quest for artistic renewal and independence, he grew in stature as an author of significance and entered the mainstream of European writing. It is the intention of this article to follow this process through an analysis of texts and to establish the most essential distinctive features of his narrative discourse or fictional world. In doing so, one ought to be aware that the transition from one stage to another is not rigid or brought into strong relief by a single work; rather, it is flexible and gradual, marked by the mutual coexistence and continuous recurrence (dynamic or passive) of some formal devices and thematic threads. Thus, for example, if some narrative characteristics of one period may have remained in its background they are strongly reactivated and come to the fore as prime formative constituents in the next. This is particularly relevant with regard to Konwicki's later writings.

From the very beginning, Konwicki's prose has been typified by a thematic triad: war, reminiscences of juvenile experience, and broad commentary on contemporary life. It is difficult to say whether any of these thematic components overwhelms the others in terms of recurrence. Rather, what we observe is their constant interaction throughout all of Konwicki's works. They are intertwined in a great number of narrative constants and appear even in his most "metaphysical" or, as he calls them, "existential" novels of the sixties such as *A Dreambook for Our Time, Wniebowstapienie (Ascension,* 1967), *Nic albo nic (Nothing or Nothing,* 1971). This thematic unity is reinforced by a quite frequent reappearance of the same situations, settings (for example, the above-mentioned valley), episodes, and characters. The reader will encounter Karnowski on the pages of *Nic albo nic, Rzeka podziemna, podziemne ptaki, Moonrise, Moonset,* and **"Kilka dni wojny o ktorej nie wiadomo, czy byla"** in *Zorze wieczorne* (**"A Few Days' War Which One Is Not Certain Happened"** in *Evening Dawns,* 1991). The same is true of other characters. Konwicki's prose, then, manifests a thematic consistency but not thematic homogeneity: with the exception of *Rojsty,* which is entirely devoted to the vicissitudes of a Polish guerrilla unit fighting the Soviets, they are always composed of the above-mentioned thematic triad. Consequently, due to this juxtaposition of themes, Konwicki's prose is basically either associative or kaleidoscopic in nature.

The Associative Chain:
The Prose of Doubt and Suspicion

In Konwicki's ample literary output *A Dreambook for Our Time* constitutes a break with his style of the fifties with its distinctive rectilinear progression of the plot. Now the author begins to disrupt this sequential unity of his prose by disregarding both its temporal and spatial "logical" order. The novel leaves the impression of being "chaotic" with many loose ends hanging untied, and the reader is challenged to unravel the mysteries of the story. This outward disorder is matched by the vagueness of the narrator's position and the protagonist's behavior. Who is Paul? After a failed suicide attempt, he awakes from unconsciousness, surrounded by people who came to his room out of curiosity rather than compassion. They are insensitive observers without any intention to help him. As it turns out later, he cannot relate to them either, although most of them are as unhappy and degraded in their social condition as he is: Regina cannot find a partner to realize her dreams for love and happy marriage; the mutual animosity between the Korsak siblings grows with age, yet they are doomed to one another forever; the former partisan Krupa is obsessed with his unfulfilled sexual desire for Regina; militiaman Glowko, a drunkard, is terrorized by his wife; roadman Debicki (to his irritation, he is often addressed by local inhabitants as Mr. Dobas) suffers because of the conflict between his excessive ambitions and his actual occupational status. This register of unhappiness and failure can be extended. The characters are all sidetracked in a small, unnamed town, and even this miserable existence is endangered. A huge dam is planned for the area, and the whole valley, including the town, is to be flooded. Everything is surrounded by an air of uncertainty. Yet in this microworld of lost individuals Paul meets one person to whom he develops an emotional attachment: Justine. She is the wife or common-law wife (in this novel nothing is certain about the personal and professional details of the characters) of Joseph Car (pronounced "czar"), spiritual leader of a religious sect. There exists, however, another impediment on the road to a true and lasting relationship between Justine and Paul: it is the latter's past, which proves to be strangely interwoven with that of Car. Consequently, their relationship turns into a series of morbid encounters leading nowhere. Paul lives in two worlds: the world of the emotionally and even physically oppressive present and the painful past. *A Dreambook for Our Time* is a narrative of alternating images or fragments reflecting Paul's frame of mind (mental distress) and his inner instability. As he reflects upon his past and tries to recall its details, he gradually arrives at the realization that Car is his former colleague from the underground resistance movement who betrayed its cause and was sentenced to death. Paul was designated to carry out the sentence. Indeed, he shot at Car but without a firm intention to kill him; Car was wounded but survived. Now their paths cross again. There is additional, unresolved mystery in the story: a rumor has it that the adjacent forests still harbor a legendary underground fighter, Huniady. Is this Car's double? The question cannot be answered, and Paul is lost in conjecture. The novel ends with his leaving town.

Similar issues of the human condition in an unfriendly environment are pursued in *Nic albo nic,* except that in this case the number of characters is reduced. The novel is focused primarily on two protagonists: the young guerrilla fighters nicknamed Stary and Darek, whose occupational affiliations are not clearly defined. The young men of Stary's partisan detachment dream about a just postwar social order, and most of them believe in a change for the better in a future in which they will be able to fulfill their dreams. The reply to these dreams can be found in the fate of Darek, who lives in a new postwar reality. His life is enveloped in grayness, marked by dreadful events and loneliness; and there

is an indication that he lives in a state of schizophrenic dissociation. The novel consists of two separate storylines or threads which do not intersect. It is unclear whether Darek is a *porte-parole* of Stary, who entered the new reality as a civilian. The reader can only guess and try to make some vague associations or to draw parallels. But if Stary indeed entered the world of Darek, it would mean that the lofty dreams of his generation have dissipated into nothingness. Darek's existential condition is even worse: if Stary had hopes about a bright future, Darek has been deprived of such comforts. The only "exit" left to him, the only solution available to him is death, which indeed befalls him toward the end of the novel. In short, the alternative to "nothing" is only "nothing," which explains the title of the novel. In its extreme pessimism *Nic albo nic* is akin to *A Dreambook for Our Time,* but the frightful description of human alienation in the former is stretched to the limits by the strong motif of death.

Konwicki's prose cannot be properly understood without attention being paid to the novel *Zwierzoczlekoupiór* (*The Anthropos-Specter-Beast,* 1969). In his conversations with Nowicki, the author claimed that *The Anthropos-Specter-Beast* was written for "the pleasure of readers and my own"; he links it with *Dziura w niebie* and *Kronika wypadków milosnych* (*Chronicle of Love Events,* 1974) into one cycle of what he calls "recreational and doleful" prose. If *The Anthropos-Specter-Beast* is indeed as docile or "innocent" as Konwicki suggests, why then was it so fiercely attacked by Party hacks and official critics shortly after its publication? It seems, therefore, that it would be much more appropriate to place this novel within a different context, namely, to discuss it as part of Konwicki's writing of the sixties in which the *associative flow of narration* reveals itself as the dominant creative principle. Konwicki's prose does not move forward by cycles, but its growing maturity and changing nature can be measured by decades, by temporal progression—the sixties being the period of camouflaged disappointment, skepticism, and suspicion. The writer himself admitted that he began to write in a code, to apply Aesopian language. In this, Konwicki was not alone. In the 1960s many Polish writers and artists began to produce works that seemingly did not relate to contemporary external reality. In this respect the novel was not only symptomatic of Konwicki's work but in many ways quite characteristic of Polish literature of the sixties.

The novel is related by a first-person narrator, a little boy named Peter who declares in his opening sentence that "This book is not meant for obedient sons and daughters." Indeed, it's not. It is a tale of a naughty boy who knows how to vex his parents and to go his own way. He considers the adults to be naive and unworthy of trust. But the significance of the novel lies not in its external layer of events but in its plot, which distinguishes itself in two ways: first, Peter befriends Sebastian, a dog who can speak his language, and second, together they embark on an adventure of liberating a little girl, Eva, who is held captive and with whom they are both in love. Thus for the first time Konwicki ushers into his prose both the fantastic and some elements of the traditional romance. The narrative unfolds as a chain of alternating images of the real versus the unreal, and above the entire novel hovers the atmosphere of a Peter Pan story but without its optimistic ending. Peter finds an escape from the dreadful reality in the unreal: it is the fantastic that allows him (or so he imagines) to realize his dreams. And vice versa: the real appears before him as something alien, irrational, something that assumes the shape of the "anthropos-specter-beast." The function of the unreal and the real are reversed, the latter being unfriendly, hostile, and even terrifying. By the end of the novel, however, one can hardly avoid asking if the fantastic world is as friendly as Peter seems to believe when he cooperates with the old dog Sebastian. After a series of bold escapades, they succeed in liberating Eva from Troip (almost the reverse spelling of the name Piotr), her captor; yet when Peter thinks that his dream of happy union with Eva is at hand, the old dog brutally throws him off and leads Eva away from him. In the end Peter has no choice but to return to his parents. In both *The Anthropos-Specter-Beast* and *Nic albo nic,* the protagonists experience a painful condition of total isolation and disappointment and reach an existential cul-de-sac.

Kaleidoscopic Variety:
The Prose of Protest and Rejection

The publication of *Kalendarz i klepsydra* in 1976 presaged change in Konwicki's writing. Distinct from everything that Konwicki had already written, it abandons plot as the means of organizing the narrative. Written in the form of a diary, *Kalendarz i klepsydra* preserves the fragmentation of the earlier prose yet is devoid of its associative ambiguity. It strikes with the directness of its discourse in which the denotative function of language comes clearly to the fore. The only principal character of the text is the author himself, and the book delights with its manifold presentation of happenings, gossip, and observations taken directly from either his personal life or the broader framework of his artistic, political, and social milieu. We are faced with a literary collage—the succession of themes, subjects, and images that occur with kaleidoscopic speed, as if the author intended to encompass the whole of reality. Thus we find here some threads that he later develops into full-scale stories (for example, about his grandmother Konwicka), comments about his previous works (both as a filmmaker and writer), confessions about his friendships, unflattering commentaries on Polish TV and the Union of Writers, and expressed frustrations caused by everyday life's inconveniences and nonsense. The register of subjects can go on. At the same time, this "essayistic prose," as the writer himself calls it, is imbued

with a pervasive sense of self-irony and irony, indicating his own limitations and helplessness. On the first page of the book he indicates that "the nicest thing would be to write the truth" and nothing but the truth. The conditional mood used in this sentence indicates, however, that there are some impediments to the fulfillment of this wish. Somewhat later in the text he strengthens this statement by referring to his book as a "simulated diary." In other words, it is not devoid of a certain degree of fictionality because the writer cannot ignore some external constraints. Paradoxically, the refusal to name these constraints directly reveals to the reader the truth about censorship. Ten years later, when Konwicki returned to "official circulation" (that is, official publishing houses) by writing *Nowy Swiat i okolice* (*New World Avenue and Vicinity,* 1986), he wrote openly that "I am writing a book for the censors." It should be pointed out, however, that in spite of these authorial limitations, *Kalendarz i klepsydra* contains some formidable pages of direct and intransigent criticism of the communist regime. When he writes about senseless life and the collective dying of a whole nation, his attack on the existing political system reaches hitherto unknown dimensions and force. In this book Konwicki came as close as possible to testing the patience and vigilance of the censor. Beyond this point lay the imminent ban on publishing. He crossed this line in his next novel, *The Polish Complex.*

> **When Konwicki writes about senseless life and the collective dying of a whole nation, his attack on the existing political system reaches hitherto unknown dimensions and force.**
>
> **—Edward Mozejko**

In Konwicki's evolution this novel constitutes a major innovation as regards both form and content. It alternates between two concerns—the present and the past—and four narrative voices. Each of them reports on a different set of events but reflects the same existential condition: individual and collective enslavement. The largest part of the novel is narrated by the author himself, who appears as a character (under the name of Tadeusz Konwicki) and who even indicates his real address in Warsaw. One Christmas Eve he stands in a queue before a jewelry store to buy Soviet gold. This leads him to a chain of unexpected adventures. The second, "historical," theme refers to the Polish insurrection of 1863 and its suppression by the Russians. It has two invariants: a second-person narrator and a third-person narrator. The fourth voice is an "I" narrator, too, who makes his presence known by a letter. In relation to the totalitarian political regime in Poland, this section of the book is most revealing in its accusatory frankness and denial. The author applies the device of misattribution: the sender of the letter, a Pole who emigrated after the war, resides in a faraway country on another continent. However, this unnamed country has been forced to accept the political system of "its omnipotent neighbor to the north." He describes the agony of its existence, its total moral and social decay, but most of all, the suffocating lack of freedom. In his letter to a Polish friend he looks up to Poland as the "homeland of freedom," as "lair of tolerance," as "big white angel in the middle of Europe." Freedoms that Polish people enjoy inspire the author of the letter with hope and hearten him. In other words, all features that have usually been ascribed to the West are now attributed to Poland and vice versa: characteristics for which the communist regime was known in Poland are bestowed upon a country the geographical location of which is indeterminable but which belongs to the Western hemisphere.

The above-mentioned device of misattribution is close to what is known in science fiction as extrapolation. Konwicki explores the possibilities of the latter device in his dystopian novel *A Minor Apocalypse,* which exploits the topoi of "a world to come" and as such rests on the use of temporal displacement. The action is set in Warsaw on the eve of Poland's joining the Soviet Union as its sixteenth republic. The capital hosts its powerful neighbor's first secretary, and he and his Polish counterpart embrace and they kiss "each other on the mouth." The masses who "support" this merger are greatly enthusiastic and Polish and red banners abound. But the Polish banners—known for white and red colors of equal width—have been altered: the white part remains only as a thin stripe, hardly visible on the top. But underneath this external and official world pulsates a troubled underground opposition that wants to organize a protest against Poland being "swallowed" by the Soviet Union. This plan is to be implemented by someone who would be ready to commit the highest act of self-sacrifice by making a burnt offering of himself, that is, by setting himself on fire in front of the Party Central Committee building. The choice falls on the narrator. When he asks for explanation ("why me?"), Hubert, one of the leading members of the dissident camp, has this to say: "You see . . . an act like this can make sense only if it shakes people here in Poland and everywhere abroad. You are known to Polish readers and you have a bit of a name in the West, too. Your life story, your personality are perfect for this situation." When the narrator responds that some other artists are better known in the West than he and therefore better suited for the sacrifice because it would make a greater impact on the world's opinion, Hubert replies: "That would be too high a price to pay. Too high a price for the country and our community. You are just right." This scene sets the tone for the whole novel. The conversation between representatives of the opposition and the narrator borders on the absurd. The matter-of-fact arguments of Hubert and Rysio trying to convince their friend to commit suicide and the use of the short phrase "you have a bit

of a name in the West, too" evoke a comic picture rather than a favorable image of the dissident movement and the way it operates. While Konwicki may have intended to settle a few personal accounts with some of his colleagues, the novel points to the abnormal conditions in which the political struggle takes place. This abnormality is also visible in, or "harmonized" with, a total decay of the external, material setting, that is, the city; its buildings are dirty, gray, falling apart. This vision of gloom and doom is further enhanced by the description of nature: "The Vistula's water was dun-colored, slimy, close to flood level"; there are "trees so small there wasn't room on them for even a single pigeon, trees which yielded miniature fruit, each one propped up by a small branch or dried stalk"; and so on. As with any dystopian fiction, *A Minor Apocalypse* is a satire. It derides the Orwellian vision of a society turned real in the seventies. Yet at the same time it is permeated with a mood of despair. In such a society everyone is bound to go through a "comic inferno" because everything deviates from the norm. As much as the writer may sympathize with the goals of the opposition and foster its cause, he shows that its mode of existence is not comparable to that of an opposition in a democratic society and casts doubt as to whether its methods of struggle in such a deviant situation make sense. Richard Lourie is right when he comments in his introduction to the English translation of the novel that Konwicki examines "tensions, both tragic and comic, generated by a situation where conscience demands sacrifice and reality offers no hope that the sacrifice will be of any value or significance."

In most cases the action of Konwicki's stories is laid at a time loaded heavy with consequences. In *A Dreambook for Our Time* Paul arrives in a small town when it is about to be flooded for the purpose of building a dam; in *Kronika wypadków miłosnych* Witek lives out his first juvenile fascination with Alina just before the outbreak of World War II; the protagonists of *The Anthropos-Specter-Beast* are seized by bewilderment at the news that a comet is heading toward the earth; *Nic albo nic* describes events preceding Darek's death; and so on. In this respect *A Minor Apocalypse* is no exception. The narrator relates the last day of his life as he decides to comply with the request of his "friends" to commit self-immolation in front of the Central Committee building. The way this story moves forward reminds us of accelerated cinematic frames: it presents a condensed review of the last day with a speedy succession of happenings, interspersed with flashbacks and reflections about art, Russia, the meaning of dissent, and so on. Thus in his final hours of wandering around the city he meets a philosopher, visits a hiding place of dissidents, makes a new acquaintance with a Russian woman named Nadezhda (meaning "hope"), and feels toward her an instant attraction. He attends his friend's film show, is arrested for a short while, and is interviewed by an arrogant but intelligent security officer. After his release, he runs, by strange coincidence, into a group of women to whom he made love in the past, and finally he reaches the site of his fateful destination. In one respect, however, this book seems to stand out against previous work: it tells us not about an individual death but about the collective death of the whole nation with its material resources and natural environment. It is a sinister memento, a warning that under communist rule Poland has drawn toward a point beyond which lies but nothingness.

In *Moonrise, Moonset* Konwicki once again resorts to diary form to convince the reader of the authenticity of narration. Written during the period of Solidarity, and with obvious disregard for censorship, his narrative strategy seems to be well suited for this purpose and the time in which it was conceived. The dramatic turn of events and their rapid succession seems to invite the author to create something that can be referred to as documentary prose. Indeed, the book runs an impressive gamut of topics. There are complaints about economic inefficiency, lack of goods, political persecution, instant snapshots of city life, reminiscences, comments on other writers and his relationships with them, encounters with the clairvoyant Father Klimuszko, and more; the book ends with a relatively short description of the imposition of martial law in December 1981. As was the case with *A Minor Apocalypse, Moonrise, Moonset* contains strong political overtones and can be read as a discursive attack on the failures of communism. However, given some details and indications in the text, I would suggest that this book should be received by the reader above all as literature. One should not lose sight of the fact that whatever has been presented in this book is rendered through a highly subjective agent—the author himself, who does not hide his sentiments. Everything is seen through the prism of his sympathies and antipathies. Vis-à-vis external reality, he remains the sole "hero" who selects the narrated material according to his whims. Konwicki does not write a document—he creates the illusion of a document. The effect of probability and verisimilitude, however, is not achieved by developing an intricate plot as in so-called "realistic" prose but by the manipulating measures of a narrator who is openly engaged in an interplay with his reader. For example, as he describes in the final section of *Moonrise, Moonset* the imposition of martial law in December 1981, the narrator tells us about meeting Tadzio Skorko, a fictional character created by him in *A Minor Apocalypse.* In the early days of martial law Konwicki was pressed by the Security organs to sign a declaration of loyalty. He was interrogated by a young security officer who bore a striking resemblance to Tadzio Skorko, the detective who spies on the narrator of *A Minor Apocalypse:* "That sleek and painstakingly created literary figure had suddenly sprung to life before my very eyes one December day in martial-law Warsaw." What we have here is fiction entering life and turning out to be as truthful as reality itself or, in short, invention becoming reality. How-

ever, this fragment is not devoid of a certain paradox: while displaying concrete referential validity, it reveals at the same time the ontological status of fiction. The author clearly declares "responsibility," so to speak, for creating the character. The boundary between reality and fiction is both blurred and maintained.

The Meaning of Form:
Konwicki as Postmodernist Writer

It would be easy, even tempting to classify Konwicki as a dissident writer. As indicated above, one can provide a sufficient number of arguments to justify such a claim. And yet one has doubts whether the author of *A Minor Apocalypse* can be contained within the category of dissident writing. The reason is quite obvious: the world described by Konwicki goes through not partial but total, global degradation. This is, of course, most evident in *A Minor Apocalypse,* but other works, particularly *Rzeka podziemna, podziemne ptaki,* attest to this perception as well. In *A Minor Apocalypse* Konwicki aims the shaft of his satire at the regime, but simultaneously he draws a political cartoon of the opposition because it is a "child" of abnormality, of a decaying system, and as such it is in a sense degenerate too. The writer's sympathy tilts clearly toward dissidents, yet in some instances he does not spare them from direct critical remarks while at the same time having some positive words to say about the officials in power. In *Moonrise, Moonset* he dares to criticize the novels of Stefan Kisielewski, one of the most prominent and respected Polish dissidents (who died in October 1991 in Warsaw), and has a few propitious comments to make about the late Janusz Wilhelmi, a critic and editor closely associated with the Party apparatus of the Central Committee. It looks as if Konwicki tries to create a certain balance, to create the illusion of reality in its manifold diversity, which in its turn does not necessarily correspond to the notion of dissident literature.

> **It looks as if Konwicki tries to create a certain balance, to create the illusion of reality in its manifold diversity, which in its turn does not necessarily correspond to the notion of dissident literature.**
> —*Edward Mozejko*

Even less convincing are attempts to label Konwicki "a very Polish writer." At first, he admits, he was quite disturbed by such qualifications but later rendered himself indifferent to these misreadings of his texts. On more than one occasion Konwicki complained, and not without justification, that Polish criticism showed little understanding of his writing. His alleged "Polishness" is a good case in point, for what does it mean to be a "Polish writer"? This quality is attributed to him just as it is to many other writers in Poland, in fact, to all of them! It also demonstrates a certain intellectual deadlock in choosing strategies for critical discourse. Konwicki's example shows clearly that it is impossible to comprehend fully the innovative nature of his writing by making use of hackneyed thinking, that it is necessary to place him against the broader background of contemporary Western culture. Indeed, Konwicki is a "Polish writer" but in the sense that he uses Polish material as pretext to tackle issues of formal, existential, and historical significance which must strike us with their modern or, perhaps, their postmodernist bent.

Let us dwell for a moment on Konwicki's tendency to write about "a little bit of everything." Most of his works constitute a conglomerate of wide-ranging happenings, feelings, and thoughts; they juxtapose various temporal and spatial narrative levels, and one is left with the impression that the writer has an almost programmatic stake in presenting nothing else but the plurality of commonplaceness. As if to confirm this observation, Konwicki writes in **New World Avenue and Vicinity,**

> I am not a philosopher, I have no philosophers in the family and suffer no pain from this calamity. I have a different affliction. What riles me is another misfortune. . . . I smart, writhe, and agonize under the curse of resemblances. I resemble all of you, bright and dumb, great and small, saints and sinners. I resemble you to the point that I have hardly formed a thought when I already find it in you. I can hardly write a word before seeing it written by somebody else. Barely do I start my death agony when I see one just like it next to me.

This passage brings to mind an association with a postmodern movie in which the principal descends from the screen to mingle with the audience and to become "one of them," to continue its existence as a "real" individual. In short, the author ostentatiously displays his populist stand.

Brian McHale, for one, reflects on possible thematic ontologies of literature. He differentiates between the paramount or shared reality of everyday life "marked by circumscribed meanings and modes of experience" and private or peripheral realities that include a wide range of topics: dreaming, playing, hobbies, sex, holidays, gambling, mass media, entertainment, games, therapy, the use of alcohol and drugs, religious conversion, Utopian alternative societies, mental disorders such as schizophrenia, and so on. The imitative realm of postmodern fiction refers exactly to this "pluralistic and anarchistic ontological landscape" typical of advanced industrial cultures. If viewed against the background of the shared, paramount reality that constitutes the common ground for interaction between people, this multiplicity of private realities is marginal and signifies an attempt to escape from it. At the same time, by depicting peripheral realities, postmodern fiction expresses an anarchistic refusal "either to accept or to reject any of a plurality of available ontological orders." McHale concludes that "postmodern fiction *does* hold the mirror up to reality but that reality, now more than ever before, is plural."

In this context such formulations as "'anarchistic ontological landscape' typical of advanced industrial cultures" or "an anarchistic refusal 'either to accept or reject any of a plurality of available ontological orders'" deserve our special attention. First, it should be pointed out that an "anarchistic ontological landscape" is typical not only of advanced industrial cultures: albeit suppressed, it was strongly present for the past twenty years or so in totalitarian communist regimes as well. On the level of literature it found its expression in so-called "jeans prose" or "little realism," which represented either a form of revolt/insubordination against the officialdom of the communist system or an exclusive preoccupation with small, everyday worries of ordinary people. Most recently, these anarchistic tendencies made themselves known in the form of unprecedented political fragmentation. With the collapse of communist power, hundreds of new parties emerged and declared their willingness to participate in free elections, which resulted, for example, in thirty parties entering the newly formed Polish parliament. Even in Czechoslovakia, where the tradition of democracy and political expediency has always been strong, there exist close to 300 political groups, some of them (as in Poland) with openly anarchistic programs and manifestos. As for Konwicki, it should be noted that in a recent interview he declared that he has remained in full sympathy with the current anarchistic movements and has taken exception to all codified values. Second, he remains faithful to the principle of "anarchistic refusal either to accept or to reject any of a plurality of available ontological orders" in that he preserved a certain moderation in criticizing what he negates and expressing lukewarm praise for what he supports. Therefore, although he has been critical of the communist state and predicted its inevitable downfall, one can find in his **Moonrise, Moonset** the following lines: "I'm not clapping my hands for joy and not whacking my thigh in delight because the totalitarian Communism practiced in our poor land will fizzle out in the end." While he does not accept communism, neither does he celebrate its fall because he is equally suspicious of what is to come in its aftermath. The writer anticipates that other problems will arise; in short, his creative attitude is underlaid by skepticism and mistrust.

McHale's characterization of postmodernism adheres so well to Konwicki's prose that one could unmistakably recognize in Konwicki an almost programmatic representative of postmodernist fiction. [Most probably some strong terminological objections prevent Polish critics from using *postmodernism* as a viable concept in relation to contemporary Polish literature. It has much to do with the way the term *modernism* (Polish: *modernizm*) is understood in Poland. This term refers strictly to a full-fledged movement that occurred in Polish literature at the end of the nineteenth century. Consequently, the introduction of the term *postmodernism* is potentially confusing and would not correspond to the meaning one attributes to it today. The term *modernism* as known in the Anglo-American cultural tradition is consistently defined in Polish literary scholarship as *avant-garde* (Polish: *awangarda*).] But this adherence goes beyond the above-mentioned specificity. Konwicki has also been perceived as one who writes in the vein of romantic tradition. Indeed, his world is populated by dreamers, lonely strangers, and detached individuals who typify the "peripheral" or "private" reality McHale has talked about. It should be noted, however, that Konwicki's link with romanticism, or more precisely, his reevaluation of it, does not end here; it is transformed into a broader confrontation with history or, one could say, bears a clear stamp of historicity.

It would be difficult to find another contemporary Polish writer who diversifies narrative perspectives with such ingenuity as Konwicki does.
—*Edward Mozejko*

Konwicki's reevaluation of romanticism makes itself known, for example, in his struggle with the tradition of romantic perception of Polish history. With references to this question, *The Polish Complex* has to be recalled. The action of this novel is frequently interrupted by temporal shifts consisting of sudden lapses of the narrative line from the remote past to closer historical events of World War II and contemporary life. These various temporal sequences are mediated through the narrator; they merge in him and represent his reincarnations at some critical turns of history. He is the preserver of collective memory. In fact, when facing the burden of romantic tradition and trying to overcome it, Konwicki makes use of palimpsest: he inscribes the contemporary experience of his narrator into history as a text shaped by a romantic worldview and, vice versa, invokes history in a modern setting stripped bare of any romantic attributes. His collective memory, placed against the background of Russia's presence, reminds one of the futility of efforts to liberate the nation from foreign oppression. This is best illustrated by one of his protagonists, Zygmunt Mineyko, the young leader of an insurgent detachment during the 1863 uprising, who dreams of defeating the Russians and regaining independence. His idealistic expectations are routed in confrontation with the harsh reality of the occupation. To make sure that this is not just an isolated event in Polish history, Konwicki applies a temporal leap, building a clasp which braces both the past and present: Wanda of 1863, who entertains Zygmunt Mineyko at her estate before his leaving to face the imperial Russian army, reminds the author-narrator (a reincarnated Zygmunt Mineyko?) of another Wanda whom he met in 1944. Both these women and fighters for independence of 1863 and 1944 (that is, Mineyko and the author-narrator) share the same lot: defeat and loss of freedom. A similar device of temporal shift can be found in ***Rzeka podziemna, podziemne ptaki.***

The above-quoted passage from *New World Avenue and Vicinity* ("I am not a philosopher . . ."), can also be interpreted as a direct challenge to Adam Mickiewicz's "Improvisation" from part 3 of the drama *Forefathers*. In his romantic ecstasy the poet wants to "embrace both past and present generations" of his countrymen, but at the same time feels himself to be above them, endowed with special powers, and therefore demands for himself the role of the nation's leader. Konwicki counters this with a modest and simple answer: "I resemble all of you, bright and dumb, great and small, saints and sinners. . . ." It should not be surprising, then, that Konwicki's grapple with romanticism comes most vividly to the fore in his recent movie *Lawa* (*Lava,* 1989), a cinematic narrative about *Forefathers*. If, as Maria Janion wants it, the current period marks a definite end of the romantic cycle in Polish culture, then it can be said that Konwicki is the one who contributed to this closure in a most interesting and effective manner. Furthermore, one can also argue that if there is any validity to the claim that "Konwicki is a Polish writer," then its concretization is to be found in the writer's polemics and rejection of romanticism. He achieves this through a recurrent application of the grotesque.

That said, a modification of the above observation is hastily needed. Konwicki's relation to romanticism is twofold: polemical or outright negative on the level of content (or its "philosophy") and positive, even creative with regard to its formal specificity and legacy. It manifests itself forcefully through the revival of *romantic irony.* Romantic irony became known for its introduction of the element of open interplay between the writer and the reader, showing that the ultimate responsibility for whatever happens in a literary work of art rests with the author or the narrator. This concept of revealing the ontological status of fiction has been acknowledged by today's critics as the prime feature of postmodern fiction.

To be sure, one should not overlook the difference between romantic irony and the postmodern foregrounding of ontological questions related to the mode of existence of literature as an artistic phenomenon, but the difference exists more in the degree of intensity with which this formal device appears in both movements than in principle. While romanticism used it on a limited basis as a hint pointing to the artful ability on the part of the writer to manipulate his/her work, postmodernism thematizes this question as an important subject.

In this respect Konwicki provides a formidable example. It would be difficult to find another contemporary Polish writer who diversifies narrative perspectives with such ingenuity as Konwicki does. He applies in his stories three pronouns, "I," "you," and "he," and most often the combination of them in a single story. He achieves extremely interesting results with the first- and second-person narrator, the latter again being a device often preferred by postmodernists. This is particularly true of his later works such as *Bohin Manor, Rzeka podziemna, podziemne ptaki,* and "Kilka dni wojny o ktorej nie wiadomo, czy byla," but it is also evident in his earlier, middle-period novels, such as *The Anthropos-Specter-Beast,* where he applies the narrative perspective of a ten- or eleven-year-old-boy. In *Bohin Manor* the narrator, who identifies himself with the author, constantly reveals his presence by commenting on the difficult task of finding the truth about his paternal grandmother who "most probably had a love affair with a young, handsome Jew" which resulted in a child born out of wedlock. Being a gentrywoman, she was repudiated for this "sinful relation" by her family. But nothing is really certain. These are only fantasy speculations of the narrator. At the outset of the story he puts into motion some events that he cannot control. The narrator is present in the same room with his grandmother, and yet he has no power to prevent her ill fortune: "I am unable to warn my grandmother Helena Konwicka; I don't have the power to restrain the course of events; and I cannot avert the finale of which I am thinking even now, concealed in a horrible solitude, gnawed by the fears of old age, racked by a sense of doom that can suddenly cause a person to shudder and shove him blindly into the black abyss of the unknown." We find this kind of narrator's interventions throughout the whole of *Bohin Manor,* and they amount to a subtheme of the novel. Parallel to the main story of the grandmother Konwicka runs the commentary of her grandson—the narrator who has difficulties in recreating her life lost in the silent past. *Rzeka podziemna, podziemne ptaki* offers yet another narrative variant: it alternates between the first-and the third-person narrator. In the opening remarks the "I" narrator states that he is flying over an ocean to reach the site of his native land. He embodies a spirit that arrives from an unknown world to discover what is happening in the place of his origin. Both his observations and memories of his youth are contrasted in separate chapters with the harsh reality depicted by the third-person narrator who talks about both the past and the present. As in Konwicki's previous works, reality is intertwined here with the fantastic which is accepted as something ordinary and is not brought into relief as being exceptional. Moreover, the autotelic and self-reflective mode of Konwicki's prose manifests itself either through the numerous comments made by protagonists about the writer's works or through direct reflections of the writer himself. The latter case is typical of what he terms "essayistic prose." The former case is most evident in *The Polish Complex,* where the author-narrator appears under his real name as both the novel's demiurge and its protagonist who often listens to what other characters have to say about his literary accomplishments.

Conclusions

Konwicki might be right in his ironic remark that he is not a philosopher, but his prose definitely spurs some philosophical reflections about literature and the position of writers in Central and Eastern Europe. Up to the present moment, the almost universally accepted opinion has been that, due to political divisions, there exists a clear-cut demarcation between the artistic conventions of the East (this usually included the so-called "people's democracies" of Central Europe and the Soviet Union) and the West. With his literary output of the last fifteen years or so, Konwicki (and in my view there are other writers like him) seems to challenge this conviction. Indeed, if Konwicki could be classified as a dissident writer, it can be equally justified to say that he attained his position via the postmodern creative process. His postmodernist sensitivity clashed, as it were, with political reality. With his comments about palimpsest, about identifying himself with the feelings and thoughts of ordinary people, about pastiche and parody, Konwicki, consciously or not, hints at his artistic affinities and makes an almost direct invitation to critics to see some aspects of his creative work in a broader cultural context, a recontextualization that would also extricate both him and the critics from such simplifications as labeling him a "Polish" or "dissident" writer. It is, of course, understandable why Polish critics have been reluctant to draw such comparisons. Close to fifty years of isolation shaped the conviction that East and West have little, if anything, in common in terms of aesthetic bonds and similarities. Such a stand was also to a great extent determined politically: any positive comparison with the Western cultural landscape could have been used to justify the legitimacy of the totalitarian regime. This was particularly true of Polish conditions. Yet in the wake of such a striking example as Konwicki, one can hardly ignore this problem any longer. In connection with this point, another question ought to be raised, too: What are the boundaries of postmodernism?

Jameson has defined postmodernism as "the cultural logic of late capitalism." Cultural models, even if based on sophisticated sociological analysis, are always thought provoking, but as a rule they leave too many unanswered questions to be trusted as adequate or unquestionable solutions. After all, feudal and backward Russia created simultaneously with the economically and politically more fully developed West the same type of "realistic" literature. It seems that the contemporary postmodernist condition transgressed far beyond its original limits and became part of the cultural scene outside the technologically advanced, capitalist West. However, it should be pointed out that Konwicki's creative experience is, first of all, of utmost significance and has its greatest innovative bearing on the shaping of modern Polish literature itself.

There exists in the Polish cultural tradition a deeply rooted conviction about "high" and "low" art. If literature is to fulfill any important function, it has to communicate a "profound" message. Consequently, modern Polish criticism assumes that the existing link between Polish literature and the more universal values of world literature is to be sought primarily through the works of such writers as Milosz, Herbert, or Herling-Grudzinski. Konwicki challenges this view not by questioning the significance of these writers but by telling his readers, either directly or indirectly, that in the modern cultural condition the difference between high and low art has been blurred. In doing so, he may claim some affinity with his great predecessor and countryman Witold Gombrowicz, who mocked pomposity and devalued in his prose some national as well as literary symbols and ideals sanctioned by tradition. Similarly, but with a tinge of tragic tension absent from the works of Gombrowicz, Konwicki demonstratively stresses his "ordinariness" and openly attacks in his conversations with Nowicki "our terrible chase for elitism and fear of commonness." He presents himself as a populist writer. In developing this artistic stand, the author of *A Minor Apocalypse* opened a new avenue by which Polish literature might be connected to the broader flow of its contemporary Western counterpart. Konwicki has modernized Polish perceptions about art and literature; he has brought them, so to speak, up to date. And in this, I believe, lies his originality and very important contribution to the Polish cultural scene of today.

FURTHER READING

Criticism

Baranczak, Stanislaw. "The Polish Complex." *Partisan Review* LI, No. 3 (Summer 1984): 433-41.
    Ruminates the themes of *The Polish Complex* and everyday life in Poland.

Beres, Stanislaw. "*Bohin Manor:* Romance with Nothingness." *Review of Contemporary Fiction* XIV, No. 3 (Fall 1994): 189-96.
    Examines narrative strategies that inform *Bohin Manor*, emphasizing Konwicki's manipulation of romance and realist conventions.

Myers, Thomas. "Training the Memory: Dystopian History in Konwicki's *A Minor Apocalypse*." *Review of Contemporary Fiction* XIV, No. 3 (Fall 1994): 180-88.
    Studies historical themes of *A Minor Apocalypse* in relation to the political, economic, and social implications of the fall of communism.

Additional coverage of Konwicki's life and career is contained in the following sources published by Gale: *Contemporary Authors*, Vol. 101; *Contemporary Authors Autobiography Series*, Vol. 9; *Contemporary Authors New Revision Series*, Vols. 39, and 59; and *Major Twentieth-Century Writers*.

Malcolm X
1925-1965

(Born Malcolm Little; changed name to Malcolm X; later adopted religious name El-Hajj Malik El-Shabazz) American autobiographer, orator, and speechwriter.

The following entry provides an overview of Malcolm X's career through 1994. For further information on his life and works, see *CLC,* Volume 82.

INTRODUCTION

An influential African-American leader, Malcolm X rose to prominence in the mid-1950s as the outspoken national minister of the Nation of Islam under Elijah Muhammad. He opposed the mainstream civil rights movement, publicly calling for black separatism and rejecting nonviolence and integration as effective means of combatting racism. In the 1960s, however, Malcolm repudiated Muhammad and the Nation of Islam and embraced conventional Islam. He documented his various experiences in *The Autobiography of Malcolm X* (1965), a work prepared with the help of American writer Alex Haley. Published after his assassination, the *Autobiography* has been called a "compelling and irreplaceable book" comparable to the autobiographies of Benjamin Franklin and Frederick Douglass.

Biographical Information

Born Malcolm Little in Omaha, Nebraska, Malcolm was exposed to white racism and the black separatist movement at an early age. His father, Earl Little, was a Baptist minister and a follower of Jamaican-born, black nationalist Marcus Garvey. When the Littles lived in Nebraska, the Ku Klux Klan tried to prevent the Reverend Little from conveying Garvey's teachings. The Littles consequently left Nebraska, eventually settling in Mason, Michigan, where they found the racial climate no better. In 1929 members of the Black Legion, a white supremacist group, reputedly burned down the Littles's home and later murdered Malcolm's father. His death, officially labeled a suicide, left Louise Little to care for the children. Unable to cope with the financial and emotional demands of single parenthood, she was placed in a mental institution, and the children were sent to separate foster homes. Despite the traumas of his early youth, Malcolm was among the best students in his class. Malcolm soon became angry toward his white teachers and friends, whom he believed viewed him not as their equal, but as their "mascot." His interest in academic study waning, he quit school after completing the eighth grade. Living in Boston, New York City, and later Detroit, he held several low-paying jobs.

To fit into his new urban environment, Malcolm altered his outward appearance, treating his hair with corrosive chemicals to straighten it and frequently wearing a zoot suit. As "Detroit Red," a name derived from his fair complexion and red hair, he made his living as a hustler, pimp, and drug dealer. Malcolm was arrested in early 1946 and sentenced to ten years in prison. Another convict, Bimbi, introduced him to the prison's extensive library, and Malcolm became an avid reader. When his siblings revealed to him that they had become followers of Elijah Muhammad—the leader of the Nation of Islam, popularly known as the Black Muslims—Malcolm pored over Muhammad's teachings and initiated a daily correspondence with the man. Upon his release from prison in 1952, Malcolm became a follower of Muhammad. He took the name "Malcolm X" to signify the loss of his true African name and to reject the "slave name" of Little. In 1953 Malcolm was appointed assistant minister of Detroit's Temple Number One of the Nation of Islam. He believed that every black person would gravitate to Muhammad's teachings, for "when he thinks about his own life, he is going to see where, to him personally, the white man sure has acted like a devil." Malcolm rose swiftly in the ranks of the Black Muslims, becoming Muhammad's national representative and, in 1954, the head of a major mosque in Harlem. There he became known as an articulate spokesperson for the radical black perspective. In addition to denouncing integration, nonviolence, and Dr. Martin Luther King, Jr., Malcolm "identified whites as the enemy of blacks and cheered at tornadoes, hurricanes, earthquakes, airplane crashes, even the Kennedy assassination—anything that might cause them anguish or pain." Malcolm termed the killing of John F. Kennedy a case of "chickens coming home to roost"—a statement that severely damaged Malcolm's career. He later explained that he meant only that "the hate in white men . . . finally had struck down the President," but he was immediately censured by Muhammad. Muhammad ordered him to refrain from public comment for ninety days, and Malcolm complied. But his remark about the Kennedy assassination gave Muhammad an opportunity to expel his national minister from the movement's hierarchy, for Malcolm had been in conflict with the leader of the Nation of Islam for some time. Malcolm had privately condemned Muhammad's materialism—his expensive cars and business suits and lavishly furnished estate—and was shocked by allegations that Muhammad had seduced several women and sired their children. Proceeding to break officially with the Nation of Islam, he made a pilgrimage to Mecca, taking the religious name El-Hajj Malik El-Shabazz. In Mecca he underwent a transformation in his beliefs: "Since I learned the truth in Mecca, my dearest friends have come to include all kinds—some Christians, Jews, Buddhists, Hindus, agnostics, and even atheists! I have friends who are called capitalists, Socialists, and Communists! Some of my friends are moderates, conservatives, extremists—some are even Uncle Toms! My friends today are black, brown, red, yellow, and white!" On a diplomatic trip to Africa, Malcolm began the work of uniting blacks across the world, later establishing the Organization of Afro-American Unity in the United States. However, Malcolm now believed that the Nation of Islam saw him as a threat. "Now I'm out," he said. "And there's the fear [that] if my image isn't shattered, the Muslims in the movement will leave." Indeed, Elijah Muhammad wrote in his periodical *Muhammad Speaks* that Malcolm was "worthy of death." On February 21, 1965, he was assassinated while addressing an audience of four hundred in the Audubon Ballroom in Harlem. Three men associated with the Nation of Islam—Talmadge Thayer, Norman 3X Butler, and Thomas 15X Johnson—were apprehended and eventually convicted of the crime.

Major Works

The Autobiography of Malcolm X, which details Malcolm X's life from infancy to the time of his assassination, was published posthumously, and although some critics questioned Alex Haley's influence over the work's production, commentators generally agreed that the story is Malcolm's own. Several of Malcolm's speeches have also been published, including *Malcolm X Speaks* (1965) and *Malcolm X: The Last Speeches* (1989), but his autobiography remains by far his most noted contribution to literature. As Malcolm X has increasingly been recognized as a leading figure in the African-American struggle for recognition and equality, *The Autobiography of Malcolm X* has grown in stature. In 1993, filmmaker Spike Lee directed a widely-known screen version of the *Autobiography.*

Critical Reception

Of the importance of Malcolm X's memoir, Charles H. Nichols asserted in 1985: "*The Autobiography of Malcolm X* is probably the most influential book read by this generation of Afro-Americans. . . . It is a fantastic success story. Paradoxically, the book, designed to be an indictment of American and European bigotry and exploitation, is a triumphant affirmation of the possibilities of the human spirit." In the decades since its initial publication, the *Autobiography* has prompted diverse critical readings, including analyses of its properties as a political and rhetorical text, as a conversion narrative reflecting Malcolm's search for identity, and as a work that both affirms and challenges the tradition of American autobiography. Truman Nelson concluded: "its manifold unsolved ambiguities will make it stand as a monument to the most painful of truths: that this country, this people, this Western world has practiced unspeakable cruelty against a race, an individual, who might have made its fraudulent humanism a reality." Malcolm X's abilities as an orator have drawn much praise from commentators who have applauded his capacity for eliciting in his audiences the intensity and dedication that he demonstrated for his beliefs. It has been noted that whether those who heard him speak agreed with his contentions did not determine whether they would be profoundly affected by the delivery of his message, if only in the sense that they marveled at the dynamic wordplay, imagery, and symbolism used by the speaker. John Illo, in an essay published in 1966, illustrated Malcolm X's skill as an orator, and asserted that Malcolm X "emerged from dope, prostitution, burglary, prison, and a fanciful sectarianism to enter a perennial humanist art, to achieve a brilliant facility in oratory and debate, in less time than many of us consume in ambling through graduate school. . . . In the full Aristotelian meaning he was a rhetorician, who, to be such, knew more than rhetoric: ethics, logic, grammar, psychology, law, history, politics; and his best speeches might be texts for students of that comprehensive science and art."

PRINCIPAL WORKS

The Autobiography of Malcolm X [with Alex Haley] (autobiography) 1965

CRITICISM

Bayard Rustin (review date 14 November 1965)

SOURCE: "Making His Mark," in *New York Herald Tribune Book Week,* November 14, 1965, pp. 1, 8, 10, 12, 16-17.

[*In the following review, Rustin offers a favorable assessment of* The Autobiography of Malcolm X, *summarizing the content and providing an analysis of some of Malcolm X's political and social beliefs and strategies.*]

[*The Autobiography of Malcolm X,* t]his odyssey of an American Negro in search of his identity and place in society, really begins before his birth 40 years ago in Omaha, Neb. He was born Malcolm Little, the son of an educated mulatto West Indian mother and a father who was a Baptist minister on Sundays and dedicated organizer for Marcus Garvey's back-to-Africa movement the rest of the week.

The first incident Malcolm recounts, as if it were his welcome to white America, occurred just before he was born. A party of Ku Klux Klanners galloped up to his house, threatened his mother and left a warning for his father "to stop spreading trouble among the good" Negroes and get out of town. They galloped into the night after smashing all the windows. A few years later the Klan was to make good on its threat by burning down the Littles' Lansing, Mich., home because Malcolm's father refused to become an Uncle Tom. These were the first in a series of incidents of racial violence, characteristic of that period, that were to haunt the nights of Malcolm and his family and hang like a pall over the lives of Negroes in the North and South. Five of Reverend Little's six brothers died by violence—four at the hands of white men, one by lynching, and one shot down by Northern police officers. When Malcolm was six, his father was found cut in two by a trolley car with his head bashed in. Malcolm's father had committed "suicide," the authorities

said. Early in his life Malcolm concluded "that I too would die by violence . . . I do not expect to live long enough to read this book."

Malcolm's early life in the Midwest was not wholly defined by race. Until he went to Boston when he was 14, after his mother suffered a mental breakdown from bringing up eight children alone, his friends were often white; there were few Negroes in the small Midwestern towns where he grew up. He recounts with pride how he was elected president of his eighth-grade class in an almost totally white school.

But the race problem was always there, although Malcolm, who was light-skinned, tried for a time to think of himself as white or just like anyone else. Even in his family life, color led to conflict that interfered with normal relationships. The Reverend Little was a fierce disciplinarian, but he never laid a hand on his light-skinned son because, unconsciously, according to Malcolm, he had developed respect for white skin. On the other hand, Malcolm's mother, whose father was a white man, was ashamed of this and favored Malcolm's darker brothers and sisters. Malcolm wrote that he spent his life trying to purge this tainted white blood of a rapist from his veins.

Race also set the limits on his youthful ambitions during what he describes as his "mascot years" in a detention home run by whites with mixed feelings of affection and superiority towards him. One of the top students in his school and a member of the debating club, Malcolm went to an English teacher he admired and told him of his ambition to become a lawyer. "Mr. Ostrowsky looked surprised and said, 'Malcolm, one of life's first needs is for us to be realistic . . . a lawyer, that's no realistic goal for a nigger . . . you're good with your hands . . . why don't you plan on carpentry?'" How many times has this scene been repeated in various forms in schoolrooms across the country? It was at this point, Malcolm writes, "that I began to change—inside. I drew away from white people."

Too many people want to believe that Malcolm "the angry black man sprang full grown from the bowels of the Harlem ghetto." These chapters on his childhood are essential reading for anyone who wants to understand the plight of American Negroes.

> **Too many people want to believe that Malcolm "the angry black man sprang full grown from the bowels of the Harlem ghetto."**
> *—Bayard Rustin*

Malcolm Little was 14 when he took the Greyhound to Boston to live with his half-sister, Ella, who had fought her way into the Boston "black bourgeoisie." The "400," as they were called, lived on "the Hill," only one step removed socially, economically and geographically from the ghetto ("the Town"). Malcolm writes that "a big percentage of the Hill dwellers were in Ella's category—Southern strivers and scramblers and West Indian Negroes, whom both the New Englanders and Southerners called 'Black Jews.'" Ella owned some real estate and her own home, and like the first Jews who arrived in the New World, she was determined to shepherd new immigrants and teach them the strange ways of city life. There were deep bonds between Ella and her younger brother, and she tried to help him live a respectable life on the Hill.

But for Malcolm the 400 were only "a big-city version of those 'successful' Negro bootblacks and janitors back in Lansing . . . 8 out of 10 of the Hill Negroes of Roxbury . . . actually worked as menials and servants. . . . I don't know how many 40- and 50-year-old errand boys went down the Hill dressed as ambassadors in black suits and white collars to downtown jobs 'in government,' 'in finance,' or 'in law.'" Malcolm instead chose "the Town," where for the first time he felt he was part of a people.

Unlike the thousands of Negro migrants who poured into the Northern ghettos, Malcolm had a choice. But from the moment he made it, the options narrowed. He got a job at the Roseland Ballroom, where all the jazz greats played. His title was shoe-shine boy but his real job was to hustle whiskey, prophylactics and women to Negroes and whites. He got his first conk and zoot suit and a new identity, "Red," and his secondary education began before he was 15. "I was . . . schooled well, by experts in such hustles as the numbers, pimping, con games of many kinds, peddling dope, and thievery of all sorts, including armed robbery."

It is significant that it was Malcolm's good qualities—his intelligence, integrity, and distaste for hypocrisy—as well as his sickness that made him choose crime rather than what passed in the Negro community for a respectable bourgeois life. Later he moved on to bigger things in Harlem, became "Detroit Red," went on dope and at one time carried three guns.

His description of the cut-throat competition between the hustlers and their fraternity is both frightening and moving. "As in the case of any jungle," he writes, "the hustler's every waking hour is lived with both the practical and the subconscious knowledge that if he ever relaxes, if he ever slows down, the other hungry, restless foxes, ferrets, wolves, and vultures out there with him won't hesitate to make him their prey." He summed up his morality at the time: "The only thing I considered wrong was what I got caught doing wrong . . . and everything I did was done by instinct to survive."

As a "steerer" of uptown rich whites to Harlem "sex specialties," he recounts perversions with racial overtones, of white men begging to be beaten by black women or paying large amounts to witness interracial sex that make Genet's "The Balcony" seem inhibited by comparison.

His "extremism" made the "mainstream" civil rights groups more respectable by comparison and helped them wrest substantial concessions from the power structure.

—Bayard Rustin

"Detroit Red" was a limited success in his trade for four years. But even in this business, success was limited by race. The big operators, the successful, respectable, and safe executives of policy, dope, and prostitution rackets, were white and lived outside the ghetto.

Malcolm left Harlem to return to Boston, and a few months later was caught as the head of a burglary gang. In February, 1946, not quite 21, he was sentenced to 10 years in prison, though the average sentence for burglary was about two years—the price for his being caught with his white girl friend and her sister.

Most of the first year in prison, Malcolm writes, he spent in solitary confinement, cursing: "My favorite targets were the Bible and God." Malcolm got a new name from the other prisoners—"Satan"—and plenty of time to think. He went through what he described as a great spiritual crisis, and, as a result, he, the man who cursed God, bowed down and prayed to Allah. It will be difficult for those readers who have never been in prison to understand the psychological torment that prisoners experience, their feelings of isolation, their need to totally commit their minds to something outside of themselves. Men without any of the external economic symbols of status seek security in a religion, philosophy or ideology. Malcolm particularly, with his great feelings of rebelliousness, hatred and internal conflict, turned to books and ideas for relief. When his brothers and sisters wrote to him that they had become followers of Elijah Muhammad and sent him Elijah's teachings, Malcolm seized on the tracts. Stimulated, he read other books on religion and philosophy voraciously. In his spiritual and psychological crisis he underwent religious conversion.

He took on a new identity and became Malcolm X, a follower of Elijah Muhammad. Now he had a God to love and obey and a white devil responsible for his plight. Many Negro prisoners accepted the "Messenger," Elijah Muhammad, for similar reasons. Excluded from American society, they are drawn to another one, the Nation of Islam. (This analysis of why Malcolm joined the Muslims is mine, for although Malcolm writes about Muslim ideas, nowhere does he discuss the reasons for his conversion beyond a surface level.)

Out of prison, Malcolm, while remaining religious, arrived at a balanced view of the more fantastic elements of Elijah's teachings and a deeper understanding of one of the driving forces: "So many of the survivors whom I knew as tough hyenas and wolves of the streets in the old days now were so pitiful. They had known all the angles, but beneath that surface they were poor, ignorant, untrained men; life had eased up on them and hyped them. . . . I was thankful to Allah that I had become a Muslim and escaped their fate."

Alex Haley, who assisted Malcolm with the book, rightly commends him for deciding not to rewrite the first parts of the book and make it a polemic against his old leader, although in the interim they had broken and now were in competition with each other. As a result, the book interestingly shows changes in Malcolm's thinking.

After seven years in prison, Detroit Red emerged as Malcolm X and was soon to be the brightest star of the Nation of Islam. But as in every conversion, the man himself was not entirely reborn. Malcolm brought with him his traits of the past—the shrewd and competitive instincts learned on the ghetto streets, combined now with the language and thoughts of the great philosophers of Western culture he applied from reading Hegel, Kant, and Nietzsche, and great Negro intellectuals like Du Bois. Remaining, too, with his burning ambition to succeed, was the rebellious anger of his youth for being denied a place in society commensurate with his abilities. But on the other side of the coin was a desire for fraternity, family and respectability.

Because of his ability, he was sent to New York, where he struck a responsive chord with a great many Harlem Negroes. The Nationalist sects provided an arena of struggle for power and status denied lower-class Negroes in the outside world.

But the same qualities that made him a successful ghetto organizer soon brought him into conflict with other Muslim leaders, especially Elijah's children and prospective heirs. They saw Malcolm as a threat to their domain and apparently were able to convince Elijah that there was a threat to himself as well. For although Malcolm always gave corollary credit to Elijah—and the limits set upon him by Elijah's demands made many underestimate the exceptional nature of his mind—he could not totally constrain his brilliance, pride or ambition. "Only by being two people could I have worked harder in the service of the Nation of Islam. I had every gratification that I wanted. I had helped bring about the progress and additional impact such that none could call

us liars when we called Mr. Muhammad the most powerful black man in America."

As Malcolm's star rose higher in the western sky, Mr. Muhammad saw his eastern star setting and grew jealous. The conflict grew, although Malcolm made efforts toward conciliation. Finally, there was a total break that can be fatal to the erring Muslim who is cast away. Malcolm was aware of the dangers. "I hadn't hustled in the streets for nothing. I knew I was being set up . . . As any official in the Nation of Islam would instantly have known, any death-talk for me could have been approved of—if not actually initiated—by only one man." Later, just before his death, Malcolm said the attempt to murder him would come from a much greater source than the Muslims; he never revealed about whom he was talking.

Under a death sentence and without money or any substantial organization, Malcolm opted for action, although it was unclear whether he was running away from or toward something as he began another phase of his odyssey—a pilgrimage to Mecca where he became El-Hajj Malik El-Shabazz. Throughout his many conversions and transformations, he never was more American than during his trip to Mecca. Because his ankles were not flexible enough, he was unable to sit properly cross-legged on the traditional Muslim rug with the others, and at first the shrank from reaching into the common food pot. Like many American tourists, he projected desires for hospitality and fraternity, frustrated at home, on the Muslims he met, most of whom he could not communicate with because of the language barrier. Back in America, he acknowledged that it would be a long time before the Negro was ready to make common struggle with the Africans and Arabs.

In Mecca, Malcolm also dramatically announced that he had changed his view on integration, because he had seen true brotherhood there between black and white Muslims. In reality he had begun changing his attitude on integration and the civil rights movement many months before as the divisions between him and Elijah Muhammad widened. Part-way through the book his attacks on the movement became muted, and in the epilogue Haley concludes that Malcolm "had a reluctant admiration for Dr. Martin Luther King."

The roots of Malcolm's ambivalence were much more profound than personal opportunism. In a touching confession of dilemma he told Haley, "'the so-called moderate' civil rights organizations avoided him as 'too militant' and the 'so-called militants' avoided him as 'too moderate.' 'They won't let me turn the corner!' he once exclaimed. 'I'm caught in a trap!'" Malcolm was moving toward the mainstream of the civil rights movement when his life was cut short, but he still had quite a way to go. His anti-Semitic comments are a symptom of this malaise.

Had he been able to "turn the corner," he would have made an enormous contribution to the struggle for equal rights. As it was, his contribution was substantial. He brought hope and a measure of dignity to thousands of despairing ghetto Negroes. His "extremism" made the "mainstream" civil rights groups more respectable by comparison and helped them wrest substantial concessions from the power structure. Malcolm himself clearly understood the complicated role he played. At a Selma rally, while Dr. King was in jail, Malcolm said, "Whites better be glad Martin Luther King is rallying the people because other forces are waiting to take over if he fails." Of course, he never frightened the racists and the reactionaries as much as he made liberals feel uncomfortable, and moderates used his extremism as an excuse for inaction.

Behind the grim visage on television that upset so many white Americans there was a compassionate and often gentle man with a sense of humor. A testament to his personal honesty was that he died broke and money had to be raised for his funeral and family.

> Malcolm was with the Negro masses, but he was not of them. His experience and ambitions separated him from working-class Negroes. But to say this is not enough. In a sense Malcolm's life was tragic on a heroic scale. He had choices but never took the easy or comfortable ones. If he had, he might today be, as he says, a successful lawyer, sipping cocktails with other members of the black bourgeoisie.
> —*Bayard Rustin*

Upset by the comments in the African and Asian press criticizing the United States government for Malcolm's fate, Carl T. Rowan, Director of the United States Information Agency, held up some foreign papers and told a Washington audience, according to Alex Haley, ". . . All this about an ex-convict, ex-dope peddler, who became a racial fanatic." Yes, all this and more, before we can understand Malcolm's autobiography, revealing little-known aspects of his life and character, makes that tortured journey more understandable.

One of the book's shortcomings is that M. S. Handler and Haley, in their sensitive and insightful supplementary comments, make no comprehensive estimate of Malcolm X as a political leader. His often conflicting roles in the civil rights movement are described rather than analyzed. Perhaps this couldn't be helped, for Haley writes that Malcolm wanted a chronicler, not an interpreter. Obviously, Malcolm was not

ready to make a synthesis of his ideas and an evaluation of his political role.

Shortly after Malcolm's death Tom Kahn and I wrote in *New America* and *Dissent:* "Now that he is dead, we must resist the temptation to idealize Malcolm X, to elevate charisma to greatness. History's judgment of him will surely be ambiguous. His voice and words were cathartic, channeling into militant verbiage emotions that otherwise might have run a violently destructive course. But having described the evil, he had no program for attacking it. With rare skill and feeling he articulated angry subterranean moods more widespread than any of us like to admit. But having blown the trumpet, he could summon, even at the very end, only a handful of followers."

Of course we cannot judge political effectiveness by numbers alone, but we cannot ignore his inability to build a movement. As a spokesman for Negro anger and frustration, he left his mark on history, but as a militant political leader he failed—and the Negro community needed both. Till the end, his program was a maze of contradictions. He was a brilliant psychologist when it came to articulating the emotions and thoughts of ghetto Negroes, but he knew virtually nothing about economics, and more important, his program had no relevance to the needs of lower-class Negroes. His conception of the economic roots of the problem is reflected in such remarks as "it is because black men do not own and control their community retail establishments that they cannot stabilize their own communities." And he advocates, as a solution, that Negroes who buy so many cars and so much expensive whiskey should own automobile franchises and distilleries. Malcolm was urging Negroes to pool their resources into small business establishments at a time when small businesses were declining under the pressure of big business and when an unplanned technological revolution is creating massive unemployment for unskilled Negroes. Malcolm's solutions were in fact almost a mirror image of many proposals made by white economic moderates; those advocates of "self-help" without a massive program for jobs remind me of no one so much as those black nationalist sects and their "build it yourself" black economy without capital. In short, Malcolm's economic program was not radical. It was, in fact, petty bourgeois.

Malcolm got a wide hearing in the ghetto because large sections of the Negro working class were being driven into the "underclass" and made part of the rootless mass by the vicissitudes of the economy. He articulated the frustration and anger of these masses, and they admired his outspoken attack on the racists and white hypocrites. But while thousands came to his funeral (I was there, too, to pay my respects), few joined his organization. Nor should it be surprising that the Negro masses did not support his proposed alliance of black Americans, Africans, and Arabs, including such leaders as Prince Faisal. For what did a Harlem Negro, let alone an Arab Bedouin, have in common with a feudal prince like Faisal? And at home Malcolm maintained an uneasy co-existence with the Harlem political machine. Today Malcolm's organization, the OAAU, hardly exists. In addition, he never clearly understood that as progress was made toward social integration, the problem for America's Negroes would become just as much one of class as of race.

Malcolm was with the Negro masses, but he was not of them. His experience and ambitions separated him from working-class Negroes. But to say this is not enough. In a sense Malcolm's life was tragic on a heroic scale. He had choices but never took the easy or comfortable ones. If he had, he might today be, as he says, a successful lawyer, sipping cocktails with other members of the black bourgeoisie. He chose instead to join the Negro masses who never had this freedom of choice. And, before his death he was working toward a more creative approach to the problems of the ghetto. Perhaps he might have been successful in "turning this corner."

After reflecting on the old days at Mosque 7, shortly before he was killed, Malcolm told Haley, "That was a bad scene, brother. The sickness and madness of those days—I'm glad to be free of them. It's a time for martyrs now. And if I'm to be one, it will be in the cause of brotherhood."

Our journey through the madness of racism continues, and there is much we can learn about both the sickness and the cure from Malcolm X.

John Henrik Clarke (review date Winter 1966)

SOURCE: "The Man and His Mission," in *Freedomways*, Winter, 1966, pp. 48-52.

[*In the following review of* The Autobiography of Malcolm X, *Clarke indicates a high regard for Malcolm X's personal accomplishments and notes while the autobiography would have benefitted from "editing and pruning," it is effective in imparting the nature of Malcolm X and his achievements.*]

The man best known as Malcolm X lived three distinct and interrelated lives under the respective names, Malcolm Little, Malcolm X and El-Hajj Malik El-Shabazz. Any honest attempt to understand the total man must begin with some understanding of the significant components that went into his making. The racist society that produced and killed Malcolm X is responsible for what he was and for destroying what he could have been. He had the greatest leadership *potential* of any person to emerge directly from the black proletariat in this country. In another time under different

circumstances he might have been a King—and a good one. He might have made a nation and he might have destroyed one.

In the introduction to this autobiography, M. S. Handler has said: "No man in our time aroused fear and hatred in the white man as did Malcolm, because in him the white man sensed an implacable foe who could not be had for any price—a man unreservedly committed to the cause of liberating the black man in American society rather than integrating the black man into that society." Malcolm X put American society on the defensive by questioning its intentions toward his people and by proving those intentions to be false. This is an act of manhood, and it is the basis for most of the trouble that Malcolm had in this country in his lifetime.

It has been said, correctly, that *The Autobiography of Malcolm X* is a book about the nature of religious conversion. The book is more precisely about a man in search of a definition of himself and his relationships to his people, his country and the world. Malcolm X knew, before he could explain it to himself and others, that he was living in a society that was engaged in the systematized destruction of his people's self-respect. His first memories are about his father and his attempts to maintain himself and his family while bigoted white policemen, Ku Klux Klansmen and Black Legionnaires were determined to teach him to stay in "his place." The father of Malcolm X was killed while fighting against the restricted place that has been assigned to his people in this country. Malcolm X continued the same fight and was killed for the same reason.

His mother was born as a result of her mother being raped by a white man in the West Indies. When he was four, the house where he and his family lived was burned down by members of the Ku Klux Klan. When he was six his father met a violent death that his family always believed was a lynching.

After the death of his father, who was a follower of the black nationalist Marcus Garvey, his family was broken up and for a number of years he lived in state institutions and boarding houses. When he finally went to school he made good marks, but lost interest and was a dropout at the age of fifteen. He went to live with his sister in Boston, and worked at the kinds of jobs available to Negro youth—mainly the jobs not wanted by white people, like: shoe-shine boy, soda jerk, hotel bus boy, member of a dining-car crew on trains traveling to New York, and waiter in a Harlem night club. From these jobs he found his way into the underworld and thought, at the time, that his position in life was advancing. In the jungle of the underworld, where the fiercest survive by fleecing the weak and the defenseless, he became a master manipulator, skilled in gambling, the selling of drugs, burglary and hustling. A friend who had helped him get his first job gave him the rationale for his actions. "The main thing you have to remember," he was told, "is that everything in the world is a hustle."

Malcolm returned to Boston, where he was later arrested for burglary and sentenced to ten years in prison. The year was 1946 and he was not quite 21 years old. Prison was another school for Malcolm. He now had time to think and plan. Out of this thinking he underwent a conversion that literally transformed his whole life. By letters and visits from his family he was introduced to the Black Muslim Movement (which calls itself officially The Lost-Found Nation of Islam).

He tested himself in the discipline of his newly chosen religion by refusing to eat pork. The event startled his fellow inmates, who had nicknamed him Satan. He describes the occasion in this manner:

> It was the funniest thing—the reaction, and the way that it spread. In prison, where so little breaks the monotonous routine, the smallest thing causes a commotion of talk. It was being mentioned all over the cell block by night that Satan didn't eat pork.

> Later I would learn, when I had read and studied Islam a good deal, that, unconsciously, my first pre-Islamic submission had been manifested. I had experienced, for the first time, the Muslim teaching, "If you take one step toward Allah—Allah will take two steps toward you." . . . My brothers and sisters in Detroit and Chicago had all become converted to what they were being taught was the "natural religion for the black man."

His description of his process of self-education in prison is an indictment of the American educational system and a tribute to his perseverance in obtaining an education after being poorly prepared in the public schools.

While in prison he devised his own method of self-education and learned how to speak and debate effectively so that he could participate in and defend the movement after his release from prison. He started by copying words from the dictionary that might be helpful to him, beginning with "A." He went through to "Z," and then he writes, "for the first time, I could pick up a book and actually understand what the book was saying."

This aspect of his story calls attention to the tremendous reservoirs of talent, and even genius, locked up in the black ghettos among the masses. It also indicates what can be accomplished when the talent of this oppressed group is respected and given hope and a purpose.

Within a few years he was to become a debater with a national reputation. He took on politicians, college professors, journalists, and anyone black or white who had the nerve to meet him. He was respected by some and feared by others.

Malcolm was released from prison in 1952, when he was twenty-seven years old. For a few weeks he took a job with his oldest brother, Wilfred, as a furniture salesman in Detroit. He went to Chicago before the end of that year to hear and meet the leader of the Nation of Islam—Elijah Muhammad. He was accepted into the movement and given the name of Malcolm X. He went back to Detroit and was made assistant minister of the Detroit Mosque. From this point on his rise in the movement and in the eyes of the public was rapid.

At the end of 1953 he went to Chicago to live with the leader of the Nation of Islam and be trained by him personally. After organizing a mosque in Philadelphia, he was sent to head the movement in Harlem in 1954 before he was thirty years old. In a few years he was able to transform the Black Muslim Movement into a national organization and himself into one of the country's best known personalities. As the public spokesman and defender of the movement, he literally put it on the map. This was the beginning of his trouble with his leader, Elijah Muhammad. When the public thought of the Black Muslim Movement they thought first of Malcolm X.

Malcolm X had appeal far beyond the movement. He was one of the most frequent speakers on the nation's campuses and the object of admiration by thousands of militant youth.

In his pamphlet, "Malcolm X—The Man and His Ideas," George Breitman gives the following description of Malcolm's appeal as a speaker:

> His speaking style was unique—plain, direct like an arrow, devoid of flowery trimming. He used metaphors and figures of speech that were lean and simple, rooted in the ordinary, daily experience of his audiences. . . . Despite an extraordinary ability to move and arouse his listeners, his main appeal was to reason, not emotion. . . . I want only to convey the idea that rarely has there been a man in America better able to communicate ideas to the most oppressed people; and that was not just a matter of technique, which can be learned and applied in any situation by almost anybody, but that it was a rare case of a man in closest communion with the oppressed, able to speak to them, because he identified himself with them.

At the Grass Roots Conference in Detroit in November 1963 Malcolm X made his last important speech as a Muslim. In this speech he took a revolutionary position in the civil rights struggle—speaking mainly for himself and not for the leader he always referred to as The Honorable Elijah Muhammad. This speech showed clearly that Malcolm X had outgrown the narrow stage of the Black Muslim Movement.

He devotes a chapter in his book to the growth of his disenchantment and his eventual suspension from the Black Muslim Movement. He says: "I had helped Mr. Muhammad and his ministers to revolutionize the American black man's thinking, opening his eyes until he would never again look in the same fearful way at the white man. . . . If I harbored any personal disappointment whatsoever, it was that privately I was convinced that our Nation of Islam could be an even greater force in the American black man's overall struggle— if we engaged in more action. By that I mean I thought privately that we should have amended, or relaxed, our general non-engagement policy. I felt that, wherever black people committed themselves, in the Little Rocks and the Birminghams and other places, militantly disciplined Muslims should also be there—for all the world to see, and respect and discuss."

The split with Elijah Muhammad finally came, as it was expected, and over a matter that seemed rather trivial. The occasion for the split was a remark by Malcolm after the death of President Kennedy in November 1963.

During the last phase of his life Malcolm X established Muslim Mosque, Inc., and a non-religious organization—The Organization of Afro-American Unity, patterned after the Organization of African Unity. He attempted to internationalize the civil rights fight by taking it to the United Nations. In several trips to Africa and one to Mecca, he sought the counsel and support of African and Asian heads of state.

In the Epilogue to this book Alex Haley has written a concise account of the last days of Malcolm X. The book, revealing as it is, reads like the first draft of what could have been the most exciting autobiography of our time. It is unfortunate that Malcolm X did not live long enough to do the necessary editing and pruning that this book needed. We have no way of knowing what liberties Alex Haley took, if any, while editing the manuscript after the assassination of Malcolm X on Sunday, February 21, 1965.

That a man who had inhabited the "lower depth" of life could rise in triumph as a reproach to its ills, and become an uncompromising champion of his people, is in itself a remarkable feat. Malcolm X went beyond this feat. Though he came from the American ghetto and directed his message to the people in the American ghetto first of all, he also became, in his brief lifetime, a figure of world importance. He died on the threshold of his potential. *The Autobiography*

of Malcolm X, written hurriedly near the end of his life, is a clear indication of what this potential could have been.

John Illo (essay date Spring 1966)

SOURCE: "The Rhetoric of Malcolm X," in *Columbia University Forum,* Vol. 9, No. 2, Spring, 1966, pp. 5-12.

[*In the following essay, Illo analyzes and applauds Malcolm X's skill as an orator.*]

In a nation of images without substances, of rehearsed emotions, in a politic of consensus where platitude replaces belief or belief is fashioned by consensus, genuine rhetoric, like authentic prose, must be rare. For rhetoric, like any verbal art, is correlative with the pristine idea of reason and justice which, if it decays with the growth of every state and jurisprudence, now has developed into an unreason that aggressively claims the allegiance of the national mind.

Jurisprudence is the prudent justification of an absurd society, of institutionalized inequity and internal contradiction. Law, and juridical logic, and grammar conspire to frustrate the original idea of a just and good society, in which all men may freely become the best that they may be. Rhetoric, like the Shelleyan poetic, returns us to primal intelligence, to the golden idea and the godly nature whose mirror is unspoiled reason. The critical and reformist function of rhetoric, apparent in processes like irony and paradox, is perceptible in the whole range of tropes and syntactic and tonal devices. Repetitions and transposals of syntax recall the emphases of nature, before civil logic; and metaphor recalls the true relations, resemblances, predications, that we have been trained to forget. Love is not a fixation but a fire, for it consumes and cleanses; and man is not a rational animal so essentially as he is dust and breath, crumbling, evanescent, and mysterious because moved invisibly.

To use schemes, figures, tropes, in a plan or plot that corresponds with the broad proceeding of the juridically logical mind, is to make an oration. Within the grammatical frame of his society, the orator, using the language of primordial reason and symbol, restores to his audience the ideas that have been obscured by imposed categories that may correspond to institution but not to reality. Rhetoric, Aristotle taught, is analogous to logic because enthymeme is related to syllogism; but, more significantly, rhetoric is related to logic as logic is related to reality. And rhetoric is also related to poetry, as Cicero observed, his prosaic Roman mind reducing poetry to ornamented language, as the lyric mind of Plato had reduced rhetoric to "cookery." Cicero and Aristotle were each half right. Rhetoric is in fact poeticized logic, logic revised by the creative and critical imagination recalling original ideas. Rhetoric, the art that could grow only in a *polis* and a system of judicature, is the art that restores the primitive value of the mystical word and the human voice. With a matured craft and a legalist's acuteness, orators contrive the free language of childlike reason, innocently reproving the unnatural and perverse, which institution, custom, law, and policy ask us to accept as the way of the world.

And so great orators, when great, have spoken for absolute justice and reason as they perceived it, in defiance of their governments or societies, accusing tyrants, protesting vicious state policies that seduced the general will, execrating the deformation of popular morality. We think of an Isaiah prophesying against the corruption of ancestral religion, of a Demosthenes against Philip, a Cicero against Antony, a Burke against a colonial war, a Garrison against slavery. At the summit of their art they recalled the language of primal intelligence and passion in defense of elemental truth; and their symbols and transposed syntax, though deliberated, were no more spurious or obtrusive than in poetry. But unlike the pure poet, the orator always holds near enough to the juridical logic, grammar, and semantic of the institution to be able to attack the institution. He never yields his reformist responsibility for the private vision that may be illusive, and may be incommunicable. The orator unlinks the mind-forged manacles, but refashions them into an armor for the innocent intelligence, the naked right.

Lesser oratory, venal, hypocritical, in defense of the indefensible, is patently factitious, its free language a cosmetic, a youthful roseate complexion arranged on an old, shrewd and degenerated visage, as in the forced prosopopoeias of Cicero appealing for a criminal Milo, or in the tediously predictable alliterated triads of Everett McKinley Dirksen. Bad morals usually produce bad rhetoric, and such is the dureful weight of institutions and their parties that *rhetoric* had been pejorated, generally, into *bad rhetoric*. Even Henry Steele Commager can regard oratory like Senator Long's as "eloquent but shameless," attributes ideally exclusive. The swelling anaphoras of a Southern Congressman are not eloquent but ludicrous, raising irrepressible images of toads and swine. Little else but bad rhetoric is possible to those within the establishment, so far from original reason, so committed to the apologetics of unreason. And those outside are conditioned by established styles, or are graceless, or are misdirected in eccentric contrariety. The poetry of Bob Dylan veers in its metaphoric texture between the more lyrical ads and the *Daily News* editorials; the new left sniffles and stumbles into the unwitting anacolutha of *uh* and *you-know*; the old left tends to rant and cant, persuasive only to the persuaded. There are clear teachers like Allen Krebs and Staughton Lynd, but as good teachers they are probably not orators.

The achievement of Malcolm X, then, though inevitable,

seems marvelous. Someone had to rise and speak the fearful reality, to throw the light of reason into the hallucinatory world of the capitalist and biracial society that thinks itself egalitarian, that thinks itself humanitarian and pacific. But it was unexpected that the speaking should be done with such power and precision by a russet-haired field Negro translated from conventional thief to zealot and at the end nearly to Marxist and humanist.

For the rhetoric of the American black outsider in this age has seldom been promising; this is not the century of Toussaint L'Ouverture or the nation of Frederick Douglass. The charismatic strength of Father Divine, or of Elijah Muhammad, did not derive from rhetoric. The language of one was hypnotically abstruse, if not perfectly unintelligible, related not to oratory or to religion but to New Thought. The oratory of the other is diffuse and halting, unornamented, solecistic, provincial, its development over-deliberate, its elocution low-keyed though rising to an affecting earnestness. Robert Williams has force but not majesty or art. Men like James Baldwin and Le Roi Jones are primarily writers, and each is deficient in the verbal and vocal size and action required in oratory, which is neither writing nor talking. The young Negro radicals are beyond criticism, the gloomy product not so much of the ghetto as of TV and the American high school. The Nobel Laureate and the Harlem Congressman have different oratorical talents, but neither is an outsider.

The rhetoric of Malcolm X was in the perennial traditions of the art, but appropriate to his audiences and purpose—perennial because appropriate. A Harlem rally is not the Senate of the Roman Republic, but Cicero would have approved Malcolm's discourses as *accommodatus, aptus, congruens,* suitable to his circumstances and subject. His exordia were properly brief, familiar, sometimes acidly realistic (". . . brothers and sisters, friends and enemies: I just can't believe everyone in here is a friend and I don't want to leave anybody out."), and he moved to his proposition within the first minute, for his audience needed relevant ideas and theses, not dignity and amplitude. His perorations were similarly succinct, sometimes entirely absorbed into the confirmations. His personal apologiae, negative or self-depreciatory, contrary to those of a Cicero or a Burke, assured his hearers that he was on the outside, like them: "I'm not a politician, not even a student of politics; in fact, I'm not a student of much of anything. I'm not a Democrat, I'm not a Republican, and I don't even consider myself an American," an ironic gradation or augmentative climax that was, in the world of Malcolm and his people, really a kind of declination or reversed climax.

His narration and confirmation were densely analytical, but perspicuous because of their familiar diction and analogies, and their catechetical repetitions: "And to show you what his [Tshombe's] thinking is—a hired killer—what's the first thing he did? He hired more killers. He went out and got the mercenaries from South Africa. And what is a mercenary? A hired killer. That's all a mercenary is. The anti-Castro Cuban pilots, what are they? Mercenaries, hired killers. Who hired them? The United States. Who hired the killers from South Africa? The United States; they just used Tshombe to do it."

Instruction was the usual purpose of Malcolm's oratory; he was primarily a teacher, his oratory of the demonstrative kind, and his speeches filled with significant matter.

—John Illo

Instruction was the usual purpose of Malcolm's oratory; he was primarily a teacher, his oratory of the demonstrative kind, and his speeches filled with significant matter. It was the substantive fullness and penetration, the honesty and closeness to reality of Malcolm's matter that imparted much of the force to his oratory.

A representative political speech in the United States is empty of content. What did President Kennedy's Inaugural Address contain that a commencement address does not? Indeed, the Inaugural displayed the meaningless chiasmus, the fatuous or sentimental metaphor, the callow hyperbaton of a valedictory. President Johnson's speeches on foreign affairs vitiate reason and intelligence as his foreign policy violates international morality: temporarily not to attack a neutral nation is a positive beneficence that should evoke gratitude and concessions, and one is ready to negotiate with any party under any conditions except the party and conditions that are relevant. But such is the tradition of vacant and meaningless political oratory in America, and such the profusion of the universally accepted and discredited rhetoric of advertising, that the public nods and acquiesces, not believes. We expect truth and substance not in open oration, but in secret conference or in caucus, "on the inside"—where we can't hear it. We assume that rhetoric is a futile and deceptive or self-deceived art, because rhetoric should persuade through rational conviction, but business and government are ruled by power and interest. And perhaps Congressional or party oratory is a facade, the votes having been decided not by analogies and metonymies but by the Dow-Jones averages.

Yet the people, closer to reason than their legislators, may still be moved by rhetoric, and popular oratory may still be a political force. We wonder how a crowd in Havana can listen to the Premier for three hours. A revolution needs people, and to explain a revolution needs time, and three

hours is little enough. To explain a self-maintaining American polity and economy while evading its real problems needs very little time, and three hours of Hubert Humphrey would be unconscionable.

Malcolm's speeches, if not so complex, not so informed or copious as those of an accomplished revolutionary, were not vacuous. The man whose secondary education began painstakingly and privately in the Norfolk Prison Colony was able to analyze for his people their immediate burden, its maintenance in a system of domestic power and its relation to colonialism, more acutely than the white and black Ph.D's with whom he debated. A man about whose life it is difficult not to sentimentalize was seldom sentimental in his oratory, and though he simplified he did not platitudinize.

Malcolm's simplifications, sometimes dangerous, though commonplace in popular oratory and less sophistic than those in establishment rhetoric, derived from the simplicity of his central message: that colored people have been oppressed by white people whenever white people have been able to oppress them, that because immediate justice is not likely ("Give it to us yesterday, and that's not fast enough"), the safest thing for all is to separate, that the liberty to "sit down next to white folks—on the toilet" is not adequate recompense for the past 400 years. Like Robert Owen or John Brown or William Lloyd Garrison, Malcolm spent the good years of his life asserting one idea and its myriad implications and its involved strategies in a society in which the black is often a noncitizen even *de jure*. And because what he said was as intelligible and obvious as a lynching, his rhetorical content was not embarrassed by the tergiversations, the sophisms, the labored evasions, the empty grandiloquence of American political oratory.

The American press attributed the preaching of violence to a man who was no political activist, who moved in the arena of words and ideas, and who usually described a condition of violence rather than urged a justifiably violent response. The obtuse *New York Times* obituary editorial was representative. At worst, Malcolm X, like St. Alphonsus Liguori, taught the ethic of self-defense. *Méchant animal!* The weakness of Malcolm, in fact, and of Elijah Muhammad, is that they were not activists; unlike Martin Luther King, neither had a "movement," for neither went anywhere. Malcolm's success in enlarging the Nation of Islam from 400 to 40,000 and in drawing "well-wishers" by the hundreds of thousands was from the ideas and the words, not from an appeal to action, and not from an appeal to license: the call to moral responsibility and the perpetual Lent of the Muslims repelled most Negroes as it would repel most whites.

But Malcolm's essential content was so simple and elemental, his arguments, like Thoreau's, so unanswerable, that the American press, even when not covertly racist, could not understand him, accustomed as it is to the settled contradictions of civil logic in a biracial country.

What answer is there to the accusations that in a large part of America, a century after the 14th Amendment, some kinds of murderers cannot be punished by law, that the law is the murderer? Is it an answer that we must tolerate injustice so that we may enjoy justice? Condemning such deformed logic, and adhering to obvious moral truths, Malcolm, like the Bogalusa Deacons, had little difficulty in understanding and explaining to his audiences the Thomistic conception of law better than the Attorney General of the United States understands it. Malcolm was always disconcerted when the powers that be and their exponents refused to recognize the legality of humanity. His strongest vocal emphases were on words like law and right: "They don't use *law*," he exclaimed of the Central Congolese Government, which was directed by outside interests, and the lawfulness of the Eastern Government was more valid, he thought, because it was of its own people.

Justice and equity and emancipation, not violence, not hatred, not retribution, and not the theology of the Muslims were the central matter of Malcolm's oratory, though that theology was useful as a repudiation of American white Christianity. He had entered the stream of sane and moral social teaching before his parting from Elijah Muhammad, and was deepening his knowledge and expression of it at the moment of the death he expected each day.

If his theses were terrible, it was because they were asserted without compromise or palliation, and because the institutional reality they challenged was terrible. How else to indicate reality and truth if not by direct challenge? Indirection is not workable, for the state has stolen irony; satire is futile, its only resource to repeat the language of the Administration. To say that the American tradition beckons us onward to the work of peace in Vietnam, or that they who reject peace overtures are great servants of peace, is to speak not ironically but authoritatively. The critical efficacy even of absurd literature is threatened by real reductions toward the absurd and beyond, and when usable, absurd statement cannot be at once terse, clear, complex, and unequivocal. The only useful attack is directness, which, opposed to outrage, is outraged and, to apologists of outrage, outrageous.

Malcolm's challenge soon implied anticolonialism, in which was implied anticapitalism. Not a doctrinal Marxist when he died, Malcolm had begun to learn a relation between racism and capitalism during his first African journey, and a relation between socialism and national liberation. Rising above the ethical limitations of many civil rights leaders, he rejected a black symbiosis in the warfare state. The black housewife may collect Green Stamps or dividends, the black paterfamilias may possess an Impala and a hi-fi, the black

student an unimpeachable graduate degree and a professorship, but what moral black or white could be happy in the world of color TV and Metrecal and napalm? If a rising Negro class could be contented by such hopes and acquirements, if it yearned for the glittering felicities of the American dream, for the Eden of *Life* and *Ebony,* Malcolm had finer longings, and so his following was small: his vision was more intense, more forbidding than that of King or Wilkins or Farmer. They preached integrated Americanism; Malcolm taught separation for goodness, the co-existence of morally contrary cultures in a geographic unit, in "America."

Because the black had been always alien in America, had been always taught to hate himself in America ("We hated our heads . . . the shape of our nose . . . the color of our skin. . . ."), he now had the freedom to despise, not embrace, a society that had grown alien to humanity, and whose profound alienation had been intimated for the black first in slavery, then in racism. Separation promised not the means to make a black image of Beverly Hills or Westchester, but the liberty to build a new Jerusalem. How might such an evangel be grasped by a social worker or a Baptist minister?

Malcolm's earlier expressions of racism, sometimes augmented or distorted in the misreporting, were a means or an error that receded after his Islamic-African pilgrimage, qualified into renouncement. Their white counterparts have been the political hardware of thousands of local American statesmen and scores of United States Congressmen, and how many have not outgrown them, are legislators because of them? An American President can admit to prior racism with little embarrassment, with becoming repentance.

It is the growth and maturing that matter, and Malcolm's ideological journey, truncated after beginning late, was leftward, enlightened, and opening toward humanitarianism and unsentimental fraternalism, contrary to that of some British lords and some Yale graduates, contrary to that of the young American Marxists of the 1930s, now darkening into polarized anticommunism. There were no saner, more honest and perspicuous analyses of the racial problem than Malcolm's last speeches and statements, beside which the pronouncements of most administrations and civic officials are calculated nonsense. Only from the outside can some truths be told.

In the rhetoric of Malcolm X, as in all genuine rhetoric, figures correspond to the critical imagination restoring the original idea and to the conscience protesting the desecration of the idea. Tropes and schemes of syntax are departures from literal meaning, *abusiones,* "abuses" of a grammar and semantic that have themselves grown into abuses of original reason. As Shelley saw, the abusion, or trope, like revolutionism, destroys conventional definitions to restore original wholeness and reality. Rhetoric, like revolution, is "a way of redefining reality."

The frequent repetitions in Malcolm X's rhetoric, like those of Cicero or St. Paul, are communications of the passion that is not satisfied by single statement, but that beats through the pulses. Good rhetorical repetition is viscerally didactic.

But it is an especially dangerous device, its potential of fraudulence proportionate to its elemental power to persuade. It may reinforce truths, it may add stones to build great lies. The anaphoras of Administration rhetoric lead successive clauses each further from reality. Abstractions in repetitions, like the "peace" and "freedom" of the Presidential addresses, are usually doubtful, because ambiguous and inaccessible to testing. War may very well be peace, and slavery freedom, if the predications are repeated often enough.

The substantives and verbs in Malcolm's repetitions were usually concrete, exposing themselves to empirical judgment:

> As long as the white man sent you to Korea, you bled. He sent you to Germany, you bled. He sent you to the South Pacific to fight the Japanese, you bled. You bleed for white people, but when it comes to seeing your own church being bombed and little black girls murdered, you haven't got any blood. You bleed when the white man says bleed; you bite when the white man says bite; and you bark when the white man says bark.

Malcolm here began with epistrophe for reinforcement of a repeated reality, combined it with anaphora to shift focus to "the man," moved to epanastrophe in the third and fourth sentences, in which "the man" and the black man share the repeating emphasis, and to epanadiplosis in the fourth for a doubled emphasis on *bleed,* while a tolling alliteration of labials and liquids instructs the outer ear, while asyndeton accelerates a tautness and indignation, and while the fullness of emotion evokes a pathetic-sardonic syllepsis or *blood.*

His rhetorical questions and percunctations with repetition, here anaphora and epistrophe, have the urgency of a Massillon convincing a noble audience of the probability of their damnation:

> Why should white people be running all the stores in our community? Why should white people be running the banks of our community? Why should the economy of our community be in the hands of the white man? Why?

The orator may redirect as well as repeat his syntactic units. Malcolm used chiasmus, or crossing of antithetic sets, not deceptively, not to confound realities, but to explore the cal-

culated fantasies of the American press, to untangle the crossing of image and reality:

> . . . you end up hating your friends and loving your enemies . . . The press is so powerful in its image-making role, it can make a criminal look like he's the victim and make the victim look like he's the criminal. . . . If you aren't careful, the newspapers will have you hating the people who are being oppressed and loving the people who are doing the oppressing.

Malcolm was attracted to chiasmus as an economy in dialectic. In the Oxford Union Society debate of December 1964, he explicated and defended Senator Goldwater's chiasmus of *extremism* and *moderation,* converting the memorable assault upon radical reform into an apology for black militancy.

As the strict clausal scheme may be varied to represent emotional thought, strict demonstration may be relieved by paradox and analogy. Paradox, here climactic and with repetitions, writes itself into any narrative of American Negro history since 1863.

> How can you thank a man for giving you what's already yours? How then can you thank him for giving you only part of what's already yours?

With an analogy Malcolm dismissed Roy Wilkins' quaver that though the black may be a second-class American, he is yet an American, with his little part of the affluent dream:

> I'm not going to sit at your table and watch you eat, with nothing on my plate, and call myself a diner. Sitting at the table doesn't make you a diner, unless you eat some of what's on that plate. Being here in America doesn't make you an American. Being born here in America doesn't make you an American.

We see a black man with half the income of a white, and think of other hungers, and the analogy works as symbol and image, like Bacon's winding stair to great place or Demosthenes' Athenian boxer defending himself from multiple blows.

Metaphor and metonymy are the symbolic image condensed and made freer from customary logic than the more explicit analogy. Like repetitions and analogies they may be recognizably fraudulent, for symbolic language is not dissociated from truth. We must know or imagine the referent before we can judge and be moved by the symbol. When an American President now says, "The door of peace must be kept wide open for all who wish to avoid the scourge of war, but the door of aggression must be closed and bolted if man himself is to survive," he is disquieting tame, weary metaphors, long since grown insipid and moribund, into a defiance of meaning, and the very antithesis emphasizes the inanity of the ghostwritten rhetoric in a linguistic culture that has not finally adopted Newspeak. If the figures are initially suspect because of the designed, limitless ambiguity and abstractness of the referents, they are contemptible when related to the realities they profess to clarify. Such metaphor is not the discovery of truth but its concealment. "When I can't talk sense," said the eighteenth-century Irish orator, John Curran, "I talk metaphor."

The metaphors of Malcolm X, sometimes ethnically conventional, sometimes original, sometimes inevitable ("I don't see an American dream. I see an American nightmare."), were rarely ambiguous in the abstract member, and were often concrete in both, lending themselves to the touch of common experience. They were infrequent, less frequent than in the elevated tradition of Pitt and Burke and Webster. Malcolm's oratory resembled rather that of the self-educated reformer Cobden in its simple, unornamented vigor, in its reduction to essential questions, in its analytic directness and clarity. In Malcolm's oratory as in Cobden's, metaphor was exceptional in a pattern of exposition by argumentation in abstract and literal diction.

And because Malcolm wished to demonstrate rather than suggest, he preferred the more fully ratiocinative structure, the analogy, to the more condensed and poetic metaphor: he had wished to be not a poet but a lawyer when his elementary school English teacher advised him to turn to carpentry. So also, Malcolm composed in the larger grammatical unit, the paragraph, which corresponds to analogy, rather than in the sentence, which corresponds to metaphor. In answering questions he often prefaced his extended expositions with the request not for one more word or one more sentence, but for "one more paragraph"—and a paragraph indeed was what he usually produced, extemporaneous and complete with counterthesis, thesis, development, synthesis and summary.

The metaphors and metonymies, restricted in number, often suggested truth, like the analogies, by fusing image and symbol, as in poetry: Blake's little black thing amid the snow is sensuously and spiritually black, the snow sensuously and spiritually white. Malcolm used the same deliberate indetermination of perception in the image by which he characterized white immigrants in America:

> Everything that came out of Europe, every blue-eyed thing is already an American.

Synecdoche and tmesis combine to refocus on generic essentials for a black audience.

In quick answer to an immoderating Stan Bernard and an uncivil Gordon Hall and trying to defend the thesis that the Muslims were a force in the Negro movement though numerically insignificant, Malcolm compared them with the Mau Mau, then condensed an implicit analogy to a metaphor and, with characteristically temerarious simplification, expanded and explicated the metaphor into analogy:

> The Mau Mau was also a minority, a microscopic minority, but it was the Mau Mau who not only brought independence to Kenya, but— . . . but it brought it—that wick. The powder keg is always larger than the wick. . . . It's the wick that you touch that sets the powder off.

By a folk metonymy in one pronoun, more convincing than the usual rhetorical patriotic genealogies, Malcolm enlarged to their real dimension the time and space of the Negro's misfortune:

> many of us probably passed through [Zanzibar] on our way to America 400 years ago.

The identification of Malcolm with his audience, not merely through the plural pronoun, was so thorough that he effected the desired harmony or union in which the speaker can disregard his audience as an object and speak his own passion and reason, when between himself and his hearers there is no spiritual division. The great orator does not play upon his audience as upon a musical instrument; his verbal structures are artful but urged from within.

Malcolm's composition and elocution were remarkable in their assimilative variety. Before the mixed or white audiences, as at college forums, the composition was more abstract and literal, austerely figured, grammatically pure, and the elocution sharper, somewhat rapid and high-pitched, near his speaking voice, enunciated precisely but not mimetic or over-articulated. Before the great black audiences Malcolm adopted a tone and ornament that were his and his audience's but that he relinquished before the white or the academic. The composition of the black speeches was rich in ethnic figuration and humor, in paronomasia, alliteration, and rhyme (the novocained patient, blood running down his jaw, suffers "peacefully"; if you are a true revolutionary "You don't do any singing, you're too busy swinging"; the Negroes who crave acceptance in white America "aren't asking for any nation—they're trying to crawl back on the plantation.") The elocution of this, Malcolm's grand style, was deeper, slower, falling into a tonal weighting and meiosis, wider in its range of pitch, dynamics, emphasis.

Always exhibiting a force of moral reason, never hectic or mainly emotional, Malcolm changed from *homo afer* to *homo europaeus* as the ambience and occasion required. In the mosques he employed the heavy vocal power of impassioned Negro discourse; in academic dialogue and rebuttal his voice sometimes resembled that of Adlai Stevenson in its east-north-central nasality, and in its hurried, thoughtful pauses, its wry humor, its rational rather than emotional emphases.

It is understandable that he was correct, intelligible, lucid, rational, for few public orators in our time have been as free as Malcolm from the need to betray their own intelligence. John Kennedy, who in January pledged a quest for peace and a revulsion from colonialism, in one week of the following April repudiated the Cuban invasion he was then assisting, in another week of the same April pugnaciously justified the intervention, and, having been rebuked by reality, reproached reality with a dialectic from the Mad Tea-Party. His audience was appropriate: American newspaper editors. Later, waving a flag in the Orange Bowl, he would promise the émigré landlords warfare and their restored rents with melodramatic and puerile metonymy. Adlai Stevenson, who twice had talked sense to the American people, denied his government's aggression in Cuba with juridical solemnity, with the noble anaphoras, the poignant metaphors, the sensitive ironies of the campaign speeches, and, fatally drawn to display *expertise,* derisively censured the oratory of Raul Roa. His indignant exposure of revolutionaries was submerged in the laughter of the black galleries of the world; he indulged himself, during the Congo debates, in the pointless metonymies of Independence Day addresses; and his recurrent denunciations of colonialism were freaks of unintended irony.

"Who would not weep, if Atticus were he?"

Malcolm, more fortunate than these, was not ordained by history to be the spokesman or the apologist of violence and unthinkable power, and so was not forced to violate reason. In his last years he was in the great tradition of rational and moral speech, consanguineous with Isaiah, with Demosthenes and Cicero, with Paine and Henry, Lincoln and Douglass, as they were allied to the primitive idea of goodness. He was not an emotionalist or a demagogue, but an orator who combined familiarity with passion, with compelling ideas and analytic clarity, and with sober force of utterance, and with a sense, now usually deficient except when depraved, of rhetoric as an art and a genre.

His feeling for the art was probably the benefit of his old-fashioned verbal and literary education in prison. As the rhetoric of Frederick Douglass, then a young slave, originated in his readings of Sheridan's oratory, so Malcolm's alma mater, he said, was "books." The methodical long-hand copying of thousands of logical definitions, his nightly labor with the dictionary in prison, left an impress of precision in diction and syntax, later tested and hardened in

hostile debate. As he learned the science and the habits of grammar, Malcolm learned the unfamiliar subtleties of the art of rhetoric within a few years. As late as 1961 he prevailed in debate more by conviction than by linguistic accuracy, and the solecisms were embarrassing to his literate admirers and probably to himself, as were the parochial pronunciations, atavistic traces of which could be heard very rarely in the last year ("influence"). But this sense of rhetoric derived also from his perception of the ideas that antedate rhetoric and that inform all moral language. His teaching, because elemental and unsophisticated in its morality, was more sane, more philosophic than the wisdom of many an academician who, detached from the facts of human pain, has the institutionalized intelligence to devise a morality to fit his institution, who can make policy his morality: Arthur Schlesinger, Jr., can regard the genocidal war in Vietnam as "an experiment, . . . something you have to try."

> **Malcolm combined magnificence and ethnic familiarity to demonstrate what he asserted: the potential majesty of the black man even in America. . . .**
>
> *—John Illo*

In his maturity, Malcolm was always aware of the centrally ethical and honest enough not to elude it, and so he soon outgrew what was doctrinally grotesque in the Nation of Islam (what native American religious movement is without such grotesqueness?). But he retained the religious commitment and the wholesome ascesis of the Muslims, and thus was helped in the exhausting work of the last years, the weeks of eighteen-hour days. A mixed seed fell in good soil.

He emerged from dope, prostitution, burglary, prison, and a fanciful sectarianism to enter a perennial humanist art, to achieve a brilliant facility in oratory and debate, in less time than many of us consume in ambling through graduate school. His developing accomplishment in the last year was, as a *New York Times* reporter exclaimed but could not write, "incredible." The Oxford Union Society, venerable, perceptive, and disinterested because unAmerican, adjudged him among the best of living orators after his debate three months before his death, a pleasant triumph ignored by the American press. Though he may be diluted, or obliterated, or forgotten by the established civil rights movement, which is built into the consensus, Malcolm was for all time an artist and thinker. In the full Aristotelean meaning he was a rhetorician, who, to be such, knew more than rhetoric: ethics, logic, grammar, psychology, law, history, politics; and his best speeches might be texts for students of that comprehensive science and art.

His controlled art, his tone of pride without arrogance, have followers if not a school, in his own Muslim Mosque and among the Nation of Islam, audible in the rational and disdainful replies of Norman 3X in the murder trial. But Malcolm is distinct rhetorically from his admirers among the surly school of Negro speakers, the oratorical equivalent of *Liberator,* who have little to offer their mixed auditory but insolence and commonplaces in broken and frenetic, in monotonous or ill-accented language. And he was remote from the misanthropic and negativist among the alienated. Malcolm, a religionist, could not be "bitter," or descend to scatology in expressing moral outrage. The laughter or chuckling, in his several oratorical styles, was, in motive and in sound, not embittered, or malicious, or frustrated, but apodictic; it was the laughter of assured rectitude, and amusement at the radical unreason of the opposition. For not he but the established structures were the opposition, dissentient to godly reason and justice, which were the authority for his teaching. Hearing Malcolm was an experience not morbid or frightening, but joyous, as Mark Van Doren said of reading *Hamlet.* Though the drama and the man were tragic, in each the confident and varied movement of language and moral ideas told us something superb about our humanity. Malcolm combined magnificence and ethnic familiarity to demonstrate what he asserted: the potential majesty of the black man even in America, a majesty idiosyncratic but related to all human greatness. And so his last ten years tell us that a man can be more fully human serving a belief, even if to serve it requires that he borrow from the society that his service and belief affront. If he and his people illustrate that the grand primal ideas and their grand expression can be spoiled for men by institutions, the whole work and life of Malcolm X declare that the good man, if he has the soul to resist the state and its courts and senates, can restore the ideal world of art and justice.

Robert Bone (review date 11 September 1966)

SOURCE: "A Black Man's Quarrel With the Christian God," in *New York Times Book Review,* September 11, 1966, pp. 3, 14.

[*In the following review, Bone demonstrates the use of Malcolm X's autobiography as a means of understanding the intentions and convictions of the proponents of the concept of "Black Power" in the civil rights movement during the latter half of the 1960s.*]

In the month of June, 1966, the Negro protest movement entered a new phase. For the first time, during the so-called "Meredith march" to Jackson, Miss., the younger activists raised the slogan of "Black Power!" In the same month, less than a year after its initial publication, Grove Press brought out a paperback edition of *The Autobiography of Malcolm X.* The two events are linked by more than a coincidence. For Malcolm's book, without a doubt, has had a major impact on the younger generation.

White liberals and Negro leaders alike have joined in condemnation of the new slogan. But before we resign *en masse* from CORE and S.N.C.C. (Student Nonviolent Coordinating Committee), and before we fill the air with charges of "nihilism" and "black nationalism," it behooves us to read, and even to reread Malcolm's book, and especially the last five chapters, which describe the transformation that took place in his mind and heart after his break with Elijah Muhammad and the Black Muslims. We might then better grasp the spirit and intent of these young men, who are in mood and outlook and political perspective nothing other than the heirs of Malcolm X.

The main events of Malcolm's life are by now familiar. His childhood in Michigan was a nightmare, replete with images of violence and misery. His adolescence in Boston, "conked" and zoot-suited, did little more than prepare him for the hustler's life he was to enter when he moved to Harlem. He became a pusher, a procurer, a gunman, and eventually was sentenced to 10 years in prison for armed robbery. There he was converted to the Nation of Islam, and for 12 years he devoted to the Muslim cause his impressive forensic and administrative talents. Not much more than a year before his death, he was "isolated indefinitely" by the Black Muslims. His last months were devoted to a pilgrimage to Mecca, and an attempt to found a splinter group called the Organization of Afro-American Unity.

Malcolm's inner history is less widely understood. His life has been from start to finish a challenge and rebuke to historic Christianity. The son of a Baptist minister, he encountered only violence and humiliation from "the good Christian white people" of his native state. He retaliated through a life of crime, which proclaimed louder than words his denial of Christian community and negation of Christian values. It was the Nation of Islam, with its anti-Christian demonology, that rescued Malcolm from criminality and elevated his rebellion to a metaphysical plane. Nor did his rupture with the Black Muslims mitigate his opposition to the Christian faith. On the contrary, it confirmed his alienation by drawing him still closer to Islam.

In the end, it is Malcolm's metaphysical revolt that matters. For around his quarrel with the Christian God clusters a series of explosive issues that are of paramount concern to Negroes of the coming generation. These include the historic relationship of Christianity to white power, the freeing of the black man's mind from the tyranny of white culture and the formation by the American Negro of an adequate self-image—or putting it another way, his conquest of shame.

To all of these issues Malcolm addressed himself with eloquence and passion from the time of his conversion to the Nation of Islam. It is to that curious sect that we must therefore turn in order to discover the sources of his personal power.

The Muslim indictment of historic Christianity might be summarized as follows. The Christian religion is the tribal religion of white Europe. Since the time of the Crusades, the Christian church has instigated, championed, and proclaimed as holy the white man's depredations into Africa. Throughout the centuries, and in every corner of the globe, the church has been the willing instrument of white power. She has been guilty of sanctifying white supremacy, blessing the white man's wars of conquest, and justifying in the name of God slavery and segregation. Without pity or remorse the Christian church has aided and abetted the white man in his criminal designs upon the colored world.

In the consolidation of white power, the church has played a crucial part. The whip and gun, although in ample evidence, remained a last resort. Far handier was the apathy, resignation, or even willing cooperation of the victim in his own enslavement. To secure this acquiescence, the blessings of the white slavemaster's religion were bestowed upon the blacks. They were taught to endure humbly and without complaint the cruelties of the slavemaster, and to look for their reward in Heaven, while the white man enjoyed the products of their labor here on earth.

The permanent effects of this indoctrination are apparent in "the brainwashed black Christian" of the present day. He has been convinced of his inferiority; his manhood has been crushed by an overwhelming sense of shame. And here again, the Muslims claim, it is the church that taught the Negro to hold his blackness in contempt, and to revere the color white.

It is difficult, for example, to believe at the bottom of one's soul that black is beautiful if one has been taught for centuries to worship a blond and blue-eyed God. For if God is man idealized, then the black man who worships a white God is through every act of worship buried deeper in a sense of worthlessness and shame. Rehabilitation, the Muslims have discovered, will require a new sense of self as well as a new concept of God.

All of this, as Malcolm never ceases to affirm, rings true to the potential Muslim convert. It corresponds to his experience, his knowledge of the white world. It comes in a package, to be sure, which also contains a good deal of magic, Puritan fanaticism, ignorance and hate. These extraneous features of the sect, Malcolm came to realize, had limited its growth and obscured its central insight. What if they were cut away? A movement might emerge shorn of racism, separatism, and blind hate, which yet preserved the explosive force and liberating energy of the Muslim myth. This is the direction in which Malcolm X was moving for a year or more before his death.

Hatred, to be sure, does not respond so readily to the imperatives of ideology. It is therefore of the utmost importance that we understand the spiritual transformation that enabled Malcolm to transcend his hate. When he returned from his pilgrimage to Mecca, he announced to the reporters, "In the past, yes, I have made sweeping indictments of *all* white people. I never will be guilty of that again—as I know now that some white people *are* truly sincere, that some truly are capable of being brotherly toward a black man." He then explained that in the Holy World his attitude was changed by virtue of the brotherhood that was extended not only to himself but to all Moslems, of whatever nationality or race.

Malcolm's explanation of his new attitude toward whites ought not to be accepted at face value. The casual encounters, however gratifying, of a visit to a foreign land, do not constitute an adequate basis for a profound personality change. What took place in Malcolm's heart was perhaps confirmed in Mecca, but initiated in Chicago: namely, his betrayal by Elijah Muhammad and expulsion from the Muslim sect. It was this experience that laid the groundwork for his new relations with co-religionists of white complexion.

What is at issue is Malcolm's education in the nature of evil. For 12 years he endorsed a demonology which proclaims that the white man is a devil. On no account is any white man to be trusted; however friendly his behavior, covertly he is plotting your betrayal. When betrayal came, however, it was by a black man and in Malcolm's world, *the* black man par excellence. Under the impact of this trauma, the simple equation of white with evil had to fall. If a man's moral nature cannot be reliably inferred from the color of his skin, then we must confront what James Baldwin has called the mysteries and conundrums of the human heart.

It was this confrontation, this inner growth, that made possible the next stage in Malcolm's political development. For want of a better term, it might be described as a *tactical* black nationalism. Toward the end of his life, Malcolm wrote that he now wanted "an all-black organization whose ultimate objective was to help create a society in which there could exist an honest white-black brotherhood."

This is as far from the separatism of the Black Muslims as Malcolm's attitude toward whites is a departure from their racism. In both instances, there remains a healthy skepticism, which places the main responsibility for brotherhood where it belongs: on the whites. The political expression of that skepticism is the transitional demand for black power.

Perhaps, in the light of Malcolm's book, we can better understand the rivalry between the youthful militants of S.N.C.C. and their erstwhile parent organization, the Southern Christian Leadership Conference. For these young men are finished with appeals to Christian conscience; that is the meaning of their new slogan. "Freedom Now!" is addressed to whites; it is a shorthand version of "Give us our freedom now!" But "Black Power!" is addressed to Negroes; it is a call to mobilize their full social weight for the achievement of specific goals. The essence of the shift is psychological. It has nothing to do with black supremacy, but much to do with manhood and self-reliance.

For centuries, the American Negro has felt the weight of white power. Now he proposes to organize a countervailing power with a base among the poorest of the poor. Those whites who are inclined to cry "Foul!" would do well to contemplate the strange career of Malcolm X. For Malcolm's ascent from the lower depths to his final vision of human brotherhood suggests that black power may be after all redemptive; and apostasy, one man's way to heaven.

Marcus H. Boulware (essay date November 1967)

SOURCE: "Minister Malcolm Orator Profundo," in *Negro History Bulletin,* Vol. 30, No. 7, November, 1967, pp. 12-14.

[*In the following essay, Boulware delineates Malcolm X's career as an orator and religious and social leader, complimenting his achievements and declaring: "People enjoyed his speaking whether or not they agreed with him, because he made speaking an appealing art."*]

The expanding prestige and stature of the Black Muslim movement attracted hundreds of adherents, and many of them were brilliant like the late Malcolm Little whose pseudonym was "Malcolm X." Opponents labelled him protestor, panelist, Muslim minister, and orator *profundo*. Numerous articles have been written about this dazzling figure who was often identified as a smooth, oily ex-convict. In his early career as a Black Muslim, Malcolm X is worthy of comparison with Plato and Aristotle of the Greeks—though his teachings were somewhat orthodox. It was rumored that Minister Malcolm X was next in line for the office of the Messenger of Allah.

At the acme of his career, Malcolm X, who split with the Black Muslims and launched his own faction, was assassinated speaking from the stage of a Harlem ballroom in mid-afternoon on February 21, 1965. It was reported that his slaying was the outgrowth of revenge by active members of the Black Muslim sect. At the trial in January, 1966, the government claimed three men stationed themselves in the audience, two started a fight to distract attention, while Thomas "15 X" Johnson shot Malcolm in the chest with a sawed-off shot gun. Then the other two men rushed to the stage and fired bullets into the prone body of Malcolm X. Before the perpetrators could escape, one was shot in the leg by an adherent of Malcolm's faction and taken into custody by the police. The other two men were arrested later.

The public remembers the late Minister Malcolm as an eloquent Muslim minister and philosopher whose trail led from a dingy prison cell to the Mount of Olives, while at the same time, he developed himself into an eloquent orator and street-corner spell-binder. People enjoyed his speaking whether or not they agreed with him, because he made speaking an appealing art. His oratorical skill was a favorite with audiences at street corners, but this did not mean that he did not have hostile listeners in his audiences. The orator's vocal style of delivery caught the fancy of numerous "avenue hangbys" who often followed him to his several speaking stations.

Like every human being, Malcolm X made mistakes and often turned his ears away from wisdom's good counsel. His courageous character led him to speak his mind in a vocabulary which the government interpreted as being treason. Unfortunately he was arrested and placed in prison. From then on, his critics never failed to forget his early career as a Harlem hoodlum nor his nickname "Big Red." In defense of himself as a youth, Malcolm X attributed his youthful delinquent habits to white people who made it difficult for a black man to earn honestly a decent living.

During his adolescent years, Malcolm became the product of the forces that molded him belatedly into a Muslim minister of the upper echelon. His life was a paradox that had to be resolved by him alone. He was born in Omaha, Nebraska, in 1925 but his family moved to Michigan. Because his father was a radical exponent of Marcus Garvey, the Ku Klux Klan drove his family to Boston by a circuitous route. There the family joined the Islamic religion. Young Malcolm never recovered fully from the tragical experiences suffered from watching his home go up in smoke, allegedly the device of a revengeful Klan. His life, therefore, was a short-changed existence.

Malcolm's life did not follow the fairy tale "happy ever after" ending, nor was it the typical success story "from rags to riches." When he was in prison in 1947, he met Elijah Muhammad from whom he learned about the religion of Islam. Then the spirit carried him upon the Mount where he made the most important decision of his life. When he descended the Mount of Temptation with the devil, there was no doubt about the work he must do. The wrestle with his unconscious mind restored his morale and gave him a new commitment for living, and the mountain experience reconstructed his integrity and manliness. However, his struggles to eke out a living during his youth and his term in prison left him without humanity for Caucasians.

Malcolm was a doer of the word, and he was effective as an organizer and speaker in the Black Muslim movement. His speaking activities were not limited to Temples and street-corner audiences, but he also spoke to audiences at colleges and universities and was a participant in radio and television discussions. He supplemented his eighth-grade education with extensive reading after affiliating with the Black Muslims. This general reading background greatly enlarged his vocabulary and refined his language style. In short, Minister Malcolm made an impression upon all whom he met. On Friday, May, 1963, he was interviewed by James Baldwin on a television broadcast. He made manifest how conversant he was with the aims and purposes of the Black Muslim movement as it was related to world issues.

The writer who viewed this telecast noticed that Malcolm X, a *confrère* of Elijah Muhammad, excelled in the rapid-fire "give-and-take" of formal discussion. His diction and vocabulary were superb: It should be added that Minister Malcolm was interviewed more than any other Negro leader during 1961 to 1963. All of the programmed interviews featuring Malcolm X revealed his personal magnetism as an orator, and he displayed a graceful vocal inflection appropriate to the meaning of what was said.

Both in speaking and writing, Malcolm opposed Dr. Martin Luther King, Jr., and the host of guerrilla chiefs who advocated non-violence as the proper approach to a solution of the racial problem in the United States. He frequently said, "We are never the aggressor. We will not attack *anyone,* but teach our people if anyone attacks you, lay down your life!" Every Muslim is counseled never to start a fight, never to look for trouble, never to stir up confusion. These statements, and others like them, often created enemies for Malcolm and this is traceable to the tone of voice employed.

Opposition to Malcolm's statements by whites resulted in name calling. C. Eric Lincoln, an authority on the Black Muslim movement, said that Malcolm wouldn't restrain himself and made utterances like this statement: "Get the white man's foot off my neck, his hands out of my pockets, and his carcass off my back. I sleep in my own bed without fear, and can look straight into his cold blue eyes and call him a liar everytime he parts his lips." Many times in speaking, Malcolm called Caucasians a devil, and he did not pass up critical Negro leaders either. Once he called Ralph Bunche "the George Washington of Israel," Thurgood Marshall a "20th century Uncle Tom." He considered the Negro race "the ugly American" for being a good Uncle Tom. He scored Martin Luther King as "the Other Cheek Man," and subtly

suggested the phrase "Galavanting Harlem Politico" as a sobriquet for Congressman Adam Clayton Powell.

In telecast interviews Malcolm X maintained an atmosphere of self-assurance, displayed dignified gestures, and attended to proper platform trivia. Tall and trim for his 40-odd years, the Muslim Minister sometimes wore a beard and the goatee of an Ivory Tower professor. In the refining fires, he learned to play this platform role. Yet, he no doubt did his best Muslim proselyting with soap-box oratory and in meeting the challenges he faced from hecklers. His effectiveness was engendered by his marvelous mental powers, his storehouse of words, his simple and lucid vocabulary, and his ability to make his audiences go home and think about his messages.

As a popular television orator, Malcolm X had the dynamics to compel people to listen. The way he carried himself behind the lectern gave his hearers an artistic experience. If one made allowances for people's dislike of all Black Muslims and the orator's ostentation of himself, the hostility he created cannot be wholly palliated. His speeches redeemed souls, but, withal of a vain orator. In spite of themselves, certain orthodox Negro leaders were impelled to hear him with thunderous approbation. This was true even when his oral discourses abound in cajolery, impetuosity, invective, and violent sarcasm—together with all that was magnificent in eloquence.

The Minister's foundation for eloquent speaking was found in his poetical faculty for setting prose to music. The soul and breath of all speaking were striking simplicity and concreteness made luminous. The Minister of Allah had good voice control, talked within a narrow band of natural pitch range in order to have great reserve whenever he needed it. Many times as a young public speaker, it was his honey-toned voice that enabled him to cope with the harassment of the rabble, as well as control his temper.

What nobler tribute could there be paid an orator than passing on to his reward while he commanded the ears and hearts of eager hearers? When the fatal shot rang out, Malcolm's talents were soaring on the climax of his address. His language was bold, fierce and strong, complementing a full round voice flowing melodiously on the atmospheric breeze. While Martin Luther King gives us poetry, Malcolm gave us prose.

"Mr. Muslim" was an active, vigorous orator who sometimes pounded the lectern softly with a clinched fist. His marvelous vocal mechanism was at its full perfection and flexible strength when he lay down his life at the hands of evil ones. Black Muslims, attending that fatal meeting when Malcolm was shot down in the theater, were compelled to surrender themselves to the magnetic pull of his proselyting rhetoric. Persons hostile to the pleas of Malcolm X were nevertheless dazzled by his persuasive language. The three perpetrators upon his life resisted his persuasion, but they can never forget his dedicated passion which was silenced when the sawed-off shotgun went off bang! Then, are there any persons who can truthfully deny that he was indeed "the called of Allah", a sobriquet he bore to the end of his natural life?

R. L. Caserio (essay date Winter 1969)

SOURCE: "Malcolm X," in *Cambridge Quarterly,* Vol. IV, No. 1, Winter, 1969, pp. 84-94.

[*In the following essay, Caserio analyzes* The Autobiography of Malcolm X, *using the works of other modern African-American writers as a means of comparing and contrasting the views expressed by Malcolm X with those of his contemporaries.*]

In 1963 Malcolm X was asked by a free-lance writer named Alex Haley to tell the story of his life, so that it could be published as a full-scale autobiography. Malcolm X was at that time the chief of staff of an American religious sect called the Nation of Islam, whose members were identified as 'Black Muslims' by the national press. Its leader was and still is a Georgia-born black man named Elijah Muhammad, who claims he has been chosen by Allah to be the saviour of American negroes. The sect requires of its members an ascetic moral discipline, and it encourages their education and their economic betterment. Its theology, or cosmology, is simple: God is black, the Devil is the white man, and a scientist named Yacub, at the beginning of recorded history, grafted the devil white race from an original black people. In 1959 a television special on the sect, entitled 'The Hate That Hate Produced', had been broadcast, and the most formidable exponent of this hate was said to be Malcolm. Originally he agreed to dictate his memories to Mr. Haley, because he thought it would help outsiders 'to appreciate better how Mr. Muhammad salvages black people'.

But during the period in which he was dictating his story Malcolm's life changed considerably. He broke with the Nation of Islam, in part because he discovered that it was not the authentic Mohammedan religion. This break seems to have thrown him into a painful and lonely self-awareness. He thought it was necessary to go on with the book, in order to justify his devotion to the Allah of Mecca. And that justification meant going in detail into what he called his 'sordid past', because he wanted to convey the sense that a pilgrimage he made to the East in 1964, and his discovery there of a larger humanity in himself and in others, had been preordained, in a sense pre-written, in all his life's experience. In spite of the popularity of the autobiography, how-

ever, the public image of Malcolm, contrived by those he frightened, endures. Without the book one would be likely to believe that Malcolm X was just a seething crackpot. He was shot down at a public rally in 1965, but he is usually not listed or mentioned in any roll call of honourable American public figures who have been assassinated.

In spite of the religious pressure which shaped the book—significantly, perhaps, because of it—I find Malcolm's life has the narrative interest of a nineteenth-century *Bildungsroman.* Malcolm was a strange, peculiarly American repetition of Pip or Julien Sorel or Eugene Rastignac, determined to become what he was, to find a vocation in which he would justify himself, and which would also suit the terms society sets to define its best men. But Malcolm became disillusioned, like his prototypes: and he had to recreate his world, at least his way of seeing it, in his own terms, so that he could believe in it again. Malcolm's father was a disciple of Marcus Garvey, and was murdered by whites. The fact represents the limits of his first expectations: he would be able to 'make it' only in the black world. He became a hip Harlem celebrity and a criminal, and he was a celebrity and a success *because* he was a criminal. In 1946, just before he was twenty-one, he was arrested for a minor robbery attempt, and was sentenced to ten years in prison. There he underwent a religious conversion, and became a follower of Mr. Muhammad, in whom he figuratively found his father (and Garvey) again. The pilgrimage to Africa curiously both rejected and vindicated his 'fathers': Malcolm brought Africa, in the form of what he believed to be its most authentic religious spirit, back with him to America. But this last step in his education kept him, I think, in the eyes of his countrymen still illegitimate, if not still criminal.

In the autobiography one sees Malcolm change continually, playing as many parts as Ralph Ellison's Rinehart in the novel *Invisible Man.* Rinehart is a kind of extraordinary Harlem politician; he seems to hold the community together by encapsulating its contradictions. He is, among other things, a pimp, a one-man general employment agency, a priest, a gigolo, a bookie, a collaborator with the white police. But this epitome of American black men incorporates too much: the narrator of *Invisible Man* wonders if Rinehart isn't the symptom of schizophrenic illness. Yet Malcolm, for all the roles he passed through—he never did ally himself with the police, however—was not schizophrenic. The autobiography illustrates how possible and yet how difficult it is for a man to unify his disparate experiences and to mature. The identity of Malcolm's assassins is not reliably certain, but I think it is reasonable to believe that he was murdered by those who couldn't accept or allow his development. Certainly Elijah Muhammad encouraged his Muslims to turn against Malcolm, and to force Malcolm's withdrawal. What one gathers from Malcolm's narrative is that Mr. Muhammad could not respond to changes taking place in himself. When he trespassed his own religion's laws concerning adultery, he told Malcolm that such was Allah's plan. To the reader he seems a split person desperately holding himself together, embodying precisely the illness he diagnosed in his people. They have not been able to grow, perhaps, because they have wanted a double existence, to be both black and white at the same time, without realising what it might mean to be either. Malcolm, although he was in anguish, could not lie about his saviour. The Muslims formally silenced him, ostensibly because of something he said to the press about the assassination of President Kennedy, and Malcolm then uncovered a Muslim plot against his life. What this betrayal crystallised compelled him to find again some new, truthful way of going forward.

Nothing in Malcolm's adventures was merely private, and one senses that he was indeed tracking down the expectations of a people. But at the same time it would be wrong to claim for certain that Malcolm's experience is *representative.* The values he actively created for himself, to justify his way of seeing us, he too conveniently attributes to Allah and to 'society'. In spite of all he shows, one is likely to feel that his diagnosis of American sickness is itself unhealthily monolithic or abstracted. Yet it is also one of the convincing wonders of his book that he can point to the sickness in the live bodies, even in the hair, of his people. When he was in his teens, Malcolm periodically straightened his hair, so that his appearance would conform to white standards of beauty. Until I read Malcolm I never realised consciously that most black Americans, at least up until the last few years, have tortured themselves with cosmetics and wigs in order to look 'better', that is, more white. The process of straightening is called 'conking'. A conk in a barbershop, even in the forties, cost up to four dollars, so Malcolm with the help of a friend conked his own hair. He describes the first time he did so as a major event. The actual conking process consisted of submitting one's scalp to a mixture of eggs, vaseline, potatoes, and lye. The lye had to be combed into the hair, and this burned fiercely, but the longer one could stand the burning, the straighter the hair would become. The lye had to be applied with rubber gloves, and rinsed off ten or twelve times, since any of it remaining would burn sores into the scalp. For years Malcolm conked faithfully, but he considered it later his 'first really big step toward self-degradation':

> I don't know which kind of self-defacing conk is the greater shame—the one you'll see on the heads of the black so-called 'middle class' and 'upper class', who ought to know better, or the one you'll see on the heads of the poorest, most down-trodden, ignorant black men. I mean the legal-minimum-wage ghetto-dwelling kind of Negro, as I was when I got my first one. It's generally among these poor fools that you'll see a black kerchief over the

man's head, like Aunt Jemima; he's trying to make his conk last longer, between trips to the barbershop. Only for special occasions is this kerchief-protected conk exposed—to show off how 'sharp' and 'hip' its owner is ... I don't see how on earth a black woman with any race pride could walk down the street with any black man wearing a conk—the emblem of his shame that he is black.

But this cosmetic enactment of social degradation is a relatively minor point in the social analysis which Malcolm opens up. Many converts to the Nation of Islam were junkies. As ex-addicts these converts went after their old friends, to reclaim *them* from addiction. Conversion took the form of the addict's breaking the habit; and at the same time breaking the white man's hold on his life:

> When the addict's withdrawal sets in, and he is screaming, cursing, and begging, 'Just one shot, Man !' the Muslims are right there talking junkie jargon to him. 'Baby, knock that monkey off your back! Kick that habit! Kick Whitey off your back!' The addict, writhing in pain, his nose and eyes running, is pouring sweat from head to foot. He's trying to knock his head against the wall, flailing his arms, trying to fight his attendants, he is vomiting, suffering diarrhea. 'Don't hold nothing back! Let Whitey go, baby! You're going to stand tall, man ! I can see you now in the Fruit of Islam !'

This is gruesome, not only because of the physical details. A reader is likely to draw back at the sight of a man exchanging a physical addiction for a spiritual one. Yet this, at the height of his preaching for Elijah Muhammad, was Malcolm's analytic method. The intimate crying-out of a sick man's nerves is at once translated into a public structure. True, in America skin can still be fate. But Malcolm tended to hide how he persuaded persons to *choose* to see that. He didn't just cleanse his converts' vision, but helped create it, as a shaping force. Malcolm's whole life proved the connection between intimate and public fact. But I come round to my doubt that the proof is representative.

Truthful descriptions of black experience and white are rare. I know how easy it is, for those of us who don't have Malcolm's very special experiences or strength, to feel we're justly getting at all the truth when we see our living exclusively in the aspect of 'issues'. I myself, a young white man, believe in the conclusions of his social analysis, and in the practical economic and political aims of the Organisation for Afro-American Unity which Malcolm founded after his return from Mecca. But in *Shadow and Act* (1966), Ralph Ellison asks, 'Are American Negroes simply the creation of white men, or have they at least helped to create themselves out of what they found around them? Men have made a way of life in caves and upon cliffs, why cannot Negroes have made a life upon the horns of the white man's dilemma'. This question was asked in a review of Gunnar Myrdal's *An American Dilemma*. We are always hearing and reading about the dilemma and its horns, and next to nothing about the life.

Malcolm's later views raise serious problems for his imitators. He did not by any means grow soft, but his condemnations changed their target, and his thinking became more flexible. His life as we have it now is what he was actively growing away from, so young people are likely to be trapped in their imitation, modelling themselves on ideas or theories he was beginning to modify, or discard.

One thing is certain: had he lived, he would not have retreated into a politics of Love. There is a euphoric moment in the story when Malcolm, in a car, has stopped for a traffic light, and a white man, stopped beside him, calls out: "'*Malcolm X* !" . . . and when I looked, he stuck his hand out of his car, across at me, grinning. "Do you mind shaking hands with a white man?" Imagine that! Just as the traffic light turned green, I told him, "I don't mind shaking hands with human beings. Are you one?"' The 'Are you one?' shows his persisting toughness. You would have to prove yourself before you dealt with him. I think this is an astonishing question to ask in America, where the commonness and omnipresence of 'humanity' is great political and diplomatic capital, yet the numberless specific and non-negotiable forms of that humanity are ignored. The last President attended a number of churches: 'aren't all gods one, and all human beings?' I expect the new President will do the same, to help create the unity that we all, for the sake of 'law and order', supposedly want. But on the basis of this totalitarian assertion of oneness, there can only develop more 'understanding' and 'love', and more disgust at the lie it makes of the life we know. I think there was in Malcolm's orthodoxy and intransigence, personal and religious, since they did not stunt him, something both holy and most significantly humane. And I say this bearing in mind the contrast of Martin Luther King, whose religion was more conventional and peaceful.

Dr. King's conventionality to be sure was more effective politically. His tactics were suitable to most of the country's belief in tolerance and fair play; before Memphis at least he never seemed to the general public to be a trouble-*maker*.. But here I cannot help expressing some bitter feelings towards the press. At times Dr. King's cunning passivity, although it was only a tactic, has struck me as similar in outward appearance to the passivity of the 'objective' news reporter, who shrewdly illuminates an 'issue' but divorces his feelings, or his passions, from it. Dr. King was indeed passionate, but his characteristic 'image' was self-effacement. And this image especially attracted newsmen, because

self-effacement characterises daily American journalism, with the result that non-feeling or stingy or 'reasonable' thinking usually become identified with wisdom and objectivity. Malcolm effaced himself before Allah, but then, the thinking seemed to go (as it did in regard to Muhammad Ali), how could a black man in America legitimately believe in Allah? And when Malcolm said that America was a sham, and spoke with hatred rather than firm and self-effacing Christian meekness in his voice, he became identified with hate, as if that emotion excluded all other feelings, and especially ruled out thought or objectivity. But the most serious injustice the newsmen do Malcolm is simply to forget him, or to believe that at best his memory is poisonous. His conviction that whites and blacks can work for common freedoms and hopes only by working separately is still behind news stories about black self-help projects, but these stories are often followed up by editorials sadly reflecting on the 'racism' implicit in separatism and self-help. But 'black power' has grown from Malcolm's book and from those who took up his work and I hardly think it sad. Maybe Malcolm opposed the nagging pressures for 'integration' because he was strongly capable of unifying his own life. Those who longed for togetherness (although most civil rights workers wanted simple justice), embarrassed even by the healthy differences between black and white, struck him as themselves fragmentary. Certainly he believed that 'giving' integration to Negroes only confirmed the white man in his specious feeling of superiority.

As a contrast with Malcolm's response to Harlem life Claude Brown's *Manchild in the Promised Land* (1965) is worth reading. Mr. Brown was also a juvenile criminal, like Malcolm he dangerously experimented with the use of drugs, and he also went through a conversion, although a very personal and not religious one, in reform school and prison. Moved especially by the hopelessness of the Harlem streets, which he saw sapping the lives of his friends and his brother, Mr. Brown went to live in lower Manhattan, and worked and studied hard enough to get into law school, and to write his best-selling autobiography. In describing his growing up Mr. Brown writes in a language which is movingly authentic, and here one does find at least as much of the real life as of the dilemma. But I find his maturity sad, it is a growing isolation from Harlem, his community, a perpetuation of a split; he seems to save himself and withdraw. In 1955, Mr. Brown remembers, he first became aware of the changes the Black Muslims were working in Harlem. He had a conversation with a street friend named Alley Bush who had become a Muslim in prison. Alley tried to convert Mr. Brown, whom he here calls by his nickname, Sonny:

> 'If you're not mad [at white men], I feel sorry for you, Sonny, because you're crazy, and you're lost, man. So there, black man, you've got to be mad, brother.'

'Alley, man, you can get mad about this shit, but if you can't do anything about it, it's gon fuck with your mind, you know? Unless you stop being mad because you realise you have to stop, for your own good.'

'How the hell are you gon stop bein' mad when you've got a foot up in your ass?'

I said, 'Look, man, if you're going to live, you got to try and take the foot out of your ass. There's some things, man, that anger doesn't mean a damn thing to. You can get mad if you want to, but why bother if nobody's going to pay any attention to you? Alley, the way I feel about it is that we—you, me, the cats we came up with, probably all the cats that were in jail with you—we were angry all our lives. That's what that shit was all about. We were having our revolution. The revolution that you're talking about, Alley, I've had it. I've had that revolution since I was six years old . . . I rebelled against school because the teachers were white. And I went downtown and robbed the stores because the store owners were white. I ran through the subways because the cats in the change booths were white.

'I was rebelling every time I went someplace like [reform school or prison] . . . But nobody was winning. That revolution was hopeless. The cats who had something on the ball and they could dig it in time, they stopped. They stopped. They didn't stop being angry. They just stopped cutting their own throats, you know?'

So Mr. Brown wasn't convinced, because he identified self-defeating criminality with social rebellion. In the final pages of his book he records a conversation with another friend, whose dream is not to be a black revolutionary, but to own two bars in Harlem, and two Cadillacs, and to be a great lover. 'You dig it?' the friend asks Sonny. 'Yeah, I dig it. It sounds like a pretty hip life.' 'I don't know, man, but that's what I want to do, Sonny.' 'Yeah, Reno, I guess that's all that matters, that a cat does what he wants to do.' But I think Malcolm's doing what something larger seems to demand of him, the *vitality* of his continuing opposition, and his faith in the persuasive power of his intellect and of his truth show themselves as more positive and more valuable.

It should be emphasised, however, that Malcolm, and the Nation of Islam, represent nothing very new; and no doubt a strong sense of this, even weariness in response to it, negatively influenced Claude Brown, and many like him. Our racial experience remains trapped in repetition. Malcolm's insights and ideas are already present in *The Souls of Black Folk* by W. E. B. DuBois, published in 1903:

The Negro is a sort of seventh son, born with a veil, and gifted with second-sight in this American world—a world which yields him no true self-consciousness, but only lets him see himself through the revelation of the other world. It is a peculiar sensation, this double-consciousness, the sense of always looking at one's self through the eyes of others, of measuring one's soul by the tape of a world that looks on in amused contempt and pity. One ever feels his twoness—an American, a Negro; two souls, two thoughts, two unreconciled strivings. . . .

The history of the American Negro is the history of this strife—this longing to attain self-conscious manhood, to merge his double self into a better and truer self. In this merging he wishes neither of the older selves to be lost. He would not Africanise America, for America has too much to teach the world and Africa. He would not bleach his Negro soul in a flood of white Americanism, for he knows that Negro blood has a message for the world. He simply wishes to make it possible to be both a Negro and an American.

This is exactly Malcolm's position after his return from Africa. A reader may ask, however, if this isn't a kind of traditional American liberal viewpoint. I doubt if it is, but DuBois' statement is special anyway, because it was written as part of a criticism of Booker T. Washington's leadership of American Negroes. Washington's leadership meant that blacks had to sacrifice political power, civil rights, and higher education, in exchange for industrial education, a chance to accumulate money, and the conciliation of whites. Now Malcolm's break with Elijah Muhammad actually repeated DuBois' break with Washington. This has been pointed out in *The Crisis of the Negro Intellectual* by Harold Cruse (1967). 'Elijah Muhammad carried out Booker T. Washington's philosophy of economic self-sufficiency and self-help', Mr. Cruse writes, 'more than any other movement'. And Malcolm's break with Elijah came when, after Mecca, Malcolm realised this was not enough; the militant self-centredness of the Nation of Islam had to be seen as part of a broader human struggle, even as part of the attempt by developing coloured nations to disengage themselves from white power. Again one is led back to DuBois. DuBois wanted to emphasise the dignity of the American Negro's African past, and to connect his condition with that of the colonial peoples of 1903. But in doing so, he did not urge emigration; he rejected Garvey. 'By the irony of fate, nothing has more effectually made this programme [of emigration] seem hopeless than the recent course of the United States toward weaker and darker peoples in the West Indies, Hawaii, and the Philippines [Malcolm would probably have added Vietnam]—for where in the world may we go and be safe from lying and brute force?' The characteristic of our age,' DuBois emphasised, 'is the contact of European civilisation with the world's undeveloped peoples.' So Malcolm finally argued that the United States would do no more than bungle its best intentions for the world, as long as it refused to recognise its blindness to the experience of an undeveloped nation within its own borders. In the last year of his life Malcolm saw very clearly, and in the chapters 'Out' and '1965' the facts and evaluations he brings forward are not marked with the crudeness of thought of the junkie episode.

> The black man in North America was economically sick and that was evident in one simple fact: as a consumer, he got less than his share, and as a producer gave least. . . . For instance, annually, the black man spends over $3 billion for automobiles, but America contains hardly any franchised black automobile dealers. For instance, forty per cent of the expensive imported Scotch whisky consumed in America goes down the throats of the status-sick black man; but the only black-owned distilleries are in bathtubs. . . . Or for instance . . . in New York City, with over a million Negroes, there aren't twenty black-owned businesses employing over ten people. It's because black men don't own and don't control their own community's retail establishments that they can't stabilise their own community.

> The black man was sickest of all politically. He let the white man divide him into such foolishness as considering himself a black 'Democrat', a black 'Republican', a black 'Conservative', or a black 'Liberal' . . . when a ten-million black vote bloc could be the deciding balance of power in American politics, because the white man's vote is almost always evenly divided. The polls are one place where every black man could fight the black man's cause with dignity, and with the power and the tools that the white man understands, and respects, and fears, and co-operates with. Listen, let me tell you something! If a black bloc committee told Washington's worst 'nigger-hater', 'We represent ten million votes', why, that 'nigger-hater' would leap up: 'Well, how *are* you? Come on *in* here!'

Malcolm still knew his enemy, but he was no longer replacing one kind of addiction with another.

I have said nothing about Malcolm's prose. Of course, the writing is Mr. Haley's, and mostly it is *Reader's Digest* writing, much of which, ironically, needs condensation. But I hope readers won't be put off by this. The sort of mind or person Malcolm was can't be gauged by scrutinising a sen-

tence or a paragraph of this prose. The significant units of the book are the chapters, and their interest is in their factualness, in what they, in spite of the mismanagement of words, make clear in broad outline about Malcolm's life. Claude Brown's writing is alive in a better way. Although Mr. Haley tried to transcribe Malcolm's speaking voice, the tone isn't personal, and the autobiography could be read suitably over loudspeakers at a rally. Mr. Brown's voice comes through without one's having the sense that a microphone needs to authenticate it. I expect English readers would find reading Mr. Brown very difficult, however, because of the specialness of the dialect, but this is the kind of daily speech one actually hears. Yet Mr. Brown doesn't seem able to connect his Harlem with his university speech; his awareness is tolerant and 'private', while Malcolm is relatively intolerant, does not believe in every man's finding his own way alone, and is decidedly 'public'. Is there no meeting ground for the two kinds of awareness? And is there a way in which the American black experience remains, at least in its completeness, inaccessible to written language? In DuBois' writing there is frequently a horrible kind of blankness and fakery. The following sentences are from *The Souls of Black Folk:*

> I sit with Shakespeare and he winces not. Across the color line I move arm in arm with Balzac and Dumas, where smiling men and welcoming women glide in gilded halls. From out the caves of evening that swing between the strong-limbed earth and the tracery of the stars, I summon Aristotle and Aurelius and what soul I will, and they come all graciously with no scorn nor condescension. So, wed with Truth, I dwell above the Veil [of colour]. Is this the life you grudge us, O knightly America? Is this the life you long to change into the dull red hideousness of Georgia?

Perhaps Mr. Haley's transcript of Malcolm, when it is insensitive and coarse, gives us only the more modern equivalent of DuBois' affectation. I trust it is only affectation, and not the symptom of a very uncertain hold on reality. DuBois was an historian, and in sorting out, for example, the history of the Freedmen's Bureau and of Negro education, his hold was strong. And Malcolm, as an historian of himself and his people, had an equal strength. But the suggestion that black experience is essentially inaccessible in writing, especially to whites, isn't very convincing. Certainly *Invisible Man* is proof against the suggestion. But that novel does bring out something more to the purpose here. In the end its narrator gives up his political activity and goes underground, realising that he has been failed by what sociology, history and politics have offered him, in the way of language and thought that can help him adequately to define and realise himself. Ellison rather explicitly points out through the narrator the large applicability of this failure, for all its specific racial conditioning. If there is a black reality which has not found its way into adequate language, then I have the feeling that this means the same is true of white reality, and that this inarticulateness and inadequacy argue our mutual condition.

Mel Watkins (review date 13 April 1969)

SOURCE: A review of *The Speeches of Malcolm X at Harvard,* in *New York Times Book Review,* April 13, 1969, pp. 24-5.

[*In the following review, Watkins asserts that* The Speeches of Malcolm X at Harvard *effectively conveys the essence of Malcolm X's "radical viewpoint" and "approach to the racial problem."*]

Malcolm X, prior to his death in 1965, found most of his support in the urban ghetto masses. His growing posthumous appeal to the élite of the black community reflects the pervasive character of the black man's militancy; Malcolm X has become, to many black Americans, the symbol of manhood. This volume, [***The Speeches of Malcolm X at Harvard,***] includes, in addition to Malcolm's Harvard speeches, an introductory "inquiry" into the validity of the militant's radical viewpoint.

The most interesting aspect of the Harvard speeches is the discernible shift in position which occurs between Malcolm's initial appearance as Muslim minister in 1961 and his last appearance, following a pilgrimage to Mecca in December of 1964. His perspective remains racist and violent (he had not yet publicly adopted the more humanitarian stance taken shortly before his assassination), but his polemics had moved from a sectarian religious foundation to a more realistic secular one. Excepting the first, the three speeches are presented in their entirety. Archie Epps's minor editing does not detract from the wit and high rhetoric of the original transcripts; and Malcolm's direct, albeit sometimes logically extenuated, approach to the racial problem is clearly shown.

Epps's long introduction, while more reasoned than the speeches, is often more obscure. He points out the ultimate uselessness of Malcolm's call to violence and shows the extent to which his early experiences, particularly his hustler background, influenced his radical viewpoint. He also incisively notes that Malcolm's true legacy is the sense of racial pride that he left with the black man.

Time (essay date 23 February 1970)

SOURCE: "Malcolm X: History as Hope," in *Time,* Vol. 95, February 23, 1970, pp. 88, 90.

[*In the following essay, published on the occasion of the fifth anniversary of Malcolm X's assassination, the critic provides a synopsis of Malcolm X's life and works, and attempts to assess his legacy.*]

He was assassinated five years ago this week. Since then, assorted parks, streets and ghetto playgrounds have been named after him. His bespectacled face, ballooned to twice life-size, gazes owlishly from the walls of innumerable schools and youth clubs. Though he is sometimes described as an apostate and a monster, these days he is more often invoked, especially by young whites and blacks, as a martyr in the cause of brotherhood, and even a kind of saint.

To whites, the apotheosis at first seems unsettling. Many Americans recall Malcolm X only as a bad guy, known mainly for preaching racism. Is the continuing Malcolm X cult just one more outrageous byproduct of the rage and rhetoric that afflict race politics and U.S. culture in general? The answer is, no. And the best way of learning why is to examine yet another post-Malcolm X phenomenon, the spate of books by or about the former Black Muslim leader that have made him a minor industry in the publishing business.

Savage Skepticism. . . . *The Autobiography* is his will and testament. The speeches [in *The Speeches of Malcolm X at Harvard,*] and *The Man and His Times,* a gathering of recollections by people who knew Malcolm X, add subtlety and substance to it. Read in retrospect, they reveal Malcolm X as the most fascinating, convincing and, in some ways, the most measured speaker and thinker that the black militant movement has yet produced.

His incitements to revolution drew a disproportionate amount of attention during his lifetime. But the angry and occasionally outrageous things that he said seemed wilder then than they do today. Malcolm X's characteristic tone was not flailing rage. It was a kind of savage, pragmatic skepticism about American liberal institutions and a sense that in the U.S., whites, collectively and historically, have been and still are a disaster for blacks. He refused to be grateful for empty favors. "I'm not going to sit at your table," he once said, "and watch you eat, with nothing on my plate, and call myself a diner." In retrospect, what seems most remarkable was the range of his intellectual change and growth. The final phase of that growth—marked by his separation from the Black Muslim movement and the founding of the Organization of Afro-American Unity—had only begun when he was shot down. Yet his last plan to start working with all civil rights and human rights groups in the U.S. shows how far beyond raw appeals to violence and references to "blue-eyed white devils" Malcolm X actually went.

Though he changed his views, he absolutely refused ever to believe that substantial change in black conditions would come about through turning the other cheek. Or through integration. Or through anything short of a relentless effort by black people themselves to take political power in their own communities, to work their own social revolution and to pull themselves up by their own bootstraps. His prolonged misgivings about the possibilities of real integration in the U.S. still seem convincing. The *Autobiography* illustrates how well-equipped X was to be successfully folded into the white man's world. One is explicitly left with the feeling that if he found integration a fraud, it was one. "You can sometimes be 'with' whites," Malcolm X concluded, "but never 'of' them." His early life was blighted by the murder of his father and poverty that eventually forced his mother to yield her children to welfare workers in Lansing, Mich., and drove her to a mental institution. Still, young Malcolm, tall, light-complexioned and smart, was elected president of his all-white junior high school class, and became a star basketball player.

His autobiography is excruciating when he recalls going to dances in the 1930s, learning to sip punch and stand around as if he did not want to dance. The devastating need of blacks to restore pride in their color and race still flames forth in Malcolm X's comment on the tragic folly of doting black parents who favored whichever child in the family was the palest. When, at age 14, Malcolm was told—like many other gifted blacks—that he should think of carpentry instead of law, he turned his back on the whole white world.

Dramatic Conversion. First in Boston, then in New York as a teenager in the early 1940s, he donned a zoot suit and painfully "conked" his hair. He graduated from show-stopping Lindy Hopper to pimp to taker and pusher of marijuana and dope. Malcolm X's scorn for authority, black or white, 30 years ago, presents remarkable parallels to youthful attitudes today. It was not merely that everyone he knew used marijuana and bitterly resented the white cops who tried to deprive them of it. They also regarded World War II as a white establishment disaster, like Viet Nam, to be avoided at all costs.

At 19, Malcolm X became a successful burglar who used two white middle-class girls as advance scouts. In 1946 he was caught and sentenced to ten years in jail. It was there, in a dramatic conversion, that he reformed his life, began copying the dictionary to improve his reading and writing, and became a disciple of Black Muslim Leader Elijah Muhammad.

Malcolm X worked twelve tireless years for the Black Muslims. It would take great cynicism to doubt that he passionately believed in and practiced what he preached—monogamy, abstinence from drugs, extramarital sex and drink, ceaseless work for the black community. But the mythology, the religion, the reexamination of history that but-

tressed the Black Muslim resolve, may still strain the credulity of new readers—even as they troubled a number of white and black men who otherwise admired Malcolm X during his life.

Today whites may still disagree with, but nevertheless understand more easily than five years ago, the Muslim's somewhat Nietzschean contention that Christianity was a white man's device that unmanned blacks by forcing them to worship a white God and taught them to be patient with any ignominy. One can disagree with but nevertheless understand the need to modify African history so that, for example, slavery appears as a unique white invention.

But what is one to make of such a personage as the prophet. W. D. Fard? According to Black Muslim dogma, Fard came from Allah to Elijah Muhammad in Detroit in the year 1931. He soon mysteriously disappeared, but only after he had explained that the white race was a cruel joke played on the black world by a satanic black named Mr. Yacub. After generations of breeding blacks for light skin on the Island of Patmos, Yacub succeeded in creating the fiendish white race, which was eventually turned loose in the desolate wastes of prehistoric Europe.

The rest, Black Muslims preached, is history: commerce, capitalism, expansion, colonialism, slavery. That cycle, they (and Fard) consolingly insisted, would soon come to an end. The black world, overcoming the white demons, would restore civilization to its pre-white peace and harmony. In a fond and perceptive preface to the autobiography, New York *Times* Correspondent M. S. Handler, who admired Malcolm X, called this kind of thing "sheer absurdity." Hostile critics have assumed that Malcolm X either didn't believe it, or if he did he was slightly cracked.

To take so literal a view is to miss one overwhelming characteristic of Malcolm X's thought, his integration of history, religion and mythology, and his profound and necessary sense of history's possibilities as a man-created aid to faith and policy. Browbeaten by the delusions of science and scholarship, white society has lately and perhaps foolishly begun to discard such conceptions. But it takes shortness of memory or lack of imagination or both not to see that W. D. Fard's cyclical vision is hardly more farfetched than the mythology of Marxism, which also explains past horrors, justifies present conflict and assumes that the story will end in peaceful victory—when the state shall wither away. The millennial curve of Christianity from the Old Testament Genesis to a vaguely predicted Judgment Day offers similar encouragements.

Human Rights. When Malcolm X broke with the Black Muslim movement in 1964 and then made his famous voyage to Mecca, he simply broadened his concept of history to include the real world of Islam with its possibilities of world brotherhood. Then he was shot.

> **Perhaps Malcolm X's most enduring legacy to black militancy was his lynx-eyed criticism of the hand-wringing but hapless efforts made by black and white liberals to wrest from the machinery of American democracy anything more than promises and paper shuffling.**
>
> —*Time*

As a man and a personality, Malcolm X seems likely to endure in literature as the subject of a classic American autobiography. The book has already sold 1.2 million copies and is used in schools and colleges all over the U.S. As a practical ideologue of black revolution and human rights, he has already been outstripped by events. The much harried Black Panthers, often the victims of their own inflammatory language, are trying to carry out a program of education, self-defense and a self-help that in some ways resembles Malcolm X's final program. Their thought, however, is tinged with a Marxian notion of solidarity, not merely of race but of economic oppression.

Perhaps Malcolm X's most enduring legacy to black militancy was his lynx-eyed criticism of the hand-wringing but hapless efforts made by black and white liberals to wrest from the machinery of American democracy anything more than promises and paper shuffling. Extremist in many ways, Malcolm X was most effectively extreme in sheer impatience. In his view, as one of his "blue-eyed" fellow citizens once remarked in another connection, "Extremism in the cause of justice is no vice."

Angela Blackwell (review date May 1970)

SOURCE: A review of *By Any Means Necessary: Speeches, Interviews and a Letter by Malcolm X,* in *Black Scholar,* Vol. 1, No. 7, May, 1970, pp. 56-7.

[*In the following review, Blackwell applauds* By Any Means Necessary, *maintaining that the volume offers insights into the spiritual and intellectual development of Malcolm X, and also illuminates aspects of "the man" himself.*]

George Breitman brings us a little more of Malcolm in the form of several previously unprinted speeches, interviews which appeared in periodicals, and a letter from Cairo. *By Any Means Necessary* is really a continuation of *Malcolm X Speaks,* also edited by George Breitman. It contains ma-

terials which were not available at the time of that printing. Everything which appears in this newest compilation was delivered by Malcolm after his break with the Black Muslims. Included with each selection are notes by the editor giving a brief background, the time and place of interviews or speeches, and references to points of interest. No interpretive attempts are made.

By Any Means Necessary is certainly an appropriate heading under which to present Malcolm's thoughts. His whole being was dedicated to the liberation of black people by any means necessary. No statement was too strong, no idea was too radical, no end was too far when it came to the cause which racism forced him to make his life. Malcolm was truly a servant to his people, and he attempted to perform that service by any means necessary.

The speeches and interviews presented in this book point to various stages of Malcolm's development. "Development" is a key word rather than "changes." Malcolm never changed his goals or his dedication to humanism, but his thinking followed a dialectical development which has had a profound effect on the struggle of the oppressed all over the world. Within the pages of this work we are examining not only Malcolm's development, but also the man. His warmth, his forcefulness, his wit, his ability to "bring it on down front" are brought to us once again.

It is doubtful whether there are any thoughts of Malcolm's included in *By Any Means Necessary* that have not, in some way, been presented elsewhere. This latest offering is not important because of its originality, but rather because it confronts us with Malcolm once more. Again we come face to face with Malcolm's challenges and his ideas. Again we are forced to feel the stab of knowing that his program and goals are not yet a reality. We are reminded of all Malcolm's aspirations and of our own failures.

The selections in this book show Malcolm before varied audiences. Several of his talks are presented to militant white groups, there are speeches before all black groups, radio interviews, and a telephone conversation. In all these circumstances, Malcolm was direct, sincere, and assured.

Malcolm's ability to express his views with pinpoint accuracy, even in impromptu situations, is demonstrated in an interview with A. B. Spellman. In one instance Spellman questioned Malcolm about his "goal of separation." Malcolm prefaced his response with an effective clarification of terms.

> This word separation is misused. The thirteen colonies separated from England but they called it a Declaration of Independence; they don't call it a Declaration of Separation . . . When you're independent of someone you can separate from them. If you

can't separate from them, it means you're not independent of them.

Malcolm was especially exciting when he spoke to black audiences. This is evidenced in four speeches which were recorded at OAAU. (Organization of Afro-American Unity) rallies. The simple, yet forceful and direct language that Malcolm used, coupled with the understanding and deep feeling which he felt for the audience, make these speeches an inspiration. At one of these rallies Malcolm was discussing the absurdity of civil rights legislation, and stated:

> The Germans, that they used to fight just a few years ago, can come here and get what you can't get. The Russians, whom they're supposedly fighting right now, can come here and get what you can't get without legislation. The Polish don't need legislation. Nobody needs it but you. Why? You should stop and ask yourself why. And when you find out why, then you'll change the direction you've been going in, and you'll change also the methods that you've been using trying to get in that direction . . . .

The effects of Malcolm's hajj to Mecca and his African tour are also revealed in these speeches by his deepened commitment to internationalize the struggle of the black man and his crystallization of the need for unity among blacks, regardless of their differences.

A letter written by Malcolm while he was in Cairo shows how aware Malcolm was of ensuing danger. He states:

> You must realize that what I am trying to do is very dangerous, because it is a direct threat to the entire international system of racist exploitation.

In this same letter, Malcolm's great humility and dedication to the cause, rather than the building up of individual personalities, is evident. After a brief discussion of dissatisfactions and infighting taking place within OAAU, Malcolm said:

> I know your grievances, much of which is just, but much of which is also based upon inability to look at the problem as a whole. It is bigger and more complicated than many of us realize. I've never sought to be anyone's leader. There are some of you there who want leadership. I've stayed away this summer and given all those who want to show what they can do the opportunity to do so. When I return I will work with anyone who thinks he can lead . . . and I only pray to Allah that you will work with me likewise.

It is refreshing and sobering to touch Malcolm's life again and to be reminded of his unparalleled rise to the forefront of the fight for black liberation. Thanks to George Breitman for compiling some additional works of the man who shaped the present struggle of the black man in America. Too many folks think that once they've read Malcolm, they've read Malcolm. To read Malcolm once is not enough; to read Malcolm twice is not enough. Malcolm should be read every morning and every evening until he is fully internalized; until his thinking is our thinking. A common phrase among black people is "it's like Malcolm says." We ought to keep reading Malcolm until Malcolm isn't saying it any more—until we're saying it.

Julius Lester (review date 16 May 1971)

SOURCE: A review of *The End of White World Supremacy: Four Speeches by Malcolm X,* in *New York Times Book Review,* May 16, 1971, pp. 4, 22.

[*In the following excerpt, Lester offers praise for* The End of White World Supremacy, *declaring that "these speeches are the best examples in print of why, even dead, [Malcolm X] is a man to measure one's self against."*]

All praises are now given to the name and memory of Malcolm X. In his person he represented the apotheosis of blackness; but, except for the last 11 months of his political career, he articulated the aims and ideals of the Nation of Islam as the number one spokesman for the Honorable Elijah Muhammad. This is important to remember because as the most important black political figure of the sixties, Malcolm X brought the thought of Elijah Muhammad to a larger audience and thereby increased its influence. That fact is not recognized or acknowledged today, but it is very evident in *The End of White World Supremacy,* a collection of four previously unpublished speeches given during 1962 and 1963, Malcolm's last year in the Nation. Here we find the concepts that, three years after his death, would be gathered under the rubric black power and forwarded as a secular philosophy: pride in blackness; the necessity to know black history; black separation; the need for black unity; black control of the political, economic and social institutions of the black community.

Malcolm X was more feared than loved by blacks while he lived, and these speeches are the best examples in print of why, even dead, he is a man to measure one's self against. One reads these four speeches from almost a decade ago and trembles. He speaks not as a political leader or social analyst (though he was both), but like one of the Old Testament prophets. He is the voice of doom from the maelstrom of American history. He does not exhort his followers or threaten his enemies. He lives in a place where such rhetorical weaknesses do not exist, for he represents Truth. He is one of the redeemed, and it is irrelevant to him if he is heeded or ignored. Being ostracized or vilified will not affect him in the least. Like Noah, he is building his ark, and if he is the only one who will be saved, then, all praises be!

It was this undoubting belief in the teachings of Elijah Muhammad, this vision of the wheat being separated from the chaff, that gave Malcolm his diamond-like integrity. He knew Armageddon was coming, and he was as sure that he was on the side of good as he was that the sun would rise each morning. I envy him his faith. For him, it was all so simple. Blacks were the chosen people, and their time had come. The white world would fall, and the black one would rise; he was one of the saved.

Unfortunately, it is not that simple, as Malcolm himself may have begun to learn in the brief months left to him after quitting the Nation. Shorn of its religious framework and the cosmological dimension Malcolm was able to give it, the thought of Elijah Muhammad is black nationalism, with all the necessary and painful contradictions that have to exist when there is no physical nation in which the nationalism can root itself, when so much of the history of the people is forever lost in the lower depths of white-sailed slave ships.

But Malcolm made an existential leap, over the abyss and into the faith of blackness. Many have made the leap with him, but there are those of us who have hesitated, knowing that there is no such thing as Truth, except the abyss itself. Faith is comforting, but it is blind. And though having sight can sometimes make one long to be blind, ultimately, it is only by seeing that we fully live. Black history reached a necessary apex through Malcolm X. It must proceed beyond that point, however, if blacks are not to become, like everyone else, hapless puppets of history, the blindest force of all. . . .

Ross Miller (essay date Summer 1972)

SOURCE: "Autobiography as Fact and Fiction: Franklin, Adams, Malcolm X," in *Centennial Review*, Vol. XVI, No. 3, Summer, 1972, pp. 221-32.

[*In the following essay, Miller uses the autobiographies of Malcolm X, Benjamin Franklin, and Henry Adams to illustrate the patterns in and the course of American autobiographies, which, he asserts, represent "a coherent American literary tradition which in addition to saying something about the country, has always challenged conservative and confining notions of what is taken to be the separate realms of fact and fiction."*]

The autobiographies which fill the bookstores today mark a departure from what I see as a classic line of autobiographical literature from Benjamin Franklin to Malcolm X. A serious metaphysical or self-reflective quality is simply missing in recent works. Using three examples of serious autobiographical art, I have chosen to reconstruct a coherent American literary tradition which in addition to saying something about the country, has always challenged conservative and confining notions of what is taken to be the separate realms of fact and fiction. But as it took Tocqueville to tell Americans about their own political institutions it is not altogether surprising that a Frenchman has brought attention to a declining American literary tradition.

André Malraux was sensitive to the failure of a profound art of autobiography in France, and his book *Anti-Memoirs* was conceived, in part, as a corrective to the dull public confessions of statesmen of his generation. He felt that there was a special vanity to those books which sought only to repeat, in an attractive context, the accomplishments of the author. Writing about oneself, Malraux thought, had to be more critical. The ongoing analogy of the autobiography to the documentary film was too mechanistic. The successful autobiography had to be reflexive, able to reflect upon its own process and organization. Writing about oneself was the archetypal activity of man, not unlike the problem he faced in trying to contemplate the implications of his own death.

> To reflect upon life—life in relation to death—is perhaps no more than to intensify one's questioning. I do not mean death in the sense of being killed, which poses few problems to anyone who has the commonplace luck to be brave; but death as it manifests itself in everything that is beyond man's control, in the aging and even the metamorphosis of the earth (the earth suggests death by its age-old torpor as well as its metamorphosis, even if this metamorphosis is the work of man) and above all the irremediable, the sense that "you'll never know what it all meant." Faced with that question, what do I care what matters only to me?

Malraux is challenging the notion that autobiographies need be personal at all and suggests that autobiographical writing involves a man in no less serious problems than are posed by living life itself. A man, as autobiographer, has the power to face his own mortality with an exorbitant power. Life to him can hold no terror, because in a sense he is already dead—facts no longer have the power to define him. He has relieved life of its temporality. And while a man always feels tangential to history, the autobiographer seems always to be at history's center. To see why this is so demands a revaluation of what we accept to be the proper relation of fact to fiction in the autobiography. I have chosen to explore the structural and methodological factors which define autobiographical literature in the works of Benjamin Franklin, Henry Adams, and Malcolm X: three writers who it would seem have nothing else in common aside from their desire to talk about themselves.

In their writing, as in all autobiographies, there is that power which comes with being one's own historian. Or the feeling that one is a *superior* historian who need not be content to painfully search out the truth from numerous sources of evidence, but rather because he is his own direct link with history the autobiographer can immediately "rethink" the past. The life of the autobiographer is the stage upon which history, that is all the history he remembers, is played out. Franklin's life spanned the period of America's movement for independence; Adams watched the country grow from an agrarian to an industrial nation; and Malcolm witnessed the resurrection of the Afro-American. Their books are records of their lives and accounts of American history they affected as well as experienced. Franklin, through his formative work in government; Adams, as a member of a great political family and as a writer; and Malcolm X as a major black leader moved the country in which they moved. In choosing to write directly from their own experience each of them encountered the central problem of autobiographical literature: how to reconcile the vanities and obsessions of the personal life with the realities of the historical past.

The problem is settled ingeniously by conflating the private and public histories with an artful narrative. Time is marked through the use of images and metaphor to insure that the reader continues to see the world centered around the writer. It is not our Philadelphia. It is young Ben Franklin's. Yes, it belongs to that boy who first walked the streets with two rolls under his arm, and a third in his mouth. It is the same way with Henry Adams's New England:

> The order of impressions retained by memory might naturally be that of color and taste, although one would rather suppose that the sense of pain would be the first to be educated. In fact, the third recollection of the child was that of discomfort. The moment he could be removed, he was bundled up in blankets and carried from the little house in Hancock Avenue to a larger one which his parents were to occupy for the rest of their lives in the neighboring Mount Vernon Street.

Or Malcolm recounting his first days in Boston:

> He peeled the potatoes and thin-sliced them into a quart-sized Mason fruit jar, then started stirring them with a wooden spoon as he gradually poured in a little over half the can of lye . . . The congolene just felt warm when Shorty started combing it in. But then my head caught fire.

> I gritted my teeth and tried to pull the sides of the kitchen table together. The comb felt as if it was raking my skin off.

> My eyes watered, my nose was running. I couldn't stand it any longer; I bolted to the washbasin. I was cursing Shorty with every name I could think of when he got the spray going and started soap-lathering my head.

In each case the intent is the same: not only to recall the past but to possess it. All three, as they view history, catalogue the senses, attempting to link themselves inextricably to the places and times they describe. Autobiographers, because they are able to see, touch, and smell their subject, write sensuous histories. They deal with the past as it is re-experienced through memory (a kind of sense itself) and conceive of history as it was lived through an individual's senses. When Franklin, Adams, and Malcolm write about themselves they use the details of their senses, not merely facts or events, to locate critical moments of the past. A silent proposition is established: the autobiographer implies that to know the world one must first know him.

All three writers use fictions to illustrate personal histories. Fictions that never lose their identity with an essentially true body of information. Personal language, metaphor, and a controlling narrative create the unique sense that the facts of the author's life are particular and yet at the same time are valid indicators of a wider history just outside or parallel to the life of the writer. Franklin's description of his entrance into Philadelphia and his subsequent success is representative of America's passage from a colony to a nation. Adams's sense of discomfort over the move to Mount Vernon Street is a sensuous mnemonic for the psychic and spiritual dislocation he felt as a victim of industrialization. His childhood change of residence is a microcosm of the larger historical displacement of towns like Quincy, Massachusetts, and other parts of pastoral America. In turn, Malcolm uses a rush of details as an emblem for a larger meaning, writing the history of his people through the landscape of his senses. His life becomes identical with the passage of the country black, "homeboy," into the world of the city Negro. It is all there in Malcolm's description of hair processing. The "conk" is the sign of the black man's humiliation, the brand of his selfhatred.

The sensuous aspect of the autobiography is really the link between the peculiarities of the autobiographer's life and broader historical currents. It affords the writer a chance to talk about the world as he talks about himself. But nowhere are the fictional devices of the autobiographer clearer than in his use of personae to respond to the complex demands of autobiographical literature.

II

Benjamin Franklin, the first major American autobiographer, understood and responded to these demands in such a way that he exemplifies the autobiographical art. Franklin employs a constant barrage of exaggeration—the hyperbole and soothsaying that D. H. Lawrence objected to. But Lawrence, among others, was deceived by Franklin's style. The man sets a trap with the didactic rhetoric of the book. *The Autobiography of Benjamin Franklin* parades as a finished document, a memoir of an aging public figure; however, the book cannot be fully understood as a *fait accompli,* but must be read in process, taken a little like we accept a man posturing in a conversation. As Franklin's autobiography is not merely a memoir, but a subtle investigation into the very act of autobiographical writing. Here is a hint of the plan.

> By my rambling digressions I perceive myself to be grown old. I us'd to write more methodically. But one does not dress for private company as for a publick ball: 'Tis perhaps only negligence.

Franklin's posture, his denial of complexity, is similar to Adams's insistence of failure, or Malcolm's pose as a bad nigger. Franklin creates a persona in his book who is human, yet always bigger than life. The *Autobiography* is as much a fable as it is a personal history. In fact the book, finally, is not personal at all. There are two Franklins: one a real historical figure; the other is a character in an elaborate fiction.

In the *Autobiography,* Franklin includes two letters. One is from Mr. Abel James and is undated; the other is from Mr. Benjamin Vaughan, dated January, 31, 1783, around the time Franklin signed the final treaty with England. Vaughan's letter is placed in the middle of the book, between Franklin's personal and public accounts of his life. It is unmistakably placed in such a strategic location to comment upon the author's method and purpose. In fact, we are tempted to question if Mr. Vaughan is really Benjamin Franklin himself, because Franklin could not have asked for a better spokesman.

> Your history is so remarkable, that if you do not give it, somebody else will certainly give it; and perhaps so as nearly to do as much harm, as your management of the same thing might do good. It will moreover present a table of the internal circumstances of your country, which will very much tend to invite to it settlers of virtuous and manly minds. And considering the eagerness with which such information is sought by them, and the extent of your reputation, I do not know of a more efficacious advertisement than your biography would give. All that has happened to you is also connected with the detail of the manners and situation of a rising

people; and in this respect I do not think that the writings of Caesar and Tacitus can be more interesting to a true judge of human nature and society.

Vaughan's "encouragement" makes explicit the link between Franklin's personal and public lives. Like a Caesar, his life is inexorably "connected with the detail of the manners and situation of a rising people." Vaughan goes on to say, "The nearest thing to having experience of one's own, is to have other people's affairs brought before us in a shape that is interesting." Franklin chooses a particular persona to describe experience in an interesting shape, a mythic embodiment of America's struggle for independence. And this need to embody and shape experience is not unique to Franklin, but is characteristic of autobiographical art. Henry Adams employs a remarkably similar metaphor to describe the plan of the *Education.*

> The object of study is the garment, not the figure. The tailor adapts the manikin as well as the clothes to his patron's wants. . . .
>
> The manikin, therefore, has the same value as any other geometrical figure of three or more dimensions, which is used for the study of relations. For that purpose it cannot be spared; it is the only measure of motion, of proportion, of human condition; it must have the air of reality; must be taken for real; must be treated as though it had life. Who knows? Possibly it had!

Franklin's personal history, like Adams's, is a manikin with which he can study relations. The life of one man becomes the key to mapping the mysteries of the race; and the wonders that are related to the one life are as important as the record of the life itself. Autobiography, at this level, is as much an exercise of will as it is a record of the past.

This posturing, the use of fictions, to get outside of oneself—to be equal to, yet, to be more than one is entitled to by birth—is the archetypal pose of the autobiographer. In Malraux's language, it is to identify yourself with no less than the eternal metamorphosis of the earth. In a word, it is that terrible reaching for immortality. Watch Malcolm struggle as he moves to identify himself with the entire black American population. Like the Sultan who dies trying to propagate the earth with his sons and daughters.

> I have given to this book so much of whatever time I have because I feel, and I hope, that if I honestly and fully tell my life's account, read objectively it might prove to be a testimony of some social value. . . .
>
> I think that an objective reader may see how when

I heard "The white man is the devil," when I played what had been my own experiences, it was inevitable that I would respond positively; the next twelve years of my life were devoted and dedicated to propagating that phrase among the black people.

I think, I hope, that the objective reader, in following my life—the life of only one ghetto-created Negro—may gain a better picture and understanding than he has previously had of the black ghettoes which are shaping the lives and the thinking of almost all of the 22 million Negroes who lives in America.

Malcolm's mythical presence, the pose of an exemplary life, just as Franklin's, is a daring simplification. They are using the autobiography, in part, as a fiction to express personal relationships to history that are true in essence, but are nevertheless suspicious in the exaggerated form they take. The personae of Malcolm and Franklin, in their autobiographies, are bigger than life because they are intended to represent many individuals. The paradox of writing in this mode is that this mythic relationship, although accepted by the writer and his audience, is illusory; it is a literary relation and not a metaphysical one. The fictive aspect of the autobiography is that result of this conflation between a first-person narrator and a naturally third-person persona who share a mutual identity. Malcolm X narrates the history of "Malcolm X," who is simultaneously himself and all black men in America, as Ben Franklin records the story of "Benjamin Franklin," who seems to be all of colonial America. This double identity is not accidental, but is intrinsic to the structure of the autobiography. It is the acting out of the quality William James called the phenomenon of the "twice born." In Franklin's words:

I should have no objection to a repetition of the same life from its beginning, only asking the advantages authors have in a second edition to correct some faults of the first. So I might, besides correcting the faults, change some sinister accidents and events of it for others more favorable. But though this were denied, I should still accepted the offer. Since such a repetition is not to be expected, the next thing most like living one's life over again seems to be a recollection as durable as possible by putting it down in writing.

Franklin could not be clearer. There is that quality to the autobiography that makes writing down the story of a life not so much reliving the past as simply living again.

What an opportunity for a man like Henry Adams. To live again. First he could arrange his marriage differently, do something about his father-in-law, and get early help for his wife. Second to that, he could write his autobiography and edit out all the painful "accidents." There did not have to be any marriage, any father-in-law, any suicide. He could leave it all out. As a result the *Education* is often more interesting for what it leaves out, at one point a full twenty years, than for what it contains. Late in the book the narrative breaks off with the year 1871 and resumes in 1892. The chapter "Twenty Years After" begins as if Adams is not conscious of his ingenious sublimation of the major emotional events of his life. Adams's style is reminiscent of those patients who awake in Swiss clinics after a month of sleep therapy (where a man is kept asleep, by the use of drugs for a protracted length of time) and who are cured by literally forgetting what was bothering them.

No doubt the world at large will always lag so far behind the active mind as to make a soft cushion of inertia to drop upon, as it did for Henry Adams: but education should try to lessen the obstacles, diminish the friction, invigorate the enemy, and should train minds to react, not a haphazard, but by choice, on the lines of force that attract their world.

Adams is not really talking about education at all. His obsession with the idea of attraction and his sense that the world always lags behind the active mind is metaphysical static generated to avoid discussing similar questions in emotional terms. He asks the impossible of education—that it should conjoin thought and action. And at the same time it reveals one of the prime motives for writing about one's life. His autobiography might, at least on paper, make life subservient to mind and, in a sense, tame it. So in the end, as it was for Franklin and Malcolm, Adams's education was in the writing of his own life.

III

Fictional methods have applied so consistently to the writing of autobiography, and historical models are now once again so fashionable in the novel, that it has become increasingly difficult to distinguish the two. Alfred Kazin has considered a variation of this problem in an essay that concerns the shifting boundary between fiction and fact in what has come to be called the "non-fiction" novel. He speaks of Truman Capote's desire, in his book *In Cold Blood,* to relieve life of its "mere factuality." Kazin's insight is correct and if expanded it could be brought to describe the activity of writing itself. But Kazin stops short of the point and is content to acknowledge yet another genre. Like the term "new journalism," the creation of the "non-fiction" novel as a separate literary entity is less helpful than it is a clever circumvention of philosophical questions that are central to writing about any subject. What is now called "new journalism" is merely the manipulation of the details of experience in the present not unlike the way Sir Walter Scott manipulates historical facts of the past to invest a situation with character and plot. Oddly enough we are inclined to believe the journalist and not the novelist because no matter how subjective the journalist's interpretation seems, it is still an interpretation of the facts. Critics have chosen to distinguish so minutely between what they feel to be works of fact and works of fiction that they find themselves continually adding new categories, like philosophers creating new links for the "Great Chain of Being," instead of challenging the need for categories at all.

This discussion of Franklin, Adams, and Malcolm attempts to show that autobiographical writing has always been an attempt to make history into a novel, and that writers like Norman Mailer have really done nothing new but have more significantly grounded themselves in an American literary tradition that moves directly from Ben Franklin.

It is appropriate that autobiography should be more than personal and factual, in the same way we expect a still-life painting to be more than a facsimile of the objects themselves; or a film to be more than the chronological development from points A to Z. Painting shows us objects from many angles at the same time; a film breaks down time and explores connections that we ordinarily do not notice. As a form, autobiography is multi-angular and able to alter perspective, to make a man bigger or smaller, like those enormous figures on a movie screen; and like the novel, its reference is explicitly self-centered. Its subject and object are identical.

The intent and method of the best autobiographies have always been literary in the broadest sense, just as conversely the novel (most obviously those in the first person closely following the writer's own experience) has reflected the intimate particulars and reflections of the writer. For example, Jack London's *Martin Eden* and Frank Conroy's *Stop-Time* disguise real situations and people through the traditional devices of the novel. London and Conroy share a central concern, to see themselves as they were. To see their lives sublimated in an elaborate fiction. The masters of this method were Proust and Colette. In both cases the fictional distance they had from their own experiences permitted self-illumination comparable to the studied self-interpretation of the autobiographer writing from hindsight. (The pose of the autobiographer as an experienced man is particularly effective because we expect to hear from someone who has a completed sense of his own life and is therefore in a position to tell what he has discovered.) The obsession with sensuous detail in Proust and Colette's writing came from their fixation upon the sensual side of their own lives. In a way, writing about themselves, through elaborate disguises, allowed them the liberation of confession and created an art which made the final significance of life (because there was no heaven or hell) solely dependent upon its telling.

Autobiography at its best has the pretensions and effects of art. Merleau-Ponty hinted at this in a different context in his essay on Cézanne, where he hoped to suggest that what makes great art move us is that it alters our basic perceptions.

> Cézanne's difficulties are those of the first word. He considered himself powerless because he was not omnipotent, because he was not God and wanted nevertheless to portray the world, to change it completely into a spectacle, to make *visible* how the world *touches* us . . . It is not enough for a painter like Cézanne, an artist, or a philosopher, to create and express an idea; they must also awaken the experiences which will make their idea take root in the consciousness of others. A successful work has the strange power to teach its own lesson.

In the same way, to write about oneself is to create a durable work of art in an attempt to freeze the process of life, for a moment, to make it visible. And it is with Franklin, Adams, and Malcolm that we feel this need to stop time, not to justify their actions in the past, but to see their lives as they might have appeared to God day by day. They use the facts of their lives, not as the historian would, but as a way of probing the limits of their own self-knowledge. Art is used in the writing of autobiography to express what cannot be understood by facts alone.

Thomas W. Benson (essay date February 1974)

SOURCE: "Rhetoric and Autobiography: The Case of Malcolm X," in *Quarterly Journal of Speech,* Vol. 60, No. 1, February, 1974, pp. 1-13.

[*In the following essay, Benson offers an analysis of Malcolm X's* Autobiography *based on the principles of rhetoric, and contends that* The Autobiography of Malcolm X *"achieves a unique synthesis of selfhood and rhetorical instrumentality."*]

Rhetoric is a way of knowing, a way of being, and a way of doing. Rhetoric is a way of knowing the world, of gaining access to the uniquely rhetorical probabilities that govern public policy and personal choice for oneself and others; it is a way of constituting the self in a symbolic act generated in a scene composed of exigencies, constraints, others, and the self; it is a way of exercising control over self, others, and by extension the scene. Taken by itself, any one of the rhetorical modes of action is incomplete. Knowledge alone becomes decadent and effete, existence alone becomes narcissistic and self-destructive, and power alone becomes dehumanized technological manipulation. Perhaps only when rhetorical knowing, being, and doing are present together can a rhetorical act truly be said to take place. In a given rhetorical event the balance among being, knowing, and doing is a function of the structure of the act and its relation to audience, scene, agent, agency, and purpose.

The constituents of rhetorical action are illustrated with special force in *The Autobiography of Malcolm X,* which, I shall argue, achieves a unique synthesis of selfhood and rhetorical instrumentality.

The general outline of Malcolm's life is familiar to many Americans. He was born Malcolm Little in 1922, the son of a Baptist minister who was later killed by the Ku Klux Klan. After a boyhood in Michigan, Malcolm moved to Boston, where he worked as a shoeshine boy, soda fountain clerk, busboy, and railroad kitchen crewman, and drifted into a life of hustling, numbers running, pimping, and burglary. Finally arrested, he was sent to prison. There he became a convert to Islam, and after his release from prison became the leading spokesman for Elijah Muhammad's Lost-Found Nation of Islam in North America (the Black Muslims), and the country's most widely heard black advocate of racial separation. Then in November of 1963, Malcolm referred to the assassination of John F. Kennedy as "chickens coming home to roost," and was publicly silenced by Elijah Muhammad. Shortly afterwards, Malcolm broke with the Muslims and undertook a pilgrimage to Mecca. He returned to America to announce that he would henceforth work for the brotherhood of all men, and set about organizing a movement to achieve his ends, hinting that violent means might be necessary.

When Malcolm X was assassinated in February of 1965, he was a much-publicized but little-understood leader who seemed temporarily to have lost his following. Cut off from the Black Muslims, spurned as a black racist by moderate Negro leaders and most of the press, Malcolm nevertheless appeared at the threshold of either national leadership or increasingly bitter notoriety. His death seemed to end all that, temporarily promoting him to a compromised martyrdom that might well, because of the seeming ambiguity of his final position, have led to a quick eradication of his influence.

But a few months later Grove Press published *The Autobiography of Malcolm X,* written "with the assistance of Alex Haley." This book quickly restored Malcolm to a position in the rank of such black leaders as Douglass, Washington, DuBois, and King. Why? Here is an autobiography, moreover an autobiography whose authorship is clouded by collaboration, exhibiting the signs of a rhetorical work, and managing to solve a rhetorical problem of great complexity. How could Malcolm meet the most serious challenges posed to his life and work? The challenges that he changed his position so abruptly, near the end of his career, that he

was without audience or program? And the challenge not only to create a place for himself in the pantheon of black leaders, but to further the development of revolutionary masses?

Let us first examine the foundation of the rhetorical problem and then try to find a reading of the *Autobiography* which illuminates his strategy.

For most of his audience, whether white or black, Malcolm's greatest needs were to establish his credibility and to explain his program. What stands in the way of satisfying these needs is the suspicion that he had no program and was not worth believing. Herbert W. Simons, for instance, sees Malcolm as impaled on the dilemma of needing to be both consistent and fresh. "When, in one year, Malcolm X broke with Elijah Muhammad, shifted positions on integration and participation in civil rights demonstrations, and confessed his uncertainties on other issues, he inevitably alienated some followers and invited charges of weakness and inconsistency from his enemies." One option for the readers of Malcolm's *Autobiography* is to explain Malcolm's apparent inconsistency by arguing that he was either a blind fanatic or an irresponsible charlatan.

One of the greatest rhetorical potentialities of the autobiographical genre lies in its ability to take a reader inside the writer's experience, and to show how early mistakes led to later enlightenment. But this very advantage also presents a danger, since later actions may be judged as variations on those earlier mistakes. In Malcolm's case, some readers may be tempted to see his conversion to Islam and his later advocacy of brotherhood as self-serving extensions of his former career as a street hustler. And there are elements of the hustler in Malcolm as he reveals himself even after his conversion to Islam.

Malcolm has an irritating propensity for opportunism in debate, cleverly setting up a situation to score a point when that point may be inconsistent with another position. For instance, late in the *Autobiography* when he is describing his visit to Africa in 1964, Malcolm tells of a press conference: "I stressed to the assembled press the need for mutual communication and support between the Africans and Afro-Americans whose struggles were interlocked. I remember that in the press conference, I used the word 'Negro,' and I was firmly corrected. "The word is not favored here, Mr. Malcolm X. The term Afro-American has greater meaning and dignity. I sincerely apologized. I don't think that I said 'Negro' again as long as I was in Africa." As it stands, this episode is unobjectionable. And yet during his ministry with the Black Muslims, Malcolm had, in his speech at Cornell University in March of 1962, for instance, repeatedly referred to America's "so-called Negroes," on the grounds that Negro was a white man's word which he refused to be ensnared by. His sincere apology of 1964, not an outright reversal, nevertheless misleads his readers for the convenience of making his point. And earlier in the *Autobiography* Malcolm makes much the same point in reporting a speech by Elijah Muhammad. The white man, says Muhammad to a group of Muslims, "has taught you, for *his* benefit, that you are a neutral, shiftless, helpless so-called 'Negro.' I say '*so-called*' because you are *not* a '*Negro.*' There is no such thing as a race of '*Negroes.*' You are members of the Asiatic nation, from the tribe of *Shabazz*! '*Negro*' is a false label forced on you by your slave-master!"

With considerable relish, Malcolm boasts of some of his debater's tactics when responding to white reporters: "I might copy a trick I had seen lawyers use, both in life and on television. It was a way that lawyers would slip in before a jury something otherwise inadmissable."

To prove that blacks did not really want integration, Malcolm said in his *Autobiography* that "the black masses prefer the company of their own kind," and as for the charge of "vain, self-exalted white people . . . that black people want to sleep in bed with them— . . . that's a lie!" And yet at Cornell in 1962, when he wanted to prove that white society had corrupted black culture, Malcolm charged that the black man in America had been made into a monster. "He is black on the outside, but you have made him white on the inside. Now he has a white heart and a white brain, and he's breathing down your throat and down your neck because he thinks he's a white man the same as you are. He thinks that he should have your house, that he should have your factory, he thinks that he should even have your school, and most of them even think that they should have your woman, and most of them are after your woman."

For some readers of the *Autobiography,* Malcolm's enormous interest in his speaking appearances at American universities may seem to betray the crude ambitions of the autodidact to establish his intellectual status.

After he left Elijah Muhammad, Malcolm undertook the traditional Hajj pilgrimage to Mecca, where among other thoughts he records the following reflection:

> Behind my nods and smiles, though, I was doing some American-type thinking and reflection. I saw that Islam's conversions around the world could double and triple if the colorfulness and true spiritualness of the Hajj pilgrimage were properly advertised and communicated to the outside world. I saw that the Arabs are poor at understanding the psychology of non-Arabs and the importance of public relations. The Arabs said "*insha Allah*" ("God willing")—then they waited for converts. Even by this means, Islam was on the march, but I

knew that with improved public relations methods the number of new converts turning to Allah could be turned into millions.

Coupled with his opportunism in debate, his inconsistencies, his earlier career as hustler, pusher, and pimp, and his ministry of millennial anti-white black nationalism, Malcolm's confession of the urge to market Islam with the tools of American public relations may seem the final proof in branding him as a charlatan. We are reminded early in the *Autobiography* that Malcolm first sees the Muslims as a hustle. His brother, Reginald, wrote to him, "Malcolm, don't eat any more pork, and don't smoke any more cigarettes. I'll show you how to get out of prison." Malcolm's first response was that his brother "had come upon some way I could work a hype on the penal authorities." Even in the last pages of his book, Malcolm speaks of how much he "cherished" his "'demagogue' role," and hints that he sees himself as another Elijah Muhammad.

Was Malcolm merely reducing Islam to a hustle, or was he a blind fanatic who was so absorbed in black racism that he would not allow logic to stand in his way?

After Malcolm's death, USIA director Carl T. Rowan called Malcolm a fanatic, and there are passages in the *Autobiography* that a judicious reader might take as evidence for fanaticism. There is, for instance, Malcolm's sense that his life is worked out according to divine guidance. While he was in prison, Malcolm had a vision:

> I prayed for some kind of relief from my confusion.
>
> It was the next night, as I lay on my bed, I suddenly, with a start, became aware of a man sitting beside me in my chair. He had on a dark suit. I remember. I could see him as plainly as I see anyone I look at. He wasn't black, and he wasn't white. He was light-brown-skinned, an Asiatic cast of countenance, and he had oily black hair.
>
> I looked right into his face.
>
> I didn't get frightened. I know I wasn't dreaming. I couldn't move, I didn't speak, and he didn't. I couldn't place him racially—other than that I knew he was a non-European. I had no idea whatsoever who he was. He just sat there. Then suddenly as he had come, he was gone.

Malcolm's own sense that he is a chosen leader is sometimes striking. He speaks of his brother Reginald, who recruited him into Islam and then was cast out by Elijah Muhammad, and was finally placed in an institution. Malcolm says of his brother: "I believe, today, that it was written, it was meant for Reginald to be used for one purpose only: as a bait, as a minnow to reach into the ocean of blackness where I was, to save me." And Malcolm says that Elijah Muhammad "virtually raised me from the dead."

Malcolm often speaks of his life as "written." After describing his arrest for robbery, Malcolm says, "I have thought a thousand times, I guess, about how I so narrowly escaped death twice that day. That's why I believe that everything is written." The incident took place before his conversion, he says, but "Allah was with me even then." Malcolm talks of having "previsions" while in prison of addressing large crowds.

Malcolm's pilgrimage to Mecca, after the break with Elijah Muhammad, is full of talk of the signs of divine guidance. On the plane from America, Malcolm's seatmates were Muslims. "Another sign!" And later, in Egypt, "I considered it another of Allah's signs, that wherever I turned, someone was there to help me, to guide me."

One curious mark of Malcolm's faith in divine guidance was his belief in the significance of numbers. He speaks of attending the Cassius Clay-Sonny Liston fight: "Among the eight thousand other seat holders in Miami's big Convention Hall, I received Seat Number Seven. Seven has always been my favorite number. It has followed me throughout my life. I took this to be Allah's message confirming to me that Cassius Clay was going to win." Variations on the theme of seven appear here and there in the *Autobiography.* For instance, on his pilgrimage he was a guest at the Jedda Palace Hotel. He is careful to report that he was in suite number 214 (the sum of whose digits is seven).

In the face of evidence that Malcolm was a hustler or a religious fanatic, how were those of Malcolm's followers who believed his descriptions of the white man as a devil to interpret the final year of his life? Malcolm quotes from speeches he made during this period: "'Since I learned the *truth* in Mecca, my dearest friends have come to include *all* kinds—some Christians, Jews, Buddhists, Hindus, agnostics, and even atheists! I have friends who are called capitalists, Socialists, and Communists! Some of my friends are moderates, conservatives, extremists—some are even Uncle Toms! My friends today are black, brown, red, yellow, and *white!*'"

How could Malcolm's diverse audiences, the audiences of his last year and beyond, of all colors and politics, be expected to understand and assent to his final appeals to them? For somehow, although he did make enemies, although his organizational following at the time of his death was smaller than during his ministry for Elijah Muhammad, Malcolm's influence has continued to grow.

For all the difficulties that Malcolm poses to credibility, the charge that he is a fanatic or a charlatan will not stick. He was too good humored for a fanatic, and in fact he spoke in his last days of the danger of assuming that anyone is divinely guided. He made more painful sacrifices than could have been borne by a charlatan. Some larger reading of his *Autobiography* is needed, one that will accept his traces of fanaticism and charlatanism without supposing that they account for the full impact of the *Autobiography* and the elevation of Malcolm to a leading role in America's tragic struggle over racial injustice.

One way out of our difficulty at this point is to find the solution in a direct refutation of charges against Malcolm's credibility. There are patterns in the *Autobiography* which support a version of Malcolm as a magnificent anti-hero, an existentialist saint, a mythic witness to America's oppressive racism.

Malcolm's existentialist credentials are strong. He often speaks as if action constitutes the man, and he was a man of action. He says, "I've never been one for inaction. Everything I've ever felt strongly about I've done something about." And again, "Our Nation of Islam could be an even greater force in the American black man's overall struggle—if we engaged in more action. . . . I felt that, wherever black people committed themselves, in the Little Rocks and Birminghams and other places, militarily disciplined Muslims should also be there—for all the world to see, respect, and discuss."

Not only did Malcolm demonstrate the virtues of courage, wit, and dedication, but he was willing to change his position when he thought it necessary. The autobiographical mode is uniquely suited to explaining and justifying how Malcolm was led from one stage of life to another, just as it is suited to keeping the focus upon Malcolm as its central figure. We are made to understand how Malcolm evolved from a troubled but promising black youth through the underworld of crime and drugs to an urgent and original agent of social redemption. Far from denying his changes, Malcolm makes "change" a major theme of his *Autobiography,* developing a pattern which tempts one to think in messianic terms. There is in the *Autobiography* a tension between the particularity of Malcolm's experience, depicted with passion and cloquence, and the sense of universal, almost mythical, patterns into which Malcolm's life is rendered, forming an archetypal cycle of innocence-initiation-corruption-salvation-disillusionment-redemption-death and, ultimately, vindication.

But to describe Malcolm as a hero or martyr, reading the *Autobiography,* in effect, as a novel or a sacred text of existential revelation, for all that the *Autobiography* suggests such patterns, especially in the context of contemporary literary and popular culture, is to detail the book as rhetoric. For if we find the principle of Malcolm's life in his existential heroism or in a repetition of universal cycles, we shall have built a monument and destroyed a leader Malcolm would be elevated above the problem posed by his inconsistencies, but his elevation would be either too personal or too universal to exercise a truly rhetorical function, that is, to contribute to the wisdom of a contemporary social movement much in need of direction. And so if Malcolm can rescue himself from the charges of fanaticism and charlatanism only by reconstituting himself in the role of hero or saint, he has allowed the autobiographical genre to triumph over its rhetorical purpose and has left the movement without any clue as to how to apply his experience to today's problems.

If Malcolm contained the principle of change within himself, how can his audience know that he would not have changed again, had he lived? Might the humanism of Malcolm's last year not be simply one more stopping place along an obscure trail whose markings only Malcolm could read? Does *The Autobiography of Malcolm X* become literature at the expense of fulfilling its rhetorical possibilities?

At this point we must pause to consider more fully the relation of rhetoric and literary forms, particularly in autobiography. Certainly it would be misleading to argue that literature and rhetoric are separated by impenetrable barriers. In the literature of experience, whether poetry, drama, journalism, fiction, or autobiography, rhetoric can provide the purpose, content, or principle of organization. In practice, literature may always be in part rhetorical. Wayne Booth has demonstrated the necessity of separating the implied from the actual author, and he has shown that where literature does not directly address an audience, at the very least it requires the audience to participate in the moral world of the literary work. And yet the language of criticism would be impoverished if we overcompensated for old dichotomies by substituting the slogan that all literature is rhetorical. Slogans are still slogans, and even if it is true that all literature is rhetorical, literature and rhetoric are not identical. In a given case such imprecise terms as literature and rhetoric must be distinguished before they can be related.

In the case of any symbolic form, a set of conventions helps to create the context for a response. What conventions operate in autobiography, and what sorts of responses do they invite? Theorists of the genre, and there are few, seem to agree that autobiography is a literary genre more important for the form it gives to felt experience than for the accuracy with which it records actual events or the extent to which it influences public or private behavior. And most theorists sharply distinguish between autobiography proper and such associated forms as reminiscence, memoir, confession, and apologia.

Roy Pascal is willing to grant that autobiography must "give us events that are symbolic of the personality as an entity unfolding not solely according to its own laws, but also in response to the world it lives in," but he is quite clear in his insistence that autobiography "is in fact not at all a suitable vehicle for the exposition of a doctrine, for by its very form we are led to appreciate the ideas and insights expounded in it (e.g., with Augustine, Wordsworth, Croce, Schweitzer) not in their objective truth but as true for this particular man, as true of him." It is this sense of the single self generated symbolically in terms of a literary genre that prompts Richard Ellmann to argue that "autobiography is essentially solitary," whereas "biography is essentially social."

The conventions of autobiography are constantly working to focus the reader's attention upon an individual, and even at that, an individual who is created in the work and not necessarily as he appeared in "real life." Where the external world is an element, it is most readily seen as a part of the author's experience, rather than as a real place shared with the reader. Indeed, the more fully realized the work as autobiography, as distinguished from such related genres as memoir, reminiscence, confession, or apologia, the more the reader may be impelled to a literary, as opposed to a rhetorical response. The literary response holds the pleasures of formal apprehension and psychological insight, whereas a fully rhetorical response ends in a responsibility which goes beyond the work. Or so, at least, the theorists of autobiography seem to tell us.

Perhaps Maurianne Adams suggests a false dichotomy when she states her preference for autobiographers when "as imaginative writers they are more concerned with the controlled articulation of subjective impressions and responses than with outer, public events and achievements." Her allegiance is given to a convention which "enables autobiography to be a form of literature that we enjoy for its own sake, not as an adjunct to our knowledge of politics, military history, or public affairs."

What may appear to Adams as the vexing intrusion of actuality into the rarified atmosphere of "authenticity, fidelity, coherence, and thematic design," is likely to appear to a rhetorical critic as a quite inevitable tension whose resolution it is up to the autobiographer to produce. In a rhetorician's view, the aim is not to purify the work of any taint of the real world. It is not how close to pure form the autobiography becomes, but how the work *relates* form to audience and external world that holds the interest of the rhetorical critic.

In Malcolm's case we can observe a reinvention and extension of the genre, recapitulating as he does the development of a literary form through religious confession and political apology to a final discovery of the self. But Malcolm does not stop with the revelation of his selfhood, and it is his ability to transcend the confines of pure literature even while meeting its formal requirements that constitutes his rhetorical genius.

For Malcolm's rhetorical purposes, either of the readings of the *Autobiography* so far proposed would amount to failure. For those who would reject Malcolm as a hustler or fanatic, the rhetorical problem is to establish credibility. For those who would promote Malcolm into a virtually fictional hero, Malcolm must avoid the more subtle failure of succeeding too well at remaining within the traditions of autobiography as literary form, and thereby isolating himself from the experimental world of the reader.

Both of the readings we have so far proposed are supportable by reference to the *Autobiography,* but both are too narrow to account fully for the work. Is it possible to develop a view of the book that acknowledges the attraction of contrasting, even inconsistent, alternate readings? Such a reading would have to accept Malcolm's opportunism and his deep commitment, his ordeal of corruption and his sacrifice in blood, his evident ambition and its accompanying self denial. The reading we seek does not lie "somewhere between" the two so far proposed, but is generated out of them. Because it must be approached in a dialectical fashion, the view now proposed takes its support not only from the direct evidence of the text, but also from the evident clash of two persuasive but conflicting readings.

At the first level, our proposed final or synthetic reading is simple: Malcolm's life is a drama of enlargement. In this view, Malcolm is a gifted but flawed man whose natural powers and sympathies undergo a gradual but powerful opening up to embrace wider scenes of action and larger groups of people. What makes Malcolm's life a drama—an enactment of conflict—rather than a mere growth, is the presence of racism, the agency of constriction, domination, and injustice. We reject the figure of growth because it is essentially passive, suggesting the involuntary fulfillment of a destiny. What is important about Malcolm is his achievement through willed action and reflection, in the face of hostile forces. Malcolm, in this view, is not a creature of circumstantial corruption, nor is he a Sisyphean figure whose life takes on a mythical distance from the immediate scene. He is a man in conflict with a condition whose nature he comes to understand and transcend as motive passes from his environment to him. Such a view, if we can accept it, gives Malcolm's life a continuity that may be extended beyond his death, and it reconciles our two previous readings.

Given this reading, the elements of fanaticism and hustlerism in his early career do not detract from Malcolm's credibility, but rather lend authenticity to a humanism which, alone, might seem anemic.

If Malcolm's life as a pimp and hustler, as a black nationalist rabble-rouser, and as a spokesman for human brotherhood can be seen as the general unfolding of a consistent pattern, then the *Autobiography* has succeeded as rhetoric, signaling the response to a human institution of which racism is the most pressing extension. Malcolm would thus not have to be dismissed as a frantic true believer or elevated—another form of dismissal—as a sainted scapegoat of racist America. Rather, he could be read as a gifted leader of men who develops a rhetoric transcending racism, a rhetoric of human purpose and brotherhood. Most importantly, perhaps, the reading gives us the principle behind Malcolm's "changes," which are now seen as consistent steps forward rather than as random and untrustworthy conversions by faith. Malcolm's readers are not reduced to admiring him; they can pick up where he left off.

As Malcolm came to understand that racism had caused him to act as he had, its power to control his actions passed over to him. Motive, previously located in his condition, was now in the hands of a conscious agent. With the *Autobiography,* Malcolm shares that motive with his readers, giving them a principle of action they can carry into the confrontation with racism as it conditions their own lives.

Thus far we have shown that to explain Malcolm's *Autobiography* as a drama of enlargement will plausibly synthesize variant readings and suggest the source of the book's power over readers. But every critical reading must pass a further test. If the notion of enlargement is to be useful, it must help us to open up the text. This it can do in a variety of ways.

First, enlargement is the pattern of Malcolm's career itself. Starting as a small-time hustler, whose power was active but restricted, Malcolm sought wider and wider stages for his actions. Moving from Michigan to Boston to Harlem to black nationalism, pan-Islamism, and the United Nations, Malcolm also enlarged his loyalties from self and family to gang, race, religion, and all mankind. Seen in this light, Malcolm's sense of brotherhood with all men is not the weakening of militancy or a softening of commitment, but an extension of potency.

The force against which Malcolm's power grew and exercised itself was racism, which Malcolm came to understand in broader terms as but the central manifestation of injustice and domination. Where racism appeared simply as the condition denying Malcolm money and prestige, he could combat it by conking his hair and resorting to a life of crime. Where racism was conceived as an institution created by white oppressors, he could turn to black nationalism. And where racism grew to appear as the symptom of a disease afflicting a social system, Malcolm could look for the healing power of revolution and social redemption.

Supporting the movement of Malcolm's life to ever larger stages is a counter-theme of thwarted growth. Before his two most important changes, Malcolm was placed temporarily in positions of impotency or confinement. It was while he was in prison that he converted to the Islamism of the Black Muslims, and later it was during an enforced silence imposed by Elijah Muhammad that Malcolm incubated his transformation into the larger world of a pilgrimage to Mecca, a political tour of Africa, and a return to America as the potential leader of an extended search for racial justice. And of course racism itself appears throughout the work in all of its forms as a constricting element that invites conflict and growth. Counter theme reinforces theme, thwarted power grows into larger power.

The pattern of enlargement is imitated in the structure of the chapters of the *Autobiography* as well as in its major movements. Typically, a chapter opens with a narrative section, which then gives way to a series of amplifications or generalizations on a theme growing out of the narrative. Chapter Three, "Home-boy," narrates Malcolm's first days in Boston and Roxbury, leading to a description of his first conk, applied by his friend Shorty. The chapter ends with an extended peroration depicting the hair-straightening process as a self-defacement, a natural product of racism. And along the way, even during the narration, there extends out from concrete particulars the larger world of values suggested by the vocabulary of a racist society: black, white, Crispus Attucks, Uncle Tom.

An early paragraph illustrates the book's movement, a movement repeated at the levels of sentence, paragraph, chapter, and section. Malcolm is describing his father, as remembered from his earliest years:

> It was in his role as a preacher that my father had most contact with the Negroes of Lansing. Believe me when I tell you that those Negroes were in bad shape then. They are still in bad shape—though in a different way. By that I mean that I don't know a town with a higher percentage of complacent and misguided so-called "middle-class" Negroes—the typical status-symbol-oriented, integration-seeking type of Negroes. Just recently, I was standing in a lobby at the United Nations talking with an African ambassador and his wife, when a Negro came up to me and said, "You know me?" I was a little embarrassed because I thought he was someone I should remember. It turned out that he was one of those bragging, self-satisfied, "middle-class" Lansing Negroes. I wasn't ingratiated. He was the type who would never have been associated with Africa, until the fad of having African friends became a status-symbol for "middle-class" Negroes.

This paragraph is worth our close attention. Here a recollection from his early childhood leads Malcolm to a larger theme which then incorporates an enlarged temporal scheme as he speaks directly from a later point in time (the incident at the United Nations did not happen, say, "many years later," in the usual formula for such things, but "just recently"). We note also that we are again in the presence of what at first appears as Malcolm's own snobbery, but by the end of the paragraph his worries about his own status, no doubt stirred by bitter memories of early snubs, have been transcended by turning the tables and by referring to the wider themes of Africa, the United Nations, and the fight against racism. The paragraph displays enlargement both as a dispositional strategy and as a struggle to confess and work from his own confining concern for status and retribution towards a principle of active change.

Malcolm's choice of figures is also governed by themes of growth and their contraries. Chapter Fifteen is climaxed by the image of Icarus, who reminds Malcolm that however high he flies his wings were supplied by Islam. Earlier in the chapter, describing a period when he was at the peak of his success as a minister of Elijah Muhammad, and therefore just about to leave the brotherhood, Malcolm devotes a section to his relations with the press: "I developed a mental image of reporters as human ferrets—steadily sniffing, darting, probing for some way to trick me, somehow to corner me in our interview exchanges." The image goes no further, and Malcolm instead continues by illustrating how he outwitted the press. Yet if the reporters were ferrets, Malcolm implies that he saw himself as a burrowing prey, retreating into a dark tunnel from which he was soon to emerge in a new form.

What bothered Malcolm most about prison were the bars, the visible sign of his confinement. "Any person who claims to have a deep feeling for other human beings should think a long, long time before he votes to have other men kept behind bars—caged. I am not saying there shouldn't be prisons, but there shouldn't be bars. Behind bars, a man never reforms. He will never forget. He never will get completely over the memory of the bars."

Later, when he had converted to Islam while in prison, Malcolm began to study, educating himself from the prison library. "Anyone who has read a great deal can imagine the new world that opened. . . . Months passed without my even thinking of being imprisoned. In fact, up to then, I had never been so truly free in my life." And still later, when Malcolm undertook his Hajj pilgrimage, he arrived in Cairo, and "the effect was as though I had just stepped out of a prison."

But there is more to the theme of enlargement and confinement than images, for Malcolm's *Autobiography* goes beyond the closed world of literary form towards the open forum of rhetorical address. The relation of the theme of confinement to the predicament of American blacks is stated clearly in the following passage: "Human rights! Respect as human beings! That's what America's black masses want. That's the true problem. The black masses want not to be shrunk from as though they are plague-ridden. They want not to be walled up in slums, in the ghettos, like animals. They want to live in an open, free society where they can walk with their heads up, like men, and women!"

When speaking to black audiences in the last year of his life, Malcolm went beyond the Islamic faith "to embrace all who sat before me." He was, he said, "for whoever and whatever benefits humanity *as a whole.*" In the face of opposition and harassment, he declared that he was against "strait-jacketed thinking, and strait-jacketed societies."

Malcolm's *Autobiography* is constructed in terms of the contradictions between open and closed, constriction and enlargement, confinement and action. The dialectical structure of the book is a major rhetorical accomplishment, since it allows Malcolm to transcend the challenges which his own life in the context of a secular and a racist society posed to his credibility and relevance.

After he left Elijah Muhammad, in the last three chapters of the *Autobiography,* Malcolm's images change, to become variations on the concept of healing, with Malcolm seeking a symbol to reconcile an intensified religiosity and a growing sense of the need for secular action. He speaks of racism as a disease, a metaphor that for him makes possible a symbolic transcendence in which violence is weighed as a radical surgery for the "cancer" which grips America—an America which he no longer hates but now seeks to mend. The image of cancer itself becomes especially meaningful when we see it in the light of Malcolm's theme of enlargement, where it takes on resonances of the perverted growth of an evil and uncontrolled malignancy. The dialectical symmetry of the cancer metaphor is, in context, unmistakable.

These final themes are not resolved, nor had Malcolm, at the end of his life, yet found a perfectly unified and straightforward synthesis for the contradictions of his life. But he had found the principle of synthesis in his actions, and had set it forth in a pattern of symbols that, like his own life, possesses the capacity to evolve.

I have not attempted a full critical exploration of the immensely rich rhetorical works of Malcolm X. Rather, I have addressed the preliminary question of how to account for Malcolm's enduring influence by suggesting the presence in *The Autobiography of Malcolm X* of a dialectical rhetoric, in which a drama of enlargement saves Malcolm from being dismissed as a fanatic, a charlatan, or an existential anti-hero, and instead renders his life as the embodiment of a principle of rhetorical action. And the form of action Malcolm achieves in the *Autobiography* transcends the rhetorical fractions of which we spoke at the beginning of this essay. If we see hustling as a parody of rhetorical Doing, fanaticism as a corruption of rhetorical Knowing, and existential sainthood as a variation of rhetorical Being, we are able to see the *Autobiography* as a synthesizing act which resolves and transcends the fractions, producing a fully rhetorical action to which Being (and becoming), Knowing, and Doing contribute equally.

Malcolm has created a work which is formally consistent, authentically autobiographical, and yet rhetorically effective. Symbolically, Malcolm continually enlarges his powers and sympathies; dialectically, Malcolm's recurrent changes are shown to be transcendent movements which reconcile his own contradictory masks as hustler, religious mystic, and existential rebel, and the polarities of America's ordeal of racism; rhetorically, Malcolm seizes motive from the scene and makes it available to his readers, who are invited to assume their roles as actors in the drama of enlargement and reconciliation.

Confinement and enlargement. In *The Autobiography of Malcolm X* these are the symbolic vehicles for an essentially rhetorical mode of knowing, being, and doing in the world. They stand as the symbols for Malcolm's discovery of himself through the act of addressing his fellow men. As Malcolm's sphere of action, a rhetorical sphere, enlarges, as he seeks in turn to rob, hustle, convert, and join in brotherhood with even larger constituencies, there is a parallel enlargement of his world view. At the end of his life, the Malcolm of the *Autobiography* stands at the threshold of both power and vision. Some men grow by appropriating the power and space of other men and women. Malcolm X, born Malcolm Little and assassinated as Brother Malcolm, El-Hajj Malik Shabazz, was one of those rare men the growth of whose power was consistently accompanied by a growing vision of freedom and brotherhood for all people.

John D. Groppe (essay date Winter 1983)

SOURCE: "From Chaos to Cosmos: The Role of Trust in *The Autobiography of Malcolm X,*" in *Soundings,* Vol. LXVI, No. 4, Winter, 1983, pp. 437-49.

[*In the following essay, Groppe employs the developmental stage theory of Erik Erikson to demonstrate Malcolm X's "growth into trust" as it is related in* The Autobiography of Malcolm X.]

The Autobiography of Malcolm X is a story of the loss, and then the regaining, of the capacity to trust. According to Erik

Erikson, trust is the foundation on which the personality is developed. The basic trust of the newborn is elaborated and refined into more conscious, more articulated, and more complex modes of relationship. In spite of the variety of modes of trust, trust is nevertheless characterized by one's confidence that his world and his own attributes can meet his needs and the needs of those he loves. In this essay I will trace Malcolm X's growth into trust by superimposing his pilgrimage upon Erikson's developmental stages.

For Malcolm X to tell his story, even to a black journalist, was an act of trust. At the beginning of his relationship to Alex Haley, he told Haley, "I don't completely trust anyone . . . not even myself. I have seen too many men destroy themselves. Other people I trust from not at all to highly, like The Honorable Elijah Muhammad. . . . You I trust about twenty-five percent." However, by listening and recording faithfully what Malcolm X said, Haley gained Malcolm X's trust. Malcolm X stepped beyond repeating the ideological formulas of the Muslim movement and began to share his life with Haley, even the moments of great shame over things like his mother's incarceration in a mental hospital. Malcolm X was conscious of whom he trusted and whom he did not trust. Haley recalls Malcolm X's affirmation of his confidence.

> One call that I will never forget came at close to four a.m., waking me; he must have just gotten up in Los Angeles. His voice said, "Alex Haley?" I said, sleepily, "Yes? Oh, *hey, Malcolm!" His voice said, "I trust you seventy percent"—and then he hung up.

Trusting a stranger with the intimate details of one's life is a violation of the code of the hustler Malcolm X lived by from 1942 to 1946.

> What I was learning was the hustling society's first rule; that you never trusted anyone outside of your own close-mouthed circle, and that you selected with time and care before you made any intimates even among them.

That group was small indeed. He encouraged his younger brother Reginald to leave the merchant marine and take up a hustle in Harlem. "I must have felt that having my kid brother around me would be a good thing. Then there would be two people I could trust—Sammy was the other." Not long afterwards Malcolm X was almost killed by Sammy for slapping Sammy's woman, and the reliable world narrowed to one. "I came to rely more and more upon my brother Reginald as the only one in my world I could completely trust."

The disintegration of the reliability of his world began early.

His home was burned when he was four. His father was assassinated when he was six. His family was treated as "*things*" by the welfare workers who destroyed family pride and sowed "seeds of division" in the minds of the children. Mrs. Little weakened under the pressure, and the children watched their "anchor giving way." His parents became causes of shame. "None of us talked much about our mother. And we never mentioned our father."

His ability to trust in his own attributes was assaulted by the same forces that defeated his mother, but the final blow was the remark by his teacher that his ambition to become a lawyer was not a "realistic goal for a nigger."

Malcolm X's move to the black worlds of Roxbury and Harlem gave him the opportunity to experience race identity and pride. "This world was where I belonged," he recalled. For one thing, it identified with him: "I still was country, I know now, but it all felt so great because I was accepted." More importantly it allowed him to express, and excel at the expression of, something he felt was deep within him and other blacks; "With alcohol and marijuana lightening my head, and that wild music wailing away on those portable players, it didn't take long to loosen up the dancing instincts in my African heritage."

Race pride, however, went hand-in-hand with race shame. It was such shame, the rejection of his own and his common blackness, that led him to straighten his hair in the painful process of conking.

> How ridiculous I was! Stupid enough to stand there simply lost in admiration of my hair now looking "white". . . . This was my first really big step toward self-degradation: when I endured all of that pain, literally burning my flesh to have it look like a white man's hair. I had joined that multitude of Negro men and women in America who are brainwashed into believing that the black people are "inferior"—and white people "superior"—that they will even violate and mutilate their God-created bodies to try to look "pretty" by white standards.

Harlem and places like Small's Paradise offered some sense of community: "Many times since, I have thought about it, and what it really meant. In one sense, we were huddled in there, bonded together in seeking security and warmth and comfort from one another, and we didn't know it." Not knowing what they needed from each other, the hustlers preyed on one another. "In this Harlem jungle people would hype their brothers." Malcolm X became physically sick from his use of opium and marijuana and spiritually, or as he puts it, "mentally dead."

The various stages of Malcolm X's life are signalled by name changes: Malcolm Little, Mascot, Sandwich Red, Harlem Red, Detroit Red. In prison he was called "Satan" because of his "antireligious attitude." But he also suggests that his resentment was directed not just at religion but also at the world. He preferred solitary confinement. He was disruptive and was punished with solitary. "I preferred the solitary that this behavior brought me. I would pace for hours like a caged leopard, viciously cursing aloud to myself." By this point Malcolm X had almost completely lost his basic trust. According to Erikson, "If you have forgotten how to trust, you may be driven to cultivate active mistrust and insist defiantly that everyone is against you."

The world he knew could not be trusted to sustain him or meet his needs, nor did there seem to be anything in himself to enable him to meet the opposition of the world and to sustain himself. However, the Satanic defiance was only a delaying tactic, not unlike the bravado of the hustling life he had lived on the streets. Just as "every criminal expects to get caught, [and] . . . stave[s] off the inevitable for as long as he can," Satan Malcolm had as yet no hope. He had to find something in himself and something in the world to trust. The convict Bimini led him to trust once again in his own mental powers. Bimini, a black burglar, could hold audiences of even white prisoners and guards spellbound by his opinions; "he was the first man [Malcolm] had ever seen command total respect . . . with his words." Bimini told him "he had some brains." A black man with some power in that restricted world spoke to him, identified his talent, and encouraged him to develop it. Malcolm began "a correspondence course in English."

He began to prepare to reenter the world, but he needed a place within it. After all, identity is characterized by mutuality. Elijah Muhammad provided that place. The role of Elijah Muhammad and the Black Muslim movement is probably the most difficult part of Malcolm X's regeneration to understand and accept. Its militant racism and its dependence on so patently absurd a foundation as "Yacub's History" of the human race suggest that Malcolm X faltered on his first regenerative step. I assume most readers are aware of Malcolm X's ultimate break with Elijah Muhammad and his movement and of his assassination by Muslims. This might prompt the reader to write off the Black Muslim experience as an unfortunate but temporary disaster. Such a reading, however, would cause the reader to fail to see how the Muslim movement aided in Malcolm X's growth. At the age of twenty-three Malcolm Little became Malcolm X and entered into the kind of relationship Erikson identifies with adolescence.

Erikson [in *Insight and Responsibility: Lectures on the Ethical Implications of Psychoanalytic Insight*] elaborates the childhood virtue of basic trust into four virtues: hope, will, purpose, and competence. Malcolm X's prison experience

rekindled hope and will and gave him a purpose. His language program (including correspondence courses, his reading of the dictionary, his letters to Elijah Muhammad, and his participation in the debate club) gave him competence. The twenty-three year old ex-con might seem to have been ready for an adult role. Erikson defines adulthood in terms of courage; "to be a person, identical with oneself, presupposes a basic trust in one's origins—and the courage to emerge from them." Malcolm had yet to reconsider his origins and to deal with the shame of being the son of an assassinated father and a mental patient mother and at the same time a Negro. Dropping his family name and assuming the unknown X immediately lifted some of the burden, and Yacub's History held open the possibility of uncovering a more dignified lineage than he was aware of.

Dropping his family name for the X was no big step. He had long since lost the name Little and much of the relatedness it entailed. He recalled making a public show of his draft notice by reading it aloud and remarking, "this was probably the only time my real name was ever heard in Harlem in those days." The names he was known by emphasized personal attributes—his red hair—or a sort of generic quality—his being from Detroit or Harlem. He had moved into a culture in which relatedness was deemphasized or almost impossible. One had no continuity with a past and, therefore, no real future. One was a creature of the present to be distinguished only by personal characteristics. Yacub's History restored a relationship to the past and made his future possible.

He needed a supportive environment to explore the unknown and to test his competence. He had to go through adolescence, the virtue of which, according to Erikson, is fidelity, a virtue which produces "a whole circle of approving eyes which makes the space [one] masters both safe and secure." The chief virtue of the Muslim movement—with its strict codes on dress, alcohol and other stimulants, sex roles and family life, cleanliness and eating habits, and its schedule that consumed almost all of the free time of its devotees—was its separatism. Such a life style created a safe and secure space by blocking out and holding off at a distance distractions and inappropriate standards of personal dignity. Malcolm X accepted that secure space Elijah Muhammad offered to him, and, being selflessly faithful to him, Minister Malcolm increased the number of approving eyes within it.

Trust grows in a stable situation and increases the stability of the relationship. It is the stability of the relationship that contributes to the growth of the persons within it. In explaining why he prefers to call the basic relationship "trust" rather than "confidence," Erikson says:

> If I prefer the word "trust," it is because there is

more naiveté and more mutuality in it: an infant can be said to be more trusting where it would go too far to say that he has confidence. The general state of trust, furthermore, implies not only that one has learned *to rely on the sameness and continuity of the other providers,* but also that one *may trust oneself* and the capacity of one's own organs *to cope with urges;* and that one is able to consider oneself trustworthy enough so that providers will not need to be on guard lest they be nipped.

In the earliest stages, the developing infant is freed by the stable provision of food, shelter, and comfort to explore and exploit his world in certain directions. The relationship is a mutual one tending toward mutual sustenance and gratification. At later stages the child plays a more definite and distinctive part in sustaining and building the stability which secures both parties of the relationship. The taken-for-grantedness of the world, the attitude of not questioning everything, allows for the growth of confidence in one's ability to manage. Though it seems fantastic, Yacub's History of the Human Race and its hope for recovery of the lost dignity of black people provided a stable center for the development of the rhetorical, administrative, philosophical, and spiritual growth of the late adolescent Minister Malcolm. Yacub's History is a story out of cosmic time, and something apparently that old and that enduring reveals a recurrent dimension of Malcolm X's search for stability. He calls it "timelessness." It was the sense of timelessness he sought in drugs.

> Going downtown to deliver the reefers, I felt sensations I cannot describe, in all those different grooves at the same time. The only word to describe it was a *timelessness.* A day might have seemed to me five minutes. Or a half-hour might have seemed a week.

The timelessness of drugs was an illusion that could be re-entered only at the cost of mental and then physical death. Accepting Yacub's History and the Black Muslim movement led Malcolm ultimately to an experience of an enduring sense of timelessness. It came in Mecca, which he called "as ancient as time itself." Two other principles of stability emerged from the Mecca experience, the oneness of God and the unity of mankind: "All ate as One, and slept as One. Everything about the pilgrimage atmosphere accepted the Oneness of Man under One God." In Mecca Malcolm X found that space and time can become one thing.

Acceptance of a world by an act of fidelity gives one the opportunity to exercise competence and to grow. Malcolm X organized mosques in Boston, Philadelphia, and New York. He was rewarded with the use of a car, which he identified as a sign of Elijah Muhammad's "trust and confidence in my efforts to help build our Nation of Islam." The New York mosque stood up to the police in a brutality case, and "a jury awarded [Brother Hinton] over $70,000, the largest police brutality judgment that New York City ever paid." He founded a newspaper. The Muslims cured drug addicts and organized many small businesses. Their membership grew. The good and faithful servant becomes in time the principle of stability for others, becomes, in other words, an adult. Minister Malcolm was rewarded for his fidelity with the trust of Elijah Muhammad. When Mr. Muhammad was convalescing in Arizona, Malcolm X went to him to discuss some public speaking requests and some administrative matters. He felt trusted:

> Mr. Muhammad evidenced the depth of his trust in me. In those areas I've described, he told me to make the decisions myself. He said that my guideline should be whatever I felt was wise—whatever was in the general good interests of our Nation of Islam.

The cared for had begun to become the career. Erikson sees the virtues of adulthood as love, care, and wisdom. Malcolm X had learned too well the meaning of Yacub's History. Black people in need of care, in need of his protective rhetoric, were not limited to the membership of the Nation of Islam, or at least those who had already declared fidelity to it. After all, Islam was for him at that time the Black Man's religion. He was willing in the name of all Black Americans to take risks that threatened the isolation and separated security of the Nation of Islam. He was soon to face another crisis of growth which would end in his emergence to full personhood or adulthood: "to be a person, identical with oneself, presupposes a basic trust in one's origins—and the courage to emerge from them." The Black Muslim movement and its familial bonds gave him a trust in his remote black origins, and his growing competence as a speaker, leader, and organizer gave him the courage to emerge from the Nation of Islam into a broader, more diverse family.

The first step toward adulthood was taking charge of some portion of the world in his own name. This step was not his marriage to Sister Betty but his helping to get his mother released from the mental hospital after over twenty years of incarceration. In fact, it was only when Alex Haley asked him to talk about his mother that Malcolm X began to tell his own life story. Haley recalled, "After that night, he never again hesitated to tell me even the most intimate details of his personal life, over the next two years. His talking about his mother triggered something." It caused Malcolm X to become Malcolm Little again and to face some unfinished business which he could now deal with, the shame of his mother's hospitalization. Later Malcolm X told Haley:

> "Ever since we discussed my mother, I've been

thinking about her. I realized that I had blocked her out of my mind. . . . It made me face something about myself. . . . My mind had closed about [my] mother. I simply didn't feel the problem could be solved, so I had shut it out."

It was, indeed, a family effort that released Mrs. Little, but perhaps Malcolm X's growth was the catalyst that freed his brothers and sisters from their own shame and impotence.

Malcolm X had to take other steps toward adulthood. When he and Haley first met, he did nothing in his own name and owned nothing. The book he contracted to do with Alex Haley was dedicated to Elijah Muhammad, and all royalties were to be paid to Mr. Muhammad's mosque in Chicago. The house he and Sister Betty and the children lived in was owned by the New York mosque. Malcolm X recalled that the only quarrel he had with his wife was about money. She wanted him to put some money away for their family, but he convinced her at that time that "the Nation of Islam would take care of her for the rest of her life, and of [their] children until they were grown." He was still a person with almost no conscious base of identity outside the Nation of Islam.

Then came the break with Elijah Muhammad. Malcolm was silenced. He found himself being made a scapegoat for the growing rift in the Nation of Islam as a result of the paternity suits against Elijah Muhammad. His life was threatened. He felt he was losing his mind, and he struggled to avoid ending like his brother Reginald, whose brain was "burned." Even Malcolm had helped to destroy Reginald's mind:

> The last time I had seen Reginald, one day he walked into the Mosque Seven restaurant. I saw him coming in the door. I went and met him. I looked into my brother's eyes; I told him he wasn't welcome among Muslims, and he turned around and left, and I haven't seen him since. I did that to my own blood brother because, years before, Mr. Muhammad had sentenced Reginald to "isolation" from all other Muslims—and I considered that I was a Muslim before I was Reginald's brother.

To survive outside the Nation of Islam, Malcolm X needed to know that his needs and, now that he was a husband and father, the needs of those he cared for could be met in that world. He had to trust, that is to identify, with that world. It was a larger, less clearly defined world than the Nation of Islam. For one thing, it included whites. He found that even white reporters were concerned about him as a result of the evident strain he was under following his silencing by Elijah Muhammad.

> Since I had been a Muslim, this was the first time

any white people really got to me in a personal way. I could tell that some of them were really honest and sincere. One of those, whose name I won't call—he might lose his job—said, "Malcolm X, the whites need your voice worse than the Negroes."

He discovered that he was a husband and father and that he could rely on Betty as he never before believed he could.

> I never would have dreamed that I would ever depend so much upon any woman for strength as I now leaned upon Betty. There was no exchange between us; Betty said nothing, being the caliber of wife that she is, with the depth of understanding that she has—but I could feel the envelopment of her comfort. I knew that she was as faithful a servant of Allah as I was, and I knew that whatever happened, she was with me.

He rewrote the contract for the book with the royalties to go to his new mosque and, in the event of his death, to his wife.

Finally, he identified with the ghetto masses. As he put it. "I could speak and understand the ghetto's language." He spoke their language because he had lived and identified with their experience, and carried the memories of it into the Muslim movement.

The Nation of Islam had separated itself from both black and white America. Malcolm X was able to find in the dream of a separated Muslim nation a cure for his own self-rejection, but there were aspects of himself that he never repudiated. To be redeemed meant not to be utterly transformed, but to allow what was good in him to emerge. He never repudiated the dancing that made him famous in Boston and Harlem. Haley recalls that when Malcolm X was retelling his dancing exploits, he "really got carried away."

> One night, suddenly, wildly, he jumped up from his chair and, incredibly, the fearsome black demagogue was scat-singing and popping his fingers, "re-bop-de-bop-blap-blam—" and then grabbing a vertical pipe with one hand (as the girl partner) he went jubilantly lindy-hopping around, his coattail and the long legs and the big feet flying as they had in those Harlem days.

In spite of the conks and zoot suits and the degradation of Laura, there was something basically good in his lindy hop experience that remained outside of the Nation of Islam and was a bond between him and the ghetto.

It pained him to see black people lost to alcohol and drugs. Haley recalls that on one of his daily walks through Harlem,

Malcolm X might tell a wino, "It's just what the white devil wants you to do, brother. . . . He wants you to get drunk so he will have an excuse to put a club up beside your head." Malcolm X did not repudiate the black hustler, even though he recognized the hell the hustler lived in. He identified with the hustler.

> "I had a jungle mind, I was living in a jungle, and everything I did was done by instinct to survive. . . .
> it was all a result of what happens to thousands upon thousands of black men in the white man's Christian world."

He did not repudiate the hustler because there was a talent in him that could have been put to greater use. The numbers runner he had bet with, West Indian Archie with his "photographic memory" for numbers, was such a lost talent. Malcolm X admitted having frequently "reflected upon such black veteran numbers men as West Indian Archie. If they had lived in another kind of society, their exceptional mathematical talents might have been better used. But they were black."

Harlem and Roxbury blacks, with their raw energies, diverse if misdirected talents, and some level of mutual acceptance and respect, were those he identified with from his first encounter with the ghetto. He continued to identify with them and yearned to serve them even as a good servant of the separatist Muslim movement, and he served them well indeed, for when he accepted the break with Elijah Muhammad, his new place was already affirmed.

> In the end, I reasoned that the decision already had been made for me. The ghetto masses already had entrusted me with an image of leadership among them. I knew the ghetto instinctively extends that trust only to one who had demonstrated that he would never sell them out to the white man. I not only had no such intention—to sell out was not in my nature.

His new mission was to be a continuation of the old one: to develop self-acceptance by developing competence and self-confidence. Part of his new vision was to continue the economic self-development he had initiated in the Muslims when the Muslims opened their own stores and services. He held that "It's because black men don't own and control their own community's retail establishments that they can't stabilize their own community." His vision was to found a new organization that would free black people from their mental, spiritual, economic, and political sickness. It would not be a separatist organization as "it would embrace all faiths of black men, and it would carry into practice what the Nation of Islam had only preached."

Acting in his own name again, he announced his new organization, The Muslim Mosque, Incorporated, at a public press conference, and then set off on the pilgrimage to Mecca. The reader who is uncomfortable with the racist statements of Minister Malcolm is relieved by the vision of unity of all races that Malcolm X had in Mecca, but to move quickly to the vision is to overlook the growth process that made the vision possible. To get to Mecca Malcolm X had to borrow money. Although he was a man conscious of the importance of language, he went to Mecca ignorant of Arabic. He had to surrender his passport at Jedda. He recalled that he "never had felt more alone and helpless" since he was a baby, yet none of his hustler self-protectiveness emerged. He was learning to trust in a different world. All during his trip he received kindnesses, each of which was "another of Allah's signs, that wherever I turned, someone was there to help me, to guide me." In such a world one could be helpless and yet not be in need. The God who cared for one cared for all humankind. He had journeyed beyond self, beyond clan, and now beyond nation and race. To the identification he shared with his family and the ghetto masses and to the care for their needs he had already amply demonstrated, he now added wisdom. He told a press conference in Cairo that what impressed him most about the Hajj was, "The *brotherhood*! The people of all races, colors, from all over the world coming together as *one*!" It had proved to him "the power of the One God." This new stage of his growth was also signalled by a name change—El-Hajj Malik El-Shabazz—that indicated that he had been fulfilled. He recalled later, "In my thirty-nine years on this earth the Holy City of Mecca had been the first time I had ever stood before the Creator of All and felt like a complete human being."

To be a complete human being is not to be separate from the world, but to be part of it. The new Malcolm X, El-Hajj Malik El-Shabazz, had acted in his own name to declare a place within the world. Yet he was also able to acknowledge his dependence on others, for example his wife. Shortly before his death, Malcolm X told Sister Betty as he was leaving the house:

> "We'll all be together. I want my family with me. Families shouldn't be separated. I'll never make another long trip without you. We'll get somebody to keep the children. I'll never leave you so long again."

He was able to admit his limitations. He told Haley that he lacked a formal education and that he had an unsatisfied thirst for knowledge:

> "You can believe me that if I had the time right now, I would not be one bit ashamed to go back into any New York City public school and start where I left

off at the ninth grade, and go on through a degree. Because I don't begin to be academically equipped for so many of the interests that I have. For instance, I love languages. I wish I were an accomplished linguist. I don't know anything more frustrating than to be around people talking something you can't understand."

He could deal openly with the fear of failure and still take the risks of defeat and shame. Haley recalls:

> A few days later, however, . . . [Malcolm X] wrote in one of his memo books this, which he let me read, "Children have a lesson adults should learn, to not be ashamed of failing, but to get up and try again. Most of us adults are so afraid, so cautious, so 'safe,' and therefore so shrinking and rigid and afraid that it is why so many humans fail. Most middle-aged adults have resigned themselves to failure."

He could rely on others without qualification. Haley recalls that when be brought Malcolm X a contract for the foreign publication rights of *The Autobiography,* Malcolm X hesitated.

> He looked suspiciously at the contract, and said, "I had better show this thing to my lawyer," and put the contract in his inside coat pocket. Driving in Harlem about an hour later, he suddenly stopped the car across the street from the 135th Street Y.M.C.A. Building. Withdrawing the contract, he signed it, and thrust it to me. "I'll trust you," he said, and drove on.

He could accept his own death.

> Anyway, now, each day I live as if I am already dead, and I tell you what I would like you to do. When I *am* dead—I say it that way because from the things I *know,* I do not expect to live long enough to read this book in its finished form—I want you to just watch and see if I'm not right in what I say: that the white man, in his press, is going to identify me with "hate."

This acceptance stance was different from the stance of the gun toting street hustler who also lived as if he were a dead man. As a hustler he was ready to die, but he was also ready to take the lives of others with his dying energies. As the leader of the Muslim Mosque, Inc., as the husband and father of a family whose home was fire bombed, he did not threaten to take others with him when he died. The hustler has only himself. When he is gone, there is nothing left. Malcolm X had come to identify with and to trust others.

He had come to accept a world larger than his own ego. Vague and indistinct though it may have been, this world participated in the timeless. Nothing could destroy it. In spite of his violent death, Malcolm Little X completed his pilgrimage from self to cosmos, each step of which was an act of ever increasing trust.

Hank Flick and Larry Powell (essay date June 1988)

SOURCE: "Animal Imagery in the Rhetoric of Malcolm X," in *Journal of Black Studies,* Vol. 18, No. 4, June, 1988, pp. 435-51.

[*In the following essay, Flick and Powell explore Malcolm X's use of animal imagery in his rhetoric as a means of changing the prevailing conceptions held by black Americans about white Americans.*]

The history of the black man in America emanates from the edifice of slavery and its subsequent effects on both white and black Americans. Over the years a number of rhetors have analyzed such a situation for the purpose of identifying those rhetorical devices that had been employed to regulate blacks to a lifelong position of servitude in America. Rhetors noted the different devices that were employed to maintain and then tighten the shackles of slavery to the limbs of blacks as they migrated from the plantations of the old South to the urban centers of America. One rhetor who analyzed such a situation was Malcolm X.

Malcolm X's rhetoric was designed to modify the image that many blacks had of white America. Such an image had white America seen as a people who were humane in their interests and treatment of other people. White America was perceived by blacks as being a moral people who had the courage to deal effectively with those injustices that had been perpetrated against blacks. In seeking to modify such an image, Malcolm faced a situation wherein he made use of several rhetorical devices. One such device was his use of animal imagery.

The rhetoric of Malcolm X was born of societal conflict. In fact, his rapid persuasive messages—dotted with short sentences and quick and cutting answers—were the means by which such conflict was perpetuated. Any examination of the rhetoric of Malcolm X might be seen as a logical result of crisis conditions that have been developing for more than a century in the black communities across America as blacks were forced to give form to their own set of experiences in the midst of a white culture.

In seeking to modify the image many blacks had of white

America, Malcolm faced a situation where one culture acted in a supraculture. Black Americans operated within a system wherein most everything was defined, given form, and controlled by white America. Malcolm envisioned the history of the United States as a personal historical chronicle of white people, written by white people, and immortalized for white people. Against such a semantic backdrop, Malcolm's words must first be heard and then understood.

The purpose of this article is to study Malcolm's use of animal imagery in relation to his goal of freeing blacks from their image of white America. In regards to this purpose, this article has (1) identified the image that many blacks had of white America, (2) identified Malcolm's paradigm for the use of animal imagery, (3) discussed this paradigm in relation to how animal imagery was employed by Malcolm to modify an image, and (4) identified what can be learned from Malcolm's discourse in terms of facing future images that are in need of change.

THE IMAGE THAT BLACKS
HAD OF WHITE AMERICA

A person's image of him- or herself, the world he or she lives in, and his or her place in that world is determined by a person's subjective knowledge. An image is nothing more than the sum total of a person's beliefs and perceptions of self and other. What a person thinks he or she is, what he or she sees others as being, what he or she thinks the world is like goes to form a person's image of the present and his or her expectations of the future. The image a person holds of him- or herself is not one-dimensional. It is a multidimensional "something" that serves to place people into a time-space relationship with other persons. This image serves to stimulate and guide people's behavior.

Over the years, white America has acquired a series of public images of their own. [K. E.] Boulding, [in *The Image,* 1956,] claims that such an image begins in the person's mind and then becomes public when it is transmitted and shared with others. One specific public image that has survived the passage of time was that white America was a humane and moral people. Within such an image whites were considered superior to others by reason of their sensitivity to the positions and needs of others.

The effect of such an image upon blacks was that many blacks came to view both black and white interests as being congruent in nature. Blacks felt that white America was concerned with their plight and were working to eradicate many of the impoverished conditions blacks faced. The trust that blacks had in white America supported and protected the image of white America. In terms of effect, by trusting in white America, blacks occupied a passive stance in terms of speaking to and dealing with their own problems.

Malcolm's rhetoric was characterized by his attempt to unify blacks. Through unification Malcolm hoped to bring blacks together so they could seek out and formulate solutions to their own problems. To accomplish this goal, Malcolm sought to modify the image blacks had of white America. For as long as the image of white America remained intact, blacks would look to others to solve their problems. So that blacks would occupy a more active stance in dealing with conditions endemic to blacks, Malcolm worked to modify the image that blacks had of white America. Malcolm sought to effect such a change through his use of animal imagery. To understand how Malcolm employed elements of animal imagery a three step paradigm is first presented and then analyzed in terms of its impact on image modification.

MALCOLM X'S PARADIGM FOR
THE USE OF ANIMAL IMAGERY

Malcolm's use of animal imagery came into being as a response to conditions blacks faced. His discourse can be judged rhetorically significant by noting the situation it spoke to, the conditions it emerged from, the change it sought to effect, and the paradigm it promulgated to effect such a change. This paradigm can be seen as a model for facing future images in need of change and the steps a rhetor might follow to effect the needed image change.

The situational nature of Malcolm's rhetoric noted those controlling devices within a situation and prescribed a series of steps a rhetor could follow to alter an image. These steps were (1) identification (method/author), (2) depiction and arousal, and (3) action.

THE USE OF ANIMAL IMAGERY AND HOW IT WAS
EMPLOYED BY MALCOLM X TO MODIFY THE
IMAGE OF WHITE AMERICA

Malcolm's paradigm for the use of animal imagery can be seen as proceeding through a series of rhetorical shifts designed to allow a rhetor's claim to maintain a balance between the familiar, reasoned analysis, vivid reductive imagery, and a call to action to effect the behavior of those people within that situation. Malcolm's use of animal imagery can be seen as a response to the situation and conditions blacks faced. It was designed to prepare blacks for future rhetorical action. Whether such action was to be immediate or delayed was not significant. What was salient was that, through this action, the future relationship between the races was to be effected to the point where black perceptions of white America were revised.

In his analysis of the conditions blacks faced, Malcolm reasoned that blacks needed to initiate specific corrective action in order that present conditions would not continue. While his use of discourse was directed toward identifying, sensitizing, and arousing blacks to the point where they would act on their own behalf, Malcolm's use of animal imagery was an attempt to invert the images that blacks had of white Americans. Malcolm's paradigm offered his auditors a design by which they could be abstracted to new positions of dignity and respect, while demoting whites to a position wherein they were recognized as active agents of evil.

IDENTIFICATION (METHOD/AUTHOR)

Malcolm's paradigm initially focused upon the identification of the method used to define blacks and of identifying the author of such tactics. His accounts were analytical in nature by reason of their examination and discussion of how images were developed and then used to regulate the behavior of self and others. Time was devoted to labeling white America as the architect of such tactics and to discussing their use of verbal artifacts to control existing and future conditions. White America was seen as having the ability to control and define the images of self and others by reason of their ownership of the rights to define the world according to their own rhetorical purposes.

Time and precedent had always allowed groups to name themselves and in turn to be named by other groups. But blacks were never afforded such an opportunity. The job of coding and defining blacks was left entirely in the hands of white America. As a result, blacks came to form their identities on the basis of what white America prescribed. This process had the effect of conditioning blacks to react to what they viewed their images and positions to be.

The coding of blacks by white America had its genus in the white belief that blacks were animals and amoral beasts of the field. Blacks were recorded as playing the role of a domesticated animal of the field with a "violence to murder, [and] ravaging sexual impulses" [A. F. Poussaint, "The Negro American: His Self-Image and Integration," *The Black Power Revolt,* 1968]. Word pictures of this kind defined blacks as being deficient in human qualities. The christening of blacks as animals abstracted blacks to a position above that of whites and sanctioned feelings of superiority in one race and inferiority in another. The fusion of idiom and imagery placed the races in polar positions. These positions served to endorse in the minds of whites their own version of apartheid and legitimized past and future perceptions of, and behavior toward, black Americans.

The importance of this process was captured by [A. L.] Smith [in *Rhetoric of Black Revolution,* 1969] when he commented that the "namer of names is always the father of things." Along with such a practice, [R. M.] Weaver maintained [in *Language Is Sermonic,* 1970] that to have the ability to define the world and the images located within,

allowed one to exert his or her influence and control over that world. Weaver contended that people's ability to manipulate symbols was their own private instrument by which they could order the relationships between people. Weaver claimed that people's overlordship of their world "begins with the naming of the world."

White America's command of language had the effect of first coding blacks and then teaching them to respond and live out such labels as if they were true. Malcolm envisioned the short-term effects of such a practice when he stated, "When you let yourself be influenced by images created by others, you'll find that oftentimes the one who creates these images can use them to mislead you and misuse you" [*The Speeches of Malcolm X at Harvard*]. Smith summarized its long-term effects when he commented, "To be defined by whites is to remain a slave."

Malcolm identified the use of image-controlling devices as not existing in its own right, isolated and independent. To Malcolm, such a process was to be seen as only a part of a larger system by which control could be exerted. Image making was objectified as a unit itself within a larger system of white control and manipulation. It was identified as a device within a system to develop an awareness of the method to be used by which a situation may be defined. Therefore, the initial step of his paradigm was to understand the situation itself and the many devices that could be employed within that system. To become cognizant of the larger system meant to understand its overall purpose and the devices within that can be employed to define and control the situation in which a person lives.

Rhetoric does not exist independent of an individual. It is a person who engineers and employs it to support his or her own rhetorical purposes. An awareness of the system or method an individual has created does not in itself constitute a complete statement of that situation. A rhetor, to be rhetorically effective, must identify and record not only the method and the purpose for which it was employed, but also its architect and against whom it is to be used. To make known one group as the causal agent of the suffering of another creates an active opposition and oppressive element that can later be vilified. The process of making known both method and architect allowed Malcolm to understand the specific forces present and to then, with the assistance of discourse, seek to modify conditions that have resulted from such conditions.

DEPICTION AND AROUSAL

Malcolm's initial step focused upon enlightening blacks as to what devices had been used to capture their presence and to imprint upon the minds of blacks who was responsible for such acts. Malcolm believed that the fusion of method and author could best be understood if it was followed by a presentation of the effects of such a merger in terms of life experiences. To Malcolm, a rhetor must develop and present his or her own "theater of the mind." Such an artifice was constructed with an appropriate and balanced blend of reasoned analysis followed by the presentation of affective imagery. A playhouse of this nature was erected for the purpose of allowing an audience the opportunity to see how such events truly applied to them. Past and present conditions under which blacks lived were vividly transported across time and set down in front of his black audience. Malcolm brought such conditions to the attention of his auditors for the purpose of awakening their feelings. The specific device he used to accomplish this task was his use of animal imagery.

Malcolm's use of animal imagery redefined both the situation in which the races lived and the images of the races. Conditions were not simply replayed for his audience but were translated into the life experiences of his auditors so that they could vicariously feel the depths of that situation. In redefining the situation and images of the races, Malcolm selectively downgraded the images of whites while he portrayed blacks as victims of a cruel and racist white society.

Malcolm's rhetoric located both races as occupying disparate positions within a jungle like atmosphere. This jungle atmosphere, Malcolm believed, had the effect of bringing out in an individual the lowest and most base parts of his or her character. Operating within such a jungle, wolves, snakes, and sheep roamed free. Survival was based upon the principle of the fiercest and strongest animals fleecing and living off the weaker animal [*The Autobiography of Malcolm X*]. Whites were coded as wolves, foxes, and snakes, while blacks were cast as sheep.

Within Malcolm's animal compound, whites were pictured as roaming free and brutalizing anything and everything that stood in their way (black Americans) [*The Autobiography of Malcolm X*]. Malcolm differentiated between the roles of whites when he stated:

> Let me tell you the only difference. The white man in the South is a wolf. You know where he stands. When he opens his mouth and you can see his teeth, he looks vicious. Well, the only difference between the white man in the South and the white man in the North is that one is a wolf and this one is a fox. The fox will lynch you and you won't even know you have been lynched. The fox will Jim Crow you and don't even know you're Jim Crowed [*The End of White World Supremacy: Four Speeches by Malcolm X*].

While noting differences between whites, Malcolm claimed

that both wolf and fox were of the same genus. Consequently, Malcolm identified both orders of canines by assigning them similar objectives. Malcolm explained, "The objective of the fox and the wolf is the same. . . . They want to exploit you, they want to take advantage of you" [*The End of White World Supremacy*]. Similarly, Malcolm claimed, "both are enemies of humanity . . . both humiliate and mutilate their victims" [J. Clarke, editor, *Malcolm X: The Man and His Times,* 1969].

Rhetoric of this nature served to debilitate whites to the point that they were no longer considered human. Having been reduced in size and power, whites were no longer considered superior to anything or anybody. In explaining the motive force behind such rhetoric, Malcolm asserted [in his *Autobiography*], "I [have] . . . participated in spreading the truths that had done so much to help the American black man rid himself of the mirage that the white race was made up of 'superior beings.'" In response to such a revelation, Malcolm requested blacks to revolutionize their own thinking so they could open their eyes and "never again look in the same fearful, worshiping way at the white man" [*The Autobiography of Malcolm X*].

Having demystified white America, Malcolm turned to arousing black anger and hatred of whites. To accomplish this task, Malcolm portrayed blacks as the victims of a cruel and ruthless white society. As sheep within an alien environment, blacks were portrayed as the constant victims of the ruthless attacks of more aggressive white wolves and foxes. Such acts of violence were labeled as criminal and cowardly in that they were perpetrated by a strong and fierce predator upon a more docile and domesticated prey. No longer did the wolf and the fox seek out prey of equal strength; instead, they gorged themselves upon the blood of the helpless. The end result of such acts of violence resulted in, claimed Malcolm, white America having its hands "dripping with blood . . . of the black man in this country" [A. L. Smith and S. Robb, editors, *The Voice of Black Rhetoric,* 1971].

The recounting of such acts, while symbolic in nature, sought to unify blacks in their hatred of white America. By his use of such vivid imagery, blacks were allowed to see themselves as victims rather than as the victimizer. This approach appeared to be effective. Smith noted [in *Rhetoric of Black Revolution*] that such statements needed no further support and documentation for blacks because such experiences had been regular segments of their daily lives within America.

In seeking to arouse his audience, Malcolm's discourse provided his auditors with a four-dimensional experience. In depicting life experiences, Malcolm sought to arouse his auditors by making use of the elements of (1) specification, (2) illumination, (3) confrontation, and (4) intensification.

Every situation contains an audience that was influenced and affected by that situation. A fixed audience had to be specified from the total corpus of hearers who merely happen to be present. To be rhetorically effective, Malcolm envisioned that this grouping must be shown how the present situation affects their lives and how such a context will continue to affect, define, and regulate future behavior if left unchecked. Real-life experiences were to be illuminated and vividly left in the minds of this audience through the use of vivid reductive imagery. Abstract situations and previously employed rhetorical devices and methods of control were to be translated through reasoned analysis and the medium of language into a series of concrete life experiences that were congruent with their own experiences.

Malcolm noted that every situation contained a series of constraints that worked within that situation to restrict the action needed to modify conditions and affect change. Malcolm identified these constraints as beliefs, attitudes, traditions, images, and self-interests. These constraints worked to perpetuate and support the status quo. When such constraints were operative, a rhetor's own call for action and change could be delayed or abated. To transcend such barriers and stimulate action, Malcolm foresaw the need for the introduction of animal imagery of a highly charged nature. In lieu of such a claim, Malcolm offered his auditors a vision of a face-to-face confrontation with those forces that sought to use and control them.

Malcolm's use of highly charged imagery was a tactic by which future adjustments to situations could be brought about, and by which disparate positions could be identified, illustrated, examined, and made more intense. In accentuating the disparate images within a situation, Malcolm stylistically displayed elements of antithesis and hyperbole. Both rhetorical devices were employed to sensitize and awaken an audience by locating opposing images within a single frame. Conflicting styles of behavior were dramatized in order to contrast and distort the relations between and images of the races.

In Malcolm's paradigm, discourse was summoned into existence for the purpose of intensifying a vision of white manipulation of blacks in the minds of his audience. Reasoned analysis, emotional appeals, and stylistic devices were conspicuously displayed to promote understanding and to provoke a response. The idiom employed to intensify experience was pictured as one that an audience could identify with, that captured their treatment within such a situation, and that unified blacks in terms of future behavioral responses. The use of vivid reductive imagery, invective, aphorisms, and caustic verbiage was employed to allow an audience an opportunity for catharsis, to vilify an alien element, and to provide life to a situation that may have had little previous meaning. The use of such imagery served to unite blacks in their anger and hatred of whites, to demystify and dehumanize white America, while resurrecting the images of blacks.

The idiom employed by Malcolm was checked by the powers of the situation itself. Imagery of this nature was presented to blacks for the purpose of producing change. It served to prescribe and legitimize Malcolm's responses to such a situation. This response came in the form of discourse. Discourse was prescribed by Malcolm as the result of previous white control and manipulation of the image-making process. This discourse was in itself a response to that situation. It became a mode of action that specified future human behavior that could effect change within that situation.

ACTION

Malcolm's words became his cues for behavior. His verbiage became his remedy, the prescribed antidote, and the answer to that situation. The labeling techniques that Malcolm employed were designed to divide the immediate world so that reality could be defined in a manner that was in line with the rhetor's own rhetorical purpose. Within this world, whites were coded as animals. Such a process, [K.] Burke claimed [in *Attitudes Toward History*, 1959], had the effect of controlling the behavior of man. Burke explained that in coding people according to your own purpose and perceptions "we form our characters, since the names embody attitudes; and implicit in the attitudes are the cues for behavior."

In the past, both blacks and whites reacted to blacks according to the language and imagery white America developed to represent blacks. Malcolm sought to use the same process to label whites according to their past deeds. This process was directed toward influencing future black responses toward the larger white community. In assigning whites the image of an animal, Malcolm lowered the white man to a base level of existence. In essence, by calling the white individual a wolf, Malcolm directed blacks to be on their guard when "the wolf" was in their presence.

Malcolm's discourse simplified reality. Alternatives were restricted that in turn directed and regulated black behavior. By calling whites animals, blacks were charged with reacting and responding to such a label. Blacks were energized to act in relation to the labels that whites were carrying. Such labels were fixed to whites by Malcolm's use of animal imagery. Burke explained this process when he said:

> Names shape our relations with our fellows. They prepare us for some functions and against others, for or against the persons representing these functions. The names go further; they suggest how you shall be for or against. Call a man a villain, and you have the choice of either attacking or cringing. Call

him mistaken, and you invite yourself to attempt setting him straight.

The imagery of past brutality in animalistic terms provided Malcolm with a vocabulary. This vocabulary was used to force his black auditors to feel the pain and view the scars they had encountered at the hands of white America. The continued repetition of experiences was recaptured and vividly presented so that no audience member could escape its grasp.

WHAT CAN BE LEARNED FROM MALCOLM'S RHETORIC IN TERMS OF FACING FUTURE IMAGES THAT ARE IN NEED OF CHANGE

Malcolm X's probe of black-white relations centered upon identifying and explaining the process of white image making and the effect it came to have on the identities, perceptions, and behavior of black Americans. Malcolm's rhetoric stressed that blacks could no longer retain an air of patience and allow themselves to be defined by extrinsic forces. Images that had been assigned to them had and would continue to condemn them to live and die trapped in an affective domain within the urban centers of America unless they would face the task of redefining the situation in which they lived and the personages located within that situation.

What can be learned from Malcolm's use of animal imagery? First, to be rhetorically effective one cannot allow another to code and define the situation in which you live. To do so is to allow rhetorical opponents the right to regulate one to positions that are advantageous to him or her. Second, the right to define oneself and the situation in which one lives is an elusive privilege. It is seldom given voluntarily by one group to another, or by exploiter to exploited. It was to be attained when a rhetor would create and present to an audience discourse of such a highly charged and vivid nature that the audience itself, in thought and action, could be so engaged in that discourse that its own experiences became the mediating agent of the needed change itself. Third, the power to act is based upon a rhetor's ability to awaken his or her auditors to the tragedies of their own lives. Action was seen as resting upon the rhetor's ability to awaken the feelings of his or her audience. Identification and depiction were identified as antecedents of action. While words were seen as static in nature, a rhetors use of those words must be active. The descriptions of the past deeds of others against another were to be objectified to the point whereby an audience could see itself in relation to these deeds. In transporting abstract life experiences across time and space, an auditor not only could identify those devices that have been employed to record his or her presence, but he or she was allowed to see the subsequent effects of such tactics. The use of animal imagery supplied an audience with a new perspective by which they could see themselves. While such

imagery had the effect of awaking and rousing feelings within an audience, it also served to transform an audience from a passive to a more active state.

Aside from these four principles, Malcolm's use of imagery illuminated two other working principles that a rhetor need consider if a rhetor hopes to employ animal imagery effectively. Malcolm's rhetoric stressed a blending of reasoned analysis and vivid reductive imagery. Within his design, reason was pictured as not having the power by itself to modify an image or to move an audience to action. Reason and emotion are noted as needing to cooperate with each other while working to evoke understanding, feeling, and dedication from an audience. To Malcolm, reason was employed to develop and help maintain an image, but it was the use of emotion that gave that image meaning and life. Finally, to affect change in the image of another, the imagery that a rhetor employs must be given a contextual meaning that identifies an agent and his or her purposes for employing rhetorical devices. Words such as *manipulation, cruelty, exploitation, violence,* and *humiliation* have a denotative meaning in themselves, but unless they are rhetorically fused to a specific agent and a series of life experiences, they will drift free and lose their meaning. This agent and context will give the words an identity of their own while identifying how each factor defined the other.

In studying Malcolm's rhetoric, several questions surface. Can a rhetor through use of imagery lessen the hurt that others have inflicted upon him or her through the use and manipulation of language? Can a rhetor through use of highly charged imagery change or reorganize the perceptions of his or her auditors toward themselves, others, and the situation in which they both live? Can a rhetor through use of imagery guide the future relationships between groups of people? Before considering the answers to these questions, let us consider another point.

As children we are told to tell other children who call us names that "sticks and stones may break our bones but words can never hurt us." While such a statement seems harmless, it does serve to reveal an important principle. By purchasing a health insurance policy, individuals find a way to protect themselves from any injuries they may endure from future extrinsic forces. But how can individuals protect themselves from semantic damage?

In probing the effects of semantic damage upon blacks, it is important to note that one can never find a proper insurance policy that will protect him or her from the verbal "sticks and stones" thrown by others. Semantic wounds, like other wounds, take time to heal. But even if time is granted, words can and do leave scars. Malcolm's use of animal imagery sought to deal with the scars that the years of white image control had left on the minds of black Americans.

While Malcolm's words could not eradicate the pains that blacks had endured at the hands of white America, it did lessen the effects of such a condition by rhetorically allowing blacks to change semantic environments. Malcolm's words imposed a new order upon the black world. Within this world, blacks occupied a more active position in defining their own humanity and the inhumanity of white America. No longer were blacks to take the verbal record of the past for their description and prescriptions of the present. To effect change, blacks were exposed to rhetoric that inverted and reorganized previous images of white Americans while adding features to the image of black Americans.

Malcolm's rhetoric attests to the proposition that an individual's behavior is dependent on his or her image of self, other, and the world they both share. One's image, in large part, can be seen as being determined by his or her subjective knowledge. His or her feelings toward self and other, what he or she knows, what he or she feels, go to make up his or her image. This image directs individuals to act and think the way they do. To control the process of image making then is to have the ability to control and direct the behavior of others.

Images can and do change. While some images are resistant to change, others can and do readily change as incoming messages are received and processed. If such incoming messages support the possessor's original image, the perceptions of those images are strengthened. But if this information is inconsistent with previous images, a degree of change may be produced. So if a man has an image of his friend Bill as trustworthy and then hears Bill lying to his boss, his image of Bill might be revised. If blacks are given an image of whites as humane and are shown through the employment of vivid reductive imagery that whites are and have been cruel in their treatment of others, such a previous image might also undergo revision.

In Malcolm's scheme of things, for change to occur, incoming information needed to be vivid in nature. Images could be modified or changed only when such incoming messages were so vivid in nature that they served to cause an auditor to reformulate his or present image of things radically. In vividly capturing what he considered to be the essence of the black/white experience, Malcolm transported life experiences across time and space to affect change in the manner blacks perceived white Americans. To modify the image that blacks had of whites meant to cause future behavioral changes that would affect the future relations between and perceptions of the races.

Lawrence B. Goodheart (essay date Autumn 1990)

SOURCE: "The Odyssey of Malcolm X: An Eriksonian Interpretation," in *Historian,* Vol. 52, No. 1, Autumn, 1990, pp. 47-62.

[*In the following essay, Goodheart examines the identity of Malcolm X—as set forth in* The Autobiography of Malcolm X—*using the theoretical framework of Erik Erikson.*]

The black search for identity in the United States has been well put by the poet Robert Penn Warren: "Alienated from the world to which he is born and from the country of which he is a citizen yet surrounded by the successful values of that world, and country, how can the Negro define himself?" At the heart of the civil rights and black power movements of the 1950s and 1960s was the defining of the individual and collective identities of members of the largest racial minority in the United States. During what recently has been labeled a "Second Reconstruction," critical constitutional, legal, and federal-state relationships were reordered to promote equality under the law regardless of race. At the same time, there was a psychological revolution, a popular transformation of African-American identity from a culturally sanctioned racial inferiority to a black assertion of pride, beauty, and power.

The odyssey of Malcolm X was a search for "a definition of himself and his relationship to his people, his country, and the world," according to sociologist John H. Clarke. When Malcolm stated that "the black man in America has been robbed by the white man of his culture, of his identity, of his soul, of his self," he conflated his own experience with that of his people; his odyssey represented the militant black search for identity in the early 1960s. His individual rage spoke directly to the frustration of other African-Americans, especially urban ghetto residents—the black underclass—for whom the promise of civil rights legislation and racial integration offered little prospect of improving their degraded living conditions.

> **[Malcolm X's] individual rage spoke directly to the frustration of other African-Americans, especially urban ghetto residents—the black underclass—for whom the promise of civil rights legislation and racial integration offered little prospect of improving their degraded living conditions.**
> —*Lawrence B. Goodheart*

Public fascination with Malcolm cut across class and racial lines: *The Autobiography of Malcolm X* (1965) has sold over two million copies and has become established as a modern classic. Together with his extensive speeches, interviews, and recollections by associates, the *Autobiography* as narrated to Alex Haley captures the dramatic changes in Malcolm's life. Haley's empathy for Malcolm served to capture the style and substance of the public man. After an initial period of suspicion and distrust, the Malcolm-Haley collaboration developed into what resembled a psychoanalytic session. As Haley patiently prompted him, Malcolm recalled his past. Despite distortion, inaccuracy, and what historian Stephen J. Whitfield calls "impression management," the *Autobiography* is useful for the psychological reality it uncovers.

Psychoanalyst Erik H. Erikson defined the psychological core of an individual as identity—"a subjective sense of an invigorating sameness and continuity." Yet he was careful to stress that the development of a person's identity over time is subject to change that must be understood within a broad cultural context. His biographies of Martin Luther and Mahatma Gandhi emphasized the interconnection between the life history of the subject and the historical moment, a linkage that could be momentous when an individual's psychic needs were resolved in a manner that crystallized communal aspirations. Similarly, the shaping of Malcolm's sense of self as a counterpart to the historic oppression of African-Americans constitutes a central theme in his life and lends itself to Eriksonian interpretation. Erikson's categories do not precisely fit Malcolm's life, particularly the months before his murder, when Malcolm was an isolated figure whom the white establishment feared, civil rights organizations shunned, and Black Muslims damned. Malcolm's resolution of his lifelong quest for a meaningful black identity in the United States was thus only partially achieved. Nevertheless the Eriksonian model, if applied selectively, illuminates the common ground where individual action, collective aspirations, and the historic possibility for change converge in the four major stages of Malcolm's identity, appropriately marked by name changes: "surrendered identity," Malcolm Little; "negative identity," Big Red; "fundamentalism," Malik El-Shabazz; and "beyond fundamentalism," El-Hajj Malik El-Shabazz.

Surrendered Identity:

Malcolm's "earliest vivid memory" was as a four-year-old in 1929 "being suddenly snatched away into a frightening confusion of pistol shots and shouting and smoke and flames." The Lansing, Michigan, equivalent of the Ku Klux Klan had burned his family's house down. Malcolm's recollection is a violent example of what Erikson termed a surrendered racial identity, historically "the fate of the black citizenry who were kept in their place so as to constitute what slaves meant besides cheap labor—the inferior identity to be superior to." Malcolm's childhood memories reveal a life representative of the collective African-American experience as he became ensnared in the racist perversion, as Erikson described it, of "light-clean-clever-white" and "dark-dirty-dumb-nigger."

His father, Earl Little—a tall, very dark-skinned man from Georgia with little formal education—used his itinerant Baptist ministry to preach the racial pride of Marcus Garvey's United Negro Improvement Association. In contrast, his mother, Louise, "looked like a white woman" and was educated. Her shame was her father, an unknown white rapist. The mark of this grandfather was visited on Malcolm; of eight children, he stood apart with his reddish-brown color.

Earl and Louise behaved towards Malcolm in antithetical ways because of his color. Of all his children, Earl took only Malcolm to Garveyite meetings, while Louise told him, "Let the sun shine on you so you can get some color." Earl saw Malcolm's complexion as a blessing in the spirit of the adage that "white is right; if you're brown, stick around; but if you're black, step back." Louise, however, favored her dark-skinned children and disparaged Malcolm's lighter color as an unwanted reminder of her white father. Malcolm's acute analysis of the effect of racism on the African-American psyche may well have developed out of his childhood experience of being alternately favored and censured for his complexion.

When Malcolm was six years old, vigilantes killed Earl, the fourth of six brothers to be killed by whites, for his Garveyite activities. As an adult, Malcolm's advocacy of the right to aggressive self-defense and his disavowal of nonviolent resistance developed from such memories of black victimization. Widowed, Louise exemplified the plight of impoverished female heads of household during the Great Depression. Racial discrimination, menial women's work, and rampant unemployment meant starvation for the Little family in 1934. As Malcolm remembered it, "We would be so hungry we were dizzy." Unable to provide for her offspring, Louise turned to state relief, a degrading condition that led to her eventual commitment to a public mental institution. Her children, including twelve-year-old Malcolm, became wards of the state.

The difficulties of growing up black in white-dominated communities provided Malcolm with a perspective that later caused him to denigrate the civil rights goal of racial integration as woefully naive and illusionary. Whites so routinely called him "nigger" that he thought it normal. Under the supervision of a white couple who ran his detention home, Malcolm was treated kindly but condescendingly. He remembered, "They didn't give me credit for having the same sensitivity, intellect, and understanding that they would have been ready and willing to recognize in a white boy in my position." He also learned as a part of a growing sexual and racial awareness, through "some kind of psychic message," that he was not to dance with white girls at school parties.

Yet he knew that furtive interracial sexual liaisons occurred in town. Malcolm was in white society but was restricted to its margins.

Nevertheless Malcolm performed well through seventh grade; he was elected class president, played basketball, and was a good student. Then his English teacher, Mr. Ostrowski, ended Malcolm's adolescent dreams of becoming a lawyer by saying, "We all here like you, you know that. But you've got to be realistic about being a nigger. A lawyer—that's no realistic goal for a nigger." The teacher suggested carpentry as the trade appropriate for Malcolm. The experience, Malcolm later reflected, was "the first major turning point of my life." Even though he believed that he was smarter than nearly all his white classmates he understood that his options were limited. The white man had initiated the black boy into a racial rite of passage. The term "nigger" predestined Malcolm's consignment to the nether world of the racial caste system of the United States.

Negative Identity:

The encounter with Ostrowski marked an identity crisis, a racist preemption of young Malcolm's self-perception. Erikson explained that the adolescent "must detect some meaningful resemblance between what he has come to see in himself and what his sharpened awareness tells him others judge and expect him to be." Knowing that his efforts to aspire to white standards were futile, Malcolm fatalistically responded to Ostrowski's pronouncement. He fled Michigan for a relative's home in the Boston ghetto, a migration route to the urban East traditionally followed by alienated Midwestern youths. During his late teenage years, he immersed himself in the hustling subculture of the Roxbury and Harlem ghettos where the lanky Malcolm was called Big Red.

The *Autobiography,* Malcolm cautioned, was not intended to "titillate" the reader with "how bad, how evil" a hustler Malcolm was but to show that "in every big city ghetto tens of thousands of yesterday's and today's drop-outs hold body and soul together by some form of hustling in the same way [he] did." The ghetto institutionalized racism, not only socially and economically but psychologically as well. High unemployment, deteriorated housing, inadequate health care, blighted schools, drug addiction, and rampant crime turned the American dream into a living nightmare. Historically, the European-American community has often defined its success by comparison with African-American failure and subordination; in effect, Northern ghettos replicate antebellum Southern plantations. Erikson discussed the nature of racial victimization: "The oppressor has a vested interest in the negative identity of the oppressed because that negative identity is a projection of his own unconscious negative identity." Blacks served whites as psychic scapegoats, readily identifiable and culturally sanctioned.

As Big Red, Malcolm embodied what Erikson termed "the evil identity of the dirty, anal-sadistic, phallic-rapist 'nigger.'" Slavemasters of the Old South had projected their own fear of racial revenge for black subjugation and wanton sexual abuse of slave women onto the black males. The exploitation of blacks in the United States created an uneasy dialectic for whites: racial degradation sowed the seeds of racial retaliation. The provocative title of Julius Lester's book, *Look Out, Whitey, Black Power's Gonna Get Your Mama* (1968), and Eldridge Cleaver's justification of the rape of white women as a "political act" in *Soul on Ice* (1968) exemplified the enduring menace of the black male in the white mind.

Barred from emulating dominant cultural ideals, the ghetto hustler of the twentieth century sought self-respect through illicit activities on the margins of society. Sixteen-year-old Malcolm spurned the hard-earned bourgeois respectability of Roxbury's Hill Negroes for the sensual pleasures of the dance-hall crowd at Roseland. Shorty, an older Michigan emigrant, instructed his young protegé in the hustler's craft. As a shoeshine boy, Malcolm not only snapped a polishing cloth but satisfied his customers' needs for alcohol, marijuana, condoms, and prostitutes. He eventually graduated into numbers running, drug selling, specialty sex, and armed robbery—all part of an underground economy based in the ghetto. Under Shorty's tutelage, Malcolm was metamorphosed into a hipster, the "Harlem jigaboo archetype." He flaunted his zoot suit with its punjab pants, dangling gold chain, and long coat. A wide-brimmed hat and pointed orange shoes completed his defiant caricature of formal dress and rejection of middle-class standards. Using a homemade concoction that included lye, he painfully straightened his kinky hair to make it look "regular," like a white man's hair. It was, he later remembered, his "first really big step toward self-degradation." On one desperate occasion when the winter cold had frozen the water pipes, he had to wash the burning lye off his scalp by dunking his head into a toilet. The image of becoming excrement itself, disgusting black refuse that should be flushed away from the sight of decent people, was not lost on the older Malcolm. Outrageous adornment served to mark Big Red's entry into an underworld and outwardly compensated for his sense of racial inferiority.

This type of negative identity, Erikson wrote, is "a desperate attempt to regain some mastery in a situation in which the available positive identity elements cancel each other out." In the absence of a culturally acceptable identity, the ghetto hustler became a symbol of heightened masculine aggressiveness and sexuality. Armed, angry Big Red used the threat of violence to gain deference, if not actual respect. In successfully resisting military conscription during World War

II, he acted out a drama for the examining army psychiatrist: "I want to get sent down South. Organize them nigger soldiers, you dig. Steal us some guns, and kill up crackers!" Big Red had the same unsettling effect on the psychiatrist as Malcolm X's advocacy of militant self-defense later had on white society and black civil rights leaders.

Further, he exploited the imagery of the "big black buck" to affirm his self-worth in a society that at once denigrated and feared him. He abandoned Laura, a sheltered and studious black girl, for Sophia, a blond white woman. Big Red then "paraded" Sophia, who was "a status symbol of the first order" among black men in the ghetto. By attracting a white woman, he had validated himself as the equal of any white man. In turn, Sophia sought the "taboo lust" personified by the ghetto hustler. Each responded eagerly to the culturally forbidden pleasures the other represented. In addition, as a "steerer" to specialty sex assignations in Harlem, Malcolm directed white "johns" to black prostitutes who catered to their clients' racial fantasies about heightened black sexual potency and promiscuity. Malcolm's experiences in the netherworld of interracial sexual liaisons led to disgust with the moral hypocrisy of whites, to the adoption of a puritanical code of conduct, and to a persistent suspicion of women.

Although Big Red defied white society, the hustler's life was short and self-destructive. The common predatory allusions in Malcolm's rhetoric and his lifelong habit of never sitting with his back to a door dated from these combative days on the ghetto streets. Pursued by police, gangsters, and Sophia's irate husband, he felt "everything was building up, closing in. . . . [He] was trapped in so many cross turns." Drug addiction muddled his thought; the ever-present pistol foreshadowed a violent end. "I had gotten to the point," he reflected, "where I was walking on my own coffin." Finally, carelessness led to his arrest. A Massachusetts court sentenced him to ten years incarceration for burglary—an excessive sentence, Malcolm believed, to punish him for his relationship with Sophia. Not quite twenty-one years old, he had "sunk to the very bottom of the American white man's society." Big Red had been walled in.

Fundamentalism:

Seven years spent in prison forced the young man to turn inward. His incarceration approximated what Erikson defined as a psychosocial moratorium, a period of delaying adult commitments and experimenting with roles in a youthful search for a social niche. Although the options offered in the penitentiary were restricted, Malcolm likened prison to an intense college experience, an environment conducive to self-education and self-examination. In 1947, Malcolm came under the influence of an older black convict, Bimbi, the prison's scholar and sage. The respect Bimbi gained with his reasoned arguments made Malcolm realize the futility of

his own thoughtless rebelliousness. With Bimbi's encouragement, he took correspondence courses to improve his command of language. In addition, Malcolm became a "fanatic fan" of Jackie Robinson, who had broken baseball's color barrier. Malcolm began to appreciate that there were more effective ways to cope with a racist society than his previous dead-end roles.

In 1948, Malcolm underwent a momentous religious conversion. His brothers and sisters gradually won him over to the teachings of the Nation of Islam, presented as the "natural religion for the black man." Malcolm said, "The first time I heard the Honorable Elijah Muhammad's statement, The white man is the devil,' it just clicked." The powerful appeal of Elijah Muhammad to the black underclass derived from the origins of the Nation of Islam in Detroit during the Great Depression. The Nation of Islam preached black supremacy, racial separatism through the formation of an African-American nation, social uplift, and economic self-reliance. Believing that divine wrath would soon destroy the evil white race, Elijah Muhammad became the savior of America's blacks trapped in a white Babylon.

Elijah Muhammad's teachings were a fusion of bourgeois aspirations with the millenniarism of racial redemption. According to the demonology of the Nation of Islam, white devils had been created to spite God and his favored people, the black tribe of Shabazz. This dogma provided an affirmation to blacks by a denigration of whites; the oppressed projected their negative identity onto the oppressor where it could be scorned. Elijah Muhammad had imaginatively inverted the axioms of white racism.

The doctrine of the Nation of Islam represented a fundamentalist world view, which Erikson called "totalism" and defined as "something you can totally identify with or against, a stable reference point against which you can know who you are." The Black Muslim's ideological certainty spurred Malcolm to turn against his past. The sense of being saved gave Malcolm the emotional strength to remake himself. He read voraciously, studied the dictionary, and devoured words to fill an internal void. He joined the prison debating society and learned to use language to expose the white conspiracy against blacks. His extraordinary rapport with audiences of the black underclass derived from the power of rhetoric, a modern example of the oral tradition of African-American culture. In his powerful oratory, words were weapons.

The doctrinal message of the Nation of Islam was accompanied by the personal regeneration of its downtrodden members, beginning with deletion of the slavemaster's surname; Malcolm Little became Malcolm X. The faithful practiced what Malcolm preached in 1960 to a Harlem street audience of several thousand: "Stop fornication, adultery, and prostitution. Elevate the black woman; respect and protect her. Let us rid ourselves of immoral habits and God will be with us to protect and guide us." Thus was created a gospel of personal cleanliness, hard work, and small business entrepreneurship that acculturated drug addicts, exconvicts, prostitutes, and others of the ghetto underclass into bourgeois behavior patterns.

After his release from prison in 1952, Malcolm increasingly served as the principal spokesman for the reclusive, asthmatic prophet, whom he revered as his personal redeemer: "He had rescued me when I was a convict; Mr. Muhammad had trained me in his home, as if I was his son." There was, however, an ambivalence in their emotionally charged relationship, which resembled that of father and son. The older man, prodded by envious leaders in the Chicago headquarters, resented Malcolm's growing prominence, while the dynamic young man had matured beyond the simple fundamentalism of his withdrawn mentor. By 1959, the mass media had discovered the electrifying presence of Minister Malcolm X and the alarming doctrine of the sect they called the Black Muslims, as exhibited in a CBS television documentary, *The Hate That Hate Produced.*

Malcolm's espousal of the Muslim doctrine of racial separation, black superiority, and the right of violent self-defense clashed with the emerging mainstream civil rights movement represented by the National Association for the Advancement of Colored People (NAACP), the National Urban League, and the Southern Christian Leadership Conference (SCLC). The image of white racists assaulting defenseless blacks who proposed "to love their enemy" and "to turn the other cheek" perpetuated in his mind the stereotype of the passive Negro, the Uncle Tom. He later explained, "Any time you know you're within the law, within your legal rights, within your moral rights, in accord with justice, then die for what you believe in. But don't die alone. Let your dying be reciprocal. This is what is meant by equality."

By the early 1960s, Malcolm was clearly frustrated with Elijah Muhammad's policy of inaction, premised on the chiliastic dogma that the chosen people needed only to await Armageddon for their redemption from racial oppression. He admitted to a journalist that "the rest of us have not seen Allah: we don't have this divine patience, and we are not going to wait on God," and that "the younger Black Muslims want to see some action." Added to the jealousy, ideological differences, and organizational rivalry was a sexual scandal. Malcolm confronted Elijah Muhammad in 1963 about a long-standing rumor that he had fathered a number of children with his young secretaries. Elijah Muhammad admitted his adultery but excused it as part of his divine fulfillment of Old Testament practices. Malcolm, who had read his own brother Reginald out of the Muslims for a similar sexual infraction, was emotionally shattered. In his words,

"My faith had been shaken in a way that I can never fully describe." The exposure of Elijah Muhammad's low moral character finally broke the fundamentalist hold that he had over Malcolm.

Beyond Fundamentalism:

The schism became formal in December 1963 when Elijah Muhammad suspended Malcolm for ninety days from speaking in public. The ostensible reason for the ban was Malcolm's unauthorized comment to the press that President Kennedy's assassination was a case of "chickens coming home to roost"—a controversial remark about endemic violence in American society. Malcolm submitted to his leader's orders until he learned that Elijah Muhammad had secretly called for his execution. The "spiritual and psychological crisis" of Elijah Muhammad's betrayal escalated into a question of survival. As Malcolm recalled, "The first direct death-order was how, finally, I began to arrive at my psychological divorce from the Nation of Islam."

The following March, Malcolm announced his break with the Nation of Islam and the creation of a rival organization, Muslim Mosque, Inc. The narrow sectarianism of the Nation of Islam had transformed the hustler but had constrained him in an ideological strait jacket. "I was a zombie then—like all Muslims—I was hypnotized," he remembered, "pointed in a certain direction and told to march." After that realization, Malcolm sought to think and act anew. From an Eriksonian perspective, the schism provided the occasion to restructure his identity from a "totalism" characterized by absolutes and conformity to a "wholeness" able to tolerate tension and diversity. He spent nearly half his last year in Africa and the Middle East, seeking solutions in the Old World to problems in the New. As a result, he abandoned Elijah Muhammad's caricature of Islam and embraced Sunni orthodoxy; he also changed his understanding of racism from a crude demonology to a sophisticated cultural analysis.

Malcolm noted: "Around 1963, if anyone had noticed, I spoke less and less of religion. I taught social doctrine to Muslims, and current events, and politics." Although he supported Elijah Muhammad's goal of a separate black nation, he was immediately concerned that "twenty-two million of our people who are still here in America need better food, clothing, housing, education and jobs *right now.*" He further modified Elijah Muhammad's doctrines by stressing the power of the black ballot in the 1964 presidential election and by extending the olive branch to other black leaders such as Martin Luther King, Jr. However, Malcolm's advocacy of the right of self-defense still prevented any alliance with the middle-class civil rights organizations. In addition, he placed the African-American struggle in the worldwide context of colonial liberation movements and demanded a

United Nations' investigation of the violation of black human rights in the United States.

Having established a tentative political credo for Muslim Mosque, Inc., Malcolm sought to anchor the new organization within the Islamic faith. In April 1964, he went on a pilgrimage to Mecca. Uncertain if he would even be accepted as a legitimate Muslim, he was overwhelmed by the gracious treatment accorded him. He wrote:

> There were tens of thousands of pilgrims, from all over the world. They were of all colors, from blue-eyed blonds to black-skinned Africans. But we were all participating in the same ritual, displaying a spirit of unity and brotherhood that my experiences in America had led me to believe never could exist between the white and non-white.

The pilgrimage experience led to "a radical alteration in [his] whole outlook about 'white men.'" The prefix El-Hajj, added to his name in honor of the hegira, marked a "spiritual rebirth." Shortly after his return to the United States, he announced, "I'm a human being first and foremost and as such I'm for whoever and whatever benefits humanity as a whole."

Denouncing Elijah Muhammad's demonology, Malcolm argued, "The white man is not inherently evil but America's racist society influences him to act evilly." He abandoned what Erikson labeled a "pseudo-species mentality," one that ignores or denigrates the humanity of others. In Erikson's words, "Nobody can really find his most adult identity by denying it to others." The challenge therefore was to change the psychology of racism and the system that nourished it, not to fantasize devils.

In June 1964, Malcolm founded the Organization of Afro-American Unity (OAAU), which captured his affinity for pan-Africanism. A subsequent eighteen-week trip to Africa and the Middle East further broadened his outlook. As he told an African summit meeting, "Our problems are your problems. It is not a Negro problem, nor an American problem. This is a world problem; a problem for humanity." Malcolm dropped the phrase black nationalism in describing the OAAU program because of its racial exclusiveness. Malcolm's desire to forge a broader African-American identity was in keeping with Erikson's observation that "the alternative to an exclusive totalism is the wholeness of a more inclusive identity."

Much of Malcolm's thought was provisional. As he told an audience in November 1964, "I don't profess to have a political, economic or social solution to a problem as complicated as the one which our people face in the States, but I am one of those who is willing to try any means necessary to bring an end to the injustices our people suffer." While skirting doctrinaire commitment, he indicted "the American 'system,'" including U.S. foreign policy in the Congo and Vietnam as he linked the government's opposition to revolutionary nationalism abroad with racial oppression at home.

During the three months remaining in his life after his return to the United States, there was further modification of his views. In contrast to his earlier distrust of women, he linked national progress in Africa with the emancipation of women. He no longer supported a black state in North America or condemned racial integration and intermarriage. He endorsed black voter registration and political involvement but emphasized that civil rights legislation had not defused the "social dynamite" in the ghetto. He correctly predicted, "1965 will be the longest, hottest, bloodiest summer of the entire black revolution."

Malcolm's remarkable evolution of thought left him alienated. Black Muslims stalked him, the FBI monitored his activities, and the "Red Squad" of the New York City police infiltrated his bodyguards. "They won't let me turn the corner," he complained of his critics. After being unexpectedly barred from France where he was to address African students, he returned to New York only to experience a firebombing of his home in the early morning of 14 February 1965. Suspecting CIA involvement, he fatalistically told a reporter on February 18, "I live like a man who's already dead." Three days later he was shot down in a hail of gunfire from assassins in the audience as he spoke to an OAAU rally at the Audubon Hall in Harlem. A jury found three Black Muslims guilty of the murder, but speculation remains about the guilt of two of the convicted men and about the complicity of the New York City police and the FBI.

> **Malcolm's success in articulating black rage was the source of both his strength and his weakness.**
> **—Lawrence B. Goodheart**

In an Eriksonian perspective, Malcolm's overall significance lay in the congruence of his life and a pivotal moment in time. Yet, such a broad generalization needs qualification where the fit between model and subject is imperfect. Erikson's concepts of "surrendered identity," "negative identity," and "fundamentalism" are more precise in describing Malcolm's earlier stages of development than is the final category, "beyond fundamentalism," because Malcolm spent the final months of his life in a state of flux: he admitted to a reporter shortly before his murder, "I won't deny I don't know where I'm at." In assessing Malcolm's legacy, it is essential to come to terms with what he accomplished and what was left unfinished during the fifty weeks that remained of his life after the break with the Nation of Islam.

Malcolm's success in articulating black rage was the source of both his strength and his weakness. The militant black identity Malcolm embodied meant the end of psychic inferiority and demanded a radical readjustment of racial relations. He taught that "a person who is fighting racism is well within his rights to fight against it by any means necessary until it is eliminated." As Erikson observed, "Revolutions have to be shocking in order to really unhinge existing identities." Malcolm's scathing indictment of racial hypocrisy and injustice made him a riveting public figure. The night of his death, his widow lamented, "He was honest—too honest for his own good."

Malcolm's candor and charisma were, however, difficult to institutionalize. The major failure of his career was that after his schism with the Nation of Islam, his evolving conception of a new black identity and the social programs needed to facilitate its emergence were not incorporated into a viable organization. The program of the OAAU was inchoate, its administration in disarray, its membership limited, and its funds minimal. Malcolm's extensive foreign travel and hectic personal schedule left little time for organizational duties. His militant posture barred cooperation with well-established groups such as SCLC, NAACP, and the Congress of Racial Equality (CORE). Martin Luther King, Jr., Roy Wilkins, and James Farmer could best use Malcolm as a foil, who, by comparison, made their civil rights programs look more palatable. Malcolm told a Harlem street rally, "They charge us with being extremists but if it was not for the extremists the white man would ignore the moderates."

In Erikson's estimation, "The best leader is the one who can realize the actual potentials in his nation, and most of all the more inclusive identities which are ready to be realized in the world." Malcolm met Erikson's prescription only in part. His spiritual enlightenment in Mecca and abandonment of the goal of black nationalism significantly broadened his world view. "I am not a racist," he said repeatedly after his break with Elijah Muhammad. "I do not subscribe to any of the tenets of racism." He also stressed the inclusive identity of the black diaspora, pan-Africanism, and ultimately human solidarity.

Malcolm was most effective as a moral critic and an exemplar of a new black identity. "When we stop always saying yes to Mr. Charlie and turning the hate against ourselves," he explained, "we will begin to be free." He lacked the systematic program—not to mention white liberal support—that the middle-class leadership of the civil rights movement had gained. A month before his death, he acknowledged, "I would be hard pressed to give a specific definition of the overall philosophy which I think is necessary for the liberation of the black people of this country." Nevertheless, he captured to a degree unattained by anyone else the frustra-

tion of the ghetto underclass whose degraded position remains largely unchanged since the Second Reconstruction. Two days before his death, Malcolm gave what in effect was his epitaph: "It's a time for martyrs now. And if I'm to be one, it will be in the cause of brotherhood. That's the only thing that can save this country."

John Locke (essay date 1993)

SOURCE: "Adapting the Autobiography," in *Cineaste,* Vol. XIX, No. 4, 1993, pp. 5-7.

[*In the following essay, Locke discusses director Spike Lee's film adaptation of* The Autobiography of Malcolm X.]

At the core of Spike Lee's [film] *Malcolm X* is **The Autobiography of Malcolm X,** a story that draws from the breadth of twentieth-century African-American experience. Like any narrative contemporaneous with a past era, the autobiography contains elements that most moviegoers today would find antiquated or irrelevant. From the outset, then, Lee's intent to tell history is at odds with the needs of a mass market, and the film's transformation of Malcolm X to meet contemporary expectations has significant consequences for historical accuracy and dramatic impact.

The story is fundamentally tripartite in structure: a man leads an aimless, self-destructive life; he experiences enlightenment; he is redeemed. Since enlightenment occurs nearer the middle of the story than the end, Malcolm's prison conversion to the Nation of Islam (NOI) becomes the fulcrum on which the story teeters. Before prison, he is Malcolm Little, humiliated beyond his comprehension by a racially prejudiced society; after prison, he becomes Malcolm X, with the prerogatives of indignation as the impetus to his claim on spiritual confession and political discourse.

For Malcolm's life to make sense in the film, his post-enlightenment anger must be evenly balanced—justified—by the cruelties of his earlier years. Indeed, his childhood is sufficiently traumatic—family harassed by the Ku Klux Klan, house burned down by the racist Black Legion, father murdered, mother driven insane. The film covers these events in flashback, however, relegating them to memory. In the film's present, the adolescent Malcolm seems to be having a pretty good time, despite his involvement in various criminal activities, so the causality between past experience and present behavior, carefully explained in the autobiography, is unclear.

Putting it another way, the film distinguishes injuries inflicted by others and those which are self-imposed. One speaks to circumstance, the other to character. Lee depicts with clarity the horrors of racism that were beyond Malcolm's control, but he minimizes what Malcolm portrays in the autobiography as self-degradation, the acts of an animal. We know Malcolm 'conks' his hair 'to be white;' we see him acting comically hip in public. More serious issues of drug addiction and criminal behavior are glamorized. In the centerpiece drug scene, West Indian Archie introduces Malcolm to cocaine, but the feel is festive, not ominous. We never see Malcolm getting high in order to face his sordid occupations. Lee dampers the gravity of crime by playing the burglary racket for amusement, as when Malcolm perilously slides a ring from his sleeping victim's finger. When the gang members are sentenced for their crimes, Malcolm warms up the scene with chuckles and Shorty delivers the punchline when he mistakes concurrent for consecutive sentences. While entertaining, the light treatment of Malcolm's purported sins undermines his future role as a man returned from the brink.

In the autobiography, Malcolm's white girlfriend, Sophia, represents his repudiation of blackness through his desire for whiteness, a manifestation of self-hatred. That she was a status symbol proved the disease was endemic among his peers. In Malcolm's view, Sophia, too, acts from psychologically suspect motives, to the point of enduring his beatings. But excepting a brief exchange in which Malcolm expresses mistrust of her intentions, the film omits the complexities of their relationship, relieving Sophia of all but her color. Had the film been made in Malcolm's day, scenes of affection between an interracial couple would have shocked the audience. Today, with the taboo diminished, the mere depiction of the otherwise cordial relationship fails as a symbol of his debasement. The meaning of the scenes is cloudy.

Is the film demonstrating a problem that Malcolm will have to overcome; is it establishing his rebelliousness; or is it praising his natural egalitarianism in order to subvert his salvation by the elitist NOI? (As a preacher, he disparages his past dating of white women, but whether that expresses some poignancy in addition to parroting NOI teachings is unclear). As their relationship ends, Malcolm notes that the white judge inflated his burglary sentence to punish him for consorting with white women, completely shifting the import of the relationship from internal to external, from Malcolm's psyche to the injustice of the legal system.

The mystique of the gun weaves thematically through the film. The occasional punctuation of gunshots on the soundtrack—as when Malcolm and Shorty play cops and robbers—ring out Malcolm's destiny, elevating his death by gunshot from circumstance to inevitability. The theme counterpoints the tired association of Malcolm X with violence. We discover throughout the film that, despite Malcolm's reputation and defiant rhetoric, he was far more scholarly than violent. But while dispelling one myth, the film falls back on Hollywood stereotypes that cast the gun as a sym-

bol of power and manhood. It begins with Malcolm's father who fires his pistol over the heads of the men who have torched his house, proclaiming, "I'm a man!" Malcolm receives his first gun in a solemn rite of passage from Archie. The gift of the weapon—Archie's first, as well—bestows the power accruing from Archie's trust and guidance. Later, Malcolm takes control of the burglary ring by bluffing his rival in Russian roulette. After the matter is resolved, and tension relieved, Sophia whispers to Malcolm, "I love you," further endowing the gun with the powers of masculinity. Rather than highlighting Malcolm's fall from civility, as the autobiography portrays this part of his life, these scenes serve the more conventional purpose of boosting the heroic stature of the role. It is not until the assassination itself that the veil of glamor falls from the gun and the prior ill-use of the theme becomes apparent. We see gunplay in all its ugliness as Malcolm is mutilated by the bullets tearing through his body.

The errant poetry of moonlit Klansmen on horseback and the other mythic images from Malcolm's childhood don't register his terror enough to establish a basis for the anger that will eventually burst forth, and what power they do contain is nullified by his guns-and-fun adolescence. For too long a period, he seems to have broken the continuum of adversity and put the past behind him. What remains is a kind of romantic victimization that protects Malcolm's image from the ravages of true degradation. We're told of his suffering but we don't have to see it. Conked hair and a white girlfriend stand in as philosophical surrogates for true pain. Lee grants Malcolm 'star quality' when the drama requires he forgo his dignity, making him special when perhaps he should be pathetically ordinary.

Rather than challenging us to oppose suffering, the glamorization of Malcolm tempts us to covet his suffering as a means toward a fabled existence. To compensate for the dearth of provocations, the film later attempts to connect Malcolm's anger with his past by having him (and others) refer to the degradations caused by his drug abuse, his pimping (which we never see), or his thievery. At one point, Baines asks Malcolm to consider whether he has ever met any whites who weren't evil. Malcolm's apparently confirming thoughts are represented by quick flashbacks of white faces, some of whom, including Sophia, have been favorably portrayed. Such techniques retroactively make his youth seem more damaging than actually shown. Pain is reduced to a debating point.

In prison, with Malcolm's rebirth looming, the film attempts to make up for lost time by putting Malcolm through the hell of solitary confinement in a bare, unlit cell. His life instantly hits bottom where the perfunctory conversion to the NOI can raise him back up. At this point, Malcolm X replaces Malcolm Little and the NOI becomes his focus.

Despite its name, the Nation of Islam is an American original and borrows little from true Islam. Its beliefs encompass an invented history of the races and the goal of self-sufficiency for African-Americans including, most abstractly, a separate black nation. Malcolm's thorough embrace of the Muslim beliefs and practices constituted much of his preaching as a minister in the organization. As in the scenes prior to Malcolm's incarceration, Lee cautiously chooses what to associate with Malcolm. Most of the NOI's more curious concepts, which include the machinations of mad scientists in the shaping of history, and which Malcolm discusses freely in his autobiography, are omitted from Malcolm's dialog. Lee does acknowledge this aspect of the NOI, however, through the words of Baines and Elijah Muhammad, men who will later discredit themselves—and thus their views—by betraying Malcolm. For example, Baines explains to Malcolm that pork should not be eaten because the pig is "a filthy beast, part cat, part rat, and the rest is dog," even though it's Malcolm's observation in the autobiography. In general, the film burdens others with the peculiarities of the NOI and leaves Malcolm with the universal messages of pride and self-discipline, though in reality Malcolm covered the spectrum.

Those who know almost nothing about Malcolm X probably know that he described Caucasians as "white devils." The oft-used term was one of the most biting expressions in his oratory. More than invective, though, the idea that all whites are devils is fundamental to Muslim doctrine. It rationalizes the plight of African-Americans and justifies separatism. Since it became so strongly identified with Malcolm X, it's interesting to see how Lee employs the term. In fact, Malcolm says "white devils" only once in the film, in a narrated letter from prison that, in other ways, amusingly demonstrates Malcolm's naiveté as a fresh convert. Afterwards we hear the term only from other Muslims. Malcolm does refer to "devils" a few times—"the devil's newspaper," "the devil's chickens" (coming home to roost)—but the closest he comes to using the term as a Muslim leader is in response to a reporter's question, "I've said white people are devils," the past tense leaving his current views ambiguous.

By separating the "white" from the "devil," Lee removes the racial philosophy underpinning the NOI's concept of evil, further distancing Malcolm from the 'religion' of the NOI. It implies his weak conviction for the NOI's counter-prejudice, thus preparing him for the idealistic high ground in his later break with the organization. Taken with the down play of Malcolm's (and the NOI's) disparagement of women and Jews by class, the overall softening of his rhetoric increases the chance that a contemporary film audience, drawn from diverse quarters, will find Malcolm appealing.

Malcolm X's departure from the NOI and its aftermath shaped the last year and a half of his life, a fittingly dramatic crisis and conclusion for the story. Superficially, Malcolm's confirmation of rumors about Muslim leader Elijah Muhammad's illegitimate children and Malcolm's tactless remarks about JFK's assassination caused the schism. But whether Malcolm 'quit' or was 'fired' is beside the point. The NOI had developed twin summits of power—Elijah Muhammad, the center of religious authority, and Malcolm X, the center of attention. Eventually one had to give way. The source of the fissure can be traced to Malcolm's mind, a division between his religious and political selves. He began as a preacher but his grass roots recruiting and lightning rod eloquence drew in many followers and the implied threat of a personal constituency. The division in his mind widened into a division in the organization. The threat might have remained benign had not his maturation as a leader within the NOI coincided with the most volatile years of the civil rights movement. While the NOI, and loyal Malcolm, eschewed political activity (calls for an unspecified black state not withstanding), the eyes of black America increasingly looked to Washington for justice. Malcolm's affiliation with the NOI threatened to render him irrelevant as an African-American spokesman. The times pressured him to make the difficult choice between his religious and political inclinations. It was his personal dilemma; it becomes the film's critical issue. If *Malcolm X* is to claim contemporary relevance, it cannot relegate its hero to a historical sideshow.

Malcolm's second conversion, to true Islam, resulting from a pilgrimage to Mecca, pulls the issue in two directions at once. It affirms his identity as a religious figure; it also allows him to forge an identity apart from the NOI and seek a secular political role. From a religious perspective, a second conversion begs a peculiar question: If God reveals His truth a second time, was He lying the first? What 'was' the vision of Elijah Muhammad, animated and speaking, that brings Malcolm to his knees for the first time? No such supernaturalism lifts the *hajj* above ritual. As shown, the principal change to Malcolm is a broadening of his outlook to recognize the fundamental equality of people. Now the seeds planted by the earlier presentation of Malcolm bear fruit. Though acknowledged as a full participant in the NOI, the film never fully dramatized his participation. Malcolm may have outgrown the absurdities of the NOI but the film never rooted him in them. He never preaches the NOI version of racial history, the theory of white devils, or any number of extreme views (although he does advocate separatism in one speech). Moreover, the film suppresses the wide differences between the NOI and true Islam. By softening the NOI and by further softening Malcolm's commitment to its philosophy, Lee 'politicizes' the second conversion by reducing it from a sweeping exchange of religions to a more palatable maturation of opinion, a maturation that moves him away from an exclusively religious perspective and towards the mainstream of the civil rights movement. The film allows

Malcolm to be seen as having represented the good in the NOI, but an impractical good given the constraints; the separation from the NOI frees him to practice the good while absolving him of a bad he never seemed to believe in anyway.

When Malcolm left the NOI, he entered a political limbo between the organization he could not return to and the civil rights movement he could hardly step into after years of denouncing its proponents. His untimely death resolves his life ambiguously, leaving open forever the question of what he might ultimately have accomplished, and freeing the film to define his potential.

The assassination itself blunts the drama of the conclusion. That Malcolm was murdered by black men is anticlimactic to his movement toward a higher political consciousness. He had been a soldier on the battle lines of race but in the end was killed by his own kind. His demise fails as an opportunity to validate his threat to entrenched white power, his longstanding pessimism toward racial relations, or his status as spokesman for the race. Lee seems to recognize this because he takes a number of steps to invite the possibility that (white) agents of the government sponsored the assassination. A pair of CIA agents trail him in Egypt; we see images of rolling tape recorders, a 'bug' in a lamp shade, FBI agents listening to his phone calls; Malcolm himself blames "larger forces" for the fire-bombing of his house, after first blaming the Muslims; he speaks of, but never specifies, a harassment beyond the NOI's capabilities. None of these facts prove the authorities had Malcolm killed but the implication further raises his viability as a civil rights leader—it sanctions him with the government's fear; it makes him look too dangerous to live.

The autobiography chronicles a series of transformations to the character of Malcolm X but, in true self-reflexive literary fashion, is itself another transformation, an attempt to redefine the past to justify a current posture. Bruce Perry's well-researched recent biography, *Malcolm: The Life of a Man Who Changed Black America,* assembles a more complete account of his life. It becomes clear from this version that the autobiography is part religious testament (to the virtues of the Muslim life) and part political tract (speaking out as an African-American Everyman), while its historical aspects have been transmuted for the purposes of the broader agenda.

Lee's *Malcolm X* does no better as history than the autobiography, but refines the book's agenda for a modern audience needing contemporary relevance and streamlined heroes. The Malcolm X of the film is less self-conscious, less square, more romantic, less dogmatic, and less divisive than the autobiographical Malcolm X. Near the end of the film, American and South African school children jump up from their desks to cry, "I am Malcolm X!," and we know they speak of the latter ecumenical man and not the Muslim separatist who came before. The film has forgiven and forgotten the hostile rhetoric of Malcolm's past as his America would not.

Then the film goes on to suggest a new transformation. As Malcolm's visit to the deteriorated, once proud Archie hinted at what an unrepentant Malcolm would have become, so does the appearance of Nelson Mandela, perhaps the world's most respected black leader, propose what Malcolm would have become had he lived to this day. Through the conceit of giving Mandela Malcolm's words rather than letting him speak his own, Mandela becomes the film's living embodiment of Malcolm X, a last-ditch effort to rescue Malcolm from history.

Henry Louis Gates, Jr. (essay date 21 February 1993)

SOURCE: "Malcolm, the Aardvark and Me," in *New York Times Book Review,* February 21, 1993, p. 11.

[*In the following essay, Gates relates his personal experience of reading* The Autobiography of Malcolm X *as a young man.*]

One of the most gratifying effects of Spike Lee's film *Malcolm X* is that its success has prompted the restoration of Malcolm's autobiography to the best-seller lists. The country is *reading* the 1965 book once again, as avidly, it seems, as it is seeing Mr. Lee's movie. For 17 weeks *The Autobiography of Malcolm X,* written with the assistance of Alex Haley, has been on the *New York Times* paperback best-seller list, and for 10 of those weeks it was No. 1. Today, on the 28th anniversary of his assassination, Malcolm's story has become as American—to borrow H. Rap Brown's famous aphorism—as violence and cherry pie.

> **One of the most gratifying effects of Spike Lee's film *Malcolm X* is that its success has prompted the restoration of Malcolm's autobiography to the best-seller lists. The country is *reading* the 1965 book once again, as avidly, it seems, as it is seeing Mr. Lee's movie.**
> **—Henry Louis Gates, Jr.**

Malcolm first came into my life some three decades ago, when I was 9 years old and Mike Wallace and CBS broadcast a documentary about the Nation of Islam. It was called

The Hate That Hate Produced, and it showed just about the scariest black people I had ever seen: black people who talked right into the faces of white people, telling them off without even blinking. While I sat in our living room, I happened to glance over at my mother. A certain radiance was slowly transforming her soft brown face, as she listened to Malcolm naming the white man us the devil. "Amen," she said, quietly at first. "All right, now," she continued, much more emphatically. All this time and I had not known just how deeply my mother despised white people. The revelation was terrifying and thrilling.

The book came into my life much later.

I was almost 17, a junior in high school, and I was slowly and pleasurably devouring *Ebony* magazine. More precisely, I was reading a profile of the Roman Catholic basketball player Lew Alcindor, who was then a star at U.C.L.A. and who later became a legend with the Los Angeles Lakers as the Muslim basketball player Kareem Abdul-Jabbar. In the profile he said that *The Autobiography of Malcolm X* had meant more to him than any other book, and that *all* black Americans should read it—*today.*

Today was not possible for me, since I lived in a village in the hills of West Virginia where nobody carried such things. I had to go down to Red Bowl's newsstand, make a deposit and wait while they sent away for it. But when the book arrived, I read it straight through the night, as struck by its sepia-colored photograph of a dangerous-looking, gesticulating Malcolm as I was by the contents, the riveting saga of a man on the run, from whites (as the son of a Garveyite father) and blacks (his former mentors and colleagues at the Nation of Islam, after his falling-out with Elijah Muhammad).

I loved the hilarious scene in which Malcolm is having his hair "conked," or "processed" ("relaxed" remains the euphemism); unable to rinse out the burning lye because the pipes in his home are frozen, he has no recourse but to dunk his head in a toilet bowl. A few months before, the benignly parochial principal of our high school had "paddled" my schoolmate Arthur Galloway when Arthur told him that his processed hairstyle was produced by a mixture of eggs, mashed potatoes and lye. "Don't lie to me, boy," the principal was heard saying above Arthur's protests.

What I remember most, though, is Malcolm's discussion of the word "aardvark":

> I saw that the best thing I could do was get hold of a dictionary—to study.... I spent two days just riffling uncertainly through the dictionary's pages. I'd never realized so many words existed! ... Funny thing, from the dictionary first page right now, that "aardvark" springs to my mind. The dictionary had

a picture of it, a long-tailed, long-eared, burrowing African mammal, which lives off termites caught by sticking out its tongue as an anteater does for ants.

Years later, near the end of his life, Malcolm found himself heading to the American Museum of Natural History in New York to learn more about that exotic creature, even while trying to figure out how to avoid an almost certain Muslim death sentence. "Boy! I never will forget that old aardvark!" he had mused to Alex Haley. What manner of politician was this, I wondered, in this the year that Stokely Carmichael and Rap Brown, Eldridge Cleaver and Huey P. Newton, Ron Karenga and Amiri Baraka, simultaneously declared themselves to be the legitimate sons of Malcolm the father, to linger with aardvarks when his world was collapsing around him?

Although Malcolm proudly avowed that he read no fiction (he says he read only one novel "since I started serious reading," and that was *Uncle Tom's Cabin*), he still loved fiction—"fiction" defined as a making, a creating, with words. His speeches—such as the oft-repeated **"Ballot or the Bullet"** or **"Bandung Conference"**—are masterpieces of the rhetorical arts. More than Martin Luther King Jr., more than any of the black nationalists or the neo-Marxists, Malcolm X was a *writer,* a wordsmith.

In 1968, my English teacher told me that in years to come, long after the civil rights struggle was a footnote in history, this man would be remembered—like St. Augustine, like Benjamin Franklin, like Henry Adams—because of his gift with words. High praise: and yet the teacher's observation, I must confess, didn't go down well with me at the time. Imagining the book stretched on the autopsy slab of purely literary analysis, I somehow felt that the overriding immediacy of Malcolm's experience—and my special relation to it—had been diminished. Despite Malcolm's cautious if heartfelt moves toward universalism, I felt that part of him would always belong to African mammals like aardvarks, like me.

Nell Irvin Painter (essay date April 1993)

SOURCE: "Malcolm X Across the Genres," in *American Historical Review,* Vol. 98, No. 2, April, 1993, pp. 432-39.

[*In the following essay, Painter examines the facts and events involved in the story of Malcolm X's life as they are presented in* The Autobiography of Malcolm X *and two films adapted from that book, both entitled* Malcolm X.]

The historian in me distrusted a dramatic early scene in Spike Lee's *Malcolm X* that is set in Omaha. The Ku Klux Klan comes pounding up to the Little family's house on horse-back. Initially, the scene seems menacingly authentic—hooded white supremacy in its most recognizable guise bent on terrorizing a helpless black family—but as soon as one recalls that this is supposed to be Omaha, Nebraska, in the 1920s, the sense of realism breaks down.

I assumed this to be yet another employment of the iconography of southern white supremacy, which Americans still think of as the *real* white supremacy, to advance a narrative of black life anywhere in the United States. Spike Lee's *Malcolm X,* like the 1972 documentary of the same name and countless other evocations of black life, uses photos and footage from southern history to hammer home the plight of black people in American life generally. Considering that in Lee's film, a still photograph from 1936 of a Florida lynch victim appears between cuts of the violence that met civil rights activists in Birmingham in 1963, it is hardly surprising that the need to show the Klan as always coming on horseback and riding off into the full moon triumphs again over regional and chronological logic. Once more in film, or so it appeared, D. W. Griffith's images cancel out the unlikelihood of twentieth-century, midwestern, urban Klansmen making their rounds by horse.

But I was wrong to think that Spike Lee had followed the dictates of film school; the image was not Lee's at all. *The Autobiography of Malcolm X* opens with this very scene. Lee and his screenwriters were following Malcolm X as though what he had said was history, which it was not. According to Bruce Perry's *Malcolm: The Life of a Man Who Changed Black America,* the story was Malcolm's own invention. This vignette encapsulates the confusion about historical truth that surrounds the figure of Malcolm X in the two genres through which he is best known: his autobiography and Spike Lee's film.

Both *The Autobiography of Malcolm X* and the film *Malcolm X* simulate history by purveying autobiographical rather than biographical truths, for the source for each representation is Malcolm's own recomposition of his life from the vantage point of 1964. Alex Haley shaped the autobiography and took it from conversation to publication. A screenplay by James Baldwin, Arnold Perl, and Spike Lee recasts the published autobiography for the 1992 film. While each of these retellings invents a new narrative, neither the book nor the film is congruent with the life that Malcolm Little/Malcolm X lived, day by day, between 1925 and 1965.

The transubstantiations work on several different levels. First of all, autobiography, even when it is not "told to" another but is written by the person who lived the life, reworks existential fragments into a meaningful new whole, as seen from a particular vantage point. Even when the autobiography is not a collaboration, the narrator passes over much in silence and highlights certain themes that become salient in light of what the narrator concludes she or he has become. When the subject is racialized, the narrative nearly always aspires to (acquires in the marketplace) metonymic stylization, as captured in the dust jacket blurb of *The Autobiography of Malcolm X* from 1965, which still serves to promote the *Autobiography* today: "In the agony of [his] self-creation [is] the agony of an entire people in their search for identity. No man has better expressed his people's trapped anguish." If Malcolm X is to work as a racial symbol, it is best not to look at him too closely.

The process of transforming an individual into a racial symbol alters the subject's life (with its false starts and, above all, with its intra-racial conflicts) into a narrative whose plot is coded in black and white. Usually, the black protagonist faces "white society" or the "white power structure." Such stark dichotomies are hardly the sign of history that is written sensitively. History grows out of evidence, the more the better, we say—or at least so we said until the late twentieth century, when evidence in absurd abundance threatened to paralyze historians by swamping the research phase of the work.

The best drama, in contrast, is spun out of the fewest number of documents, the least amount of detail and nuance. For the sake of theater, the less we know of thoroughly racialized figures like Malcolm X, the better. When we know enough about a man to analyze his childhood family dynamics, as Bruce Perry has done, then we know enough to realize that what happened between self, parents, and siblings counts as much as—more than?—the oppressiveness of segregation in the public sphere. It is hardly surprising that Spike Lee's movie has reached millions, while Bruce Perry's debunking biography, a 1991 imprint by a small publishing house called Station Hill, is hardly known at all. Even though the makers of Spike Lee's film conducted many interviews, for the purpose of the drama they chose to use a univocal source: *The Autobiography of Malcolm X.* The movie should have borne the same title, for it is autobiography rather than history.

As a means of buttressing the historical claims of his film, Spike Lee takes the process of stylization a step further and plays havoc with the distinction between feature and documentary. The results are mind boggling. At crucial junctures, the narrative, which is shot in color, is punctuated with scenes in which Denzel Washington, the actor who plays Malcolm X, appears in black and white—in the press conference in which Malcolm announces his departure from the Nation of Islam, as well as on the stretcher that bears his bullet-ridden body away from the Audubon ballroom and to the hospital. This faux footage replicates documentary technique like that in the 1972 documentary of Malcolm X by Marvin Worth and Arnold Perl, whose authority was also

The Autobiography of Malcolm X. Spike Lee is so skilled at fabricating documentation that when Nelson Mandela appeared at the end of *Malcolm X,* I questioned *his* authenticity! The movie's credits reveal more faux footage, as in the black-and-white scene of the Kennedy assassination that is cross-cut poststructurally with Denzel Washington's/Malcolm's reaction to the assassination.

This movie is not a documentary, but it wraps itself in manufactured images of documentary truth. When the images are real—as in footage of Martin Luther King, Jr.'s remarks after the assassination of Malcolm X, the effect can be chilling, for viewers know that King would be the victim of assassination three years later. The verisimilitude of Spike Lee's faux footage is intensified by the cameo appearances of the Reverend Al Sharpton and former Black Panther Bobby Seale. Their roles as street-corner speakers establish a continuity of black nationalist leadership from Malcolm X in the 1960s to the Panthers in the 1970s to Sharpton in the 1980s and 1990s. Given the relative stability of black political grievances, notably police brutality and official harassment, this film may well reopen questions about the role of police and government in Malcolm X's assassination. If so, such an inquiry would underscore the political role of film in African-American life and further blur the line between art and life, between symbolism and history.

Viewed as an artifact of this time rather than of the 1960s, *Malcolm X* subordinates certain aspects of the problem of realism and accentuates others. Spike Lee's film heightens Malcolm's confrontation with the police over the beating of Brother Johnson, as though it were a major turning point rather than one of many steps (sideways and backward as well as forward) in the emergence of the Nation of Islam. For a 1993 audience, Denzel Washington is a good-enough Malcolm X: he looks and talks like Malcolm did in the 1960s; and, from this vantage point, it only matters slightly that Washington is significantly darker-skinned than Little/X and much older than Malcolm during much of the action. Although Washington is in his mid-thirties, Malcolm was a teenager during his years as a hustler. He went to prison before turning twenty and was only twenty-seven when he emerged from incarceration in Massachusetts and went to work as an organizer for the Nation of Islam. These are trivialities in racialized drama, where the conflict is posed mainly in terms of black and white and other questions are less intelligible. When what happens outside the black-white nexus is not of much interest, the black protagonist needs only enough family influence and youthful experience to foreshadow the anguish that will come of being black.

In the movie, Malcolm X's siblings lose the roles they played in his personal and intellectual trajectory, roles that were clearly acknowledged in the *Autobiography.* In life, four of his siblings joined the Nation of Islam before he did, and

his family, particularly his brothers Philbert and Reginald, brought him into the fold while he was still in prison. Later on, when Malcolm was acting as Elijah Muhammad's national representative and building the Nation of Islam from 400 to 40,000 adherents, part of the hostility he encountered derived from the fear that by promoting the interests of his brothers, who were also ministers in the Nation, he was building a family dynasty intended to rival that of Elijah Muhammad. After Malcolm left the Nation of Islam in early 1964, his half-sister Ella, a businesswoman in Boston, underwrote his pilgrimage to Mecca. While he spent months on end abroad in 1964-1965, Ella Little took over the leadership of his ephemeral new organizations, the Muslim Mosque, Inc., and the Organization of Afro-American Unity, continuing to head them after his assassination. Given the kind of roles allotted to women in the Nation of Islam and in this and Spike Lee's other films, the effacement of the strong and complicated figure of Ella Little is hardly surprising.

Even though their roles are circumscribed, the female characters in Spike Lee's film have bigger parts than they did in *The Autobiography of Malcolm X.* His girlfriend Laura's place in the autobiography is narrowly circumscribed, although Alex Haley notes in his epilogue that Malcolm blamed his own shoddy treatment of Laura for her eventual ruin (which seems unlikely unless his role in her life was far larger than the autobiography or Perry's biography indicates). In the feature film, the figure of Laura reappears at several junctures, first as the proper young black woman whom the teenaged Malcolm deserts for a white woman named Sophia. Laura sharpens the point that the *Autobiography* makes obliquely by telling Malcolm, "I'm not white and I don't put out, so why would you want to call me, Malcolm?" Young Laura's purity contrasts with the figure she presents as the film progresses. When Malcolm arouses her sexually, she becomes willing to jettison her grandmother's prohibitions. Later, she is naïvely vulnerable to the manipulation of a freeloading junkie boyfriend. Finally, as a prostitute at the bottom of the pit of degradation, Laura is seen giving a white john a blow-job in a Harlem doorway. (Spike Lee does not explain how she gets from Boston to New York.)

At other points, Lee phrases succinctly the patriarchal gender values of the Nation of Islam. Malcolm admonishes his wife Betty not to raise her voice in *his* home. A scene at a Savior's Day Rally hammers home the message, as the audience sees a banner stretched across the balcony in which the sisters are sequestered. It reads: "We must protect our women, our most valuable possession." Is Spike Lee using this prop ironically? I'm not sure, for popular black nationalism, in the 1990s as in the 1960s, often espouses precisely this sort of gender ideal. Lee may be using the Nation of Islam to preach a gospel that he also finds appealing.

Spike Lee's *Malcolm X* captures the strengths of the Nation of Islam in redeeming poor, black incarcerated men for useful lives. Elijah Muhammad wrote to black inmates, many of whom lacked Malcolm's family, and the Nation played a unique role in educating and empowering the most vulnerable men in American society. The content of the Nation's beliefs is not well explained, however, and Lee's film (like the biography and documentary film) glosses over the weirder themes in Elijah Muhammad's doctrine, which he learned from Master W. D. Fard in Detroit in 1931. (Fard's portrait appears on the walls of Elijah Muhammad's house in the feature film. Fard was even more light-skinned than Muhammad.) Fard taught that when blacks separated from whites, they would enter heaven on earth, after four hundred years of hell on earth under the control of white devils. Fard and Muhammad said that the black man was the original man, and that whites had been purposefully bred out of the original man six thousand years earlier in order to put black people through hell. The end of time was near, and on a day of judgment Allah would defeat whites and vindicate blacks through racial separation.

Both the feature and the documentary films mention the Nation of Islam's apocalyptic vision of racial redemption, but neither fleshes it out. The Nation's solution to American racism, the creation of a black state out of Georgia and Alabama, is similarly phrased in terms that are suitably vague. Spike Lee's film reveals why so many black Americans were drawn to the Nation of Islam through Malcolm X's preaching of black beauty and power; but, by deleting the inane portions of the creed, it eliminates the mystery of why so intelligent a person as Malcolm X would stay twelve years in such a narrow-minded movement. Answering that question means stepping outside the framework of Spike Lee's film.

The Nation of Islam is a combination of two intellectual traditions: first, holiness religion of the sort that is commonly found in working-class black neighborhoods and that appeals primarily to women and, second, the masculinist tradition of black nationalism continued by the Black Panthers in the late 1960s and early 1970s. Within urban Afro-American life, the first tradition is strongly class-based, the second is highly gendered.

Holiness religion is perfectionist and apocalyptic, maintaining that the end is near and the faithful must prepare for judgment by purifying their thoughts, behavior, and bodies. Black Muslims, like acolytes of holiness churches, must take baths frequently, dress modestly, and eat healthfully (little or no meat, no pork, lots of fresh fruits and vegetables); they must not smoke, drink alcohol, use drugs, curse, gamble, steal, or fornicate. Men wear white shirts and suits, women wear long dresses, head coverings, and no make-up. Both holiness

Christianity and the Nation of Islam have saved thousands of poor blacks from the snares of vice-ridden neighborhoods.

Critics of the Nation of Islam have sometimes remarked on the paradox of black nationalists' adopting the trappings of "the white middle-class," but that designation is flawed. Muslims, like many other people of color in similar clothing, are dressing for respectability, not for racial transmogrification. Respectability, like the putative characteristics of economic class, are for many Americans color-coded: the stereotypical vices of the poor (intemperance, laziness, fecklessness, immorality) are in the United States the stereotypical vices of blacks; the supposed virtues of the middle class (thrift, hard work, sobriety, moral rectitude) are associated with whites.

Racial stereotype, which has long tended to lump all blacks together, regardless of their class, gender, or region, deeded black nationalism an intellectual inheritance with many of white supremacy's serious flaws. Malcolm X, in autobiography, documentary film, and feature film, exhibits one such weakness, a preoccupation with whiteness, in three different guises. On the most obvious level, whiteness provides the measure of beauty and desirability for young Malcolm Little, who undergoes excruciating pain in order to conk (straighten) his hair. In the film and in *The Autobiography of Malcolm X.* Malcolm and his composite sidekick, Shorty, display white girlfriends like trophies. In Malcolm's case, whiteness alone does not quite suffice. In the *Autobiography,* he emphasizes Sophia's elegant clothing. Her relatively elevated class standing is also indicated in the feature film, as Sophia presents herself as a classy dame who is better than the trashy poor white women, "harps" (Irish-Americans) with whom black men were more likely to associate.

In the Nation of Islam, Malcolm X outgrows the aesthetic of whiteness, but the gaze of the superego figure he terms "the white man" remains steady. While "the white man" is the devil and "the white man" has done only evil in this world, Malcolm X seems to agree with the judgment of "the white man" with regard to the self-destructive behavior of poor blacks. Minister Malcolm X hectors his audience for ingesting the white man's poisons: pork, cigarettes, white women. "The white man sees you and laughs," says Malcolm, calling on the scorn of strange white people to induce dietary and sexual reform.

At the very end of the Spike Lee film, "the white man" goes from stern parent to Islamic brother. After his pilgrimage to Mecca in 1964, El-Hajj Malik El-Shabazz/Malcolm X wrote an open letter to the Muslim Mosque, Inc., in New York that is quoted in both films and reproduced in the *Autobiography.* In the letter, Malcolm marvels at the color blindness he encounters in Mecca and reports that he has prayed and eaten and slept with brother Muslims whose skin was the whitest white and whose eyes were the bluest blue and whose hair was the blondest blonde. (Those white Muslims may have been Bosnians, the very people whom Serbs are slaughtering and raping today in the name of "ethnic cleansing.") The geography of the Muslim world is such that fair-skinned pilgrims in Saudi Arabia would have formed a small minority, who were remarkable to Malcolm X because the figure of "the white man" had acquired such salience in his own ideology. The great majority in Mecca would have been more or less brownish people from Asia and Africa.

In 1964 and early 1965, as Malcolm traveled widely and came into contact with pan-Africanism and anti-imperialism, he grew intellectually and began to situate American racial issues within a broader context. Had he lived, he might well have outgrown the intellectually constricting aspects of black nationalism. But in 1964, he knew he would not live much longer. The Nation of Islam (with official support?) assassinated him, in a spectacular and tragic example of black nationalism's inability to tolerate intra-racial diversity. During most of his public life, Malcolm X, too, subscribed to the unifying tenets of the Nation, which lacked language with which to manage dissent or conceive of difference within the race.

The rhetoric of the Nation as preached so effectively by Malcolm X dwelled endlessly on "the white devil" and "the black man." Interracial conflict was not nearly so dramatic in Malcolm's own life, for he was as much the victim of poverty as of racism. Spike Lee emphasizes the dramatic parallel between the burning of the Little family's home in Lansing, Michigan, and the fire-bombing of Malcolm's family home in New York, but the parallel, no matter how spectacular, is flawed: Malcolm called the Lansing fire a white-on-black crime, while he blamed the conflagration in New York on the Nation of Islam.

The leading theme in Malcolm's life was actually intra-racial conflict, which, in the last analysis, took his life. Like Americans who lack a conceptual category for black respectability, Malcolm X (and black nationalists generally) found it difficult to envision a Negro race made up of people of different classes and clashing convictions. Malcolm much preferred to speak in the singular, as though all twenty-two million African Americans had identical interests and needs. The Nation of Islam offered solutions to "the black man," no matter what "his" education or income. Women in the Nation were to accept the interests of Muslim men as their own.

Racial unity is the great ideal of the various strains of black nationalism, and it is usually considered an attainable goal. If black people were united, so the reasoning goes, they could challenge racial oppression effectively; if black people were united, they could advance economically; if black people were united, they would represent a potent political influence. In this ideology, the impediment to unity is not the implausibility of tens of millions of people without their own governmental institutions or police power acting together in unison. Instead, racial unity is seen as being prevented by the actions of traitors who are in cahoots with whites. Malcolm X identified race traitors as educated blacks and house Negroes, and he usually treated these two kinds of people as one.

While he was proud of his own self-education and wanted young black people to educate themselves, Malcolm X denied that formal education was good for African Americans. He labeled black Ph.D.s "Uncle Thomases" and called them fakes and traitors, asking his audiences what a black man with a Ph.D. was called. Answer: "A n—er!" As if to say that for a black person, formal education serves for naught.

For Malcolm X before 1964, formal education served for less than naught, because he saw a close connection between blacks with education and what he called "the house Negro," the slave who loved his master better than himself or other black people, that is, the traitor to his race. These lines always got a laugh when Malcolm appeared on television or on college campuses, and they still do in the movies that have appeared since his assassination. Even those who were skewered managed to laugh at their own expense, for, despite his harsh rhetoric, Malcolm X remained a good-humored man whose razor wit never became personal. This, at least, is my memory of seeing him in the early 1960s.

When he spoke at the University of California at Berkeley, I was one of a handful of black students in his audience, and I recall my realization that he was not really talking to us. Malcolm X spoke around us to white people, even though educated blacks like us were his rhetorical *bête blanche*. Like "the white man," we were a stereotype, but we were not nearly so interesting. As stereotype, we had a part to play in the drama of foiled race unity, but his real engagement was with the vast majority of his audience, whom he could bait and smile at with devastating effectiveness. As sidelined players in his American drama, we nevertheless relished Malcolm's appearance, for he was able to discomfort white people with an enviable skill that we did not possess. He was smart, assertive, funny, and, all in all, very entertaining. After he left the Nation of Islam, he realized what we had hoped, that he could do better than tailor his analysis to fit the demands of the Honorable Elijah Muhammad's creed.

The second and last time I saw Malcolm X was in West Africa in the fall of 1964. Perhaps because ideologically he was becoming more like us—the well-educated Afro-American community sheltering in Kwame Nkrumah's Ghana—our existence seemed to annoy him no longer. He was at home intellectually, but he was also utterly exhausted physically.

When he returned to New York, Malcolm tried to implement what he had learned by founding new organizations that were still black nationalist. He also moved to the left politically, which, had he lived, would have ultimately strained his racial ideals.

Given the Nation of Islam's willingness to shed blood, I doubt it would have been possible for Malcolm X to survive much longer. He certainly felt, when he finished his work with Alex Haley, that he would not live to see the publication of *The Autobiography of Malcolm X,* and he did not. Had he somehow managed to preserve his life, his intellectual trajectory would probably have continued leftward and away from black nationalism. Would he still have inspired Huey Newton and Bobby Seale to found the Black Panther Party, which repeated much of the Nation of Islam's tragic history? Probably not, for by 1966-1967, Malcolm X would have seen the danger inherent in a fascination with guns and come to resemble the Nelson Mandela of the late 1980s. Nelson Mandela, another symbol of race and manhood, is the figure with whom Spike Lee closes his film. The vision—still pan-African—raises hopes for another round of consciousness-raising among black nationalists.

Chris Roark (essay date Fall 1994)

SOURCE: "Hamlet, Malcolm X, and the Examined Education," in *CEA Critic,* Vol. 57, No. 1, Fall, 1994, pp. 111-22.

[*In the following essay, Roark outlines the use of* The Autobiography of Malcolm X *and William Shakespeare's* Hamlet *as a means of illustrating to students the effect of external influences on their perceptions of the world.*]

Shakespeare's *Hamlet* and *The Autobiography of Malcolm X,* taught in conjunction, are useful texts for encouraging first-year writing students to examine how their educations are often a mix of conflicting influences. Both works can be used to provoke not only arguments and counter arguments regarding those influences but also practical action on the insights derived from such study. The usually debilitating "double consciousness" that permeates the thoughts of both Hamlet and Malcolm X can also suggest attitudes and techniques useful for student argumentative writing, especially when such a habit pushes both students and teachers to confront contradictory evidence, thus undermining the urge to distort or simplify experience. After briefly reviewing the unusual ways these two works mirror each other, I will discuss how passages that offer conflicting evidence imply a structure for class discussions. This approach in class also offers a method for student autobiographical and argumentative writing, which in turn aims at self-examination and right action. I'll conclude by describing what are, admittedly,

the idealistic aims of the project, discussing how such work can lead to the possibility of more autonomous and informed behavior by students. Like the two figures under consideration—who must reconcile their complex perceptions of the world with their desire to take direct action against wrongs—the difficulties and yet the necessity of moving from reflective, critical thought to action can hardly receive too much attention.

Though my purpose here is not to dwell on a comparison of the two works, a few of the parallels between *Hamlet* and *The Autobiography* deserve mention. Both Hamlet and Malcolm X grapple with archetypal problems of violence and political action inextricably tied to family experiences; each struggles with the unexplained death of a father and betrayal by a substitute father who seeks his death; each experiences the appearance of a ghost who seems to offer direction; each rejects a female figure and, it could be argued, drives her to self-destruction; and both have premonitions of death that, when played out, partially resemble suicide. The two men also possess a keen sense of self-presentation, viewing their worlds as theaters in which a public self driven to achieve or complete an action often hides and conflicts with a private self. Thus, both sometimes self-consciously project public images of themselves as madmen with the potential to undertake imminent violent action, using these images to manipulate various audiences.

Yet both figures also struggle privately with substantial psychological problems. Both also, finally, depend on mediators, Horatio and Alex Haley, to tell their stories aright to the unsatisfied, raising again the problem of presenting the self to various public audiences. Indeed, when Ossie Davis eulogizes Malcolm X as "our own black shining prince" [in *The Autobiography of Malcolm X*], he echoes Horatio's eulogy of Hamlet, the "sweet prince." The often-private, confessional nature of Hamlet's soliloquies parallels the confessional nature of parts of *The Autobiography,* suggesting similarities in the two different forms of self-presentation and self-analysis. Thus, within the frameworks of poetic tragedy and conversion narrative, the two figures sometimes partially escape consideration of an immediate public audience and its influence and yet still remain aware that they are offering a "show" for others. Both also experience moments when identity and evidence seem clear, so that action can seem right. Yet these moments are exceptions, and for the most part we see both figures in the fullness of warring influences (for example, conflicting religious beliefs) that resist understanding and impede action.

Rather than lecturing to students about such things, I let these issues arise in discussions based on passages students select and prepare for class. The approach to the two works takes place within the context of argument and counterargument, and class discussion introduces the methods required in later argumentative writing. Students prepare for class by selecting two passages from one text that offer conflicting evidence about an idea or issue. For example, one student juxtaposed these two passages from *The Autobiography:*

> They were good people. Mrs. Swerlin was bigger than her husband, I remember, a big buxom, robust, laughing woman, and Mr. Swerlin was thin, with black hair, and a black mustache and a red face, quiet and polite, even to me.

> They liked me right away, too. Mrs. Swerlin showed me to my room, my own room—the first in my life.

> The devil white man cut these black people (slaves) off from all knowledge of their own kind, and cut them off from any knowledge of their own language, religion, and past culture, until the black man in America was the earth's only race of people who had absolutely no knowledge of his true identity.

This student's selection focuses on a consistent conflict in the work: evidence that sometimes offers a sympathetic view of whites in contrast to evidence that defines the "white man" as the devil. I asked the student whether she thought Malcolm X's behavior could be influenced more by what is described in one passage than by what is reflected in the other. Her response was to begin to contextualize the quotations, arguing that his earlier age at the time of the first passage could make it a greater influence. Another student suggested that "good people" (here white) can also be part of what cuts Malcolm X off from his "true identity." We also discussed his early life with the Swerlins in contrast to what he learns later from books. After more remarks about the context and specifics of these quotations, along with passages prepared by other students, we moved on to the section that describes Malcolm X's learning in prison and continued to discuss the influence of books versus the impact of actual experience on his behavior.

Discussions based on student selections can take many paths, but often the paths intersect, and always our remarks are ordered by efforts to seek details that counter an idea from an initial passage. Here, working to understand the development of Malcolm X's shifting perceptions of whites is crucial not only to interpreting *The Autobiography*'s final chapters but also to the debate about his final political philosophy. This contrastive approach also invites the students to review details and consciously seek, with each new passage, to argue even as they immediately complicate initial perceptions with contrary evidence. It becomes clear that Malcolm X is often inconsistent and self-contradictory. We can argue that the contradictions potentially undermine the work for us or that they seem to humanize Malcolm X and point to his attempts to change, find the truth, and take right action.

Hamlet and *The Autobiography,* as their critical history shows, invite a focus on the nuclear family to understand the central figure's problems with his identity and actions. Yet to assume that this is the heart of the mystery for both men is to ignore pervasive problems with, for one thing, conflicting religious beliefs that are also very much a part of these texts. Students often touch on these ideas with their passages. A student pointed out that much of Hamlet's first soliloquy focuses on his mother ("Frailty, thy name is woman"). Searching for a possible counterargument, he noted that Hamlet also thinks about Christianity here ("that the Everlasting had not fixed / His cannon 'gainst self-slaughter"). I asked which influence seems to have the greater effect on Hamlet's behavior here, his family or his religious beliefs. After more discussion, a student noted that Haley describes Malcolm X's initial inability to speak about his family, yet this is eventually broken down when Malcolm X is asked about his mother. I asked, "Do the troubling family structures in *The Autobiography* and in *Hamlet* seem more or less important than uncertainty about religious beliefs, especially as these things influence the two figures' actions?"

As students seek contradictory evidence, they also begin to confront problems with methodology important to literary critics and biographers, who themselves privilege certain influences over others, or one above all. Considering conflicting evidence offers not only a structure for class discussion but also a structure for student essays, in which each passage supporting one view can be confronted not just with a counterargument but with specific textual evidence that complicates or, again, contradicts that initial evidence. Crucially, because students seek evidence that both supports and contradicts an argument, they learn that there are no certain or facile answers to questions regarding primary influence or methodological issues. As others have argued, too often we "aid in their educated self-deception" by not making this point repeatedly and forcefully to students [James S. and Tita French Baumlin, "Knowledge, Choice, and Consequence: Reading and Teaching *Hamlet,*" *CEA Critic,* Vol. 52, Nos. 1-2, 1989]. Thus, requiring students to argue for the relative importance of various influences, such as religious belief versus the nuclear family, means they must qualify their arguments in light of contradictory evidence, continually grapple with the details of the works, and understand that such questions do not lead to single answers so much as to more questions and the necessary habit of review.

As the example of the two mothers' influence implies, the works mirror each other in ways that are useful for classroom discussion. For problems students raise from *Hamlet,* parallel issues arise from *The Autobiography,* and the class begins to see how such diverse and different texts "talk" to each other. Usually, the class works for two weeks on *Hamlet,* begins to read *The Autobiography* during the second week of *Hamlet,* and for a third and fourth week finishes reading *The Autobiography* as well as working on comparing the texts in class. After the students find conflicting evidence about a problem in one work, I have them find passages for a similar problem and conflicting evidence in the other work, and I ask whether the texts offer any mutual illumination. One student compared the difficulties both men have with women. She noted that Hamlet's tendency to generalize—"Frailty, thy name is woman"—seems like Malcolm X's generalization that "a woman's true nature is to be weak," even though his admiration of his half-sister Ella offers one instance of substantial counterevidence to this habit of mind. For many issues in both works, the central tension is between a generalization the figure makes and evidence regarding a specific person or problem that contradicts or complicates that generalization and throws doubt upon related action.

Indeed, problems that both Hamlet and Malcolm X face reflect a central dilemma for first-year writers as well as for most other writers. Both figures share with writing students the wish to simplify the evidence of experience, sometimes with generalizations, so that a path of action or argument will seem clearer. Therefore, my aim is to put problems to students in a manner that compels them to respond to the complexity of those problems. Thus, in conjunction with studying these two figures, I ask students first to write their own "autobiographies," works that narrate their day-to-day lives in school for a month, and then to write an argumentative paper based exclusively on evidence from their autobiographies. Though the initial writing is also like a journal, I use the term "autobiography" to lend more seriousness to the undertaking and to invite students to see the relationship between their writing and *The Autobiography.* That is, I encourage students to be opinionated, to reflect on causes, and to pinpoint events that seem to have meaning for them. With their autobiographies, students narrate responses to their current classes, their studies, and other related experiences; then, in the argumentative essay, they attempt to get out of their skins and analyze their autobiographies. With this follow-up essay, they must argue for the value, or lack thereof, of their current college education. So that the evidence in the autobiography will not consciously be slanted toward one argument or the other, I don't tell them they will eventually write arguments based on their autobiographies until this initial writing is completed.

As with the approach to the works in class, students must build their arguments on evidence that presents both sides of various issues. To encourage attitudes that are both exploratory and argumentative in the follow-up essay, I require students first to state a thesis based on questions before stating which way they will argue. For example, "What evidence from the autobiography suggests that the (student's) education helps develop discipline, risktaking, unrestricted questioning, and self-confrontation—things that characterize

Malcolm X's and Hamlet's pursuits? What evidence implies that their education is failing to develop such habits?" After viewing their experience from the inside by writing autobiographies, students examine the evidence from the outside by constructing arguments, with their autobiographical texts as their evidence.

Periodically, when they are writing their autobiographies and before they turn to argument, I have students write in response to these questions and directions: (1) "How is your perception of the material in a given class different from, or similar to, your teacher's views?" (2) "How are influences (such as religious or political beliefs) that you observe in *The Autobiography* and *Hamlet* like or unlike influences acting in your own life?" (3) "Identify places in your autobiography where these influences could affect your descriptions of your education, or perception of 'facts,' as we often see happening with Hamlet and Malcolm X." These questions are meant to make students think about the myth of objective consciousness, to begin to see that "often we invent the world around us" [David Schuman, *A Preface to Politics,* 1981]. Their reading of *Hamlet* encourages such reflection. Hamlet, at one point, desires to know the world and himself from the mirrorlike, and thus seemingly objective, reflection of drama. So he offers:

> . . . the purpose of playing, whose end, both at first
> and now, was and is to hold, as 'twere, the mirror
> up to nature, to show virtue her own feature, scorn
> her own image.

Yet he later seems to question this, when, regarding his conflict with Laertes, he remarks that "by the image of my cause I see / The portraiture of his." Here, "image" and "portraiture" imply that Hamlet, while striving to know himself and Laertes, senses the subjective and interpretive aspects mediating this process.

Janet Varner Gunn comments on the important influence of autobiography on the self-awareness of readers:

> The reader experiences the autobiographical text as
> an occasion for discovery: of seeing in the text the
> heretofore unexpressed depth of the reader's self—
> not as a mirror image, nor even as a particular mani-
> festation of some shared idea of selfhood, but as
> instance of interpretive activity that risks display.

Hamlet and Malcolm X offer habits of mind and perception that need to be interpreted because they are often in conflict. Similarly, each student's autobiography displays not a true mirror reflection of the student but a self-in-depth that demands interpretation. As Hamlet and Malcolm X both strive to know themselves but often are also conscious of the limits of their perceptions, so also students begin to see that the perceived selves and education described in their autobiographies are something they are as much *making* with their biases and *uses* of evidence as *finding* in the "facts." David Schuman, following William James, clarifies this point:

> Nothing—no part of our experience—has self-evident meaning. Once we are conscious of something, we add meaning to it. Not only that, we *get* those meanings from our surroundings. The myths of our society, the values of our parents and peers, the kind of day we're having, all contribute to how we make sense and meaning of events around us. We make meaning *within* in the context of meaning; we make history within history.

Schuman's clear and no-nonsense approach to James and epistemology, combined with Plato's "Allegory of the Cave," is a useful introduction for students first studying these issues. In a later work, Schuman outlines epistemological positions that encourage students to reflect critically on the evidence of their day-to-day education. He quotes Alfred Schutz:

> Philosophers as different as James, Bergson, Dewey, Husserl, and Whitehead agree that the common-sense knowledge of everyday life is the unquestioned but always questionable background within which inquiry starts and within which alone it can be carried out. [David Schuman, *Policy Analysis, Education, and Everyday Life: An Empirical Reevaluation of Higher Education in America,* 1982]

Perhaps what unites Hamlet and Malcolm X as much as anything else is their habit of questioning what we take to be common-sense knowledge of everyday life.

After students determine the questions for their argumentative essays, I ask them to speculate, in view of the evidence from their autobiographies and the influence of teaching techniques, both about problems and about ways to improve their day-to-day education: "What helps and what inhibits developing a thirst for critical understanding in your classes?" "What would you change about a class and your own behavior that would enable you to recapture (since most have it as children) 'the craving to be mentally alive,' as Malcolm X describes it?" "Considering Malcolm X's self-education in prison or Hamlet's isolation, how much should learning be a painful and often solitary struggle (as Plato seems to argue in his 'Allegory'); how much pleasurable and communal?" I assume that students need to examine such questions and that the snapshots of their autobiographies become clearer when pasted on the wider backdrop of such issues.

Even the most rudimentary recording of experiences when combined with an argumentative essay reveals vexing conflicts and evidence that cannot be easily resolved. One student's autobiography had short entries, many of which simply listed the days' events. This lack of effort in itself could be evidence against the value of the student's current education. But when the student reflected on his autobiography, he realized that the argumentative paper, in contrast to the autobiography, revealed that his education encourages him to confront himself, to question the value of his education, and to argue from day-to-day evidence that is hardly abstract. Another student argued against the usefulness of her current education, questioning institutional practices (especially a writing class whose procedures are so regimented!). According to an article in *College English,* the most useful arguments are often conscious of the institutional context in which an essay is produced, rebelling against the usual model of student as apprentice and demystifying institutional authority [Ronald Strickland, "Confrontational Pedagogy and Traditional Literary Studies," *College English,* Vol. 52, No. 3, 1990]. Ironically, therefore, the student who sees this creates an argument that can, to the extent it is persuasive, be evidence for a valuable education based on self-confrontation, since the writing class offers the means for this critique. My comments on this second student's essay encouraged her to revise her arguments, considering the essay itself as evidence in the analysis. Likewise, other students discover they have difficulty writing convincing arguments if their autobiographies present only *positive* descriptions of classes and study, since the subsequent essay would probably argue that there is no significant conflicting evidence about the student's education in the autobiography. Yet this lack of conflict itself may testify that the student is not being encouraged to know the limits of his or her classroom experience and that there may be important problems with that experience.

I enjoy using the students' own evidence and arguments against them when commenting on their essays and consciously aim to do so. In a course evaluation, one student wrote, "His comments agitated me so much that in my revision I quoted and attacked them as much as they attacked my argument." The structure of the autobiography/argument exercise—similar to the structure of *The Autobiography* as conversion narrative and to the structure of poetic tragedy—thus creates a situation in which the exercise "informs against" the students, a situation in which conflicting evidence regarding the value of their actions and environment exists and requires argument. In other words, the autobiography combined with an argument about the value of one's education puts students in a paradoxical situation that makes them conscious of their medium, like our two figures.

I assume that most students live with a double consciousness, similar to but less intense than that described by W.

E. B. DuBois for black Americans. That is, in college, students often slip into uncomfortable roles that seem to bear little relation to how they perceive themselves or their needs; instead of finding Dewey's crucial continuity of experience, a student finds that a semester can seem more like "five courses, five truths, five selves" [John Dewey, *Experience and Education,* 1938; and Schuman, *Policy Analysis*]. This double consciousness can be debilitating; DuBois writes of "the longing . . . to merge his double self into a truer self," echoing Hamlet's desire to express "that within which passes show," a substantial identity beyond the roles one plays for others. Yet the examples of Malcolm X and Hamlet not only imply this desire for a united self but also show how the double consciousness can be transformed into a positive quality to encourage "knowing" and "objectivity," as Richard Wright suggests. In response to DuBois, Wright comments, in his novel *The Outsider,*

> They are going to be self-conscious; they are going to be gifted with a double vision, for, being Negroes, they are going to be both inside and outside of our culture at the same time.

Part of the aim of the autobiography/argument assignments is to take the students' unrealized position that they are by turns both inside and outside of their education and to make this position a site for critical reflection. Instead of trying to resolve each student's divided self, the purpose is to use a student's conflicting experiences to encourage more objective understanding through documenting and arguing about that conflicting evidence.

Thus, one student asked, like Hamlet and Malcolm X, "Am I more trapped or liberated by these different roles I play at school?" Here, the essential question is not so much "Who am I?" as "Where am I?; where do I belong?" As Gunn comments, "The question of the self's identity becomes a question of the self's location in the world." James Baldwin, writing about students in his essay "A Question of Identity," remarks,

> [T]he American confusion seem[s] to be based on the very unconscious assumption that it is possible to consider the person apart from the forces that produced him.

Is it not foolish, if we fail to encourage students to question the education working to form them and to know the limits of that education, to profess that we educate students toward self-knowledge? Indeed, it is through a knowledge of both the limitations imposed by their worlds and their own shortcomings that Hamlet and Malcolm X, albeit briefly, rise above those limitations.

The process outlined here hinges on the paradox that students, in order to assess evidence from which they can begin to develop a greater objectivity that can lead to more informed actions, need first to confront themselves and to see evidence as inevitably contradictory. I should emphasize that "greater objectivity," if it is achieved, is also developed paradoxically, by repeatedly seeing that our perceptions are value-laden and always subject to revision. As the class works to understand the contradictory details of Malcolm X's life and Hamlet's tragedy, they simultaneously see the details of their own experience as equally messy, and are inspired, I hope, with a thirst for learning and right action similar to that shared by Hamlet and Malcolm X. One student wrote, "Because it was accepted that questions didn't have certain answers, I was willing to raise harder questions." Ideally, I provoke students to pursue the questions that inhabit their own thoughts and emotions. I say "ideally" here because trying to do such things inevitably makes me self-conscious of the long distance between one's ideas about teaching and putting those ideas into action in class, as well as the short distance, as one colleague puts it, between the lesson plan and the garbage can. To be sure, an assessment of my plans-in-action may reveal results as mixed as the students' assessments of their education.

In this respect, I also have students consider their experience in my writing class—its problems and limitations. Is it best that received institutional practices (tests, essays, etc.) in this class often encourage students to think alone? Should class discussions be the kind of polemical exchanges that characterize Malcolm X's public appearances and parts of *The Autobiography*? Or should the class be more collaborative, as we see in the friendship between Malcolm X and Haley, a relationship that began as confrontational but evolved into what was arguably a mutual confrontation with racism? How much and in what context should the teacher/student relationship take the form of a master/slave relationship, with students as receptacles of a teacher's ideas or techniques—a relationship similar to Malcolm's relationship to Elijah Muhammad? When does the regimentation of the autobiography/argument assignment seem to pay off, and when is it too restrictive? Does the evidence suggest we can change the master/slave relationship between teacher and student by assessing such a thing? And how much with this particular assignment are the students at the mercy of a manipulative teacher and thus, perhaps, only playing the game to get the desired grade rather than grappling with the evidence to honestly learn? The limitations of the class itself provide some of the best sites for recognizing conflicting evidence and undertaking critical thinking.

Because of these limitations, I view the classroom and our work less as a site for change and action than as a place to play with possibilities. Yet, within this play, as the students work on their journals and arguments, I posit as a goal the possibility of changing, to the extent we can, the passive role students often take toward teachers and education. What can the students teach me, in class discussions and as they write their autobiographies and arguments, about what it means to be a student from a specific ethnic or social background and with particular goals at this university? How can they overcome a passive approach to education so that their writing and thoughts become a means of changing and bettering this class, or any class, making themselves not just *in* a class, but *of* it? As Hamlet and Malcolm X struggle to unite thought with purposeful action, the students' work with these exercises can be a first step toward a clarification of consciousness. And this clarification, in turn, can lead to attitudes that foster practical action in the present, addressing students' limitations as well as those of the environment, and influencing, for example, their curriculum choices, their behavior and effort in classes, and even the decision whether higher education is right for them at this point.

Here again, though, there is a paradox: Students gain some autonomy through a recognition of their close relationship to the strong and sometimes negative influences of their education, which are themselves constantly in flux. I suspect that some of our best students have more energy because they sense that a class is not just a place where they learn but a place of drama where they are both making themselves and being made. Hamlet and Malcolm X recognize that they must struggle to understand how they are being made by their respective worlds while simultaneously attempting to create themselves to take action in those worlds. Both also show an intense consciousness of their limitations when it comes to addressing wrongs, and yet they also understand the necessity of action against those wrongs, though they know that no course of action is certain, much less guaranteed. Furthermore, both works cut to the heart of many of our puzzling experiences with race, family, the opposite sex, and school, a place where a humanly purposeful identity is something students often work for in spite of our institutional condition. Both works inspire me to re-examine myself and what it means to attempt teaching when the aim is to help students explore who, what, and where they are now, encouraging practical habits so they may rethink their perceptions, actions, and relationships to others. To be sure, attempts to court and badger students to live lives based on critical understanding are useless unless we also offer the techniques to do so. Fusing autobiographical writing with argument offers students a chance to evaluate themselves and to critique their education while it develops attitudes necessary for both argument and research, especially a conscious search for contradictory evidence that undermines the urge to simplify. By examining the conflicting details of their own experiences along with those of Malcolm X and Hamlet, students begin to see the difference between self-serving and more objective reasoning, as well as to develop a respect for, and doubt of, both words and facts. Perhaps they also develop a hunger for freedom—defined as the need

for dignity and responsibility—that is the heart of a living university community.

FURTHER READING

Criticism

Abbott, Philip. "Hustling: Benjamin Franklin, Malcolm X, Abbie Hoffman." *States of Perfect Freedom: Autobiography and Political Thought,* pp. 27-57. Amherst: The University of Massachusetts Press, 1987.
> Asserts that "taken together" the autobiographies of Benjamin Franklin, Malcolm X, and Abbie Hoffmann—to whom Abbott refers as "hustlers"—exhibit a particular type of personality and also provide insights into the nature of American politics and society.

Barbour, John D. "Christianity and 'The White Man's Religion.'" *Versions of Deconversion: Autobiography and the Loss of Faith,* pp. 85-105. Charlottesville and London: University Press of Virginia, 1994.
> Compares the autobiographies of early Christian African-American and Native-American writers to the autobiographies of the non-Christian Malcolm X and Lame Deer to illustrate that the latter two writers adapted the earlier writers' strategy of "show[ing] the reader the difference between Christianity and 'the white man's religion,' which is the religious justification of white superiority."

Hareven, Tamara K. "Step-Children of the Dream." *History of Education Quarterly* IX, No. 4 (Winter 1969): 505-14.
> Examines the objectives of African-American autobiographers in a discussion of the works of Malcolm X, James Baldwin, Richard Wright, Claude Brown, Eldridge Cleaver, and Anne Moody.

Taylor, Gordon O. "Voices from the Veil: W. E. B. DuBois to Malcolm X." *Chapters of Experience: Studies in 20th Century American Autobiography,* pp. 41-65. New York: St. Martin's Press, 1983.
> Considers how in the autobiographical works of such African-American authors as W. E. B. DuBois, Richard Wright, James Baldwin, and Malcolm X "narrative consciousness of the personal present is both invaded and informed, threatened and sustained, by a sense of dissolution within the racial past."

Terry, Eugene. "Black Autobiography—Discernible Forms." *Okike,* No. 19 (September 1981): 6-10.
> Posits that there is a similarity between the autobiographical works of "Afro-Americans of as varied experience and vision as Frederick Douglass, W. E. B.

DuBois, and Malcolm X" which is "best explained by the way of life foisted upon blacks since the days of slavery."

"Voices from Black America." *Times Literary Supplement,* No. 3,613 (28 May 1971): 605-06.

Brief, favorable assessment of *By Any Means Necessary: Speeches, Interviews, and A Letter by Malcolm X,* which the reviewer asserts "bears the powerful impress of that formidable personality."

Additional coverage of Malcolm X's life and career is contained in the following sources published by Gale: *Black Literature Criticism,* **Vol. 2;** *Black Writers; Contemporary Authors,* **Vols. 111, and 125;** *DISCovering Authors; DISCovering Authors: British; DISCovering Authors: Canadian; DISCovering Authors Modules: Most-Studied and Multicultural;* **and** *Major Twentieth-Century Writers;* **and** *World Literature Criticism Supplement.*

Mary Stewart
1916-

(Full name Mary Florence Elinora Stewart) English novelist, poet, and author of children's books.

The following entry presents an overview of Stewart's career through 1997. For further information on her life and works, see *CLC,* Volumes 7 and 35.

INTRODUCTION

Stewart is credited with bringing higher standards to the genre of romantic suspense novels, and with adding a fresh perspective to the tradition of the Arthurian legends. In her novels of mystery and historical romance, Stewart has provided carefully developed characterizations and vivid recreations of locales such as Delphi, Corfu, and various sites around Great Britain. Her retelling of the story of King Arthur's court are considered highly respectable additions to that genre.

Biographical Information

Born in 1916 in Sunderland, Durham, England, Stewart received her B.A. in 1938 and her M.A. in 1941, from the University of Durham, where she went on to teach English literature until 1955. In 1945 Stewart married Frederick Henry Stewart, a renowned geologist who was knighted in 1974 for his devotion to science. In 1956 Stewart moved to Edinburgh, Scotland, where her husband accepted a professorship at the University of Edinburgh. It was then that Stewart decided to give up her own university career to concentrate on writing full-time. Beginning with her first published novel, *Madam, Will You Talk?* (1955), Stewart was a best-selling author. Stewart has continued to produce widely acclaimed novels, juvenile stories, and most recently, poetry.

Major Works

Stewart's works of suspense and historical romance usually center on a charming young woman inadvertently caught in extraordinary, sometimes life-threatening, events. With the aid of the hero, her love interest, Stewart's heroine solves a mystery or survives an adventure. According to Stewart, her characters "observe certain standards of conduct, of ethics, a somewhat honorable behavior pattern." All of Stewart's novels in this genre follow similar plots, and all are set in exotic or romantic locations around the world. This "predictability," rather than diminishing the success of the novels, is the key to their popularity. Readers find Stewart's char-

acters and plots familiar and her themes—which never diverge from the conventional—comforting and stabilizing. In 1970 Stewart began a series of novels retelling the Arthurian legend. *The Crystal Cave* (1970), *The Hollow Hills* (1973), and *The Last Enchantment* (1979) are notable for several variations from standard versions of the legend: they are told from the viewpoint of Merlin the magician rather than from that of King Arthur; they are set in the more accurate fifth century, rather than the twelfth, where most writers place them; and Stewart adheres to historical fact in describing places, customs, and clothing, unlike many chroniclers of the Arthurian legend. In *The Wicked Day* (1983), the fourth book in the series, Mordred, Arthur's illegitimate son, is depicted as a sensitive, ill-fated youth instead of the purely evil figure of traditional legend who singlehandedly destroys his father.

Critical Reception

Although Stewart's novels usually fall into the category of popular fiction, they almost consistently receive praise from reviewers. Particularly acclaimed is Stewart's ability to evoke the proper moods for her settings, describing them as she does in great detail, and always historically accurate. But it is Stewart's Arthurian cycle that has received the highest acclaim from critics. Her authentic fifth-century setting has been widely considered a welcome variation from earlier versions of the story, and the shift of focus from King Arthur to Merlin—as well as more strongly defined characters from Mordred to Queen Guenevere—is also seen as a enhancement to the traditional versions of this story.

PRINCIPAL WORKS

Madam, Will You Talk? (novel) 1955
Wildfire at Midnight (novel) 1956
Thunder on the Right (novel) 1957
Nine Coaches Waiting (novel) 1958
My Brother Michael (novel) 1960
The Ivy Tree (novel) 1962
The Moon-Spinners (novel) 1962
This Rough Magic (novel) 1964
Airs above the Ground (novel) 1965
The Gabriel Hounds (novel) 1967
The Wind off the Small Isles (novel) 1968
The Crystal Cave (novel) 1970
The Little Broomstick (juvenile) 1971
The Hollow Hills (novel) 1973
Ludo and the Star Horse (juvenile) 1974
Touch Not the Cat (novel) 1976
The Last Enchantment (novel) 1979
A Walk in Wolf Wood (novel) 1980
The Wicked Day (novel) 1983
Thornyhold (novel) 1988
Frost on the Window and Other Poems (poetry) 1990
The Stormy Petrel (novel) 1991
The Prince and the Pilgrim (novel) 1995
Rose Cottage (novel) 1997

CRITICISM

Kirkus Reviews (review date 1 February 1960)

SOURCE: Review of *My Brother Michael*, in *Kirkus Reviews*, Vol. XXVIII, No. 3, February 1, 1960, p. 107.

[*In the following review, the critic praises* My Brother Michael *as an improbable but well-written and fully absorbing mystery.*]

[*My Brother Michael* is a] fast moving suspense novel set against the background of Delphi, which affords the reader even more hair-raising nightmarish adventures than in ear-

lier novels. Mary Stewart has hit upon a successful basic pattern:—a young Englishwoman, escaping herself in travel, becomes involved in a succession of tense experiences, skirting death, and playing with dangerous characters who stop at nothing. This time the sense of inevitable disaster colors every incident:—her first rather hair-brained acceptance of the challenge of delivering a car, ordered by an unknown woman for an unknown man in Delphi, where she wants to go; her facile meeting with the Simon to whom the car was assigned—only he knew nothing about it—and his involving her in his own mission, to run down the truth of his brother Michael's violent death some fourteen years earlier, when he was in the Greek underground. Just how the mystery is solved—what the explanation of a curious letter received after Michael's death—and how Cemilla finds herself a pawn in a dangerous game build up to an incredible but absorbing climax of passion and death. The Delphi setting is unique, and the story takes on the echoes of the classic tragedies centuries ago. Mary Stewart writes vividly, she conveys an extraordinary sense of place, she tells a first rate story.

Mary Byerly (review date Spring 1965)

SOURCE: "Lucy in Corfu," in *The North American Review*, Vol. 2, No. 1, Spring 1965, pp. 55-6.

[*In the following review, Byerly offers a favorable appraisal of* This Rough Magic, *noting in particular Stewart's wide range of subject matter synthesized into a single plot.*]

[In ***This Rough Magic,***] Lucy Waring, whose first major appearance on the London stage is cut short by an early closing, comes to the beautiful isle of Corfu to visit her wealthy sister. Almost immediately her disappointment is forgotten, as she is caught up in a series of puzzling and alarming events: the carefully secluded presence of the great English actor, Sir Julian Gale; mysterious shots at a playful dolphin in the bay; the drowning of two island boys within a week; and, finally, discovery of the true nature of Godfrey Manning's photographic expeditions.

Mary Stewart spins a good yarn, and this one is no exception, magically woven as it is from such diverse elements as the contemporary London theater and the intelligence of dolphins; the benevolence of Corfu's patron, St. Spiridion, and the political climate of Albania. Shakespeare's *The Tempest* is skillfully blended into both setting and plot, while vivid description, suspense, and lively tempo, with just the right touch of romance, are combined to provide the kind of excellent entertainment Miss Stewart's readers have come to expect.

R. F. Grady (review date 1 October 1967)

SOURCE: Review of *The Gabriel Hounds,* in *Best Sellers,* Vol. 27, No. 13, October 1, 1967, p. 253.

[In the following review, Grady offers a favorable assessment of Stewart's complex and colorful plot and writing in The Gabriel Hounds.*]*

Christabel Mansel, a spirited and pretty English girl on a tour of the Near East (Syria and Lebanon) had planned to leave the tour group in Beirut to do a little sightseeing on her own before returning home. In the back of her mind was an intent to try to see her Great-Aunt Harriet who for years had lived in splendor in the former sultan's palace called Dar Ibrahim, built on a promontory in the gorge of the El Saq'h river, an eccentric woman who modeled herself on historic Lady Hester Stanhope, wore the clothes of an Arab prince and hunted at times through the countryside mounted on a handsome chestnut horse with two saluki dogs. Aunt Harriet now was over eighty and supposed to be more or less a recluse, but still in complete control of her faculties.

Quite by chance Christabel mets her second cousin Charles Mansel in the bazaar in Damascus and he quickened her interest in Aunt H. (as he called her) promising to meet her in Beirut so that both could call on their ancient relative, Charles having been Aunt H.'s favorite great-nephew. She had, in fact, promised him two porcelain dogs of considerable value which were called "the Gabriel Hounds" only because they seemed, as did the salukis, to be associated with an old legend that the Gabriel Hounds ran with Death (although Gabriel was not the angel of death) and would be heard howling above a house if someone were going to die there. Much like the Irish legend of the banshees, or similar legends of hounds baying at the death of someone nearby.

Christabel decides to make an attempt to visit her aunt on her own before Charles arrives, succeeds in having an interview at midnight and stays the night in the seraglio quarter of the sprawling and rundown castle, only to be forced to prolong the stay when a heavy rainstorm swells the river and its tributary into flood conditions. The household is small—gone are the many servants The Lady of Lebanon had formerly employed; there are now only the English John Lethman, presumably a psychologist attending Aunt H.; the Arab girl Halide and her brother Nasirulla; and a very old and almost mute gateman named Jissom. There are, however, the two saluki dogs which are supposed to be fierce guardians of Dar Ibrahim, let loose only at nightfall.

This is but the background of the story, the beginning, one might say; for adventure piles on adventure and it would be unfair to outline the entire story. But this is every bit as fine a piece of writing and plotting as Mary Stewart's previous and best novels. That it will also, like them, be a best-seller is easy to predict. The setting and color is fabulous, probably attributable to Mrs. Stewart's travels with her husband who is head of the Geology Department of Edinburgh University.

Sara Blackburn (review date 16 August 1970)

SOURCE: "Wizard Briton," in *Book World,* August 16, 1970, p. 2.

[In the following review, Blackburn presents a brief outline of the plot of The Crystal Cave *and praises the book as a "colorful romance."]*

Fifth-century Britain is the setting of Miss Stewart's new novel [*The Crystal Cave*], and its hero is the magical Merlin, seen here from his youth as a court bastard in Wales through the far-flung adventures that lead to his hand in the birth of King Arthur, whose destiny he is to guide as he rules Britain. It is as the author notes, not a work of scholarship, but "a work of the imagination," and its hero offers Miss Stewart fine opportunity for building the kind of colorful romance that has made her books so widely read in this country.

In Miss Stewart's version, Merlin is a solitary but game little boy whose Sight is kept secret during the difficult childhood he spends in the court of his grandfather, the King of Wales, where he is recognized as the result of a dark coupling between the King's daughter and the devil himself. After clandestine seminars in the cave of an old and learned wizard, and the acquisition of five languages, he escapes by necessity to "Less Britain" and the protection of kindly Count Ambrosius, where he not only learns his true and proud identity, but becomes a trusted participant and even initiator in the struggle which is to unite all of Britain. There is an impressive cast of characters and many of them are drawn in considerable dimension, so that Miss Stewart makes it easy for us to imagine that this is what life might have been like in a still-divided Britain as it moved to free itself from the effects of Roman rule. It is perhaps unnecessary to add that the novel is peppered throughout with the regulation political intrigues, formidable nunneries, fierce battle scenes and secret ceremonies—there is even a bit of Druid rite and human sacrifice—so necessary to the atmosphere of such romances. But Miss Stewart brings them off with an easy talent for making them real elements of the plot, not mere sideshow devices, and her Merlin makes a narrator quite worthy of the large audience that will doubtless be following his adventures this summer. She is no Zoë Oldenbourg, nor does she pretend to be.

Mary Cadogan (review date 18 July 1980)

SOURCE: "Spells that Bind," in *Times Literary Supplement,* July 18, 1980, p. 806.

[*In the following review, Cadogan questions several inconsistencies in the plot of* A Walk in Wolf Wood *but praises the novel overall for its subtlety and cleverness.*]

In *A Walk in Wolf Wood* Mary Stewart continues her preoccupation with issues that have been central to her recent Arthurian novels for adults. The eerie events that overtake two down-to-earth twentieth-century children become the vehicle for an incisive exploration of magic, savagery and the mis-uses of power.

On holiday with their parents in Germany, John and Margaret Begbie are suddenly projected from the drowsy stillness of a perfectly ordinary summer's afternoon into a stark world of medieval sorcery and intrigue. They are in the Black Forest and their slip backwards in time takes place when curiosity and concern prompt them to follow a distressed man into the woods. He is "weeping bitterly"—and with good cause. The children discover that the stranger, Lord Mardian, is in the grip of a terrible enchantment put upon him by a rival at the ducal court. By day he is a sensitive, tormented and guilt-ridden man who lives in hiding from his sorcerer enemy, and at night he has to roam the forest, transformed into a slavering, bloodlusting wolf.

At first John and Margaret think that they are acting out a dream, but they are soon made aware of being caught up, although only peripherally, in the spell that binds Mardian. They come to the awesome realization that by voluntarily grappling with great and unspecified dangers they may be able to release him from his enchantment. Of course they do not hesitate; they prove, as so many other fictional heroes and heroines have done, that two plucky and resourceful children can be a match for the most malevolent of medieval sorcerers. But *A Walk in Wolf Wood* is not by any means all magic and moonshine. Once the basic premise has been accepted the characters are skilfully manipulated through a series of challenges, and from one level of apparent reality to another, without irritating or mind-bending complexities. The trappings of another time like jousts and hunts, terraces and towers, are vivid and atmospheric but not overdone. They are harnessed with other energized effects to create a convincing buildup of suspense, and at the right moments the gothic mood of dark green forest gloom is lightened by wit and warmth.

This is, in a sense, a holiday-adventure story and appropriately the main narrative movement is vigorous and direct. There are also, however, satisfying descriptions of natural beauty and of resonances between the children's inner experiences and the externals that they observe. (A bird's sudden flight out of a clump of trees, for example, heightens a not quite definable sense of psychological unease and menace.)

There is no doubt about the power and persuasiveness of *A Walk in Wolf Wood,* but it is slightly flawed by inconsistencies in the time-shift from which the action of the story derives. John and Margaret accept this startling process in a low-key and very practical manner. They are concerned about the kind of clothes they should wear to enable them best to fit into their new surroundings; after some initial shocks they take werewolves, sinister magicians and palace settings in their stride; they adopt the speech and manners of the time without conscious effort, although they are a little surprised at their fluency in a foreign tongue—and a medieval one at that. They occasionally discuss the anomalous aspects of their adventures, but explain these away by concluding that they are all part of the spell. It is possible, however, that some readers may not so easily be able to dismiss some of the inconsistencies—although these in themselves suggest several stimulating areas of speculation and enquiry.

Harold J. Herman (essay date Spring 1984)

SOURCE: "The Women in Mary Stewart's Merlin Trilogy," in *Interpretations: A Journal of Idea, Analysis, and Criticism,* Vol. 15, No. 2, Spring, 1984, pp. 101-14.

[*In the following essay, Herman argues that Stewart's portrayal of women in her Merlin trilogy is the most sympathetic and groundbreaking in Arthurian legend because of her rejection of feminine stereotypes.*]

With the publication of *The Crystal Cave, The Hollow Hills,* and *The Last Enchantment* Mary Stewart has made a significant contribution to the development of the Arthurian legend, for her trilogy is not merely a retelling but a reworking of earlier Arthurian material. Claiming that, though firmly based in both history and legend, her novels are works of the imagination, she has nonetheless provided explanatory notes for the benefit of those readers who wish to "trace for themselves the seeds of certain ideas and the origins of certain references." Because she has specified some of her sources, one may also examine them to see how she used earlier works to create her trilogy on Merlin. Obviously many of the changes, deletions, and additions were necessitated by her concept of Merlin as basically a human being with the god-given gift of sight.

The focus of this study, however, is not Merlin but Mary Stewart's female characters. A student of the Arthurian legend is struck by her vivid portrayal of women who are not frightened, submissive creatures content to satisfy their men's lustful appetites and blind to everything except bearing and rearing children. Rather than being toys of men, for use or abuse, they themselves often select the men they wish to bed and wed. They frequently dominate the men around them, for they are stronger and cleverer than most men, and they are ambitious, demanding more out of life than marriage and children. It is this concept of women that distinguishes Stewart's trilogy from the earlier Arthurian works she used as her sources.

Stewart's ideal woman is Igerne, Duchess of Cornwall, whose portrayal in two of Stewart's major sources, Geoffrey of Monmouth's *Historia Regum Britanniae* and Malory's *Morte d'Arthur,* is here examined. According to Geoffrey, Uther orders all his barons to assemble in London to celebrate his coronation. Among those gathered there is Gorlois, Duke of Cornwall, a loyal supporter of Ambrosius and Uther, with his young wife Igerne, the most beautiful woman in the realm. Uther falls in love with Igerne and openly displays his affection for her, whereupon Gorlois, in anger, takes his wife and retires from the court. Enraged, Uther commands Gorlois to return and appear in his court so that he may take lawful satisfaction for the affront. When Gorlois fails to obey the summons, Uther with his army invades Cornwall and besieges Dimilioc, the castle Gorlois occupies after placing Igerne in the invincible castle of Tintagel. A week later, Uther, overcome with the love of Igerne, declares to Ulfin, one of his familiars, that he will die if he cannot possess her. At Ulfin's counsel, Merlin is summoned; and, moved by the sight of Uther's suffering, Merlin declares that to fulfill Uther's wish, he must call upon acts new and unheard of in their day. Through the use of "mendicaminibus" (i.e., "leechcraft" or "mendicaments"), he transforms the king into the likeness of Gorlois and Ulfin and himself into those of Jordan and Brithael, Gorlois's retainers, in such a manner that none could tell them from the originals. In this transformed appearance, they are admitted to Tintagel Castle; Uther enjoys the love of Igerne, who believes him to be her husband, and that night Arthur is conceived. Meanwhile, Uther's men attack Dimilioc; Gorlois, with his comrades, sallies forth and is killed; messengers arrive at Tintagel to inform Igerne of Gorlois's death and are amazed to see the duke sitting beside the duchess. Smiling at their tiding, Uther, as Gorlois, declares that he is very much alive, but is fearful that the king will overtake them there and make them prisoners in the castle. Hence he resolves to make peace with the king. Leaving Tintagel, he puts off the semblance of Gorlois and joins his army. Grieved at the death of Gorlois but glad that Igerne is released from the bonds of matrimony, he returns to Tintagel, takes the castle, and makes Igerne his wife. Geoffrey says that Uther and Igerne are thereafter linked together in no little mutual love. In short, Geoffrey's Igerne is a beautiful but passive woman, obedient to her husband,

duped into having sex with Uther, and eventually united with the king in wedded bliss.

Malory begins his Book I, "The Tale of King Arthur," with Uther as King of England and the Duke of Tintagel as Uther's enemy, who warred against the king for a long time. Summoned by Uther, Gorlois and his wife, "a fair lady and a passynge wyse," arrive at court, and Uther lusts after Igerne, who, as a "passing good woman," rejects him. As a faithful wife, she tells her husband of Uther's lust and suggests that they quickly depart from the court and ride all night to their castle. Angered, Uther invades Cornwall. The story continues as in Geoffrey, but Malory's Merlin is already on his way to the king when he, as a beggar, meets Ulfin, for Merlin has foreknowledge of Ulfin's mission. Shortly after Ulfin has ridden back to Uther, Merlin is magically there, promising to fulfill Uther's desire on the condition that the child who will be conceived that night should, upon birth, be turned over to him. Uther agrees and, magically transformed into Gorlois, beds Igerne. The child is conceived, and the next morning Merlin, transformed as Brithael, arrives and takes "Gorlois" away. When Igerne hears that her husband was killed three hours before Uther came to her, "she merveilled who that myghte be that laye with her in lykenes of her lord. So she mourned pryvely and held hir pees." With the assent of all the barons, Uther makes Igerne his queen. When, six months later, Uther asks her to name the father of the child within her body, the queen truthfully explains, and Uther tells her it was he who came to her in the likeness of Gorlois and "the cause how it was by Merlyns counceil." Then the queen "made grete joye" when she knew Uther was the father of her child. At this point there is no mention of Uther's telling his wife of his promise to turn over the child to Merlin; rather, we are merely told that when the child is born, it is delivered to Merlin, who takes it to Ector and has it christened Arthur. Later in the tale, when Igerne is brought to court to meet her son for the first time, she is accused by Ulfin of falseness and treachery because she did not proclaim Arthur as her and Uther's child and thus prevent the civil war. Igerne defends herself, saying that when the child was born Uther commanded it be given to Merlin, that she did not know the child's name, and that she never saw him thereafter. When Merlin declares that Igerne is Arthur's mother and Ector testifies that he fostered Arthur according to Uther's order, Arthur embraces his mother. Thus, Igerne is portrayed by Malory as the faithful wife, first to Gorlois and then, in spite of the duplicity, to Uther; her only concern is to serve her lord and husband. Indeed, Ulfin speaks the truth when he says to Merlin, "Year than more to blame than the queene."

Mary Stewart's treatment of this episode is vastly different from Geoffrey's and Malory's because of her different concept of Merlin and of Igerne. Unlike Malory's Merlin, Stewart's Emrys has no foreknowledge of Uther's love for

Igerne; he learns of it from Cadal, who reports the gossip at the inn. And it takes four days for Merlin to get to the king in London. When Uther asks him to bring Igerne secretly to him and make her love him, Merlin replies that his magic cannot do what the king desires. Significantly, he does not magically transform Uther into Gorlois. Stewart's Merlin, of course, has prophetic sight, but unlike Malory, whose Merlin states outright that a child will be conceived when Uther lies with Igerne, Stewart parcels out this particular prophecy bit by bit in the form of Merlin's vague visions. In fact, it is not until Merlin is outside Tintagel waiting for Uther disguised as Gorlois that Stewart has Merlin clearly explain to Cadal and to the reader that Merlin is merely an instrument of fate, Uther a tool, and Igerne a vessel to bring forth the "past and future king." Moreover, Merlin's prophetic sight is not complete, for although he earlier saw Cadal's death, he has no foreknowledge of his own physical injuries or of Uther's anger and refusal to acknowledge the "bastard" he begot that night. Such a treatment of Merlin's sight, especially the earlier vague visions, is necessary to enable Stewart to create suspense, but it also enables her to focus on the human side of Merlin's character and to develop other characters, especially Igerne.

Unlike Geoffrey's and Malory's Igerne, who is a weak, unsuspecting, innocent dupe of Uther and Merlin, Mary Stewart's Igerne is a proud, strong-willed, politically astute, clever woman.
—Harold J. Herman

Unlike Geoffrey's and Malory's Igerne, who is a weak, unsuspecting, innocent dupe of Uther and Merlin, Mary Stewart's Igerne is a proud, strong-willed, politically astute, clever woman. It is she who, feigning illness, gets her husband to fetch Merlin to her. And, unlike other women, she is not in awe of Merlin, although she does believe he can see the future. To her, he is a wise, cold person who loves no woman, is committed to no man, and thus is a good judge of her situation. So to Merlin she declares that she loves and desires Uther but that she is a proud woman. She is the daughter of a king, married at sixteen to the Duke of Cornwall; and, although she does not say that she loves the old duke, she declares that Gorlois is a good man whom she honors and respects. Until she saw Uther, she was half content, she says, to starve and die in Cornwall. She knows what she must have, but it is beyond her. So she waits and is silent, for upon her silence hangs not only the honor of herself, Gorlois, and her house but also the safety of the kingdom that Ambrosius died for and that Uther sealed with blood and fire. She is no trashy Helen for men to fight, die, and burn down a kingdom for, she declares. She cannot dishonor Gorlois and the king in the eyes of men, and she can-

not go to him secretly and dishonor herself in her own eyes. "I am a lovesick woman, yes. But I am also Ygraine of Cornwall," she concludes.

> I [Merlin] said coldly: "So you intend to wait until you can go to him in honour, as his Queen?"
>
> "What else can I do?"
>
> "Was this the message I had to give him?"
>
> She was silent.
>
> I said: "Or did you get me here to read you the future? To tell you the length of your husband's life?"
>
> Still she said nothing.
>
> "Ygraine," I said, "the two are the same. If I give Uther the message that you love him and desire him, but that you will not come to him while your husband is alive, what length of life would you prophesy for Gorlois?"
>
> Still she did not speak. The gift of silence, too, I though.

Igerne intends to be queen, and she certainly has the qualifications. Indeed, throughout this scene Merlin refers to this fact. For example, standing over Igerne in bed, he notes that though she is only a woman and young, she acts as if she is a queen giving an audience. Looking at the lovely duchess, he notes her proud mouth, perceives that she is no man's toy, and concludes that if Uther wants her he will have to make her his queen. She is clearheaded, for, getting up from her "sick bed," she does not walk in front of the window to be seen from the courtyard. When Merlin asks her if she will go to Uther on the condition that he will tell her how she may have the king's love on her terms, with no dishonor to herself, Uther, or Gorlois, she takes time to think before answering. Moreover, she refuses to promise to obey Merlin until she knows what she is committed to. Merlin remarks that for the first time he has met a woman with whom he does not have to choose his words, to whom he can speak as he would to another man. Moreover, Igerne's concern is not only for herself and Gorlois and her family name but also for Uther and the kingdom: When Merlin outlines his plot—for her to inform Gorlois that she is pregnant and then to flee with him to Cornwall without the king's leave—Igerne interrupts and, with acute political insight, declares that the angry king will follow and there will be war, when Uther "should be working and mending, not breaking and burning." She then declares that Uther cannot win, for even if he should be the victor in the field, he would lose the loyalty of the West. Merlin observes at this point that Igerne indeed will be queen; though she desires Uther as much as he desires her, she can still think—is cleverer than Uther, clearer of mind and stronger too. Even her final speech to Merlin—if he brings bloodshed to Cornwall through her or death to Gorlois, then she will spend the rest of her life praying to any gods there are that Merlin shall die betrayed by a woman—reveals her concern for her people. So Igerne is not duped into having sex with Uther transformed as Gorlois, and there is no need of Merlin's magical transformations; for it is Igerne who arranges for the admission to Tintagel of the king, merely disguised as the Duke of Cornwall.

This portrayal of Igerne as a strong woman is maintained throughout the trilogy. In *The Hollow Hills* Merlin, secretly meeting with the pregnant queen, finds her as direct as a man, with the same high pride and fire as before. Unlike Uther, who blames himself, Merlin, and even the child for Gorlois's death, Igerne pragmatically dismisses the matter with What's done is done, for her immediate concern is her child. Uther refuses to acknowledge the child as his heir, planning to send him to King Budec of Brittany to be reared. But the queen (unlike Malory's Igerne) wants Merlin to take the child, rear him as a king's son, and bring him back fully grown to take his place at Uther's side. She, of course, wants Merlin to reassure her of the prophecy concerning her child and of the possibility of her having more children. When Merlin takes leave of Igerne, he reveals that when the time comes, the child will be taken not from a regretful, weeping woman but from a queen who is content to let him go to his destiny. In *The Last Enchantment* Igerne is present for the funeral of Uther; and although mourning the loss of her beloved husband and terminally ill herself, she plays the role of a queen, richly furnishing her quarters as an appropriate setting for her to meet her son. Also, there is evidence of her ability to judge people and of her political astuteness: She is aware of the ambitions of Lot and of the political necessity of betrothing her daughter Morgan to him. Later she sees the political advantage of marrying her to Urbgen. Moreover, she truly understands, though she dislikes, Morgause, Uther's illegitimate daughter, who tried to teach black arts to Morgan. And she marries Arthur to her lady-in-waiting, the first Guenevere, who unfortunately dies in childbirth.

And so here is Mary Stewart's Igerne, the finest portrayal of this character in the entire body of Arthurian literature. Stewart's remaking of Igerne, as already noted, is partly due to her concept of Merlin as basically a human being with the gift of sight, but it is also a manifestation of her basic concept of women, for her trilogy on Merlin abounds with strong females. Note, for example, Niniane, Merlin's mother, who in Geoffrey's *Historia* is the nameless daughter of a king of Demetia, a nun at St. Peter's who informs Vortigern that Merlin's father was an incubus. Stewart's Niniane is not a lifeless character but a headstrong woman who refuses to tell her father the name of the man who fathered her child, even though she is beaten so badly that the women believe she will miscarry. Refusing to marry Gorlan, she cooly withstands her father's anger and later bravely confronts her brother Camlach, the new King of South Wales, because of her determination to go to St. Peter's as a nun, even suppressing her gift of sight because the church is opposed to soothsaying.

Moravik, Merlin's governess, is another strong-willed woman. When Merlin's grandfather orders the women to leave the room so that he and Camlach can talk to Niniane, Moravik stands her ground, puffed up with bravery like a partridge, and then leaves with a sniff. Though Merlin is merely a bastard, she obviously regards herself to be superior to the other servants; and when Olwen's baby and Camlach's son are born, she firmly establishes herself in the royal nursery as its official ruler. After Vortigern's sacking of Maridunum, Moravik returns to Brittany and marries Brand, a retired army man who runs her father's tavern. As Merlin tells Hoel, Brand will do as Moravik bids him: "I never knew a man who didn't except perhaps my grandfather." Later, when Merlin arrives at the inn with Ralf and Branwen, there is Moravik, fists on her hips, a creature of bulk and commanding voice, surrounded by an aura of authority. She quickly takes command of Branwen and the child and throughout this scene treats Merlin not as a man, the renowned son of King Ambrosius, but as the wayward small boy from her nursery.

Similar to Moravik is Maeve, another innkeeper and a dominant, earthy woman. When Merlin and Ralf, disguised as an eye doctor and his assistant, arrive at the inn, Maeve eyes them up and down, assessing their sexual potential, until she realizes who they are. Maeve assures Merlin, who is to stay at the inn until Uther leaves Tintagel and the pregnant queen sends for him, that they will be safe there and that they should have no fear of her husband Caw, who is loyal to Igerne and always does as his wife tells him except "some things he don't do near often enough for my liking." Later when Marcia, Ralf's grandmother, riding as straight as a man, arrives at the inn, Maeve chases everyone out of the room, including her husband, so that Marcia can speak privately with her grandson.

Even Marcia, Igerne's maid and confidante, is a strong woman. Because Uther regards Ralf's service to him as a betrayal of his master the Duke of Cornwall, Marcia is concerned about her grandson's safety and sends him to serve Merlin and later Igerne's child, for she believes Merlin's prophecy to Igerne about the crown and the sword standing in an altar. When Merlin leaves the pregnant queen, Marcia, aware of her mistress's plans, confronts Merlin and demands reassurances that he will take possession of the child and keep him safe. Obviously claiming the birth of Arthur as her province of concern, she resents any interference, complaining to Merlin that Gandar, an army surgeon, is to deliver the baby and worrying about wet nurses and related matters. Note that it is she who delivers the baby to Merlin.

Rejecting the traditional role of women as merely sex objects and mothers, Stewart admires strong-willed women who seek other positions in society to fulfill their lives.
—Harold J. Herman

Even Keri is a strong woman. The daughter of a prostitute, Keri is brought up at St. Peter's. It is she who pursues Merlin, waiting outside his mother's room to talk to him, pretending to have a toothache, placing his hand against her cheek to effect a cure. Later, fleeing from the nunnery, she goes to Bryn Myrdin, lures Merlin into her arms, and, when he is unable to complete the sex act because of his fear of losing the sight, demands payment for the torn gown. She is no common whore, for she knows that Merlin is a prince, and among her clients she can boast of Uther.

Obviously, with the exception of Marcia, an aged woman who nonetheless bears herself as straight as a young girl, none of these strong-willed women is a man's toy, content merely to satisfy a man's lust. Igerne, married young to old Gorlois, is fortunate to have a kind man as a husband. Yet when she meets Uther, she refrains from sex with Gorlois and physically desires Uther as much as he desires her, so that it is only with her consent that Uther beds her. Even Niniane, according to Merlin's vision of her last meeting with Ambrosius, initiates the sex act by declaring that they must not waste their last two hours together and by heading toward the cave. And one can be certain that Cerdic the groom would not have been permitted to sleep with Moravik without her consent, for Moravik, as does Maeve, dominates the men with whom she wishes to bed.

Indeed, Mary Stewart has little sympathy for women who are willing victims of sexual lust and childbearing. Such a one is Olwen, who, within a month after the death of Merlin's grandfather's second wife, has taken the dead queen's place in the royal bed. This young, dark, silent, "rather stupid" girl can sing like a bird and do fine needlework but little else. She is afraid of her husband, and although she secretly teaches Merlin to play the harp when his grandfather is not around, Merlin says that she was always kind to him in her "vague, placid way." Another is Branwen, Arthur's wet nurse, whose devotion to the baby, following the loss of her own, blinds her to all else. According to Merlin, she is the kind of woman whose life is in the bearing and rearing of children, and she is described as "weak and biddable to the point of stupidity." One should also note that she is of little interest to her companion Ralf, who later falls in love with and marries another girl.

This disdain for women whose lives are devoted solely to the bearing and rearing of children is evidenced elsewhere in the trilogy. In fact, Merlin declares to Ector that Igerne is not a woman for a family, any more than Uther is a family man. Their concern is for each other, and outside their bed they are king and queen. Also, one cannot imagine Morgause's being blind to everything except the bearing and rearing of her sons. And Niniane, who protects her son by remaining silent about his father's identity and later by lying to Vortigern, nonetheless turns him over to Moravik's care and pursues her own desire to become a nun at St. Peter's.

Rejecting the traditional role of women as merely sex objects and mothers, Stewart admires strong-willed women who seek other positions in society to fulfill their lives. Obviously, lower class women, like Moravik, Marcia, Maeve, and Keri, have limited opportunities, but Moravik is a governess, firmly established in the nursery as a figure of authority; Maeve is in charge of a clean, well-run inn; Marcia is not merely a maid but Igerne's closest servant confidante; and Keri rejects the convent to enter the oldest profession. Women of nobility have greater opportunities and are more ambitious. Granted, Niniane rejects the world to become a nun, but Igerne is determined to be queen, and she gets what she wants.

Morgause and Morgan are also ambitious women who end up as queens, but unlike Igerne, they and Rowena use their power for selfish, often destructive, purposes, and consequently there is no sympathy in Stewart's portrayal of these women. Let us first look at Rowena, Vortigern's Saxon queen. According to Geoffrey of Monmouth, Vortigern, upon first meeting Rowena, lusted after her, and Hengist gave his daughter in marriage to him in exchange for Kent. Hengist later demanded and received more concessions of land from his son-in-law, but eventually Vortigern turned against Hengist, Rowena remaining faithful to her husband. This account is absent from Mary Stewart's work, whose unsympathetic treatment of Rowena includes her large, milk-white breasts bulging above a tight blue bodice and her beringed fingers thick and ugly like a servant's. She apparently shares her husband's power, for she is seated beside the high king in a chair which, though smaller, is as elaborately carved as Vortigern's. She questions the head magician about Niniane's story, and it is she who orders Ambrosius's messenger's hands to be severed and tied in a bloody cloth to the belt at his waist. Clearly the Saxon witch deserves to be burned alive along with her traitorous husband.

Uther's illegitimate daughter, Morgause, fully aware that the youthful Arthur is her half-brother, lures him to her bed, so that she will conceive a child and thereby retain her position of power at court after the demise of Uther. When her plans are foiled by Merlin, she turns to Lot and marries him, usurping the place of Morgan, the daughter of Uther and Igerne. Realizing that Lot will know her child is not his, she substitutes a newborn bastard of Lot's for Modred, whom she sends away. She then taunts Lot into murdering his own child and ordering his soldiers to kill all the newborn babies in the town, on pretense of orders from Arthur. Morgause and Lot then go to bed laughing and sate their sexual appetites. At the wedding festivities for Morgan and Urbgen, Morgause drugs Merlin's wine—the cause of his insanity and his wandering for seven months in the woods with a pig for companion. Morgause is Stewart's prime villainess, Merlin's and Arthur's enemy, a powerful, evil woman. Indeed, Morgause's only good act is withholding from Modred who his real father is. Arthur has her confined in a religious house, perhaps for her own good but definitely for the good of others.

Unlike Morgause, Stewart's Morgan is not vividly portrayed, her actions being reported rather than directly presented. Morgan, betrothed in her youth to Lot, is happy to be freed of him when Morgause becomes his wife. Not to be outdone by Morgause, Morgan marries the King of Rheged, though, interestingly, it is not until Morgan shows an interest in Urbgen that Igerne and Arthur acknowledge the political advantages of the match. Whether Morgan desires or merely uses the love-struck Accolon is not clear in Stewart's work, but Morgan is obviously in control of him. In the belief that her brother will be killed, she has Accolon steal Arthur's sword Caliburn, substitute a copy, and then challenge Arthur to a fight. Morgan believes that because of her possession of Caliburn her husband will be crowned high king and she queen, but her plans are foiled. Arthur's fake sword breaks, but he kills Accolon, and Urbgen confines his wife in the same nunnery that houses Morgause.

The three queens are contrasted with Igerne, for Morgause and Morgan seek positions of power for purely selfish reasons, and they, along with Rowena, misuse their power for destructive purposes. In this respect they are like their counterparts, Vortigern and Lot, who are contrasted with Ambrosius, Merlin, Uther, and Arthur, who serve the higher goals of ridding Britain of the traitorous Vortigern; containing the Saxons; repelling the Picts, the Scots, and the Irish; establishing peace and stability in Britain and freedom and prosperity for her people. And it is because Igerne shares in and selflessly contributes to the fulfillment of these ideals that she is an admirable woman.

Another such is Nimuë. As Mary Stewart points out in her "Author's Note" to *The Last Enchantment,* Nimuë's be-

trayal of Merlin springs from the need to explain the death or disappearance of the all-powerful enchanter. According to Malory, Nimuë is one of the ladies of the lake brought to the court by King Pellinore. Doting on her, Merlin will let her have no rest. She makes Merlin "good chere" until she has learned from him all that she desires. Warning Arthur to take care of his sword and scabbard because they will be stolen by a woman he most trusts (Morgan), Merlin tells the king that his own days are numbered, that he will be buried alive, and that he cannot circumvent his fate. When Nimuë leaves the court, Merlin follows; and because Merlin would have transported her away privily by his subtle craft, she makes him swear not to use any enchantment on her. They travel abroad, Merlin showing her many wonders. Upon returning to Cornwall, she is tired of him and his desire to have her maidenhead, but she is afraid to act against him because he is the devil's son. Nonetheless, when Merlin shows her a marvelous rock under a great stone, she asks him to go under the stone—ostensibly to let her know of the marvels there but really to confine him forever "with her subtle working." Freed of Merlin, she marries Pelleas and serves Arthur, saving the king's life three times. Needless to say, this portrayal of Merlin as a dirty old man lusting after a young, beautiful girl is degrading.

Such a portrayal of Merlin was unsuitable to Stewart, and although Tennyson, whom Stewart mentions, is more sympathetic in his treatment of Merlin as a man of intellect overcome by sexual passion, the poet laureate's Vivian is such a vile harlot that Stewart rejected *Idylls of the King* and turned to another source, "Summer Country," in which Merlin, growing old, wants to pass on his magical powers to someone who can be Arthur's advisor after his death. For this he chooses as his pupil Nimuë. As Stewart says, this tale not only allows Merlin his dignity and a degree of common sense but also explains Nimuë's subsequent influence over Arthur, who would otherwise have hardly kept her near him or accepted her help against his enemies. Stewart prepares for Nimuë's (Niniane's) appearance in *The Last Enchantment* by having Merlin recognize in Ninian, Beltane the goldsmith's boy slave, the qualities of a prospective disciple who can carry on his work; Ninian, however, is drowned, much to the sage's grief. Ten years later, returning to Applegarth after Guenevere is rescued from Melwas's lodge, Merlin mistakes Nimuë of the Lake (Niniane), one of the ancillae of the goddess, for the boy Ninian and begs "him" to come along and be tutored. When Nimuë, disguised as a boy, finally arrives, Merlin accepts the youth as god-sent. Nimuë quickly learns, and even though Merlin realizes that his powers are being diminished as they are transferred to the "boy," he is content. He knows that because of the recurrent falling sickness his days are numbered and that Nimuë must be prepared to serve as Arthur's prophet. Moreover, Merlin is in love with him. Not until nine months after Nimuë came to live with Merlin does he learn from

Arthur that Nimuë is a girl. Although he has foreseen his end, he knows that love cannot be gainsaid and believes that if Nimuë has any part in his end, it will be merciful. So, toward the end of his life Merlin finds a new beginning in love, a love for both of them. He takes her on a trip to visit the places where he passed his life. At Galava, where he tells her of Macsen's treasures of the grail and spear, he has another spell of passing sickness and, pronounced dead, is entombed alive in his cave. He recovers, escapes with the aid of his servant Stilicho, and is reunited with Arthur and later with Nimuë, now established as the king's enchantress. The meeting between Merlin and Nimuë absolves Nimuë of any guilt in Merlin's "death" and entombment and shows that, while they truly cared for one another, they now realize that the love they once shared is gone. At the end of their meeting, Merlin kisses her, once with passion and once with love, and then lets her go—to Pelleas, her husband, who later tells Merlin that Nimuë belongs first to the king and then to her spouse.

Nimuë is, of course, another of Stewart's strong women. She has no fear of Merlin, and she is not in awe of the king. And she is ambitious. She is not content merely to be another servant of the goddess but is driven by the god to serve Merlin and to acquire his powers. Merlin willingly teaches her, for he loves her and she loves him. Granted, she exults in her newly acquired powers, and one may even say that she is ruthless: as Merlin is slipping into the deathlike sleep, she takes the last of his strength by forcing him to yield the last of his powers to her. But even this action is defensible, for Merlin has instructed her to learn all that he had to tell her, to build on every detail of his life, because after his death she must be Merlin. Moreover, Merlin's "death" is attributed not to Nimuë but to Morgause, for his malady is an aftereffect of the drug that Morgause put into Merlin's wine during Morgan's wedding. And unlike Morgause, who uses her power for selfish and destructive purposes, Nimuë, by taking Merlin's place, uses her power for the higher goal of faithfully serving Arthur and Britain.

But what of Guenevere? Because she is the wife of Arthur and the beloved of Lancelot (Bedwyr in Stewart's *The Last Enchantment*), one can best examine Guenevere in terms of the various writers' attitudes toward this love affair. At the one extreme is Chrétien de Troyes, who in accord with the dictates of Marie de Champagne, his patroness, glorifies Lancelot and Guenevere as ideal courtly lovers and portrays Arthur as an uncaring husband and an incompetent fool. At the other extreme is Malory, who, although he declares that Lancelot and Guenevere are one of the two greatest pairs of lovers in the world, nonetheless characterizes her in unflattering terms. As T. H. White remarks, Malory has no love for Guenevere. And neither does Tennyson, who places the blame for the moral decay of Arthur's court clearly on Guenevere.

Mary Stewart is more sympathetic. Melwas does abduct the queen, and Bedwyr, with Merlin's aid, does rescue her before Arthur's arrival; but it is Arthur, not Bedwyr, who defeats Melwas in singlehanded combat and is thus avenged. Arthur's dignity is restored, and the queen is blameless. That Guinevere was not blameless was Merlin's original deduction, but several days later he realizes his mistake when he learns from Arthur of Guenevere's true account of what happened. Pointing out that Merlin has declared several times that he knows nothing of women, Arthur, in his defense of Guenevere, offers a strong defense of women: "Does it never occur to you," Arthur remarks to Merlin, "that they lead lives of dependence so complete as to breed uncertainty and fear? That their lives are like those of slaves, or of animals that are used by creatures stronger than themselves, and sometimes cruel? Why, even royal ladies are bought and sold, and are bred to lead their lives far from their homes and their people, as the property of men unknown to them." Merlin recalls that he has seen women suffer from the whims of men, even those women who, like Morgause, were stronger and cleverer than most men. He also notes that, except for the lucky ones who find men they can rule or who love them, women suffer from men's use.

Arthur truly loves Guenevere, but unlike the majority of Stewart's female characters, Guenevere is not a strong woman. Although she is not afraid of her husband, she is afraid of the people around her, afraid of Melwas, and especially afraid of Merlin. Indeed, Arthur tells Merlin that at times he thinks Guenevere is afraid of life itself. When Merlin goes to Ynys Witrin to escort the queen back to Arthur, he realizes that Arthur has been right about her; for he sees that Guenevere, although a queen in composure and courage, is really a timid, lonely, frightened girl and that her youthful gaiety is merely the mask of an exile's eager search for friendship among the strangers of a court vastly different from the homely hearth in her father's kingdom. Because Arthur is frequently away from court on state affairs, she has no husband to stand between her and the flatterers, the power-hungry schemers, the enviers of her rank and beauty, and the young men ready to worship her. Moreover, being barren, she is tormented by those who tell her of the first Guenevere, who conceived the first time Arthur bedded her and for whom he grieved so bitterly. Consequently, Merlin—like the reader—pities the queen.

Guenevere and Bedwyr, of course, are lovers, but, again, Stewart is sympathetic. Because of their love for Arthur, both Guenevere and Bedwyr struggle against their desires. Moreover, Arthur is aware of this love affair long before Merlin informs him of it; he accepts it as fated and leaves Bedwyr with Guenevere when he travels north to Strathclyde in order "to let them have something, however little." Arthur explains that he is a king, not a cottager with nothing in his life except a wife and a bed to be jealous of, like a cock on a dunghill. His life is that of a king, whose principal concern is the safety and well-being of his people. Guenevere is queen, but because she is childless, her life is less than a woman's. Because of his duties he cannot be there at court with her, and, realizing that Guenevere is a young woman who needs companionship and love, he is thankful that of all the men she could have taken as a lover she chose Bedwyr. He refuses to say anything; to do so would be to no avail, for, as Merlin has noted, love cannot be gainsaid. And, most important, Arthur does not wish to destroy the trust and friendship that he and Bedwyr share. Merlin is overwhelmed by Arthur's wisdom, and thus Stewart has achieved two purposes: to increase Arthur's stature and to defend the queen in one of the most sympathetic treatments of Guenevere in Arthurian literature.

In conclusion, even in the case of Guenevere, a weak woman, Mary Stewart has both Merlin and Arthur defend and forgive her. Such a treatment of Guenevere is consistent with Stewart's overall theme of strong, dominant women who reject traditional feminine roles.

Jeanie Watson (essay date Spring 1987)

SOURCE: "Mary Stewart's Merlin: Word of Power," *Arthurian Interpretations,* Vol. 1, No. 2, Spring, 1987, pp. 70-83.

[*In the following essay, Watson examines the ways in which Merlin symbolizes the "word of power" in that he is a visionary who is privy to the knowledge and wisdom of the gods.*]

The Merlin of Mary Stewart's trilogy—*The Crystal Cave, The Hollow Hills,* and *The Last Enchantment*—is a man of many roles: prophet, prince, enchanter, king-maker, teacher, engineer, physician, poet, and singer. But in all of these, he is first and foremost a man of power. Merlin's power is the power of knowledge, knowledge revealed progressively through active preparation and wise waiting. "Power," says Merlin, "is doing and speaking with knowledge; it is bidding without thought, and knowing that one will be obeyed". This kind of knowledge and power is of the spirit, coming from the god, as the god wills, and resulting in the word of prophecy. In addition to embodying this word of power, Merlin also represents a kind of "bidding without thought" that comes from the confidence of acquired knowledge.

Merlin's word of power in the historical and naturalistic realm and the word of power that comes from the god—the nature of the word, its source, limitation, consequences, and progressive revelation—are intrinsic themes in Stewart's

books. Each of the progressions toward truth in the trilogy emphasizes a general movement from partiality to wholeness: the unity of one God and one King, the truth of lineage, and the androgynous wholeness of the word of power.

> **Each of the progressions toward truth in the trilogy emphasizes a general movement from partiality to wholeness: the unity of one God and one King, the truth of lineage, and the androgynous wholeness of the word of power.**
> —*Jeanie Watson*

Mary Stewart's trilogy is historical fiction, set, not in the usual, romantic Middle Ages of Malory, but in the historically more accurate Dark Ages of fifth-century Celtic Britain. Characters, place names, and events in the story carefully accord with actual historical facts. Similarly, Stewart's Merlin is not a mysterious magician inhabiting the misty peripheries of action; he is, instead, in this story, a real man, who narrates his own role in the Matter of Britain as he sees the events unfold. Because he is a man, Merlin experiences ordinary human emotions. For instance, as a child, he suffers the taunts and humiliation aimed at a bastard child, and he learns to live by his wits. As an old man, he learns about love in his relationships with Arthur and Nimuë. And Merlin is capable of being mistaken, especially in his interpretations of the actions of women. Morgause's intentions toward Arthur, for example, escape him entirely until it is too late:

> I have said men with god's sight are often human-blind: when I exchanged my manhood for power it seemed I had made myself blind to the ways of women. If I had been a simple man instead of a wizard I would have seen the way eye answered eye back there at the hospital, have recognized Arthur's silence later, and known the woman's long assessing look for what it was.

In the course of the trilogy, Merlin tells us his personal history, from the night Ambrosius and Niniane conceive him in the cave at Bryn Myrddin to his burial alive in the same cave by Nimuë.

Because Stewart's Merlin is a man very much grounded in the natural world, much of his knowledge is knowledge of the physical world, a knowledge that makes him the best of engineers and physicians. Although the range and depth of Merlin's knowledge in these areas are so far beyond that of most people that his accomplishments seem supernatural, there are, in fact—as Merlin is always at pains to point out—perfectly natural explanations for these feats of power. The primary example of such a feat is the raising of the Hanging Stones of the Giant's Dance outside Amsbury. Ambrosius tells Merlin he wants "the chaos of giant stones in a lonely place where the sun and the winds strike" to become a monument to the "making of one kingdom under one King." For this it is necessary that the stones be raised. Ambrosius tells Merlin:

> "I have talked of this to Tremorinus. He says that no power of man could raise those stones."
>
> I smiled. "So you sent for me to raise them for you?"
>
> "You know they say it was not men who raised them, but magic."
>
> "Then," I said, "no doubt they will say the same again."
>
> His eyes narrowed. "You are telling me you can do it?"
>
> "Why not?"
>
> He was silent, merely waiting. It was a measure of his faith in me that he did not smile.
>
> I said: "Oh, I've heard all the tales they tell, the same tales they told in Less Britain of the standing stones. But the stones were put there by men, sir. And what men put there once, men can put there again."
>
> "Then if I don't possess a magician, at least I possess a competent engineer."
>
> "That's it."

And it is the engineer who goes to work to raise the stones and make the Dance. Using his knowledge of engineering, the guidance of the songs learned from the blind singer of Kerrec, and the strength of two hundred men, Merlin raises the stones and fits them together:

> I heard it said, long afterwards, that I moved the stones of the Dance with magic and with music. I suppose you might say that both are true. I have thought, since, that this must have been how the story started that Phoebus Apollo built with music the walls of Troy. But the magic and the music that moved the Giant's Dance, I shared with the blinder singer of Kerrec.

Mathematics and music work the magic that once more links the circle of the Giant's Dance, symbol of the unity and harmony of the kingdom.

Much earlier, when he is still a boy living as a bastard at his grandfather's court, Merlin has the power that comes from listening and observing. His first "cave" of knowledge is in the tunnels of the unused underground heating system, a "secret labyrinth" which the six-year-old finds "a curiously strong pleasure in exploring", mostly because it provides him a place "to be alone in the secret dark". But it also provides him a hiding place in which to learn information that gives him power over events that affect his life. At this early age, Merlin learns the value of letting others believe his knowledge comes from magic, even though there is a reasonable, natural explanation:

> One night, creeping beneath his bed chamber on the way to my "cave," I chanced to hear [Dinias] and his pack-follower Brys laughing over a foray of that afternoon when the pair of them had followed Camlach's friend Alun to his tryst with one of the servant-girls, and stayed hidden, watching and listening to the sweet end. When Dinias waylaid me next morning I stood my ground and—quoting a sentence or so—asked if he had seen Alun yet that day. He stared, went red and then white (for Alun had a hard hand and a temper to match it) and then sidled away, making the sign behind his back. If he liked to think it was magic rather than simple blackmail, I let him. After that if the High King himself had ridden in claiming parentage for me, none of the children would have believed him. They left me alone.

Later, the twelve-year-old Merlin is able to escape to Ambrosius because he tells Ambrosius's men, "Oh, yes, there's a lot I could tell you". He offers Ambrosius "valuable information and five languages" and, eventually, dreams and prophecies. When Merlin is seventeen, Vortigern, the High King opposed to Ambrosius, is trying to build fortifications against Ambrosius at King's Fort; however, the foundations keep collapsing. Vortigern's soothsayers tell him that only the sacrificial blood of one who is no man's son will hold the foundation. Hearing the story of Merlin's demon ancestry, Vortigern intends to sacrifice Merlin. However, from his own exploration of the caves at King's Fort when he was a boy, Merlin knows the answer to the problem:

> If I had no power to use, I had knowledge. I cast my mind back to the day at King's Fort, and to the flooded mine in the core of the crag, to which the dream led me. I would certainly be able to tell them why their foundations would not stand. It was an engineer's answer, not a magician's. But, I thought, meeting the oyster eyes of Maugan as he dry-

washed those long dirty hands before him, if it was a magician's answer they wanted, they should have it.

King Vortigern, following Merlin's bidding to the cave within the hill, hears the engineer's answer. But as Merlin and the king and the king's people stand at the edge of the pool, the cave becomes like Galapas's crystal cave "come alive and moving and turning . . . like the starred globe of midnight whirling and flashing" as Merlin speaks the word of power that comes from the god:

> I stopped. The light had changed. Nobody had moved, and the air was still, but the torchlight wavered as men's hands shook. I could no longer see the King: the flames ran between us. Shadows fled across the streams and staircases of fire, and the cave was full of eyes and wings and hammering hoofs and the scarlet rush of a great dragon stooping on his prey. . . .

> A voice was shouting, high and monotonous, gasping. I could not get my breath. Pain broke through me, spreading from groin and belly like blood bursting from a wound. I could see nothing. I felt my hands knotting and stretching. My head hurt, and the rock was hard and streaming wet under my cheekbone. I had fainted, and they had seized me as I lay and were killing me: this way my blood seeping from me to spread into the pool and shore up the foundations of their rotten tower. I choked on breath like bile. My hands tore in pain at the rock, and my eyes were open, but all I could see was the whirl of banners and wings and wolves' eyes and sick mouths gaping, and the tail of a comet like a brand, and stars shooting through a rain of blood.

> Pain went through me again, a hot knife into the bowels. I screamed, and suddenly my hands were free. I threw them up between me and the flashing visions and I heard my own voice calling, but could not tell what I called. In front of me the visions whirled, fractured, broke open in intolerable light, then shut again into darkness and silence.

What Merlin prophesies is the victory of Ambrosius and the coming of Arthur. Several things about the power are made clear in this incident. First, there is mystery in power. The god comes when and as it will, in its own time and its own way. Second, there is a price to be paid for the word of power; pain and suffering are necessary accompaniments. Third, Merlin is the *word* of power, the medium, the vehicle for the god. Often, he does not know the meaning of what he has said at the time of speaking, and the revelation must be a gradual unfolding. Finally, when Merlin becomes the word of power, what he speaks is truth. As he says to Cadal after the Vortigern prophecy:

> There will be something there. Don't ask me what, I don't know, but if I said so. . . . It's true, you know. The things I see this way are true. . . I'm not on my own. Remember that; and if you can't trust me, trust what is in me. I have learned too. I've learned that the god comes when he will, and how he will, rending your flesh to get into you, and when he has done, tearing himself free as violently as he came. Afterwards—now—one feels light and hollow and like an angel flying. . . No, they can do nothing to me, Cadal. Don't be afraid. I have the power.

Throughout the three books, the presence of the god is imaged as the wind. After Merlin enters the crystal cave of vision for the first time, he tells Galapas, "I feel all right, only a headache, but—empty, like a shell with the snail out of it. No, like reed with the pith pulled out." "A whistle for the winds. Yes", responds Galapas. And as Merlin leaves to go home, he says, "I'm still in the god's path. I can feel the wind blowing". The blowing wind of the natural world is often the foreshadowing of the word of power. As in one of the scenes with Vortigern, there will be a gust of wind and then another gust until, in this case, Vortigern's banner streams out "like a sail holding the full weight of the wind" and then tears free to sink into a pool of water at the king's feet. The wind dies, and Merlin says, "Can any doubt the god has spoken?". Another time, planning for Arthur's safe-keeping after his birth, Merlin says, "Something was moving; there was a kind of breathing brightness in the air, the wind of God brushing by, invisible in sunlight. Even for men who cannot see or hear them, the gods are still there, and I was not less than a man." The wind is blowing the night Arthur is born, and Merlin says to Ralf that in Arthur's crowning, "We whistled up a strong wind".

There is, in addition, a cluster of images that denote the presence of God. Like the "breathing brightness" of the wind of God, references to wind are often accompanied by references to fire and to music, particularly harp music. It is this cluster of images that authenticates Arthur's role when Merlin takes Arthur to Ector. "And this is the one," says Merlin to Ector.

> "Your stars tell you this?"

> "It has been written there, certainly, and who writes among the stars but God?"

> "What's that? That sound?"

> "Only the wind in the bowstrings."

"I thought it was a harp sounding. Strange. What is it, boy? Why do you look so?"

"Nothing." He looked at me doubtfully for a moment longer, then grunted and fell silent, and behind us the long humming stretched out, a cold music, something from the air itself. I remembered how, as a child, I had lain watching the stars and listening for the music which (I had been told) they made as they moved. This must, I thought, be how it sounded.

It is the breath and light of God that made the harmony of the world.

And it is this harmony for which Merlin is the hollow reed, the medium for the Word. As Merlin speaks the word of power from the god, he becomes the Word. Speaking to Cadal, Merlin is explicit: "I am a spirit, a word, a thing of air and darkness, and I can no more help what I am doing than a reed can help the wind of God blowing through it." In *The Last Enchantment,* Merlin explains to Nimuë that when one becomes a word of power, one is "merely a seer, an eye and a voice for a most tyrannous god." The god is tyrannous; it comes and goes as it will. Merlin says, "I would not importune God for the smallest breath of the great wind. If he came to me, he came. It was for him to choose the time, and for me to go with it." God often chooses the least expected time, and where Merlin goes in vision is into the Otherworld of spirit. When Guinevere disappears with Melwas, Merlin looks into the fire and finds himself suddenly carried away: "I did not hear him go. I was already far from the firelit room, borne on the cool and blazing river that dropped me, light as a leaf loosened by the wind, in the darkness at the gates of the Otherworld." In the Otherworld, Merlin finds himself in caves that go "on and on for ever," dreaming of the "legendary hall of Llud-Nautha, King of the Otherworld". Then this dream dissolves, and Merlin sees Guinevere where Melwas has her hidden away.

Caves of one sort or another abound in the trilogy. Merlin is conceived in the cave at Bryn Myrddin; he is buried alive in the same cave; and it is there that he first visits Galapas and later makes his home for much of his life. Within that cave is a smaller crystal cave, the crystal cave of vision. The cave represents the mind, the power of thought and sight and insight. The crystals of the cave throw light into darkness and bring the god-vision. Truth is often hidden, underground, invisible, and there is some form of cave present in almost every instance of vision in the trilogy. For example, there are the "caves" of the hypocaust and the mining cavern at King's Fort—which Merlin sees once in vision and twice in actuality. As the boy Merlin wakes outside Ambrosius's military camp to see Mithras (who was born in a cave) and the bull, he first sees that "the brilliant arch of stars about [him]

was like a curved roof of the cave with the light flashing off the crystals". Again, in a temple of Mithras which is below ground, cave-like, Merlin finds Macsen's sword and the grail. As Merlin replaces the grail, the plaster from the apse tumbles down and buries it, and the wall shows "blank, like the wall of a cave". The sword he takes and hides in a deep cavern on Caer Bannog, the Castle in the Mountains "said to be haunted by Bilis the dwarf king of the Otherworld. It was reputed to appear and disappear at will, sometimes floating invisible, as if made of glass". The place is called the "isle of glass," and the cavern is another crystal cave:

> The place was a temple, pillared in pale marble and floored with glass. Even I, who was here by right, and hedged with power, felt my scalp tingle. *By land and water shall it go home, and lie hidden in the floating stone until by fire it shall be raised again.* So had the Old Ones said, and they would have recognized this place as I did; as the dead fisherman did who came back from the Otherworld raving of the halls of the dark King. Here, in Bilis' antechamber, the sword would be safe till the youth came who had the right to life it.

The Old Ones, "keeping faith in their cold caves with the past and the future", live in the hollow hills of faery, speak the Old Tongue, and are the guardians of the knowledge of the sword. They live in the woods, so much a part of nature that they come to look like the trees around them. Almost entirely at one with the natural world, they consider themselves descended from the Gods. They, like Merlin, eat the offerings people leave for the gods, and, again like Merlin, they know that knowledge is power. Their leader says, "There are things we must know. Knowledge is the only power we have". When Merlin, gone crazy from Morgause's poison, wanders the woods, the Old Ones look after him. Merlin speaks the Old Tongue, as does Arthur. The hollow hills in which the Old Ones live are the gates to the Otherworld, and "it is not possible to keep secrets from the Old Ones". The Otherworld is the world of dream, myth, and spirit. "Magic," explains Merlin, "is the door through which mortal man may sometimes step, to find the gates in the hollow hills, and let himself through into the halls of that other world".

At its deepest level, the suffering that comes from knowledge is not physical, but spiritual. Merlin learns this as a child. . . .
                                        —*Jeanie Watson*

One does not enter the halls of the Otherworld with impunity; there is a price to be paid: "There is no power without knowledge, and no knowledge without suffering". "Moments of vision have always to be paid for, first with the pain of the vision itself"—what Merlin calls "Nails of pain" —then "afterwards in the long trance of exhausted sleep". Those who have had to do with the Gods know that when those Gods make promises they hide them in light, and a smile on a God's lips is not always a sign that you may take his favor for granted. Men have a duty to make sure. The Gods like the taste of salt; the sweat of human effort is the savour of their sacrifices. Merlin knows he is "not immune from the God's fire" , and he likens the physical "whirling pain" to the last pains of childbirth, the pain necessary to complete creation: "Prophecy . . . is like being struck through the entrails by that whip of God that we call lightning. But even as my flesh winced from it I welcomed it as a woman welcomes the final pang of childbirth". The vision and the suffering are one. After Arthur has taken the sword of Macsen from the stone, Merlin remembers "How my body ached, and how at length, when I knelt again, my sight blurred and darkened as if still blind with vision, or with tears.

At its deepest level, the suffering that comes from knowledge is not physical, but spiritual. Merlin learns this as a child, when, coming to Merlin in the garden, his uncle offers him, in seeming innocence, a piece of fruit, an Edenic apricot filled with poison. Camlach urges Merlin to eat it, but Merlin says, "I don't want it. It's black inside." Camlach hurls the apricot against the wall where

> . . . it burst in a golden splash of flesh against the brick. . . . I stood where I was, watching the juice of the apricot trickle down the hot wall. A wasp alighted on it, crawled stickily, then suddenly fell, buzzing on its back to the ground. Its body jackknifed, the buzz rose to a whine as it struggled, then it lay still. I hardly saw it, because something had swelled in my throat till I thought I would choke, and the golden evening swam, brilliant, into tears. This was the first time in my life that I remember weeping.

The knowledge that there is evil which would betray innocence brings suffering. The major betrayal of innocence in the story, with its attendant and inevitable suffering, is, of course, Morgause's seduction of the innocent Arthur. The rosegold Morgause carries the poison:

> This morning she wore red, the color of cherries, and over the shoulders of the gown her hair looked rosy fair, larch buds in spring, the color of apricots. Her scent was heavy and sweet, apricots and honeysuckle mixed. . . . But death was here, in a form and with a smell I did not know. A smell like treachery, something remembered dimly from my childhood, when my uncle planned to betray his father's kingdom, and to murder me.

Modred is the seed of suffering engendered by the betrayal of innocence. Morgause is even able to use her treachery on Merlin, poisoning his wine at Morgan's wedding feast:

> I must have drunk far more than I was accustomed to, because I well remember how the torchlight beat and swelled, bright and dark alternately, while talk and laughter surged and broke in gusts and with it the woman's scent, a thick sweetness like honeysuckle, catching and trapping the sense as a lime twig holds a bee. The fumes of the wine rose through it. A gold jug tilted, and my goblet brimmed again. Someone said, smiling "Drink, my lord." There was a taste of apricots in my mouth, sweet and sharp; the skin had a texture like the fur of a bee, or a wasp dying in sunlight on a garden wall. . . . And all the while eyes watching me, in excitement and wary hope, then in contempt, and in triumph.

The result is that Merlin spends seven months "stark crazy," wandering in the woods, his words garbled. Poisoned magic brings madness, not vision.

No one is exempt from suffering, nor is it clear what the price will be. "It is God who keeps the price secret, Uther, not I," Merlin tells Uther. It is God who exacts the price, and he does so for his own purposes. Men are merely vehicles through whom the purpose is accomplished. "The gods sit over the board, but it is men who move under their hands for the mating and the kill". As Merlin explains to Moravick: "'I don't know if I can make you understand, Moravick: Visions and prophecies, gods and stars and voices speaking in the night . . . things seen cloudy in the flames and in the stars, but real as pain in the blood, and piercing the brain like ice. But now . . .' I paused again. '. . .Now it is no longer a god's voice or a vision, it is a small human child with lusty lungs, a baby like any other baby, who cries and sucks milk, and soaks his swaddling clothes. One's visions do not take account of this'". Merlin speaks of himself as one "who had been used by the driving god for thirty years" for the god's own purposes. What those purposes are is usually revealed only gradually.

The progressive revelation of Truth, or the searching after final truth, can be seen in a number of ways throughout the course of the novels. In each of the progressions, there is a movement from division to unification, from partiality to wholeness. Merlin's personal search is for the source of his power. He says his power comes from the god, but there are many religions and many gods in Merlin's world: "And dreamed again . . . a dream half-waking, broken and uneasy, of the small gods of small places; gods of hills and woods and streams and crossways; the gods who still haunt their broken shrines, waiting in the dust beyond the lights of the busy Christian churches, and the dogged rituals of the greater gods of Rome". Mithras, the druids, Roman gods, the Christian God—Merlin says, "I believe in giving due honour to whatever god confronts you. . . . That's common sense in these days, as well as courtesy. Sometimes I think the gods themselves have not yet got it clear". Merlin explains to Ambrosius: "My lord, when you are looking for . . . what I am looking for, you have to look in strange places. Men can never look at the sun, except downwards, at his reflection in things of earth. If he is reflected in a dirty puddle, he is still the sun. There is nowhere I will not look, to find him"). One of the first gods Merlin traffics with is Mithras, Mithras, who, as Ambrosius says, is another face of Christ: "'For,' said my father to me afterwards when we were alone, 'as you will find, all gods who are born of the light are brothers, and in this land, if Mithras who gives us victory is to bear the face of Christ, why, then, we worship Christ"). Mithras is:

> the soldier's god, the Word, the Light, the Good Shepherd, the mediator between the one God and man. I had seen Mithras, who had come out of Asia a thousand years ago. He had been born, Ambrosius told me, in a cave at mid-winter, while shepherds watched and a star shone; he was born of earth and light, and sprang from the rock with a torch in his left hand and a knife in his right. He killed the bull to bring life and fertility to the earth with its shed blood, and then, after his last meal of bread and wine, he was called up to heaven. He was the god of strength and gentleness, of courage and self-restraint.

But Merlin is neither a worshipper of Mithras nor a Christian. Galapas tells Merlin in their first meeting: "[Myrddin] lends me his spring, and his hollow hill, and his heaven of woven light, and in return I give him his due. It does not do to neglect the gods of a place, whoever they may be. In the end, they are all one"). And this is also Merlin's belief: "I think there is only one. Oh, there are gods everywhere, in the hollow hills, in the wind and the sea, in the very grass we walk on and the air we breathe, and in the blood stained shadows where men like Belasius wait from them. But I believe there must be one who is God Himself, like the great sea, and all the rest of us, small gods and men and all, like rivers, we all come to Him in the end"). Throughout the story, Merlin respects each of the individual gods, but the word of power which he speaks in from the one God, the god who is the light: "I only know that God is the source of all the light which has lit the world, and that his purpose runs through the world and past each one of us like a great river, and we cannot check or turn it, but can only drink from it while living, and commit our bodies to it when we die".

Merlin's word of power and his movement toward one God parallels the word of power spoken by a king. The Matter of Britain is a movement from many kings to one King, from divided kingdoms to one, unified Kingdom within which there can be harmony. The idea of one country and one king is first instilled in Merlin by Galapas: "He spoke as if it were all one country, though I could have told him the names of the kings of a dozen places that he mentioned. I only remember this because of what came after". It is Merlin's role to establish Arthur as the one King, and just as there is one God of light and truth, so, prophesies Merlin at Ambrosius's burial, there will be in Britain one King:

> And while the King lies there under the stone the Kingdom shall not fall. For as long and longer than it had stood before, the Dance shall stand again, with the light striking it from the living heaven. And I shall bring back the great stone to lay upon the grave-place, and this shall be the heart of Britain, and from this time on all the kings shall be one King and all the gods one God. And you shall live again in Britain, and for ever, for we will make between us a King whose name will stand as long as the Dance stands, and who will be more than a symbol; he will be a shield and a living sword.

When this has been accomplished, God's purpose for Merlin is also accomplished, and Merlin says, "The god, who was God, has indeed dismissed his servant, and was letting him go in peace".

There are two other progressions in the novels that emphasize the general movement from partiality to wholeness. The first has to do with the issue of lineage, and the second involves the role of Nimuë. Just as there is a succession of gods, each heirs of the former, and just as one king succeeds another in search for one King, so do individual characters search for the truth of their origins. There are a good number of bastard children in the novels: Merlin, Morgause, Modred, and—for much of his life—Arthur. The search for legitimacy is an overriding one for Merlin and for Arthur, and the two cases have many parallels. Neither is conceived in wedlock, but each is finally proclaimed the legitimate heir by a father who is king. They are enough alike that Arthur for a time believes that Merlin is his father. And Merlin is Arthur's father in spirit and in love, a fact which Arthur never forgets. He calls Merlin "the man who was more to me than my own father" ; and when Merlin tells Arthur the truth about his parentage and of his own role in bringing Arthur to the throne, Arthur responds: "'You,' he said quietly, 'you, from the very beginning. I wasn't so far wrong after all, was I? I'm as much yours as the King's—more; and Ector's too'". Cador says to Merlin of Arthur: "Did you know he was more like you than ever like the King?". There are many kinds of fathers. Galapas and Ambrosius are father to Merlin; Merlin and Ector and Ralf and Uther are father to Arthur; and Merlin is father to Niniane.

Ninian, as Niniane is called when Merlin thinks she is a boy, or Nimuë, once she becomes the King's enchantress, is first the "son" Merlin could have had in no other way and then the only lover he could ever have had. And, finally, Nimuë becomes the heir of Merlin's word of power. That Merlin comes to see her as that heir denotes a movement from partial to whole truth on his part. Merlin begins by making a clear distinction between the magic of women and his own power. His mother, Niniane, has the Sight and something of power, but she loses it. Merlin explains to Ambrosius that he gets his Sight from his mother, "but it is different. She saw only women's things, to do with love. Then she began to fear the power, and let it be". When Merlin sees his mother after a five year absence, he says: "I found her much changed. She was pale and quiet, and had put on weight, and with it a kind of heaviness of the spirit that she had not had before. It was only after a day or two, jogging north with the escort through the hill, that it suddenly came to me what this was; she had lost what she had had of power. Whether time had taken this, or illness, or whether she had abnegated it for the power of the Christian symbol that she wore on her breast, I had no means of guessing. But it had gone". Morgause also has something of the power, but when she asks Merlin to teach her his arts, he refuses:

> I've told you it isn't possible. You will have to take my word for that. You are too young. I'm sorry, child. I think that for power like mine you will always be too young. I doubt if any woman could go where I go and see what I see. It is not as easy art. The god I serve is a hard master. . . . He only lends his power for his own ends. When they are achieved, who knows? If he wants you, he will take you, but don't walk into the flames, child. Content yourself with such magic as young maids use.

While it is true that if Morgause knows nothing of the god and wants to use the power for her own ends rather than being used by the god, she could never speak the word of power, it is also true that at this point, and for most of his life, Merlin doubts that any woman could go where he goes and see what he sees. He believes in women's magic—distinct from his own power—and in women's power over men because of their ability to incite physical desire. He himself, "knowing what a girl could do to rob a man of power", avoids relationships with women: "I had known, that day at twenty when I fled from the girl's angry and derisive laughter, that for me there had been a cold choice between manhood and power, and I had chosen power". Merlin is eager to teach Niniane because he believes her at first to be the drowned Ninian returned:

The boy Ninian—so young and quiet, and with a grace in look and motion that gave lie to the ugly slave-burn on his arm—he had had about him the mark of coming death. This, once seeing, any man might have wept for, but I was weeping, too, for myself; for Merlin the enchanter, who saw and could do nothing; who walked his own lonely heights where it seemed that none would ever come near to him. In the boy's still face and listening eyes, that night on the moor when the birds had called, I had caught a glimpse of what might have been. For the first time, since those days long ago when I had sat at Galapas' feet to learn the arts of magic, I had seen someone who might have learned worthily from me. Not as others had wanted to learn, for power or excitement, or for the prosecution of some enmity or private greed; but because he had seen, darkly with a child's eyes, how the gods move with the winds and speak with the sea and sleep in the gentle herbs; and how God himself is the sum of all that is on the face of the lovely earth.

Merlin is lonely; the very power which is the force of his life also isolates him, separates him from others. What Nimuë brings him is wholeness. She allows him to love, to be a lover, and to share his knowledge and power. They become one in body and in spirit: "At last I was free to give, along with all the rest of the power and effort and glory, the manhood that until now had been the god's alone. The abdication I had feared, and feared to grudge, would not be a loss, but rather a new joy gained". The similarities between Merlin and Nimuë become apparent as Arthur questions Nimuë about her desire to study magic and Nimuë says of that desire, with "a look straight at [Arthur], equal to equal. 'You must have known it. I was still unborn, hammering at the egg, to get out into the air'". The "burning to be free," the desire to be bound by no man, is something both Arthur and Merlin understand.

What Merlin learns is that freedom is finally not a matter of isolation and separation but a matter of unification and wholeness. Merlin and Nimuë have chosen to live outside the traditional masculine and feminine roles which they view as confining to their spirits. Thus, both have become, not sexless, but androgynous. The two remain individuals, yet the two become one:

> So, toward the end of my life, I found a new beginning. A beginning it was in love, for both of us. . . . Between myself and Nimuë was a bond stronger than any between the best-matched pair in the flower of their age and strength. We were the same person. We were part of each other as are night and daylight, dark and dawn, sun and shadow. When we lay together we lay at the edge of life

where opposites fuse and make new entities, not of the flesh, but of the spirit, the issue as much of the ceaseless traffic of mind with mind, as of the body's pleasure.

We did not marry. Looking back now, I doubt if either of us even thought of cementing the relationship in this way; it was not clear what rites we could have used, what faster bond we could have hoped for. With the passing of the days and nights of that sweet summer, we found ourselves closer and yet more close, as if cast in a common mould: we would wake in the morning and know we had shared the same dream; meet at evening and each know what the other had learned and done that day. And all the time, as I believed, each of us harboured our own private and growing joy: I to watch her trying the wings of power like a strong young bird feeling for the first time the mastery of air; she to receive this waxing strength, and to know, with love but without pity, that at the same time the power was leaving me.

And so, Merlin gives Nimuë the sum of his life on which to build her own. She will inherit the word of power which is Merlin's word and the word of the god. The quest for the sword and the grail, the quest for the truth of one Kingdom and the quest for the one God are all one in the end: "It is time the gods became one god, and there in the grail is the oneness for which men will seek, and die, and dying, live". Successful in his own quest, Merlin can echo the words of Christ's fulfillment: "I said to the ghosts, to the voices, to the empty moonlight: 'It was time. Let me go in peace.' Then, commending myself and my spirit to God who all these years had held me in his hand, I composed myself for sleep".

In the course of the novels . . . Merlin, who is the word of power, becomes so closely associated with the Word that is God that he also becomes that Word and, thus, is a maker, a creator of the story of history.
—*Jeanie Watson*

There is a final thing to be said about Merlin as word of power. Merlin explains that he is "a spirit, a word", a voice through which the god can speak. In the course of the novels, however, Merlin, who is the word of power, becomes so closely associated with the Word that is God that he also becomes that Word and, thus, is a maker, a creator of the story of history. The identification of Merlin with divinity begins with his name and comes for the first time in the revelation scene between Merlin and Ambrosius:

"Emrys, she called you. Child of the light. Of the immortals. Divine. You knew that's what it meant?"

"Yes."

"Didn't you know it was the same as mine?"

"My name?" I asked, stupidly.

He nodded. "Emrys. . . . Ambrosius; it's the same word. Merlinus Ambrosius—she called you after me."

I stared at him. "I—yes, of course. It never occurred to me." I laughed.

"Why do you laugh?"

"Because of our names. Ambrosius, prince of light. . . . She told everyone that my father was the prince of darkness. I've even heard a song about it. We make songs of everything, in Wales."

Merlin Emrys, "Child of the light. Of the immortals. Divine," has from the beginning been the occasion of song and legend. Merlin lives in a cave of legend, Bryn Myrddin, a hollow "hill sacred to the sky-god Myrddin, he of the light and the wild air", a hill the people associate with Merlin "rather than with the god, calling it Merlin's Hill"), a hill Merlin is willing to share with the god, becoming "their god made flesh" and taking the people's offering to the god as his own:

> I know that the wine and bread, like the thrown coins, had been left as much as an offering to the god as to me; in the minds of the simple folk I had already become part of the legend of the hill, their god made flesh who came and went as quietly as the air, and brought with him the gifts of healing.

Merlin, like Myrddin, is associated with the light and the wind. Merlin once says of a dog that barks at him that the dog is wise since "he's one who can see the wind". And, again, Merlin observes: "So the year went by, and the lovely month came, September, my birth-month, the wind's month, the month of the raven, and of Myrddin himself, that wayfarer between heaven and earth". As the word and the Word, Merlin can say to Ninian, "'You will be welcome.' I added, softly, as much to myself as to him: 'By God himself, you will be welcome'". Because he is the Word of power, Merlin can say to Morgause—when she curses him, saying, "In the end you will only be a shadow and a name"—"I am nothing, yes; I am air and darkness, a word, a promise. I watch in the crystal and I wait in the hollow hills. But out there in the light I have a young king and a bright sword to do my work for me". As Word of power, Merlin uses Arthur to build the one Kingdom, a kingdom whose legend will last forever.

A legend is itself a word of power, a story which has the power to capture the imagination of the listener. Mary Stewart's Merlin is a man very much aware of his own legend in the making and of his part in creating and fostering that legend. Throughout the trilogy, Merlin carefully explains the "supernatural" events in which he participates. His explanations revise and reinterpret the stories of Mary Stewart's sources, while becoming in that very process the source of his own legend. Who could be a more authoritative narrator of the events than Merlin himself? Because he is seer, he knows how the stories will be passed down in the future, but because he is Merlin, word of power, he is the word of truth, telling us the truth of the legend—a legend which, over time, assumes its own truth and power. The stories of Stewart's sources—Merlin's demon origins, the red and white dragons beneath Vortigern's tower, the magical transformation of Uther into the shape of Gorlois, the story of the hanging Stones of the Giant's Dance, the sword in the stone, Nimuë's betrayal and Merlin's death-in-life—all have, as Merlin testifies, perfectly natural and reasonable explanations based on boyhood escapades, mathematics, the superstitious credulity of the general populace, and the emotion of human love. At the same time, there is still mystery in each of these "truths," so that the explanation is not, nor ever can be, the whole truth. There is mystery in truth; and it is out of this mystery, which is ultimately the god, that the word of power comes. And it is for this power that Merlin is the word.

Kirkus Reviews (review date 15 July 1991)

SOURCE: Review of *The Stormy Petrel*, in *Kirkus Reviews,* Vol. LIX, No. 14, July 15, 1991, p. 887.

[*In the following review, the critic praises Stewart's ability to evocatively portray the setting of her novel* The Stormy Petrel.]

By the English author of *Thornyhold* (1988), etc., more atmospheric romance, but here in a slight, mere wisp of a novel [*The Stormy Petrel*] set in Scotland's Western Islands. The scenery, however, is grand.

Rose Fenemore is a tutor of English at one of the Cambridge colleges; she also writes poetry and now needs an "ivory tower" retreat. Brother Crispin promises to join her for a holiday on the Scottish island of Moila but is delayed. Alone in her cottage, Rose is at first terrified, then angry and puzzled, by the night arrivals—separately—of two men. Both are strangers to her. Ewen Mackay, who lets himself

in with a key, claims that the cottage was his childhood home and hints that he was the love-child of the now-deceased Colonel Hamilton, owner of the nearby "Big House." But the man who calls himself John Parsons turns out to be the Hamilton heir. There are curious break-ins at the Hamilton house, and odd movements of Ewen's boat, the *Stormy Petrel.* As Rose puzzles, and enjoys the scenic wonders of the island, others arrive—including two of her students; Crispin; a Mr. Bagshaw (ex-con and developer!); and, at the finale, two policemen. Before the crowd thins, the island is saved from development, and a romantic interest is hinted. But all this is a mere puff beside the cries of birds, boom of sea, and ancient artifacts.

For Stewart's many followers, a pleasant armchair holiday in a wild and lovely landscape.

Christopher Dean (essay date 1991)

SOURCE: "The Metamorphosis of Merlin: An Examination of the Protagonist of *The Crystal Cave* and *The Hollow Hill,*" in *Comparative Studies in Merlin from the Vedas to C. G. Jung,* edited by James Gollnick, 1991, pp. 63-75.

[*In the following essay, Dean argues that a successful literary representation of the character Merlin requires that modern readers be able and willing to suspend their skepticism and accept Merlin as half human and half divine.*]

In medieval times, the problem of presenting the supernatural was easier than it is today. The dominant form of medieval fiction was romance, and there, the naturalistic existed very comfortably side by side with the supernatural. Havelock the Dane, for example, who earns his living by day in the most humdrum manner, catching fish and selling them in the market town of Lincoln, goes to sleep at night and has a light as bright as a sunbeam play magically about his head as an indication of his royal rank.

It is the newly respectable genre of fantasy literature which carries on this tradition today. Ursula Le Guin begins *A Wizard of Earthsea* with the disarmingly frank statement: "The Island of Gont, a single mountain that lifts its peak a mile above the storm-wracked Northeast Sea, is a land famous for wizards." Tolkien's *The Lord of the Rings* has gone no more than five pages before we meet "an odd-looking waggon . . . driven by outlandish folk, singing strange songs: dwarves with long beards and deep hoods . . . [and] an old man . . . [with] a tall pointed blue hat, a long grey cloak, and a silver scarf . . . the old man was Gandalf the wizard."

But most of our fiction today is realistic and deals with the people and the facts of the everyday world about us. The supernatural cannot easily appear in such a context. If realistic fiction takes Arthurian themes as its subject matter, the supernatural should not enter the story. It can be hinted at or invoked as superstition, but in the end, there always has to be a rational explanation. Rosemary Sutcliff's *Sword at Sunset* is a good illustration of the point.

When the birth of Guenhumara's daughter comes on unexpectedly at the height of a great storm, Arthur in desperation finds her a place of safety in the village of Druim Dhu, the leader of the Old Race, the Little Dark Ones. Guenhumara begs not to be left in the Fairy Hills, and later when her baby dies, she accuses the Dark People of having drawn the life out of it to save a weak child of their own. But Arthur will not accept this, protesting that her fear was nothing but an "ill dream." In the same way, when Arthur lies with Ygerna, he talks of "the magic mist," he finds the air filled with the "bloom of enchantment," and he calls her "a witch," but the rational explanation is clear enough. Ygerna drugged his wine, and it was under the influence of that that the seduction took place. *Sword at Sunset* is realistic fiction albeit that it is set in the distant past. There is no magic in it.

It seems to me that of all the current writers, she has gone the farthest in trying to make Merlin as realistic a character as possible.
—Christopher Dean

The original question that I intended to address in this paper was: How must modern writers adapt the supernatural side of the Arthurian legend in order to make it acceptable to contemporary readers? I proposed in particular to see what happened to Merlin as he passed from the middle ages to our own times, hence the paper's title. But the task is obviously far too big for a single paper.

Consequently, I have limited myself to seeing what a single writer, Mary Stewart, in her first two Arthurian novels *The Crystal Cave* and *The Hollow Hills* does with Merlin, for it seems to me that of all the current writers, she has gone the farthest in trying to make Merlin as realistic a character as possible. A study of her methods and her degree of success will be a significant step in answering the question I originally posed.

In both novels, Stewart's emphasis is totally on the realistic. She begins by placing the events of her narrative as firmly as she can into what is known of the historical framework of the period. Thus, for example, we have an account of Magnus Maximus that is near enough to the truth to be quite convincing:

The facts were these. Maximus, a Spaniard by birth, had commanded the armies in Britain under his general Theodosius at a time when Saxons and Picts were raiding the coasts constantly, and the Roman province of Britain looked like crumbling to its fall. Between them the commanders repaired the Wall of Hadrian, and held it, and Maximus himself rebuilt and garrisoned the great fortress at Segontium in Wales . . . Then in the year that Ector had called the Flood Year . . . 'Prince Macsen' . . . was declared Emperor by his troops . . . and marched on Rome itself. He never came back . . . He was defeated there, and later executed.

In the same way we have references to Stilicho, who restored order in Britain at the end of the fourth century, to the practice of using foreign mercenaries in Britain to keep back the Picts, to the recognition and settlement of independent Saxon kingdoms in the south and east of the island—what Stewart calls the Federated States—and even to the British settlement on the continent in what is now Brittany.

Next, Stewart makes her background authentic by describing the ordinary people of the novels in a detached, almost scientific, way. Here, for example, is her account of the people who lived in the low-lying marshes that surrounded the River Severn and the tributaries that run into it:

The marsh folk always needed medicine, living as they do at the edge of the fetid bogland, with agues and swollen joints and the fear of fever. They built their huts right on the borders of the scummed pools, just clear of the deep black mud at the edge, or even set them on stilts right over the stagnant water. The huts crack and rot and fall to pieces every year, and have to be patched each spring, but in spring and autumn the flocks of travelling birds fly down to drink, in summer the waters are full of fish and the forest game, and in winter the folk break the ice and lie in wait for the deer to come and drink . . . So the folk of the marshes cling to their stinking cabins, and eat well and drink the standing water, and die of fever. . . .

Most important of all, however, is the almost tangible texture of all the settings in which the actions take place. This is achieved by a meticulous use of concrete details that are both photographically exact and at the same time poetically evocative.

Merlin describes his return to Bryn Myrddin:

In the lower reaches of the valley the woods were thick; the oaks still rustled their withered leaves, chestnut and sycamore crowded close, fighting for the light, and hollies showed black and glinting between the beeches. Then the trees thinned, and the path climbed along the side of the valley, with the stream running deep down on the left, and to the right slopes of grass, broken by scree, rising sharply to the crags that crowned the hill. The grass was still bleached with winter, but among the rusty drifts of last year's bracken the bluebell showed glossy green, and blackthorn was budding.

The same technique equally makes man-built structures vividly real. This is Dimilioc, where Gorlois' body lies in state:

The place was cold, silent but for the sounds of wind and sea. The wind had changed and now blew from the north-west, bringing with it the chill and promise of rain. There was neither glazing nor horn in the windows, and the draught stirred the torches in their iron brackets, sending them sideways, dim and smoking, to blacken the walls. It was a stark, comfortless place, bare of paint, or tiling, or carved wood. . . The ashes in the hearth were days old, the half-burnt logs dewed with damp.

Just as important, however, are the people of the story. They are made of real flesh and blood and they feel the passions and emotions that we do, and they know the same happinesses and disappointments. We understand, for example, the anger and resentment of Ralf, dismissed from the court of the queen and banished, as he thinks, unfairly to the services of Merlin in his cave. We watch his faithful, loyal service as the vigilant keeper of Arthur as a boy, but all the while chafing to get back to the mainstream of action at the court, and we experience his joy and delight when Arthur is ultimately acknowledged as the next High King. Igraine is another character vividly portrayed as she sacrifices everything—her first husband and then her baby—as the price she must pay for her love of Uther. And then there is King Lot, crafty and scheming, untrustworthy and ambitious, a dangerous rival to Arthur and playing desperately for high stakes.

It is into this entirely convincing, realistic world that Mary Stewart places Merlin. How does she go about making him acceptable at the realistic level too?

From the earliest times, tradition had made Merlin the son of the devil; it had made him move the stones of Stonehenge from Ireland to Britain by magic; and it had made him bring about Arthur's conception at Tintagel by means of enchantment. Stewart cuts away all this medieval supernatural inheritance.

From the opening pages of *The Crystal Cave* we know that Merlin is a man begotten in the usual manner. In the very

first vision reported to us, we see his father, "a young man, sword in hand, at the edge of the trees". His actual identity is concealed until late in the book, but there is never any question that he had existed. The idea of the devil as Merlin's father comes in only where we might realistically have expected it. It is either used as an oath, such as when Camlach, after his attempt to poison Merlin has failed, says, "Keep away from me after this, you devil's brat" or it is used to indicate in a contemptuous way Merlin's difference from other children, "Your sister's bastard," said the king. "There he is. Six years old this month, grown like a weed, and no more like any of us than a damned devil's whelp would be". Or it is the occasion of a deliberate lie such as when Niniane fabricates the story of the incubus as the father of her child.

Stewart emphatically makes Merlin's building of Stonehenge no more than a feat of skillful engineering. When Uther says that Merlin has power because he did what Tremorinus could not do, Merlin could not have poured colder water on the idea. "My mathematics are better, that is all". The superstition that later surrounded the event is dismissed by Merlin as "a lot of nonsense".

On the third matter, the bringing of Uther to Igraine's bed, Merlin is equally emphatic. It is true that he does say to the agitated duchess, "This is where we come to magic" but this is nothing more than his pacifying her apprehension at that moment. Later he tells us:

My plan was simply to disguise Uther, Ulfin and myself to pass, if we were seen, as Gorlois and his companions and servant.

The means were saddle cloths, suitably blazoned, a cloak belonging to the duke, a grey dye for Uther's beard, a bandage over his face, a ring for his finger and a knowledge of the password. Months later, when Merlin talks to the queen, he says clearly that there was no magic in the ruse that brought the king to her.

Leaving aside for the moment the crucial question of what supernatural powers, if any, Merlin has, let us ask ourselves how an author would go about passing off a purely human figure as an enchanter or wizard.

The first requirement would be to construct a world in which a man of supernatural power would seem at home. In other words, Stewart needs a world that seems to be filled with the supernatural. Hence, in her novels, there is a multiplicity of gods of all kinds, ranging from the institutionalized one of Christianity, Mithraism, Druidism and the classical deities down to the local gods such as the god of Merlin's hill and the "old goddess of the crossways, the Nameless One, who sits staring from her hollowed log like the owl who is her creature". And because the people of the story believe in these gods, it is not surprising that they are ready to accept and believe in anyone who claims to be a servant of any of these gods.

Stewart's world has a second supernatural strain to it. It is filled with superstition and ignorance which again leads to a ready acceptance of magicians. Thus, we meet stories about "the spirit in the shape of a huge white bird that flies in men's faces if they venture too far up the track". We are told about "the white owl haunting the place as if it waited to convey his spirit home", and we hear of the power of the druids to "send a knife after you that'll hunt you down for days, and all you know is the whistling noise in the air behind you just before it strikes". The well-known belief that "enchanters can't cross water" has its place in this superstitious world. At a more mundane level even than this, we have love potions such as "every old woman swears she can concoct" and spells for protection in childbed.

How does this kind of background establish Merlin, a naturalistic man, as an enchanter? It does so because the people who live in such a credulous world genuinely believe in magicians and will of their own accord build stories about anyone who seems at all unusual. The reputation of such a man will grow and eventually take over from the reality. The legend will supplant the man behind it. And such is the case with Merlin. Much of his power comes from what people believe about him whether there are grounds for those beliefs or not.

Some, such as Hoel, can laugh when saying, "Oh, the usual stories that follow you as closely as your cloak flapping in the wind. Enchantments, flying dragons, men carried through the air and through walls invisibly", but for others the awe and the fear is very real. Crinas' men, for instance, are in mortal fear of Merlin when they waylay him in his cave; Llyd's men have heard that "he is a giant, with eyes that freeze you to the marrow".

As a consequence, even when the facts of the situations are capable of rational explanation—even when Merlin tells people what the explanation is—it is the magical account that is remembered. Thus a legend grows independently of the events. This happens in the matter of Uther coming to Igraine:

> Arthur told me once himself, the story that was current about the 'rape at Tintagel.' The legend had lost nothing in the telling. By now, it seemed, men believed that Merlin had spirited the King's party, horses and all, invisibly within the walls of the stronghold, and out again in the broad light of the next morning.

> 'And they say,' finished Arthur, 'that a dragon

curled on the turrets all night, and in the morning Merlin flew off on him, in a trail of fire.'

In a like manner, Crinas and his men believe that the music they heard in Merlin's cave was magically made:

> 'Music all around us,' said the man. 'Soft, like whispering, running round and round the wall of the cave in an echo. I'm not ashamed, my lord, we came out of that cave, and we did not dare go in again.'

Merlin knows this, of course, and deliberately plays up to it, encouraging his reputation to grow. Thus, even as a young boy, he deceives Dinias in order to stop his bullying:

> When Dinias waylaid me next morning I stood my ground and—quoting a sentence or so—asked if he had seen Alun yet that day . . . If he like to think it was magic rather than simple blackmail, I let him.

On a more serious occasion, when his life is threatened by Vortigern unless he can convince the king that he knows why the castle keeps falling down, he says:

> I could tell them the truth, coldly. I could take the torch and clamber up into the dark workings and point out faults which were giving way under the weight of the building work. . .but what Vortigern needed was not logic and an engineer; he wanted magic.

And so he leads them underground to the cave and points to a rock shaped like a dragon in the water:

> This is the magic, King Vortigern, that lies beneath your tower. This is why your walls cracked as fast as they could build them. Which of your soothsayers could have showed you what I show you now?

At other times he plays up to the people's credulity and claims by silence powers that he does not have. So, after visiting Queen Igraine, when trapped by the king's messengers who are seeking him, he pretends that he knew their mission and was already riding to meet them. The officer speaks:

> You—you knew the King was travelling north to Viroconium? How not? I asked him. From the edge of my eye I saw the nods and head-turning among the men, that also asked *How not?*

The element of coincidence also comes into play. Merlin seems to have been led to the crystal cave the first time by a bird, and he similarly finds the cavern that lies under the crag upon which Vortigern will later build his castle when he follows a falcon that attacks a ring dove. He discovers the island where Belasius is because a wild boar dashes across his path and throws him from his horse.

At other times, Merlin deliberately capitalizes on these co-incidental happenings. The heavy rain stops and the sun comes out at the very moment when he makes his prophecy to Vortigern:

> As I spoke, like the turning off of a tap, the down-pour stopped. In the sudden quiet, men's mouths gaped. Even Maugan was dumb. Then like the pulling aside of a dark curtain, the sun came out.

On another occasion, he blatantly turns a natural event to his own advantage:

> I jumped off the platform in front of them all and threw up my arms.

> "Can any doubt the god has spoken? Look up from the ground, and see where he speaks again!"

> Across the dark east, burning white hot with a trail like a young comet, went a shooting star, the star men called the firedrake or dragon of fire.

> "There is runs," I shouted. "There it runs! The Red Dragon of the West."

But a little later, Merlin laughs at Cadal for being impressed by this event saying, "Cadal . . . It was only a shooting star".

What I have tried to show is how in a world of superstition and ignorance any man who is quick-witted enough and a bit of a charlatan to boot could pass himself off quite convincingly as an enchanter. And to some extent, this is the way that Mary Stewart portrays Merlin. But it is even easier for him to pass as an enchanter because he has so much more than just quick wits. Stewart has made him genuinely skillful in surgery and in the use of drugs. He has mathematical and engineering skills, he has real ability with languages, he is a gifted musician and he has travelled widely acquiring an impressive amount of general knowledge. But all of this is within the power of any real man who has ability and a devotion to studying.

Does Merlin have anything else? Does he have powers that excel the capabilities of a realistic human being? More than anything else, he claims to be a prophet. But we should notice that even his prophecies are of two different kinds. There is first the wild kind of frenzy that Cadal tells Merlin he cried out in the presence of Vortigern:

> All wrapped up, it was, with eagles and wolves and lions and boars and as many other beasts as they've ever had in the arena and a few more besides, dragons and such—and going hundreds of years forward, which is safe enough.

This kind of prophecy is not specific; it is capable of many interpretations; it can even be forgotten if it does not turn out to be true. It does not need to be accounted for because it is the very kind of thing that an imposter would try when his back was to the wall.

But there are other visions that are not put on in order to deceive a gullible audience. They are private, and they turn out to be true. A typical example is Merlin's foreknowledge that he will be given Arthur to care for:

> Someone was coming softly down the stairs; a woman, shrouded in a mantle, carrying something. She came without a sound, and there had been neither sound nor movement from Ulfin. I stepped out onto the landing, and the light from the guardroom came after me, firelight and shadow.

> It was Marcia. I saw the tears glisten on her cheeks as she bent her head over what lay in her arms. A child, wrapped warm against the winter night. She saw me and held her burden out to me. "Take care of him," she said, and through the shine of the tears I saw the treads of the stairway outline themselves again behind her.

Similar to this is his knowledge of things that have happened far away—his awareness while still in Galapas' cave that Cerdic was dead, his knowing the moment that his mother died, and, even more startling, his premonition of danger when Camlach handed him the poisoned apricot.

This kind of knowledge cannot be dismissed as coincidence or as a lucky guess. It has to be accepted as genuine revelation. Certainly Merlin believes that it is and this, in part, convinces us too that it is real. Merlin has a ready explanation. He has what he calls the Sight, and he believes that he is the agent through whom the god speaks: "The voice that had said so now in the musty dark of Camlach's room, was not mine; it was the god's. He uses the analogy of "an empty shell with something working through him", and later, he calls himself "a reed" with "the wind of God blowing through it".

Here Stewart seems to be getting the best of two worlds. She has found a way to work the supernatural into her story without making Merlin himself anything but human. She makes him a human agent for something else that is genuinely supernatural.

For people who fully accept the idea of a god co-existing

with their everyday real world, Stewart's answer solves the problem. Even her refusal to name the god does not matter because, as Merlin explains to Cadal, all the gods in the end are one and the same.

In this way, therefore, Stewart can pretend to stay within the genre of realistic fiction and maintain that Merlin is no more than a man, albeit a special kind of man, by postulating a god who acts through Merlin. And if this were the end and full extent of Merlin's powers, we might perhaps settle for this kind of uneasy reconciliation.

But Merlin has one more power which goes beyond prophecy and foreknowledge. Two examples will suffice:

> Areth had managed to set the damp stuff smouldering, but it gave neither heat nor light, only an intermittent gusting of smoke, acrid and dirty . . . It was time, I thought, that I made an end . . . I said . . . 'Stand back from the fire, Areth.' . . . And as easily as a breath taken . . . the power ran through me, cool and free.

> Something dropped through the dark, like a fire arrow, or a shooting star. With a flash, a shower of white sparks that looked like burning sleet, the logs caught, blazing.

And again:

> I stretched out my hands. From the air the pale fire came, running down the blade, so that runes—quivering and illegible—shimmered there. Then the fire spread, engulfing it, till, like a brand too brightly flaring, the flames died, and when they had gone, there stood the altar, pale stone, with nothing against it but the stone sword.

For this kind of power, there can be no word but 'magic.' We have no sense here of a god acting through Merlin. These are actions that he decides to do and it is he who has the power to do it. This is magic, pure and simple. It is very much akin to the action of Gandalf of Mount Caradhras when the fire will not catch and he thrust the end of his staff into the midst of it. 'At once a great sprout of . . . flame sprang out, and the wood flared and sputtered'.

Narratively, of course, Stewart's episodes are right. They are appropriate dramatic climaxes to the incidents in which they are related and readers are swept up by them in the excitement of the moment. But later, when we look at the novels analytically, we recognize that Stewart has overstepped her boundaries and left the realistic novels that she seemed to be at such pains to write.

To return then, finally, to the question with which we started. Accepting that modern readers demand characters who are explicable in human terms, who are swayed by human emotions and who are psychologically plausible, what metamorphosis does Merlin have to undergo to be credible to twentieth-century readers, while still retaining those fundamental qualities that are part of his very nature?

Different critics have suggested different answers to account for his powers. Raymond Thompson in his recent *The Return from Avalon* talks of credible magic, but I see 'credible magic' as a contradiction in terms. Beverley Taylor and Elizabeth Brewer in *The Return of King Arthur* say that Merlin's powers 'are derived from the application of exceptional intelligence' and that 'magic is introduced under the naturalistic guise of psychic phenomena or even ESP.' But this at best covers only Merlin's prophetic powers. It does not account for the crucial kind of case where Merlin brings fire from the air.

The reality is otherwise. In order to be presented to modern readers, Merlin needs no metamorphosis. He can be the same figure he has always been—half human and half divine, exercising magic powers in his own right. *What the modern reader has to do is accept that a realistic presentation of him is not possible.* There has to be a sense of mystery to him, and everything cannot be explained.

She has found a way to work the supernatural into her story without making Merlin himself anything but human. She makes him a human agent for something else that is genuinely supernatural.
—Christoper Dean

From the beginning, Merlin has been a creature of fantasy, and the genre to which he belongs is fantasy. Realism and Merlin are contradictory ideas. Realism in novels about Merlin, therefore, exists only to make credible that which is patently unrealistic. Mary Stewart's novels may have been intended to be historical fiction, but in the end, became an epic fantasy trilogy which, in its own way, out-rivals the greatest of all epic fantasies, Tolkien's *The Lord of the Rings*.

Marilyn Jurich (essay date 1992)

SOURCE: "Mithraic Aspects of Merlin in Mary Stewart's *The Crystal Cave*," in *The Celebration of the Fantastic: Selected Papers from the Tenth Anniversary International Conference on the Fantastic in the Arts,* edited by Donald E.

Morse, Marshall B. Tymn, and Csilla Bertha, 1992, pp. 91-101.

[In the following essay, Jurich explains Stewart's use of the ancient figure Mithras, from the Zoroastrian religion, in the creation of her Merlin.]

The figure of Merlin is a fascinating palimpsest of myth, legend, and history; this sage-magician-trickster prophet, wild man of the forest, and protector of kings has spanned fourteen centuries. He has performed his sleight of hand and necromancy in poems, novels, and plays, enchanting both children and adults in his many roles. Nowhere, however, except in Mary Stewart's fantasy *The Crystal Cave* has Merlin been cast as a Mithraic figure—as the force of light and truth, the messenger of Zoroastrian Ahura-Mazda, Mithras who came to Britain with the Romans and whose more ancient roots go back to Persia and India. In her brief note on historical sources that follows her novel, Mary Stewart says little of Mithraism, a religion whose practice in the Roman Empire can only be surmised from bas-reliefs, sculptures, and objects discovered in the grotto chapels or "caves" where Mithras was worshipped by Roman men, soldiers, and business men. Stewart's statement is cagey or better "cave-y": "Mithraism has been (literally) underground for years. I have postulated a local revival for the purpose of my story. . . ." She postulates that Merlin's father, Ambrosius, has Roman leanings and favors the worship of Mithra, the god most favored by Roman warriors during the first four centuries A.D. Yet if it be, as Stewart tells us, that King Arthur's birth occurred around 470 A.D., the practice of the Mithraic religion had already been prohibited in the Roman Empire some seventy years before. While historically Mithraism is perhaps somewhat anachronistic in the novel, artistically it forms a crucial layer of *The Crystal Cave* as Mithras illumines two alluring possibilities: Mithras may represent the god who guides Merlin, and he may also signify Merlin himself. After all, what god can be more appropriate for the mythic dimension of a fantasy about Merlin—Mithras, born in a cave, bringer of light?

To understand the subtleties of Mithra and Mithraism in relation to the novel, some religious background is valuable. Mithra, originating in the mythological Mitra in the fourteenth century B.C. *Vedas* of India, is the servant of the sky god, Varuna, whose great power is "binding". This quality the Persian god Mithras will inherit, to enforce the "binding" of contracts and, more generally, justice. in the *Rig-Veda*, Mitra is also considered one of the twelve Adityas, gods of the months of the year headed by Aditya, the Hindu sun goddess. Later, as Mithras, as the supreme God in the "Mazdean Pantheon," he is considered to be "boundless Time"; his statue may display the signs of the zodiac engraved on his body. In particular, Mitra is a deity of light in the *Vedas,* connected to fertilizing warmth, as well as to truth

and to oath keeping. These qualities are suggested in etymology: *Mithras* derives from the Assyrian *metru* meaning "rain" and the Sanskrit *metru* meaning "friend". Thus, the god Mithras is the light that nurtures both earth and man—and can these functions, perhaps, also be ascribed to Merlin?

> **While historically Mithraism is perhaps somewhat anachronistic in the novel, artistically it forms a crucial layer of *The Crystal Cave* as Mithras illumines two alluring possibilities: Mithras may represent the god who guides Merlin, and he may also signify Merlin himself.**
> **—Marilyn Jurich**

The ritual re-enactment in Mithraism of the slaying of the bull by Mithras confirms the god's role in assuring fertility. Whereas in ancient Indian texts Mitra is sometimes depicted as the unwilling participant in the sacrifice of the god Soma, the god of Immortality depicted either as a bull or as the moon, it is the Mithras of the Hellenistic period (331 B.C. to 324 A.D.) who is predominantly known as Tauroctonus, the Slayer of the Primeval Bull. The older Persian Mithraism had declined in the time of Zoroaster (c. 550 B.C.) who, objecting to the Persian polytheism, sought to restore the one god, Ahura Mazdah, but by 8 B.C. the Iranian Mithras was known as "a celestial soldier at Ahura's side": like Ahura-Mazda, god of light and justice, Mithras was "undeceivable and omniscient". Mithra's ascendancy relative to Ahura-Mazda seems to have derived literally from Mithras' "taking the bull by the horns," for after wrestling the bull down, Mithras drags the exhausted animal into a cave, and after deliberately allowing the bull to escape and recapturing it, in the cave he ritually plunges a dagger into its throat.

By the first century B.C. these rituals of Mithraism were prominent among the Romans. By the second century A.D., even though a religion confined to males solely, Mithraism was stronger in the Roman Empire than was Christianity ("Mithraism,"; in the third century A.D. it became so prominent as to be regarded a world religion. Mithraism at mid-third century had reached its apogee of power before Theodosius I (r. 379-395 A.D.) assured its decline by his edict prohibiting it, though some worship seemed to have persisted into the fifth century in remote parts of the Alps and Vosges mountains.

Why did Mithraism have such appeal to its followers and offer such imaginative possibilities to Mary Stewart, who incorporates its mythology, ritual, and the qualities of its divinity into *The Crystal Cave*? The answer, of course, must derive from some understanding of Mithraic beliefs and practices and from the particular sense of how the god, Mithras, was perceived and understood.

Like all gods and heroes, Mithras had a miraculous birth. Emerging mysteriously from a rock, he came as "the new begetter of light." Even at his birth, he is fully attired with a Phrygian cap (that worn during the ritual bull sacrifice) and is holding a dagger and a torch. Often flames are shown blazing from the rock from which he appears and his cap is studded with stars. The parallel to Merlin as depicted in *The Crystal Cave* is clear—Merlin Emyrs is conceived in a cave, and recognizing his destiny through fire and light, frames a "new cosmogony" with Arthur as the unifying force. This application has even greater resonance when bas-reliefs of Mithras' birth are viewed where the god is shown holding a globe in one hand as he touches the circle of the zodiac with the other.

The bull has a place in the cosmic scene as well. Often considered a god, especially among the Aryans, and often related to kings, the bull was considered the bringer of new life. The Mithraic bull sacrifice closely resembles the bull sacrifice of the Phrygians commemorating the resurrection of Attis in the spring. Dionysus often took the shape of a bull to embody vegetation or the spirit of the corn. The reader of *The Crystal Cave* may find in Merlin qualities associated with the Mithraic bull, and perhaps more distinctly qualities associated with Mithras the slayer of the bull.

Mithras is assigned the sacrifice of the bull by Sol, who appoints the raven as messenger to tell Mithras what he must do. In the novel Merlin often serves as spokesman, that is, messenger, of the god and is named for a bird, the corwalch falcon: often directed by qualities of birds, the dove's wariness, the merlin's aggressive persistence, Merlin must transform himself from being like a dove to being a merlin, the bird of his name, for he will have to participate in violent acts; like a soldier, he will have to slay his bull.

Stewart's fantasy makes use of animals as symbolic and transforming agents, especially the bull, in some other ways. In Mithraic ritual at the death of the bull the cloak of Mithras becomes the vault of heaven covered with planets and stars; the bull himself is transformed through this "holy deed," in some versions becoming the moon, while the tail (or spinal chord) changes to ears of corn and the blood rises to form a vine. A seed issues from the bull, which generates all of life. Thus, the sacrifice influences earth as well as the heaven. Such a sacrifice Merlin, too, will have to make to secure the birth of Arthur.

Those initiated into the Mithraic mysteries descend into a pit, the *taurobolium,* where they are baptized in the blood of the bull sacrificed above them, a "blood bath". If the sacrifice of the bull relates the forces of light overcoming dark-

ness (in earlier myths Angra Mainyu, the Zoroastrian Antagonist, afflicts the bull) the purification of the initiate through blood rite symbolizes man's overcoming his dark instinctual drives. Now he will be able to transcend to a higher sphere of being. Yet, by participating in this "ritual killing," it seems evident that the initiate loses "light" even as he gains it. The Mithras figure often appears regretful, expressing compassion or remorse. In *The Crystal Cave* Merlin, an initiate in the Mithraic faith, later takes on the function of Mithras himself; he, too, experiences simultaneous joy in the coming of Arthur and loss in having to bring about the deaths of guiltless others, in the loss of his own "innocence."

Other elements in Mithraism are significant in the fantasy for supplying historical background as well as for enhancing the fantasy elements and deepening the mystery in the narrative. The sanctuary in which Mithraic rites were observed was a "mysterious" place. Worshipers congregated underground in caves that resembled the Mithraeum at Camuntum near Vienna, an oblong sanctuary approached by a stairway through a square hall. At the center of the sanctuary the bull ritual is sculpturally depicted. On either side of the central aisle is a row of benches, while at the beginning of the aisle are paired pillars, each extending a torch bearer. Sometimes the vault of the sanctuary represented the sky and various lighting devices might be manipulated to create "fitful flashes of light"—like in Stewart's "crystal cave." The celebrants in costumes symbolizing their grades sat on the benches. Just as the chapel had seven steps and seven altars, so the worshipers represented seven planets, each defined by a designated animal or other symbolic mask and assigned a special hierarchy. While authorities disagree as to the planet represented by each animal (for example, [M. J.] Vermaseren sees the Raven as air, while [Joseph] Campbell identifies it with the moon), most agree on the order prescribed for the celebrants. The servitors comprised the lower grades in this ascending sequence: Raven, Bridegroom, Soldier. The upper grades were known as Participants and included in ascending sequence Lion, Persian, Courier of the Sun, and Father. In addition, [Mercia] Eliade regards the participants as climbing on a seven-runged ladder, each rung of a different metal associated with the particular planet—such as gold for the sun. Thus, the initiate gains the empyrean by going through "the seven heavens". (Perhaps we derive from this the expression "I'm in seventh heaven"?)

The central mystery performed by the initiates was the journey of the soul from birth to immortality. At birth, according to this doctrine, the soul passes through the seven planetary spheres: at each planet the soul becomes tainted with the vice associated with the planet (for example, at Mars, anger). Once arrived on earth, the soul has the opportunity to cast off these impurities, aided by Mithras, who reveals a special moral discipline. After the person dies,

Mithras has yet another function; he is arbiter in the struggle between the *devas* (demons) and angels for the soul. If the soul's good qualities outweigh the bad, it rises again, this time passing the planets in reverse order and shedding all of its impurities. If, as some authorities believe, Mithra once formed a link between Ahura-Mazda (light) and Angra-Mainyu (darkness), his capacity for acting as mediator has another relevance in his role as the Roman soldier's god. In acting for the good of the emperor, in regulating the conduct of the army, in sanctioning oaths among the brotherhood of believers, the soldier, like Mithras, brings divine sanction to the nation. Such, too, is Merlin's role in *The Crystal Cave.*

During Roman times Mithras represented the power of the emperor, and emperors were actually represented as Mithras in statuary and coinage, also identified as *Sol Invictus,* the invincible Sun god. Aurelian (r. 270-275 A.D.), seeking to find a new power that would unite the Eastern and Western Empires, built in Rome in 274 A.D. a magnificent temple to the Sun god. On the side of the angels and the Roman emperors, Mithras is a more complex mythic hero in his relationship to the sun. "A sun hero will always present . . . a 'dark side,' a connection with the world of the dead". The destruction of the bull here occurs in a new context as Mithras, the sun hero, succeeds in opening up a new era, in fact "a new organization in the universe". For when Ahriman (spirit of darkness, evil) will succeed in destroying life, suddenly a marvelous bull will appear on the earth and Mithra will descend again, this time to awaken the dead. He will immolate the divine bull to provide the righteous with a substance that confers immortality and will lead the resurrected into paradise. Merlin's affinity to Mithras, the sun hero, is unmistakable; as arbiter and faithful supporter of the sovereign, Ambrosius, his father, as commentator on moral codes, and finally as the mentor he will become for Arthur—in all these roles, he will guide men on a spiritual journey and recreate Britain as an earthly paradise.

Mithraism functions in several ways in *The Crystal Cave:* as historical background, as a religion defined by ritual and ethical codes affecting Merlin and others, and as a mythology. The presence of Mithraism and the hero Mithras in Stewart's fantasy creates a texture and tonality that make the narrative glow and its hero Merlin a radiant figure, both realistic and luminous, pragmatic and prophetic.

In the novel Mithras first appears as a figure carved on the wooden chest that holds Merlin's clothing at the palace in Maridinum. The child Merlin is intrigued by the representation of a cave scene in which appear a bull, a man with a knife, someone holding some corn, and in one corner "some figure, rubbed almost away, with rays round his head, like the sun. . . ." When Merlin is twelve and hiding in a cow shed near Ambrosius' headquarters, he has vision of that same scene. In the winter landscape the sky is a "black dome" and the arch of stars "like the curved roof of the cave with the light flashing off the crystals, and the passing shadows flying, chased by the fire." When the shadows lift, Merlin sees the god himself dressed in the ritual costume—cross-bound trousers, thongs, low-girded tunic, Phrygian cap, and wide cape. Then, from the charging of the bull to the final plunge of the knife into its neck, Merlin observes the great sacrifice. This powerful vision Merlin, in a situation of peril in which his identity cannot be established, describes to Uther and his followers, and to Ambrosius; and because the vision reveals secret Mithraic knowledge the listeners are persuaded not to arrest, not to harm the ill-dressed unknown youth who tells it, for he apparently has supernatural powers.

Later Ambrosius explains the vision to Merlin as of "the soldier's god, the Word, the Light, the Good Shepherd, the Mediator between the one God and man." Mithras, says Ambrosius, represents courage and self-restraint, is both strong and gentle. Ambrosius describes Merlin's birth in a cave and interprets the ritual sacrifice. Merlin, who comes to be characterized by the qualities of Mithras, had also been conceived in a cave; and he, too, must commit a form of ritual sacrifice. The parallels between god and prophet become increasingly evident.

When Ambrosius becomes King of all Britain, Merlin is almost eighteen. The taking of York marks a special victory for the king, and it is in York on June 16, the feast day of the god, that Merlin is initiated into Mithraism. Stewart describes the cave sanctuary—with the long benches to either side of the central aisle, the torch bearers, the star studded roof of the cave, the masked believers—a historically accurate description. Mithras on the bas-relief is correctly depicted by Stewart as an unwilling participant in the bull slaying, his head "turned away in sorrow." Eight days after Merlin's initiation as Raven (the first level of Mithraic initiation), Ambrosius celebrates a Christian ceremony, reconciling Christ with Mithras: "As you will find, all gods who are born of the light are brothers, and in this land, if Mithras who gives us victory is to bear the face of Christ, why, then, we worship Christ."

Like those Christians who become members of religious orders, some devout believers in Mithraism practiced absolute continence. Merlin, a vessel of the god, must remain a virgin if he is to keep his power. When the young temptress Keridwen entices him to lie with her, he feels strangled in her embrace; he sees terrifying images and feels crushed inside a cave where the breathing walls take away his breath. But he tears himself away from her and saves his power. The cave symbol is used here by Stewart to image the dark fear of sexuality experienced by the dedicated celibate hero, Mithraic or Christian, bound to the code of the brotherhood of male warriors or priests.

The Mithraic aspects of Merlin are most clearly demonstrated in his special relationship to caves and in his magical ability to use fire and light. Often he is clairvoyant. Yet his powers begin naturally enough. In childhood, while he still lives in his grandfather's palace, his first "cave" serves as retreat where, unknown to others, he can listen to people conversing, learn their feelings, gain information about the adult world that would otherwise be held back from him. This boy seems to be supernaturally knowing, although he has gained his knowledge by going down into the tunnels under the palace floor, the system of tunnels once use for heating called the hypocaust, and there listening to conversations above. He is "alone in the secret dark, where a man is his own master, except for death." A particular area within the hypocaust, where a chimney shaft had once crumbled, the six year old calls his "cave." From a vantage point there he can look up at night to see the stars, to sense the magical design in the universe.

As a young boy, Merlin experiences a spiritual rebirth in "Myrddin's cave," the cave of Galapas, the seer, a sanctuary overhung by oak and rowan where water springs from the rock. Merlin's birth had been that of a hero-god, in his mother Niniane's legend the son of a "virgin" (Niniane) and a supernatural being ("demon"), in reality the son of princess Niniane and prince Ambrosius. But Galapas is his first true father, teacher, and role model. From him Merlin learns natural science, geography, healing, and spells; he learns how to use "the sight." Finally in this special cave of Galapas he is provided with the moral convictions and spiritual courage to put himself in the path of the gods.

Through a gap in the rock of Galapas' cave, Merlin discovers the "crystal cave," torchlight refracted from a mirror of bronze that creates a conflagration of flames and the illusion of a "whole globe" floored, roofed, lined with crystals. In the "crystal cave" he sees burning diamonds, "rainbows and rivers and bursting stars and a shape like a crimson dragon clawing up the wall, while below it a girl's face swimming faintly with closed eyes." The light drives into Merlin's body as if it would break him open. The phantasmagoric splendor Stewart ascribes to the "crystal cave" must hold either promise or peril depending on how the seer makes use of his vision. In this setting Merlin views the events following his grandfather's death and gains knowledge that will ultimately save his life as well as lead him to Ambrosius and the discovery of his real identity as no "devil's whelp" but the son of Ambrosius.

While in the crystal cave, Merlin has a vision of another cave, that beneath the King's Fort at Segontium which, the vision reveals, has a crack on the rock face; he will use this knowledge later to escape the priests of his father's enemy, Vortimer, who would have Merlin's blood to pour into the foundations being built for the King's Fort, blood to strengthen mortar. To prove that his magic is greater than the soothsayers', Merlin descends into the cave where he plans to contrive some "magic" to convince the King that Merlin can strengthen the Fort better than the priests, but once in the cave he is overwhelmed by flame and light that glitter like crystals—it is "the crystal cave come alive," the starred globe of the cosmos. Through the dazzling haze he sees images of wings and wolves' eyes, "stars shooting through a rain of blood." In a great voice, he prophesies the combat between the white dragon of the Saxons and the red dragon of Ambrosius. A bear shall come out of Cornwall. These visions are so impressive, his delivery so thrilling that even the sceptics are convinced; and he becomes known as "Vortigern's prophet," commanding awe and respect. Later he appears as the great cloaked figure atop the rocky crag at Caerleon, the symbol and assurance of certain triumph to Ambrosius' soldiers.

More than the place that gives him birth and later contributes to his reputation, the cave is for Merlin a retreat, his true home; even after he is acknowledged as prince, he chooses to live not in a palace but in Galapas' cave. The cave, Merlin knows, will also be the site where he dies. To Cadal, his servant and friend, he confides that Belasius, the menacing Druid, cannot harm him, for Merlin sees another death. "I shall come to the cave in the end. . . ." Yet, as Merlin recognizes, the cave is also "birth or a gate of vision or a dark limbo of sleep. . . ." Thus, the cave becomes a cosmos, the very globe Mithras holds when he is born, as well as the dome that the soul ascends on the way to its ultimate rebirth.

While the cave defines and influences Merlin, as well as suggests his Mithraic affinity, it is light itself in the form of crystals, fire, and stars that gives Merlin his magical power and that, once again, realizes his proximity to Mithras, god of light. When as a child Merlin first met his uncle Camlach who asked his name, he had responded with "'myrrdin Emyrs,'" Camlach retorted, "'Emyrs? Child of light, belonging to the gods. . . ? That hardly seems the name for a demon's whelp'." Scarcely "the demon's whelp," Merlin comes to have the supernatural power that can blind. Merlin admits to Cadal that his visionary experiences often frighten him, for when he is in a trance-like state, he is detached from his body, has no control over what he says, becomes only "a horn being blown through to make the sound carry." Yet one day Merlin knows for certain that he "shall command this part [of himself] that knows and sees, this god, and that really will be power." For the truth this God sends is shadowed—is incomplete. To use it fully, it is imperative that Merlin discover God's identity. Ambrosius once suggests that Mithras might be the god who guides him. The reader sees Merlin himself as Mithras, who is "all-seeing," knows the moment of Niniane's death, can perceive Ambrosius' death, recognizes that Arthur's coming will be a "shield and a living sword for a united Britain," however fraught with danger and death. As Mithras, the god of "binding," Merlin, while he recognizes perils, must keep his oath to the memory of Ambrosius, must assure the union and prosperity of Britain.

Mithras-Merlin is an ambivalent figure, for the sun is only light against the dark, and Mithras is the "divinity who formed a link between the Ahura Mazda and the Angra Mainyu of Zoroaster." In this sense, Merlin regulates the cycle of light and darkness, comes in darkness to Tintagel disguised as Brithael, Gorlois' captain and friend. His mission is "dark"—he is an accomplice in an act of betrayal, the betrayal of the loyal Gorlois, and the deviser of adultery, for he must make possible Uther's adultery with Gorlois' wife so that Arthur may be conceived. Yet for Merlin these dark deeds are not immoral, only essential. Merlin asserts to Cadal that on this night when Uther lies with Ygraine, Gorlois' wife, Uther is no King—only a ruler in a procession of rulers and "even less than that: he is a tool, and she is a vessel and I . . . I am a spirit, a word, a thing of air and darkness. . . ." In order to safeguard Uther and Ygraine, he must kill his "other self," the real Brithael who unexpectedly comes to the castle to report Gorlois' death at Dimilioc. Cadal, who is with Merlin at Tintagel, also dies on this night, having been mortally wounded by Brithael. Merlin has endangered Uther and has drenched himself in the blood of many others.

To Uther's accusations that he has brought disaster through this night's contriving, Merlin replies that he could not have known the price of the night's work, for God keeps his price secret. When Uther demands to know the identity of this God, Merlin responds by naming many gods—"Mithras, Apollo, Arthur, Christ. . . ." The name is irrelevant, Merlin concludes. It is "what men call the light. . . ." It is this light that all men must live by or die. Yet Merlin might have added that light does not exist without shadow, and the god who uses man to consummate divine intention also corrupts his vessel, as indeed Mithras was tainted when he killed the bull. Slaying the sacred bull, however, was necessary for fertility, for human consciousness, for the possibility of moral evolution and eternal life. In the view of Stewart's novel, Merlin's "sacrifice" of others accomplishes the same mission—the growth of human civilization through a united Britain and the possibility for spiritual immortality through another deity of light, a Christian King.

As *The Crystal Cave* ends, Merlin, still steeped in blood, watches the star directly overhead become enveloped in gold. Then as the pale sky brightens, a wave of brilliant light bursts forth. The "young sun" covers the heavens. To secure cosmic order and the promise of its continual renewal, Merlin as mediator, Logos, and savior sacrifices a portion of himself. Like Mithras, he intercedes for the good of Britain. By murdering the innocent Brithael whose coming into Uther's chamber would have prevented the conception of Arthur, Merlin suffers for his people to attain for them a life where moral sanctions are upheld, where death need not be final—can, indeed, be the promise of spiritual regeneration.

Kirkus Reviews (review date 15 August 1997)

SOURCE: Review of *Rose Cottage*, in *Kirkus Reviews*, Vol. LXV, No. 16, August 15, 1997, p. 1255.

[*In the following review, the critic assesses* Rose Cottage *as familiar Stewart material—"mild doings in enchanting surroundings."*]

For the frazzled Anglophile, the countryside-enamored reader, here's a bit of romance, light mystery, and the reassuring stability of a timeless English village—in short, another Stewart comforter.

Here, [in *Rose Cottage*], a young widow returns in 1947 to her childhood home and the enigma of her parentage. Kate Herrick, née Welland, who lost her husband in the war, is summoned to Scotland by her beloved grandmother, formerly a cook in the household of Sir James Brandon. She asks Kate to return to their native village in the north of England, where Kate was raised by Gran and severe Aunt Betsy. Kate's mother Lilias, who'd become pregnant while serving at the Brandons' estate, had left Kate at six, never to return. Gran had told Kate that she had "gone with the gipsies," but some years later Kate learned that her mother and new husband had been killed in Ireland in a bus accident. Now, Kate is to come again to Gran's Rose Cottage, long shuttered, charged with shipping some of Gran's belongings to her in Scotland and with locating a neatly hidden safe containing family items of sentimental value. But someone has broken into the cottage, ripped out the safe, and removed its contents. Then there are strange rumors of odd appearances, generated mainly by the "Witches Corner"—comprised of two gossipy ladies, as well as a feathery individual who's sure she has "the sight" and has seen a dead woman digging in the cottage yard and piling flowers on the grave of mean Aunt Betsy. With the help of young Davey, son of old family friends, and scraps of information from neighbors, Kate will at last discover an absent mother and a name for an unknown father.

Soothing as a warm brew on a cold night are Stewart's satisfying denouements—and environs: ". . . willows and wild roses, cuckoo-pint and king cups, and a wood pigeon crooning in the elm." Mild doings in enchanting surroundings.

Additional coverage of Stewart's life and career is contained in the following sources published by Gale: *Contemporary Authors*, Vols. 1-4R; *Contemporary Authors New Revision Series*, Vols. 1, and 59; *DISCovering Authors: British*; and *Something about the Author*, Vol. 12.

□ Contemporary Literary Criticism

Indexes

Literary Criticism Series
Cumulative Author Index
Cumulative Topic Index
Cumulative Nationality Index
Title Index, Volume 117

How to Use This Index

The main references

Camus, Albert
  1913-1960 . . . . . . .CLC 1, 2, 4, 9, 11,
  14, 32, 69; DA; DAB; DAC; DAM
  DRAM, MST, NOV; DC2; SSC 9;
  WLC

list all author entries in the following Gale Literary Criticism series:

BLC = *Black Literature Criticism*
BLCS = *Black Literature Criticism Supplement*
CLC = *Contemporary Literary Criticism*
CLR = *Children's Literature Review*
CMLC = *Classical and Medieval Literature Criticism*
DA = *DISCovering Authors*
DAB = *DISCovering Authors: British*
DAC = *DISCovering Authors: Canadian*
DAM = *DISCovering Authors Modules*
  DRAM = *dramatists;* *MST* = *most-studied*
  authors; *MULT* = *multicultural authors;* *NOV* =
  novelists; *POET* = *poets;* *POP* = *popular/genre*
  writers; *DC* = *Drama Criticism*
HLC = *Hispanic Literature Criticism*
LC = *Literature Criticism from 1400 to 1800*
NCLC = *Nineteenth-Century Literature Criticism*
PC = *Poetry Criticism*
SSC = *Short Story Criticism*
TCLC = *Twentieth-Century Literary Criticism*
WLC = *World Literature Criticism, 1500 to the Present*
WLCS = *World Literature Criticism Supplement*

The cross-references

See also CA 89-92; DLB 72; MTCW

list all author entries in the following Gale biographical and literary sources:

AAYA = *Authors & Artists for Young Adults*
AITN = *Authors in the News*
BEST = *Bestsellers*
BW = *Black Writers*
CA = *Contemporary Authors*
CAAS = *Contemporary Authors Autobiography Series*
CABS = *Contemporary Authors Bibliographical Series*
CANR = *Contemporary Authors New Revision Series*
CAP = *Contemporary Authors Permanent Series*
CDALB = *Concise Dictionary of American Literary Biography*
CDBLB = *Concise Dictionary of British Literary Biography*

DLB = *Dictionary of Literary Biography*
DLBD = *Dictionary of Literary Biography Documentary Series*
DLBY = *Dictionary of Literary Biography Yearbook*
HW = *Hispanic Writers*
JRDA = *Junior DISCovering Authors*
MAICYA = *Major Authors and Illustrators for Children and Young Adults*
MTCW = *Major 20th-Century Writers*
NNAL = *Native North American Literature*
SAAS = *Something about the Author Autobiography Series*
SATA = *Something about the Author*
YABC = *Yesterday's Authors of Books for Children*

See Adams, Henry (Brooks)

Amory, Thomas .... 1691(?)-1788
LC 48

Anand, Mulk Raj 1905-
CLC 23, 93; DAM NOV
See also CA 65-68; CANR 32, 64; MTCW 1

Anatol
See Schnitzler, Arthur

Anaximander .... c. 610B.C.-c. 546B.C.
CMLC 22

Anaya, Rudolfo A(lfonso) 1937-
CLC 23; DAM MULT, NOV; HLC
See also AAYA 20; CA 45-48; CAAS 4; CANR 1, 32, 51; DLB 82, 206; HW 1; MTCW 1

Andersen, Hans Christian 1805-1875
NCLC 7; DA; DAB; DAC; DAM MST, POP; SSC 6; WLC
See also CLR 6; MAICYA; SATA 100; YABC 1

Anderson, C. Farley
See Mencken, H(enry) L(ouis); Nathan, George Jean

Anderson, Jessica (Margaret) Queale 1916-
CLC 37
See also CA 9-12R; CANR 4, 62

Anderson, Jon (Victor) 1940-
CLC 9; DAM POET
See also CA 25-28R; CANR 20

Anderson, Lindsay (Gordon) 1923-1994
CLC 20
See also CA 125; 128; 146

Anderson, Maxwell 1888-1959
TCLC 2; DAM DRAM
See also CA 105; 152; DLB 7

Anderson, Poul (William) 1926-
CLC 15
See also AAYA 5; CA 1-4R; CAAS 2; CANR 2, 15, 34, 64; DLB 8; INT CANR-15; MTCW 1; SATA 90; SATA-Brief 39

Anderson, Robert (Woodruff) 1917-
CLC 23; DAM DRAM
See also AITN 1; CA 21-24R; CANR 32; DLB 7

Anderson, Sherwood 1876-1941
TCLC 1, 10, 24; DA; DAB; DAC; DAM MST, NOV; SSC 1; WLC
See also CA 104; 121; CANR 61; CDALB 1917-1929; DLB 4, 9, 86; DLBD 1; MTCW 1

Andier, Pierre
See Desnos, Robert

Andouard
See Giraudoux, (Hippolyte) Jean

Andrade, Carlos Drummond de .... **CLC 18**
See also Drummond de Andrade, Carlos

Andrade, Mario de 1893-1945
TCLC 43

Andreae, Johann V(alentin) 1586-1654
LC 32
See also DLB 164

Andreas-Salome, Lou 1861-1937
TCLC 56
See also DLB 66

Andress, Lesley
See Sanders, Lawrence

Andrewes, Lancelot 1555-1626
LC 5
See also DLB 151, 172

Andrews, Cicily Fairfield
See West, Rebecca

Andrews, Elton V.
See Pohl, Frederik

Andreyev, Leonid (Nikolaevich) . 1871-1919

TCLC 3
See also CA 104

Andric, Ivo 1892-1975
CLC 8
See also CA 81-84; 57-60; CANR 43, 60; DLB 147; MTCW 1

Androvar
See Prado (Calvo), Pedro

Angelique, Pierre
See Bataille, Georges

Angell, Roger 1920-
CLC 26
See also CA 57-60; CANR 13, 44, 70; DLB 171, 185

Angelou, Maya 1928-
CLC 12, 35, 64, 77; BLC 1; DA; DAB; DAC; DAM MST, MULT, POET, POP; WLCS
See also Johnson, Marguerite (Annie)
See also AAYA 7, 20; BW 2; CA 65-68; CANR 19, 42, 65; CLR 53; DLB 38; MTCW 1; SATA 49

Anna Comnena 1083-1153
CMLC 25

Annensky, Innokenty (Fyodorovich)
1856-1909 .... **TCLC 14**
See also CA 110; 155

Annunzio, Gabriele d'
See D'Annunzio, Gabriele

Anodos
See Coleridge, Mary E(lizabeth)

Anon, Charles Robert
See Pessoa, Fernando (Antonio Nogueira)

Anouilh, Jean (Marie Lucien Pierre)
1910-1987 **CLC 1, 3, 8, 13, 40, 50; DAM DRAM; DC 8**
See also CA 17-20R; 123; CANR 32; MTCW 1

Anthony, Florence
See Ai

Anthony, John
See Ciardi, John (Anthony)

Anthony, Peter
See Shaffer, Anthony (Joshua); Shaffer, Peter (Levin)

Anthony, Piers 1934-
CLC 35; DAM POP
See also AAYA 11; CA 21-24R; CANR 28, 56, 73; DLB 8; MTCW 1; SAAS 22; SATA 84

Anthony, Susan B(rownell) 1916-1991
TCLC 84
See also CA 89-92; 134

Antoine, Marc
See Proust, (Valentin-Louis-George-Eugene-) Marcel

Antoninus, Brother
See Everson, William (Oliver)

Antonioni, Michelangelo 1912-
CLC 20
See also CA 73-76; CANR 45

Antschel, Paul 1920-1970
See Celan, Paul
See also CA 85-88; CANR 33, 61; MTCW 1

Anwar, Chairil 1922-1949
TCLC 22
See also CA 121

Apess, William .... 1798-1839(?)
NCLC 73; DAM MULT
See also DLB 175; NNAL

Apollinaire, Guillaume 1880-1918
TCLC 3, 8, 51; DAM POET; PC 7
See also Kostrowitzki, Wilhelm Apollinaris de
See also CA 152

Appelfeld, Aharon 1932-

CLC 23, 47
See also CA 112; 133

Apple, Max (Isaac) 1941-
CLC 9, 33
See also CA 81-84; CANR 19, 54; DLB 130

Appleman, Philip (Dean) 1926-
CLC 51
See also CA 13-16R; CAAS 18; CANR 6, 29, 56

Appleton, Lawrence
See Lovecraft, H(oward) P(hillips)

Apteryx
See Eliot, T(homas) S(tearns)

Apuleius, (Lucius Madaurensis) 125(?)-175(?)
CMLC 1

Aquin, Hubert 1929-1977
CLC 15
See also CA 105; DLB 53

Aragon, Louis 1897-1982
CLC 3, 22; DAM NOV, POET
See also CA 69-72; 108; CANR 28, 71; DLB 72; MTCW 1

Arany, Janos 1817-1882
NCLC 34

Aranyos, Kakay
See Mikszath, Kalman

Arbuthnot, John 1667-1735
LC 1
See also DLB 101

Archer, Herbert Winslow
See Mencken, H(enry) L(ouis)

Archer, Jeffrey (Howard) 1940-
CLC 28; DAM POP
See also AAYA 16; BEST 89:3; CA 77-80; CANR 22, 52; INT CANR-22

Archer, Jules 1915-
CLC 12
See also CA 9-12R; CANR 6, 69; SAAS 5; SATA 4, 85

Archer, Lee
See Ellison, Harlan (Jay)

Arden, John 1930-
CLC 6, 13, 15; DAM DRAM
See also CA 13-16R; CAAS 4; CANR 31, 65, 67; DLB 13; MTCW 1

Arenas, Reinaldo 1943-1990
CLC 41; DAM MULT; HLC
See also CA 124; 128; 133; CANR 73; DLB 145; HW

Arendt, Hannah 1906-1975
CLC 66, 98
See also CA 17-20R; 61-64; CANR 26, 60; MTCW 1

Aretino, Pietro 1492-1556
LC 12

Arghezi, Tudor 1880-1967
CLC 80
See also Theodorescu, Ion N.
See also CA 167

Arguedas, Jose Maria 1911-1969
CLC 10, 18
See also CA 89-92; CANR 73; DLB 113; HW

Argueta, Manlio 1936-
CLC 31
See also CA 131; CANR 73; DLB 145; HW

Ariosto, Ludovico 1474-1533
LC 6

Aristides
See Epstein, Joseph

Aristophanes .... 450B.C.-385B.C.
CMLC 4; DA; DAB; DAC; DAM DRAM, MST; DC 2; WLCS
See also DLB 176

See also CA 104; 155

Babits, Mihaly 1883-1941
TCLC 14
See also CA 114

Babur 1483-1530
LC 18

Bacchelli, Riccardo 1891-1985
CLC 19
See also CA 29-32R; 117

Bach, Richard (David) 1936-
CLC 14; DAM NOV, POP
See also AITN 1; BEST 89:2; CA 9-12R; CANR 18; MTCW 1; SATA 13

Bachman, Richard
See King, Stephen (Edwin)

Bachmann, Ingeborg 1926-1973
CLC 69
See also CA 93-96; 45-48; CANR 69; DLB 85

Bacon, Francis 1561-1626
LC 18, 32
See also CDBLB Before 1660; DLB 151

Bacon, Roger .... 1214(?)-1292
CMLC 14
See also DLB 115

Bacovia, George .... TCLC 24
See also Vasiliu, Gheorghe

Badanes, Jerome 1937-
CLC 59

Bagehot, Walter 1826-1877
NCLC 10
See also DLB 55

Bagnold, Enid 1889-1981
CLC 25; DAM DRAM
See also CA 5-8R; 103; CANR 5, 40; DLB 13, 160, 191; MAICYA; SATA 1, 25

Bagritsky, Eduard 1895-1934
TCLC 60

Bagrjana, Elisaveta
See Belcheva, Elisaveta

Bagryana, Elisaveta .... CLC 10
See also Belcheva, Elisaveta
See also DLB 147

Bailey, Paul 1937-
CLC 45
See also CA 21-24R; CANR 16, 62; DLB 14

Baillie, Joanna 1762-1851
NCLC 71
See also DLB 93

Bainbridge, Beryl (Margaret) 1933-
CLC 4, 5, 8, 10, 14, 18, 22, 62; DAM NOV
See also CA 21-24R; CANR 24, 55, 75; DLB 14; MTCW 1

Baker, Elliott 1922-
CLC 8
See also CA 45-48; CANR 2, 63

Baker, Jean H. .... TCLC 3, 10
See also Russell, George William

Baker, Nicholson 1957-
CLC 61; DAM POP
See also CA 135; CANR 63

Baker, Ray Stannard 1870-1946
TCLC 47
See also CA 118

Baker, Russell (Wayne) 1925-
CLC 31
See also BEST 89:4; CA 57-60; CANR 11, 41, 59; MTCW 1

Bakhtin, M.
See Bakhtin, Mikhail Mikhailovich

Bakhtin, M. M.
See Bakhtin, Mikhail Mikhailovich

Bakhtin, Mikhail
See Bakhtin, Mikhail Mikhailovich

Bakhtin, Mikhail Mikhailovich ... 1895-1975
CLC 83
See also CA 128; 113

Bakshi, Ralph .... 1938(?)-
CLC 26
See also CA 112; 138

Bakunin, Mikhail (Alexandrovich) 1814-1876
NCLC 25, 58

Baldwin, James (Arthur) 1924-1987
CLC 1, 2, 3, 4, 5, 8, 13, 15, 17, 42, 50, 67, 90; BLC 1; DA; DAB; DAC; DAM MST, MULT, NOV, POP; DC 1; SSC 10, 33; WLC
See also AAYA 4; BW 1; CA 1-4R; 124; CABS 1; CANR 3, 24; CDALB 1941-1968; DLB 2, 7, 33; DLBY 87; MTCW 1; SATA 9; SATA-Obit 54

Ballard, J(ames) G(raham) 1930-
CLC 3, 6, 14, 36; DAM NOV, POP; SSC 1
See also AAYA 3; CA 5-8R; CANR 15, 39, 65; DLB 14; MTCW 1; SATA 93

Balmont, Konstantin (Dmitriyevich)
1867-1943 .... TCLC 11
See also CA 109; 155

Baltausis, Vincas
See Mikszath, Kalman

Balzac, Honore de 1799-1850
NCLC 5, 35, 53; DA; DAB; DAC; DAM MST, NOV; SSC 5; WLC
See also DLB 119

Bambara, Toni Cade 1939-1995
CLC 19, 88; BLC 1; DA; DAC; DAM MST, MULT; WLCS
See also AAYA 5; BW 2; CA 29-32R; 150; CANR 24, 49; DLB 38; MTCW 1

Bamdad, A.
See Shamlu, Ahmad

Banat, D. R.
See Bradbury, Ray (Douglas)

Bancroft, Laura
See Baum, L(yman) Frank

Banim, John 1798-1842
NCLC 13
See also DLB 116, 158, 159

Banim, Michael 1796-1874
NCLC 13
See also DLB 158, 159

Banjo, The
See Paterson, A(ndrew) B(arton)

Banks, Iain
See Banks, Iain M(enzies)

Banks, Iain M(enzies) 1954-
CLC 34
See also CA 123; 128; CANR 61; DLB 194; INT 128

Banks, Lynne Reid .... CLC 23
See also Reid Banks, Lynne
See also AAYA 6

Banks, Russell 1940-
CLC 37, 72
See also CA 65-68; CAAS 15; CANR 19, 52, 73; DLB 130

Banville, John 1945-
CLC 46
See also CA 117; 128; DLB 14; INT 128

Banville, Theodore (Faullain) de 1832-1891
NCLC 9

Baraka, Amiri 1934-
CLC 1, 2, 3, 5, 10, 14, 33, 115; BLC 1; DA; DAC; DAM MST, MULT, POET, POP; DC 6; PC 4; WLCS
See also Jones, LeRoi
See also BW 2; CA 21-24R; CABS 3; CANR

27, 38, 61; CDALB 1941-1968; DLB 5, 7, 16, 38; DLBD 8; MTCW 1

Barbauld, Anna Laetitia 1743-1825
NCLC 50
See also DLB 107, 109, 142, 158

Barbellion, W. N. P. .... TCLC 24
See also Cummings, Bruce F(rederick)

Barbera, Jack (Vincent) 1945-
CLC 44
See also CA 110; CANR 45

Barbey d'Aurevilly, Jules Amedee 1808-1889
NCLC 1; SSC 17
See also DLB 119

Barbusse, Henri 1873-1935
TCLC 5
See also CA 105; 154; DLB 65

Barclay, Bill
See Moorcock, Michael (John)

Barclay, William Ewert
See Moorcock, Michael (John)

Barea, Arturo 1897-1957
TCLC 14
See also CA 111

Barfoot, Joan 1946-
CLC 18
See also CA 105

Baring, Maurice 1874-1945
TCLC 8
See also CA 105; 168; DLB 34

Baring-Gould, Sabine 1834-1924
TCLC 88
See also DLB 156, 190

Barker, Clive 1952-
CLC 52; DAM POP
See also AAYA 10; BEST 90:3; CA 121; 129; CANR 71; INT 129; MTCW 1

Barker, George Granville 1913-1991
CLC 8, 48; DAM POET
See also CA 9-12R; 135; CANR 7, 38; DLB 20; MTCW 1

Barker, Harley Granville
See Granville-Barker, Harley
See also DLB 10

Barker, Howard 1946-
CLC 37
See also CA 102; DLB 13

Barker, Jane 1652-1732
LC 42

Barker, Pat(ricia) 1943-
CLC 32, 94
See also CA 117; 122; CANR 50; INT 122

Barlach, Ernst 1870-1938
TCLC 84
See also DLB 56, 118

Barlow, Joel 1754-1812
NCLC 23
See also DLB 37

Barnard, Mary (Ethel) 1909-
CLC 48
See also CA 21-22; CAP 2

Barnes, Djuna 1892-1982
CLC 3, 4, 8, 11, 29; SSC 3
See also CA 9-12R; 107; CANR 16, 55; DLB 4, 9, 45; MTCW 1

Barnes, Julian (Patrick) 1946-
CLC 42; DAB
See also CA 102; CANR 19, 54; DLB 194; DLBY 93

Barnes, Peter 1931-
CLC 5, 56
See also CA 65-68; CAAS 12; CANR 33, 34, 64; DLB 13; MTCW 1

Baroja (y Nessi), Pio 1872-1956

TCLC 3
See also CA 104; 130; DLB 72

Bernard, April 1956-
CLC 59
See also CA 131

Berne, Victoria
See Fisher, M(ary) F(rances) K(ennedy)

Bernhard, Thomas 1931-1989
CLC 3, 32, 61
See also CA 85-88; 127; CANR 32, 57; DLB
85, 124; MTCW 1

Bernhardt, Sarah (Henriette Rosine)
1844-1923 .... TCLC 75
See also CA 157

Berriault, Gina 1926-
CLC 54, 109; SSC 30
See also CA 116; 129; CANR 66; DLB 130

Berrigan, Daniel 1921-
CLC 4
See also CA 33-36R; CAAS 1; CANR 11, 43;
DLB 5

Berrigan, Edmund Joseph Michael, Jr.
1934-1983
See Berrigan, Ted
See also CA 61-64; 110; CANR 14

Berrigan, Ted .... CLC 37
See also Berrigan, Edmund Joseph Michael, Jr.
See also DLB 5, 169

Berry, Charles Edward Anderson 1931-
See Berry, Chuck
See also CA 115

Berry, Chuck .... CLC 17
See also Berry, Charles Edward Anderson

Berry, Jonas
See Ashbery, John (Lawrence)

Berry, Wendell (Erdman) 1934-
CLC 4, 6, 8, 27, 46; DAM POET
See also AITN 1; CA 73-76; CANR 50, 73; DLB
5, 6

Berryman, John 1914-1972
CLC 1, 2, 3, 4, 6, 8, 10, 13, 25, 62; DAM
POET
See also CA 13-16; 33-36R; CABS 2; CANR
35; CAP 1; CDALB 1941-1968; DLB 48;
MTCW 1

Bertolucci, Bernardo 1940-
CLC 16
See also CA 106

Berton, Pierre (Francis Demarigny) .. 1920-
CLC 104
See also CA 1-4R; CANR 2, 56; DLB 68; SATA
99

Bertrand, Aloysius 1807-1841
NCLC 31

Bertran de Born .... c. 1140-1215
CMLC 5

Besant, Annie (Wood) 1847-1933
TCLC 9
See also CA 105

Bessie, Alvah 1904-1985
CLC 23
See also CA 5-8R; 116; CANR 2; DLB 26

Bethlen, T. D.
See Silverberg, Robert

Beti, Mongo ... CLC 27; BLC 1; DAM MULT
See also Biyidi, Alexandre

Betjeman, John 1906-1984
CLC 2, 6, 10, 34, 43; DAB; DAM MST,
POET
See also CA 9-12R; 112; CANR 33, 56; CDBLB
1945-1960; DLB 20; DLBY 84; MTCW 1

Bettelheim, Bruno 1903-1990
CLC 79

See also CA 81-84; 131; CANR 23, 61; MTCW
1

Betti, Ugo 1892-1953
TCLC 5
See also CA 104; 155

Betts, Doris (Waugh) 1932-
CLC 3, 6, 28
See also CA 13-16R; CANR 9, 66; DLBY 82;
INT CANR-9

Bevan, Alistair
See Roberts, Keith (John Kingston)

Bey, Pilaff
See Douglas, (George) Norman

Bialik, Chaim Nachman 1873-1934
TCLC 25
See also CA 170

Bickerstaff, Isaac
See Swift, Jonathan

Bidart, Frank 1939-
CLC 33
See also CA 140

Bienek, Horst 1930-
CLC 7, 11
See also CA 73-76; DLB 75

Bierce, Ambrose (Gwinett) ...... 1842-1914(?)
TCLC 1, 7, 44; DA; DAC; DAM MST; SSC
9; WLC
See also CA 104; 139; CDALB 1865-1917;
DLB 11, 12, 23, 71, 74, 186

Biggers, Earl Derr 1884-1933
TCLC 65
See also CA 108; 153

Billings, Josh
See Shaw, Henry Wheeler

Billington, (Lady) Rachel (Mary) 1942-
CLC 43
See also AITN 2; CA 33-36R; CANR 44

Binyon, T(imothy) J(ohn) 1936-
CLC 34
See also CA 111; CANR 28

Bioy Casares, Adolfo 1914-1984
CLC 4, 8, 13, 88; DAM MULT; HLC; SSC
17
See also CA 29-32R; CANR 19, 43, 66; DLB
113; HW; MTCW 1

Bird, Cordwainer
See Ellison, Harlan (Jay)

Bird, Robert Montgomery 1806-1854
NCLC 1
See also DLB 202

Birkerts, Sven 1951-
CLC 116
See also CA 128; 133; CAAS 29; INT 133

Birney, (Alfred) Earle 1904-1995
CLC 1, 4, 6, 11; DAC; DAM MST, POET
See also CA 1-4R; CANR 5, 20; DLB 88;
MTCW 1

Biruni, al .... 973-1048(?)
CMLC 28

Bishop, Elizabeth 1911-1979
CLC 1, 4, 9, 13, 15, 32; DA; DAC; DAM
MST, POET; PC 3
See also CA 5-8R; 89-92; CABS 2; CANR 26,
61; CDALB 1968-1988; DLB 5, 169;
MTCW 1; SATA-Obit 24

Bishop, John 1935-
CLC 10
See also CA 105

Bissett, Bill 1939-
CLC 18; PC 14
See also CA 69-72; CAAS 19; CANR 15; DLB
53; MTCW 1

Bitov, Andrei (Georgievich) 1937-

CLC 57
See also CA 142

Biyidi, Alexandre 1932-
See Beti, Mongo
See also BW 1; CA 114; 124; MTCW 1

Bjarme, Brynjolf
See Ibsen, Henrik (Johan)

Bjoernson, Bjoernstjerne (Martinius)
1832-1910 .... TCLC 7, 37
See also CA 104

Black, Robert
See Holdstock, Robert P.

Blackburn, Paul 1926-1971
CLC 9, 43
See also CA 81-84; 33-36R; CANR 34; DLB
16; DLBY 81

Black Elk 1863-1950
TCLC 33; DAM MULT
See also CA 144; NNAL

Black Hobart
See Sanders, (James) Ed(ward)

Blacklin, Malcolm
See Chambers, Aidan

Blackmore, R(ichard) D(oddridge) 1825-1900
TCLC 27
See also CA 120; DLB 18

Blackmur, R(ichard) P(almer) 1904-1965
CLC 2, 24
See also CA 11-12; 25-28R; CANR 71; CAP 1;
DLB 63

Black Tarantula
See Acker, Kathy

Blackwood, Algernon (Henry) 1869-1951
TCLC 5
See also CA 105; 150; DLB 153, 156, 178

Blackwood, Caroline 1931-1996
CLC 6, 9, 100
See also CA 85-88; 151; CANR 32, 61, 65; DLB
14; MTCW 1

Blade, Alexander
See Hamilton, Edmond; Silverberg, Robert

Blaga, Lucian 1895-1961
CLC 75
See also CA 157

Blair, Eric (Arthur) 1903-1950
See Orwell, George
See also CA 104; 132; DA; DAB; DAC; DAM
MST, NOV; MTCW 1; SATA 29

Blais, Marie-Claire 1939-
CLC 2, 4, 6, 13, 22; DAC; DAM MST
See also CA 21-24R; CAAS 4; CANR 38, 75;
DLB 53; MTCW 1

Blaise, Clark 1940-
CLC 29
See also AITN 2; CA 53-56; CAAS 3; CANR
5, 66; DLB 53

Blake, Fairley
See De Voto, Bernard (Augustine)

Blake, Nicholas
See Day Lewis, C(ecil)
See also DLB 77

Blake, William 1757-1827
NCLC 13, 37, 57; DA; DAB; DAC; DAM
MST, POET; PC 12; WLC
See also CDBLB 1789-1832; CLR 52; DLB 93,
163; MAICYA; SATA 30

Blasco Ibanez, Vicente 1867-1928
TCLC 12; DAM NOV
See also CA 110; 131; HW; MTCW 1

Blatty, William Peter 1928-
CLC 2; DAM POP
See also CA 5-8R; CANR 9

Bleeck, Oliver

See Thomas, Ross (Elmore)

Blessing, Lee 1949-
CLC 54

Blish, James (Benjamin) 1921-1975
CLC 14
See also CA 1-4R; 57-60; CANR 3; DLB 8;
MTCW 1; SATA 66

Bliss, Reginald
See Wells, H(erbert) G(eorge)

Blixen, Karen (Christentze Dinesen)
1885-1962
See Dinesen, Isak
See also CA 25-28; CANR 22, 50; CAP 2;
MTCW 1; SATA 44

Bloch, Robert (Albert) 1917-1994
CLC 33
See also CA 5-8R; 146; CAAS 20; CANR 5;
DLB 44; INT CANR-5; SATA 12; SATA-Obit
82

Blok, Alexander (Alexandrovich) 1880-1921
TCLC 5; PC 21
See also CA 104

Blom, Jan
See Breytenbach, Breyten

Bloom, Harold 1930-
CLC 24, 103
See also CA 13-16R; CANR 39, 75; DLB 67

Bloomfield, Aurelius
See Bourne, Randolph S(illiman)

Blount, Roy (Alton), Jr. 1941-
CLC 38
See also CA 53-56; CANR 10, 28, 61; INT
CANR-28; MTCW 1

Bloy, Leon 1846-1917
TCLC 22
See also CA 121; DLB 123

Blume, Judy (Sussman) 1938-
CLC 12, 30; DAM NOV, POP
See also AAYA 3, 26; CA 29-32R; CANR 13,
37, 66; CLR 2, 15; DLB 52; JRDA;
MAICYA; MTCW 1; SATA 2, 31, 79

Blunden, Edmund (Charles) 1896-1974
CLC 2, 56
See also CA 17-18; 45-48; CANR 54; CAP 2;
DLB 20, 100, 155; MTCW 1

Bly, Robert (Elwood) 1926-
CLC 1, 2, 5, 10, 15, 38; DAM POET
See also CA 5-8R; CANR 41, 73; DLB 5;
MTCW 1

Boas, Franz 1858-1942
TCLC 56
See also CA 115

Bobette
See Simenon, Georges (Jacques Christian)

Boccaccio, Giovanni 1313-1375
CMLC 13; SSC 10

Bochco, Steven 1943-
CLC 35
See also AAYA 11; CA 124; 138

Bodel, Jean .... 1167(?)-1210
CMLC 28

Bodenheim, Maxwell 1892-1954
TCLC 44
See also CA 110; DLB 9, 45

Bodker, Cecil 1927-
CLC 21
See also CA 73-76; CANR 13, 44; CLR 23;
MAICYA; SATA 14

Boell, Heinrich (Theodor) 1917-1985
**CLC 2, 3, 6, 9, 11, 15, 27, 32, 72; DA; DAB;
DAC; DAM MST, NOV; SSC 23; WLC**
See also CA 21-24R; 116; CANR 24; DLB 69;
DLBY 85; MTCW 1

Boerne, Alfred
See Doeblin, Alfred

Boethius .... 480(?)-524(?)
CMLC 15
See also DLB 115

Bogan, Louise 1897-1970
CLC 4, 39, 46, 93; DAM POET; PC 12
See also CA 73-76; 25-28R; CANR 33; DLB
45, 169; MTCW 1

Bogarde, Dirk ....**CLC 19**
See also Van Den Bogarde, Derek Jules Gaspard
Ulric Niven
See also DLB 14

Bogosian, Eric 1953-
CLC 45
See also CA 138

Bograd, Larry 1953-
CLC 35
See also CA 93-96; CANR 57; SAAS 21; SATA
33, 89

Boiardo, Matteo Maria 1441-1494
LC 6

Boileau-Despreaux, Nicolas 1636-1711
LC 3

Bojer, Johan 1872-1959
TCLC 64

Boland, Eavan (Aisling) 1944-
CLC 40, 67, 113; DAM POET
See also CA 143; CANR 61; DLB 40

Boll, Heinrich
See Boell, Heinrich (Theodor)

Bolt, Lee
See Faust, Frederick (Schiller)

Bolt, Robert (Oxton) 1924-1995
CLC 14; DAM DRAM
See also CA 17-20R; 147; CANR 35, 67; DLB
13; MTCW 1

Bombet, Louis-Alexandre-Cesar
See Stendhal

Bomkauf
See Kaufman, Bob (Garnell)

Bonaventura ....**NCLC 35**
See also DLB 90

Bond, Edward 1934-
CLC 4, 6, 13, 23; DAM DRAM
See also CA 25-28R; CANR 38, 67; DLB 13;
MTCW 1

Bonham, Frank 1914-1989
CLC 12
See also AAYA 1; CA 9-12R; CANR 4, 36;
JRDA; MAICYA; SAAS 3; SATA 1, 49;
SATA-Obit 62

Bonnefoy, Yves 1923-
CLC 9, 15, 58; DAM MST, POET
See also CA 85-88; CANR 33, 75; MTCW 1

Bontemps, Arna(ud Wendell) 1902-1973
**CLC 1, 18; BLC 1; DAM MULT, NOV,
POET**
See also BW 1; CA 1-4R; 41-44R; CANR 4,
35; CLR 6; DLB 48, 51; JRDA; MAICYA;
MTCW 1; SATA 2, 44; SATA-Obit 24

Booth, Martin 1944-
CLC 13
See also CA 93-96; CAAS 2

Booth, Philip 1925-
CLC 23
See also CA 5-8R; CANR 5; DLBY 82

Booth, Wayne C(layson) 1921-
CLC 24
See also CA 1-4R; CAAS 5; CANR 3, 43; DLB
67

Borchert, Wolfgang 1921-1947
TCLC 5

See also CA 104; DLB 69, 124

Borel, Petrus 1809-1859
NCLC 41

Borges, Jorge Luis 1899-1986
**CLC 1, 2, 3, 4, 6, 8, 9, 10, 13, 19, 44, 48,
83; DA; DAB; DAC; DAM MST, MULT;
HLC; PC 22; SSC 4; WLC**
See also AAYA 26; CA 21-24R; CANR 19, 33,
75; DLB 113; DLBY 86; HW; MTCW 1

Borowski, Tadeusz 1922-1951
TCLC 9
See also CA 106; 154

Borrow, George (Henry) 1803-1881
NCLC 9
See also DLB 21, 55, 166

Bosman, Herman Charles 1905-1951
TCLC 49
See also Malan, Herman
See also CA 160

Bosschere, Jean de .... 1878(?)-1953
TCLC 19
See also CA 115

Boswell, James 1740-1795
LC 4; DA; DAB; DAC; DAM MST; WLC
See also CDBLB 1660-1789; DLB 104, 142

Bottoms, David 1949-
CLC 53
See also CA 105; CANR 22; DLB 120; DLBY
83

Boucicault, Dion 1820-1890
NCLC 41

Boucolon, Maryse .... 1937(?)-
See Conde, Maryse
See also CA 110; CANR 30, 53

Bourget, Paul (Charles Joseph) .. 1852-1935
TCLC 12
See also CA 107; DLB 123

Bourjaily, Vance (Nye) 1922-
CLC 8, 62
See also CA 1-4R; CAAS 1; CANR 2, 72; DLB
2, 143

Bourne, Randolph S(illiman) 1886-1918
TCLC 16
See also CA 117; 155; DLB 63

Bova, Ben(jamin William) 1932-
CLC 45
See also AAYA 16; CA 5-8R; CAAS 18; CANR
11, 56; CLR 3; DLBY 81; INT CANR-11;
MAICYA; MTCW 1; SATA 6, 68

Bowen, Elizabeth (Dorothea Cole) 1899-1973
**CLC 1, 3, 6, 11, 15, 22; DAM NOV; SSC 3,
28**
See also CA 17-18; 41-44R; CANR 35; CAP 2;
CDBLB 1945-1960; DLB 15, 162; MTCW
1

Bowering, George 1935-
CLC 15, 47
See also CA 21-24R; CAAS 16; CANR 10; DLB
53

Bowering, Marilyn R(uthe) 1949-
CLC 32
See also CA 101; CANR 49

Bowers, Edgar 1924-
CLC 9
See also CA 5-8R; CANR 24; DLB 5

Bowie, David ....**CLC 17**
See also Jones, David Robert

Bowles, Jane (Sydney) 1917-1973
CLC 3, 68
See also CA 19-20; 41-44R; CAP 2

Bowles, Paul (Frederick) 1910-
CLC 1, 2, 19, 53; SSC 3
See also CA 1-4R; CAAS 1; CANR 1, 19, 50,

75; DLB 5, 6; MTCW 1

Box, Edgar
See Vidal, Gore

Boyd, Nancy
See Millay, Edna St. Vincent

Boyd, William 1952-
CLC 28, 53, 70
See also CA 114; 120; CANR 51, 71

Boyle, Kay 1902-1992
CLC 1, 5, 19, 58; SSC 5
See also CA 13-16R; 140; CAAS 1; CANR 29,
61; DLB 4, 9, 48, 86; DLBY 93; MTCW 1

Boyle, Mark
See Kienzle, William X(avier)

Boyle, Patrick 1905-1982
CLC 19
See also CA 127

Boyle, T. C. 1948-
See Boyle, T(homas) Coraghessan

Boyle, T(homas) Coraghessan 1948-
CLC 36, 55, 90; DAM POP; SSC 16
See also BEST 90:4; CA 120; CANR 44; DLBY
86

Boz
See Dickens, Charles (John Huffam)

Brackenridge, Hugh Henry 1748-1816
NCLC 7
See also DLB 11, 37

Bradbury, Edward P.
See Moorcock, Michael (John)

Bradbury, Malcolm (Stanley) 1932-
CLC 32, 61; DAM NOV
See also CA 1-4R; CANR 1, 33; DLB 14;
MTCW 1

Bradbury, Ray (Douglas) 1920-
CLC 1, 3, 10, 15, 42, 98; DA; DAB; DAC;
DAM MST, NOV, POP; SSC 29; WLC
See also AAYA 15; AITN 1, 2; CA 1-4R; CANR
2, 30, 75; CDALB 1968-1988; DLB 2, 8;
MTCW 1; SATA 11, 64

Bradford, Gamaliel 1863-1932
TCLC 36
See also CA 160; DLB 17

Bradley, David (Henry, Jr.) 1950-
CLC 23; BLC 1; DAM MULT
See also BW 1; CA 104; CANR 26; DLB 33

Bradley, John Ed(mund, Jr.) 1958-
CLC 55
See also CA 139

Bradley, Marion Zimmer 1930-
CLC 30; DAM POP
See also AAYA 9; CA 57-60; CAAS 10; CANR
7, 31, 51, 75; DLB 8; MTCW 1; SATA 90

Bradstreet, Anne .... 1612(?)-1672
LC 4, 30; DA; DAC; DAM MST, POET;
PC 10
See also CDALB 1640-1865; DLB 24

Brady, Joan 1939-
CLC 86
See also CA 141

Bragg, Melvyn 1939-
CLC 10
See also BEST 89:3; CA 57-60; CANR 10, 48;
DLB 14

Brahe, Tycho 1546-1601
LC 45

Braine, John (Gerard) 1922-1986
CLC 1, 3, 41
See also CA 1-4R; 120; CANR 1, 33; CDBLB
1945-1960; DLB 15; DLBY 86; MTCW 1

Bramah, Ernest 1868-1942
TCLC 72
See also CA 156; DLB 70

Brammer, William .... 1930(?)-1978
CLC 31
See also CA 77-80

Brancati, Vitaliano 1907-1954
TCLC 12
See also CA 109

Brancato, Robin F(idler) 1936-
CLC 35
See also AAYA 9; CA 69-72; CANR 11, 45;
CLR 32; JRDA; SAAS 9; SATA 97

Brand, Max
See Faust, Frederick (Schiller)

Brand, Millen 1906-1980
CLC 7
See also CA 21-24R; 97-100; CANR 72

Branden, Barbara ....CLC 44
See also CA 148

Brandes, Georg (Morris Cohen) . 1842-1927
TCLC 10
See also CA 105

Brandys, Kazimierz 1916-
CLC 62

Branley, Franklyn M(ansfield) 1915-
CLC 21
See also CA 33-36R; CANR 14, 39; CLR 13;
MAICYA; SAAS 16; SATA 4, 68

Brathwaite, Edward Kamau 1930-
CLC 11; BLCS; DAM POET
See also BW 2; CA 25-28R; CANR 11, 26, 47;
DLB 125

Brautigan, Richard (Gary) 1935-1984
CLC 1, 3, 5, 9, 12, 34, 42; DAM NOV
See also CA 53-56; 113; CANR 34; DLB 2, 5,
206; DLBY 80, 84; MTCW 1; SATA 56

Brave Bird, Mary 1953-
See Crow Dog, Mary (Ellen)
See also NNAL

Braverman, Kate 1950-
CLC 67
See also CA 89-92

Brecht, (Eugen) Bertolt (Friedrich)
1898-1956TCLC 1, 6, 13, 35; DA; DAB;
DAC; DAM DRAM, MST; DC 3; WLC
See also CA 104; 133; CANR 62; DLB 56, 124;
MTCW 1

Brecht, Eugen Berthold Friedrich
See Brecht, (Eugen) Bertolt (Friedrich)

Bremer, Fredrika 1801-1865
NCLC 11

Brennan, Christopher John 1870-1932
TCLC 17
See also CA 117

Brennan, Maeve 1917-1993
CLC 5
See also CA 81-84; CANR 72

Brent, Linda
See Jacobs, Harriet A(nn)

Brentano, Clemens (Maria) 1778-1842
NCLC 1
See also DLB 90

Brent of Bin Bin
See Franklin, (Stella Maria Sarah) Miles
(Lampe)

Brenton, Howard 1942-
CLC 31
See also CA 69-72; CANR 33, 67; DLB 13;
MTCW 1

Breslin, James 1930-1996
See Breslin, Jimmy
See also CA 73-76; CANR 31, 75; DAM NOV;
MTCW 1

Breslin, Jimmy .... CLC 4, 43
See also Breslin, James

See also AITN 1; DLB 185

Bresson, Robert 1901-
CLC 16
See also CA 110; CANR 49

Breton, Andre 1896-1966
CLC 2, 9, 15, 54; PC 15
See also CA 19-20; 25-28R; CANR 40, 60; CAP
2; DLB 65; MTCW 1

Breytenbach, Breyten .... 1939(?)-
CLC 23, 37; DAM POET
See also CA 113; 129; CANR 61

Bridgers, Sue Ellen 1942-
CLC 26
See also AAYA 8; CA 65-68; CANR 11, 36;
CLR 18; DLB 52; JRDA; MAICYA; SAAS
1; SATA 22, 90

Bridges, Robert (Seymour) 1844-1930
TCLC 1; DAM POET
See also CA 104; 152; CDBLB 1890-1914;
DLB 19, 98

Bridie, James .... TCLC 3
See also Mavor, Osborne Henry
See also DLB 10

Brin, David 1950-
CLC 34
See also AAYA 21; CA 102; CANR 24, 70; INT
CANR-24; SATA 65

Brink, Andre (Philippus) 1935-
CLC 18, 36, 106
See also CA 104; CANR 39, 62; INT 103;
MTCW 1

Brinsmead, H(esba) F(ay) 1922-
CLC 21
See also CA 21-24R; CANR 10; CLR 47;
MAICYA; SAAS 5; SATA 18, 78

Brittain, Vera (Mary) .... 1893(?)-1970
CLC 23
See also CA 13-16; 25-28R; CANR 58; CAP 1;
DLB 191; MTCW 1

Broch, Hermann 1886-1951
TCLC 20
See also CA 117; DLB 85, 124

Brock, Rose
See Hansen, Joseph

Brodkey, Harold (Roy) 1930-1996
CLC 56
See also CA 111; 151; CANR 71; DLB 130

Brodskii, Iosif
See Brodsky, Joseph

Brodsky, Iosif Alexandrovich 1940-1996
See Brodsky, Joseph
See also AITN 1; CA 41-44R; 151; CANR 37;
DAM POET; MTCW 1

Brodsky, Joseph 1940-1996
CLC 4, 6, 13, 36, 100; PC 9
See also Brodskii, Iosif; Brodsky, Iosif
Alexandrovich

Brodsky, Michael (Mark) 1948-
CLC 19
See also CA 102; CANR 18, 41, 58

Bromell, Henry 1947-
CLC 5
See also CA 53-56; CANR 9

Bromfield, Louis (Brucker) 1896-1956
TCLC 11
See also CA 107; 155; DLB 4, 9, 86

Broner, E(sther) M(asserman) 1930-
CLC 19
See also CA 17-20R; CANR 8, 25, 72; DLB 28

Bronk, William 1918-
CLC 10
See also CA 89-92; CANR 23; DLB 165

Bronstein, Lev Davidovich

See Trotsky, Leon

Bronte, Anne 1820-1849
   NCLC 71
   See also DLB 21, 199

Bronte, Charlotte 1816-1855
   NCLC 3, 8, 33, 58; DA; DAB; DAC; DAM
   MST, NOV; WLC
   See also AAYA 17; CDBLB 1832-1890; DLB
   21, 159, 199

Bronte, Emily (Jane) 1818-1848
   NCLC 16, 35; DA; DAB; DAC; DAM
   MST, NOV, POET; PC 8; WLC
   See also AAYA 17; CDBLB 1832-1890; DLB
   21, 32, 199

Brooke, Frances 1724-1789
   LC 6, 48
   See also DLB 39, 99

Brooke, Henry ....: 1703(?)-1783
   LC 1
   See also DLB 39

Brooke, Rupert (Chawner) 1887-1915
   TCLC 2, 7; DA; DAB; DAC; DAM MST,
   POET; PC 24; WLC
   See also CA 104; 132; CANR 61; CDBLB
   1914-1945; DLB 19; MTCW 1

Brooke-Haven, P.
   See Wodehouse, P(elham) G(renville)

Brooke-Rose, Christine .... 1926(?)-
   CLC 40
   See also CA 13-16R; CANR 58; DLB 14

Brookner, Anita 1928-
   CLC 32, 34, 51; DAB; DAM POP
   See also CA 114; 120; CANR 37, 56; DLB 194;
   DLBY 87; MTCW 1

Brooks, Cleanth 1906-1994
   CLC 24, 86, 110
   See also CA 17-20R; 145; CANR 33, 35; DLB
   63; DLBY 94; INT CANR-35; MTCW 1

Brooks, George
   See Baum, L(yman) Frank

Brooks, Gwendolyn 1917-
   CLC 1, 2, 4, 5, 15, 49; BLC 1; DA; DAC;
   DAM MST, MULT, POET; PC 7; WLC
   See also AAYA 20; AITN 1; BW 2; CA 1-4R;
   CANR 1, 27, 52, 75; CDALB 1941-1968;
   CLR 27; DLB 5, 76, 165; MTCW 1; SATA 6

Brooks, Mel .... CLC 12
   See also Kaminsky, Melvin
   See also AAYA 13; DLB 26

Brooks, Peter 1938-
   CLC 34
   See also CA 45-48; CANR 1

Brooks, Van Wyck 1886-1963
   CLC 29
   See also CA 1-4R; CANR 6; DLB 45, 63, 103

Brophy, Brigid (Antonia) 1929-1995
   CLC 6, 11, 29, 105
   See also CA 5-8R; 149; CAAS 4; CANR 25,
   53; DLB 14; MTCW 1

Brosman, Catharine Savage 1934-
   CLC 9
   See also CA 61-64; CANR 21, 46

Brossard, Nicole 1943-
   CLC 115
   See also CA 122; CAAS 16; DLB 53

Brother Antoninus
   See Everson, William (Oliver)

The Brothers Quay
   See Quay, Stephen; Quay, Timothy

Broughton, T(homas) Alan 1936-
   CLC 19
   See also CA 45-48; CANR 2, 23, 48

Broumas, Olga 1949-

CLC 10, 73
   See also CA 85-88; CANR 20, 69

Brown, Alan 1950-
   CLC 99
   See also CA 156

Brown, Charles Brockden 1771-1810
   NCLC 22, 74
   See also CDALB 1640-1865; DLB 37, 59, 73

Brown, Christy 1932-1981
   CLC 63
   See also CA 105; 104; CANR 72; DLB 14

Brown, Claude 1937-
   CLC 30; BLC 1; DAM MULT
   See also AAYA 7; BW 1; CA 73-76

Brown, Dee (Alexander) 1908-
   CLC 18, 47; DAM POP
   See also CA 13-16R; CAAS 6; CANR 11, 45,
   60; DLBY 80; MTCW 1; SATA 5

Brown, George
   See Wertmueller, Lina

Brown, George Douglas 1869-1902
   TCLC 28
   See also CA 162

Brown, George Mackay 1921-1996
   CLC 5, 48, 100
   See also CA 21-24R; 151; CAAS 6; CANR 12,
   37, 67; DLB 14, 27, 139; MTCW 1; SATA
   35

Brown, (William) Larry 1951-
   CLC 73
   See also CA 130; 134; INT 133

Brown, Moses
   See Barrett, William (Christopher)

Brown, Rita Mae 1944-
   CLC 18, 43, 79; DAM NOV, POP
   See also CA 45-48; CANR 2, 11, 35, 62; INT
   CANR-11; MTCW 1

Brown, Roderick (Langmere) Haig-
   See Haig-Brown, Roderick (Langmere)

Brown, Rosellen 1939-
   CLC 32
   See also CA 77-80; CAAS 10; CANR 14, 44

Brown, Sterling Allen 1901-1989
   CLC 1, 23, 59; BLC 1; DAM MULT, POET
   See also BW 1; CA 85-88; 127; CANR 26, 74;
   DLB 48, 51, 63; MTCW 1

Brown, Will
   See Ainsworth, William Harrison

Brown, William Wells 1813-1884
   NCLC 2; BLC 1; DAM MULT; DC 1
   See also DLB 3, 50

Browne, (Clyde) Jackson .... 1948(?)-
   CLC 21
   See also CA 120

Browning, Elizabeth Barrett 1806-1861
   NCLC 1, 16, 61, 66; DA; DAB; DAC; DAM
   MST, POET; PC 6; WLC
   See also CDBLB 1832-1890; DLB 32, 199

Browning, Robert 1812-1889
   NCLC 19; DA; DAB; DAC; DAM MST,
   POET; PC 2; WLCS
   See also CDBLB 1832-1890; DLB 32, 163;
   YABC 1

Browning, Tod 1882-1962
   CLC 16
   See also CA 141; 117

Brownson, Orestes Augustus 1803-1876
   NCLC 50
   See also DLB 1, 59, 73

Bruccoli, Matthew J(oseph) 1931-
   CLC 34
   See also CA 9-12R; CANR 7; DLB 103

Bruce, Lenny .... CLC 21

See also Schneider, Leonard Alfred

Bruin, John
   See Brutus, Dennis

Brulard, Henri
   See Stendhal

Brulls, Christian
   See Simenon, Georges (Jacques Christian)

Brunner, John (Kilian Houston) . 1934-1995
   CLC 8, 10; DAM POP
   See also CA 1-4R; 149; CAAS 8; CANR 2, 37;
   MTCW 1

Bruno, Giordano 1548-1600
   LC 27

Brutus, Dennis 1924-
   CLC 43; BLC 1; DAM MULT, POET; PC
   24
   See also BW 2; CA 49-52; CAAS 14; CANR 2,
   27, 42; DLB 117

Bryan, C(ourtlandt) D(ixon) B(arnes) 1936-
   CLC 29
   See also CA 73-76; CANR 13, 68; DLB 185;
   INT CANR-13

Bryan, Michael
   See Moore, Brian

Bryant, William Cullen 1794-1878
   NCLC 6, 46; DA; DAB; DAC; DAM MST,
   POET; PC 20
   See also CDALB 1640-1865; DLB 3, 43, 59,
   189

Bryusov, Valery Yakovlevich 1873-1924
   TCLC 10
   See also CA 107; 155

Buchan, John 1875-1940
   TCLC 41; DAB; DAM POP
   See also CA 108; 145; DLB 34, 70, 156; YABC
   2

Buchanan, George 1506-1582
   LC 4
   See also DLB 152

Buchheim, Lothar-Guenther 1918-
   CLC 6
   See also CA 85-88

Buchner, (Karl) Georg 1813-1837
   NCLC 26

Buchwald, Art(hur) 1925-
   CLC 33
   See also AITN 1; CA 5-8R; CANR 21, 67;
   MTCW 1; SATA 10

Buck, Pearl S(ydenstricker) 1892-1973
   CLC 7, 11, 18; DA; DAB; DAC; DAM
   MST, NOV
   See also AITN 1; CA 1-4R; 41-44R; CANR 1,
   34; DLB 9, 102; MTCW 1; SATA 1, 25

Buckler, Ernest 1908-1984
   CLC 13; DAC; DAM MST
   See also CA 11-12; 114; CAP 1; DLB 68; SATA
   47

Buckley, Vincent (Thomas) 1925-1988
   CLC 57
   See also CA 101

Buckley, William F(rank), Jr. 1925-
   CLC 7, 18, 37; DAM POP
   See also AITN 1; CA 1-4R; CANR 1, 24, 53;
   DLB 137; DLBY 80; INT CANR-24; MTCW
   1

Buechner, (Carl) Frederick 1926-
   CLC 2, 4, 6, 9; DAM NOV
   See also CA 13-16R; CANR 11, 39, 64; DLBY
   80; INT CANR-11; MTCW 1

Buell, John (Edward) 1927-
   CLC 10
   See also CA 1-4R; CANR 71; DLB 53

Buero Vallejo, Antonio 1916-

Calisher, Hortense 1911-
   CLC 2, 4, 8, 38; DAM NOV; SSC 15
   See also CA 1-4R; CANR 1, 22, 67; DLB 2;
   INT CANR-22; MTCW 1
Callaghan, Morley Edward 1903-1990
   CLC 3, 14, 41, 65; DAC; DAM MST
   See also CA 9-12R; 132; CANR 33, 73; DLB
   68; MTCW 1
Callimachus .... c. 305B.C.-c. 240B.C.
   CMLC 18
   See also DLB 176
Calvin, John 1509-1564
   LC 37
Calvino, Italo 1923-1985
   **CLC 5, 8, 11, 22, 33, 39, 73; DAM NOV;
   SSC 3**
   See also CA 85-88; 116; CANR 23, 61; DLB
   196; MTCW 1
Cameron, Carey 1952-
   CLC 59
   See also CA 135
Cameron, Peter 1959-
   CLC 44
   See also CA 125; CANR 50
Campana, Dino 1885-1932
   TCLC 20
   See also CA 117; DLB 114
Campanella, Tommaso 1568-1639
   LC 32
Campbell, John W(ood, Jr.) 1910-1971
   CLC 32
   See also CA 21-22; 29-32R; CANR 34; CAP 2;
   DLB 8; MTCW 1
Campbell, Joseph 1904-1987
   CLC 69
   See also AAYA 3; BEST 89:2; CA 1-4R; 124;
   CANR 3, 28, 61; MTCW 1
Campbell, Maria 1940-
   CLC 85; DAC
   See also CA 102; CANR 54; NNAL
Campbell, (John) Ramsey 1946-
   CLC 42; SSC 19
   See also CA 57-60; CANR 7; INT CANR-7
Campbell, (Ignatius) Roy (Dunnachie)
   1901-1957 .... TCLC 5
   See also CA 104; 155; DLB 20
Campbell, Thomas 1777-1844
   NCLC 19
   See also DLB 93; 144
Campbell, Wilfred .... TCLC 9
   See also Campbell, William
Campbell, William .... 1858(?)-1918
   See Campbell, Wilfred
   See also CA 106; DLB 92
Campion, Jane .... CLC 95
   See also CA 138
Campos, Alvaro de
   See Pessoa, Fernando (Antonio Nogueira)
Camus, Albert 1913-1960
   **CLC 1, 2, 4, 9, 11, 14, 32, 63, 69; DA; DAB;
   DAC; DAM DRAM, MST, NOV; DC 2;
   SSC 9; WLC**
   See also CA 89-92; DLB 72; MTCW 1
Canby, Vincent 1924-
   CLC 13
   See also CA 81-84
Cancale
   See Desnos, Robert
Canetti, Elias 1905-1994
   CLC 3, 14, 25, 75, 86
   See also CA 21-24R; 146; CANR 23, 61; DLB
   85, 124; MTCW 1
Canfield, Dorothea F.

See Fisher, Dorothy (Frances) Canfield
Canfield, Dorothea Frances
   See Fisher, Dorothy (Frances) Canfield
Canfield, Dorothy
   See Fisher, Dorothy (Frances) Canfield
Canin, Ethan 1960-
   CLC 55
   See also CA 131; 135
Cannon, Curt
   See Hunter, Evan
Cao, Lan 1961-
   CLC 109
   See also CA 165
Cape, Judith
   See Page, P(atricia) K(athleen)
Capek, Karel 1890-1938
   **TCLC 6, 37; DA; DAB; DAC; DAM
   DRAM, MST, NOV; DC 1; WLC**
   See also CA 104; 140
Capote, Truman 1924-1984
   **CLC 1, 3, 8, 13, 19, 34, 38, 58; DA; DAB;
   DAC; DAM MST, NOV, POP; SSC 2;
   WLC**
   See also CA 5-8R; 113; CANR 18, 62; CDALB
   1941-1968; DLB 2, 185; DLBY 80, 84;
   MTCW 1; SATA 91
Capra, Frank 1897-1991
   CLC 16
   See also CA 61-64; 135
Caputo, Philip 1941-
   CLC 32
   See also CA 73-76; CANR 40
Caragiale, Ion Luca 1852-1912
   TCLC 76
   See also CA 157
Card, Orson Scott 1951-
   CLC 44, 47, 50; DAM POP
   See also AAYA 11; CA 102; CANR 27, 47, 73;
   INT CANR-27; MTCW 1; SATA 83
Cardenal, Ernesto 1925-
   **CLC 31; DAM MULT, POET; HLC; PC
   22**
   See also CA 49-52; CANR 2, 32, 66; HW;
   MTCW 1
Cardozo, Benjamin N(athan) 1870-1938
   TCLC 65
   See also CA 117; 164
Carducci, Giosue (Alessandro Giuseppe)
   1835-1907 .... TCLC 32
   See also CA 163
Carew, Thomas .... 1595(?)-1640
   LC 13
   See also DLB 126
Carey, Ernestine Gilbreth 1908-
   CLC 17
   See also CA 5-8R; CANR 71; SATA 2
Carey, Peter 1943-
   CLC 40, 55, 96
   See also CA 123; 127; CANR 53; INT 127;
   MTCW 1; SATA 94
Carleton, William 1794-1869
   NCLC 3
   See also DLB 159
Carlisle, Henry (Coffin) 1926-
   CLC 33
   See also CA 13-16R; CANR 15
Carlsen, Chris
   See Holdstock, Robert P.
Carlson, Ron(ald F.) 1947-
   CLC 54
   See also CA 105; CANR 27
Carlyle, Thomas 1795-1881
   NCLC 70; DA; DAB; DAC; DAM MST

See also CDBLB 1789-1832; DLB 55; 144
Carman, (William) Bliss 1861-1929
   TCLC 7; DAC
   See also CA 104; 152; DLB 92
Carnegie, Dale 1888-1955
   TCLC 53
Carossa, Hans 1878-1956
   TCLC 48
   See also CA 170; DLB 66
Carpenter, Don(ald Richard) 1931-1995
   CLC 41
   See also CA 45-48; 149; CANR 1, 71
Carpenter, Edward 1844-1929
   TCLC 88
   See also CA 163
Carpentier (y Valmont), Alejo 1904-1980
   CLC 8, 11, 38, 110; DAM MULT; HLC
   See also CA 65-68; 97-100; CANR 11, 70; DLB
   113; HW
Carr, Caleb .... 1955(?)-
   CLC 86
   See also CA 147; CANR 73
Carr, Emily 1871-1945
   TCLC 32
   See also CA 159; DLB 68
Carr, John Dickson 1906-1977
   CLC 3
   See also Fairbairn, Roger
   See also CA 49-52; 69-72; CANR 3, 33, 60;
   MTCW 1
Carr, Philippa
   See Hibbert, Eleanor Alice Burford
Carr, Virginia Spencer 1929-
   CLC 34
   See also CA 61-64; DLB 111
Carrere, Emmanuel 1957-
   CLC 89
Carrier, Roch 1937-
   CLC 13, 78; DAC; DAM MST
   See also CA 130; CANR 61; DLB 53
Carroll, James P. .... 1943(?)-
   CLC 38
   See also CA 81-84; CANR 73
Carroll, Jim 1951-
   CLC 35
   See also AAYA 17; CA 45-48; CANR 42
Carroll, Lewis ...... NCLC 2, 53; PC 18; WLC
   See also Dodgson, Charles Lutwidge
   See also CDBLB 1832-1890; CLR 2, 18; DLB
   18, 163, 178; JRDA
Carroll, Paul Vincent 1900-1968
   CLC 10
   See also CA 9-12R; 25-28R; DLB 10
Carruth, Hayden 1921-
   CLC 4, 7, 10, 18, 84; PC 10
   See also CA 9-12R; CANR 4, 38, 59; DLB 5,
   165; INT CANR-4; MTCW 1; SATA 47
Carson, Rachel Louise 1907-1964
   CLC 71; DAM POP
   See also CA 77-80; CANR 35; MTCW 1; SATA
   23
Carter, Angela (Olive) 1940-1992
   CLC 5, 41, 76; SSC 13
   See also CA 53-56; 136; CANR 12, 36, 61; DLB
   14; MTCW 1; SATA 66; SATA-Obit 70
Carter, Nick
   See Smith, Martin Cruz
Carver, Raymond 1938-1988
   CLC 22, 36, 53, 55; DAM NOV; SSC 8
   See also CA 33-36R; 126; CANR 17, 34, 61;
   DLB 130; DLBY 84, 88; MTCW 1
Cary, Elizabeth, Lady Falkland . 1585-1639
   LC 30

Charyn, Jerome 1937-
CLC 5, 8, 18
See also CA 5-8R; CAAS 1; CANR 7, 61;
DLBY 83; MTCW 1
Chase, Mary (Coyle) 1907-1981
DC 1
See also CA 77-80; 105; SATA 17; SATA-Obit
29
Chase, Mary Ellen 1887-1973
CLC 2
See also CA 13-16; 41-44R; CAP 1; SATA 10
Chase, Nicholas
See Hyde, Anthony
Chateaubriand, Francois Rene de 1768-1848
NCLC 3
See also DLB 119
Chatterje, Sarat Chandra .... 1876-1936(?)
See Chatterji, Saratchandra
See also CA 109
Chatterji, Bankim Chandra 1838-1894
NCLC 19
Chatterji, Saratchandra .... TCLC 13
See also Chatterje, Sarat Chandra
Chatterton, Thomas 1752-1770
LC 3; DAM POET
See also DLB 109
Chatwin, (Charles) Bruce 1940-1989
CLC 28, 57, 59; DAM POP
See also AAYA 4; BEST 90:1; CA 85-88; 127;
DLB 194
Chaucer, Daniel
See Ford, Ford Madox
Chaucer, Geoffrey .... 1340(?)-1400
LC 17; DA; DAB; DAC; DAM MST,
POET; PC 19; WLCS
See also CDBLB Before 1660; DLB 146
Chaviaras, Strates 1935-
See Haviaras, Stratis
See also CA 105
Chayefsky, Paddy .... CLC 23
See also Chayefsky, Sidney
See also DLB 7, 44; DLBY 81
Chayefsky, Sidney 1923-1981
See Chayefsky, Paddy
See also CA 9-12R; 104; CANR 18; DAM
DRAM
Chedid, Andree 1920-
CLC 47
See also CA 145
Cheever, John 1912-1982
CLC 3, 7, 8, 11, 15, 25, 64; DA; DAB; DAC;
DAM MST, NOV, POP; SSC 1; WLC
See also CA 5-8R; 106; CABS 1; CANR 5, 27;
CDALB 1941-1968; DLB 2, 102; DLBY 80,
82; INT CANR-5; MTCW 1
Cheever, Susan 1943-
CLC 18, 48
See also CA 103; CANR 27, 51; DLBY 82; INT
CANR-27
Chekhonte, Antosha
See Chekhov, Anton (Pavlovich)
Chekhov, Anton (Pavlovich) 1860-1904
TCLC 3, 10, 31, 55; DA; DAB; DAC; DAM
DRAM, MST; DC 9; SSC 2, 28; WLC
See also CA 104; 124; SATA 90
Chernyshevsky, Nikolay Gavrilovich
1828-1889 .... NCLC 1
Cherry, Carolyn Janice 1942-
See Cherryh, C. J.
See also CA 65-68; CANR 10
Cherryh, C. J. .... CLC 35
See also Cherry, Carolyn Janice
See also AAYA 24; DLBY 80; SATA 93

Chesnutt, Charles W(addell) 1858-1932
TCLC 5, 39; BLC 1; DAM MULT; SSC 7
See also BW 1; CA 106; 125; DLB 12, 50, 78;
MTCW 1
Chester, Alfred .... 1929(?)-1971
CLC 49
See also CA 33-36R; DLB 130
Chesterton, G(ilbert) K(eith) 1874-1936
TCLC 1, 6, 64; DAM NOV, POET; SSC 1
See also CA 104; 132; CANR 73; CDBLB
1914-1945; DLB 10, 19, 34, 70, 98, 149,
178; MTCW 1; SATA 27
Chiang, Pin-chin 1904-1986
See Ding Ling
See also CA 118
Ch'ien Chung-shu 1910-
CLC 22
See also CA 130; CANR 73; MTCW 1
Child, L. Maria
See Child, Lydia Maria
Child, Lydia Maria 1802-1880
NCLC 6, 73
See also DLB 1, 74; SATA 67
Child, Mrs.
See Child, Lydia Maria
Child, Philip 1898-1978
CLC 19, 68
See also CA 13-14; CAP 1; SATA 47
Childers, (Robert) Erskine 1870-1922
TCLC 65
See also CA 113; 153; DLB 70
Childress, Alice 1920-1994
CLC 12, 15, 86, 96; BLC 1; DAM DRAM,
MULT, NOV; DC 4
See also AAYA 8; BW 2; CA 45-48; 146; CANR
3, 27, 50, 74; CLR 14; DLB 7, 38; JRDA;
MAICYA; MTCW 1; SATA 7, 48, 81
Chin, Frank (Chew, Jr.) 1940-
DC 7
See also CA 33-36R; CANR 71; DAM MULT
Chislett, (Margaret) Anne 1943-
CLC 34
See also CA 151
Chitty, Thomas Willes 1926-
CLC 11
See also Hinde, Thomas
See also CA 5-8R
Chivers, Thomas Holley 1809-1858
NCLC 49
See also DLB 3
Chomette, Rene Lucien 1898-1981
See Clair, Rene
See also CA 103
Chopin, Kate TCLC 5, 14; DA; DAB; SSC 8;
WLCS
See also Chopin, Katherine
See also CDALB 1865-1917; DLB 12, 78
Chopin, Katherine 1851-1904
See Chopin, Kate
See also CA 104; 122; DAC; DAM MST, NOV
Chretien de Troyes .... c. 12th cent. -
CMLC 10
Christie
See Ichikawa, Kon
Christie, Agatha (Mary Clarissa) 1890-1976
CLC 1, 6, 8, 12, 39, 48, 110; DAB; DAC;
DAM NOV
See also AAYA 9; AITN 1, 2; CA 17-20R;
61-64; CANR 10, 37; CDBLB 1914-1945;
DLB 13, 77; MTCW 1; SATA 36
Christie, (Ann) Philippa
See Pearce, Philippa
See also CA 5-8R; CANR 4

Christine de Pizan .... 1365(?)-1431(?)
LC 9
Chubb, Elmer
See Masters, Edgar Lee
Chulkov, Mikhail Dmitrievich 1743-1792
LC 2
See also DLB 150
Churchill, Caryl 1938-
CLC 31, 55; DC 5
See also CA 102; CANR 22, 46; DLB 13;
MTCW 1
Churchill, Charles 1731-1764
LC 3
See also DLB 109
Chute, Carolyn 1947-
CLC 39
See also CA 123
Ciardi, John (Anthony) 1916-1986
CLC 10, 40, 44; DAM POET
See also CA 5-8R; 118; CAAS 2; CANR 5, 33;
CLR 19; DLB 5; DLBY 86; INT CANR-5;
MAICYA; MTCW 1; SAAS 26; SATA 1, 65;
SATA-Obit 46
Cicero, Marcus Tullius .... 106B.C.-43B.C.
CMLC 3
Cimino, Michael 1943-
CLC 16
See also CA 105
Cioran, E(mil) M. 1911-1995
CLC 64
See also CA 25-28R; 149
Cisneros, Sandra 1954-
CLC 69; DAM MULT; HLC; SSC 32
See also AAYA 9; CA 131; CANR 64; DLB 122,
152; HW
Cixous, Helene 1937-
CLC 92
See also CA 126; CANR 55; DLB 83; MTCW
1
Clair, Rene .... CLC 20
See also Chomette, Rene Lucien
Clampitt, Amy 1920-1994
CLC 32; PC 19
See also CA 110; 146; CANR 29; DLB 105
Clancy, Thomas L., Jr. 1947-
See Clancy, Tom
See also CA 125; 131; CANR 62; INT 131;
MTCW 1
Clancy, Tom . CLC 45, 112; DAM NOV, POP
See also Clancy, Thomas L., Jr.
See also AAYA 9; BEST 89:1, 90:1
Clare, John 1793-1864
NCLC 9; DAB; DAM POET; PC 23
See also DLB 55, 96
Clarin
See Alas (y Urena), Leopoldo (Enrique Garcia)
Clark, Al C.
See Goines, Donald
Clark, (Robert) Brian 1932-
CLC 29
See also CA 41-44R; CANR 67
Clark, Curt
See Westlake, Donald E(dwin)
Clark, Eleanor 1913-1996
CLC 5, 19
See also CA 9-12R; 151; CANR 41; DLB 6
Clark, J. P.
See Clark, John Pepper
See also DLB 117
Clark, John Pepper 1935-
CLC 38; BLC 1; DAM DRAM, MULT; DC
5
See also Clark, J. P.

See also BW 1; CA 65-68; CANR 16, 72

Clark, M. R.
See Clark, Mavis Thorpe

Clark, Mavis Thorpe 1909-
CLC 12
See also CA 57-60; CANR 8, 37; CLR 30;
MAICYA; SAAS 5; SATA 8, 74

Clark, Walter Van Tilburg 1909-1971
CLC 28
See also CA 9-12R; 33-36R; CANR 63; DLB
9; SATA 8

Clark Bekederemo, J(ohnson) P(epper)
See Clark, John Pepper

Clarke, Arthur C(harles) 1917-
CLC 1, 4, 13, 18, 35; DAM POP; SSC 3
See also AAYA 4; CA 1-4R; CANR 2, 28, 55,
74; JRDA; MAICYA; MTCW 1; SATA 13,
70

Clarke, Austin 1896-1974
CLC 6, 9; DAM POET
See also CA 29-32; 49-52; CAP 2; DLB 10, 20

Clarke, Austin C(hesterfield) 1934-
CLC 8, 53; BLC 1; DAC; DAM MULT
See also BW 1; CA 25-28R; CAAS 16; CANR
14, 32, 68; DLB 53, 125

Clarke, Gillian 1937-
CLC 61
See also CA 106; DLB 40

Clarke, Marcus (Andrew Hislop) 1846-1881
NCLC 19

Clarke, Shirley 1925-
CLC 16

Clash, The
See Headon, (Nicky) Topper; Jones, Mick;
Simonon, Paul; Strummer, Joe

Claudel, Paul (Louis Charles Marie)
1868-1955 .... TCLC 2, 10
See also CA 104; 165; DLB 192

Clavell, James (duMaresq) 1925-1994
CLC 6, 25, 87; DAM NOV, POP
See also CA 25-28R; 146; CANR 26, 48;
MTCW 1

Cleaver, (Leroy) Eldridge 1935-1998
CLC 30; BLC 1; DAM MULT
See also BW 1; CA 21-24R; 167; CANR 16, 75

Cleese, John (Marwood) 1939-
CLC 21
See also Monty Python
See also CA 112; 116; CANR 35; MTCW 1

Cleishbotham, Jebediah
See Scott, Walter

Cleland, John 1710-1789
LC 2, 48
See also DLB 39

Clemens, Samuel Langhorne 1835-1910
See Twain, Mark
See also CA 104; 135; CDALB 1865-1917; DA;
DAB; DAC; DAM MST, NOV; DLB 11, 12,
23, 64, 74, 186, 189; JRDA; MAICYA; SATA
100; YABC 2

Cleophil
See Congreve, William

Clerihew, E.
See Bentley, E(dmund) C(lerihew)

Clerk, N. W.
See Lewis, C(live) S(taples)

Cliff, Jimmy .... CLC 21
See also Chambers, James

Clifton, (Thelma) Lucille 1936-
CLC 19, 66; BLC 1; DAM MULT, POET;
PC 17
See also BW 2; CA 49-52; CANR 2, 24, 42;
CLR 5; DLB 5, 41; MAICYA; MTCW 1;

SATA 20, 69

Clinton, Dirk
See Silverberg, Robert

Clough, Arthur Hugh 1819-1861
NCLC 27
See also DLB 32

Clutha, Janet Paterson Frame 1924-
See Frame, Janet
See also CA 1-4R; CANR 2, 36; MTCW 1

Clyne, Terence
See Blatty, William Peter

Cobalt, Martin
See Mayne, William (James Carter)

Cobb, Irvin S. 1876-1944
TCLC 77
See also DLB 11, 25, 86

Cobbett, William 1763-1835
NCLC 49
See also DLB 43, 107, 158

Coburn, D(onald) L(ee) 1938-
CLC 10
See also CA 89-92

Cocteau, Jean (Maurice Eugene Clement)
1889-1963CLC 1, 8, 15, 16, 43; DA; DAB;
DAC; DAM DRAM, MST, NOV; WLC
See also CA 25-28; CANR 40; CAP 2; DLB
65; MTCW 1

Codrescu, Andrei 1946-
CLC 46; DAM POET
See also CA 33-36R; CAAS 19; CANR 13, 34,
53

Coe, Max
See Bourne, Randolph S(illiman)

Coe, Tucker
See Westlake, Donald E(dwin)

Coen, Ethan 1958-
CLC 108
See also CA 126

Coen, Joel 1955-
CLC 108
See also CA 126

The Coen Brothers
See Coen, Ethan; Coen, Joel

Coetzee, J(ohn) M(ichael) 1940-
CLC 23, 33, 66, 117; DAM NOV
See also CA 77-80; CANR 41, 54, 74; MTCW
1

Coffey, Brian
See Koontz, Dean R(ay)

Cohan, George M(ichael) 1878-1942
TCLC 60
See also CA 157

Cohen, Arthur A(llen) 1928-1986
CLC 7, 31
See also CA 1-4R; 120; CANR 1, 17, 42; DLB
28

Cohen, Leonard (Norman) 1934-
CLC 3, 38; DAC; DAM MST
See also CA 21-24R; CANR 14, 69; DLB 53;
MTCW 1

Cohen, Matt 1942-
CLC 19; DAC
See also CA 61-64; CAAS 18; CANR 40; DLB
53

Cohen-Solal, Annie .... 19(?)-
CLC 50

Colegate, Isabel 1931-
CLC 36
See also CA 17-20R; CANR 8, 22, 74; DLB
14; INT CANR-22; MTCW 1

Coleman, Emmett
See Reed, Ishmael

Coleridge, M. E.

See Coleridge, Mary E(lizabeth)

Coleridge, Mary E(lizabeth) 1861-1907
TCLC 73
See also CA 116; 166; DLB 19, 98

Coleridge, Samuel Taylor 1772-1834
NCLC 9, 54; DA; DAB; DAC; DAM MST,
POET; PC 11; WLC
See also CDBLB 1789-1832; DLB 93, 107

Coleridge, Sara 1802-1852
NCLC 31
See also DLB 199

Coles, Don 1928-
CLC 46
See also CA 115; CANR 38

Coles, Robert (Martin) 1929-
CLC 108
See also CA 45-48; CANR 3, 32, 66, 70; INT
CANR-32; SATA 23

Colette, (Sidonie-Gabrielle) 1873-1954
TCLC 1, 5, 16; DAM NOV; SSC 10
See also CA 104; 131; DLB 65; MTCW 1

Collett, (Jacobine) Camilla (Wergeland)
1813-1895 .... NCLC 22

Collier, Christopher 1930-
CLC 30
See also AAYA 13; CA 33-36R; CANR 13, 33;
JRDA; MAICYA; SATA 16, 70

Collier, James L(incoln) 1928-
CLC 30; DAM POP
See also AAYA 13; CA 9-12R; CANR 4, 33,
60; CLR 3; JRDA; MAICYA; SAAS 21;
SATA 8, 70

Collier, Jeremy 1650-1726
LC 6

Collier, John 1901-1980
SSC 19
See also CA 65-68; 97-100; CANR 10; DLB
77

Collingwood, R(obin) G(eorge) 1889(?)-1943
TCLC 67
See also CA 117; 155

Collins, Hunt
See Hunter, Evan

Collins, Linda 1931-
CLC 44
See also CA 125

Collins, (William) Wilkie 1824-1889
NCLC 1, 18
See also CDBLB 1832-1890; DLB 18, 70, 159

Collins, William 1721-1759
LC 4, 40; DAM POET
See also DLB 109

Collodi, Carlo 1826-1890
NCLC 54
See also Lorenzini, Carlo
See also CLR 5

Colman, George 1732-1794
See Glassco, John

Colt, Winchester Remington
See Hubbard, L(afayette) Ron(ald)

Colter, Cyrus 1910-
CLC 58
See also BW 1; CA 65-68; CANR 10, 66; DLB
33

Colton, James
See Hansen, Joseph

Colum, Padraic 1881-1972
CLC 28
See also CA 73-76; 33-36R; CANR 35; CLR
36; MAICYA; MTCW 1; SATA 15

Colvin, James
See Moorcock, Michael (John)

Colwin, Laurie (E.) 1944-1992

CLC 5, 13, 23, 84
See also CA 89-92; 139; CANR 20, 46; DLBY 80; MTCW 1

Comfort, Alex(ander) 1920-
CLC 7; DAM POP
See also CA 1-4R; CANR 1, 45

Comfort, Montgomery
See Campbell, (John) Ramsey

Compton-Burnett, I(vy) .... 1884(?)-1969
CLC 1, 3, 10, 15, 34; DAM NOV
See also CA 1-4R; 25-28R; CANR 4; DLB 36; MTCW 1

Comstock, Anthony 1844-1915
TCLC 13
See also CA 110; 169

Comte, Auguste 1798-1857
NCLC 54

Conan Doyle, Arthur
See Doyle, Arthur Conan

Conde, Maryse 1937-
CLC 52, 92; BLCS; DAM MULT
See also Boucolon, Maryse
See also BW 2

Condillac, Etienne Bonnot de 1714-1780
LC 26

Condon, Richard (Thomas) 1915-1996
CLC 4, 6, 8, 10, 45, 100; DAM NOV
See also BEST 90:3; CA 1-4R; 151; CAAS 1; CANR 2, 23; INT CANR-23; MTCW 1

Confucius .... 551B.C.-479B.C.
CMLC 19; DA; DAB; DAC; DAM MST; WLCS

Congreve, William 1670-1729
LC 5, 21; DA; DAB; DAC; DAM DRAM, MST, POET; DC 2; WLC
See also CDBLB 1660-1789; DLB 39, 84

Connell, Evan S(helby), Jr. 1924-
CLC 4, 6, 45; DAM NOV
See also AAYA 7; CA 1-4R; CAAS 2; CANR 2, 39; DLB 2; DLBY 81; MTCW 1

Connelly, Marc(us Cook) 1890-1980
CLC 7
See also CA 85-88; 102; CANR 30; DLB 7; DLBY 80; SATA-Obit 25

Connor, Ralph .... TCLC 31
See also Gordon, Charles William
See also DLB 92

Conrad, Joseph 1857-1924
TCLC 1, 6, 13, 25, 43, 57; DA; DAB; DAC; DAM MST, NOV; SSC 9; WLC
See also AAYA 26; CA 104; 131; CANR 60; CDBLB 1890-1914; DLB 10, 34, 98, 156; MTCW 1; SATA 27

Conrad, Robert Arnold
See Hart, Moss

Conroy, Pat
See Conroy, (Donald) Pat(rick)

Conroy, (Donald) Pat(rick) 1945-
CLC 30, 74; DAM NOV, POP
See also AAYA 8; AITN 1; CA 85-88; CANR 24, 53; DLB 6; MTCW 1

Constant (de Rebecque), (Henri) Benjamin 1767-1830 .... NCLC 6
See also DLB 119

Conybeare, Charles Augustus
See Eliot, T(homas) S(tearns)

Cook, Michael 1933-
CLC 58
See also CA 93-96; CANR 68; DLB 53

Cook, Robin 1940-
CLC 14; DAM POP
See also BEST 90:2; CA 108; 111; CANR 41; INT 111

Cook, Roy
See Silverberg, Robert

Cooke, Elizabeth 1948-
CLC 55
See also CA 129

Cooke, John Esten 1830-1886
NCLC 5
See also DLB 3

Cooke, John Estes
See Baum, L(yman) Frank

Cooke, M. E.
See Creasey, John

Cooke, Margaret
See Creasey, John

Cook-Lynn, Elizabeth 1930-
CLC 93; DAM MULT
See also CA 133; DLB 175; NNAL

Cooney, Ray ....CLC 62

Cooper, Douglas 1960-
CLC 86

Cooper, Henry St. John
See Creasey, John

Cooper, J(oan) California .... CLC 56; DAM MULT
See also AAYA 12; BW 1; CA 125; CANR 55

Cooper, James Fenimore 1789-1851
NCLC 1, 27, 54
See also AAYA 22; CDALB 1640-1865; DLB 3; SATA 19

Coover, Robert (Lowell) 1932-
CLC 3, 7, 15, 32, 46, 87; DAM NOV; SSC 15
See also CA 45-48; CANR 3, 37, 58; DLB 2; DLBY 81; MTCW 1

Copeland, Stewart (Armstrong) 1952-
CLC 26

Copernicus, Nicolaus 1473-1543
LC 45

Coppard, A(lfred) E(dgar) 1878-1957
TCLC 5; SSC 21
See also CA 114; 167; DLB 162; YABC 1

Coppee, Francois 1842-1908
TCLC 25
See also CA 170

Coppola, Francis Ford 1939-
CLC 16
See also CA 77-80; CANR 40; DLB 44

Corbiere, Tristan 1845-1875
NCLC 43

Corcoran, Barbara 1911-
CLC 17
See also AAYA 14; CA 21-24R; CAAS 2; CANR 11, 28, 48; CLR 50; DLB 52; JRDA; SAAS 20; SATA 3, 77

Cordelier, Maurice
See Giraudoux, (Hippolyte) Jean

Corelli, Marie 1855-1924
TCLC 51
See also Mackay, Mary
See also DLB 34, 156

Corman, Cid 1924-
CLC 9
See also Corman, Sidney
See also CAAS 2; DLB 5, 193

Corman, Sidney 1924-
See Corman, Cid
See also CA 85-88; CANR 44; DAM POET

Cormier, Robert (Edmund) 1925-
CLC 12, 30; DA; DAB; DAC; DAM MST, NOV
See also AAYA 3, 19; CA 1-4R; CANR 5, 23; CDALB 1968-1988; CLR 12, 55; DLB 52; INT CANR-23; JRDA; MAICYA; MTCW 1;

SATA 10, 45, 83

Corn, Alfred (DeWitt III) 1943-
CLC 33
See also CA 104; CAAS 25; CANR 44; DLB 120; DLBY 80

Corneille, Pierre 1606-1684
LC 28; DAB; DAM MST

Cornwell, David (John Moore) 1931-
CLC 9, 15; DAM POP
See also le Carre, John
See also CA 5-8R; CANR 13, 33, 59; MTCW 1

Corso, (Nunzio) Gregory 1930-
CLC 1, 11
See also CA 5-8R; CANR 41; DLB 5, 16; MTCW 1

Cortazar, Julio 1914-1984
CLC 2, 3, 5, 10, 13, 15, 33, 34, 92; DAM MULT, NOV; HLC; SSC 7
See also CA 21-24R; CANR 12, 32; DLB 113; HW; MTCW 1

CORTES, HERNAN 1484-1547
LC 31

Corvinus, Jakob
See Raabe, Wilhelm (Karl)

Corwin, Cecil
See Kornbluth, C(yril) M.

Cosic, Dobrica 1921-
CLC 14
See also CA 122; 138; DLB 181

Costain, Thomas B(ertram) 1885-1965
CLC 30
See also CA 5-8R; 25-28R; DLB 9

Costantini, Humberto .... 1924(?)-1987
CLC 49
See also CA 131; 122; HW

Costello, Elvis 1955-
CLC 21

Cotes, Cecil V.
See Duncan, Sara Jeannette

Cotter, Joseph Seamon Sr. 1861-1949
TCLC 28; BLC 1; DAM MULT
See also BW 1; CA 124; DLB 50

Couch, Arthur Thomas Quiller
See Quiller-Couch, SirArthur (Thomas)

Coulton, James
See Hansen, Joseph

Couperus, Louis (Marie Anne) ... 1863-1923
TCLC 15
See also CA 115

Coupland, Douglas 1961-
CLC 85; DAC; DAM POP
See also CA 142; CANR 57

Court, Wesli
See Turco, Lewis (Putnam)

Courtenay, Bryce 1933-
CLC 59
See also CA 138

Courtney, Robert
See Ellison, Harlan (Jay)

Cousteau, Jacques-Yves 1910-1997
CLC 30
See also CA 65-68; 159; CANR 15, 67; MTCW 1; SATA 38, 98

Coventry, Francis 1725-1754
LC 46

Cowan, Peter (Walkinshaw) 1914-
SSC 28
See also CA 21-24R; CANR 9, 25, 50

Coward, Noel (Peirce) 1899-1973
CLC 1, 9, 29, 51; DAM DRAM
See also AITN 1; CA 17-18; 41-44R; CANR 35; CAP 2; CDBLB 1914-1945; DLB 10; MTCW 1

Cowley, Abraham 1618-1667
    LC 43
    See also DLB 131, 151
Cowley, Malcolm 1898-1989
    CLC 39
    See also CA 5-8R; 128; CANR 3, 55; DLB 4,
    48; DLBY 81, 89; MTCW 1
Cowper, William 1731-1800
    NCLC 8; DAM POET
    See also DLB 104, 109
Cox, William Trevor 1928-
    CLC 9, 14, 71; DAM NOV
    See also Trevor, William
    See also CA 9-12R; CANR 4, 37, 55; DLB 14;
    INT CANR-37; MTCW 1
Coyne, P. J.
    See Masters, Hilary
Cozzens, James Gould 1903-1978
    CLC 1, 4, 11, 92
    See also CA 9-12R; 81-84; CANR 19; CDALB
    1941-1968; DLB 9; DLBD 2; DLBY 84, 97;
    MTCW 1
Crabbe, George 1754-1832
    NCLC 26
    See also DLB 93
Craddock, Charles Egbert
    See Murfree, Mary Noailles
Craig, A. A.
    See Anderson, Poul (William)
Craik, Dinah Maria (Mulock) 1826-1887
    NCLC 38
    See also DLB 35, 163; MAICYA; SATA 34
Cram, Ralph Adams...................... 1863-1942
    TCLC 45
    See also CA 160
Crane, (Harold) Hart 1899-1932
    TCLC 2, 5, 80; DA; DAB; DAC; DAM
    MST, POET; PC 3; WLC
    See also CA 104; 127; CDALB 1917-1929;
    DLB 4, 48; MTCW 1
Crane, R(onald) S(almon) 1886-1967
    CLC 27
    See also CA 85-88; DLB 63
Crane, Stephen (Townley) 1871-1900
    TCLC 11, 17, 32; DA; DAB; DAC; DAM
    MST, NOV, POET; SSC 7; WLC
    See also AAYA 21; CA 109; 140; CDALB
    1865-1917; DLB 12, 54, 78; YABC 2
Cranshaw, Stanley
    See Fisher, Dorothy (Frances) Canfield
Crase, Douglas 1944-
    CLC 58
    See also CA 106
Crashaw, Richard..................... 1612(?)-1649
    LC 24
    See also DLB 126
Craven, Margaret 1901-1980
    CLC 17; DAC
    See also CA 103
Crawford, F(rancis) Marion 1854-1909
    TCLC 10
    See also CA 107; 168; DLB 71
Crawford, Isabella Valancy 1850-1887
    NCLC 12
    See also DLB 92
Crayon, Geoffrey
    See Irving, Washington
Creasey, John 1908-1973
    CLC 11
    See also CA 5-8R; 41-44R; CANR 8, 59; DLB
    77; MTCW 1
Crebillon, Claude Prosper Jolyot de (fils)
    1707-1777 .... LC 1, 28

Credo
    See Creasey, John
Credo, Alvaro J. de
    See Prado (Calvo), Pedro
Creeley, Robert (White) 1926-
    CLC 1, 2, 4, 8, 11, 15, 36, 78; DAM POET
    See also CA 1-4R; CAAS 10; CANR 23, 43;
    DLB 5, 16, 169; DLBD 17; MTCW 1
Crews, Harry (Eugene) 1935-
    CLC 6, 23, 49
    See also AITN 1; CA 25-28R; CANR 20, 57;
    DLB 6, 143, 185; MTCW 1
Crichton, (John) Michael 1942-
    CLC 2, 6, 54, 90; DAM NOV, POP
    See also AAYA 10; AITN 2; CA 25-28R; CANR
    13, 40, 54; DLBY 81; INT CANR-13; JRDA;
    MTCW 1; SATA 9, 88
Crispin, Edmund ....CLC 22
    See also Montgomery, (Robert) Bruce
    See also DLB 87
Cristofer, Michael............................. 1945(?)-
    CLC 28; DAM DRAM
    See also CA 110; 152; DLB 7
Croce, Benedetto 1866-1952
    TCLC 37
    See also CA 120; 155
Crockett, David 1786-1836
    NCLC 8
    See also DLB 3, 11
Crockett, Davy
    See Crockett, David
Crofts, Freeman Wills 1879-1957
    TCLC 55
    See also CA 115; DLB 77
Croker, John Wilson 1780-1857
    NCLC 10
    See also DLB 110
Crommelynck, Fernand 1885-1970
    CLC 75
    See also CA 89-92
Cromwell, Oliver 1599-1658
    LC 43
Cronin, A(rchibald) J(oseph) 1896-1981
    CLC 32
    See also CA 1-4R; 102; CANR 5; DLB 191;
    SATA 47; SATA-Obit 25
Cross, Amanda
    See Heilbrun, Carolyn G(old)
Crothers, Rachel .... 1878(?)-1958
    TCLC 19
    See also CA 113; DLB 7
Croves, Hal
    See Traven, B.
Crow Dog, Mary (Ellen) .... (?)-
    CLC 93
    See also Brave Bird, Mary
    See also CA 154
Crowfield, Christopher
    See Stowe, Harriet (Elizabeth) Beecher
Crowley, Aleister .... TCLC 7
    See also Crowley, Edward Alexander
Crowley, Edward Alexander 1875-1947
    See Crowley, Aleister
    See also CA 104
Crowley, John 1942-
    CLC 57
    See also CA 61-64; CANR 43; DLBY 82; SATA
    65
Crud
    See Crumb, R(obert)
Crumarums
    See Crumb, R(obert)
Crumb, R(obert) 1943-

CLC 17
    See also CA 106
Crumbum
    See Crumb, R(obert)
Crumski
    See Crumb, R(obert)
Crum the Bum
    See Crumb, R(obert)
Crunk
    See Crumb, R(obert)
Crustt
    See Crumb, R(obert)
Cryer, Gretchen (Kiger) 1935-
    CLC 21
    See also CA 114; 123
Csath, Geza 1887-1919
    TCLC 13
    See also CA 111
Cudlip, David 1933-
    CLC 34
Cullen, Countee 1903-1946
    TCLC 4, 37; BLC 1; DA; DAC; DAM
    MST, MULT, POET; PC 20; WLCS
    See also BW 1; CA 108; 124; CDALB
    1917-1929; DLB 4, 48, 51; MTCW 1; SATA
    18
Cum, R.
    See Crumb, R(obert)
Cummings, Bruce F(rederick) 1889-1919
    See Barbellion, W. N. P.
    See also CA 123
Cummings, E(dward) E(stlin) 1894-1962
    CLC 1, 3, 8, 12, 15, 68; DA; DAB; DAC;
    DAM MST, POET; PC 5; WLC
    See also CA 73-76; CANR 31; CDALB
    1929-1941; DLB 4, 48; MTCW 1
Cunha, Euclides (Rodrigues Pimenta) da
    1866-1909 .... TCLC 24
    See also CA 123
Cunningham, E. V.
    See Fast, Howard (Melvin)
Cunningham, J(ames) V(incent) . 1911-1985
    CLC 3, 31
    See also CA 1-4R; 115; CANR 1, 72; DLB 5
Cunningham, Julia (Woolfolk) 1916-
    CLC 12
    See also CA 9-12R; CANR 4, 19, 36; JRDA;
    MAICYA; SAAS 2; SATA 1, 26
Cunningham, Michael........................ 1952-
    CLC 34
    See also CA 136
Cunninghame Graham, R(obert) B(ontine)
    1852-1936 .... TCLC 19
    See also Graham, R(obert) B(ontine)
    Cunninghame
    See also CA 119; DLB 98
Currie, Ellen .... 19(?)-
    CLC 44
Curtin, Philip
    See Lowndes, Marie Adelaide (Belloc)
Curtis, Price
    See Ellison, Harlan (Jay)
Cutrate, Joe
    See Spiegelman, Art
Cynewulf .... c. 770-c. 840
    CMLC 23
Czaczkes, Shmuel Yosef
    See Agnon, S(hmuel) Y(osef Halevi)
Dabrowska, Maria (Szumska) 1889-1965
    CLC 15
    See also CA 106
Dabydeen, David 1955-
    CLC 34

Author Index

5, 193; DLBD 7; DLBY 82, 93, 96, 97; INT
CANR-10; MTCW 1
Dickey, William 1928-1994
CLC 3, 28
See also CA 9-12R; 145; CANR 24; DLB 5
Dickinson, Charles 1951-
CLC 49
See also CA 128
Dickinson, Emily (Elizabeth) 1830-1886
**NCLC 21; DA; DAB; DAC; DAM MST,
POET; PC 1; WLC**
See also AAYA 22; CDALB 1865-1917; DLB
1; SATA 29
Dickinson, Peter (Malcolm) 1927-
CLC 12, 35
See also AAYA 9; CA 41-44R; CANR 31, 58;
CLR 29; DLB 87, 161; JRDA; MAICYA;
SATA 5, 62, 95
Dickson, Carr
See Carr, John Dickson
Dickson, Carter
See Carr, John Dickson
Diderot, Denis 1713-1784
LC 26
Didion, Joan 1934-
CLC 1, 3, 8, 14, 32; DAM NOV
See also AITN 1; CA 5-8R; CANR 14, 52;
CDALB 1968-1988; DLB 2, 173, 185;
DLBY 81, 86; MTCW 1
Dietrich, Robert
See Hunt, E(verette) Howard, (Jr.)
Difusa, Pati
See Almodovar, Pedro
Dillard, Annie 1945-
CLC 9, 60, 115; DAM NOV
See also AAYA 6; CA 49-52; CANR 3, 43, 62;
DLBY 80; MTCW 1; SATA 10
Dillard, R(ichard) H(enry) W(ilde) 1937-
CLC 5
See also CA 21-24R; CAAS 7; CANR 10; DLB
5
Dillon, Eilis 1920-1994
CLC 17
See also CA 9-12R; 147; CAAS 3; CANR 4,
38; CLR 26; MAICYA; SATA 2, 74;
SATA-Obit 83
Dimont, Penelope
See Mortimer, Penelope (Ruth)
Dinesen, Isak .... **CLC 10, 29, 95; SSC 7**
See also Blixen, Karen (Christentze Dinesen)
Ding Ling .... **CLC 68**
See also Chiang, Pin-chin
Diphusa, Patty
See Almodovar, Pedro
Disch, Thomas M(ichael) 1940-
CLC 7, 36
See also AAYA 17; CA 21-24R; CAAS 4;
CANR 17, 36, 54; CLR 18; DLB 8;
MAICYA; MTCW 1; SAAS 15; SATA 92
Disch, Tom
See Disch, Thomas M(ichael)
d'Isly, Georges
See Simenon, Georges (Jacques Christian)
Disraeli, Benjamin 1804-1881
NCLC 2, 39
See also DLB 21, 55
Ditcum, Steve
See Crumb, R(obert)
Dixon, Paige
See Corcoran, Barbara
Dixon, Stephen 1936-
CLC 52; SSC 16
See also CA 89-92; CANR 17, 40, 54; DLB 130

Doak, Annie
See Dillard, Annie
Dobell, Sydney Thompson 1824-1874
NCLC 43
See also DLB 32
Doblin, Alfred .... **TCLC 13**
See also Doeblin, Alfred
Dobrolyubov, Nikolai Alexandrovich
1836-1861 ....**NCLC 5**
Dobson, Austin 1840-1921
TCLC 79
See also DLB 35; 144
Dobyns, Stephen 1941-
CLC 37
See also CA 45-48; CANR 2, 18
Doctorow, E(dgar) L(aurence) 1931-
**CLC 6, 11, 15, 18, 37, 44, 65, 113; DAM
NOV, POP**
See also AAYA 22; AITN 2; BEST 89:3; CA
45-48; CANR 2, 33, 51; CDALB 1968-1988;
DLB 2, 28, 173; DLBY 80; MTCW 1
Dodgson, Charles Lutwidge 1832-1898
See Carroll, Lewis
See also CLR 2; DA; DAB; DAC; DAM MST,
NOV, POET; MAICYA; SATA 100; YABC 2
Dodson, Owen (Vincent) 1914-1983
CLC 79; BLC 1; DAM MULT
See also BW 1; CA 65-68; 110; CANR 24; DLB
76
Doeblin, Alfred 1878-1957
TCLC 13
See also Doblin, Alfred
See also CA 110; 141; DLB 66
Doerr, Harriet 1910-
CLC 34
See also CA 117; 122; CANR 47; INT 122
Domecq, H(onorio) Bustos
See Bioy Casares, Adolfo; Borges, Jorge Luis
Domini, Rey
See Lorde, Audre (Geraldine)
Dominique
See Proust, (Valentin-Louis-George-Eugene-)
Marcel
Don, A
See Stephen, SirLeslie
Donaldson, Stephen R. 1947-
CLC 46; DAM POP
See also CA 89-92; CANR 13, 55; INT
CANR-13
Donleavy, J(ames) P(atrick) 1926-
CLC 1, 4, 6, 10, 45
See also AITN 2; CA 9-12R; CANR 24, 49, 62;
DLB 6, 173; INT CANR-24; MTCW 1
Donne, John 1572-1631
**LC 10, 24; DA; DAB; DAC; DAM MST,
POET; PC 1; WLC**
See also CDBLB Before 1660; DLB 121, 151
Donnell, David .... 1939(?)-
CLC 34
Donoghue, P. S.
See Hunt, E(verette) Howard, (Jr.)
Donoso (Yanez), Jose 1924-1996
CLC 4, 8, 11, 32, 99; DAM MULT; HLC
See also CA 81-84; 155; CANR 32, 73; DLB
113; HW; MTCW 1
Donovan, John 1928-1992
CLC 35
See also AAYA 20; CA 97-100; 137; CLR 3;
MAICYA; SATA 72; SATA-Brief 29
Don Roberto
See Cunninghame Graham, R(obert) B(ontine)
Doolittle, Hilda 1886-1961
CLC 3, 8, 14, 31, 34, 73; DA; DAC; DAM

MST, POET; PC 5; WLC
See also H. D.
See also CA 97-100; CANR 35; DLB 4, 45;
MTCW 1
Dorfman, Ariel 1942-
CLC 48, 77; DAM MULT; HLC
See also CA 124; 130; CANR 67, 70; HW; INT
130
Dorn, Edward (Merton) 1929-
CLC 10, 18
See also CA 93-96; CANR 42; DLB 5; INT
93-96
Dorris, Michael (Anthony) 1945-1997
CLC 109; DAM MULT, NOV
See also AAYA 20; BEST 90:1; CA 102; 157;
CANR 19, 46, 75; DLB 175; NNAL; SATA
75; SATA-Obit 94
Dorris, Michael A.
See Dorris, Michael (Anthony)
Dorsan, Luc
See Simenon, Georges (Jacques Christian)
Dorsange, Jean
See Simenon, Georges (Jacques Christian)
Dos Passos, John (Roderigo) 1896-1970
**CLC 1, 4, 8, 11, 15, 25, 34, 82; DA; DAB;
DAC; DAM MST, NOV; WLC**
See also CA 1-4R; 29-32R; CANR 3; CDALB
1929-1941; DLB 4, 9; DLBD 1, 15; DLBY
96; MTCW 1
Dossage, Jean
See Simenon, Georges (Jacques Christian)
Dostoevsky, Fedor Mikhailovich . 1821-1881
**NCLC 2, 7, 21, 33, 43; DA; DAB; DAC;
DAM MST, NOV; SSC 2, 33; WLC**
Doughty, Charles M(ontagu) 1843-1926
TCLC 27
See also CA 115; DLB 19, 57, 174
Douglas, Ellen ....**CLC 73**
See also Haxton, Josephine Ayres; Williamson,
Ellen Douglas
Douglas, Gavin .... 1475(?)-1522
LC 20
See also DLB 132
Douglas, George
See Brown, George Douglas
Douglas, Keith (Castellain) 1920-1944
TCLC 40
See also CA 160; DLB 27
Douglas, Leonard
See Bradbury, Ray (Douglas)
Douglas, Michael
See Crichton, (John) Michael
Douglas, (George) Norman 1868-1952
TCLC 68
See also CA 119; 157; DLB 34, 195
Douglas, William
See Brown, George Douglas
Douglass, Frederick .... 1817(?)-1895
**NCLC 7, 55; BLC 1; DA; DAC; DAM
MST, MULT; WLC**
See also CDALB 1640-1865; DLB 1, 43, 50,
79; SATA 29
Dourado, (Waldomiro Freitas) Autran 1926-
CLC 23, 60
See also CA 25-28R; CANR 34
Dourado, Waldomiro Autran
See Dourado, (Waldomiro Freitas) Autran
Dove, Rita (Frances) 1952-
**CLC 50, 81; BLCS; DAM MULT, POET;
PC 6**
See also BW 2; CA 109; CAAS 19; CANR 27,
42, 68; DLB 120
Doveglion

CLC 13, 46
　　See also CA 89-92; 150; CANR 17, 46; DLB
　　40; MTCW 1
Ewers, Hanns Heinz 1871-1943
　　TCLC 12
　　See also CA 109; 149
Ewing, Frederick R.
　　See Sturgeon, Theodore (Hamilton)
Exley, Frederick (Earl) 1929-1992
　　CLC 6, 11
　　See also AITN 2; CA 81-84; 138; DLB 143;
　　DLBY 81
Eynhardt, Guillermo
　　See Quiroga, Horacio (Sylvestre)
Ezekiel, Nissim 1924-
　　CLC 61
　　See also CA 61-64
Ezekiel, Tish O'Dowd 1943-
　　CLC 34
　　See also CA 129
Fadeyev, A.
　　See Bulgya, Alexander Alexandrovich
Fadeyev, Alexander .... TCLC 53
　　See also Bulgya, Alexander Alexandrovich
Fagen, Donald 1948-
　　CLC 26
Fainzilberg, Ilya Arnoldovich 1897-1937
　　See Ilf, Ilya
　　See also CA 120; 165
Fair, Ronald L. 1932-
　　CLC 18
　　See also BW 1; CA 69-72; CANR 25; DLB 33
Fairbairn, Roger
　　See Carr, John Dickson
Fairbairns, Zoe (Ann) 1948-
　　CLC 32
　　See also CA 103; CANR 21
Falco, Gian
　　See Papini, Giovanni
Falconer, James
　　See Kirkup, James
Falconer, Kenneth
　　See Kornbluth, C(yril) M.
Falkland, Samuel
　　See Heijermans, Herman
Fallaci, Oriana 1930-
　　CLC 11, 110
　　See also CA 77-80; CANR 15, 58; MTCW 1
Faludy, George 1913-
　　CLC 42
　　See also CA 21-24R
Faludy, Gyoergy
　　See Faludy, George
Fanon, Frantz 1925-1961
　　CLC 74; BLC 2; DAM MULT
　　See also BW 1; CA 116; 89-92
Fanshawe, Ann 1625-1680
　　LC 11
Fante, John (Thomas) 1911-1983
　　CLC 60
　　See also CA 69-72; 109; CANR 23; DLB 130;
　　DLBY 83
Farah, Nuruddin 1945-
　　CLC 53; BLC 2; DAM MULT
　　See also BW 2; CA 106; DLB 125
Fargue, Leon-Paul .... 1876(?)-1947
　　TCLC 11
　　See also CA 109
Farigoule, Louis
　　See Romains, Jules
Farina, Richard .... 1936(?)-1966
　　CLC 9
　　See also CA 81-84; 25-28R

Farley, Walter (Lorimer) 1915-1989
　　CLC 17
　　See also CA 17-20R; CANR 8, 29; DLB 22;
　　JRDA; MAICYA; SATA 2, 43
Farmer, Philip Jose 1918-
　　CLC 1, 19
　　See also CA 1-4R; CANR 4, 35; DLB 8; MTCW
　　1; SATA 93
Farquhar, George 1677-1707
　　LC 21; DAM DRAM
　　See also DLB 84
Farrell, J(ames) G(ordon) 1935-1979
　　CLC 6
　　See also CA 73-76; 89-92; CANR 36; DLB 14;
　　MTCW 1
Farrell, James T(homas) 1904-1979
　　CLC 1, 4, 8, 11, 66; SSC 28
　　See also CA 5-8R; 89-92; CANR 9, 61; DLB 4,
　　9, 86; DLBD 2; MTCW 1
Farren, Richard J.
　　See Betjeman, John
Farren, Richard M.
　　See Betjeman, John
Fassbinder, Rainer Werner 1946-1982
　　CLC 20
　　See also CA 93-96; 106; CANR 31
Fast, Howard (Melvin) 1914-
　　CLC 23; DAM NOV
　　See also AAYA 16; CA 1-4R; CAAS 18; CANR
　　1, 33, 54; DLB 9; INT CANR-33; SATA 7
Faulcon, Robert
　　See Holdstock, Robert P.
Faulkner, William (Cuthbert) 1897-1962
　　CLC 1, 3, 6, 8, 9, 11, 14, 18, 28, 52, 68;
　　DA; DAB; DAC; DAM MST, NOV; SSC
　　1; WLC
　　See also AAYA 7; CA 81-84; CANR 33;
　　CDALB 1929-1941; DLB 9, 11, 44, 102;
　　DLBD 2; DLBY 86, 97; MTCW 1
Fauset, Jessie Redmon .... 1884(?)-1961
　　CLC 19, 54; BLC 2; DAM MULT
　　See also BW 1; CA 109; DLB 51
Faust, Frederick (Schiller) ...... 1892-1944(?)
　　TCLC 49; DAM POP
　　See also CA 108; 152
Faust, Irvin 1924-
　　CLC 8
　　See also CA 33-36R; CANR 28, 67; DLB 2,
　　28; DLBY 80
Fawkes, Guy
　　See Benchley, Robert (Charles)
Fearing, Kenneth (Flexner) 1902-1961
　　CLC 51
　　See also CA 93-96; CANR 59; DLB 9
Fecamps, Elise
　　See Creasey, John
Federman, Raymond 1928-
　　CLC 6, 47
　　See also CA 17-20R; CAAS 8; CANR 10, 43;
　　DLBY 80
Federspiel, J(uerg) F. 1931-
　　CLC 42
　　See also CA 146
Feiffer, Jules (Ralph) 1929-
　　CLC 2, 8, 64; DAM DRAM
　　See also AAYA 3; CA 17-20R; CANR 30, 59;
　　DLB 7, 44; INT CANR-30; MTCW 1; SATA
　　8, 61
Feige, Hermann Albert Otto Maximilian
　　See Traven, B.
Feinberg, David B. 1956-1994
　　CLC 59
　　See also CA 135; 147

Feinstein, Elaine 1930-
　　CLC 36
　　See also CA 69-72; CAAS 1; CANR 31, 68;
　　DLB 14, 40; MTCW 1
Feldman, Irving (Mordecai) 1928-
　　CLC 7
　　See also CA 1-4R; CANR 1; DLB 169
Felix-Tchicaya, Gerald
　　See Tchicaya, Gerald Felix
Fellini, Federico 1920-1993
　　CLC 16, 85
　　See also CA 65-68; 143; CANR 33
Felsen, Henry Gregor 1916-
　　CLC 17
　　See also CA 1-4R; CANR 1; SAAS 2; SATA 1
Fenno, Jack
　　See Calisher, Hortense
Fenton, James Martin 1949-
　　CLC 32
　　See also CA 102; DLB 40
Ferber, Edna 1887-1968
　　CLC 18, 93
　　See also AITN 1; CA 5-8R; 25-28R; CANR 68;
　　DLB 9, 28, 86; MTCW 1; SATA 7
Ferguson, Helen
　　See Kavan, Anna
Ferguson, Samuel 1810-1886
　　NCLC 33
　　See also DLB 32
Fergusson, Robert 1750-1774
　　LC 29
　　See also DLB 109
Ferling, Lawrence
　　See Ferlinghetti, Lawrence (Monsanto)
Ferlinghetti, Lawrence (Monsanto)　1919(?)-
　　CLC 2, 6, 10, 27, 111; DAM POET; PC 1
　　See also CA 5-8R; CANR 3, 41, 73; CDALB
　　1941-1968; DLB 5, 16; MTCW 1
Fernandez, Vicente Garcia Huidobro
　　See Huidobro Fernandez, Vicente Garcia
Ferrer, Gabriel (Francisco Victor) Miro
　　See Miro (Ferrer), Gabriel (Francisco Victor)
Ferrier, Susan (Edmonstone) 1782-1854
　　NCLC 8
　　See also DLB 116
Ferrigno, Robert .... 1948(?)-
　　CLC 65
　　See also CA 140
Ferron, Jacques 1921-1985
　　CLC 94; DAC
　　See also CA 117; 129; DLB 60
Feuchtwanger, Lion 1884-1958
　　TCLC 3
　　See also CA 104; DLB 66
Feuillet, Octave 1821-1890
　　NCLC 45
　　See also DLB 192
Feydeau, Georges (Leon Jules Marie)
　　1862-1921 ...... TCLC 22; DAM DRAM
　　See also CA 113; 152; DLB 192
Fichte, Johann Gottlieb 1762-1814
　　NCLC 62
　　See also DLB 90
Ficino, Marsilio 1433-1499
　　LC 12
Fiedeler, Hans
　　See Doeblin, Alfred
Fiedler, Leslie A(aron) 1917-
　　CLC 4, 13, 24
　　See also CA 9-12R; CANR 7, 63; DLB 28, 67;
　　MTCW 1
Field, Andrew 1938-
　　CLC 44

See also CA 97-100; CANR 25
Field, Eugene 1850-1895
    NCLC 3
See also DLB 23, 42, 140; DLBD 13; MAICYA;
SATA 16
Field, Gans T.
See Wellman, Manly Wade
Field, Michael 1915-1971
    TCLC 43
See also CA 29-32R
Field, Peter
See Hobson, Laura Z(ametkin)
Fielding, Henry 1707-1754
    **LC 1, 46; DA; DAB; DAC; DAM DRAM,
    MST, NOV; WLC**
See also CDBLB 1660-1789; DLB 39, 84, 101
Fielding, Sarah 1710-1768
    LC 1, 44
See also DLB 39
Fields, W. C. 1880-1946
    TCLC 80
See also DLB 44
Fierstein, Harvey (Forbes) 1954-
    CLC 33; DAM DRAM, POP
See also CA 123; 129
Figes, Eva 1932-
    CLC 31
See also CA 53-56; CANR 4, 44; DLB 14
Finch, Anne 1661-1720
    LC 3; PC 21
See also DLB 95
Finch, Robert (Duer Claydon) 1900-
    CLC 18
See also CA 57-60; CANR 9, 24, 49; DLB 88
Findley, Timothy 1930-
    CLC 27, 102; DAC; DAM MST
See also CA 25-28R; CANR 12, 42, 69; DLB
53
Fink, William
See Mencken, H(enry) L(ouis)
Firbank, Louis 1942-
See Reed, Lou
See also CA 117
Firbank, (Arthur Annesley) Ronald
    1886-1926 .... **TCLC 1**
See also CA 104; DLB 36
Fisher, Dorothy (Frances) Canfield
    1879-1958 .... **TCLC 87**
See also CA 114; 136; DLB 9, 102; MAICYA;
YABC 1
Fisher, M(ary) F(rances) K(ennedy)
    1908-1992 .... **CLC 76, 87**
See also CA 77-80; 138; CANR 44
Fisher, Roy 1930-
    CLC 25
See also CA 81-84; CAAS 10; CANR 16; DLB
40
Fisher, Rudolph 1897-1934
    TCLC 11; BLC 2; DAM MULT; SSC 25
See also BW 1; CA 107; 124; DLB 51, 102
Fisher, Vardis (Alvero) 1895-1968
    CLC 7
See also CA 5-8R; 25-28R; CANR 68; DLB 9
Fiske, Tarleton
See Bloch, Robert (Albert)
Fitch, Clarke
See Sinclair, Upton (Beall)
Fitch, John IV
See Cormier, Robert (Edmund)
Fitzgerald, Captain Hugh
See Baum, L(yman) Frank
FitzGerald, Edward 1809-1883
    NCLC 9

See also DLB 32
Fitzgerald, F(rancis) Scott (Key)   1896-1940
    **TCLC 1, 6, 14, 28, 55; DA; DAB; DAC;
    DAM MST, NOV; SSC 6, 31; WLC**
See also AAYA 24; AITN 1; CA 110; 123;
CDALB 1917-1929; DLB 4, 9, 86; DLBD 1,
15, 16; DLBY 81, 96; MTCW 1
Fitzgerald, Penelope 1916-
    CLC 19, 51, 61
See also CA 85-88; CAAS 10; CANR 56; DLB
14, 194
Fitzgerald, Robert (Stuart) 1910-1985
    CLC 39
See also CA 1-4R; 114; CANR 1; DLBY 80
FitzGerald, Robert D(avid) 1902-1987
    CLC 19
See also CA 17-20R
Fitzgerald, Zelda (Sayre) 1900-1948
    TCLC 52
See also CA 117; 126; DLBY 84
Flanagan, Thomas (James Bonner) 1923-
    CLC 25, 52
See also CA 108; CANR 55; DLBY 80; INT
108; MTCW 1
Flaubert, Gustave 1821-1880
    **NCLC 2, 10, 19, 62, 66; DA; DAB; DAC;
    DAM MST, NOV; SSC 11; WLC**
See also DLB 119
Flecker, Herman Elroy
See Flecker, (Herman) James Elroy
Flecker, (Herman) James Elroy .. 1884-1915
    TCLC 43
See also CA 109; 150; DLB 10, 19
Fleming, Ian (Lancaster) 1908-1964
    CLC 3, 30; DAM POP
See also AAYA 26; CA 5-8R; CANR 59;
CDBLB 1945-1960; DLB 87, 201; MTCW
1; SATA 9
Fleming, Thomas (James) 1927-
    CLC 37
See also CA 5-8R; CANR 10; INT CANR-10;
SATA 8
Fletcher, John 1579-1625
    LC 33; DC 6
See also CDBLB Before 1660; DLB 58
Fletcher, John Gould 1886-1950
    TCLC 35
See also CA 107; 167; DLB 4, 45
Fleur, Paul
See Pohl, Frederik
Flooglebuckle, Al
See Spiegelman, Art
Flying Officer X
See Bates, H(erbert) E(rnest)
Fo, Dario 1926-
    CLC 32, 109; DAM DRAM; DC 10
See also CA 116; 128; CANR 68; DLBY 97;
MTCW 1
Fogarty, Jonathan Titulescu Esq.
See Farrell, James T(homas)
Folke, Will
See Bloch, Robert (Albert)
Follett, Ken(neth Martin) 1949-
    CLC 18; DAM NOV, POP
See also AAYA 6; BEST 89:4; CA 81-84; CANR
13, 33, 54; DLB 87; DLBY 81; INT
CANR-33; MTCW 1
Fontane, Theodor 1819-1898
    NCLC 26
See also DLB 129
Foote, Horton 1916-
    CLC 51, 91; DAM DRAM
See also CA 73-76; CANR 34, 51; DLB 26; INT

CANR-34
Foote, Shelby 1916-
    CLC 75; DAM NOV, POP
See also CA 5-8R; CANR 3, 45, 74; DLB 2, 17
Forbes, Esther 1891-1967
    CLC 12
See also AAYA 17; CA 13-14; 25-28R; CAP 1;
CLR 27; DLB 22; JRDA; MAICYA; SATA
2, 100
Forche, Carolyn (Louise) 1950-
    CLC 25, 83, 86; DAM POET; PC 10
See also CA 109; 117; CANR 50, 74; DLB 5,
193; INT 117
Ford, Elbur
See Hibbert, Eleanor Alice Burford
Ford, Ford Madox 1873-1939
    TCLC 1, 15, 39, 57; DAM NOV
See also CA 104; 132; CANR 74; CDBLB
1914-1945; DLB 162; MTCW 1
Ford, Henry 1863-1947
    TCLC 73
See also CA 115; 148
Ford, John .... 1586-(?)
    DC 8
See also CDBLB Before 1660; DAM DRAM;
DLB 58
Ford, John 1895-1973
    CLC 16
See also CA 45-48
Ford, Richard 1944-
    CLC 46, 99
See also CA 69-72; CANR 11, 47
Ford, Webster
See Masters, Edgar Lee
Foreman, Richard 1937-
    CLC 50
See also CA 65-68; CANR 32, 63
Forester, C(ecil) S(cott) 1899-1966
    CLC 35
See also CA 73-76; 25-28R; DLB 191; SATA
13
Forez
See Mauriac, Francois (Charles)
Forman, James Douglas 1932-
    CLC 21
See also AAYA 17; CA 9-12R; CANR 4, 19,
42; JRDA; MAICYA; SATA 8, 70
Fornes, Maria Irene 1930-
    CLC 39, 61; DC 10
See also CA 25-28R; CANR 28; DLB 7; HW;
INT CANR-28; MTCW 1
Forrest, Leon (Richard) 1937-1997
    CLC 4; BLCS
See also BW 2; CA 89-92; 162; CAAS 7; CANR
25, 52; DLB 33
Forster, E(dward) M(organ) 1879-1970
    **CLC 1, 2, 3, 4, 9, 10, 13, 15, 22, 45, 77;
    DA; DAB; DAC; DAM MST, NOV; SSC
    27; WLC**
See also AAYA 2; CA 13-14; 25-28R; CANR
45; CAP 1; CDBLB 1914-1945; DLB 34, 98,
162, 178, 195; DLBD 10; MTCW 1; SATA
57
Forster, John 1812-1876
    NCLC 11
See also DLB 144, 184
Forsyth, Frederick 1938-
    CLC 2, 5, 36; DAM NOV, POP
See also BEST 89:4; CA 85-88; CANR 38, 62;
DLB 87; MTCW 1
Forten, Charlotte L. .... **TCLC 16; BLC 2**
See also Grimke, Charlotte L(ottie) Forten
See also DLB 50

Gautier, Theophile 1811-1872
    NCLC 1, 59; DAM POET; PC 18; SSC 20
    See also DLB 119
Gawsworth, John
    See Bates, H(erbert) E(rnest)
Gay, Oliver
    See Gogarty, Oliver St. John
Gaye, Marvin (Penze) 1939-1984
    CLC 26
    See also CA 112
Gebler, Carlo (Ernest) 1954-
    CLC 39
    See also CA 119; 133
Gee, Maggie (Mary) 1948-
    CLC 57
    See also CA 130
Gee, Maurice (Gough) 1931-
    CLC 29
    See also CA 97-100; CANR 67; SATA 46, 101
Gelbart, Larry (Simon) 1923-
    CLC 21, 61
    See also CA 73-76; CANR 45
Gelber, Jack 1932-
    CLC 1, 6, 14, 79
    See also CA 1-4R; CANR 2; DLB 7
Gellhorn, Martha (Ellis) 1908-1998
    CLC 14, 60
    See also CA 77-80; 164; CANR 44; DLBY 82
Genet, Jean 1910-1986
    CLC 1, 2, 5, 10, 14, 44, 46; DAM DRAM
    See also CA 13-16R; CANR 18; DLB 72;
    DLBY 86; MTCW 1
Gent, Peter 1942-
    CLC 29
    See also AITN 1; CA 89-92; DLBY 82
Gentlewoman in New England, A
    See Bradstreet, Anne
Gentlewoman in Those Parts, A
    See Bradstreet, Anne
George, Jean Craighead 1919-
    CLC 35
    See also AAYA 8; CA 5-8R; CANR 25; CLR 1;
    DLB 52; JRDA; MAICYA; SATA 2, 68
George, Stefan (Anton) 1868-1933
    TCLC 2, 14
    See also CA 104
Georges, Georges Martin
    See Simenon, Georges (Jacques Christian)
Gerhardi, William Alexander
    See Gerhardie, William Alexander
Gerhardie, William Alexander ... 1895-1977
    CLC 5
    See also CA 25-28R; 73-76; CANR 18; DLB
    36
Gerstler, Amy 1956-
    CLC 70
    See also CA 146
Gertler, T. .... CLC 34
    See also CA 116; 121; INT 121
Ghalib .... NCLC 39
    See also Ghalib, Hsadullah Khan
Ghalib, Hsadullah Khan 1797-1869
    See Ghalib
    See also DAM POET
Ghelderode, Michel de 1898-1962
    CLC 6, 11; DAM DRAM
    See also CA 85-88; CANR 40
Ghiselin, Brewster 1903-
    CLC 23
    See also CA 13-16R; CAAS 10; CANR 13
Ghose, Aurabinda 1872-1950
    TCLC 63
    See also CA 163

Ghose, Zulfikar 1935-
    CLC 42
    See also CA 65-68; CANR 67
Ghosh, Amitav 1956-
    CLC 44
    See also CA 147
Giacosa, Giuseppe 1847-1906
    TCLC 7
    See also CA 104
Gibb, Lee
    See Waterhouse, Keith (Spencer)
Gibbon, Lewis Grassic .... TCLC 4
    See also Mitchell, James Leslie
Gibbons, Kaye 1960-
    CLC 50, 88; DAM POP
    See also CA 151
Gibran, Kahlil 1883-1931
    TCLC 1, 9; DAM POET, POP; PC 9
    See also CA 104; 150
Gibran, Khalil
    See Gibran, Kahlil
Gibson, William 1914-
    CLC 23; DA; DAB; DAC; DAM DRAM,
    MST
    See also CA 9-12R; CANR 9, 42; DLB 7; SATA
    66
Gibson, William (Ford) 1948-
    CLC 39, 63; DAM POP
    See also AAYA 12; CA 126; 133; CANR 52
Gide, Andre (Paul Guillaume) 1869-1951
    TCLC 5, 12, 36; DA; DAB; DAC; DAM
    MST, NOV; SSC 13; WLC
    See also CA 104; 124; DLB 65; MTCW 1
Gifford, Barry (Colby) 1946-
    CLC 34
    See also CA 65-68; CANR 9, 30, 40
Gilbert, Frank
    See De Voto, Bernard (Augustine)
Gilbert, W(illiam) S(chwenck) 1836-1911
    TCLC 3; DAM DRAM, POET
    See also CA 104; SATA 36
Gilbreth, Frank B., Jr. 1911-
    CLC 17
    See also CA 9-12R; SATA 2
Gilchrist, Ellen 1935-
    CLC 34, 48; DAM POP; SSC 14
    See also CA 113; 116; CANR 41, 61; DLB 130;
    MTCW 1
Giles, Molly 1942-
    CLC 39
    See also CA 126
Gill, Eric 1882-1940
    TCLC 85
Gill, Patrick
    See Creasey, John
Gilliam, Terry (Vance) 1940-
    CLC 21
    See also Monty Python
    See also AAYA 19; CA 108; 113; CANR 35;
    INT 113
Gillian, Jerry
    See Gilliam, Terry (Vance)
Gilliatt, Penelope (Ann Douglass) 1932-1993
    CLC 2, 10, 13, 53
    See also AITN 2; CA 13-16R; 141; CANR 49;
    DLB 14
Gilman, Charlotte (Anna) Perkins (Stetson)
    1860-1935 .... TCLC 9, 37; SSC 13
    See also CA 106; 150
Gilmour, David 1949-
    CLC 35
    See also CA 138, 147
Gilpin, William 1724-1804

NCLC 30
Gilray, J. D.
    See Mencken, H(enry) L(ouis)
Gilroy, Frank D(aniel) 1925-
    CLC 2
    See also CA 81-84; CANR 32, 64; DLB 7
Gilstrap, John .... 1957(?)-
    CLC 99
    See also CA 160
Ginsberg, Allen 1926-1997
    CLC 1, 2, 3, 4, 6, 13, 36, 69, 109; DA; DAB;
    DAC; DAM MST, POET; PC 4; WLC
    See also AITN 1; CA 1-4R; 157; CANR 2, 41,
    63; CDALB 1941-1968; DLB 5, 16, 169;
    MTCW 1
Ginzburg, Natalia 1916-1991
    CLC 5, 11, 54, 70
    See also CA 85-88; 135; CANR 33; DLB 177;
    MTCW 1
Giono, Jean 1895-1970
    CLC 4, 11
    See also CA 45-48; 29-32R; CANR 2, 35; DLB
    72; MTCW 1
Giovanni, Nikki 1943-
    CLC 2, 4, 19, 64, 117; BLC 2; DA; DAB;
    DAC; DAM MST, MULT, POET; PC 19;
    WLCS
    See also AAYA 22; AITN 1; BW 2; CA 29-32R;
    CAAS 6; CANR 18, 41, 60; CLR 6; DLB 5,
    41; INT CANR-18; MAICYA; MTCW 1;
    SATA 24
Giovene, Andrea 1904-
    CLC 7
    See also CA 85-88
Gippius, Zinaida (Nikolayevna) .. 1869-1945
    See Hippius, Zinaida
    See also CA 106
Giraudoux, (Hippolyte) Jean 1882-1944
    TCLC 2, 7; DAM DRAM
    See also CA 104; DLB 65
Gironella, Jose Maria 1917-
    CLC 11
    See also CA 101
Gissing, George (Robert) 1857-1903
    TCLC 3, 24, 47
    See also CA 105; 167; DLB 18, 135, 184
Giurlani, Aldo
    See Palazzeschi, Aldo
Gladkov, Fyodor (Vasilyevich) 1883-1958
    TCLC 27
    See also CA 170
Glanville, Brian (Lester) 1931-
    CLC 6
    See also CA 5-8R; CAAS 9; CANR 3, 70; DLB
    15, 139; SATA 42
Glasgow, Ellen (Anderson Gholson)
    1873-1945 .... TCLC 2, 7
    See also CA 104; 164; DLB 9, 12
Glaspell, Susan .... 1882(?)-1948
    TCLC 55; DC 10
    See also CA 110; 154; DLB 7, 9, 78; YABC 2
Glassco, John 1909-1981
    CLC 9
    See also CA 13-16R; 102; CANR 15; DLB 68
Glasscock, Amnesia
    See Steinbeck, John (Ernst)
Glasser, Ronald J. .... 1940(?)-
    CLC 37
Glassman, Joyce
    See Johnson, Joyce
Glendinning, Victoria 1937-
    CLC 50
    See also CA 120; 127; CANR 59; DLB 155

See also DLB 98, 135, 174
Graham, Robert
See Haldeman, Joe (William)
Graham, Tom
See Lewis, (Harry) Sinclair
Graham, W(illiam) S(ydney) 1918-1986
CLC 29
See also CA 73-76; 118; DLB 20
Graham, Winston (Mawdsley) 1910-
CLC 23
See also CA 49-52; CANR 2, 22, 45, 66; DLB 77
Grahame, Kenneth 1859-1932
TCLC 64; DAB
See also CA 108; 136; CLR 5; DLB 34, 141, 178; MAICYA; SATA 100; YABC 1
Grant, Skeeter
See Spiegelman, Art
Granville-Barker, Harley 1877-1946
TCLC 2; DAM DRAM
See also Barker, Harley Granville
See also CA 104
Grass, Guenter (Wilhelm) 1927-
CLC 1, 2, 4, 6, 11, 15, 22, 32, 49, 88; DA; DAB; DAC; DAM MST, NOV; WLC
See also CA 13-16R; CANR 20; DLB 75, 124; MTCW 1
Gratton, Thomas
See Hulme, T(homas) E(rnest)
Grau, Shirley Ann 1929-
CLC 4, 9; SSC 15
See also CA 89-92; CANR 22, 69; DLB 2; INT CANR-22; MTCW 1
Gravel, Fern
See Hall, James Norman
Graver, Elizabeth 1964-
CLC 70
See also CA 135; CANR 71
Graves, Richard Perceval 1945-
CLC 44
See also CA 65-68; CANR 9, 26, 51
Graves, Robert (von Ranke) 1895-1985
CLC 1, 2, 6, 11, 39, 44, 45; DAB; DAC; DAM MST, POET; PC 6
See also CA 5-8R; 117; CANR 5, 36; CDBLB 1914-1945; DLB 20, 100, 191; DLBD 18; DLBY 85; MTCW 1; SATA 45
Graves, Valerie
See Bradley, Marion Zimmer
Gray, Alasdair (James) 1934-
CLC 41
See also CA 126; CANR 47, 69; DLB 194; INT 126; MTCW 1
Gray, Amlin 1946-
CLC 29
See also CA 138
Gray, Francine du Plessix 1930-
CLC 22; DAM NOV
See also BEST 90:3; CA 61-64; CAAS 2; CANR 11, 33; INT CANR-11; MTCW 1
Gray, John (Henry) 1866-1934
TCLC 19
See also CA 119; 162
Gray, Simon (James Holliday) 1936-
CLC 9, 14, 36
See also AITN 1; CA 21-24R; CAAS 3; CANR 32, 69; DLB 13; MTCW 1
Gray, Spalding 1941-
CLC 49, 112; DAM POP; DC 7
See also CA 128; CANR 74
Gray, Thomas 1716-1771
LC 4, 40; DA; DAB; DAC; DAM MST; PC 2; WLC

See also CDBLB 1660-1789; DLB 109
Grayson, David
See Baker, Ray Stannard
Grayson, Richard (A.) 1951-
CLC 38
See also CA 85-88; CANR 14, 31, 57
Greeley, Andrew M(oran) 1928-
CLC 28; DAM POP
See also CA 5-8R; CAAS 7; CANR 7, 43, 69; MTCW 1
Green, Anna Katharine 1846-1935
TCLC 63
See also CA 112; 159; DLB 202
Green, Brian
See Card, Orson Scott
Green, Hannah
See Greenberg, Joanne (Goldenberg)
Green, Hannah .... 1927(?)-1996
CLC 3
See also CA 73-76; CANR 59
Green, Henry 1905-1973
CLC 2, 13, 97
See also Yorke, Henry Vincent
See also DLB 15
Green, Julian (Hartridge) 1900-1998
See Green, Julien
See also CA 21-24R; 169; CANR 33; DLB 4, 72; MTCW 1
Green, Julien .... CLC 3, 11, 77
See also Green, Julian (Hartridge)
Green, Paul (Eliot) 1894-1981
CLC 25; DAM DRAM
See also AITN 1; CA 5-8R; 103; CANR 3; DLB 7, 9; DLBY 81
Greenberg, Ivan 1908-1973
See Rahv, Philip
See also CA 85-88
Greenberg, Joanne (Goldenberg) 1932-
CLC 7, 30
See also AAYA 12; CA 5-8R; CANR 14, 32, 69; SATA 25
Greenberg, Richard .... 1959(?)-
CLC 57
See also CA 138
Greene, Bette 1934-
CLC 30
See also AAYA 7; CA 53-56; CANR 4; CLR 2; JRDA; MAICYA; SAAS 16; SATA 8, 102
Greene, Gael ....CLC 8
See also CA 13-16R; CANR 10
Greene, Graham (Henry) 1904-1991
CLC 1, 3, 6, 9, 14, 18, 27, 37, 70, 72; DA; DAB; DAC; DAM MST, NOV; SSC 29; WLC
See also AITN 2; CA 13-16R; 133; CANR 35, 61; CDBLB 1945-1960; DLB 13, 15, 77, 100, 162, 201; DLBY 91; MTCW 1; SATA 20
Greene, Robert 1558-1592
LC 41
See also DLB 62, 167
Greer, Richard
See Silverberg, Robert
Gregor, Arthur 1923-
CLC 9
See also CA 25-28R; CAAS 10; CANR 11; SATA 36
Gregor, Lee
See Pohl, Frederik
Gregory, Isabella Augusta (Persse) 1852-1932
TCLC 1
See also CA 104; DLB 10
Gregory, J. Dennis

See Williams, John A(lfred)
Grendon, Stephen
See Derleth, August (William)
Grenville, Kate 1950-
CLC 61
See also CA 118; CANR 53
Grenville, Pelham
See Wodehouse, P(elham) G(renville)
Greve, Felix Paul (Berthold Friedrich)
1879-1948
See Grove, Frederick Philip
See also CA 104; 141; DAC; DAM MST
Grey, Zane 1872-1939
TCLC 6; DAM POP
See also CA 104; 132; DLB 9; MTCW 1
Grieg, (Johan) Nordahl (Brun) ... 1902-1943
TCLC 10
See also CA 107
Grieve, C(hristopher) M(urray) . 1892-1978
CLC 11, 19; DAM POET
See also MacDiarmid, Hugh; Pteleon
See also CA 5-8R; 85-88; CANR 33; MTCW 1
Griffin, Gerald 1803-1840
NCLC 7
See also DLB 159
Griffin, John Howard 1920-1980
CLC 68
See also AITN 1; CA 1-4R; 101; CANR 2
Griffin, Peter 1942-
CLC 39
See also CA 136
Griffith, D(avid Lewelyn) W(ark)
1875(?)-1948 .... TCLC 68
See also CA 119; 150
Griffith, Lawrence
See Griffith, D(avid Lewelyn) W(ark)
Griffiths, Trevor 1935-
CLC 13, 52
See also CA 97-100; CANR 45; DLB 13
Griggs, Sutton Elbert .... 1872-1930(?)
TCLC 77
See also CA 123; DLB 50
Grigson, Geoffrey (Edward Harvey)
1905-1985 .... CLC 7, 39
See also CA 25-28R; 118; CANR 20, 33; DLB 27; MTCW 1
Grillparzer, Franz 1791-1872
NCLC 1
See also DLB 133
Grimble, Reverend Charles James
See Eliot, T(homas) S(tearns)
Grimke, Charlotte L(ottie) Forten
1837(?)-1914
See Forten, Charlotte L.
See also BW 1; CA 117; 124; DAM MULT, POET
Grimm, Jacob Ludwig Karl 1785-1863
NCLC 3
See also DLB 90; MAICYA; SATA 22
Grimm, Wilhelm Karl 1786-1859
NCLC 3
See also DLB 90; MAICYA; SATA 22
Grimmelshausen, Johann Jakob Christoffel von
1621-1676 .... LC 6
See also DLB 168
Grindel, Eugene 1895-1952
See Eluard, Paul
See also CA 104
Grisham, John 1955-
CLC 84; DAM POP
See also AAYA 14; CA 138; CANR 47, 69
Grossman, David 1954-
CLC 67

See also CA 1-4R; CANR 4, 55; DLB 13
Hasegawa Tatsunosuke
See Futabatei, Shimei
Hasek, Jaroslav (Matej Frantisek) 1883-1923
TCLC 4
See also CA 104; 129; MTCW 1
Hass, Robert 1941-
CLC 18, 39, 99; PC 16
See also CA 111; CANR 30, 50, 71; DLB 105;
SATA 94
Hastings, Hudson
See Kuttner, Henry
Hastings, Selina .... **CLC 44**
Hathorne, John 1641-1717
LC 38
Hatteras, Amelia
See Mencken, H(enry) L(ouis)
Hatteras, Owen .... **TCLC 18**
See also Mencken, H(enry) L(ouis); Nathan,
George Jean
Hauptmann, Gerhart (Johann Robert)
1862-1946 .... **TCLC 4; DAM DRAM**
See also CA 104; 153; DLB 66, 118
Havel, Vaclav 1936-
CLC 25, 58, 65; DAM DRAM; DC 6
See also CA 104; CANR 36, 63; MTCW 1
Haviaras, Stratis .... **CLC 33**
See also Chaviaras, Strates
Hawes, Stephen .... 1475(?)-1523(?)
LC 17
See also DLB 132
Hawkes, John (Clendennin Burne, Jr.)
1925-1998 CLC 1, 2, 3, 4, 7, 9, 14, 15, 27,
49
See also CA 1-4R; 167; CANR 2, 47, 64; DLB
2, 7; DLBY 80; MTCW 1
Hawking, S. W.
See Hawking, Stephen W(illiam)
Hawking, Stephen W(illiam) 1942-
CLC 63, 105
See also AAYA 13; BEST 89:1; CA 126; 129;
CANR 48
Hawkins, Anthony Hope
See Hope, Anthony
Hawthorne, Julian 1846-1934
TCLC 25
See also CA 165
Hawthorne, Nathaniel 1804-1864
**NCLC 39; DA; DAB; DAC; DAM MST,
NOV; SSC 3, 29; WLC**
See also AAYA 18; CDALB 1640-1865; DLB
1, 74; YABC 2
Haxton, Josephine Ayres 1921-
See Douglas, Ellen
See also CA 115; CANR 41
Hayaseca y Eizaguirre, Jorge
See Echegaray (y Eizaguirre), Jose (Maria
Waldo)
Hayashi, Fumiko 1904-1951
TCLC 27
See also CA 161; DLB 180
Haycraft, Anna
See Ellis, Alice Thomas
See also CA 122
Hayden, Robert E(arl) 1913-1980
**CLC 5, 9, 14, 37; BLC 2; DA; DAC; DAM
MST, MULT, POET; PC 6**
See also BW 1; CA 69-72; 97-100; CABS 2;
CANR 24; CDALB 1941-1968; DLB 5, 76;
MTCW 1; SATA 19; SATA-Obit 26
Hayford, J(oseph) E(phraim) Casely
See Casely-Hayford, J(oseph) E(phraim)
Hayman, Ronald 1932-

CLC 44
See also CA 25-28R; CANR 18, 50; DLB 155
Haywood, Eliza .... 1693(?)-1756
LC 44
See also DLB 39
Haywood, Eliza (Fowler) .... 1693(?)-1756
LC 1, 44
Hazlitt, William 1778-1830
NCLC 29
See also DLB 110, 158
Hazzard, Shirley 1931-
CLC 18
See also CA 9-12R; CANR 4, 70; DLBY 82;
MTCW 1
Head, Bessie 1937-1986
CLC 25, 67; BLC 2; DAM MULT
See also BW 2; CA 29-32R; 119; CANR 25;
DLB 117; MTCW 1
Headon, (Nicky) Topper .... 1956(?)-
CLC 30
Heaney, Seamus (Justin) 1939-
**CLC 5, 7, 14, 25, 37, 74, 91; DAB; DAM
POET; PC 18; WLCS**
See also CA 85-88; CANR 25, 48; CDBLB
1960 to Present; DLB 40; DLBY 95; MTCW
1
Hearn, (Patricio) Lafcadio (Tessima Carlos)
1850-1904 .... **TCLC 9**
See also CA 105; 166; DLB 12, 78, 189
Hearne, Vicki 1946-
CLC 56
See also CA 139
Hearon, Shelby 1931-
CLC 63
See also AITN 2; CA 25-28R; CANR 18, 48
Heat-Moon, William Least .... **CLC 29**
See also Trogdon, William (Lewis)
See also AAYA 9
Hebbel, Friedrich 1813-1863
NCLC 43; DAM DRAM
See also DLB 129
Hebert, Anne 1916-
CLC 4, 13, 29; DAC; DAM MST, POET
See also CA 85-88; CANR 69; DLB 68; MTCW
1
Hecht, Anthony (Evan) 1923-
CLC 8, 13, 19; DAM POET
See also CA 9-12R; CANR 6; DLB 5, 169
Hecht, Ben 1894-1964
CLC 8
See also CA 85-88; DLB 7, 9, 25, 26, 28, 86
Hedayat, Sadeq 1903-1951
TCLC 21
See also CA 120
Hegel, Georg Wilhelm Friedrich 1770-1831
NCLC 46
See also DLB 90
Heidegger, Martin 1889-1976
CLC 24
See also CA 81-84; 65-68; CANR 34; MTCW
1
Heidenstam, (Carl Gustaf) Verner von
1859-1940 .... **TCLC 5**
See also CA 104
Heifner, Jack 1946-
CLC 11
See also CA 105; CANR 47
Heijermans, Herman 1864-1924
TCLC 24
See also CA 123
Heilbrun, Carolyn G(old) 1926-
CLC 25
See also CA 45-48; CANR 1, 28, 58

Heine, Heinrich 1797-1856
NCLC 4, 54; PC 25
See also DLB 90
Heinemann, Larry (Curtiss) 1944-
CLC 50
See also CA 110; CAAS 21; CANR 31; DLBD
9; INT CANR-31
Heiney, Donald (William) 1921-1993
See Harris, MacDonald
See also CA 1-4R; 142; CANR 3, 58
Heinlein, Robert A(nson) 1907-1988
CLC 1, 3, 8, 14, 26, 55; DAM POP
See also AAYA 17; CA 1-4R; 125; CANR 1,
20, 53; DLB 8; JRDA; MAICYA; MTCW 1;
SATA 9, 69; SATA-Obit 56
Helforth, John
See Doolittle, Hilda
Hellenhofferu, Vojtech Kapristian z
See Hasek, Jaroslav (Matej Frantisek)
Heller, Joseph 1923-
**CLC 1, 3, 5, 8, 11, 36, 63; DA; DAB; DAC;
DAM MST, NOV, POP; WLC**
See also AAYA 24; AITN 1; CA 5-8R; CABS
1; CANR 8, 42, 66; DLB 2, 28; DLBY 80;
INT CANR-8; MTCW 1
Hellman, Lillian (Florence) 1906-1984
**CLC 2, 4, 8, 14, 18, 34, 44, 52; DAM
DRAM; DC 1**
See also AITN 1, 2; CA 13-16R; 112; CANR
33; DLB 7; DLBY 84; MTCW 1
Helprin, Mark 1947-
CLC 7, 10, 22, 32; DAM NOV, POP
See also CA 81-84; CANR 47, 64; DLBY 85;
MTCW 1
Helvetius, Claude-Adrien 1715-1771
LC 26
Helyar, Jane Penelope Josephine 1933-
See Poole, Josephine
See also CA 21-24R; CANR 10, 26; SATA 82
Hemans, Felicia 1793-1835
NCLC 71
See also DLB 96
Hemingway, Ernest (Miller) 1899-1961
**CLC 1, 3, 6, 8, 10, 13, 19, 30, 34, 39, 41,
44, 50, 61, 80; DA; DAB; DAC; DAM MST,
NOV; SSC 1, 25; WLC**
See also AAYA 19; CA 77-80; CANR 34;
CDALB 1917-1929; DLB 4, 9, 102; DLBD
1, 15, 16; DLBY 81, 87, 96; MTCW 1
Hempel, Amy 1951-
CLC 39
See also CA 118; 137; CANR 70
Henderson, F. C.
See Mencken, H(enry) L(ouis)
Henderson, Sylvia
See Ashton-Warner, Sylvia (Constance)
Henderson, Zenna (Chlarson) 1917-1983
SSC 29
See also CA 1-4R; 133; CANR 1; DLB 8; SATA
5
Henley, Beth .... **CLC 23; DC 6**
See also Henley, Elizabeth Becker
See also CABS 3; DLBY 86
Henley, Elizabeth Becker 1952-
See Henley, Beth
See also CA 107; CANR 32, 73; DAM DRAM,
MST; MTCW 1
Henley, William Ernest 1849-1903
TCLC 8
See also CA 105; DLB 19
Hennissart, Martha
See Lathen, Emma
See also CA 85-88; CANR 64

See Hostos (y Bonilla), Eugenio Maria de
Hostos, Eugenio M. de
See Hostos (y Bonilla), Eugenio Maria de
Hostos, Eugenio Maria
See Hostos (y Bonilla), Eugenio Maria de
Hostos (y Bonilla), Eugenio Maria de
1839-1903 .... **TCLC 24**
See also CA 123; 131; HW
Houdini
See Lovecraft, H(oward) P(hillips)
Hougan, Carolyn 1943-
CLC 34
See also CA 139
Household, Geoffrey (Edward West)
1900-1988 .... **CLC 11**
See also CA 77-80; 126; CANR 58; DLB 87;
SATA 14; SATA-Obit 59
Housman, A(lfred) E(dward) 1859-1936
TCLC 1, 10; DA; DAB; DAC; DAM MST,
POET; PC 2; WLCS
See also CA 104; 125; DLB 19; MTCW 1
Housman, Laurence 1865-1959
TCLC 7
See also CA 106; 155; DLB 10; SATA 25
Howard, Elizabeth Jane 1923-
CLC 7, 29
See also CA 5-8R; CANR 8, 62
Howard, Maureen 1930-
CLC 5, 14, 46
See also CA 53-56; CANR 31; DLBY 83; INT
CANR-31; MTCW 1
Howard, Richard 1929-
CLC 7, 10, 47
See also AITN 1; CA 85-88; CANR 25; DLB 5;
INT CANR-25
Howard, Robert E(rvin) 1906-1936
TCLC 8
See also CA 105; 157
Howard, Warren F.
See Pohl, Frederik
Howe, Fanny (Quincy) 1940-
CLC 47
See also CA 117; CAAS 27; CANR 70;
SATA-Brief 52
Howe, Irving 1920-1993
CLC 85
See also CA 9-12R; 141; CANR 21, 50; DLB
67; MTCW 1
Howe, Julia Ward 1819-1910
TCLC 21
See also CA 117; DLB 1, 189
Howe, Susan 1937-
CLC 72
See also CA 160; DLB 120
Howe, Tina 1937-
CLC 48
See also CA 109
Howell, James .... 1594(?)-1666
LC 13
See also DLB 151
Howells, W. D.
See Howells, William Dean
Howells, William D.
See Howells, William Dean
Howells, William Dean 1837-1920
TCLC 7, 17, 41
See also CA 104; 134; CDALB 1865-1917;
DLB 12, 64, 74, 79, 189
Howes, Barbara 1914-1996
CLC 15
See also CA 9-12R; 151; CAAS 3; CANR 53;
SATA 5
Hrabal, Bohumil 1914-1997

CLC 13, 67
See also CA 106; 156; CAAS 12; CANR 57
Hroswitha of Gandersheim .... c. 935-c. 1002
CMLC 29
See also DLB 148
Hsun, Lu
See Lu Hsun
Hubbard, L(afayette) Ron(ald) ... 1911-1986
CLC 43; DAM POP
See also CA 77-80; 118; CANR 52
Huch, Ricarda (Octavia) 1864-1947
TCLC 13
See also CA 111; DLB 66
Huddle, David 1942-
CLC 49
See also CA 57-60; CAAS 20; DLB 130
Hudson, Jeffrey
See Crichton, (John) Michael
Hudson, W(illiam) H(enry) 1841-1922
TCLC 29
See also CA 115; DLB 98, 153, 174; SATA 35
Hueffer, Ford Madox
See Ford, Ford Madox
Hughart, Barry 1934-
CLC 39
See also CA 137
Hughes, Colin
See Creasey, John
Hughes, David (John) 1930-
CLC 48
See also CA 116; 129; DLB 14
Hughes, Edward James
See Hughes, Ted
See also DAM MST, POET
Hughes, (James) Langston 1902-1967
CLC 1, 5, 10, 15, 35, 44, 108; BLC 2; DA;
DAB; DAC; DAM DRAM, MST, MULT,
POET; DC 3; PC 1; SSC 6; WLC
See also AAYA 12; BW 1; CA 1-4R; 25-28R;
CANR 1, 34; CDALB 1929-1941; CLR 17;
DLB 4, 7, 48, 51, 86; JRDA; MAICYA;
MTCW 1; SATA 4, 33
Hughes, Richard (Arthur Warren) 1900-1976
CLC 1, 11; DAM NOV
See also CA 5-8R; 65-68; CANR 4; DLB 15,
161; MTCW 1; SATA 8; SATA-Obit 25
Hughes, Ted 1930-
CLC 2, 4, 9, 14, 37; DAB; DAC; PC 7
See also Hughes, Edward James
See also CA 1-4R; CANR 1, 33, 66; CLR 3;
DLB 40, 161; MAICYA; MTCW 1; SATA
49; SATA-Brief 27
Hugo, Richard F(ranklin) 1923-1982
CLC 6, 18, 32; DAM POET
See also CA 49-52; 108; CANR 3; DLB 5
Hugo, Victor (Marie) 1802-1885
NCLC 3, 10, 21; DA; DAB; DAC; DAM
DRAM, MST, NOV, POET; PC 17; WLC
See also DLB 119, 192; SATA 47
Huidobro, Vicente
See Huidobro Fernandez, Vicente Garcia
Huidobro Fernandez, Vicente Garcia
1893-1948 .... **TCLC 31**
See also CA 131; HW
Hulme, Keri 1947-
CLC 39
See also CA 125; CANR 69; INT 125
Hulme, T(homas) E(rnest) 1883-1917
TCLC 21
See also CA 117; DLB 19
Hume, David 1711-1776
LC 7
See also DLB 104

Humphrey, William 1924-1997
CLC 45
See also CA 77-80; 160; CANR 68; DLB 6
Humphreys, Emyr Owen 1919-
CLC 47
See also CA 5-8R; CANR 3, 24; DLB 15
Humphreys, Josephine 1945-
CLC 34, 57
See also CA 121; 127; INT 127
Huneker, James Gibbons 1857-1921
TCLC 65
See also DLB 71
Hungerford, Pixie
See Brinsmead, H(esba) F(ay)
Hunt, E(verette) Howard, (Jr.) 1918-
CLC 3
See also AITN 1; CA 45-48; CANR 2, 47
Hunt, Kyle
See Creasey, John
Hunt, (James Henry) Leigh 1784-1859
NCLC 1, 70; DAM POET
See also DLB 96, 110, 144
Hunt, Marsha 1946-
CLC 70
See also BW 2; CA 143
Hunt, Violet .... 1866(?)-1942
TCLC 53
See also DLB 162, 197
Hunter, E. Waldo
See Sturgeon, Theodore (Hamilton)
Hunter, Evan 1926-
CLC 11, 31; DAM POP
See also CA 5-8R; CANR 5, 38, 62; DLBY 82;
INT CANR-5; MTCW 1; SATA 25
Hunter, Kristin (Eggleston) 1931-
CLC 35
See also AITN 1; BW 1; CA 13-16R; CANR
13; CLR 3; DLB 33; INT CANR-13;
MAICYA; SAAS 10; SATA 12
Hunter, Mollie 1922-
CLC 21
See also McIlwraith, Maureen Mollie Hunter
See also AAYA 13; CANR 37; CLR 25; DLB
161; JRDA; MAICYA; SAAS 7; SATA 54
Hunter, Robert .... (?)-1734
LC 7
Hurston, Zora Neale 1903-1960
CLC 7, 30, 61; BLC 2; DA; DAC; DAM
MST, MULT, NOV; SSC 4; WLCS
See also AAYA 15; BW 1; CA 85-88; CANR
61; DLB 51, 86; MTCW 1
Huston, John (Marcellus) 1906-1987
CLC 20
See also CA 73-76; 123; CANR 34; DLB 26
Hustvedt, Siri 1955-
CLC 76
See also CA 137
Hutten, Ulrich von 1488-1523
LC 16
See also DLB 179
Huxley, Aldous (Leonard) 1894-1963
CLC 1, 3, 4, 5, 8, 11, 18, 35, 79; DA; DAB;
DAC; DAM MST, NOV; WLC
See also AAYA 11; CA 85-88; CANR 44;
CDBLB 1914-1945; DLB 36, 100, 162, 195;
MTCW 1; SATA 63
Huxley, T(homas) H(enry) 1825-1895
NCLC 67
See also DLB 57
Huysmans, Joris-Karl 1848-1907
TCLC 7, 69
See also CA 104; 165; DLB 123
Hwang, David Henry 1957-

CLC 55; DAM DRAM; DC 4
See also CA 127; 132; INT 132

Hyde, Anthony 1946-
CLC 42
See also CA 136

Hyde, Margaret O(ldroyd) 1917-
CLC 21
See also CA 1-4R; CANR 1, 36; CLR 23; JRDA; MAICYA; SAAS 8; SATA 1, 42, 76

Hynes, James .... 1956(?)-
CLC 65
See also CA 164

Ian, Janis 1951-
CLC 21
See also CA 105

Ibanez, Vicente Blasco
See Blasco Ibanez, Vicente

Ibarguengoitia, Jorge 1928-1983
CLC 37
See also CA 124; 113; HW

Ibsen, Henrik (Johan) 1828-1906
TCLC 2, 8, 16, 37, 52; DA; DAB; DAC; DAM DRAM, MST; DC 2; WLC
See also CA 104; 141

Ibuse, Masuji 1898-1993
CLC 22
See also CA 127; 141; DLB 180

Ichikawa, Kon 1915-
CLC 20
See also CA 121

Idle, Eric 1943-
CLC 21
See Monty Python
See also CA 116; CANR 35

Ignatow, David 1914-1997
CLC 4, 7, 14, 40
See also CA 9-12R; 162; CAAS 3; CANR 31, 57; DLB 5

Ihimaera, Witi 1944-
CLC 46
See also CA 77-80

Ilf, Ilya .... TCLC 21
See also Fainzilberg, Ilya Arnoldovich

Illyes, Gyula 1902-1983
PC 16
See also CA 114; 109

Immermann, Karl (Lebrecht) 1796-1840
NCLC 4, 49
See also DLB 133

Inchbald, Elizabeth 1753-1821
NCLC 62
See also DLB 39, 89

Inclan, Ramon (Maria) del Valle
See Valle-Inclan, Ramon (Maria) del

Infante, G(uillermo) Cabrera
See Cabrera Infante, G(uillermo)

Ingalls, Rachel (Holmes) 1940-
CLC 42
See also CA 123; 127

Ingamells, Reginald Charles
See Ingamells, Rex

Ingamells, Rex 1913-1955
TCLC 35
See also CA 167

Inge, William (Motter) 1913-1973
CLC 1, 8, 19; DAM DRAM
See also CA 9-12R; CDALB 1941-1968; DLB 7; MTCW 1

Ingelow, Jean 1820-1897
NCLC 39
See also DLB 35, 163; SATA 33

Ingram, Willis J.
See Harris, Mark

Innaurato, Albert (F.) .... 1948(?)-
CLC 21, 60
See also CA 115; 122; INT 122

Innes, Michael
See Stewart, J(ohn) I(nnes) M(ackintosh)

Innis, Harold Adams 1894-1952
TCLC 77
See also DLB 88

Ionesco, Eugene 1909-1994
CLC 1, 4, 6, 9, 11, 15, 41, 86; DA; DAB; DAC; DAM DRAM, MST; WLC
See also CA 9-12R; 144; CANR 55; MTCW 1; SATA 7; SATA-Obit 79

Iqbal, Muhammad 1873-1938
TCLC 28

Ireland, Patrick
See O'Doherty, Brian

Iron, Ralph
See Schreiner, Olive (Emilie Albertina)

Irving, John (Winslow) 1942-
CLC 13, 23, 38, 112; DAM NOV, POP
See also AAYA 8; BEST 89:3; CA 25-28R; CANR 28, 73; DLB 6; DLBY 82; MTCW 1

Irving, Washington 1783-1859
NCLC 2, 19; DA; DAB; DAC; DAM MST; SSC 2; WLC
See also CDALB 1640-1865; DLB 3, 11, 30, 59, 73, 74, 186; YABC 2

Irwin, P. K.
See Page, P(atricia) K(athleen)

Isaacs, Jorge Ricardo 1837-1895
NCLC 70

Isaacs, Susan 1943-
CLC 32; DAM POP
See also BEST 89:1; CA 89-92; CANR 20, 41, 65; INT CANR-20; MTCW 1

Isherwood, Christopher (William Bradshaw)
1904-1986 . CLC 1, 9, 11, 14, 44; DAM DRAM, NOV
See also CA 13-16R; 117; CANR 35; DLB 15, 195; DLBY 86; MTCW 1

Ishiguro, Kazuo 1954-
CLC 27, 56, 59, 110; DAM NOV
See also BEST 90:2; CA 120; CANR 49; DLB 194; MTCW 1

Ishikawa, Hakuhin
See Ishikawa, Takuboku

Ishikawa, Takuboku .... 1886(?)-1912
TCLC 15; DAM POET; PC 10
See also CA 113; 153

Iskander, Fazil 1929-
CLC 47
See also CA 102

Isler, Alan (David) 1934-
CLC 91
See also CA 156

Ivan IV 1530-1584
LC 17

Ivanov, Vyacheslav Ivanovich 1866-1949
TCLC 33
See also CA 122

Ivask, Ivar Vidrik 1927-1992
CLC 14
See also CA 37-40R; 139; CANR 24

Ives, Morgan
See Bradley, Marion Zimmer

J. R. S.
See Gogarty, Oliver St. John

Jabran, Kahlil
See Gibran, Kahlil

Jabran, Khalil
See Gibran, Kahlil

Jackson, Daniel

See Wingrove, David (John)

Jackson, Jesse 1908-1983
CLC 12
See also BW 1; CA 25-28R; 109; CANR 27; CLR 28; MAICYA; SATA 2, 29; SATA-Obit 48

Jackson, Laura (Riding) 1901-1991
See Riding, Laura
See also CA 65-68; 135; CANR 28; DLB 48

Jackson, Sam
See Trumbo, Dalton

Jackson, Sara
See Wingrove, David (John)

Jackson, Shirley 1919-1965
CLC 11, 60, 87; DA; DAC; DAM MST; SSC 9; WLC
See also AAYA 9; CA 1-4R; 25-28R; CANR 4, 52; CDALB 1941-1968; DLB 6; SATA 2

Jacob, (Cyprien-)Max 1876-1944
TCLC 6
See also CA 104

Jacobs, Harriet A(nn) .... 1813(?)-1897
NCLC 67

Jacobs, Jim 1942-
CLC 12
See also CA 97-100; INT 97-100

Jacobs, W(illiam) W(ymark) 1863-1943
TCLC 22
See also CA 121; 167; DLB 135

Jacobsen, Jens Peter 1847-1885
NCLC 34

Jacobsen, Josephine 1908-
CLC 48, 102
See also CA 33-36R; CAAS 18; CANR 23, 48

Jacobson, Dan 1929-
CLC 4, 14
See also CA 1-4R; CANR 2, 25, 66; DLB 14; MTCW 1

Jacqueline
See Carpentier (y Valmont), Alejo

Jagger, Mick 1944-
CLC 17

Jahiz, al- .... c. 780-c. 869
CMLC 25

Jakes, John (William) 1932-
CLC 29; DAM NOV, POP
See also BEST 89:4; CA 57-60; CANR 10, 43, 66; DLBY 83; INT CANR-10; MTCW 1; SATA 62

James, Andrew
See Kirkup, James

James, C(yril) L(ionel) R(obert) . 1901-1989
CLC 33; BLCS
See also BW 2; CA 117; 125; 128; CANR 62; DLB 125; MTCW 1

James, Daniel (Lewis) 1911-1988
See Santiago, Danny
See also CA 125

James, Dynely
See Mayne, William (James Carter)

James, Henry Sr. 1811-1882
NCLC 53

James, Henry 1843-1916
TCLC 2, 11, 24, 40, 47, 64; DA; DAB; DAC; DAM MST, NOV; SSC 8, 32; WLC
See also CA 104; 132; CDALB 1865-1917; DLB 12, 71, 74, 189; DLBD 13; MTCW 1

James, M. R.
See James, Montague (Rhodes)
See also DLB 156

James, Montague (Rhodes) 1862-1936
TCLC 6; SSC 16
See also CA 104; DLB 201

James, P. D. 1920-
    CLC 18, 46
    See also White, Phyllis Dorothy James
    See also BEST 90:2; CDBLB 1960 to Present;
    DLB 87; DLBD 17
James, Philip
    See Moorcock, Michael (John)
James, William 1842-1910
    TCLC 15, 32
    See also CA 109
James I 1394-1437
    LC 20
Jameson, Anna 1794-1860
    NCLC 43
    See also DLB 99, 166
Jami, Nur al-Din 'Abd al-Rahman 1414-1492
    LC 9
Jammes, Francis 1868-1938
    TCLC 75
Jandl, Ernst 1925-
    CLC 34
Janowitz, Tama 1957-
    CLC 43; DAM POP
    See also CA 106; CANR 52
Japrisot, Sebastien 1931-
    CLC 90
Jarrell, Randall 1914-1965
    CLC 1, 2, 6, 9, 13, 49; DAM POET
    See also CA 5-8R; 25-28R; CABS 2; CANR 6,
    34; CDALB 1941-1968; CLR 6; DLB 48, 52;
    MAICYA; MTCW 1; SATA 7
Jarry, Alfred 1873-1907
    TCLC 2, 14; DAM DRAM; SSC 20
    See also CA 104; 153; DLB 192
Jarvis, E. K.
    See Bloch, Robert (Albert); Ellison, Harlan
    (Jay); Silverberg, Robert
Jeake, Samuel, Jr.
    See Aiken, Conrad (Potter)
Jean Paul 1763-1825
    NCLC 7
Jefferies, (John) Richard 1848-1887
    NCLC 47
    See also DLB 98, 141; SATA 16
Jeffers, (John) Robinson 1887-1962
    CLC 2, 3, 11, 15, 54; DA; DAC; DAM
    MST, POET; PC 17; WLC
    See also CA 85-88; CANR 35; CDALB
    1917-1929; DLB 45; MTCW 1
Jefferson, Janet
    See Mencken, H(enry) L(ouis)
Jefferson, Thomas 1743-1826
    NCLC 11
    See also CDALB 1640-1865; DLB 31
Jeffrey, Francis 1773-1850
    NCLC 33
    See also DLB 107
Jelakowitch, Ivan
    See Heijermans, Herman
Jellicoe, (Patricia) Ann 1927-
    CLC 27
    See also CA 85-88; DLB 13
Jen, Gish .... CLC 70
    See also Jen, Lillian
Jen, Lillian .... 1956(?)-
    See Jen, Gish
    See also CA 135
Jenkins, (John) Robin 1912-
    CLC 52
    See also CA 1-4R; CANR 1; DLB 14
Jennings, Elizabeth (Joan) 1926-
    CLC 5, 14
    See also CA 61-64; CAAS 5; CANR 8, 39, 66;

DLB 27; MTCW 1; SATA 66
Jennings, Waylon 1937-
    CLC 21
Jensen, Johannes V. 1873-1950
    TCLC 41
    See also CA 170
Jensen, Laura (Linnea) 1948-
    CLC 37
    See also CA 103
Jerome, Jerome K(lapka) 1859-1927
    TCLC 23
    See also CA 119; DLB 10, 34, 135
Jerrold, Douglas William 1803-1857
    NCLC 2
    See also DLB 158, 159
Jewett, (Theodora) Sarah Orne .. 1849-1909
    TCLC 1, 22; SSC 6
    See also CA 108; 127; CANR 71; DLB 12, 74;
    SATA 15
Jewsbury, Geraldine (Endsor) 1812-1880
    NCLC 22
    See also DLB 21
Jhabvala, Ruth Prawer 1927-
    CLC 4, 8, 29, 94; DAB; DAM NOV
    See also CA 1-4R; CANR 2, 29, 51, 74; DLB
    139, 194; INT CANR-29; MTCW 1
Jibran, Kahlil
    See Gibran, Kahlil
Jibran, Khalil
    See Gibran, Kahlil
Jiles, Paulette 1943-
    CLC 13, 58
    See also CA 101; CANR 70
Jimenez (Mantecon), Juan Ramon 1881-1958
    TCLC 4; DAM MULT, POET; HLC; PC
    7
    See also CA 104; 131; CANR 74; DLB 134;
    HW; MTCW 1
Jimenez, Ramon
    See Jimenez (Mantecon), Juan Ramon
Jimenez Mantecon, Juan
    See Jimenez (Mantecon), Juan Ramon
Jin, Ha 1956-
    CLC 109
    See also CA 152
Joel, Billy .... CLC 26
    See also Joel, William Martin
Joel, William Martin 1949-
    See Joel, Billy
    See also CA 108
John, Saint .... 7th cent. -
    CMLC 27
John of the Cross, St. 1542-1591
    LC 18
Johnson, B(ryan) S(tanley William)
    1933-1973 .... CLC 6, 9
    See also CA 9-12R; 53-56; CANR 9; DLB 14,
    40
Johnson, Benj. F. of Boo
    See Riley, James Whitcomb
Johnson, Benjamin F. of Boo
    See Riley, James Whitcomb
Johnson, Charles (Richard) 1948-
    CLC 7, 51, 65; BLC 2; DAM MULT
    See also BW 2; CA 116; CAAS 18; CANR 42,
    66; DLB 33
Johnson, Denis 1949-
    CLC 52
    See also CA 117; 121; CANR 71; DLB 120
Johnson, Diane 1934-
    CLC 5, 13, 48
    See also CA 41-44R; CANR 17, 40, 62; DLBY
    80; INT CANR-17; MTCW 1

Johnson, Eyvind (Olof Verner) ... 1900-1976
    CLC 14
    See also CA 73-76; 69-72; CANR 34
Johnson, J. R.
    See James, C(yril) L(ionel) R(obert)
Johnson, James Weldon 1871-1938
    TCLC 3, 19; BLC 2; DAM MULT, POET;
    PC 24
    See also BW 1; CA 104; 125; CDALB
    1917-1929; CLR 32; DLB 51; MTCW 1;
    SATA 31
Johnson, Joyce 1935-
    CLC 58
    See also CA 125; 129
Johnson, Lionel (Pigot) 1867-1902
    TCLC 19
    See also CA 117; DLB 19
Johnson, Marguerite (Annie)
    See Angelou, Maya
Johnson, Mel
    See Malzberg, Barry N(athaniel)
Johnson, Pamela Hansford 1912-1981
    CLC 1, 7, 27
    See also CA 1-4R; 104; CANR 2, 28; DLB 15;
    MTCW 1
Johnson, Robert .... 1911(?)-1938
    TCLC 69
Johnson, Samuel 1709-1784
    LC 15; DA; DAB; DAC; DAM MST; WLC
    See also CDBLB 1660-1789; DLB 39, 95, 104,
    142
Johnson, Uwe 1934-1984
    CLC 5, 10, 15, 40
    See also CA 1-4R; 112; CANR 1, 39; DLB 75;
    MTCW 1
Johnston, George (Benson) 1913-
    CLC 51
    See also CA 1-4R; CANR 5, 20; DLB 88
Johnston, Jennifer 1930-
    CLC 7
    See also CA 85-88; DLB 14
Jolley, (Monica) Elizabeth 1923-
    CLC 46; SSC 19
    See also CA 127; CAAS 13; CANR 59
Jones, Arthur Llewellyn 1863-1947
    See Machen, Arthur
    See also CA 104
Jones, D(ouglas) G(ordon) 1929-
    CLC 10
    See also CA 29-32R; CANR 13; DLB 53
Jones, David (Michael) 1895-1974
    CLC 2, 4, 7, 13, 42
    See also CA 9-12R; 53-56; CANR 28; CDBLB
    1945-1960; DLB 20, 100; MTCW 1
Jones, David Robert 1947-
    See Bowie, David
    See also CA 103
Jones, Diana Wynne 1934-
    CLC 26
    See also AAYA 12; CA 49-52; CANR 4, 26,
    56; CLR 23; DLB 161; JRDA; MAICYA;
    SAAS 7; SATA 9, 70
Jones, Edward P. 1950-
    CLC 76
    See also BW 2; CA 142
Jones, Gayl 1949-
    CLC 6, 9; BLC 2; DAM MULT
    See also BW 2; CA 77-80; CANR 27, 66; DLB
    33; MTCW 1
Jones, James 1921-1977
    CLC 1, 3, 10, 39
    See also AITN 1, 2; CA 1-4R; 69-72; CANR 6;
    DLB 2, 143; DLBD 17; MTCW 1

Kavanagh, Patrick (Joseph) 1904-1967
   CLC 22
   See also CA 123; 25-28R; DLB 15, 20; MTCW
   1

Kawabata, Yasunari 1899-1972
   CLC 2, 5, 9, 18, 107; SSC 17
   See also CA 93-96; 33-36R; DLB 180

Kaye, M(ary) M(argaret) 1909-
   CLC 28
   See also CA 89-92; CANR 24, 60; MTCW 1;
   SATA 62

Kaye, Mollie
   See Kaye, M(ary) M(argaret)

Kaye-Smith, Sheila 1887-1956
   TCLC 20
   See also CA 118; DLB 36

Kaymor, Patrice Maguilene
   See Senghor, Leopold Sedar

Kazan, Elia 1909-
   CLC 6, 16, 63
   See also CA 21-24R; CANR 32

Kazantzakis, Nikos .... 1883(?)-1957
   TCLC 2, 5, 33
   See also CA 105; 132; MTCW 1

Kazin, Alfred 1915-
   CLC 34, 38
   See also CA 1-4R; CAAS 7; CANR 1, 45; DLB
   67

Keane, Mary Nesta (Skrine) 1904-1996
   See Keane, Molly
   See also CA 108; 114; 151

Keane, Molly .... **CLC 31**
   See also Keane, Mary Nesta (Skrine)
   See also INT 114

Keates, Jonathan .... 1946(?)-
   CLC 34
   See also CA 163

Keaton, Buster 1895-1966
   CLC 20

Keats, John................................... 1795-1821
   NCLC 8, 73; DA; DAB; DAC; DAM MST,
   POET; PC 1; WLC
   See also CDBLB 1789-1832; DLB 96, 110

Keene, Donald 1922-
   CLC 34
   See also CA 1-4R; CANR 5

Keillor, Garrison .... **CLC 40, 115**
   See also Keillor, Gary (Edward)
   See also AAYA 2; BEST 89:3; DLBY 87; SATA
   58

Keillor, Gary (Edward) 1942-
   See Keillor, Garrison
   See also CA 111; 117; CANR 36, 59; DAM
   POP; MTCW 1

Keith, Michael
   See Hubbard, L(afayette) Ron(ald)

Keller, Gottfried 1819-1890
   NCLC 2; SSC 26
   See also DLB 129

Keller, Nora Okja .... **CLC 109**

Kellerman, Jonathan 1949-
   CLC 44; DAM POP
   See also BEST 90:1; CA 106; CANR 29, 51;
   INT CANR-29

Kelley, William Melvin 1937-
   CLC 22
   See also BW 1; CA 77-80; CANR 27; DLB 33

Kellogg, Marjorie 1922-
   CLC 2
   See also CA 81-84

Kellow, Kathleen
   See Hibbert, Eleanor Alice Burford

Kelly, M(ilton) T(erry) 1947-

   CLC 55
   See also CA 97-100; CAAS 22; CANR 19, 43

Kelman, James 1946-
   CLC 58, 86
   See also CA 148; DLB 194

Kemal, Yashar 1923-
   CLC 14, 29
   See also CA 89-92; CANR 44

Kemble, Fanny 1809-1893
   NCLC 18
   See also DLB 32

Kemelman, Harry 1908-1996
   CLC 2
   See also AITN 1; CA 9-12R; 155; CANR 6, 71;
   DLB 28

Kempe, Margery .... 1373(?)-1440(?)
   LC 6
   See also DLB 146

Kempis, Thomas a 1380-1471
   LC 11

Kendall, Henry 1839-1882
   NCLC 12

Keneally, Thomas (Michael) 1935-
   CLC 5, 8, 10, 14, 19, 27, 43, 117; DAM
   NOV
   See also CA 85-88; CANR 10, 50, 74; MTCW
   1

Kennedy, Adrienne (Lita) 1931-
   CLC 66; BLC 2; DAM MULT; DC 5
   See also BW 2; CA 103; CAAS 20; CABS 3;
   CANR 26, 53; DLB 38

Kennedy, John Pendleton 1795-1870
   NCLC 2
   See also DLB 3

Kennedy, Joseph Charles 1929-
   See Kennedy, X. J.
   See also CA 1-4R; CANR 4, 30, 40; SATA 14,
   86

Kennedy, William 1928-
   CLC 6, 28, 34, 53; DAM NOV
   See also AAYA 1; CA 85-88; CANR 14, 31;
   DLB 143; DLBY 85; INT CANR-31; MTCW
   1; SATA 57

Kennedy, X. J. .... **CLC 8, 42**
   See also Kennedy, Joseph Charles
   See also CAAS 9; CLR 27; DLB 5; SAAS 22

Kenny, Maurice (Francis) 1929-
   CLC 87; DAM MULT
   See also CA 144; CAAS 22; DLB 175; NNAL

Kent, Kelvin
   See Kuttner, Henry

Kenton, Maxwell
   See Southern, Terry

Kenyon, Robert O.
   See Kuttner, Henry

Kepler, Johannes 1571-1630
   LC 45

Kerouac, Jack .... **CLC 1, 2, 3, 5, 14, 29, 61**
   See also Kerouac, Jean-Louis Lebris de
   See also AAYA 25; CDALB 1941-1968; DLB
   2, 16; DLBD 3; DLBY 95

Kerouac, Jean-Louis Lebris de ... 1922-1969
   See Kerouac, Jack
   See also AITN 1; CA 5-8R; 25-28R; CANR 26,
   54; DA; DAB; DAC; DAM MST, NOV,
   POET, POP; MTCW 1; WLC

Kerr, Jean 1923-
   CLC 22
   See also CA 5-8R; CANR 7; INT CANR-7

Kerr, M. E. .... **CLC 12, 35**
   See also Meaker, Marijane (Agnes)
   See also AAYA 2, 23; CLR 29; SAAS 1

Kerr, Robert .... **CLC 55**

Kerrigan, (Thomas) Anthony 1918-
   CLC 4, 6
   See also CA 49-52; CAAS 11; CANR 4

Kerry, Lois
   See Duncan, Lois

Kesey, Ken (Elton) 1935-
   CLC 1, 3, 6, 11, 46, 64; DA; DAB; DAC;
   DAM MST, NOV, POP; WLC
   See also AAYA 25; CA 1-4R; CANR 22, 38,
   66; CDALB 1968-1988; DLB 2, 16; MTCW
   1; SATA 66

Kesselring, Joseph (Otto) 1902-1967
   CLC 45; DAM DRAM, MST
   See also CA 150

Kessler, Jascha (Frederick) 1929-
   CLC 4
   See also CA 17-20R; CANR 8, 48

Kettelkamp, Larry (Dale) 1933-
   CLC 12
   See also CA 29-32R; CANR 16; SAAS 3; SATA
   2

Key, Ellen 1849-1926
   TCLC 65

Keyber, Conny
   See Fielding, Henry

Keyes, Daniel 1927-
   CLC 80; DA; DAC; DAM MST, NOV
   See also AAYA 23; CA 17-20R; CANR 10, 26,
   54, 74; SATA 37

Keynes, John Maynard 1883-1946
   TCLC 64
   See also CA 114; 162, 163; DLBD 10

Khanshendel, Chiron
   See Rose, Wendy

Khayyam, Omar 1048-1131
   CMLC 11; DAM POET; PC 8

Kherdian, David 1931-
   CLC 6, 9
   See also CA 21-24R; CAAS 2; CANR 39; CLR
   24; JRDA; MAICYA; SATA 16, 74

Khlebnikov, Velimir .... **TCLC 20**
   See also Khlebnikov, Viktor Vladimirovich

Khlebnikov, Viktor Vladimirovich 1885-1922
   See Khlebnikov, Velimir
   See also CA 117

Khodasevich, Vladislav (Felitsianovich)
   1886-1939 .... **TCLC 15**
   See also CA 115

Kielland, Alexander Lange 1849-1906
   TCLC 5
   See also CA 104

Kiely, Benedict 1919-
   CLC 23, 43
   See also CA 1-4R; CANR 2; DLB 15

Kienzle, William X(avier) 1928-
   CLC 25; DAM POP
   See also CA 93-96; CAAS 1; CANR 9, 31, 59;
   INT CANR-31; MTCW 1

Kierkegaard, Soren 1813-1855
   NCLC 34

Killens, John Oliver 1916-1987
   CLC 10
   See also BW 2; CA 77-80; 123; CAAS 2; CANR
   26; DLB 33

Killigrew, Anne 1660-1685
   LC 4
   See also DLB 131

Kim
   See Simenon, Georges (Jacques Christian)

Kincaid, Jamaica 1949-
   CLC 43, 68; BLC 2; DAM MULT, NOV
   See also AAYA 13; BW 2; CA 125; CANR 47,
   59; DLB 157

King, Francis (Henry) 1923-
    CLC 8, 53; DAM NOV
    See also CA 1-4R; CANR 1, 33; DLB 15, 139;
    MTCW 1
King, Kennedy
    See Brown, George Douglas
King, Martin Luther, Jr. 1929-1968
    CLC 83; BLC 2; DA; DAB; DAC; DAM
    MST, MULT; WLCS
    See also BW 2; CA 25-28; CANR 27, 44; CAP
    2; MTCW 1; SATA 14
King, Stephen (Edwin) 1947-
    CLC 12, 26, 37, 61, 113; DAM NOV, POP;
    SSC 17
    See also AAYA 1, 17; BEST 90:1; CA 61-64;
    CANR 1, 30, 52; DLB 143; DLBY 80;
    JRDA; MTCW 1; SATA 9, 55
King, Steve
    See King, Stephen (Edwin)
King, Thomas 1943-
    CLC 89; DAC; DAM MULT
    See also CA 144; DLB 175; NNAL; SATA 96
Kingman, Lee .... CLC 17
    See also Natti, (Mary) Lee
    See also SAAS 3; SATA 1, 67
Kingsley, Charles 1819-1875
    NCLC 35
    See also DLB 21, 32, 163, 190; YABC 2
Kingsley, Sidney 1906-1995
    CLC 44
    See also CA 85-88; 147; DLB 7
Kingsolver, Barbara 1955-
    CLC 55, 81; DAM POP
    See also AAYA 15; CA 129; 134; CANR 60;
    INT 134
Kingston, Maxine (Ting Ting) Hong .. 1940-
    CLC 12, 19, 58; DAM MULT, NOV;
    WLCS
    See also AAYA 8; CA 69-72; CANR 13, 38,
    74; DLB 173; DLBY 80; INT CANR-13;
    MTCW 1; SATA 53
Kinnell, Galway 1927-
    CLC 1, 2, 3, 5, 13, 29
    See also CA 9-12R; CANR 10, 34, 66; DLB 5;
    DLBY 87; INT CANR-34; MTCW 1
Kinsella, Thomas 1928-
    CLC 4, 19
    See also CA 17-20R; CANR 15; DLB 27;
    MTCW 1
Kinsella, W(illiam) P(atrick) 1935-
    CLC 27, 43; DAC; DAM NOV, POP
    See also AAYA 7; CA 97-100; CAAS 7; CANR
    21, 35, 66; INT CANR-21; MTCW 1
Kipling, (Joseph) Rudyard 1865-1936
    TCLC 8, 17; DA; DAB; DAC; DAM MST,
    POET; PC 3; SSC 5; WLC
    See also CA 105; 120; CANR 33; CDBLB
    1890-1914; CLR 39; DLB 19, 34, 141, 156;
    MAICYA; MTCW 1; SATA 100; YABC 2
Kirkup, James 1918-
    CLC 1
    See also CA 1-4R; CAAS 4; CANR 2; DLB 27;
    SATA 12
Kirkwood, James .... 1930(?)-1989
    CLC 9
    See also AITN 2; CA 1-4R; 128; CANR 6, 40
Kirshner, Sidney
    See Kingsley, Sidney
Kis, Danilo 1935-1989
    CLC 57
    See also CA 109; 118; 129; CANR 61; DLB
    181; MTCW 1
Kivi, Aleksis 1834-1872

NCLC 30
Kizer, Carolyn (Ashley) 1925-
    CLC 15, 39, 80; DAM POET
    See also CA 65-68; CAAS 5; CANR 24, 70;
    DLB 5, 169
Klabund 1890-1928
    TCLC 44
    See also CA 162; DLB 66
Klappert, Peter 1942-
    CLC 57
    See also CA 33-36R; DLB 5
Klein, A(braham) M(oses) 1909-1972
    CLC 19; DAB; DAC; DAM MST
    See also CA 101; 37-40R; DLB 68
Klein, Norma 1938-1989
    CLC 30
    See also AAYA 2; CA 41-44R; 128; CANR 15,
    37; CLR 2, 19; INT CANR-15; JRDA;
    MAICYA; SAAS 1; SATA 7, 57
Klein, T(heodore) E(ibon) D(onald) ... 1947-
    CLC 34
    See also CA 119; CANR 44
Kleist, Heinrich von 1777-1811
    NCLC 2, 37; DAM DRAM; SSC 22
    See also DLB 90
Klima, Ivan 1931-
    CLC 56; DAM NOV
    See also CA 25-28R; CANR 17, 50
Klimentov, Andrei Platonovich ... 1899-1951
    See Platonov, Andrei
    See also CA 108
Klinger, Friedrich Maximilian von 1752-1831
    NCLC 1
    See also DLB 94
Klingsor the Magician
    See Hartmann, Sadakichi
Klopstock, Friedrich Gottlieb 1724-1803
    NCLC 11
    See also DLB 97
Knapp, Caroline 1959-
    CLC 99
    See also CA 154
Knebel, Fletcher 1911-1993
    CLC 14
    See also AITN 1; CA 1-4R; 140; CAAS 3;
    CANR 1, 36; SATA 36; SATA-Obit 75
Knickerbocker, Diedrich
    See Irving, Washington
Knight, Etheridge 1931-1991
    CLC 40; BLC 2; DAM POET; PC 14
    See also BW 1; CA 21-24R; 133; CANR 23;
    DLB 41
Knight, Sarah Kemble 1666-1727
    LC 7
    See also DLB 24, 200
Knister, Raymond 1899-1932
    TCLC 56
    See also DLB 68
Knowles, John 1926-
    CLC 1, 4, 10, 26; DA; DAC; DAM MST,
    NOV
    See also AAYA 10; CA 17-20R; CANR 40, 74;
    CDALB 1968-1988; DLB 6; MTCW 1;
    SATA 8, 89
Knox, Calvin M.
    See Silverberg, Robert
Knox, John .... c. 1505-1572
    LC 37
    See also DLB 132
Knye, Cassandra
    See Disch, Thomas M(ichael)
Koch, C(hristopher) J(ohn) 1932-
    CLC 42

See also CA 127
Koch, Christopher
    See Koch, C(hristopher) J(ohn)
Koch, Kenneth 1925-
    CLC 5, 8, 44; DAM POET
    See also CA 1-4R; CANR 6, 36, 57; DLB 5;
    INT CANR-36; SATA 65
Kochanowski, Jan 1530-1584
    LC 10
Kock, Charles Paul de 1794-1871
    NCLC 16
Koda Shigeyuki 1867-1947
    See Rohan, Koda
    See also CA 121
Koestler, Arthur 1905-1983
    CLC 1, 3, 6, 8, 15, 33
    See also CA 1-4R; 109; CANR 1, 33; CDBLB
    1945-1960; DLBY 83; MTCW 1
Kogawa, Joy Nozomi 1935-
    CLC 78; DAC; DAM MST, MULT
    See also CA 101; CANR 19, 62; SATA 99
Kohout, Pavel 1928-
    CLC 13
    See also CA 45-48; CANR 3
Koizumi, Yakumo
    See Hearn, (Patricio) Lafcadio (Tessima Carlos)
Kolmar, Gertrud 1894-1943
    TCLC 40
    See also CA 167
Komunyakaa, Yusef 1947-
    CLC 86, 94; BLCS
    See also CA 147; DLB 120
Konrad, George
    See Konrad, Gyoergy
Konrad, Gyoergy 1933-
    CLC 4, 10, 73
    See also CA 85-88
Konwicki, Tadeusz 1926-
    CLC 8, 28, 54, 117
    See also CA 101; CAAS 9; CANR 39, 59;
    MTCW 1
Koontz, Dean R(ay) 1945-
    CLC 78; DAM NOV, POP
    See also AAYA 9; BEST 89:3, 90:2; CA 108;
    CANR 19, 36, 52; MTCW 1; SATA 92
Kopernik, Mikolaj
    See Copernicus, Nicolaus
Kopit, Arthur (Lee) 1937-
    CLC 1, 18, 33; DAM DRAM
    See also AITN 1; CA 81-84; CABS 3; DLB 7;
    MTCW 1
Kops, Bernard 1926-
    CLC 4
    See also CA 5-8R; DLB 13
Kornbluth, C(yril) M. 1923-1958
    TCLC 8
    See also CA 105; 160; DLB 8
Korolenko, V. G.
    See Korolenko, Vladimir Galaktionovich
Korolenko, Vladimir
    See Korolenko, Vladimir Galaktionovich
Korolenko, Vladimir G.
    See Korolenko, Vladimir Galaktionovich
Korolenko, Vladimir Galaktionovich
    1853-1921 .... TCLC 22
    See also CA 121
Korzybski, Alfred (Habdank Skarbek)
    1879-1950 .... TCLC 61
    See also CA 123; 160
Kosinski, Jerzy (Nikodem) 1933-1991
    CLC 1, 2, 3, 6, 10, 15, 53, 70; DAM NOV
    See also CA 17-20R; 134; CANR 9, 46; DLB
    2; DLBY 82; MTCW 1

Levi, Primo 1919-1987
    CLC 37, 50; SSC 12
    See also CA 13-16R; 122; CANR 12, 33, 61,
    70; DLB 177; MTCW 1
Levin, Ira 1929-
    CLC 3, 6; DAM POP
    See also CA 21-24R; CANR 17, 44, 74; MTCW
    1; SATA 66
Levin, Meyer 1905-1981
    CLC 7; DAM POP
    See also AITN 1; CA 9-12R; 104; CANR 15;
    DLB 9, 28; DLBY 81; SATA 21; SATA-Obit
    27
Levine, Norman 1924-
    CLC 54
    See also CA 73-76; CAAS 23; CANR 14, 70;
    DLB 88
Levine, Philip 1928-
    CLC 2, 4, 5, 9, 14, 33; DAM POET; PC 22
    See also CA 9-12R; CANR 9, 37, 52; DLB 5
Levinson, Deirdre 1931-
    CLC 49
    See also CA 73-76; CANR 70
Levi-Strauss, Claude 1908-
    CLC 38
    See also CA 1-4R; CANR 6, 32, 57; MTCW 1
Levitin, Sonia (Wolff) 1934-
    CLC 17
    See also AAYA 13; CA 29-32R; CANR 14, 32;
    CLR 53; JRDA; MAICYA; SAAS 2; SATA
    4, 68
Levon, O. U.
    See Kesey, Ken (Elton)
Levy, Amy 1861-1889
    NCLC 59
    See also DLB 156
Lewes, George Henry 1817-1878
    NCLC 25
    See also DLB 55, 144
Lewis, Alun 1915-1944
    TCLC 3
    See also CA 104; DLB 20, 162
Lewis, C. Day
    See Day Lewis, C(ecil)
Lewis, C(live) S(taples) 1898-1963
    **CLC 1, 3, 6, 14, 27; DA; DAB; DAC; DAM
    MST, NOV, POP; WLC**
    See also AAYA 3; CA 81-84; CANR 33, 71;
    CDBLB 1945-1960; CLR 3, 27; DLB 15,
    100, 160; JRDA; MAICYA; MTCW 1; SATA
    13, 100
Lewis, Janet 1899-
    CLC 41
    See also Winters, Janet Lewis
    See also CA 9-12R; CANR 29, 63; CAP 1;
    DLBY 87
Lewis, Matthew Gregory 1775-1818
    NCLC 11, 62
    See also DLB 39, 158, 178
Lewis, (Harry) Sinclair 1885-1951
    **TCLC 4, 13, 23, 39; DA; DAB; DAC; DAM
    MST, NOV; WLC**
    See also CA 104; 133; CDALB 1917-1929;
    DLB 9, 102; DLBD 1; MTCW 1
Lewis, (Percy) Wyndham .... 1882(?)-1957
    TCLC 2, 9
    See also CA 104; 157; DLB 15
Lewisohn, Ludwig 1883-1955
    TCLC 19
    See also CA 107; DLB 4, 9, 28, 102
Lewton, Val 1904-1951
    TCLC 76
Leyner, Mark 1956-

CLC 92
    See also CA 110; CANR 28, 53
Lezama Lima, Jose 1910-1976
    CLC 4, 10, 101; DAM MULT
    See also CA 77-80; CANR 71; DLB 113; HW
L'Heureux, John (Clarke) 1934-
    CLC 52
    See also CA 13-16R; CANR 23, 45
Liddell, C. H.
    See Kuttner, Henry
Lie, Jonas (Lauritz Idemil) ..... 1833-1908(?)
    TCLC 5
    See also CA 115
Lieber, Joel 1937-1971
    CLC 6
    See also CA 73-76; 29-32R
Lieber, Stanley Martin
    See Lee, Stan
Lieberman, Laurence (James) 1935-
    CLC 4, 36
    See also CA 17-20R; CANR 8, 36
Lieh Tzu .... fl. 7th cent. B.C.-5th cent. B.C.
    CMLC 27
Lieksman, Anders
    See Haavikko, Paavo Juhani
Li Fei-kan 1904-
    See Pa Chin
    See also CA 105
Lifton, Robert Jay 1926-
    CLC 67
    See also CA 17-20R; CANR 27; INT CANR-27;
    SATA 66
Lightfoot, Gordon 1938-
    CLC 26
    See also CA 109
Lightman, Alan P(aige) 1948-
    CLC 81
    See also CA 141; CANR 63
Ligotti, Thomas (Robert) 1953-
    CLC 44; SSC 16
    See also CA 123; CANR 49
Li Ho 791-817
    PC 13
Liliencron, (Friedrich Adolf Axel) Detlev von
    1844-1909 .... TCLC 18
    See also CA 117
Lilly, William 1602-1681
    LC 27
Lima, Jose Lezama
    See Lezama Lima, Jose
Lima Barreto, Afonso Henrique de
    1881-1922 .... TCLC 23
    See also CA 117
Limonov, Edward 1944-
    CLC 67
    See also CA 137
Lin, Frank
    See Atherton, Gertrude (Franklin Horn)
Lincoln, Abraham 1809-1865
    NCLC 18
Lind, Jakov .... CLC 1, 2, 4, 27, 82
    See also Landwirth, Heinz
    See also CAAS 4
Lindbergh, Anne (Spencer) Morrow . 1906-
    CLC 82; DAM NOV
    See also CA 17-20R; CANR 16, 73; MTCW 1;
    SATA 33
Lindsay, David 1878-1945
    TCLC 15
    See also CA 113
Lindsay, (Nicholas) Vachel 1879-1931
    **TCLC 17; DA; DAC; DAM MST, POET;
    PC 23; WLC**

See also CA 114; 135; CDALB 1865-1917;
    DLB 54; SATA 40
Linke-Poot
    See Doeblin, Alfred
Linney, Romulus 1930-
    CLC 51
    See also CA 1-4R; CANR 40, 44
Linton, Eliza Lynn 1822-1898
    NCLC 41
    See also DLB 18
Li Po 701-763
    CMLC 2
Lipsius, Justus 1547-1606
    LC 16
Lipsyte, Robert (Michael) 1938-
    CLC 21; DA; DAC; DAM MST, NOV
    See also AAYA 7; CA 17-20R; CANR 8, 57;
    CLR 23; JRDA; MAICYA; SATA 5, 68
Lish, Gordon (Jay) 1934-
    CLC 45; SSC 18
    See also CA 113; 117; DLB 130; INT 117
Lispector, Clarice .... 1925(?)-1977
    CLC 43
    See also CA 139; 116; CANR 71; DLB 113
Littell, Robert .... 1935(?)-
    CLC 42
    See also CA 109; 112; CANR 64
Little, Malcolm 1925-1965
    See Malcolm X
    See also BW 1; CA 125; 111; DA; DAB; DAC;
    DAM MST, MULT; MTCW 1
Littlewit, Humphrey Gent.
    See Lovecraft, H(oward) P(hillips)
Litwos
    See Sienkiewicz, Henryk (Adam Alexander
    Pius)
Liu, E 1857-1909
    TCLC 15
    See also CA 115
Lively, Penelope (Margaret) 1933-
    CLC 32, 50; DAM NOV
    See also CA 41-44R; CANR 29, 67; CLR 7;
    DLB 14, 161; JRDA; MAICYA; MTCW 1;
    SATA 7, 60, 101
Livesay, Dorothy (Kathleen) 1909-
    CLC 4, 15, 79; DAC; DAM MST, POET
    See also AITN 2; CA 25-28R; CAAS 8; CANR
    36, 67; DLB 68; MTCW 1
Livy .... c. 59B.C.-c. 17
    CMLC 11
Lizardi, Jose Joaquin Fernandez de
    1776-1827 .... NCLC 30
Llewellyn, Richard
    See Llewellyn Lloyd, Richard Dafydd Vivian
    See also DLB 15
Llewellyn Lloyd, Richard Dafydd Vivian
    1906-1983 .... CLC 7, 80
    See also Llewellyn, Richard
    See also CA 53-56; 111; CANR 7, 71; SATA
    11; SATA-Obit 37
Llosa, (Jorge) Mario (Pedro) Vargas
    See Vargas Llosa, (Jorge) Mario (Pedro)
Lloyd, Manda
    See Mander, (Mary) Jane
Lloyd Webber, Andrew 1948-
    See Webber, Andrew Lloyd
    See also AAYA 1; CA 116; 149; DAM DRAM;
    SATA 56
Llull, Ramon .... c. 1235-c. 1316
    CMLC 12
Lobb, Ebenezer
    See Upward, Allen
Locke, Alain (Le Roy) 1886-1954

SSC 15; WLC
See also AAYA 16; CA 5-8R; 118; CABS 1;
CANR 28, 62; CDALB 1941-1968; DLB 2,
28, 152; DLBY 80, 86; MTCW 1

Malan, Herman
See Bosman, Herman Charles; Bosman, Herman
Charles

Malaparte, Curzio 1898-1957
TCLC 52

Malcolm, Dan
See Silverberg, Robert

Malcolm X .... **CLC 82, 117; BLC 2; WLCS**
See also Little, Malcolm

Malherbe, Francois de 1555-1628
LC 5

Mallarme, Stephane 1842-1898
NCLC 4, 41; DAM POET; PC 4

Mallet-Joris, Francoise 1930-
CLC 11
See also CA 65-68; CANR 17; DLB 83

Malley, Ern
See McAuley, James Phillip

Mallowan, Agatha Christie
See Christie, Agatha (Mary Clarissa)

Maloff, Saul 1922-
CLC 5
See also CA 33-36R

Malone, Louis
See MacNeice, (Frederick) Louis

Malone, Michael (Christopher) 1942-
CLC 43
See also CA 77-80; CANR 14, 32, 57

Malory, (Sir) Thomas .... 1410(?)-1471(?)
**LC 11; DA; DAB; DAC; DAM MST;
WLCS**
See also CDBLB Before 1660; DLB 146; SATA
59; SATA-Brief 33

Malouf, (George Joseph) David 1934-
CLC 28, 86
See also CA 124; CANR 50

Malraux, (Georges-)Andre 1901-1976
CLC 1, 4, 9, 13, 15, 57; DAM NOV
See also CA 21-22; 69-72; CANR 34, 58; CAP
2; DLB 72; MTCW 1

Malzberg, Barry N(athaniel) 1939-
CLC 7
See also CA 61-64; CAAS 4; CANR 16; DLB
8

Mamet, David (Alan) 1947-
CLC 9, 15, 34, 46, 91; DAM DRAM; DC 4
See also AAYA 3; CA 81-84; CABS 3; CANR
15, 41, 67, 72; DLB 7; MTCW 1

Mamoulian, Rouben (Zachary) .. 1897-1987
CLC 16
See also CA 25-28R; 124

Mandelstam, Osip (Emilievich)
1891(?)-1938(?) .... **TCLC 2, 6; PC 14**
See also CA 104; 150

Mander, (Mary) Jane 1877-1949
TCLC 31
See also CA 162

Mandeville, John .... fl. 1350-
CMLC 19
See also DLB 146

Mandiargues, Andre Pieyre de .... **CLC 41**
See also Pieyre de Mandiargues, Andre
See also DLB 83

Mandrake, Ethel Belle
See Thurman, Wallace (Henry)

Mangan, James Clarence 1803-1849
NCLC 27

Maniere, J.-E.
See Giraudoux, (Hippolyte) Jean

Mankiewicz, Herman (Jacob) 1897-1953
TCLC 85
See also CA 120; 169; DLB 26

Manley, (Mary) Delariviere .... 1672(?)-1724
LC 1, 42
See also DLB 39, 80

Mann, Abel
See Creasey, John

Mann, Emily 1952-
DC 7
See also CA 130; CANR 55

Mann, (Luiz) Heinrich 1871-1950
TCLC 9
See also CA 106; 164; DLB 66

Mann, (Paul) Thomas 1875-1955
**TCLC 2, 8, 14, 21, 35, 44, 60; DA; DAB;
DAC; DAM MST, NOV; SSC 5; WLC**
See also CA 104; 128; DLB 66; MTCW 1

Mannheim, Karl 1893-1947
TCLC 65

Manning, David
See Faust, Frederick (Schiller)

Manning, Frederic .... 1887(?)-1935
TCLC 25
See also CA 124

Manning, Olivia 1915-1980
CLC 5, 19
See also CA 5-8R; 101; CANR 29; MTCW 1

Mano, D. Keith 1942-
CLC 2, 10
See also CA 25-28R; CAAS 6; CANR 26, 57;
DLB 6

Mansfield, Katherine **TCLC 2, 8, 39; DAB; SSC
9, 23; WLC**
See also Beauchamp, Kathleen Mansfield
See also DLB 162

Manso, Peter 1940-
CLC 39
See also CA 29-32R; CANR 44

Mantecon, Juan Jimenez
See Jimenez (Mantecon), Juan Ramon

Manton, Peter
See Creasey, John

Man Without a Spleen, A
See Chekhov, Anton (Pavlovich)

Manzoni, Alessandro 1785-1873
NCLC 29

Mapu, Abraham (ben Jekutiel) ... 1808-1867
NCLC 18

Mara, Sally
See Queneau, Raymond

Marat, Jean Paul 1743-1793
LC 10

Marcel, Gabriel Honore 1889-1973
CLC 15
See also CA 102; 45-48; MTCW 1

Marchbanks, Samuel
See Davies, (William) Robertson

Marchi, Giacomo
See Bassani, Giorgio

Margulies, Donald .... **CLC 76**

Marie de France .... c. 12th cent. -
CMLC 8; PC 22

Marie de l'Incarnation 1599-1672
LC 10

Marier, Captain Victor
See Griffith, D(avid Lewelyn) W(ark)

Mariner, Scott
See Pohl, Frederik

Marinetti, Filippo Tommaso 1876-1944
TCLC 10
See also CA 107; DLB 114

Marivaux, Pierre Carlet de Chamblain de

1688-1763 .... **LC 4; DC 7**

Markandaya, Kamala .... **CLC 8, 38**
See also Taylor, Kamala (Purnaiya)

Markfield, Wallace 1926-
CLC 8
See also CA 69-72; CAAS 3; DLB 2, 28

Markham, Edwin 1852-1940
TCLC 47
See also CA 160; DLB 54, 186

Markham, Robert
See Amis, Kingsley (William)

Marks, J
See Highwater, Jamake (Mamake)

Marks-Highwater, J
See Highwater, Jamake (Mamake)

Markson, David M(errill) 1927-
CLC 67
See also CA 49-52; CANR 1

Marley, Bob .... **CLC 17**
See also Marley, Robert Nesta

Marley, Robert Nesta 1945-1981
See Marley, Bob
See also CA 107; 103

Marlowe, Christopher 1564-1593
**LC 22, 47; DA; DAB; DAC; DAM DRAM,
MST; DC 1; WLC**
See also CDBLB Before 1660; DLB 62

Marlowe, Stephen 1928-
See Queen, Ellery
See also CA 13-16R; CANR 6, 55

Marmontel, Jean-Francois 1723-1799
LC 2

Marquand, John P(hillips) 1893-1960
CLC 2, 10
See also CA 85-88; CANR 73; DLB 9, 102

Marques, Rene 1919-1979
CLC 96; DAM MULT; HLC
See also CA 97-100; 85-88; DLB 113; HW

Marquez, Gabriel (Jose) Garcia
See Garcia Marquez, Gabriel (Jose)

Marquis, Don(ald Robert Perry) 1878-1937
TCLC 7
See also CA 104; 166; DLB 11, 25

Marric, J. J.
See Creasey, John

Marryat, Frederick 1792-1848
NCLC 3
See also DLB 21, 163

Marsden, James
See Creasey, John

Marsh, (Edith) Ngaio 1899-1982
CLC 7, 53; DAM POP
See also CA 9-12R; CANR 6, 58; DLB 77;
MTCW 1

Marshall, Garry 1934-
CLC 17
See also AAYA 3; CA 111; SATA 60

Marshall, Paule 1929-
CLC 27, 72; BLC 3; DAM MULT; SSC 3
See also BW 2; CA 77-80; CANR 25, 73; DLB
157; MTCW 1

Marshallik
See Zangwill, Israel

Marsten, Richard
See Hunter, Evan

Marston, John 1576-1634
LC 33; DAM DRAM
See also DLB 58, 172

Martha, Henry
See Harris, Mark

Marti, Jose 1853-1895
NCLC 63; DAM MULT; HLC

Martial .... c. 40-c. 104

Author Index

CMLC 9; DAM DRAM; DC 3
See also DLB 176

Mencken, H(enry) L(ouis) 1880-1956
TCLC 13
See also CA 105; 125; CDALB 1917-1929;
DLB 11, 29, 63, 137; MTCW 1

Mendelsohn, Jane .... 1965(?)-
CLC 99
See also CA 154

Mercer, David 1928-1980
CLC 5; DAM DRAM
See also CA 9-12R; 102; CANR 23; DLB 13;
MTCW 1

Merchant, Paul
See Ellison, Harlan (Jay)

Meredith, George 1828-1909
TCLC 17, 43; DAM POET
See also CA 117; 153; CDBLB 1832-1890;
DLB 18, 35, 57, 159

Meredith, William (Morris) 1919-
CLC 4, 13, 22, 55; DAM POET
See also CA 9-12R; CAAS 14; CANR 6, 40;
DLB 5

Merezhkovsky, Dmitry Sergeyevich
1865-1941 .... TCLC 29
See also CA 169

Merimee, Prosper 1803-1870
NCLC 6, 65; SSC 7
See also DLB 119, 192

Merkin, Daphne 1954-
CLC 44
See also CA 123

Merlin, Arthur
See Blish, James (Benjamin)

Merrill, James (Ingram) 1926-1995
CLC 2, 3, 6, 8, 13, 18, 34, 91; DAM POET
See also CA 13-16R; 147; CANR 10, 49, 63;
DLB 5, 165; DLBY 85; INT CANR-10;
MTCW 1

Merriman, Alex
See Silverberg, Robert

Merriman, Brian 1747-1805
NCLC 70

Merritt, E. B.
See Waddington, Miriam

Merton, Thomas 1915-1968
CLC 1, 3, 11, 34, 83; PC 10
See also CA 5-8R; 25-28R; CANR 22, 53; DLB
48; DLBY 81; MTCW 1

Merwin, W(illiam) S(tanley) 1927-
CLC 1, 2, 3, 5, 8, 13, 18, 45, 88; DAM
POET
See also CA 13-16R; CANR 15, 51; DLB 5,
169; INT CANR-15; MTCW 1

Metcalf, John 1938-
CLC 37
See also CA 113; DLB 60

Metcalf, Suzanne
See Baum, L(yman) Frank

Mew, Charlotte (Mary) 1870-1928
TCLC 8
See also CA 105; DLB 19, 135

Mewshaw, Michael 1943-
CLC 9
See also CA 53-56; CANR 7, 47; DLBY 80

Meyer, June
See Jordan, June

Meyer, Lynn
See Slavitt, David R(ytman)

Meyer-Meyrink, Gustav 1868-1932
See Meyrink, Gustav
See also CA 117

Meyers, Jeffrey 1939-

CLC 39
See also CA 73-76; CANR 54; DLB 111

Meynell, Alice (Christina Gertrude Thompson)
1847-1922 .... TCLC 6
See also CA 104; DLB 19, 98

Meyrink, Gustav .... TCLC 21
See also Meyer-Meyrink, Gustav
See also DLB 81

Michaels, Leonard 1933-
CLC 6, 25; SSC 16
See also CA 61-64; CANR 21, 62; DLB 130;
MTCW 1

Michaux, Henri 1899-1984
CLC 8, 19
See also CA 85-88; 114

Micheaux, Oscar 1884-1951
TCLC 76
See also DLB 50

Michelangelo 1475-1564
LC 12

Michelet, Jules 1798-1874
NCLC 31

Michels, Robert 1876-1936
TCLC 88

Michener, James A(lbert) .... 1907(?)-1997
CLC 1, 5, 11, 29, 60, 109; DAM NOV, POP
See also AAYA 27; AITN 1; BEST 90:1; CA
5-8R; 161; CANR 21, 45, 68; DLB 6; MTCW
1

Mickiewicz, Adam 1798-1855
NCLC 3

Middleton, Christopher 1926-
CLC 13
See also CA 13-16R; CANR 29, 54; DLB 40

Middleton, Richard (Barham) 1882-1911
TCLC 56
See also DLB 156

Middleton, Stanley 1919-
CLC 7, 38
See also CA 25-28R; CAAS 23; CANR 21, 46;
DLB 14

Middleton, Thomas 1580-1627
LC 33; DAM DRAM, MST; DC 5
See also DLB 58

Migueis, Jose Rodrigues 1901-
CLC 10

Mikszath, Kalman 1847-1910
TCLC 31
See also CA 170

Miles, Jack .... CLC 100

Miles, Josephine (Louise) 1911-1985
CLC 1, 2, 14, 34, 39; DAM POET
See also CA 1-4R; 116; CANR 2, 55; DLB 48

Militant
See Sandburg, Carl (August)

Mill, John Stuart 1806-1873
NCLC 11, 58
See also CDBLB 1832-1890; DLB 55, 190

Millar, Kenneth 1915-1983
CLC 14; DAM POP
See also Macdonald, Ross
See also CA 9-12R; 110; CANR 16, 63; DLB
2; DLBD 6; DLBY 83; MTCW 1

Millay, E. Vincent
See Millay, Edna St. Vincent

Millay, Edna St. Vincent 1892-1950
TCLC 4, 49; DA; DAB; DAC; DAM MST,
POET; PC 6; WLCS
See also CA 104; 130; CDALB 1917-1929;
DLB 45; MTCW 1

Miller, Arthur 1915-
CLC 1, 2, 6, 10, 15, 26, 47, 78; DA; DAB;
DAC; DAM DRAM, MST; DC 1; WLC

See also AAYA 15; AITN 1; CA 1-4R; CABS
3; CANR 2, 30, 54; CDALB 1941-1968;
DLB 7; MTCW 1

Miller, Henry (Valentine)............. 1891-1980
CLC 1, 2, 4, 9, 14, 43, 84; DA; DAB; DAC;
DAM MST, NOV; WLC
See also CA 9-12R; 97-100; CANR 33, 64;
CDALB 1929-1941; DLB 4, 9; DLBY 80;
MTCW 1

Miller, Jason .... 1939(?)-
CLC 2
See also AITN 1; CA 73-76; DLB 7

Miller, Sue 1943-
CLC 44; DAM POP
See also BEST 90:3; CA 139; CANR 59; DLB
143

Miller, Walter M(ichael, Jr.) 1923-
CLC 4, 30
See also CA 85-88; DLB 8

Millett, Kate 1934-
CLC 67
See also AITN 1; CA 73-76; CANR 32, 53;
MTCW 1

Millhauser, Steven (Lewis) 1943-
CLC 21, 54, 109
See also CA 110; 111; CANR 63; DLB 2; INT
111

Millin, Sarah Gertrude 1889-1968
CLC 49
See also CA 102; 93-96

Milne, A(lan) A(lexander) 1882-1956
TCLC 6, 88; DAB; DAC; DAM MST
See also CA 104; 133; CLR 1, 26; DLB 10, 77,
100, 160; MAICYA; MTCW 1; SATA 100;
YABC 1

Milner, Ron(ald) 1938-
CLC 56; BLC 3; DAM MULT
See also AITN 1; BW 1; CA 73-76; CANR 24;
DLB 38; MTCW 1

Milnes, Richard Monckton 1809-1885
NCLC 61
See also DLB 32, 184

Milosz, Czeslaw 1911-
CLC 5, 11, 22, 31, 56, 82; DAM MST,
POET; PC 8; WLCS
See also CA 81-84; CANR 23, 51; MTCW 1

Milton, John 1608-1674
LC 9, 43; DA; DAB; DAC; DAM MST,
POET; PC 19; WLC
See also CDBLB 1660-1789; DLB 131, 151

Min, Anchee 1957-
CLC 86
See also CA 146

Minehaha, Cornelius
See Wedekind, (Benjamin) Frank(lin)

Miner, Valerie 1947-
CLC 40
See also CA 97-100; CANR 59

Minimo, Duca
See D'Annunzio, Gabriele

Minot, Susan 1956-
CLC 44
See also CA 134

Minus, Ed 1938-
CLC 39

Miranda, Javier
See Bioy Casares, Adolfo

Mirbeau, Octave 1848-1917
TCLC 55
See also DLB 123, 192

Miro (Ferrer), Gabriel (Francisco Victor)
1879-1930 .... TCLC 5
See also CA 104

Mishima, Yukio 1925-1970
    CLC 2, 4, 6, 9, 27; DC 1; SSC 4
    See also Hiraoka, Kimitake
    See also DLB 182
Mistral, Frederic 1830-1914
    TCLC 51
    See also CA 122
Mistral, Gabriela .... **TCLC 2; HLC**
    See also Godoy Alcayaga, Lucila
Mistry, Rohinton 1952-
    CLC 71; DAC
    See also CA 141
Mitchell, Clyde
    See Ellison, Harlan (Jay); Silverberg, Robert
Mitchell, James Leslie 1901-1935
    See Gibbon, Lewis Grassic
    See also CA 104; DLB 15
Mitchell, Joni 1943-
    CLC 12
    See also CA 112
Mitchell, Joseph (Quincy) 1908-1996
    CLC 98
    See also CA 77-80; 152; CANR 69; DLB 185;
    DLBY 96
Mitchell, Margaret (Munnerlyn) 1900-1949
    TCLC 11; DAM NOV, POP
    See also AAYA 23; CA 109; 125; CANR 55;
    DLB 9; MTCW 1
Mitchell, Peggy
    See Mitchell, Margaret (Munnerlyn)
Mitchell, S(ilas) Weir 1829-1914
    TCLC 36
    See also CA 165; DLB 202
Mitchell, W(illiam) O(rmond) 1914-1998
    CLC 25; DAC; DAM MST
    See also CA 77-80; 165; CANR 15, 43; DLB
    88
Mitchell, William 1879-1936
    TCLC 81
Mitford, Mary Russell 1787-1855
    NCLC 4
    See also DLB 110, 116
Mitford, Nancy 1904-1973
    CLC 44
    See also CA 9-12R; DLB 191
Miyamoto, Yuriko 1899-1951
    TCLC 37
    See also CA 170; DLB 180
Miyazawa, Kenji 1896-1933
    TCLC 76
    See also CA 157
Mizoguchi, Kenji 1898-1956
    TCLC 72
    See also CA 167
Mo, Timothy (Peter) .... 1950(?)-
    CLC 46
    See also CA 117; DLB 194; MTCW 1
Modarressi, Taghi (M.) 1931-
    CLC 44
    See also CA 121; 134; INT 134
Modiano, Patrick (Jean) 1945-
    CLC 18
    See also CA 85-88; CANR 17, 40; DLB 83
Moerck, Paal
    See Roelvaag, O(le) E(dvart)
Mofolo, Thomas (Mokopu) ...... 1875(?)-1948
    TCLC 22; BLC 3; DAM MULT
    See also CA 121; 153
Mohr, Nicholasa 1938-
    CLC 12; DAM MULT; HLC
    See also AAYA 8; CA 49-52; CANR 1, 32, 64;
    CLR 22; DLB 145; HW; JRDA; SAAS 8;
    SATA 8, 97

Mojtabai, A(nn) G(race) 1938-
    CLC 5, 9, 15, 29
    See also CA 85-88
Moliere 1622-1673
    **LC 10, 28; DA; DAB; DAC; DAM DRAM,
    MST; WLC**
Molin, Charles
    See Mayne, William (James Carter)
Molnar, Ferenc 1878-1952
    TCLC 20; DAM DRAM
    See also CA 109; 153
Momaday, N(avarre) Scott 1934-
    **CLC 2, 19, 85, 95; DA; DAB; DAC; DAM
    MST, MULT, NOV, POP; PC 25; WLCS**
    See also AAYA 11; CA 25-28R; CANR 14, 34,
    68; DLB 143, 175; INT CANR-14; MTCW
    1; NNAL; SATA 48; SATA-Brief 30
Monette, Paul 1945-1995
    CLC 82
    See also CA 139; 147
Monroe, Harriet 1860-1936
    TCLC 12
    See also CA 109; DLB 54, 91
Monroe, Lyle
    See Heinlein, Robert A(nson)
Montagu, Elizabeth 1720-1800
    NCLC 7
Montagu, Mary (Pierrepont) Wortley
    1689-1762 .... **LC 9; PC 16**
    See also DLB 95, 101
Montagu, W. H.
    See Coleridge, Samuel Taylor
Montague, John (Patrick) 1929-
    CLC 13, 46
    See also CA 9-12R; CANR 9, 69; DLB 40;
    MTCW 1
Montaigne, Michel (Eyquem) de   1533-1592
    LC 8; DA; DAB; DAC; DAM MST; WLC
Montale, Eugenio 1896-1981
    CLC 7, 9, 18; PC 13
    See also CA 17-20R; 104; CANR 30; DLB 114;
    MTCW 1
Montesquieu, Charles-Louis de Secondat
    1689-1755 .... **LC 7**
Montgomery, (Robert) Bruce 1921-1978
    See Crispin, Edmund
    See also CA 104
Montgomery, L(ucy) M(aud) 1874-1942
    TCLC 51; DAC; DAM MST
    See also AAYA 12; CA 108; 137; CLR 8; DLB
    92; DLBD 14; JRDA; MAICYA; SATA 100;
    YABC 1
Montgomery, Marion H., Jr. 1925-
    CLC 7
    See also AITN 1; CA 1-4R; CANR 3, 48; DLB
    6
Montgomery, Max
    See Davenport, Guy (Mattison, Jr.)
Montherlant, Henry (Milon) de .. 1896-1972
    CLC 8, 19; DAM DRAM
    See also CA 85-88; 37-40R; DLB 72; MTCW
    1
Monty Python
    See Chapman, Graham; Cleese, John
    (Marwood); Gilliam, Terry (Vance); Idle,
    Eric; Jones, Terence Graham Parry; Palin,
    Michael (Edward)
    See also AAYA 7
Moodie, Susanna (Strickland) 1803-1885
    NCLC 14
    See also DLB 99
Mooney, Edward 1951-
    See Mooney, Ted

    See also CA 130
Mooney, Ted .... **CLC 25**
    See also Mooney, Edward
Moorcock, Michael (John) 1939-
    CLC 5, 27, 58
    See also AAYA 26; CA 45-48; CAAS 5; CANR
    2, 17, 38, 64; DLB 14; MTCW 1; SATA 93
Moore, Brian 1921-
    **CLC 1, 3, 5, 7, 8, 19, 32, 90; DAB; DAC;
    DAM MST**
    See also CA 1-4R; CANR 1, 25, 42, 63; MTCW
    1
Moore, Edward
    See Muir, Edwin
Moore, George Augustus 1852-1933
    TCLC 7; SSC 19
    See also CA 104; DLB 10, 18, 57, 135
Moore, Lorrie .... **CLC 39, 45, 68**
    See also Moore, Marie Lorena
Moore, Marianne (Craig) 1887-1972
    **CLC 1, 2, 4, 8, 10, 13, 19, 47; DA; DAB;
    DAC; DAM MST, POET; PC 4; WLCS**
    See also CA 1-4R; 33-36R; CANR 3, 61;
    CDALB 1929-1941; DLB 45; DLBD 7;
    MTCW 1; SATA 20
Moore, Marie Lorena 1957-
    See Moore, Lorrie
    See also CA 116; CANR 39
Moore, Thomas 1779-1852
    NCLC 6
    See also DLB 96, 144
Morand, Paul 1888-1976
    CLC 41; SSC 22
    See also CA 69-72; DLB 65
Morante, Elsa 1918-1985
    CLC 8, 47
    See also CA 85-88; 117; CANR 35; DLB 177;
    MTCW 1
Moravia, Alberto 1907-1990
    CLC 2, 7, 11, 27, 46; SSC 26
    See also Pincherle, Alberto
    See also DLB 177
More, Hannah 1745-1833
    NCLC 27
    See also DLB 107, 109, 116, 158
More, Henry 1614-1687
    LC 9
    See also DLB 126
More, Sir Thomas 1478-1535
    LC 10, 32
Moreas, Jean .... **TCLC 18**
    See also Papadiamantopoulos, Johannes
Morgan, Berry 1919-
    CLC 6
    See also CA 49-52; DLB 6
Morgan, Claire
    See Highsmith, (Mary) Patricia
Morgan, Edwin (George) 1920-
    CLC 31
    See also CA 5-8R; CANR 3, 43; DLB 27
Morgan, (George) Frederick 1922-
    CLC 23
    See also CA 17-20R; CANR 21
Morgan, Harriet
    See Mencken, H(enry) L(ouis)
Morgan, Jane
    See Cooper, James Fenimore
Morgan, Janet 1945-
    CLC 39
    See also CA 65-68
Morgan, Lady .... 1776(?)-1859
    NCLC 29
    See also DLB 116, 158

Morgan, Robin (Evonne) 1941-
CLC 2
See also CA 69-72; CANR 29, 68; MTCW 1;
SATA 80
Morgan, Scott
See Kuttner, Henry
Morgan, Seth .... 1949(?)-1990
CLC 65
See also CA 132
Morgenstern, Christian 1871-1914
TCLC 8
See also CA 105
Morgenstern, S.
See Goldman, William (W.)
Moricz, Zsigmond 1879-1942
TCLC 33
See also CA 165
Morike, Eduard (Friedrich) 1804-1875
NCLC 10
See also DLB 133
Moritz, Karl Philipp 1756-1793
LC 2
See also DLB 94
Morland, Peter Henry
See Faust, Frederick (Schiller)
Morley, Christopher (Darlington) 1890-1957
TCLC 87
See also CA 112; DLB 9
Morren, Theophil
See Hofmannsthal, Hugo von
Morris, Bill 1952-
CLC 76
Morris, Julian
See West, Morris L(anglo)
Morris, Steveland Judkins .... 1950(?)-
See Wonder, Stevie
See also CA 111
Morris, William 1834-1896
NCLC 4
See also CDBLB 1832-1890; DLB 18, 35, 57,
156, 178, 184
Morris, Wright 1910-1998
CLC 1, 3, 7, 18, 37
See also CA 9-12R; 167; CANR 21; DLB 2;
DLBY 81; MTCW 1
Morrison, Arthur 1863-1945
TCLC 72
See also CA 120; 157; DLB 70, 135, 197
Morrison, Chloe Anthony Wofford
See Morrison, Toni
Morrison, James Douglas 1943-1971
See Morrison, Jim
See also CA 73-76; CANR 40
Morrison, Jim .... **CLC 17**
See also Morrison, James Douglas
Morrison, Toni 1931-
**CLC 4, 10, 22, 55, 81, 87; BLC 3; DA;
DAB; DAC; DAM MST, MULT, NOV,
POP**
See also AAYA 1, 22; BW 2; CA 29-32R;
CANR 27, 42, 67; CDALB 1968-1988; DLB
6, 33, 143; DLBY 81; MTCW 1; SATA 57
Morrison, Van 1945-
CLC 21
See also CA 116; 168
Morrissy, Mary 1958-
CLC 99
Mortimer, John (Clifford) 1923-
CLC 28, 43; DAM DRAM, POP
See also CA 13-16R; CANR 21, 69; CDBLB
1960 to Present; DLB 13; INT CANR-21;
MTCW 1
Mortimer, Penelope (Ruth) 1918-

CLC 5
See also CA 57-60; CANR 45
Morton, Anthony
See Creasey, John
Mosca, Gaetano 1858-1941
TCLC 75
Mosher, Howard Frank 1943-
CLC 62
See also CA 139; CANR 65
Mosley, Nicholas 1923-
CLC 43, 70
See also CA 69-72; CANR 41, 60; DLB 14
Mosley, Walter 1952-
CLC 97; BLCS; DAM MULT, POP
See also AAYA 17; BW 2; CA 142; CANR 57
Moss, Howard 1922-1987
CLC 7, 14, 45, 50; DAM POET
See also CA 1-4R; 123; CANR 1, 44; DLB 5
Mossgiel, Rab
See Burns, Robert
Motion, Andrew (Peter) 1952-
CLC 47
See also CA 146; DLB 40
Motley, Willard (Francis) 1909-1965
CLC 18
See also BW 1; CA 117; 106; DLB 76, 143
Motoori, Norinaga 1730-1801
NCLC 45
Mott, Michael (Charles Alston) 1930-
CLC 15, 34
See also CA 5-8R; CAAS 7; CANR 7, 29
Mountain Wolf Woman 1884-1960
CLC 92
See also CA 144; NNAL
Moure, Erin 1955-
CLC 88
See also CA 113; DLB 60
Mowat, Farley (McGill) 1921-
CLC 26; DAC; DAM MST
See also AAYA 1; CA 1-4R; CANR 4, 24, 42,
68; CLR 20; DLB 68; INT CANR-24; JRDA;
MAICYA; MTCW 1; SATA 3, 55
Mowatt, Anna Cora 1819-1870
NCLC 74
Moyers, Bill 1934-
CLC 74
See also AITN 2; CA 61-64; CANR 31, 52
Mphahlele, Es'kia
See Mphahlele, Ezekiel
See also DLB 125
Mphahlele, Ezekiel 1919-1983
CLC 25; BLC 3; DAM MULT
See also Mphahlele, Es'kia
See also BW 2; CA 81-84; CANR 26
Mqhayi, S(amuel) E(dward) K(rune Loliwe)
1875-1945 ..... **TCLC 25; BLC 3; DAM
MULT**
See also CA 153
Mrozek, Slawomir 1930-
CLC 3, 13
See also CA 13-16R; CAAS 10; CANR 29;
MTCW 1
Mrs. Belloc-Lowndes
See Lowndes, Marie Adelaide (Belloc)
Mtwa, Percy .... (?)-
CLC 47
Mueller, Lisel 1924-
CLC 13, 51
See also CA 93-96; DLB 105
Muir, Edwin 1887-1959
TCLC 2, 87
See also CA 104; DLB 20, 100, 191
Muir, John 1838-1914

TCLC 28
See also CA 165; DLB 186
Mujica Lainez, Manuel 1910-1984
CLC 31
See also Lainez, Manuel Mujica
See also CA 81-84; 112; CANR 32; HW
Mukherjee, Bharati 1940-
CLC 53, 115; DAM NOV
See also BEST 89:2; CA 107; CANR 45, 72;
DLB 60; MTCW 1
Muldoon, Paul 1951-
CLC 32, 72; DAM POET
See also CA 113; 129; CANR 52; DLB 40; INT
129
Mulisch, Harry 1927-
CLC 42
See also CA 9-12R; CANR 6, 26, 56
Mull, Martin 1943-
CLC 17
See also CA 105
Muller, Wilhelm .... **NCLC 73**
Mulock, Dinah Maria
See Craik, Dinah Maria (Mulock)
Munford, Robert .... 1737(?)-1783
LC 5
See also DLB 31
Mungo, Raymond 1946-
CLC 72
See also CA 49-52; CANR 2
Munro, Alice 1931-
**CLC 6, 10, 19, 50, 95; DAC; DAM MST,
NOV; SSC 3; WLCS**
See also AITN 2; CA 33-36R; CANR 33, 53;
DLB 53; MTCW 1; SATA 29
Munro, H(ector) H(ugh) 1870-1916
See Saki
See also CA 104; 130; CDBLB 1890-1914; DA;
DAB; DAC; DAM MST, NOV; DLB 34, 162;
MTCW 1; WLC
Murasaki, Lady .... **CMLC 1**
Murdoch, (Jean) Iris 1919-
**CLC 1, 2, 3, 4, 6, 8, 11, 15, 22, 31, 51; DAB;
DAC; DAM MST, NOV**
See also CA 13-16R; CANR 8, 43, 68; CDBLB
1960 to Present; DLB 14, 194; INT CANR-8;
MTCW 1
Murfree, Mary Noailles 1850-1922
SSC 22
See also CA 122; DLB 12, 74
Murnau, Friedrich Wilhelm
See Plumpe, Friedrich Wilhelm
Murphy, Richard 1927-
CLC 41
See also CA 29-32R; DLB 40
Murphy, Sylvia 1937-
CLC 34
See also CA 121
Murphy, Thomas (Bernard) 1935-
CLC 51
See also CA 101
Murray, Albert L. 1916-
CLC 73
See also BW 2; CA 49-52; CANR 26, 52; DLB
38
Murray, Judith Sargent 1751-1820
NCLC 63
See also DLB 37, 200
Murray, Les(lie) A(llan) 1938-
CLC 40; DAM POET
See also CA 21-24R; CANR 11, 27, 56
Murry, J. Middleton
See Murry, John Middleton
Murry, John Middleton 1889-1957

Author Index

TCLC 4, 29; DA; DAB; DAC; DAM DRAM, MST; DC 5; SSC 22; WLC
See also CA 104; 153

Pirsig, Robert M(aynard) 1928-
CLC 4, 6, 73; DAM POP
See also CA 53-56; CANR 42, 74; MTCW 1; SATA 39

Pisarev, Dmitry Ivanovich 1840-1868
NCLC 25

Pix, Mary (Griffith) 1666-1709
LC 8
See also DLB 80

Pixerecourt, (Rene Charles) Guilbert de
1773-1844 .... **NCLC 39**
See also DLB 192

Plaatje, Sol(omon) T(shekisho) ... 1876-1932
TCLC 73; BLCS
See also BW 2; CA 141

Plaidy, Jean
See Hibbert, Eleanor Alice Burford

Planche, James Robinson 1796-1880
NCLC 42

Plant, Robert 1948-
CLC 12

Plante, David (Robert) 1940-
CLC 7, 23, 38; DAM NOV
See also CA 37-40R; CANR 12, 36, 58; DLBY 83; INT CANR-12; MTCW 1

Plath, Sylvia 1932-1963
CLC 1, 2, 3, 5, 9, 11, 14, 17, 50, 51, 62, 111; DA; DAB; DAC; DAM MST, POET; PC 1; WLC
See also AAYA 13; CA 19-20; CANR 34; CAP 2; CDALB 1941-1968; DLB 5, 6, 152; MTCW 1; SATA 96

Plato .... 428(?)B.C.-348(?)B.C.
CMLC 8; DA; DAB; DAC; DAM MST; WLCS
See also DLB 176

Platonov, Andrei .... **TCLC 14**
See also Klimentov, Andrei Platonovich

Platt, Kin 1911-
CLC 26
See also AAYA 11; CA 17-20R; CANR 11; JRDA; SAAS 17; SATA 21, 86

Plautus .... c. 251B.C.-184B.C.
CMLC 24; DC 6

Plick et Plock
See Simenon, Georges (Jacques Christian)

Plimpton, George (Ames) 1927-
CLC 36
See also AITN 1; CA 21-24R; CANR 32, 70; DLB 185; MTCW 1; SATA 10

Pliny the Elder .... c. 23-79
CMLC 23

Plomer, William Charles Franklin 1903-1973
CLC 4, 8
See also CA 21-22; CANR 34; CAP 2; DLB 20, 162, 191; MTCW 1; SATA 24

Plowman, Piers
See Kavanagh, Patrick (Joseph)

Plum, J.
See Wodehouse, P(elham) G(renville)

Plumly, Stanley (Ross) 1939-
CLC 33
See also CA 108; 110; DLB 5, 193; INT 110

Plumpe, Friedrich Wilhelm 1888-1931
TCLC 53
See also CA 112

Po Chu-i 772-846
CMLC 24

Poe, Edgar Allan 1809-1849
NCLC 1, 16, 55; DA; DAB; DAC; DAM

MST, POET; PC 1; SSC 1, 22; WLC
See also AAYA 14; CDALB 1640-1865; DLB 3, 59, 73, 74; SATA 23

Poet of Titchfield Street, The
See Pound, Ezra (Weston Loomis)

Pohl, Frederik 1919-
CLC 18; SSC 25
See also AAYA 24; CA 61-64; CAAS 1; CANR 11, 37; DLB 8; INT CANR-11; MTCW 1; SATA 24

Poirier, Louis 1910-
See Gracq, Julien
See also CA 122; 126

Poitier, Sidney 1927-
CLC 26
See also BW 1; CA 117

Polanski, Roman 1933-
CLC 16
See also CA 77-80

Poliakoff, Stephen 1952-
CLC 38
See also CA 106; DLB 13

Police, The
See Copeland, Stewart (Armstrong); Summers, Andrew James; Sumner, Gordon Matthew

Polidori, John William 1795-1821
NCLC 51
See also DLB 116

Pollitt, Katha 1949-
CLC 28
See also CA 120; 122; CANR 66; MTCW 1

Pollock, (Mary) Sharon 1936-
CLC 50; DAC; DAM DRAM, MST
See also CA 141; DLB 60

Polo, Marco 1254-1324
CMLC 15

Polonsky, Abraham (Lincoln) 1910-
CLC 92
See also CA 104; DLB 26; INT 104

Polybius .... c. 200B.C.-c. 118B.C.
CMLC 17
See also DLB 176

Pomerance, Bernard 1940-
CLC 13; DAM DRAM
See also CA 101; CANR 49

Ponge, Francis (Jean Gaston Alfred)
1899-1988 ...... **CLC 6, 18; DAM POET**
See also CA 85-88; 126; CANR 40

Pontoppidan, Henrik 1857-1943
TCLC 29
See also CA 170

Poole, Josephine .... **CLC 17**
See Helyar, Jane Penelope Josephine
See also SAAS 2; SATA 5

Popa, Vasko 1922-1991
CLC 19
See also CA 112; 148; DLB 181

Pope, Alexander 1688-1744
LC 3; DA; DAB; DAC; DAM MST, POET; WLC
See also CDBLB 1660-1789; DLB 95, 101

Porter, Connie (Rose) .... 1959(?)-
CLC 70
See also BW 2; CA 142; SATA 81

Porter, Gene(va Grace) Stratton 1863(?)-1924
TCLC 21
See also CA 112

Porter, Katherine Anne 1890-1980
CLC 1, 3, 7, 10, 13, 15, 27, 101; DA; DAB; DAC; DAM MST, NOV; SSC 4, 31
See also AITN 2; CA 1-4R; 101; CANR 1, 65; DLB 4, 9, 102; DLBD 12; DLBY 80; MTCW 1; SATA 39; SATA-Obit 23

Porter, Peter (Neville Frederick) 1929-
CLC 5, 13, 33
See also CA 85-88; DLB 40

Porter, William Sydney 1862-1910
See Henry, O.
See also CA 104; 131; CDALB 1865-1917; DA; DAB; DAC; DAM MST; DLB 12, 78, 79; MTCW 1; YABC 2

Portillo (y Pacheco), Jose Lopez
See Lopez Portillo (y Pacheco), Jose

Post, Melville Davisson 1869-1930
TCLC 39
See also CA 110

Potok, Chaim 1929-
CLC 2, 7, 14, 26, 112; DAM NOV
See also AAYA 15; AITN 1, 2; CA 17-20R; CANR 19, 35, 64; DLB 28, 152; INT CANR-19; MTCW 1; SATA 33

Potter, (Helen) Beatrix 1866-1943
See Webb, (Martha) Beatrice (Potter)
See also MAICYA

Potter, Dennis (Christopher George)
1935-1994 .... **CLC 58, 86**
See also CA 107; 145; CANR 33, 61; MTCW 1

Pound, Ezra (Weston Loomis) 1885-1972
CLC 1, 2, 3, 4, 5, 7, 10, 13, 18, 34, 48, 50, 112; DA; DAB; DAC; DAM MST, POET; PC 4; WLC
See also CA 5-8R; 37-40R; CANR 40; CDALB 1917-1929; DLB 4, 45, 63; DLBD 15; MTCW 1

Povod, Reinaldo 1959-1994
CLC 44
See also CA 136; 146

Powell, Adam Clayton, Jr. 1908-1972
CLC 89; BLC 3; DAM MULT
See also BW 1; CA 102; 33-36R

Powell, Anthony (Dymoke) 1905-
CLC 1, 3, 7, 9, 10, 31
See also CA 1-4R; CANR 1, 32, 62; CDBLB 1945-1960; DLB 15; MTCW 1

Powell, Dawn 1897-1965
CLC 66
See also CA 5-8R; DLBY 97

Powell, Padgett 1952-
CLC 34
See also CA 126; CANR 63

Power, Susan 1961-
CLC 91

Powers, J(ames) F(arl) 1917-
CLC 1, 4, 8, 57; SSC 4
See also CA 1-4R; CANR 2, 61; DLB 130; MTCW 1

Powers, John J(ames) 1945-
See Powers, John R.
See also CA 69-72

Powers, John R. .... **CLC 66**
See also Powers, John J(ames)

Powers, Richard (S.) 1957-
CLC 93
See also CA 148

Pownall, David 1938-
CLC 10
See also CA 89-92; CAAS 18; CANR 49; DLB 14

Powys, John Cowper 1872-1963
CLC 7, 9, 15, 46
See also CA 85-88; DLB 15; MTCW 1

Powys, T(heodore) F(rancis) 1875-1953
TCLC 9
See also CA 106; DLB 36, 162

Prado (Calvo), Pedro 1886-1952
TCLC 75

Rexroth, Kenneth 1905-1982
    CLC 1, 2, 6, 11, 22, 49, 112; DAM POET;
    PC 20
        See also CA 5-8R; 107; CANR 14, 34, 63;
        CDALB 1941-1968; DLB 16, 48, 165;
        DLBY 82; INT CANR-14; MTCW 1
Reyes, Alfonso 1889-1959
    TCLC 33
        See also CA 131; HW
Reyes y Basoalto, Ricardo Eliecer Neftali
        See Neruda, Pablo
Reymont, Wladyslaw (Stanislaw)
        1868(?)-1925 .... TCLC 5
        See also CA 104
Reynolds, Jonathan 1942-
    CLC 6, 38
        See also CA 65-68; CANR 28
Reynolds, Joshua 1723-1792
    LC 15
        See also DLB 104
Reynolds, Michael Shane 1937-
    CLC 44
        See also CA 65-68; CANR 9
Reznikoff, Charles 1894-1976
    CLC 9
        See also CA 33-36; 61-64; CAP 2; DLB 28, 45
Rezzori (d'Arezzo), Gregor von .. 1914-1998
    CLC 25
        See also CA 122; 136; 167
Rhine, Richard
        See Silverstein, Alvin
Rhodes, Eugene Manlove 1869-1934
    TCLC 53
Rhodius, Apollonius .... c. 3rd cent. B.C.-
    CMLC 28
        See also DLB 176
R'hoone
        See Balzac, Honore de
Rhys, Jean .... 1890(?)-1979
    CLC 2, 4, 6, 14, 19, 51; DAM NOV; SSC
    21
        See also CA 25-28R; 85-88; CANR 35, 62;
        CDBLB 1945-1960; DLB 36, 117, 162;
        MTCW 1
Ribeiro, Darcy 1922-1997
    CLC 34
        See also CA 33-36R; 156
Ribeiro, Joao Ubaldo (Osorio Pimentel)
        1941- .... CLC 10, 67
        See also CA 81-84
Ribman, Ronald (Burt) 1932-
    CLC 7
        See also CA 21-24R; CANR 46
Ricci, Nino 1959-
    CLC 70
        See also CA 137
Rice, Anne 1941-
    CLC 41; DAM POP
        See also AAYA 9; BEST 89:2; CA 65-68; CANR
        12, 36, 53, 74
Rice, Elmer (Leopold) 1892-1967
    CLC 7, 49; DAM DRAM
        See also CA 21-22; 25-28R; CAP 2; DLB 4, 7;
        MTCW 1
Rice, Tim(othy Miles Bindon) 1944-
    CLC 21
        See also CA 103; CANR 46
Rich, Adrienne (Cecile) 1929-
    CLC 3, 6, 7, 11, 18, 36, 73, 76; DAM POET;
    PC 5
        See also CA 9-12R; CANR 20, 53, 74; DLB 5,
        67; MTCW 1
Rich, Barbara

See Graves, Robert (von Ranke)
Rich, Robert
        See Trumbo, Dalton
Richard, Keith .... CLC 17
        See also Richards, Keith
Richards, David Adams 1950-
    CLC 59; DAC
        See also CA 93-96; CANR 60; DLB 53
Richards, I(vor) A(rmstrong) 1893-1979
    CLC 14, 24
        See also CA 41-44R; 89-92; CANR 34, 74; DLB
        27
Richards, Keith 1943-
        See Richard, Keith
        See also CA 107
Richardson, Anne
        See Roiphe, Anne (Richardson)
Richardson, Dorothy Miller 1873-1957
    TCLC 3
        See also CA 104; DLB 36
Richardson, Ethel Florence (Lindesay)
        1870-1946
        See Richardson, Henry Handel
        See also CA 105
Richardson, Henry Handel .... TCLC 4
        See also Richardson, Ethel Florence (Lindesay)
        See also DLB 197
Richardson, John 1796-1852
    NCLC 55; DAC
        See also DLB 99
Richardson, Samuel 1689-1761
    LC 1, 44; DA; DAB; DAC; DAM MST,
    NOV; WLC
        See also CDBLB 1660-1789; DLB 39
Richler, Mordecai 1931-
    CLC 3, 5, 9, 13, 18, 46, 70; DAC; DAM
    MST, NOV
        See also AITN 1; CA 65-68; CANR 31, 62; CLR
        17; DLB 53; MAICYA; MTCW 1; SATA 44,
        98; SATA-Brief 27
Richter, Conrad (Michael) 1890-1968
    CLC 30
        See also AAYA 21; CA 5-8R; 25-28R; CANR
        23; DLB 9; MTCW 1; SATA 3
Ricostranza, Tom
        See Ellis, Trey
Riddell, Charlotte 1832-1906
    TCLC 40
        See also CA 165; DLB 156
Riding, Laura .... CLC 3, 7
        See also Jackson, Laura (Riding)
Riefenstahl, Berta Helene Amalia 1902-
        See Riefenstahl, Leni
        See also CA 108
Riefenstahl, Leni .... CLC 16
        See also Riefenstahl, Berta Helene Amalia
Riffe, Ernest
        See Bergman, (Ernst) Ingmar
Riggs, (Rolla) Lynn 1899-1954
    TCLC 56; DAM MULT
        See also CA 144; DLB 175; NNAL
Riis, Jacob A(ugust) 1849-1914
    TCLC 80
        See also CA 113; 168; DLB 23
Riley, James Whitcomb 1849-1916
    TCLC 51; DAM POET
        See also CA 118; 137; MAICYA; SATA 17
Riley, Tex
        See Creasey, John
Rilke, Rainer Maria 1875-1926
    TCLC 1, 6, 19; DAM POET; PC 2
        See also CA 104; 132; CANR 62; DLB 81;
        MTCW 1

Rimbaud, (Jean Nicolas) Arthur   1854-1891
    NCLC 4, 35; DA; DAB; DAC; DAM MST,
    POET; PC 3; WLC
Rinehart, Mary Roberts 1876-1958
    TCLC 52
        See also CA 108; 166
Ringmaster, The
        See Mencken, H(enry) L(ouis)
Ringwood, Gwen(dolyn Margaret) Pharis
        1910-1984 .... CLC 48
        See also CA 148; 112; DLB 88
Rio, Michel .... 19(?)-
    CLC 43
Ritsos, Giannes
        See Ritsos, Yannis
Ritsos, Yannis 1909-1990
    CLC 6, 13, 31
        See also CA 77-80; 133; CANR 39, 61; MTCW
        1
Ritter, Erika .... 1948(?)-
    CLC 52
Rivera, Jose Eustasio 1889-1928
    TCLC 35
        See also CA 162; HW
Rivers, Conrad Kent 1933-1968
    CLC 1
        See also BW 1; CA 85-88; DLB 41
Rivers, Elfrida
        See Bradley, Marion Zimmer
Riverside, John
        See Heinlein, Robert A(nson)
Rizal, Jose 1861-1896
    NCLC 27
Roa Bastos, Augusto (Antonio) 1917-
    CLC 45; DAM MULT; HLC
        See also CA 131; DLB 113; HW
Robbe-Grillet, Alain 1922-
    CLC 1, 2, 4, 6, 8, 10, 14, 43
        See also CA 9-12R; CANR 33, 65; DLB 83;
        MTCW 1
Robbins, Harold 1916-1997
    CLC 5; DAM NOV
        See also CA 73-76; 162; CANR 26, 54; MTCW
        1
Robbins, Thomas Eugene 1936-
        See Robbins, Tom
        See also CA 81-84; CANR 29, 59; DAM NOV,
        POP; MTCW 1
Robbins, Tom .... CLC 9, 32, 64
        See also Robbins, Thomas Eugene
        See also BEST 90:3; DLBY 80
Robbins, Trina 1938-
    CLC 21
        See also CA 128
Roberts, Charles G(eorge) D(ouglas)
        1860-1943 .... TCLC 8
        See also CA 105; CLR 33; DLB 92; SATA 88;
        SATA-Brief 29
Roberts, Elizabeth Madox 1886-1941
    TCLC 68
        See also CA 111; 166; DLB 9, 54, 102; SATA
        33; SATA-Brief 27
Roberts, Kate 1891-1985
    CLC 15
        See also CA 107; 116
Roberts, Keith (John Kingston) 1935-
    CLC 14
        See also CA 25-28R; CANR 46
Roberts, Kenneth (Lewis) 1885-1957
    TCLC 23
        See also CA 109; DLB 9
Roberts, Michele (B.) 1949-
    CLC 48

See also CA 115; CANR 58

Robertson, Ellis
See Ellison, Harlan (Jay); Silverberg, Robert

Robertson, Thomas William 1829-1871
NCLC 35; DAM DRAM

Robeson, Kenneth
See Dent, Lester

Robinson, Edwin Arlington 1869-1935
TCLC 5; DA; DAC; DAM MST, POET;
PC 1
See also CA 104; 133; CDALB 1865-1917;
DLB 54; MTCW 1

Robinson, Henry Crabb 1775-1867
NCLC 15
See also DLB 107

Robinson, Jill 1936-
CLC 10
See also CA 102; INT 102

Robinson, Kim Stanley 1952-
CLC 34
See also AAYA 26; CA 126

Robinson, Lloyd
See Silverberg, Robert

Robinson, Marilynne 1944-
CLC 25
See also CA 116

Robinson, Smokey .... CLC 21
See also Robinson, William, Jr.

Robinson, William, Jr. 1940-
See Robinson, Smokey
See also CA 116

Robison, Mary 1949-
CLC 42, 98
See also CA 113; 116; DLB 130; INT 116

Rod, Edouard 1857-1910
TCLC 52

Roddenberry, Eugene Wesley 1921-1991
See Roddenberry, Gene
See also CA 110; 135; CANR 37; SATA 45;
SATA-Obit 69

Roddenberry, Gene .... CLC 17
See also Roddenberry, Eugene Wesley
See also AAYA 5; SATA-Obit 69

Rodgers, Mary 1931-
CLC 12
See also CA 49-52; CANR 8, 55; CLR 20; INT
CANR-8; JRDA; MAICYA; SATA 8

Rodgers, W(illiam) R(obert) 1909-1969
CLC 7
See also CA 85-88; DLB 20

Rodman, Eric
See Silverberg, Robert

Rodman, Howard .... 1920(?)-1985
CLC 65
See also CA 118

Rodman, Maia
See Wojciechowska, Maia (Teresa)

Rodriguez, Claudio 1934-
CLC 10
See also DLB 134

Roelvaag, O(le) E(dvart) 1876-1931
TCLC 17
See also CA 117; DLB 9

Roethke, Theodore (Huebner) 1908-1963
CLC 1, 3, 8, 11, 19, 46, 101; DAM POET;
PC 15
See also CA 81-84; CABS 2; CDALB
1941-1968; DLB 5; MTCW 1

Rogers, Samuel 1763-1855
NCLC 69
See also DLB 93

Rogers, Thomas Hunton 1927-
CLC 57

See also CA 89-92; INT 89-92

Rogers, Will(iam Penn Adair) 1879-1935
TCLC 8, 71; DAM MULT
See also CA 105; 144; DLB 11; NNAL

Rogin, Gilbert 1929-
CLC 18
See also CA 65-68; CANR 15

Rohan, Koda .... TCLC 22
See also Koda Shigeyuki

Rohlfs, Anna Katharine Green
See Green, Anna Katharine

Rohmer, Eric .... CLC 16
See also Scherer, Jean-Marie Maurice

Rohmer, Sax .... TCLC 28
See also Ward, Arthur Henry Sarsfield
See also DLB 70

Roiphe, Anne (Richardson) 1935-
CLC 3, 9
See also CA 89-92; CANR 45, 73; DLBY 80;
INT 89-92

Rojas, Fernando de 1465-1541
LC 23

**Rolfe, Frederick (William Serafino Austin
Lewis Mary)** 1860-1913
TCLC 12
See also CA 107; DLB 34, 156

Rolland, Romain 1866-1944
TCLC 23
See also CA 118; DLB 65

Rolle, Richard .... c. 1300-c. 1349
CMLC 21
See also DLB 146

Rolvaag, O(le) E(dvart)
See Roelvaag, O(le) E(dvart)

Romain Arnaud, Saint
See Aragon, Louis

Romains, Jules 1885-1972
CLC 7
See also CA 85-88; CANR 34; DLB 65; MTCW
1

Romero, Jose Ruben 1890-1952
TCLC 14
See also CA 114; 131; HW

Ronsard, Pierre de 1524-1585
LC 6; PC 11

Rooke, Leon 1934-
CLC 25, 34; DAM POP
See also CA 25-28R; CANR 23, 53

Roosevelt, Theodore 1858-1919
TCLC 69
See also CA 115; 170; DLB 47, 186

Roper, William 1498-1578
LC 10

Roquelaure, A. N.
See Rice, Anne

Rosa, Joao Guimaraes 1908-1967
CLC 23
See also CA 89-92; DLB 113

Rose, Wendy 1948-
CLC 85; DAM MULT; PC 13
See also CA 53-56; CANR 5, 51; DLB 175;
NNAL; SATA 12

Rosen, R. D.
See Rosen, Richard (Dean)

Rosen, Richard (Dean) 1949-
CLC 39
See also CA 77-80; CANR 62; INT CANR-30

Rosenberg, Isaac 1890-1918
TCLC 12
See also CA 107; DLB 20

Rosenblatt, Joe .... CLC 15
See also Rosenblatt, Joseph

Rosenblatt, Joseph 1933-

See Rosenblatt, Joe
See also CA 89-92; INT 89-92

Rosenfeld, Samuel
See Tzara, Tristan

Rosenstock, Sami
See Tzara, Tristan

Rosenstock, Samuel
See Tzara, Tristan

Rosenthal, M(acha) L(ouis) 1917-1996
CLC 28
See also CA 1-4R; 152; CAAS 6; CANR 4, 51;
DLB 5; SATA 59

Ross, Barnaby
See Dannay, Frederic

Ross, Bernard L.
See Follett, Ken(neth Martin)

Ross, J. H.
See Lawrence, T(homas) E(dward)

Ross, John Hume
See Lawrence, T(homas) E(dward)

Ross, Martin
See Martin, Violet Florence
See also DLB 135

Ross, (James) Sinclair 1908-
CLC 13; DAC; DAM MST; SSC 24
See also CA 73-76; DLB 88

Rossetti, Christina (Georgina) 1830-1894
NCLC 2, 50, 66; DA; DAB; DAC; DAM
MST, POET; PC 7; WLC
See also DLB 35, 163; MAICYA; SATA 20

Rossetti, Dante Gabriel 1828-1882
NCLC 4; DA; DAB; DAC; DAM MST,
POET; WLC
See also CDBLB 1832-1890; DLB 35

Rossner, Judith (Perelman) 1935-
CLC 6, 9, 29
See also AITN 2; BEST 90:3; CA 17-20R;
CANR 18, 51, 73; DLB 6; INT CANR-18;
MTCW 1

Rostand, Edmond (Eugene Alexis) 1868-1918
TCLC 6, 37; DA; DAB; DAC; DAM
DRAM, MST; DC 10
See also CA 104; 126; DLB 192; MTCW 1

Roth, Henry 1906-1995
CLC 2, 6, 11, 104
See also CA 11-12; 149; CANR 38, 63; CAP 1;
DLB 28; MTCW 1

Roth, Philip (Milton) 1933-
CLC 1, 2, 3, 4, 6, 9, 15, 22, 31, 47, 66, 86;
DA; DAB; DAC; DAM MST, NOV, POP;
SSC 26; WLC
See also BEST 90:3; CA 1-4R; CANR 1, 22,
36, 55; CDALB 1968-1988; DLB 2, 28, 173;
DLBY 82; MTCW 1

Rothenberg, Jerome 1931-
CLC 6, 57
See also CA 45-48; CANR 1; DLB 5, 193

Roumain, Jacques (Jean Baptiste) 1907-1944
TCLC 19; BLC 3; DAM MULT
See also BW 1; CA 117; 125

Rourke, Constance (Mayfield) 1885-1941
TCLC 12
See also CA 107; YABC 1

Rousseau, Jean-Baptiste 1671-1741
LC 9

Rousseau, Jean-Jacques 1712-1778
LC 14, 36; DA; DAB; DAC; DAM MST;
WLC

Roussel, Raymond 1877-1933
TCLC 20
See also CA 117

Rovit, Earl (Herbert) 1927-
CLC 7

See also CA 128; 109; DLB 69

Schmitz, Aron Hector 1861-1928
See Svevo, Italo
See also CA 104; 122; MTCW 1

Schnackenberg, Gjertrud 1953-
CLC 40
See also CA 116; DLB 120

Schneider, Leonard Alfred 1925-1966
See Bruce, Lenny
See also CA 89-92

Schnitzler, Arthur 1862-1931
TCLC 4; SSC 15
See also CA 104; DLB 81, 118

Schoenberg, Arnold 1874-1951
TCLC 75
See also CA 109

Schonberg, Arnold
See Schoenberg, Arnold

Schopenhauer, Arthur 1788-1860
NCLC 51
See also DLB 90

Schor, Sandra (M.) .... 1932(?)-1990
CLC 65
See also CA 132

Schorer, Mark 1908-1977
CLC 9
See also CA 5-8R; 73-76; CANR 7; DLB 103

Schrader, Paul (Joseph) 1946-
CLC 26
See also CA 37-40R; CANR 41; DLB 44

Schreiner, Olive (Emilie Albertina)
1855-1920 .... TCLC 9
See also CA 105; 154; DLB 18, 156, 190

Schulberg, Budd (Wilson) 1914-
CLC 7, 48
See also CA 25-28R; CANR 19; DLB 6, 26,
28; DLBY 81

Schulz, Bruno 1892-1942
TCLC 5, 51; SSC 13
See also CA 115; 123

Schulz, Charles M(onroe) 1922-
CLC 12
See also CA 9-12R; CANR 6; INT CANR-6;
SATA 10

Schumacher, E(rnst) F(riedrich). 1911-1977
CLC 80
See also CA 81-84; 73-76; CANR 34

Schuyler, James Marcus 1923-1991
CLC 5, 23; DAM POET
See also CA 101; 134; DLB 5, 169; INT 101

Schwartz, Delmore (David) 1913-1966
CLC 2, 4, 10, 45, 87; PC 8
See also CA 17-18; 25-28R; CANR 35; CAP 2;
DLB 28, 48; MTCW 1

Schwartz, Ernst
See Ozu, Yasujiro

Schwartz, John Burnham 1965-
CLC 59
See also CA 132

Schwartz, Lynne Sharon 1939-
CLC 31
See also CA 103; CANR 44

Schwartz, Muriel A.
See Eliot, T(homas) S(tearns)

Schwarz-Bart, Andre 1928-
CLC 2, 4
See also CA 89-92

Schwarz-Bart, Simone 1938-
CLC 7; BLCS
See also BW 2; CA 97-100

Schwob, Marcel (Mayer Andre) . 1867-1905
TCLC 20
See also CA 117; 168; DLB 123

Sciascia, Leonardo 1921-1989
CLC 8, 9, 41
See also CA 85-88; 130; CANR 35; DLB 177;
MTCW 1

Scoppettone, Sandra 1936-
CLC 26
See also AAYA 11; CA 5-8R; CANR 41, 73;
SATA 9, 92

Scorsese, Martin 1942-
CLC 20, 89
See also CA 110; 114; CANR 46

Scotland, Jay
See Jakes, John (William)

Scott, Duncan Campbell 1862-1947
TCLC 6; DAC
See also CA 104; 153; DLB 92

Scott, Evelyn 1893-1963
CLC 43
See also CA 104; 112; CANR 64; DLB 9, 48

Scott, F(rancis) R(eginald) 1899-1985
CLC 22
See also CA 101; 114; DLB 88; INT 101

Scott, Frank
See Scott, F(rancis) R(eginald)

Scott, Joanna 1960-
CLC 50
See also CA 126; CANR 53

Scott, Paul (Mark) 1920-1978
CLC 9, 60
See also CA 81-84; 77-80; CANR 33; DLB 14;
MTCW 1

Scott, Sarah 1723-1795
LC 44
See also DLB 39

Scott, Walter 1771-1832
NCLC 15, 69; DA; DAB; DAC; DAM
MST, NOV, POET; PC 13; SSC 32; WLC
See also AAYA 22; CDBLB 1789-1832; DLB
93, 107, 116, 144, 159; YABC 2

Scribe, (Augustin) Eugene 1791-1861
NCLC 16; DAM DRAM; DC 5
See also DLB 192

Scrum, R.
See Crumb, R(obert)

Scudery, Madeleine de 1607-1701
LC 2

Scum
See Crumb, R(obert)

Scumbag, Little Bobby
See Crumb, R(obert)

Seabrook, John
See Hubbard, L(afayette) Ron(ald)

Sealy, I. Allan 1951-
CLC 55

Search, Alexander
See Pessoa, Fernando (Antonio Nogueira)

Sebastian, Lee
See Silverberg, Robert

Sebastian Owl
See Thompson, Hunter S(tockton)

Sebestyen, Ouida 1924-
CLC 30
See also AAYA 8; CA 107; CANR 40; CLR 17;
JRDA; MAICYA; SAAS 10; SATA 39

Secundus, H. Scriblerus
See Fielding, Henry

Sedges, John
See Buck, Pearl S(ydenstricker)

Sedgwick, Catharine Maria 1789-1867
NCLC 19
See also DLB 1, 74

Seelye, John (Douglas) 1931-
CLC 7

See also CA 97-100; CANR 70; INT 97-100

Seferiades, Giorgos Stylianou 1900-1971
See Seferis, George
See also CA 5-8R; 33-36R; CANR 5, 36;
MTCW 1

Seferis, George ....CLC 5, 11
See also Seferiades, Giorgos Stylianou

Segal, Erich (Wolf) 1937-
CLC 3, 10; DAM POP
See also BEST 89:1; CA 25-28R; CANR 20,
36, 65; DLBY 86; INT CANR-20; MTCW 1

Seger, Bob 1945-
CLC 35

Seghers, Anna ....CLC 7
See also Radvanyi, Netty
See also DLB 69

Seidel, Frederick (Lewis) 1936-
CLC 18
See also CA 13-16R; CANR 8; DLBY 84

Seifert, Jaroslav 1901-1986
CLC 34, 44, 93
See also CA 127; MTCW 1

Sei Shonagon .... c. 966-1017(?)
CMLC 6

Sejour, Victor 1817-1874
DC 10
See also DLB 50

Sejour Marcou et Ferrand, Juan Victor
See Sejour, Victor

Selby, Hubert, Jr. 1928-
CLC 1, 2, 4, 8; SSC 20
See also CA 13-16R; CANR 33; DLB 2

Selzer, Richard 1928-
CLC 74
See also CA 65-68; CANR 14

Sembene, Ousmane
See Ousmane, Sembene

Senancour, Etienne Pivert de 1770-1846
NCLC 16
See also DLB 119

Sender, Ramon (Jose) 1902-1982
CLC 8; DAM MULT; HLC
See also CA 5-8R; 105; CANR 8; HW; MTCW
1

Seneca, Lucius Annaeus 4B.C.-65
CMLC 6; DAM DRAM; DC 5

Senghor, Leopold Sedar 1906-
CLC 54; BLC 3; DAM MULT, POET; PC
25
See also BW 2; CA 116; 125; CANR 47, 74;
MTCW 1

Serling, (Edward) Rod(man) 1924-1975
CLC 30
See also AAYA 14; AITN 1; CA 162; 57-60;
DLB 26

Serna, Ramon Gomez de la
See Gomez de la Serna, Ramon

Serpieres
See Guillevic, (Eugene)

Service, Robert
See Service, Robert W(illiam)
See also DAB; DLB 92

Service, Robert W(illiam) .... 1874(?)-1958
TCLC 15; DA; DAC; DAM MST, POET;
WLC
See also Service, Robert
See also CA 115; 140; SATA 20

Seth, Vikram 1952-
CLC 43, 90; DAM MULT
See also CA 121; 127; CANR 50, 74; DLB 120;
INT 127

Seton, Cynthia Propper 1926-1982
CLC 27

See also CA 5-8R; 108; CANR 7

Seton, Ernest (Evan) Thompson . 1860-1946
  TCLC 31
    See also CA 109; DLB 92; DLBD 13; JRDA;
    SATA 18

Seton-Thompson, Ernest
  See Seton, Ernest (Evan) Thompson

Settle, Mary Lee 1918-
  CLC 19, 61
    See also CA 89-92; CAAS 1; CANR 44; DLB
    6; INT 89-92

Seuphor, Michel
  See Arp, Jean

**Sevigne, Marie (de Rabutin-Chantal) Marquise
  de** 1626-1696
  LC 11

Sewall, Samuel 1652-1730
  LC 38
    See also DLB 24

Sexton, Anne (Harvey) 1928-1974
    **CLC 2, 4, 6, 8, 10, 15, 53; DA; DAB; DAC;
    DAM MST, POET; PC 2; WLC**
    See also CA 1-4R; 53-56; CABS 2; CANR 3,
    36; CDALB 1941-1968; DLB 5, 169;
    MTCW 1; SATA 10

Shaara, Michael (Joseph, Jr.) 1929-1988
    CLC 15; DAM POP
    See also AITN 1; CA 102; 125; CANR 52;
    DLBY 83

Shackleton, C. C.
  See Aldiss, Brian W(ilson)

Shacochis, Bob .... **CLC 39**
    See also Shacochis, Robert G.

Shacochis, Robert G. 1951-
  See Shacochis, Bob
    See also CA 119; 124; INT 124

Shaffer, Anthony (Joshua) 1926-
    CLC 19; DAM DRAM
    See also CA 110; 116; DLB 13

Shaffer, Peter (Levin) 1926-
    **CLC 5, 14, 18, 37, 60; DAB; DAM DRAM,
    MST; DC 7**
    See also CA 25-28R; CANR 25, 47, 74; CDBLB
    1960 to Present; DLB 13; MTCW 1

Shakey, Bernard
  See Young, Neil

Shalamov, Varlam (Tikhonovich)
    1907(?)-1982 .... **CLC 18**
    See also CA 129; 105

Shamlu, Ahmad 1925-
  CLC 10

Shammas, Anton 1951-
  CLC 55

Shange, Ntozake 1948-
    **CLC 8, 25, 38, 74; BLC 3; DAM DRAM,
    MULT; DC 3**
    See also AAYA 9; BW 2; CA 85-88; CABS 3;
    CANR 27, 48, 74; DLB 38; MTCW 1

Shanley, John Patrick 1950-
  CLC 75
    See also CA 128; 133

Shapcott, Thomas W(illiam) 1935-
  CLC 38
    See also CA 69-72; CANR 49

Shapiro, Jane .... **CLC 76**

Shapiro, Karl (Jay) 1913-
    CLC 4, 8, 15, 53; PC 25
    See also CA 1-4R; CAAS 6; CANR 1, 36, 66;
    DLB 48; MTCW 1

Sharp, William 1855-1905
    TCLC 39
    See also CA 160; DLB 156

Sharpe, Thomas Ridley 1928-

See Sharpe, Tom
  See also CA 114; 122; INT 122

Sharpe, Tom .... **CLC 36**
    See also Sharpe, Thomas Ridley
    See also DLB 14

Shaw, Bernard .... **TCLC 45**
    See also Shaw, George Bernard
    See also BW 1

Shaw, G. Bernard
  See Shaw, George Bernard

Shaw, George Bernard 1856-1950
    **TCLC 3, 9, 21; DA; DAB; DAC; DAM
    DRAM, MST; WLC**
    See also Shaw, Bernard
    See also CA 104; 128; CDBLB 1914-1945;
    DLB 10, 57, 190; MTCW 1

Shaw, Henry Wheeler 1818-1885
    NCLC 15
    See also DLB 11

Shaw, Irwin 1913-1984
    CLC 7, 23, 34; DAM DRAM, POP
    See also AITN 1; CA 13-16R; 112; CANR 21;
    CDALB 1941-1968; DLB 6, 102; DLBY 84;
    MTCW 1

Shaw, Robert 1927-1978
    CLC 5
    See also AITN 1; CA 1-4R; 81-84; CANR 4;
    DLB 13, 14

Shaw, T. E.
  See Lawrence, T(homas) E(dward)

Shawn, Wallace 1943-
  CLC 41
    See also CA 112

Shea, Lisa 1953-
  CLC 86
    See also CA 147

Sheed, Wilfrid (John Joseph) 1930-
    CLC 2, 4, 10, 53
    See also CA 65-68; CANR 30, 66; DLB 6;
    MTCW 1

Sheldon, Alice Hastings Bradley 1915(?)-1987
    See Tiptree, James, Jr.
    See also CA 108; 122; CANR 34; INT 108;
    MTCW 1

Sheldon, John
  See Bloch, Robert (Albert)

Shelley, Mary Wollstonecraft (Godwin)
    1797-1851 **NCLC 14, 59; DA; DAB; DAC;
    DAM MST, NOV; WLC**
    See also AAYA 20; CDBLB 1789-1832; DLB
    110, 116, 159, 178; SATA 29

Shelley, Percy Bysshe 1792-1822
    **NCLC 18; DA; DAB; DAC; DAM MST,
    POET; PC 14; WLC**
    See also CDBLB 1789-1832; DLB 96, 110, 158

Shepard, Jim 1956-
  CLC 36
    See also CA 137; CANR 59; SATA 90

Shepard, Lucius 1947-
  CLC 34
    See also CA 128; 141

Shepard, Sam 1943-
    **CLC 4, 6, 17, 34, 41, 44; DAM DRAM; DC
    5**
    See also AAYA 1; CA 69-72; CABS 3; CANR
    22; DLB 7; MTCW 1

Shepherd, Michael
  See Ludlum, Robert

Sherburne, Zoa (Morin) 1912-
  CLC 30
    See also AAYA 13; CA 1-4R; CANR 3, 37;
    MAICYA; SAAS 18; SATA 3

Sheridan, Frances 1724-1766

LC 7
    See also DLB 39, 84

Sheridan, Richard Brinsley 1751-1816
    **NCLC 5; DA; DAB; DAC; DAM DRAM,
    MST; DC 1; WLC**
    See also CDBLB 1660-1789; DLB 89

Sherman, Jonathan Marc .... **CLC 55**

Sherman, Martin .... 1941(?)-
  CLC 19
    See also CA 116; 123

Sherwin, Judith Johnson 1936-
  CLC 7, 15
    See also CA 25-28R; CANR 34

Sherwood, Frances 1940-
  CLC 81
    See also CA 146

Sherwood, Robert E(mmet) 1896-1955
    TCLC 3; DAM DRAM
    See also CA 104; 153; DLB 7, 26

Shestov, Lev 1866-1938
    TCLC 56

Shevchenko, Taras 1814-1861
    NCLC 54

Shiel, M(atthew) P(hipps) 1865-1947
    TCLC 8
    See Holmes, Gordon
    See also CA 106; 160; DLB 153

Shields, Carol 1935-
    CLC 91, 113; DAC
    See also CA 81-84; CANR 51, 74

Shields, David 1956-
  CLC 97
    See also CA 124; CANR 48

Shiga, Naoya 1883-1971
    CLC 33; SSC 23
    See also CA 101; 33-36R; DLB 180

Shilts, Randy 1951-1994
    CLC 85
    See also AAYA 19; CA 115; 127; 144; CANR
    45; INT 127

Shimazaki, Haruki 1872-1943
    See Shimazaki Toson
    See also CA 105; 134

Shimazaki Toson 1872-1943
    TCLC 5
    See also Shimazaki, Haruki
    See also DLB 180

Sholokhov, Mikhail (Aleksandrovich)
    1905-1984 .... **CLC 7, 15**
    See also CA 101; 112; MTCW 1; SATA-Obit
    36

Shone, Patric
  See Hanley, James

Shreve, Susan Richards 1939-
  CLC 23
    See also CA 49-52; CAAS 5; CANR 5, 38, 69;
    MAICYA; SATA 46, 95; SATA-Brief 41

Shue, Larry 1946-1985
    CLC 52; DAM DRAM
    See also CA 145; 117

Shu-Jen, Chou 1881-1936
    See Lu Hsun
    See also CA 104

Shulman, Alix Kates 1932-
  CLC 2, 10
    See also CA 29-32R; CANR 43; SATA 7

Shuster, Joe 1914-
  CLC 21

Shute, Nevil .... **CLC 30**
    See also Norway, Nevil Shute

Shuttle, Penelope (Diane) 1947-
  CLC 7
    See also CA 93-96; CANR 39; DLB 14, 40

CLC 3, 5, 14, 36, 44; BLC 3; DA; DAB;
DAC; DAM DRAM, MST, MULT; DC 2;
WLC
See also BW 2; CA 13-16R; CANR 27, 39; DLB
125; MTCW 1

Spackman, W(illiam) M(ode) 1905-1990
CLC 46
See also CA 81-84; 132

Spacks, Barry (Bernard) 1931-
CLC 14
See also CA 154; CANR 33; DLB 105

Spanidou, Irini 1946-
CLC 44

Spark, Muriel (Sarah) 1918-
CLC 2, 3, 5, 8, 13, 18, 40, 94; DAB; DAC;
DAM MST, NOV; SSC 10
See also CA 5-8R; CANR 12, 36; CDBLB
1945-1960; DLB 15, 139; INT CANR-12;
MTCW 1

Spaulding, Douglas
See Bradbury, Ray (Douglas)

Spaulding, Leonard
See Bradbury, Ray (Douglas)

Spence, J. A. D.
See Eliot, T(homas) S(tearns)

Spencer, Elizabeth 1921-
CLC 22
See also CA 13-16R; CANR 32, 65; DLB 6;
MTCW 1; SATA 14

Spencer, Leonard G.
See Silverberg, Robert

Spencer, Scott 1945-
CLC 30
See also CA 113; CANR 51; DLBY 86

Spender, Stephen (Harold) 1909-1995
CLC 1, 2, 5, 10, 41, 91; DAM POET
See also CA 9-12R; 149; CANR 31, 54; CDBLB
1945-1960; DLB 20; MTCW 1

Spengler, Oswald (Arnold Gottfried)
1880-1936 .... TCLC 25
See also CA 118

Spenser, Edmund .... 1552(?)-1599
LC 5, 39; DA; DAB; DAC; DAM MST,
POET; PC 8; WLC
See also CDBLB Before 1660; DLB 167

Spicer, Jack 1925-1965
CLC 8, 18, 72; DAM POET
See also CA 85-88; DLB 5, 16, 193

Spiegelman, Art 1948-
CLC 76
See also AAYA 10; CA 125; CANR 41, 55, 74

Spielberg, Peter 1929-
CLC 6
See also CA 5-8R; CANR 4, 48; DLBY 81

Spielberg, Steven 1947-
CLC 20
See also AAYA 8, 24; CA 77-80; CANR 32;
SATA 32

Spillane, Frank Morrison 1918-
See Spillane, Mickey
See also CA 25-28R; CANR 28, 63; MTCW 1;
SATA 66

Spillane, Mickey .... CLC 3, 13
See also Spillane, Frank Morrison

Spinoza, Benedictus de 1632-1677
LC 9

Spinrad, Norman (Richard) 1940-
CLC 46
See also CA 37-40R; CAAS 19; CANR 20; DLB
8; INT CANR-20

Spitteler, Carl (Friedrich Georg) 1845-1924
TCLC 12
See also CA 109; DLB 129

Spivack, Kathleen (Romola Drucker) 1938-
CLC 6
See also CA 49-52

Spoto, Donald 1941-
CLC 39
See also CA 65-68; CANR 11, 57

Springsteen, Bruce (F.) 1949-
CLC 17
See also CA 111

Spurling, Hilary 1940-
CLC 34
See also CA 104; CANR 25, 52

Spyker, John Howland
See Elman, Richard (Martin)

Squires, (James) Radcliffe 1917-1993
CLC 51
See also CA 1-4R; 140; CANR 6, 21

Srivastava, Dhanpat Rai .... 1880(?)-1936
See Premchand
See also CA 118

Stacy, Donald
See Pohl, Frederik

Stael, Germaine de 1766-1817
See Stael-Holstein, Anne Louise Germaine
Necker Baronn
See also DLB 119

**Stael-Holstein, Anne Louise Germaine Necker
Baronn** 1766-1817
NCLC 3
See also Stael, Germaine de
See also DLB 192

Stafford, Jean 1915-1979
CLC 4, 7, 19, 68; SSC 26
See also CA 1-4R; 85-88; CANR 3, 65; DLB 2,
173; MTCW 1; SATA-Obit 22

Stafford, William (Edgar) 1914-1993
CLC 4, 7, 29; DAM POET
See also CA 5-8R; 142; CAAS 3; CANR 5, 22;
DLB 5; INT CANR-22

Stagnelius, Eric Johan 1793-1823
NCLC 61

Staines, Trevor
See Brunner, John (Kilian Houston)

Stairs, Gordon
See Austin, Mary (Hunter)

Stannard, Martin 1947-
CLC 44
See also CA 142; DLB 155

Stanton, Elizabeth Cady 1815-1902
TCLC 73
See also DLB 79

Stanton, Maura 1946-
CLC 9
See also CA 89-92; CANR 15; DLB 120

Stanton, Schuyler
See Baum, L(yman) Frank

Stapledon, (William) Olaf 1886-1950
TCLC 22
See also CA 111; 162; DLB 15

Starbuck, George (Edwin) 1931-1996
CLC 53; DAM POET
See also CA 21-24R; 153; CANR 23

Stark, Richard
See Westlake, Donald E(dwin)

Staunton, Schuyler
See Baum, L(yman) Frank

Stead, Christina (Ellen) 1902-1983
CLC 2, 5, 8, 32, 80
See also CA 13-16R; 109; CANR 33, 40;
MTCW 1

Stead, William Thomas 1849-1912
TCLC 48
See also CA 167

Steele, Richard 1672-1729
LC 18
See also CDBLB 1660-1789; DLB 84, 101

Steele, Timothy (Reid) 1948-
CLC 45
See also CA 93-96; CANR 16, 50; DLB 120

Steffens, (Joseph) Lincoln 1866-1936
TCLC 20
See also CA 117

Stegner, Wallace (Earle) 1909-1993
CLC 9, 49, 81; DAM NOV; SSC 27
See also AITN 1; BEST 90:3; CA 1-4R; 141;
CAAS 9; CANR 1, 21, 46; DLB 9; DLBY
93; MTCW 1

Stein, Gertrude 1874-1946
TCLC 1, 6, 28, 48; DA; DAB; DAC; DAM
MST, NOV, POET; PC 18; WLC
See also CA 104; 132; CDALB 1917-1929;
DLB 4, 54, 86; DLBD 15; MTCW 1

Steinbeck, John (Ernst) 1902-1968
CLC 1, 5, 9, 13, 21, 34, 45, 75; DA; DAB;
DAC; DAM DRAM, MST, NOV; SSC 11;
WLC
See also AAYA 12; CA 1-4R; 25-28R; CANR
1, 35; CDALB 1929-1941; DLB 7, 9; DLBD
2; MTCW 1; SATA 9

Steinem, Gloria 1934-
CLC 63
See also CA 53-56; CANR 28, 51; MTCW 1

Steiner, George 1929-
CLC 24; DAM NOV
See also CA 73-76; CANR 31, 67; DLB 67;
MTCW 1; SATA 62

Steiner, K. Leslie
See Delany, Samuel R(ay, Jr.)

Steiner, Rudolf 1861-1925
TCLC 13
See also CA 107

Stendhal 1783-1842
NCLC 23, 46; DA; DAB; DAC; DAM
MST, NOV; SSC 27; WLC
See also DLB 119

Stephen, Adeline Virginia
See Woolf, (Adeline) Virginia

Stephen, SirLeslie 1832-1904
TCLC 23
See also CA 123; DLB 57, 144, 190

Stephen, Sir Leslie
See Stephen, SirLeslie

Stephen, Virginia
See Woolf, (Adeline) Virginia

Stephens, James .... 1882(?)-1950
TCLC 4
See also CA 104; DLB 19, 153, 162

Stephens, Reed
See Donaldson, Stephen R.

Steptoe, Lydia
See Barnes, Djuna

Sterchi, Beat 1949-
CLC 65

Sterling, Brett
See Bradbury, Ray (Douglas); Hamilton,
Edmond

Sterling, Bruce 1954-
CLC 72
See also CA 119; CANR 44

Sterling, George 1869-1926
TCLC 20
See also CA 117; 165; DLB 54

Stern, Gerald 1925-
CLC 40, 100
See also CA 81-84; CANR 28; DLB 105

Stern, Richard (Gustave) 1928-

CLC 4, 39
See also CA 1-4R; CANR 1, 25, 52; DLBY 87;
INT CANR-25

Sternberg, Josef von 1894-1969
CLC 20
See also CA 81-84

Sterne, Laurence 1713-1768
LC 2, 48; DA; DAB; DAC; DAM MST,
NOV; WLC
See also CDBLB 1660-1789; DLB 39

Sternheim, (William Adolf) Carl   1878-1942
TCLC 8
See also CA 105; DLB 56, 118

Stevens, Mark 1951-
CLC 34
See also CA 122

Stevens, Wallace 1879-1955
TCLC 3, 12, 45; DA; DAB; DAC; DAM
MST, POET; PC 6; WLC
See also CA 104; 124; CDALB 1929-1941;
DLB 54; MTCW 1

Stevenson, Anne (Katharine) 1933-
CLC 7, 33
See also CA 17-20R; CAAS 9; CANR 9, 33;
DLB 40; MTCW 1

Stevenson, Robert Louis (Balfour) 1850-1894
NCLC 5, 14, 63; DA; DAB; DAC; DAM
MST, NOV; SSC 11; WLC
See also AAYA 24; CDBLB 1890-1914; CLR
10, 11; DLB 18, 57, 141, 156, 174; DLBD
13; JRDA; MAICYA; SATA 100; YABC 2

Stewart, J(ohn) I(nnes) M(ackintosh)
1906-1994 .... CLC 7, 14, 32
See also CA 85-88; 147; CAAS 3; CANR 47;
MTCW 1

Stewart, Mary (Florence Elinor) 1916-
CLC 7, 35, 117; DAB
See also CA 1-4R; CANR 1, 59; SATA 12

Stewart, Mary Rainbow
See Stewart, Mary (Florence Elinor)

Stifle, June
See Campbell, Maria

Stifter, Adalbert 1805-1868
NCLC 41; SSC 28
See also DLB 133

Still, James 1906-
CLC 49
See also CA 65-68; CAAS 17; CANR 10, 26;
DLB 9; SATA 29

Sting 1951-
See Sumner, Gordon Matthew
See also CA 167

Stirling, Arthur
See Sinclair, Upton (Beall)

Stitt, Milan 1941-
CLC 29
See also CA 69-72

Stockton, Francis Richard 1834-1902
See Stockton, Frank R.
See also CA 108; 137; MAICYA; SATA 44

Stockton, Frank R. .... TCLC 47
See also Stockton, Francis Richard
See also DLB 42, 74; DLBD 13; SATA-Brief
32

Stoddard, Charles
See Kuttner, Henry

Stoker, Abraham 1847-1912
See Stoker, Bram
See also CA 105; 150; DA; DAC; DAM MST,
NOV; SATA 29

Stoker, Bram 1847-1912
TCLC 8; DAB; WLC
See also Stoker, Abraham

See also AAYA 23; CDBLB 1890-1914; DLB
36, 70, 178

Stolz, Mary (Slattery) 1920-
CLC 12
See also AAYA 8; AITN 1; CA 5-8R; CANR
13, 41; JRDA; MAICYA; SAAS 3; SATA 10,
71

Stone, Irving 1903-1989
CLC 7; DAM POP
See also AITN 1; CA 1-4R; 129; CAAS 3;
CANR 1, 23; INT CANR-23; MTCW 1;
SATA 3; SATA-Obit 64

Stone, Oliver (William) 1946-
CLC 73
See also AAYA 15; CA 110; CANR 55

Stone, Robert (Anthony) 1937-
CLC 5, 23, 42
See also CA 85-88; CANR 23, 66; DLB 152;
INT CANR-23; MTCW 1

Stone, Zachary
See Follett, Ken(neth Martin)

Stoppard, Tom 1937-
CLC 1, 3, 4, 5, 8, 15, 29, 34, 63, 91; DA;
DAB; DAC; DAM DRAM, MST; DC 6;
WLC
See also CA 81-84; CANR 39, 67; CDBLB
1960 to Present; DLB 13; DLBY 85; MTCW
1

Storey, David (Malcolm) 1933-
CLC 2, 4, 5, 8; DAM DRAM
See also CA 81-84; CANR 36; DLB 13, 14;
MTCW 1

Storm, Hyemeyohsts 1935-
CLC 3; DAM MULT
See also CA 81-84; CANR 45; NNAL

Storm, Theodor 1817-1888
SSC 27

Storm, (Hans) Theodor (Woldsen) 1817-1888
NCLC 1; SSC 27
See also DLB 129

Storni, Alfonsina 1892-1938
TCLC 5; DAM MULT; HLC
See also CA 104; 131; HW

Stoughton, William 1631-1701
LC 38
See also DLB 24

Stout, Rex (Todhunter) 1886-1975
CLC 3
See also AITN 2; CA 61-64; CANR 71

Stow, (Julian) Randolph 1935-
CLC 23, 48
See also CA 13-16R; CANR 33; MTCW 1

Stowe, Harriet (Elizabeth) Beecher
1811-1896 NCLC 3, 50; DA; DAB; DAC;
DAM MST, NOV; WLC
See also CDALB 1865-1917; DLB 1, 12, 42,
74, 189; JRDA; MAICYA; YABC 1

Strachey, (Giles) Lytton 1880-1932
TCLC 12
See also CA 110; DLB 149; DLBD 10

Strand, Mark 1934-
CLC 6, 18, 41, 71; DAM POET
See also CA 21-24R; CANR 40, 65; DLB 5;
SATA 41

Straub, Peter (Francis) 1943-
CLC 28, 107; DAM POP
See also BEST 89:1; CA 85-88; CANR 28, 65;
DLBY 84; MTCW 1

Strauss, Botho 1944-
CLC 22
See also CA 157; DLB 124

Streatfeild, (Mary) Noel .... 1895(?)-1986
CLC 21

See also CA 81-84; 120; CANR 31; CLR 17;
DLB 160; MAICYA; SATA 20; SATA-Obit
48

Stribling, T(homas) S(igismund)   1881-1965
CLC 23
See also CA 107; DLB 9

Strindberg, (Johan) August 1849-1912
TCLC 1, 8, 21, 47; DA; DAB; DAC; DAM
DRAM, MST; WLC
See also CA 104; 135

Stringer, Arthur 1874-1950
TCLC 37
See also CA 161; DLB 92

Stringer, David
See Roberts, Keith (John Kingston)

Stroheim, Erich von 1885-1957
TCLC 71

Strugatskii, Arkadii (Natanovich) 1925-1991
CLC 27
See also CA 106; 135

Strugatskii, Boris (Natanovich) 1933-
CLC 27
See also CA 106

Strummer, Joe .... 1953(?)-
CLC 30

Stuart, Don A.
See Campbell, John W(ood, Jr.)

Stuart, Ian
See MacLean, Alistair (Stuart)

Stuart, Jesse (Hilton) 1906-1984
CLC 1, 8, 11, 14, 34; SSC 31
See also CA 5-8R; 112; CANR 31; DLB 9, 48,
102; DLBY 84; SATA 2; SATA-Obit 36

Sturgeon, Theodore (Hamilton) .. 1918-1985
CLC 22, 39
See also Queen, Ellery
See also CA 81-84; 116; CANR 32; DLB 8;
DLBY 85; MTCW 1

Sturges, Preston 1898-1959
TCLC 48
See also CA 114; 149; DLB 26

Styron, William 1925-
CLC 1, 3, 5, 11, 15, 60; DAM NOV, POP;
SSC 25
See also BEST 90:4; CA 5-8R; CANR 6, 33,
74; CDALB 1968-1988; DLB 2, 143; DLBY
80; INT CANR-6; MTCW 1

Su, Chien 1884-1918
See Su Man-shu
See also CA 123

Suarez Lynch, B.
See Bioy Casares, Adolfo; Borges, Jorge Luis

Suckow, Ruth 1892-1960
SSC 18
See also CA 113; DLB 9, 102

Sudermann, Hermann 1857-1928
TCLC 15
See also CA 107; DLB 118

Sue, Eugene 1804-1857
NCLC 1
See also DLB 119

Sueskind, Patrick 1949-
CLC 44
See also Suskind, Patrick

Sukenick, Ronald 1932-
CLC 3, 4, 6, 48
See also CA 25-28R; CAAS 8; CANR 32; DLB
173; DLBY 81

Suknaski, Andrew 1942-
CLC 19
See also CA 101; DLB 53

Sullivan, Vernon
See Vian, Boris

See also CA 129; 125
Tchicaya U Tam'si
  See Tchicaya, Gerald Felix
Teasdale, Sara 1884-1933
  TCLC 4
  See also CA 104; 163; DLB 45; SATA 32
Tegner, Esaias 1782-1846
  NCLC 2
Teilhard de Chardin, (Marie Joseph) Pierre
  1881-1955 .... **TCLC 9**
  See also CA 105
Temple, Ann
  See Mortimer, Penelope (Ruth)
Tennant, Emma (Christina) 1937-
  CLC 13, 52
  See also CA 65-68; CAAS 9; CANR 10, 38,
  59; DLB 14
Tenneshaw, S. M.
  See Silverberg, Robert
Tennyson, Alfred 1809-1892
  NCLC 30, 65; DA; DAB; DAC; DAM
  MST, POET; PC 6; WLC
  See also CDBLB 1832-1890; DLB 32
Teran, Lisa St. Aubin de .... **CLC 36**
  See also St. Aubin de Teran, Lisa
Terence .... 195(?)B.C.-159B.C.
  CMLC 14; DC 7
Teresa de Jesus, St. 1515-1582
  LC 18
Terkel, Louis 1912-
  See Terkel, Studs
  See also CA 57-60; CANR 18, 45, 67; MTCW
  1
Terkel, Studs .... **CLC 38**
  See also Terkel, Louis
  See also AITN 1
Terry, C. V.
  See Slaughter, Frank G(ill)
Terry, Megan 1932-
  CLC 19
  See also CA 77-80; CABS 3; CANR 43; DLB 7
Tertullian .... c. 155-c. 245
  CMLC 29
Tertz, Abram
  See Sinyavsky, Andrei (Donatevich)
Tesich, Steve .... 1943(?)-1996
  CLC 40, 69
  See also CA 105; 152; DLBY 83
Tesla, Nikola 1856-1943
  TCLC 88
Teternikov, Fyodor Kuzmich 1863-1927
  See Sologub, Fyodor
  See also CA 104
Tevis, Walter 1928-1984
  CLC 42
  See also CA 113
Tey, Josephine .... **TCLC 14**
  See also Mackintosh, Elizabeth
  See also DLB 77
Thackeray, William Makepeace . 1811-1863
  NCLC 5, 14, 22, 43; DA; DAB; DAC; DAM
  MST, NOV; WLC
  See also CDBLB 1832-1890; DLB 21, 55, 159,
  163; SATA 23
Thakura, Ravindranatha
  See Tagore, Rabindranath
Tharoor, Shashi 1956-
  CLC 70
  See also CA 141
Thelwell, Michael Miles 1939-
  CLC 22
  See also BW 2; CA 101
Theobald, Lewis, Jr.

See Lovecraft, H(oward) P(hillips)
Theodorescu, Ion N. 1880-1967
  See Arghezi, Tudor
  See also CA 116
Theriault, Yves 1915-1983
  CLC 79; DAC; DAM MST
  See also CA 102; DLB 88
Theroux, Alexander (Louis) 1939-
  CLC 2, 25
  See also CA 85-88; CANR 20, 63
Theroux, Paul (Edward) 1941-
  CLC 5, 8, 11, 15, 28, 46; DAM POP
  See also BEST 89:4; CA 33-36R; CANR 20,
  45, 74; DLB 2; MTCW 1; SATA 44
Thesen, Sharon 1946-
  CLC 56
  See also CA 163
Thevenin, Denis
  See Duhamel, Georges
Thibault, Jacques Anatole Francois
  1844-1924
  See France, Anatole
  See also CA 106; 127; DAM NOV; MTCW 1
Thiele, Colin (Milton) 1920-
  CLC 17
  See also CA 29-32R; CANR 12, 28, 53; CLR
  27; MAICYA; SAAS 2; SATA 14, 72
Thomas, Audrey (Callahan) 1935-
  CLC 7, 13, 37, 107; SSC 20
  See also AITN 2; CA 21-24R; CAAS 19; CANR
  36, 58; DLB 60; MTCW 1
Thomas, D(onald) M(ichael) 1935-
  CLC 13, 22, 31
  See also CA 61-64; CAAS 11; CANR 17, 45,
  74; CDBLB 1960 to Present; DLB 40; INT
  CANR-17; MTCW 1
Thomas, Dylan (Marlais) 1914-1953
  TCLC 1, 8, 45; DA; DAB; DAC; DAM
  DRAM, MST, POET; PC 2; SSC 3; WLC
  See also CA 104; 120; CANR 65; CDBLB
  1945-1960; DLB 13, 20, 139; MTCW 1;
  SATA 60
Thomas, (Philip) Edward 1878-1917
  TCLC 10; DAM POET
  See also CA 106; 153; DLB 19
Thomas, Joyce Carol 1938-
  CLC 35
  See also AAYA 12; BW 2; CA 113; 116; CANR
  48; CLR 19; DLB 33; INT 116; JRDA;
  MAICYA; MTCW 1; SAAS 7; SATA 40, 78
Thomas, Lewis 1913-1993
  CLC 35
  See also CA 85-88; 143; CANR 38, 60; MTCW
  1
Thomas, Paul
  See Mann, (Paul) Thomas
Thomas, Piri 1928-
  CLC 17
  See also CA 73-76; HW
Thomas, R(onald) S(tuart) 1913-
  CLC 6, 13, 48; DAB; DAM POET
  See also CA 89-92; CAAS 4; CANR 30;
  CDBLB 1960 to Present; DLB 27; MTCW 1
Thomas, Ross (Elmore) 1926-1995
  CLC 39
  See also CA 33-36R; 150; CANR 22, 63
Thompson, Francis Clegg
  See Mencken, H(enry) L(ouis)
Thompson, Francis Joseph 1859-1907
  TCLC 4
  See also CA 104; CDBLB 1890-1914; DLB 19
Thompson, Hunter S(tockton) 1939-
  CLC 9, 17, 40, 104; DAM POP

See also BEST 89:1; CA 17-20R; CANR 23,
  46, 74; DLB 185; MTCW 1
Thompson, James Myers
  See Thompson, Jim (Myers)
Thompson, Jim (Myers) .... 1906-1977(?)
  CLC 69
  See also CA 140
Thompson, Judith .... **CLC 39**
Thomson, James 1700-1748
  LC 16, 29, 40; DAM POET
  See also DLB 95
Thomson, James 1834-1882
  NCLC 18; DAM POET
  See also DLB 35
Thoreau, Henry David 1817-1862
  NCLC 7, 21, 61; DA; DAB; DAC; DAM
  MST; WLC
  See also CDALB 1640-1865; DLB 1
Thornton, Hall
  See Silverberg, Robert
Thucydides .... c. 455B.C.-399B.C.
  CMLC 17
  See also DLB 176
Thurber, James (Grover) 1894-1961
  CLC 5, 11, 25; DA; DAB; DAC; DAM
  DRAM, MST, NOV; SSC 1
  See also CA 73-76; CANR 17, 39; CDALB
  1929-1941; DLB 4, 11, 22, 102; MAICYA;
  MTCW 1; SATA 13
Thurman, Wallace (Henry) 1902-1934
  TCLC 6; BLC 3; DAM MULT
  See also BW 1; CA 104; 124; DLB 51
Ticheburn, Cheviot
  See Ainsworth, William Harrison
Tieck, (Johann) Ludwig 1773-1853
  NCLC 5, 46; SSC 31
  See also DLB 90
Tiger, Derry
  See Ellison, Harlan (Jay)
Tilghman, Christopher .... 1948(?)-
  CLC 65
  See also CA 159
Tillinghast, Richard (Williford) 1940-
  CLC 29
  See also CA 29-32R; CAAS 23; CANR 26, 51
Timrod, Henry 1828-1867
  NCLC 25
  See also DLB 3
Tindall, Gillian (Elizabeth) 1938-
  CLC 7
  See also CA 21-24R; CANR 11, 65
Tiptree, James, Jr. .... **CLC 48, 50**
  See also Sheldon, Alice Hastings Bradley
  See also DLB 8
Titmarsh, Michael Angelo
  See Thackeray, William Makepeace
Tocqueville, Alexis (Charles Henri Maurice
  Clerel, Comte) de 1805-1859
  NCLC 7, 63
Tolkien, J(ohn) R(onald) R(euel) 1892-1973
  CLC 1, 2, 3, 8, 12, 38; DA; DAB; DAC;
  DAM MST, NOV, POP; WLC
  See also AAYA 10; AITN 1; CA 17-18; 45-48;
  CANR 36; CAP 2; CDBLB 1914-1945; DLB
  15, 160; JRDA; MAICYA; MTCW 1; SATA
  2, 32, 100; SATA-Obit 24
Toller, Ernst 1893-1939
  TCLC 10
  See also CA 107; DLB 124
Tolson, M. B.
  See Tolson, Melvin B(eaunorus)
Tolson, Melvin B(eaunorus) .... 1898(?)-1966
  CLC 36, 105; BLC 3; DAM MULT, POET

See also BW 1; CA 124; 89-92; DLB 48, 76

Tolstoi, Aleksei Nikolaevich
See Tolstoy, Alexey Nikolaevich

Tolstoy, Alexey Nikolaevich 1882-1945
TCLC 18
See also CA 107; 158

Tolstoy, Count Leo
See Tolstoy, Leo (Nikolaevich)

Tolstoy, Leo (Nikolaevich) 1828-1910
**TCLC 4, 11, 17, 28, 44, 79; DA; DAB;
DAC; DAM MST, NOV; SSC 9, 30; WLC**
See also CA 104; 123; SATA 26

Tomasi di Lampedusa, Giuseppe 1896-1957
See Lampedusa, Giuseppe (Tomasi) di
See also CA 111

Tomlin, Lily .... **CLC 17**
See also Tomlin, Mary Jean

Tomlin, Mary Jean .... 1939(?)-
See Tomlin, Lily
See also CA 117

Tomlinson, (Alfred) Charles 1927-
CLC 2, 4, 6, 13, 45; DAM POET; PC 17
See also CA 5-8R; CANR 33; DLB 40

Tomlinson, H(enry) M(ajor) 1873-1958
TCLC 71
See also CA 118; 161; DLB 36, 100, 195

Tonson, Jacob
See Bennett, (Enoch) Arnold

Toole, John Kennedy 1937-1969
CLC 19, 64
See also CA 104; DLBY 81

Toomer, Jean 1894-1967
**CLC 1, 4, 13, 22; BLC 3; DAM MULT;
PC 7; SSC 1; WLCS**
See also BW 1; CA 85-88; CDALB 1917-1929;
DLB 45, 51; MTCW 1

Torley, Luke
See Blish, James (Benjamin)

Tornimparte, Alessandra
See Ginzburg, Natalia

Torre, Raoul della
See Mencken, H(enry) L(ouis)

Torrey, E(dwin) Fuller 1937-
CLC 34
See also CA 119; CANR 71

Torsvan, Ben Traven
See Traven, B.

Torsvan, Benno Traven
See Traven, B.

Torsvan, Berick Traven
See Traven, B.

Torsvan, Berwick Traven
See Traven, B.

Torsvan, Bruno Traven
See Traven, B.

Torsvan, Traven
See Traven, B.

Tournier, Michel (Edouard) 1924-
CLC 6, 23, 36, 95
See also CA 49-52; CANR 3, 36, 74; DLB 83;
MTCW 1; SATA 23

Tournimparte, Alessandra
See Ginzburg, Natalia

Towers, Ivar
See Kornbluth, C(yril) M.

Towne, Robert (Burton) .... 1936(?)-
CLC 87
See also CA 108; DLB 44

Townsend, Sue .... **CLC 61**
See also Townsend, Susan Elaine
See also SATA 55, 93; SATA-Brief 48

Townsend, Susan Elaine 1946-
See Townsend, Sue

See also CA 119; 127; CANR 65; DAB; DAC;
DAM MST

Townshend, Peter (Dennis Blandford)   1945-
CLC 17, 42
See also CA 107

Tozzi, Federigo 1883-1920
TCLC 31
See also CA 160

Traill, Catharine Parr 1802-1899
NCLC 31
See also DLB 99

Trakl, Georg 1887-1914
TCLC 5; PC 20
See also CA 104; 165

Transtroemer, Tomas (Goesta) 1931-
CLC 52, 65; DAM POET
See also CA 117; 129; CAAS 17

Transtromer, Tomas Gosta
See Transtroemer, Tomas (Goesta)

Traven, B. .... (?)-1969
CLC 8, 11
See also CA 19-20; 25-28R; CAP 2; DLB 9,
56; MTCW 1

Treitel, Jonathan 1959-
CLC 70

Tremain, Rose 1943-
CLC 42
See also CA 97-100; CANR 44; DLB 14

Tremblay, Michel 1942-
CLC 29, 102; DAC; DAM MST
See also CA 116; 128; DLB 60; MTCW 1

Trevanian .... **CLC 29**
See also Whitaker, Rod(ney)

Trevor, Glen
See Hilton, James

Trevor, William 1928-
CLC 7, 9, 14, 25, 71, 116; SSC 21
See also Cox, William Trevor
See also DLB 14, 139

Trifonov, Yuri (Valentinovich) 1925-1981
CLC 45
See also CA 126; 103; MTCW 1

Trilling, Lionel 1905-1975
CLC 9, 11, 24
See also CA 9-12R; 61-64; CANR 10; DLB 28,
63; INT CANR-10; MTCW 1

Trimball, W. H.
See Mencken, H(enry) L(ouis)

Tristan
See Gomez de la Serna, Ramon

Tristram
See Housman, A(lfred) E(dward)

Trogdon, William (Lewis) 1939-
See Heat-Moon, William Least
See also CA 115; 119; CANR 47; INT 119

Trollope, Anthony 1815-1882
**NCLC 6, 33; DA; DAB; DAC; DAM MST,
NOV; SSC 28; WLC**
See also CDBLB 1832-1890; DLB 21, 57, 159;
SATA 22

Trollope, Frances 1779-1863
NCLC 30
See also DLB 21, 166

Trotsky, Leon 1879-1940
TCLC 22
See also CA 118; 167

Trotter (Cockburn), Catharine ... 1679-1749
LC 8
See also DLB 84

Trout, Kilgore
See Farmer, Philip Jose

Trow, George W. S. 1943-
CLC 52

See also CA 126

Troyat, Henri 1911-
CLC 23
See also CA 45-48; CANR 2, 33, 67; MTCW 1

Trudeau, G(arretson) B(eekman) 1948-
See Trudeau, Garry B.
See also CA 81-84; CANR 31; SATA 35

Trudeau, Garry B. .... **CLC 12**
See also Trudeau, G(arretson) B(eekman)
See also AAYA 10; AITN 2

Truffaut, Francois 1932-1984
CLC 20, 101
See also CA 81-84; 113; CANR 34

Trumbo, Dalton 1905-1976
CLC 19
See also CA 21-24R; 69-72; CANR 10; DLB
26

Trumbull, John 1750-1831
NCLC 30
See also DLB 31

Trundlett, Helen B.
See Eliot, T(homas) S(tearns)

Tryon, Thomas 1926-1991
CLC 3, 11; DAM POP
See also AITN 1; CA 29-32R; 135; CANR 32;
MTCW 1

Tryon, Tom
See Tryon, Thomas

Ts'ao Hsueh-ch'in .... 1715(?)-1763
LC 1

Tsushima, Shuji 1909-1948
See Dazai Osamu
See also CA 107

Tsvetaeva (Efron), Marina (Ivanovna)
1892-1941 .... **TCLC 7, 35; PC 14**
See also CA 104; 128; CANR 73; MTCW 1

Tuck, Lily 1938-
CLC 70
See also CA 139

Tu Fu 712-770
PC 9
See also DAM MULT

Tunis, John R(oberts) 1889-1975
CLC 12
See also CA 61-64; CANR 62; DLB 22, 171;
JRDA; MAICYA; SATA 37; SATA-Brief 30

Tuohy, Frank .... **CLC 37**
See also Tuohy, John Francis
See also DLB 14, 139

Tuohy, John Francis 1925-
See Tuohy, Frank
See also CA 5-8R; CANR 3, 47

Turco, Lewis (Putnam) 1934-
CLC 11, 63
See also CA 13-16R; CAAS 22; CANR 24, 51;
DLBY 84

Turgenev, Ivan 1818-1883
**NCLC 21; DA; DAB; DAC; DAM MST,
NOV; DC 7; SSC 7; WLC**

Turgot, Anne-Robert-Jacques 1727-1781
LC 26

Turner, Frederick 1943-
CLC 48
See also CA 73-76; CAAS 10; CANR 12, 30,
56; DLB 40

Tutu, Desmond M(pilo) 1931-
CLC 80; BLC 3; DAM MULT
See also BW 1; CA 125; CANR 67

Tutuola, Amos 1920-1997
CLC 5, 14, 29; BLC 3; DAM MULT
See also BW 2; CA 9-12R; 159; CANR 27, 66;
DLB 125; MTCW 1

Twain, MarkTCLC 6, 12, 19, 36, 48, 59; SSC 6,

See also CA 115; 165

Vega, Lope de 1562-1635
LC 23

Venison, Alfred
See Pound, Ezra (Weston Loomis)

Verdi, Marie de
See Mencken, H(enry) L(ouis)

Verdu, Matilde
See Cela, Camilo Jose

Verga, Giovanni (Carmelo) 1840-1922
TCLC 3; SSC 21
See also CA 104; 123

Vergil .... 70B.C.-19B.C.
**CMLC 9; DA; DAB; DAC; DAM MST,
POET; PC 12; WLCS**

Verhaeren, Emile (Adolphe Gustave)
1855-1916 .... **TCLC 12**
See also CA 109

Verlaine, Paul (Marie) 1844-1896
NCLC 2, 51; DAM POET; PC 2

Verne, Jules (Gabriel) 1828-1905
TCLC 6, 52
See also AAYA 16; CA 110; 131; DLB 123;
JRDA; MAICYA; SATA 21

Very, Jones 1813-1880
NCLC 9
See also DLB 1

Vesaas, Tarjei 1897-1970
CLC 48
See also CA 29-32R

Vialis, Gaston
See Simenon, Georges (Jacques Christian)

Vian, Boris 1920-1959
TCLC 9
See also CA 106; 164; DLB 72

Viaud, (Louis Marie) Julien 1850-1923
See Loti, Pierre
See also CA 107

Vicar, Henry
See Felsen, Henry Gregor

Vicker, Angus
See Felsen, Henry Gregor

Vidal, Gore 1925-
**CLC 2, 4, 6, 8, 10, 22, 33, 72; DAM NOV,
POP**
See also AITN 1; BEST 90:2; CA 5-8R; CANR
13, 45, 65; DLB 6, 152; INT CANR-13;
MTCW 1

Viereck, Peter (Robert Edwin) 1916-
CLC 4
See also CA 1-4R; CANR 1, 47; DLB 5

Vigny, Alfred (Victor) de 1797-1863
NCLC 7; DAM POET
See also DLB 119, 192

Vilakazi, Benedict Wallet 1906-1947
TCLC 37
See also CA 168

Villa, Jose Garcia 1904-1997
PC 22
See also CA 25-28R; CANR 12

Villaurrutia, Xavier 1903-1950
TCLC 80
See also HW

**Villiers de l'Isle Adam, Jean Marie Mathias
Philippe Auguste, Comte de** 1838-1889
NCLC 3; SSC 14
See also DLB 123

Villon, Francois .... 1431-1463(?)
PC 13

Vinci, Leonardo da 1452-1519
LC 12

Vine, Barbara .... **CLC 50**
See also Rendell, Ruth (Barbara)

See also BEST 90:4

Vinge, Joan (Carol) D(ennison) 1948-
CLC 30; SSC 24
See also CA 93-96; CANR 72; SATA 36

Violis, G.
See Simenon, Georges (Jacques Christian)

Virgil
See Vergil

Visconti, Luchino 1906-1976
CLC 16
See also CA 81-84; 65-68; CANR 39

Vittorini, Elio 1908-1966
CLC 6, 9, 14
See also CA 133; 25-28R

Vivekenanda, Swami 1863-1902
TCLC 88

Vizenor, Gerald Robert 1934-
CLC 103; DAM MULT
See also CA 13-16R; CAAS 22; CANR 5, 21,
44, 67; DLB 175; NNAL

Vizinczey, Stephen 1933-
CLC 40
See also CA 128; INT 128

Vliet, R(ussell) G(ordon) 1929-1984
CLC 22
See also CA 37-40R; 112; CANR 18

Vogau, Boris Andreyevich .... 1894-1937(?)
See Pilnyak, Boris
See also CA 123

Vogel, Paula A(nne) 1951-
CLC 76
See also CA 108

Voigt, Cynthia 1942-
CLC 30
See also AAYA 3; CA 106; CANR 18, 37, 40;
CLR 13, 48; INT CANR-18; JRDA;
MAICYA; SATA 48, 79; SATA-Brief 33

Voigt, Ellen Bryant 1943-
CLC 54
See also CA 69-72; CANR 11, 29, 55; DLB 120

Voinovich, Vladimir (Nikolaevich) 1932-
CLC 10, 49
See also CA 81-84; CAAS 12; CANR 33, 67;
MTCW 1

Vollmann, William T. 1959-
CLC 89; DAM NOV, POP
See also CA 134; CANR 67

Voloshinov, V. N.
See Bakhtin, Mikhail Mikhailovich

Voltaire 1694-1778
**LC 14; DA; DAB; DAC; DAM DRAM,
MST; SSC 12; WLC**

von Aschendrof, BaronIgnatz
See Ford, Ford Madox

von Daeniken, Erich 1935-
CLC 30
See also AITN 1; CA 37-40R; CANR 17, 44

von Daniken, Erich
See von Daeniken, Erich

von Heidenstam, (Carl Gustaf) Verner
See Heidenstam, (Carl Gustaf) Verner von

von Heyse, Paul (Johann Ludwig)
See Heyse, Paul (Johann Ludwig von)

von Hofmannsthal, Hugo
See Hofmannsthal, Hugo von

von Horvath, Odon
See Horvath, Oedoen von

von Horvath, Oedoen
See Horvath, Oedoen von

von Liliencron, (Friedrich Adolf Axel) Detlev
See Liliencron, (Friedrich Adolf Axel) Detlev
von

Vonnegut, Kurt, Jr. 1922-

**CLC 1, 2, 3, 4, 5, 8, 12, 22, 40, 60, 111;
DA; DAB; DAC; DAM MST, NOV, POP;
SSC 8; WLC**
See also AAYA 6; AITN 1; BEST 90:4; CA
1-4R; CANR 1, 25, 49; CDALB 1968-1988;
DLB 2, 8, 152; DLBD 3; DLBY 80; MTCW
1

Von Rachen, Kurt
See Hubbard, L(afayette) Ron(ald)

von Rezzori (d'Arezzo), Gregor
See Rezzori (d'Arezzo), Gregor von

von Sternberg, Josef
See Sternberg, Josef von

Vorster, Gordon 1924-
CLC 34
See also CA 133

Vosce, Trudie
See Ozick, Cynthia

Voznesensky, Andrei (Andreievich) 1933-
CLC 1, 15, 57; DAM POET
See also CA 89-92; CANR 37; MTCW 1

Waddington, Miriam 1917-
CLC 28
See also CA 21-24R; CANR 12, 30; DLB 68

Wagman, Fredrica 1937-
CLC 7
See also CA 97-100; INT 97-100

Wagner, Linda W.
See Wagner-Martin, Linda (C.)

Wagner, Linda Welshimer
See Wagner-Martin, Linda (C.)

Wagner, Richard 1813-1883
NCLC 9
See also DLB 129

Wagner-Martin, Linda (C.) 1936-
CLC 50
See also CA 159

Wagoner, David (Russell) 1926-
CLC 3, 5, 15
See also CA 1-4R; CAAS 3; CANR 2, 71; DLB
5; SATA 14

Wah, Fred(erick James) 1939-
CLC 44
See also CA 107; 141; DLB 60

Wahloo, Per 1926-1975
CLC 7
See also CA 61-64; CANR 73

Wahloo, Peter
See Wahloo, Per

Wain, John (Barrington) 1925-1994
CLC 2, 11, 15, 46
See also CA 5-8R; 145; CAAS 4; CANR 23,
54; CDBLB 1960 to Present; DLB 15, 27,
139, 155; MTCW 1

Wajda, Andrzej 1926-
CLC 16
See also CA 102

Wakefield, Dan 1932-
CLC 7
See also CA 21-24R; CAAS 7

Wakoski, Diane 1937-
CLC 2, 4, 7, 9, 11, 40; DAM POET; PC 15
See also CA 13-16R; CAAS 1; CANR 9, 60;
DLB 5; INT CANR-9

Wakoski-Sherbell, Diane
See Wakoski, Diane

Walcott, Derek (Alton) 1930-
**CLC 2, 4, 9, 14, 25, 42, 67, 76; BLC 3;
DAB; DAC; DAM MST, MULT, POET;
DC 7**
See also BW 2; CA 89-92; CANR 26, 47; DLB
117; DLBY 81; MTCW 1

Waldman, Anne (Lesley) 1945-

SATA-Obit 26

Weber, Max 1864-1920
  TCLC 69
  See also CA 109

Webster, John .... 1579(?)-1634(?)
  LC 33; DA; DAB; DAC; DAM DRAM, MST; DC 2; WLC
  See also CDBLB Before 1660; DLB 58

Webster, Noah 1758-1843
  NCLC 30

Wedekind, (Benjamin) Frank(lin) 1864-1918
  TCLC 7; DAM DRAM
  See also CA 104; 153; DLB 118

Weidman, Jerome 1913-
  CLC 7
  See also AITN 2; CA 1-4R; CANR 1; DLB 28

Weil, Simone (Adolphine) 1909-1943
  TCLC 23
  See also CA 117; 159

Weininger, Otto 1880-1903
  TCLC 84

Weinstein, Nathan
  See West, Nathanael

Weinstein, Nathan von Wallenstein
  See West, Nathanael

Weir, Peter (Lindsay) 1944-
  CLC 20
  See also CA 113; 123

Weiss, Peter (Ulrich) 1916-1982
  CLC 3, 15, 51; DAM DRAM
  See also CA 45-48; 106; CANR 3; DLB 69, 124

Weiss, Theodore (Russell) 1916-
  CLC 3, 8, 14
  See also CA 9-12R; CAAS 2; CANR 46; DLB 5

Welch, (Maurice) Denton 1915-1948
  TCLC 22
  See also CA 121; 148

Welch, James 1940-
  CLC 6, 14, 52; DAM MULT, POP
  See also CA 85-88; CANR 42, 66; DLB 175; NNAL

Weldon, Fay 1931-
  CLC 6, 9, 11, 19, 36, 59; DAM POP
  See also CA 21-24R; CANR 16, 46, 63; CDBLB 1960 to Present; DLB 14, 194; INT CANR-16; MTCW 1

Wellek, Rene 1903-1995
  CLC 28
  See also CA 5-8R; 150; CAAS 7; CANR 8; DLB 63; INT CANR-8

Weller, Michael 1942-
  CLC 10, 53
  See also CA 85-88

Weller, Paul 1958-
  CLC 26

Wellershoff, Dieter 1925-
  CLC 46
  See also CA 89-92; CANR 16, 37

Welles, (George) Orson 1915-1985
  CLC 20, 80
  See also CA 93-96; 117

Wellman, John McDowell 1945-
  See Wellman, Mac
  See also CA 166

Wellman, Mac 1945-
  CLC 65
  See also Wellman, John McDowell; Wellman, John McDowell

Wellman, Manly Wade 1903-1986
  CLC 49
  See also CA 1-4R; 118; CANR 6, 16, 44; SATA 6; SATA-Obit 47

Wells, Carolyn .... 1869(?)-1942
  TCLC 35
  See also CA 113; DLB 11

Wells, H(erbert) G(eorge) 1866-1946
  TCLC 6, 12, 19; DA; DAB; DAC; DAM MST, NOV; SSC 6; WLC
  See also CA 110; 121; CDBLB 1914-1945; DLB 34, 70, 156, 178; MTCW 1; SATA 20

Wells, Rosemary 1943-
  CLC 12
  See also AAYA 13; CA 85-88; CANR 48; CLR 16; MAICYA; SAAS 1; SATA 18, 69

Welty, Eudora 1909-
  CLC 1, 2, 5, 14, 22, 33, 105; DA; DAB; DAC; DAM MST, NOV; SSC 1, 27; WLC
  See also CA 9-12R; CABS 1; CANR 32, 65; CDALB 1941-1968; DLB 2, 102, 143; DLBD 12; DLBY 87; MTCW 1

Wen I-to 1899-1946
  TCLC 28

Wentworth, Robert
  See Hamilton, Edmond

Werfel, Franz (Viktor) 1890-1945
  TCLC 8
  See also CA 104; 161; DLB 81, 124

Wergeland, Henrik Arnold 1808-1845
  NCLC 5

Wersba, Barbara 1932-
  CLC 30
  See also AAYA 2; CA 29-32R; CANR 16, 38; CLR 3; DLB 52; JRDA; MAICYA; SAAS 2; SATA 1, 58

Wertmueller, Lina 1928-
  CLC 16
  See also CA 97-100; CANR 39

Wescott, Glenway 1901-1987
  CLC 13
  See also CA 13-16R; 121; CANR 23, 70; DLB 4, 9, 102

Wesker, Arnold 1932-
  CLC 3, 5, 42; DAB; DAM DRAM
  See also CA 1-4R; CAAS 7; CANR 1, 33; CDBLB 1960 to Present; DLB 13; MTCW 1

Wesley, Richard (Errol) 1945-
  CLC 7
  See also BW 1; CA 57-60; CANR 27; DLB 38

Wessel, Johan Herman 1742-1785
  LC 7

West, Anthony (Panther) 1914-1987
  CLC 50
  See also CA 45-48; 124; CANR 3, 19; DLB 15

West, C. P.
  See Wodehouse, P(elham) G(renville)

West, (Mary) Jessamyn 1902-1984
  CLC 7, 17
  See also CA 9-12R; 112; CANR 27; DLB 6; DLBY 84; MTCW 1; SATA-Obit 37

West, Morris L(anglo) 1916-
  CLC 6, 33
  See also CA 5-8R; CANR 24, 49, 64; MTCW 1

West, Nathanael 1903-1940
  TCLC 1, 14, 44; SSC 16
  See also CA 104; 125; CDALB 1929-1941; DLB 4, 9, 28; MTCW 1

West, Owen
  See Koontz, Dean R(ay)

West, Paul 1930-
  CLC 7, 14, 96
  See also CA 13-16R; CAAS 7; CANR 22, 53; DLB 14; INT CANR-22

West, Rebecca 1892-1983
  CLC 7, 9, 31, 50

See also CA 5-8R; 109; CANR 19; DLB 36; DLBY 83; MTCW 1

Westall, Robert (Atkinson) 1929-1993
  CLC 17
  See also AAYA 12; CA 69-72; 141; CANR 18, 68; CLR 13; JRDA; MAICYA; SAAS 2; SATA 23, 69; SATA-Obit 75

Westermarck, Edward 1862-1939
  TCLC 87

Westlake, Donald E(dwin) 1933-
  CLC 7, 33; DAM POP
  See also CA 17-20R; CAAS 13; CANR 16, 44, 65; INT CANR-16

Westmacott, Mary
  See Christie, Agatha (Mary Clarissa)

Weston, Allen
  See Norton, Andre

Wetcheek, J. L.
  See Feuchtwanger, Lion

Wetering, Janwillem van de
  See van de Wetering, Janwillem

Wetherald, Agnes Ethelwyn 1857-1940
  TCLC 81
  See also DLB 99

Wetherell, Elizabeth
  See Warner, Susan (Bogert)

Whale, James 1889-1957
  TCLC 63

Whalen, Philip 1923-
  CLC 6, 29
  See also CA 9-12R; CANR 5, 39; DLB 16

Wharton, Edith (Newbold Jones) 1862-1937
  TCLC 3, 9, 27, 53; DA; DAB; DAC; DAM MST, NOV; SSC 6; WLC
  See also AAYA 25; CA 104; 132; CDALB 1865-1917; DLB 4, 9, 12, 78, 189; DLBD 13; MTCW 1

Wharton, James
  See Mencken, H(enry) L(ouis)

Wharton, William (a pseudonym) CLC 18, 37
  See also CA 93-96; DLBY 80; INT 93-96

Wheatley (Peters), Phillis .... 1754(?)-1784
  LC 3; BLC 3; DA; DAC; DAM MST, MULT, POET; PC 3; WLC
  See also CDALB 1640-1865; DLB 31, 50

Wheelock, John Hall 1886-1978
  CLC 14
  See also CA 13-16R; 77-80; CANR 14; DLB 45

White, E(lwyn) B(rooks) 1899-1985
  CLC 10, 34, 39; DAM POP
  See also AITN 2; CA 13-16R; 116; CANR 16, 37; CLR 1, 21; DLB 11, 22; MAICYA; MTCW 1; SATA 2, 29, 100; SATA-Obit 44

White, Edmund (Valentine III) 1940-
  CLC 27, 110; DAM POP
  See also AAYA 7; CA 45-48; CANR 3, 19, 36, 62; MTCW 1

White, Patrick (Victor Martindale)
  1912-1990 **CLC 3, 4, 5, 7, 9, 18, 65, 69**
  See also CA 81-84; 132; CANR 43; MTCW 1

White, Phyllis Dorothy James 1920-
  See James, P. D.
  See also CA 21-24R; CANR 17, 43, 65; DAM POP; MTCW 1

White, T(erence) H(anbury) 1906-1964
  CLC 30
  See also AAYA 22; CA 73-76; CANR 37; DLB 160; JRDA; MAICYA; SATA 12

White, Terence de Vere 1912-1994
  CLC 49
  See also CA 49-52; 145; CANR 3

White, Walter F(rancis) 1893-1955

TCLC 15
See also White, Walter
See also BW 1; CA 115; 124; DLB 51

White, William Hale 1831-1913
See Rutherford, Mark
See also CA 121

Whitehead, E(dward) A(nthony) 1933-
CLC 5
See also CA 65-68; CANR 58

Whitemore, Hugh (John) 1936-
CLC 37
See also CA 132; INT 132

Whitman, Sarah Helen (Power) .. 1803-1878
NCLC 19
See also DLB 1

Whitman, Walt(er) 1819-1892
NCLC 4, 31; DA; DAB; DAC; DAM MST,
POET; PC 3; WLC
See also CDALB 1640-1865; DLB 3, 64; SATA
20

Whitney, Phyllis A(yame) 1903-
CLC 42; DAM POP
See also AITN 2; BEST 90:3; CA 1-4R; CANR
3, 25, 38, 60; JRDA; MAICYA; SATA 1, 30

Whittemore, (Edward) Reed (Jr.) 1919-
CLC 4
See also CA 9-12R; CAAS 8; CANR 4; DLB 5

Whittier, John Greenleaf 1807-1892
NCLC 8, 59
See also DLB 1

Whittlebot, Hernia
See Coward, Noel (Peirce)

Wicker, Thomas Grey 1926-
See Wicker, Tom
See also CA 65-68; CANR 21, 46

Wicker, Tom .... CLC 7
See also Wicker, Thomas Grey

Wideman, John Edgar 1941-
CLC 5, 34, 36, 67; BLC 3; DAM MULT
See also BW 2; CA 85-88; CANR 14, 42, 67;
DLB 33, 143

Wiebe, Rudy (Henry) 1934-
CLC 6, 11, 14; DAC; DAM MST
See also CA 37-40R; CANR 42, 67; DLB 60

Wieland, Christoph Martin 1733-1813
NCLC 17
See also DLB 97

Wiene, Robert 1881-1938
TCLC 56

Wieners, John 1934-
CLC 7
See also CA 13-16R; DLB 16

Wiesel, Elie(zer) 1928-
CLC 3, 5, 11, 37; DA; DAB; DAC; DAM
MST, NOV; WLCS
See also AAYA 7; AITN 1; CA 5-8R; CAAS 4;
CANR 8, 40, 65; DLB 83; DLBY 87; INT
CANR-8; MTCW 1; SATA 56

Wiggins, Marianne 1947-
CLC 57
See also BEST 89:3; CA 130; CANR 60

Wight, James Alfred 1916-1995
See Herriot, James
See also CA 77-80; SATA 55; SATA-Brief 44

Wilbur, Richard (Purdy) 1921-
CLC 3, 6, 9, 14, 53, 110; DA; DAB; DAC;
DAM MST, POET
See also CA 1-4R; CABS 2; CANR 2, 29; DLB
5, 169; INT CANR-29; MTCW 1; SATA 9

Wild, Peter 1940-
CLC 14
See also CA 37-40R; DLB 5

Wilde, Oscar (Fingal O'Flahertie Wills)

1854(?)-1900 ... TCLC 1, 8, 23, 41; DA;
DAB; DAC; DAM DRAM, MST, NOV;
SSC 11; WLC
See also CA 104; 119; CDBLB 1890-1914;
DLB 10, 19, 34, 57, 141, 156, 190; SATA 24

Wilder, Billy .... CLC 20
See also Wilder, Samuel
See also DLB 26

Wilder, Samuel 1906-
See Wilder, Billy
See also CA 89-92

Wilder, Thornton (Niven) 1897-1975
CLC 1, 5, 6, 10, 15, 35, 82; DA; DAB;
DAC; DAM DRAM, MST, NOV; DC 1;
WLC
See also AITN 2; CA 13-16R; 61-64; CANR
40; DLB 4, 7, 9; DLBY 97; MTCW 1

Wilding, Michael 1942-
CLC 73
See also CA 104; CANR 24, 49

Wiley, Richard 1944-
CLC 44
See also CA 121; 129; CANR 71

Wilhelm, Kate .... CLC 7
See also Wilhelm, Katie Gertrude
See also AAYA 20; CAAS 5; DLB 8; INT
CANR-17

Wilhelm, Katie Gertrude 1928-
See Wilhelm, Kate
See also CA 37-40R; CANR 17, 36, 60; MTCW
1

Wilkins, Mary
See Freeman, Mary Eleanor Wilkins

Willard, Nancy 1936-
CLC 7, 37
See also CA 89-92; CANR 10, 39, 68; CLR 5;
DLB 5, 52; MAICYA; MTCW 1; SATA 37,
71; SATA-Brief 30

Williams, C(harles) K(enneth) 1936-
CLC 33, 56; DAM POET
See also CA 37-40R; CAAS 26; CANR 57; DLB
5

Williams, Charles
See Collier, James L(incoln)

Williams, Charles (Walter Stansby)
1886-1945 .... TCLC 1, 11
See also CA 104; 163; DLB 100, 153

Williams, (George) Emlyn 1905-1987
CLC 15; DAM DRAM
See also CA 104; 123; CANR 36; DLB 10, 77;
MTCW 1

Williams, Hank 1923-1953
TCLC 81

Williams, Hugo 1942-
CLC 42
See also CA 17-20R; CANR 45; DLB 40

Williams, J. Walker
See Wodehouse, P(elham) G(renville)

Williams, John A(lfred) 1925-
CLC 5, 13; BLC 3; DAM MULT
See also BW 2; CA 53-56; CAAS 3; CANR 6,
26, 51; DLB 2, 33; INT CANR-6

Williams, Jonathan (Chamberlain) 1929-
CLC 13
See also CA 9-12R; CAAS 12; CANR 8; DLB
5

Williams, Joy 1944-
CLC 31
See also CA 41-44R; CANR 22, 48

Williams, Norman 1952-
CLC 39
See also CA 118

Williams, Sherley Anne 1944-

CLC 89; BLC 3; DAM MULT, POET
See also BW 2; CA 73-76; CANR 25; DLB 41;
INT CANR-25; SATA 78

Williams, Shirley
See Williams, Sherley Anne

Williams, Tennessee 1911-1983
CLC 1, 2, 5, 7, 8, 11, 15, 19, 30, 39, 45, 71,
111; DA; DAB; DAC; DAM DRAM, MST;
DC 4; WLC
See also AITN 1, 2; CA 5-8R; 108; CABS 3;
CANR 31; CDALB 1941-1968; DLB 7;
DLBD 4; DLBY 83; MTCW 1

Williams, Thomas (Alonzo) 1926-1990
CLC 14
See also CA 1-4R; 132; CANR 2

Williams, William C.
Williams, William Carlos

Williams, William Carlos 1883-1963
CLC 1, 2, 5, 9, 13, 22, 42, 67; DA; DAB;
DAC; DAM MST, POET; PC 7; SSC 31
See also CA 89-92; CANR 34; CDALB
1917-1929; DLB 4, 16, 54, 86; MTCW 1

Williamson, David (Keith) 1942-
CLC 56
See also CA 103; CANR 41

Williamson, Ellen Douglas 1905-1984
See Douglas, Ellen
See also CA 17-20R; 114; CANR 39

Williamson, Jack .... CLC 29
See also Williamson, John Stewart
See also CAAS 8; DLB 8

Williamson, John Stewart 1908-
See Williamson, Jack
See also CA 17-20R; CANR 23, 70

Willie, Frederick
See Lovecraft, H(oward) P(hillips)

Willingham, Calder (Baynard, Jr.) 1922-1995
CLC 5, 51
See also CA 5-8R; 147; CANR 3; DLB 2, 44;
MTCW 1

Willis, Charles
See Clarke, Arthur C(harles)

Willy
See Colette, (Sidonie-Gabrielle)

Willy, Colette
See Colette, (Sidonie-Gabrielle)

Wilson, A(ndrew) N(orman) 1950-
CLC 33
See also CA 112; 122; DLB 14, 155, 194

Wilson, Angus (Frank Johnstone) 1913-1991
CLC 2, 3, 5, 25, 34; SSC 21
See also CA 5-8R; 134; CANR 21; DLB 15,
139, 155; MTCW 1

Wilson, August 1945-
CLC 39, 50, 63; BLC 3; DA; DAB; DAC;
DAM DRAM, MST, MULT; DC 2; WLCS
See also AAYA 16; BW 2; CA 115; 122; CANR
42, 54; MTCW 1

Wilson, Brian 1942-
CLC 12

Wilson, Colin 1931-
CLC 3, 14
See also CA 1-4R; CAAS 5; CANR 1, 22, 33;
DLB 14, 194; MTCW 1

Wilson, Dirk
See Pohl, Frederik

Wilson, Edmund 1895-1972
CLC 1, 2, 3, 8, 24
See also CA 1-4R; 37-40R; CANR 1, 46; DLB
63; MTCW 1

Wilson, Ethel Davis (Bryant) .. 1888(?)-1980
CLC 13; DAC; DAM POET
See also CA 102; DLB 68; MTCW 1

Wilson, John 1785-1854
NCLC 5

Wilson, John (Anthony) Burgess 1917-1993
See Burgess, Anthony
See also CA 1-4R; 143; CANR 2, 46; DAC;
DAM NOV; MTCW 1

Wilson, Lanford 1937-
CLC 7, 14, 36; DAM DRAM
See also CA 17-20R; CABS 3; CANR 45; DLB 7

Wilson, Robert M. 1944-
CLC 7, 9
See also CA 49-52; CANR 2, 41; MTCW 1

Wilson, Robert McLiam 1964-
CLC 59
See also CA 132

Wilson, Sloan 1920-
CLC 32
See also CA 1-4R; CANR 1, 44

Wilson, Snoo 1948-
CLC 33
See also CA 69-72

Wilson, William S(mith) 1932-
CLC 49
See also CA 81-84

Wilson, (Thomas) Woodrow 1856-1924
TCLC 79
See also CA 166; DLB 47

Winchilsea, Anne (Kingsmill) Finch Counte
1661-1720
See Finch, Anne

Windham, Basil
See Wodehouse, P(elham) G(renville)

Wingrove, David (John) 1954-
CLC 68
See also CA 133

Wintergreen, Jane
See Duncan, Sara Jeannette

Winters, Janet Lewis .... CLC 41
See also Lewis, Janet
See also DLBY 87

Winters, (Arthur) Yvor 1900-1968
CLC 4, 8, 32
See also CA 11-12; 25-28R; CAP 1; DLB 48;
MTCW 1

Winterson, Jeanette 1959-
CLC 64; DAM POP
See also CA 136; CANR 58

Winthrop, John 1588-1649
LC 31
See also DLB 24, 30

Wiseman, Frederick 1930-
CLC 20
See also CA 159

Wister, Owen 1860-1938
TCLC 21
See also CA 108; 162; DLB 9, 78, 186; SATA 62

Witkacy
See Witkiewicz, Stanislaw Ignacy

Witkiewicz, Stanislaw Ignacy 1885-1939
TCLC 8
See also CA 105; 162

Wittgenstein, Ludwig (Josef Johann)
1889-1951 .... TCLC 59
See also CA 113; 164

Wittig, Monique .... 1935(?)-
CLC 22
See also CA 116; 135; DLB 83

Wittlin, Jozef 1896-1976
CLC 25
See also CA 49-52; 65-68; CANR 3

Wodehouse, P(elham) G(renville) 1881-1975

CLC 1, 2, 5, 10, 22; DAB; DAC; DAM
NOV; SSC 2
See also AITN 2; CA 45-48; 57-60; CANR 3,
33; CDBLB 1914-1945; DLB 34, 162;
MTCW 1; SATA 22

Woiwode, L.
See Woiwode, Larry (Alfred)

Woiwode, Larry (Alfred) 1941-
CLC 6, 10
See also CA 73-76; CANR 16; DLB 6; INT
CANR-16

Wojciechowska, Maia (Teresa) 1927-
CLC 26
See also AAYA 8; CA 9-12R; CANR 4, 41; CLR
1; JRDA; MAICYA; SAAS 1; SATA 1, 28,
83

Wolf, Christa 1929-
CLC 14, 29, 58
See also CA 85-88; CANR 45; DLB 75; MTCW
1

Wolfe, Gene (Rodman) 1931-
CLC 25; DAM POP
See also CA 57-60; CAAS 9; CANR 6, 32, 60;
DLB 8

Wolfe, George C. 1954-
CLC 49; BLCS
See also CA 149

Wolfe, Thomas (Clayton) 1900-1938
TCLC 4, 13, 29, 61; DA; DAB; DAC; DAM
MST, NOV; SSC 33; WLC
See also CA 104; 132; CDALB 1929-1941;
DLB 9, 102; DLBD 2, 16; DLBY 85, 97;
MTCW 1

Wolfe, Thomas Kennerly, Jr. 1930-
See Wolfe, Tom
See also CA 13-16R; CANR 9, 33, 70; DAM
POP; DLB 185; INT CANR-9; MTCW 1

Wolfe, Tom .... CLC 1, 2, 9, 15, 35, 51
See also Wolfe, Thomas Kennerly, Jr.
See also AAYA 8; AITN 2; BEST 89:1; DLB
152

Wolff, Geoffrey (Ansell) 1937-
CLC 41
See also CA 29-32R; CANR 29, 43

Wolff, Sonia
See Levitin, Sonia (Wolff)

Wolff, Tobias (Jonathan Ansell) 1945-
CLC 39, 64
See also AAYA 16; BEST 90:2; CA 114; 117;
CAAS 22; CANR 54; DLB 130; INT 117

Wolfram von Eschenbach ..... c. 1170-c. 1220
CMLC 5
See also DLB 138

Wolitzer, Hilma 1930-
CLC 17
See also CA 65-68; CANR 18, 40; INT
CANR-18; SATA 31

Wollstonecraft, Mary 1759-1797
LC 5
See also CDBLB 1789-1832; DLB 39, 104, 158

Wonder, Stevie .... CLC 12
See also Morris, Steveland Judkins

Wong, Jade Snow 1922-
CLC 17
See also CA 109

Woodberry, George Edward 1855-1930
TCLC 73
See also CA 165; DLB 71, 103

Woodcott, Keith
See Brunner, John (Kilian Houston)

Woodruff, Robert W.
See Mencken, H(enry) L(ouis)

Woolf, (Adeline) Virginia 1882-1941

TCLC 1, 5, 20, 43, 56; DA; DAB; DAC;
DAM MST, NOV; SSC 7; WLC
See also CA 104; 130; CANR 64; CDBLB
1914-1945; DLB 36, 100, 162; DLBD 10;
MTCW 1

Woolf, Virginia Adeline
See Woolf, (Adeline) Virginia

Woollcott, Alexander (Humphreys)
1887-1943 .... TCLC 5
See also CA 105; 161; DLB 29

Woolrich, Cornell 1903-1968
CLC 77
See also Hopley-Woolrich, Cornell George

Wordsworth, Dorothy 1771-1855
NCLC 25
See also DLB 107

Wordsworth, William 1770-1850
NCLC 12, 38; DA; DAB; DAC; DAM
MST, POET; PC 4; WLC
See also CDBLB 1789-1832; DLB 93, 107

Wouk, Herman 1915-
CLC 1, 9, 38; DAM NOV, POP
See also CA 5-8R; CANR 6, 33, 67; DLBY 82;
INT CANR-6; MTCW 1

Wright, Charles (Penzel, Jr.) 1935-
CLC 6, 13, 28
See also CA 29-32R; CAAS 7; CANR 23, 36,
62; DLB 165; DLBY 82; MTCW 1

Wright, Charles Stevenson 1932-
CLC 49; BLC 3; DAM MULT, POET
See also BW 1; CA 9-12R; CANR 26; DLB 33

Wright, Frances 1795-1852
NCLC 74
See also DLB 73

Wright, Jack R.
See Harris, Mark

Wright, James (Arlington) 1927-1980
CLC 3, 5, 10, 28; DAM POET
See also AITN 2; CA 49-52; 97-100; CANR 4,
34, 64; DLB 5, 169; MTCW 1

Wright, Judith (Arandell) 1915-
CLC 11, 53; PC 14
See also CA 13-16R; CANR 31; MTCW 1;
SATA 14

Wright, L(aurali) R. 1939-
CLC 44
See also CA 138

Wright, Richard (Nathaniel) 1908-1960
CLC 1, 3, 4, 9, 14, 21, 48, 74; BLC 3; DA;
DAB; DAC; DAM MST, MULT, NOV;
SSC 2; WLC
See also AAYA 5; BW 1; CA 108; CANR 64;
CDALB 1929-1941; DLB 76, 102; DLBD
2; MTCW 1

Wright, Richard B(ruce) 1937-
CLC 6
See also CA 85-88; DLB 53

Wright, Rick 1945-
CLC 35

Wright, Rowland
See Wells, Carolyn

Wright, Stephen 1946-
CLC 33

Wright, Willard Huntington 1888-1939
See Van Dine, S. S.
See also CA 115; DLBD 16

Wright, William 1930-
CLC 44
See also CA 53-56; CANR 7, 23

Wroth, LadyMary .... 1587-1653(?)
LC 30
See also DLB 121

Wu Ch'eng-en .... 1500(?)-1582(?)

Literary Criticism Series
Cumulative Topic Index

This index lists all topic entries in Gale's *Classical and Medieval Literature Criticism, Contemporary Literary Criticism, Literature Criticism from 1400 to 1800, Nineteenth-Century Literature Criticism,* and *Twentieth-Century Literary Criticism.*

Topic Index

Topic Index

Contemporary Literary Criticism
Cumulative Nationality Index

Nationality Index

Nationality Index

Nationality Index

Nationality Index

Nationality Index

ISBN 0-7876-3192-2

90000